D0022804

Social Psychology

Goals in Interaction

SIXTH EDITION

Douglas T. Kenrick
Arizona State University

Steven L. Neuberg
Arizona State University

Robert B. Cialdini
Arizona State University

Boston   Columbus   Indianapolis   New York   San Francisco
Amsterdam   Cape Town   Dubai   London   Madrid   Milan   Munich   Paris   Montréal   Toronto
Delhi   Mexico City   São Paulo   Sydney   Hong Kong   Seoul   Singapore   Taipei   Tokyo

VP, Product Development: Dickson Musslewhite
Senior Acquisitions Editor: Amber Chow
Editorial Assistant: Luke Robbins
Director, Project Management Services:
    Lisa Iarkowski
Project Team Lead: Linda Behrens
Project Manager: Shelly Kupperman
Program Team Lead: Amber Mackey
Program Manager: Diane Szulecki
VP, Director of Product Marketing: Maggie Moylan
Director of Field Marketing: Jonathan Cottrell
Senior Product Marketer: Lindsey Prudhomme Gill
Executive Field Marketer: Kate Stewart
Marketing Assistant, Field Marketing: Paige Patunas

Marketing Coordinator, Product Marketing:
    Jessica Warren
Procurement Manager: Mary Fischer
Procurement Specialist: Diane Peirano
Associate Director of Design: Blair Brown
Interior Designer: Kathryn Foot
Cover Design: Pentagram
Digital Media Project Manager: Pamela Weldin
Full-Service Project Management: Jenna Vittorioso,
    Lumina Datamatics Ltd.
Cover Printer: Phoenix Color/Hagerstown
Printer/Binder: RR Donnelley/Willard
Cover Image: Oliver Sved/Shutterstock
Text Font: Palatino LT Std 9.5 pt/12 pt

Credits and acknowledgments borrowed from other sources and reproduced, with permission, in this textbook appear on the appropriate page of appearance or in the Credits on pages 545–549.

Copyright © 2015, 2010, 2007 by Pearson Education, Inc. or its affiliates. All Rights Reserved. Printed in the United States of America. This publication is protected by copyright, and permission should be obtained from the publisher prior to any prohibited reproduction, storage in a retrieval system, or transmission in any form or by any means, electronic, mechanical, photocopying, recording, or otherwise. For information regarding permissions, request forms and the appropriate contacts within the Pearson Education Global Rights & Permissions department, please visit www.pearsoned.com/permissions/.

Library of Congress Cataloging-in-Publication Data

Kenrick, Douglas T.
  Social psychology / Douglas T. Kenrick, Arizona State University, Steven
L. Neuberg, Arizona State University, Robert B. Cialdini, Arizona State
University.—Sixth Edition.
      pages cm
  Includes bibliographical references and index.
  ISBN 978-0-13-381018-9 (alk. paper)—ISBN 0-13-381018-6 (alk. paper)
  1. Social psychology. I. Neuberg, Steven L. II. Cialdini, Robert B. III. Title.
  HM1033.K46 2014
  302—dc23
                                            2014014799

3   17

Student Edition
ISBN-10:   0-13-381018-6
ISBN-13: 978-0-13-381018-9

Books a lá Carte
ISBN-10:   0-13-381034-8
ISBN-13: 978-0-13-381034-9

To David, Liam, Carol, Finian, and Greta

To Erika, Rachel, Zachary, and Elliot

To Bobette, Christopher, and Jason

Brief Contents

Contents

Welcome from the Authors

Social psychology is intrinsically fun. Indeed, to students assigned a typical social psychology textbook, the field must sometimes seem like an amazing three-ring circus, where every turn of the eye reveals a dizzying assortment of attention-demanding performances. A different show unfolds in each ring—awe-inspiring acts of altruism, shocking deeds of aggression, persuasive tricks from magicians' hats, human pyramids of cooperation, and mysterious feats of self-delusion. At the center of it all stands the course instructor, the ringmaster, calling students' attention alternately to one then another facet of the spectacle—*And now, ladies and gentlemen, I invite you to shift your gaze from the clownish antics of self-deception to the daring men and women attempting to traverse the tightrope of romantic love, and then back down to the wild lion pit of aggression.*

The Need for an Integrative Approach to Social Psychology

But there's a problem with the three-ring circus presentation of social psychology. It masks a critically important point: Human social behaviors are woven together in related, interconnected patterns. To present an array of separate, disjointed chapter topics—aggression here, persuasion, prejudice, and personal relationships there, there, and there—offers a sorely inadequate view of the field. Hidden beneath all the dazzling aspects of human social behavior, there are a central set of common concepts, dimensions, and principles. We are convinced that students benefit greatly from discovering those underlying principles. After all, a primary rule of learning and memory is that people grasp and retain more material, more easily, when the various parts can be connected by organizing principles.

As entertaining and stimulating as a circus may be, it is not a good arena for learning. Much better, and equally engaging, is a well-constructed work of theater, cinema, or literature. The field of social psychology should be presented to students as a captivating and coherent chronicle, not a bewildering circus. It's an intricate chronicle to be sure, rich in twists and variations. But it is coherent nonetheless, with recurring characters, scenes, and themes linking its elements. Our major purpose in writing this text is to offer students and instructors a cohesive framework that retains social psychology's renowned ability to captivate student interest but that adds the more intellectually helpful (and satisfying) feature of integration.

How Do We Accomplish the Integration?

For a full year before deciding to write this book, we met for an afternoon every week to try to develop a truly integrative framework for the course. We knew that we had one ironic advantage: In a basic way, we disagreed with one another. Each of us had approached the task with a different one of the major, sometimes opposing, theoretical perspectives in social psychology today—social cognition, social learning, and evolutionary psychology. We realized that if we could find an overarching framework that would bridge our diverse approaches, it would provide an especially broad foundation for integrating the course material—one that allowed and incorporated a full range of theoretical starting points.

Those meetings were an exhilarating mix of good-natured conflicts, eye-opening insights, false starts, blind alleys, and gratifying breakthroughs—always accompanied by the shared sense that our understanding of social psychology was growing. The effort would have been worthwhile even if no book had come of it. At the end of that year of discussion and debate, not only did we have an invaluable mid-career learning experience under our belts, but, as well, we had consensus on an integrative framework about which we were all genuinely enthusiastic.

The text's subtitle, "Goals in Interaction," reflects the two key themes that we use to tie together the text material within and across chapter topics:

1. The goal-directed nature of social behavior. First, we stress that social responding is goal directed. People might not even be able to consciously describe their goals, but when they obey an authority figure, begin a new relationship, or raise a fist against another, they do so in the service of some goal—perhaps to gain another's approval, verify a self-image, or acquire social status. In Chapter 1, we describe how everyday goals flow from fundamental social motives, such as establishing social ties, attracting mates, and understanding ourselves and those around us. In Chapter 2, we examine how goals work. In each succeeding chapter, we reestablish this emphasis on goals by asking the question "What particular goals are served by aggression, conformity, prejudice (or whichever particular behaviors we consider in that chapter)?"

2. The interaction of the person and the situation. Second, to understand fully the causes of a person's social behavior, we need to consider how aspects of that person interact with aspects of his or her situation. How do features inside the individual—attitudes, traits, expectations, attributions, moods, goals, stereotypes, and emotions—work together with features of the situation to influence social behavior? Beginning with Kurt Lewin, this interactionist theme has been prominent in our field. Unfortunately, introductory social psychology texts have rarely engaged the full explanatory power of interactionism. In contrast, in this book, we continuously invite readers to consider the interplay of influences inside and outside the person.

Bridging Perspectives: Cognition, Culture, and Evolution

For the last two decades, social psychologists have profitably mined the cognitive perspective for insights into how humans process information about their social situations. These insights added to a foundation of findings discovered within the social learning perspective. In recent years, as researchers have made fascinating discoveries about social behavior in different human cultures and different animal species, the sociocultural and evolutionary perspectives have increasingly contributed to the mix.

The sociocultural perspective has emphasized how our social thoughts and behaviors are encompassed within the larger context of the societies we live in. Cultural influences can change the answer to questions about which techniques of persuasion will be effective, whether a person will define herself in terms of her group memberships or her individual qualities, or whether that person will marry one partner or many. The study of culture is fascinating because it often highlights differences, and reminds us that "our way" isn't always the only way.

But cross-cultural research has also taught us that humans the world over have some common ways of thinking and behaving around one another. The evolutionary perspective has helped us understand why there are similarities not only across human cultures, but even across different species. Initial forays into evolutionary psychology emphasized the darker side of human nature—"selfish genes" driving aggression, sexuality, and the battle between the sexes. But evolutionary analyses have revealed that our ancestors survived not just by selfish competition but also by positive behaviors: forming friendships, cooperating with other members of their groups, and forging loving family bonds.

It has become clear that these various perspectives are not "alternatives" to one another. Instead, they work together to enable a fuller understanding of the social world. As long-term students of cognition, culture, and evolutionary psychology, we have woven these threads together into the unique interactionist tapestry of this book. In this edition, we emphasize how social psychology is an important bridge discipline, connecting different areas of psychology (such as neuroscience, developmental, and clinical psychology) as well as other behavioral sciences (such as anthropology, economics, political science, and zoology).

What's New in the Sixth Edition?

1. Videos to accompany the opening mysteries. In this edition, David Lundberg Kenrick has lent his film production talents to developing a short animated video at the beginning of each chapter, in which the text authors introduce the mysteries of social life we will try to unravel in the chapter. Chapter 1 begins with the story of a formerly destitute single mom who, once her luck turned around, began giving away millions and millions of her hard-earned dollars. The question of why some people hoard their wealth, while others become generous philanthropists, connects to a fascinating series of studies of social psychologist Elizabeth Dunn and her colleagues, on the psychological benefits of giving to others. J.K. Rowling is the formerly destitute single mom in this story, and her case also helps raise questions about the relative influences of social learning, culture, cognition, and biology on our social decisions. Throughout the book, we introduce other mysteries of social behavior, in the stories of people as diverse as Martin Luther King, the Dalai Lama, and Charles Manson, in each case, to introduce questions that have been addressed by scientific research in social psychology.

2. Original research videos. Social psychologists not only probe into some of the most fascinating mysteries of social life, but they do so with scientific methods that are, in themselves, quite fascinating. For this edition, we also introduce researchers from around the world, who briefly describe one of the questions they were able to answer with their research. For example, to accompany the first chapter's opening mystery, Liz Dunn from the University of British Columbia describes her work on the benefits of giving money away, including some fascinating new cross-cultural and developmental twists on the topic. In the chapter on groups, Mark Van Vugt from VU Amsterdam describes his work on leadership, explaining how, contrary to stereotypes, people are much more likely to choose female leaders over males under the right circumstances. In the chapter on social dilemmas, Texas Christian University's Sarah Hill describes some fascinating research demonstrating how economic factors can influence White people's tendencies to perceive a "mixed-race" person as either Black or White. And for the chapter on self-presentation, University of Queensland's Bill Von Hippel describes some research he conducted in a skateboard park, demonstrating how the mere presence of a beautiful young woman boosted male skateboarders' testosterone levels, which in turn led them to literally risk their necks doing more dangerous tricks.

3. *Learning Objectives.* Each major section of every chapter begins with a set of explicit learning objectives that serve as road-maps to focus the reader on the central concepts in upcoming sections.

4. *Quick Quiz* Self-Tests. Following each major section, we present a short series of multiple-choice questions, to give you a chance to check your understanding of the material and practice for exams.

5. New and expanded coverage. There are a wide range of new and expanded topics covered in this edition, including many new findings linking social psychology, culture, and neuroscience. In Chapter 7, for example, we present new findings suggesting that your brain responds differently to your wins versus those of your friends, unless your culture encourages you to think about yourself as part of a collective. Many other new findings build bridges between social psychology and other disciplines, such as findings showing that you respond very differently to economic losses when you are in mating-motivated frame of mind (Chapter 14). In fact, almost three hundred new references have been added to the sixth edition, the majority of which come from new research papers published in 2011 or later.

The Structure of Each Chapter

After introducing social psychology (Chapter 1) and taking a closer look at the person and the social situation (Chapter 2), we organize the remaining chapters around a common structure:

1. The Mystery

Each chapter begins with an account of a baffling pattern of human behavior—an incident or a set of incidents that seems beyond understanding. For example:

- Why did the beautiful and talented artist Frida Kahlo fall for the much older, and much less attractive, Diego Rivera, and then tolerate his numerous extramarital affairs?

- What forces could persuade a young man to sign a confession saying he'd killed his own mother, when later evidence suggested he could not possibly have done it?

- How did a Black civil rights advocate and a member of the Ku Klux Klan turn around and become friends with one another?

Later, as the chapter progresses, we introduce general principles of human behavior that, when put together properly, resolve the mystery. These mysteries are more than simple devices for engaging readers' interest. They are designed to convey something basic about how we approach the text material: Our approach is heavily research based, and research is akin to good detective work. Researchers, like detectives,

begin their search with an interesting or perplexing question, then examine clues, gather evidence, test hypotheses, eliminate alternatives and—if things fall into place—uncover the right answer. To mine these instructive parallels, we return often in the text to the concept of researcher-as-detective.

2. The Goals

Next we introduce readers to the set of goals underlying the behavior covered in the chapter, by asking "What purposes does this behavior (e.g., aggression or helping or conformity) serve for an individual?" and "Which factors lead an individual to use this behavior to achieve those goals?" Taking each goal of the set in turn, we consider factors in the person, in the situation, and in their interaction:

PERSON **The person.** Here, we present research showing which factors inside the individual trigger each particular goal. So, which traits motivate people to seek social approval through conformity? Which moods influence people to think deeply in order to understand themselves and others more accurately?

SITUATION **The situation.** Here, we consider evidence of situational factors that trigger each goal. How do personal threats engage self-protective prejudices? How do cultural norms influence the desire to seek sexual gratification through casual relationships? How does time pressure affect the inclination to think deeply before deciding what a stranger's personality is like?

INTERACTION **The person–situation interaction.** In this section, we present data demonstrating how personal and situational factors interact. Social psychologists are used to thinking about how people with different attitudes, expectations, and traits act differently in the same situation. But interactions are much richer than this: People choose their life situations, change situations they do not like, and are themselves rejected from some situations and changed by others. For example, lonely people sometimes act in needy ways that alienate others. In turn, others may avoid them and stop inviting them to social events, further enhancing their inner feelings of social isolation. By systematically showing students the importance of person–situation interactions, we hope to illustrate the limitations of the usual single-factor explanations—such as putting all the blame for aggression or blind obedience on the person or the converse error of viewing people as interchangeable pawns on a giant interpersonal chess board.

3. Special Features

Several of social psychology's messages and themes are highlighted in each chapter's special features:

Investigation. Building on our metaphor of social psychologist as detective, we invite students to connect themselves to the concepts in the "Investigation" feature. These questions encourage students to enter an investigation, either by piecing together the concepts and findings in the book with what they know about themselves or other people, or by using their own powers of logical analysis to critically analyze the evidence just covered. "Investigation" questions are designed not only to emphasize the relevance of social psychology to students' lives but also to help students study more effectively. Research on learning and memory shows we learn material more easily if we connect it to ourselves, think critically about it, and actively rehearse what we've just read.

INVESTIGATION

Consider two people you know whose cultural backgrounds differ from yours (another country, a different social class, ethnicity, or religion). In what ways do the norms of your different cultures lead you to behave differently in your interactions with each other?

Bridging Theory and Application. Here, we discuss how a specific experimental finding or body of findings relates to real-world issues—how research insights can be used to create less-prejudiced classrooms, help married couples stay together, or reduce violence.

Bridging Function and Dysfunction. Psychology students are fascinated by disordered behavior. In this feature, we tap that fascination to demonstrate broader principles. We examine how normally healthy social behaviors can, if taken too far, produce unhealthy consequences—for example, how the usually adaptive tendency to develop strong bonds between lovers can underlie obsessive relationships.

4. Revisiting the Mystery

The final section of each chapter returns to the opening mystery to help students pull together the various research findings discussed in the chapter. For example, we return to the puzzle of the boy who falsely confessed to a heinous crime and the relationship between Frida Kahlo and Diego Rivera, in light of research findings on persuasion and relationships (and we pull together the new clues we revealed in the chapter). In this way, we hope not only to capitalize on curiosity but also to tap another general principle of learning and memory—the principle that students recall more facts when they are connected to vivid cases.

5. Chapter Summary

The Chapter Summary feature at the end of each chapter includes a number of useful review tools for students: a chart that revisits how factors in the person, in the situation, and in their interaction relate to the chapter's goals (in Chapters 3–14); and a numbered summary of text content organized by A-head.

Weaving Methods and Applications into the Story

A glance at the table of contents shows that we have included no separate applications chapters on such topics as health, business, or the law. This is not because of any lack of regard for their importance within social psychology. Quite the reverse. Rather than giving these topics a tagged-on, stand-alone status in the book, we want to emphasize their frequent connections to the mainstream topics of the field. Consequently, we point out these links as they occur naturally within the text discussion, and (when special elaboration is appropriate) in the *Bridging Theory and Application* features found in the chapters. In this way, we hope to convey to students the inherent relationship between the principles of social psychology and the behaviors of people in workplaces, schoolrooms, and other applied settings.

For similar reasons, there is no isolated chapter or appendix on methodology. Although we do expose the reader to the major methodological issues of social psychological research in Chapter 1, we blend the discussion of methods with the puzzling research questions that inspire those methods, so the student learns the details of the methods that can answer them (for example, we introduce the idea of meta-analysis alongside the many studies of media influences on aggression). Additionally, the student learns to appreciate that one cannot be fully confident in the results of a study without understanding how those results were obtained.

Last, and once again reflecting our emphasis on integration, the chapters are not grouped and divided into separate sections, such as social knowing, social influence, and social relationships. Instead, the chapter topics flow in a continuum from phenomena occurring primarily inside the individual to those occurring primarily outside. However, there is no imperative to this ordering and, with the exception of the first and last chapters, instructors may sequence the chapters to fit their own preferences without harm to student understanding.

One reason for this adaptability is that the integration we have proposed does not depend on any lock-step, building-block progress through the course material. Rather, that integration comes from a pair of concepts, *goals* and the *person–situation interaction*, that apply generally to the topics of the course. Although the goals may not be the same, the ways that goals function—the mechanisms by which they develop and operate—are similar in the case of aggression or attraction or self-presentation or any of the social behaviors we consider. And, although the particular factors may differ depending on the behavior under study, understanding how factors in the person interact with factors in the situation provides the most informed insights into the causes of everyday social behaviors—whatever the behaviors, in whichever order they are considered. Our two central concepts, then, allow an organization that we think is both integrative and flexible.

In the pages that follow, readers will find everyday social behaviors depicted as something more tightly woven and interconnected than a three-ring circus. Beyond being "the greatest *show* on earth," social psychology may well be the greatest *story*—breathtaking, coherent, and, most of all, instructive. We hope you will agree.

REVEL™

REVEL™ is Pearson's newest way of delivering our respected content. Fully digital and highly engaging, REVEL offers an immersive learning experience designed for the way today's students read, think, and learn. Enlivening course content with media interactives and assessments, REVEL empowers educators to increase engagement with the course, and to better connect with students.

For more information, please contact your local Pearson representative or visit www.pearsonhighered.com/revel.

For the Instructor

Download Instructor Resources at the Instructor's Resource Center

Register or log in to the Instructor Resource Center to download supplements from our online catalog. Go to http://www.pearsonhighered.com/educator.

For technical support for any of your Pearson products, you and your students can contact http://247.pearsoned.com.

Instructor's Resource Manual (ISBN 0133984974)

This rich collection of teaching materials can be used by first-time or experienced teachers to enrich class presentations. For each chapter of the text, the instructor's manual includes an At-a-Glance Grid with detailed pedagogical information linking chapter topics to other available resources, learning objectives targeting specific goals for each chapter, a comprehensive chapter overview, a list of key terms, detailed lecture outlines, lecture and discussion suggestions, classroom learning activities, and other detailed pedagogical information. In addition, this manual includes a preface and a sample syllabus. Available for download on the Instructor's Resource Center at www.pearsonhighered.com.

Test Bank (ISBN 0133984982)

Our comprehensive test bank contains over 100 challenging items per chapter, in multiple-choice, true/false, and essay format. Each question is correlated to a learning objective, skill level, and a difficulty rating to allow customization of the assessment materials to best fit your needs. Available for download on the Instructor's Resource Center at www.pearsonhighered.com.

MyTest Test Bank (ISBN 0133972720)

This powerful assessment-generation program helps instructors easily create and print quizzes and exams. Questions and tests can be authored online, allowing instructors ultimate flexibility and the ability to efficiently manage assessments anytime, anywhere. For more information, go to www.PearsonMyTest.com.

PowerPoint Presentation (0133984958)

Each chapter's PowerPoint presentation contains key points covered in the textbook, images from the textbook, and questions to provoke effective classroom discussion and add life to lectures. Available for download on the Instructor's Resource Center at www.pearsonhighered.com.

MyPsychLab™ (ISBN 0133972526)

Available at www.mypsychlab.com, MyPsychLab™ is an online homework, tutorial, and assessment program that truly engages students in learning. It helps students better prepare for class, quizzes, and exams—resulting in better performance in the course. It provides educators a dynamic set of tools for gauging individual and class performance:

- *Customizable.* MyPsychLab is customizable. Instructors choose what students' course looks like. Homework, applications, and more can easily be turned on and off.

- *Blackboard Single Sign-On.* MyPsychLab can be used by itself or linked to any course management system. Blackboard single sign-on provides deep linking to all new MyPsychLab resources.

- *Pearson eText and Chapter Audio.* Like the printed text, students can highlight relevant passages and add notes. The Pearson eText can be accessed through laptops, iPads, and tablets. Download the free Pearson eText app to use on tablets. Students can also listen to their text with the Audio eText.

- *Assignment Calendar.* A drag and drop assignment calendar makes assigning and completing work easy.

Acknowledgments

We would like to acknowledge the many reviewers who read this sixth edition, as well as those who examined earlier editions. We greatly appreciate their thoughtful feedback.

Sixth Edition Reviewers

Linda Bastone, Purchase College, SUNY
Kiersten Baughman, University of Oklahoma
Gordon Bear, Ramapo College of New Jersey
James Benjamin, University of Arkansas-Fort Smith
Alex Czopp, Western Washington University

Michele Delucia, Gateway Community College
Heidi English, College of the Siskiyous
Stacy Fambro, Wesleyan University
Carey Fitzgerald, Oakland University
Omri Gillath, University of Kansas
Sheldon Helms, Ohlone College
Alishia Huntoon, Oregon Institute of Technology
Jill Lorenzi, Virginia Tech
Julie Luker, The College of St. Scholastica
Katy Neidhardt, Cuesta Community College
Karyn Plumm, University of North Dakota
Joanna Schug, College of William & Mary
Dylan Selterman, University of Maryland, College Park
Heather Terrell, University of North Dakota
Anre Venter, University of Notre Dame
Edward Witt, Michigan State University

Previous Edition Reviewers and Survey Respondents

Jeffrey M. Adams, High Point University; William Adler, Colin County Community College; David W. Alfano, Community College of Rhode Island; Scott T. Allison, University of Richmond; Michael L. Atkinson, University of Western Ontario; Anita P. Barbee, University of Louisville; Jennifer Barber, University of Michigan; John Bargh, Yale University; Bruce Bartholow, University of North Carolina, Chapel Hill; Deborah Belle, Boston University; Roy Baumeister, Case Western Reserve University; Gordon Bear, Ramapo College; Susan E. Beers, Sweet Briar College; Frank Bernieri, University of Toledo; John Bickford, University of Massachusetts, Amherst; Victor L. Bissonnette, Southeastern Louisiana University; Melinda Blackman, California State University–Fullerton; Galen Bodenhausen, Northwestern University; Martin Bolt, Calvin College; Nyla Branscombe, University of Kansas; Martin Bourgeois, University of Wyoming; Fred B. Bryant, Loyola University Chicago; Jeff Bryson, San Diego State University; Cheri Budzynski, Heidelberg College; Brad J. Bushman, Iowa State University; Delia Cioffi, Dartmouth College; Lisa N. Coates-Shrider, McMurry University; Diana Cordova, Yale University; Traci Craig, University of Idaho; Robert Cramer, California State University, San Bernadino; Christian Crandall, University of Kansas; Michael Crow, Southern Methodist University; Cynthia Crown, Xavier University; Virginia Cylke, Sweet Briar College; Deborah Davis, University of Nevada-Reno; Joseph Davis, San Diego State University; Mark H. Davis, Eckerd College; Carl Denti, Dutchess Community College; Bella DePaulo, University of California-Santa Barbara; Virginia DeRoma, The Citadel; Patricia Devine, University of Wisconsin, Madison; Joan DiGiovanni, Western New England College; Kenneth I. Dion, University of Toronto; William Dragon, Cornell College; Steve Duck, University of Iowa; Michael G. Dudley,

Southern Illinois University, Edwardsville; Joshua Duntley, Florida Institute of Technology; Nancy F. Dye, Humboldt State University; Kelli England, Virginia Polytechnic Institute; Victoria Esses, University of Western Ontario; Robert Fern, Mesa Community College; Joseph R. Ferrari, DePaul University; Phillip Finney, Southeast Missouri State University; Barry Friedman, Lebanon Valley College; Robert W. Fuhrman, University of Texas—San Antonio; Grace Galliano, Kennesaw State College; Stella Garcia, University of Texas—San Antonio; Bill Garris, Cumberland College; Bryan Gibson, Central Michigan University; Noah Goldstein, Arizona State University; Sheldon W. Helms, Ohlone College; Marti Hope Gonzales, University of Minnesota; Kenneth J. Good, Minnesota State University, Mankato; Mark Hartlaub, Texas A & M University at Corpus Christi; John Harvey, University of Iowa; Cindy Hazan, Cornell University; Edward Hirt, Indiana University; David Houston, University of Memphis; Lisa Hollis-Sawyer, Northeastern Illinois University; Robert Hymes, University of Michigan—Dearborn; Blair Johnson, University of Connecticut; Heide Island, University of Central Arkansas; Craig A. Johnson, Hofstra University; Mike Jordan, Francis Marion University; Pat Kalata, Burlington County College; Martin Kaplan, Northern Illinois University; Rich Keefe, Scottsdale Community College; Suzanne Keiffer, University of Houston; Bruce Kelly, Lindenwood University; Cyndi Kernahan, University of Wisconsin; Michael Kitchens, Lebanon Valley College; Linda Kline, California State University–Chico; Roger J. Kreuz, The University of Memphis; Joachim Krueger, Brown University; Robin Kowalski, Clemson University; Catherine T. Kwantes, Eastern Michigan University; Sherri Lantinga, Dordt College; Mark Leary, Wake Forest University; Michael R. Leippe, St. Louis University; Richard Leo, University of California at Irvine; Heather Lench, Texas A&M University; Angela Lipsitz, Northern Kentucky University; Chris Loersch, Ohio State University; Keith Maddox, Tufts University; Paul Magro, Saint Joseph's College; Heike I. M. Mahler, California State University at San Marcos; Robyn Mallett, University of Virginia; Alan Marks, Morehouse College; David Marx, San Diego State University; Rene Martin, University of Iowa; Pam McAuslan, University of Michigan–Dearborn; Larry Messé, Michigan State University; Sarah A. Meyers, Simpson College; Rowland Miller, Sam Houston State University; Jeffrey Scott Mio, California State Polytechnic University, Pomona; Paul A. Mongeau, Miami University; Paul Nail, Southwestern Oklahoma State University; Roderick Neal, Bluefield State College; Joseph S. Neuschab, Roger Williams University; Cindy Nordstrom, Southern Illinois University, Edwardsville; Carol K. Oyster, University of Wisconsin at La Crosse; Ernest Park, Michigan State University; Miles L. Patterson,

University of Missouri—St. Louis; Lou Penner, University of South Florida; Alison Pfent, Ohio State University; Lawrence Pervin, Rutgers University; Jacqueline Pope-Tarrence, Western Kentucky University; Felicia Pratto, University of Connecticut; Diane Quinn, University of Connecticut; Brandon Randolph-Seng, Texas Tech University; Cynthia K. S. Reed, Tarrant County College; Pamela Regan, California State University-Los Angeles; Robert Reeves, Augusta State University; Pamela Regan, California State University, Los Angeles; John W. Reich, Arizona State University; Harry Reis, University of Rochester; Nancy Rhodes, Texas A & M University; Robert Ridge, Brigham Young University; Robert Riedel, Lynn University; James Roney, University of California-Santa Barbara; Martin Rosenman, Morehouse College; Alexander Rothman, University of Minnesota; Dan Sachau, Minnesota State University, Mankato; Brad Sagarin, Northern Illinois State University; Catherine Salmon, Redlands University (CA); Eric Sambolec, Michigan State University; Mark Schaller, University of British Columbia; Connie Schick, Bloomsburg University, Pennsylvania; P. Wesley Schultz, California State University, San Marcos; Bill Scott, Oklahoma State University; Chris Segrin, University of Kansas; Charles F. Seidez, Mansfield University; Todd K. Shackelford, Florida Atlantic University; James Shepperd, University of Florida; Robert Short, Arizona State University; Laura S. Sidorowicz, Nassau Community College; Jeff Simpson, Texas A & M University; Jessi Smith, Ohio State University; Jana Spain, High Point University; Kari Terzino, Iowa State University; Dianne Tice, Case Western Reserve University; David M. Tom, Columbus State Community College; Timothy P. Tomczak, Genesee Community College; David Trafimow, New Mexico State University; Stephen Trotter, Tennessee State University; Robin Vallacher, Florida Atlantic University; Paul van Lange, Free University (Amsterdam); James Clay Vaughn, Western Michigan University; Anre Venter, University of Notre Dame; Terri Vescio, Pennsylvania State University; Cheri Vetter, Glendale Community College; T. Joel Wade, Bucknell University; Karly Way-Schramm, Yavapi College; Ann Weber, University of North Carolina—Asheville; Anne Weiher, University of Colorado; James Whyte, Grandview College; David Wilder, Rutgers University; Kevin Woller, Rogers State University; Wilhelmina Wosinska, Arizona State University; Margaret Zimmerman, Virginia Wesleyan College; and Anthony Zoccolillo, DeVry College of Technology.

Our home in the psychology department at Arizona State University is intellectually stimulating and interpersonally collegial, for which we have always been grateful. We wish to thank, in particular, our colleagues and students who commented on early drafts of this book: Terrilee Asher, Dan Barrett, Adam Cohen, Linda Demaine, Nancy Eisenberg, Rosanna Guadagno, Sara Gutierres, Carol Luce, Greg Neidert, John Reich, Kelton Rhoads, Ed Sadalla, Brad Sagarin, Delia Saenz, Melanie Trost, and Wilhemina Wosinska. The last four editions also profited greatly from the help of Andy Delton, Andreana Kenrick (no relation), Jean Luce, Andy Menzel, Megan Ringel, Kristopher Smith, and Josh Tybur. Ariana Ehuan and Kelly Morford provided invaluable assistance in preparing the animations for the new video series for the 6th edition. Finally, Carol Luce and Jean Luce provided editorial assistance, advice, and social support to the first author.

We would especially like to thank the students in our social psychology classes for providing invaluable insights from the perspective of the readers that most matter—undergraduate students.

In writing this book, we have searched for interesting real-world events and stories to help illustrate the concepts of social psychology. Several people were able to help us go beyond what was already available in published books and articles, and we greatly appreciate their efforts: Dr. Avrum Bluming, Lenell Geter, Steven Hassan, Bradley Henry, Cindy Jackson, Darlene and Bob Krueger, Eric Saul, and Rabbi Marvin Tokayer.

Turning a set of ideas into a textbook is a long, complex task, and Jim Anker was there at the beginning to offer great advice. Much thanks.

About the Authors

For over ten years, Douglas Kenrick, Steven Neuberg, and Robert Cialdini met weekly over enchiladas, shwarma, or pasta to design experiments and debate the big issues in social psychology. Over time, they came to realize that they agreed on several important things and that these ideas could form the foundation of an integrative and exciting social psychology textbook. The authors each have years of experience teaching social psychology to undergraduate and graduate students, in environments ranging from small private colleges to large public universities. They have published research in the field's most prestigious journals on a wide range of topics, including social cognition, self-presentation, persuasion and social influence, friendship and romance, helping, aggression, and prejudice and stereotyping. Each is independently recognized for integrative research that, when combined, inspires the two major themes of the book. This textbook brings together their many teaching and research interests.

Douglas T. Kenrick is a professor at Arizona State University. He received his B.A. from Dowling College and his Ph.D. from Arizona State University. He taught at Montana State University for four years before returning to ASU. His research has been published in a number of prestigious outlets, including *Psychological Review, Behavioral and Brain Sciences, American Psychologist, Handbook of Social Psychology, Journal of Personality and Social Psychology, Current Directions in Psychological Science, Perspectives on Psychological Science*, and *Personality and Social Psychology Review*. He is author of the 2011 book: *Sex, Murder, and the Meaning of Life: A psychologist investigates how evolution, cognition, and complexity are revolutionizing our view of human nature*, and in 2013, with Vlad Griskevicius, he wrote *The Rational Animal: How evolution made us smarter than we think*. He has taught a graduate course on teaching psychology, and he thoroughly enjoys teaching undergraduate sections of social psychology, for which he has won several teaching awards.

Steven L. Neuberg is Foundation Professor of Psychology at Arizona State University. He received his undergraduate degree from Cornell University and his graduate degrees from Carnegie-Mellon University. He spent a postdoctoral year at the University of Waterloo in Canada and has since taught at ASU. Neuberg's research has been published in outlets such as *Advances in Experimental Social Psychology, Journal of Personality and Social Psychology, Psychological Science, Handbook of Social Psychology*, and *Perspectives on Psychological Science*, and has been supported by the National Institute of Mental Health and the National Science Foundation. He has received a half dozen teaching honors, including his college's Outstanding Teaching Award and the ASU Honors College Outstanding Honors Disciplinary Faculty Award. He has served on federal grant review panels and as associate editor of the *Journal of Experimental Social Psychology* and teaches a graduate course on teaching social psychology.

Robert B. Cialdini is Regents' Professor Emeritus at Arizona State University, where he has also been named Graduate Distinguished Professor. He received his undergraduate degree from the University of Wisconsin and his graduate degrees from the University of North Carolina. He is a past president of the *Society of Personality and Social Psychology* and has received the Society's award for *Distinguished Scientific Contributions*. His research has appeared in numerous publications, including *Handbook of Social Psychology, Advances in Experimental Social Psychology*, and *Journal of Personality and Social Psychology*. His book, *Influence: Science and Practice*, has sold over 2 million copies and has appeared in 28 languages.

Social Psychology

Chapter 1

Introduction to Social Psychology

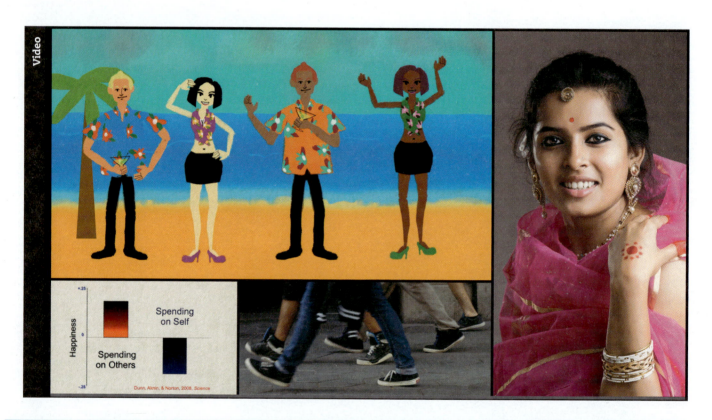

Learning Objectives

LO 1.1 Define social psychology and explain why it relies on scientific description and theory.

LO 1.2 Explain why social psychology is considered a bridge discipline.

LO 1.3 Summarize the four major theoretical perspectives of social psychology.

LO 1.4 Discuss how the four major perspectives work together to explain human social behavior.

LO 1.5 Describe the five fundamental motives behind goal-oriented social behavior.

LO 1.6 Explain what is meant by the person, the situation, and person–situation interactions.

LO 1.7 List the strengths and weaknesses of each of the different descriptive methods (e.g., naturalistic observation, case study) and experimental methods, and explain why researchers find value in combining them.

LO 1.8 Explain why it is difficult to infer causality from correlation.

LO 1.9 Discuss some of the ethical risks that social psychologists face.

LO 1.10 Discuss the links between social psychology and other disciplines of psychology.

LO 1.11 Explain why an understanding of social psychology is valuable to disciplines outside of psychology.

The Mysteries of Social Life

A few years after graduating from college, things were not going well for Joyce R. As she describes it:

> I had failed on an epic scale. An exceptionally short-lived marriage had imploded, and I was jobless, a lone parent, and as poor as it is possible to be in modern Britain, without being homeless. The fears that my parents had had for me, and that I had had for myself, had both come to pass, and by every usual standard, I was the biggest failure I knew.

In the face of all this personal and economic failure, many people might have stopped trying. But Joyce didn't passively accept her fate. Besides struggling to put bread on the table for her young daughter, she worked long hours into the night, using her knowledge of classic literature, to write a children's novel.

Writing a novel is not a very practical formula for economic success. There are approximately 493,000 books published in English every year, and many more that are written but never find a publisher. In fact, Joyce's novel seemed to be just another one of her life's failures: It was rejected by 12 publishers.

But an editor at the thirteenth publishing house accepted the book and offered her a £1,500 advance as well as some practical advice: He gently informed her that she was not likely to make any money writing children's books and suggested that she instead get a day job (Blais, 2005). But Joyce's book defied the unfavorable odds and did quite well in the bookstores. Joyce, rather than taking a day job, wrote a series of follow-up books, which also sold handsomely. Indeed, in a few short years the formerly poverty-stricken single mom was listed on *Fortune* magazine's list of billionaires.

You may know Joyce as J.K. Rowling, author of the Harry Potter series.

It might not have been surprising if Ms. Rowling, having experienced poverty, had hoarded her hard-earned cash. Many people who start making a lot of money are suddenly shocked at how many dollars they pay in taxes and begin to seek tax shelters, or to consider migrating to a place with lower taxes. But not J.K. Rowling. Not only did she proudly pay her taxes, she began giving large portions of the rest of her money away. In just one single contribution, she once wrote a check for $15,000,000. And there were many, many more such checks. Indeed, she was giving away so much that she was removed from *Fortune* magazine's list of billionaires.

After her great financial success, Ms. Rowling was invited to give a speech to the graduates of Harvard University, amongst whom were many future millionaires and world leaders. She implored them to use their intelligence, capacity for hard work, and education to work not just for themselves, but to improve the plight of the thousands and millions of powerless people suffering throughout the world.

J.K. Rowling's story raises a number of interesting mysteries. One view of human nature foundational to many of the social sciences is that our minds are designed to be selfish—to make decisions that serve our own self-interest. If so, why are some people, like J.K. Rowling, so generous with their money and so concerned about the welfare of others?

In this book we will explore not only broad questions about human nature, but also everyday mysteries about love and hatred, generosity and aggression, and heroism and betrayal. Why do we react generously and lovingly toward some of the people we meet (and in some situations), but defensively or aggressively toward others? What are the roots of romance versus parental love? What causes some marriages, like J.K. Rowling's, to implode after a few months, and others to flourish for a lifetime? How can we get our coworkers to cooperate with us? Why do some people make better leaders? How are our reactions to other people affected by our cultural background, by our early experiences, by our sex, and by neurochemical events in our brains?

Most of us try to solve mysteries like these in our minds, by devouring news stories and books and chatting with friends about our feelings and opinions. Social psychologists go a step further in their detective work; they apply the systematic methods of scientific inquiry.

What Is Social Psychology?

LO 1.1   Define social psychology and explain why it relies on scientific description and theory.

LO 1.2   Explain why social psychology is considered a bridge discipline.

Social psychology is the scientific study of how people's thoughts, feelings, and behaviors are influenced by other people. What does it mean, though, to say that social psychology is "scientific"?

Describing and Explaining Social Behavior

We can divide the tasks of a scientific social psychology into two general categories: *description* and *explanation*. As a first step toward a scientific account of any phenomenon (bird migrations, earthquakes, or intertribal warfare), we need an objective and reliable description. Part of what scientists do is to develop reliable and valid methods to help them avoid careless or biased descriptions.

Careful description is a first step, but it is not, in itself, enough to satisfy scientific curiosity. Social psychologists also seek to explain *why* people influence one another in the ways they do. A good scientific explanation can connect many thousands of unconnected observations into an interconnected, coherent, and meaningful pattern. The philosopher Jules Henri Poincaré compared scientific facts to the stones used to build a house, but he also observed that without a theory those facts are merely a pile of stones, rather than a well-formed house. Scientific explanations that connect and organize existing observations are called **theories**.

In addition to organizing what we already know, scientific theories give us hints about where to look next. What causes some people, like J.K. Rowling, to be especially

Social psychology The scientific study of how people's thoughts, feelings, and behaviors are influenced by other people.

Theory Scientific explanation that connects and organizes existing observations and suggests fruitful paths for future research.

likely to extend help, and others to be more selfish? Without a good theory, we would not know where to start searching for an answer. Maybe an inclination to help others is caused by the arrangement of the planets under which altruists are born or by something in the water they drank as children. Social psychological theories are more likely to suggest searching elsewhere for the causes of social behavior—in a person's interpretation of his or her immediate social environment, in his or her family background, in the broader culture, or in general predispositions humans share with baboons and other social animals. And, as we'll see, social psychologists have developed some intriguing research methods designed to sort out those different sources of influence.

Finally, scientific theories can help us make predictions about future events and control previously unmanageable phenomena. Scientific theories have led to the electric light bulb, the personal computer, the space shuttle, and the control of diseases such as smallpox. As we will see, social psychological theories have provided useful information about the roots of prejudice, kindness, and love; about why people join rioting mobs or religious cults; and about a host of other puzzling phenomena.

Social Psychology Is an Interdisciplinary Bridge

Psychologists aren't the only ones pondering the mysteries of human social behavior. Anthropologists puzzle over why people in some societies have social customs that would seem radically inappropriate in others (in Chapter 8, we will talk about societies in which one woman marries multiple men, for example). Evolutionary biologists search for common patterns linking human social behavior with the behaviors of chimpanzees, hyenas, and indigo buntings (in Chapter 10, we will see that the hormone testosterone is similarly linked to aggression, and to sex roles, across a wide range of species). Political scientists and historians search for the determinants of warfare and intergroup conflicts, of the sort we will explore in Chapters 11 and 13. And economists search for the roots of people's decisions about whether to contribute to their group's welfare, or hoard their resources to themselves, topics we will investigate in Chapters 9 and 13.

How do the perspectives of all these disciplines fit together into a bigger picture? How does what you are learning in your biology class link up with what you're learning in your anthropology class? How do the factoids of history connect with recent discoveries in neuroscience? What are the links between geography, economics, and marriage patterns? It turns out all these things are profoundly connected, and in ways that affect not only the course of your personal life but also the course of world affairs and major social problems. Evolutionary biology, neurochemistry, history, culture, and geography, all have important implications for how people socially interact with one another; those social interactions, in turn, affect which moral and religious sentiments are enforced as laws, how children are educated, and even how medical doctors treat their patients.

Because all of these influences converge to influence social behavior, social psychologists consider social behavior at many different levels of analysis. For example, a recent series of studies of societies around the world found that cultural differences in friendliness and sociability are linked to geographic variations in disease prevalence—where there is more disease, people have traits that lead them to avoid contact with others (Murray et al., 2011; Schaller & Park, 2011). Other studies we'll discuss have examined how our relationships with other people can be affected by historical factors, hormone levels, phase of the menstrual cycle, and brain activity, and how all these influences can, in turn, affect our physical and mental health, as well as our economic behavior and political beliefs (e.g., Apicella et al., 2008; Cantú et al., 2014; Gelfand et al., 2011; Little et al., 2008; Uskul, Kitayama, & Nisbett, 2008; Varnum et al., 2014). Thus, social psychology is in many ways the ultimate bridge discipline. Throughout this text, we will encounter many such interdisciplinary bridges, often considering findings that reflect culture, evolutionary biology, neuroscience, and that connect with applied disciplines from business to law to medicine.

Quick Quiz

1 Social psychology is the scientific study of:
  - a. How people's reactions to others develop over the life cycle.
  - b. How people's thoughts, feelings, and behaviors are influenced by other people.
  - c. How societal forces contribute to the development of mental illness.
  - d. How the brain influences the development of social reactions.

2 Which of the following best describes scientific theories?
  - a. Theories are based on hypothetical conjecture as opposed to established evidence.
  - b. Theories explain the cause of specific behaviors.
  - c. Theories are a collection of facts.
  - d. Theories are scientific explanations that connect and organize existing observations.

3 To say that social psychology is the ultimate bridge discipline means that the field:
  - a. Connects laboratory findings with clinical applications.
  - b. Bridges careful description with theoretical explanation.
  - c. Links sociology and psychology.
  - d. Connects multiple perspectives on social behavior, from biology, anthropology, economics, and other disciplines.

Major Theoretical Perspectives of Social Psychology

LO 1.3 Summarize the four major theoretical perspectives of social psychology.

LO 1.4 Discuss how the four major perspectives work together to explain human social behavior.

Social psychological theories have been influenced by intellectual developments ranging from the discovery of DNA to the emergence of artificial intelligence. Four major perspectives (or families of theories) have dominated the field: sociocultural, evolutionary, social learning, and social cognitive.

The Sociocultural Perspective

The year 1908 saw the publication of the first two major textbooks titled *Social Psychology*. One of these was written by sociologist Edward Alsworth Ross. Ross argued that the wellsprings of social behavior reside not in the individual but in the social group. He argued that people were carried along on "social currents," such as "the spread of a lynching spirit through a crowd . . . [or] an epidemic of religious emotion" (Ross, 1908, 1–2). Ross analyzed incidents such as the Dutch tulip bulb craze of 1634, in which people sold their houses and lands to buy flower roots that cost more than their weight in gold, but that instantly became worthless when the craze stopped. To explain these crazes, Ross looked at the group as a whole rather than at the psyche of the individual group member. He viewed crazes and fads as products of "mob mind . . . that irrational unanimity of interest, feeling, opinion, or deed in a body of communicating individuals, which results from suggestion and imitation" (Ross, 1908, 65).

Like Ross, other sociologically based theorists emphasized larger social groupings, from neighborhood gangs to ethnic groups and political parties (e.g., Sumner, 1906). That emphasis continues in the modern **sociocultural perspective**—the view that a person's prejudices, preferences, and political persuasions are affected by factors that work at the level of the group, factors such as nationality, social class, and current historical trends (Gelfand et al., 2014; Heine, 2010). For example, compared to her working-class Irish grandmother, a modern-day Manhattan executive probably has different attitudes about premarital sex and women's roles in business (Roberts & Helson, 1997). Sociocultural theorists focus on the central importance of **social norms**, or rules about appropriate behavior, such as *Don't eat with your hands, Don't wear shorts*

Sociocultural perspective The theoretical viewpoint that searches for the causes of social behavior in influences from larger social groups.

Social norm A rule or expectation for appropriate social behavior.

to a wedding, and so on. At the center of this perspective is the concept of **culture**, which we can broadly define as a set of beliefs, customs, habits, and languages shared by the people living in a particular time and place. People in Italy and France regard it as appropriate to kiss acquaintances on both cheeks when they meet in public, a custom that can make a visiting American feel awkward, who might be more comfortable with a high five.

Culture includes all the human-engineered features of the environment, from subjective features, such as rules of etiquette, to objective features, such as houses and clothing (Fiske, 2002; Triandis, 1994). The technological features of our culture can have powerful effects on our social behaviors, as evidenced in recent years in the phenomena of iPhones and social networking Internet sites—technologies that profoundly influence how and when people can communicate with one another (Crabb, 1996a, 1996b, 1999; Guadagno et al., 2008; McKenna & Bargh, 2000).

Each of us has been exposed to different cultural norms depending on our ethnicity, our socioeconomic status, the geographical region in which we were raised, and our religion (Cohen, 2009; Iyengar & Lepper, 1999; Johnson et al., 2013; Krauss et al., 2011; Sanchez-Burks, 2002). Someone who grew up poor in the Southern United States, for example, is more likely to listen to country and western music, whereas someone who grew up in an upper-middle-class city on the West Coast is more likely to listen to rock. The lyrics in these two types of music emphasize very different cultural values: Rock lyrics stress doing your own thing, going against the grain, and changing the world. Country lyrics emphasize adapting yourself to the world's challenges, being resilient, and maintaining your integrity (Snibbe & Markus, 2005). As another example, Asian Americans differ in some ways from European Americans, placing a relatively low value on self-expression, personal choice, and the inclination to "think out loud" (Kim, 2002; Kim & Sherman, 2007). As you will see, the study of groups, cultures, and social norms continues as a major thrust in social psychology (e.g., Adams, 2005; Alter & Kwan, 2009; Chen, 2008; Matsumato et al., 2008; Ross et al., 2005; Shiota et al., 2010). We will consider these sociocultural influences in every chapter of this text.

A psychologist adopting a sociocultural perspective might observe that as a college student J.K. Rowling kept company with left-wing coffeehouse intellectuals. In that subculture, social action is highly valued and individual greed is scorned. After college Rowling went to work for Amnesty International, an agency dedicated to social action and also peopled by liberal-minded intellectuals fighting to save the world's poor and downtrodden underdogs. Hoarding her wealth would have thus violated the norms of J.K. Rowling's social set, whereas giving it to needy others would have been considered highly appropriate.

INVESTIGATION

Consider two people you know whose cultural backgrounds differ from yours (another country, a different social class, ethnicity, or religion). In what ways do the norms of your different cultures lead you to behave differently in your interactions with each other?

The Evolutionary Perspective

There was another text called *Social Psychology* released in 1908, and that one was written by a British psychologist originally trained in biology. William McDougall took an **evolutionary perspective**, adopting the view that human social behaviors are rooted in physical and psychological predispositions that helped our ancestors survive and reproduce. McDougall followed Charles Darwin's (1873) suggestion that human social behaviors (such as smiling, sneering, and other emotional expressions) had evolved along with physical features (such as upright posture and grasping thumbs).

The central driving force of evolution is **natural selection**, the process whereby animals pass to their offspring those characteristics that help them survive and

Culture The beliefs, customs, habits, and languages shared by the people living in a particular time and place.

Evolutionary perspective A theoretical viewpoint that searches for the causes of social behavior in the physical and psychological predispositions that helped our ancestors survive and reproduce.

Natural selection The process by which characteristics that help animals survive and reproduce are passed on to their offspring.

Expressions of happiness across human cultures. In the first book on evolutionary psychology, Charles Darwin argued that some emotional expressions might be universal patterns of communication inherited from our ancestors.

reproduce. New characteristics that are well suited to particular environments—called **adaptations**—will come to replace characteristics that are less well suited to the demands and opportunities those environments present. Dolphins are mammals closely related to cows, but their legs evolved into fins because that shape is better suited to life under water. Darwin assumed that just as an animal's body is shaped by natural selection, so is an animal's brain.

Psychologists once assumed that evolution could only produce inflexible "instincts" that were "wired in" at birth and not much influenced by the environment. Most experts on evolution and behavior now understand that biological influences on humans and other animals are usually flexible and responsive to the environment (e.g., Gangestad et al., 2006; Kenrick & Gomez-Jacinto, 2014; O'Gorman et al., 2008; Robinson et al., 2008). Consider fear, for example. There is good evidence that fear is an evolved psychological reaction that helped our ancestors respond rapidly to threats such as poisonous insects, snakes, and other people who might pose a danger to them (Ohman, Lundqvist, & Esteves, 2001). Because it would exhaust our bodies to be on continuous high alert, the so-called fight-or-flight response (which makes us want to run or defend ourselves in frightening situations) is exquisitely sensitive to cues in a situation that suggest when we are and are not likely to be in danger (Cannon, 1929).

One team of researchers examined how this evolutionary perspective on fear might help us understand potentially volatile prejudices between different groups of people (Schaller, Park, & Mueller, 2003). The researchers asked white and Asian Canadian college students to rate their reactions to photographs of black men. Some of the students did the ratings in a brightly lit room; others were in a completely dark room. Students who viewed the world as a dangerous place were particularly prone to see the black men as threatening if they rated the photos in a dark room. Furthermore, these effects were stronger when the raters were men than when they were women. The researchers interpreted these data in terms of an evolutionary perspective on intergroup relationships (Kurzban & Leary, 2001; Navarrete et al., 2009; Sidanius & Pratto, 1998). From this viewpoint it might have been useful to our ancestors to be especially fearful of strangers under certain circumstances. The possibility of dangerous conflict between two different groups of men who encountered one another after dark would have led to wariness on the part of men who found themselves in this type of situation. The researchers note that in modern multicultural societies the tendency to respond with these primitive self-protective reactions can lead to adverse consequences, including bullying, gang warfare, and intergroup conflict.

On the one hand, as we noted earlier, sociocultural theorists have been intrigued by differences in behavior from one culture to another. On the other hand, evolutionary

Adaptation A characteristic that is well designed to help an animal survive and reproduce in a particular environment.

theorists have searched for common patterns in human social behaviors around the world because they are interested in general characteristics of our species (e.g., Dunn et al., 2010; Kenrick & Keefe, 1992; Matsumoto & Willingham, 2006; Schmitt, 2006). Men and women in every human society, for example, establish long-term marriage bonds in which the man helps the woman raise a family (Geary, 2000; Hrdy, 1999). This might seem unsurprising until one looks at most of our furry relatives. Mothers in 95 to 97% of other mammalian species go it alone without any help from the male. Why are family values so rare among mammalian males? That may be because after fertilization fathers just aren't all that necessary. Paternal care becomes useful, though, in species like coyotes and human beings, whose young are born helpless (Geary, 2005).

Besides the broad commonalities of human nature, evolutionary psychologists are also interested in differences between individuals (e.g., Boothroyd et al., 2008; Duncan et al., 2007; Feinberg et al., 2008; Griskevicius, Delton et al., 2011; Jackson & Kirkpatrick, 2008). Within any species there are often multiple strategies for survival and reproduction. For example, some male sunfish grow large, defend territories, and build nests, which attract females. Other males are smaller and impersonate females, darting in to fertilize the eggs just as the female mates with a large territorial male (Gould & Gould, 1989). Although people in all societies form some type of long-term parental bond, they also vary considerably in their mating strategies: Some men and women are monogamous, whereas others join in marriages that involve more than one husband, as in Tibet, or more than one wife, as in Afghanistan (Schmitt, 2005). As we shall see in later chapters, social psychologists are just beginning to explore how biological predispositions and culture interact to shape complex social behaviors, from violence and prejudice to altruism, love, and religiosity (e.g., Cottrell & Neuberg, 2005; Elfenbein & Ambady, 2002; Weeden, Cohen, & Kenrick, 2008).

Paternal investment. Unlike males in 95 percent of other mammalian species, human fathers invest a great deal of time, energy, and resources in their offspring.

The Social Learning Perspective

During the decades following 1908, Ross's group-centered perspective and McDougall's evolutionary approach declined in popularity. Instead, many psychologists adopted a **social learning perspective**, which viewed social behavior as driven by each individual's past learning experiences with reward and punishment (e.g., Allport, 1924; Hull, 1934).

On this view, whether we love or hate another person or group of people, whether we are gregarious or reserved, and whether we desire to be a leader or a follower, are all determined by the rewards and punishments we receive from our parents, our teachers, and our peers. We don't need to learn everything from our own trials and errors though; we can observe what happens to the other people around us and the people we read about in books and magazines, or hear about on television. In a classic series of experiments, Albert Bandura and his colleagues showed how children learn to imitate aggressive behavior after seeing another child or adult rewarded for beating an inflatable Bobo doll (e.g., Bandura, Ross, & Ross, 1961). Bandura expressed concern because his own research had suggested that movies and television often teach young people that violent behavior can be heroic and rewarding. These concerns have been validated by numerous examples of life imitating art. For example, on April 8, 2000, the *Arizona Republic* reported the story of a group of boys in a local high school who started a "fight club" modeled after one started by Brad Pitt's character in a 1999 movie of the same name. As modeled by the characters in the movie, the teenage boys would gather together to trade gloveless punches with one another (Davis, 2000). In a related vein, as we will discuss in Chapter 10, there is evidence that violent video games, which often give players additional points every time they kill or maim a lifelike opponent, may desensitize young boys to violence and teach them to associate hurting others with rewards (Anderson & Dill, 2000; Bartholow et al., 2006; Englehardt et al., 2011).

Social learning perspective A theoretical viewpoint that focuses on past learning experiences as determinants of a person's social behaviors.

Social learning. Venus Williams's father began teaching her to play tennis when she was just a young child. According to social learning theory, whether a person ends up as a successful athlete, a criminal, or a doctor depends on modeling experiences and rewards from parents and others in the child's environment.

In attempting to explain J.K. Rowling's generosity and social activism as an adult, a social learning theorist would be interested in her response to one young reader who asked if Rowling had a role model. She responded that her heroine was Jessica Mitford, a social rights activist. As a young teenage girl, Rowling had a great-aunt who taught classics and from whom she received a copy of Jessica Mitford's autobiography. Mitford was a rebellious woman who left behind a very wealthy and conservative upper-crust British family and moved to America to become a muckraking journalist and social activist. In America she spent a good part of her life working to help poor African-Americans. The young Joyce Rowling was moved by Mitford's story and went on to read all of Mitford's books. A few years later Rowling followed in her unconventional aunt's footsteps by defying her own parents' wishes and choosing to study classic literature in college. J.K. Rowling's aunt thus provided a direct role model for a rewarding life studying and teaching literature and pointed her toward the writings of another woman, who provided a role model for Rowling's later life as a writer and egalitarian social activist.

The social learning perspective is similar to the sociocultural perspective in that it searches for the causes of social behavior in a person's environment. The two perspectives are slightly different in their breadth of focus over time and place, however. Social learning theorists emphasize the individual's unique experiences in a particular family, school, or peer group. Sociocultural theorists are not as concerned with specific individuals or their unique experiences but instead look at larger social aggregates, such as Asian Canadians, Hispanic Americans, college students in sororities, Protestants, or members of the upper class (e.g., Cohen, Malka, Hill, et al., 2009; Hoshino-Browne et al., 2005; Vandello & Cohen, 2003). Also, sociocultural theorists lean toward the assumption that norms, like clothing styles, can change relatively quickly, whereas social learning theorists have generally assumed that habits learned early in life may be difficult to break.

INVESTIGATION

Think of someone whose behavior has been prominent in the news of late. How might this person's actions be explained differently from the sociocultural, evolutionary, and social learning perspectives?

The Social Cognitive Perspective

Despite their differences, the sociocultural, evolutionary, and social learning perspectives all emphasize the objective environment. Each assumes that our social behaviors are influenced by real events in the world. During the 1930s and 1940s Kurt Lewin brought a different perspective to social psychology, arguing that social behavior is driven by each person's subjective interpretations of events in the social world. For example, whether you decide to work toward the goal of becoming class president would depend on (1) your subjective guess about your chances of winning the office and (2) your subjective evaluation of the benefits of being class president (Higgins, 1997). If you don't *think* it would be personally rewarding to be class president, or if you want to be president but don't *expect* to win, you won't bother to run for election—regardless of whether it would objectively be a winnable or enjoyable post for you.

By emphasizing subjective interpretations, Lewin did not mean to imply that no objective reality existed. Instead, he emphasized the interaction between events in the situation and the person's interpretations. Lewin believed that a person's interpretation of a situation was also related to his or her goals at the time. If a teenage boy is itching for a fight, he might interpret an accidental bump as an aggressive shove.

The emphasis on an interaction between inner experience and the outside world led naturally to a close association between social psychology and cognitive psychology (Ross, Lepper, & Ward, 2010). Cognitive psychologists study the mental processes involved in noticing, interpreting, judging, and remembering events in the environment. During the 1950s the advent of computers helped lead a "cognitive revolution"—a rebirth of interest in the workings of the mind. During the 1970s and 1980s an increasing number of social psychologists adopted a **social cognitive perspective**, which focuses on the processes involved in people's choice of which social events to pay attention to, which interpretations to make of these events, and how to store these experiences in memory (e.g., Andersen & Chen, 2002; Carlston, 2013; Plant et al., 2004; Roese & Summerville, 2005).

Researchers have conducted a host of fascinating experiments to explore how your reactions to any social situation can be influenced by cognitive factors such as attention and memory (e.g., Donders et al., 2008; Sharif & Norenzayan, 2007; Trawalter et al., 2008). In one such experiment, high school students were asked how important they thought it was to make a lot of money in their future jobs (Roney, 2003). Some of the students answered the question in a room with members of the opposite sex; some were around only members of their own sex. As you can see in Figure 1.1, the presence of boys made no difference in the way that high school girls answered the question. But being around girls led high school boys to inflate the value they placed on wealth. The researcher also found that seeing ads with young, attractive models (as opposed to ads depicting older people) stimulated college men at the University of Chicago to rate themselves as more ambitious and to place more value on being financially successful. The researcher explained the results in terms of a simple cognitive mechanism—seeing attractive young women activates thoughts about dating in young men. This, in turn, triggers associated thoughts about "what women want," including the tendency for women to place more emphasis on financial success in a mate (e.g., Li, Bailey, et al., 2002; Li, Yong, et al., 2013).

One problem we face in processing social information is that there is so much of it. It's virtually impossible to remember everyone you passed as you walked across campus this morning, much less all the social interactions you had over the last week or the last year. Because we can't focus on everything we see and hear, social information processing is selective. As we'll see in later chapters, sometimes we put our minds on automatic, focusing on a superficial detail or two that will help us come to a quick decision about what to do next (such as when you're in a rush and have to decide whether to give 50 cents to a homeless woman with her hand out). At other times, we pay careful attention to particular details and search, like scientists, for particular types of social information that will allow us to make accurate decisions (when you're thinking of dating someone, for example) (Chaiken & Trope, 1999; Strack et al., 2006).

Social psychologists have found that people have a very hard time keeping a completely fair and open mind to new social information, even when we're trying to do so (e.g., Lord et al., 1979). Rather than operating like scientists seeking the truth, we often process social information more like lawyers defending a client (Haidt, 2001). Consider this question: What are you like now, and how are you different now from what you were like when you were 16 years old? When one team of researchers asked Canadian college students this question, the students had lots of positive things to say about their present selves and more negative things to say about their former selves. Of course, it might be that people simply become better human beings as they age. When the researchers, however, asked another group of students to rate acquaintances of the same age, the students did not perceive their acquaintances as growing into better and better people (Wilson & Ross, 2001). The tendency to view ourselves (but not others) as having changed "from chumps to champs" fits with a number of other findings suggesting that people tend to process social information in a way that tends to flatter themselves (Greenwald et al., 2002; Kurzban, 2012; Vohs et al., 2005).

As we will describe in several later chapters, most of us tend to find it unpleasant when our behaviors are not consistent with our beliefs (Gawronski, 2012).

Figure 1.1   Social context and decision making

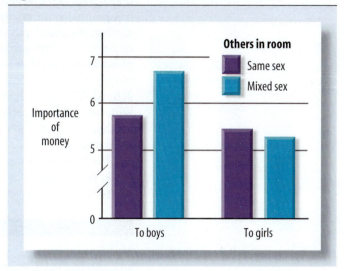

When high school students were asked to rate "How important is having lots of money to your life?" boys' answers were different if they answered the question around high school girls.

Social cognitive perspective A theoretical viewpoint that focuses on the mental processes involved in paying attention to, interpreting, and remembering social experiences.

As a consequence, we will sometimes go to great lengths to avoid inconsistency (Festinger, 1957). When asked whether she resented paying high taxes, J.K. Rowling has pointed out that she herself benefited from welfare when she was a poor single mother. To avoid paying taxes when she herself became wealthy would be rather hypocritical. Furthermore, Rowling had worked for Amnesty International and had publicly declared her identification with Jessica Mitford, the woman who had scorned her family's upper-crust wealthy society and emigrated to America to work as a social activist. If Rowling had started hoarding her wealth, it would have been inconsistent with her publicly declared self-image as a left-wing social activist. However, spending her money to help out various social causes is completely consistent with that self-image.

Because of the central importance of the social cognitive perspective in modern social psychology, it will provide an essential component throughout this text as we discuss the many mysteries of social behavior.

INVESTIGATION

Think of the different people you've passed on the street or on campus or had interactions with anywhere else today. In what ways might the cognitive processes we have discussed in this section affect which people come to mind more easily?

Combining Perspectives

Table 1.1 summarizes the four major theoretical perspectives in social psychology. Although these perspectives are sometimes viewed as competing, each actually focuses on different parts of the mysteries of social life.

Because a single traditional perspective focuses on only part of the picture, we need to combine and integrate the different approaches to see the full picture. The processes of attention and memory studied by cognitive researchers are shaped by people's learning histories and cultures, which are, in turn, the products of an evolutionary past in which humans have created, and have been created by, their social groups (Kenrick, Nieuweboer, & Buunk, 2010; Klein et al., 2002). Consider the topic of prejudice—to some extent, prejudices against members of other groups are related to evolved aversions to strangers, who were often sources of physical danger and new diseases for our ancestors (e.g., Schaller et al., 2003). However, aversions to outsiders always involved tradeoffs because members of different groups engaged in trade and exchanged mates with one another (Faulkner et al., 2004; Navarette et al., 2007). Hence, human beings have always had to learn who were their friends and who were their enemies, and which members of different outgroups to fear and which to trust

Table 1.1 Major Theoretical Perspectives in Social Psychology

Perspective	What Drives Social Behavior?	Example
Sociocultural	Forces in larger social groups	Employees working at IBM in the 1960s wore blue dress shirts (as opposed to white); employees working for Apple in 2015 are more likely to wear colorful T-shirts and jeans to work.
Evolutionary	Inherited tendencies to respond to the social environment in ways that would have helped our ancestors survive and reproduce	Human infants the world over are born with a set of behavioral mechanisms (sucking, crying, cooing) that induce hormonal changes in their mothers, increasing the likelihood they will be nursed and cared for.
Social learning	Rewards and punishments; observing how other people are rewarded and punished for their social behaviors	A teenage boy decides to become a musician after watching an audience scream in admiration of the lead singer at a concert.
Social cognitive	What we pay attention to in a social situation, how we interpret it, and how we connect the current situation to related experiences in memory	If you pass a homeless person on the street, you may be more likely to help if you interpret his plight as something beyond his control and if he reminds you of the parable of the Good Samaritan.

(e.g., Phelps et al., 2000). As relationships between different groups change with historical events, the cultural norms also change accordingly. For example, in the 1950s many African Americans were still being denied the right to vote; 50 years later, things changed so much that an African American could become president of the United States. To fully understand the mysteries of social life, then, it is necessary to piece together clues from several different perspectives.

Quick Quiz

1 A(n) _____ theorist would be relatively more interested in similarities between people in different societies, whereas a _____ theorist would likely focus more on differences across societies.

    a. Social cognitive, social learning
    b. Social learning, evolutionary
    c. Evolutionary, sociocultural
    d. Sociocultural, social learning

2 Which of the following definitions is correct?

    a. Evolutionary perspective focuses on social behaviors as evolved adaptations that helped our ancestors survive and reproduce.
    b. Sociocultural perspective focuses on how social behavior is influenced by group level factors, such as social class and nationality.
    c. Social learning perspective focuses on past experiences with direct and indirect rewards and punishments.
    d. Social cognitive perspective focuses on the mental processes involved in paying attention to, interpreting, and remembering social experiences.
    e. All of the above

Basic Principles of Social Behavior

LO 1.5 Describe the five fundamental motives behind goal-oriented social behavior.

LO 1.6 Explain what is meant by the person, the situation, and person–situation interactions.

Despite their differences, all the major perspectives in social psychology share a pair of key assumptions. First, people interact with one another to achieve some goal or satisfy some inner motivation. Cognitive psychologists emphasize conscious goals triggered by the current situation, as when an ad saying "Father's Day is just around the corner!" reminds you to rush out and buy your father another one of those Hawaiian print ties he appreciated so much last year. Learning theorists emphasize how past rewards encourage us to approach some goals and avoid others. For example, if your parents smile proudly every time you share your toys with your sister but grimace every time you talk about money, you may set the goal of joining the Peace Corps instead of a Wall Street brokerage firm. Evolutionary theorists emphasize social motivations rooted in our ancestral past: People who were motivated to get along with other members of their social groups, for instance, were more likely to survive and pass on their genes than were self-centered hermits.

A second common theoretical thread is a focus on the interaction between the person and the situation. All the major perspectives assume that motivations inside each of us interact with events in the outside situations we encounter. For example, the evolutionary perspective emphasizes how internal reactions such as anger, fear, or sexual arousal are triggered by situations related to survival or reproduction (hungry-looking predators or flirtatious glances, for example). Social learning theorists study how learned responses within the individual are linked to rewards and punishments in the social setting. And cognitive theorists examine how a person's thought processes are linked with moment-to-moment changes in the social situation.

Throughout this book, then, we will emphasize two broad principles shared by the different perspectives.

1. Social behavior is *goal oriented*. People interact with one another to achieve some goal or satisfy some inner motivation.
2. Social behavior represents a continual *interaction* between the person and the situation.

In the following sections, we take a closer look at these two principles.

Social Behavior Is Goal Oriented

Goals affect our social behaviors on several levels. At the surface level, we can enumerate a long list of day-to-day goals: to find out the latest office gossip, to make a good impression on a teacher, or to get a date for next Saturday night. At a somewhat broader level, we can talk about longer-term goals: to gain a reputation as being competent, to be seen as likable, to feel good about oneself, or to develop a romantic relationship. Those broader goals often tie together several other day-to-day goals: Developing a romantic relationship incorporates shorter-term goals such as getting a date for Saturday night and being comforted by your partner after an exam.

At the broadest level, we can ask about fundamental motives—the ultimate functions of our social behavior (Kenrick, Griskevicius, Neuberg, & Schaller, 2010). So, for example, succeeding in one's career and making connections with people in high places could both be incorporated into a fundamental motive of "gaining and maintaining status." To better understand these fundamental motives, let's consider several that have been investigated by social psychologists.

TO ESTABLISH SOCIAL TIES In J.K. Rowling's Harry Potter novels, Harry triumphs over the forces of evil. But he could not have done so without the help of his close friends Hermione Granger and Ron Weasley, and the protection of Albus Dumbledore, the headmaster of Hogwarts School of Witchcraft and Wizardry. It works the same way out here in the real world for us non-magical Muggles. In the case of almost every goal you ever reach, you get there more easily when there are others helping you along. Some goals, like building a school or even moving a couch up a flight of stairs, would not happen at all if not for teamwork.

When psychologists enumerate the most basic motives underlying human behavior, the desire to establish ties with other people is usually high on the list (e.g., Bugental, 2000; McAdams, 1990). People are exquisitely sensitive to rejection and go to great lengths to reconnect with others if they feel excluded (Anthony et al., 2007; Maner et al., 2007; Williams & Nida, 2011). One team of researchers observed brainwave patterns in people as they played a virtual ball-tossing game with two other players. When the two other players threw the ball to one another and excluded the participant, the person who was ostracized showed a pattern of activity in two different areas of the cortex usually associated with physical injury (Eisenberger et al., 2003). Other research suggests that the agony of social separation can be reduced by opiates, drugs normally used to quell the agony of a bleeding wound (Panksepp, 2005). Why does social isolation tap into the same neural mechanisms as physical pain? Perhaps because, without their friends, our ancestors would not have survived (Hill & Hurtado, 1996; MacDonald & Leary, 2005). Hence social rejection may trigger a primitive physiological emergency reaction.

TO UNDERSTAND OURSELVES AND OTHERS People gossip, they read profiles of criminal personalities in the newspaper, and they seek feedback from their friends about their chances of getting a date with a charming new classmate. The importance of such information is obvious—by understanding ourselves and our relationships with others we are able to manage our lives more effectively. Someone who is "out of touch" with these realities will have a harder time surviving in a social group (Leary & Baumeister, 2000; Sedikides & Skowronski, 2000). Because social knowledge is so fundamental to all human relationships, social psychologists have devoted a great deal of attention to the topic of social cognition (which, as noted earlier, refers to the mental processes involved in attending to, interpreting, and remembering other people). In Chapter 3, we explore this topic in depth, and we return to it throughout the chapters that follow.

TO GAIN AND MAINTAIN STATUS Part of what made Harry Potter so popular is that he rises from being an absolute loser (an orphan living in a closet with relatives who mistreat him) to the heights of heroism. Winning and losing are matters of profound importance, to gradeschoolers competing for places on Little League all-star teams, college students fighting for grades, middle managers striving for executive positions, and senators and governors campaigning to win the presidency. And humans aren't alone in struggling for status. Baboons are social primates who, like us, pay close attention to where they stand in the social hierarchy. An intensive study of baboons' physiological responses to social events revealed that a loss of status led to a particularly disruptive set of hormonal alarm responses (Sapolsky, 2001).

The advantages of attaining status include not only immediate material payoffs such as access to food but also the less tangible social benefits that follow from other people's (or other baboons') respect and admiration (Henrich & Gil-White, 2001; Maner & Mead, 2010). So it makes sense that most of us go to great lengths not only to present ourselves in a positive light to others, but also to convince ourselves that we have reason to hold our heads up high (e.g., Sedikides et al., 2003; Tesser, 2000). Throughout this book, we will see that the motivation to gain and maintain status underlies a wide range of social behaviors.

TO DEFEND OURSELVES AND THOSE WE VALUE At the local level, people build fences around their houses, put up Keep Out signs on their streets, join gangs, and buy attack dogs to protect themselves. At the national level, countries build armies to protect themselves against the armies of other countries. People are extremely motivated to defend themselves when their reputations, their resources, or their families are threatened. People can recognize an angry expression in just a fraction of a second and do so significantly faster if the angry expression is on a man's face (Becker et al., 2007). Why? Men generally pose more of a physical threat than do women, particularly if those men are strangers or members of outgroups (Ackerman, Shapiro, et al., 2007; Neel et al., 2012).

The motivation to defend ourselves can have obvious benefits, promoting our survival and that of our family members, but it can also lead to escalating violence and racism (Duntley, 2005; Schaller et al., 2003). We will discuss the sometimes frightening power of self-protective motivation in the chapters that deal with aggression, prejudice, and intergroup conflict.

TO ATTRACT AND RETAIN MATES Rajinder Singh, sixth maharajah of the state of Patiala in India, took 350 spouses; most North Americans will take at least one. People often go to great lengths to find and keep these partners, writing lengthy love letters, having long phone calls at 2 A.M., or joining computer dating services. An initial flirtation with a pleasant acquaintance in your psychology class could lead to feelings of attraction, romantic love, and even a lifelong family bond. From an evolutionary perspective, these are all connected (Kenrick, Maner, & Li, 2014). Indeed, evolutionary theorists believe that the goal of reproduction underlies all the other social goals. From this perspective, we affiliate, we seek social information, we strive for status, and we act in aggressive and self-protective ways all toward the ultimate end of reproducing our genes (Buss, 2004; Hill et al., 2012; Neuberg et al., 2010).

The motive to gain and maintain status. Sarah Jessica Parker was one of eight siblings born to relatively poor parents in a small Ohio town. She personifies the rags-to-riches fantasy, having progressed from a struggling rural girl to an awkward adolescent to an internationally famous winner of several Golden Globes. Though not everyone has such high aspirations, most of us are motivated to gain regard in the eyes of others.

INVESTIGATION

Recall one pleasant and one unpleasant interaction you've had with another person or group. How do those interactions link up with the different goals we just discussed?

The Interaction between the Person and the Situation

If an attractive stranger on your left begins to flirt with you, you may stop trying to impress your boss, who is standing on your right. If you later notice that a third person—a large male dressed in black leather—has started to sneer at you and to stand possessively close to the flirtatious stranger, you may shift to thoughts of self-protection. In contrast, a coworker who is a more devoted social climber may be so desperately trying to impress the boss as to be oblivious to flirtation opportunities or physical dangers.

In other words, the fundamental motives and specific goals active at any one time reflect the continual interaction between factors inside the person and factors outside in the world. Because we will examine these interactions in some detail throughout the book, let us briefly consider what we mean by "the person" and "the situation" and how the two become interwoven through "person–situation interactions."

PERSON   **THE PERSON**   When we talk about the **person**, we will typically be referring to features or characteristics that individuals carry into social situations. If asked to describe yourself, you might mention physical characteristics (your height or your gender, for example), chronic attitudes or preferences (your tendency to vote Republican, Democrat, or Libertarian, for example), and psychological traits (whether you are extraverted or introverted, emotional or calm, and so on). These characteristics may be based on genetic or physiological factors that make you different from others, or they may be based on past learning experiences and maintained by particular ways you have of thinking about yourself or the other people you encounter on a day-to-day basis. Other aspects of the person may be more temporary, such as your current mood or sense of self-worth. Throughout the text, when we want to focus specifically on a feature of the person, we will signify this by using the yellow Person icon.

SITUATION   **THE SITUATION**   When we talk about the social **situation**, we are referring to events or circumstances outside the person. These can range from fleeting events in the immediate social context (as when a stranger winks at you) to long-lasting influences, such as growing up on an isolated rural farm in Montana or a multiethnic neighborhood in New York City. When we want to focus specifically on a feature of the situation, we will signify this by using the blue Situation icon.

INTERACTION   **PERSON–SITUATION INTERACTIONS**   Neither the person nor the situation is a fixed entity. As William James observed, "Many a youth who is demure enough before his parents and teachers, swears and swaggers like a pirate among his 'tough' young friends" (1890, p. 294). Different social situations trigger different goals—sometimes we want to be liked, sometimes we want to be feared, and so on (Griskevicius, Tybur, et al., 2009; Maner & Gerend, 2007). Because there is often quite a bit going on in a single situation, your goal at any given moment may depend on what you are paying attention to. And depending on your current goals and your lifelong traits, you may respond differently to a situation from the way others do (e.g., Graziano et al., 2007). Think of a party where some people are dancing, some are having a philosophical discussion, and still others are sharing raunchy jokes.

As we discuss in detail in Chapter 2, people and situations interact in several different ways. For example, we tend to interpret ambiguous situations in ways that fit with our personal motives (Dunning & Balcetis, 2013; Huang & Bargh, 2014). Whether you think someone was flirting with you or just being friendly depends on your sex and whether you are in a romantic frame of mind (Maner et al., 2003). Our personalities also affect which situations we choose to enter (Roberts et al., 2003; Snyder & Ickes, 1985). If you are an introvert, you might decline an invitation to a party; an extravert might crash the party, even if he wasn't invited.

Just as people choose their situations, so social situations may choose certain types of people to enter them. The high school freshman who is taller than average may be recruited for basketball training, for example, whereas a friend who is better than average at math and science may be recruited for honors classes. And small initial differences between people may get magnified by situations (such as basketball training

Person Features or characteristics that individuals carry into social situations.

Situation Environmental events or circumstances outside the person.

sessions and honors classes). Thus situation and person shape and choose one another in a continuing cycle.

When we want to focus specifically on a person–situation interaction, we will signify this by using the green Interaction icon.

Quick Quiz

1 According to the text, what is the connection between everyday goals (such as making an impression on the boss or getting a date) and fundamental motives (such as gaining status or establishing social ties)?

    a. Everyday goals often conflict with fundamental motives.
    b. Everyday goals are more important in determining our behavior than are fundamental motives.
    c. Fundamental motives are more important influences on our behavior than are everyday goals.
    d. Fundamental goals link our everyday goals to their ultimate functions.

2 Which example demonstrates a person–situation interaction?

    a. A woman in a sad mood donates to a charity to make herself feel better.
    b. A man is more likely to honk his horn on a hot humid day than on a comfortable day.
    c. Men are more likely to help in emergencies that require heroic action, whereas women are more likely to help when emotional support is needed.
    d. None of the above

How Psychologists Study Social Behavior

LO 1.7   List the strengths and weaknesses of each of the different descriptive methods (e.g., naturalistic observation, case study) and experimental methods, and explain why researchers find value in combining them.

LO 1.8   Explain why it is difficult to infer causality from correlation.

LO 1.9   Discuss some of the ethical risks that social psychologists face.

Scientific research is a bit like detective work. A detective begins with a mystery and a set of procedures for solving that mystery: interview witnesses, look for a motive, try to rule out various suspects, examine the material evidence, and so on. There are pitfalls at every step: Witnesses may lie or base their testimony on unfounded assumptions, some motives may be hidden, and the evidence may have been tampered with. Like detectives, social psychologists begin with mysteries. We opened this chapter with several, including: What might cause a woman to give away large portions of her money? What causes some marriages to end in early divorces, and others to flourish for a lifetime? Why do some people make better leaders? Social psychologists have a set of procedures for solving such mysteries and, like detectives, they must also be aware of potential pitfalls involved in using these procedures.

Psychologists begin their detective work with **hypotheses**—educated guesses about how the evidence is likely to turn out. If you wanted to search for evidence about some interesting social behavior, how would you come up with a viable hypothesis to lead your search? You might start with one of the theoretical perspectives we discussed earlier. For example, adopting a social learning perspective on J.K. Rowling's philanthropy and social activism, you might note that her aunt gave her a biography of a famous British woman who had left her wealthy family to become a social activist and Civil Rights worker in the United States. One hypothesis, which we will consider in Chapter 9, is that prosocial behavior in adulthood is linked to having altruistic role models during one's developing years. An alternative hypothesis (which we will also consider in Chapter 9) is that people inherit genetic tendencies toward altruism from their parents.

But not all social psychological hypotheses are logically derived from a scientific theory. You might draw an interesting hypothesis from an odd event that seems to contradict common sense, such as when a person becomes more committed to a religious

Hypothesis A researcher's prediction about what he or she will find.

cult after the leader's predictions about the end of the world do not come true (Festinger, Reicken, & Schachter, 1956). Or you might search for exceptions to some established psychological principle, such as when a reward causes a child to stop working on a task (e.g., Lepper, Green, & Nisbett, 1973). Social psychologist William McGuire (1997) enumerated 49 different ways to go about generating a research hypothesis.

Many people stop looking once they come up with a plausible-sounding explanation for why another person appeared generous, zealous, aggressive, or loving. But concocting a plausible-seeming hypothesis is only the beginning of a scientific search. Sometimes even the most plausible hypotheses prove to be dead wrong. For example, raising students' self-esteem has been touted by educators and politicians as a cure for everything from premarital sex to assault, rape, and murder (see Baumeister, Smart, & Boden, 1996). On the surface it seems quite reasonable that people who feel bad about themselves might be more likely to act out in a sexual or violent way, perhaps to boost their fragile self-esteem. But when psychologists look at the actual research evidence, it appears that the hypotheses about the dangers of low self-esteem, however logical they sound, are often wrong. After reviewing the research evidence on self-esteem, social psychologists Roy Baumeister, Brad Bushman, and Keith Campbell (2000) concluded that we have little to fear from people with low self-esteem and more to fear from those who have an inflated view of themselves. These contrary findings make sense if we think of low self-esteem as humility and high self-esteem as conceit and arrogance.

The detective tools psychologists use to gather data about their hypotheses can be roughly divided into two categories: descriptive and experimental. **Descriptive methods** are used to measure or record behaviors, thoughts, or feelings in their natural state. When psychologists use descriptive methods, they hope to record behaviors without changing them in any way. **Experimental methods**, in contrast, are used to uncover the causes of behavior by systematically varying some aspect of the situation.

Descriptive Methods

Before we can understand the causes of any phenomenon, it helps to have a careful description of what it is we're talking about. How does one go about carefully describing social behavior? Social psychologists use five major types of descriptive methods: naturalistic observation, case studies, archives, surveys, and psychological tests.

NATURALISTIC OBSERVATION Perhaps the most straightforward descriptive method is **naturalistic observation**. It involves, quite simply, observing behavior as it unfolds in its natural setting. As one example, psychologist Monica Moore (1985) went to a setting where she expected women to naturally show a lot of nonverbal flirtation behaviors—a singles bar. Sitting out of view, she counted various gestures displayed by women toward men and compared these to behaviors displayed in a library or women's center meeting. Women flirting with men in the singles bar gestured in certain ways that were very uncommon in the other settings. For instance, a woman in the bar would frequently glance at a man for a few seconds, smile, flip her hair, and tilt her head at a 45-degree angle so her neck was exposed.

Naturalistic observation has a number of advantages as a research method. For one, behavior in a natural setting is spontaneous rather than artificial and contrived. In contrast, imagine the difficulties of asking students to demonstrate flirtation gestures in a laboratory. For one thing, people might not be consciously aware of the bodily movements and gestures they make when they are actually flirting. For another, people might feel too uncomfortable to flirt when they know researchers with notepads are watching them.

Despite its strengths, naturalistic observation also has its pitfalls. Researchers need to ensure that their subjects do not know they are being observed. Otherwise, they might not act normally. As we discuss in the chapter on Social Influence, social psychologists have discovered some clever ways to observe behavior without making people self-conscious. Another problem with naturalistic observation is that some

Studying flirtation gestures.
Monica Moore wanted to study the gestures women use to flirt. To do so, she conducted a naturalistic observation, recording women's spontaneous behaviors in a singles' bar, a library, or a women's center meeting. She found that women in a singles bar were more likely to exhibit nonverbal gestures such as a direct glance accompanied with a hair flip, a smile, and a slight tilt of the neck.

Descriptive method Procedure for measuring or recording behaviors, thoughts, and feelings in their natural state (including naturalistic observations, case studies, archival studies, surveys, and psychological tests).

Experimental method Procedure for uncovering causal processes by systematically manipulating some aspect of a situation.

Naturalistic observation Recording everyday behaviors as they unfold in their natural settings.

behaviors researchers want to study are rare. Imagine waiting around on a street corner for a homicide to occur. Even in the worst of neighborhoods you would spend a long time waiting for your first observation.

A final problem is that, unless the observation is conducted very systematically, biased expectations may lead the observer to ignore some influences on behavior and exaggerate others. A researcher's hypothesis may lead that researcher to search for supportive information but fail to notice inconsistent evidence. This problem is called **observer bias**. For instance, if you expected to see flirtatious behaviors in a bar, you might misinterpret a woman's hair-flip as flirtation, when all she was really trying to do was keep her hair from falling into her beer mug.

CASE STUDIES   Another observational method is the **case study**, an intensive examination of one individual or group. A researcher could study a completely normal individual or group but often selects a case because it represents some unusual pattern of behavior. Imagine that you were interested in studying how people respond when they are catapulted from social obscurity into the ranks of the rich and famous. If you sampled a random group of the population at a shopping mall or in a psychology class, you might not find anyone famous. However, you could interview J.K. Rowling or Michelle Obama.

Case studies are sometimes used by psychologists when they want to better understand a rare or unusual individual or group. For example, social psychologist Mark Schaller (1997) was interested in studying what happens to people's feelings about themselves when they suddenly become famous. Schaller examined case materials from the lives and writings of several famous individuals, including rock star Kurt Cobain, who committed suicide at the peak of his fame during the 1990s. As Cobain's story illustrates, the case materials suggested that fame isn't always good fortune and can actually lead some people to unpleasantly high levels of self-concern.

Case studies can be rich sources of hypotheses. For example, psychologists have proposed many hypotheses about why Vincent van Gogh cut off his ear, wrapped it, and presented it as a gift to a prostitute (Runyan, 1981). According to one hypothesis, he did it to express his anger because she had slept with his friend Paul Gauguin. According to another, he did it because he had unconscious and unacceptable homosexual feelings toward Paul Gauguin and wanted to symbolically emasculate himself. Unfortunately, psychologists who limit themselves to case study material often allow their hypotheses to bias their search through the evidence in a person's life, picking and choosing events to support their favored hunch (Runyan, 1981). On the basis of a single case study, we simply have no way of telling which events in the case have actually *caused* the event of interest and which are irrelevant. A case study can suggest any number of interesting hypotheses. It cannot, however, tell us much about why an event occurred.

Another problem in using case studies has to do with **generalizability**, the extent to which a particular research finding applies to other similar circumstances. After examining only a single case, such as Vincent Van Gogh or J.K. Rowling, we simply cannot know which of the specifics generalize to other similar cases.

ARCHIVES   One solution to the problem of generalizability is to examine a number of similar cases. Consider a study of police reports for 512 homicides committed in Detroit during 1972. Here is one:

> Case 185: Victim (male, age 22) and offender (male, age 41) were in a bar when a mutual acquaintance walked in. Offender bragged to victim of "this guy's" fighting ability and that they had fought together. Victim replied "you are pretty tough" and an argument ensued over whether victim or offender was the better man. Victim then told offender "I got mine" (gun) and the offender replied "I got mine too," both indicating

Observer bias Error introduced into measurement when an observer overemphasizes behaviors he or she expects to find and fails to notice behaviors he or she does not expect.

Case study An intensive examination of an individual or group.

Generalizability The extent to which the findings of a particular research study extend to other similar circumstances or cases.

The problems of the case study method. Psychologists have used details of Vincent Van Gogh's life to support dozens of different hypotheses about why he cut off his own ear. However, a single case does not allow clear cause-and-effect conclusions.

their pockets. The victim then said "I don't want to die and I know you don't want to die. Let's forget about it." But the offender produced a small automatic, shot the victim dead, and left the bar. (Wilson & Daly, 1985, p. 64)

Although the details of this particular case may be unique, Margo Wilson and Martin Daly found a number of similar details across the hundreds of homicide cases they examined. First, offenders and their victims tended to be males, particularly males in their early twenties. Second, the homicides were often instigated by a conflict over social dominance.

Wilson and Daly's study of homicides is an example of the **archival method**, in which researchers test hypotheses using data that was originally collected for other purposes (police reports, marriage licenses, newspaper articles, and so on). Another archival study found that during G. W. Bush's first term as U.S. president (during which he initiated wars with Afghanistan and Iraq) people became more supportive of him after government-issued terror warnings (Willer, 2004). Still other studies have looked at the relationship between daily temperatures in a given city and the number of violent crimes reported on the same day (e.g., Bell, 2005; Bushman et al., 2005; Cohn & Rotton, 2005). The advantage of archives is that they provide easy access to an abundance of real-world data. The disadvantage is that many interesting social phenomena do not get recorded. Both the beginning and end of a two-month-long marriage make it to the public records. However, a five-year-long live-in relationship that breaks up over an argument about whom to invite to the wedding never registers in the archives.

SURVEYS Some very interesting behaviors are unlikely to be recorded in public records or to be demonstrated in natural settings. For instance, back in the 1940s biologist Alfred Kinsey became curious about the prevalence of sexual behaviors such as masturbation and premarital intercourse. Because these behaviors are rarely done in public, naturalistic observation would not do. Likewise, individual case studies of convicted sex offenders or prostitutes, for example, would be uninformative about normal sexual behavior. Kinsey, therefore, chose the **survey method**, in which the researcher simply asks respondents a series of questions about their behaviors, beliefs, or opinions.

The survey has one very important advantage: It allows a researcher to collect a great deal of data about phenomena that may rarely be demonstrated in public. Like other methods, surveys have drawbacks. First, the respondent may not give accurate information, because of either dishonesty or memory biases. For instance, it is puzzling that men answering surveys often report more heterosexual experiences than do women. Men in Britain, France, and the United States report 10 to 12 sexual partners in their lives, whereas women in all these countries report just over 3 (Einon, 1994). The discrepancy could be due to **social desirability bias**, or the tendency for people to say what they believe is appropriate or acceptable (whether it is true or not). Sexual activity is more socially approved for men (Hyde, 1996). Hence men may thus be more inclined to talk about their sexual escapades or more likely to remember them, or women may be inclined to downplay theirs (Alexander & Fisher, 2003).

Another potential problem with the survey method is obtaining a **representative sample**. A sample is representative when the participants, as a group, have characteristics that match those of the larger population the researcher wants to describe. A representative sample of North American executives would include percentages of men, women, blacks, Hispanics, Canadians, Midwesterners, and Southerners that reflect the total population of executives on the continent. A small group of male bank executives from Toronto or of Hispanic female executives in the New York fashion industry would not represent North American executives as a whole. The sample for Kinsey's sex survey was composed largely of volunteers from community organizations, which means that many segments of U.S. society were not well represented.

Kinsey's survey may have also faced a problem in which some people selected themselves into, or out of, his sample. Many potential respondents are simply unwilling to volunteer to discuss topics such as their sex lives. Others might relish the opportunity to regale the survey researchers with their wild erotic experiences. If those

Archival method Examination of systematic data originally collected for other purposes (such as marriage licenses or arrest records).

Survey method A technique in which the researcher asks people to report on their beliefs, feelings, or behaviors.

Social desirability bias The tendency for people to say what they believe is appropriate or acceptable.

Representative sample A group of respondents having characteristics that match those of the larger population the researcher wants to describe.

who do or do not participate are different from the norm in their sexual activities, the researcher might draw erroneous conclusions about the whole population. Carefully constructed surveys can reduce some of these problems. But not all surveys are to be trusted, particularly when they allow subjects to select themselves for participation.

PSYCHOLOGICAL TESTS Are some people more socially skillful than others? Are some people inclined to think critically before allowing themselves to be persuaded by an argument? **Psychological tests** are instruments for assessing differences between people in abilities, cognitions, or chronic motivations. They differ from surveys in that surveys typically aim to get at specific attitudes or behaviors, whereas tests aim to uncover broader underlying traits. Most of us have taken a variety of psychological tests. College aptitude tests (such as the SATs) are designed to distinguish people according to their ability to do well in college. Vocational interest tests (such as the Strong Vocational Interest Blank) are designed to distinguish people in terms of their likely enjoyment of various professions.

Psychological tests are not always perfect indications of the things they are designed to measure. A test of "your ability to get along with your lover" published in a popular magazine, for example, may be a poor predictor of your actual skills at relationships. There are two criteria a psychological test must meet before it is useful—reliability and validity.

Reliability is the consistency of the test's results. If a test of social skills indicates that you are highly charismatic the first time you take it but socially inept when you take it a week later, your score is unreliable. To measure anything, it is essential that the measurement instrument be consistent. Some psychological tests, such as the famous Rorschach inkblots, do not provide very reliable measurements; others, such as IQ tests, yield much more consistent scores. Even if a test is reliable, however, it may not be valid.

Validity is the extent to which the test measures what it is designed to measure. To use a rather unlikely example, we could theoretically use eye color as a measure of desirability to the opposite sex. Our test would be very reliable—trained observers would agree well about who had blue, hazel, and brown eyes; and subjects' eye color would certainly not change very much if we measured it again a month or two later. Yet eye color would probably not be a valid index of attractiveness—it would probably not relate to the number of dates a person had in the last year, for instance. However, if judges rated the attractiveness of the whole face, or a videotape of the person engaged in conversation, the scores might be a little less reliable but more valid as predictors of dating desirability.

Reliability and validity can be issues for all methods. For instance, archival records of men's and women's age differences at marriage are reasonably consistent across different cultures and time periods (Campos et al., 2002; Kenrick & Keefe, 1992). Hence they give a reliable estimate (several times as many women as men get married in their teens, for example). Yet the marriage records from one month in one small town would probably be unreliable (perhaps two teenage boys and only one teenage girl got married that particular month). With regard to validity, three different environmental surveys might agree that people are doing more recycling and driving less. Yet those survey responses, though reliable, might not be valid: People might consistently misrepresent their recycling or driving habits. It is thus important to ask about any research study: Are the results reliable? That is, would we get the same results if the measurement was done in a different way or by a different observer? And are the results valid? That is, is the researcher really studying what he or she intends to study?

INVESTIGATION

Imagine that you work for a magazine and you have been assigned to write a series of articles on how a particular interesting group of people (Utah polygynists, New York gang members, or Hollywood superstars, for example) differs from the prototypical American suburbanite. Which of the different descriptive methods could you use to address this question, and what problems would you run into in drawing confident conclusions?

Psychological test Instrument for assessing a person's abilities, cognitions, or motivations.

Reliability The consistency of the score yielded by a psychological test.

Validity The extent to which a test measures what it is designed to measure.

Correlation and Causation

Data from descriptive methods can reveal **correlation**, or the extent to which two or more variables occur together (psychologists use the term "variable" to refer broadly to any factor that fluctuates, such as daily temperature, people's height, hair color, the size of a crowd, or the amount of alcohol consumed on different college campuses). Leon Mann (1981) was interested in investigating which variables might be linked to the puzzling phenomenon of suicide baiting, in which onlookers encourage a suicidal person to jump to his or her death. In one case, a nighttime crowd of 500 onlookers not only urged Gloria Polizzi to jump off a 150-foot water tower but also screamed obscenities and threw stones at the rescue squad. Using newspaper archives to study the topic, Mann discovered that suicide baiting was correlated with the size of the crowd. As crowds got larger, they were more likely to taunt someone perched on the edge of life.

A correlation between two variables is often expressed mathematically in terms of a statistic called **correlation coefficient**. Correlation coefficients can range from +1.0, indicating a perfect positive relationship between two variables, through 0, indicating absolutely no relationship, to –1.0, indicating a perfect negative relationship. A positive correlation means that as one variable goes up or down, the other goes up or down with it. As crowds got larger, for example, the amount of suicide baiting increased.

A negative correlation indicates a reverse relationship—as one variable goes up or down, the other goes in the opposite direction. For instance, women who are *more* committed to, and more satisfied with, their current partners generally spend *less* time paying attention to other attractive men (Maner et al., 2003; Miller, 1997).

Correlations can provide important hints, but they do not enable a researcher to draw conclusions about cause and effect. Consider the case of crowd size and suicide baiting. Large crowds are associated with many forms of otherwise inappropriate behavior, as can often be observed at a rock concert, a Halloween block party, or when fans take to the streets after a major sporting event. It seemed plausible to conclude, as Mann did in his study of suicide baiting, that large crowds led onlookers to feel anonymous. This, in turn, could reduce their concern about being identified as the perpetrators of such a cruel and nasty deed. However, it is important to keep in mind that correlation does not equal causation.

Why doesn't correlation equal causation? For one thing, it is always possible that the presumed direction of causality is reversed—that B causes A rather than A causing B (see Figure 1.2). For instance, once the suicide baiting started, it may have been reported on the radio, inspiring nearby listeners to go view the spectacle (thus suicide baiting would have caused crowds, rather than the other way around). Another problem is that correlations can be found when there is no causal relationship at all, as when a third variable C is causing both A and B. For instance, Mann also found that suicide baiting occurred more frequently at night. Perhaps people are more likely to be drinking alcohol at night, and drunks are more likely to be gregarious (hence to join crowds) and unruly (hence to taunt potential suicides). If so, neither darkness nor the size of the crowd was a direct cause of suicide baiting; each was related only incidentally.

Correlation The extent to which two or more variables are associated with one another.

Correlation coefficient A mathematical expression of the relationship between two variables.

Figure 1.2   Explaining correlations

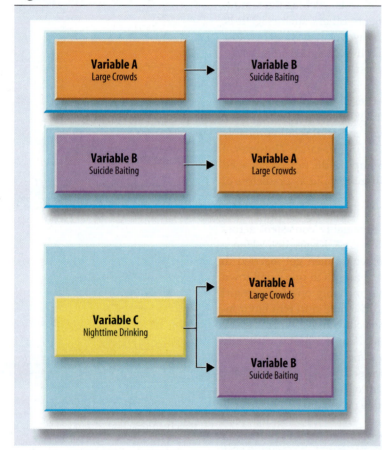

When two variables (such as crowd size and suicide baiting) are correlated, it is possible that variable A (crowd size, in this example) leads to changes in variable B (suicide baiting, in this case). It is also possible, however, that variable B causes variable A, or that a third variable C (such as nighttime drinking, in this example) causes both A and B independently.

Because of the different possible connections between correlated variables, then, it is difficult to draw clear causal conclusions from correlations. To make conclusions about cause and effect, researchers turn to the experimental method, in which variables are teased apart from the other factors that normally co-occur with them.

Experimental Methods

When using descriptive methods, researchers try to avoid interfering with the phenomenon they are studying. A researcher using naturalistic observation hopes his subjects don't notice that they are being observed, for example, and a survey researcher tries not to word questions so as to lead people to misrepresent their true feelings or behaviors. In an **experiment**, however, the researcher actually sets out to alter people's behavior by systematically manipulating one aspect of the situation while controlling others. If a researcher wanted to know whether anonymity of the sort that occurs in large crowds actually *causes* people to act more antisocially, that researcher could vary the situation so that some people felt especially anonymous while others felt especially identifiable. In fact, Philip Zimbardo (1969) did just that, while asking students in a laboratory experiment to deliver electric shocks to a fellow student. Half the participants wore name tags and remained in their own clothes and were thus made easily identifiable. To make the other participants anonymous, they were outfitted with oversized white coats and hoods that completely covered their faces. These anonymous subjects delivered twice as much shock as did those who were left identifiable.

MANIPULATING VARIABLES   The variable manipulated by the experimenter is called the **independent variable**. In Zimbardo's experiment, the independent variable was the type of clothing worn (anonymous versus identifiable). The variable that is measured is called the **dependent variable**. In this case, the experimenter measured the amount of shock delivered by the subject.

There are several things to note about experiments. A key feature of Zimbardo's experiment is that participants were randomly assigned to the anonymous and nonanonymous conditions. **Random assignment** means each participant has an equal probability of being in the different conditions. By assigning participants to the two groups on the basis of a coin flip, for instance, a researcher reduces the chances that the groups are different in terms of mood, personality, social class, or other factors that might affect the outcomes. In this way the researcher minimizes any systematic differences between the groups, such as those that might have characterized suicide observers in nighttime versus daytime crowds. Although large suicide-baiting crowds could have differed from small nonbaiting crowds in other ways related to antisocial tendencies, such systematic differences are not a problem when participants are randomly assigned. In Zimbardo's study, the only differences among subjects were due to random variations in the population (which are reduced in importance as the experimenter runs large groups of subjects). It was also important that only the anonymity of clothing (the independent variable) varied from one group of subjects to another. All other aspects of the situation were the same— the experimenter, the setting, the victim, and the task. This also reduces the likelihood that these other variables might have influenced the antisocial behavior. Finally, aggressiveness was measured in an identical fashion for the high- and low-anonymity subjects, enabling the experimenter to quantify reliably the exact amount of shock that the different subjects delivered in each condition.

By randomly assigning subjects and controlling extraneous variables, the experimenter gains an important advantage—the ability to make statements about causal relationships. Zimbardo could be fairly confident that it was something about his manipulation of anonymity, rather than something about the different subjects in the anonymous condition, that led to the higher level of aggression.

POTENTIAL LIMITATIONS OF THE EXPERIMENTAL METHOD   Despite its advantage over descriptive methods in making causal statements, the experiment has its own

Experiment   A research method in which the researcher sets out to systematically manipulate one source of influence while holding others constant.

Independent variable   The variable manipulated by the experimenter.

Dependent variable   The variable measured by the experimenter.

Random assignment   The practice of assigning participants to treatments so each person has an equal chance of being in any condition.

Experimenting with deindividuation. In Zimbardo's experiment, half the subjects dressed in clothing making them anonymous and the other half stayed in their normal clothes and were visible to others. That difference constituted the independent variable. The dependent variable was the amount of shock delivered to a fellow subject.

drawbacks. For one, the laboratory settings used in most experiments are artificial. Is the anonymity created by wearing a big coat and hood really the same as that experienced in a large crowd on a dark night? Is the tendency to deliver shock really the same as the tendency to throw rocks at suicide rescue squads?

We discussed the concept of validity in psychological tests—whether a test measures what it intends to measure. The same question can be asked of experiments (Aronson, Wilson, & Brewer, 1998). **Internal validity** is the extent to which an experiment allows confident conclusions about cause and effect. Was the independent variable the sole cause of any systematic variations in the participants' behaviors? Imagine if in Zimbardo's deindividuation experiment all the subjects in the anonymous condition were met by an obnoxious male experimenter, whereas all the subjects in the nonanonymous condition were met by a pleasant female. If the subjects in the anonymous condition behaved more aggressively, we would not know whether it was because the subject was anonymous or because the experimenter was obnoxious. A variable that systematically changes along with the independent variable is called a **confound**. In this imaginary case, the sex and temperament of the experimenter are both confounded with anonymity. Such confounding variables are like the invisible third variables in correlations—they make it difficult to know what caused the subject's behavior.

External validity is the extent to which the results of an experiment can be generalized to other circumstances. We mentioned earlier that studying a single case raises a problem of generalizability. The same problem comes up with regard to laboratory experiments as well. Does delivering shock in an anonymous laboratory experiment tap the same processes as being in a large mob on a dark night, for instance? Perhaps not. Certainly, no two situations are identical, but experimenters try to pick variables that tap the same mental and emotional processes as those operating in the wider world outside.

One problem in generalizing from laboratory studies to natural behavior is that participants know they are being observed in the lab. As we noted with naturalistic observation, people sometimes act differently when they know they are being watched. **Demand characteristics** are cues in the experiment that make subjects aware of how the experimenter expects them to behave. Experimenters try to avoid this problem by distracting participants from an experiment's true purpose. For instance, an experimenter would not tell subjects, "We are examining how long you hold down the shock button, as an index of hostility." Instead, the experimenter would offer a plausible reason for administering shock—to study how punishment affects learning, for example. This shifts attention from the participant's use of shock to the recipient's "learning responses." As you will see, social psychologists have developed some rather skillful methods of engaging subjects' natural reactions. But it is always important to be on the lookout for these possible confounds. For example, do you think that having students in the anonymity experiment wear oversized white coats and hoods (not unlike those worn by members of the Ku Klux Klan) might have communicated an expectation to act antisocially?

FIELD EXPERIMENTS One way to overcome the hurdles of artificiality and demand characteristics is to bring the experiment out of the laboratory and into an everyday setting. This approach of using experimental manipulations on unknowing participants in natural settings is called **field experimentation**.

Consider a study in which the researchers took advantage of a naturally occurring manipulation of anonymity—the disguises worn by Halloween trick-or-treaters (Diener, Fraser, Beaman, & Kelem, 1976). Participants were children in costumes who arrived to trick-or-treat at a house in Seattle. The trick-or-treaters were greeted by a research assistant who pointed to a bowl of candies alongside a bowl of pennies. She told them to take *one* of the candies each and then she hurried off, claiming to be busy. Unbeknownst to the children, the researchers were watching from a hidden location and recording whether the little angels and superheroes took extra candies or filched some coins from the money bowl.

What made this an experiment is that the researchers randomly assigned groups of children to different levels of anonymity. Anonymity was manipulated by the way in which the experimenter greeted the children. In half the cases, she asked each child his or

Internal validity The extent to which an experiment allows confident statements about cause and effect.

Confound A variable that systematically changes along with the independent variable, potentially leading to a mistaken conclusion about the effect of the independent variable.

External validity The extent to which the results of an experiment can be generalized to other circumstances.

Demand characteristic Cue that makes participants aware of how the experimenter expects them to behave.

Field experimentation The manipulation of independent variables using unknowing participants in natural settings.

her name, thus removing the identity shield of the costume. In the other half, she allowed them to remain anonymous. The results supported the correlational findings obtained by Mann and the laboratory findings obtained by Zimbardo. When left anonymous, the majority of little devils grabbed more than they had been told to take. When they had been asked to identify themselves, however, most of them acted more angelically.

Why Social Psychologists Combine Different Methods

Table 1.2 summarizes the different methods and their main strengths and limitations. If each method has weaknesses, is the pursuit of social psychological knowledge

Table 1.2	Summary of Research Methods Used by Social Psychologists		
Method	**Description**	**Strengths**	**Weaknesses**
Descriptive Correlational Methods			
Naturalistic observation	Inconspicuous recording of behavior as it occurs in a natural setting **Example:** Moore's study of flirtation behavior in women	• Taps into people's spontaneous real world behaviors • Doesn't rely on people's ability to report on their own experiences	• Researcher may interfere with ongoing behavior • Some interesting behaviors are very rare. • Researcher may selectively attend to certain events and ignore others (observer bias)
Case studies	Intensive examination of a single person or group **Example:** Schaller's study of fame and self-awareness	• Provides a source of hypotheses • Allows study of rare behaviors	• Observer bias • Difficult to generalize findings from a single case • Impossible to reconstruct causes from complexity of past events
Archives	Examination of public records for multiple cases **Example:** Wilson and Daly's study of police homicide reports	• Easy access to large amounts of prerecorded data	• Many interesting social behaviors are never recorded.
Surveys	Researcher asking people direct questions **Example:** Kinsey's study of sexual behavior	• Allows study of difficult-to-observe behaviors, thoughts, and feelings	• People who respond may not be representative. • Participants may be biased or untruthful in responses.
Psychological tests	Researcher attempting to assess an individual's abilities, cognitions, motivations, or behaviors **Example:** Strong Vocational Interest Blank; SATs	• Allows measurement of characteristics that are not always easily observable	• Tests may be unreliable (yielding inconsistent scores). • Tests may be reliable but not valid (not measuring the actual characteristic they are designed to measure).
Experimental Methods			
Laboratory experiment	Researcher directly manipulating variables and observing their effects on the behavior of laboratory participants **Example:** Zimbardo's study of aggression and anonymity	• Allows cause–effect conclusions • Allows control of extraneous variables	• Artificial manipulations may not represent relevant events as they naturally unfold. • Participants' responses may not be natural, because they know they are being observed.
Field experiment	Same as laboratory experiment, but subjects in natural settings **Example:** Diener et al.'s study of trick-or-treaters	• Allows cause–effect conclusions • Participants give more natural responses.	• Manipulations may not be natural. • Less control of extraneous factors than in a laboratory experiment

hopeless? Not at all. The weaknesses of one method are often the strengths of another. For instance, experiments allow researchers to make cause–effect conclusions but have problems of artificiality. In contrast, archival methods and naturalistic observations do not allow cause–effect conclusions (because they are correlational), but the data they provide are not at all artificial. By *combining the different methods*, social psychologists can reach more trustworthy conclusions than any single method can provide (McGrath, Martin, & Kukla, 1982).

Consider a recent program of research that used multiple methods to examine the hypothesis that giving to others makes us happier (Aknin et al., 2013; Dunn & Norton, 2013). Elizabeth Dunn and her colleagues first conducted a survey to test this hypothesis (Dunn et al., 2008). In an initial correlational study, they asked a nationally representative sample of 632 Americans to rate their general happiness and to estimate what percentage of their income they spent on bills, on themselves personally, on gifts for others, and on donations to charity. Spending money on gifts for themselves was not related to respondents' happiness, but spending on other people was. Because this result is a correlation, we can't be sure whether spending on others caused people to be happier, or whether unhappy people simply tend also to be less generous (and might be made even less happy if they spent money on others). The researchers then conducted a longitudinal study of people who received an unexpected bonus at work and measured their happiness both before the bonus and six to eight weeks later. Those who had spent more of their bonus on other people experienced a significant boost in happiness; those who had spent more on themselves did not. This longitudinal study allowed the researchers to control for initial levels of happiness, but it still does not nail down a cause-and-effect relationship (besides chronic happiness levels, there might have been something else different about the people who chose to spend their money on others). So the researchers conducted an experimental study in which they asked a group of college students to rate their happiness in the morning, then gave them an envelope containing $5 or $20, and randomly assigned them to spend the money either on themselves or on others (by buying someone a gift or giving the money to charity). At the end of the day, the students again reported how happy they were. Those who had spent their money on themselves had not changed since the morning, but those who spent their money on others were happier. Interestingly, when asked to predict what would make them happier, other students (incorrectly) thought that they would be happiest if they got $20 to spend on themselves. Perhaps, one could argue, the experiment was not natural because participants might have guessed that the researchers were interested in their happiness and had obviously given them money between two measurements of happiness. However, because the results converge nicely with the other two correlational studies, showing a similar relationship in natural contexts, the researchers could be much more confident than if they had used only one method. For some interesting new findings on giving and happiness, see this chapter's research video.

The psychologist's situation is analogous to that of a detective confronted with stories from several witnesses to a murder, each less than perfect. The blind woman overheard the argument but couldn't see who pulled the trigger. The deaf man saw someone enter the room just before the murder but didn't hear the shot. The child was there to see and hear but tends to mix up the details. Despite the problems presented by each witness, if they all agree that the butler did it, it would be wise to check his fingerprints against those on the gun. Like the detective, the social psychologist is always confronted with bits of evidence that are, by themselves, imperfect but together may add up to a compelling case.

Just as detectives go back and forth between evidence and hunches—using evidence to educate their hunches and hunches to lead the search for new evidence— so, too, social psychologists go full cycle between the laboratory and the natural world (Cialdini, 1995). Evidence from descriptive studies conducted in the real world leads to theories that researchers test with rigorous experiments. The results of these theory-testing experiments lead back to new hunches about natural events in the real world. By combining different kinds of evidence, then, it is possible to come to more confident conclusions.

WATCH THE VIDEO: *Professor Dunn describes the program of research on spending money and happiness, including some recent updates.*

INVESTIGATION

You are a member of a research team, and you've been assigned to answer the following questions: How does alcohol affect our memory for the faces of new people we meet? How would you use a correlational approach to explore this question? How would you use an experimental approach? What are the greatest strengths and weaknesses of each approach likely to be?

Ethical Issues in Social Psychological Research

In reading about Zimbardo's study of aggression and anonymity, you might have wondered how the participants ended up feeling about themselves after delivering shocks to fellow students. Unlike geology or chemistry, social psychological research is conducted with living, breathing, feeling human beings (and sometimes other living creatures). This makes it important to consider another question: Is the research ethically justifiable?

ETHICAL RISKS IN SOCIAL PSYCHOLOGICAL RESEARCH Consider some of the research that we, the authors of this text, have conducted. One of us induced students to give up some of their blood using the following deceptive technique: "Would you be willing to join our long-term blood donor program and give a pint of blood every six weeks for a minimum of three years? No? Then how about just a single pint tomorrow?" (Cialdini & Ascani, 1976). Another one of us asked students whether they had ever had a homicidal fantasy, and, if so, to describe it in detail (Kenrick & Sheets, 1994). And in another investigation, we asked people to level with us about any prejudicial emotional reactions they felt toward different groups (including feminists, Christians, European Americans, African-Americans, and gay men) (Cottrell & Neuberg, 2005).

These studies yielded potentially useful information about charitable contributions, violent impulses, and prejudicial emotions. Yet each raised the sort of ethical questions that social psychologists confront frequently. Asking people about homicidal fantasies or prejudicial feelings constitutes a potential *invasion of privacy*. The invasion may not be egregious, because participants were volunteers who had the right to refrain from sharing any information if they so wished. But are researchers still violating social conventions by even asking? The problem of invasion of privacy becomes even

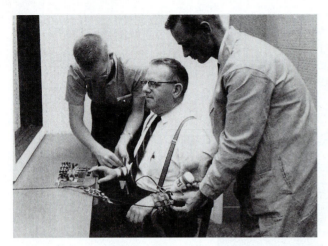

A scene from an ethically controversial experiment. In Milgram's research on obedience to authority, subjects were led to believe that they were delivering electric shocks to a man (shown here) who said that he had a heart condition. The research raised questions about exposing subjects to psychological discomfort.

more acute with naturalistic observations and field experiments, in which participants may not know that they are disclosing information about themselves. In one controversial study, unknowing participants were approached by a private detective who offered them an opportunity to help the government gather evidence by illegally breaking into an office (West, Gunn, & Chernicky, 1975). Is this sort of invasion of privacy justified in the interest of finding out about human behavior? The general rule of thumb psychologists follow is that using unwitting subjects is acceptable if they are left completely anonymous and if they will not be induced to perform behaviors that they would not otherwise (no actual break-ins occurred, for example).

In experiments people's behavior is manipulated, which raises another question: Will this research produce physical or psychological injury to the subject? Social psychological studies sometimes involve unpleasant physical manipulations, including strenuous exercise (Allen et al., 1989), injections of drugs such as adrenaline (Schachter & Singer, 1962), exposure to uncomfortable heat (Rule, Taylor, & Dobbs, 1987), or ingestion of alcohol (MacDonald, Fong, Zanna, & Martineau, 2000).

Physical dangers are generally less of a problem in social psychology than in medical research (in which the manipulations may actually lead to illness or death), but there are discomforts and slight risks nevertheless. Social psychological research is more likely to involve psychological injury, ranging from embarrassment (from being "taken in" by a deceptive cover story, for example) through guilt (for thoughts about homicidal fantasies or alternative romantic partners) to anxiety (produced by the threat of electric shock).

In perhaps the most controversial study in social psychology, Stanley Milgram (1963) led participants to think that they were delivering painful electric shocks to an older man who had a heart condition. Part way through the experiment, the older man completely stopped responding, yet the experimenter insisted that subjects continue to deliver higher and higher levels of shock. Subjects in this study showed extreme levels of anxiety, including "profuse sweating, trembling, and stuttering." Although this study was the subject of a rousing ethical controversy, Milgram (1964) defended it by pointing out that no participant showed evidence of lasting harm. In fact, 74% thought that they had learned something important. A year later, one subject wrote: "This experiment has strengthened my belief that man should avoid harm to his fellow man even at the risk of violating authority" (Milgram, 1964, 850). Milgram argued that researchers study controversial topics in the sincere hope that it "will lead to human betterment, not only because enlightenment is more dignified than ignorance, but because new knowledge is pregnant with human consequences."

ETHICAL SAFEGUARDS IN SOCIAL PSYCHOLOGICAL RESEARCH Social psychological research holds the promise of potential benefits—as any knowledge about love, prejudice, or homicidal violence could be used to better society. Yet the benefits must be weighed against the costs. How much discomfort for the participant is acceptable?

Fortunately, there are safeguards against abuses of scientific inquiry. For one, the American Psychological Association (APA) has a set of ethical guidelines for research. According to these guidelines, participants in psychological studies are told they are free to withdraw before consenting to any potentially injurious procedures, and they are debriefed after the research is completed. **Debriefing** involves discussing procedures and hypotheses with the participants, addressing any negative reactions they had and alleviating any problems before they leave. The APA guidelines also encourage psychologists to ask about costs and benefits: Does the research have the potential to produce useful knowledge that might justify temporary discomforts? For instance, Milgram argued that his study of obedience gave us insights into the horrible events in Nazi Germany.

Debriefing A discussion of procedures, hypotheses, and participant reactions at the completion of the study.

As another ethical safeguard, any institution applying for federal research funding (as do most colleges and universities) is required to have an institutional review board that evaluates the potential costs and benefits of research. Members of this board have no stake in the studies under consideration. They commonly ask researchers to revise manipulations, consent forms, or debriefing procedures. Using these safeguards, psychologists hope to optimize the tradeoff between subject discomfort and potential knowledge.

Quick Quiz

1 Which of the following are types of *experimental* methods?
   a. Case study
   b. Naturalistic observation
   c. Survey
   d. Field experiment
   e. All of the above

2 Which of these methods uncover correlations but do <u>not</u> establish causes?
   a. Archival method
   b. Naturalistic observation
   c. Case studies
   d. Surveys
   e. All of the above

3 Which of these factors is a limitation of an experiment?
   a. High internal validity
   b. Low external validity
   c. No confounding variables
   d. The absence of demand characteristics

4 Which of the following are examples of correlation *without* necessary causation?
   a. As ice cream consumption increases, the number of reported shark bites increases.
   b. Women who are highly satisfied with their partners spend less time noticing other attractive men.
   c. Regions with a high number of churches also report a high rate of alcoholism.
   d. All of the above

5 Which of the following is <u>not</u> an ethical risk in social psychological research?
   a. Invasion of privacy
   b. Psychological discomfort
   c. Debriefing
   d. None of the above

Social Psychology's Bridges with Other Areas of Knowledge

LO 1.10 Discuss the links between social psychology and other disciplines of psychology.

LO 1.11 Explain why an understanding of social psychology is valuable to disciplines outside of psychology.

As we have noted, social psychology is in many ways the ultimate bridging discipline. Social psychologists share many theories, methods, and research findings with researchers in other disciplines. Thus, you can make better sense of social psychology if you understand how it fits with other areas of knowledge.

Social Psychology and Other Areas of Psychology

Social psychology has direct bridges to all the other areas of psychology. Consider two central areas of experimental psychology—*cognitive psychology* (the study of mental processes) and *behavioral neuroscience* (the study of how biochemistry and neural structures relate to behavior). Social psychologists are increasingly studying how other people affect our physiological processes such as blood pressure, heart rate, and eye-blink responses (e.g., Amodio et al., 2003; Fritz, Nagurney, & Hegelson, 2003; Mendes et al., 2003). A new subdiscipline emerging from this work is called *social neuroscience* (the study of how social behavior is linked to events in the brain and other branches of the nervous system) (e.g., Berntson & Cacioppo, 2000; Dickerson et al., 2004; Lieberman, 2007; Varnum et al., 2012). For example, one study used magnetic resonance imagining (MRI) to study brainwave activity in white college students while they were exposed to faces of black men. Negative feelings toward black males were linked to activity in the amygdala (an area linked to emotional evaluation) when students were shown black strangers, but not when they were shown familiar and positively regarded blacks (such as Martin Luther King Jr., Will Smith, and Denzel Washington) (Phelps et al., 2000). Another facet of social neuroscience involves studying brain-damaged patients for clues about how the brain, cognition, and social behavior are interlinked (Stone et al., 2002). One particular form of brain damage leads to a disorder called prosopagnosia—the inability to recognize human faces (Rossion et al., 2003).

Social psychology also has close connections with *clinical psychology*—the study of behavioral dysfunction and treatment (e.g., Snyder & Forsyth, 1991; Snyder, Tennen, Affleck, & Cheavens, 2000). Understanding social relationships is essential if a psychologist wants to treat depression or loneliness or hopes to teach people how to deal with everyday stress, for instance (Dandeneau, Baldwin, Baccus, Sakellaropoulo, & Pruessner, 2007; Fredrickson et al., 2003; Simpson et al., 2003). Furthermore, many behavioral disorders are defined by their devastating effects on a person's social life. Throughout this text we will include a special feature, "Bridging Function and Dysfunction," in which we will examine problems rooted in, or causing disruptions for, social relationships. In this feature, we will consider how the social world can affect the disordered individual, and how normal group processes can sometimes go awry, from obsessive love relationships to paranoid distrust of "outsiders."

Clinical psychology has traditionally focused on suffering, weakness, and disorder, in hopes of alleviating these problems (Seligman, Steen, Park, & Peterson, 2005). In contrast, some social psychologists have also become increasingly involved in research on *positive psychology*—the study of factors leading to positive emotions, virtuous behaviors, and optimal performance in people and groups (e.g., Diener & Biswas-Diener, 2008; Gable & Haidt, 2005; Hogan & Kaiser, 2005). For example, several psychologists have examined the factors that cause some people to be happy with their social lives (e.g., Lyubomirsky et al., 2005; Myers, 2000; Van Boven, 2005).

Many social psychologists have also been involved in the area of *health psychology*—the study of behavioral and psychological factors that affect illness and physical well-being. Our relationships with other people can have direct consequences for our health, providing buffers against stress when they are going well and leading to health problems when they are going poorly (e.g., Stinson et al., 2008; Taylor et al., 2008). Social psychologists have also been applying knowledge about social influence to increase healthy behaviors, such as condom use among delinquent youth at risk for HIV (e.g., Bryan, Aiken, & West, 2004).

Positive Psychology Balancing psychologists' traditional interest in clinical disorders and negative behaviors, positive psychologists study the virtuous side of human behavior.

Researchers in the field of *developmental psychology* consider how lifetime experiences combine with predispositions and early biological influences to produce the adult's feelings, thoughts, and behaviors. Social relationships are central to development. For example, social development researchers study how infants become attached to their parents and how these early experiences affect relationships among adults (e.g., Del Giudice, 2009; Rom & Mikulincer, 2003; Sharpsteen & Kirkpatrick, 1997).

Personality psychology addresses differences between people and also examines how individual psychological components add up to a whole person. Many important personality differences are intimately tied to social relationships (e.g., Biesanz et al., 2007; Joireman et al., 2003; Pratto et al., 2013; Webster & Bryan, 2007). For example, two of the characteristics people use most often to describe one another—extraversion and agreeableness—are largely defined by social relationships (e.g., Aron & Aron, 1997; Graziano et al., 1997).

Environmental psychology is the study of people's interactions with the physical and the social environment (e.g., Aarts & Dijksterhuis, 2003). Environmentally oriented social psychologists study many important societal issues, including why people destroy the physical environment or how they respond to heat spells, water shortages, and urban crowding, and what motivates people to work toward energy conservation (e.g., Campbell et al., 2005; Griskevicius, Tybur, & Van den Bergh, 2010; Schroeder, 1995b; Van Vugt, 2009). These environmental issues will be a major focus of Chapter 13, which addresses global social dilemmas.

INVESTIGATION

Think about your plans following college (or graduate school). In what ways will a better understanding of the principles and findings of social psychology be beneficial to you?

Social Psychology and Other Disciplines

Social psychology is intimately linked not only to other areas of psychology, but also to other domains of knowledge. One of the first textbooks in social psychology was written by a sociologist, and the connections with the field of sociology continue to this day. Social psychologists have traditionally focused more on the *individual's* thoughts, feelings, and behaviors, whereas sociologists focus on the level of the group. However, like sociologists, social psychologists often consider how variables such as social class and shared social norms affect behaviors such as prejudice and aggression (e.g., Barnes et al., 2012; Jackson & Esses, 1997; Vandello & Cohen, 2003). Social psychologists have begun to consider how group processes may naturally emerge from individual thoughts and behaviors (Kerr & Tindale, 2004; Vallacher et al., 2002).

Social psychology is likewise linked with anthropology, a field concerned with the links between human culture and human nature (e.g., Fiske, 2000; Henrich et al., 2006). Anthropologists study cultures around the world for hints about which human social arrangements are universal and which ones vary by culture. Social psychology is also linked to several areas of biology, including genetics and zoology (e.g., Campbell, 1999; Gangestad & Simpson, 2000). In recent years, social psychologists have begun to use the methods of neuroscience to examine how hormones and brain structures affect parenting, love relationships, and responses to social stress (e.g., Berntson & Cacioppo, 2000; Diamond, 2003; Lieberman, 2007).

In addition to the bridges linking social psychology with other basic scientific disciplines, the field is also connected to several applied sciences, including law, medicine, business, education, and political science (e.g., Caprara et al., 2003; Kay et al., 2008; Kenrick & Griskevicius, 2013; McCann, 1997). Many of our interactions with other people take place in school and the workplace, and understanding social psychology can have practical payoffs in those settings. *Industrial/organizational psychology* integrates social psychology and business to understand social relationships in organizations (Pfeffer, 1998; Roberts et al., 2003; Van Vugt, Hogan, & Kaiser, 2008). In the political realm, many of the most pressing problems facing the world today—from environmental destruction to overpopulation to international conflict—are directly linked to social interactions. In our "Bridging Theory and Application" features, we discuss how social psychology can help us understand, and sometimes alleviate, practical problems in arenas ranging from the small classroom to the global ecosystem.

These connections highlight an important point: Although each course in the curriculum focuses on one area of knowledge, all of them are bridged together into a larger network. Your university education can be viewed as one long course designed to answer several big questions:

- What logical and methodological tools can we use to generate useful knowledge and to distinguish fact from fiction?
- What are the important ideas previous thinkers have had about human nature and our place in the universe, and what is the evidence for those ideas?
- How are those important ideas connected to one another?

Quick Quiz

1 Which of the following is true?

    a. Whereas clinical psychologists focus on pathology, social psychologists emphasize normal healthy behavior.

    b. Unlike positive psychologists, social psychologists focus on problematic behaviors such as aggression and prejudice.

    c. Unlike environmental psychologists, social psychologists focus on personality determinants of behavior.

    d. Social psychologists are increasingly using the tools of neuroscience to study the links between social behavior and changes happening inside the brain and body.

    e. All of the above

2 The study of virtuous behaviors and optimal group performance directly links social psychology with:

    a. Clinical psychology.

    b. Cognitive neuroscience.

    c. Environmental psychology.

    d. Positive psychology.

Revisiting The Mysteries of Social Life

We opened the chapter with several mysteries. Why would a previously poverty-stricken woman who suddenly struck it rich as a writer start giving away a large portion of her hard-earned wealth to help people she had never met? At the more general level, we asked about the factors that lead to charitable behavior, prejudice, divorce, and other social behaviors.

In this first chapter, we have not yet delved into the evidence social psychologists have uncovered about charitable behavior, heroism, prejudice, or leadership. However, the theoretical and methodological principles we discussed in this chapter have started us on the search for more informed answers. To begin with, by understanding the limitations of case studies we should realize that we can only go so far in reconstructing the particular causes of J.K. Rowling's decision to give away her hard-earned money rather than selfishly hoarding it for herself. Perhaps her experience as a struggling single mother on welfare gave her an extra dose of empathy for her fellow human beings

(indeed, much of her charitable work has aimed to help children in one-parent families). Or maybe her generosity traces back to her time working for Amnesty International, where she was exposed first-hand to people from other countries who had suffered harsh poverty and cruel injustices at the hands of wealthy and powerful despots (the real-life equivalent of Lord Voldemort and his Death-Eaters, who personify evil and greed in Rowling's novels). Perhaps it was the pain of losing her own beloved mother (the check for $15 million we mentioned at the outset went to fight multiple sclerosis, the disease that killed her mother at an early age). Yet another possibility is that she inherited a genetic proclivity toward generosity from her mom. Cases can inspire theoretical speculations, but hypotheses based on case studies ultimately need to be tested with more rigorous data from diverse and controlled methods. Going full circle, theoretical principles drawn from rigorous research can inspire new ways to think about particular cases in the real world.

Social psychology's theories and methods also provide a set of practical detective tools to address the more general questions raised by particular cases. Theoretical perspectives such as the sociocultural and cognitive approaches give social psychologists clues about probable places to begin their investigations. Research methods such as surveys and experiments provide tools that, like fingerprint kits for a detective, can help researchers see beyond the limitations of the unaided eye. In later chapters, we will review how these different theories and methods have already yielded a wealth of information about the broader questions we raised in this beginning chapter. As we shall see, social psychologists have learned quite a bit about why and how people help, hurt, love, and hate one another, and about the motivations behind charitable and heroic behaviors. We are also beginning to learn about how and why biological factors influence our relationships with other people and about how human biology and human culture interact with one another in dynamic and interesting ways.

Not everyone who reads a social psychology text aspires to a career as a behavioral researcher. But all of us are profoundly affected in our thoughts, feelings, and behaviors by the actions of other people—relatives, friends, lovers, coworkers, and even strangers on the street. A basic understanding of social psychology gives you a new set of lenses through which to view the people in your life who affect you so profoundly. As we will see, our everyday intuitions about social behavior are often slightly biased, and sometimes deeply wrong. If you try to be aware of other people's deeper motivations, and of your own cognitive biases, it can keep you from being blinded by the seemingly "obvious" and also help you appreciate the complexity that lies beneath the surface.

Besides providing potential clues about how to get along with the other people you encounter every day, the principles of social psychology can help you become a more informed citizen. As a voter and perhaps even a potential leader, you will be called on to make important decisions about education, criminal behavior, urban development, and race relations. It is hard to make a good decision if you do not know to evaluate the evidence. Finally, studying social psychology and understanding how its findings and theories bridge with other areas of knowledge can provide satisfaction at a purely intellectual level. We are entering a century in which many of the mysteries of social life will be solved, and the educated mind will be best prepared to marvel at those discoveries.

Chapter Summary

What Is Social Psychology?

1. Social psychology is the scientific study of how people's thoughts, feelings, and behaviors are influenced by other people. Social psychologists aim to describe social behavior carefully and to explain its causes.
2. Theories help connect and organize existing observations and suggest fruitful paths for future research.

Major Theoretical Perspectives of Social Psychology

1. Researchers who adopt a sociocultural perspective consider how behavior is influenced by factors that operate in larger social groups, including social class, nationality, and cultural norms.
2. The evolutionary perspective focuses on social behaviors as evolved adaptations that helped our ancestors survive and reproduce.
3. The social learning perspective focuses on past learning experiences as determinants of a person's social behavior.
4. The social cognitive perspective focuses on the mental processes involved in paying attention to, interpreting, and remembering social experiences.

Basic Principles of Social Behavior

1. Social behavior is goal oriented. People enter social situations with short-term immediate goals, and these are linked to broader long-term goals and ultimately to more fundamental motives (such as establishing social ties, understanding ourselves and others, gaining and maintaining status, defending ourselves and those we value, and attracting and retaining mates).
2. Social behavior represents a continual interaction between features within the person and events in the situation. People and their social situations choose, respond to, and alter one another.

How Psychologists Study Social Behavior

1. Descriptive methods (including naturalistic observations, case studies, archival studies, surveys, and psychological tests) involve recording behaviors, thoughts, and feelings in their natural state. These methods can uncover correlations, but they do not pin down causes.
2. Experimental methods search for causal processes by systematically manipulating some aspect of the situation (called the independent variable). Experiments allow conclusions about cause and effect but are more artificial than many descriptive methods.
3. Ethical issues for researchers include invasion of privacy and potential harm to subjects. These potential dangers must be weighed against the benefits of possibly useful knowledge.

Social Psychology's Bridges with Other Areas of Knowledge

1. Social psychology is closely connected to other sub-disciplines of psychology, including developmental, personality, clinical, cognitive, and physiological psychology.

2. Social psychology also connects to other disciplines, including basic research sciences like biology and sociology, as well as applied fields like organizational behavior and education.

Key Terms

Adaptation, 8

Archival method, 20

Case study, 19

Confound, 24

Correlation, 22

Correlation coefficient, 22

Culture, 7

Debriefing, 28

Demand characteristic, 24

Dependent variable, 23

Descriptive method, 18

Evolutionary perspective, 7

Experiment, 23

Experimental method, 18

External validity, 24

Field experimentation, 24

Generalizability, 19

Hypothesis, 17

Independent variable, 23

Internal validity, 24

Natural selection, 7

Naturalistic observation, 18

Observer bias, 19

Person, 16

Psychological test, 21

Random assignment, 23

Reliability, 21

Representative sample, 20

Situation, 16

Social cognitive perspective, 11

Social desirability bias, 20

Social learning perspective, 9

Social norm, 6

Social psychology, 4

Sociocultural perspective, 6

Survey method, 20

Theory, 4

Validity, 21

Chapter 2

The Person and the Situation

Video

Learning Objectives

LO 2.1   Understand the distinctions between motives and goals, and between automatic and conscious goal pursuit.

LO 2.2   Distinguish between exemplars and schemas, and between priming and chronic accessibility.

LO 2.3   Define and describe self-concepts, self-esteem, self-regulation, and self-presentation.

LO 2.4   Summarize the different types of situational influence, and discuss the distinction between strong and weak situations.

LO 2.5   Describe the differences between individualistic and collectivistic cultures.

LO 2.6   Explain the different types of person–situation interactions.

LO 2.7   Discuss the importance of person–situation fit in the workplace.

The Enigma of an Ordinary and Extraordinary Man

According to his sister, he was an "ordinary man." He grew up in a middle-class home, where his youth was happy but uneventful (Branch, 1988; Garrow, 1986). M. L., as he was known then, was obviously intelligent, but neither his family nor his friends considered him gifted.

His college years were also unspectacular. He earned mediocre grades, and his coworkers on a summer job gave him a "laziness" award. After receiving a graduate degree in theology, M. L. moved with his wife to take a job in Montgomery, Alabama. The "ordinary" young preacher had settled into an ordinary preacher's life.

But his settled life did not last long. Several weeks after the birth of his first child, the police in Montgomery arrested Rosa Parks, an African American woman, for refusing to give up her seat on a bus to a white man. The rest, as they say, is history. M.L., the "ordinary man," better known as Reverend Martin Luther King Jr., was catapulted into fame when he led the successful Montgomery bus boycott of 1955–1956, the first of his many triumphs for the U.S. Civil Rights movement.

For the next 12 years, King endured arrests, imprisonments, and attempts on his life. Despite these great obstacles, King marched on. Under his leadership the Civil Rights movement successfully overturned long-entrenched laws that barred blacks from having equal opportunities in education, employment, voting, and housing. King won the respect of people of all races for his willingness to assume huge personal burdens for the benefit of the greater good. And when an assassin's bullet cut short his life at the age of 39, King became to many a martyr, his death symbolizing both all that was wrong with race relations in the United States and the hope that the future could be so much better.

How can an "ordinary man" perform such extraordinary deeds? How can he have such a huge impact on his world?

Some argue that people's actions are determined by their personalities. From this perspective, King must have possessed a remarkable personality even before his role in the Montgomery bus boycott. Should we assume, then, that the perceptions of his family, friends, colleagues, and teachers were in error? Perhaps. But if the people who knew him best couldn't discern his true personality, who could? Moreover, if King's actions flowed from an extraordinary personality—one embodying special values and talents—how can we explain those times when these personal forces apparently abandoned him? In light of his powerful Christian beliefs and commitment to family, for instance, how does one explain his numerous marital infidelities? If his personality prior to the Rosa Parks incident was responsible for his actions afterward, it surely wasn't the neatly structured personality that people so easily attribute to him.

An "Ordinary Man"? Martin Luther King Jr. is viewed as heroic for his extraordinary actions on behalf of the Civil Rights movement. Yet, according to friends and family, he was in many ways "ordinary." How does an ordinary man perform extraordinary deeds? In this chapter, we explore how features of the person and of the situation work together to create the fascinating ways in which people relate to their social world.

Others argue that a person's actions are determined by the situation. Perhaps, then, we should assume that the situations in which King found himself were so powerful that virtually anyone would have responded as he did. King himself liked this explanation. He wasn't leading the movement at all, he would say. Instead, the people were pushing him along ahead of them. But this, too, is an oversimplification. After all, there were other potential leaders in Montgomery at the time who failed to assume the same burden of responsibility. And huge numbers of people throughout the nation had witnessed similar incidents of racial discrimination without taking action. The situation hadn't captured them as it had King.

It seems that, alone, neither King's personality nor his situation was enough to account for his conduct. How, then, do we explain Martin Luther King Jr.'s remarkable deeds?

The story of Martin Luther King Jr. illustrates one of the fundamental principles of modern social psychology: Neither the person nor the situation alone determines social behavior. Instead, features of the person and the situation *work together* in interesting and often complex ways to influence how people relate to their social world (Snyder & Cantor, 1998). In this chapter we begin to explore this fascinating interplay of person and situation, introducing what social psychologists mean when they discuss "the person," "the situation," and "person–situation interactions."

PERSON   The Person

LO 2.1   Understand the distinctions between motives and goals, and between automatic and conscious goal pursuit.

LO 2.2   Distinguish between exemplars and schemas, and between priming and chronic accessibility.

LO 2.3   Define and describe self-concepts, self-esteem, self-regulation, and self-presentation.

We open our examination of social behavior by peering inside the individual, asking "Who *is* the person as he or she enters the social situation?" As we'll see, the person is the social individual—a dynamic combination of motivations, knowledge, and feelings, all of which work with one another to produce the fascinating range of social thought and behavior we'll discover throughout this book.

Motivation: What Drives Us

Motivation is the driving force, the energy that moves people toward their desired outcomes. Confronted with a crime to be solved and seeking to discover *why* their criminal predator might have perpetrated the dastardly deed, police detectives ask questions about motive. Throughout this book, we provide answers to many mysteries of motivation: Why do people help others even when it places their own lives in jeopardy? Why are people prejudiced against those they don't even know? Why do people sometimes buy products they don't want and for which they have no use?

MOTIVES AND GOALS Think for a moment about what you want to accomplish over the next few weeks. Do you hope to get together with your old roommate for dinner next Saturday night? Do you want to study for an upcoming test in your math class? What are your **goals**? What do you want to achieve or accomplish?

If you're like most people, your list includes many goals having to do with everyday projects or concerns, such as looking attractive for a date, borrowing a classmate's notes for a lecture you missed, or cleaning your apartment (e.g., Emmons, 1989; Little, 1989). Now think about why you want to accomplish these goals. Why, for example, might you want to make yourself attractive, keep up with chemistry notes, or maintain a clean apartment? Many of your goals are *subgoals*—steps toward a larger goal. For instance, making yourself attractive may help you get a date, whereas borrowing class notes may help you earn good grades. And if you ask yourself why finding a date and getting good grades are important, you might conclude that a date could lead to a desired long-term relationship, whereas doing well in school could help you achieve social and economic status. As Figure 2.1 illustrates, we have goals at multiple levels and many of those goals enable us to reach other, more important, goals (e.g., Chulef, Read, & Walsh, 2001; Murray, 1938; Vallacher & Wegner, 1987). **Motives** are goals with a broad scope, such as the desires to gain status, protect family members from harm, and so on.

CONSCIOUS AND AUTOMATIC GOAL PURSUIT Achieving our goals sometimes requires considerable attention—we need to consider alternative strategies, decide which ones to pursue, closely monitor their effectiveness, and then adjust them if necessary (e.g., Duval & Wicklund, 1972; Heatherton, 2011; Mischel et al., 1996; Scheier & Carver, 1988). **Attention** is the process through which people consciously focus on what's going on within and around them. What we pay attention to is greatly influenced by our goals (e.g., Maner et al., 2007; Moskowitz, 2002). You can think of attention as a spotlight that illuminates the information we need to accomplish our goals. When we are interested in romance, we shine our attentional beam on the appealing classmate and his or her reactions to us; when we are concerned about safety, we focus our attention instead on burly strangers, dark alleys, and fast-moving cars.

Sometimes our strategies are so well practiced they become "automatized" and no longer require our attention (e.g., Bargh & Williams, 2006). **Automaticity** refers to the ability of a behavior or thought process to operate without conscious guidance once it's put into motion (Huang & Bargh, 2014; Wood & Neal, 2007). Once an experienced driver decides to drive her car, for example, she generally does not need to pay attention to coordinating the pedals, stick shift, and steering wheel.

Attention is a limited resource—we can only pay attention to a small amount of information at any one time (e.g., Pashler, 1994). But by

Motivation The force that moves people toward desired outcomes.

Goal A desired outcome; something one wishes to achieve or accomplish.

Motive A high-level goal fundamental to social survival.

Attention The process of consciously focusing on aspects of our environment or ourselves.

Automaticity The ability of a behavior or cognitive process to operate without conscious guidance once it's put into motion.

Figure 2.1 Multiple levels of goals

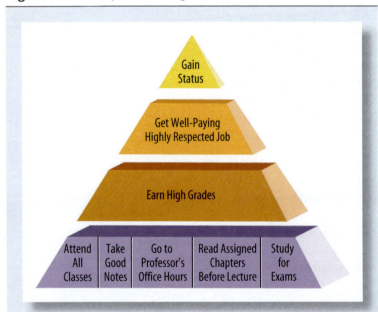

A person's fundamental motive to gain status may involve the goal of getting a good job, which may have a subordinate goal of achieving high grades, which itself may have a number of subordinate goals such as wanting to attend class, go to office hours, and so forth.

automatizing one task, we can devote our limited attention to other tasks. If you are an experienced driver, you have attention to spare for chatting with a passenger or changing the radio station. By automatizing the ways we think about and interact with others, we can efficiently move toward our goals.

There are clear benefits to moving through life without having to pay close attention to every single decision we make. But there are costs to such automaticity as well: We sometimes make "mindless" mistakes. Picture the following: You're about to use the copy machine in the library when a stranger walks up and asks if she can jump ahead of you to copy five pages. Participants in one study were more likely to grant this favor when the person provided a reason ("May I use the Xerox machine, *because I'm in a rush*") than when no excuse was offered (94% versus 60%). This appears to be a sensible strategy—after all, if the request is small and the person has a justifiable rationale, why not be nice and help her out? Surprisingly, however, people were also likely to grant the request (93%) even when the reason offered no new information ("May I use the Xerox machine, *because I have to make copies*?") (Langer, Blank, & Chanowitz, 1978). These subjects mindlessly activated their usual strategy—to be helpful and grant the request as soon as they heard the person say "because." As "because" suggests there's a reason, we may rarely register that the reason isn't really a justifiable one (After all, don't we *all* use the Xerox machine to make copies?). Sometimes people don't pay much attention to what they are doing and why they are doing it (Langer & Moldoveneau, 2000).

THOUGHT SUPPRESSION   We sometimes try to reach difficult goals by suppressing thoughts incompatible with those goals. Dieters may try not to think of tasty desserts and individuals recovering from failed relationships may attempt to avoid thinking about former lovers. Unfortunately, trying *not* to do something can be quite difficult. Let's perform a short experiment: Take out a piece of paper, a pen, and a watch. Clear your mind, and don't continue reading until it feels relatively unjumbled.

For the next three minutes, you are *not* to think about white bears. That's right, *white bears*. Don't think about polar bears; don't think about cute, little, fuzzy-white teddy bears; don't think about any kind of white bear at all. If you *do* happen to think about white bears, scribble a little tick mark on the paper. But this shouldn't happen often, because you are going to work hard at *not* thinking about them. Ready? Remember, no white bears. Okay. Begin the three minutes now. . .

How did you do? Did you think of white bears at all? If you are like the participants in a study by Daniel Wegner and his colleagues (Wegner et al., 1987), white bears probably ambled into your mind at least several times. Some individuals even find their thoughts totally inundated with images of the furry creatures. Moreover, now that you're no longer guarding against them, white bears will likely come to mind even more often than if you hadn't tried to suppress your images of them in the first place (Wegner & Erber, 1992).

If it can be hard to stop frivolous thoughts about bears from "rebounding" back into mind, might it also be difficult to suppress other, more important thoughts? When on a diet, for example, might attempts to keep thoughts of food out of mind focus us even more on the joys of potato chips, Big Macs, and hot fudge sundaes? Might attempts to suppress our fear of spiders make it even more likely that we will feel fearful of those eight-legged arachnids? Might attempts to suppress your stereotypes of a disliked ethnic group actually increase the likelihood that you'll negatively stereotype this group? The answer to these questions seems to be a resounding yes (e.g., Hooper et al., 2011; Macrae et al., 1996; Monteith, Sherman, & Devine, 1998; Wenzlaff & Wegner, 2000). Trying not to think about something often backfires.

Thus our first peek into the person reveals that we are motivated creatures. We have goals, and we pursue them. Goal pursuit sometimes requires attention and willpower, but it often operates automatically. This automaticity frees us to focus our attention and willpower elsewhere. We turn now to explore a second key component of the person—knowledge.

INVESTIGATION

Most of us have made resolutions—at New Year's, for instance—to change something about our lives. Think back to a resolution that didn't work out for you or an important goal you didn't achieve. Given what you've learned about reaching goals, why do you think your resolution failed? What can you do in the future to increase the chances you'll achieve your goals?

Knowledge: Our View of the World

Knowledge comes in many rich and varied forms. As Figure 2.2 illustrates, we have *sensory memories* of visual images, smells, sounds, tastes, and touches. For example, based on films you've seen, you may have an image of what Martin Luther King Jr. looked and sounded like as he gave his rousing "I have a dream" speech at the Lincoln Memorial. We also have *beliefs* about people's behaviors, traits, abilities, goals, preferences, relationships, and usual activities. For instance, your impression of Martin Luther King Jr. may include the beliefs that he was a minister, a Civil Rights activist, and a skilled orator. Our knowledge also includes *explanations* for why people, groups, or situations are the way they are (e.g., Kunda, Miller, & Claire, 1990; Sedikides & Anderson, 1994). For example, we may explain King's pursuit of egalitarian goals by pointing to his religious values.

How is all this knowledge organized in memory? As an example, take out a pen and a piece of paper and list everything that occurs to you when you think about *great leaders*. Be free and open with your listing—write down everything that comes to mind.

Figure 2.2 A mind's-eye view of Dr. King

Mental representations hold and organize the information we have about people, objects, and events. A hypothetical mental representation of Dr. Martin Luther King Jr. might contain information of the sorts illustrated here.

Based on research, we suspect that your list might include some *specific* examples of great leaders—perhaps Martin Luther King Jr., Abraham Lincoln, or Queen Victoria. We call knowledge of a specific episode, event, or individual an **exemplar** (e.g., Smith & Zárate, 1992). We also suspect that your list included some *general characteristics* that great leaders, as a group, tend to possess. For example, perhaps you believe that great leaders want to better the lives of those around them and use their charisma to influence others for the better. Knowledge that represents generalized information of this sort is called a **schema** (e.g., Bartlett, 1932; Taylor & Crocker, 1981). Our views of the social world contain both exemplars and schemas. And we'll see in just a few pages that people also possess knowledge of social situations and how they fit into them.

WHAT DOES KNOWLEDGE DO? Knowledge provides the "raw material" for many social judgments. Just as a builder uses bricks, wood, and concrete to create a house, people use their knowledge to form impressions, make decisions, and so on.

Knowledge also tells us what to expect from our encounters with the world. To believe that college professors as a group are absent-minded is to expect that the next professor you come across will be a bit flaky; to believe that fine restaurants employ servers is to expect that you will be waited on in the next nice restaurant you visit. Knowledge guides our expectations, preparing us for our social encounters by suggesting what we ought to be paying attention to, how we should interpret ambiguous situations, and how we ought to behave.

Consider a classic study by Harold Kelley (1950): College students learned one day that a substitute instructor would be teaching their class. Some students were led to believe the substitute would be generally warm and friendly, whereas others were led to believe he would be somewhat cold and distant. After the class period, all students evaluated the teacher. Even though both sets of students viewed the *same* lecture, those expecting the teacher to be nice formed more favorable impressions of him than did those expecting him to be unfriendly. Why? Their expectation led them to focus on somewhat different behaviors and, even when focused on the same behaviors, to interpret them differently. The knowledge we bring with us as we observe social events influences how we understand them (e.g., Bruner, 1957; Higgins et al., 1977; Sinclair et al., 1987). In Chapter 3, we continue to explore the important roles that expectations play as people try to make sense of their social world.

PRIMED KNOWLEDGE Throughout our lives we accumulate a huge amount of knowledge. Do we use all of it, all of the time, for making all judgments? If we only use some of it, what do we use, and why? Is some knowledge more "ready" for use than other knowledge?

One of the authors earned money as teenagers by cutting his neighbors' grass with a lawn mower. Before he could start the engine, he needed to "prime" it—to pump a little gas in before pulling the ignition cord. Just as priming the engine was a process for making it ready to use, **priming** in the psychological sense is the process of activating knowledge or goals—of making them ready to use (Wheeler & DeMarree, 2009).

Knowledge is primed by the situations we're in. The thoughts that come to mind while sitting in math class are different from those that come to mind while sitting around the family dinner table. Situational priming is extremely useful, as it greatly increases the chance that the most relevant knowledge will be accessible to us when we need it. After all, the knowledge you need to understand a math lesson differs greatly from the knowledge you need to understand why your brother and sister are arguing.

Knowledge is also primed by related knowledge. When you think of your brother, for instance, a visual image may pop to mind, as may your beliefs about his goals, personality, and typical behaviors. Thinking about your brother will also make it more likely that you'll start thinking about other family members. Because knowledge is interconnected, as one thought becomes active, it primes related knowledge as well.

Exemplar A mental representation of a specific episode, event, or individual.

Schema A mental representation capturing the general characteristics of a particular class of episodes, events, or individuals.

Priming The process of activating knowledge or goals, of making them ready for use.

Finally, some thoughts come to mind more readily than others: These thoughts are **chronically accessible**, ready to "leap into action" with only the slightest encouragement. For example, if you are especially involved in your new job, images of your coworkers may present themselves with relative ease; if you are trying to remember your first-grade classmates, their images may be less accessible (e.g., Bargh & Pratto, 1986; Higgins, King, & Mavin, 1982; Wyer & Srull, 1986). Again, this is very useful. For a person who spends a lot of time at work, it's important that work-related knowledge be accessible and ready for use.

Throughout the book, we will explore how our knowledge of the social world influences how we think about it, feel toward it, and act within it.

Feelings: Attitudes, Emotions, and Moods

The nasty-looking thug on a lonely street fills us with fear. A magical first encounter with that "special" person incites us to romance and desire. And Martin Luther King Jr.'s "I have a dream" speech reverberates through us, echoing sadness and hope. Feelings are the music of life.

Social psychologists consider three general types of feelings—attitudes, emotions, and moods. **Attitudes** are favorable or unfavorable evaluations of particular people, objects, events, or ideas (Bohner & Dickel, 2011; Eagly & Chaiken, 1998; Petty & Wegener, 1998). You may dislike politicians, like double fudge ice cream sundaes, and be in favor of capital punishment. Attitudes are relatively basic feelings, simple evaluations along a positive–negative continuum—we feel positively or negatively, favorably or unfavorably, approvingly or disapprovingly about something.

Emotions—feelings such as fear, joy, anger, and guilt—are richer, more complex, and more intense than attitudes. In addition to their positivity/negativity component, they also have a physiological arousal component. When people are fearful, for example, their hearts begin to pound, their respiration quickens, their facial expressions change, and their bodies start pumping adrenaline. Moreover, emotions are often accompanied by complex thoughts, as when feelings of shame trigger memories of childhood inadequacy and social sins we committed as adolescents.

Finally, **moods** are feelings that are less focused and longer lasting than emotions. When we're in a bad mood, everything about the morning seems gray; when we're in a good mood, everything is rosy; when we're anxious, the sight of our own shadows can make us nervous. A mood colors all our experiences, not just the particular event that brought it about initially.

Because social behavior is powerfully influenced by feelings, measuring those feelings is crucial. It can be difficult to figure out what's going on inside another person, but, as we see next, psychologists have developed some useful techniques for reading people's feelings.

ASSESSING FEELINGS   If you want to know how a friend felt about breaking up with her boyfriend, what would you do? To start, you might just ask her. Researchers often do the same, although in a more systematic, sophisticated way . *Self-report measures* can be as straightforward as asking a simple series of questions. For example, "On a 9-point scale—with 1 = extremely sad and 9 = extremely happy—how do you feel right now?"

It often makes good sense simply to ask people to report their feelings. After all, feelings are personal experiences and the person having them will usually know them best. There can be problems associated with this method, however. For instance, people may hesitate to report feelings they believe to be socially inappropriate or undesirable. As one example, your friend may be reluctant to admit that she felt no sadness at all after splitting with her old boyfriend.

Because people sometimes have reason to hide their true feelings or may have difficulty expressing feelings in words, social psychologists also look toward *behavior* for clues. This, of course, is similar to what nonpsychologists do when they don't trust what others are telling them. For example, you might presume that a person with

Chronically accessible The state of being easily activated, or primed, for use.

Attitudes Favorable or unfavorable evaluations of a particular person, object, event, or idea.

Emotions Relatively intense feelings characterized by physiological arousal and complex cognitions.

Moods Relatively long-lasting feelings that are diffuse and not directed toward particular targets.

glaring eyes, tightened jaw, and clenched fists is angry. Indeed, detailed analyses of facial expressions can often provide a fascinating window on a person's feelings (Ekman, 1982; Keltner & Ekman, 1994). However, this isn't foolproof either. People can sometimes manipulate their emotional expressions, pretending to be angry, for instance, when they're really not. Moreover, different people may respond to the same feeling in very different ways (e.g., Gross, John, & Richards, 2000). Whereas some people fly into a rage when angry, others become icy calm and calculating. Nonetheless, psychologists interested in assessing people's feelings can obtain very useful information by observing their behavior.

Finally, social psychologists have several tools at their disposal that ordinary people do not. For instance, researchers can use instruments designed to gather *physiological measures* of blood pressure, heart rate, respiration, sweating, and biochemical production. People who are anxious, for instance, often get sweaty palms and pounding hearts, and specialized instruments can pick these up (Blascovich & Kelsey, 1990). Similarly, different facial expressions characterize emotions such as anger, fear, disgust, and joy, and these expressions can be assessed with the use of facial electrodes sensitive to even tiny changes in facial muscles (Cacioppo et al., 1993). And emotion-relevant brain activity can be observed with modern technologies such as positron emission tomography (PET) scans and functional magnetic resonance imaging (fMRI). For example, it appears that different areas of the brain become active when we are happy as opposed to disgusted or angry, or when we feel good about a friend winning a reward (e.g., Davidson et al., 1990; Varnum et al., 2014).

Physiological measures have their weaknesses too, however. Different people often exhibit different biological responses to the same emotional state; when aroused, some people show increases in heart rate, whereas others show increases in skin conductance. Moreover, physiological measures are influenced by processes other than emotion. For example, your heart rate goes up when you are angry, but also when you exercise. Most important, researchers have yet to discover any physiological pattern that maps perfectly onto any particular emotion. Indeed, this problem contributes to the controversy over the effectiveness of lie-detector machines, an issue we explore in Chapter 4.

Nonetheless, physiological instruments can be quite valuable, particularly when used in conjunction with other kinds of measures. If a person says she's afraid, displays the usual facial expressions and bodily postures, and has a racing heart and sweaty palms, she is probably fearful ("If it looks like a duck, walks like a duck, and quacks like a duck, it's probably a duck!"). Indeed, this seems to be the most important lesson: To the extent that self-report measures, behavioral indicators, and physiological measures all provide *converging* evidence, we can be confident that we indeed know what the person is feeling.

GENETIC AND CULTURAL FOUNDATIONS OF FEELINGS Is there a genetic basis to what we feel and how we express those feelings? How would we know? First, because humans share the vast majority of their genes with one another, we might expect many aspects of feelings to be universal. Consistent with this hypothesis, people from many different societies express and experience emotions in surprisingly similar ways (e.g., Ekman & Friesen, 1971; Hejmadi, Davidson, & Rozin, 2000; Mauro, Sato, & Tucker, 1992). For example, people from various cultures—including

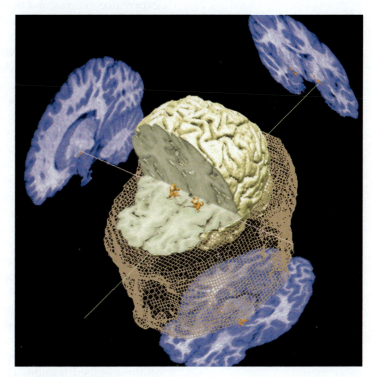

Mapping emotions. How do psychologists know what others are feeling? fMRI imaging techniques scan the brain to reveal changes in blood flow related to different activation patterns. In the image above, the orange "clouds" reveal areas of the brain that become especially active when people view negative images such as weapons or horrible accidents. Together with self-report measures and behavioral observations, physiological measures such as fMRI help researchers identify others' emotions.

nonliterate cultures unexposed to Western influences—agree strongly on which facial expressions reflect happiness, sadness, fear, disgust, and anger, and they also report very similar feelings, physiological symptoms, and emotion-related behaviors (Scherer & Wallbott, 1994). Second, if there is a strong genetic component to certain feelings, they should be experienced and expressed even in individuals who haven't had the opportunity to learn how and when to experience and express them. Indeed, when they win or lose, athletes who were born blind produced the exact same facial expressions of agony and ecstasy as did athletes whose vision was intact (Matsumoto & Willingham, 2009). Finally, if genes influence feelings, then people who differ from one another genetically should differ in their feelings. This, too, is the case (e.g., Gabbay, 1992): Genetic heredity influences our emotional expressions, our moods, and even some of our everyday attitudes (e.g., Kim et al., 2011; Lykken & Tellegen, 1996; Plomin et al., 1990; Tesser, 1993; Waller et al., 1990). It's clear that genes contribute greatly to feelings.

It's also clear that culture and learning play a large role. For instance, in addition to cross-cultural similarities in how we experience and express our feelings, there are important cross-cultural differences as well (e.g., Eid & Deiner, 2001; Kobayashi et al., 2003; Marsh et al., 2003; Mesquita, 2001; Russell, 1994, 1995; Wong et al., 2008). For instance, although European Americans, Asian Americans, and Hong Kong Chinese all want to experience positive feelings, European Americans especially value feeling excited, Hong Kong Chinese especially value feeling calm, and Asian Americans value both (Tsai, Knutson, & Fung, 2006). As another example, whereas Utku Eskimos rarely express anger, even when provoked, the men of the Awlad 'Ali Bedouin tribe of western Egypt are quick to respond angrily to even the remote appearance of an insult (Abu-Lughod, 1986; Briggs, 1970). And people from different cultures often look to different cues in the face and surrounding situation to infer others' emotions (Masuda et al., 2008; Yuki et al., 2007). It's clear that cultures teach their members when and how to experience, express, and understand feelings (e.g., Lewis, 1993; Saarni, 1993). Genes and culture, together, create the foundation for our experience and expression of feelings.

PHYSIOLOGICAL AND COGNITIVE INFLUENCES ON FEELINGS   Genes give us the capability to experience certain emotions, moods, and attitudes, and these capabilities are modified, differentiated, and developed through learning and cultural processes. So what is it that determines what a person feels in any single moment? Part of the answer is relatively simple—some feelings are automatically triggered by the perception of a particular event (e.g., Zajonc, 1980; Ohman & Mineka, 2001). For example, the simple perception of a wasp flying rapidly toward one's head will be enough to arouse fear. We'll consider two other proximate contributors to feelings: current physiological states and thoughts.

Try the following: (a) *Gently* hold the end of a pen between your teeth, making sure it doesn't touch your lips (Figure 2.3); what does this feel like? (b) After a while remove the pen and replace it, this time gripping the end of it firmly with your lips (no teeth) and making sure it doesn't droop downward (Figure 2.3); what is this sensation like?

Fritz Strack, Leonard Martin, and Sabine Stepper (1988) used this task in an experiment with student volunteers. The students were led to believe the researchers were investigating ways for people with physical impairments to perform everyday tasks like writing or phone dialing. They were then asked to hold a pen with their teeth, with their lips, or in their nondominant hand. While they grasped the pen in the designated fashion, students performed a connect-the-dots exercise and an underlining task. Finally, the students were asked to evaluate the funniness of several cartoons by circling with the pen the appropriate number on a rating scale, still grasping the pen in the assigned fashion. This last task was what the investigators were really interested in. They expected to observe differences in the funniness ratings across the three pen-grasping conditions. What do you think they discovered? Why?

Recall your experience of holding the pen in your mouth the two different ways. Also, look again at the photos in Figure 2.3. Holding the pen gently between the teeth causes the facial muscles to contract into something like a smile; in contrast, holding the pen firmly between the lips creates a facial expression incompatible with smiling and similar to an angry grimace. Because different facial expressions are associated with

Figure 2.3 The pen-holding experiment

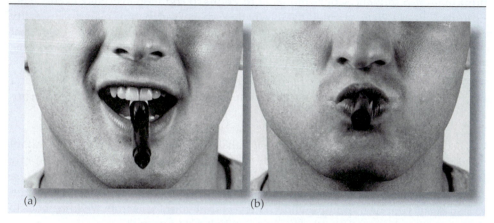

(a)   (b)

Hold a pen in your mouth as the model in (a) is doing. What is this sensation like? Now hold the pen as the model in (b) is doing. What is this sensation like? Do you notice a difference between the two? How might these different facial expressions influence your feelings?

different emotional states—for instance, we often smile when we are happy or amused—the researchers hypothesized that students holding the pen with their teeth (facilitating a smile) should rate the cartoons the funniest, whereas students holding the pen with their lips (inhibiting a smile) should find the cartoons less funny. These were indeed the students' reactions. Others have observed similar patterns (McCanne & Anderson, 1987), and researchers now believe that the contraction and relaxation of certain facial muscles can influence the emotions people experience (e.g., Cacioppo et al., 1993; Kleck et al., 1976).

Just as changes in facial muscles can alter feelings, changes in other aspects of our physiology—for example, in the neurochemistry and the autonomic nervous system (i.e., the heart, visceral organs, and endocrine glands)—can do the same (Lewis, 2000; Plutchik, 1994). Changes in ongoing thinking also affect our feelings. In particular, our feelings are influenced strongly by how we interpret—or *appraise*—our situations (e.g., Lazarus & Folkman, 1984; Neumann, 2000; Siemer, Mauss, & Gross, 2007; Sinclair et al., 1994). Guilty feelings, for example, arise from the perception that we have harmed a person whom we care about and who cares about us (Baumeister et al., 1994; Tangney, 1992). Thus we might feel guilty when we fail to return a phone call from mom, but not when we ignore a call from an annoyingly persistent salesperson. Although our action—not returning the call—is identical in both cases, our different appraisals of the two situations create quite different feelings.

Victoria Medvec, Scott Madey, and Thomas Gilovich (1995) cleverly demonstrated how ongoing thought can affect feelings. Before reading about their study, though, answer the following question: Who is happier after their Olympic performances: silver medalists, who finish in second place, or bronze medalists, who finish third? The researchers analyzed film of athletes from the 1992 Summer Olympics and discovered that bronze medalists were happier than the silver medalists, even though the silver medalists did better. Why? It's relatively easy for silver medalists to imagine improving their performances enough to earn the gold medal and all its associated fame and glory. As a result, they were somewhat disappointed in their performances. In contrast, it's easy for bronze medalists to imagine making even tiny mistakes that would have left them in fourth place or worse—leaving them with no medal at all. As a result, they felt relieved and happy to have won the bronze.

The thrill of bronze, the agony of silver. Who should be happier—athletes who finish second or athletes who finish third? Research by Victoria Medvec, Scott Madey, and Thomas Gilovich (1995) reveals that bronze medalists are generally happier than the more successful silver medalists, such as the woman pictured here. Why might this be?

This kind of "what might have been" thinking—labeled **counterfactual thinking**—also influences our emotional reactions to common everyday events (e.g., Epstude & Roese, 2008; Mandel, 2003). Whether we feel sad, happy, regretful, or guilty may depend on whether we imagine happier, sadder, or prouder alternatives to what really happened (e.g., McMullen & Markman, 2002; Niedenthal, Tangney, & Gavanski, 1994; Tykocinski & Steinberg, 2005).

Thus the foundations of our feelings are determined by our genes and culture, and our more proximate reactions are heavily influenced by current physiological states and how we interpret our surroundings and label our feelings.

WHY FEELINGS ARE IMPORTANT   As you walk on campus after class, thinking about your friend's upcoming wedding, you notice out of the corner of your eye a rapidly looming object. Even before you realize it's an automobile (and certainly before you're able to identify its make and model for the police report), your body tenses, you begin to lean away, your heart pumps wildly, and you shift your focus from wedding bells to the impending danger. Energized by fear, you bolt out of its path.

This illustrates one of the primary functions of emotions: to alert us when something isn't normal. When our ongoing activities are interrupted—as when the barreling car interferes with your thoughts of your friend's wedding—we become physiologically aroused, and this arousal signals us to shift our attention from our current activities to the new, emerging concern (e.g., Berscheid, 1983; Frijda, 1986; Tomkins, 1980).

When we notice the oncoming hunk of steel, we don't become joyous, sad, or amused; none of these states helps us take evasive action. Rather, we feel fear—a high-adrenaline state compatible with quick movement. This illustrates an important point: It makes no sense to sound the same emotional alarm every time something unexpected happens. Rather, different emotions accompany different circumstances (Carver & Scheier, 1998; Frijda, 1988; Gonnerman et al., 2000; Izard, 2007; Shiota et al., 2006). When our security is threatened, we become fearful; when we learn of an unanticipated low grade, we are saddened; and when we get an even bigger raise than expected, we feel joyous.

Attitudes and moods are useful as well. Attitudes enable us to make quick approach/avoidance judgments about things, without having to think too much about them (e.g., Cacioppo, Gardner, & Berntson, 1999; Chen & Bargh, 1999). When seeing a friend, we approach her; upon encountering a burly stranger clad in leather and chains, we avert our eyes and try to pass unnoticed. And moods, which are often carryover feelings from emotional responses, prepare us to deal with our current circumstances (Schwarz & Clore, 1996). If we hear of layoffs at work, we remain anxiously attuned to signs of being fired; if we've recently been praised by a boss, we stay happily alert for other rewards from the company.

Feelings have longer-term benefits as well. Positive emotions reduce the physical stress brought on by negative life events and enable people to think more broadly, creatively, and openly (e.g., Fredrickson & Levenson, 1998; Isen, 2002; Zautra et al., 2005). As a result, they help us develop more effective ways to cope with the crises in our lives (Fredrickson, 2001). Americans' reactions to the September 11, 2001, terrorist attacks on New York City and Washington, D.C., provide a case in point. The events of that tragic day took a great emotional toll: Many Americans experienced strong anger, fear, and sadness, and had difficulty sleeping and concentrating. Data collected in the weeks following September 11 revealed, however, that those who supplemented their negative emotions with positive emotions coped better than those who did not. It wasn't that these resilient individuals reported fewer attack-related negative emotions, but rather that they *also* reported feeling hope, pride, and other positive emotions (Fredrickson et al., 2003). These folks managed to find something positive in the aftermath of the attack—perhaps a greater appreciation for friendships and family or a sense that the United States could pull together. Positive emotions serve an important, adaptive role: In both the short and long term, they help us deal better with the negative events and crises that confront us.

Counterfactual thinking The process of imagining alternative, "might have been" versions of actual events.

Thus feelings are an essential component of the person. They tell us when we're moving nicely toward our goals and when we're not. They also prepare us to deal with our circumstances and make whatever adjustments appear useful. In contrast to popular views suggesting that feelings are irrational sources of human error and misery, we see instead that they are quite functional and necessary (Keltner, Haidt, & Shiota, 2006; Parrott, 2002).

Introducing the Self

Are you a "good" person? What could you do to reach your long-term goals? Why do you think others view you as they do? Although we all struggle to find the right answers to questions like these, we ask them of ourselves easily and naturally. Unlike other animals, we humans are self-reflective: We think about ourselves . . . a lot.

Self-Reflection. People spend a lot of time assessing their strengths and weaknesses, contemplating how to reach their goals, and wondering how they come across to others.

Why are we so self-obsessed? Self-reflection enables us to know about ourselves, control our actions, and present ourselves more effectively to others (e.g., Leary & Tangney, 2003). We explore the effects of the self throughout the book. Here, we briefly introduce some of the main ideas.

WHO AM I AND HOW DO I FEEL ABOUT MYSELF?: SELF-CONCEPT AND SELF-ESTEEM

Who are you? Take a minute and write about yourself: List whatever comes to mind.

Although the content of your list likely differs from your earlier description of great leaders, the *types* of things you listed were probably similar. You may have listed examples of past behavior, and you almost certainly listed some general characteristics you believe describe you. Indeed, just as we possess knowledge about others, we also possess knowledge of ourselves—the **self-concept**. Like other people and social events, you yourself are an "object" to be understood by your mind (James, 1890).

You may also have described your attitude toward yourself—your **self-esteem**. People who feel favorably about themselves are said to have high self-esteem; people who feel negatively about themselves have low self-esteem. Your self-esteem—how high it is, how stable it is, and how much it's threatened by social events—greatly influences how you think, feel, and act.

Multiple selves. Is there just one of you, or several? Just as your thoughts of "great leaders" likely include multiple exemplars, your self-concept includes multiple selves. Some of your selves are linked to the roles you play and the relationships you have (e.g., Chen, Boucher, & Tapias, 2006; Markus & Wurf, 1987). For instance, Martin Luther King Jr. probably saw himself as a husband, a father, a leader, and a preacher. Some selves are linked to your current goals in life (Kenrick & Griskevicius, 2013).

Other selves are linked to the future—they represent what you ideally hope to become, what you think you ought to become, and what you fear becoming (e.g., Markus & Nurius, 1986; Oyserman et al., 2004). King hoped to be a strong, effective champion of Civil Rights, thought he ought to be a better husband to his wife and a better father to his children, and feared becoming a glory-seeking leader out of touch with the people. Future selves like these are important because they help define our goals and direct our actions. When we believe, for example, that our "actual selves" (who we think we actually are) fall short of our "ought selves" (who we think we ought to be), we become anxious and that anxiety motivates us to work harder toward our goals (Higgins, 1996). Most of us, like Martin Luther King Jr., "have a dream," and in that dream of a better future world we may also imagine a better future "me."

Finally, most of us possess, to some degree, a group or *collective self*. Just as King saw himself as being a black American, you might view yourself as being a New Yorker, a woman, or a Unitarian (e.g., Deaux et al., 1995; Triandis, 1989). We'll see

Self-concept A mental representation capturing our views and beliefs about ourselves.

Self-esteem Our attitude toward ourselves.

later in the chapter that who you are in any moment—which of your selves dominates—often depends on what aspect of your self is made salient by your current situation.

Where self-concept and self-esteem come from.   Where do our beliefs and feelings about ourselves come from? Sometimes we learn about ourselves through **social comparison**—by comparing our abilities, attitudes, and beliefs with those of others (Festinger, 1954; Wood & Wilson, 2003). By seeing, for example, how well your exam grades compare to a classmate's, you may learn something about your academic abilities.

We also come to know ourselves through a **reflected appraisal process**—by observing or imagining what others think of us (e.g., Cooley, 1902; Mead, 1934; Tice & Wallace, 2003). A child may come to think of herself as talented, amusing, difficult, or overweight, based on her observations of how her parents and fellow students respond to her.

Finally, sometimes we come to understand ourselves in the same way we come to understand others. If you see, for instance, a neighbor viciously reprimanding his child, you might guess that he's insensitive or cruel. We may learn about ourselves in a similar way, by "stepping outside ourselves" and observing our own actions (Bem, 1967, 1972). By engaging in this **self-perception process**—the process through which people observe their own behavior to infer their own internal characteristics—you may come to believe that you are or are not a very good parent.

Consider an experiment conducted by Jerry Burger and David Caldwell (2003). While participating in a study ostensibly exploring issues related to personality, some college students were asked by another student to sign a petition encouraging politicians to work harder to end homelessness. Participants in a second condition were offered $1 for signing the petition, and those in a third condition were told after signing: "It's great to see someone who cares about people in need."

Social comparison The process through which people come to know themselves by comparing their abilities, attitudes, and beliefs with those of others.

Reflected appraisal process The process through which people come to know themselves by observing or imagining how others view them.

Self-perception process The process through which people observe their own behavior to infer internal characteristics such as traits, abilities, and attitudes.

Two days later, a new experimenter phoned all these participants (as well as a control group of students who hadn't been asked previously to sign the petition) and asked whether they'd be willing to volunteer two hours during the upcoming weekend to box canned goods for a local homeless shelter. What do you think they found? Which students were especially likely to volunteer their time?

As Figure 2.4 reveals, students who signed the petition and were labeled by the confederate as a caring person were especially likely to donate their time. Why? They had two things going for them. First, they had observed themselves choosing to sign the petition and so, via a self-perception process, they likely came to view themselves as helpful people. Moreover, they had been labeled as helpful by the other student and so, via a reflected appraisal process, had a second reason to see themselves as helpful. Indeed, after signing the petition, these participants in particular reported that they were the kind of people who support needy others.

But what of those who signed the petition and also received $1 for doing so? Shouldn't they have been especially likely to volunteer later? After all, don't rewards increase the likelihood of doing similar behaviors in the future? Not in this case. In line with what we'd expect from self-perception processes, "watching" themselves sign for money likely led them to infer that they were not really signing for prosocial reasons, but rather for the money. Indeed, just as these students exhibited very little enhanced volunteering, they also exhibited very little evidence of an enhanced prosocial self-concept.

Figure 2.4   "I'm the kind of person who helps."

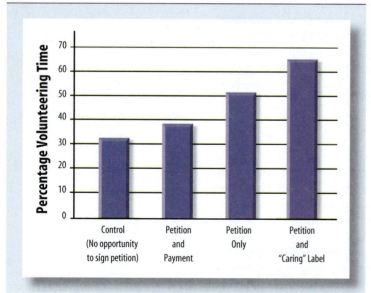

Consistent with what social psychologists have learned about self-perception and reflected appraisal processes, college students who freely chose to sign a petition to help the homeless, and who were afterward labeled as "caring," were most likely to volunteer time at a homeless shelter. Those who were paid to sign, however, were no more likely to volunteer than were control participants who never signed the petition in the first place.

Source: Based on Burger, J. M., & Caldwell, D. F. (2003). Table 3, p. 239. The effects of monetary incentives and labeling on the foot-in-the-door effect: Evidence for a self-perception process. *Basic and Applied Social Psychology*, 25, 235–231.

In Chapter 6, you'll read about the "foot-in-the-door" influence technique—about how and why getting people to do something small (like signing a petition) often makes it more likely they will subsequently do something large (like volunteering two hours of their valuable time). For now, however, the lesson of this study is straightforward: Not only do we come to know ourselves by comparing ourselves to others but also by seeing how others view us and by observing our own actions.

What we want to believe about ourselves. When someone else gives you feedback, do you want it to be accurate even if it means learning about your weaknesses and negative characteristics? Do you want it to fit with what you already believe about yourself, thereby enabling you to validate your existing self-concept? Or do you want the feedback to be favorable and self-enhancing, so you can feel good about yourself? As we'll see in Chapter 3, people often go through great cognitive efforts to enhance their sense of self—by comparing themselves with people worse off than themselves, taking personal credit for successes while blaming others for failures, and so forth (e.g., Crocker & Park, 2003; Sedikides, Skowronski, & Gaertner, 2004).

Nonetheless, people sometimes do seek out accurate information about themselves. And people also seek from others information that confirms their self-conceptions (e.g., Bosson & Swann, 1999; Swann, Rentfrow, & Guinn, 2003). This desire to verify what we already believe about ourselves can influence who we choose to spend time with. In one study, married people were more committed to spouses who saw them as they saw themselves—even when the spouse's evaluations were *negative* (Swann, Hixon, & De La Ronde, 1992b). The desire to have others view us as we view ourselves seems especially important for those of us who are highly certain of our self-images (Pelham, 1991): If we truly believe we know who we are, we want others to see us similarly.

WHAT DO I WANT, AND HOW DO I GET IT?: SELF-REGULATION Imagine yourself at a friend's party, where you discover a charming student from class loitering near the sound system, inspecting the stack of CDs. Your heart leaps! You've wanted to meet Pat all semester and you begin to contemplate how you might make this happen. What do you do? You first sort through different strategies ("Should I wait for Pat to notice me?" "Should I ask my friend to introduce us?" "Should I just saunter on over and pretend to be interested in the CDs?"). Generating the courage, you select a strategy, try it out, assess whether it's working, and, if necessary (and if you're still motivated), go to plan B (or C or D or...). This is the **self-regulation** process in action—the process through which people select, monitor, and adjust their strategies in an attempt to reach their goals (Heatherton, 2011).

As we learned just a few pages ago, self-regulation can require a lot of attention (when one learns to drive a stick shift for the first time), can use up a lot of willpower (when one tries to ignore a craving for yummy but unhealthy food), and can—even then—fail miserably (we hope those white bears are gone by now!). Most often, however, we regulate and control our behavior quite effectively, as evidenced by the fact that so much of our goal-directed activity has become automatized—thus enabling us to daydream while driving, avoid the candy aisle when shopping, and contemplate issues more pressing than white bears.

HOW DO I WANT OTHERS TO VIEW ME?: SELF-PRESENTATION As soon as you got Pat to notice you, you'd probably start working on getting Pat to view you favorably. Do you want Pat to like you? If so, how would you present yourself to make yourself likable? Perhaps you want Pat to see you as competent or as having high status? How would you present yourself to create those impressions?

Self-presentation—the process through which we try to control the impressions people form of us—colors much of our social lives (e.g., Leary, 1995; Schlenker, 2003). The clothes you choose to wear before leaving your home on a Saturday night, the manner in which you behave at a job interview, and the way you change your behavior when a grandparent enters the room, all reflect something about how you want others to view you. And it's no surprise that we're often so concerned about the impressions

Self-regulation The process through which people select, monitor, and adjust their strategies in an attempt to reach their goals.

Self-presentation The process through which we try to control the impressions people form of us.

others have of us. After all, others frequently have something we want, such as friendships or jobs. Moreover, as we just learned, our views of ourselves are influenced by our own behaviors—either directly, through self-perception processes, or indirectly, through reflected appraisal processes. How we decide to present ourselves publicly, then, will also influence how we view ourselves.

INVESTIGATION

Think about who you are—what characteristics you believe you possess (and want to possess), how you feel about yourself, what your values are, and how you want to come across to others. How have these aspects of your "self" influenced your planning for the future and your long-term aspirations?

We've seen in this brief introduction that the self is greatly intertwined with what we've learned about motivation, knowledge, and feelings. As we turn in this chapter from the person to the situation to person–situation interactions, and in following chapters to the rich and varied nature of social life, we will observe time and again the self's influences on how people think, feel, and behave toward themselves and others.

Quick Quiz

1 Knowledge of a specific episode, event, or individual is a(n) _____, whereas a(n) _____ is knowledge of the general characteristics of a particular class of episodes, events, or individuals.
   a. schema, exemplar
   b. exemplar, primed knowledge
   c. exemplar, schema
   d. schema, primed knowledge

2 _____ are long-lasting feelings that are diffuse and not directed toward particular targets; _____ are relatively intense feelings that involve physiological arousal and complex cognitions; favorable or unfavorable evaluations of particular people, objects, events or ideas are known as _____.
   a. Emotions, moods, attitudes
   b. Moods, emotions, attitudes
   c. Moods, attitudes, emotions
   d. Attitudes, moods, emotions

3 Which of the following are sources of self-knowledge?
   a. Reflected appraisal
   b. Self-perception
   c. Social comparison
   d. All of the above

4 Which of the following is an example of self-regulation?
   a. Impressing a potential date by mentioning your high-status job.
   b. Dressing in a professional suit for an important interview.
   c. Sticking to your diet by not ordering dessert at a restaurant.
   d. None of the above

SITUATION The Situation

LO 2.4 Summarize the different types of situational influence, and discuss the distinction between strong and weak situations.

LO 2.5 Describe the differences between individualistic and collectivistic cultures.

Where have you been so far today? Who else was there, and how much did you interact with them?

As you think about your day, you'll notice that you're embedded in your physical and social world. You are *situated*, and the situations in which you find yourself greatly affect how you think, feel, and behave.

Consider your physical environment. It may be noisy or serene, warm or cold, confined or spacious, ugly or aesthetically pleasing. And these features influence you (e.g., Guinote, 2008). Noise, for example, is stressful. Long-term exposure to noise via automobile traffic, airplanes flying overhead, or poorly designed buildings can harm your health, stifle reading skills, and dampen your motivation to work hard on difficult tasks (e.g., Maxwell & Evans, 2000). Or consider the interior design of your home. If its layout makes it easy for housemates to intrude on you unpredictably, you are more likely to become psychologically distressed and socially withdrawn than if you were living in a better designed home (e.g., Evans, Lepore, & Schroeder, 1996). In one interesting experiment, Andrew Baum and Glenn Davis (1980) found that by merely changing the way a dorm floor was arranged they could increase the number of friendships among the students who lived there (see Figure 2.5).

Like physical environments, social situations can shape our thoughts, feelings, and behavior. Humans are a highly social species, and much of our time is spent in the presence of others. Indeed, while working on this chapter one of us thought it would be interesting to count the number of people he encountered that day. The task quickly became overwhelming: the wife and three kids in the morning; the five people on the telephone before leaving home; the hundreds of folks passed during the morning drive; the hundred or so university students and employees encountered on the walk from car to office; the 14 email and three phone messages waiting at work; the dozen or so departmental staff and colleagues met while getting the morning's mail; the 40 people passed while walking to the library, the 50 or so in the library, and the 30 passed on the walk back. By 10 A.M., he had encountered hundreds of people and had talked to and closely interacted with over 30 of them.

On the surface, many social encounters seem unimportant. After all, how many of the hundreds of people we might encounter every morning really influence us? More than you might guess, actually. Indeed, we'll see that even subtle, short-lived social encounters can have powerful consequences. People can even influence us when they're not present, as when we are inspired to do the "right thing" by simply imagining how a police officer, or our mother back in Pittsburgh, might react if we didn't.

In the sections that follow, we explore the rich and varied nature of situations more deeply, previewing the types of situational influence we will see throughout the book.

Persons as Situations: Mere Presence, Affordances, and Descriptive Norms

Martin Luther King Jr.'s "I have a dream" speech at the 1963 Civil Rights March on Washington deeply affected those in the large crowd. By focusing on King, though, we lose sight of the fact that the crowd was also a prominent part of the situation for him. So it goes in all social situations, where the influences of people on one another are to some extent reciprocal. When dining with a friend, your situation is defined largely by your friend and your friend's situation is defined largely by you. People are situations for one another.

Figure 2.5 Interior design and dormitory life

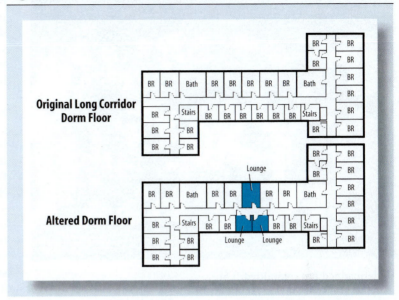

By adding just two doors to a long corridor floor and changing three bedrooms into communal lounges, Andrew Baum and Glenn Davis (1980) altered the social life of dormitory residents: Although the residents on the two floors were initially comparable, those on the altered floor made more friends, were more social, and reported fewer problems with their floormates.

Source: Baum, A., & Davis, G. E. (1980). Reducing the stress of high-density living: An architectural intervention. *Journal of Personality and Social Psychology, 38,* 471–481. Fig. 1, p. 475.

Undermanned but committed. On March 20, 1954, the boys from tiny Milan High School (enrollment 162) defeated in a shocking upset the much larger, big-city team from Muncie Central to win the Indiana State High School Basketball Championship—a feat so inspirational that it was immortalized by Hollywood in the film *Hoosiers.* Although students in "understaffed" schools like Milan High are disadvantaged in some ways, they benefit greatly in others. In particular, they tend to participate in more school activities, have more opportunities for leadership, and take on more challenges.

MERE PRESENCE OF OTHERS The very presence of others creates situations that affect how we think, feel, and behave. Consider how the number of students at your high school—whether it had a large versus a small student body—may have influenced your experiences there. Roger Barker and his colleagues (e.g., Barker & Gump, 1964) explored this very issue by comparing 13 high schools in eastern Kansas. Even though these schools were generally equivalent to one another, their students differed in interesting ways. To understand why, it helps to recognize that schools, regardless of their size, try to make similar activities and tasks available to their students. For example, even relatively small schools usually have athletic teams, choirs, student government, and school dances. This means that schools with small student bodies are "understaffed"—they have a difficult time getting enough students to participate in each activity. In contrast, large schools are often "overstaffed"—they have more students than they need for each activity.

Because of this, each student is needed to a greater extent in a small school than in a large school and so we might expect students in small schools to be more tolerant of differences among students and to try harder to convince and encourage their classmates to participate. In contrast, we might expect students in large schools to be less tolerant of differences and to "veto out" classmates on the social fringes, isolating them and turning them into uninvolved spectators.

The research supported these hypotheses (Barker & Gump, 1964). Moreover, compared to students in the larger schools, students in small schools were more strongly motivated, participated in more activities, had more positions of responsibility, and felt more challenged. And it's easy to see how gaining leadership experience and participating in multiple activities might benefit students when they're older. Although there are advantages of being in larger groups (e.g., the ability to accomplish larger tasks), there are also advantages of being in smaller ones.

Barker's research showed that the mere number of people in one's environment creates different situations. And it's not just the number of people that affects us but also where those people are. In one study, the stress levels of commuters on an urban passenger train were not influenced by the total number of passengers on their train car but rather by the number of passengers sitting close to them (Evans & Wener, 2007). Many of our air-travel experiences corroborate how sitting in the middle seat is stressful!

We've seen that the number of people around can influence our social behaviors in important ways. We'll see two particularly prominent examples of this in Chapter 12: We'll learn that the mere presence of other people can enhance a person's job performance in well-mastered, simple tasks but hurt performance in unmastered, complex tasks. And we'll see that the mere presence of an anonymous crowd can lead people to lose sight of their inner values and standards and thus lead them to act in antisocial ways.

AFFORDANCES: OPPORTUNITIES AND THREATS Different people provide us with different things. Your boss at the company picnic provides an opportunity for advancement, and the attractive stranger across the picnic table provides an opportunity for romance. People are more than just positive opportunities, however. They are also possible threats (Baron & Misovich, 1993). A drunken driver provides a chance of bodily harm, and the new budget-cutting manager at work may provide a severance check. Even the desirable stranger who provides you an opportunity for romance also presents the threat of an embarrassing rejection. The opportunities and threats that people and situations provide are called **affordances** (Baron & Boudreau, 1987; Gibson, 1979; McArthur & Baron, 1983).

People are pretty proficient at assessing the potential opportunities and threats others might provide (e.g., Ambady & Rosenthal, 1992; Kenny et al., 1994; Matsumoto & Hwang, 2011; Zebrowitz & Collins, 1997). On the basis of just facial photographs or short silent videos, for instance, people are able to assess with a reasonable degree of accuracy the extent to which others are dominant, extraverted, conscientious, aggressive, and sexually available. In one striking study, participants were able to judge accurately the effectiveness of teachers after watching just a two-second soundless film of each in action (Ambady & Rosenthal, 1993). Thus the people we encounter provide us various kinds of opportunities and threats, which we often discern quite effectively and with little effort.

Affordances. What do these individuals afford one another? Friendship, or perhaps back-stabbing in the office? Romance, or maybe a humiliating rejection? Even a simple conversation in the park can provide both intriguing opportunities and imposing threats.

DESCRIPTIVE NORMS People influence others through their mere presence and through the opportunities and threats they provide. They also wield influence by communicating **descriptive norms**—information about what most people commonly do in a situation. Descriptive norms can help us make the right choices. In the first class meeting of your college career, for instance, if your classmates stop talking when the instructor approaches the lectern, there's a pretty good chance you too would do well by ending your conversation. Descriptive norms are powerful: Among their other effects, they influence whether we help, express our prejudices, cheat on our taxes, commit adultery, gamble, and conserve energy (e.g., Buunk & Baker, 1995; Larimer & Neighbors, 2003; Latané & Darley, 1970; Nolan et al., 2008; Steenbergen et al., 1992).

When customers line up outside a dance club, it usually means they think the place is worth the wait. Sometimes, however, there is a mismatch between the norm suggested by people's behavior and what they actually believe or feel. Consider a classroom lecture in which the teacher presents the material in a confusing way—no doubt a rare occurrence! Despite being confused, you may be reluctant to raise your hand and question the teacher. Why? Perhaps you will feel embarrassed to have the other students think you don't understand. So, hoping to find social validation for the belief that the lecture is dense and confusing, you scan the room for befuddled looks on the faces of your classmates—all the while masking your own befuddlement. Unfortunately, as you scan the room, all you see are faces exhibiting confident understanding. So you keep your hand down, not wanting to embarrass yourself. What you don't realize is that other students are doing the same thing: They too are masking their confusion while looking to see if others appear baffled. No one questions the teacher, all because you and the others have hidden your actual beliefs from one another (Miller & McFarland, 1987).

This common occurrence in the classroom is an example of **pluralistic ignorance**—the phenomenon in which people in a group misperceive the beliefs of others because everyone acts inconsistently with their beliefs (e.g., Miller & Nelson, 2002). In the classroom example, the students are ignorant of the others' confusion because everyone is concealing it. We see, next, that pluralistic ignorance can contribute to a dangerous form of recreation popular on college campuses: binge drinking.

Affordance An opportunity or threat provided by a situation.

Descriptive norm A norm that defines what is commonly done in a situation.

Pluralistic ignorance The phenomenon in which people in a group misperceive the beliefs of others because everyone acts inconsistently with their beliefs.

Bridging Function and Dysfunction:

Descriptive Norms, Pluralistic Ignorance, and Binge Drinking on Campus

Scott Krueger was smart, athletic, and a natural leader. He was also well liked and considered by many to be a strong role model. He was full of promise, an all-American boy.

His promise would never be realized. Just weeks into his freshman year at the highly selective Massachusetts Institute of Technology, Scott Krueger lay comatose in a hospital bed. An inexperienced drinker pledging a fraternity, he had consumed enough beer and rum during a mandatory hazing event to raise his blood alcohol level to a toxic 0.41%—more than five times the legal limit for drivers in Massachusetts. For three days medical experts heroically used all the miracle-producing technologies at their disposal, but to no avail. His brain never responded. Scott Krueger was dead.

Binge drinking—defined as consuming five or more drinks in a row for men, and four or more in a row for women—is common on college campuses (Wechsler et al., 2000; Wechsler & Nelson,

2008). A survey of more than 14,000 students at 119 four-year colleges in 39 states revealed that:

- 45% of students binge when they drink.
- 47% of students drink to get drunk.
- Students in fraternities and sororities are much more likely to binge drink (79%) than are students living in dorms (45%) or off campus (44%).
- Male students (51%) are more likely than female students (40%) to binge drink.
- White students are more likely to binge drink (49%) than are students from other ethnic groups (e.g., Hispanics, 40%; Asians, 23%; African Americans, 16%).
- Frequent binge drinkers are much more likely than non-bingers to skip class, get behind in schoolwork, do things they regret, damage property, get into trouble with police, get hurt or injured, and engage in unplanned, unprotected sexual activity.

Given the amount of drinking on campus, it would be easy for a newcomer and inexperienced drinker to believe that the students really like to drink a lot and think that doing so is a good thing (e.g., Borsari & Carey, 2003; Segrist et al., 2007; Suls & Green, 2003). However, this belief may reflect a troubling demonstration of pluralistic ignorance. Deborah Prentice and Dale Miller (1993) found, for instance, that the typical student erroneously believed he or she was relatively alone in being uncomfortable with the alcohol use on campus. This misperception had especially significant implications for the men in this study: They shifted their own attitude over the course of the semester to be more in line with their mistaken perceptions of others' views. Over time, they became more comfortable with heavy drinking.

Pluralistic ignorance can be dangerous. In the case of alcohol, students may drink more than they're comfortable with. Why? "It must be safe, because others are drinking heavily." This thinking is especially likely to characterize inexperienced drinkers like Scott Krueger, who don't know how much drinking is too much. This heavy drinking then further communicates a message that few students privately endorse—that heavy drinking is safe. Thus students unintentionally encourage others to drink heavily, and the cycle of pluralistic ignorance continues.

Did pluralistic ignorance kill Scott Krueger? We'll never know for sure. There's a good chance, though, it would be convicted of being an active accomplice.

Pluralistic Ignorance and Drinking Norms. New college students sometimes observe heavy drinking, and presume that everyone else must be more comfortable with drinking than they are. Over time, they may shift their opinions and behaviors to match what they think is considered appropriate.

Rules: Injunctive Norms and Scripted Situations

Look at the grid in Figure 2.6. Along the top are several behaviors people sometimes do (e.g., talk, laugh, fight). Along the left side are a few situations in which people sometimes find themselves (e.g., own bedroom, public restroom, job interview). In each box, indicate how appropriate the relevant behavior is for the situation. How appropriate would it be, for instance, to talk in a public restroom or to fight in a house of worship?

Figure 2.6   How appropriate would it be to . . . ?

Behaviors						
Situations	Talk	Laugh	Fight	Cry	Belch	Read
Date						
Restroom						
Job Interview						
Religious Service						
Dorm Lounge						
Own Room						

In each square of the grid above, rate the *appropriateness* of doing the specific behavior in the specific situation. For instance, in the top-left square, assess the appropriateness of talking on a date, using a scale ranging from 0 ("the behavior is *extremely inappropriate* in this situation") to 9 ("the behavior is *extremely appropriate* in this situation").

What do you see when you look at your ratings? Are some behaviors more (or less) appropriate regardless of the situations in which they're performed? And are some situations more constraining—that is, "allow" fewer behaviors—than others?

Source: Adapted Price, R. H., & Bouffard, D. L. (1974). Behavioral appropriateness and situational constraint as dimensions of social behavior. *Journal of Personality and Social Psychology*, 30, 579–586. P. 581.

Richard Price and Dennis Bouffard (1974) had students at Indiana University perform this task for 15 behaviors in 15 situations. Several of their findings stand out. First, some behaviors (e.g., talking and laughing) were seen as appropriate across many different situations, whereas others (e.g., fighting) were seen as generally inappropriate (Figure 2.6). More important, however, was the finding that situations differ in how much they limit what we can do in them. In some situations—like your own room, a park, or a dorm lounge—you are "allowed" to act in lots of different ways. In other situations—like places of worship and job interviews—you are drastically limited in the kinds of behavior you are allowed to do.

Indeed, many situations, such as religious services and job interviews, have "rules" that tell us what we're allowed to do and what we're not. These rules are called **injunctive norms**, and they define what is typically approved and disapproved of in the situation. Injunctive norms are different from descriptive norms: Whereas descriptive norms communicate what people typically do, injunctive norms communicate what people *should* (and *should not*) do (Cialdini, Kallgren, & Reno, 1991). One example of an important injunctive norm is the norm of reciprocity, which obligates us to repay others for the favors they do for us. If you scratch my back, it is expected that I'll scratch yours. We'll explore the reciprocity norm in Chapters 6 and 9.

Injunctive norms contribute to the extent to which particular situations are "scripted." That is, in some situations there is a script—a list of events that happen in a predictable order. Such situations are called **scripted situations**. For instance, in the 1980s the script for getting a date in college typically went something like this (Pryor & Merluzzi, 1985):

- The two people notice each other.
- They get caught staring at each other, and they smile.
- They find out about one another from friends.
- They attempt to "accidentally" come across one another again.
- They get a friend to introduce them.
- They begin a conversation, looking for common interests.
- One *finally* asks the other out.

There are also scripts for what to do—and when to do it—on a date (e.g., Morr Serewicz & Gale, 2008; Rose & Frieze, 1993). There are scripts for how a relationship

Injunctive norm A norm that describes what is commonly approved or disapproved in a situation.

Scripted situation A situation in which certain events are expected to occur in a particular sequence.

should progress, from the first date to becoming engaged (Holmberg & Mackenzie, 2002). There are scripts describing the activities involved in satisfying sexual experiences (Seal et al., 2008). There are even scripts for breaking off a romantic relationship (Battaglia, Richard, Datteri, & Lord, 1998). These mental scripts help us to both coordinate our behaviors with the behaviors of others and avoid violating the injunctive norms of the situation (Abelson, 1981; Forgas, 1979; Schank & Abelson, 1977). To understand how frequently we rely on our mental scripts, consider how quickly and easily you notice it when someone violates a script. Wouldn't you be surprised, for example, if a waitress sat down next to you and started plucking food off your plate, or if a neighbor showed up at a Presbyterian funeral in Maine wearing Bermuda shorts and a Hawaiian shirt?

INVESTIGATION

The dating script we just presented was common 20 years ago. Does this script still hold today? If not, how is it different? And how does the currently dominant script make pursuing your romantic interests easier or more difficult?

Strong versus Weak Situations

On the basis of what we've seen so far, some situations are "stronger" than others (Snyder & Ickes, 1985). Whereas some situations (onrushing trucks, funerals) demand that people behave in particular ways, other situations (nightclubs, empty living rooms) allow people to behave in many different ways. Strong situations tend to afford a narrower range of opportunities and threats for the people in them. For instance, onrushing trucks provide few opportunities—except, perhaps, for heroism—and one very clear threat (to physical preservation). Strong situations also tend to have obvious injunctive and descriptive norms: For instance, it's very clear which behaviors are appropriate at funerals and which are not; in case a mourner can't discern the norm on the basis of the actions of others, stern stares and sharp elbow nudges will correct the errors. Finally, strong situations are frequently scripted. At funerals, for instance, there's a typical sequence of events and this sequence usually does not leave much room for other activities.

In contrast, weak situations tend to afford a relatively wide range of opportunities and threats. Nightclubs, for instance, not only allow for socializing with friends, finding romance, and dancing, but also for saying something stupid to a friend, getting rejected by a desired love interest, and demonstrating clumsiness on the dance floor. Weak situations are also characterized by a lack of clear descriptive norms, as the behaviors of others in them will vary greatly. For example, some nightclub visitors may be talking intimately, others drinking heavily, and still others unashamedly flirting and flattering; this range of behaviors provides social license for an equally wide range of behavior on your part. Weak situations also communicate few injunctive norms: Nightclubs don't have as many "rules" of behavior as do funerals. Finally, weak situations tend not to be as scripted—in a nightclub there is more flexibility in what you do and when you do it than there is at a funeral.

Of course, most situations provide people a reasonable amount of behavioral flexibility, falling somewhere between strong situations like job interviews and weak situations like picnics in the park.

Culture

If you were raised in rural China, many of your friends are cousins, aunts, and uncles. What you do is heavily influenced by what they want you to do. In contrast, if you were raised in suburban southern California, you have many people you consider friends. Most of them are not members of your family, and the preferences of your relatives have less impact on your life decisions. Culture—the beliefs, customs, habits, and languages shared by people living in a particular time and place—can influence the circumstances we're in (e.g., how much time we spend with relatives) and how these circumstances influence us (e.g., whether our relatives strongly influence what we do).

In recent years, social psychologists have become increasingly interested in how culture influences the ways people think, feel, and behave (e.g., A. Cohen, 2009; Kitayama & D. Cohen, 2007; Lehman, Chiu, & Schaller, 2004; Oyserman & Lee, 2008; Smith, Bond, & Kağitçibasi, 2006). The reason for this is straightforward: Although people from the world's cultures are clearly similar to one another in many ways—after all, we all share a common biology and basic human needs—they also sometimes differ from one another in fascinating ways. Throughout the book, we'll explore both these commonalities and differences as we unravel the mysteries of social behavior. In this chapter's research video, Michael Varnum describes some of the research he did with Shinobu Kitayama on how your parents' cultural background may have influenced their decision about whether to give you a common name (such as Sarah or Michael), or an unusual name (such as Zaharah or Ezra) (Varnum & Kitayama, 2011).

WATCH THE VIDEO: *How your parents' cultural background may have influenced the name they chose for you.*

Much of the research on culture has focused on differences in the extent to which cultures are individualistic versus collectivistic (see Table 2.1) (Chinese Cultural Connection, 1987; Hofstede, 1980/2001; Triandis, 1989). **Individualistic cultures** (e.g., the United States, Australia, Great Britain) predominantly socialize their members to view themselves as unique individuals and to prioritize their personal goals. In contrast, **collectivistic cultures** (e.g., Guatemala, South Korea, Taiwan) predominantly socialize their members to view themselves in terms of their relationships and as members of the larger social group, and to prioritize the concerns of their relationship partners and groups before their own (Brewer & Chen, 2007). Although cultures vary along other dimensions as well, most research has focused on this individualism–collectivism dimension, particularly as it's represented by North American and European cultures, on the one hand, and East Asian cultures on the other. So, to illustrate how cultures provide a broad situational context for their members, we'll focus in this chapter on the individualism–collectivism dimension.

CULTURAL AFFORDANCES Different cultures provide different opportunities for their members. For example, individualistic cultures afford great opportunities for people to assert independence and personal control. One way individualistic

Individualistic culture A culture that socializes its members to think of themselves as individuals and to give priority to their personal goals.

Collectivistic culture A culture that socializes its members to think of themselves in terms of their relationships and as members of the larger social group, and to prioritize the concerns of their relationship partners and groups before their own.

Table 2.1 Individualistic and Collectivistic Nations

Hofstede (1980, 2001) analyzed data from more than 80,000 employees of a large, multinational corporation about their work-related goals and values. As the rankings reveal, Western nations tended to encourage greater individualism, especially compared to nations in Latin America and Asia.

Rank on Individualism	Selected National Cultures	Rank on Individualism	Selected National Cultures
# 1	United States	#32	Mexico
# 2	Australia	#34	Portugal and East African region
# 3	Great Britain	#40	Singapore, Thailand, and West African region
# 4	Canada and Netherlands	#43	Taiwan
#10	France	#44	South Korea
#15	West Germany	#45	Peru
#20	Spain	#49	Colombia
#22	Japan	#50	Venezuela
#25	Jamaica	#51	Panama
#26	Arab region and Brazil	#52	Ecuador
#30	Greece	#53	Guatemala

Source: Based on J. Deregewski et al. (1983), *Expications in Cross-Cultural Psychology*, pp. 335–355, Fig. 2 © Swets & Zeitlinger Publishers.

cultures do this is by giving their members many choices (Fiske et al., 1998). For instance, one American belief is that any person can become president (or an astronaut, professional athlete, or famous musician): "Just work hard," the story goes, "and you can become whatever you choose to become—all opportunities are open to you." "Have it your way™"—the choice is yours—advertises a popular fast food restaurant. Even the simple purchase of milk at the local market provides Americans with a myriad of choices: Whole milk, 2%, 1%, or skim? Regular milk, buttermilk, acidophilus? Lactose-free? Soy-based milk substitute? Calcium-enriched? Chocolate? Strawberry? A gallon, half gallon, quart, or pint? Paper carton or plastic jug? Amazingly, the average supermarket in our hometown of Phoenix carries more than 20,000 different items, whereas the very concept of a *super*market might seem ridiculous and unnecessary to those in some collectivistic nations. By providing many choices to their members, individualistic cultures allow people to express their individuality and take personal control in meeting their own needs. We see, then, that different cultures provide different opportunities for those who live in them (Bond, 2004; Morling, Kitayama, & Miyamoto, 2002).

CULTURE AND NORMS "Be all that you can be,™" sang the catchy U.S. Army recruitment ad. "Don't be wishy-washy," people sneer at those who act inconsistently from one time to another. The norms of individualistic societies communicate a clear message: Stand out from the crowd! Be true to your self!

On the other hand, the Malay adage warns that "one drop of indigo spoils the bucket of milk." And the Chinese maxim states that "if one finger is sore, the whole hand will hurt." These East Asian proverbs represent the very different belief of collectivistic cultures—the belief that group members ought to seek harmony and not stand out from others. And just as individualistic societies communicate norms encouraging independent behavior, collectivistic societies communicate norms encouraging interdependence and discouraging independence.

Consistent with this orientation toward harmony and interdependence, people in collectivistic cultures are especially likely to adjust their behaviors to fit the behaviors of others, especially if the others are people they know. Consider the famous "line judging" studies initially performed in the United States, in which participants often conform to obviously wrong choices if the rest of group unanimously gives the wrong answer (Asch, 1956). This pattern of conformity is even more prevalent in collectivistic societies (Smith & Bond, 1994). It is not that people in collectivist societies never strive to distinguish themselves. But in contrast to individualists, who strive to be different and separate from their groups, collectivists strive to excel in ways that will elevate them within their groups (Becker et al., 2012).

Cultures may also differ in how they enforce norms (Tinsley & Weldon, 2003). For instance, American parents often reprimand wayward children by withholding rights and privileges—"you're grounded for a week . . . no TV for you!" In contrast, Japanese and Chinese parents are more likely to threaten the standing of their children's social ties: "People will laugh at you if you behave like that" (Miller, Fung, & Mintz, 1996; Okimoto & Rohlen, 1988). These different styles of punishment make sense from the perspectives of the different cultures: People in individualistic cultures place great value on personal freedom, so punishments that take away freedom should be especially effective; members of collectivistic cultures place great value on their relationships, so punishments that threaten social ties should be especially effective.

CULTURAL SCRIPTS We saw earlier that the presence of social scripts enables people to better coordinate their behaviors with others. How might culture influence the use of such scripts?

First, it's possible that social scripts are more pervasive and more strongly enforced in some cultures than others. For example, the Japanese have formal and elaborate cultural scripts for events ranging from family meals to piano lessons to social greetings (Hendry, 1993)—events that are usually much less ordered in the United States. Cultural psychologists have distinguished between cultures that are "tight" (where the norms are strong and there is little tolerance of deviance) and those that are "loose" (where norms are more relaxed and informal, and deviation is relatively more acceptable) (Gelfand, 2013; Pelto, 1968; Triandis, 1989). If you grew up in Singapore or Malaysia (relatively "tight" societies), you would be expected to closely follow the rules and not deviate. On the other hand, if you grew up in the Netherlands or Brazil (relatively "loose" societies), you would have a lot more latitude in choosing which rules to follow (Gelfand et al., 2011).

Second, even when cultures script the same events, their contents may differ considerably. Consider funerals. Although funerals in most cultures share common features—disposal of the body, grieving—they also differ in fascinating ways (Matsunami, 1998). In North America, for instance, the typical funeral is a quiet, low-key affair (although there are interesting variations due to ethnicity, religion, and region). People tend to dress conservatively, speak quietly, listen respectfully to those speaking, and control their public expressions of grief. We might contrast this type of ceremony with the funerals held by the Berawan people of the island of Borneo (Metcalf & Huntington, 1991). The Berawan hold two ceremonies that are separated by a period of at least eight months and sometimes as much as five years. The first ceremony begins immediately after death occurs. The corpse is displayed on a specially built seat for a day or two until all the close kin have seen it. When the time comes to perform the second ceremony, guests are summoned from far and wide to attend and for four to ten days there is a boisterous evening party on the veranda adjacent to the jar or coffin. Drinking and socializing are encouraged, and the general hubbub from the carousing, music, games, and shotgun blasts can be heard half a mile away through the thick forest. Not exactly the type of funeral we're used to seeing! Culture influences not only the extent to which everyday situations are governed by socially accepted scripts but also the content of those scripts.

In this section, we've seen that people are situated in their physical and social environments and that these situations affect thoughts, feelings, and behavior. We turn now to consider the person and the situation together.

Quick Quiz

1 People can act as situations in which of the following ways:
  a. The mere number of people in an environment creates different situations.
  b. People can act as affordances, providing threats and opportunities.
  c. People communicate descriptive norms.
  d. All of the above

2 A(n) _____ norm describes what is commonly done in a situation, whereas a(n) _____ norm describes what is commonly approved or disapproved in a situation.
  a. Descriptive, associative
  b. Descriptive, injunctive
  c. Injunctive, descriptive
  d. Injunctive, associative

3 Which of the following represents a "strong" situation?
  a. A funeral
  b. A friend's house party
  c. Spending time alone in your garage
  d. None of the above

4 _____ cultures socialize members to view themselves as individuals and prioritize personal goals, whereas _____ cultures socialize members to view themselves as members of the larger social group and prioritize the group's concerns.
  a. Collectivistic, individualistic
  b. Hedonistic, collectivistic
  c. Individualistic, collectivistic
  d. Individualistic, hedonistic

INTERACTION The Person and the Situation Interact

LO 2.6 Explain the different types of person–situation interactions.

LO 2.7 Discuss the importance of person–situation fit in the workplace.

If someone asks you to describe the personalities of your two best friends, you might mention that one is outgoing whereas the other is shy, that one is unreliable whereas the other is dependable, and so forth. As the conversation deepens, however, you will likely find yourself saying things such as "she's the kind of person who is nervous and quiet with strangers but comfortable and a bit wild with her friends," or "he may not be all that motivated and reliable at his job, but he's a perfectly committed, dependable friend."

Statements like these reveal an intuitive understanding that our personalities are partially defined by how we react to situations—by the particular sets of goals, thoughts, feelings, and behaviors that emerge in the different situations we confront (e.g., Mischel, Shoda, & Mendoza-Denton, 2002). Such statements also accord with a fundamental tenet of social psychology—that the person and the situation *work together* to influence how people think, feel, and behave (e.g., Kenrick & Funder, 1988; Ozer, 1986; Shoda, Lee Tiernan, & Mischel, 2002; Snyder & Ickes, 1985). In the remainder of this chapter, we consider six ways in which the person and situation influence one another and interact to shape social life.

Different Persons Respond Differently to the Same Situation

Imagine you've agreed to participate in an experiment studying the effects of video games on the ability to rapidly make decisions. First, you and another participant separately play video games. Then you and the other participant play a competitive game in which you have to respond rapidly when you hear a certain tone through your headphones. If you press the computer key before your opponent, a large "YOU WON" appears on the computer screen. If you are slower, "YOU LOST" appears, followed by a blast of noise through your headphones. Prior to each trial, you set the intensity level and duration of the blast that your opponent will receive if you win; these settings could range from no noise at all to a 2.5-second blast at 105 decibels (equivalent to hearing a car horn blaring in your ear from a distance of a few feet). How much noise would you force your opponent to endure each time you win?

As Bruce Bartholow, Marc Sestir, and Edward Davis (2005) discovered, it would depend on the video game you just played—violent or nonviolent—and on the amount of experience you've had playing violent video games in the past. They randomly assigned some students to play a graphically realistic "shooter" game in which success was determined solely by the number of characters they killed. Other students instead played a nonviolent puzzle-solving game. For participants with relatively little experience playing violent video games, the type of game they played strongly influenced how aggressively they blasted their opponents: Demonstrating the power of the situation, less experienced participants playing the violent game blasted their opponents more aggressively than did those playing the nonviolent game. In contrast, the type of game did not influence those participants who had more experience playing violent video games: They loudly blasted their opponents regardless (see Figure 2.7).

These findings illustrate one important type of person–situation interaction: *Different people respond differently to the same situation.* Person–situation interactions of this sort can occur because different people are attuned to different parts of a situation, or because the same situation means different things to different people. In this experiment, even though all participants received equivalent punishments—the "opponent" was really just the computer following an assigned script—those who were experienced at playing violent video games were especially likely to interpret their opponent's actions as hostile, even after playing the *non*violent game. In contrast, those with little experience playing violent video games only perceived their opponents as hostile after playing the violent game. Because the nonviolent context meant something different to the experienced and inexperienced participants, they responded to it differently.

Person–situation fit refers to the extent to which a person and a situation are compatible. Just as keys don't work unless inserted into the correct locks, people can't reach their goals unless their situations provide appropriate opportunities. Indeed, if we find ourselves in ill-fitting situations we're likely to feel dissatisfied and to be unsuccessful. For example, students who see their values as fitting well with the values of their college environment tend to be more satisfied than students who perceive a poorer fit (e.g., Pervin & Rubin, 1967; Sagiv & Schwartz, 2000). We see next that the degree of person–situation fit also has important implications for people's work lives.

Figure 2.7 "Different people behave differently in the same situation."

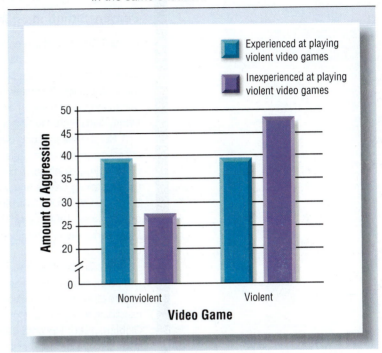

Students with relatively little experience playing violent video games blasted their opponents more aggressively after playing a violent game than after playing a nonviolent game. In contrast, participants with greater experience playing violent video games aggressively blasted their opponents regardless.

Source: Based on Bartholow, B. D., Sestir, M. A., & Davis, E. B. (2005). Correlates and consequences of exposure to video game violence: Hostile personality, empathy, and aggressive behavior. *Personality and Social Psychology Bulletin*, 31, 1573–1586. Figure 2, p. 1581.

Person–situation fit The extent to which a person and a situation are compatible.

Bridging Theory and Application:
Person–Situation Fit in the Workplace

Michael Ovitz was the premier deal maker in an industry known for deal making. As the agent of megastars like Tom Cruise and as the chairman of the Creative Artists Agency, Ovitz could make or break new films by providing or withholding star directors and actors. So when the Walt Disney Company needed to replace its president, it recruited Ovitz as second-in-command to its chairman, Michael Eisner, a business superstar himself. With Eisner and Ovitz, Disney had created an executive Dream Team.

But the dream soon became a nightmare. The characteristics that made Ovitz such an effective power broker—his hands-on style, his ability to take command and control those around him—didn't serve him well in his role as a corporate administrator. Moreover, he wasn't used to taking orders and wasn't very good at it. So a mere 16 months after headlines had trumpeted his arrival, Ovitz admitted the mistake and resigned—with Disney's blessing (*Ovitz & out at Disney*, 1996; *Ovitz, Hollywood power broker, resigns from no. 2 job at Disney*, 1996). Despite his savvy, energy, and talent, Michael Ovitz was the wrong person for the job. He didn't fit.

The Greek philosopher Plato, writing in the fourth century B.C., proposed that people should be assigned jobs according to their abilities and personalities. Because different jobs require different skills and personal characteristics, he reasoned, not everyone will be a good candidate for each job. Contemporary theorists agree (e.g., Driskell et al., 1987; Hackman & Oldham, 1980; Holland, 1997), as do the data: When people's personal characteristics—interests, goals, abilities, traits—fit with the demands and opportunities of their occupations, they are happier and more likely to stay in their jobs (e.g., Ambrose et al., 2008; Gardner et al., 2012). In one study, business students whose personal characteristics better matched a profile of a "successful young manager" received more job offers upon graduating one year later. Moreover, four years after graduating they were earning higher salaries, were more likely to be working full time, and had changed jobs less frequently (Chatman et al., 1999).

Other research illustrates the value of having the person fit not just the job but also the organization's culture. Employees who fit their organization's culture tend to be more satisfied, more committed to the company, and less likely to leave for other jobs (e.g., Adkins & Caldwell, 2004; Silva et al., 2010).

There are clear advantages, then, of creating a good fit between workers and their jobs and workplaces. Individuals can enhance their employment "fitness" and work satisfaction by identifying their personal qualities and seeking job types compatible with them. Workplaces can interview workers and attempt to screen out those whose values don't mesh with the company's. And organizations can attempt to increase fit by socializing new recruits into the workplace's values (Chatman, 1991).

Should Ovitz and Eisner have seen their mistake coming? Perhaps. In any case, this mistake was an expensive one for all parties: Personal reputations were greatly damaged, and Disney was forced to buy out Ovitz with a severance package worth nearly $90 million. All because a single worker was ill matched to his job and work environment.

Situations Choose the Person

Each year, after competing to gain admission into the college of their choice, thousands of students around the world "rush" sororities, fraternities, and dining clubs. Others try to win roles in the casts of theater groups, positions in student government, and spots on athletic teams. Or they seek recognition in honors societies and deans' lists. And when they graduate, they compete for jobs and admission into graduate school.

As the great behavioral scientist Mick Jagger observed, we can't always get what we want. Not everyone gets to enter his or her preferred situations. Students are rejected by their first-choice colleges, they're ignored by popular sororities, and they pound the pavement looking for jobs. This is because *situations choose the person*, another type of person–situation interaction. We'll see in Chapter 8, for instance, that women across the globe prefer as romantic partners men who tend to be their age or a bit older (Kenrick & Keefe, 1992; Dunn et al., 2010). As a result, 14-year-old boys will rarely get dates with 21-year-old women. Much as the boys might desire such an opportunity, the women aren't going to choose them. And just as young boys don't get chosen by older women, socially awkward women don't get chosen by desirable sororities, new employees don't get chosen to lead corporations, and lazy students don't get into the best graduate programs.

Indeed, most situations limit "enrollment"—not everyone gets in. Athletic teams have slots for only so many players, and people have time and energy for only so many friends. Because of these limits, even casual situations typically have "entrance requirements" of one sort or another. To demonstrate this for yourself, stop bathing and brushing your hair for two weeks and then try to make new friends.

Persons Choose Their Situations

Just as situations choose people, *people choose their situations*. You may choose to spend next Saturday evening at the local movie theater; your roommate may choose the library. You may choose to marry and start a family; your best friend may choose to stay single. Situations don't always just happen *to* us. Rather, we play a large part in determining our own situations.

We choose situations based on the opportunities they provide. If your goal is to forget about your upcoming exam, the movie theater might be a better choice than the library. If you have a migraine headache, a quiet evening at home might be better than the crowded arena rock concert. When different situations provide different opportunities, we tend to choose those whose opportunities appear to fit well with our desires and goals (Buss, 1987; Caspi & Bem, 1990; Emmons, Diener, & Larsen, 1986; Snyder & Ickes, 1985). The movie theater affords distraction, so the person hoping to escape thoughts of the upcoming exam will choose it over the library. The rock concert poses the threat of noise, so the person hoping to alleviate a headache will choose the living room couch instead.

Different Situations Prime Different Parts of the Person

We suspect that most of you know someone who is *bicultural*—someone who has internalized two cultures and feels like both are "alive within." You may be such a person yourself. Bicultural individuals often say that the two internalized cultures "take turns" influencing their actions (LaFromboise, Coleman, & Gerton, 1993; Phinney & Devich-Navarro, 1997): "At school . . . everyone was American, including me. Then I would go home in the afternoon and be Mexican again" (quoted in Padilla, 1994, 30).

We saw earlier that a situation can prime, or make more ready, knowledge relevant to it. For the Mexican American student quoted above, the language spoken in the different settings probably primed her different cultural orientations—the Spanish spoken at home by her parents and grandparents made her psychologically Mexican, and the English used at school made her psychologically American (Ross, Xun, & Wilson, 2002). Many studies have used the idea of priming to see if features of the situation can indeed elicit one cultural orientation over the other

Changing situation, changing person. Is Barack Obama the same person in an Irish bar as he is at home with his daughters? Not likely. As circumstances change, certain features of who we are flow into prominence and others ebb into the background. Different situations prime different parts of the person.

(e.g., Pouliasi & Verkuyten, 2007; Zou, Morris, & Benet-Martinez, 2008; Zhang et al., 2013). In one study, Chinese university students in Hong Kong—who tend to possess both Chinese and Western self-conceptions—were found to think more collectivistically after viewing Chinese cultural icons (e.g., a Chinese dragon or the Great Wall) and more individualistically after viewing American cultural icons (e.g., the U.S. flag, the U.S. Capitol) (Hong, Chiu, & Kung, 1997). Cultural symbols can even prime styles of thinking among members of other cultures (Clobert & Saraglou, 2012). The yin-yang symbol represents the East Asian understanding of the continuous life dynamic of change and balance—that good follows bad, that light follows dark, and the like. In an interesting series of studies, Adam Alter and Virginia Kwan (2009) demonstrated that subtly exposing European Americans to the yin-yang symbol (as opposed to control symbols) led them to think less like European Americans and more like East Asians—to be more likely to predict that successful stocks will lose value whereas poorly performing stocks will gain value, and that after a string of sunny days will come rainy days and that after a string of rainy days will come sunny days.

Findings such as these illustrate another type of person–situation interaction: *Different situations prime different parts of the person.* For instance, seeing an attractive person smile at you may prime thoughts of romance, whereas hearing the same person yell at you raises concerns about safety. The situations we're in bring to mind goals and beliefs that influence how we think, feel, and behave—even when we're not in the same situation anymore (e.g., Higgins, 1996). You are likely to interpret and react to an ambiguous collision with a stranger outside the movie theater differently after leaving a slapstick comedy ("How clumsy of us!") versus a blow-'em-up action thriller ("He can't do that to me. I'll show him!").

Even features of the situation of which we are unaware can powerfully influence our actions (Ferguson & Bargh, 2004). Students in an experiment by John Bargh, Mark Chen, and Lara Burrows (1996) were asked to create four-word sentences out of scrambled sets of five words. By design, some of the sets included words related to rudeness, others included words related to politeness, and others contained words unrelated to rudeness or politeness. After completing the task, the participants left the lab to get the experimenter so they could prepare for a second study. They found the experimenter engaged in a conversation with another subject, and the experimenter continued this conversation until interrupted by the participant (or until 10 minutes had passed). Which participants were more likely to interrupt the conversation within the 10-minute time limit—those previously primed by the rude words, the polite words, or the neutral words?

If you guessed those primed by the rude words, you're correct: 63% of these participants interrupted, compared to 38% of those in the neutral condition, and only 17% of those in the polite condition. Even small features of our situations can prime goals, beliefs, feelings, and habits. Because of this, we may act politely in one situation and rudely in another.

Persons Change the Situation

If a clumsy person runs into a brick wall, the wall stays pretty much the same and only the person is changed. But social situations are rarely brick walls, and *each person who enters a situation has the ability to change it.* Add a competitive person to a relaxed game of touch football at the company picnic, and "touch" soon turns to "tackle." Add a socially skilled teacher to an awkward classroom of first-day kindergartners, and the kids will soon shed their shyness and begin making friends.

Sometimes people change their situations for the same reason they might choose a situation: to better achieve their goals. A person hoping to clean up a littered neighborhood might recruit others to form a cooperative team, and the kindergarten teacher certainly wants her pupils getting along comfortably.

But people also change their situations inadvertently. Depressed college students don't desire to depress their roommates, but they may—and their roommates may start avoiding them (Hames, Hagan, & Joiner, 2013; Strack & Coyne, 1983). The cheery roommate doesn't necessarily try to raise others' spirits, but she does—and they may start looking for her when needing a boost. Throughout the book we'll see many instances of people changing their situations—of leaders increasing the effectiveness of their groups, of lonely people bringing about social isolation, of people with unpopular views changing the minds of others, and the like.

Situations Change the Person

Neglectful parents can turn infants with calm dispositions into anxious toddlers. The people we marry can change our views toward politics and social issues. Watching violent pornography can desensitize you to aggression against women. Just as people change their situations, *situations can change people.*

Sometimes this change is obvious: We were one way "then," and we're different now. An infant is overwhelmed by a rambunctious Irish setter and suddenly comes to fear dogs. But sometimes situations shape us in slower and less obvious ways.

Socialization is the process through which a culture teaches its members about its beliefs, customs, habits, and languages. In our discussion of culture, we saw that individualistic cultures socialize their children into adults who strive for independence, personal success, and high self-esteem. In contrast, collectivistic cultures socialize their young into adults who seek interdependence and relationships, group success, and harmony within their groups. How do cultures do this? Cultures have core ideas about what is good, and these values are represented in the customs, norms, politics, and institutions of the culture. For instance, the individualistic value of personal achievement is represented in American law (e.g., as an emphasis on personal property rights), in education (e.g., as the way to enable every motivated child to achieve his or her potential), and in the media (e.g., with its portrayals of entrepreneurs and their successes). And these forces influence the way people interact with one another on a day-to-day basis (e.g., American children are frequently given their own rooms from a very early age and taught to "stand up for themselves").

INVESTIGATION

Think about a close friend of yours and his or her sibling. In what ways are they alike, and in what ways are they different? How might you account for these similarities and differences in terms of the six types of person–situation interactions you've just learned about?

Socialization The process whereby a culture teaches its members about its beliefs, customs, habits, and language.

Cultures exist at many "levels" (A. Cohen, 2009). Within the United States, cultures differ somewhat depending on region (e.g., we'll discuss the "southern culture of honor" in Chapter 10). Cultures also differ between urban and rural areas; big cities tend to foster somewhat less collectivism than do small towns and farm country. Cultures also differ as a function of ethnicity and religion. Colleges possess their own cultures—a student who spends four years at the Naval Academy is likely to confront different norms, rules, and customs than he or she would at U.C. Berkeley. And there are even family cultures—the lessons taught in your house will differ somewhat from the lessons taught in your neighbor's. So even within the most individualistic country in the world, there are many cultural influences that help shape who we become. Situations, whether short-lived or long-lasting, isolated or linked with related situations, can change who we are.

As we've seen, then, the person and the situation interact in interesting ways to influence what we think, feel, and do (see Table 2.2).

Table 2.2 Different Types of Person–Situation Interactions

Interaction	Example
• Different persons respond differently to the same situation.	• Some students think college life is fun and exciting; others find it dull and nerdy.
• Situations choose the person.	• Your college doesn't admit everyone who wants to enroll.
• Persons choose their situations.	• You may choose to live in a sorority or fraternity; your dorm-mate may choose to stay in the dorms.
• Different situations prime different parts of the person.	• You may see yourself as studious while in class but as fun-loving when at a party.
• Persons change the situation.	• An energetic, knowledgeable teacher can turn a quiet, passive classroom into an active, interested one.
• Situations change the person.	• If one student goes off to school at the Naval Academy, while an initially similar friend goes to U.C. Berkeley, they are likely to be less similar four years later.

Quick Quiz

1 Which of these is an example of a situation choosing the person?
   a. A student spends the night in the library rather than at a friend's party.
   b. A law school applicant gets rejected from his first-choice college.
   c. A woman decides to start a family after finishing college.
   d. None of the above

2 Which of these is an example of how different situations prime different parts of the person?
   a. Person thinks more individualistically after viewing an American flag, but thinks more collectivistically after viewing a Chinese flag
   b. Person primed with words related to politeness is more likely to act polite in a subsequent social interaction than if she were primed with words related to rudeness
   c. Student feels outgoing and talkative when hanging out with his friends but shy and reticent in the classroom
   d. All of the above

3 Which of these is an example of a situation changing the person?
   a. A person who grew up in New York City moves to a rural area and learns to be strongly connected to a small-town community.
   b. A person starts a community garden to strengthen the community's social ties and health.
   c. A person contributes to her community by volunteering at an animal shelter.
   d. All of the above

Revisiting The Enigma of an Ordinary and Extraordinary Man

Although he was indeed ordinary in many ways, Dr. Martin Luther King Jr. arrived in Montgomery, Alabama, with several of the features that would later characterize him as the leader of the Civil Rights movement. His desire to see African Americans treated with respect had been instilled in him by his father, who left a lasting impression on his young son by walking out of a shoe store when the clerk refused to serve him in the "white" section.

King's motivations and beliefs were accompanied by powerful feelings. Capable of strong passions, even as a boy, he exhibited great sympathy for the poor he observed standing in Depression-era breadlines. This capacity for powerful emotion later revealed itself in King's commitment to his causes and in the force of his speeches. By focusing on the person—on King's motives, beliefs, and feelings—we begin to see the makings of the Martin Luther King Jr. the world would come to know.

These personal characteristics, however, weren't the only factors that set him on his course. First, he was in the right place at the right time. Rosa Parks, the brave woman who placed herself at great personal risk by violating Montgomery's segregation ordinance, was the secretary of the local NAACP, on whose board the young Martin Luther King Jr. served. His connection to her put him in close contact with the local controversy. Moreover, as a newcomer to town, he must have felt flattered by the request to lead his community in the boycott of the bus system. And it would have been difficult for him to refuse the request, given the local expectations that preachers be community leaders.

These features of the situation placed him in an early position of leadership, but they certainly didn't guarantee his success. Indeed, King's meteoric rise almost never was. His speech to announce the boycott, which would set the tone for the protest, began with little of the power for which he later became known. Energized by years of inequality and discrimination, however, his audience would not allow King to fall short of its lofty expectations. The audience *needed* a big moment, and its responsiveness and passion pulled it from him.

King was energizing the crowd, proving to both himself and them that he was capable of leading. The situation had chosen him, and King had accepted the challenge.

King was changed into a leader, and he, in turn, gave the people increased hope.

The person and situation continued to interact throughout the boycott. The people's enthusiasm and favorable endorsements fortified him when his faith and confidence began to waver. The police department's decision to jail him for a bogus speeding violation increased his visibility and credibility, as did the firebombing of his home. And the common people's willingness to sacrifice made the boycott a success, leading to the *Time* magazine cover story on King that elevated him to national prominence.

Dr. Martin Luther King Jr. brought to his situation a powerful commitment to egalitarian principles, the nonviolent style of protest espoused by Gandhi, and magnificent oratory skills. The situation provided him with self-confidence and energy and bestowed upon him a wealth of opportunity. His truly extraordinary accomplishments were brought about not merely by the strength of his personality but by the interaction of that personality with the powerful situational forces in his life. Like all of us, he had his personal strengths and weaknesses. Like all of us, his actions—and his character—were shaped by the situations he encountered. And like all of us, he, in turn, shaped his world. This is the essence of social psychology.

We have seen that the fit between King and his circumstances facilitated his great successes and helped push forward the Civil Rights movement. Indeed, the social-psychological concept of person–situation fit has proved itself to be valuable for understanding many arenas of everyday life, from productivity on the factory floor to achievements at the highest reaches of politics. The research reviewed in this chapter shows that the findings of social psychology bridge well beyond the disciplines of industrial/organizational behavior and political science, however. For instance, we have seen how social psychology bridges genetics, neuroscience, and anthropology in the mapping and understanding of emotions, their origins, and their effects and how social psychology relates to sociology and other cultural studies as it helps explain how descriptive and injunctive norms shape both simple and complex social actions.

We have taken the first step of our journey to understand the fascinating world of social behavior. The following chapters pick up where this one leaves off—exploring in greater depth the thought processes and behaviors people use to traverse their social landscapes.

Chapter Summary

The Person

1. The person is a dynamic combination of motivations, knowledge, and feelings, all of which work with one another to help produce social behavior.

2. Motivation is the energy that moves people toward their goals.

3. Achieving goals sometimes requires considerable attention. With practice, however, strategies for reaching some goals can become automatized, enabling us to devote our limited amount of attention to other tasks.

4. Goals can be difficult to achieve. A goal of *not* doing something may be especially difficult to achieve, as the thoughts we suppress may later rebound into awareness with even greater frequency and intensity.

5. Knowledge is the information we take away from our life experiences and store in memory. We organize this information in mental structures, such as exemplars and schemas.

6. Knowledge that is primed is especially likely to influence what we pay attention to, how we interpret ambiguous social situations, and how we behave.

7. Feelings include attitudes, emotions, and moods. Social psychologists have various ways of measuring a person's feelings, including self-report, behavioral observation, and physiological techniques.

8. The way in which we experience and express our feelings is influenced by our genetic and cultural backgrounds. The feelings we experience at any one moment are determined by proximate physiological changes (e.g., facial feedback) and interpretations of our circumstances.

9. Feelings are extremely functional. Emotions signal us that something isn't normal, so we can shift our attention from our current activities to the new, emerging concern. Attitudes enable us to make quick approach/avoidance judgments about things we encounter. And moods keep us prepared to deal with our recent and current circumstances.

10. People think about themselves a lot—about who they are, how they are going to reach their goals, and how they can manage the impressions that others have of them.

11. Self-concept is the knowledge we have about ourselves. Self-esteem is the attitude we have toward ourselves. We learn about ourselves by observing or imagining how others view us (reflected appraisal), comparing ourselves to others (social comparison), and observing our own behavior (self-perception).

12. People attempt to reach their goals through a process of self-regulation and attempt to manage the impressions that others have of them by presenting themselves in ways consistent with their desired public images.

The Situation

1. People are situated in their physical and social environments, and these situations affect their thoughts, feelings, and behavior.

2. The number of people in our environment can have a great influence. For example, students in small, "understaffed" high schools were more strongly motivated, participated in more activities, had more positions of responsibility, and felt more challenged.

3. Different situations provide us with different opportunities and threats. These are called affordances, and we often detect them effectively and with little effort.

4. People communicate descriptive norms—information about what most people commonly do in a situation—and these help us make correct choices about what to do in new situations. Descriptive norms usually represent what people really believe or feel. When people behave in ways different from what they actually believe or feel, they can create a state of pluralistic ignorance, which can contribute to dangerous behaviors like binge drinking.

5. Many situations have "rules" that tell us what we're allowed to do and what we're not. These rules are called injunctive norms, and they define what is typically approved and disapproved of in these situations. Moreover, some situations are scripted in that there is a general sequence of behaviors expected of people in them. Injunctive norms and scripts guide people toward appropriate and expected behavior.

6. Some situations are "stronger" than others. Strong situations afford the people in them fewer opportunities, have clear injunctive and descriptive norms, and are more likely to be scripted. Weak situations afford many opportunities, have less clear norms, and are less likely to be scripted.

7. Culture can influence the circumstances we're in and how these circumstances influence us. Individualistic cultures socialize members to view themselves as individuals and to prioritize their personal goals. Collectivistic cultures socialize their members to view themselves as members of the larger social group and to place the group's concerns before their own.

8. Different cultures often afford somewhat different opportunities for their members. They may also have different norms and script their situations differently.

The Person and the Situation Interact

1. The person and the situation interact in various interesting ways to influence what we think, feel, and do.

2. Different people respond differently to the same situation. When a person "fits" well with the situation, he or she is likely to be more satisfied and effective.

3. Situations choose the people who enter them; not everyone can be in the situations of their choice.

4. People can often choose which situations to enter, and they pick those they believe provide the best opportunities to reach their goals.

5. Different situations prime different goals, beliefs, and feelings in each person's repertoire.

6. People change their situations.

7. Situations change people.

Key Terms

Affordance, 53

Attention, 38

Attitudes, 42

Automaticity, 38

Chronically accessible, 42

Collectivistic culture, 57

Counterfactual thinking, 46

Descriptive norm, 53

Emotions, 42

Exemplar, 41

Goal, 38

Individualistic culture, 57

Injunctive norm, 55

Moods, 42

Motivation, 38

Motive, 38

Person–situation fit, 61

Pluralistic ignorance, 53

Priming, 41

Reflected appraisal process, 48

Schema, 41

Scripted situation, 55

Self-concept, 47

Self-esteem, 47

Self-perception process, 48

Self-presentation, 49

Self-regulation, 49

Social comparison, 48

Socialization, 65

Chapter 3

Social Cognition: Understanding Ourselves and Others

Outline

Learning Objectives

LO 3.1 Identify the four core processes of social cognition.

LO 3.2 Describe the goals of social cognition.

LO 3.3 Identify and describe the cognitive strategies we use to conserve mental effort.

LO 3.4 Identify the different types of heuristics that influence our social judgments.

LO 3.5 Describe the features of the person and situation that increase or decrease our inclinations to use cognitive shortcuts.

LO 3.6 Summarize the cognitive strategies we use to enhance and protect our self-images.

LO 3.7 Understand how self-esteem influences the ways in which we seek to maintain a positive self-regard.

LO 3.8 Discuss the types of threats that can lead people to enhance or protect their self-esteem.

LO 3.9 Identify the cognitive strategies people use when seeking an accurate understanding of themselves and others.

LO 3.10 Describe the features of Jones and Davis' correspondent inference theory and Kelley's covariation model of attribution.

LO 3.11 Explain the features of the person and situation that increase the desire to make accurate decisions and judgments.

Portraits of Hillary Rodham Clinton

She was a Conservative Republican who became a liberal Democrat. She grew up in the Midwest, went to college and law school in the Northeast, and lived in the Deep South. She's a mother, an accomplished attorney, and a compelling advocate for the poor. She was the First Lady, a U.S. Senator, and Secretary of State, responsible for U.S. foreign policy. She seems to be a perennial presidential contender. She's been accused of serious crimes and ethical lapses but has never been formally charged. She endured her husband's marital infidelities, public scandal, and impeachment. It would be hard to deny that Hillary Rodham Clinton has led a remarkable and interesting life.

As much as any figure in recent history, Hillary Rodham Clinton has elicited strongly polarized reactions—adored by so many, reviled by so many others. She has become more popular in recent years, but when she was running for president in 2008, 84% of Republicans had an unfavorable opinion of her (Cohen & Blake, 2013). Consider just a small sampling of what intelligent and experienced observers of politics and politicians have written or said about her:

- "She possesses an extraordinary intelligence and toughness, and a remarkable work ethic. Hillary's appointment is a sign to friend and foe of the seriousness of my commitment to renew American diplomacy and restore our alliances." (Soon-to-be President Barack Obama, announcing in late 2008 his choice of Hillary Clinton as his Secretary of State)
- "I had no idea how dangerous she would become. . . . Neither she nor Bill loves America. They don't want the presidency to help the country but to use it as a platform to power." (Peggy Noonan, former speech writer for Presidents Ronald Reagan and George H. W. Bush, cited in Wakefield, 2002)
- "Hillary Clinton is the kind of person who offers little girls a model for their lives, and little boys an understanding of the promises and opportunities that exist for women." (Karen Burstein, 2000, former New York state senator and family court judge)

Hillary Rorschach Clinton. As with a Rorschach inkblot test, different people "see" different things in Hillary Rodham Clinton. Is she an idealistic, talented public servant worthy of role-model status? Or is she a dangerous, deceitful, anti-American power seeker? How can it be that people view the same woman so differently?

- "Our First Lady—a woman of undoubted talents who was a role model for many in her generation—is a congenital liar." (William Safire, 1996, Pulitzer Prize–winning author and journalist for the *New York Times*)
- "[Hillary Clinton's] decision to land in New York in order to be elected to the Senate represents a fundamental assault on our most basic idea of representative democracy. . . . Hillary does not want to join us. She will agree to live with us only if we send her to Washington. We are no more than a launching pad. When Hillary poses in a Yankee hat, it turns our stomachs." (Dick Morris, 1999, former Bill Clinton political strategist)
- "Hillary Clinton can lay claim to the effective blend of idealism and tenacity that has characterized generations of progressive reformers in New York. And surely these ties should qualify her as a native as much as a lifetime of rooting for the Yankees." (Ellen Chesler, 1999, author and advocate for reproductive health and rights)

Given that Hillary Clinton has led much of her life in the public eye and that the major facts of her life are well known, one might have expected these observers to agree on what she is like. People's thoughts about her have diverged wildly, however. Indeed, even those who have worked closely with her, and who thus presumably share even more knowledge about her than do typical observers, have sometimes painted contrary cognitive portraits of her.

Differences in public opinion don't just apply to Hillary Rodham Clinton but to many of the people we know and encounter each day. Your roommate thinks her new boyfriend is deeply sensitive and charming; her parents think he's a boring and shallow loser. You think your brother's funny; your girlfriend thinks he's offensive. How can we explain this? What is it about the way we think about others that allows such different impressions to emerge, not only when we contemplate the actions and lives of public figures like Hillary Rodham Clinton but also when we consider, each day, the actions and lives of those around us?

The Social Thinker

LO 3.1 Identify the four core processes of social cognition.

LO 3.2 Describe the goals of social cognition.

When someone does something unexpected, one often hears the question: "What could he have been thinking?" We're interested not only in what people do, but also in what goes on in their minds—in that "black box" inside their heads. Because how you think about your social world influences how you act, we devote this chapter to **social cognition**—to the process through which people think about and make sense of themselves and others (Moskowitz, 2005).

Four Core Processes of Social Cognition

By now, most of you have had a couple of weeks to observe and interact with your social psychology professor. What do you think of him or her? How did you arrive at this impression? To begin answering questions such as these, we need to consider the four core processes of social cognition: attention, interpretation, judgment, and memory.

ATTENTION: SELECTING INFORMATION We learned in Chapter 2 that attention—the process of consciously focusing on aspects of one's environment or oneself—is limited; people can pay attention to only a tiny fraction of the information available to them. Moreover, depending on our goals, we pay more attention to some people and to some aspects of their behavior than we do to others (see Figure 3.1).

Because different people expose themselves to different information, and because people select the information they pay attention to, you might base your impression

Social cognition The process of thinking about and making sense of oneself and others.

of your professor on a somewhat different set of information than will your classmates. Some of you have gone to office hours or bumped into your professor at a local coffee house. Some of you, in contrast, know nothing of your instructor beyond what seems apparent in the classroom. Of course, if you pay attention to different information you may well form a very different impression of the same person (e.g., Maner et al., 2003; Sanbonmatsu, Akimoto, & Biggs, 1993; Taylor & Fiske, 1978). If you missed the class period during which your professor talked emotionally about his new baby, you might not think of him as warm, though other students might. Throughout this chapter, we'll explore how features of the person and situation influence what we pay attention to and, thus, the impressions we form of ourselves and others.

INTERPRETATION: GIVING INFORMATION MEANING

Once we pay attention to something, we still need to determine what that information *means*—we need to interpret it. Does your professor's upbeat style reflect a natural enthusiasm, or is it just contrived to make you more interested in the course material?

Most social behaviors can be interpreted in multiple ways. When Hillary Clinton published her memoirs, for example, political liberals accused the media of being too harsh in their critiques, whereas political conservatives believed that the media were reacting too positively to her and her book. Diverging interpretations like this

Figure 3.1   I can't take my eyes off of you

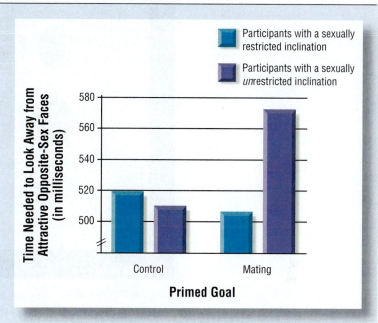

In one experiment, heterosexuals who were dispositionally favorable toward short-term sexual encounters (i.e., sexually unrestricted) *and* primed to think about mating—a combination of forces that would make one especially interested in having a sexual relationship—found it especially difficult to look away from attractive opposite-sex individuals (Maner, Gailliot, Rouby, & Miller, 2007).

Source: Maner, J. K., Gailliot, M. T., Rouby, D. A., & Miller, S. L. (2007). Can't take my eyes off you: Attentional adhesion to mates and rivals. *Journal of Personality and Social Psychology, 93,* 389–401.

aren't unusual. Strong advocates of social and political causes often believe that the mainstream media favor the opposing view (Matheson & Dursun, 2001; Vallone, Ross, & Lepper, 1985). In one study by Roger Giner-Sorolla and Shelley Chaiken (1994), people with either pro-Israeli or pro-Palestinian views watched identical news broadcasts of an Israeli–Palestinian confrontation. The pro-Israeli students interpreted the broadcasts as favoring the Palestinians, whereas pro-Palestinian students thought the same presentations favored the Israelis. Throughout this chapter, we'll encounter various factors that influence how people interpret events.

JUDGMENT: USING INFORMATION TO FORM IMPRESSIONS AND MAKE DECISIONS   Why do we gather and interpret information about people? Because we need to form impressions of them if we are to make important decisions. We want to determine how helpful a teacher will be outside of class, whether a new acquaintance will become a trustworthy friend, or which sales strategy will work best on an unfamiliar customer. Sometimes, the decision process is straightforward and simple. For example, if you want to know how tall your professor is, you could stand him or her against a wall and pull out your tape measure. Social impressions and decisions tend to be more difficult, however, because they usually involve a fair amount of uncertainty. It's often unclear how to weigh the information we do have. If your professor tells you you'll have a hard time getting into graduate school, is that because he is helpful and honest or because he is blunt and insensitive? As a result, many of our impressions and decisions are "best guesses"—the best we can do given the information we have to work with. In this chapter's video link, University of Iowa's Rebecca Neel describes some research demonstrating how our best guesses about who is likely to be happy or angry can lead us to make errors if we have to make snap judgments about men's and women's emotions (Neel et al., 2012).

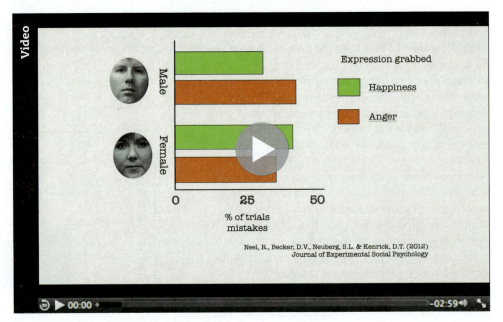

WATCH THE VIDEO: *Who was that angry person? How your expectations can throw off your judgments about other people's emotions.*

MEMORY: STORING INFORMATION FOR FUTURE USE   If you pay enough attention to any event, it will be registered in your memory. Memories can directly contribute to new judgments, as when you recall a friendly encounter with a professor and then seek advice from him or her in the future. Memories can also indirectly influence our impressions and decisions by affecting what we pay attention to and how we interpret it, as when your memory of the pleasant encounter increases the odds you will interpret future interactions with your professor as supportive. As we learned in Chapter 2, existing memories are especially influential when they've been "standing at the ready"—when they either have been recently primed or are chronically accessible.

To understand how people think about themselves and others, then, we need to take into account certain fundamental cognitive processes—attention, interpretation, judgment, and memory. Considering these processes may help explain the widely divergent judgments people have formed about Hillary Rodham Clinton. Her supporters focus their attention on her efforts to help children, interpret her stint as Secretary of State as reflecting her desire to serve, and are less likely to bring to mind her political failures. In contrast, her detractors focus on her alleged role in various political scandals, interpret her public service as reflecting her desire for raw political power, and are less likely to bring to mind her successes on behalf of children. Throughout this chapter, we will return to these four processes, exploring how they (1) are influenced by our goals, knowledge, and feelings and (2) influence what we think of ourselves and others.

INVESTIGATION

Think about the last disagreement you had with a roommate, friend, or family member. Why did you disagree? To what extent did differences in your cognitive processes—for example, differences in what the two of you focused on and in how you interpreted the event—contribute to your disagreement?

The Goals of Social Cognition

Social thought needs to be flexible. It makes little sense, for instance, for you to devote as much mental effort to a passing stranger as to a romantic partner. Fortunately, your thought processes are well equipped to adapt to a wide range of circumstances. We'll see, for instance, that sometimes people want to be more mentally efficient, forming quick impressions and making effortless decisions that are "good enough." At other times, people want to think well of themselves—to boost or protect their self-image. And sometimes people want to be quite accurate in their judgments, when they need to avoid potentially costly errors and mistakes. Because these goals are very different, different "styles" of thought are sometimes needed to achieve them. People are motivated tacticians: As their goals change, they adopt different styles of thought (Fiske & Taylor, 1991; Smith & Semin, 2007). In the remainder of this chapter, we will explore how such goals influence the ways people think about themselves and others.

Quick Quiz

1 Which of the following best describes *judgment* (one of the main social-cognitive processes)?
   a. The process of consciously focusing on aspects of one's environment or oneself.
   b. The process of storing information for future use.
   c. The process of interpreting information.
   d. The process of using information to form impressions or make decisions.

2 Which of the following best describes what it means for people to act as "motivated tacticians"?
   a. People are motivated to maintain a single, "all-purpose" style of thinking that best suits their personality type.
   b. People's motivational tactics often lead them to miscalculate the goals of a given situation.
   c. People's flexibly adopt different styles of thought to achieve different goals.
   d. None of the above

Conserving Mental Effort

LO 3.3   Identify and describe the cognitive strategies we use to conserve mental effort.

LO 3.4   Identify the different types of heuristics that influence our social judgments.

LO 3.5   Describe the features of the person and situation that increase or decrease our inclinations to use cognitive shortcuts.

You spend much of your life in complex social environments—classrooms, shopping malls, dormitories, and the like—in which you encounter people who vary in their ethnicity, gender, attractiveness, behavioral demeanor, age, clothing style, and so on. How do you deal with the huge amount of information available to you in any single moment?

Recall from Chapter 2 that we can think consciously about only a few things at once. This wouldn't be a limitation if we happened upon people and events one at a time—and could thoughtfully consider each new situation and then, when satisfied, move on to the next. Unfortunately, the social world is not only information rich but also relentless in its pace. Social events don't wait for an invitation; they come upon us rapidly.

Because of this, we don't always have the mental resources for effortful, "rational" processing. So we need cognitive strategies that free up scarce mental resources for other important tasks. In short, we need simple ways of understanding the world—strategies that help us make "good enough" judgments while expending only a minimal amount of mental effort (e.g., Goldstein & Gigerenzer, 2002; Haselton & Funder, 2006). We explore several such strategies next (see Figure 3.2).

Expectations

We saw in Chapter 2 that our beliefs about the world function as *expectations*—they tell us what we may expect from the people and situations around us, thus saving us the effort of having to evaluate each new situation from scratch. For example, you may have stereotypes about fraternity men. Upon learning that a classmate belongs to a fraternity, then, you may already "know" quite a bit about the person, even whether you think you'll like him. This knowledge prepares you to think about him without having

Figure 3.2   Keeping it simple

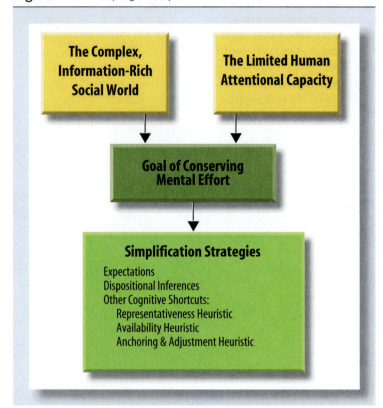

The information-rich social environment, together with our limited attentional resources, creates the need for simplifying, low-effort cognitive strategies that nonetheless let us form impressions and make decisions that are "good enough."

to expend effort to learn about the specific individual behind the label (Sedikides & Skowronski, 1991). Indeed, expectations such as these are so useful that we are reluctant to see them proven wrong.

To maintain the benefits of our expectations, we often think in ways that tend to preserve them. For example, people pay special attention to behaviors and events relevant to their expectations and often even seek information that confirms their expectations (e.g., Trope & Thompson, 1997). Believing that a classmate belongs to a fraternity, you may be especially likely to notice when he arrives late to class—a characteristic that is likely compatible with your beliefs about fraternity men.

Moreover, we tend to interpret ambiguous events and behaviors in ways that support our expectations. You might thus presume that the tired-looking fraternity member spent last night partying, as opposed to studying diligently for the upcoming midterm.

Finally, we tend to remember people and events that are consistent with our expectations (e.g., Hirt, McDonald, & Erikson, 1995). Indeed, you would probably better recall the time a fraternity member boasted of his passion for cheap beer than the time he revealed his longings for jamoca almond fudge ice cream. Although people sometimes also have very good memory for events inconsistent with their expectations—because such events can receive lots of attention—they almost always have a strong memory for events consistent with their expectations (e.g., Sherman & Frost, 2000; Stangor & McMillan, 1992).

Expectations, then, not only provide a cognitively inexpensive way of understanding people and events, but they also validate their own use and greatly simplify our cognitive life (e.g., Macrae, Milne, & Bodenhausen, 1994). Moreover, when our expectations are accurate, as they often are, using them enables decision making that is not only efficient but also correct (Jussim, 1991).

Regrettably, our expectations are sometimes inaccurate. For instance, although people's common stereotypes of fraternity men may indeed contain a substantial kernel of truth, they nonetheless fail to represent many fraternity members. Some fraternity members, for example, actually go on to earn Ph.Ds and become second authors of social psychology textbooks. Unfortunately, acting upon inaccurate expectations can lead to poor decisions and judgments, as when a manager fails to hire a highly qualified applicant because he holds exaggerated negative stereotypes about fraternity men. Even more problematic, inaccurate expectations sometimes create *self-fulfilling prophecies*, in which the expectations actually come true.

Bridging Function and Dysfunction:

The Self-Fulfilling Prophecy

In the early 1930s, thousands of U.S. banks went out of business, losing billions of dollars of their customers' money. Not surprisingly, depositors in other locales became jittery, fearing that the same could happen to them. Rumors of impending bank failures spread like wildfire. In some cases, hordes of customers rushed to remove their savings, a move that proved disastrous. Well-managed,

responsible banks don't keep their deposits locked away in vaults but rather recirculate this money throughout the community in the form of long-term investments such as home mortgages and business loans. As a result, they're unable to meet concentrated requests for large cash withdrawals. These stampedes of fearful depositors wishing to close their accounts overwhelmed even

From potential to performance. A student with parents and teachers who expect her to do well—and who, therefore, provide her with appropriate challenges and encouragement—is more likely to perform to her potential. The same student is likely to underperform her potential, however, if faced with the diminished opportunities that accompany negative expectations. Expectations not only change the way we think about people, but can also change the people we think about.

those banks that were thriving and solvent the day before. Banks went broke in hours, and late-arriving depositors lost their life savings. Bank customers, in their panic, unwittingly made their initially unfounded fears a reality.

With this and other examples, sociologist Robert Merton (1948) introduced the concept of the **self-fulfilling prophecy**, in which inaccurate expectations lead to actions that cause those expectations to come true. Children who are erroneously expected by their teachers to be bright may perform better in school because teachers are warmer to them, challenge them with more material, and interact with them more (e.g., Harris & Rosenthal, 1985; Madon et al., 2001). Job applicants who are inaccurately expected to be unqualified may perform less well because

interviewers ask them less favorable questions, conduct shorter sessions, and "leak" negative nonverbal behaviors (e.g., Neuberg, 1989; Word, Zanna, & Cooper, 1974). People who we erroneously believe to be introverted may indeed behave more shyly because we treat them less warmly (Stukas & Snyder, 2002). By acting on our inaccurate expectations, we may make them true.

When mistaken expectations are negative, the damage they create can be substantial. Imagine an intelligent, friendly 14-year-old who settles with his immigrant family in a small town where everyone expects people of "his kind" to be thieves. On the streets, he is treated with suspicion by passersby and police officers; in the classroom, he is ignored by teachers, who erroneously presume that he has little academic potential; and in the neighborhood, he is viewed by the local toughs as a potential recruit to their gangs. With relatively few opportunities for legitimate accomplishment, he may indeed flirt with criminal activity—thereby confirming the expectations of the community.

Are self-fulfilling prophecies inevitable? Fortunately not. Self-fulfilling prophecies are most likely to occur when (1) the people holding the erroneous expectations control the social encounter and (2) the targets of the expectations defer to this control (e.g., Smith et al., 1997; Snyder & Haugen, 1995). For example, when people who hold expectations have more power in the social encounter—as we might see in teacher–student, interviewer–applicant, and therapist–client relationships—self-fulfilling prophecies become more likely (Copeland, 1994). Indeed, low-power individuals in the educational system—students who are African American, of low socioeconomic status, or female—may be particularly vulnerable to their teachers' expectations (Jussim, Eccles, & Madon, 1995).

As useful as expectations are when they're accurate, then, they can be quite dysfunctional when they aren't. Not only may they lead us to misjudge people and situations, but they can limit the achievements of others and lead us to unwittingly create the very realities we most fear.

Dispositional Inferences

Imagine coming home one evening to discover your new roommate screaming at her father over the phone. How would you explain her behavior? Would you see the cause of the tantrum as residing in her personality (perhaps she's characteristically disrespectful and spoiled)? Would you instead attribute her actions to a feature of the situation (perhaps her father was continuing his unfair criticism of her boyfriend)? Or might you view the behavior as caused by some interaction of the two (perhaps your friend's short temper together with her dad's negativity combined to lead to the confrontation)?

Later in the chapter, we will see how people use information about both the person and the situation when they are motivated to understand accurately why a person behaved as he or she did. When people want to simplify and conserve mental effort, however, they tend to see other peoples' behaviors as stemming primarily from their personality (Gilbert & Malone, 1995; Jones, 1990). For instance, it doesn't take much thinking to simply presume that someone who is yelling at a stranger on the street is hostile. Indeed, these **dispositional inferences**—judgments that a person's behavior is caused by his or her disposition, or personality—seem to occur spontaneously and with little effort. That is, when we observe another's behavior, we often leap first to

Self-fulfilling prophecy When an initially inaccurate expectation leads to actions that cause the expectation to come true.

Dispositional inference The judgment that a person's behavior has been caused by an aspect of that person's personality.

assume it was caused by some characteristic within the person (e.g., Carlston, Skow-ronski, & Sparks, 1995; Kressel & Uleman, 2010; Moskowitz & Roman, 1992; Uleman, Saribay, & Gonzalez, 2008).

CORRESPONDENCE BIAS: THE FUNDAMENTAL ATTRIBUTION ERROR Because it's so easy to see others' behaviors as corresponding to their dispositions, we may under-estimate the importance of forces within the situation. Indeed, this **correspondence bias**—the tendency to attribute behavior to a person's disposition more than is jus-tified (Jones, 1979)—occurs so frequently that one social psychologist labeled it the **fundamental attribution error** (Ross, 1977). Participants in a classic study conducted by Edward Jones and Victor Harris (1967) were shown essays, ostensibly written by students on a debate team, either supporting or opposing Cuba's then-president, Fidel Castro. Some participants were told that the student author had freely cho-sen to present the viewpoint, whereas others were told that the student was forced by the debate coach to defend the position. When told that the essays were freely written, participants reasonably assumed that the essay reflected the writer's actual attitudes—that the writer of the pro-Castro essay was indeed strongly pro-Castro and that the writer of the anti-Castro essay was strongly anti-Castro. Surprisingly, however, participants made this dispositional inference even when they were told the authors had no choice as to which side to take. To a large extent, then, partici-pants ignored the influence that the situation—the debate coach's instructions—had on the author's behavior.

Thus, not only do we have a tendency to see others' behavior as arising from their personality, but this tendency sometimes leads us to underappreciate the role of situa-tional influences. Why? In general, it may be simpler to assume a personality influence than to assume a situational one (Gilbert & Malone, 1995). Situations that influence be-havior are often "invisible" to observers. For instance, watching your new roommate yell at her father, you may be unaware that he is unfairly criticizing her boyfriend. And, being unaware of this situational influence, your attributions for her behavior are likely to be dispositional ("she's disrespectful").

People also tend toward dispositional inferences because they're often correct. People outside the laboratory are rarely assigned randomly to social situations. In-stead, as we observed in Chapter 2, people choose situations that fit their personalities, and situations choose people that fit their requirements. Because people and situations often fit together nicely—professional athletes tend to be concerned with their phys-ical fitness and college professors tend to be intellectually curious—the dispositional inference may be not only a simple way of understanding another's behavior but also an accurate way.

CULTURE AND THE "FUNDAMENTAL ATTRIBUTION ERROR" In November 1991, Dr. Gang Lu went on a shooting rampage at the University of Iowa, killing five people and critically wounding another before fatally shooting himself. Lu, who had recently received his PhD from the physics department, had been upset that another student had defeated him in a competition for a prestigious academic award. In a period of 10 terrifying minutes, he moved through two buildings, methodically seeking his victims—the winner of the prize, the chairman of the physics department and two of its professors, the associate vice-president of student affairs, and her receptionist. The carnage complete, Lu turned the revolver on himself.

Two weeks later, outside Detroit, Michigan, Thomas McIlvane stormed into a postal service center with a semiautomatic rifle. For the next six minutes, the re-cently fired postal worker sprayed scores of bullets at his former colleagues, killing four supervisors and wounding five more. When the police arrived, he shot himself. McIlvane, previously dismissed for insubordination, had lost his final appeal to regain his job just six days earlier.

Why did Lu and McIlvane each embark on such a deadly path? In light of the discussion above, we might expect observers' explanations to be mostly dispositional, having to do with the killers' personal characteristics. Indeed, reporters for the *New York Times* stressed such factors in their articles: Lu was "darkly disturbed," had a "very

Correspondence bias (fundamental attribution error) The tendency for observers to overestimate the causal influence of personality factors on behavior and to underestimate the causal role of situational influences.

bad temper," and had a "psychological problem with being challenged"; McIlvane was "mentally unstable," a "martial arts enthusiast," and "had a short fuse." In contrast, as Michael Morris and Kaiping Peng (1994) discovered, the causes attributed to these mass murders by writers for the *World Journal*, a Chinese-language newspaper, were quite different. According to reporters for this paper, Lu had been "isolated from the Chinese community" and his actions could be "traced to the availability of guns." Likewise, McIlvane "had been recently fired," his supervisor had been "his enemy," and he was following "the example of a recent mass slaying in Texas." Whereas writers for the American newspaper had focused on dispositional causes, as the fundamental attribution error would suggest, writers for the Chinese newspaper focused on situational causes. How do we explain these differences? And if such differences are reliable, how fundamental could the "fundamental attribution error" truly be?

In Chapter 2, we learned that some cultures tend to be *individualistic* whereas others are more *collectivistic*. In highly individualistic cultures such as the United States, people are defined as individuals and are socialized to act independently—to take personal responsibility for their successes and failures. In collectivistic societies such as China, in contrast, people are defined in terms of their relations with others, and they are socialized to act *inter*dependently—to consider what others expect of them as well. Given this important distinction, we might expect people from these cultures to differ as well in their beliefs about where behavior typically comes from. Individualists should believe that aspects within a person, such as traits and attitudes, are particularly strong causes of behavior. Collectivists, in contrast, should have a greater appreciation for how aspects of the situation, such as norms and social pressures, influence behavior. Thus, the differences between cultures in the way people understand the causes of behavior may arise from broader differences in the importance that cultures place on people as individuals versus as members of social groups (e.g., Norenzayan & Nisbett, 2000; Oyserman & Lee, 2008). Indeed, even though members of both individualistic and collectivistic societies easily see dispositional causes of behavior, those from collectivistic societies are more likely to presume situational causes of behavior (Krull et al., 1999; Lieberman, Jarcho, & Obayashi, 2005; Miyamoto & Kitayama, 2002; Norenzayan, Choi, & Nisbett, 2002). Within the United States, there are sub-cultural differences in attributing people's behaviors to internal traits: Protestants, who are especially taught the importance of individual responsibility, are also more likely than Catholics to attribute others' behaviors to causes inside the individual (Li, Johnson, Cohen et al., 2012).

When viewed from a cross-cultural perspective, then, the fundamental attribution error seems far from fundamental.

Other Cognitive Shortcuts: Heuristics

To this point, we've discussed two strategies for understanding the social world while at the same time conserving mental effort—(1) people use their expectations in confirmatory ways and (2) they make dispositional inferences for others' behaviors (especially in individualistic cultures). Here, we explore several other frequently used shortcuts—known as **cognitive heuristics**.

REPRESENTATIVENESS HEURISTIC Jim drinks a lot of beer and spends many hours reading sports magazines. Is he more likely a member of Delta House Fraternity or of the Sierra Club? All else being equal, most people would guess Delta House. After all, people expect fraternity men to exhibit such behaviors. This use of our expectations is sometimes called the **representativeness heuristic**—because our judgment of which group Jim belongs to is based simply on how well his characteristics fit with, or represent, the different groups (Kahneman & Tversky, 1972). Because Jim's characteristics fit with belonging to a fraternity, we guess that he does.

AVAILABILITY HEURISTIC Let's try an exercise: See Table 3.1 and rank in order the likelihood that a U.S. citizen will die from the causes listed there.

Done? Let's see how you did. If you're like most people, you overestimated the threats from homicide.

Cognitive heuristic A mental shortcut used to make a judgment.

Representativeness heuristic A mental shortcut people use to classify something as belonging to a certain category to the extent that it is similar to a typical case from that category.

Table 3.1	Selected Causes of Death		
Place a number next to each cause of death, ordering them according to the likelihood that a U.S. citizen will die from them.			
Estimated Rank	**Cause of Death**	**Estimated Rank**	**Cause of Death**
_____	Chronic Lower Respiratory Diseases	_____	Heart disease
_____	Alzheimer's	_____	Homicide
_____	Diabetes	_____	Influenza and Pneumonia
_____	Kidney Disease	_____	Accidents
_____	Septicimia	_____	Liver Disease
_____	Parkinson's Disease	_____	Hypertension
_____	Pneumonitis	_____	Suicide
_____	Cancer	_____	Stroke

(1) Heart disease; (2) Cancer; (3) Chronic Lower Respiratory Diseases; (4) Stroke; (5) Accidents; (6) Alzheimer's; (7) Diabetes (8) Kidney Disease; (9) Influenza and Pneumonia; (10) Suicide; (11) Septicimia (blood poisoning); (12) Liver disease; (13) Hypertension; (14) Parkinson's Disease; (15) Pneumonitis; (16) Homicide.

Source: Estimates based on 2010 U.S. Cause of Death data, reported by the Centers for Disease Control.

To understand why, think about how you performed the task. Without the statistics in hand, your guess was probably based on how easy it felt to remember particular instances of each of these fatal events, a strategy psychologists label the **availability heuristic** (Caruso, 2008; Schwarz et al., 1991; Tversky & Kahneman, 1973). If it feels easier to recall murders than, say, deaths from diabetes, it would be reasonable to guess that homicides occur more often. After all, events that come to mind more easily usually *are* those that occur more often. Unfortunately, the media are biased toward reporting impactful and visual stories—like murders—thereby skewing our perceptions of what actually happens out there in the world. As a consequence, we tend to overestimate the likelihood of "newsworthy" causes of death and underestimate the likelihood of less newsworthy causes of death.

ANCHORING AND ADJUSTMENT HEURISTIC   Do you think college admissions affirmative action programs are a good idea? Why or why not? If we were to poll your social psychology classmates, what would they say? What percentage of them would share your opinion?

When people make judgments like this, they tend to overestimate the extent to which others agree with them—they fall prey to the **false consensus effect** (e.g., Kulig, 2000; Mussweiler & Strack, 2000; Ross, Greene, & House, 1977). The false consensus effect results from yet another useful simplifying strategy—the **anchoring and adjustment heuristic**. When we have a novel judgment to make, we often start with a rough estimate as an *anchor*, or starting point, and then *adjust* it to account for the possibility that it is imperfect (Janiszewski & Uy, 2008; Tversky & Kahneman, 1974). If you want to guess how well you'll do on your social psychology final exam, you may start with an estimate based on your midterm grades and then adjust it to take into account some unique characteristics of the final. (It may, for instance, have more essay questions on it; you may have two other finals that same day.)

Like other cognitive heuristics, the anchoring and adjustment heuristic saves us time and effort: Instead of having to gather lots of information before making a decision, we can just start with a useful approximation and adjust from there. Indeed, if we select a good anchor and make appropriate adjustments, the strategy will be both efficient and effective (Dawes, 1989; Krueger, 2007). Unfortunately, we sometimes pick poor anchors or adjust insufficiently (Epley & Gilovich, 2004; Kruger, 1999). The false consensus effect results from an anchoring-and-adjustment process in which a person uses his or her own views as the anchor and then inappropriately adjusts (Alicke & Largo, 1995; Fenigstein & Abrams, 1993).

Availability heuristic A mental shortcut people use to estimate the likelihood of an event by the ease with which instances of that event come to mind.

False consensus effect The tendency to overestimate the extent to which others agree with us.

Anchoring and adjustment heuristic A mental shortcut through which people begin with a rough estimation as a starting point and then adjust this estimate to take into account unique characteristics of the present situation.

Consider, for instance, your own judgment about what others would think about college admissions affirmative action programs. Because you probably didn't actually know how others would answer our question, you probably used your own opinion as an anchor and then assumed that many of your classmates would think similarly. You probably also realized, however, that at least some others might disagree—not having thought the issue through as carefully as you had! So you adjusted your estimate down from the presumption that 100% of your classmates would agree with you, although probably not far enough. Of course, you could have instead put off answering our question until you had a chance to poll all your classmates yourself or at least scientifically question a representative sample of them. But these alternative strategies would have taken a lot of time, and you probably didn't care all that much about getting the answer to this question perfectly correct anyway. So your simple intuitive estimation, using the anchoring and adjustment heuristic, seemed appropriate enough.

Circadian rhythms and judgment. Are you a "morning person" or an "evening person"? If you don't think it matters, think again: People are more likely to use cognitive shortcuts to make decisions during their "off" times than during the peak times of their circadian cycles.

We've explored several strategies that people use to simplify their understandings of the social world. These strategies serve the goal of mental economy quite well: They can be implemented quickly, require relatively few cognitive resources, and generally lead to reasonably accurate judgments and decisions. In the sections below, we explore when people seek mental economy, beginning with those factors residing within the person.

PERSON   Arousal and Circadian Rhythms

Jogging, riding a bicycle, and watching a horror movie all increase physiological arousal. You might be surprised to discover, however, that these activities also change the way we think (Mather & Sunderland, 2011). Specifically, arousal often prompts us to rely on our cognitive shortcuts. For example, aroused individuals are especially likely to rely on existing beliefs and expectations (Wilder & Shapiro, 1989), to succumb to the availability heuristic (Kim & Baron, 1988), and to ignore alternative possibilities when making decisions (Keinan, 1987). Why?

Arousal may lead us to simplify by distracting us. If you pay attention to your pounding heart while playing tennis, for instance, you will have less attention available for understanding why your opponent is trouncing you so badly. Arousal may alternatively lead us to simplify because it narrows the beam of our attentional spotlight, making it difficult to employ more comprehensive cognitive strategies (like those we explore later in the chapter). In either case, arousal makes it more difficult to think in complex ways and leads us to rely instead on low-effort shortcuts.

In a related vein, Galen Bodenhausen (1990) noted that individuals lose attentional resources during certain periods of their circadian—that is, their daily biological—cycle. He thus hypothesized that people who report reaching the peak of their cognitive functioning early in the day ("morning people") would use cognitive shortcuts (e.g., the representativeness heuristic) more at night, whereas people who report peaking later in the day ("evening people") would rely more on these shortcuts in the morning. In studies of social judgment, subjects were randomly assigned to participate at either 9:00 A.M. or 8:00 P.M. For some of the participants, then, the experiments occurred during their peak times, whereas for the others, they occurred during their "off" times. As Bodenhausen suspected, morning people were more likely to use cognitive shortcuts at night, whereas evening people were more likely to use their shortcuts in the morning.

In sum, when we enter a situation with a shortage of attentional resources—because we're either highly aroused or because it's our circadian down time—we're more likely to rely on simplifying strategies.

PERSON Need for Structure

It would be a mistake to think that simplifying the world is something that only other—less intelligent—folks do. For example, when people are aroused, they're more likely to simplify—and, of course, all of us are aroused at times. Nonetheless, there is a stable personality trait that also influences whether we use simple or more complex cognitive strategies: It's been labeled *need for structure*, and it reflects the extent to which people are motivated to organize their mental and physical worlds in simple ways. To assess this motivation, Megan Thompson, Michael Naccarato, and Kevin Parker (1989) designed the *Personal Need for Structure Scale*. People high in need for structure tend to agree strongly with items like "I enjoy having a clear and structured mode of life" and "I don't like situations that are uncertain." They are also more likely to engage in all sorts of cognitive shortcuts. For instance, they rely on preexisting expectations when judging others, form stereotypes especially easily, and attribute others' behaviors to their dispositions (Moskowitz, 1993; Neuberg & Newsom, 1993; Schaller et al., 1995; Webster, 1993).

In sum, physiological arousal and a dispositional need for structure increase the desire for mental economy and thus encourage individuals to take cognitive shortcuts. As the next section reveals, certain *situations* also lead people to simplify.

SITUATION Complex Situations and Time Pressure

It's finals week, and chaos reigns! You have four final exams and a term paper in biochemistry, and you need to move out of your apartment. On top of it all, your boss at Howard's House of Hot Dogs wants you to interview 18 people for two server openings. With all these things on your mind, are you likely to probe in great depth the past experiences, character, and background of each applicant, carefully comparing each of their strengths and weaknesses, as they apply to their intended part-time career as waiters or waitresses? Or might you instead rely more than usual on "quick-and-dirty" shortcuts? Research suggests the latter: Because each additional concern draws resources from your limited attentional pool, it becomes increasingly difficult for you to engage in careful thought as situations become more complex (Biesanz et al., 2001; Bodenhausen & Lichtenstein, 1987; Gilbert, Pelham, & Krull, 1988; Pratto & Bargh, 1991). One series of studies found that when people were rapidly adding numbers in their heads, they perceived an angry facial expression as being on a man when it was actually on a nearby woman, and on a black man when it was actually on a white man—they saw what their stereotypes suggested would be there (Becker, Neel, & Anderson, 2010; Neel et al., 2012).

We're also especially likely to rely on cognitive shortcuts when we're under time pressure (De Dreu, 2003; Epley et al., 2004; Rieskamp & Hoffrage, 2008). Indeed, imagine if two of your finals and the term paper were due tomorrow and you had yet to finish the paper and begin studying. Would this affect your willingness to use cognitive shortcuts in evaluating those job applicants?

In one experiment, Israeli teachers read an essay presented as coming from a student of high-status descent or from a student of low-status heritage. Some teachers had one hour to grade the essay (low time pressure) whereas others had only 10 minutes (high time pressure). Not only did the high-status student receive higher grades than the low-status student for the identical essay when time pressures were low (73% versus 64%), but this stereotyping effect was exaggerated when the teachers were rushed (80% versus 64%)—the teachers under time pressure further benefited the high-status student by two-thirds of a grade level (Kruglanski & Freund, 1983).

In sum, people are more likely to use simplifying cognitive strategies when situations are complex and when time is short.

INTERACTION When the World Doesn't Fit Our Expectations

From our discussion thus far, you might get the impression that people arrive on the social scene with a toolbox full of favorite cognitive shortcuts and rarely use anything more complex. It's true that we use a lot of simplification strategies. It's also true, however, that there's a real world out there, and to survive we must be flexible enough to go beyond simplification when the situation calls for it. For example, when we feel accountable for our judgments—when we have to justify them to others—we're less likely to rely on simple ways of judging our social world (e.g., Bodenhausen et al., 1994; Pendry & Macrae, 1996; Schaller et al., 1995). Indeed, later in the chapter, we explore in depth those circumstances that motivate us to go beyond our cognitive shortcuts. For now, it will do merely to illustrate that people will indeed put aside their shortcuts when the situation calls for it.

Imagine that, over coffee, a friend describes a new acquaintance—Pablo, an artist. You immediately envision a creative, nonconforming, somewhat idealistic individual, so you're not surprised in the least to hear her describe the funny hours he keeps and his strange style of dress. Pablo fits with your expectations, so you picture him as you would many other artists. Imagine instead, however, that she describes Pablo as meticulously neat, scientific, and politically conservative. This doesn't accord with your expectations. *A scientific artist? And meticulously neat?* Will you stick with your initial expectations and view him as a typical artist? Sometimes you will—if your initial expectations and beliefs are very important to you. Other times, however, you'll probably search for a better way of understanding Pablo, one that accounts more easily for his apparent complexities (e.g., Biek, Wood, & Chaiken, 1996; Edwards & Smith, 1996; Fiske & Neuberg, 1990).

INVESTIGATION

Think about a time when you stereotyped someone—that is, when you viewed him or her not as a complex individual but as a typical member of his or her social group. To what extent did the factors we've discussed so far contribute to this? And, given what you've learned, what might you do next time to reduce the chance that you'll rely on your stereotypes to understand someone?

Our expectations, then, don't always result in the confirming processes we've discussed. Rather, our expectations interact with the information available to us to determine whether we seek to confirm our expectations or instead seek greater accuracy. When our expectations are clearly out of sync with the world, we often go beyond them (McNulty & Swann, 1994).

Quick Quiz

1   Which of the following are consequences of holding expectations?

  a. We tend to remember people and events that are consistent with our expectations.
  b. We often think in ways that preserve our expectations.
  c. We tend to interpret ambiguous events in ways that support our expectations.
  d. All of the above
  e. (a) and (c)

2   Which of the following statements is *correct* regarding the correspondence bias?

  a. When evaluating others' behavior, people in individualistic cultures, compared to those in collectivist cultures, tend to attribute behavior mostly to situational forces.
  b. It is similar to what is called the fundamental attribution error.
  c. People tend to attribute behavior to a person's disposition, but when informed that a person did not freely choose the behavior, observers are quick to take into account the influence of the situation.
  d. All of the above

3   Which of the following best defines the *representativeness heuristic*?

  a. A mental shortcut used to estimate the likelihood of an event by the ease with which instances of that event come to mind.
  b. A mental shortcut used to classify something as belonging to a certain category based on how similar it is to a typical case from that category.
  c. The tendency to overestimate the extent to which others agree with us.
  d. A mental shortcut in which people start with a rough estimate and then adjust it to accommodate unique characteristics of the present situation.

> **4** Which of the following examples highlight features of the *person* (rather than the situation) that increase the tendency to use cognitive simplification strategies?
>
> a. A time-pressured graduate student rushes through the grading of essays and gives much higher marks to students she assumes are native English speakers.
> b. A busy parent of three small children glances at a mail-in ballot and chooses only her preferred party's politicians rather than taking the extra time to research all of the candidates.
> c. A manager who typically feels most energized at night had to conduct an interview early in the morning; consequently, he didn't feel awake enough to ask the candidate deep questions that would have helped him make the best hiring decision possible.
> d. None of the above

Managing Self-Image

LO 3.6 Summarize the cognitive strategies we use to enhance and protect our self-images.

LO 3.7 Understand how self-esteem influences the ways in which we seek to maintain a positive self-regard.

LO 3.8 Discuss the types of threats that can lead people to enhance or protect their self-esteem.

Are your recent grades good or bad? Why? Have your relationships been going well? If not, who's to blame? As we contemplate questions like these, quick-and-easy answers may not be enough. Instead, we often strive to find answers that help us feel good about ourselves. "I found those courses too dull to take seriously," we tell ourselves, "and that man was just *impossible* to get along with."

If thoughts like these come to mind, you're not alone. Consider, for instance, that most Americans report having high self-esteem, view their future prospects optimistically, see their negative behaviors as caused by external forces, and believe they possess more favorable characteristics and abilities than the average person (e.g., Alicke & Govorun, 2005; Helweg-Larsen & Shepperd, 2001; Malle, 2006; Weinstein & Klein, 1996; Williams & Gilovich, 2008). To put it simply, most people want to feel good about themselves.

We desire positive self-regard for several reasons. First, with positive self-regard comes the belief that we're effective—that we can accomplish our goals—and such beliefs help us summon the willpower and energy we need to achieve. Finding ways to improve your self-regard can thus improve your ability to accomplish important tasks (McFarlin et al., 1984). Second, self-regard indicates how we're doing in our social lives. When our social interactions and friendships are going well, we feel better about ourselves (e.g., Anthony, Holmes, & Wood, 2007; Denissen et al., 2008). Thus, when we're feeling lousy about ourselves, that may be a signal that we need to assess our interpersonal relationships and improve them (e.g., Leary et al., 1995). As a consequence, finding ways to boost your self-regard should also reduce your anxiety about personal relationships. Third, self-regard may indicate how successfully we're living up to society's standards of value. When self-regard is low, then, it may signal that we need to affirm our society's values. Thus, finding ways to boost your self-regard may also reduce your anxiety about not being a "good person" in the eyes of your society (Pyszczynski et al., 2004).

Enhancing your view of yourself can also have health benefits (Stinson et al., 2008). Consider, for example, the potential trauma experienced by residents of New York City who lived or worked near the World Trade Center in the days and months following the terrorist attacks of September 11, 2001. Indeed, the attacks took their psychological toll on many residents. Those who had self-enhancing personalities, however—who made a habit of boosting their self-regard—experienced fewer symptoms of depression and posttraumatic stress disorder both 7 and 18 months after the attack (Bonanno, Rennicke, & Dekel, 2005).

This isn't to say that we want to blindly delude ourselves. It certainly wouldn't be adaptive to believe that things are great when, in reality, they stink. When positive self-regard is unjustified and exaggerated to the point of conceit and narcissism, it can harm relationships, contribute to bullying, and create other significant problems

(Baumeister et al., 2003; Colvin, Block, & Funder, 1995; Crocker & Park, 2004). Indeed, the high self-enhancers who had *personally* adjusted so well to the attacks were viewed by their friends and family as being less *socially* adjusted and honest (Bonanno et al., 2005). Moreover, a somewhat weaker form of this self-deception—one that's a bit more sensitive to feedback—may help us work toward our goals and, at the same time, alleviate some everyday worries (e.g., Sedikides & Luke, 2008; Taylor et al., 2003b). In this section, we discuss some of the cognitive strategies people use to enhance and protect their self-images and then explore the factors in the person and the situation that lead people to employ such strategies.

Cognitive Strategies for Enhancing and Protecting the Self

We'll see in other chapters that people sometimes use actual behaviors to affirm desired self-images. For instance, coming to another's aid can help people feel good about themselves. But sometimes our minds can do the work without our bodies having to spring into action. In this section, we focus on some of the cognitive strategies people use to enhance and protect their self-image (see Figure 3.3).

SOCIAL COMPARISON How smart are you? How do you know? Are your political opinions reasonable? Again, how do you know? In his landmark 1954 paper, Leon Festinger argued that people have a fundamental drive to evaluate their abilities and

Figure 3.3 Maintaining a desirable self-image

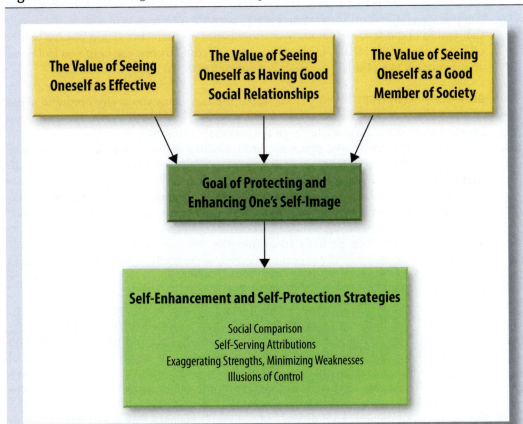

Social survival often requires that we assert ourselves. We need to approach our social environment to secure from it what we need. To believe we are effective, have good social relationships, and are good members of our society gives us the confidence to make this approach. For this reason, people use various cognitive strategies to enhance and protect their self-images.

opinions and often do so by comparing themselves with others. To assess your intelligence, you might see how your SAT scores stack up against those of your classmates; to evaluate whether your opinion of the president is reasonable, you may compare your views with your neighbor's. Festinger's (1954) social comparison theory focused on the drive to *accurately* assess one's abilities and the legitimacy of one's opinions. We examine this part of the theory in Chapters 7 and 12, when we explore who people choose as their friends and why people join groups.

People also compare themselves with others for the purpose of self-enhancement (e.g., Suls, Martin, & Wheeler, 2002; Wood, 1989). How might you use social comparisons to elevate your self-image? First, you might engage in **downward social comparison**—that is, you might compare yourself to someone who is less fortunate than yourself, has lesser abilities, and so on. For example, a study of breast cancer patients revealed that a large majority spontaneously compared themselves with others in even worse condition (Wood, Taylor, & Lichtman, 1985). As one woman said, "I just had a comparatively small amount of surgery on the breast, and I was so miserable, because it was so painful. How awful it must be for women who have had a mastectomy." Because downward comparisons can increase self-esteem and reduce stress, this woman may be better able to cope with her own difficult situation (Gibbons & Gerrard, 1989; Lemyre & Smith, 1985).

Second, people can sometimes create positive self-regard through **upward social comparison**—by comparing themselves to those better off (Collins, 1996; Lockwood et al., 2012). This is a somewhat dangerous strategy. On the one hand, comparing yourself to the really sharp student in your math class might prove beneficial by motivating you toward self-improvement (Blanton et al., 1999; Helgeson & Taylor, 1993; Vrugt & Koenis, 2002). On the other hand, such a strategy carries a risk, as you're likely to realize that you're not as smart as the other person. Indeed, if you select your upward comparisons haphazardly, the strategy may backfire. The trick is to convince yourself that you're in the *same general range* as those better off than you. If you believe you're on a trajectory to succeed as others have, upward comparisons can help you feel good about yourself (e.g., Burleson, Leach, & Harrington, 2005).

SELF-SERVING ATTRIBUTIONS Think about the last exam you really aced and write down the reasons you performed so well. Done? Now think back to the last exam you performed poorly on and write down the reasons for this, too.

If you're like most folks, you sometimes exhibit a **self-serving bias**: You take personal credit for your successes and blame external forces for your failures (Shepperd, Malone, & Sweeny, 2008). For instance, students often attribute their A grades to something within themselves—a special understanding of the material, perhaps, or serious studying effort—and their poorer showings to causes outside their control—an unfair teacher or the cold they caught the night before.

The self-serving bias partially arises from the expectations we have for our performances: Because we generally expect to succeed, we're likely to interpret our successes as reflecting our abilities and efforts; because we don't expect to fail, we're likely to look for external events that "got in the way" (Miller & Ross, 1975). More fundamentally, however, the self-serving bias enhances self-image. Taking credit for our successes helps us feel good about ourselves (e.g., Miller, 1976; Sicoly & Ross, 1979; Weary, 1980).

Making self-serving attributions after failure—that is, blaming one's failure on external influences—occurs easily, perhaps even automatically. The brain activity of participants in one study was measured as they received feedback while performing a very difficult task (having to identify whether rapidly presented faces were the same as one another). After each piece of experimentally manipulated feedback—that they had made a correct or incorrect judgment—participants selected a reason for their success or failure while their brain activity was being monitored. Internal reasons included statements such as "I am smart" or "I didn't try hard"; external reasons included statements such as "It was hard" or "It was bad luck." Unlike when they took credit for successes and blamed external forces for their failures—the self-serving set of responses—when participants blamed themselves for their failures and credited external forces for their

Downward social comparison The process of comparing ourselves with those who are less well off.

Upward social comparison The process of comparing ourselves with those who are better off.

Self-serving bias The tendency to take personal credit for our successes and to blame external factors for our failures.

successes, activity levels increased in the part of their brains that engage when people need to work to control their automatic, usual responses (Krusemark, Campbell, & Clementz, 2008). Whereas unbiased attributions require enhanced mental control, these findings suggest that self-serving attributions come easily.

EXAGGERATING OUR STRENGTHS, DIMINISHING OUR WEAKNESSES   Let's try an exercise (you can also try this on your friends): Rank the six traits below in order of importance. If you think it most important that people be intelligent, you should rank intelligence first; if you think it least important that people be sensitive, you should rank sensitivity sixth, and so on.

- Creativity
- Industriousness
- Intelligence
- Kindness
- Sense of humor
- Sensitivity

Now rank the characteristics again, this time in terms of how well they represent you. That is, if you think creativity is your strong suit, you should rank it first. What do you find when you compare your two rankings?

If you're like most people, your two rankings will look similar. That is, if you see yourself as pretty smart, you will also place a high value on intelligence; if you believe yourself to be funny, you will put more weight on sense of humor. In general, people tend to value quite highly—in both themselves and others—those characteristics and abilities they happen to possess (e.g., Dunning, Perie, & Story, 1991; Harackiewicz, Sansone, & Manderlink, 1985; Schmader & Major, 1999). Similarly, people tend to *devalue* the traits and abilities they don't have. In one study, for instance, intellectually gifted boys who thought they hadn't done well in class minimized the importance of academics and boosted the importance of other pursuits (Gibbons, Benbow, & Gerrard, 1994).

From the self-regard perspective, the reasons for this are clear: By manipulating the relative importance of different traits and abilities, we can boost our self-image (Greve & Wentura, 2003). "I have what's important," we think to ourselves, thus increasing our sense of worth. Moreover, by using our strengths to evaluate others, we're more likely to compare favorably to them, also helping to enhance our self-image.

BELIEVING WE HAVE CONTROL   Often, enhancing or protecting our self-image involves believing we have control over certain situations and events in our lives. Some time ago, the payout for the multistate Powerball lottery had reached $110 million. One of the authors of this textbook, disregarding the daunting odds, overheard the following conversation while waiting in line to buy his ticket.

Person 1: "What are you going to do? Pick your own numbers or let the computer pick for you?"

Person 2: "Pick my own. I figure it gives me a better chance of winning."

A better chance of winning?! Our "logical" minds reject such a supposition. After all, because lottery numbers are selected randomly, all numbers have an equally dismal chance of being a winner. Nonetheless, allowing the computer to pick our ticket leaves the outcome of such a potentially important event—$110 million!—totally outside our control. So what do we do? Along with our tendency to roll our own dice at the craps table and to wear lucky T-shirts while watching the big game, we personally choose our lottery numbers, creating for ourselves the *perception* of control (e.g., Biner et al., 1995; Langer, 1975; Thompson, 1999).

To some extent, the perception of control is adaptive. Without it, we may lack the confidence needed to work toward potentially difficult goals. For instance, if you don't think you'll be able to convince a corporate recruiter to hire you, you may not even interview for the job, thus guaranteeing you won't get it. Indeed, young people who lack a sense of personal control tend to achieve less in school and are more likely to engage in delinquent behavior. A 40-year trend is thus quite disturbing in its implications: American youth are much less likely these days to believe they control what happens to them (Twenge, Zhang, & Im, 2004).

Having a sense of personal control is so important that people react strongly when it's taken away (Brehm & Brehm, 1981). For example, when we reward people for doing what they already like to do, we may kill their interest in the activity because such rewards are often seen by their recipients as attempts to control them (e.g., Deci, Koestner, & Ryan, 2001; Lepper, Greene, & Nisbett, 1973). Society's practice, then, of rewarding students for the learning that most kids naturally enjoy may actually turn them off to self-education. Of course, if a child just isn't interested in reading, rewards may be necessary (e.g., Hidi & Harackiewicz, 2000). Nonetheless, praise and other rewards can have seriously detrimental effects, especially if these rewards are perceived as an attempt to control one's actions (Deci, Koestner, & Ryan, 1999; Henderlong & Lepper, 2002).

Feeling that we're no longer in control may do more than just reduce our motivation to achieve and our interest in previously enjoyable activities. It may also have crucial health implications, as we see next.

Bridging Theory and Application:

Control Beliefs and Health

When people perceive a loss of control, they cope less effectively with stress and their health suffers. Residents of nursing homes who perceive little opportunity to control their lives are generally worse off than those who see themselves as having more control (Rodin, 1986), and cancer patients having little sense of personal control are generally more poorly adjusted (Taylor, Lichtman, & Wood, 1984; Thompson et al., 1993).

It would seem, then, that programs designed to increase people's perceptions of control should enhance their ability to cope with stress. This is indeed the case. Nursing home residents given greater control over their everyday lives tend to be happier, more active, and healthier than other residents (Langer & Rodin, 1976; Rodin & Langer, 1977; Schulz, 1976). Moreover, when

postoperative hospital patients are given responsibility for self-administering pain-killing drugs, they often experience reduced pain and sometimes even recover faster—even though such patients typically give themselves *less* painkiller than their physicians prescribe (Egan, 1990; Ferrante, Ostheimer, & Covino, 1990).

Are increased perceptions of personal control beneficial for all individuals? Apparently not. Rather, perceptions of control help *internals*—people who like to be in control of their environments—but may actually harm *externals*—people who like to have others in control. In one study, middle-aged "external" women with rheumatoid arthritis became *more distressed* if their husbands encouraged them to take personal control (Reich & Zautra, 1995). The relationship between control and well-being also seems to vary across cultures. For example, the link between external locus of control and anxiety is stronger individualistic cultures than in collectivistic societies (Cheng et al., 2013).

Finally, when perceptions of control are a mere illusion—when we don't in reality have control over important events in our lives—such perceptions can be maladaptive (e.g., Colvin & Block, 1994). For example, unrealistic perceptions of control held by cardiac patients and rheumatoid arthritis sufferers are associated with poor adjustment (Affleck et al., 1987; Helgeson, 1992). It may be, however, that we have more control over our health than we often think. For example, even people who are HIV-positive can increase their longevity by adhering to their drug regimen, engaging in better health habits, maintaining supportive relationships, and avoiding other life stresses. And research indicates that positive beliefs about control can help such individuals do just that (Taylor et al., 2000a). In sum, it seems that perceptions of control can be quite beneficial to mental and physical health when the exercise of control is actually possible, which is frequently the case. However, when one no longer has the ability to influence events, psychological well-being may benefit more from the acceptance of this loss.

Control and health. Perceptions of control can contribute greatly to one's mental and physical health. For instance, residents of nursing homes who perceive opportunities to control their lives (like these senior fellows playing chess) are generally better off than those who see themselves as having limited control.

We've seen that people have a wide range of cognitive strategies for feeling good about themselves—they compare themselves with others, are quick to take personal credit for their successes, view their strengths as being especially important, and inflate their perceptions of control. Of course, the desires for self-enhancement and self-protection are stronger for some people than others. We turn, then, to explore the person and situation factors that motivate people toward positive self-regard.

INVESTIGATION

Think back to a time when a good friend was rejected socially (for a date perhaps) or did more poorly on an exam than he or she wanted. Did your friend exhibit any of the biases you've just learned about—such as downward social comparison or self-serving attributions? Why? In what ways was this response productive, and in what ways not?

PERSON Self-Esteem

People who have high self-esteem—who feel good about themselves as individuals—are especially likely to engage in self-enhancing strategies. They're more likely than their counterparts with low self-esteem to boost themselves through social comparison, and they appear to be better skilled at using both upward and downward comparison strategies (Buunk et al., 1990). They're more likely to put down others to improve their own feelings of self-worth (e.g., Crocker et al., 1987; Gibbons & McCoy, 1991). They're also more likely to exhibit the self-serving bias (Blaine & Crocker, 1993; Taylor & Brown, 1988), to inflate the importance of their own traits and successes (Harter, 1993), and to exaggerate their sense of control (Alloy & Abramson, 1979). All told, people who have high self-esteem use many cognitive strategies to improve the way they feel about themselves.

What about people with lower self-esteem? Are they immune to such self-enhancement practices? Are they uninterested in positive self-regard? Actually, most individuals, regardless of the level of self-esteem, want to feel good about themselves (Baumeister, 1993; Pelham, 1993). Self-esteem does seem to influence, however, the strategies people use to create a positive self-image. People who have high self-esteem are bold and tend to engage in direct self-*enhancing* strategies. People who have only moderate or low self-esteem, however, tend to be more cautious in how they go about gaining positive self-regard (e.g., Shepperd, Ouellette, & Fernandez, 1996). They focus instead on *protecting* the esteem they already possess (Bernichon, Cook, & Brown, 2003; Spencer, Josephs, & Steele, 1993; Tice, 1993). There is sometimes an upside to a negative self-image, though. Some recent research suggests that people with negative views of themselves are relatively better at coping with negative feedback (Ayduk et al., 2013).

SITUATION Threats to Self-Esteem

Threats to self-esteem spur people to enhance and protect their self-image. As part of a study assessing student impressions of standardized IQ tests, participants attempted a set of problems depicted as basic to creativity and intelligence (Greenberg, Pyszczynski, & Solomon, 1982). The test was further described as an excellent predictor of future academic and financial success. Some participants were led to believe they had performed poorly; others were led to believe they had performed quite well. When later asked to appraise the test, the opinions of the groups diverged quite dramatically: Students who thought they had done poorly not only minimized the importance of good performance but also were likely to attribute their low scores to bad luck, unclear instructions, and the invalidity of the test—apparently everything but their own ability! This type of self-protective bias is not limited to the laboratory. Students at the University of Florida, for instance, were more likely to see the Scholastic Aptitude Test (SAT) as invalid if they had performed poorly on it (Shepperd, 1993b).

Findings like these are quite common: Situational threats to self-image frequently lead to efforts to restore that self-image (e.g., Guenther & Alicke, 2008; Jordan & Monin, 2008; Shepperd, Arkin, & Slaughter, 1995). Besides poor test performances, self-image

Death threat. After thinking about death, people favor those who affirm their cherished values and derogate those who don't, seek support for their social attitudes and beliefs, and engage in other cognitive strategies to affirm their views of the world—all to protect themselves from threatening thoughts of their own mortality.

can also be threatened by negative interpersonal feedback ("Don't you think you could lose a few pounds?"), a serious illness like cancer, or even our own actions, as when we feel terrible about ourselves for being insensitive to someone we love. To deal with such threats, we may use the same strategies described earlier; that is, we may compare ourselves with others less fortunate, derogate those who give us negative feedback, and so forth (e.g., Dunning, Leuenberger, & Sherman, 1995; Kernis et al., 1993; Wood, Giordano-Beech, & Ducharme, 1999).

One particularly interesting form of self-image threat is *mortality salience*—the awareness that one will, at some point, die. Tom Pyszczynski, Jeff Greenberg, and Sheldon Solomon (1999) propose that thinking about the possibility of one's own demise is extremely threatening to the self-image. To remedy this challenge, the argument goes, we should look for ways to protect or enhance our self-views. Consistent with the hypothesis, thinking about their own death makes people more likely to exhibit the self-serving bias and leads college students to become especially optimistic about their financial circumstances 15 years in the future (Kasser & Sheldon, 2000; Mikulincer & Florian, 2002).

These researchers further propose that, because it's frightening to own up to the fact that we are mortal and will eventually die, we adopt spiritual and cultural views that provide additional meaning to our lives (and sometimes even suggest the possibility of a heavenly immortality). We should be especially likely to reaffirm those views when made aware of our mortality—to bolster individuals who agree with our cherished views and put down those who challenge them.

In one study, students with Christian beliefs were made highly aware of their own mortality—they were asked to write about what will happen to them as they die and how they feel about thinking about their own death. Other Christian students completed an otherwise identical questionnaire that made no mention of death. Later, all provided their impressions of a previously unknown person presented as either Christian or Jewish. Consistent with the hypothesis, this person was evaluated more favorably when Christian than when Jewish—that is, when she shared the students' religious values—but only by those subjects made aware of their own mortality (Greenberg et al., 1990). When thoughts of death threaten our self-image, we become more favorable toward those who validate our values and unfavorable to those who challenge them (Greenberg et al., 2001).

In sum, situational threats to self-image—whether in the form of apparent failure, negative feedback from others, serious illness, one's own negative behaviors, or thoughts of one's own mortality—lead to greater self-protection efforts.

INTERACTION ## When Self-Esteem Is Fragile

The self-esteem of some of your friends is probably very stable from day to day—they feel good about themselves today, they felt good about themselves yesterday, and they will feel good about themselves tomorrow—whereas, for others, self-esteem seems to fluctuate quite dramatically over even short periods of time (Kernis et al., 2000).

People with unstable self-esteem are greatly concerned with the self-implications of life's everyday events and are particularly likely to respond to these events with attempts to enhance or protect the self. In one study, students with unstable self-esteem were more likely than their stable counterparts to generate excuses to explain their grades on a psychology exam ("I didn't care enough to study very hard for this exam"). Indeed, the tendency for students with high self-esteem to use excuses to boost their self-image and for students with low self-esteem to use excuses to protect their self-image occurred mostly for those students who had unstable self-esteem (Kernis, Grannemann, & Barclay, 1992). We see, then, that the stability of self-esteem interacts with level of self-esteem to influence how people maintain a positive self-regard.

These interactive influences of self-esteem and self-esteem instability are particularly apparent when a person feels that his or her self-esteem is under threat. In one study, subjects were given either positive or negative feedback on a speech. Individuals who had unstable high self-esteem were most likely of all subjects to generate excuses for their poor performance after receiving negative feedback ("I didn't try very hard") and least likely of all subjects to make excuses after receiving positive feedback (Kernis et al., 1993). Self-esteem, self-esteem instability, and threat all work together to influence how we go about viewing ourselves.

How Culturally Universal Is the Need for Positive Self-Regard?

The desire for positive self-regard has traditionally been assumed to be a universal need—everyone's interested in viewing himself or herself favorably, or so it seems. But is this the case? Clearly, the findings we've explored so far suggest so: People compare themselves with others, manage how they view their successes and failures, exaggerate their strengths and minimize their weaknesses, and create illusions of control—usually to feel good about themselves. However, most of the research we've explored in this section has studied Americans, Canadians, and northern Europeans. Might people from other cultures be less motivated to elevate their personal self-esteem?

Recall that people in individualistic cultures are taught to focus on the *me*—to stand out and pursue their own goals and interests. Their esteem is predominantly grounded in their personal or independent self-concepts—in their view of themselves as autonomous individuals. In contrast, people in collectivistic cultures are taught to focus on the *we*—to fit in and seek harmony with others. Their esteem is predominantly grounded in their social or interdependent self-concepts—in their view of themselves in relation to others (Markus & Kitayama, 1991). People with interdependent selves should thus be less motivated to enhance and protect a personal self-image. After all, "sticking out" from others is potentially damaging to harmonious relations with others, and self-enhancement promotes sticking out (recall the Japanese adage from Chapter 2: "If a nail sticks up, hammer it down!").

Indeed, research contrasting Japanese with North Americans suggests that members of collectivistic cultures *are* less likely to demonstrate biases like the ones we've been exploring (e.g., Chang & Asakawa, 2003; Heine & Hamamura, 2007; Ross et al., 2005). For example, Americans tend to blame their failures on the situation, whereas Japanese attribute their failures to their own personal inadequacies (Kitayama, Takagi, & Matsumoto, 1995). Similarly, Canadians appear to be more unrealistically optimistic than Japanese (Heine & Lehman, 1995).

It seems, then, that the desire for positive self-regard characterizes those in individualistic cultures more than those in collectivistic cultures. Or does it? Recent research on university students from China, Japan, and the United States reveals that all self-enhance on implicit, subtle measures of self-esteem (Yamaguchi et al., 2007). Other research suggests that members of collectivistic cultures self-enhance just as much as those from individualistic cultures, but do so in different ways (e.g., Dalsky et al., 2008; Kudo & Numazaki, 2003; Kurman, 2001; Sedikides, Gaertner, & Vevea, 2005). For example, as Figure 3.4 suggests, Americans may be particularly likely to self-enhance

Figure 3.4 Self-enhancement in the United States and Japan

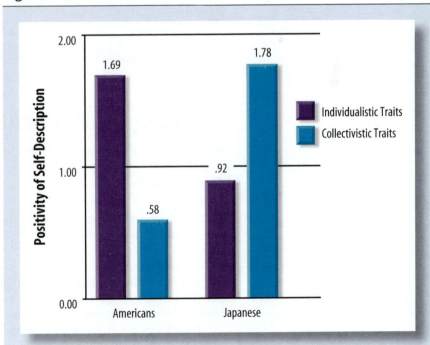

Some research suggests that Americans (and members of more individualistic societies) are more likely to self-enhance than are Japanese (and members of more collectivistic societies). Other studies suggest, however, that both Americans and Japanese self-enhance, but in different ways. In this study, Americans presented themselves especially favorably on individualistic characteristics such as self-reliance, whereas Japanese presented themselves especially favorably on collectivistic characteristics such as cooperation.

Source: Based on data reported in Sedikides, C., Gaertner, L., & Toguchi, Y. (2003). Pancultural self-enhancement. *Journal of Personality & Social Psychology,* 84, 60–79. Table 3.

when describing themselves on traits highly valuable to their individualistic culture (e.g., independence, uniqueness, self-reliance), whereas Japanese may be particularly likely to self-enhance when describing themselves on traits highly valuable to their collectivistic culture (e.g., loyal, compromising, cooperative) (Sedikides, Gaertner, & Toguchi, 2003).

So is there a universal need for positive self-regard? Some say yes (Sedikides & Gregg, 2008), but the jury's still out on this interesting question. Regardless, it's clear that creating and maintaining a positive sense of self is important to many, if not all, of us, and that this desire often greatly affects how we think about ourselves and others.

Quick Quiz

1 Which of the following is *not* a reason that people desire positive self-regard?

   a. High positive self-regard, to the point of narcissism, was once evolutionarily adaptive; thus, people in modern societies retained this desire.
   b. Self-regard may indicate how successfully we're living up to society's standards of value.
   c. Self-regard indicates how we're doing in our social lives.
   d. Positive self-regard indicates that we are effective in accomplishing our goals.
   e. None of the above

2 Which of these are strategies people use to enhance and protect their self-image?

   a. Taking responsibility for failure and eschewing personal credit for success
   b. Downward social comparison
   c. Minimizing their perception of control
   d. Magnifying the importance of things they do poorly and minimizing the importance of things they do well

3 Which of the following is NOT true regarding people with high self-esteem?

   a. They are more likely to engage in self-enhancing strategies.
   b. They are less likely to use downward social comparison strategies.
   c. They are more likely to emphasize the importance of their own traits when they succeed.
   d. They are more likely to exaggerate their sense of control.

4 People in collectivist cultures:

   a. Have higher need for self-regard than those in individualist cultures.
   b. Score higher on explicit self-esteem, but lower on implicit self-esteem.
   c. Show no evidence of a drive for self-regard.
   d. Enhance on group-valued traits such as cooperation rather than traits such as self-reliance.

Seeking an Accurate Understanding

LO 3.9   Identify the cognitive strategies people use when seeking an accurate understanding of themselves and others.

LO 3.10   Describe the features of Jones and Davis' correspondent inference theory and Kelley's covariation model of attribution.

LO 3.11   Explain the features of the person and situation that increase the desire to make accurate decisions and judgments.

To this point, you've seen that human judgment is shaded by all manner of simplifying and self-enhancing strategies. At first glance, this seems to paint a less than flattering portrait of the human social thinker, especially because some of these shortcuts can lead to biases in judgment and behavior.

Recall, though, that our mental shortcuts are designed to provide "good enough" answers, given the socially complex and cognitively taxing circumstances we often find ourselves in (Haselton & Funder, 2006). Indeed, such shortcuts often work quite well, leading us to be pretty accurate judges of others even when the information we have about them is fleeting or sparse (Ambady, Bernieri, & Richeson, 2000; Funder, 1999; Johnson, Gill, Reichman, & Tassinary, 2007; Kenny, 1994; Yamagishi et al., 2003). Moreover, attempts to go beyond our simplifying heuristics sometimes lead us to think too much, thereby reducing accuracy (e.g., Wilson & LeFleur, 1995). This certainly isn't to say that our mental shortcuts enable us to be perfect judges of ourselves and others, but they do provide a "fast and frugal" leap toward a potentially high level of understanding (Goldstein & Gigerenzer, 2002).

Recall, too, that our self-enhancing strategies have their useful functions. Perhaps most important, thought processes that enhance our sense of being effective also increase the likelihood that we'll risk failure to approach opportunities with desirable payoffs—that we'll compete against hundreds of others in applying for a high-paying job, ask out a desirable classmate who appears to be outside our reach, or invest extra effort to accomplish a difficult task. Although we won't always succeed, one thing is clear: "You can't win if you don't play." Having an elevated self-regard—to a point—may thus be quite adaptive.

Nonetheless, we don't simplify and self-enhance indiscriminately. After all, to survive certain challenges of the social world, it will sometimes be useful to take an unflinching, hard look at ourselves and others. We turn, then, to explore some of the strategies people employ when they hope to gain a more accurate understanding of their social world (see Figure 3.5).

Unbiased Information Gathering

When we're motivated to be accurate in daily life, we gather more information than usual. For instance, if we want to form an accurate impression of another person, we tend to listen more and ask more questions (Darley et al., 1988; Neuberg, 1989). We also seem to value information that will help us go beyond our initial biases. In a study by Ralph Erber and Susan Fiske (1984), student participants believed that they would be working with an education major to create new games for children and that they could win a cash reward if they did well. Before starting, they all privately completed and then exchanged personal profiles describing themselves. For half the participants, the education major—actually a confederate of the experimenters—presented herself as very creative; for the other half, she described herself as noncreative. Finally, students were given a chance to read the confederate's teaching evaluations. Half these evaluations were quite favorable and half were unfavorable, and the experimenter secretly timed how long participants read each type.

Where did the students focus their attention? Note that evaluations *in*consistent with what you expect should be particularly useful—after all, only these contain new information. Indeed, when the confederate presented herself positively, subjects focused on the unfavorable evaluations; when the confederate presented herself negatively, they focused on the favorable evaluations. When people are motivated to be accurate—as in this case, in which participants depended on each other to win the money—they pay special attention to information that enables them to go beyond their initial conceptions (Fiske & Neuberg, 1990).

Considering Alternatives

Even after people collect lots of information, they may make poor decisions because they don't seriously assess alternative possibilities. This is why groups facing difficult decisions sometimes assign a member the role of "devil's advocate." This person's task is to argue *against* the popular view, whatever it might be. Such a position is valuable

Figure 3.5 Seeking accuracy

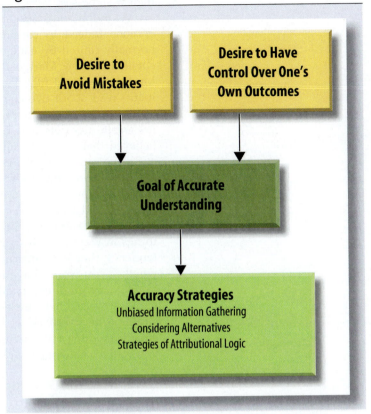

When people have a special desire to have control over their lives, or when they want to avoid making mistakes, they sometimes put aside their simplifying and self-enhancing strategies in the hope of gaining a more accurate understanding of themselves and others.

because it increases the probability the group will consider alternatives and expose their weaknesses.

As individuals, we can adopt a similar orientation in our own cognitive deliberations. Indeed, by considering alternative possibilities, we are able to avoid errors normally caused by using the anchoring and adjustment heuristic and other shortcuts (e.g., Hirt & Markman, 1995; Mussweiler et al., 2000). A study by Charles Lord, Mark Lepper, and Elizabeth Preston (1984) nicely illustrates how this works. Participants read about two competing research studies—one that suggested that capital punishment deters future murders and one that suggested that capital punishment is not an effective deterrent. Consistent with research on expectation biases, participants believed that the study supporting their own views was methodologically stronger and more compelling than the study opposing their views: Supporters of capital punishment favored the study demonstrating its deterrent effects; opponents favored the study showing a lack of deterrent effects.

A second set of participants underwent the same procedure, but with an important change. Prior to reading the studies, they were taught that people often interpret things in ways that fit with their expectations and desires. To counter this natural tendency, they were instructed to consider the opposite: "Ask yourself at each step whether you would have made the same high or low evaluations had exactly the same study produced results on the *other* side of the issue" (p. 1233). In essence, they were asked to be their own devil's advocates. As the researchers suspected, this strategy effectively reduced the bias: These participants evaluated the two studies as equally credible and convincing. When desiring to be evenhanded, it will often serve you well to challenge your own initial views and to consider alternative possibilities.

Attributional Logic: Seeking the Causes of Behavior

People also attempt to increase the accuracy of their judgments by working to better understand the causes of others' actions. This is no simple feat, and social psychologists have long been interested in figuring out how people do this (e.g., Heider, 1958; Malle, 1999, 2004). We saw earlier that people sometimes approach this task by trying to attribute the causes of behavior to forces either *internal* to the actor (e.g., features of his or her personality) or *external* to the actor (e.g., features of the social situation). When motivated to simplify, Westerners especially tend toward internal, dispositional attributions. When motivated to be accurate, however, people move more into the role of an impartial detective, considering more carefully both internal (dispositional) and external (situational) causes.

But how should we decide whether the cause of a behavior is internal to the actor, external to the actor, or some combination of the two? **Attribution theories** were specifically designed to answer this question. Two attribution theories have been especially prominent. First, Edward Jones and Keith Davis (1965; Jones, 1990) presented **correspondent inference theory**, which described how a person might logically determine whether a particular behavior *corresponds* to an enduring characteristic of the actor. Second, Harold Kelley (1973, 1973) advanced his **covariation model**, which proposes that people pick among several possible causes by weighting most heavily the potential cause that best covaries—or correlates—with the event. From these, and related, perspectives, several general principles emerged.

ANALYZING BEHAVIOR IN ITS SOCIAL CONTEXT Arriving at school one morning, you learn that Jack, a classmate, proposed to Jill. Although your initial inclination might be to presume that Jack loves Jill—thereby making an internal, dispositional inference—your curiosity motivates you to think a bit harder, to try to be accurate. After all, there could be other reasons why Jack might propose. How, then, might you determine whether his marriage proposal reflects a true underlying love for her?

When confronted with a behavior to be explained, a good detective might begin by looking for clues in the immediate surroundings—in the circumstances in which the behavior occurred. This type of analysis is the focus of correspondent inference theory. According to the theory, we might begin by contemplating whether the behavior was

Attribution theories Theories designed to explain how people determine the causes of behavior.

Correspondent inference theory The theory that proposes that people determine whether a behavior corresponds to an actor's internal disposition by asking whether (1) the behavior was intended, (2) the behavior's consequences were foreseeable, (3) the behavior was freely chosen, and (4) the behavior occurred despite countervailing forces.

Covariation model The theory that proposes that people determine the cause of an actor's behavior by assessing whether other people act in similar ways (consensus), the actor behaves similarly in similar situations (distinctiveness), and the actor behaves similarly across time in the same situation (consistency).

intended and its consequences *foreseeable*. If, for instance, Jack was merely mimicking lines spoken by a character on a television movie and didn't realize that Jill had just returned to the room, we should probably view Jack's proposal as an accident. In the absence of intention and foreseeability, we can infer little about stable aspects of an actor's personality or about powerful features of the situation.

If we conclude that a behavior was both intended and the consequences foreseeable—for instance, if we determine that Jack proposed to Jill, knowing that she would take his proposal seriously—we should then consider whether the behavior occurred with *free choice*. For instance, if Jack was forced to propose by Jill's heavily armed brother, we're unlikely to infer that the proposal was driven by his deep affection for her. Only behaviors that occur with free choice can reflect dispositions that correspond with the behavior.

Even if we determine, however, that Jack has freely chosen to propose to Jill, knowing full well the consequences (e.g., that she might hear him and say yes), we still can't know whether the proposal corresponded to something specific within Jack or whether it was because of some aspect of Jack's situation. Here the analysis gets more complicated, as there may exist multiple possibilities within each of these categories. For example, perhaps Jack's buddies really like Jill, perhaps she lives in a stunning mansion on a hill, or perhaps she is the only woman Jack has ever known who will tolerate his bad habits. This large cast of possibilities makes it difficult to place great stock in any specific one of them. It may indeed be that Jack's proposal was driven by love alone—but maybe not. Our reluctance, under these circumstances, to bet our own house on the love explanation follows from the **discounting principle**: As the number of possible causes increases, we become less sure that any particular cause is the true one (Kelley, 1973; Oppenheimer, 2004).

Or consider an alternative set of circumstances: Jack's friends despise Jill, she's dirt poor, and she's always trying to change his bad habits. If Jack proposes *despite* these restraining forces, this suggests that internal influences—Jack's love—might be extremely strong. This reasoning illustrates the **augmenting principle**: If an event occurs despite powerful countervailing or opposing forces, we can view the event's probable cause as especially potent (Kelley, 1973; see Figure 3.6).

EXTENDING THE ANALYSIS: THE COVARIATION MODEL

Kelley's covariation model proposes that the effective detective might extend the analysis even further by considering available information from *outside* the immediate situation. For instance, we might ask whether other men have also proposed to Jill: If there's a lack of *consensus*—that is, if few, if any, men besides Jack are interested in marrying Jill—we might attribute more of the causal responsibility to factors within Jack. In contrast, if there is a large consensus—that is, if many men want to marry Jill—we should attribute more of the causal responsibility for Jack's proposal to external factors, such as Jill's desirability.

We might further ask whether Jack has acted similarly toward other women. That is, if Jack's behavior has shown no *distinctiveness*—if he proposes to every woman he dates—we should view his proposal as coming from internal sources (e.g., his desperation). In contrast, if Jack is acting distinctively toward Jill—proposing only to her, and not other women—at least part of the cause underlying his proposal likely lies externally (with Jill's favorable characteristics).

Discounting principle The judgmental rule that states that as the number of possible causes for an event increases, our confidence that any particular cause is the true one should decrease.

Augmenting principle The judgmental rule that states that if an event occurs despite the presence of strong opposing forces, we should give more weight to those possible causes that lead toward the event.

Figure 3.6 Discounting and augmenting

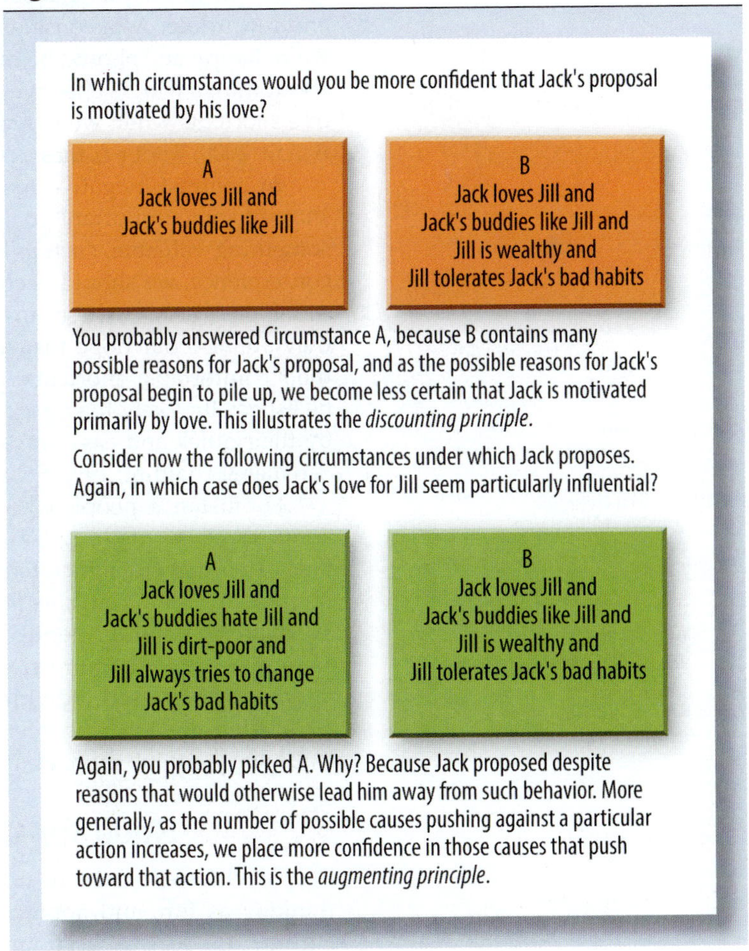

In which circumstances would you be more confident that Jack's proposal is motivated by his love?

A
Jack loves Jill and
Jack's buddies like Jill

B
Jack loves Jill and
Jack's buddies like Jill and
Jill is wealthy and
Jill tolerates Jack's bad habits

You probably answered Circumstance A, because B contains many possible reasons for Jack's proposal, and as the possible reasons for Jack's proposal begin to pile up, we become less certain that Jack is motivated primarily by love. This illustrates the *discounting principle*.

Consider now the following circumstances under which Jack proposes. Again, in which case does Jack's love for Jill seem particularly influential?

A
Jack loves Jill and
Jack's buddies hate Jill and
Jill is dirt-poor and
Jill always tries to change
Jack's bad habits

B
Jack loves Jill and
Jack's buddies like Jill and
Jill is wealthy and
Jill tolerates Jack's bad habits

Again, you probably picked A. Why? Because Jack proposed despite reasons that would otherwise lead him away from such behavior. More generally, as the number of possible causes pushing against a particular action increases, we place more confidence in those causes that push toward that action. This is the *augmenting principle*.

Consider the following event: Jack asks Jill to marry him. One possible cause for Jack's proposal, of course, is his love for Jill. But let's consider circumstances A and B in the figure.

Finally, we might ask whether Jack had proposed to Jill at other times. A high level of *consistency*—he proposes every weekend—would suggest the stability of the underlying cause, whereas a low level of consistency—one week he wants to get married, the next week not—would make it difficult to draw any firm conclusions.

By pulling all this together, we can see that different combinations of consensus, distinctiveness, and consistency information should lead us to draw different conclusions about why people act as they do. Figure 3.7 illustrates how three patterns in particular are useful to us as we try to determine why people have acted as they have.

We've seen that people use a variety of strategies when they want to be particularly accurate. They can gather information in a comprehensive way, they can consider alternatives, and they can engage in logical attributional thought. We turn now to explore the forces within the person and situation that lead people to think carefully about themselves and others.

INVESTIGATION

Life throws tons of information at us, but we can process only a small amount of it. It's sometimes important, though, that we think hard about things and do our best to be accurate. When is it especially important to you that you be accurate? Given what you've learned, what can you do—to change your frame of mind or your immediate circumstances—to better your chances of making more accurate judgments and decisions?

PERSON Mood

As we saw in Chapter 2, feeling happy signals that "all is well"—that the world is safe and rewarding. As a consequence, we have less need to be vigilant and careful when we're happy and should be more confident that our "tried and true" ways of thinking about things will be effective. Indeed, we're especially likely to use simplifying cognitive shortcuts when we're happy (e.g., Bodenhausen, Kramer, & Süsser, 1994; Park & Banaji, 2000; Ruder & Bless, 2003).

In contrast, negative feelings signal that things aren't well—that we're falling short of some important goals (Frijda, 1988). Sadness, for instance, signals the loss of something valuable, such as a friendship, a good grade, or a prized possession. As a consequence, we should become particularly aware of our social surroundings when sad. Not only have these surroundings made it difficult for us to reach our goals, but they are also our hope for reaching our goals in the future. Instead of sticking with their comfortable shortcuts, people experiencing mild to moderate sadness should be especially likely to engage in thought about their circumstances that is less biased by their quick and easy ways of understanding the world (Forgas, 1995; Isbell, 2004; Schaller & Cialdini, 1990; Schwarz, 1990).

For instance, people who are mildly depressed are more thorough when thinking about social events (e.g., Gannon, Skowronski, & Betz, 1994). Consider, for example, how carefully you might interview potential roommates after learning that your current roommate no longer wants to live with you. In a study by John Edwards and Gifford Weary (1993), mildly depressed students were less likely to rely on their academic stereotypes to form impressions of other students. Careful and comprehensive thought apparently helps sad individuals deal with uncertainty and lost control (Weary et al., 1993). Thus, it appears that feeling sad can have some positive side effects, occasionally leading us to think more clearly (Forgas, 2013).

PERSON Need for Cognition

People who are high in the need for cognition—who enjoy solving life's puzzles, view thinking as fun, and appreciate discovering the strengths and weaknesses of their arguments—seek an accurate understanding of the world. Such individuals are less likely to use simplifying heuristics and more willing to expend instead the extra effort needed to assess their circumstances fully (e.g., Cacioppo et al., 1996).

Figure 3.7 Using consensus, distinctiveness, and consistency information to understand why a person acted as he or she did

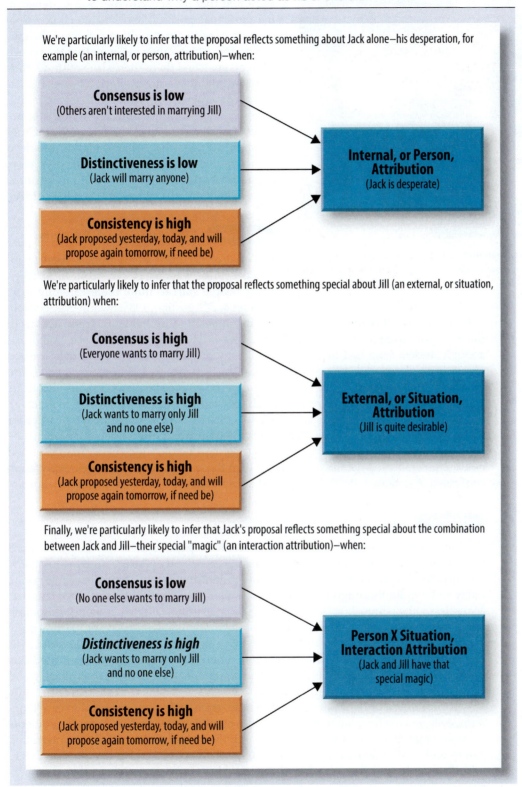

We're particularly likely to infer that the proposal reflects something about Jack alone—his desperation, for example (an internal, or person, attribution)—when:

Consensus is low
(Others aren't interested in marrying Jill)

Distinctiveness is low
(Jack will marry anyone)

Consistency is high
(Jack proposed yesterday, today, and will propose again tomorrow, if need be)

Internal, or Person, Attribution
(Jack is desperate)

We're particularly likely to infer that the proposal reflects something special about Jill (an external, or situation, attribution) when:

Consensus is high
(Everyone wants to marry Jill)

Distinctiveness is high
(Jack wants to marry only Jill and no one else)

Consistency is high
(Jack proposed yesterday, today, and will propose again tomorrow, if need be)

External, or Situation, Attribution
(Jill is quite desirable)

Finally, we're particularly likely to infer that Jack's proposal reflects something special about the combination between Jack and Jill—their special "magic" (an interaction attribution)—when:

Consensus is low
(No one else wants to marry Jill)

Distinctiveness is high
(Jack wants to marry only Jill and no one else)

Consistency is high
(Jack proposed yesterday, today, and will propose again tomorrow, if need be)

Person X Situation, Interaction Attribution
(Jack and Jill have that special magic)

Kelley's covariation model proposes that different configurations of consensus, distinctiveness, and consistency information lead us to different conclusions about the reasons underlying a person's actions. Three configurations are particularly clear in their implications (McArthur, 1972). Consider the event in Figure 3.6: Jack asks Jill to marry him.

Source: McArthur, L. A. (1972). The how and what of why: Some determinants and consequences of causal attribution. *Journal of Personality and Social Psychology*, 22, 171–193.

Thinking hard about friends and classmates. When we depend on people—when their actions can determine our own outcomes—we think about them in more comprehensive, systematic ways.

Subjects in one study read a speech either opposing or favoring legalized abortion and were told that the speechwriter was assigned to the particular position and had no choice. People low in need for cognition exhibited the correspondence bias—they believed that the speech contents matched the writer's true attitude, thus disregarding the author's lack of free choice. In contrast, people high in need for cognition correctly took into account the writer's situation (D'Agostino & Fincher-Kiefer, 1992). Other research suggests that subjects high in the need for cognition are better at detecting deception, because they pay careful attention to more of the clues that might give away liars (Reinhard, 2010).

SITUATION Unexpected Events

The goal of accuracy stems from a need to increase control. When personal control is taken away, people start to think more carefully (e.g., Pittman & D'Agostino, 1985; Swann, Stephenson, & Pittman, 1981). Because unexpected events threaten control, they typically lead us to think in more complex ways (e.g., Clary & Tesser, 1983). Participants in one study read about a student who had done either well or poorly in high school and then learned about the student's college grades. For some participants, their expectations were confirmed. For example, the good student in high school received good grades in college. For others, their expectations were violated. For example, the poor student in high school did unexpectedly well in college. Participants then retold the story into a tape recorder as if they were relaying it to a friend. Those who learned of the unexpected outcome considered many more causal attributions ("perhaps he did much better than expected because he finally learned how to study") than those who simply had their expectation confirmed (Kanazawa, 1992). Unexpected events increase our search for explanations.

SITUATION Social Interdependence

We think carefully about others when our outcomes depend on them—when their actions have important implications for us. This is the case when we're accountable to others. For instance, if you know your boss is going to scrutinize your hiring decisions, you're likely to be quite thorough in your evaluations of the applicants (e.g., Kruglanski & Mayseless, 1988; Tetlock & Kim, 1987). This is also the case when we're competing with people or when they have power over us. Junior managers, for example, are more likely to pay attention to their bosses than vice versa (Hall, Carter, & Horgan, 2001; Ruscher & Fiske, 1990). And this is also true when we have cooperative relationships with other people. When we rely on our friends, spouses, and project coworkers, we're quite thorough in our deliberations about them (Brewer, 1988; Fiske & Neuberg, 1990).

In one study, students participated in a program ostensibly designed to ease long-term, college-aged hospital patients back into everyday life. As an ice-breaker, students were told that they would work together with the former patients to create interesting games and could win cash prizes for particularly creative ideas. Some students were told they could win the prize based only on their *individual* efforts, whereas others were told that their *joint* efforts with the former patient would be critical. All students learned that their partner, "Frank," had been hospitalized as a schizophrenic. They then read a personal statement he had written and provided their initial impressions of him.

When students' fates were tied to the patient, their impressions of him were affected less by their stereotypes of schizophrenics. Instead, they paid extra attention to his personal statement and adjusted their impressions of him accordingly (Neuberg & Fiske, 1987).

When we're interdependent on others, we think about them more thoroughly and reduce our reliance on cognitive shortcuts.

INTERACTION ## Accuracy Motivation Requires Cognitive Resources

No matter how motivated we are to be accurate, we won't be able to think deeply if we lack the necessary attentional resources (Ferreira et al., 2012; E. P. Thompson et al., 1994; Wyer, Sherman, & Stroessner, 2000). Gathering a lot of information, being your own devil's advocate, and engaging in complex attributional reasoning are difficult. They require a large amount of mental resources. Even if you really want to decide on the best person for a job, for instance, you may fail if you're simultaneously distracted by a pending loan approval, dinner plans with your girlfriend's parents, or rumored layoffs at your company.

In one study, Louise Pendry and Neil Macrae (1994) informed participants that they would be working with "Hilda," a 65-year-old, on a problem-solving task. As in the "Frank" study described earlier, some participants were told they could receive a monetary prize for working well with Hilda; they were *interdependent* with her and thus motivated to form an accurate impression of her. The remaining participants were told they would be rewarded solely on the basis of their own individual performance; their performance was *independent*, and so they were not especially motivated to be accurate in their impression of Hilda. Moreover, because the experimenters were ostensibly interested in how people could perform multiple tasks concurrently, half the participants in each condition were asked to hold in mind an eight-digit number. These participants were thus cognitively busy: They had to split their attention between the tasks of understanding Hilda and remembering the long number. All then read a personality profile that presented Hilda in a way partially consistent with stereotypes about the elderly and partially inconsistent with them. Finally, just prior to meeting her, participants provided their impressions of Hilda.

As Figure 3.8 demonstrates, the participants unmotivated by accuracy used their stereotypes of the elderly to evaluate Hilda, as did the accuracy-motivated participants who were cognitively busy. Only those who were both nonbusy *and* motivated to be accurate were able to reduce their reliance on the elderly stereotypes. This study demonstrates, then, that the desire to be accurate isn't enough—only when a desire for accuracy is combined with sufficient cognitive resources can people move beyond their tendency to simplify.

Figure 3.8 Is the desire to be accurate enough?

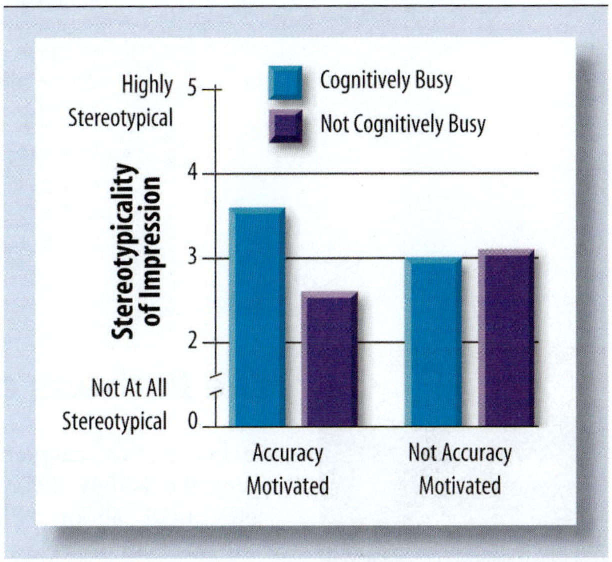

In the Pendry and Macrae (1994) study, participants were either motivated to form accurate impressions or not, and were either made cognitively busy or not. Only those who were both accuracy-motivated and cognitively nonbusy reduced their reliance on stereotypes.

Source: Adapted from Pendry, L. F., & Macrae, C. N. (1994). Stereotypes and mental life: The case of the motivated but thwarted tactician. *Journal of Experimental Social Psychology*, 30, 303–325. Table 1.

Quick Quiz

1 Which of the following strategies serve the goal of accurate understanding?

    a. Playing "devil's advocate"
    b. Unbiased information gathering
    c. Attributional logic
    d. All of the above

2 The _____ principle states that if an event occurs despite the presence of strong opposing forces, we should give more weight to the event's possible causes, whereas the _____ principle states that as the number of possible causes increases, we become less sure that any particular cause is the true one.

    a. Discounting, augmenting
    b. Augmenting, covariation
    c. Augmenting, discounting
    d. Discounting, augmenting

3 According to Kelley's covariation model, people are more likely to make a *person attribution* when which of the following criteria are met?

    a. Consensus is high

    b. Consistency is low

    c. Distinctiveness is high

    d. None of the above

4 Which factor increases the desire to make accurate judgments?

    a. Low need for cognition

    b. Unexpected events

    c. Sad mood

    d. Low social interdependence

    e. Both b and c

5 People require _____ to move beyond their tendency to simplify.

    a. Attentional resources

    b. Positive mood

    c. Independence from their groups

    d. None of the above

Revisiting

The Portraits of Hillary Rodham Clinton

We began this chapter by noting the widely diverging views held about Hillary Rodham Clinton. How do the lessons of this chapter help us understand how observers of Clinton could view her so differently?

Decades of research have demonstrated how our expectations and perspectives influence how we attend to, interpret, judge, and remember the world around us. Consider, for instance, that in 2003 Democrats held opinions of Clinton that were much more favorable than unfavorable (75% to 13%), whereas Republicans held opinions that were as strongly biased in the opposite direction (72% to 18%). Registered independents, on the other hand, were evenly split (Gallup, 2003), suggesting a powerful bias on the part of members of both parties.

Consider also the individual commentators we quoted: Whereas two of the most critical (Peggy Noonan and William Safire) are well-known conservatives who had at earlier points in their lives been highly effective speechwriters for Republican presidents, two of Clinton's most supportive commentators (Burstein and Chesler) are well-known liberals. For committed political conservatives to view Hillary Rodham Clinton favorably, and for committed political liberals to view her unfavorably, would create cognitive confusion—a state of mind most of us hope to avoid. Fortunately, for our miserly cognitive system, much of human behavior is ambiguous in its meaning, making it relatively easy to interpret events as we'd like. "How might one explain how Clinton turned a $1,000 commodities investment into a $100,000 profit in a matter of months?" you ask. "Illegal favors given her by investment managers wanting to influence government policy," say those wanting to maintain a negative impression of her. "Lucky timing and savvy investing," answer those wanting to maintain a positive impression of her. The fact of this financial success is straightforward. The meaning of it is not. People very often see what they want to see.

Self-serving interpretations aren't limited to preserving cherished values and ideologies. Dick Morris, who strongly criticized Hillary Rodham Clinton on a number of grounds, had, at the time, nothing against Democrats. Indeed, he had been a highly paid political consultant to both Democratic and Republican candidates and worked for Bill Clinton for a while—before apparently being fired. One might reasonably entertain the possibility that his considerable prior access to the former First Lady gave him privileged access to her motives; perhaps he was correct in his accusation, then, that she was merely using New Yorkers to gain a place in the Senate. However, one might also reasonably wonder whether his firing and claimed mistreatment by the Clintons might play some role in the positions he took. Could it be that he believed he would restore his tarnished image by tarnishing, in turn, the image of the woman partially responsible for his firing? Of course, our choice of alternatives likely reveals something about ourselves: Those of us who dislike Hillary Clinton will prefer the former possibility; those of us who like her will prefer the latter.

It should be clear, then, that Hillary Rodham Clinton is a canvas upon which each of us can paint a portrait and that the nature of these portraits are colored by our own beliefs, goals, and social circumstances. We paint many such portraits each day—of people and events we encounter, and, of course, of ourselves.

It's likely that many who purchased copies of her autobiography, *Living History*, hoped to see yet more evidence to support their portraits of Hillary Clinton—and would, in any case, interpret her writings in ways so they could do just that. Many thousands of others, however, stood in long lines upon the book's release and paid their $28 because they were curious about how Clinton herself viewed the events of her life. "How does she explain the Whitewater and Travelgate

Scandals?" folks wondered. "How did she react to learning about her husband's affair with Monica Lewinsky?" Unfortunately, as the great writer Daphne du Maurier noted in her own autobiography, "all autobiography is self-indulgent" (du Maurier, 1977). And so we should not be surprised when Clinton attributed the allegations against her and Bill Clinton not to legitimate concerns but rather to "a vast right-wing conspiracy" aimed at bringing down her husband's presidency. People want to feel good about themselves and possess a natural—if sometimes distressing—tendency to seek flattering explanations for unflattering events.

We also see in Clinton's memoirs, however, evidence of thought processes associated with a desire to understand things accurately. We learn, for instance, about how a simple "consider the opposite" position taken in a high school debate—a position strikingly similar to the one assigned to students in the study reported just a few pages back—began to push her away from her Republican leanings and toward more Democratic positions. We learn that she explored many competing views as she sought a political philosophy she felt comfortable with. We learn also of how she consulted with a select group of 100 politically astute New Yorkers and traveled through that state on a "listening tour," in an attempt to thoroughly gather information before making her decision to run for the Senate.

Like Hillary Rodham Clinton, we have a great number of tools in our cognitive toolbox—tools that help us reach our goals of the moment. When concerned with mental efficiency, we reach for those strategies that usually buy us "good enough" judgments for minimal effort. When concerned with self-image, we reach for strategies useful for enhancing and protecting our self-regard. And, when circumstances become important enough, we reach in deep for those effortful strategies we hope will lead to accurate understanding.

As we leave this chapter, the strong and plentiful bridges between social psychology and cognitive science should be particularly salient. People think, and much of that cognition is *social* cognition. As a social animal, our well-being and fitness depends on our ability to effectively and efficiently manage our many interdependent relationships with others—with passersby on the street, clerks at the grocery store, coworkers on the job, and family members at home. This requires that we pay close attention to some people (but, for efficiency's sake, ignore others), understand their intentions and dispositions, strategize about how to interact with them, and the like. To truly understand social behavior, then, one must appreciate the role that cognition plays and understand how the mind works. Yet, as cutting-edge research is beginning to reveal, to understand why the mind works as it does, one also must understand the complex and fascinating challenges that humans face as social and cultural creatures. The bridges between social psychology and the cognitive sciences are indeed two-way thoroughfares, carrying steady streams of traffic in both directions.

Chapter Summary

Summary of the Goals Influencing Social Cognition and the Factors Related to Them

The Goal	Person	Situation	Interaction
Conserving mental effort	• Arousal and circadian rhythms • Need for structure	• Situational complexity • Time pressure	• When expectations are clearly incompatible with the information available to us, we often rely on them less.
Managing self-image	• Self-esteem	• Threats to self-esteem	• Self-esteem, self-esteem instability, and threat all work together to influence how people manage their self-image. People who possess unstable high self-esteem and who see that esteem as being threatened are particularly likely to respond strongly with self-protective strategies in defense of their selves.
Seeking an accurate understanding	• Mood • Need for cognition	• Unexpected events • Social interdependence	• When people seek to form accurate impressions, they are often able to reduce the biasing impact of their stereotypes and expectations. The desire to be accurate is not enough, however. Only when the desire for accuracy is combined with sufficient cognitive resources can people move beyond their tendency to simplify.

The Social Thinker

1. People's actions are critically affected by their social cognition—by how they think about the social events and people they encounter. Four social-cognitive processes are fundamental: attention, interpretation, judgment, and memory.

Conserving Mental Effort

1. The social environment is amazingly complex, and humans have only a limited attentional capacity. As a result, people often use simplifying strategies that require few cognitive resources and that provide judgments that are generally "good enough."

2. People use their existing beliefs as expectations, which makes understanding new events much easier. When our expectations are accurate, using them leads to good judgments at little cost. When they are inaccurate, however, they may lead to erroneous judgments and self-fulfilling prophecies.

3. People—at least those in Western, individualistic cultures—make dispositional inferences to simplify the task of understanding the causes of others' actions. In the process, they may underestimate the impact of situational forces (the correspondence bias or fundamental attribution error), although this tendency is less prominent when people judge their own behavior (the actor–observer difference).

4. People have other cognitive shortcuts to choose from as well, including the representativeness heuristic, the availability heuristic, and the anchoring and adjustment heuristic.

5. People who are aroused or dispositionally high in need for structure are particularly likely to use cognitive shortcuts.

6. When situations are particularly complex or people are under time pressure, they are also more likely to use simplifying cognitive shortcuts.

7. Sometimes people go beyond these simplification strategies, however, as when their situational realities just don't fit with their expectations.

Managing Self-Image

1. Positive self-regard is valuable because it equips us with the confidence needed to meet challenges, and suggests that our social relationships are going well and that we are good members of our society.

2. The strategies people use to enhance and protect their self-image include both downward and upward social comparisons; taking credit for success and minimizing responsibility for failure; magnifying the importance of things they do well and minimizing the importance of things they do poorly; and exaggerating their perception of control.

3. People having high self-esteem are especially likely to engage in brazen attempts to enhance their self-regard.

People having moderate to low self-esteem also desire positive self-regard but are more cautious in their strategies—they focus instead on protecting their existing level of self-regard.

4. Situations that threaten self-esteem increase the tendency to self-enhance or self-protect. Such situations include poor task performance, negative interpersonal feedback, a serious illness, one's own negative behaviors, or thinking about one's own death (mortality salience).

5. Self-esteem, self-esteem instability, and situational threat interact to promote self-enhancement and self-protection.

6. Is the desire for positive self-regard universal? Some studies suggest that this desire is stronger in Western, individualistic societies, although other evidence suggests that people from Eastern, collectivistic societies also work to boost their self-regard, although primarily on characteristics valued by those societies.

Seeking an Accurate Understanding

1. When seeking accuracy, people often gather social information in a more thorough, comprehensive way and consider alternatives to their current view.

2. The desire for accuracy may lead people to apply a "rational" attributional logic toward understanding why certain events happened as they did. As people consider the relative contributions of forces within the person and forces within the situation, they ask whether a person's behavior was intended and the consequences foreseeable and whether he or she behaved with free choice. They are also likely to use the discounting and augmenting principles and to use information regarding consensus, distinctiveness, and consistency.

3. Accuracy-motivated strategies are employed more frequently by people who are mildly sad or who have a high need for cognition.

4. When events happen unexpectedly or when people's outcomes depend on the actions of others, people are more likely to seek accuracy.

5. Because accuracy-seeking strategies are relatively thoughtful, people are less able to use them when they are under a high cognitive load.

Key Terms

Anchoring and adjustment
  heuristic, 80

Attribution theories, 94

Augmenting principle, 95

Availability heuristic, 80

Cognitive heuristic, 79

Correspondence bias (fundamental
  attribution error), 78

Correspondent inference
  theory, 94

Covariation model, 94

Discounting principle, 95

Dispositional inference, 77

Downward social comparison, 86

False consensus effect, 80

Representativeness
  heuristic, 79

Self-fulfilling prophecy, 77

Self-serving bias, 86

Social cognition, 72

Upward social comparison, 86

Chapter 4

Presenting the Self

Outline

Learning Objectives

LO 4.1   Understand why and when we self-present.

LO 4.2   Describe examples of self-presentation failure and its relationship to social anxiety.

LO 4.3   Explain why most people are poor at lie detection and why the polygraph isn't very useful.

LO 4.4   Identify the four main strategies we use to get others to like us.

LO 4.5   Discuss gender differences in ingratiation strategies.

LO 4.6   Describe how people manage the multiple-audience dilemma.

LO 4.7   Identify the four main strategies we use to get others to view us as competent.

LO 4.8   Understand why shy people have difficulty promoting their competence.

LO 4.9   Explain the situational factors that influence our desire to appear competent.

LO 4.10   Identify the four main strategies we use to convey high status and power.

LO 4.11   Explain who is most likely to display high status and power and why.

LO 4.12   Summarize the gender differences associated with self-presentational strategies.

Ferdinard Waldo DeMara, Jr. The Great Imposter.

The Amazing Lives of Fred Demara

The air was chilly and the winds blowing hard that Valentine's Day morning as the Maine state troopers crossed Penobscot Bay on their way to small North Haven Island. Their quarry was Martin Godgart. When he wasn't teaching high school English, Latin, and French, Godgart was leading a troop of teenage Sea Scouts, supervising Sunday school at the Baptist Church, and playing Santa Claus to the island's poor children. In his short time on the island, Godgart had earned the respect and admiration of a community normally wary of strangers.

He was captured without a struggle—fighting wasn't his way—and was escorted via Coast Guard cutter back to the mainland. On the day of his trial, the courtroom was packed. What was his horrific crime? Murder? Rape? Hardly. The charge was "cheating by false premises," punishable by up to seven years in prison. The man who had been calling himself Martin Godgart, it turns out, was no more Martin Godgart than you or I. He was Ferdinand ("Fred") Waldo Demara, Jr., who for the previous 20-odd years had been "The Great Impostor."

Consider just a few of The Great Imposter's exploits:

- As Robert Linton French, Ph.D., Demara was a science teacher in Arkansas; dean of the School of Philosophy at Gannon College; and a teacher, head of the psychology center, and deputy sheriff at St. Martin's College.
- As Cecil Boyce Hamann, Ph.D., he entered law school at Northeastern University, trained to become a priest, and helped found LeMennais College in Maine.
- As Joseph Cyr, M.D., he joined the Royal Canadian Navy during the Korean War and performed heroic life-saving surgeries—despite never having before viewed the inside of a living, breathing human body.
- As Ben W. Jones, he got a job as a guard at the notoriously dangerous Huntsville prison in Texas and, in little more than a month, was promoted to assistant warden of the maximum security wing, where he earned respect for his ability to peacefully defuse perilous confrontations.

All of this—and more—from a high school dropout who had no training or legitimate credentials in any of his adopted careers (Allen, 1989; Crichton, 1959, 1961; McCarthy, 1952).

Demara's successes as an impostor were astounding in several ways. First, he had an extraordinary ability to present himself as someone he was not, and to do so convincingly and for long periods of time. Second, despite his lack of formal background for the jobs he assumed, he managed to avoid making job-related mistakes. Although he was uncovered many times, it was either because he was recognized as Demara (as when a prisoner in Huntsville identified him from a story that *Life* magazine had written years before) or because he had become so good in his new role that the publicity reached the ears of the owner of his borrowed identity (as when the real Dr. Cyr read in the newspaper of his wartime surgical miracles). Finally—and amazingly—many of the people he duped nonetheless wanted him back. People usually feel ripped off by impostors. Not in this case: His fiancée said she loved him no matter who he really was. The warden of Huntsville said he'd be proud to hire him again if only Demara had some legitimate credentials. And the nice folks of North Haven Island convinced the judge to set him free, even urging Demara to continue teaching their children.

Why was Fred Demara willing to go to such lengths to present himself as Martin Godgart, Robert French, Joseph Cyr, Ben Jones, and the others? And how was he able to present himself so effectively under so many different guises?

Demara's acts of deception were dramatic, incredible, and extreme. Yet, just as exploring the bizarrely rapid, aberrational growth of cancerous cells helps medical researchers better understand the normal growth patterns of healthy cells, exploring the actions of a great impostor like Demara helps illustrate why and how people like you and I try to manage how others view us. What do we do to make others see us as likable, worthy of respect, or intelligent? In this chapter, we explore why people want to control their public images, which images they most want to present, what strategies they use to do so effectively, and when they bring these strategies to bear.

What Is Self-Presentation?

LO 4.1 Understand why and when we self-present.

LO 4.2 Describe examples of self-presentation failure and its relationship to social anxiety.

LO 4.3 Explain why most people are poor at lie detection and why the polygraph isn't very useful.

Self-presentation, sometimes called *impression management*, is the process through which we try to control the impressions people form of us (Leary, Allen, & Terry, 2011; Schlenker & Pontari, 2000). Although few people are as adventurous or successful in their self-presentations as Demara, self-presentation is pervasive in everyday life. Take yourself as an example. Why do you dress the way you do? Do you have an image or a style you want to communicate? Do you sunbathe? Work out? For what purpose? Do you have a profile on Facebook? What do you reveal about yourself, and what do you keep private? Do you alter your posture or facial expressions when a potential love interest wanders by? Of course, not all public behaviors are determined by self-presentational concerns. Wearing clothes, for instance, serves functions well beyond making us look good to others. Nonetheless, most people are quite aware that their public behaviors influence the way others view them—leading most of us, for instance, to spend perhaps too much time deciding exactly which clothes to buy.

Why Do People Self-Present?

Self-presentation is an integral part of human nature. But why should people be so concerned with how others view them?

First, people self-present to obtain desirable resources from others. Because others often have things we want or need, we must "convince" them to share. The man who wants a job or who hopes to date a particular woman must convey the impression to

Self-presentation The process through which we try to control the impressions people form of us; synonymous with impression management.

What images are these people trying to convey? People frequently try to control the images others have of them by managing their public behaviors—by self-presenting.

his interviewer or love interest that he's indeed worthy. Self-presentation, then, is a way of strategically gaining control over one's life, a way of increasing one's rewards and minimizing one's costs (Jones & Pittman, 1982; Schlenker, 1980). Rather than trying to actively deceive others, most of self-presentation involves putting our best foot forward, to ensure that others accurately view our strengths and abilities (Human et al., 2012; Leary et al., 2011). In fact, we may even go out of our way to display our weaknesses or downplay our positive characteristics (Holoien & Fiske, 2012).

Second, self-presentation is a way of "constructing" a self-image. As we saw in Chapter 2, our images of ourselves—our self-concepts—are influenced partially by how we think others view us. It's easier to see ourselves as having a good sense of humor if others validate that view by laughing at all the right times. One interesting implication of this is that we often choose to spend time with those who see us as we see ourselves. For instance, people who have positive self-views prefer interacting with those who evaluate them favorably, and people who have negative self-views often prefer interacting with those who evaluate them unfavorably (Swann, Stein-Seroussi, & Giesler, 1992). By managing the impressions others have of us, we are able to manage the impressions we have of ourselves.

Some researchers suggest another, more direct way in which self-presentation can influence a person's self-image. In line with the *self-perception process* explored in Chapter 2, there may be times when people serve as their own audiences—when they present not only to others but to themselves as well (e.g., Hogan, Jones, & Cheek, 1985). To put it simply, if you want to see yourself in a certain way, you need to act the part. Because each time you make a witty remark you reinforce your self-image as a humorous person, you may indeed be motivated to joke a lot in public (e.g., Rhodewalt & Agustsdottir, 1986; Schlenker et al., 1994; Tice, 1992).

Self-presentations, then, help us get what we want and help us create desired self-images. They also serve a social purpose: They help others know how we *expect* to be treated, enabling social encounters to run more smoothly. Erving Goffman (1959) introduced the **dramaturgical perspective**, likening self-presentation to theater, with actors, performances, settings, scripts, props, roles, backstage areas, and the like. For the play to go smoothly—for people's interactions with each other to be comfortable—performances must follow general social scripts, and the actors must respect and go

Dramaturgical perspective The perspective that much of social interaction can be thought of as a play, with actors, performances, settings, scripts, props, roles, and so forth.

along with each other's presentations. For instance, if high-status people expect to be treated with respect, Goffman reasoned, they must do more than merely *possess* the status. They must also *play the part* by dressing appropriately, associating with the correct people, maintaining the proper distance from those of lesser status, and so forth.

Smooth social interaction is important to all of us. For this reason, we're usually reluctant to challenge others' presentations. Instead, we allow them to "save face," to get away with public presentations that may be less than perfectly true. For instance, we may publicly let slide a friend's slight boasts, knowing that to point out the exaggerations would not only embarrass the friend but make everyone else uncomfortable as well. Indeed, being sensitive to face-saving social conventions is valued in most cultures (e.g., Holtgraves & Yang, 1990).

In sum, self-presentation helps us obtain those things we need and value, helps us create and maintain desired self-identities, and enables our social encounters to run more smoothly. Applying these lessons to Fred Demara's youth, we can begin to unravel the mystery of why he embarked on the life of an impostor. For Demara, more than most, public reputation mattered. As the gifted son of a popular and prosperous businessman, Fred not only learned the value of a favorable public image but also grew to like it. He was devastated, then, when his family's good fortune took a turn for the worse, taking with it his positive public reputation and shaking the foundations of his favorable self-image. Unable to stand the public and private humiliation of being poor, Demara ran away from home at age 16. He trained to be a monk, then a priest, but succeeded in neither. In frustration, he "borrowed" a car from the Catholic Boys Home where he worked, got drunk for the first time in his life, and, on a whim, joined the army. He soon realized that the army, too, was not for him, and he promptly went AWOL.

By age 20, Fred Demara was on the run, his public reputation shattered beyond repair. To the folks in his hometown, he was the son of a failed businessman; to the Catholic Church he loved so much, he was a failure and a thief; and to the U.S. Army, he was a deserter. For a person to whom appearances mattered so much, public life was essentially over. Or was it? The logic that emerged in Demara's mind seems straightforward enough: (1) he wanted success; (2) a good reputation is central to a person's success; (3) the reputation of the man known as Demara was forever spoiled; therefore, (4) he could no longer be Demara! So he shed his tarnished identity and, assuming the reputable identities of others, began his new journey as the Great Impostor.

The theater of everyday life.
Erving Goffman likened social interaction to theater. Social interactions go more smoothly when people present themselves in ways that make their roles and parts clear to others, when they follow conventional social scripts, and when they accept and respect the performances of others.

When Do People Self-Present?

People are more likely to present to others when they perceive themselves to be in the "public eye." When you pose for a photograph, dine in front of a mirror, or meet your lover's parents for the first time, you become aware of yourself as a public figure and become more likely to self-present, perhaps by fixing your hair, bringing out your best table manners, or being extra polite.

Indeed, we often see ourselves in the public eye even when we're not—a phenomenon dubbed the *spotlight effect*. In one experiment, college students were asked to don a T-shirt bearing the picture of the outdated and decidedly uncool Barry Manilow, and then enter a room where others were working. When later asked to estimate how many of the observers noticed the likeness on the T-shirt, the students greatly overestimated: They predicted that nearly 50% noticed, whereas only about 25% actually noticed (Gilovich, Medvec, & Savitsky, 2000). People often don't pay as much attention to us as we think they do.

Some people are more sensitive to how they come across than are others. Consider, for instance, a sole woman working in an otherwise male office. As a "token," she actually *does* stand out relative to others, and she will generally be more concerned with public appearances than if she worked with other women (Cohen & Swim, 1995;

Saenz, 1994). People can also stand out because of a physical disability, exceptional attractiveness, or obesity. They, too, are particularly mindful of how others view them (Frable, Blackstone, & Scherbaum, 1990). More generally, people differ in their **public self-consciousness**—in the degree to which they characteristically believe others pay attention to them (Carver & Scheier, 1985; Fenigstein, 1979). People high in public self-consciousness are especially attuned to how others view them, respond negatively to rejection, and focus to a greater degree on their reputation and appearance (e.g., Baldwin & Main, 2001; Culos-Reed et al., 2002; Doherty & Schlenker, 1991).

Just because we see ourselves as a focus of attention, however, doesn't mean we always self-present. For example, if you don't care what a particular observer thinks of you, you have little reason to spend much effort self-presenting. We become more concerned with strategic self-presentation (1) when observers can influence whether or not we obtain our goals, (2) when these goals are important to us, and (3) when we think observers have impressions different from the ones we want to project.

First, we're more likely to self-present to observers when they control something we want. For instance, we're more interested in presenting ourselves favorably when observed by a boss than by a stranger, because our boss will usually have more power over whether we reach our goals (e.g., Bohra & Pandey, 1984; Hendricks & Brickman, 1974).

Second, the more important our goal, the more likely we are to step up our presentational efforts. In one study, prospective job applicants were led to believe either that they were competing with many others for just a few jobs or that there were more than enough jobs to go around. Applicants facing the greater competition reported being more likely to adjust their opinions and attitudes to conform to those of their interviewers, presumably because winning the job became increasingly important as the number of opportunities dwindled (Pandey & Rastagi, 1979). In this chapter's research video, University of Queensland's Bill Von Hippel describes some fascinating research examining how young male skateboarders change their self-presentation strategies in potentially dangerous ways when a beautiful young woman is watching them perform their tricks.

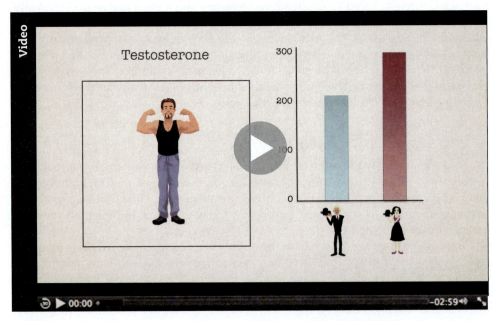

WATCH THE VIDEO: *How an attractive woman boosts testosterone and risk-taking in young men.*

Public self-consciousness The tendency to have a chronic awareness of oneself as being in the public eye.

And third, if we believe that important observers hold undesired impressions of us, we'll become motivated to change their views (Barreto et al., 2003). If you feel that an interviewer, for instance, sees you as unqualified for a job you really want, you will

Figure 4.1 How important is self-presentation to you?

1. I guess I put on a show to impress or entertain others.

2. In different situations and with different people, I often act like very different persons.

3. I'm not always the person I appear to be.

4. I may deceive people by being friendly when I really dislike them.

5. At parties and social gatherings, I do not attempt to do or say things that others will like.

6. I would not change my opinions (or the way I do things) in order to please someone or win his or her favor.

Some people are especially interested in managing their public images. The items above are from Mark Snyder's (1974) Self-Monitoring Scale. These items assess *other-directed self-presentation*, the extent to which people alter their behavior to influence how others view them (Briggs, Cheek, & Buss, 1980; Gangestad & Snyder, 1985). If you tend to agree with statements 1 through 4 and disagree with statements 5 and 6, you are probably a high self-monitor.

Source: From Snyder, M. (1974). Self-monitoring of expressive behavior. *Journal of Personality and Social Psychology, 30,* 526–537. Reprinted by permission of Mark Snyder.

be more motivated to present yourself favorably than when you think the interviewer already believes you to be qualified (Leary & Kowalski, 1990).

Although social circumstances like these motivate most of us to manage our public impressions, people do differ in the strength of this motivation (e.g., Nezlek & Leary, 2002). For instance, people identified as high in **self-monitoring** are almost always motivated to manage how others view them (see Figure 4.1). High self-monitors are adept both at assessing what others want and at tailoring their behavior to meet those demands (Turnley & Bolino, 2001). For instance, high self-monitors are quite skilled at reading others' emotional expressions and detecting when others are being manipulative (Geizer, Rarick, & Soldow, 1977). They are more likely to mimic others' behavior—for instance, laughing when others laugh and yawning when they yawn (e.g., Estow, Jamieson, & Yates, 2007). Moreover, because high self-monitors are more comfortable acting in ways inconsistent with their attitudes and beliefs, they are also better at customizing their presentations to fit the situation (Cheng & Chartrand, 2003; Klein, Snyder, & Livingston, 2004). Perhaps because of these skills, high self-monitors are somewhat more likely to rise to leadership positions (e.g., Day et al., 2002).

Of course, as we discussed in Chapter 2, certain behaviors can occur mindlessly, and self-presentations are no exception (Schlenker & Pontari, 2000; Tyler, 2012). As people shower and dress each morning, combing their hair and applying their makeup, they may be unaware that they're performing these cosmetic rituals for presentational reasons. Similarly, a city dweller who learns to carry herself so as to appear confident and in control may unintentionally walk through an unpopulated scenic redwood forest with the same determined gait. Finally, we should note that not all public actions are self-presentational. As you walk from one class to another, absorbed by thoughts of an upcoming exam or where to have lunch, your actions may have little or nothing to do with conveying a certain image.

The Nature of Self-Presentation

When we prepare for a date, particularly a first date, we strive to "put our best foot forward." We brush our hair and teeth, choose flattering clothes, and try to arrive on time. We steer the conversation toward our strengths (say, our knowledge of music) and try to avoid mentioning weaknesses (such as failed past relationships). As

Self-monitoring The tendency to be chronically concerned with one's public image and to adjust one's actions to fit the needs of the current situation.

this example suggests, self-presentation generally entails the strategic "editing" of information. Because people have multiple selves—for instance, husband, father, professor, musician, sports fan—self-presentation usually takes the form of displaying those selves most appropriate to immediate goals and then, perhaps, exaggerating them a bit. The adventures of Fred Demara aside, self-presentation rarely consists of blatant fabrications of information. Few of us, after all, falsely claim to be rock 'n' roll stars or international spies.

INVESTIGATION

Think for a few minutes about your behaviors so far today. How much of what you've done has been influenced by self-presentational concerns? To whom were you presenting? What images did you want to convey? Why?

Despite our best efforts, self-presentation sometimes fails. Even Demara couldn't get *everyone* to like him. Sometimes, we're unable to create the desired image. It takes focus and effort to create certain impressions, so if we are preoccupied with other concerns or have recently performed a difficult task, we may not have the mental resources needed to lead others to see us as we'd like (e.g., Vohs, Baumeister, & Ciarocco, 2005; von Hippel & Gonsalkorale, 2005). Other times, we accidentally acquire undesired reputations, as when a young suitor trying to impress his date with his sophistication spills his wine glass at a fine restaurant, staining himself as a klutz. When much is riding on a particular impression, self-presentational failures can carry heavy costs. Some costs are tangible, such as lost employment or dating opportunities. Other costs are psychological. For example, presentational failures threaten self-concept and self-esteem and can also be embarrassing (e.g., Miller, 1995).

The fear of self-presentational failure has been labeled **social anxiety**. Social anxiety is quite common, for example, when we're on a first date or have to speak in front of a large group (Leary & Kowalski, 1995). Although some amount of social anxiety is probably useful, too much may lead people to avoid social situations entirely, to withdraw from them once there, or to inhibit their behavior if escape isn't possible (e.g., DePaulo, Epstein, & LeMay, 1990). Thirty to forty percent of Americans label themselves as *shy*—they experience social anxiety on a regular basis—and approximately 2% of the U.S. population experiences social anxiety severely enough to be classified as *socially phobic* (Cheek & Briggs, 1990; Pollard & Henderson, 1988).

When people worry that simply putting their best foot forward might not be enough to achieve their goals, they may be tempted to manufacture false presentations (Feldman, Forrest, & Happ, 2002). Indeed, most of us occasionally present ourselves in ways that could be considered "false advertising"—perhaps "forgetting" to tell your mom or dad of a failing grade on an exam or pretending to be interested in a boss's vacation photos. Such deceptions may even be well-intentioned, as when we feign excitement over a hideous birthday gift so as not to hurt the feelings of the person giving it. People lie to one another with some frequency, and many of these lies are told for the recipient's own benefit (DePaulo et al., 1996).

Being untruthful carries with it the risk of perhaps the most devastating of unintended impressions. When one is caught "presenting" instead of just "being," people typically mark the presenter as dishonest, insincere, hypocritical, or immoral. The costs of a reputation soiled in this way are great, as people labeled as untrustworthy are avoided and isolated by others. Understanding this, Demara was horrified by the prospect of being viewed as a fraud. Indeed, despite his fiancée's desire to marry him after discovering his true identity, and despite his consuming love for her, Demara fled from her in shame. Her protestations to the contrary, Demara believed her view of him had been forever sullied.

Demara's extreme reaction sharply illustrates the importance people place on having a reputation for honesty. It's no surprise, then, that people will go to great lengths to present themselves as honest and to disguise their dishonest acts. As a result, we sometimes go to equally great lengths to see if others are presenting themselves truthfully. Unfortunately, we are not very good at detecting lies.

Social anxiety The fear people experience while doubting that they'll be able to create a desired impression.

Bridging Theory and Application:

Detecting Lies

Aldrich Ames was a long-time employee of the U.S. Central Intelligence Agency (CIA) and had access to top-secret, highly sensitive information. Despite this, he was viewed by his colleagues as barely competent, as an alcoholic with little ambition who would never do anything meaningful. They were wrong. For nine years, he'd sold information to the Soviet Union, leading directly to the deaths of at least 10 CIA agents (Adams, 1995; Weiner et al., 1995). He was a traitor to his country and, by many definitions, a mass murderer. Aldrich Ames had worked right under the noses of the very people whose job it was to stop spies like him, which raises interesting and important questions about people's ability to detect deception.

Most of us just aren't very good lie detectors, especially regarding strangers. Controlled laboratory studies reveal success rates not much better than what one would expect by chance (Bond & DePaulo, 2006; Hartwig & Bond, 2011). Why are we so easily duped? Part of the difficulty lies in our tendency to trust others and to initially believe what they say and how they present themselves (Gilbert, Tafarodi, & Malone, 1993; O'Sullivan et al., 1988). This usually makes sense: Most people do indeed tell the truth most of the time. Because we trust what people say, however, we often fail to pay attention to those cues that turn out to be most useful for differentiating lies from truth: Liars, for example, provide fewer details when describing an event, tell their stories in less engaging ways, raise their chins more, exhibit dilating pupils, and seem a bit more nervous or tense (DePaulo et al., 2003). Even these behaviors, however, are only weak indicators of deception, and so using them would still lead us to make lots of mistakes.

Are we better at detecting the lies of our friends and lovers than we are of strangers? We do seem to do a reasonable job detecting our lovers' lies—but only when we suspect them of lying beforehand (McCornack & Levine, 1990). Of course, this also means that we'll be more likely to see them as lying even when they're telling the truth. And although we improve over time at detecting the lies of our close friends, we still don't do that much better than how we would perform by chance (Anderson, DePaulo, & Ansfield, 2002).

So ordinary people aren't very good at detecting deception. But what about people whom we'd expect to be "experts": federal law enforcement agents, police interrogators, and the like? The findings from some studies suggest that such professionals, when working within their professional contexts, may indeed be better than most of us at detecting lies (O'Sullivan, 2008). Others, looking across a wide range of experiments and studies, suggest that such abilities are usually more apparent than real—less about professionals possessing special skills and more about chance (e.g., even mediocre baseball batters sometimes hit Game 7 home runs to win the World Series for their team); their analyses suggest that detecting a lie depends more on the cues given off by liars than on any special abilities that some perceivers have and others don't (Bond & DePaulo, 2008). One thing is clear: Detecting strangers' lies is very difficult, and very few people are (even minimally) good at it. Given these findings, it's not surprising that Ames's CIA colleagues failed to suspect his illicit activities. It's also not surprising that organizations whose job it is to catch liars and criminals often turn to technical means of assessing deceit, such as the polygraph.

The polygraph machine records physiological arousal in the form of electrodermal activity, blood pressure, heart rate, and respiration. Polygraphic examiners explore whether a suspect's arousal levels increase more when he or she is questioned about potentially suspicious activities (about which a guilty suspect would likely lie) compared to when he or she is asked control questions about unrelated issues (about which even a guilty suspect would likely tell the truth). The assumption underlying the polygraph examination is that people become physiologically aroused when lying.

Unfortunately, no specific pattern of heart rate, skin conduction, and the like maps directly onto dishonesty. Anger and fear also increase arousal, and an innocent suspect may become truthfully indignant or anxious when asked about whether he or she has engaged in illicit activities. As a consequence, polygraph examinations run a great risk of inaccurately identifying innocent people as guilty. In general, studies of polygraph interrogations reveal accuracy rates running from a dismal 25% to highs of around 90% (Ford, 1996; Saxe, 1994).

The usefulness of polygraphic testing decreases further when the suspect doesn't believe that the test is effective, because such doubts reduce anxiety. Guilty suspects can also foil the test—as many intelligence officers are trained to do—by

(Don't) Lie to Me. People lie, often to avoid creating an unfavorable impression. We need to trust one another for social life to run smoothly, however, so we view quite unfavorably those we believe to be lying. Inspired by the research discoveries of deception scientists, including Dr. Paul Ekman (left), the television show *Lie to Me* follows the fictional Dr. Cal Lightman and his team as they attempt to uncover the lies of criminals and others who threaten society. Unfortunately, very few of us—including those we'd expect to be experts—approach the success rate depicted in this TV show.

Lie detector? Polygraph examinations are used frequently by law enforcement and security organizations to catch murderers in their false alibis, employees suspected of selling company secrets, and spies believed to be working for the other side. Unfortunately, these "lie detector" exams often falsely identify innocent suspects as guilty and guilty perpetrators as innocent.

increasing anxiety levels in response to control questions by tightening their anal sphincters, biting their tongues, or pressing their toes hard against the floor (Gudjonsson, 1988; Honts, Raskin, & Kircher, 1994). Moreover, some of the best cues to deception are related to *what* people say and *how* they say it—the details they provide, the logical structure of their statements—and the polygraph does not assess these (DePaulo et al., 2003). Finally, people who experience little guilt and anxiety are unlikely to be detected through techniques like the polygraph that measure only arousal (e.g., Verschuere et al., 2005). Aldrich Ames benefited greatly from these weaknesses of the test: He passed two polygraph examinations while secretly spying for the Soviet Union, enabling him to continue his deadly activities.

We see, then, that the polygraph exam, as typically conducted in the field by inadequately trained interrogators, is a poor device for detecting lies (e.g., Fiedler, Schmid, & Stahl, 2002; National Research Council, 2003). Because of this, researchers seeking high-tech means of detecting deception have been exploring alternative approaches. One such approach measures those brain waves that occur when people recognize something they've experienced previously, reasoning that only guilty suspects will exhibit these responses when an item specific to the crime is mentioned (e.g., Rosenfeld, 2002). Others use thermal-imaging techniques, hoping to detect deceit by recording the patterns of heat emanating from faces (Pavlidis, Eberhardt, & Levine, 2002), or fMRI imaging techniques, hoping to track particular patterns of brain activation thought to be associated with lying (Langleben et al., 2002; Lee et al., 2002). None of these new techniques, however, has yet to prove practically useful (e.g., Sip et al., 2008; Spence, 2008).

In all, our ability to detect lies—using intuition or mechanical devices, on everyday occasions or when trying to detect criminal wrongdoing—is mediocre at best. We are fortunate, then, that maintaining a lie is very difficult to do (e.g., Bond, Thomas, & Paulson, 2004). Different stories often need to be told to different people, each lie requires other lies to back it up, and it's easy to trip oneself up by being a bit too clever. This was Aldrich Ames's downfall, and we should be relieved. Otherwise, our lie detection abilities being what they are, he would have—literally—continued to get away with murder.

In light of our discussion, we hope you haven't concluded that self-presentation is always deceptive. As we mentioned earlier, self-presentation is typically more about strategically *revealing* aspects of oneself than about *manufacturing* aspects of oneself (Leary, 1995). This shouldn't be surprising. After all, because we must ultimately live up to our presentations, gross exaggeration will harm us in the long run. If your affections for another are discovered to be false, you will gain a reputation as a phony, and future friendships may be difficult to come by. If you pretend to be tougher than you really are and your bluff is called, you may be forced to retreat in humiliation or fight a battle you're likely to lose. For these reasons, it usually makes little sense to create public presentations that stray far from our personal realities (Schlenker & Weigold, 1992; Toma, Hancock, & Ellison, 2008).

In the remainder of this chapter, we discuss the kinds of images people frequently want to present. Most people want to be viewed as honest and trustworthy, as we've just seen. Most people also want to be viewed as stable—as consistent and predictable. Even negative self-presentations are helpful in some circumstances (Kowalski & Leary, 1990). For instance, women in bars and other nightspots who don't want men "hitting on them" may go out of their way to be dislikable, by not smiling, avoiding eye contact, and cutting conversations short (Snow, Robinson, & McCall, 1991). People may feign incompetence to avoid tedious chores or heavy responsibilities, or to lull opponents into a false sense of security (e.g., Gibson & Sachau, 2000; Shepperd & Socherman, 1997). Or they may look confused in order to receive more information from others (Rozin & Cohen, 2003). Most of the time, however, we hope to be viewed favorably. Three public images are especially useful: People want to appear *likable,* to appear *competent*, and to convey *high status* and *power*. In the following pages, we describe the strategies people use to reach these goals and the person and situation factors that bring these goals to prominence.

Quick Quiz

1 Which of the following is one of the reasons that we self-present?
   a. To acquire desirable resources
   b. To help construct our self-images
   c. To enable our social encounters to run more smoothly
   d. All of the above

2 In one study college students were asked to wear a T-shirt bearing a picture of an unhip older pop star (Barry Manilow). The study demonstrated:
   a. The anonymity effect, in that people underestimate how much others pay attention to them.
   b. The spotlight effect, in which people overestimate how much others pay attention to them.
   c. The self-monitoring effect, in which people forget what others are saying when they focus too heavily on self-presentation.
   d. The overpopularity effect, in which people overestimate the extent to which others share their own tastes.

3 Which of the following are problems associated with the validity of the polygraph test?
   a. No specific physiological pattern (e.g., heart rate, skin conduction) maps directly onto honesty.
   b. The polygraph only measures arousal, so people who feel little shame or anxiety about their behavior can pass the test regardless of whether they are guilty of a crime.
   c. The polygraph is less accurate when the suspect doubts the test's effectiveness.
   d. All of the above
   e. (b) and (c)

Appearing Likable

LO 4.4   Identify the four main strategies we use to get others to like us.

LO 4.5   Discuss gender differences in ingratiation strategies.

LO 4.6   Describe how people manage the multiple-audience dilemma.

Most cultures seriously punish impostors, and for good reason. To present oneself deceptively, to claim unearned credentials and unowned abilities, challenges the established social order and may place observers at risk. So it was to Demara's considerable credit that, despite being caught in his deceptions on numerous occasions, he served little jail time. Amazingly, the victims of his fabrications—those who should have been the most upset—frequently bailed Demara out of trouble and jail.

Fred Demara survived these unmaskings because he understood the importance of being liked. To be liked is to belong, to share the ample benefits of being tied into a social network. When we're liked, others will go the extra yard for us, excuse our mistakes, and generally make our lives easier. As a consequence, we want others to like us, and the lengths to which we go to be liked are quite impressive.

Strategies of Ingratiation

Ingratiation is an attempt to get others to like us. We have many ways to ingratiate ourselves with others. To ingratiate yourself with a new neighbor, for instance, you may do her a favor, become friends with one of her friends, or tell funny jokes. Four ingratiation strategies seem particularly effective (see Figure 4.2), and we explore them now.

EXPRESSING LIKING FOR OTHERS   "Flattery will get you nowhere," claims the cultural maxim. Untrue. Complimenting others can be an effective technique for getting others to like us, if handled delicately. For instance, in one experiment a simple compliment by female servers after taking a meal order ("You made a good choice!") increased their

Ingratiation An attempt to get others to like us.

Figure 4.2 Strategies of ingratiation

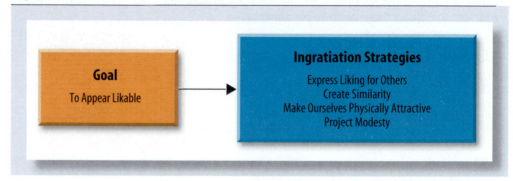

People use a variety of strategies to get others to like them.

tips, compared to a control condition (Seiter, 2007). Having a coworker subtly mention to your boss how much you respect him can be a particularly successful form of flattery, because your boss is less likely to see the compliment as manipulative when it comes from a third party (Liden & Mitchell, 1988; Wortman & Linsenmeier, 1977). Asking others for advice is also often effective, as it implies respect for their expertise and knowledge.

Flattery, as an ingratiation technique, appears to emerge during the preschool years (Fu & Lee, 2007) and is often quite successful: Although we're quick to interpret as insincere the flattering statements people make toward others, we tend to accept quite readily compliments directed toward us (e.g., Gordon, 1996; Vonk, 2002). And why not? After all, in *our* particular case, the compliments are clearly well deserved!

People express their liking for others through nonverbal means as well (DePaulo, 1992; Edinger & Patterson, 1983). For instance, when we want others to like us, we may nonconsciously mimic their behavior with our own—crossing our legs when they cross theirs, rubbing our chin when they rub theirs, and the like (Chartrand & Lakin, 2013). And it works: People like us more when we subtly imitate their nonverbal behaviors (Chartrand & Bargh, 1999; Likowski et al., 2008); they even allow us more favorable terms in negotiated deals (Maddux, Mullen, & Galinsky, 2008). Indeed, research participants immersed in a virtual environment even formed more favorable impressions of artificial, *computer-generated* characters with which they were interacting when these characters were programmed to subtly mimic the participants' own head movements (Bailenson & Yee, 2005). As another example, those of you who truly like your social psychology professor probably smile and nod more during lectures, pay focused attention, and seek more eye contact (e.g., Lefebvre, 1975; Purvis, Dabbs, & Hopper, 1984). As professors, we must admit that such behaviors make us feel good, and they probably lead us to like those students in return. Smiling, in particular, is a powerful tool for getting others to like us. This is probably because, when natural smiles occur spontaneously, they usually indicate that the smiler is sociable and willing to act prosocially (Mehu, Grammer, & Dunbar, 2007). In *How to Win Friends and Influence People*—over 15 million copies sold worldwide—Dale Carnegie (1936/1981) wrote, "A smile says 'I like you. You make me happy. I am glad to see you' " (p. 66). Carnegie was so taken by the impact of a well-placed smile that he even provided tips on how to smile when we don't feel like it. Is this good advice? After all, it assumes that people are able to manipulate their facial expressions without appearing insincere and fake. Are people any good at doing this? And how would we know?

After carefully analyzing the movement of various facial muscles during emotional expressions, Paul Ekman and Wallace Friesen (1978) discovered that false smiles indeed differ from true enjoyment smiles. The enjoyment smile involves the movement of two major facial muscles: The zygomatic major pulls up the corners of the lips toward the cheekbones, while the orbicularis oculi raises the cheek, narrows the eye, and produces "crows-feet" wrinkles at the corners of the eyes, as shown in Figure 4.3(a). This would seem easy to imitate. Not so. Although we can effectively manipulate the zygomatic major and turn up the corners of our mouths, most of us are

Figure 4.3 Felt and false smiles

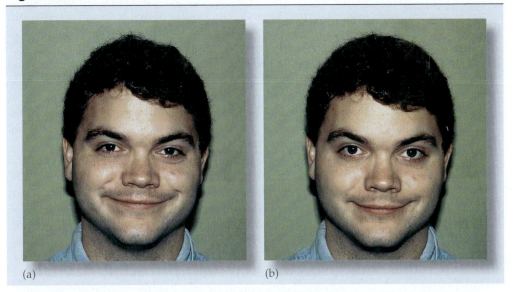

(a)   (b)

Not all smiles are the same. The natural smile we express when feeling happy is characterized by both turning up the muscles at the corners of the mouth (called the zygomatic major) and by "crinkling" of the muscles around the eyes (called the obicularis oculi) (a). Although most people can consciously manipulate the zygomatic major, approximately 80% of us are unable to contract the orbicularis oculi voluntarily. As a result, the area around the eyes can often reveal the false smile (b).

unable to contract the orbicularis oculi voluntarily. This muscle just doesn't respond easily to our will. As a consequence, a close look around the eyes will often reveal a false smile, as shown in Figure 4.3(b).

False smiles differ in other ways as well. They tend to be less symmetrical, meaning that the muscle movements on the two sides of the face aren't precisely the same. In addition, the muscle movements during false smiles are jerkier, less smooth. And false smiles are often held longer than natural (Frank & Ekman, 1993). Such differences in facial dynamics—in the *movement* of the facial muscles—make it relatively easy for researchers analyzing videotaped expressions to distinguish a false smile from an enjoyment smile (Krumhuber & Kappas, 2005).

But what about the rest of us? Can we discriminate between enjoyment smiles and false smiles as we observe people smiling in the natural flow of social interaction? The research says that we often can, although we're not great at it (Frank & Ekman, 1993). Flashing a false smile to ingratiate yourself with another is a risky strategy, then. You'll sometimes succeed—usually when you're merely exaggerating an existing enjoyment smile with people who don't know you. But, unless you're a "natural liar," you'll fail with some frequency. And when you do, the cost will be great: You'll come across as an insincere fake, perhaps the worst presentation of all.

CREATING SIMILARITY   Imagine yourself at a party, deeply engaged in a conversation with a person with whom you want to start a relationship. So far, the conversation has been enjoyable and safe—you've discussed common friends, the recent lousy weather, and the writing professor you both despise—and you think the person likes you. Then the topic gets political—"What do you think of traditional gender norms? Should men work while women stay home and take care of the kids?"—and your heart skips a beat. "How should I answer?" you think. "Should I tailor my response somewhat to fit with what I think the other person believes? If we disagree, will I become less desirable?"

This was the dilemma faced by female students at Princeton University in a study exploring how people form impressions of one another (Zanna & Pack, 1975). In the

Figure 4.4 Opinion conformity as an ingratiation strategy

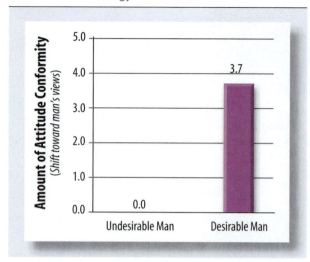

In one experiment, women about to interact with a desirable man adjusted their opinions to match his more closely; they showed no such opinion conformity, however, when about to interact with an undesirable man.

Source: Reprinted from *Journal of Experimental Social Psychology,* 11, Mark P. Zanna1, Susan J. Pack, On the self-fulfilling nature of a apparent sex differences in behavior, 583–591, 1975, with permission from Elsevier.

Becoming Barbie, then Bardot. Cindy Jackson never liked the way she looked. So through cosmetic surgery and procedures—around 60 in all—she began to transform herself into her physical ideal, Barbie, and then Brigitte Bardot, a cultural icon of the 1960s and 1970s. Is Jackson's quest to make herself physically attractive extreme? By everyday standards, yes. From a pragmatic perspective, is it entirely misguided? Perhaps not. Research demonstrates that, whether we like it or not, it often pays to be physically attractive.

first stage of the study, the women received information from a male student whom they expected to meet later. The information suggested that he was either quite desirable (a tall, 21-year-old Princeton senior who had a car and who was athletic, unattached, and interested in meeting women) or not (a short, 18-year-old, unathletic non-Princeton freshman who had a girlfriend and no car). The women additionally learned that he was either quite traditional in his beliefs about women (believing that the ideal woman is emotional, concerned with how she looks, passive, and the like) or nontraditional in his beliefs (believing that the ideal woman is independent, ambitious, and so forth).

The women then completed several questionnaires for the male student to peruse, including one reporting their own attitudes about gender roles. As Figure 4.4 reveals, when the partner was desirable, the women modified their opinions to match his. Other research demonstrates that men do the same when presenting their views to desirable women (Morier & Seroy, 1994). The bottom line? We often adjust our public opinions when we want people to like us. But why?

All else being equal, people like those who are similar to them and dislike those who are different from them—and we know it! People like others who dress like them, who share their tastes in movies and foods, who hold similar opinions—and even those who share such trivial similarities as having a few of the same letters in their last name (Byrne, 1971; Jones et al., 2004; see Chapter 7). It makes sense, then, that we often *create* similarity to ingratiate ourselves with others by altering our dress, activities, our public opinions, and even our levels of alcohol consumption (O'Grady, 2013). It also makes sense that we try to avoid coming across as different from those we wish to ingratiate, because to be different—to have a very different style, to do very different things, or to hold incompatible opinions—decreases the chances they will like us (e.g., Dodd et al., 2001; Swim & Hyers, 1999). When we make ourselves like others, they tend to like us more.

MAKING OURSELVES PHYSICALLY ATTRACTIVE "I didn't have the right clothes and I didn't have the right face and I would sit back and notice how much easier it was for the girls who had those things. This is what life rewards. Life will reward you if you have the right look" ("Becoming Barbie," 1995). With this observation, and a new inheritance, Cindy Jackson decided to transform herself physically, from a woman whom no one "would look at twice" to her physical ideal, Barbie. At age 33, she began to sculpt herself through plastic surgery: two nose jobs, a lip enhancement, a chin reduction, breast implants (which were later removed), multiple liposuctions, cheek implants, chemical peels, hair transplants, three face lifts, permanent make-up, and more—47 procedures in all, including nine operations. More recently, Jackson underwent another series of nine surgeries and procedures to reinvent her physical self again—this time as the iconic French actress of the 1960s and 1970s, Brigitte Bardot.

We do not know whether the benefits to Cindy Jackson of these procedures outweighed their costs, both physical and financial (she's spent well over $100,000). We do know, however, that physically attractive people are indeed liked more and viewed more favorably than unattractive people (Eagly et al., 1991; Feingold, 1992; Langlois et al., 2000). Attractive people are seen as more honest (Zebrowitz, Voinesco, & Collins, 1996). They are more likely to be hired for managerial positions and elected to public office, even though interviewers and voters deny any influence of physical appearance (e.g., Budesheim & DePaola, 1994; Mack & Rainey, 1990). They receive lesser fines and bail judgments in misdemeanor cases and shorter sentences in felony cases (Downs & Lyons, 1991; Stewart, 1980, 1985). They find it easier to get jobs and they get paid more (Benzeval, Green, & Macintyre, 2013). Compared to being of average attractiveness, there's an approximately 7% penalty for being unattractive and a 5% premium for being highly attractive (Hamermesh & Biddle, 1994). All other things being equal, this 12% income difference is the same gap you'd expect to find between one employee and another having an extra 1.5 years of education! Physically attractive people are more desirable for romantic relationships, as we'll see in Chapter 8. Even newborn infants receive more affection from their mothers when they're cute (Langlois et al., 1995). It clearly pays to be physically attractive.

Realizing this, most people try to make themselves more attractive. Consider the following:

- In 2013, Americans had over 11 million cosmetic surgical and nonsurgical procedures—an increase of 8% from 2006 (American Society for Aesthetic Plastic Surgery, 2009).
- The most popular cosmetic procedure—performed over 3.7 million times in 2013—was the Botox injection, which involves injecting a paralyzing toxin into the facial muscles responsible for creating wrinkle lines around the eyes, mouth, and forehead.
- Worldwide, cosmetics are a $20 billion-per-year industry, and perfume and cologne makers sell $10 billion worth of fragrances.
- Five million Americans currently wear braces or other orthodontic devices—nearly 1 million of them adults—mostly to improve the look of their smile.
- Americans spend $6-plus billion on diet foods, supplements, books, and weight-loss programs each year.

Consider, also, the time and money we spend styling our hair, adorning ourselves with jewelry and tattoos, and buying clothes that will hide our weaker physical features and show off our more attractive ones. And let's not forget our more dangerous—even life-threatening—attractiveness-seeking activities, such as roasting ourselves in the sun, going on severe diets, and using muscle-building steroids (Leary, Tchividjian, & Kraxberger, 1994; Martin & Leary, 2001).

We want others to like us; we know that being physically attractive helps, so we're apparently willing to absorb the many costs to buy, in Cindy Jackson's words, the "right look."

PROJECTING MODESTY If you aced an exam, receiving the highest grade in the class, would you immediately announce it to others? Not if you want to be liked! People who downplay their successes are generally liked more than people who boast of them (e.g., Rosen, Cochran, & Musser, 1990; Wosinska et al., 1996). As a consequence, we often give public credit to others for aiding in our successes and gently point to weaknesses we have in other—less important—areas (e.g., Baumeister & Ilko, 1995; Miller & Schlenker, 1985).

Being modest has its risks, however. If people don't know of your successes, they may believe you when you profess a lack of talent. If you are too modest, people may think you have horribly low self-esteem or little self-insight (Robinson, Johnson, & Shields, 1995). And if you appear insincere in minimizing the importance of what you've done ("Oh, the award is no big deal"), people may view you as smug and arrogant (Pin & Turndorf, 1990). These risks aside, modest individuals tend to be liked.

Although modesty is valued across the globe, there are some interesting cultural variations. Consider the case of Muhammad Ali, the finest heavyweight boxer of his era and perhaps of all time. His boastful claims—"I am the greatest!"—did not always endear him to boxing fans, however. In particular, Ali was disliked by many white Americans. Although some of this opposition was racist in nature, other African American boxers who fought during the 1970s and 1980s—Joe Frazier, for instance—were well liked. In part, Ali's image problem among whites was probably attributable to his penchant for bragging, for his immodest style of self-presentation.

"I am the greatest!" And perhaps he was. But Muhammad Ali's bold self-proclamations did little to endear him to many white Americans, among whom even truthful verbal immodesty is disliked.

This illustration points to a cultural disparity between blacks and whites in the social acceptability of boastfulness. In a study exploring this difference, African American and European American college students read short biographies of three male students and then read a transcription of a conversation these students had about travel experiences, academic achievements, sports prowess, and the like. One of the students was portrayed as a *nonbragger*, who understated his strengths; a second student was depicted as an *untruthful bragger*, who boasted of things that weren't true; and the third student was presented as a *truthful bragger*, whose boasts reflected his actual accomplishments. Black and white students equally liked the nonbragger and disliked the untruthful bragger. They differed, however, in their impressions of the truthful bragger. Black students liked the truthful bragger more than the white students did (Holtgraves & Dulin, 1994). Immodesty, when truthful, is apparently tolerated more by African Americans than by European Americans.

This is not to say that European Americans are particularly modest. Indeed, compared to Americans of Asian descent, European Americans come across as quite boastful (e.g., Fry & Ghosh, 1980; Yamagishi et al., 2012). Across the globe, Asians are particularly modest in their self-presentations, living one of Confucius's maxims: "The superior man is modest in his speech" (e.g., Fu et al., 2001; Furnham, Hosoe, & Tang, 2002).

We should be careful not to overgeneralize from these data, however. It's unlikely that race per se can explain the differences in verbal modesty among Asian Americans, African Americans, and European Americans. For instance, in a study of Nigerians, Boski (1983) discovered a wide range of modesty norms across the different tribes: The Hausa stress modesty, whereas the Igbo allow for more self-promotion. Moreover, because most of the research on modesty has explored verbal self-presentation, we know little about cultural differences in what we might call material modesty (e.g., the display of expensive cars, jewelry, and the like).

In sum, modesty norms are like most other norms—interesting similarities and differences exist across cultures. Whereas all cultures appear to frown upon deceptive self-promotion, some cultures encourage modesty more than others.

To this point, we've described four tactics people use to ingratiate themselves with others: People try to convince others that they like them, using flattery and certain nonverbal expressions; they point out their similarities to others; they make themselves more physically attractive; and they act modestly. Now let's explore the characteristics of the person and situation that encourage people to be ingratiating.

PERSON Gender and Ingratiation

On an afternoon jaunt to the library, one of us came across a collection of "advice" books for young men and women, written in the eighteenth and nineteenth centuries. In general, the recommendations for men concerned such things as industriousness, accomplishment, and status seeking. The advice for "ladies" differed considerably, focusing instead on the importance of being likable and proper. In his *Lectures on Female Education*, for example, John Barton (1794) told the students of a girls' school "to please and to captivate" (p. 72). And after extolling the benefits of cheerfulness, gentleness, modesty, and beauty, he counseled the girls that "a conduct regulated by these agreeable qualities will not only be pleasing in its appearance, but useful in its effects" (p. 162). Female writers of the time made similar suggestions, focusing in particular on the advantages of appropriate dress and manners (e.g., Farrar, 1838). The implication of such writings was clear: Women should present themselves in ways that are likable to others.

Of course, these prescriptions were written long ago, in a society different in many ways from the present one. It may surprise some of you to learn, then, that even today the desire to be liked seems generally more important to women than to men (DePaulo, 1992; Forsyth et al., 1985). As a result, women are somewhat more likely than men to use the ingratiation tactics we just explored. In social situations, women smile more than men (e.g., Hall & Friedman, 1999; LaFrance, Hecht, & Paluck, 2003) and are more likely to adjust their opinions to match those held by others (Becker, 1988; Eagly & Carli, 1981). They are more concerned with their physical attractiveness than are men (e.g., Dion et al., 1990; Hart et al., 1989) and account for around 91% of cosmetic surgeries and procedures (American Society for Aesthetic Plastic Surgery, 2009). And women present themselves more modestly, especially in public (e.g., Berg et al., 1981; Daubman et al., 1992).

This doesn't mean that men are uninterested in ingratiating themselves with others. Far from it. It's important for almost everyone to be liked, and men can be as ingratiating as women (Vrugt & VanEechoud, 2002). In fact, when young Black men are worried about racial stereotypes, they report going out of their way to smile, to defuse any concerns that they might be dangerous (Neel, Neufeld, & Neuberg, 2013). But, in general, other self-presentational goals—such as the desire to be viewed as powerful and dominant—are more prominent for men than for women, a difference we explore later in this chapter.

Why is ingratiation relatively more important for women? One explanation suggests that women in particular are rewarded for presenting themselves in agreeable and likable ways (e.g., Deaux & Major, 1987). Consistent with this, girls become more nonverbally agreeable as they move through adolescence, presumably because they learn how society expects them to behave (Blanck et al., 1981). Biological factors may also be important. Compared to men, women usually have much lower levels of *testosterone*, a hormone responsible for important aspects of sexual development. People who have high levels of testosterone use more confrontational, hardened ways of getting what they want from others, they are less friendly, they are less concerned about others' welfare, and they smile less (e.g., Cashdan, 1995; Dabbs et al., 1996). In contrast, people who have lower levels of testosterone are friendlier and are more likely to use politeness and social graces to achieve their goals. Thus, both socialization and biological factors may contribute to women's greater concern with ingratiation.

Charming. Books of etiquette have long taught young women about the value and effectiveness of presenting themselves as likable. Although the times have changed in many ways, and etiquette manuals and "charm schools" are no longer in vogue, even women today focus more on being liked than do men.

SITUATION Potential Friends and Power-Holders

Personal characteristics alone don't create the desire to ingratiate oneself with others. When people hope to form or maintain friendships or when they interact with people in positions of higher status, they're also particularly likely to be ingratiating.

FRIENDSHIP SETTINGS It almost goes without saying that we should be especially concerned with ingratiating ourselves with those people with whom we want to develop or maintain positive relationships. Participants in one study were interviewed by either a good friend or a total stranger and asked to evaluate and discuss their prospects for a successful career, satisfying relationships, and so on. The participants presented themselves more modestly to their friends than to the strangers (Tice et al., 1995). And just as we're careful not to toot our own horns too loudly when we are fostering friendships, we're also more likely to smile, say nice things about the other person, make ourselves more attractive, and so on (e.g., Bohra & Pandey, 1984; Daly et al., 1983).

INTERACTING WITH PEOPLE IN POWERFUL POSITIONS Those who occupy positions of power are often less focused on getting others to like them. After all, these individuals can exercise their power to get what they want—"If your productivity doesn't improve, Smithers, you'll be out on the street collecting unemployment!" Intimidation, of course, isn't a compelling option for those having little actual power. Instead, people in positions of little power focus more on getting others to like them. For example, members of lower social classes are especially likely to adjust their public opinions and provide socially appropriate answers to interviewer questions (Ross & Mirowsky,

1983), and employees seeking better relationships with their supervisors are especially likely to flatter them (Kacmar, Carlson, & Bratton, 2004). In another study, women modified their physical appearance to match what they thought their interviewer would like: Women expecting to interview with a traditional man showed up wearing more makeup and jewelry than did women expecting to interview with a man who had nontraditional views (von Baeyer, Sherk, & Zanna, 1981).

Indeed, ingratiating oneself with the holders of power is quite effective, especially in the business world (Vilela et al., 2007). In one study of college graduates, attempts to ingratiate themselves with supervisors—by praising them or pretending to agree with them, for instance—was the fourth largest factor contributing to career success, after hours worked per week, years of job experience, and marital status (married people are more successful) (Judge & Bretz, 1994). Similarly, workers who are liked by their supervisors tend to be paid more—according to one study, being liked was worth a pay increase of 4% to 5% over and beyond the impact of job performance (Deluga & Perry, 1994).

Although people in powerful positions possess more tools of influence and thus need to rely less on ingratiation, they too want to be liked. Interestingly, they tend to use different ingratiation tactics than do their less powerful counterparts. Because they are unlikely to be perceived as "brown-nosing" their subordinates, it is less risky for them to seek affection by rendering favors and giving out compliments (Jones & Wortman, 1973). In contrast, people in positions of power rarely seek liking by conforming their opinions to match their subordinates', as to do so might threaten their status.

INTERACTION Multiple Audiences

Getting others to like us becomes particularly tricky when we want to simultaneously ingratiate ourselves with two audiences having opposing values. Consider, for example, the dilemma faced by the student who wants to "butter up" the professor while other students are nearby or by the politician giving a nationally televised speech who wants the support of voters on both sides of the pro-life/pro-choice divide. To flatter the professor blatantly will earn the dislike of one's peers, who frown on such behaviors, and to support the pro-life position will cost the politician the affections of the pro-choice voters. How do people manage such **multiple audience dilemmas**?

If at all possible, we segregate our different audiences. Thus, the flattering student may wait to ply his tricks until he reaches the privacy of the professor's office, while the politician may state one set of views during a meeting of pro-lifers and a different set of views at a gathering of pro-choicers. Alternatively, we might determine that one audience is more important to us than the other, as when the student decides that he'd rather have the friendship of his classmates than of his professor.

These options are sometimes unavailable, however. We can't always separate our audiences and we sometimes need the positive regard of both audiences. Even so, people are remarkably good at managing multiple audiences (Fleming & Darley, 1991). They may finesse the competing desires of multiple audiences by "moderating" their presentations—by presenting their opinions as falling somewhere between the contrasting opinions held by the two audiences (Braver et al., 1977; Snyder & Swann, 1976). Of course, an ingratiator using this strategy runs the risk of being disliked by both audiences, as might happen if a presidential candidate waffles on his or her views of the abortion issue. People may also try to present different messages on the different "channels" of communication. A student telephoning a professor to request an extension on a paper may mention flattering aspects of the class while simultaneously grimacing for the benefit of his roommates (Fleming & Rudman, 1993).

Finally, we can manage the multiple audience dilemma by capitalizing on the different information the audiences may have about us. In one study, students were asked to present themselves to one conversation partner as a "nerd" and to a second partner as a "party animal." After speaking separately with each partner, the students were asked to maintain these opposing images in a conversation with both partners at once. They

Multiple audience dilemma A situation in which a person needs to present different images to different audiences, often at the same time.

were able to do so effectively, partially because they made statements that would mean different things to the two partners. For example, by saying that "it's like I said before, Saturdays are good for one thing and one thing only," the students reinforced their images as nerds to the first partner and party animals to the second (Van Boven et al., 2000).

The values held by multiple audiences interact, then, to influence how we go about getting others to like us. If everyone in the audience holds the same values, we can readily sculpt our presentations to conform with them. When the audience is made up of people having differing and incompatible values, however, effective ingratiation becomes trickier, and self-presenters must become more creative to pull it off.

INVESTIGATION

Why is it so important to people that they be liked? We'll learn in Chapter 7 about some of the benefits of friendships and about some of the costs of being excluded. What do you think these benefits and costs are?

Quick Quiz

1 Which of the following is *not* an ingratiation strategy that supports the goal of appearing likable?
   a. Projecting modesty
   b. Making oneself physically attractive
   c. Expressing liking for others
   d. Showing off your unique talents

2 A true enjoyment smile involves the movement of the muscles controlling _____, whereas false smiles are usually _____.
   a. Both lips and eyes; jerky and asymmetrical
   b. Lips but not the eyes; smooth and symmetrical
   c. Eyes but not the lips; jerky and symmetrical
   d. Lips but not the cheeks; jerky and open-mouthed

3 Which of the following statements is true?
   a. Men are more likely to ingratiate themselves to be seen as likable to others.
   b. Men are more driven than women to be viewed as powerful and dominant.
   c. Because of recent power shifts in the business world, women are now more likely than men to present themselves as socially dominant.
   d. Testosterone and other biological factors have little to do with gender differences in ingratiation.
   e. All of the above

4 Which of the following statements best defines the *multiple audience dilemma*?
   a. A situation in which a person needs to present different images to different audiences, often simultaneously.
   b. A situation in which a person on TV needs to present different images to different audiences, often simultaneously.
   c. A feature of the person whereby those who have a high preference for consistency struggle to present a consistent image across all situations.
   d. A situation in which a person needs to present different images at different times—to family, friends, and coworkers.

Appearing Competent

LO 4.7 Identify the four main strategies we use to get others to view us as competent.

LO 4.8 Understand why shy people have difficulty promoting their competence.

LO 4.9 Explain the situational factors that influence our desire to appear competent.

If Demara had posed as a postal employee, garbage collector, or waiter, his life would have been much easier—he was quite smart and socially skilled and would have learned quickly the tricks of those trades. But he decided, instead, to pass himself off as a college professor, an accountant, and a surgeon, among other learned professions. To escape detection in these more technical fields, Demara had to convince others that he was competent—that he possessed the knowledge and abilities of someone who had been trained and had received the proper certifications.

Even nonimpostors have to convince others of their competence. Physicians must appear competent if they are to acquire and retain patients, salespeople must appear competent if they are to be promoted into the managerial ranks, and children must appear competent if they are to be chosen by classmates to play kickball during recess. Indeed, people are sometimes so concerned with appearing competent that they may be too distracted from the task at hand to perform it well (e.g., Lord, Saenz, & Godfrey, 1987; Osborne & Gilbert, 1992; Steele & Aronson, 1995). In this section, we explore the strategies people use to communicate their competence and the features of the person and situation that make such communications more likely.

Strategies of Self-Promotion

The occupations Demara chose required years of specialized training, and we can't help but wonder why Demara's colleagues never caught him in the act, never realized that he was a fraud. It helped Demara that he was well liked, as this reduced the likelihood that people would suspect that he was incompetent (e.g., Wayne & Ferris, 1990). It also helped that he was a hard worker and a quick study. But Demara had several tricks up his sleeves as well. Although Demara's tactics for **self-promotion**—behaviors intended to create the image of competence—were, at times, outrageously bold, they usefully highlight the principles underlying the everyday strategies people employ (see Figure 4.5).

STAGING PERFORMANCES A legitimate reputation for competence requires that a person actually *be* competent. Unfortunately, one's achievements can go unobserved. Perhaps your dad's head was turned the moment you made that picture-perfect dive into the community pool or your mom was working in the yard when you finally mastered the difficult piano piece. Because successes are sometimes overlooked, we may seek and create opportunities to *stage* our performances, to demonstrate our competence in public—to subtly scream, "Lookit, Pa!" as we're about to leap off the metaphorical high dive (Goffman, 1959; Jones, 1990). For instance, if you're a skilled dancer and want to impress a new love interest with your talent, you might feel tempted to arrange an evening not far from music and a dance floor.

Of course, this staging tactic has its flip side—if you're *in*competent at something (if you have the physical graces of a rhinoceros), you're likely to avoid public stagings. Demara understood both lessons well. On the one hand, he often chose professions like teaching and medicine, in which the audiences—students and patients—possessed little technical knowledge and thus could be easily impressed. On the other hand, he did his best to avoid demonstrating his dubious skills when other professionals were around, by making himself scarce when necessary.

Figure 4.5 Strategies of self-promotion

| Goal
To Appear Competent | → | **Self-Promotional Strategies**
Stage Performances
Claim Competence
Use the Trappings of Competence
Make Excuses or Claim Obstacles |

Self-promotion An attempt to get others to see us as competent.

People use a variety of strategies to get others to see them as competent.

Staging performances can be as simple as moving one's body into the spotlight of public attention. In one study, participants who expected to perform well on a simulated game show chose a seat that placed them front and center. Not surprisingly, students who expected to perform poorly chose to seat themselves off to the side (Akimoto, Sanbonmatsu, & Ho, 2000).

Sometimes it's not possible to stage performances of competence, nor is it possible to avoid public displays of incompetence. The boss isn't always around while we're generating valuable insights, and we may get dragged onto the dance floor against our will. So we rely on other tactics as well to convince others of our competence.

CLAIMING COMPETENCE Sometimes we just *tell* others about our accomplishments when we want them to see us as competent. Indeed, verbal declarations of competence work well when they're "invited." For instance, if you're being interviewed for a job, verbal self-promotion is both appropriate and effective for communicating competence (Holtgraves & Srull, 1989; Kacmar et al., 1992). We especially benefit from verbal claims of competence made by others on our behalf (Giacalone, 1985). This was one of Demara's favorite tricks: He would forge reference letters from highly credible sources, all glowing in their praise of his competence.

Verbal claims of competence can be risky, however. They can easily come across as immodest—and immodest people are often disliked, as we just learned (Godfrey, Jones, & Lord, 1986). Moreover, people generally believe that truly competent individuals don't need to claim it—that their performances will "speak for themselves." As a result, when people *do* boldly highlight their abilities or accomplishments, they may inadvertently imply to us the opposite—that they're really not all that skilled (Jones & Pittman, 1982). Because self-promoting statements come across as immodest and are only marginally credible, then, they may actually harm one's professional success if not delivered delicately (Judge & Bretz, 1994; Wayne & Ferris, 1990).

USING THE TRAPPINGS OF COMPETENCE Many advisors in the self-promotion industry recommend that people surround themselves with the props and habits usually associated with competence (e.g., Bly et al., 1986). For instance, self-promoters are advised to look busy—by writing a lot in their calendar books or taking a while to return phone calls—because very successful individuals usually have little free time on their hands. Demara was skilled at using clothing and professional-appearing stationery to convey the image of competence. If a person looks like a physician, he correctly reasoned, he or she is more likely to be accepted as such. The use of props for self-presentational purposes is frequent, and we discuss them further when we explore the ways people try to convey images of status and power.

MAKING EXCUSES, CLAIMING OBSTACLES "The sun was in my eyes," claims the outfielder after badly misjudging the lazy fly ball. "The dog ate it," pleads the sixth-grader late once again with his homework. These classic gems point to the ease with which people generate excuses after poor performances. Indeed, people may even make excuses *before* performing, anticipating for their audiences the obstacles that could get in the way of success. Although such excuses are valid at times, at other times they serve less to explain poor performance than to make the excuse-makers feel better about their performances and to help them influence the way they are viewed (e.g., Schlenker, Pontari, & Christopher, 2001).

Excuses, excuses. To maintain a reputation for competence, we sometimes make excuses for our failures and indiscretions. Douglas Bernstein (1993) compiled a list of amazing, strange, and unusual—but actual—excuses students have used to avoid taking exams, turning in term papers, and other failures to live up to standards: "My paper is late because my parrot crapped into my computer" (the contemporary version of "my dog ate my homework"?). "I can't finish my paper because I just found out my girlfriend is a nymphomaniac." And one from our own campus, in usually sunny Arizona: "I couldn't make the exam yesterday because it was cloudy and I drive a convertible."

The self-promotional value of excuses and claimed obstacles follows from the *discounting* and *augmenting* principles we discussed in Chapter 3. If others believe that the sun truly was in your eyes, they may discount the relevance of your softball ability in determining your botched attempt. And if you manage to catch the ball despite the sun's glare, your reputation for competence will be augmented. So making excuses and claiming obstacles may shield us from images of incompetence following failure and create images of competence following success (e.g., Erber & Prager, 2000; Giacalone & Riordan, 1990; Snyder & Higgins, 1988).

Of course, excuses also carry with them great self-presentational risks (Schlenker et al., 2001). For example, excuses designed to preserve an image of competence may make you appear unreliable or uncommitted (e.g., "I couldn't finish the assignment on time because my sister invited me to spend the weekend with her in Las Vegas."). If your excuses involve blaming others, you are likely to be seen as self-centered. And if you get caught making a phony excuse, you will be viewed as untrustworthy. Making excuses, then, can be risky (Tyler & Feldman, 2007).

It's one thing to claim an obstacle to success; it's quite another to *create* such an obstacle for oneself (Arkin & Baumgardner, 1985; Hirt, Deppe, & Gordon, 1991; Leary & Shepperd, 1986). However, people sometimes do just that. By **self-handicapping**—by creating circumstances for ourselves that actually obstruct our ability to demonstrate true competence—we may reduce the likelihood that people will attribute our failures to incompetence and increase the likelihood that people will attribute our successes to some outstanding ability.

Self-handicapping The behavior of withdrawing effort or creating obstacles to one's future successes.

Bridging Function and Dysfunction:

The Paradox of Self-Handicapping

A famous news anchor, successful beyond her dreams, starts abusing drugs and throws away her career in the process. A high school student voted "most likely to succeed" attends a prestigious university, becomes uncharacteristically negligent in his studies, and flunks out.

Do you know people like this—people who, after early successes, begin to act in ways that make future successes less likely? Self-handicapping is especially likely to occur when people doubt that previous achievements accurately reflect their personal abilities and efforts (Berglas & Jones, 1978). For instance, the television anchor may believe her rapid attainment to be the result of beauty and luck, and the student may attribute his academic accomplishments to the advantages of his family's prosperous background.

The result of such beliefs is the fear that similar high-level performances will be difficult to sustain and that the private and public esteem built upon past successes will crumble. So to maintain a public image of competence, and to preserve their fragile competence beliefs, self-handicappers withdraw effort or create obstacles to future performance. If they succeed despite the impediment, people would reasonably conclude (via the augmenting principle) that they are especially skilled; if they fail, people would reasonably conclude (via the discounting principle) that the obstacle caused the failure. In either case, by withdrawing effort or forcing themselves to hurdle daunting obstacles, self-handicappers can maintain a public and private image of competence (McCrea & Hirt, 2001).

Certain people are more likely than others to self-handicap. Individuals who have a fragile sense of their effectiveness are especially likely to self-handicap, as are those who have a strong desire to demonstrate their competence (Coudevylle et al., 2008; Harris & Snyder, 1986). Interestingly, men place more obstacles in the paths to their own achievements, although both sexes are quite adept at claiming obstacles following failures (e.g., Ferrari, 1991; McCrea, Hirt, & Milner, 2008; Rhodewalt & Hill, 1995). And although both persons high and persons low in self-esteem self-handicap to some extent, they seem to do so for different reasons. People who have high self-esteem want to enhance their already favorable images, whereas people who have low self-esteem want to protect their less favorable images from failure (Tice, 1991).

How do college students—perhaps like people you know?—self-handicap when confronted with difficult tasks? Let us begin to count the ways:

- By taking cognition-impairing drugs before or during the task (e.g., Kolditz & Arkin, 1982)
- By not practicing when given the opportunity (e.g., Alter & Forgas, 2007)
- By consuming alcohol prior to a performance (Higgins & Harris, 1988)
- By listening to loud, distracting music during the task (e.g., Shepperd & Arkin, 1989)
- By choosing unattainable goals (Greenberg, 1985)

Our choices of self-handicaps are wide and varied, indeed, and we suspect that you've seen at least several of these in action.

The self-handicapping strategy carries with it heavy, long-term costs. By placing significant obstacles in their paths, people actually reduce their chances for future success (e.g., Elliot & Church, 2003; Zuckerman, Kieffer, & Knee, 1998). Moreover, over time, people who habitually self-handicap exhibit worse health and report increased alcohol, marijuana, and other illegal drug use (Zuckerman & Tsai, 2005). That people will go so far to sabotage both future achievements and broader images points to the importance they place on the image of competence. And therein lies the great paradox of self-handicapping: Our great desire to appear competent leads us under some circumstances to engage in behaviors that make competent performances less likely.

INVESTIGATION

Do you know anyone who self-handicaps? What were the consequences? Knowing what you do about why people self-handicap—to maintain a public and private image of competence—what might you do to help someone reduce this destructive behavior?

In sum, people can project an image of competence by staging performances, making verbal claims, taking on the trappings of success, providing excuses for their failures and claiming or creating obstacles for their success. We turn now to explore the kinds of persons for whom an image of competence is especially important and the circumstances that create in most of us the desire to be seen as competent.

PERSON Competence Motivation and Shyness

Demara hated to fail. He was determined, once he applied his considerable abilities to a task, to succeed at it. He needed to do more than just "pass"; he wanted to be among the best. He also wanted to be *seen* as one of the best. Demara was high in **competence motivation**—the desire to perform effectively (e.g., Deci & Ryan, 1985). People may be high in competence motivation for intrinsic reasons, that is, because gaining mastery is interesting and challenging. This is typically called *achievement motivation* (e.g., McClelland et al., 1953). Alternatively, people may possess a strong competence motivation because they know that success can boost their public- or self-images. In this case, achievement is driven by the extrinsic desire to be seen (or to see oneself) as competent (Koestner & McClelland, 1990). Although only a few research studies have explored the effects of competence motivation on self-presentation, the evidence supports the idea that the two are associated. For instance, those who score high on measures of this second, extrinsic type of competence motivation are quick to claim personal credit for successes (Kukla, 1972). These individuals are also especially likely to display the trappings of competence by dressing professionally in their work settings (Ericksen & Sirgy, 1989). For certain people—those focused on public achievement—presenting a competent image may be particularly important.

Even though most people want to be seen as competent in at least some circumstances, some are unwilling to get there by adopting the competence tactics we've discussed. Some folks experience frequent or chronic **shyness**—they tend to feel tense, worried, or awkward in unfamiliar social interactions, even while merely imagining or anticipating social interaction (Cheek et al., 1986; Leary, 1986b). Shy people are anxiously self-preoccupied: In social situations, they spend a lot of time thinking about their feelings, their behaviors, and how they come across to others ("Why am I so nervous? Is it really important what she thinks of me? I have no idea what I'm going to say next") (Cheek & Melchior, 1990).

Compared with nonshy individuals, shy people are less likely to promote their competence boldly. Instead, their self-presentations tend to be protective: Rather than trying to acquire favorable public images, shy people focus on preventing unfavorable public images. To be safe, shy people try to avoid unfamiliar social encounters, date less frequently, prefer to work alone rather than with others, and tend to occupy seats in college classrooms toward the rear and sides (Curran, 1977; Dykman & Reis, 1979). By keeping themselves out of the attentional spotlight, they reduce the risk of coming across as incompetent. When they do find themselves in the company of others, shy people try to reduce the social pressure to appear competent. They may

Competence motivation The desire to perform effectively.

Shyness The tendency to feel tense, worried, or awkward in novel social situations and with unfamiliar people.

To be shy in a self-promoting world. Shy people become anxious even imagining themselves in unfamiliar social situations. Because of this, they may miss opportunities for personal and professional advancement that staging performances, claims of competence, excuse-making, and other bold self-promotional tactics make available. Shyness hurts in more ways than one.

even purposely fail, to lower the expectations others hold of them (Baumgardner & Brownlee, 1987). They are on the other hand likely to self-handicap their performances (Shepperd & Arkin, 1990).

It's not that shy people don't want to be viewed as competent. Rather, they are just wary of promoting themselves when they know they may have to prove their competence in the future. Thus, whereas shy people are hesitant to create self-handicaps for themselves, if an obvious excuse for a potentially poor performance already exists in the situation, they will take advantage of it to increase the boldness of their self-promotional claims (Arkin & Baumgardner, 1988; Leary, 1986a).

The reluctance of shy people to promote themselves actively may carry with it significant costs. For instance, some studies suggest that shy individuals tend to be underemployed and relatively unsuccessful in their careers (e.g., Caspi, Elder, & Bem, 1988; Gilmartin, 1987). Skillful self-promotion creates benefits that shy people are less likely to receive.

SITUATION When Competence Matters

We are more concerned with whether we come across as competent in some settings than in others. For instance, your desire to be appreciated as a good dancer is more likely to come to mind when in a nightclub than when sitting through a psychology lecture. Similarly, certain people are more likely to arouse concerns about competence than are others. For example, you're likely to prefer being viewed as a good dancer by a romantic partner than by your chemistry professor. Of course, there are times and places where we have few self-promotional concerns of any sort, such as when a father finds himself lost in the joys of playing with his child—which probably explains the goofy gestures and expressions such situations often evoke, most of which would be quite embarrassing (not to mention damaging to one's reputation) if displayed in the corporate boardroom.

Failure, or a fear of impending failure, amplifies the concern with appearing competent. If you want others to think you're smart, failing an exam will be a very threatening experience for you—one that may lead you to reach into your self-promotional bag of tricks. In one experiment, students who were informed they had performed poorly on a test of social sensitivity were especially likely to present themselves afterward as well adjusted. In comparison, students who had succeeded on the test engaged in a more modest self-presentation; because their social competence was validated by the test, they could focus instead on being liked (Schneider, 1969). In another study, some of the participants were led to believe that they did worse than their assigned partners on an academic achievement test, and that their partners would later see their scores and evaluate them. To counteract the effects of their relatively unfavorable performances, these participants were especially likely to lie to their partners about their past academic performances—exaggerating their high school GPA, bragging about their writing skills, and the like (Tyler & Feldman, 2005). The desire to appear competent may be particularly strong in ambiguous settings, in which individuals are unsure of their standing (Yun et al., 2007), and in pressure-filled, competitive circumstances. Ironically, such circumstances also increase the chance that a performer will "choke," or perform well below potential (Baumeister & Showers, 1986; Beilock & Carr, 2001).

INTERACTION Competence Checks

Unlike shy individuals, socially confident people often take advantage of opportunities to promote their competence, especially after a public failure. Do these individuals self-promote with reckless abandon, without considering their present circumstances? Probably not. As James Shepperd, Robert Arkin, and Jean Slaughter (1995) demonstrated, even socially confident individuals are attuned to the riskiness of self-promotion. Participants in their study were led to believe either that they had performed poorly on an intelligence test or that they had done quite well. Moreover, some participants were told they would be tested again shortly. All then completed a short questionnaire. Regardless of conditions, shy participants were quite modest when estimating their future performance on the test and tests like it, showing no inclination to boast of future successes. Socially confident individuals, in contrast, were quick to jump at the opportunity to claim future success after they had failed. But this was only true when they wouldn't be immediately retaking the test. When they knew their second performance would be evaluated, they became more modest in their predictions. This finding illustrates, then, one kind of person–situation interaction: Certain people (those who are socially confident), when confronted with a particular situation (failure on an important test that won't be retaken), are especially likely to act in certain ways to restore the damage done to their reputations (by claiming future success).

INTERACTION ## The Interpersonal Cycle of Self-Promotion

As we've learned, people can change their situations. An experiment conducted by Roy Baumeister, Debra Hutton, and Dianne Tice (1989) explored how one person's self-promotions can create a social situation in which others also feel compelled to self-promote. Pairs of students were recruited for a study exploring the nature of group interviews. One of these students—labeled the "protagonist"—was instructed prior to the interview (and out of earshot of the partner) either (1) to promote him- or herself as strongly as possible or (2) to present him- or herself modestly. The interviewer proceeded to ask the students questions about their career prospects, relationships with members of the opposite sex, and so forth, always beginning with the protagonist. As expected, protagonists instructed to self-promote provided more favorable answers than did those instructed to be modest. Interestingly, however, the *partners* of the self-promoters presented themselves more favorably than did the partners of the modest self-presenters. Illustrating the power of people to alter their situations, these self-promoters created an environment in which their partners felt compelled to self-promote as well.

INVESTIGATION

Recall a time when you got into a self-promotional "contest" with someone: "I did this." "Well, *I* did this . . ." "Well, *I* did this . . ." How did this contest come about? Can you recall a time when you got into a self-*deprecating* contest with someone: "I did this, I'm so stupid." "If you think *that's* bad, listen to the stupid thing *I* did . . .?" Why did *this* happen? In what ways might these two "contests" be related?

....

Quick Quiz

1 Taking your date to an ice-skating rink so you can display your figure-skating skills is an example of _____, whereas talking about your professional skills during an interview is an example of _____.

    a. Using the trappings of competence; claiming competence
    b. Claiming competence; staging performances
    c. Staging performances; claiming competence
    d. Staging performances; using the trappings of competence

2 Which of the following statements about self-handicapping is true?

    a. People with low self-esteem are more likely to self-handicap than people with high self-esteem.
    b. People are more likely to self-handicap when they have a strong desire to demonstrate their competence.
    c. Women are more likely than men to place obstacles in the paths to their own achievements.
    d. None of the above

3 Which of the following is true regarding shy people and self-promotion?

    a. Shy people tend to have less of a desire to be viewed as competent.

    b. Shy people focus more on preventing unfavorable public images than trying to acquire favorable public images.

    c. Despite the differences in shy people's self-promotion strategies, long-term employment outcomes for shy persons do not differ significantly.

    d. Shy people are more likely to self-handicap their performances.

4 The interpersonal cycle of self-promotion refers to _____.

    a. A social situation in which one person's self-promotions makes others feel compelled to self-promote

    b. A good example of a person-situation interaction

    c. Both of the above

    d. None of the above

Conveying Status and Power

LO 4.10 Identify the four main strategies we use to convey high status and power.

LO 4.11 Explain who is most likely to display high status and power and why.

LO 4.12 Summarize the gender differences associated with self-presentational strategies.

One event of his early childhood long stood out in Fred Demara's mind. His father was at that time a prosperous businessman, the owner of several movie theaters, and the well-to-do family lived in a large home in a fancy part of town. It was Demara's fourth birthday, and his father assembled the house staff in front of the large winding staircase, under the shimmering glass chandelier. "Today my son is four years old, and on this day he becomes a little man," he announced. "From this day on I shall expect all of you to address the young master with the respect due him. Beginning tonight he is to be called Mr. Demara. I will expect it of you and so shall he." And then, as if on cue, each servant stepped forward and bowed—"Happy birthday, *Mr.* Demara" (Crichton, 1959).

Seven years later, when the family was forced to vacate its glorious home after a business setback, Demara noticed the disrespect of the moving men as they unloaded the family's possessions into a rundown house on the edge of town. Young Fred was now poor, and the loss of status it implied pained him greatly. Should we be surprised, then, that as an impostor he would almost always choose to step into the shoes of men of respect and status—the physician Joseph Cyr, the famous professor Robert Linton French, and others like them?

Demara's cons were extraordinary. His desire to be held in high regard, however, was quite normal. Why *shouldn't* a person want a reputation for status and power, given the benefits that come with it? Individuals who have high status and power gain access to greater educational opportunities and material resources. They're more likely to be accepted into influential social circles that offer opportunities to make money, find desirable mates, and wield political power. And they're less likely to be bothered and hassled by others. With a reputation of high status and power comes not only the metaphorical carrot for enticing others to do your bidding but also the stick with which to intimidate them into doing so.

Strategies for Conveying Status and Power

How do people create for themselves the appearance of high status and power? Having a reputation for competence helps, as certain kinds of status are based heavily on one's achievements. In this section, we explore a range of other tactics that people frequently use to convey an image of status and power (see Figure 4.6).

DISPLAYING THE ARTIFACTS OF STATUS AND POWER When we enter a physician's office, we immediately know where we are—thanks to the telltale waiting room, the

Figure 4.6   Strategies for conveying status and power

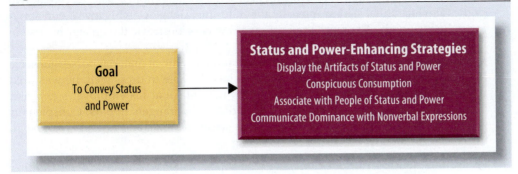

People wield several strategies to convince others of their high status and power.

receptionist behind the counter, and the diplomas, board certifications, and organizational stamps of approval on the walls. These are among the artifacts of the medical profession, and when in their midst, we just "know" we're at the doctor's office. Similarly, a corporate CEO is likely to occupy a top-floor corner office with large windows, imposing desk, fancy phone, and little clutter. The message? Decisions of magnitude are made here. People often display artifacts associated with high status or power so they will be accorded the respect and reputation they believe they have earned.

Unfortunately, people who have no legitimate credentials sometimes misappropriate these artifacts to gain respect. Indeed, some businesses exist for the sole purpose of manufacturing purely artificial artifacts. One of us was recently invited to have his biography, photograph, and essay published in the first edition of a heavy, leather-bound book entitled "One Thousand Great Intellectuals." Moreover, to commemorate his (obviously well-deserved) inclusion in such an esteemed international volume, he would also receive a gold-finished medal and framed certificate. And all he had to do to receive this honor was . . . pay $1,125!!! How flattering.

Your author saw this "invitation" for what it was—a (not so) cheap attempt to help folks create the appearance of status. But for individuals like Demara, the opportunity to exploit for his own gain artifacts of status was usually too good to pass up. For example, to impress upon people his worldliness and social standing, Demara traveled with a trunk he had purchased from a secondhand store—a trunk already plastered with stickers from expensive hotels and resorts across the globe, like the luggage owned by world travelers of that era. If Demara possessed such a trunk, observers reasoned, he must be a wealthy world traveler.

CONSPICUOUS CONSUMPTION The impression of status may also be conveyed by the amounts of money and resources people are able to expend. In fact, much of material consumption serves the purpose of communicating status (Fussell, 1983; Veblen, 1899). Rich people may communicate their high status through the ability to spend lavishly on houses in the "right" neighborhoods, automobiles, and jewels; less wealthy folks often do the same on a smaller scale, buying designer clothes and national-brand-name products instead of local brands or "generics" (e.g., Bushman, 1993).

Cacophony of conspicuous consumption! Costing over $25,000, this diamond-encrusted iPhone is conspicuous consumption on steroids. "But it must at least perform much better than the usual iPhone," you wonder. Nope. It's just a regular, off-the-shelf iPhone embellished with jewels and precious metals.

Although few can spend lavishly on jeweled electronics, many of us can—and do—spend more than we need to own "better" (although no more accurate) watches, to wear designer (but no more practical) fashions, and to, more generally, purchase for ourselves a little bit of extra status.

Giving things away and wasting money are also forms of consumption. As we'll discuss in Chapter 9, high-status members of some societies hold *potlatches*, ceremonial parties at which tribal leaders move up the status hierarchy by giving away or destroying valuable goods. The more the host gives away or destroys, the greater his rise in status (Murdock, 1923/1970).

Demara certainly understood the presentational value of material possessions. He ran scams on salesmen in clothing stores so he'd be able to dress well; he was fired from one job after exquisitely furnishing his new office at his employer's expense; and he had the expensive habit of buying drinks for strangers in bars. Conspicuous consumption, like the appropriation of high-status symbols and artifacts, can be an effective way to enhance one's social standing.

PERSONAL ASSOCIATIONS Managing one's personal associations is yet another self-presentational tool. In the fall of 1973, researchers at universities having major football teams discovered that fans were more likely to wear their team logos after victories than after defeats (Cialdini et al., 1976). Follow-up studies revealed that students were also more likely to use the pronoun *we* to describe victories ("*We* won!") than defeats ("*They* lost."). By **basking in the reflected glory** of their triumphant teams, by associating themselves with known winners, students could use the victories to strengthen their own public images. On the other side of the coin, people may **cut off reflected failure** (Snyder, Lassegard, & Ford, 1986)—that is, distance themselves from known "losers"—fearing that unfavorable public associations may leave their reputations tarnished. Filip Boen and his colleagues (2002) observed this very pattern among politically active citizens of Flanders, Belgium—citizens who had advertised their political preferences with posters in their front windows. After the election, nearly 60% of those who supported the winning parties kept their posters up, compared to only 19% of those who supported the losing parties. People associate themselves with winners and distance themselves from losers (End et al., 2002).

Demara understood the power of associations. For example, he always arrived at job interviews well "papered"—that is, with a handful of forged letters from men of acknowledged status and power testifying to his position and character. These letters served two purposes. First, as we learned earlier, they helped establish Demara's competence. They also, however, conferred status on him. After all, would such prestigious men write such glowing letters for a nobody? By using such connections, by linking himself to people of status or power, Demara was able to create high public regard for himself.

STATUS AND POWER IN NONVERBAL EXPRESSIONS Much as we might smile to convey the impression that we are likable, we adopt other forms of **body language** (Fast, 1970)—the popular term for nonverbal signals such as facial expressions, postures, body orientations, and hand gestures—to communicate images of status and power (e.g., Hall, Coats, & LeBeau, 2005; Tiedens & Fragale, 2003). For instance, people who feel secure in their high status tend to adopt more relaxed, "open" postures—postures that take up more space and lay claim to greater territory. Some research suggests that expansive dominance poses like this not only alter others' views but also boost the poser's testosterone levels and feelings of power (Carney et al., 2010).

High-status individuals also demand attention from others but seem relatively unconcerned with others and what they are doing. This is demonstrated in *visual dominance behavior*, whereby high-status individuals maintain eye contact with their audiences when speaking but pay less visual attention when listening. In contrast, low-status people orient toward those who have higher status, both with their body positions and with their eyes (e.g., Exline, 1972). High-status individuals are also more likely to interrupt others and place themselves in positions of prominence, such as in the head chair in the corporate boardroom (e.g., Goldberg, 1990; Heckel, 1973; Reiss & Rosenfeld, 1980; Russo, 1966).

Although high-status persons look relaxed when their status is secure, their posturing may change dramatically when that status is threatened. To communicate power, for instance, we may act angry—because angry people are potentially

Basking in reflected glory The process of associating ourselves with successful, high-status others or events.

Cutting off reflected failure The process of distancing ourselves from unsuccessful, low-status others or events.

Body language The popular term for nonverbal behaviors like facial expressions, posture, body orientation, and hand gestures.

dangerous people (Olson, Hafer, & Taylor, 2001). Indeed, threats to status often result in *dominance displays* remarkably similar to those exhibited by other animals. Like gorillas, we may puff ourselves up to full size, stiffen our backs, tighten our brows, thrust our chins forward, and lean toward the challenger. These displays often suffice to convince others of our power (e.g., Keating et al., 1977; Schwartz et al., 1982).

For some people, the image of status and power is so important, the fear of being seen as weak so great, that they resort to actual aggression to communicate their power (e.g., Felson & Tedeschi, 1993). For instance, a child who wants a reputation as a bruiser may beat up weaker children, especially when others are around to watch (Besag, 1989; Toch, 1969). And, unfortunately, bullying often pays: Highly aggressive boys can be among the most popular and socially connected boys in elementary school classrooms (Rodkin et al., 2000). Self-presentational aggression becomes more likely when a person's reputation for status or power is publicly insulted (Bushman & Baumeister, 1998; Felson, 1982). In Chapter 10, we explore how self-presentational concerns contribute to aggressive behavior.

PERSON Gender, Status, and Power

Are some people more likely than others to use strategies for conveying status and power? We learned earlier that women are more likely than men to present themselves as likable: They smile more in social situations, pay more attention to their physical attractiveness, and behave more modestly. This is not because men don't care about whether others like them. Indeed, they care a lot and often exhibit similar behaviors. Women just tend to care more. We see a similar pattern, but reversed, when we look at presentations of status and power: Men, more than women, present themselves as having status and power.

GENDER DIFFERENCES Men claim larger zones of personal space and are more likely to violate the space of lower-status others (Henley, 1973; Leibman, 1970). Men are better at gaining control over conversations and arguments, often by interrupting and drowning out others (Frieze & Ramsey, 1976). Men are also more likely to engage in high-status visual dominance behavior. That is, they tend to maintain eye contact with their audience when speaking but pay less attention when listening. Women show the opposite pattern, minimizing eye contact when speaking and paying rapt attention when listening (e.g., Dovidio et al., 1988). Men are more likely than women to present their professional status and financial standing in personal ads (Cicerello & Sheehan, 1995; Deaux & Hanna, 1984; Koestner & Wheeler, 1988). Men are more likely than women to signal their status by conspicuously spending on luxurious and publicly observable goods, especially when in a romantic frame of mind (Griskevicius et al., 2007; Sundie et al., 2011). And men are more likely than women to respond to an insult with physical aggression (Felson, 1982).

What accounts for this gender difference? Socialization practices clearly play a role: Males seem to be "trained" to present themselves as dominant and ascendant. In addition to learning early that the spoils of childhood go to those who have the power either to provide rewards or to inflict pain, boys also learn that girls—and, when older, women—prefer socially ascendant and financially secure men as dating and marriage partners (Kenrick, Maner, & Li, 2014). We discuss this cross-cultural female preference for socially dominant males in Chapter 8.

A complementary answer, however, rests in the biology of males and females. In many animal species, females choose to mate with those males best able to provide territory, food, and protection (Alcock, 1989). As a result, males in such species compete with one another, presenting themselves as strong, hardy, and powerful. Not only do men, compared to women, invest greater effort in building upper-body muscle, but men are also able to effectively assess others' physical strength and fighting ability (Jonason, 2007; Sell et al., 2008). Like male bullfrogs, elephant seals, and baboons, an ambitious man can't afford to have others view him as weak, or else, the argument

Aspiring women want to know. Hillary Rodham Clinton is successful and powerful. What kinds of self-presentational difficulties have her achievements posed for her? Why is it so hard for her to maintain a favorable public image?

goes, he is likely to lose his assets and the opportunity to land the woman of his dreams (Sadalla, Kenrick, & Vershure, 1987).

Consistent with the biological perspective is the fact that men who have high levels of the hormone testosterone behave more aggressively toward one another and, like male members of other primate species, generally become more dominant than those who have lower levels of testosterone (Dabbs, 1996). Interestingly, women with relatively high levels of testosterone (for women) exhibit some of the same dominance-seeking and aggressive behaviors, further revealing a role for biology (Baker, Pearcey, & Dabbs, 2002; Dabbs et al., 2001).

We see, then, that biology and socialization each contribute to men's tendency to present themselves as having high status and power. Of course, this does not mean that such concerns are foreign to women. For example, there are no apparent gender differences in the human use of status artifacts or personal associations; women, as well as men, take advantage of these tactics. Indeed, women in one study were more likely than men to display nonverbal dominance behaviors in cross-sex conversations about pattern sewing, a domain where the women possessed much more expertise (Dovidio et al., 1988). In general, however, presentations of status and power are more important to men.

THE SELF-PRESENTATIONAL DILEMMA OF ASPIRING WOMEN   Women who seek positions of high status and power face special self-presentational roadblocks (Phelan & Rudman, 2010). Consider the case of Hillary Rodham Clinton, former first lady, U.S. Senator, presidential candidate, and Secretary of State. Hillary Clinton was the president of her college class. She attended an Ivy League law school, became a partner in a prestigious law firm, and was acclaimed as one of the 100 most important attorneys in the United States. She is known to commit her talents to charitable work, to be religious, and to be a loving and protective mother. Why, then, has she been so disliked by so many for so long?

Hillary Clinton's problems stem partially from her success. Women in traditionally male fields, like the law, are often penalized for doing their jobs well—perhaps even *because* they do their jobs well (Coulomb-Cabagno, Rascle, & Souchen, 2005; Heilman et al., 2004). Moreover, Clinton's communication style is direct. She is often seen as blunt and to the point, and as wasting little time on niceties. Although this style is generally acceptable (and sometimes even desirable) in achieving men, it is not as easily accepted in similarly achieving women. For instance, although men allow themselves to be influenced by direct, assertive, task-oriented men, they are les influenced by women who use this same style (Carli, 2001). Similarly, whereas assertive body language communicates status quite effectively when used by men, it is less effective when displayed by women (Henley & Harmon, 1985). And whereas expressing anger in a professional context enhances status for men, it decreases status for women (Brescoll & Uhlmann, 2008).

It seems unfair that some of the most effective power and status tactics used by men are unsuccessful when used by aspiring women. Indeed, the problem compounds itself when one considers the secondary impressions people form of women who use these tactics. Women who exhibit task-oriented or domineering styles are generally disliked, partially because they are perceived to be insufficiently nurturing and socially sensitive; these strategies are usually less costly for men (Bowles et al., 2007; Heilman & Okimoto, 2007; Rudman & Glick, 2001). Moreover, women who display high-status body language run a risk of being seen as sexually aggressive (Henley & Harmon, 1985).

These research findings suggest, then, that Hillary Clinton's assertive style, in concert with her great successes, contributes to her image among some as a stereotypical "Iron Maiden"—as a cold, conniving, abrasive female achiever (Deaux & Lewis, 1984; Heilman, Block, & Martell, 1995).

You might not be surprised that many men dislike ambitious women. You might also expect women to be different—to readily accept other women who present themselves assertively. This is often not the case, however (Parks-Stamm et al., 2008). Indeed, women sometimes derogate achieving and ambitious women *more* than do men. Why? Some research suggests that, although women are more likely to support women who promote the causes of *others*, they may be less likely than men to support women who promote *themselves* (e.g., Janoff-Bulman & Wade, 1996; Rudman, 1998).

Two points stand out. First, we see again the importance of being liked: People who are liked find it easier to achieve status and power. Second, ambitious women face much greater self-presentational hurdles than do their equally ambitious male counterparts. That women still need to hide their ambitions and successes attests to the lasting power of sex-role stereotypes.

SITUATION Threatened Images, New Resources

People are especially likely to display status and power when they perceive tangible threats to their images as powerful, high-status individuals. For instance, men who have their toughness insulted are particularly likely to respond with verbal and physical aggression (Felson, 1982). Similarly, people take more risks with their health when they're challenged to be brave and gutsy (Martin & Leary, 1999). In-line skaters, for example, often refuse to wear pads to avoid being viewed by others as "overly cautious" or "wimpy" (Williams-Avery & Mackinnon, 1996). Such challenges may also lead people to drive too fast, refuse to wear seatbelts, and drink too much at a single sitting.

INVESTIGATION

Recall the last time you saw a real fight, one involving physical violence. Who was fighting, how did it start, and what were they (really) fighting about? How do your answers to these questions relate to what you've learned so far about the self-presentation of status and power?

People are also more likely to display status and power when valuable resources become newly available. Bullfrogs do it by bellowing loudly upon discovering an unclaimed, nutrient-rich location in the marsh; siblings do it with threatening glances upon receiving from Grandma the hottest new video game; and young men do it by adopting a high-status persona when around desirable, and potentially unattached, women (e.g., Renninger, Wade, & Grammer, 2004; Roney, 2003). Indeed, these are often effective strategies. Bullfrogs and children who make the most noise will usually gain special access to the marsh and new toys, whereas men subtly playing up their status will usually attract the attentions of desirable women.

INTERACTION Different Strategies for Different Audiences

Presentations of status and power can be complex. How people attempt to create such images and even whether they make such an attempt depend partially on an interaction between the gender of the presenter and the gender of his or her audience. Men, for instance, present differently to other men than to women. Although men are particularly likely to respond aggressively when insulted in front of an audience, this self-presentational aggression is strongest when the observers are also male (Borden, 1975). In fact, female audiences often inhibit male self-presentational violence. This is not because women frown upon male displays of status and power. Indeed, women greatly value status and power in their male partners and, as a result, men boast of their professional status and height in personal ads (e.g., Cicerello & Sheehan, 1995; Deaux & Hanna, 1984; Gonzales & Meyers, 1993), purchase more charity raffle tickets when with women than when alone (Rind & Benjamin, 1994), and so forth. Instead, women are just generally less approving than men of physical aggression. Thus, although men present their status and power to both male and female audiences, they texture their tactics to fit with the different preferences of these audiences.

Quick Quiz

1 Which of the following is a strategy for conveying status and power?

    a. Associating with people of status and power

    b. Communicating dominance with nonverbal expressions

    c. Displaying artifacts of status and power

    d. All of the above

2 Wearing your favorite team's t-shirt the day after they win a big game is an example of _____, whereas removing the pro-candidate bumper sticker on your car after your chosen political candidate loses the election is an example of _____.

    a. Basking in reflected glory; social ingratiation

    b. Basking in reflected glory; cutting off reflected failure

    c. Social ingratiation; multiple audience dilemma

    d. Conspicuous consumption; social ingratiation

3 Which of the following statements is false?

    a. Women are less likely than men to respond to an insult with physical aggression.

    b. Men are better than women at gaining control over conversations and arguments.

    c. Men and women are equally likely to convey their status through conspicuous consumption.

    d. Men maintain more eye contact with an audience when speaking but pay less attention while listening.

Revisiting

The Amazing Lives of Fred Demara

By any standard, the accomplishments of Fred Demara were astounding. For more than 20 years, he lived a series of theatrical productions, reserving all the lead roles for himself: the famous, life-saving surgeon; the highly respected college professor; the courageous prison warden; and many others. He convinced thousands that he was someone he was not. But why? What motivated him to become an impostor? And what made him so successful?

The research findings presented in this chapter provide useful tools for understanding Demara's life. In the small factory town where he grew up, Demara was, in his early years, a center of attention: He was physically large, he was the son of one of the town's leading citizens, and his intellect was superior. Demara learned quickly that he was special and believed himself worthy of respect. From his father, a dapper dresser and creative showman, Demara learned a second critical lesson: Appearance matters. How early these lessons took root, we cannot know, but they were firmly established by the time his father's business went bust. Image meant so much to Demara and, in a period of just a few days—the time needed to move from the family mansion to the small hovel on the edge of town—his image was in tatters.

Demara, however, had been taught that his destiny was special, that he was the master of his own future. Rebutting the actual circumstances at home, he would show everyone—even himself—that he had "class." On the way to school each morning, he would secretly change from the practical, inexpensive workboots his mother had bought to the shiny black shoes he had surreptitiously purchased with pinched pennies. On Valentine's Day, he somehow managed to buy fancy boxed chocolates for his class. For an 11-year-old boy, his public reputation under attack and his self-concept uncertain, an excursion into self-presentation hardly seems strange. After all, who among us hasn't wanted to prove our desirability after having a relationship end, to demonstrate our competence after a work failure, or to display our toughness when mocked?

These small presentations did little to restore Demara's reputation, however. And so on the day his father finally admitted that the family would never again be rich, that they would never move back to the big house, Demara realized that his reputation in town was forever spoiled; people would never again accord him the respect he craved. So he ran away from home, seeking, perhaps, a new audience. Still, it would be a mistake to view even this action as falling outside the range of normal social conduct. After all, seeking the opportunity to create new, unspoiled images, many students choose to attend college far from home and once-poor professionals retreat to the suburbs, hoping to escape their roots.

But Demara bungled his opportunities badly. Frustrated with his training for the priesthood, he stole a car, and hating the regimentation of the army, he deserted. Demara had become a wanted man. Having a criminal record meant that he could no longer take the "Fred Demara Show" on the road. And so he took that one huge self-presentational leap that most of us would never consider and could never pull off: Demara disposed of himself, discarded his past.

In this bold choice, we see again the power of the person–situation interaction. A person with Demara's drive for public recognition but without the threat created by the failure of his father's business and the dilemma created by his crimes would probably live normally among his neighbors, recognized only for his abilities and slightly inflated ego. A person confronted with Demara's family failure and criminal predicament but without his great need to be respected would probably hide himself from others, living unobtrusively on the run. These factors converged, however, in Demara, and from them emerged someone unique—the Great Impostor.

At this fork in Demara's road it becomes too easy to pass off his actions as aberrational, as the dysfunctional behaviors of some self-presentational freak. What can a closer look at Demara possibly tell us about *ourselves*, we wonder? Plenty. We all share with Demara not only similar presentational goals—to appear likable, to appear competent, and to convey status and power—but also similar ways of creating these desired images. Indeed, Demara's great success as an impostor was rooted in his skillful use of *common* presentational strategies. When he wanted to be liked, he would flatter others, adjust his opinions, make himself attractive, and display a dignified modesty. When he wanted people to respect his talents, he would work hard, stage performances, and get others to boast for him. And when he wanted others to respect his status, he would dress the part, surround himself with worldly objects, associate himself with high-status others, and carry himself with poise and dignity. These are precisely the self-presentational tactics we use to manage the impressions others have of us.

Demara was expert in the everyday tactics of self-presentation, and so we see in his life many lessons on how to manage one's reputation successfully. But we also see the costs. As an impostor, Demara was constantly afraid of making a mistake, of saying something that could cause his whole edifice of deception to crumble. He was also painfully aware that he was a fraud. Perhaps worse, he had begun to lose himself: "Every time I take a new identity, some part of the real me dies, whatever the real me is" (Crichton, 1959, p. 10).

In Demara's journey, then, we see much of what science has taught us about why and how people present themselves as they do. Like Demara, most of us care deeply about how others view us. Like Demara, we often find ourselves in circumstances that threaten our desired reputations. Like Demara, we reach into our oft-used presentational bag of tricks when people don't view us the way we want to be viewed. And like Demara, we fear the costs of undesired reputations. It seems fair to say that there's just a bit of Demara in each of us.

In studying Demara's journey, we see some of social psychology's many bridges to other disciplines. For instance, how people come across to others at work greatly influences their levels of success and accomplishment; not surprisingly, then, those hoping to understand management processes and organizational behavior have imported much of what social psychologists have learned about self-presentation. Similarly, marketing and communication researchers and practitioners have leveraged many of the findings we've explored here to sell their products and ideas. We've also seen bridges to biology and animal behavior (e.g., the dominance and submissiveness displays of humans exhibit striking similarities to those of many other animals), to medical practice (e.g., a large portion of the specialty of plastic surgery is fundamentally driven by patients' self-presentational desires), and to health and disease (e.g., a range of behaviors designed to make one more desirable—for instance, sunbathing and taking steroids—can have devastating health consequences). As social beings we want to impress others, so it's not surprising the social psychology of self-presentation bridges to many different disciplines.

Ferdinand Waldo Demara Jr. died of heart failure at the age of 60. The many obituaries published nationwide noted that he had lived under his own name for almost 23 years, trying, it seemed, to make up for his past. Returning to his religious roots, he had worked at youth camps, a rescue mission for the poor, and as a bona fide Baptist minister and hospital chaplain. We suspect that, of all people, Demara would have found comfort in the knowledge that his final reviews were favorable.

Chapter Summary

Summary of the Goals Served by Self-Presentation and the Factors Related to Them

The Goal	Person	Situation	Interaction
Appearing likable	• Gender	• Audiences of potential friends • Audiences of power-holders	• The values held by multiple audiences interact to influence how people get others to like them. If everyone in the audience holds the same values, people can readily sculpt their self-presentations to conform with them. When the audience is composed of people having differing and incompatible values, however, more creative ingratiation tactics become necessary.

The Goal	Person	Situation	Interaction
Appearing competent	• Competence motivation • Shyness	• Competence settings • Impending or actual failure	• Compared to shy people, socially confident individuals promote themselves in exaggerated ways after their public reputation for competence has been shaken by failure but not if their true competence can be easily checked by others. • Self-promoters can create an environment in which others feel compelled to self-promote.
Conveying status and power	• Gender	• Image threat • Availability of unclaimed resources	• The gender of the presenter interacts with the gender of the audience to determine which tactics work best to convey images of status and power. Men typically use more direct, physical tactics when presenting to men than to women.

What Is Self-Presentation?

1. Self-presentation, sometimes called impression management, is the process through which we try to control the impressions people form of us.
2. We self-present to acquire desirable resources, to help "construct" our self-images, and to enable our social encounters to run more smoothly.
3. We are more likely to focus on self-presentation when we think others are paying attention to us, when they can influence whether we reach our goals, when these goals are important to us, and when we think these observers have impressions of us different from the ones we desire.
4. Some people are more likely to self-present than are others. Although people generally overestimate the extent to which they're in the public eye (the spotlight effect), individuals who are high in public self-consciousness are especially aware of how they are coming across to others. People who are high self-monitors care about how others view them and often adjust their actions to fit the behaviors of the people around them.
5. Self-presentation is sometimes deceptive, but usually not. Instead, our self-presentations typically focus on emphasizing our strengths and minimizing our weaknesses.
6. Because liars threaten the trust needed to maintain social relationships, people often go to great lengths to detect them. Unfortunately, people are mediocre lie detectors at best. Polygraph exams don't fare much better.

Appearing Likable

1. Perhaps more than any other self-presentational goal, we want others to like us.
2. To create an image of likability, we may express our liking for others, using both verbal flattery and nonverbal behaviors such as smiling; point out or create similarities with others; make ourselves physically attractive; and act modestly.
3. Women, more than men, focus on getting others to like them.

4. We are generally interested in being liked by people with whom we want to start or maintain a friendship and by people who are in positions of power.
5. We sometimes find ourselves in circumstances in which we want to be liked by multiple audiences, who differ in what they value. These multiple audience dilemmas are difficult, and we try to manage them by segregating the audiences, moderating our presentations, presenting different messages on different communication channels, or texturing messages so they mean different things to the different audiences.

Appearing Competent

1. We frequently want others to view us as competent.
2. To create an image of competence, we may stage performances so that others have an opportunity to view our skills and abilities, make verbal claims of competence, surround ourselves with the trappings of competence, and make excuses for our failures or claim obstacles to possible success. People may even self-handicap by withdrawing effort or placing real obstacles in the way of future successes.
3. People high in competence motivation are especially concerned with how they come across in public. Shy people are less likely than nonshy individuals to engage in bold self-promotion.
4. Competitive settings such as workplaces, classrooms, and athletic fields often increase our desires to appear competent.
5. Recent failures increase the desire to appear competent.
6. Compared to shy people, socially confident individuals are especially likely to promote themselves in exaggerated ways after their public reputations for competence have been shaken by failure, but not if their true competence can be easily checked by others. Also, self-promoters often create a social environment in which others feel compelled to self-promote.

Conveying Status and Power

1. We sometimes want others to view us as having status and power.
2. To create an image of status and power, we may display the artifacts of status and power, conspicuously consume material resources, associate ourselves with others who already possess status and power, use body language to convey status and power, and even behave aggressively.
3. Men, more than women, focus on presenting themselves as having status and power.
4. Women face an especially difficult self-presentational dilemma: When presenting their status and power, they are frequently disliked by both men and women.
5. People try to present themselves as having status and power when their images are threatened and when newly available resources lie unclaimed.
6. The gender of the presenter interacts with the gender of the audience to determine which tactics work best to convey images of status and power. Men typically use more direct, physical tactics when presenting to men than to women.

Key Terms

Basking in reflected glory, 130

Body language, 130

Competence motivation, 125

Cutting off reflected failure, 130

Dramaturgical perspective, 106

Ingratiation, 113

Multiple audience dilemma, 120

Public self-consciousness, 108

Self-handicapping, 124

Self-monitoring, 109

Self-presentation, 105

Self-promotion, 122

Shyness, 125

Social anxiety, 110

Chapter 5

Attitudes and Persuasion

Outline

Learning Objectives

LO 5.1 Describe the four sources of attitude formation.

LO 5.2 Identify the two components of a strong attitude that make it resistant to change.

LO 5.3 Summarize the factors that influence attitude–behavior consistency.

LO 5.4 Define persuasion and understand how attitude change is measured.

LO 5.5 Explain the cognitive response model and the significance of self-talk.

LO 5.6 Compare the two basic kinds of attitude change processes within the dual process models of persuasion.

LO 5.7 Identify and explain the three sources of shortcut evidence that people often use when trying to hold accurate attitudes.

LO 5.8 Understand the circumstances under which people are most motivated to hold accurate views.

LO 5.9 Describe the factors that push people to hold less accurate views.

LO 5.10 Explain balance theory and cognitive dissonance theory.

LO 5.11 Summarize the factors that affect our desire for cognitive consistency.

LO 5.12 Discuss how Western and Eastern cultures differ in their preference for consistency.

LO 5.13 Compare high self-monitors to low self-monitors.

LO 5.14 Identify how men and women differ in opinion change when they desire social approval.

LO 5.15 Explain how the expectation of discussion with another person can affect persuasion.

The Changing Story of Peter Reilly

In 1973, an 18-year-old Peter Reilly returned home after an evening church meeting to find his mother lying on the floor, murdered. Though reeling from the sight, he had the presence of mind to phone for help immediately.

At five feet seven inches and 121 pounds and with not a speck of blood on his body, clothes, or shoes, Peter Reilly seemed an unlikely killer. Yet from the start, when they found him staring blankly outside the room where his mother lay dead, the police suspected that Reilly was responsible for her murder. The reason for that suspicion had less to do with what they knew about him than with what they knew about the victim. She took delight in irritating the people she met—men especially—belittling, confronting, and challenging them. By any measure, she was a difficult woman to get along with. Thus, it did not seem unreasonable to police officials that Reilly, fed up with his mother's constant antagonisms, would fly off the handle and slaughter her in a spasm of rage.

At the scene and even when taken in for questioning, Reilly waived his right to an attorney, thinking that if he told the truth, he would be believed and released in short order. That was a serious miscalculation. Over a period of 16 hours, he was interrogated by a rotating team of four police officers, including a polygraph operator who confidently informed Reilly that, according to the lie detector, he had killed his mother. The chief interrogator told Reilly, falsely, that additional evidence proving his guilt had been obtained. He also suggested to the boy how he could have done the crime without remembering any such thing: Reilly had become furious with his mother, had erupted into a murderous fit during which he slaughtered her, and now had repressed the horrible memory. It was their job,

If you admit, we won't acquit. Police interrogators used powerful principles of social influence to get Peter Reilly to admit to a heinous crime (despite the fact that later evidence suggested strongly that he was completely innocent).

Reilly's and the interrogator's, to "dig, dig, dig" at the boy's subconscious until the memory was recovered.

Dig, dig, dig they did, exploring every way to bring that memory to the surface, until Reilly did begin to recall—dimly at first but then more vividly—slashing his mother's throat and stomping on her body. Analyzing, reanalyzing, and reviewing these images convinced him that they betrayed his guilt. Along with his interrogators, who pressed him relentlessly to break through his "mental block," Reilly pieced together from the scenes in his head an account of his actions that fit the details of the murder. Finally, a little more than 24 hours after the grisly crime, though still uncertain of many specifics, Peter Reilly formally confessed in a signed, written statement. That statement conformed closely to the explanation that had been proposed by his interrogators and that he had come to accept as accurate—even though he believed none of it at the outset of his questioning and even though, as later events demonstrated, none of it was true.

When Reilly awoke in a jail cell the next day, with the awful fatigue and the persuasive onslaught of the interrogation room gone, he no longer believed his confession. Like the victims of high-pressure sales tactics who find that they no longer want their purchase once the salesperson has gone, Reilly found that when his interrogators left, he no longer wanted the confession they'd "sold" him. But he couldn't retract it convincingly. To almost every official in the criminal justice system, the confession remained compelling evidence of his guilt: A judge rejected a motion to suppress it at Reilly's trial, ruling it voluntarily made; the police were so satisfied that it incriminated Reilly that they stopped considering other suspects; the prosecuting attorneys made it the centerpiece of their case; and the jury members who ultimately convicted Reilly of killing his mother relied on it heavily in their deliberations.

As is the case in many such instances (Kassin, 2008), these individuals did not believe that a normal person could be made to confess falsely to a crime without the use of threats, violence, or torture. But they were wrong: Two years later, evidence was found hidden in the chief prosecutor's files that placed Reilly at a time and in a location on the night of the crime that established his innocence and that led to the repeal of his conviction and to the dismissal of all charges.

Through what mysterious methods and extraordinary circumstances could the police convince a wholly innocent man of his guilt? The methods were not so mysterious nor the circumstances so extraordinary. In fact, they embodied the features of everyday persuasion—the kind of persuasion you are exposed to hundreds of times a day (Davis & Leo, 2006). Some persuasion attempts occur in conversations with friends and acquaintances; others appear on billboards or in radio, magazine, or television ads; still others ambush you on the Internet (Mandel & Johnson, 2002). In the remainder of this chapter, we consider how those appeals can generate attitude and belief change, how that change can be measured, and what goals are served by the change.

By far, the majority of persuasion research has focused on attitude change. So, before beginning our exploration of how they are changed, let's examine the nature of attitudes.

The Nature of Attitudes

LO 5.1   Describe the four sources of attitude formation.

LO 5.2   Identify the two components of a strong attitude that make it resistant to change.

LO 5.3   Summarize the factors that influence attitude–behavior consistency.

As we noted in Chapter 2, **attitudes** are positive or negative evaluations of particular things. But how are they formed in the first place? What makes them strong or weak? And to what extent do they predict behavior? Let's start at the beginning with the topic of attitude formation.

Attitude A favorable or unfavorable evaluation of a particular thing.

Attitude Formation

Where do attitudes come from? They spring from several sources.

CLASSICAL CONDITIONING   Through the process of classical conditioning, we come to like or dislike new objects or events merely because they are associated with objects or events we already like or dislike. For instance, when we associate people with something positive—like receiving good news—we like them more, even though they didn't cause the good news (Manis, Cornell, & Moore, 1974). Conversely, when we associate people with something negative—like being with them in a hot, humid room—we like them less (Griffitt, 1970). Even associations of which we are unaware can shape our attitudes (Gibson, 2008; Olson & Fazio, 2002). In one study, students viewed a series of slides of a woman going about her daily routine and were asked to form an impression of her. Just before each slide presentation, however, they were subliminally exposed to photos of either positive or negative objects (e.g., a bridal couple, a bloody shark). As expected, students exposed to the positive photographs formed a more favorable attitude toward the woman in the slides (Krosnick et al., 1992).

OPERANT CONDITIONING   Through the process of operant conditioning, people learn by being rewarded or punished. Operant conditioning is an important source of our attitudes. In one experiment, students at the University of Hawaii were contacted by phone and surveyed about their attitudes toward the creation of a Springtime Aloha Week. Half the students were rewarded whenever they expressed a favorable attitude toward the idea; the interviewer said "good" each time a student's views supported the event. The remaining students were rewarded with a "good" each time they expressed an unfavorable attitude. One week later, all students completed a questionnaire on local issues, and buried within the questionnaire was an item assessing their feelings toward Springtime Aloha Week. As expected, students previously rewarded for favoring the event expressed more positive attitudes toward it than did students rewarded for opposing it (Insko, 1965). Recent brain-imaging research shows that, like the classical conditioning of attitudes, the operant conditioning of attitudes can also occur without awareness (Pessiglione et al., 2008).

OBSERVATIONAL LEARNING   We do not need to experience rewards and punishments firsthand to learn lessons from them. Instead, we often learn by observing others. When we see others punished, we learn to avoid their behaviors and attitudes. When we see others rewarded, we engage in those behaviors and adopt their attitudes. For instance, children with fearful feelings toward dogs became significantly more positive toward them after simply watching movie clips of other children enjoying their interactions with a variety of dogs (Bandura & Menlove, 1968).

HEREDITY   Psychologists once assumed that attitudes developed exclusively through the learning process. Although it is undeniably true that experience plays a role, more recent evidence indicates that there is also an unlearned, genetic component to many attitudes, such as those involving political and religious issues (Brandt & Wetherell, 2012; Olson et al., 2001). For instance, attitudes toward the death penalty or censorship are much more likely to be influenced by heredity than are attitudes toward teenage drivers or the wisdom of learning Latin (Alford et al., 2005). Research by Abraham Tesser (1993) indicates that these genetically influenced attitudes are particularly strong and influential in social life. Not only can people tell you more quickly what they prefer on these issues, they are more likely to resist your attempts to change them, and they will dislike you more if you hold an opposing position on these issues.

Attitude Strength

Not all attitudes are equally strong. Why should we care whether an attitude is strong or weak? One reason is that strong attitudes accurately predict behavior, such as who will register to vote in a presidential election (Farc & Sagarin, 2009). A second reason is that strong attitudes resist change (Bassili, 1996; Visser & Mirabile, 2004). This is true in two senses. First, strong attitudes are more stable than weaker ones; they are more likely to remain unchanged as time passes. Second, strong attitudes are better able to withstand persuasive attacks. Let's say you now hold a strong attitude toward gun control. Not only is your attitude likely to be the same next month, but also if someone tried to change your mind on the issue at that point, you would probably not be influenced.

What are the components of a strong attitude that make it unlikely to change? Research by Eva Pomeranz, Shelly Chaiken, and Rosalind Tordesillas (1995) suggests two main reasons to show that strong attitudes resist change: *commitment* and *embeddedness*.

People are more *committed* to a strongly held attitude. That is, they are more certain that it is correct (Petrocelli et al., 2007; Tormala & Petty, 2002). In addition, a strongly held attitude is more *embedded in* (connected to) other features of the person, such as the individual's self-concept, values, and social identity (Boninger, Krosnick, & Berent, 1995). For example, officers of the National Rifle Association are both committed to an antigun control position and typically make that position a central part of their social identities. Consequently, they are unlikely to change their attitudes on this topic.

So both commitment and embeddedness make strong attitudes more resistant to change (Visser & Krosnick, 1998). But, they do so in different ways (see Figure 5.1). Being committed to a particular attitude causes people to review relevant information

Figure 5.1 Why strong attitudes resist change

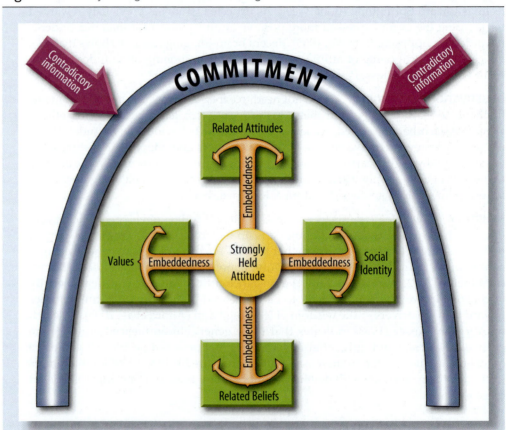

Commitment—one quality of strong attitudes—shields attitudes against contradictory information, whereas embeddedness—a second quality of strong attitudes—anchors them to a variety of other change-resistant features of the self.

in a biased fashion and to intensify their opinions. All this leads them to dismiss evidence that goes against their initial attitude. For example, in one experiment, participants who already had strong attitudes about capital punishment were shown an essay and a research study that opposed their position on the issue. They reacted by rejecting this information, deciding that the essay's arguments were weak and the study's methods were flawed (Pomeranz, Chaiken, & Tordesillas, 1995).

Embeddedness restricted change in another way—by simply tying the attitude to so many other features of the person (beliefs, values, additional attitudes) that it became difficult to move in any direction. That is, because changing an embedded attitude would mean changing all sorts of other aspects of the self, people are reluctant to undertake the process (O'Brian & Jacks, 2000).

On the surface, the evidence that people are unlikely to change strong attitudes and beliefs makes the phenomenon of persuaded false confessions—such as Peter Reilly's—even more mystifying. Surely, a blameless person has strongly held attitudes and beliefs regarding his or her own innocence. Indeed, because this is the case, experienced criminal interrogators typically do not try to attack such a belief directly until they have first weakened it.

A favorite tactic used to weaken a belief of innocence is to convince suspects that they don't remember doing the deed because they were powerfully affected by alcohol or drugs or, in the case of Peter Reilly, a blind rage, while performing it (Leo, 2008). During his interrogation, Reilly reported being greatly alarmed by the idea—planted well before the interrogation began—that he could have suppressed the memory of the murder of his mother, because that idea sent the first tremors of self-doubt through him.

This tactic works so well for interrogators because it undercuts both of the aspects of strong attitudes and beliefs that resist change. First, it reduces suspects' commitment to their innocence by undermining the certainty of their belief in that innocence: Suspects cannot be sure that they haven't perpetrated the crime if it is possible that they don't remember it. Second, the tactic decreases the embeddedness of the belief by unhooking the crime from the self-concept of the person who committed it: The view of oneself as someone who could not have done such a thing simply does not apply if it was the alcohol or drugs or blind rage that did it.

Attitude–Behavior Consistency

To what extent does your attitude toward gun control affect your behavior with regard to gun control legislation? Although it sounds like a simple question, it's more complicated than you might think. Several factors influence the likelihood that a person's attitude will be consistent with his or her behavior.

KNOWLEDGE   The more knowledge we have about something, the more likely it is that our pertinent attitudes and actions will be consistent with one another (Kallgren & Wood, 1986; Wyer, 2008). Therefore, the more you know about gun control laws, the greater the chance that your evaluation of such laws will predict your conduct in support of or in opposition to them. In addition, if you came to this greater knowledge through direct contact with the effects of the laws—perhaps you were harmed (or rescued) by someone with a gun—your attitude would be even more predictive of your behaviors toward these laws, as firsthand experience creates stronger attitude–behavior consistency than does secondhand exposure (Glasman & Albarracin, 2006; Millar & Millar, 1996). So, two aspects of knowledge intensify the link between attitudes and related actions—the *amount* of knowledge acquired on the subject and the *direct (versus indirect) nature* of the knowledge (Davidson et al., 1985).

PERSONAL RELEVANCE   When government officials proposed raising the legal drinking age from 18 to 21, nearly all the students at Michigan State were opposed to the plan. Yet, when asked to act consistently with their negative attitudes by campaigning against the proposal, those who were under 20 (and, consequently, would be personally affected by the new law) were much more likely to volunteer (Sivacek & Crano,

1982). This result fits with many others indicating that one's attitude on a topic will be a better predictor of one's deeds when the topic is personally relevant (Leary et al., 2011; Lehman & Crano, 2002). Therefore, your attitude toward gun control legislation would be more likely to govern your actions if someone close to you was thinking of purchasing a gun.

ATTITUDE ACCESSIBILITY   An attitude is accessible to the degree that it springs to mind quickly. And, a highly accessible attitude is likely to stimulate actions that are consistent with it (Glasman & Albarracin, 2006). To demonstrate this point in a political campaign, Russell Fazio and Carol Williams (1986) asked potential voters to express their attitudes toward then presidential candidates Ronald Reagan and Walter Mondale by pressing keys on a handheld recording device. The speed with which the citizens began punching in their responses was the measure of attitude accessibility. Although this measure was taken during the summer of the 1984 presidential race, the researchers didn't assess consistent behavior until immediately after Election Day (November 4th) when they phoned participants to ask how they voted. Remarkably, the quicker participants had indicated their preferences in June and July, the more likely they were to act in line with those preferences in the voting booth four to five months later. In like manner, if you asked each of your friends about their attitudes toward gun control laws, you should be able to tell which of them would act consistently with their responses by judging how quickly they offered those responses.

BEHAVIORAL INTENTIONS   Your attitude is likely to be consistent with your behavior when that attitude is also consistent with your intentions to act. In fact, Icek Ajzen and Martin Fishbein claim that attitudes influence action by first influencing a person's *behavioral intentions* (specific aims to act in a certain way) and that these intentions

Figure 5.2   The theory of planned behavior

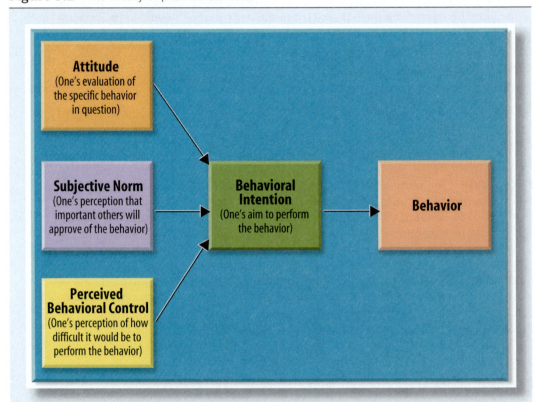

According to this theory, attitudes aren't the best predictors of behavior; behavioral intentions are. However, these intentions are influenced by attitudes as well as by subjective norms and perceived behavioral control.

are more likely than the attitudes themselves to predict behavior. Of course, attitudes aren't the only factors that influence actions. In their *theory of reasoned action* (Fishbein & Ajzen, 1975) and in a modified version called the **theory of planned behavior** (Ajzen, 2011; McLachlan & Hagger, 2011), these researchers identified two additional factors (besides attitudes) said to influence behavior through their impact on behavioral intentions. First is what they called *subjective norms*, which refer to a person's perception that important others would approve or disapprove of the behavior in question. For example, your intention to campaign for changes in gun control laws should be influenced by your view that the important people in your life would respect or disrespect you as a result. The second additional factor is *perceived behavioral control*, which refers to a person's perception of how difficult it is to perform the behavior in question. Even if you'd really like to campaign for gun control changes (attitude) and even if the significant people in your life would respect you for it (subjective norm), you probably wouldn't intend to do it if time limitations or other circumstances made it seem unrealistic. Quite a lot of research has supported the theory (see Figure 5.2), especially for behaviors that require deliberation and planning (Albarracin et al., 2001; Armitage & Connor, 2001).

Quick Quiz

1. Which of the following statements is false?
   a. People can learn to hold attitudes by being rewarded or punished.
   b. There is a genetic component to many attitudes, including those related to political and religious issues.
   c. Unlike classical conditioning, operant conditioning cannot occur without conscious awareness.
   d. Classical conditioning is a process in which we come to like or dislike new objects or events because we associate them with other objects or events we already like or dislike.

2. _____ makes strong attitudes more resistant to change by tying the attitude to multiple features of the person, whereas _____ makes strong attitudes more resistant to change by leading people to evaluate relevant information in a biased fashion.
   a. Consistency, commitment
   b. Embeddedness, commitment
   c. Commitment, embeddedness
   d. Consistency, embeddedness

3. Which of the following factors *increase* the likelihood that a person's attitude will be consistent with his or her behavior?
   a. Low attitude accessibility
   b. Low personal relevance
   c. Indirect knowledge
   d. None of the above

What Is Persuasion?

LO 5.4 Define persuasion and understand how attitude change is measured.

LO 5.5 Explain the cognitive response model and the significance of self-talk.

LO 5.6 Compare the two basic kinds of attitude change processes within the dual process models of persuasion.

If we are to blame the persuasion process for Peter Reilly's false confession, we had best establish what we mean by the concept. Although social scientists have defined **persuasion** in a variety of ways, we view it as change in a *private* attitude or belief resulting from the receipt of a message. As we discussed in Chapter 2, *attitudes* are favorable or unfavorable evaluations of particular things. *Beliefs*, in contrast, are thoughts (cognitions) about these things. In this chapter, we will examine how both can be changed through the persuasion process.

Theory of planned behavior A theory stating that the best predictor of a behavior is one's behavioral intention, which is influenced by one's attitude toward the specific behavior, the subjective norms regarding the behavior, and one's perceived control over the behavior.

Persuasion Change in a private attitude or belief as a result of receiving a message.

Our efforts will be aided greatly by a large body of research into the factors that make for an effective persuasive message. Indeed, beginning in earnest with government information and propaganda programs enacted during World War II (Hovland et al., 1949; Stouffer et al., 1949), social psychologists have been studying the persuasion process for over half a century. As a result, social psychologists often hold positions in advertising and marketing firms.

Measuring Attitude Change

Clever persuaders have developed many techniques for changing attitudes and beliefs, even initially strong ones. In the process of trying to understand whether and when these various techniques are effective, researchers have had to confront the knotty question of how to measure persuasion accurately. After all, we can't claim a persuasion tactic works if we can't tell how much change it creates. And correctly measuring change is often no simple task. You've no doubt recognized that your actions change if someone is recording them. Of course, scientists studying persuasion want to record it in its truest, least altered form. Consequently, they frequently rely on certain proven methods for reducing the impact of the act of measurement on their data.

We briefly discussed one such method in Chapter 2, in which we described how researchers sometimes measure attitudes unobtrusively (covertly), without asking subjects to give self-reports of these attitudes. In these cases, the researcher judges the attitude in question by simply observing an attitude-relevant behavior. For instance, Cialdini and Baumann (1981) were able to predict the outcome of a presidential election by observing the littering of campaign ads. Voters at the polls were less likely to litter flyers they found on the windshields of their cars if the flyers' message supported their favored candidate. In fact, before official voting totals were announced, this measure correctly predicted the winner at all nine voting locations where it was used.

In general, researchers have found that these covert techniques are more accurate than self-report measures only when people have a good reason to be less than honest about their true feelings—for example, when they want to appear more fair-minded or unprejudiced than they actually are (Fazio et al., 1995; Nowicki & Manheim,

Pervasive persuasion. Persuasive appeals are everywhere in our daily lives.

1991). Under these circumstances, covert techniques are preferred because they are a more **nonreactive measurement** than are self-reports; that is, using them to record a response is less likely to distort the response. When there is no good reason for people to hide their feelings, however, self-reports are usually preferred because they inquire about attitudes more directly (Dunton & Fazio, 1997).

Cognitive Responses: Self-Talk Persuades

Early approaches to attitude change emphasized the importance of the message itself—its clarity, logic, memorability, and so on—because researchers believed that the target's comprehension and learning of the message content were critical to persuasion (Hovland et al., 1953; McGuire, 1966). Although this is often true, Anthony Greenwald's (1968) **cognitive response model** of persuasion offered a subtle but critical shift in thinking about attitude change. Greenwald proposed that the best indication of how much change a communicator will produce lies not in what the communicator says to the persuasion target but, rather, in what the target says to him- or herself as a result of receiving the communication. According to this model, the message is not directly responsible for change. Instead, the direct cause is the *self-talk*—the internal cognitive responses or thinking—people engage in after being exposed to the message. A great deal of research supports the model by showing that persuasion is powerfully affected by the amount of self-talk that occurs in response to a message (Eagly & Chaiken, 1993), by the degree to which the self-talk supports the message (Killeya & Johnson, 1998), and by the confidence that recipients express in the validity of that self-talk (Petty, Briñol, & Tormala, 2002).

POSITIVE SELF-TALK   Suppose that you belong to a group that wants to save lives by reducing the speed limit on state highways and that you have been assigned the job of writing a persuasive letter on this issue that will be mailed to all the citizens of your town. Does the cognitive response model have implications for the way you might fashion a persuasive attempt? A key implication is that you ought to consider what your audience members are likely say to themselves in response to your arguments. You want to find ways to stimulate positive cognitive responses to your message.

This means that besides considering features of your intended message (e.g., the strength and logic of the arguments), you should take into account an entirely different set of factors that are likely to enhance positive cognitive responses to your message. For instance, you may want to delay your message until your local newspaper reports a rash of highway speeding deaths; that way, when your message will gain validity in the minds of the recipients because it will fit with prominent other information (Anderson, 1991; van der Plight & Eiser, 1984). Or you might want to increase the favorability of cognitive responses to your letter by printing the message professionally on high-quality paper, because people assume that the more care and expense a communicator has put into a persuasion campaign, the more the communicator believes in its validity (Kirmani, 1990; Kirmani & Wright, 1989).

COUNTERARGUMENTS   Besides trying to ensure that your message creates positive cognitive responses in your audience members, you should also think about how to avoid negative cognitive responses—especially **counterarguments**, which weaken the impact of a persuasive message by arguing against it (Bernard, Maio, & Olson, 2003). Indeed, when Julia Jacks and Kimberly Cameron (2003) tried to change attitudes toward the death penalty, they found counterarguing to be the most frequent and effective tactic their subjects used to resist persuasion. Thus, you might want to include in your letter a quotation from a traffic safety expert asserting that higher speed limits increase automobile fatalities because, typically, people generate fewer counterarguments against a position if they learn that an expert holds it (Sternthal, Dholakia, & Leavitt, 1978). Other tactics for reducing counterarguing

Nonreactive measurement Measurement that does not change a subject's responses while recording them.

Cognitive response model A theory that locates the most direct cause of persuasion in the self-talk of the persuasion target.

Counterargument An argument that challenges and opposes other arguments.

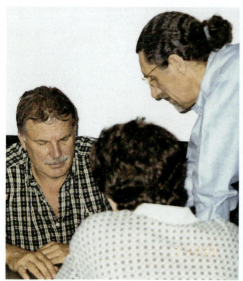

Exhaustive questioning. Pushing suspects to defend themselves when they are physically and cognitively depleted is a notorious practice among some criminal interrogators.

have also proven effective: Giving audience members little time to formulate counterarguments or giving them distracting or overburdening tasks that drain their ability to counterargue makes audience members more susceptible to persuasion (Burkley, 2008; Romero et al., 1996). In one study, subjects who could not counterargue (because their cognitive capacities were overburdened by a taxing task) were persuaded by information even though they knew the information was false (Gilbert, Tafarodi, & Malone, 1993).

Peter Reilly's interrogators employed each of these tactics to persuade a wholly innocent young man that he was a murderer. First, Reilly was informed that the polygraph operator was an expert in his field and that the polygraph machine could not be wrong in implicating him.

Reilly: Does that actually read my brain?
Polygraph operator: Definitely. Definitely.
Reilly: Would it definitely be me? Could it have been someone else?
Polygraph operator: No way from these reactions.

In fact, as we discussed in Chapter 4, the results of polygraph examinations are far from infallible, even in the hands of practiced operators; because of their unreliability, they are banned as evidence in the courts of many states and countries (Gudjonsson, 2003).

Second, Reilly was never given the time to form counterarguments to the theories and accusations of guilt directed at him incessantly during eight consecutive hours of interrogation; a tag-team of four interrogators took turns peppering him in rapid succession with questions, allegations, and denunciations. Third, even if he had been afforded the time to generate counterarguments, events before the interrogation had probably drained him of the ability to do so: At the start of formal questioning, he was mentally and emotionally spent and hadn't eaten or slept in 24 hours. During the interrogation, the police ignored Reilly's repeated claims that he was exhausted and unable to think straight.

In sum, the same counterargument-suppressing factors that have increased persuasion in scientific research—communicator expertise and insufficient time and ability to formulate counterarguments—were used by Peter Reilly's interrogators. Peter eventually came to believe their message, even though he knew it to be false at the time. Such miscarriages of justice are far from unique to the Reilly case. They occur regularly, frequently, and via the same interrogation practices (Bennett, 2005; Leo, 2008).

INVESTIGATION

If you were accused of a crime you didn't commit, what would you do to avoid what happened to Peter Reilly?

....

DEFEATING A MESSAGE THROUGH INOCULATION AND COUNTERARGUING   Factors that stimulate counterarguing decrease persuasion (Bernard, Maio, & Olson, 2003; Bizer, Larsen, & Petty, 2011). You can use this fact to neutralize an opponent's message. One clever way to stimulate counterarguing in an audience is to send an unconvincing message favoring your opponent's position, which will cause the audience to think of all sorts of arguments against that rival position. Then, when your opponent delivers a stronger version of his or her message, the audience will already have a set of counterarguments to attack it. William McGuire (1964) named this the **inoculation procedure**—because of its similarity to disease inoculation procedures in which a weakened form of a virus is injected into healthy individuals.

You might use this technique in your campaign to reduce highway speed limits by including in your persuasive letter a few of your opponents' weaker arguments

Inoculation procedure A technique for increasing individuals' resistance to a strong argument by first giving them weak, easily defeated versions of it.

(e.g., "in some countries, they don't even have speed limits") and asking recipients to consider the validity of those arguments. This should lead recipients to develop counterarguments against your opponents' view and should protect them from stronger attacks by your rivals.

Although the inoculation procedure offers an ingenious and effective approach (Eagly & Chaiken, 1993), by far the most common tactic for reducing the persuasiveness of an opponent's message is simply to give audience members direct counterarguments against the strongest versions of that message. In the advertising arena, this tactic can be highly effective, as we will see in the following section.

Bridging Theory and Application:

Smoking the Tobacco Companies with Counterarguments

Something extraordinary happened on July 22, 1969, during U.S. congressional hearings on tobacco regulation: Representatives of the tobacco industry argued vigorously in favor of a proposal to ban all advertising of their own products on radio and television. The unexpected tobacco company support for the ban enabled legislation that has prohibited tobacco advertising on the airwaves in the United States since 1971.

What could account for this unprecedented action on the part of Big Tobacco? Could it be that company executives became concerned about the health of the nation? Hardly. They didn't reduce their intensive ad campaign for smokers after the ban. They simply shifted their advertising dollars from the airwaves to other places such as magazines, sports sponsorships, promotional giveaways, and movie product placements. For example, secret documents of one tobacco firm included a letter from movie actor/director Sylvester Stallone agreeing to use its cigarettes in several films in return for $500,000 (Massing, 1996).

So it was only on the airwaves that the tobacco industry wanted to bar the advertising of its products. But this deepens

the mystery of their motives even further: In the year they proposed the ban, tobacco executives had been spending four out of five advertising dollars on television because advertisers recognized it as "by far the most effective way to reach people, especially young people" (L. C. White, 1988, p. 145). What could have made them want to abandon their most persuasive route to new customers?

The answer lies in something equally remarkable that occurred two years earlier: Against all odds, a young attorney named John Banzhaf successfully argued to the Federal Communications Commission (FCC) that it should apply its "fairness doctrine" to the issue of tobacco advertising. The fairness doctrine acknowledged the power and importance of counterargument in a free society by requiring that when positions on controversial topics of public importance are broadcast, free air time must be made available to citizens wishing to state opposing views. The FCC's ruling made an enormous difference, allowing antitobacco forces such as the American Cancer Society to air ads that punctured and parodied the tobacco ads' images of health, attractiveness, and rugged independence—often by satirizing the tobacco companies' own ads and showing that, in truth, tobacco use led to ill health, damaged attractiveness, and dependence. In one counterad, tough Marlboro Man-like characters were rendered weak and helpless by spasms of hacking, wheezing, and coughing.

The tobacco industry reacted predictably by increasing its television advertising budgets to meet this new challenge, but to no avail—because, by the rules of the fairness doctrine, the more ads they ran, the more time had to be given to the counterarguing messages.

When the logic of the situation finally hit them, the tobacco companies maneuvered masterfully. They supported a ban on the advertising of their products on the air—*only* on the air—where the fairness doctrine applied. With these ads prohibited, the antitobacco forces could no longer receive free air time for their counterads. In the first year after the ban on tobacco ads went into effect, cigarette consumption in the United States jumped more than 3%, even though the tobacco companies were able to reduce their advertising expenditures by 30% (Fritschler, 1975; McAlister et al., 1989).

Coughing up the truth. Counterarguments like this one can be very effective against the persuasive appeals of tobacco companies.

Tobacco opponents found that they could use counterarguments to undercut tobacco ad effectiveness. But the tobacco executives learned (and profited from) a related lesson: One of the best way to reduce resistance to a message is to reduce the availability of counterarguments to it. Of course, the counterarguments that people have at their disposal don't come only from others. People are sometimes spurred to think about a message and to generate their own counterarguments (Albarracin & Mitchell, 2004). When they are willing and able to do so is the topic of the next section.

Dual Process Models of Persuasion: Two Routes to Change

Dual process model of persuasion
A model that accounts for the two basic ways that attitude change occurs—with and without much thought.

Elaboration likelihood model A model of persuasive communication that holds that there are two routes to attitude change—the central route and the peripheral route.

Central route to persuasion The way people are persuaded when they focus on the quality of the arguments in a message.

Peripheral route to persuasion The way people are persuaded when they focus on factors other than the quality of the arguments in a message, such as the number of arguments.

In studying people's cognitive responses to persuasion, researchers have recognized that folks don't always process the information carefully after receiving a message; sometimes they accept or reject it without much thought at all (Chaiken & Trope, 1999; Evans, 2008). This recognition led to the development of **dual process models of persuasion** (Chaiken & Ledgerwood, 2012; Petty & Cacioppo, 1986), which incorporate two basic kinds of attitude change processes—those that involve a focus on the arguments in a message and those that involve a focus on other factors such as the attractiveness of the communicator (Smith & DeCoster, 2000). The first and still most prevalent dual process model is the **elaboration likelihood model** of Richard Petty and John Cacioppo (1986), which proposes two routes that people can take to be persuaded—the **central route** and the **peripheral route to persuasion**.

Message recipients will take the central route—paying close attention to the quality of its arguments—when they have both the *motivation* and the *ability* to do so. If either of these conditions is missing, recipients will take the peripheral route—focusing on some factor other than quality, such as the mere number of arguments or the status or attractiveness of the communicator (see Figure 5.3).

Figure 5.3   Elaboration likelihood model: Dual routes to successful persuasion

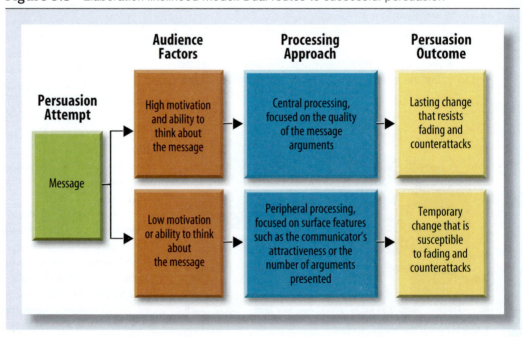

Depending on whether they have the motivation and ability to think hard about a message, people will process it either centrally or peripherally. Although both processing approaches can lead to persuasion, central processing produces more enduring change.

MOTIVATION Two factors influence a person's motivation to process a message centrally. The first is the personal relevance of the topic: The more an issue directly affects you, the more willing you are to think hard about it. The second is the tendency to think hard about *any* topic, called need for cognition. Let's examine these factors in turn.

Suppose that in tomorrow's edition of your campus newspaper you read an article describing a plan by university administrators that would require each student to pass a comprehensive exam covering all prior class work before graduation. Suppose as well that the administrators were proposing that the plan go into effect immediately so that, if approved, it would apply to you! Because of this direct *personal relevance*, you would be motivated to consider the administrators' arguments carefully before deciding whether to support or oppose the plan, no doubt mulling over those arguments and analyzing them in terms of their quality. Now, imagine the same set of events with one change: the policy is designed to go into effect not this year but in 10 years; so it would not apply to you. Under these conditions, the dual processing models would predict that you would respond quite differently to the article. No longer would you be motivated to pore over its points, working up arguments and counterarguments in response. Instead, you might process the administrators' arguments lightly, deciding whether to support or oppose the proposal based on something as superficial as the number of arguments the administrators listed favoring their plan.

A study done by Richard Petty and John Cacioppo (1984) confirmed these predictions. College students read either three or nine arguments favoring comprehensive exams. Those arguments were either of high quality ("Average starting salaries are higher for graduates of schools with exams.") or of low quality ("The exams would allow students to compare performance against students at other schools."). Figure 5.4 shows the outcome of the study. When students thought the policy would apply to them, they processed the message centrally, becoming more favorable after reading

Figure 5.4 The effects of personal relevance

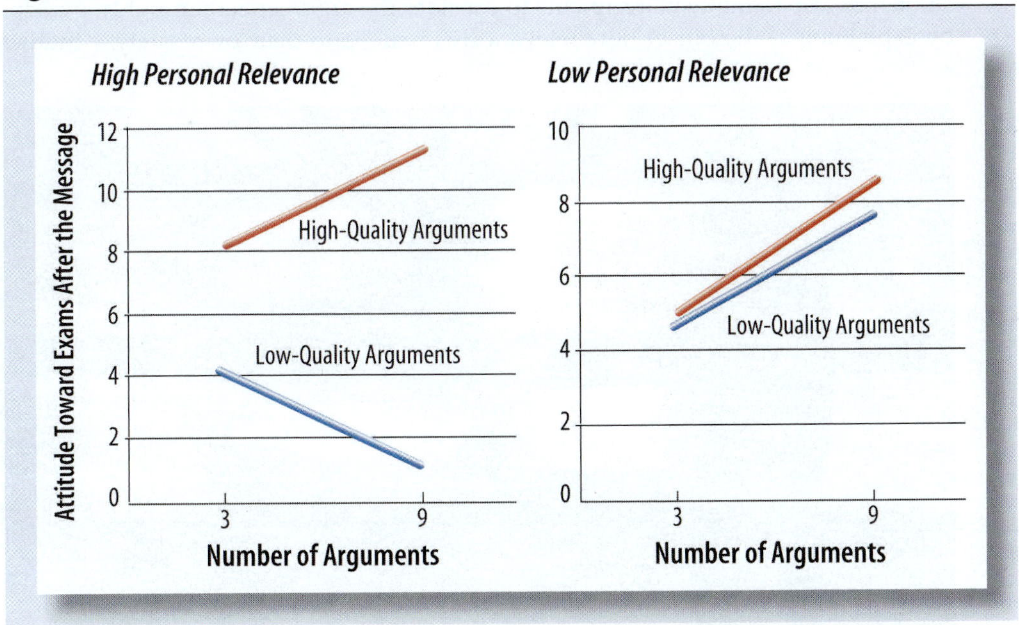

When the topic was personally relevant, students responded to a message by taking into account the quality of its arguments. When the topic was not personally relevant, the students processed the message peripherally, responding not to the quality of the arguments but to the sheer number. Thus, both central and peripheral message processing can lead to persuasion, but in different ways.

Source: Adapted from Petty, R. E., & Cacioppo, J. T. (1984). The effects of involvement on responses to argument quantity and quality: Central and peripheral routes to persuasion. *Journal of Personality and Social Psychology, 46*, 69–81.

strong arguments and less favorable after reading weak ones. However, when they thought the policy would not cover them, because it would not go into effect for 10 years, students based their opinions on the number rather than the quality of the arguments.

Another motivating factor resides less in the topic than in the individuals themselves: *need for cognition*. As we discussed in Chapter 3, some people simply prefer to think more fully and deeply than others about almost any issue. These people have a high **need for cognition**, the preference for engaging in central route, deliberative thinking. This need can be measured by questions inquiring how much a person likes to think deliberatively about things in general (Cacioppo et al., 1996). Individuals who have a high need for cognition are motivated to think in a deliberative way even about issues that are not personally relevant to them. For example, in one study, University of Iowa undergraduates read a communication containing either strong or weak arguments in favor of a tuition increase that would go into effect a decade later. Thus, the issue was not personally relevant to these students. Yet those who had a high need for cognition expended more effort thinking about the communication's points and were more swayed by the quality of those points than were those who had a low need for cognition (Cacioppo et al., 1986).

In sum, people can be motivated to think deeply about a topic by such factors as the personal relevance of the topic and their natural preference for deliberative thought (need for cognition). When this motivation is high, people base their opinions on a careful analysis of the quality of the arguments for and against the issue. When this motivation is low, people don't focus so much on the strengths and weaknesses of the arguments; rather, they often base their opinions on peripheral considerations—simply counting the number of arguments, for example. Although these peripheral factors can produce as much initial attitude change as strong arguments, the change fades more quickly and is more vulnerable to persuasive attempts to change the attitude back again (Haugtvedt & Petty, 1992).

Thus, in your letter designed to convince people to support lower speed limits, you would be well advised not just to provide strong arguments favoring your position, but also to motivate recipients to consider the arguments thoroughly, perhaps by explaining at the outset how relevant this issue is to their own safety. ("Studies

Need for cognition The tendency to enjoy and engage in deliberative thought.

Slipping by. Because the message points of TV ads stream past us rapidly, it is difficult to assess their quality using central processing.

show that lowered highway speed limits would prevent hundreds of deaths next year. Yours could be one of them.") That way, the change your letter generates is more likely to last.

ABILITY Having a strong desire to process a message centrally may not be sufficient. A person must also have the ability to follow through. If you were motivated to think thoroughly about a communication—let's say an ad for a camera you wanted to buy— what could prevent you from weighing the points of the ad carefully? Researchers have uncovered several ways of limiting your ability to deliberate fully: providing distractions to take your mind off the ad (Albarracin & Wyer, 2001); providing you with information insufficient to let you know what to think about the ad's points (Wood, Kallgren, & Preisler, 1985); and providing insufficient time for you to consider those points completely (Ratneswar & Chaiken, 1991).

A study conducted by Joseph Alba and Howard Marmorstein (1987) showed how this last factor, insufficient time, can affect consumers' reactions to camera advertisements. Subjects were given information about two comparably priced camera brands, A and B. The information described 12 separate features that the cameras had in common. Brand A was described as superior to brand B on just three of these features, but they were the most important features to consider in purchasing a camera (they directly involved the quality of the camera and the pictures you could take with it). Brand B, on the other hand, was described as superior on eight of the features, but they were relatively unimportant aspects of a camera purchase (e.g., the presence of a shoulder strap). In one study condition, subjects were exposed to each feature for only two seconds. In a second condition, subjects were given five seconds to consider each feature. Finally, a last group of subjects had as much time as they wanted to study the information about the 12 features. Later, subjects rated their favorability toward the cameras.

The results were striking. When given only two seconds per feature to evaluate the cameras, few subjects preferred the higher-quality camera (17%); the majority opted for the camera that had a greater number of unimportant advantages. When given five seconds per feature, this pattern changed somewhat; but, still, fewer than half (38%) preferred the quality choice. It wasn't until subjects had unlimited time to consider the alternatives that the pattern reversed and the majority of subjects (67%) favored the camera that had fewer, but more important, advantages.

Does the idea of having insufficient time to analyze the points of a communication remind you of how you have to respond to typical, rapid-fire advertisements? Think about it for a second (better still, think about it for an unlimited time): Isn't this the way radio and television commercials operate? In contrast to print ads, the points in their messages speed past in a stream that can't be slowed or reversed to give you the chance to process any of it centrally. As a result, you focus not on the quality of the advertiser's case but on peripheral aspects of the case, such as the likability or attractiveness of the people in the ads (Chaiken & Eagly, 1983). This is also true of much of the other information you receive through the broadcast media (political opinions, interviews with public figures, and so on).

In summary, dual processing models of persuasion recognize two ways in which people process persuasive communications. Central processing involves paying attention to the quality of the arguments in the communication, which results in focused thinking about those arguments and in change that is based on their strengths and weaknesses. Peripheral processing involves paying attention to other aspects of the communication besides argument quality, such as the mere number of arguments or the communicator's likability. This leads people to change their attitudes and beliefs on the basis of these secondary factors. People are likely to engage in central processing of

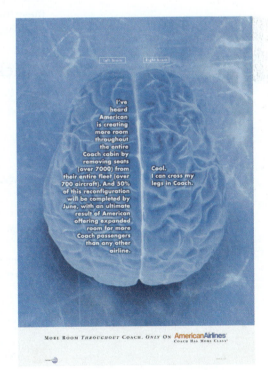

A dual-brainer. This advertiser has cleverly arranged to appeal simultaneously to both central and peripheral information processors in the market.

a message when they have both the motivation and the ability to do so. If either is missing, they are more likely to process the message peripherally.

No matter which kind of processing is used, people change their attitudes and beliefs to achieve personal goals. Let's consider what they are.

The Goals of Persuasion: Why People Change Their Attitudes and Beliefs

Without much strain, you could probably think of several reasons why one person might want to persuade another, as all manner of goals can be realized by changing another's attitudes and beliefs. But why would an individual choose to *become* persuaded? What goals would be served by such change? This seems the more intriguing and instructive question (Snyder & DeBono, 1989).

To understand the functions of attitude change, we should first consider what the functions of attitude might be. Psychologists have proposed several: Through their attitudes, people can gain rewards and avoid punishments, organize information efficiently, express themselves to others, maintain self-esteem, and fit in with their groups (Herek, 1986; Maio & Olson, 1995; Shavitt, 1990).

Combining these various functions and applying them to the issue of attitude change, we can see three major persuasion goals. Individuals may yield to a persuasive message to

1. hold a more accurate view of the world,
2. be consistent within themselves, or
3. gain social approval and acceptance.

Sometimes, a single shift of attitude can serve more than one goal. For example, when you move closer to a friend's position on an issue after your friend makes an excellent point, this move should promote both accuracy and social approval. Although these three goals don't always operate consciously, in the remainder of this chapter, we will consider how they motivate people to change.

Quick Quiz

1 Which of the following statements correctly defines *persuasion*?

   a. A change in a public attitude or belief as a result of receiving a message.
   b. A change in a private attitude or belief as a result of receiving a message.
   c. A change in a public or private belief as a result of receiving a message.
   d. None of the above

2 Which of the following strategies qualifies as a nonreactive measurement of attitudes?

   a. Self-report measures
   b. Interviews with an experimenter
   c. Littering a political candidate's political pamphlet
   d. All of the above

3 According to the _____ model, the most direct determinant of persuasion is the _____ in response to the persuasive message.

   a. Cognitive response; number of favorable counterarguments
   b. Dual process; amount of self-talk
   c. Dual process; number of counterarguments
   d. Cognitive response; amount of self-talk

4 According to the dual process model of persuasion, which of the following statements are true?

   a. High motivation and ability to think about the message are associated with temporary attitude change.
   b. Peripheral processing of the persuasive message is associated with lasting attitude change.
   c. High motivation and low ability to reflect on the message are associated with more permanent attitude change.
   d. All of the above
   e. None of the above

Having an Accurate View of the World

LO 5.7   Identify and explain the three sources of shortcut evidence that people often use when trying to hold accurate attitudes.

LO 5.8   Understand the circumstances under which people are most motivated to hold accurate views.

LO 5.9   Describe the factors that push people to hold less accurate views.

Silver-tongued politicians, smooth-talking salespeople, and sensationalizing advertisers can often mislead their audiences. It should come as no surprise, then, that to avoid costly mistakes, people want to orient themselves to the world as it truly is. Holding accurate attitudes and beliefs offers one way to do so. In this section, we explore some of the shortcuts people use to try to achieve accuracy. We then examine those features in the person and those in the situation that influence the accuracy goal.

Good Shortcuts to Accuracy

As we have already seen, when individuals want to be accurate in their views of an issue—for example, when the issue is personally important—they spend considerable time and effort analyzing the relevant evidence (Lundgren & Prislin, 1998; Petty & Cacioppo, 1979). But we must be careful not to suppose that only those thinking deeply about a topic want to hold accurate views of it. Frequently, people want to be accurate but don't have the time or ability to analyze the evidence closely. What then? They often rely on a different kind of evidence to help them choose correctly—shortcut evidence of accuracy. This shortcut evidence can be gathered from three sources: credible communicators, others' responses, and ready ideas.

INVESTIGATION

Accuracy is usually a good thing. But is it always what we want? Think of a time when you convinced yourself to believe something that wasn't true. What was your real goal in that case?

CREDIBLE COMMUNICATORS HAVE EXPERTISE AND TRUSTWORTHINESS   When circumstances don't allow you to thoroughly examine a persuasive communication, you can increase your accuracy by basing your opinion on the credibility of the communicator (Chaiken & Maheswaran, 1994; Smith, De Houwer, & Nosek, 2013). What are the characteristics of a credible communicator? Over many years of research, two have emerged: A credible communicator is expert and trustworthy (Perloff, 1993).

When the media present an expert's views on a topic, the effect on public opinion is dramatic. A single expert opinion news story in the *New York Times* is associated with a 2% shift in public opinion nationwide; when the expert's statement is aired on national television, the impact nearly doubles (Jorden, 1993; Page et al., 1987).

What does this tell you about how to increase the effectiveness of your highway speed reduction letter? If there are public statements by transportation safety experts that support your position, you would make a mistake if you didn't include them, especially when your intended audience doesn't initially favor your proposal (Aronson et al., 1963). Still, you won't be optimally persuasive by just convincing your audience that you are a source of expert information. Research indicates that you must also demonstrate that you are a trustworthy source of that information (Van Overwalle & Heylighen, 2006). In the research video for this chapter, Robert Cialdini tells us about a study that validates the importance of these two elements (of expertise and trustworthiness) and shows how consumers can be taught to employ them wisely when making decisions about purchases.

Whereas expertise refers to a communicator's knowledge and experience, *trustworthiness* refers to the communicator's honesty and lack of bias. How can communicators

WATCH THE VIDEO: *That's an Actor, Not a Doctor! Recognizing False Credibility.*

appear to be honest and unbiased when delivering a persuasive message? They can do so by conveying the impression that their message is intended not to change attitudes to serve the communicators' own interests but instead to serve the audience members' interests by informing them accurately about the issues (M. C. Campbell, 1995; Davis & O'Donohue, 2004). Advertisements promising "straight talk" about a problem or product illustrate one approach often taken to establish trustworthiness. Another is trickier: Rather than arguing only in their own favor, communicators sometimes make a show of providing both sides of the argument—the pros and the cons—which gives the impression of honesty and impartiality. Researchers have long known that communicators who present two-sided arguments and who appear to be arguing against their own interests can gain the trust of their audiences and become more influential (Eagly et al., 1978), especially when the audience initially disagrees with the communicator (Hovland et al., 1949). Indeed, children as young as second-graders increase their belief in communications that run counter to the communicator's self-interest; for instance, they're more likely to believe the story of a child who said he placed second rather than first in a footrace (Mills & Keil, 2005).

Advertisers have hit on one particularly effective way of seeming to argue against their own interests. They mention a minor weakness or drawback of their product in the ads promoting it. That way, they create a perception of honesty from which they can be more persuasive about the strengths of the product (see Figure 5.5). Advertisers are not alone in the use of this tactic. Attorneys are taught to "steal the opponent's thunder" by mentioning a weakness in their own case before the opposing lawyer does, thereby establishing a perception of honesty in the eyes of jury members. Experiments have demonstrated that this tactic works. When jurors heard an attorney bring up a weakness in his own case first, jurors assigned him more honesty and were more favorable to his overall case in their final verdicts because of that perceived honesty (Williams, Bourgeois, & Croyle, 1993).

OTHERS' RESPONSES   When people want to react correctly to a persuasive message but don't have the motivation or ability to think about it deeply, there is another kind of shortcut they can take. They can observe the responses of others to the message (Saporito, 2005; Westerwick, 2013). For example, if you heard a political speech and everyone in the audience around you responded enthusiastically to it, you might well conclude that the speech was a good one and become persuaded in its direction

(Axsom, Yates, & Chaiken, 1987). In addition, the more consensus you witnessed among audience members, the more likely you would be to follow their lead, even if you didn't initially agree with them (Betz, Skowronski, & Ostrom, 1996; Surowiecki, 2004). It's for this reason that interrogators are taught to say to a suspect "We believe you are guilty" rather than "I believe you are guilty" (Inbau et al., 2001).

Although consensus among audience members increases the impact of their responses, a lone other's response to a message can sometimes greatly influence an observer's response to it as well. Criminal interrogators understand this and often support their claim that a suspect is guilty by telling the suspect that they have an eyewitness who agrees with them. What is worrisome about this tactic is that interrogators frequently employ it when no such witness exists. Not only is the use of false evidence in police interrogations legal, according to sociologist Richard Leo (1996), who watched 182 interrogations, but also, after false evidence was presented, suspects made incriminating admissions in the majority of these cases. Is it possible that some of these admissions were made by suspects who were truly innocent but convinced of their guilt by the falsified evidence? And, if so, what would be the circumstances that would lead to this remarkable form of persuasion?

Saul Kassin and Katherine Kiechel (1996) devised a study to answer precisely these questions. College students performing a computer task in an experiment were accused by the researcher of a wrongdoing that they had not committed—pressing a specific key that they had been warned to avoid, which erased all of the data. Upset, the researcher demanded a signed confession from the student. How many of the students signed even though not one was guilty? That depended importantly on two features of the study. First, those individuals who had been cognitively overloaded while performing the computer task (they had to process information at a frenzied pace) were more likely to admit guilt than were those who were not overloaded by the task (83% versus 62%). As we have seen before, when people are made to feel confused and uncertain, they are more vulnerable to influence.

Second, half of the students heard a fellow subject (actually an experimental confederate) claim that she had seen the student press the forbidden key. The individuals implicated by the bogus eyewitness testimony were significantly more likely to confess than were those who were not (94% versus 50%). So powerful was the combination of these two factors that those students who were both overloaded by the situation and falsely accused by a witness admitted their guilt 100% of the time.

Figure 5.5   When something bad makes something good

Ugly is only skin-deep.

It may not be much to look at, but beneath that humble exterior beats an air-cooled engine. It won't boil over and ruin your piston rings. It won't freeze over and ruin your life. It's in the back of the car, where the weight on the rear wheels makes the traction very good in snow and sand. And it will give you about 29 miles to a gallon of gas.

After a while you get to like so much about the VW, you even get to like what it looks like.

You find that there's enough legroom for almost anybody's legs. Enough headroom for almost anybody's head. With a hat on it. Snug-fitting bucket seats. Doors that close so well you can hardly close them. (They're so airtight, it's better to open the window a crack first.)

Those plain, unglamorous wheels are each suspended independently. So when a bump makes one wheel bounce, the bounce doesn't make the other wheel bump.

It's things like that you pay the $1663 for, when you buy a VW. The ugliness doesn't add a thing to the cost of the car. That's the beauty of it.

Forty-five years ago, the advertising firm of Doyle, Dane, Bernbach was given the task of introducing a small German car to the U.S. market, where no little cars were selling and no import had ever thrived. It responded with legendary success in a series of ads that imparted overall credibility to the car and to the company by pointing to small liabilities. You may have to strain to see it, but in the ad copy, a negative comment precedes each set of positive comments.

Crowd control. When others, especially many others, respond in a positive way to an idea, we're likely to see the idea as more valid and to respond similarly.

An even more frightening aspect of these particular students' mental states is that, apparently, most of them truly believed their confessions. When waiting alone outside the laboratory afterward, they were approached by another student (actually a second experimental confederate) who asked what had happened. Sixty-five percent of them responded by admitting their guilt to this unknown person, saying things such as "I hit the wrong button and ruined the program." Obviously, the impact of other people's views—even the views of a single person—can greatly affect our susceptibility to persuasion, especially when we have first been made to feel unsure of ourselves. These factors fit disturbingly well with Peter Reilly's confession. During his interrogation, he was cognitively overloaded to the point of confusion and was then assured by others (his interrogators and the polygraph operator) that he was guilty.

READY IDEAS According to the *availability heuristic* we discussed in Chapter 3, one shortcut people use to decide on the validity or likelihood of an idea is how easily they can picture it or instances of it (Bacon, 1979; Tversky & Kahneman, 1973). This gives communicators a subtle way to get an audience to accept an idea—by making the idea more *cognitively ready*, that is, easier to picture or to bring to mind.

Communicators can use two methods to make an idea more cognitively ready. The first is to present the idea several times. Much research shows that repeated assertions are seen as more valid (Hertwig, Gigerenzer, & Hoffrage, 1997). Moreover, after an idea is encountered several times, it becomes more familiar and easier to picture, which makes it seem more true (Arkes et al., 1989; Boehm, 1994).

Asking an audience to imagine an idea or event is a second method for increasing its readiness and believability (Frye, Lord, & Brady, 2012; Garry & Polaschek, 2000). After you have once imagined something, it becomes easier to picture the next time you consider it, thus appearing more likely.

In one study, after imagining themselves in a car accident, students at New Mexico State University became significantly more willing to support traffic safety initiatives (Gregory, Burroughs, & Ainslie, 1985). You no doubt see the relevance of these findings to your letter advocating lower speed limits: You might ask readers to take a minute and *just imagine* how easy it would be to get involved in an accident when traffic is traveling at high rates of speed.

Thus, ideas can be made to seem more valid by increasing their cognitive readiness, which can be accomplished by presenting the ideas more than once and by arranging for the audience to imagine or picture the ideas. In retrospect, it is clear that Peter Reilly's interrogators used both of these methods. He was assaulted by repeated assertions that he had murdered his mother and was incessantly pushed to imagine how he could have done it. By the time the interrogation was over, these imaginations had become reality for both the interrogators and Reilly.

Interrogator: But you recall cutting her throat with a straight razor.

Reilly: It's hard to say. I think I recall doing it. I mean, I imagine myself doing it. It's coming out of the back of my head . . .

Interrogator: How about her legs? What kind of vision do we get there? . . . Can you remember stomping her legs?

Reilly: You say it, then I imagine I'm doing it.

Interrogator: You're not imagining anything. I think the truth is starting to come out. You want it out.

Reilly: I know . . .

What Affects the Desire for Accuracy?

The desire for an accurate perspective on a topic is not always the same. At some times and in certain people, it can be particularly intense. At other times and in other individuals, it can drop drastically. Let's explore a set of factors that affect when and how the goal for accuracy operates to influence persuasion.

PERSON **ISSUE INVOLVEMENT** You probably have opinions on thousands of issues. Although it would be nice to hold accurate views on them all, you are more motivated to be correct concerning those that involve you directly. Political differences in a remote part of the world may spark important events there—war, revolution, and social change. But you would probably be less motivated to hold informed opinions on such issues than on a plan for a sales tax increase in your home town. As we've seen, you'll want to have more accurate attitudes and beliefs on issues that are *personally* important. Consequently, you'll be more likely to think hard about messages concerning these issues, becoming persuaded only when the arguments are strong (Petty et al., 2005).

One study showed how easy it is for advertisers to get you more involved with a topic so that you will pay careful attention to their messages. The researchers wrote advertising copy—for disposable razors—that either used the self-referencing pronoun *you* exclusively ("You might have thought that razor technology could never be improved.") or did not. Individuals who saw the self-referencing ads thought more thoroughly about the information and were only influenced by it when it contained strong arguments (Burnkrant & Unnava, 1989). Can *you* see how *you* could incorporate this device into *your* letter concerning highway speed limits—and that it would be wise to do so only if *you* had good arguments to support *your* cause? Of course, textbook writers would never stoop to using this tactic.

PERSON **MOOD** Being in a happy or sad mood does more than give you a positive or negative feeling; it also gives you information about the nature of your immediate situation (Schwarz & Clore, 1996). If you are feeling happy at the moment, it is likely that your current environment has recently been receptive and rewarding. If you are feeling sad, on the other hand, chances are that the environment has recently yielded something unfortunate; it will seem a riskier place, and you will feel more vulnerable (Salovey & Birnbaum, 1989). No doubt you would want to make sure you react correctly to a persuasion attempt in this insecure environment. Thus, when in a sad versus a happy mood, you will be especially motivated to acquire accurate attitudes and beliefs that pertain to the situation at hand—because of what your mood says about the potential danger of making errors in the immediate environment (Forgas & East, 2008; Isbell, 2004; Schwarz, Bless, & Bohner, 1991). More recent research shows that a positive mood can sometimes lead you to scrutinize a message, if that message goes against your existing attitude (Ziegler, 2013).

SITUATION **DONE DEALS** The Bible says that there is a time for all things, "a time to every purpose under heaven." The goal of accuracy is not excused from this rule. For example, Peter Gollwitzer and his coworkers have shown that there is a particular time when people are most motivated to be accurate—when they are deciding what to feel, believe, or do. *After* that decision is made, however, the desire to see things as they really are can give way to the desire to get on with the now-made decision (Armor & Taylor, 2003; Gollwitzer et al., 1990). As Napolean advised his generals, "Take time to deliberate; but, when the time for action has arrived, stop thinking and go in."

SITUATION **UNWELCOME INFORMATION** Under certain circumstances, people choose to believe only what they want to believe, usually what fits with their self-interests and personal preferences (Johnson & Eagly, 1989; Kunda, 1999). This tendency can affect persuasion. For example, people see information that contradicts what they prefer to believe as less valid than information that supports these beliefs; as a result, such evidence is less persuasive (Lord et al., 1979;). People who receive persuasive information that fits with their personal interests, preferences, and positions feel content and typically don't expend the cognitive effort needed to look for flaws. However, those who encounter information that doesn't fit become upset and search it for weaknesses they can use to form counterarguments (Giner-Sorolla & Chaiken, 1994; Munro & Ditto, 1997). Although it is not necessarily harmful to scrutinize and resist information at odds with one's preferred traits and beliefs, it can be self-destructive if overdone, as we see in the following section.

Bridging Function and Dysfunction:

Defeating Defensiveness and Denial

Do people take a biased approach, trying to challenge and undermine negative (but not positive) information, even when the information concerns the vital matter of their own health? Indeed they do (Kunda, 1987; Lench & Ditto, 2008). For example, drivers with a history of hospitalization for auto accidents nonetheless continue to believe that they are better and safer drivers than most (Guerin, 1994; Svenson, 1981).

Suppose you were participating in an experiment using a new saliva test to detect an enzyme deficiency that predicted pancreatic disease in later life. How much would you believe in the accuracy of the new test? According to a study done by Peter Ditto and David Lopez (1992), that would depend on whether the test identified you as possessing the worrisome deficiency. Like the majority of those students, you would likely downgrade the accuracy of the test if it informed you that pancreas problems were in your future. A second study showed how you might go about it. Ditto and Lopez asked subjects if there were any irregularities in their diet, sleep, or activity patterns over the last 48 hours that might have affected the accuracy of the test. Those who got health-threatening results listed three times more "irregularities" than did those receiving health-confirming results. Thus, they searched for ways to undercut evidence contradicting their preferred image of healthiness.

How ads can overcome defensiveness. Advertising appeals like this one can be effective when they alert recipients to a danger and then provide clear steps for reducing the danger.

On the surface, this tendency seems potentially harmful. And it can be, as it involves finding fault with information that can warn of physical danger. However, a study by John Jemmott and his coworkers (1986) suggests that most people are not so foolish as to ignore the warning entirely. Participants in that experiment were told that an enzyme deficiency test either did or did not identify them as candidates for future pancreatic disorders. Those who were informed that they had the deficiency judged the test's validity as significantly lower than did those informed that they were deficiency free. Nonetheless, 83% of the deficiency-present individuals asked to receive information about services available to people who had the deficiency. Thus, although they tried to defend against the threat in the test results, the great majority did not simply brush the matter aside; instead, they made arrangements to get more information and, if need be, assistance.

Hence, for most people, the tendency to reject unwelcome information is tempered by the accuracy motive, especially when important aspects of the self are at stake.

It is when people place no reasonable limits on their desire to view the world according to their beliefs and preferences that a serious problem arises (Armor & Taylor, 1998). This sort of reaction is more than healthy skepticism toward incongruous information. It might be characterized as *denial*, and it can be self-destructive (Gladis et al., 1992; Lazarus, 1983).

Who are these individuals who engage in denial when confronted with troubling information? They are not merely optimists—individuals who believe that, as a rule, good things are likely to happen to them (Carver, Scheier & Segerstrom, 2010). They are better termed *chronic unrealistic optimists*—individuals who refuse to believe that they are vulnerable to bad events in general and who, therefore, fail to take precautions against them (Davidson & Prkachin, 1997; Thompson & Schlehofer, 2008). Apparently, such individuals are so upset by the possibility of harm that they repress relevant information and deny that they are vulnerable to the harm (Taylor et al., 1989). The irony is that by repressing and denying the existence of distressing dangers, these individuals make the very same dangers more real (Radcliffe & Klein, 2002; Robins & Beer, 2001).

This tendency to deal with threat by ignoring or denying the problem can appear in normal individuals, too, but only under certain conditions. For the most part, fear-arousing communications

Figure 5.6 Fear is not enough; you have to have a plan

Students read a public health pamphlet on the dangers of tetanus infection that either was or was not laden with frightening images of the consequences of contracting tetanus. In addition, they either did or did not receive a specific plan for how to arrange to get a tetanus shot. Finally, there was a control group of students who got no tetanus message but did get a plan. The high-fear message spurred recipients to get a shot only if it included a plan identifying the specific actions they could take to secure a shot and thereby reduce their fear of tetanus.

Source: Based on Leventhal, H., & Cameron, L. (1994). Persuasion and health attitudes. In S. Shavitt & T. C. Brock (Eds.), *Persuasion* (pp. 219–249). Boston: Allyn & Bacon.

usually stimulate recipients to take actions to reduce the threat (Boster & Mongeau, 1984; Robberson & Rogers, 1988). For instance, a lecture to French teenagers about the dangers of alcohol was more effective in changing attitudes and behaviors toward drinking when it was accompanied by fear-arousing pictures (Levy-Leboyer, 1988). However, there is an exception to this general rule: When the danger described in the fear-producing message is severe but the recipients are told of no effective means of reducing the danger—self-restraint, medication, exercise, diet, or the like—they may deal with the fear by "blocking out" the message or denying that it applies to them. As a consequence, they may take no preventive action (Rogers & Mewborn, 1976).

This helps explain why it is important to accompany high-fear messages with specific recommendations for behavior that will diminish the danger: The more clearly people see behavioral means for ridding themselves of the fear, the less they will need to resort to psychological means such as denial (Leventhal & Cameron, 1994) (see Figure 5.6 and photo on page 165). The lesson: Don't try to persuade people through fear without giving them specific steps to handle the fear (Das, deWit, & Stroebe, 2003). This applies to your letter designed to convince citizens of the dangers of high speed limits. Vividly describing the highway mayhem these high speed limits allow should be effective as long as you also describe specific steps recipients can take to reduce the danger, such as contributing to relevant political action groups or calling relevant legislators (whose phone numbers you should provide).

INTERACTION **EXPERTISE AND COMPLEXITY** Suppose you are sitting on a jury deciding how much money to award a man who claims that he contracted cancer as a result of exposure to a chemical while on the job. His employer, a manufacturing firm, admits that he was exposed to this chemical but disputes that it caused his cancer. One piece of evidence you hear is the testimony of an expert witness, Dr. Thomas Fallon, who states that scientific data show that the chemical does indeed lead to cancer in a variety of species, including humans. How swayed are you likely to be by this expert? According to a study done by Joel Cooper, Elizabeth Bennett, and Holly Sukel (1996), that would depend not just on how expert you think he is but also on how complex his testimony was.

In that study, mock jurors heard Dr. Fallon described as either highly expert or only moderately expert on the topic. Some of the jurors then heard him give his testimony in ordinary language, saying simply that the chemical causes liver cancer, several other diseases of the liver, and diseases of the immune system. Other jurors heard him give his testimony in complex, almost incomprehensible language, saying that the chemical led to "tumor induction as well as hepatomegaly, hepatomegalocytosis, and lymphoid atrophy of the spleen and thymus." The most interesting finding of the study was that the highly expert witness was more successful in swaying the jury only when he spoke in complex, difficult-to-understand terms. Why? The study's authors think that when Dr. Fallon used simple language, jurors could judge the case on the basis of the evidence itself. They didn't need to use his expertise as a shortcut to accuracy. However, when his testimony was too obscure to understand, they had to rely on his reputation as an expert to tell them what to think. These results suggest an interesting but discomforting irony: Acknowledged experts may be most persuasive when people can't understand the details of what they are saying! A more recent study finds that complex language enhances an expert witness's credibility more so when the expert is a man; female experts were more convincing when they used simple language (McKimmie et al., 2012).

Quick Quiz

1 What are the two primary characteristics of a credible communicator?
a. Expertise and likability
b. Expertise and trustworthiness
c. Likability and trustworthiness
d. Attractiveness and expertise

2 People are most motivated to hold accurate views when . . .
a. they feel personally involved with the issue.
b. they're in a happy mood.
c. they've already made an important decision.
d. All of the above

3 People are least motivated to hold accurate views when . . .
a. they're in a sad mood.
b. new information fits with what they already believe.
c. they feel personally involved with the issue.
d. None of the above

Being Consistent in One's Attitudes and Actions

LO 5.10 Explain balance theory and cognitive dissonance theory.

LO 5.11 Summarize the factors that affect our desire for cognitive consistency.

LO 5.12 Discuss how Western and Eastern cultures differ in their preference for consistency.

The giant of nineteenth-century British science Michael Faraday was once asked about a long-hated academic rival, "Is the professor always wrong, then?" Faraday glowered at his questioner and replied, "He's not that consistent."

In Faraday's dismissive description of his opponent's intellect, we find a pair of insights relevant to the goal of consistency. The first is straightforward: Like most people, Faraday considered consistency an admirable trait that ought to appear in one's behavior. When it doesn't, there is cause for scorn (Allgeier et al., 1979). Finding the second insight requires a bit more digging. Why did Faraday feel the need to deflate his rival's occasional accomplishments at all? A social psychologist might answer the question by suggesting that Faraday himself was a victim of the workings of the **consistency principle**, which states that people are motivated toward cognitive consistency and will change their attitudes, beliefs, perceptions, and actions to achieve it. To maintain consistency within his unfavorable view of his rival, Faraday had to find a way to negate the successes of the man—hence the characterization of his opponent's accomplishments as inconsistencies.

Although we can't be certain that a desire to be personally consistent motivated Faraday's response (he's been unavailable for questioning since 1867), we can review the evidence for the causes of similar responses in modern-day individuals. In the process, we will first examine the two main consistency theories—balance and cognitive dissonance—that have guided the investigations of persuasion researchers. Then, we will consider the features in the person and in the situation that affect the goal of being consistent.

Consistency principle The principle that people will change their attitudes, beliefs, perceptions, and actions to make them consistent with each other.

Balance Theory

According to Fritz Heider (1946, 1958), who proposed **balance theory**, we all prefer to have harmony and consistency in our views of the world. We want to agree with the people we like and disagree with those we dislike; we want to associate good things with good people and bad things with bad people; we want to see things that are alike in one way as alike in other ways, too. Heider says that such harmony creates a state of cognitive balance in us. When we are in a state of balance—perhaps finding ourselves agreeing on a political issue with someone we truly like—we are content; there is no need to change. But if our cognitive system is out of balance—for example, when finding ourselves disagreeing on an issue with the person we like so much—we will experience uncomfortable tension. To remove this tension, we will have to change something in the system. Let's take a closer look at balance theory to see how this pressure to change can affect persuasion.

Name your favorite celebrity. Now, suppose you heard this person advocating a political position that you opposed. The theory states that your cognitive system would be out of balance because you would be disagreeing with someone you liked. What could you do to relieve the resulting tension and bring the system into balance? One maneuver would be to change your feelings about the celebrity; that way you would then disagree with someone you dislike. A second approach would be to change your attitude toward the topic; that way you would then agree with someone you like. In both instances, harmony would again reign.

Which approach you would take would likely depend on the strength of your attitudes. For example, if you had very deep feelings about the political topic—let's say gun control—you would probably achieve balance by changing your opinion of the celebrity who disagreed with you. If, however, you didn't have a strong attitude toward the topic, you would be more likely to achieve balance by changing that attitude to agree with the liked individual. A great deal of research has supported the predictions of balance theory as it applies to attitude change (Gawronski, Walther, & Blank, 2005; Greenwald et al., 2002; Priester & Petty, 2001). In general, people do change their views in order to keep the connections involving themselves, communicators, and communication topics in harmony.

Advertisers frequently try to make use of this tendency—by choosing famous spokespeople for their products. The willingness of manufacturers to pay enormous sums to celebrities (whose talents may be unrelated to their products) suggests that the business community has determined that the pull of cognitive balance makes the investment worthwhile. Evidence of the potential return on investment to business of being associated with positive people and things can be seen in the results of a poll indicating that 76% of consumers would switch to a corporate brand or product connected to favorably viewed causes such as the Olympics (Kadlec, 1997). According to the credit card company Visa, which is an Olympic sponsor, if a store displays a Visa sign featuring the Olympics rings symbol, Visa card purchases rise by 15 to 25% (Emert, 2000) and, Tsingtao Brewery, China's largest beer seller, reported a 32% profit jump during and immediately after sponsoring the Beijing Olympics (China, 2008).

Balance theory Heider's theory that people prefer harmony and consistency in their views of the world.

Success in the balance. When Oprah Winfrey, one of America's most positively rated celebrities, joined Barack Obama on the presidential campaign trail, his approval ratings jumped in the polls.

INVESTIGATION

Before basketball star Kobe Bryant was charged with sexual assault, he was a spokesperson for an Italian company (Nutella), which trumpeted the fact that Bryant had spent years in Italy while growing up. After he was charged, this company was the first to drop his contract. How does all this fit balance theory?

Cognitive Dissonance Theory

By far, the theoretical approach that has generated the most evidence for the motivation to be consistent is Leon Festinger's (1957) cognitive dissonance theory. Like balance theory, its basic assumption is that when people recognize an inconsistency among their attitudes, beliefs, or behaviors, they will feel a state of uncomfortable psychological arousal (termed **cognitive dissonance**) and will be motivated to reduce the discomfort by reducing the inconsistency. In addition, Festinger stated that people will be motivated to reduce an inconsistency only to the extent that it involves something important. For example, if you perceive an inconsistency in your beliefs about the wisdom of riding motorcycles—on the one hand they seem economical but on the other dangerous—you should feel strong dissonance only if riding motorcycles is a real and important issue for you, perhaps because you are thinking of buying one. This helps explain why strong dissonance effects rarely occur unless the self is involved (Aronson, 1969; Stone, 2003). When the inconsistency includes something about yourself, it becomes more important, and your need to resolve it increases.

Before dissonance theory came to prominence, persuasion theorists had focused mainly on changing attitudes and beliefs first, assuming that these shifts would then cause behavior change. One of the valuable contributions of dissonance theory has been to show that the reverse can also occur—changing a behavior first can spur an individual to change related attitudes and beliefs in an attempt to keep them consistent with the action (Cooper, Mirabile, & Scher, 2005).

Many dissonance experiments have been performed through the years, but the one published by Leon Festinger and J. Merrill Carlsmith in 1959 is easily the most famous. In the study, subjects who had performed a boring task (turning pegs on a board) were paid either $1 or $20 to tell the next subject that the task was interesting and a lot of fun. When later asked their attitudes toward the boring task, those who received the $1 payment had come to see it as more enjoyable than had those who got $20, who hadn't changed their attitudes at all.

How can we explain this strange result? Dissonance theory offers an answer. Subjects who paid only $1 had to confront two inconsistent cognitions about themselves: "I am a generally truthful person" (something that almost everyone believes) and "I just told a lie for no good reason." The easiest way for them to reduce the inconsistency was to change their attitudes toward the enjoyableness of the task; that way, they would no longer have to view themselves as lying about its being fun. In contrast, subjects who paid $20 had no dissonance to reduce because they had a good reason (*sufficient justification*) for what they did—the $20. After all, even a generally truthful person will tell a white lie for $20 (note that 20 1959 dollars would be worth more than $100 today). So, because of the substantial payment, what they did was not inconsistent with their views of themselves as generally truthful; hence, they didn't feel any pull to change their attitudes toward the task.

COUNTERATTITUDINAL BEHAVIOR   This explanation of the Festinger and Carlsmith study underscores a fundamental assertion of dissonance theory: A **counterattitudinal action**—behavior that is inconsistent with an existing attitude—will produce change in that attitude only when there is *insufficient justification* (i.e., no strong additional motivation for taking the action). It is for this reason that contrary behavior leads to attitude

Cognitive dissonance The unpleasant state of psychological arousal resulting from an inconsistency within one's important attitudes, beliefs, or behaviors.

Counterattitudinal action A behavior that is inconsistent with an existing attitude.

change principally when the actor feels that he or she has had *free choice* in performing it (Eisenstadt et al., 2005). For example, if you signed a petition supporting a disliked politician because your boss at work insisted on it, you would not be likely to feel a strain to become more positive toward the politician because you would probably see yourself as having little choice in the matter, given your boss's strong pressure. When potent external forces (threats, bribes, requirements) take away one's sense of personal choice in counterattitudinal behavior, dissonance rarely results (Eagly & Chaiken, 1993); see Figure 5.7.

POSTDECISIONAL DISSONANCE Counterattitudinal behavior isn't the only way that dissonance can be aroused. Another source of dissonance was examined in a study conducted at a Canadian racetrack, where bettors at the $2 window were approached and asked what chance they thought their favored horse had to win (Knox & Inkster, 1968). Half were asked immediately before placing their bets, and half were asked immediately after. In two separate studies, those asked after laying down their money were significantly more confident of their horse's chances. How odd. After all, nothing about the race, field, track, or weather had changed in the few seconds from before to after the bet. Perhaps not, but according to dissonance theory, something about the bettors had changed: They had experienced **postdecisional dissonance**, which is the conflict between the knowledge that you have made a decision and the possibility that the decision may be wrong. To reduce the unpleasant conflict, the bettors persuaded themselves that their horses really would win.

In general, soon after making a decision, people come to view their selections more favorably and all the alternative selections less favorably. This is particularly so

Postdecisional dissonance The conflict one feels about a decision that could possibly be wrong.

Figure 5.7 From dissonance induction to dissonance reduction

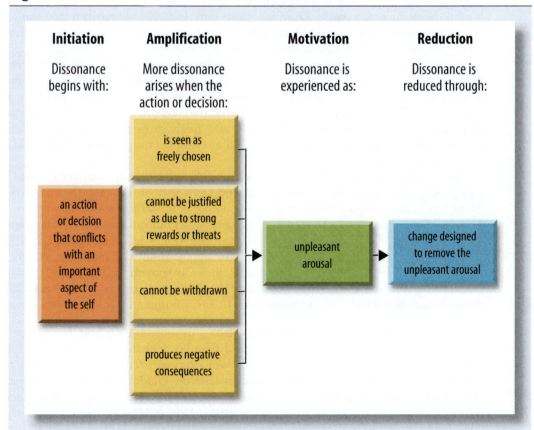

A number of factors initiate, amplify, motivate, and reduce cognitive dissonance.

when they feel highly committed (personally tied) to the decision (Brehm & Cohen, 1962; Eagly & Chaiken, 1993). In the case of the racetrack bettors, they became committed once they placed their bets and could no longer change their choices. At that point, they became irrevocably tied to their selections and had to reduce their postdecisional dissonance by convincing themselves that they had chosen correctly. The same process applies to political races where, immediately after casting a ballot, voters believe more strongly that their candidate will win (Regan & Kilduff, 1988). Recall that, earlier in this chapter, we said that after an irreversible decision, the desire to see things accurately is no longer paramount (Taylor & Gollwitzer, 1995); dissonance theory tells us that it is replaced by the desire to see things consistently (Harmon-Jones & Harmon-Jones, 2002). Moreover, as we will see in the following section, the dissonance will be particularly strong when the irreversible decision is likely to have negative consequences (Harmon-Jones et al., 1996).

What Affects the Desire for Cognitive Consistency?

The goal of achieving (or simply maintaining) cognitive consistency has been the subject of considerable research within social psychology (Albarracin & Wyer, 2000). That research has uncovered several features of the person and of the situation that play a role in determining how the desire for consistency affects persuasion. Most of the evidence for the impact of these features comes from explorations of dissonance theory.

PERSON **AROUSAL** Festinger (1957) claimed that inconsistency produces unpleasant arousal and that people will frequently change their attitudes to be rid of the discomfort. In general, research has supported both components of Festinger's claim.

First, there is good evidence that inconsistency does result in increased arousal (Elkin & Leippe, 1986; Harmon-Jones et al., 1996). In one study, researchers set up a typical dissonance procedure: Princeton University students were given free choice to write an essay contrary to their attitudes toward a total ban of alcohol on campus. The researchers said that they needed an essay that was in favor of the ban and asked for such an essay, saying, "We would appreciate your help, but we want to let you know that it's completely up to you." When these students agreed to write the counterattitudinal essay, their arousal (as measured by physiological recordings) jumped compared to similar students who were given no free choice in the matter. Thus, just as dissonance theory would expect, individuals who freely chose to act contrary to their existing attitudes experienced elevated tension as a result of the personal inconsistency (Croyle & Cooper, 1983).

Second, there is also good evidence to support the other part of Festinger's claim—that people will modify an inconsistent attitude as a way of reducing the accompanying unpleasant arousal (Fazio et al., 1977). Other studies have found that it is not just general arousal that is crucial to the change process but rather the particular variety that Festinger first suggested—*unpleasant* arousal (Elliot & Devine, 1994; Losch & Cacioppo, 1990). It is the annoying quality of that arousal that motivates change, discomforting inconsistent individuals until they do something to restore consistency. In all, research has implicated uncomfortable arousal as a critical factor in inconsistency-based attitude and belief shifts (Jonas, Graupmann, & Frey, 2006).

PERSON **PREFERENCE FOR CONSISTENCY** In introducing the consistency goal, we reported a quotation from Michael Faraday that indicated his value for consistency. Most people would agree, but not everyone. Consider the following statements by various other famous persons: Ralph Waldo Emerson: "A foolish consistency is the hobgoblin of little minds"; Oscar Wilde: "Consistency is the last refuge of the unimaginative"; and our favorite, Aldous Huxley: "The only truly consistent people are dead." Obviously, the concept of consistency is not held in universally high regard (Staw & Ross, 1980).

This insight led one of the authors of this textbook and two colleagues to develop a Preference for Consistency scale by asking subjects to agree or disagree with such statements as "It is important to me that my actions are consistent with my beliefs" and "I make an effort to appear consistent to others" (Cialdini, Trost, & Newsom, 1995). They found that individuals who scored low on preference for consistency didn't show typical consistency effects such as cognitive dissonance. As one might expect, the motive to be self-consistent doesn't apply to those who don't value consistency (Bator & Cialdini, 2006; Nail et al., 2001; Newby-Clark, McGregor, & Zanna, 2002).

INVESTIGATION

How would you rate yourself on preference for consistency, high or low? Why do you think you feel the way you do about personal consistency?

SITUATION **CONSEQUENCES** Ironically, the negative outcomes of an act can increase the amount of positive attitude change it creates. Because we are especially reluctant to perform *consequential* behaviors that conflict with our attitudes or beliefs, it stands to reason that the more impact our behavior has had on the world, the more motivated we will be to change our attitudes and beliefs to fit the behavior, especially when we feel responsible for those consequences (Harmon-Jones et al., 1996). For example, consider what happened at a corporate retreat for a group of 100 Burger King managers who were urged to walk barefoot over hot coals (as hot as 1,200 degrees) as part of a group "bonding experience." Despite the fact that a dozen of the managers received first- and second-degree burns as a result, a Burger King vice-president expressed no regrets about the event. Indeed, she praised it highly, even though she herself was burned. Perhaps dissonance theory can help explain her bewilderingly positive response when we recognize that (1) the consequences of the experience were clearly negative—one walker's burns required hospitalization, a doctor had to be brought in to treat the others, some of the injured had to use wheelchairs the next day—and that (2) she was responsible for organizing it ("Burger King fire-walkers," 2001).

SITUATION **SALIENCE OF THE INCONSISTENCY** If, as we have suggested, people change their attitudes and beliefs to be rid of an inconsistency, then aspects of the situation that make the inconsistency salient (prominent) to them should produce greater change (Blanton et al., 1997; Stone & Cooper, 2001). One way to make an inconsistency salient is through the use of the *Socratic method*—an approach for shifting a person's position on a topic by posing questions that reveal hidden contradictions between it and the person's position on related topics. Socrates, the author of the method, felt that once the discrepancies were made obvious, the person would try to eliminate them. Research on persuasion has supported Socrates' prediction: Most people react to messages that reveal their inconsistencies by moving toward consistency (McGuire & McGuire, 1996).

In fact, an effective way to get people to perform socially beneficial acts is to make salient the discrepancy between what they value and what they do (Harmon-Jones, Peterson, & Vaughn, 2003). Suppose that a survey-taker called and inquired into your attitude toward recycling and that you expressed a high opinion of it. Suppose that she then asked you to recall the times in the past month that you had failed to recycle (a newspaper or soft drink can). Most likely, after being confronted with this mismatch between your beliefs and actions, you would resolve to be more supportive of recycling in the future. This tactic of getting people to express their commitment to a good cause and then pointing out that they have not always lived up to that commitment has successfully reduced energy consumption in Australian households (Kantola, Syme, & Campbell, 1984). In the United States, researchers have employed the tactic to increase water conservation, recycling, and condom use (see Stone & Fernandez, 2008).

Think how a salient inconsistency could have pushed Peter Reilly to admit to a murder someone else committed. At first, he had no memory of the crime. But, after hours of mind-draining interrogation, he began to accept the "expert" evidence against him in his polygraph test, began to defer to the assurances of authority figures that he was guilty, and began to see the imagined scenes of his involvement as real. Is it any surprise that his failure to recall any specifics, which had become the single, salient inconsistency in the case, couldn't stand for long? Soon thereafter, he began not simply to admit to the killing but to add details. When these specifics didn't match with the facts the interrogators knew, they would claim that Reilly was being evasive, and he would offer different specifics. In one instructive exchange, after being chastised for remembering incorrect details, he plaintively asked his interrogator for "some hints" so he could make everything fit.

What happened to Reilly is remarkably similar to what happened in the earlier-discussed Kassin and Kiechel (1996) study, in which innocent people were accused of hitting a computer key that ruined data. Many of those who came to believe (on the basis of false evidence) that they were guilty remembered details of how and when the (non)event occurred, saying things such as "I hit it with the side of my hand right after you called out the A." Evidence like this aligns well with a conclusion drawn by psychologists studying other kinds of responding (for instance, eyewitness testimony in court and "recovered" memories in therapy sessions): So wide-ranging is the desire for consistency that it can reach into one's memory and change the features of recalled events to make them conform to a newly installed belief (Davis & Follette, 2001; Loftus & Ketcham, 1994).

INTERACTION Consistency and Culture

Although most people strive to be consistent with their prevailing self-concept, not everyone shares the same view of self. Consequently, the desire for consistency often

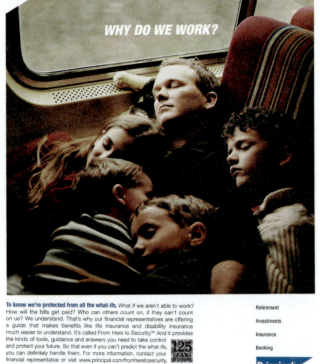

I am the one. We are the world. Ads like that on the left, which connect to an individualized sense of self, are more successful in the United States. Ads like that on the right, which connect to a collective sense of self, are more successful in Korea.

results in different types of behaviors in different cultures, because what people want to be consistent with differs in these cultures.

When advertisements for the U.S. military tempt recruits by challenging them to become "Power of One" and when ads for L'Oreal cosmetics urge women to ignore the products' high prices because "You're worth it," they are appealing to a type of personal self-enhancement that would seem foreign to many people in non-Western cultures (Morling & Lamoreaux, 2008). As we first discussed in Chapter 2, in North America and Western Europe, the prevailing sense of self is different from that of much of the rest of the world. Primarily, it involves the individual, the single person; hence, it is this individualized version of the self that is enhanced or protected by attitude and belief change.

In many other cultures, however, the prevailing conception of the self is not so narrow. Rather, it is a collective self, expanded to include one's group (Cohen & Gunz, 2002; Markus & Kitayama, 1991). For citizens of these cultures, performing an act that doesn't fit with a personal belief doesn't necessarily threaten the most important (collective) conception of self. Consequently, such personal inconsistencies may not be especially motivating. This may explain why residents of Eastern communal cultures appear to show traditional dissonance effects much less often than do Westerners: Traditional dissonance procedures typically engage only the individualized self (Heine & Lehman, 1997).

This is not to say that citizens of communal societies fail to enhance or protect important aspects of themselves through attitude and belief change. However, the emphasis is on the collective version of self (English & Chen, 2011; Hoshino-Browne et al., 2005; Sedikides, Gaertner, & Vevea, 2005). For example, a message should be more effective in a communal society if it promises group rather than personal enhancement. But the opposite should be true in an individualistic society (Morling & Lamoreaux, 2008). To test this reasoning, Sang-Pil Han and Sharon Shavitt (1994) examined advertisements in two nations characterized by either an individualized or a collective sense of self—the United States and Korea, respectively. First, they evaluated the advertisements that appeared in popular U.S. and Korean magazines over a two-year period. They found that in Korea, the ads appealed more to group and family benefits and harmony, whereas in the United States, they appealed more to individual benefits, success, and preferences.

Just because advertisers in the two cultures use different kinds of appeals, does that mean that they work as intended? To answer this question, Han and Shavitt conducted a second study. They created ads for products (for instance, chewing gum) that emphasized either personal or group benefits ("Treat yourself to a breath-freshening experience" versus "Share a breath-freshening experience"). Next, they showed the ads to potential consumers of the products in Korea and the United States and asked for reactions. In Korea, people were more positive toward the ad, the product, and a purchase when the ad focused on group gain; in the United States, the reverse occurred (see Figure 5.8). Thus, ads that emphasized advantages to the group or to the individual were more successful when the emphasis matched and promoted the culture's predominant version of self.

Figure 5.8 Selling the self in two cultures

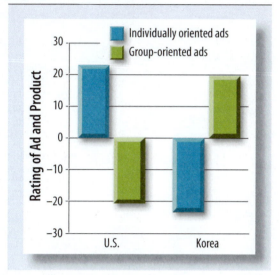

In the United States, where an individualized sense of self predominates, raters had more favorable reactions to ads appealing to individual benefits. But in Korea, where a collective sense of self predominates, the group-oriented ads were better received.

Source: Adapted from Han, S-P., & Shavitt, S. (1994). Persuasion and culture: Advertising appeals in individualistic and collectivistic societies. *Journal of Experimental Social Psychology, 30,* 326–350.

Quick Quiz

1 According to balance theory, if you discover that a likeable celebrity holds a view on abortion that contradicts your own strongly cherished opinion, you are likely to respond by _____.

    a. Changing your view of the celebrity
    b. Changing your opinion on abortion
    c. Experiencing post decisional dissonance
    d. Decreasing your preference for consistency

2 According to cognitive dissonance theory, a _____ action will only produce attitude change when there is _____.

    a. counterattitudinal; insufficient justification
    b. counterattitudinal; little choice
    c. pro-attitudinal; little choice
    d. pro-attitudinal; insufficient justification

3 Which of these factors increases the desire to achieve or maintain cognitive consistency?

    a. Low preference for consistency
    b. Performing an inconsequential behavior
    c. Unpleasant arousal
    d. None of the above

4 Which of the following ads would likely be more effective in a Western (as opposed to Eastern) culture?

    a. An ad for health insurance that depicts a woman parasailing above the crowd sitting on a beach.
    b. An ad for chewing gum that shows a person getting along better with friends because of the gum's breath-freshening properties.
    c. An ad for insurance that depicts grandparents planning for their grandchildren's financial future.
    d. An ad for chewing gum that shows a person benefiting from the gum's tooth-whitening properties.
    e. (a) and (d) only

Gaining Social Approval

LO 5.13 Compare high self-monitors to low self-monitors.

LO 5.14 Identify how men and women differ in opinion change when they desire social approval.

LO 5.15 Explain how the expectation of discussion with another person can affect persuasion.

If you learned that a close friend was offended by your opinion on gun control, would you consider changing your position somewhat? People sometimes shift their positions to gain approval from those around them. Holding the right position can project a public image that opens doors to desired social exchanges, whereas holding the wrong position can lead to social rejection. The motivation to achieve approval is called **impression motivation**, because its goal is to make a good impression on others (Chaiken, Giner-Sorolla, & Chen, 1996). This tendency can sometimes conflict with the pursuit of the other two persuasion-related goals we have discussed—those of accuracy and consistency (Chen, Shechter, & Chaiken, 1996). Let's explore which features of the person and situation tend to make the third goal, social approval, rise above the others.

PERSON   Self-Monitoring

If social gains motivate attitude change, we might expect those who are most attuned to relationships and interpersonal settings to change their attitudes most in response to such rewards.

    Certain individuals are especially adaptable in their opinions as they move from situation to situation. Like attitudinal chameleons, they are able to adjust their "colors" to those that are favored in each new environment. As we discussed in Chapter 4, these individuals are called high self-monitors because they constantly monitor and modify their public selves (how others see them) to fit what is socially appropriate (Snyder, 1987). In contrast, low self-monitors are much more likely to rely on their own standards in deciding how to respond in a new situation. Thus, high self-monitors are more motivated by the social approval goal than are low self-monitors, who are more motivated by the consistency goal (DeBono, 1987).

Impression motivation The motivation to achieve approval by making a good impression on others.

If high self-monitors are especially sensitive to what others think of them, might they be especially susceptible to advertising that promises a desired image in the eyes of others? Several studies suggest the answer is yes. High self-monitors were more persuaded by ads that promoted socially appealing images (prestige, sophistication) associated with particular brands of coffee, whiskey, and cigarettes than they were by ads touting the quality of the same brands (Snyder & DeBono, 1985). Other research finds that high self-monitors are more influenced by image-oriented product names, such as "Fast Track" (Smidt & DeBono, 2011); and they are more persuaded by attractive communicators (Evans & Clark, 2011).

PERSON Gender: Women, Men, and Persuasion

Like high self-monitors, women tend to be sensitively attuned to relationships and interpersonal issues. This sensitivity affects the way they respond to persuasive appeals. When Wendy Wood and Brian Stagner (1994) examined the research investigating differences in persuadability between men and women, they reported a surprising conclusion: Women seem to be more readily influenced than men. What might account for this tendency in women? One hint comes from evidence that the tendency is strongest in group pressure contexts, in which a person's position is out of line with those of the rest of the group. Under these conditions, women are most likely to yield to influence attempts (Eagly & Carli, 1981). An even more instructive insight comes from work showing that if others in the situation cannot observe whether change has taken place, women don't change any more than men (Eagly & Chrvala, 1986; Eagly, Wood, & Fishbaugh, 1981). Thus, you shouldn't expect your letter concerning highway speed limits to generate more change in women, as there is no evidence that women are more persuaded than men under private circumstances.

Why would the presence and surveillance of others in the situation affect women's willingness to agree? Wood and Stagner think the reason lies in the approved gender role for women in most societies. In social contexts, it often falls to women to cultivate positive relationships, to build interpersonal bridges, and to assure social harmony—all of which can be accomplished by shifting toward agreement. To do less is to risk the social disapproval that goes with failing to live up to societal expectations. After all, if women are expected to perform the vital task of fostering cohesiveness and consensus, they are likely to be rewarded for finding ways to agree rather than disagree, especially in social contexts (Carli, 1989; Stiles et al., 1997).

SITUATION The Expectation of Discussion and Self-Monitoring

Earlier, we reviewed research showing that when an issue is personally relevant, people think hard about it and are persuaded only by messages containing strong arguments (Petty & Cacioppo, 1986). These tendencies reflect the desire for accuracy in one's opinions: If an issue affects you personally, you will want to change your position only if provided with good reasons. Persuasion researchers Michael Leippe and Roger Elkin (1987) wondered what would happen if they pitted this accuracy goal against the goal of gaining social approval.

To find out, they exposed Adelphi University undergraduates to a recorded message arguing for the implementation of comprehensive exams at their school in the next year. Half heard strong arguments, and half heard weak arguments. As in prior research, these personally involved students thought deeply about the message arguments, and were much more persuaded when its arguments were strong versus weak.

Fender-bender. Gender-tender. Because of accepted gender roles, women often try to find grounds for agreement in social interactions.

Other subjects in the study were treated similarly, except for one difference: They were told that, after hearing the message, they would have to *discuss* their views on the topic with another student whose position was unknown. With this difference, the researchers introduced another consideration to their subjects. Not only did they have to be concerned about the accuracy of their opinions but also they had to consider the impression their opinions would make on their future discussion partner. Among these subjects, the strength of the message arguments made much less of a difference in determining their attitudes. Rather than changing a lot when the arguments were strong and very little when they were weak, these subjects chose to hold moderate opinions no matter which arguments they heard.

When do these admissions of persuasion reflect actual changes in attitude? It appears that opinion shifts designed to create a good impression on another can become lasting when the process of shifting causes people to think about the topic in a different way from before—for example, by taking the perspective on the topic of the person one is trying to impress. If, instead, the shifts don't cause people to think differently or deeply about the issues, the changes don't last, and people "snap back" to their original positions as soon as they think they don't have to impress anyone any longer (Cialdini et al., 1976; McFarland, Ross, & Conway, 1984; Wood & Quinn, 2003).

INTERACTION

As we have seen, the goal of social approval becomes more relevant when people expect to have to discuss their views with another. However, this expectation does not have equally powerful effects in all people and all situations. For example, it is particularly influential among high self-monitors. Earlier, we differentiated high self-monitors, who focus on the goal of social approval in deciding when to be persuaded, from low self-monitors, who focus more on the goal of self-consistency. One team of researchers (Chen, Schechter, & Chaiken, 1996) reasoned that it should be the approval-oriented, high self-monitors whose attitudes would be most affected by the expectation of discussion. In an experiment testing this reasoning, subjects received a communication arguing that the media should reduce its coverage of terrorist hijackings. Half expected that, after reading the communication, they would have to discuss their views on the topic with another subject whose opinion was unknown. The other half also read the communication but anticipated no later discussion. As predicted, only the high self-monitoring subjects were influenced by the expectation of discussion, becoming significantly more moderate in their positions when they thought they would have to defend those positions. Thus, making approval relevant to the persuasion situation influenced the attitudes of just those individuals who act primarily to achieve the social approval goal.

Our consideration of the impact of the desire for approval on attitude change provides yet another way to understand Peter Reilly's baseless confession. At the time he made it, he had a strong respect for the police (he had hoped to become an officer some day), had just lost his only family, and had been informed, falsely, that his friends had expressed no interest in his well-being—all of which were likely to make him crave the approval of those in that room. Tragically, for Reilly, they were his persuaders, and the one sure way to gain their approval was to agree with them.

INVESTIGATION

Can you recall an instance when you agreed with others on an issue just to gain their approval? What do you think the effect was on your true attitude?

....

Quick Quiz

1 _____ self-monitors are more motivated by the _____ goal, whereas _____ self-monitors are more motivated by the desire for consistency.

    a. Low; social approval; high

    b. High; social approval; low

    c. High; accuracy; low

    d. Low; accuracy; high

2 When are women more likely than men to be influenced by a persuasive appeal?

    a. When a woman's position is out of line with the rest of the group.
    b. Under private circumstances when the appeal comes from a male persuader.
    c. Under private circumstances when the appeal comes from an authority figure.
    d. All of the above

3 Who is more likely to be persuadable when there is an expectation of discussion with another person?

    a. Individually oriented persons
    b. Persons with a high preference for consistency
    c. Low self-monitors
    d. High self-monitors

The Story of Peter Reilly

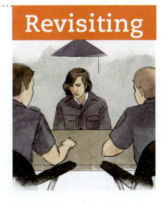

Revisiting

When Peter Reilly was interviewed about his life 20 years after the murder, the damage was still evident. At 38, he was disillusioned, divorced, unemployed, and recently back in Connecticut after bouncing through a series of low-paying jobs in other states (O'Brien, 1993). At the end of that interview, Reilly revealed what it was about the entire affair that most puzzled and distressed him.

Interestingly, it was not the puzzle of how he could have been persuaded to confess falsely to a murder. Comments he made at a conference two years later demonstrated that he understood quite well how it could and did happen:

> To be kept awake for many hours, confused, fatigued, shocked that your only family was gone, in a strange and imposing place, surrounded by police who continue to tell you that you must have done this horrible thing and that nobody cares or has asked about you, . . . assured by authorities you don't remember things, being led to doubt your own memory, having things suggested to you only to have those things pop up in a conversation a short time later but from your own lips . . . under these conditions you would say and sign anything they wanted. (Reilly, 1995, p. 93)

If Peter was aware of precisely how he was led to confess, what was the mystery that still confounded him 20 years after the fact? It was the puzzle of why the police had never changed their minds about him. Despite strong evidence of his innocence, those who extracted his admission of guilt and who used it to convict and imprison him still believed it, insisting that "the subsequent reinvestigation did nothing to change the fact [of Reilly's guilt] as far as we are concerned" (Connery, 1995, p. 92).

Why haven't the police and prosecutors in the case been swayed by the uncovered evidence pointing clearly to Reilly's innocence? The answer to this question allows us to construct an instructive bridge between a real-life incident and a psychological theory that can help us understand it—in this case the theory of cognitive dissonance. Consider the intense cognitive dissonance they would feel if they permitted themselves to believe that they had trapped, convicted, and imprisoned an innocent boy who never fully recovered from the ordeal, while the real killer continued to roam free. Because that belief would be so inconsistent with the central conception of themselves as champions of fairness and justice, it makes sense that they would deny validity to the idea and to any evidence that supported it. To do otherwise would invite heavy psychological costs.

Does psychological self-protection really explain the inflexibility of these individuals? Perhaps any police official or prosecutor looking at the totality of the evidence would judge Reilly guilty. However, that possibility does not fit with the answer to the last mystery we will consider in the Reilly case: How did information hidden for years in the chief prosecutor's files surface to exonerate Reilly after the verdict? Death led to Reilly's rebirth. The prosecutor died of a heart attack, and his successor (who had not been involved in the conviction) came across some startling evidence in the case files—eyewitness reports of two people, including an off-duty state trooper, placing Reilly in another location at the time of the crime. He quickly recognized the need to serve justice by disclosing the evidence and freeing Reilly.

Indeed, every court officer who has seen the evidence and who was not part of the prosecution team decided similarly. It is telling that those officials who were in some way responsible for the harm to Reilly remain adamant that the evidence implicates him. But those looking at the same evidence and having no personal responsibility for past harm see things very differently.

What can we think about the motives of the first prosecutor? By all accounts, he believed fervently in Reilly's guilt until the day he died, sure that he was acting fairly and righteously (Connery, 1977). He no doubt dismissed the critical evidence as unreliable and a hindrance to true justice. And what should we say about the character of the other officials involved who have committed and recommitted themselves to their initial positions in the face of contrary information? If terms such as *immoral* or *malevolent* don't seem appropriate, what label would best apply? We can offer a suggestion: *Human.*

Chapter Summary

Summary of the Goals Served by Persuasion and the Factors Related to Them

The Goal	Person	Situation	Interaction
Seeking accuracy	• Issue involvement • Mood	• Done deals • Unwelcome information	• When striving for accuracy, people rely on the expertise of a communicator principally when the message is highly complex.
Being consistent	• Arousal • Preference for consistency	• Consequences • Salience	• People are more likely to be persuaded by messages that are consistent with the predominant sense of self in their culture.
Gaining social approval	• Self-monitoring • Gender	• Expectation of discussion	• High self-monitors (who pay more attention to social rewards) shift their attitudes and beliefs more than do low self-monitors when expecting a discussion.

The Nature of Attitudes

1. An attitude is a favorable or unfavorable evaluation of a particular thing.
2. Attitudes spring from several sources, including classical conditioning, operant conditioning, observational learning, and heredity.
3. Strongly held attitudes are resistant to persuasion because of two properties: commitment and embeddedness.
4. Factors influencing the likelihood that a person's attitude will be consistent with his or her behavior include knowledge, personal relevance, attitude accessibility, and behavioral intentions.

What Is Persuasion?

1. Persuasion is a change in a private attitude or belief resulting from the receipt of a message.
2. Researchers use covert methods to try to measure persuasion in a nonreactive manner.
3. According to the cognitive response model, the most direct determinant of persuasion is not the persuasive message itself but what the recipient says to him- or herself in response (self-talk).
4. Dual process models of persuasion recognize that attitude change can occur through either deep or superficial processing of the message arguments.
5. Recipients of a message process it deeply when they have both the motivation and the ability to do so; otherwise, they process it superficially.

Having an Accurate View of the World

1. Most of the time, people want to hold accurate attitudes and beliefs. One way to achieve this goal is to

process persuasive messages deeply, thinking carefully about the arguments. However, a second path to this goal is a superficial route in which recipients use shortcut evidence of accuracy.
2. Three sources of shortcut evidence are credible communicators, the responses of others to the message, and ready ideas.
3. People are more motivated to be accurate in their views when the issue involves them personally and when they are in a sad mood.
4. People mostly want to hold accurate attitudes and beliefs before a decision. After the decision is made, they may prefer to be biased in favor of their choice.
5. Sometimes people resist information because it conflicts with what they prefer to believe. When individuals take this to an extreme by denying the validity of threatening information, they put themselves at risk.
6. People are most likely to use communicator expertise as a shortcut to accuracy when the communication is complex.

Being Consistent in One's Attitudes and Actions

1. According to the consistency principle, we are motivated toward cognitive consistency and will change our attitudes and beliefs to have it.
2. Heider's balance theory and Festinger's cognitive dissonance theory both propose that inconsistency produces an uncomfortable tension that pushes people to reduce the inconsistency.
3. Heider asserted that individuals want to experience balance in their cognitive systems and will change their attitudes and opinions to keep the systems in harmony.
4. According to Festinger, inconsistencies on important issues lead to dissonance (a state of uncomfortable

psychological arousal). Research has shown that dissonance is most likely to occur when a counterattitudinal action conflicts with an important aspect of the self, is viewed as freely chosen, cannot be justified as due to strong rewards or threats, cannot be withdrawn, and produces negative consequences.

5. Features of the person and situation that affect the desire for cognitive consistency include level of arousal, preference for consistency, consequences of an action, and salience of the inconsistency.

6. People are more likely to be persuaded by messages that are consistent with the predominant sense of self in their culture—an individualized sense of self in Western cultures and a collective sense of self in Eastern cultures.

Gaining Social Approval

1. People sometimes change their attitudes and beliefs to gain approval.

2. High self-monitors are focused on making a good impression; consequently, they are more likely to be persuaded by advertisements that promise a desirable image in the eyes of others.

3. Women, too, seem more responsive to interpersonal considerations in changing their positions, but not for reasons of image. Instead, the feminine gender role assigns them the task of creating social harmony, which they can often accomplish by finding ways to agree, especially in groups.

4. When expecting to have to discuss one's position on an issue, individuals move toward the center if the position of their discussion-partner is unknown; if it is known, they move toward the partner's position. These tactical shifts, designed to achieve social approval, can lead to genuine, lasting attitude change when the shifts cause people to think differently or more deeply about the issue than before.

5. When the goal of social approval is salient, high self-monitors, who prioritize social approval, are especially likely to change their attitudes toward another when they anticipate a discussion with that other.

Key Terms

Attitude, 140

Balance theory, 163

Central route to persuasion, 150

Cognitive dissonance, 164

Cognitive response model, 147

Consistency principle, 162

Counterargument, 147

Counterattitudinal action, 164

Dual process model of persuasion, 150

Elaboration likelihood model, 150

Impression motivation, 170

Inoculation procedure, 148

Need for cognition, 152

Nonreactive measurement, 147

Peripheral route to persuasion, 150

Persuasion, 145

Postdecisional dissonance, 165

Theory of planned behavior, 145

Chapter 6

Social Influence: Conformity, Compliance, and Obedience

Learning Objectives

LO 6.1   Define conformity, compliance, and obedience.

LO 6.2   Identify the six principles of influence.

LO 6.3   Describe the two powerful principles we use to help us choose correctly and *why* we use them.

LO 6.4   Explain how *consensus, similarity*, and *uncertainty* increase the impact of social validation.

LO 6.5   Explain how a group's injunctive norms can change members' behavior.

LO 6.6   Describe how the norm of reciprocity operates to change behavior.

LO 6.7   Discuss the factors that affect a person's willingness to be influenced by others.

LO 6.8   Describe the four commitment-initiating tactics and how they differ from one another.

LO 6.9   Discuss the two situational features of commitments that make them most enduring.

The Extraordinary Turnaround (and Around) of Steve Hassan

Steve Hassan claims that a high-speed collision with a semitrailer truck battered, hospitalized, nearly killed . . . and saved him.

At the time, Hassan was a member of the Unification Church—an organization better known as the Moonies—whose leader was the Reverend Sun Myung Moon. Although critics described Moon (who died in 2012) as a multimillionaire Korean businessman intent on creating a religious cult to enrich and empower himself and his family, his followers considered him the new Messiah whose mission was to establish a kingdom of God on Earth. As Hassan drove headlong toward the collision that would shatter and "save" him, he was one of Reverend Moon's most fervent followers.

It hadn't always been so. Barely two years earlier, he was a normal 19-year-old college student from a supportive, loving home life and middle-class upbringing. Although not intensely religious, he participated regularly in his Jewish faith along with his family. He was doing well in school and intended to become a teacher and writer after graduation. Despite a desire to improve the world, he was neither obsessed with the idea nor depressed by an inability to make a big difference. In all, there seemed little about him to predict the startling turnaround he would soon make.

After a breakup with his girlfriend left him feeling lonely, things changed quickly. Hassan was approached on campus by three attractive young women who invited him to a discussion-group dinner, made up of young people like himself. He agreed and in the course of a few days he was recruited, indoctrinated, and inducted into Moon's organization.

Over the next two years, he became wholly dedicated to the group and to his role in it—so dedicated that he moved in with the Moonies, turned over his bank account to them, and renounced all sexual relations until his marriage, which would occur only at a time and to a woman chosen by Reverend Moon. He broke off contact with his family and quit school to work full-time raising funds for the organization by selling candles, mints, and flowers on the streets. He allowed himself to be relocated to distant cities, where he labored without pay for long periods with only three to four hours of sleep a night. He never informed his parents or former friends of his whereabouts because he had come to see them, like most other outsiders, as

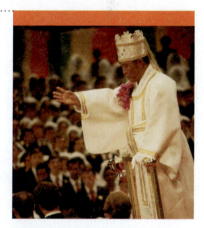

Wedding masses. If he had remained a member of the Unification Church, Steve Hassan may have been part of a mass wedding like this one, dutifully encountering his bride for the first time.

carriers of Satan's message. The work itself was tedious, arduous, and dangerous: Twice, he fought and escaped armed robbers on dark city streets rather than give up the night's proceeds—because, as he explained, "I would never let anyone steal God's money" (Hassan, 1990, p. 24).

Ironically, Hassan's devotion to the Unification Church led to his separation from it. Exhausted from 48 hours of nonstop efforts, he fell asleep at the wheel of the Moonie-owned van he was driving to his next task. After crashing into an 18-wheel truck, he was pinned in the wreckage for nearly an hour while rescue crews struggled to free him. Through the searing pain, he still thought only of his shame at failing his mission. Chanting over and over "Father, forgive me," he blamed himself and worried about the effect of the crash on the group's finances. But a delayed—and revolutionary—reaction to the accident was about to occur.

Following extensive surgery and hospitalization, he was released to visit his sister's home, where he encountered his father and several strangers who said they wanted to discuss his association with the Unification Church. From the start, Hassan knew that the strangers were "deprogrammers" retained by his family to convince him to desert the Messiah. He resisted fiercely. In one harrowing incident, while being driven to an apartment where the deprogramming would take place, he considered reaching over and snapping his father's neck, thinking it better to kill the father who had raised him than to betray the one who had inspired him. Hassan decided against this course of action only because he was sure he could never be moved from his dedication to Reverend Moon.

INVESTIGATION

People seem to be most susceptible to joining a cult relatively soon after some sort of life transition such as a romantic break-up, high school graduation, or a move to a new city. Why would you suppose this is the case?

He was entirely mistaken. Within days, he had rejected Moonie doctrine, expressing deep embarrassment that he had embraced it so completely. He felt bewildered that he had been willing to give up everything—faith, family, and future—to a wealthy businessman who claimed to be the new Messiah. Hassan's turnabout was complete. He became an active opponent of the Unification movement, and today makes his living counseling families on how to help their loved ones escape the control of the Moonies and similar groups. How could Steve Hassan have been so quickly influenced to join and devote himself to this strange religious sect? And, after years of escalating commitment, how was he just as quickly influenced to abandon his deep personal investment in it?

The answers to both puzzles lie in the same set of psychological principles. They are the principles of social influence that we consider in this chapter. *Social influence* can be defined as a change in behavior caused by real or imagined pressure from others. Defining influence as a change in behavior distinguishes it from *persuasion*, which, as we discussed in Chapter 5, refers to a change in private attitudes or beliefs and which may not necessarily lead to behavior change.

The most effective social influence attempts succeed in changing a person's attitudes, beliefs, and behavior, as in Steve Hassan's experience with the Moonies. But shifting someone's attitudes or beliefs isn't necessary for social influence to occur; all that's required is behavior change. For example, a pair of your friends might influence you to come with them to a particular movie without even trying to persuade you that the movie is one you'll enjoy. Instead, they might make you feel obligated to comply simply by pointing out that you chose the movie last week. Although a feeling of obligation is a powerful tool of social influence (Garner, 2005), it's hardly the only one. We will encounter many equally powerful tools in the process of examining, first, the major categories of social influence (conformity, compliance, and obedience) and, next, the major goals of social influence (choosing correctly, gaining social approval, and managing self-image).

Categories of Social Influence: Conformity, Compliance, and Obedience

LO 6.1   Define conformity, compliance, and obedience.

LO 6.2   Identify the six principles of influence.

Social psychologists have considered three major categories of **social influence**: conformity, compliance, and obedience. As one moves from conformity to compliance and, finally, to obedience, the amount of overt social pressure escalates. **Conformity** involves changing one's behavior to match the responses or actions of others, to fit in with those around us. Before a party or concert, you might ask "What will people be wearing?" Imagine showing up in torn shorts and a tie-died T-shirt when everyone else is wearing tuxedos and evening gowns. The discomfort most of us would feel in such situations gives you some sense of the strength of the desire to fit in. Conformity can occur without overt social pressure; no one may ever have to take you aside to say "You're dressed inappropriately," but you may still voluntarily leave to change into an outfit that looks less out of place.

 Compliance refers to the act of changing one's behavior in response to a direct request. The request may come from sources as distinct as friends ("C'mon, have a beer and forget your studying!"), salespeople ("You should sign now because we can't guarantee this model will be here tomorrow."), charities ("St. Mary's Food Bank needs your contributions to feed the poor this Thanksgiving. Please give."), or panhandlers on the street ("Hey buddy, can you spare any change?"). As in the case of a restroom sign asking you to wash your hands before leaving, the requester need not be physically present to exert pressure to comply.

 Obedience is a special type of compliance that involves changing one's behavior in response to a directive from an authority figure. A boss may require employees to work overtime, or a police officer may order drivers to take a detour. In directing others to obey, authority figures typically exert the most overt attempts at influence.

 Before considering the factors that motivate us to yield to social influence pressures, let's explore conformity, compliance, and obedience in greater depth by examining a classic piece of research into each process. These pieces of research are noteworthy in that each revealed more impact of social influence than nearly anyone expected and each stimulated a tradition of investigation that continues today (Cialdini, 2008; Packer, 2008; Pratkanis, 2007).

Conformity: Asch's Research on Group Influence

When Steve Hassan joined the Unification organization, he was pressured to separate himself from the dissenting views of his family and friends, and he was surrounded constantly by believers, a practice common to many extreme religious sects:

> In many cults people eat together, work together, have group meetings, and sometimes sleep together in the same room. Individualism is discouraged. People may be assigned a constant "buddy" or be placed in a small unit of a half dozen members. (Hassan, 1990, p. 60)

 It makes sense that a group's unanimity can influence something as subjective as a person's religious beliefs. After all, whether Reverend Sun Myung Moon was or was not the Messiah can't be tested with hard data. What seems more remarkable is that group pressure can lead people to conform even when contradictory evidence is right before their eyes. This phenomenon was investigated in a series of experiments conducted by Solomon Asch (1956). Asch was interested not only in the submission of individuals to group forces but also in the capacity of people to act independent of conformity pressures.

Social influence A change in overt behavior caused by real or imagined pressure from others.

Conformity Behavior change designed to match the actions of others.

Compliance Behavior change that occurs as a result of a direct request.

Obedience Compliance that occurs in response to a directive from an authority figure.

Figure 6.1 Asch's line-judging task

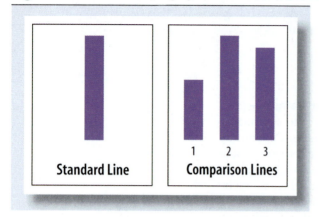

Standard Line   Comparison Lines

In Asch's conformity studies, subjects were shown a standard line like that on the left and three comparison lines like those on the right. Their task was to choose the comparison line that matched the length of the standard line. It was an easy task—until the other group members began choosing incorrectly.

Figure 6.2 Effects of incorrect group judgments on conformity

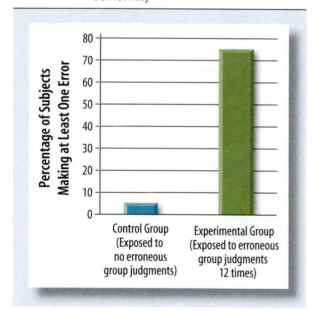

Subjects estimated the length of lines either after the other group members had made no errors in their own estimates (control group) or after the other group members had all judged the line lengths incorrectly (experimental group). Only 5% of control group subjects made any errors. But 75% of experimental group subjects made at least one mistake.

Source: Adapted from Asch, S. E. (1956). Studies of independence and conformity: A minority of one against a unanimous majority. *Psychological Monographs, 70* (9, Whole number 416).

To investigate these processes of conformity and independence, Asch asked college students in groups of eight to match the lengths of different lines. You can see a typical line-matching problem in Figure 6.1. The task was not difficult. In the control condition, when there was no group pressure pushing toward wrong choices, 95% of the participants got all of 12 line matches right. For people in the experimental condition, however, the situation changed. They faced a social consensus that contradicted their own eyes. Before making their own judgments, they heard five other students (who were actually confederates of the experimenter) unanimously agree on an answer that was clearly wrong. Did they stick to their guns and give the right answers or did they go along with the crowd? As shown in Figure 6.2, 75% went against the evidence of their senses and conformed to some extent. Although no one went along every single time, one individual conformed on 11 of the 12 choices.

What was going on in the minds of the participants when they heard the whole group make judgments that seemed plainly wrong? The participant who conformed 11 out of 12 times (more than any other participant) claimed later that he was swayed by the seeming confidence of the other group members. He said he actually came to believe that they were right, thinking that he alone had fallen victim to some sort of "illusion." Asch's research demonstrated that people faced with strong group consensus sometimes go along even though they think that the others may be wrong. In addition, they sometimes believe that the others are right, doubting the evidence of their own senses if the members of their group seem confident enough.

More recently, researchers have examined what happens inside our brains when we find ourselves in disagreement with the group (e.g., Mori & Arai, 2010; Trautmann-Lengsfeld & Hermann, 2013). In one study, the researchers added an interesting twist: The external information came either from four other study participants or from four computers (Berns et al., 2005). Over a series of 32 separate choices, conformity to the external information was significantly greater when it came from a set of peers rather than a set of computers, even though participants rated the peers' and the computers' judgments as equally accurate. If participants viewed the reliability of the two sources of information as the same, why did they conform more to their peers' choices? The answer seems to lie in what occurred whenever they resisted the consensus of the other participants. The area of their brains associated with negative emotion (the amygdala) became activated, reflecting what the researchers called "the pain of independence." It seems that defying one's peers produced a painful emotional state that caused participants to avoid subsequent nonconformity. Defying a set of computers didn't have the same emotional or behavioral consequences, most likely because it wouldn't have the same social consequences (Hodges & Geyer, 2006).

If people will conform to the opinions of strangers convened for a short experiment, think how potent the pressures might be when the other people are members of one's own circle, whose goodwill is treasured. And imagine how much more potent the pressure might become within groups like religious cults, in which the members are taught to suppress their individuality and warned about the importance of blind faith in the group's beliefs. Two months before the Heaven's Gate commune members committed mass suicide in 1997, they spent several thousand dollars for a high-powered telescope because they had heard rumors about a small object (which they suspected was a spaceship) that appeared to be trailing Comet Hale–Bopp. When they complained to the salesman that the telescope showed them no trace of the mysterious object, he explained that there never was a trailing object, only a rumor based on a blip of static in one very early and poor-quality image of the comet. How did they respond to this direct evidence against their group's unanimous and firmly held beliefs about a spaceship carrying their extraterrestrial contacts? They decided to continue believing in the spaceship's existence but to stop looking at the evidence: They turned in the telescope for a refund (Ferris, 1997).

Compliance: The "Foot-in-the-Door" Technique

It seems unlikely that a recruiter for the Unification Church would have had much success if he had walked up to Steve Hassan on campus and asked, "How would you like to drop out of school, break off all ties to your family, and dedicate yourself entirely to collecting money for a cultlike group led by a Korean multimillionaire?" Hassan's recruiters were much more subtle than that. First, he was invited to meet a group of other young people interested in "combating social problems." Next, he was invited to what he was told was a weekend workshop, only to learn later that it went on for three days. Following the more intense recruiting efforts at the workshop, he was urged to attend another workshop, and later—in an ever-escalating order—he was encouraged to become a full member, live in the church house, and donate his bank account to the church. This approach—starting with a small request and advancing to larger requests—is the basis of a commonly used compliance technique called the **foot-in-the-door technique**.

The term *foot-in-the-door* refers to door-to-door salespeople getting one foot in the door as a way to gain full entry. The psychological underpinnings of this technique were investigated in a clever series of experiments by Jonathan Freedman and Scott Fraser (1966). To address their question, "How can a person be induced to do something he would rather not do?" Freedman and Fraser left the laboratory to conduct field experiments.

In one experiment, 156 housewives in Palo Alto, California, were called on the phone and asked to do something the researchers guessed that most people would rather not do: allow a team of six men from a consumer group to come into their home for two hours "to enumerate and classify all the household products you have." The women were told that the men would need full freedom to go through the house exploring cupboards and storage spaces. Only 22% of the women complied. However, another group of women was contacted twice, once with a small request designed simply to get a "foot in the door"—they were asked to answer a series of eight short questions about household soaps (such as "What brand of soap do you use in your kitchen sink?"). It was such a minor favor that nearly everyone agreed. Three days later, these women were contacted by the same consumer group, but now with the larger, home-visit request. Under these circumstances, 52% of the women agreed to allow the team of men to rummage through their cupboards and closets for two hours (Freedman & Fraser, 1966).

Together forever. Being surrounded by like-minded people can have a powerful effect on interpretations of reality. Members of the Heaven's Gate cult were required to disassociate from all family and friends and to consult only with other group members before making any decision. The group's unanimity led members to accept their leader's belief that a spaceship was coming to "take them to the next level." The group was so united, and thereby confident, in this belief that in March 1997, 39 members committed joint suicide to allow their spirits to board that ship.

Obedience: Milgram's Shock(ing) Procedure

In July 1983, 2,075 identically dressed couples were married by Reverend Sun Myung Moon in Madison Square Garden. Most partners were strangers to one another. Why marry a total stranger? In this case, it was because Reverend Moon had chosen the partners and directed them to marry each other. Obeying such an unusual command

Foot-in-the door technique A technique that increases compliance with a large request by first getting compliance with a smaller, related request.

Infiltrating the Influence Professions

A few years ago, one of your textbook authors, Robert Cialdini, was facing a dilemma. He was interested in the reasons people comply with requests of all sorts. Furthermore, he thought that studying the tactics of a wide variety of *successful* "compliance pros" would be especially instructive because these individuals have learned what makes people say yes to requests—otherwise, they wouldn't be successful. But he recognized that few influence practitioners would want him tagging along to record their secrets. To resolve his dilemma, Cialdini engaged in a distinct type of systematic natural observation: **participant observation**. Rather than simply watching from the side, the participant observer becomes an internal spy of sorts. Often with disguised identity and intent, the researcher infiltrates the setting of interest to examine it from within.

To get the insider's view, Cialdini (2008) enrolled in the training programs of a broad range of compliance professions—sales, advertising, fundraising, and so on—learning the same lessons that successful influence practitioners regularly pass on to trainees. He looked for parallels, common principles of influence that rose to the surface and persisted in each of the professions. Six widely used and successful principles of influence, to which we'll refer throughout this chapter, emerged from this program of participant observation:

- *Reciprocation.* People are more willing to comply with requests (for favors, information, and concessions) from other people who previously did them a good turn. Because people feel an obligation to reciprocate, Cialdini found that free samples in supermarkets, free home inspections by exterminating companies, and free gifts through the mail from marketers or fundraisers were all highly effective ways to increase compliance with a follow-up request. For example, according to the Disabled American Veterans organization, mailing out a simple appeal for donations produces an 18% success rate, but enclosing a small gift—personalized address labels— boosts the success rate to 35% (Smolowe, 1990).
- *Commitment/Consistency.* People are more willing to be moved in a particular direction if they see it as consistent with an existing commitment. For instance, high-pressure

Rare value. Marketers have found that making an item seem scarce increases its perceived value.

door-to-door sales companies are plagued by some buyers' tendency to cancel the deal after the salesperson has left and the pressure to buy is no longer present. In training sessions Cialdini attended, several of the door-to-door sales companies claimed that they had significantly reduced this problem with a trick that heightens the customer's sense of personal commitment to the sale: Rather than having the sales representative write in the details of the contract, they have the customer do it.

- *Authority.* People are more willing to follow the recommendations of someone they view as an authority. So automatic is the tendency to follow an authority, Cialdini noted, that many times advertisers try to—and do— succeed merely by employing actors dressed to look like experts (scientists, physicians, police officers, and so on) (Sagarin et al., 2002).
- *Social validation.* People are more willing to take a recommended step if they see evidence that many others, especially similar others, are taking it. Manufacturers make use of this principle by claiming that their products are the fastest growing or largest selling in the market. Cialdini found that the strategy of providing evidence of others who had already complied was the most widely used of the six principles he encountered.
- *Scarcity.* People find objects and opportunities more attractive to the degree that they are scarce, rare, or dwindling in availability. Hence, newspaper ads are filled with warnings to potential customers regarding the folly of delay: "Limited time offer" or "One week only sale." One particularly single-minded movie theater owner managed to load three separate appeals to the scarcity principle into just five words of advertising copy that read: "Exclusive, limited engagement, ends soon."
- *Liking/friendship.* People prefer to say yes to those they know and like. If you doubt this, consider the remarkable success of the Tupperware Home Party Corporation, which has generated billions of dollars in sales by arranging for customers to buy its products not from a stranger across a counter, but from the neighbor, friend, or relative who has sponsored a Tupperware party and gets a percentage of its profits. According to interviews done by Cialdini, many people attend the parties and purchase the products, not out of a need for more containers but out of a sense of liking or friendship for the party sponsor.

Before we can feel secure in the conclusions of participant observation studies, we usually need to find support for their conclusions elsewhere—for example, in experimental research or in additional natural observations by other scientists. Fortunately, as we'll see in this chapter, experimental evidence and additional observations have validated the role of each of these principles in compliance decisions. For instance, in one study, each of the principles, when applied in the sales presentations of department store clerks, produced a significant increase in retail clothing purchases (Cody, Seiter, & Montagne-Miller, 1995).

may make more sense when we realize that Moon's followers regarded him as a divine Messiah on earth. For most of us, however, effective orders can come from decidedly lesser authorities than such beings: Political leaders, military commanders, police officers, high school principals, store managers, and parents issue commands that produce obedience on a daily basis. Social psychologist Stanley Milgram wanted to see how far the obedience-inducing power of authority could be extended. Would you obey orders from a researcher you had never before met if he or she asked you to deliver painful, potentially deadly electric shocks to an innocent victim? And if so, what would the victim have to say to get you to stop obeying such orders?

Mean machine. Milgram's subjects delivered shocks by operating the levers of this intimidating piece of equipment.

In a well-known series of studies done decades ago (see Chapter 1), Milgram (1974) placed advertisements in local newspapers to solicit participants for a "memory experiment" at Yale University. Suppose you signed up to participate in such a study today. Here's what you'd encounter: Upon your arrival at the laboratory, you'd be introduced to another participant (actually a confederate of the experimenter). After hearing that the research would examine the effects of punishment on memory, you'd be assigned to the Teacher role and the other participant to the Learner role in the study. You'd be informed that, as part of your duties, you'd have to deliver a series of electric shocks to the Learner. At this point, the Learner would mention that he had been treated for a heart condition and express concern about the dangers of receiving electric shocks. To this, the experimenter would reply that, although painful, the shocks would produce "no permanent tissue damage."

The experimenter would then take you both to the next room, where the nervous Learner would be strapped into an apparatus looking eerily like an electric chair. That accomplished, you'd be ushered into an experimental room and shown a menacing shock-delivery machine with shock levers ascending from 15 to 450 volts. Each group of four shock levers would be assigned a progressively more frightening label, ranging from "Slight shock" through "Moderate," "Strong," "Very strong," "Intense," "Extreme intensity," to "Danger: Severe shock." A final pair of levers (for the 435- and 450-volt shocks) would apparently deliver shocks so intense that the English language had no words to describe them adequately; they carried only the stark label "XXX."

Before beginning, you would receive an unpleasant sample shock of 45 volts to give you an idea of what the Learner would be experiencing. You'd then be instructed to deliver a shock to the Learner every time he erred on a memory task, advancing to the next higher shock lever with every new mistake. With each error and each more punishing shock, the confederate would voice increasingly desperate cries of pain. At first, he'd simply cry out, "Ugh." At 120 volts, he would shout out, "Hey, this really hurts!" At 150 volts, he'd plead to be released:

> That's all! Get me out of here. I told you I had heart trouble. My heart's starting to bother me now. Get me out of here, please. My heart's starting to bother me. I refuse to go on. Let me out.

Would you continue or stop? If you tried to stop, the experimenter would prod you by saying, "Please continue." If you failed to obey, the experimenter would insist, "The experiment requires that you continue." If you persisted in your disobedience, he'd state, "It is absolutely essential that you continue." Finally, he would demand, "You have no choice; you must go on."

If you continued to follow orders and deliver the shocks, the Learner's appeals would become more agonized and desperate. Finally, he'd burst into a litany of pleas, demands, and shrieks:

> Let me out of here. Let me out of here. My heart's bothering me. Let me out, I tell you. Let me out of here. Let me out of here. You have no right to hold me here. Let me out! Let me out! Let me out! Let me out of here! Let me out! Let me out!

Should that not be enough to convince you to resist the experimenter's orders, things would suddenly change. When you delivered the next shock, you'd hear nothing from the Learner's chamber. If you asked the experimenter to see if the Learner was all right, he'd refuse, saying instead, "Treat no response as a wrong response, and deliver the next

Participant observation A research approach in which the researcher infiltrates the setting to be studied and observes its workings from within.

higher level of shock." For the final eight shocks—into the "Danger" category and the region marked "XXX"—the Learner, once so vocal in his pain, would be deadly silent.

How likely would you and other participants like you be to follow orders to go all the way to 450 volts? Before publishing his study, Milgram described the procedures to 40 psychiatrists at a leading medical school and asked them to predict the results. They expected that fewer than 4% of Milgram's subjects would continue once the Learner stopped answering and that only 0.01% would go all the way to the end. Sadly, the psychiatrists greatly underestimated the power of obedience to authority. Around 75% of the participants continued past the Learner's refusal to answer. Even more remarkably, 65% persisted to the end—defying an innocent victim's repeated screams and enduring his subsequent ominous silence—simply because the "boss" of the study commanded it (see Figure 6.3). What's more, these high levels of obedience have remained steady when researchers have repeated Milgram's procedures in more recent years (Blass, 1999; Burger, 2009).

How do we know that it was authority influence rather than some other factor—the desire to release pent-up aggression, for instance—that caused Milgram's subjects to behave so cruelly? First, it's clear that, without the researcher's directive to continue, the participants would have ended the experiment quickly. They hated what they were doing and agonized over their victim's agony. They implored the researcher to let them stop. When he refused, they went on, but in the process they trembled, perspired, shook, and stammered protests and additional pleas for the victim's release. In addition to these observations, Milgram provided even more convincing evidence for the interpretation of his results in light of obedience to authority. In a later experiment, for instance, he had the researcher and the victim switch scripts so that the researcher told the Teacher to stop delivering shocks to the victim, while the victim insisted bravely that the Teacher continue. The result couldn't have been clearer: 100% of the participants refused to give one additional shock when it was merely the fellow participant who demanded it. These results would hardly be expected if participants' principal motive was to release aggressive energy rather than to follow an authority.

If, as Milgram's research indicates, a majority of people will deliver painful shocks to a heart patient on the orders of a research scientist who has no real authority over

Figure 6.3   Obedience in the Milgram study

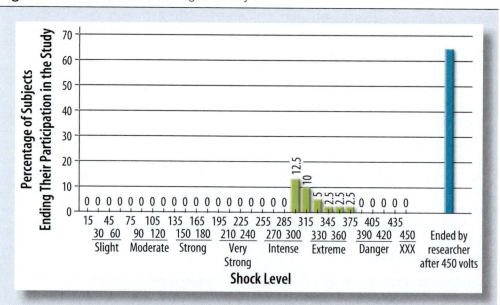

Despite predictions to the contrary from psychiatrists at Yale Medical School, the majority (65%) of subjects obeyed a researcher's commands to deliver every available shock through 450 volts, to an innocent fellow subject.

Source: Based on data from Milgram, S. (1963). Behavioral study of obedience. *Journal of Abnormal and Social Psychology, 67,* 371–378.

them, it becomes less surprising that soldiers will kill innocent civilians and that cult members will kill themselves at the direction of more personally relevant authority figures. But *why* do people obey? What goals are served by this and the other forms of social influence?

INVESTIGATION

In the years following Milgram's studies, some critics faulted him on ethical grounds, saying that he should not have subjected his participants to the stress of thinking they were harming the Learner. Others have defended Milgram, arguing that the importance of his findings outweighed this discomfort. What's your position on this controversy?

The Goals of Social Influence

Notice that conformity, compliance, and obedience all refer not to the act of wielding influence but to the act of yielding to it. When it comes to understanding human motivation, yielding questions are more interesting—and more instructive—than wielding questions. Think of the obvious, self-serving reasons Moonie leaders had for wanting to get Steve Hassan to conform, comply, and obey: They got the benefits of his money, time, energy, and support. In general, it's not difficult to imagine why people would want to influence others to do their bidding. Much more intriguing is why people would agree to *be* influenced. Consequently, that is the question we address. Just as in Chapter 5, in which we emphasized the goals of individuals who choose to alter their attitudes and beliefs, in this chapter we emphasize the goals of those who choose to conform, comply, and obey. As we will see, people yield to social influence to achieve one or more of three basic goals: choosing correctly, gaining social approval, and managing self-image.

Quick Quiz

1. Wearing formal clothing to a friend's wedding is an example of _____, whereas agreeing to a fellow student's request to sign a petition is an example of _____.
   - a. Conformity, obedience
   - b. Obedience, compliance
   - c. Compliance, obedience
   - d. Conformity, compliance

2. Which of the following is one of the six principles of influence described in your text?
   - a. Scarcity
   - b. Liking/friendship
   - c. Reciprocation
   - d. All of the above

3. Which of the following is one of the three basic goals of social influence?
   - a. Gaining social approval
   - b. Choosing correctly
   - c. Managing self-image
   - d. All of the above

Choosing Correctly: Yielding to Be Right

LO 6.3 Describe the two powerful principles we use to help us choose correctly and *why* we use them.

LO 6.4 Explain how *consensus*, *similarity*, and *uncertainty* increase the impact of social validation.

According to Robert W. White (1959), we all have a motive for *competence*, a motive to master our environments so we consistently gain desired rewards and resources. Of course, to do well, we must choose well. From a profusion of possibilities, we must make the choices most likely to bring us the rewards and resources we seek. It's for this reason that influence practitioners are forever trying to convince us that, if we select their products or services we will have chosen well and gotten a "good deal." But how can we know beforehand whether a choice for a particular toothpaste or political candidate will prove wise and effective? Frequently, we rely on two powerful principles to steer us correctly in our influence decisions—authority and social validation.

Authority

The most striking research evidence for the influence of legitimate authority comes from the Milgram obedience study. But the tendency to defer to an authority arises in many more situations than the laboratory setting that Milgram constructed (Blass, 1991; Miller, Collins, & Brief, 1995). What's more, the behaviors influenced in these situations range from the ordinary to the dramatic. In the realm of ordinary behaviors, we can find deference to authority in something as commonplace as the tone of voice one uses in a conversation. Communication researchers have learned that people shift their conversational voice and speech style toward the style of individuals in positions of power and authority (Pittam, 1994). One study explored this phenomenon by analyzing interviews on the *Larry King Live* television show. When King interviewed guests with wide social recognition (for instance, a former president), his voice style changed to match theirs. But when he interviewed guests with less social recognition (for instance, an independent film director), he remained unmoved, and their voice styles shifted to match his (Gregory & Webster, 1996).

As Milgram's findings demonstrated, people also follow an authority's lead in situations with more dramatic consequences. Consider, for example, the catastrophic consequences of a phenomenon that airline industry officials have labeled "captainitis" (Foushee, 1984). Accident investigators from the Federal Aviation Administration have recognized that an obvious error by a flight captain often goes uncorrected by other crew members and results in a crash. It seems that, because of the captain's authority position, crew members either fail to notice or fail to challenge the mistake. They appear to assume that if the captain said it, it must be right.

In light of the remarkable power of authority over human behavior, we can better understand Steve Hassan's actions as a member of the Unification organization. To devoted members, the Reverend Moon was the wisest being on earth, and high-ranking church officials were viewed as intermediaries carrying out his wishes. To fail to follow the directions of any of these individuals would be to disobey ultimate authority. Indeed, when anthropologist Geri-Ann Galanti (1993) secretly infiltrated a Moonie introductory weekend, she found that the group's authoritarian structure was instilled in recruits from the outset:

We were continually made to feel like children rather than adults. Lecturers take on a position of authority because they are the ones in possession of the knowledge. Until we've learned it all, we must remain unquestioning children/students. (p. 91)

It's clear that authorities have a potent impact on the choices and actions of others. What is it about authorities that make them so influential? The teacher role assumed by leaders at the Moonie recruitment weekend provides some clues.

The catastrophic consequences of captainitis.
Minutes before this airliner crashed into the Potomac River near National Airport in Washington, D.C., an alarming exchange occurred between pilot and copilot, concerning the wisdom of taking off with ice on the wings. Their conversation was recorded on the plane's "black box."

Copilot: Let's check those tops [wings] again since we've been sitting awhile.

Captain: No, I think we get to go in a minute.

Copilot: [Referring to an instrument reading] That doesn't seem right, does it? Uuh, that's not right.

Captain: Yes, it is . . .

Copilot: Oh, maybe it is. [Sound of plane straining unsuccessfully to gain altitude]

Copilot: Larry, we're going down.

Captain: I know it! [Sound of impact that killed the captain, copilot, and 67 passengers]

Think back. Throughout your schooling, when your English teachers corrected your writing style, you probably took their criticisms into account in your next paper. That was no doubt the case for multiple reasons. First, like many authorities, teachers have power over you. They can affect your grade in the class, your standing in school, your chances for a good position after graduation, and so on. For such reasons alone, it makes good sense to follow their directions. But there's a second reason. Like many authorities, teachers are experts on the subject at hand. If they say that a sentence you've written is awkward, you're likely to *believe* it and to change in order to improve your writing in general. In short, just as we learned in Chapter 5, following the advice of authorities helps us choose rapidly and correctly. Although some authorities are in a position to force us into obedience, it's more interesting to consider how effective they can be without the power to reward or punish—when what they have instead is **expert power**, the power that comes from acknowledged competence in the matter at hand (French & Raven, 1959).

AUTHORITIES AS EXPERTS   An authority's expert power can have a strong effect on compliance because it serves our strong motivation to choose correctly. Milgram (1965, p. 74) claimed that his subjects' obedience occurred not simply through overt pressure but, as well, "by the uncritical acceptance of the experimenter's definition of the situation." When authorities are presumed to know best, following their lead becomes a sensible thing. This helps explain why less educated individuals are more obedient to authority figures (Hamilton, Sanders, & McKearney, 1995; Milgram, 1974): They tend to presume that authorities know more than they do.

Because following an expert's direction is normally wise, and because authorities are frequently experts, we often use authority as a decision-making heuristic (short-cut). Assuming that an authority knows best can be an efficient way of deciding, because we don't have to think hard about the issues ourselves; all we have to do to be right is accept the authority's advice. But unthinking reliance on authority can be dangerous, too. This shortcut approach can lead us to respond to the symbols rather than the substance of genuine authority.

The results of a study conducted by a team of physicians and nurses revealed the force that one such symbol—the mere title *Dr.*—has in the medical arena. Hospital nurses received a phone call from a man they'd never met but who identified himself as the doctor of a patient on their floor. He then ordered them to give twice the maximum acceptable dosage of a drug to that patient. Ninety-five percent of the nurses obeyed and had to be stopped on their way to the patient's room with the unsafe drug dosage in their hands (Hofling et al., 1966). A follow-up study asked nurses to recall a time when they'd obeyed a doctor's order that they considered inappropriate and potentially harmful to a patient. Those who admitted such incidents (46%) attributed their actions to their beliefs that the doctor was a legitimate and expert authority in the matter—the same two features of authority that appear to account for obedience in the Milgram procedure (Krackow & Blass, 1995). Incidents of this deference to the symbols of authority continue to occur. A 17-year-old convinced nurses at a Virginia hospital to carry out 12 treatments on six patients by misrepresenting himself as a doctor on the phone (Teenager, 2000).

AUTHORITIES AS AGENTS OF INFLUENCE   It should come as no surprise that influence professionals frequently try to harness the power of authority by touting their experience, expertise, or scientific recognition—"Fashionable clothiers since 1841," "Babies are our business, our only business," "Four out of five doctors recommend the ingredients in . . . ," and so on. There's nothing wrong with such claims when they're real, because we usually want to know who is the authority on a topic and who isn't; it helps us choose correctly. The problem comes when we are subjected to phony claims of this sort (Rampton & Stauber, 2001). When we aren't thinking hard, as is often the case when confronted by authority symbols, we can be easily steered in the wrong direction by false authorities—those who aren't authorities at all but who merely present the aura of authority (Sagarin et al., 2002). For instance, people

Expert power The capacity to influence other people as a function of a person's presumed wisdom or knowledge.

are more willing to perform a variety of unusual actions (to pick up a paper bag on the street, stand on the other side of a bus stop sign, put money in someone else's parking meter) if they are directed to do so by someone wearing a security guard's or firefighter's uniform; moreover, they are more likely to do so unquestioningly (Bickman, 1974; Bushman, 1984).

In sum, authorities are formidable sources of social influence. One reason is that they are often expert. Consequently, following their directions offers us a shortcut route to choosing correctly. However, when we defer to authority orders or advice too readily, we risk performing actions that may be unethical or unwise. One recent study found that the vast majority of Dutch college students predicted that they personally would disobey an authority who asked them to do something unethical (write a false testimonial for an experimental method that was likely to potentially traumatize other students). But when students from the same university were actually asked by an experimenter to do that very same unethical act, their behaviors told a less optimistic story—almost 80% went along unquestioningly (Bocchiaro, Zimbardo, & Van Lange, 2012).

Let's turn now to a second major principle that people use to help them achieve the goal of choosing correctly, social validation.

Social Validation

Just as following the advice of an authority is normally a shortcut to good decisions, so is following the lead of most of one's peers (Surowiecki, 2004). If all your friends are raving about a new restaurant, you'll probably like it, too. If the vast majority of online commentaries are raving about a product, then you're likely to feel more confident about clicking the "purchase" button (Guadagno et al., 2013). We use the actions of these others as a means of **social validation**, as an interpersonal way to locate and validate the correct choice (Baron et al., 1996; Festinger, 1954).

Because the desire to choose correctly is powerful, the tendency to follow the crowd is both strong and widespread. On the basis of what their peers are doing, bystanders decide whether to help an emergency victim (Latané & Darley, 1970), juveniles decide whether to commit a wide range of crimes (Kahan, 1997), spouses decide whether to have an extramarital affair (Buunk & Baker, 1995), and homeowners decide whether to conserve energy (Allcott, 2011). In one study, residents of a Los Angeles suburb received information describing the regular curbside recycling behavior of many of their neighbors. This information produced an immediate boost in recycling. And a month

Social validation An interpersonal way to locate and validate the correct choice.

WATCH THE VIDEO: *Using Social Validation to Motivate Environmental Conservation.*

later, they were recycling more trash than ever. These improvements did not occur, however, for residents who received only a plea to recycle but no evidence of others' regular recycling (Schultz, 1999). In this chapter's research video, Robert Cialdini describes how the social validation technique produced a dramatic effect on recycling behavior in hotels, where hotel managers had previously tried numerous ineffective methods to get people to re-use their towels rather than toss them in a pile on the floor.

Whenever influence practitioners identify a psychological principle that people use to reach their goals, the practitioners are sure to use it to advance their own goals. We saw that this was the case for the authority principle, and it is no less the case for the principle of social validation. Sales and marketing professionals make a special point of informing us when a product is the "largest selling" or "fastest growing" in its market. Television commercials depict crowds rushing into stores and hands depleting shelves of the advertised item. Consider the advice offered more than 350 years ago by the Spaniard Balthazar Gracian (1649/1945) to anyone wishing to sell goods and services: "Their intrinsic worth is not enough, for not all turn the goods over or look deep. Most run where the crowd is—because the others run" (p. 142). This tendency to run because others are running affects more than product sales. Indeed, it accounts for some of the most bizarre forms of human conduct on record. In the Bridging Function and Dysfunction feature, we examine one such form, contagious delusions.

Bridging Function and Dysfunction:

Contagious Delusions and Solutions

Throughout history, people have been subject to extraordinary collective delusions—irrational sprees, manias, and panics of various sorts. In his 1841 text, Charles MacKay listed hundreds of examples of "the madness of crowds." It is noteworthy that many shared an instructive characteristic—contagiousness. Often, they began with a single person or group and then swept rapidly through whole populations. Action spread to observers, who then acted and thereby validated the correctness of the action for still other observers, who acted in turn.

For instance, in 1761, London experienced two moderate-sized earthquakes exactly a month apart. Convinced by this coincidence that a third, much larger quake would occur in another month, a soldier named Bell began spreading his prediction that the city would be destroyed on April 5. At first, few paid him any heed. But those who did took the precaution of moving their families and possessions to surrounding areas. The sight of this small exodus stirred others to follow, which, in cascading waves over the next week, led to near panic and a large-scale evacuation. Great numbers of Londoners streamed into nearby villages, paying outrageous prices for any accommodations. Included in the terrified throngs were "hundreds who had laughed at the prediction a week before, [but who] packed up their goods, when they saw others doing so, and hastened away" (MacKay, 1841/1932, p. 260).

After the designated day dawned and died without a tremor, the fugitives returned to the city furious at Bell for leading them astray. As MacKay's description makes clear, however, their anger was misdirected. It wasn't the crackpot Bell who was most convincing. It was the Londoners themselves, each to the other. In all, most people feel that behaviors become more valid when many others are performing them. In instances of mass delusion, this social validation extends to wildly irrational acts that seem to reflect correct choices not because of any hard evidence in their favor but merely because multiple others have chosen them.

Although the tendency to follow the lead of our peers can lead to misguided behavior, most of the time it doesn't. Most of the time it sends us in right directions, toward healthy choices. For example, it has long been known that cigarette smoking is a contagious activity, springing up in clusters among friends, family members, and coworkers. Fortunately, more recent evidence shows that the same contagious quality applies to the process of quitting. Researchers found that whole groups of people quit smoking in concert. When one of their number stopped, smoking among siblings dropped 25%; for coworkers, the drop was 34%; and among friends, it was 36% (Christakis & Fowler, 2008).

Which are the factors that spur people to use the actions of others in the process of trying to choose correctly? Social psychologists have uncovered several. We begin with two that reside in the situation: consensus and similarity.

Consensus and Similarity

While Steve Hassan was a group member, he and other Moonies used a tactic during their introductory recruitment weekends that increased the chance that at least some first-time visitors would return for more training. Likely candidates for Church

Figure 6.4 Looking up

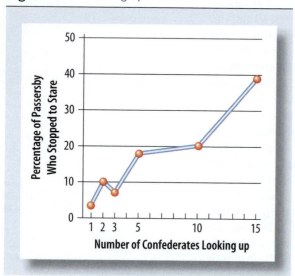

What could motivate pedestrians on a wintry day in New York City to stop, stand, and stare at little of obvious interest or importance? Researchers had sent confederates to stare upward for 60 seconds. The more confederates staring upward at nothing in particular, the more passersby joined the group.

Source: Based on data from Milgram, S., Bickman, L., & Berkowitz, L. (1969). Note on the drawing power of crowds of different size. *Journal of Personality and Social Psychology*, Vol. 13(2), Oct. 1969, 79–82.

membership were grouped with similar likely candidates; they were labeled "sheep." Others who asked too many questions or showed signs of stubborn individualism were labeled "goats" and were quickly separated from the sheep so as not to contaminate them with doubt. Various cultlike groups around the world do the same thing at their introductory sessions. This particular tactic is effective because it incorporates two factors that people rely on to choose correctly: consensus and similarity.

SITUATION **CONSENSUS** Remember Asch's (1956) conformity research? It showed that people would make obvious errors on a line-judging task merely because everybody in their group had already chosen to make that error. Imagine the pressure you would feel in such a situation if *everyone* else chose an answer that looked wrong to you. With perfect agreement among the others, you'd probably trust the group more and yourself less. In your desire to choose correctly, you might well conform because you believed that the group was right. In addition, the more group members who were in agreement, the stronger would be your tendency to conform (Bond & Smith, 1996; Insko et al., 1985) (see Figure 6.4).

In contrast, imagine a slightly different situation: Before you have to give your answer, the consensus of the group is broken by one individual who chooses the line that looks right to you. Now, when it's your turn to speak, what would you do—go along with the majority or join the rebel? Most likely, you'd become much less likely to agree with the majority. Even a single visible dissenter from the group's position emboldens others to resist conformity (Morris & Miller, 1975). Why should that be? One reason is that dissenters reduce confidence that the group has *the* right answer (Allen & Levine, 1969; Gordijn, DeVries, & DeDreu, 2002); therefore, people seeking to select accurately begin looking beyond the group's choice to other possibilities.

Because of the conformity-cracking power of diverse points of view, nearly all cultlike groups try to suppress communication with outside sources of information, including family and friends (Brandis, 2004). According to Steve Hassan (1990), the factor that separates those who leave such groups on their own ("walk-aways") from those who stay is that only the walk-aways have managed to maintain contact with outsiders. For the most part, though, cult members are enveloped by consensus about the teachings of the group, making even wrongheaded beliefs appear correct. Margaret Singer, who spent a lifetime studying cults, frequently asked former members why they remained in their often-abusive groups for as long as they did. Here's a typical answer: "I'd look around and I'd think, 'Well, Joe's still doing it. Mary's still doing it. It must be me; it must be me. *I* just don't get it' " (Singer & Lalich, 1995, p. 273).

SITUATION **SIMILARITY** If people follow the lead of others to make good choices for themselves, it stands to reason that most of the time they would want to follow the actions of individuals similar to themselves (Platow et al., 2005). Suppose you were trying to decide which of the two classes to take next term. Wouldn't you be more likely to seek out and accept the advice of individuals like you, who match your background, interests, and goals? If they think one class is better than the other, the chances are good that you would too (Suls, Martin, & Wheeler, 2000).

Heightened sensitivity to the responses of similar can sometimes be taken to surprising lengths. Take the phenomenon of copycat suicides. After highly publicized suicide stories appear in the media, the suicide rate jumps in those areas that have been exposed to the stories (Phillips, 1989; Sisask & Värnik, 2012). Apparently, certain troubled individuals imitate the actions of other troubled individuals in the act of suicide. What's the evidence that this increase in self-inflicted deaths comes from the tendency to look to similar others for direction? Copycat suicides are more prevalent among people who are similar in age and sex to the victim in the previously publicized suicide story (Schmidtke & Hafner, 1988).

Although similar others can lead us down dark, deadly paths, they can also take us in positive directions. For example, Noah Goldstein and his coworkers wondered if they could increase the willingness of hotel guests to reuse their towels by changing the typical wording of a sign in the room, which urged guests to do so "for the environment." When consensus information was added to the sign—stating that the majority of guests who'd stayed at the hotel did reuse their towels—towel reuse increased by 19%. But when similarity information was added as well—stating that the majority of guests who'd stayed "in this room" had reused their towels—towel reuse jumped by 32% (Goldstein, Cialdini, & Griskevicius, 2008).

In sum, we are more likely to match our actions to those of others when those others are in agreement with one another and akin to us. Both of these factors—consensus and similarity—stimulate conformity because they give us confidence that the others' choices represent good choices for us, too.

INVESTIGATION

Suppose two charity volunteers came to your door and, before asking you to contribute to their cause, they showed you a long list of your neighbors who had already donated. How would they have used consensus and similarity to influence your decision?

....

PERSON ## Uncertainty

When we don't trust our own judgments, we may look to others for evidence of how to choose correctly (Wooten & Reed, 1998). This self-doubt may come about because the situation is ambiguous, as in a classic series of experiments conducted by the Turkish social psychologist Muzafer Sherif (1936). Sherif projected a dot of light on the wall of a darkened room and asked subjects to indicate how much the light moved while they watched it. Actually, the light never moved at all; but, because of an optical illusion termed the *autokinetic effect*, it seemed to shift constantly about, although to a different extent for each subject. When participants announced their movement estimates in groups, these estimates were strongly influenced by what the other group members estimated; nearly everyone changed toward the group average. Sherif concluded that when there's no objectively correct response, people are likely to doubt themselves and, thus, are especially likely to assume that "the group must be right" (p. 111). Many studies have supported his conclusion (Bond & Smith, 1996; Zitek & Hebl, 2007).

Another source of uncertainty is lack of familiarity with a situation. In a novel situation, people are especially likely to follow the lead of others there. Consider how this simple insight allowed one man to become a multimillionaire. His name was Sylvan Goldman. After acquiring several small grocery stores in 1934, he noticed that his customers stopped buying when their hand-held shopping baskets got too heavy. This inspired him to invent the shopping cart, which in its earliest form was a folding chair equipped with wheels and a pair of heavy metal baskets. The contraption was so unfamiliar-looking that, at first, none of Goldman's customers was willing use one— even after he built a more-than-adequate supply, placed several in a prominent place in the store, and erected signs describing their uses and benefits. Frustrated and about to give up, he tried one more trick to reduce his customers' uncertainty—one based on social validation: He hired fake shoppers to wheel the carts through the store. As a result, his real customers soon began following suit, his invention swept the nation, and he died a very wealthy man with an estate of over $400 million (Dauten, 2004).

People also feel unsure of themselves when they face a task that is difficult to solve. Hence, when researchers at Wayne State University gave students the opportunity to conform to the majority position on the answers to math problems, the problems that generated the most conformity were those that were most difficult to answer (Lucas, Alexander, Firestone, & Baltes, 2006). In many cults, knowing what to believe at any given moment is an especially difficult problem to solve—because the answer depends on the ambiguous and constantly changing opinions of the leaders. In addition, cult groups

Figure 6.5 Conformity and uncertainty

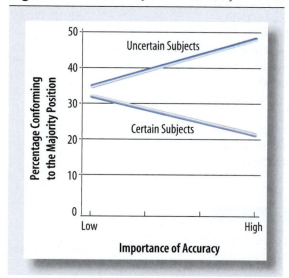

Subjects who were uncertain of their judgments on a face-identification task conformed to the unanimous majority position more often when being accurate was especially important to them. However, those who were certain of their judgments conformed less often when accuracy was especially important. Thus, only the uncertain individuals chose conformity as the best route to accuracy.

Source: Adapted from Baron, R. S., Vandello, J., & Brunsman, B. (1996). The forgotten variable in conformity research: Impact of task importance on social influence. *Journal of Personality and Social Psychology, 71,* 915–927.

often add to their members' sense of disorientation by using tactics such as exhaustion and sleep deprivation (Baron, 2000). As Steve Hassan (1990) reports, "in such an environment, the tendency within most people is to doubt themselves and defer to the group" (p. 68).

When people feel unsure of their grasp on reality, they're more likely to defer to authority figures, too. In field tests of combat artillery units, teams that are fully rested often refuse to fire on hospitals and other civilian targets, but after 36 sleepless hours, they obey orders to fire at anything without question (Schulte, 1998).

INTERACTION Now that it seems clear that one reason people conform to the majority is to choose accurately, wouldn't you agree that the more someone wants to be accurate, the more he or she will conform to what everyone else has decided? If you do agree, you would be right. But sometimes you would be wrong, because uncertainty interacts with one's desire for accuracy, and it can change everything.

To examine how uncertainty and the desire for accuracy can interact, Robert S. Baron, Joseph Vandello, and Bethany Brunsman (1996) created a variation of the Asch line-judging procedure. Instead of choosing correct line lengths, University of Iowa undergraduates had to choose the correct suspect in criminal lineups. First, they saw a picture of a single criminal suspect. Then, they saw a picture of a lineup containing four suspects, including the one they had previously seen. Their task was to pick out of the lineup the previously seen suspect. This was repeated 13 times with 13 different pairs of pictures. To make accuracy especially important for one group of students, the researchers promised a $20 prize to those who made the most correct choices. But, for some students, there was an added complication—the pictures were flashed on a screen so quickly (half a second each) that they couldn't be very certain of their judgments. Other students did not encounter this uncertainty because, for them, the pictures were left on the screen for five seconds each.

How did the students choose when, on seven separate occasions, they heard confederates unanimously identifying the wrong suspects in the lineups? Did they conform to the majority or stay with their own judgments? That depended on how uncertain they were of their private judgments and on how important accuracy was for them on the task. Those who were unsure of their judgments became more likely to conform to the majority when accuracy was important; but those who were sure of their judgments became less likely to conform when accuracy was important (see Figure 6.5). Although the sure and unsure individuals moved in opposite directions, their movement was motivated by the same goal: to choose correctly. The critical difference between them was whether they felt that relying on themselves or on others offered the best route to choosing correctly. The motivation to be accurate pushes us toward conformity only when we are unsure of our own judgments.

Quick Quiz

1 The phenomenon that airline officials describe as "captainitis" demonstrates the effect of _____.

    a. social validation

    b. authority

    c. reciprocity

    d. liking/friendship

2 A saleswoman on a shopping network telling viewers she is offering a "bestselling" necklace is using the _____ principle to increase her sales.

    a. scarcity

    b. expert power

    c. consensus

    d. social validation

3   Which of the following statements is true?
  a. When a situation is ambiguous for all group members, conformity tends to decrease.
  b. People are more likely to conform when they are motivated to be accurate, regardless of their certainty in their own judgments.
  c. People are more likely to conform when they feel uncertain of their own judgment and are motivated to be accurate.
  d. None of the above

Gaining Social Approval: Yielding to Be Liked

LO 6.5   Explain how a group's injunctive norms can change members' behavior.

LO 6.6   Describe how the norm of reciprocity operates to change behavior.

LO 6.7   Discuss the factors that affect a person's willingness to be influenced by others.

Most everyone wants to be correct. But it's not easy. Part of the difficulty comes from the fact that the term *correct* can have two different and sometimes opposing meanings. So far in this chapter, we've emphasized just one of these meanings—accuracy. We've focused on the willingness to be influenced in order to be *right*. But the second meaning of being correct—being socially appropriate or approved—can also leave people open to influence (Insko et al., 1983). For example, after being ignored and excluded in an Internet game, participants (from 14 different countries) conformed more to the group opinion on a subsequent task (Williams, Cheung, & Choi, 2000). Thus, people frequently change to be more accepted in their group or culture—in other words, to belong (Baumeister & Leary, 1995; Williams, 2007).

Take, for example, the account by Irving Janis (1997) of what happened in a group of heavy smokers who came to a clinic for treatment. During the group's second meeting, nearly everyone took the position that, because tobacco is so addicting, no one could be expected to quit all at once. But one man disputed the group's view, announcing that he had stopped smoking completely since joining the group the week before and that others could do the same. In response, the other group members banded against him, delivering a series of angry attacks on his position. At the following meeting, the dissenter reported that, after careful thought, he had come to an important decision: "I have gone back to smoking two packs a day; and won't make any effort to stop again until after the last meeting" (p. 334). The other group members immediately welcomed him back into the fold, greeting his decision with applause.

This account illustrates the old dictum that "it's easier to get along if you go along." In a classic set of studies, Stanley Schachter (1951) observed how groups pressure members who deviate from the consensus. In newly formed discussion teams, Schachter planted a male confederate who asserted an opinion different from the other members. The group's reaction typically followed a three-step sequence. First, the others directed a large number of comments to the deviate, arguing heatedly with him. Next, when he failed to come into line with the group mind, the other members began to ignore him and to treat him with disdain. Finally, when he held firm through the shift from hot attack to cold shoulder, he was rejected outright with a vote to expel him from the group.

However, Schachter found that groups can respond with affection to opinion deviates, provided the dissenters admit the error of their ways and adopt the group's view. In some discussion groups, the confederate was programmed to be a "slider"—someone who began by disagreeing, but who gradually yielded to group pressure. What happened to the slider? He, too, received an initial barrage of comments designed to convert him to the group position. But, because he yielded, he never experienced the disdain and rejection that the unbending deviate did. In fact, the slider was embraced as fully into the group as any other member. For a deviate in a group, then, the unforgivable sin is not to be different; it is to *stay* different. As a result, many dissenting individuals shift toward group consensus to be accepted and to avoid rejection.

Wheel deal. Carpooling is an example of the norm of reciprocity. Each member receives the favor of a free ride and then feels obligated to return the favor.

Coffee sweetener. Small amounts of food or drink are often given away to spur purchases.

These twin needs to foster social acceptance and escape social rejection help explain why cults can be so effective in recruiting and retaining members. An initial showering of affection on prospective members, called "love bombing," is typical of cult induction practices. It accounts for some of the success of these groups in attracting new members, especially those feeling lonely or disconnected. Later, the threatened withdrawal of that affection accounts for the willingness of some members to remain in the groups: After having cut their bonds to outsiders, as the cults invariably urge, members have nowhere else to turn for social acceptance.

Social Norms: Codes of Conduct

How can people know which behaviors will lead to social acceptance? The message is carried in the social norms of the group or culture. As we discussed in Chapter 2, **descriptive norms** define what is typically done; and **injunctive norms** define what is typically approved and disapproved (Cialdini, Kallgren, & Reno, 1991; Jacobson, Mortensen, & Cialdini, 2011). Although what is usually done and what is usually approved are frequently the same, this is not always so. For instance, the great majority of holiday shoppers may pass by a Salvation Army charity kettle without giving a donation, even though that same majority may nevertheless approve of giving to the organization.

Descriptive norms can inform people of what is likely to be effective action for them. Thus, these norms connect to the first goal we discussed in this chapter, the goal of choosing correctly (accurately). By following what most people do in a setting, one can usually make an accurate choice. Injunctive norms, on the other hand, inform people of what is likely to be acceptable to others. These norms connect to the second goal of social influence, the goal of social approval (Crandall, Eshleman, & O'Brien, 2002). If you want to enhance the extent to which you are appreciated and wanted in a group, you would be best advised to pay special attention to injunctive norms.

One particular injunctive norm that is renowned for its favorable effect on social relationships is the norm for reciprocity. It produces potent forms of social influence. According to the sociologist Alvin Gouldner (1960), every human society abides by the **norm of reciprocity**, which obligates people to give back the type of behavior they have received.

The norm of reciprocity creates one of the great benefits of social life. If you do me a favor today, you have the right to expect a favor from me tomorrow (Pilluta, Malhotra, & Murnighan, 2003). Those traded favors allow us to accomplish tasks we could not do alone (moving a heavy dresser, for example) and help us all survive through uneven times (buy me lunch today when I'm broke, and I'll buy you lunch when my paycheck comes in). Through the obligated repayment of gifts, favors, and services, people become connected to one another in ongoing relationships. The future reach of this obligation is nicely connoted in a Japanese word for thank you, *sumimasen*, which means "this will not end" in its literal form. Anyone who violates the norm by taking without giving in return invites social disapproval and risks the relationship (Cotterell, Eisenberger, & Speicher, 1992; Meleshko & Alden, 1993). Most people feel uncomfortable receiving without giving in return because they don't want to be labeled as "takers" or "moochers."

Descriptive norm A norm that defines what behaviors are typically performed.

Injunctive norm A norm that defines what behaviors are typically approved or disapproved.

Norm of reciprocity The norm that requires that we repay others with the form of behavior they have given us.

RECIPROCAL FAVORS   The reciprocity norm is often exploited by influence professionals who begin by giving us something before asking for compliance with their request. Businesses do it all the time by offering "free gifts" for simply listening to a sales pitch, "free workouts" at health spas, "free weekends" at resorts, "free inspections" in the home, and so on. Such techniques are often effective in getting people to buy products and services that they would not have purchased without the powerful social pressure produced by having accepted a gift (Gruner, 1996). Waiters and waitresses can significantly increase the size of their tips by giving diners something as small as a single piece of candy (Lynn & McCall, 1998; Strohmetz et al., 2002).

RECIPROCAL CONCESSIONS   Gifts, favors, and services are not the only actions governed by the reciprocity norm; so, too, are the *concessions* people make to one another in negotiations. After receiving a concession from another, most people feel an obligation to make a concession in return. A compliance tactic designed to exploit this felt obligation is called the reciprocal concessions or **door-in-the-face technique** (Cialdini et al., 1975). Rather than starting with a small request designed to get a yes and then advancing to the desired favor (as occurs in the foot-in-the-door technique), someone using the door-in-the-face technique begins with a large request intended, of all things, to get the target person to say no! After the target rejects the first request, however, the requester *retreats* to the desired favor. By retreating from a large first favor to a smaller one, the requester appears to make a concession to the target, who—through the norm of reciprocity—feels obligated to provide a return concession by agreeing to the reduced favor. Several years ago, a resourceful Boy Scout selling tickets to the circus used the technique on one of this text's authors:

"*How much would you pay for all the secrets of the universe? Wait, don't answer yet. You also get this six-quart covered combination spaghetti pot and clam steamer. Now how much would you pay?*"

The that's-not-all technique.

Source: Michael Maslin The New Yorker Collection/The Cartoon Bank

> He asked if I wished to buy any tickets at $5 apiece. . . . I declined. "Well," he said, "if you don't want to buy any tickets, how about buying some of our big chocolate bars? They're only $1 each." I bought a couple and, right away, realized that something noteworthy had happened. I knew this to be the case because: (a) I do not like chocolate bars; (b) I do like dollars; (c) I was standing there with two of his chocolate bars; and (d) he was walking away with two of my dollars. (Cialdini, 2008, p. 36)

Related to the door-in-the-face technique but somewhat different is the **that's-not-all technique**. An important procedural difference between the two techniques is that in the that's-not-all tactic, the target person does not turn down the first offer before a better second offer is provided. After making the first offer but before the target can respond, the requester betters the deal with an additional item or a price reduction.

Jerry Burger (1986) found this approach useful for selling bakery goods during a campus bake sale. After first citing a price of $1 a piece for cupcakes and before customers responded, the salesperson added two cookies to the deal at no extra cost. This produced more purchases than simply offering a cupcake and two cookies at a $1 price from the outset (76% versus 40%). One reason this technique works is that the target person feels a need to reciprocate the receipt of the improved deal.

NORMS OF OBLIGATION ACROSS CULTURES   Although the obligation to reciprocate what one has received exists in all human societies (Gouldner, 1960), it may not apply with the same strength in each (Shen, Wan, & Wyer, 2011). Michael Morris, Joel Podolny, and Sheira Ariel (2001) gained access to a multinational bank (Citibank) that had branches in 195 countries. The researchers selected four societies for examination: the United States, China, Spain, and Germany. They surveyed multiple Citibank branches

Door-in-the-face technique A technique that increases compliance by beginning with a large favor likely to be rejected and then retreating to a more moderate favor.

That's-not-all technique A technique that increases compliance by "sweetening" an offer with additional benefits.

within each society and measured employees' willingness to comply voluntarily with a request from a coworker for assistance with a task. The main reason employees felt obligated to comply differed in the four nations. Each of these reasons reflected a different normative approach to obligation.

- *In the United States.* Employees in the United States took a *market-based* approach to the obligation to comply. They offered assistance on the basis of the norm for a reciprocal exchange of favors between two individuals. In deciding to comply, they asked, "What has this person done for me recently?" They felt most obligated to comply if they owed the requester a favor.

- *In China.* Employees in China took a *family-based* approach. They offered assistance on the basis of ingroup/outgroup norms that encourage loyalty only to those within one's small group. In addition, they felt especially loyal to those of high status within their small group. In deciding to comply, they asked, "Is this requester connected to someone in my unit, especially someone of high ranking?" If the answer was yes, they felt obligated to yield to the request.

- *In Spain.* Spanish personnel took a *friendship-based* approach. They offered assistance on the basis of friendship norms that encourage loyalty to one's friends, regardless of the friend's position or status. They decided to comply by asking, "Is this requester connected to my friends?" If the answer was yes, they felt obligated to say yes.

- *In Germany.* German employees took a *system-based* approach to obligation. They offered assistance on the basis of the existing norms and rules of the organization. Rather than feeling obligated to specific individuals or groups, they felt obligated to support the system that governed these individuals and groups. They decided to comply by asking, "According to official rules and categories, am I supposed to assist this requester?" If the answer was yes, the obligation to grant the request was high.

Clearly, different norms of obligation to comply with requests predominate in different cultures. This is not to say that these cultures are entirely different from one another in this regard. No doubt, obligations to prior benefactors, to ingroup members, to friends, and to legitimate systems exist in all four of the cultures studied by Morris, Podolny, and Ariel. But, as their findings make clear, the relative potency of these different norms of obligation varies from culture to culture.

<hr/>

INVESTIGATION

On the basis of Morris, Podolny, and Ariel's (2001) findings, how would you structure a request (differently) to a person from each of the cultures they studied?

<hr/>

 PERSON — ## What Personal Factors Affect the Impact of Social Approval?

Imagine that before going to dinner with friends, there is divided opinion about whether to eat Mexican or Italian food. At the restaurant, opinions diverge in a discussion of a hot political topic. After dinner, there is another difference of opinion, this time over whether to go to a crowded bar for a drink or to a quiet coffee shop for intellectual conversation. Do you have a friend who would be especially likely to go along with the group in each instance to keep things operating smoothly? Can you think of another friend who would be willing to resist to the bitter end? What might be the psychological differences between the two people? In other words, what factors inside the person affect the tendency to "go along to get along," the willingness to be influenced in order to be socially approved? Let's explore three person factors that affect whether an individual is likely to accommodate to the group position—approval, collectivism versus individualism, and resistance—beginning with approval.

DESIRE FOR APPROVAL   Certain individuals are very concerned with social approval and seem highly motivated to gain the respect of those around them. In an early study of personality and conformity, researchers measured people's need for social approval before observing how these same people responded to group pressure to make in-correct choices (as in the Asch line-judging experiments we described earlier). Just as would be expected if need for social approval motivates people to yield to others, those whose personality test scores indicated a high need for approval were more likely to go along with the group (Strickland & Crowne, 1962). Similarly, college students who feel a need for social support are more likely to match their alcohol consumption patterns to those of their peers (Cullum et al., 2011).

Treating the desire for approval as a need frames it in a somewhat negative way, implying that going along with others is based in some personality weakness. How-ever, there is another way to view it. The desire for approval is at the center of the "nicest" of the major personality factors—agreeableness. Agreeableness is made up of a host of positive characteristics, including warmth, trust, and helpfulness. In addition, agreeable people are described as accommodating and compliant. They are inclined to go along with others in their groups to avoid conflict (Suls, Martin, & David, 1998). Psychologists who have studied personality and social behavior have suggested that agreeableness may have been vitally important to our ancestors' survival in groups (Graziano & Eisenberg, 1997; Hogan, 1993). According to this perspective, yielding in order to be agreeable should be regarded positively, as a valued personal trait. Af-ter all, it would be impossible for groups to function efficiently without a substantial amount of member conformity (Tyler & Degoey, 1995).

COLLECTIVE SENSE OF SELF   Earlier, we said that the injunctive norms of a group or culture tell people which of their behaviors will be met with social approval. However, some individuals in these groups and cultures are more likely than others to live up to these norms. What determines this tendency to respond to social norms rather than to personal preferences? One cause is a person's definition of self. Some people character-ize themselves in personal and individualized terms, focusing on features that distin-guish them from others: "I am an avid outdoors person with a strong spiritual nature." Other people characterize themselves in collective terms, identifying themselves by the groups to which they belong: "I am a member of the Sierra Club and am active in the Campus Interfaith Council." David Trafimow and Krystina Finlay (1996) found that people who defined themselves in individualistic ways made their decisions on the basis of their personal attitudes rather than group norms. However, those who defined themselves through their groups were more affected by what they thought others felt than by what they felt. Cultures that differ in the extent to which they are individualistic or collectivistic also produce this effect. In the Asch line-judging proce-dure, citizens of the more collectivistic societies of the East conform to a greater extent than do citizens of the more individualistic societies of the West (Bond & Smith, 1996).

RESISTANCE   Perhaps you've noticed that almost all of the processes and tactics cov-ered in this chapter—for example, authority, social validation, the foot-in-the-door technique—cause people to *yield* to social influence. Eric Knowles and his colleagues (Davis & Knowles, 1999; Knowles & Linn, 2003) have argued that just as important as these influence-enhancing factors (which they have termed *Alpha forces*) are factors that lead people to resist social influence (which they have termed *Omega forces*). Thus, a relatively underappreciated way to get people to say yes is to reduce the power of the (Omega) forces causing them to resist your influence attempt. One such tactic is the **disrupt-then-reframe technique**. For instance, consider the problem facing Charlie, a door-to-door solicitor selling greeting cards at an excellent price. Part of his difficulty is that most customers feel resistant when asked to buy anything by someone who appears uninvited at their door, because they view the event as a potential scam. If Charlie could somehow disrupt the customers' perception of his offer as a scam and replace it with a more favorable conception of the offer, that should increase purchases by decreasing customers' resistance. To see if this was the case, researchers posing as salespeople went door-to-door offering a packet of eight high-quality greeting cards for an attractive price ("They're $3."); with this wording, only 35% of the prospects bought any cards. Adding a favorable label to the deal ("They're $3. It's a bargain."), didn't help the salespeople at all, as once again only 35% of the prospects bought cards.

Disrupt-then-reframe technique
A tactic that operates to increase compliance by disrupting one's initial, resistance-laden view of a request and quickly reframing the request in more favorable terms.

Non Sequitur by Wiley Miller

Backpedaling. According to reactance theory, people want to resist influence attempts that reduce their freedoms.

Source: Universal UClick

However, wording designed to confuse and disrupt customers' initial representation of the event and then quickly to reframe the event in favorable terms ("These cards sell for 300 pennies . . . that's $3. It's a bargain."), pushed the success rate to 65% (Davis & Knowles, 1999). Apparently, saying something unexpected ("These cards sell for 300 pennies.") temporarily disrupted customers' typical, resistance-laden thinking about door-to-door sales, which allowed the salespeople to strike swiftly and reframe the exchange as a bargain. Perhaps the most instructive point in all this is that, besides human tendencies to say yes to social pressure, there are equally important tendencies to say no. To fully understand the social influence process, we must consider processes that affect each type.

Various tendencies to resist social influence exist to some degree in most people. For example, according to **reactance theory** (Brehm & Brehm, 1981), we all value our freedom to decide how to act. When something (such as social pressure) threatens to take away that freedom, we often respond by doing the opposite of what we are being pressured to do. For instance, one study found that drivers who returned to their parked cars were slower at leaving their parking spaces if another driver was waiting to take the space. In addition, they moved even more slowly if the waiting driver honked to pressure them to leave faster (Ruback & Juieng, 1997).

Of course, some people respond against threats to their freedoms more strongly than do others (Nail & Van Leeuvan, 1993; Nail, McDonald, & Levy, 2000). These reactant individuals can be identified by a personality scale that includes items such as "If I am told what to do, I often do the opposite" (Bushman & Stack, 1996; Dowd, Milne, & Wise, 1991). Studies have found that highly reactant individuals are more likely to defy the advice of even their therapists and physicians (Dowd et al., 1988; Graybar et al., 1989).

Suppose you wanted to reduce the negative effects of reactance on the likelihood that someone would comply with your request. A simple way might be to end your request by stating, "Of course, it's up to you" (Gueguen et al., 2010). In one study, such a statement increased compliance with a panhandler's request for money by 400% (Gueguen & Pascual, 2000).

SITUATION ## What Situational Factors Affect the Impact of Social Approval?

Which features of a person's social situation are likely to alter the motivation to go along to get along? One factor is the appeal of the group or individual pressuring for change. For example, if you found yourself among people you didn't much care for, you would be unlikely to try to dress like them, comply with their requests, or obey their directives. In contrast, you would be much more receptive to the influence efforts of people you liked or valued (Platow et al., 2005). A second factor is the observability of the behavior in question. People are more likely to act in socially approved ways when their actions are visible to others. Let's look at each of these factors in turn.

OTHERS' APPEAL Would you choose a political decision maker simply because he or she was good-looking? Although you might think not, candidates' looks have a deceptively strong impact on elections (Budesheim & DePaola, 1994; White, Kenrick, & Neuberg, 2013; Zebrowitz, 1994). For example, voters in a Canadian federal election gave physically attractive candidates several times as many votes as they gave unattractive ones—while insisting that their choices would never be influenced by something as superficial as appearance (Efran & Patterson, 1974, 1976). Looks are influential in other domains as well. Good-looking fundraisers for the American Heart Association

Reactance theory Brehm's theory that we react against threats to our freedoms by reasserting those freedoms, often by doing the opposite of what we are being pressured to do.

generated nearly twice as many donations (42% versus 23%) as other requesters (Reingen & Kernan, 1993). It is not surprising, then, that when Steve Hassan accepted an invitation to his first Unification Church weekend, it was at the urging of three attractive young women he met on campus.

In addition, we are more attracted to—and more influenced by—those with whom we share connections and group memberships, especially when these similarities have been made prominent (Burn, 1991; Turner, 1991). Thus, salespeople often search for (or fabricate) a connection between themselves and their customers: "Well, no kidding, you're from Minneapolis? My wife's from Minnesota!" Fundraisers do the same, with good results. In one study (Aune & Basil, 1994), on-campus donations to charity more than doubled when the requester claimed a shared group identity with the target person by saying "I'm a student, too."

Hat trick. Influence professionals of all sorts recognize the compliance-producing power of common group membership.
Source: Cartoonbank

PUBLIC OBSERVABILITY   Just as we would expect, if social influence is sometimes based on the desire for acceptance and approval, conformity is less prevalent in private. When people can keep their decisions secret, they don't have to worry about the loss of connection and respect that an independent opinion might create.

Chester Insko and his colleagues (1985) demonstrated this point by presenting groups of University of North Carolina students with an ambiguous problem: judging whether a blue-green color was more blue or more green. When the students had to announce their judgments aloud and in public (rather than writing them down privately), they conformed more to what the other group members had said. Other studies have shown similar effects with judgments as trivial as evaluations of the taste of coffee and as serious as decisions about how to handle racist propaganda on campus (Blanchard, Lilly, & Vaughn, 1991; Cohen & Golden, 1972). After learning what others have said, people are especially likely to go along if their own responses are observable to the group (Campbell & Fairey, 1989). Cults appear to recognize that conformity is stronger when behavior is observable: Many such groups keep members under the unrelenting gaze of other members. For example, the Heaven's Gate cultists, who committed joint suicide in 1997, were required to perform their daily activities with a "partner" from the group.

In sum, people are more likely to go along with the influence attempts of appealing individuals because they are more motivated to gain the approval of those individuals. Two important situational sources of personal appeal are physical attractiveness and common group membership. Because the increased yielding comes from a desire to get along with these others, their influence is most pronounced when they can see whether yielding occurred.

INTERACTION   Who's Strong Enough to Resist Strong Group Norms?

Norms don't always steer people in beneficial directions. What the people in one's group typically do and approve can be unhealthy. For example, among certain subgroups of young people, peer norms may support such dangers as alcohol and tobacco use. When these potentially harmful norms are strong, is there any psychological factor that will help resist them? Alan Stacy and his coworkers (1992) investigated several possible factors that might reduce high school students' vulnerability to peer norms for cigarette smoking. Only one proved effective: the students' belief that they possessed the ability to resist their peers' influence. A student who held this belief was significantly more

Figure 6.6   Message pollution

Gross National Product.

This year
Americans will
produce more
litter and
pollution
than ever before.

If you don't do
something
about it,
who will?

**Give A Hoot.
Don't Pollute.**

Forest Service-USDA

In an attempt to dramatize the problem of littering, the developers of this public service announcement have contaminated their message with a potentially harmful countermessage: "Littering is what we Americans do."

Bridging Theory and Application:

Doing Wrong by Trying to Do Right

In many schools, it has become common to give students resistance training intended to equip them with the skills necessary to reject the influence efforts of peers who try to tempt them into unhealthy habits. The resistance-skills education often takes the form of "just say no" training, in which students repeatedly practice how to deflect the negative influence of classmates. These resistance-skills-only programs have produced an entirely unexpected result: Despite coming to see themselves as more able to resist peer influence, the students in the programs often become more likely to engage in the unhealthy habits!

How could this be? A study done in the Los Angeles and San Diego County public school systems offers an answer. It examined the impact of junior high school programs for limiting adolescent alcohol use. After participating in multiple "just say no" skits and exercises intended to bolster their resistance to peer pressure to drink, students came to believe that drinking was more common among their peers than they had previously thought (Donaldson, Graham, Piccinin, & Hansen, 1995). By giving students resistance skills through repeated "just say no" trials, the program inadvertently conveyed an unintended message—"A lot of your peers do this and want you to do this." Thus, although these students became more able to resist peer influence, they became less motivated to do so because they perceived that drinking was the norm for people their age.

Alcohol-reduction programs are not the only ones that have backfired in this way. After participating in an eating disorder program at Stanford University, college women exhibited more eating disorder symptoms than before. Why? A key feature of the program was the testimony of classmates about their own harmful eating behaviors, which made such behaviors seem more prevalent to participants (Mann et al., 1997). Similarly, a suicide-prevention program administered to New Jersey teenagers informed participants of the alarmingly high number of teenage suicides. As a consequence, participants became more likely to see suicide as a possible solution to their problems (Shaffer et al., 1991).

In all, there seems to be an understandable but misguided tendency of health educators to call attention to a problem by depicting it as regrettably frequent. It is easy to forget that the statement "Look at all the people like you who are doing this *unhealthy* thing" contains the powerful and potentially undercutting message "Look at all the people like you who *are* doing it" (see Figure 6.6).

What can program designers do to avoid these boomerang effects? Health educators must structure their programs so participants see the unwanted behavior as the exception rather than the rule. That way, the power of norms will work for the program rather than against it. Indeed, when resistance-skills training is included as part of a program that shows participants that healthy behavior is the norm, the resistance-skills training no longer reduces program effectiveness but instead enhances it (Donaldson et al., 1995). Under these circumstances, young people acquire both the ability to resist a peer's unhealthy influence and the desire to do so, because they recognize that *most* of their peers prefer the healthier route. As a result, the program is more likely to be successful.

likely to withstand even strong group norms—for example, when most of the student's small group of friends smoked and approved of smoking. Other research has found similar results among students in every ethnic group examined: white, black, Hispanic, and Asian (Sussman et al., 1986). Thus, even strong group norms don't sway everyone.

These findings may offer a way to reduce negative social influence in schools. If the belief in one's own capacity to resist peer pressure can protect a person from such pressure, instilling this belief in schoolchildren should safeguard them from dangerous peer norms, right? Right, but research suggests that the way in which this belief is instilled is crucial to the success of the strategy, as the Bridging Theory and Application feature shows.

A second factor interacts with norms to affect their impact on group members' behavior: the degree to which the member identifies with the group (Reed et al., 2007). Chances are, if you are reading this book, you are a college student. But not everyone who is taking college classes identifies him- or herself primarily in that way. If asked "Who are you?" many college students would describe themselves first in terms of religious, family, or ethnic group memberships. For these individuals, college student norms may not be especially influential because they don't identify strongly with the group, even though they are members of it.

Deborah Terry and Michael Hogg (1996) found good support for this idea in a study of Australian university students. The researchers measured subjects' views of the strength of the student norm on campus for regular exercise by asking them to estimate the amount of approval for regular exercise among their peers at the university. The students also indicated how much they identified themselves with their university peer group. When asked about their own intentions to exercise regularly during the upcoming weeks, only those individuals who identified themselves strongly as university students planned to follow the norms of the group. Those who held little identification with the group didn't let the approval of other group members affect their exercise plans at all. In sum, even strong group norms won't guide the behavior of members of the group who don't identify themselves psychologically as group members.

Quick Quiz

1. _____ norms connect to the goal of _____; in contrast, _____ norms connect more closely to the goal of _____.
   a. Reciprocity, choosing correctly; descriptive, social approval
   b. Consensus, choosing correctly; similarity, social approval
   c. Descriptive, social approval; injunctive, choosing correctly
   d. Injunctive, social approval; descriptive, choosing correctly

2. A salesperson handing you a free makeup sample before pitching the rest of the product line to you is an example of _____, whereas a Girl Scout who first asks you to buy several boxes of cookies before changing her request to just one box demonstrates _____.
   a. Reciprocal favors, the door-in-the-face technique
   b. That's-not-all technique, reciprocal concessions
   c. Reciprocal concessions, the door-in-the-face technique
   d. Reciprocal favors, the norm of reciprocity

3. Which of the following factors *increase* people's willingness to be influenced by others?
   a. When a person's decision is publicly observable
   b. When a person has an individualistic sense of self
   c. When a person tends to be highly reactant
   d. Both (a) and (c)

Managing Self-Image: Yielding to Be Consistent

LO 6.8 Describe the four commitment-initiating tactics and how they differ from one another.

LO 6.9 Discuss the two situational features of commitments that make them most enduring.

Restaurant owners typically face a big problem with callers who make reservations but fail to appear. Tables that could have been filled by paying customers stand empty, causing substantial economic loss. However, Gordon Sinclair, who was the proprietor of Gordon's restaurant in Chicago, hit on a highly effective tactic. He instructed his receptionists to stop saying, "Please call us if you change your plans" and to start asking

"Will you call us if you change your plans?" and to wait for a response. As a result, his no-show rate dropped from 30% to 10% (Grimes, 1997).

What is it about this subtle shift that leads to such a dramatic difference? The receptionist specifically asks for and waits for the customer's affirmative response. By inducing customers to make a personal commitment to a behavior, this approach increases the chance that they will perform the behavior.

A **personal commitment** ties an individual's identity to a position or course of action, making it more likely that he or she will follow through. This is so because most individuals prefer to be consistent and have a strong desire to see themselves as the kind of person who lives up to promises and commitments (Kerr, Garst, Lewandowski, & Harris, 1997). As a consequence, even seemingly insignificant commitments can lead to large behavior changes. For instance, getting people to answer a five-question survey about organ donation increases their willingness to become organ donors (Carducci, Deuser, Bauer, Large, & Ramaekers, 1989).

Commitment-Initiating Tactics

Because of the desire to be consistent with their existing behaviors, promises, and self-images, people are often vulnerable to a simple request strategy. This basic strategy—first initiating a commitment and then making a request that is consistent with it—is at the core of numerous compliance techniques used regularly by influence professionals. Let's look at several that differ primarily in the way they obtain the initial commitment.

REVISITING THE FOOT-IN-THE-DOOR TECHNIQUE   Earlier in this chapter, we described the foot-in-the-door technique, which increases compliance with a particular request by first gaining compliance with a smaller, related request (Dolinski, 2012). The power of the technique can be seen in a study in which Israeli researchers went to a local apartment district, knocked on half the doors, and asked residents to sign a petition favoring the establishment of a recreation center for the mentally handicapped. Because the cause was good and the request was small, almost everyone agreed to sign. Residents in the other apartments did not receive a visit and, consequently, did not make a commitment to the mentally handicapped. Two weeks later, on National Collection Day for the Mentally Handicapped, all neighborhood residents were approached at home and asked to give money to this cause. Only about half (53%) of those who had not been previously asked to sign a petition made a contribution, but nearly all (92%) of those who had signed two weeks earlier gave a donation (Schwartzwald, Bizman, & Raz, 1983).

What is it about saying yes to a minor charity request that causes people to say yes to a larger, related one? According to Jonathan Freedman and Scott Fraser (1966), who first investigated the foot-in-the-door technique, compliance with the initial request changes people's self-images: They come to see themselves as more helpful, public-spirited individuals. Then, to be consistent with this modified self-identity, they are more willing to comply with other charitable requests. A study by Jerry Burger and Rosanna Guadagno (2003) offers support for the idea that the foot-in-the-door technique works by changing self-concept. They found that the technique was successful only on individuals who scored high on *self-concept clarity*, which reflects the extent to which people alter their self-concepts on the basis of new information. Thus, the more a person was likely to change self-concept as a result of agreeing to a small charity request, the more that person was then likely to agree to a larger charity request.

THE LOW-BALL TECHNIQUE   Someone using the **low-ball technique** first gets a commitment from another by offering a good deal, then—after the commitment is obtained— raises the cost of completing the deal (Cialdini et al., 1978; Gueguen & Pascual, 2013). The tactic can be surprisingly effective. For example, French cigarette smokers were asked to participate in a study in which they would fill out a short questionnaire. After committing to a date and time, they were informed that the study required them to refrain from smoking for 18 hours before the experiment. Even though they were given the chance to back out after hearing of the nonsmoking requirement, an astounding 85% agreed to

Personal commitment Anything that connects an individual's identity more closely to a position or course of action.

Low-ball technique Gaining a commitment to an arrangement and then raising the cost of carrying out the arrangement.

participate anyway—many more than the 12% who agreed to participate if informed of the nonsmoking requirement before they committed to a date and time (Joule, 1987).

Automobile salespeople "throw the low-ball" regularly: First, they induce a customer to choose a particular car by offering a low price on that model. After the selection has been made—and, at times, after commitment to the car is enhanced by allowing the customer to take it home overnight or arrange financing with the bank—something happens to remove the attractive price before the final papers are signed. Perhaps a calculation error is "discovered" or the sales manager disallows the deal because "we'd be losing money at that price." By this time, though, many customers have experienced a strong internal commitment to that automobile. Consequently, they often proceed with the purchase.

How could it be that car shoppers would forge ahead with a purchase after the reason they chose it had been removed? After making an active choice for something, people see it more positively and are reluctant to relinquish it (Cioffi & Garner, 1996; Kahneman, Knetsch, & Thaler, 1991). This is especially the case when they think they have come to own it, because once they have taken "mental possession" of

Customer friendly. To attract customers who don't want to expose themselves to influence tactics, some auto dealers have adopted a one-price, no-haggling approach to sales. How might this constitute a consistency-based influence tactic itself?

an important object, it becomes part of self-concept (Ball & Tasaki, 1992; Beggan & Allison, 1997). Hence, the behavior of car buyers who fall for the low-ball technique makes good psychological, if not good economic, sense. Despite the increased cost, many car shoppers decide to buy anyway, saying, "It's worth a few hundred dollars extra to get the car I really like because it fits who I am." Rarely do they realize that it wasn't these positive feelings toward the car that caused their commitment to it. Instead, it was their commitment to the car (launched by the low-ball technique) that caused the positive feelings.

THE BAIT-AND-SWITCH TECHNIQUE A somewhat similar practice sometimes employed by car dealers is called the **bait-and-switch technique**. Initially, an automobile is advertised at a special low price to get customers to decide that they can afford to purchase a new car. They make the commitment to buying a car by visiting the dealership to secure the deal. When they arrive, however, they find that the advertised model is sold and no longer available or is of low quality, possessing none of the features people typically want. However, because they have made an active commitment to getting a new car from that dealer, they are more willing to agree to examine and buy a more expensive model there. Vehicles are not the only merchandise sold through the bait-and-switch tactic; appliance and furniture stores are notorious for relying on it.

French researchers Robert Joule, Fabienne Gouilloux, and Florent Weber (1989), who called it the "lure" procedure, demonstrated how the technique worked at their university. Students were recruited for an interesting study involving movie clips that would pay 30 francs (about $6) for their participation. However, when they appeared for the experiment, they were informed that it had been cancelled. They were also told that, as long as they were there, they could volunteer for a different experiment, which offered no pay and was less interesting than the first one—it involved memorizing lists of numbers. The researchers knew that the second experiment was not attractive enough to get many volunteers by itself: When it was described to another group of students, only 15% agreed to participate without pay. But the bait-and-switch procedure tripled the number of volunteers: About 47% of the students who had made a commitment of time and effort to come to participate in an attractive experiment that was cancelled were then willing to take part in a much less attractive experiment.

Like the low-ball tactic, the bait and switch works by first getting people to commit to a desirable arrangement. Once the commitment is in place, they are willing

Bait-and-switch technique Gaining a commitment to an arrangement, then making the arrangement unavailable or unappealing and offering a more costly arrangement.

Table 6.1   Commitment-Initiating Compliance Techniques

TECHNIQUE	THE FIRST STEP		THE SECOND STEP	
	Initiating the Commitment by:	**Example:**	**Taking Advantage of the Initial Commitment by:**	**Example:**
Foot-in-the-door	Gaining the target person's compliance with a small request	Getting the target to sign a petition for a charitable cause	Requesting compliance with a related, larger request	Asking for a donation to support the cause
Low-ball	Obtaining the target person's agreement to a specific arrangement	Negotiating a deal with the target on a new car	Changing the terms of the arrangement	Saying that the original deal contained a calculation error
Bait-and-switch	Spurring the target person to take a course of action	Getting the target to decide to buy a new car by advertising a very low price	Describing the chosen action as impossible or unwise and suggesting a related action instead	Referring to the advertised car as sold or inferior and offering a more expensive model
Labeling	Assigning the target person a trait label	Describing the target as above average in citizenship	Seeking compliance with a request that is consistent with the label	Asking the target to vote in the next election

to accept a less attractive arrangement—one they would have likely bypassed before being tricked into making the commitment.

THE LABELING TECHNIQUE   Another way to induce a commitment to a course of action is to give a person a label that is consistent with the action, a procedure called the **labeling technique**. For instance, elementary schoolchildren who were told by an adult "You look to me like the kind of girl (or boy) who understands how important it is to write correctly" became more likely to choose to work on a penmanship task three to nine days later in private (Cialdini, Eisenberg, Green, Rhoads, & Bator, 1998). Alice Tybout and Richard Yalch (1980) demonstrated how labeling tactics could be used to spur adults to vote. They interviewed 162 voters and, at random, told half that, according to their interview responses, they were "above-average citizens likely to vote and participate in political events." The other half were told that they appeared to be average in these activities. As a result, those given the above-average label not only saw themselves as better citizens than those given the average label but also were more likely to vote in a local election held a week later.

In sum, because of a desire in most people to live up to their commitments, it is possible to increase a target person's performance of an action by using any of several commitment-initiating techniques (see Table 6.1). Although these techniques differ in the way they bring about the commitment, they have in common the establishment of an early commitment that ties the target person's identity to the desired action. In the process of performing the action, the target person achieves the goal of managing (i.e., enhancing, confirming, or protecting) self-image. Let's look more closely at some of the factors of the person and of the situation that affect when and how people live up to their commitments so as to manage their self-images.

INVESTIGATION

Suppose you were about to start a negotiation with someone you wanted to treat you fairly. How could you use the labeling technique to increase the likelihood that your opponent would do so?

PERSON   ## Harnessing Existing Commitments

So far, we have focused on commitments that have been initiated by outside pressures—requests for small favors, induced choices or decisions, and external labels. But certain commitments reside within a person in the form of existing values. Sometimes

Labeling technique   Assigning a label to an individual and then requesting a favor that is consistent with the label.

people can be influenced toward a course of action because they recognize that the action is consistent with a value—let's say fairness—that they already possess or wish to possess. Thus, those who value fairness may go along with something not because they want what is being offered but because they want to be fair.

People often align their behaviors to fit with values such as good health, world peace, religious faith, and so on. These deep-seated commitments keep individuals working at the important personal projects in their lives, causing them to persevere through time, toil, and adversity (Lydon & Zanna, 1990; Sheldon & Elliot, 1999). Thus, marketers who can create a link between our personal values and their products or services will likely have us as long-term customers. This form of influence can be quite ethical and beneficial, but it can also be used to bind people to activities and organizations that are not in their best interests. Cultlike groups, for instance, recruit and retain members by linking the group's (declared) purposes to such widely held values as spiritual salvation, personal enlightenment, and social justice (Zimbardo, 1997). Steve Hassan says that before he joined the Unification Church, he felt committed to reducing social problems but didn't know how to go about it. During his first visit to a Moonie gathering, he was assured that the group was dedicated to combating "just such social problems as the ones I was concerned about" (Hassan, 1990, p. 13).

SITUATION Active and Public Commitments

When it comes to spurring future consistent behavior, not all commitments are created equal. The most enduring commitments are those that most clearly connect a desired course of action to an individual's self-concept. Two situational features of commitments work successfully in this regard: Lasting commitments are active and public.

ACTIVE COMMITMENTS Perhaps you have noticed that an important piece of information is missing from ads for popular rock music concerts—ticket prices. Why should concert promoters try to hide the cost of a ticket from fans? Even if the figure is high, people will find out the price of a seat as soon as they call or visit a ticket outlet, right? True, but promoters have recognized that potential concertgoers are more likely to purchase tickets after that call or visit than before. Even making a phone call to inquire about ticket prices constitutes an active personal commitment to the concert, which makes the caller more favorable to the idea of attending.

The impact of action on future action can be seen in research investigating the effect of active versus passive commitments (Allison & Messick, 1988). For instance, in a study by Delia Cioffi and Randy Garner (1996), college students volunteered for an AIDS education project in the local schools. The researchers arranged for half to volunteer actively by filling out a form stating that they wanted to participate. The other half volunteered passively by failing to fill out a form stating that they didn't want to participate. Three to four days later, when asked to begin their involvement in the project, the great majority (74%) who appeared as scheduled came from the ranks of those who had actively agreed to participate.

What was it about active commitment that caused these individuals to follow through? One way people come to perceive and define themselves is through an examination of their actions (Bem, 1967; Vallacher & Wegner, 1985). The evidence is strong that we think our actions tell us more about ourselves than do our non-actions (Fazio, 1987; Nisbett & Ross, 1980). Indeed, compared to those who volunteered passively for the AIDS education project in the Cioffi and Garner (1996) study, those who volunteered actively were more likely to explain their decisions by implicating their personal values, preferences, and traits. Thus, active commitments give us the kind of information we use to shape our self-images, which then shape our future behavior (Burger & Caldwell, 2003; Dolinski, 2000).

Figure 6.7 The staying power of different types of commitments

Individuals who made active and public commitments to an initial set of judgments were most likely to stay loyal to those judgments when they were later attacked. Those who made neither active nor public commitments were least loyal.

Source: Adapted from Deutsch, M., & Gerard, H. B. (1955). A study of normative and informational social influences upon individual judgment. *Journal of Abnormal and Social Psychology, 51, 629–636.*

PUBLIC COMMITMENTS In addition to active commitments, public commitments to a course of action increase the chance that people will maintain that course of action into the future. Morton Deutsch and Harold Gerard (1955) performed a classic experiment that examined how both types of commitments operate. The researchers had subjects estimate the lengths of lines in an Asch-type procedure. One group of subjects left these length judgments in their minds, not committing to them either actively or publicly. A second group wrote down their estimates privately for just a second—thereby making the commitment active—and then immediately erased them. A third group wrote down their judgments and turned them over to the experimenter, making an active and public commitment to their decisions. At this point, all subjects received information that their judgments were wrong—they learned that the other subjects in the study (actually confederates) had estimated the lines differently. Deutsch and Gerard wanted to find out which of the three groups would be most inclined to stay with their initial choices after receiving feedback that the choices were incorrect. The results were clear. Those whose judgments had never left their heads, having been neither written down nor made public, were least loyal to them. Those who had made an active commitment to their initial choices were less willing to change their minds when confronted with contradictory evidence. But, by far, it was those who had connected themselves publicly to their first estimates who most resolutely refused to shift from those positions later (see Figure 6.7).

We can think of two reasons why public commitments were the most resistant to change. First, participants who had gone on record may not have wanted to be seen by the experimenter as easily influenced or inconsistent. This is a real possibility, as most people prefer to be seen as resolute and stable (Baumeister, 1982). But there is a second reason as well. Once people have made a public pronouncement, they come to believe it more (Schlenker, Dlugolecki, & Doherty, 1994; Schlenker & Trudeau, 1990). For example, in research conducted by Diane Tice (1992), subjects agreed to play the role of an extraverted person and then did so under either public or private circumstances. Much more than subjects in the private condition, those who played the extraverted role in public incorporated extraversion into their real self-concepts, describing themselves later as truly more outgoing and sociable. This new extraverted identity showed itself in subjects' behavior after the study was over and they were left in a waiting room with a confederate: Those who had publicly portrayed themselves earlier as extraverted sat closer and talked more to the confederate. Tice also found that the effect of public self-presentations was strongest when subjects felt that they had free choice in deciding to make them. In sum, like active commitments, public commitments—especially when freely chosen—alter self-image (Kelly, 1998; Kelly & McKillop, 1996; Schlenker, 1980). These altered self-images then guide further actions accordingly.

INTERACTION ## Gender and Public Conformity

Because public commitments have the ability to change not just social image but also self-image, people may try to protect their self-concepts by being careful about when they publicly admit that they have been influenced. But which aspects of self-concept people choose to protect in this way can differ for men and women (Smith et al., 2013).

The Deutsch and Gerard (1955) experiment demonstrated that, in the face of conformity pressures, people are more loyal to their public decisions than to their private decisions. However, one study showed that men may be especially reluctant to conform under public conditions (Eagly, Wood, & Fishbaugh, 1981). In that study, male and female participants conformed to the group opinion to about the same extent when their responses were privately made, but males conformed less than females to the group opinion when they had to do so in public.

Why would men resist public conformity more than women? The researchers suggest that the males' nonconformity may have represented conformity at a higher level—with an image of independence that is socialized into the identity of most men (Eagly, 1987). Men prefer to see themselves as independent, unique, and self-sufficient. Election surveys over the last 40 years have found that men are even more likely than women to announce their political category as Independent (Norrander, 1997). A man who expresses nonconformity communicates a picture of himself as self-reliant, as a leader rather than a follower. To whom is he communicating this picture? It appears that he is sending the message as much to himself as to others. One series of studies found that men base self-esteem on factors that make them unique and independent, whereas women are more likely to base self-esteem on factors that connect them to members of their groups (Josephs, Markus, & Tarafodi, 1992). Thus, because of the potent impact of public pronouncements on private image, men may resist public conformity in an effort to stay true to a view of themselves as possessing independence.

Roy Baumeister and Kristin Sommer (1997) have suggested a further twist to the plot: Men's public nonconformity might be motivated not by a desire to be independent of the group but by a desire to belong. They contend that men want to be accepted by their groups as much as women do; however, women seek acceptance from close cooperative relationships, whereas men aim to be accepted by demonstrating a unique ability or by showing the potential for leadership. After all, a leader is importantly interconnected with group members. In all, it appears that women and men don't differ much in their basic social influence goals—for example, to be accepted and to validate their self-images—but that they do differ in the routes they take to reach those goals.

Quick Quiz

1 Which of the following examples demonstrates the low-ball technique?

    a. Negotiating a deal on a used car, then finding out the salesperson threw in a set of new tires to "sweeten" the deal.

    b. After deciding on a used car to buy, the salesperson discloses that the car was once in an accident and not worth the money, then tries to sell you a more expensive model.

    c. Negotiating a "bundle" deal with your cable company so you can lower the price of your Internet bill; after you agree to the deal you find out there are extra fees and taxes that make the price higher than you were originally told.

    d. All of the above

2 Which of the following examples demonstrates the bait-and-switch technique?

    a. After a salesperson convinces you to buy a new sweater, she makes the offer more attractive by telling you that you can get an additional sweater for 50% off.

    b. You make a special trip to a store that advertises a great deal on your favorite shampoo; a salesperson tells you they are sold out but recommends a similar shampoo that costs slightly more.

    c. A salesperson gives you an acceptable price on the used car you want to buy, but right before signing the final papers you're told a calculation error was made and the car will actually cost $1000 more.

    d. All of the above

3 Which of these commitments is most likely to be resistant to change?

    a. A commitment that does not arise from free choice.

    b. A commitment with little connection to one's self-concept.

    c. A commitment that is active and private.

    d. A commitment that is both active and public.

The Turnaround of Steve Hassan

We promised at the beginning of this chapter that by the end, you'd understand the causes of Steve Hassan's remarkably rapid switch from normal college student to fully committed follower of the Reverend Moon. Furthermore, we promised that, in the process, you'd also understand the causes of his subsequent, equally rapid shift away from the Unification organization—because the causes are the same. They are the principles of social influence that drive all of us to conform, comply, and obey. They may get us to vote for a candidate, purchase a product, or donate to a cause. In Hassan's case, they got him to change his life dramatically, twice.

Let's examine how these principles worked in terms of the three goals of social influence that we've described. Like the rest of us, in making any important changes, Hassan wanted to achieve the goal of *choosing correctly*. The Unification organization accommodated him by providing information from both of the sources people normally use to make correct decisions—authorities and peers. The authorities were Reverend Moon himself, the new Messiah, and officials of the group who took the role of teachers. The peers were young people just like Hassan who had decided to devote themselves to the purposes of the organization because, just like him, they shared similar concerns about the world. Among these peers, the consensus about the correctness of their actions was total.

Moreover, Hassan was pressured to cut off contact with voices from outside the group that could undermine this consensus. Under these conditions, the opinions and norms of the group forged a compelling sense of reality for him.

When Hassan was deprogrammed out of the Unification organization, the deprogrammers relied on these same principles of social influence. They, too, portrayed themselves as experts and teachers on the matter at hand, demonstrating intricate knowledge of the group's doctrines, dynamics, and deceptions. They, too, revealed themselves to be just like him, recounting how each had been subjected to the same recruitment and persuasion tactics that he had experienced and exhibiting an

As the world turns. As he was when he joined the Moonies, Steve Hassan is still striving to make the world a better place. Today, he does so not as a cult member but as a cult fighter.

unshakable consensus that they were right in their decisions to leave the group. And by hiding him from the Unification organization for five days in a secret apartment, they, too, cut him off from his customary reference group.

In recruiting and retaining Hassan as a member, the Moonies also saw to it that he could achieve the goal of *gaining social approval* by yielding to the group's wishes. At the beginning, he was approached by appealing young people whose acceptance he found desirable. Not long after, at recruitment workshops, he was the focus of great positive attention and affection. Then, once he was a full-fledged member, his only approval came from those who shared his group membership; and, of course, that approval came exclusively for doing things that advanced the group's purposes. Hassan's deprogramming experience proceeded similarly. He was quickly impressed with how personally appealing the deprogrammers were, describing them as warm, caring, and spiritually minded individuals. He was also gratified by the sympathetic and respectful attention they gave him. And, in the isolation of the apartment where he was being held, his only approval came from responses that fit the deprogrammers' purposes.

When members of the Unification organization tried to influence Hassan toward the group, they made certain that by yielding, he could achieve the goal of *managing his self-image*, assuring him that his inner commitment to solving social problems could be met by joining the group. His deprogrammers did the same, except that they allowed him to see that leaving the group was the way to achieve this goal. They pressed him to get in touch with his deep-seated values for honesty, family, and freedom—all of which were incompatible with what he had experienced in the Unification organization.

But most tellingly, after Hassan recognized for himself that the group had deceived and trapped him into an unhealthy environment, he saw how he could recommit himself to a life of social service: He could help others extricate themselves from these prisonlike organizations. He could become a cult exit counselor and reduce the social problems that cults create in our world. In all, the deprogramming experience was successful because it provided Hassan with a substituted reference group, set of values, and sense of purpose—just as the Moonie recruitment and indoctrination experience had done years before.

Steve Hassan has since remained committed to his vision, emerging to become one of the country's leading cult exit counselors and explaining his effective techniques (Hassan, 2000) in ways that rely on insights from the scientific study of social influence—insights that you, too, now possess, at a fraction of the cost. But, truth be told, those insights are not enough. As is always the case when bridging between information and application, the bridge must be built with specific plans for how to implement new knowledge into our lives. If we don't think specifically and protectively about how that knowledge can be used successfully for us, it is likely only to be used successfully on us.

Chapter Summary

Summary of the Goals Served by Social Influence and the Factors Related to Them

The Goal	Person	Situation	Interaction
Choosing correctly	• Uncertainty	• Consensus • Similarity	• The desire for accuracy increases conformity only when people are unsure of their judgments.
Gaining social approval	• Desire for approval • Collective sense of self • Resistance	• Others' appeal • Public observability	• Even strong forms of group approval and disapproval can be resisted by people who believe they can withstand group pressure and are not highly identified with the group.
Being consistent with commitments	• Existing commitments	• Active commitments • Public commitments	• When conformity threatens one's identity as an independent person, one may conform less in public situations. This is especially true of men who see independence as an important part of self-concept.

1. Social influence is defined as a change in behavior caused by real or imagined pressure from others. It is different from persuasion in that it refers to shifts in overt actions rather than in private attitudes and beliefs.

Categories of Social Influence: Conformity, Compliance, and Obedience

1. Social psychologists have investigated three major types of social influence: conformity, compliance, and obedience.
2. Conformity refers to behavior change designed to match the actions of others.
3. Compliance refers to behavior change that occurs as a result of a direct request.
4. Obedience is a special type of compliance that occurs as a result of a directive from an authority figure.

Choosing Correctly: Yielding to Be Right

1. People often rely on two powerful psychological principles to help them choose correctly: authority and social validation. Thus, they are more willing to be influenced by authority figures on the one hand and similar peers on the other.
2. One reason authorities are influential is that they are often expert, and, by following an authority's directives, people can usually choose correctly without having to think hard about the issue themselves.

3. Just as following an authority is normally a shortcut to choosing correctly, so is following the lead of most of one's peers. The choices of these others provide social validation for the correctness of that choice.
4. When others share a consensus about the correct way to act, they are especially influential to observers.
5. In addition, observers are more likely to be influenced by others who are similar to them and who, therefore, provide better evidence about what the observers should do.
6. People are most likely to allow themselves to be influenced by others when they are uncertain about how to respond in the situation—because when uncertainty and ambiguity reign, people lose confidence in their own ability to choose well.
7. When choosing accurately is important, only uncertain individuals are more likely to follow the crowd; those who are already sure of the validity of their judgments are less willing to conform.

Gaining Social Approval: Yielding to Be Liked

1. Frequently, people change in order to be more accepted and approved by their groups and to avoid the social rejection that often comes from resisting group pressure for change.
2. Injunctive norms of a group or culture inform people as to the behaviors that are likely to get them accepted or rejected there.
3. One such norm is that of reciprocity, which obligates people to give back to those who have given first.

Anyone who violates this norm risks social disapproval and rejection, which makes people more willing to comply with requests of those who have provided an initial favor or concession.

4. The door-in-the-face technique engages the tendency to reciprocate concessions. It begins with a large favor likely to be rejected and then retreats to a smaller favor.

5. The desire for social approval and a collective self-definition both increase one's willingness to submit to social influence in order to gain acceptance. But a tendency for reactance decreases one's susceptibility to social influence, especially when the influence is seen as threatening one's freedom to decide.

6. Two features of a person's social situation increase the motivation to go along to get along: the appeal of the group or individual pressing for change and the public observability of the person's actions.

7. Even strong group norms can be resisted when members feel that they have the ability to withstand group influence or when members don't feel highly identified with the group.

Managing Self-Image: Yielding to Be Consistent

1. People can manage their self-image by yielding to requests for action that fit or enhance their identity.

2. Influence professionals can increase compliance by linking their requests to the values to which people feel committed.

3. Several influence techniques (foot-in-the-door, low-ball, bait-and-switch, and labeling) work by establishing an early commitment that links a person's identity to a desired course of action.

4. These commitments are most effective when actively and publicly made, particularly when they are also made with free choice.

5. To maintain the image of self-reliance, men are less likely than women to conform publicly to the group opinion.

Key Terms

Bait-and-switch technique, 203

Compliance, 179

Conformity, 179

Descriptive norm, 194

Disrupt-then-reframe technique, 197

Door-in-the-face technique, 195

Expert power, 187

Foot-in-the-door technique, 181

Injunctive norm, 194

Labeling technique, 204

Low-ball technique, 202

Norm of reciprocity, 194

Obedience, 179

Participant observation, 183

Personal commitment, 202

Reactance theory, 198

Social influence, 179

Social validation, 188

That's-not-all technique, 195

Chapter 7

Affiliation and Friendship

Video

Outline

Learning Objectives

LO 7.1 Compare and contrast friendships to relationships with relatives and lovers.

LO 7.2 Summarize the differences between domain-specific and domain-general models.

LO 7.3 Explain how the "tend and befriend" response to stress differs from "fight or flight."

LO 7.4 Identify the kinds of threats that lead people to seek or avoid others.

LO 7.5 Describe how loneliness and depression can lead to a negative, self-perpetuating cycle and how attachments with others can break that cycle.

LO 7.6 Summarize social comparison theory and how it relates to our tendency to be attracted to similar others.

LO 7.7 Discuss the type of person who is more likely to make self-disclosures and understand the consequences of self-disclosure.

LO 7.8 Explain how social comparisons are linked to self-evaluation and happiness.

LO 7.9 Describe the consequences of sex differences in seeking status versus affection on relationships.

LO 7.10 Understand how status motives contribute to our tendencies to approach or avoid others.

LO 7.11 Identify the four categories of social exchange rules used in different relationships.

LO 7.12 Explain the difference between a communal relationship and an exchange relationship and how exchange relationships differ between Western and non-Western cultures.

LO 7.13 Discuss how proximity is linked to social capital.

Friends for life. At left, the real Heinrich Harrer greets the Dalai Lama half a century after they befriended one another in Tibet. At right, a scene from the movie depicting the very unlikely friendship between a German prison-camp escapee and the young Dalai Lama.

The Fugitive Who Befriended the God-King

Heinrich Harrer arrived in Tibet's Forbidden City of Lhasa a penniless and starving fugitive. Harrier and his companion, Peter Aufschnaiter, escapees from a British prisoner-of-war camp in India, had been trudging over the mountains of Tibet for almost two years. They were forced to skulk through bandit-infested highlands, evading Tibetan authorities who repeatedly ordered them to leave the country. Tibetans had seen few Europeans, and these two renegades, dressed in increasingly ragged garments, were openly scorned even by poor peasants.

Nevertheless, Harrer and Aufschnaiter pushed onward, walking over a thousand miles through snowy mountain passes regarded as impassable even by Tibetan highlanders. When he and his companion finally reached the Forbidden City of Lhasa, the two vagabonds again met a chilly reception. They refused to go on, however, and threw their packs down in front of a large house, ignoring the servants who harassed them and tried to shoo them away.

The Forbidden City was the home of the Dalai Lama, regarded by Tibetans as the incarnation of Buddha. This 13-year-old god-king, revered by all Tibetans, was surrounded by an army of monks who kept him isolated even from the wealthiest and most powerful citizens of Lhasa. When he rode through town on his throne, even the heads of noble families cast their eyes to the ground, not daring to gaze upon the living deity. One could hardly imagine a person more different from Heinrich Harrer.

Given Harrer's dishonorable entry into Lhasa, it seems almost inconceivable that he would go on to become friends with this most revered of all Tibetans. Yet despite the Dalai Lama's isolation and their immensely different backgrounds and social stations, these two men formed a bond that lasted for the rest of their lives.

Heinrich Harrer's friendship with the Dalai Lama was made famous in his book *Seven Years in Tibet* (1996). In contrast, most of our friendships may not seem to merit a movie starring Brad Pitt. As we'll see, though, unraveling the mystery of the unlikely coalition between Harrer and the Dalai Lama reveals many of the motivations that bring all of us together into everyday companionships. In this chapter, we will explore the general question: What factors cause us to befriend some people and not others?

What Is a Friend?

LO 7.1 Compare and contrast friendships to relationships with relatives and lovers.

LO 7.2 Summarize the differences between domain-specific and domain-general models.

Webster's dictionary defines **friend** as "someone on terms of affection and regard for another who is neither relative nor lover." Students asked for their personal definitions tend to agree on a number of features of friendship (Bukowski et al., 1994; Davis & Todd, 1985). These include:

- Friends participate as equals.
- Friends enjoy each other's company.
- Friends trust one another to act in their best interest.
- Friends help each other in times of need.
- Friends act themselves around one another and do not "wear masks."
- Friends share similar interests and values.

Of course, these are ideal characteristics. Any particular friendship may contain only a few of these features (Davis & Todd, 1985).

Unlike our relationships with relatives, friendships are more voluntary (Adams & Bleiszner, 1994). We pick our friends and can change them but not so for our relatives. Though *Webster's* excludes relatives from the category of friends, the line real people draw is fuzzier than the one in the dictionary. In many societies, your closest friends are frequently genetically related to you (Daly, Salmon, & Wilson, 1997). Although the high monks of Tibet kept the young Dalai Lama insulated from everyday people, he was allowed to maintain a close personal relationship with his brother, Lobsang Samten. The modern industrialized world differs from the Tibet of 1940, and indeed from any place at any other period in history, in that we modern people spend less time than ever in the company of our relatives (Adams & Bleiszner, 1994).

Webster's also excludes lovers from the friendship category. Love relationships involve romantic or sexual feelings, and marriages involve legal rules and exclusive "rights." Friendships, in contrast, do not (Ackerman, Kenrick, & Schaller, 2007; Rawlins, 1992). Again, the distinction sometimes gets fuzzy, and the majority of married people pick their spouse as their "best friend" (Myers, 2000). In this chapter, we focus mainly on the "platonic" aspects of friendship and affiliation, leaving love and romance for Chapter 8.

Friend Someone with whom we have an affectionate relationship.

Reinforcement-affect model The theory that we like people with whom we associate positive feelings and dislike those with whom we associate negative feelings.

Goals of Affiliation and Friendship

What makes us want to affiliate with others? Social psychologists have advanced several general theories designed to answer that question.

LIKING THOSE WHO MAKE US FEEL GOOD The **reinforcement-affect model** assumes people are motivated by one very simple goal—the desire to feel good

Friendship. When students are asked to describe the features of friendship, they include mutual enjoyment, support, openness, trust, and equality. Although the dictionary distinguishes friends from relatives and lovers, actual friendships do not involve such a neat distinction.

(Byrne & Clore, 1970). The central premise is this: We affiliate with, and come to like, people we associate with positive feelings. Conversely, we come to dislike, and to avoid, people we associate with negative feelings.

The reinforcement-affect model has been used to explain a wide range of findings: why people like others who agree with their attitudes and are repelled by those who disagree with them, why people are drawn to others who possess desirable characteristics such as physical attractiveness, and even why we may come to like other people who just happen to be around when we hear good news (Byrne, London, & Reeves, 1968; Veitch & Griffitt, 1976). According to simple principles of classical conditioning, good or bad feelings in any situation will automatically rub off on any person who happens to be there. Just as salivation was elicited by the bell Pavlov's dogs heard when they were fed, so a good feeling is elicited by someone who's around when something nice happens.

The reinforcement-affect model is a **domain-general model**—one that attempts to explain all behavior using some simple rule: in this case, "do it if it feels good." The advantage of the domain-general approach is that it seeks to use a minimum number of presumptions to explain a broad range of phenomena. The limitation is that it doesn't tell us why some things feel good and others bad. For instance, sometimes we like people more when we meet them under unpleasant circumstances, provided they're in the same boat and aren't causing the unpleasant feelings (Kenrick & Johnson, 1979). And sometimes the very same experience, such as seeing someone beautiful or handsome, can make one person feel good while it makes another person feel bad (Kenrick et al., 1993).

LIKING THOSE WHO OFFER US A GOOD DEAL   **Social exchange** theory also presumes that affiliation and friendship are motivated by a simple and general goal—to maximize the ratio of benefits to costs (Thibaut & Kelly, 1959). This theory shares with reinforcement theory the assumption that we seek rewards. However, social exchange theory presumes that, rather than being like Pavlov's dogs, people are more calculating and rational in approaching their relationships. The model is derived from economic assumptions and, in its simplest form, presumes we approach relationships like a stockbroker approaches a financial transaction—buy when it looks as if we'll make a profit, sell if it looks like we'll take a loss.

An influential exchange-based model assumes we're drawn to relationships in which we experience **equity**—a state of affairs in which your benefits and costs from the relationship are proportional to the benefits and costs incurred by your partner (e.g., Hatfield et al., 1985). To understand how equity works, pick one friend and list the rewards and benefits each of you gets from your relationship. Your friend may be a good study partner, a source of compliments, and the host of really fun parties. You may provide the same benefits for your friend, minus the parties, but he may also get to borrow your car when his old junker is in the repair shop.

Next list the costs you both incur from the relationship. Perhaps your friend occasionally distracts you with irrelevant jokes during study sessions, beats you mercilessly at tennis, and criticizes your choice of romantic partners. As costs to your friend, you may make him feel dumb by getting better grades on the same exams, and maybe you get grouchy when you lose at tennis. If you add up all your benefits and costs and compare them to his, the relationship is equitable if you both seem to get a similar value. However, if he gets somewhat more out of the relationship, you'll feel underbenefitted. Conversely, if you get more out of the friendship, you'll feel overbenefitted. In line with the idea that people are rational economists seeking a good deal for themselves, people are generally less happy if they are underbenefitted than if they are overbenefitted (Buunk et al., 1993; Hatfield et al., 1982).

Domain-general model A model that attempts to explain a wide range of different behaviors according to a simple general rule (such as: do it if it's rewarding).

Social exchange The trading of benefits within relationships.

Equity A state of affairs in which one person's benefits and costs from a relationship are proportional to the benefits and costs incurred by his or her partner.

INVESTIGATION

List the rewards you get from your relationships with a parent, a friend, and your most recent romantic interest. How are they different? Which rewards would not be rewarding if they came from a different person?

Social exchange theories also take a domain-general approach. The simple and powerful assumption is that we seek to optimize the ratio of costs to benefits in all our relationships—with friends, relatives, lovers, or coworkers. As with reinforcement-affect theory, social exchange theories do not typically address why the same outcome may seem more costly or beneficial, depending on which relationship we are considering. If your best friend asked you to spot him a couple of hundred thousand dollars, drive him to school every day for a decade, cook his meals, and do his laundry, you'd probably start looking for a new companion. Yet many parents will tell you that their relationships with their children are the most rewarding experiences in their lives. As we'll see, social psychologists have begun to consider how our calculation of costs and benefits varies systematically depending on the type of relationship we are considering (e.g., Ackerman & Kenrick, 2008; Clark & Monin, 2006; Haslam & Fiske, 1999).

DOMAIN-SPECIFIC SOCIAL MOTIVATIONS We aspire to very different goals in relationships with lovers, business associates, relatives, friends, and strangers (Cann, 2004; Reis, Collins, & Berscheid, 2000). What feels good and what feels like a good deal depends importantly on who's involved and what we want from them. Sometimes it feels good to get a hug from someone else (if we are with a close friend and feeling lonely), sometimes we prefer their advice rather than affection (if we are talking to an auto mechanic about our transmission), and at still other times it feels best to be left completely alone (if a stranger calls on the phone to sell us something). **Domain-specific models** presume we think and feel very differently depending on the adaptive problem posed by particular kinds of relationships (Kenrick, Sundie, & Kurzban, 2008; Overall, Fletcher, & Friesen, 2003; Sedikides & Skowronski, 2000). In line with our focus on the different goals of social behavior, we will explore those different relationship motivations throughout this chapter and the next.

We'll consider affiliation and friendship in terms of four specific, and sometimes competing, social goals: getting social support, getting information, gaining status, and exchanging material benefits.

Quick Quiz

1 Which of the following statements are true?

    a. Similar to the dictionary definition of "friend," most psychologists contend that true friendships only exist with people who are not related to or romantically involved with one another.

    b. In the vast majority of human societies, people's closest friends are not genetic relatives.

    c. From an evolutionary perspective, it makes sense that people would only form close friendships with non-relatives.

    d. None of the above

2 Which of the following is true?

    a. The reinforcement-affect model is a domain-general model, whereas social exchange theory constitutes a domain-specific model.

    b. Social exchange theory focuses on associations with positive and negative feelings, and assumes that people do not use rational criteria when forming associations and friendships.

    c. The reinforcement-affect model assumes that people come to like those with whom they associate positive feelings and dislike those with whom they associate negative feelings.

    d. All of the above

3 A model that explains a wide range of behaviors using a simple general rule can be described as _____, whereas a model that assumes we think and feel differently depending on different situations is considered _____.

    a. Domain-general, domain-specific

    b. Domain-specific, domain-general

    c. Domain-relative, domain-specific

    d. Domain-general, domain-relative

Domain-specific model A model that presumes that the governing principles vary from one domain of behavior to another (such as friendship versus romance versus parent–child relationships).

Social support and stress. After the September 11 attacks on the World Trade Center, many people turned to their friends and family members for emotional support. Research suggests that such support enhances physical and psychological health for those under stress.

Social support Emotional, material, or informational assistance provided by other people.

Health psychology The study of behavioral and psychological factors that affect illness.

Getting Social Support

LO 7.3 Explain how the "tend and befriend" response to stress differs from "fight or flight."

LO 7.4 Identify the kinds of threats that lead people to seek or avoid others.

LO 7.5 Describe how loneliness and depression can lead to a negative, self-perpetuating cycle and how attachments with others can break that cycle.

Although it might seem like a dream to live a life in which everyone bows in your presence and turns his or her eyes to the ground as you ride through town on a throne, the truth is that, the Dalai Lama was lonely before he met Heinrich Harrer. Except for rare visits from his brother Lobsang Samten, the Dalai Lama was kept isolated from playmates and family members for most of his childhood and early adolescence. The adulation of worshipers staring at the ground in his presence simply left him deprived of everyday conversation.

Harrer met the Dalai Lama after having first befriended his brother Lobsang Samten. Having been declared the next incarnation of Buddha as a very young boy, the Dalai Lama rarely encountered anyone who treated him normally. As Harrer observed, "For everyone except myself, he was not a lonely boy but a god." It must have been extremely refreshing for the lonely young teenager to have someone talk to him as another human being, and their first conversation lasted for five hours. Afterward, the Dalai Lama asked Harrer to instruct him in English and math, and would call Harrer onto the temple grounds frequently. The young monarch took great joy in these visits, often running to meet Harrer and getting extremely anxious if the German was a few minutes late. He delighted in teasing Harrer and occasionally play-boxing with him, something he could not do with the monks who cared for him.

Despite his great wealth and status, the young god-king had been deprived of something we all crave—emotional support. Emotional support is one aspect of **social support**, defined as the emotional, informational, or material assistance provided by other people. We focus this section on emotional support—the affection, caring, and nurturance people provide for one another (Gottlieb, 1994). Because unique factors affect how people exchange information and material resources, we'll address these forms of social support in later sections of the chapter.

The tendency to turn to others when we are emotionally distressed may be linked to a basic feature of human nature: Humans fare better in numbers (Cacioppo et al., 2005; Taylor, 2006). People in groups can protect one another in times of trouble. And having another shoulder to huddle against may even have medical benefits.

Bridging Theory and Application:

Health Psychology and Emotional Support

Is having friends good for your health? This is the sort of question asked by health psychologists. **Health psychology** is the study of behavioral and psychological factors that affect illness (Salovey, Rothman, & Rodin, 1998; Taylor, 2002). Health psychologists assume that the physical condition of our bodies is intimately connected with how we think and how we behave. One of the more intriguing conclusions to emerge from health psychology research is that nurturing contact with other people is linked to a longer and happier life (Loucks et al., 2005; Ryff & Singer, 2000).

Consider first the harmful properties of social isolation. Loneliness has been tied to drug and alcohol abuse, sleep disturbances, headaches, lowered immune response, suicidal thoughts, and even mortality in nursing homes (Bearman & Moody, 2004; Jaremka et al., 2013; Jones & Carver, 1991). Over time, the increased vulnerability caused by loneliness can take a serious toll. One team of researchers searched out physicians who had, during medical school, described themselves as "loners." Several decades later, those lone wolves had significantly higher rates of cancer than did their more gregarious classmates (Shaffer et al., 1987). Another study found that, after a heart attack, 16% of patients living alone, versus 9% of those living with someone else, had another heart attack (Case et al., 1992). In contrast, people who have strong social ties are less upset by stressful life events, are more resistant to disease, and even live longer after being diagnosed with life-threatening diseases (e.g., Buunk & Verhoeven, 1991; Sarason et al., 1997). Indeed, just having someone to talk to about stressful events can enhance your emotional and physical well-being (Lepore, Ragan, & Jones, 2000; Pennebaker et al., 1987, 1989; Reis et al., 2000). A recent neuropsychological study indicates that social support is associated with lowered cortisol responses to stressful tasks and a pattern of brain activity indicating enhanced ability to regulate bodily reactions to stress (Taylor et al., 2008).

Studies showing a relationship between stress resistance and social support are correlational. They highlight a statistical association between having friendship and health but do not prove a causal link. Perhaps people with certain types of personalities are both more likely to have friends and to be physically healthy. Extraverts, for example, might be more likely to exercise or less likely to sit around and dwell on every unpleasant event that befalls them. The reverse might be true of highly anxious people. Niall Bolger and John Eckenrode (1991) set out to eliminate these sources of confusion by testing students the month before they took medical entrance examinations. The researchers measured students' levels of extraversion and emotional instability and also measured the students' daily stresses as well as their contacts with others. Even when students' preexisting traits were taken into account, contact with other people still served as a buffer against anxiety: Students with more social contacts were less traumatized by the exams.

Some research suggests the best source of emotional support may come not from other people but from "man's best friend," the dog. Karen Allen, Jim Blascovich, Joe Tomaka, and Robert Kelsey (1991) subjected women to stressful tasks under one of three conditions—alone, with a friend, or with their pet dogs. The researchers measured the women's heart rate, blood pressure, and skin conductance. To induce stress, subjects were asked to count backward by 13s and 17s rapidly.

A human's best friend in times of stress.
Research discussed in the text suggests that, under some circumstances, the company of a pet dog may be more stress-reducing than the company of a friend.

The physiological measures indicated that having a human friend present only served to increase anxiety. (The anxiety-arousing effect of friends in this experiment was probably because of the particular type of task, which involved possible embarrassment. As we discover later, embarrassment is one stressor that is made worse, rather than better, by the presence of others.) However, having their dogs at their sides significantly reduced physiological distress. And the helpful canine effects are not limited to short-term experiments. Over a period of years, elderly people who have dogs are less likely to visit doctors and more likely to survive heart attacks (Friedmann et al., 1980; Siegel, 1990).

We see, then, that companionship is generally good for your mental and physical health. But this isn't equally true for all of the people all of the time. The consequences of social support depend both on the person and on the situation. What kind of person turns to others for social support, and which situations arouse the need for such support?

PERSON **Do Women Tend and Befriend While Men Fight or Take Flight?**

In Irven DeVore's classic documentary *The Baboon Troop*, there is a vivid moment when a leopard approaches the troop. In response to this threat, a group of agitated adult baboons forms a tight circle facing the leopard, each baring a set of knifelike teeth as a warning to the feline predator. These baboons are vividly demonstrating the more aggressive half of the classic "fight or flight" response (Cannon, 1932). This response involves activation of the adrenal medulla and massive secretion of hormones such as adrenaline and noradrenaline. Interestingly, every one of the baboons lined up to fight off the leopard was a male. According to social psychologist Shelley Taylor and her colleagues (2000b; Taylor & Gonzaga, 2006), there may be a good reason for this. The females are more likely to be quietly huddled in a group with other female relatives

Sex differences in response to stress. As discussed in the text, social psychologist Shelly Taylor and her colleagues review evidence that women are more likely to "tend and befriend" when confronted with stress, whereas men are more likely to show the classic "fight or flight" reaction.

protecting their offspring, demonstrating what Taylor calls a "tend and befriend" rather than a "fight or flight" response.

Taylor and her colleagues reviewed an impressive body of literature to support their conclusion that females are less likely to respond to stress with fight-or-flight behavior. Instead, they "tend" (get their offspring out of harm's way) and "befriend" (pull closer to other females). As the researchers note, most classic studies on the fight-or-flight reaction, in humans and other animals, were conducted using male subjects. Females were less frequently studied because their cyclic hormonal fluctuations posed problems for measuring stress responses. When female stress reactions have been studied, however, they look very different from those of males. Whereas males under stress are likely to secrete androgens (associated with aggressive behavior), stressed-out females are more likely to secrete oxytocin (associated with nurturing maternal behaviors and attachment). A recent study found that administering a dose of oxytocin led to a substantial boost in men's willingness to trust others, which led in turn to increased cooperation (Kosfeld et al., 2005). Taylor and her colleagues interpret these findings in evolutionary terms, suggesting that ancestral male and female mammals would have been served by different responses to stress. For females, fighting or running would probably have endangered their offspring, who are completely dependent on their mothers for care. Quietly gathering up their dependent young when trouble threatens, and seeking supportive contact with other group members, on the other hand, would have better served offspring survival.

Other research suggests that, compared to men, women are generally more supportive of one another and more attentive to their relationships with close friends (Oswald, Clark, & Kelly, 2004). Among adolescents, female friendships are more intimate and involving than males', and a teenage girl's self-esteem is tied more closely to having an intimate friend (Townsend, McCracken, & Wilton, 1988). Social inclusion is so critical that excluding a girl from a social group is the primary method teenage girls use to hurt one another (Owens, Shute, & Slee, 2000). In college, the sex difference in social support continues. College women, as compared to men, have more same-sex friends and are closer to those friends (Nezlek, 1993; Wheeler, Reis, & Nezlek, 1983).

Women have a host of personal characteristics that facilitate supportive relations with others. Compared to men, women tend to be more agreeable, more empathic, more skilled in nonverbal communication, and better at smoothing interactions in social groups (Bank & Hansford, 2000; Klein & Hodges, 2001). Women are more attentive to their friends and more direct in showing their appreciation of one another (Carli, 1989; Helgeson et al., 1987). When girls and women are under stress, they are, compared to men, more likely to seek out support (Benenson & Koulnazarian, 2008; Tamres et al., 2002). And women nonverbally invite support and intimacy by smiling substantially more than men (Hall & Halberstadt, 1986; LaFrance, Hecht, & Paluck, 2003).

It's important not to jump to the conclusion that men don't care about getting social support from others. Indeed, men depend on other group members, so tending and befriending can play a part in male response to stress as well (Geary & Flinn, 2002; Li et al., 2008). Heinrich Harrer and his friend Aufschnaiter, for example, depended on each other in numerous ways as they struggled to survive against the elements and then to be accepted by the Tibetans in the Forbidden City. And recalling the male baboons, remember it was not a lone individual that stood against the leopard but a unified group. Thus, the sex difference in social supportiveness is relative rather than absolute. In fact, studies of children and adolescents suggest that girls are more likely to end their friendships than are boys (Benensen & Alavi, 2004). As we will discuss in more detail later, men may simply have different ways of relating to their friends.

SITUATION   Threats: Why Misery (Sometimes) Loves Company

The term *emotional support* is implicitly tied to certain situations: People seek the support of others when they're feeling threatened or isolated. When a realistic radio report of Martians invading New Jersey led to a massive panic on October 30, 1938, social psychologist Hadley Cantril (1940) recorded many touching stories of people going to great lengths to be near friends and family members. And when terrorists actually did attack the United States on September 11, 2001, many students told us that the first thing they did was telephone their relatives in distant cities. Physical dangers and social isolation both increase our motivation to get solace from others.

IMPERSONAL DANGER AND THE FEAR OF DEATH   Students in one study were asked to ponder a rather unpleasant question: "Describe what you think will happen when you physically die." After a few minutes pondering their own death, the students were sent into a room for group discussion. When they arrived, they faced a seating choice—they could either sit by themselves in the lone seat on one side of the table, or with the rest of the group in a set of clustered chairs on the other side. Students who had been pondering their own deaths overwhelmingly chose to be sociable—80% sat in one of the clustered chairs. The majority of students in the control condition, who had just spent a few minutes pondering their feelings about watching television, showed a preference for sitting alone. The researchers, who replicated the effect in three different studies, believe the tendency to affiliate under threat is connected to a basic human motivation we discussed earlier—people are safer in groups, and thinking about death prompts us to seek the security of a crowd (Wisman & Koole, 2003).

It doesn't take the threat of death to trigger our affiliative tendencies; lesser threats have the same effect. For example, female undergraduates were paired up for an experiment and told it involved "ischemia," the restriction of normal blood flow. Some were led to believe that the experiment would be painless—a blood pressure cuff would be partially inflated around their arms. Other women were led to expect they'd be strapped into a torturous device that would squeeze around their arm and below the rib cage, to produce a sharp pain similar to the angina felt by heart patients. The researchers measured affiliative tendencies by recording the time spent looking at another woman in the room. When both women expected to suffer the torturous pain, they spent twice as much time looking at one another as when they were expecting no suffering (Gump & Kulik, 1997).

SOCIAL ISOLATION   In his classic *Principles of Psychology*, William James (1890) noted social isolation as the cruelest of tortures. "To one long pent up on a desert island," James observed, "the sight of a human footprint or a human form in the distance would be the most tumultuously exciting of experiences." Warren Jones and his colleagues (1985) summarized a number of factors that boost feelings of social isolation. These include having recently moved, starting college, losing a job, living alone, and having inadequate transportation. Simply pondering the possibility that they might end up alone later in life is enough to lead students to think illogically and act in irrational, self-defeating ways (Baumeister et al., 2005; Twenge et al., 2002).

The physical presence of other people isn't enough to alleviate feelings of social isolation. Sometimes being in a crowd can be the loneliest of experiences, if the other crowd members are ignoring you (e.g., van Beest & Williams, 2006). Students in one study were led to believe they were participating in an experimental chat room. After a round of introductions, they were left out in the cold by the other group members, who ignored them in favor of talking about marching bands or a (made-up) rock group called "Hoodoo Meatbucket." This rejection experience seemed to fuel students' need to belong, making them particularly attentive to social information about strangers (Gardner, Pickett, & Brewer, 2000). In another study, students tossed around a ball as part of a three-person group. Imagine how you'd react if the other two people ignored you and started tossing the ball back and forth only to one another. As we mentioned in Chapter 1, students who were excluded from a social interaction showed a pattern of brain activity similar to that found when people are experiencing physical pain (Eisenberger, Lieberman, & Williams, 2003). People generally respond to social exclusion by working hard to enhance their social bonds, showing more interest in making new friends, volunteering to work with others, and saying nice things about other people (Maner et al., 2007).

INTERACTION Pushing Support Away

If it's so good for your health, you might expect everyone to invite as much social support as possible. But sometimes people actively reject support from others (Buunk et al., 1993). For one thing, we don't always perceive social support as a good thing, especially when we can't reciprocate (e.g., Greenberg & Westcott, 1983). As we discuss more fully in Chapter 9, when someone does you a favor you can't return, it may be a source of embarrassment, marking you as a "charity case."

The potential for embarrassment erodes any motivation to seek support from others. When we have to perform on a task we're not very good at, for example, the presence of other people simply adds to the stress (Blascovich et al., 1999).

Imagine that, like subjects in a classic experiment conducted by Irving Sarnoff and Philip Zimbardo (1961), you were told that you were about to suck on various objects related to Freud's "oral" period of development, including pacifiers and nipples from baby bottles. Would you want to wait with others or alone? If you're like the subjects in this study, you'd probably choose to wait alone under these potentially embarrassing conditions. Friends' supportive function seems to disappear when their presence might lead you to feel evaluated. When female students in one experiment worked on a stressful math test, their blood pressure was lower if they had a close friend around, unless the friend was in an evaluative role, in which case it was just as well to be alone or among strangers (Kors, Linden, & Gerin, 1997). As we noted earlier, at times like these a better companion would be a dog, who is unlikely to make any snide remarks about your intelligence!

Some people push away support inadvertently. Indeed, the very people most in need of emotional support may unintentionally shut off the flow of social nurturance they crave, as we see next.

Bridging Function and Dysfunction:

The Self-Perpetuating Cycle of Loneliness and Depression

Researchers have discovered that depression and loneliness may work hand in hand to drive away social support. To begin with, depressed people are less effective in coping with stress in their lives (Marx, Williams, & Claridge, 1992). They complain more about the unsatisfying quality of their interactions with other people, and they are less able to use humor as a coping mechanism (Nezlek & Derks, 2001; Nezlek, Hampton, & Shean, 2000). And then they make things worse by acting in ways that may increase the stress. When they turn to their friends and roommates for help, their depressive focus on the negative aspects of their lives tends to alienate the very people who could provide support. Even the most sympathetic friends eventually tire of hearing repetitions on the theme of "life is miserable, nothing ever goes my way, it's all hopeless." As a consequence, depressed people get less support from others (Gracia & Herrero, 2004).

To further compound matters, depressive individuals may seek out relationships with people who view them unfavorably (Swann et al., 1992). When friends of depressed people do try to help, they themselves may become depressed (Joiner, 1994). In the long run, other people find the interactions unpleasant enough that they begin to avoid the depressive person (Joiner et al., 1992; Strack & Coyne, 1983).

Loneliness shows some of the same self-perpetuating characteristics, and is sometimes directly linked to depression (see Figure 7.1). Lonely students are, compared to their more gregarious counterparts, more nervous, more depressed, and more likely to criticize themselves (Russell et al., 1980). They tend to think about themselves in self-defeating ways—making internal and stable attributions for interpersonal problems ("I can never do anything right") even when there are obvious external explanations for their problems (Peplau et al., 1979). For instance, a student who has just moved away to college and who lacks a car to visit friends may ignore his problematic situation and decide he is lonely only because others find him unattractive and boring.

Instead of inviting others over or going out to a public event, lonely students tend to cope with their isolation in counterproductive ways, by eating, taking drugs, or watching TV, for instance (Paloutzian & Ellison, 1982). When lonely students are around others, they may act in ways that make them less attractive—they may talk more about themselves, change the topic more frequently, ask fewer questions about their conversational partners, and make more inappropriate self-disclosures than students who are not lonely (Jones et al., 1982; Solano et al., 1982).

To make things worse, lonely people set unrealistically high expectations for both themselves and others (Rawlins, 1992). After talking to others, lonely students rate themselves and others more negatively and show less interest in seeing the partners again (Gable & Reis, 1999; Jones, Freemon, & Goswick, 1981; Jones, Sansone, & Helm, 1983). And even when their conversational partners perceive them positively, the lonely students walk away from the interaction feeling as if they've done poorly (Christensen & Kashy, 1998).

So what can you do if you're stuck in this self-perpetuating cycle? It would help to tell yourself things will get better, because those who confront stress with an optimistic frame of mind do cope better (Abend & Williamson, 2002; Brissette et al., 2002). But unfortunately, we're least able to look on the bright side when we're feeling depressed (Forgas, 1995). The research we

Figure 7.1 The self-perpetuating cycle of loneliness

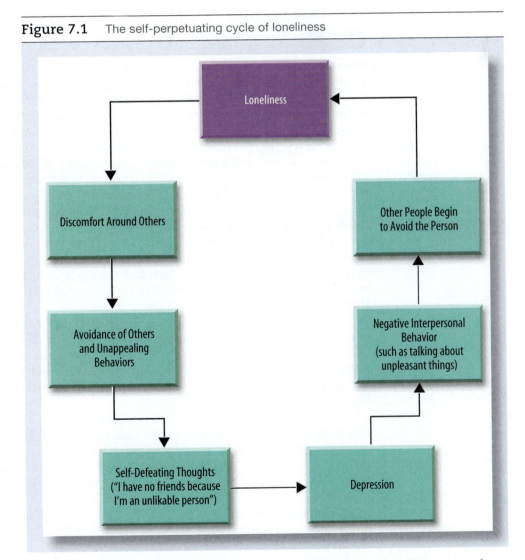

Lonely people are uncomfortable around others and act in ways that reduce their sources of social support. This may in turn lead not only to more feelings of loneliness but also to self-defeating thoughts and, in turn, to depression. Depression itself leads to behaviors that further act to turn off others thereby contributing to additional loneliness.

just discussed suggests a couple of things you don't want to do: You don't want to start avoiding others, and, if others do try to give you support, you don't want to bring them down with complaints about how miserable life can be. Instead, you might want to get involved in some active and positive social interactions with others who share your interests (Lyubomirsky, Sheldon, & Schkade, 2005). Rather than drinking or watching television, something that involves group physical movement, like a yoga class or an aerobic class, could help. Aerobic exercise can act as a mood-enhancing drug for teenagers and senior citizens alike

(Kircaldy et al., 2002; Pennix et al., 2002; Salmon, 2001). Moreover, as we'll see in the remainder of this chapter, your friends and associates will react more positively to you to the extent that you find similar interests to theirs, give them feedback about their own strengths, and provide them with useful resources or information. And although it's nice to make new friends, keeping the old can also help reduce stress. College students who make the effort to maintain their contacts with high school friends seem to reap the benefit of being buffered against loneliness (Oswald & Clark, 2003).

INVESTIGATION

Based on the research we've just reviewed, what three bits of advice could you give a friend who is caught in the cycle of loneliness and depression?

INTERACTION Attachment and Social Development

Whereas depression leads to a negative cycle, strong attachments to others can lead to a positive cycle in our interactions with other people. In his book *Attachment*, British psychologist John Bowlby (1969) suggested that people whose parents provided a secure relationship are better suited to handle stresses later in life. This may be because those who had secure attachments to their mothers are better equipped to get support. In one study, researchers followed children from infancy through their later experiences in preadolescent summer camps (Shulman, Elicker, & Sroufe, 1994). Compared to those whose maternal attachments had been insecure, children who had been securely attached to their mothers later showed more skill in dealing with their peers. Children who are securely attached to their parents are also less likely to develop behavioral problems later (Rohner, Khaleque, & Cournoyer, 2005). And as adults, those with a secure attachment style have more intimate and satisfying relationships with others, and feel that the other people in their lives are more responsive to their needs (Dykas & Cassidy, 2011; Kafetsios & Nezlek, 2002). In an ironic twist on the depressive cycle, then, those with the least need may be the most able to get support!

As children grow into their teenage years, they may rebuff their parents' offers of emotional support. Adolescents increasingly turn from their parents to their peers (Aseltine, Gore, & Colten, 1994), a trend that continues in college (Fraley & Davis, 1997). In fact, contact with their parents does not seem to reduce feelings of loneliness in college students; only contact with friends helps (Cutrona, 1982; Davis, Morris, & Kraus, 1998).

However, parental support is not irrelevant, even for college students. People who have reassuring relationships with their parents have less negative moods and get better grades in school, whereas friends aren't particularly helpful in these domains (Cutrona et al., 1994; Davis et al., 1998). So, if you someday find yourself in the role of a parent with a teenager who spurns your well-intentioned offers of support, you will probably help him or her most by keeping the offer open. And if you are on the other side, it is probably best for your mental health and happiness (not to mention your grade point average) to accept the offer of a parental shoulder to lean on.

In recent years, there have been many studies of the role of attachment in adult romantic relationships (e.g., Campbell et al., 2001; McGowan, 2002). In Chapter 8, which deals with romantic love, we will return to examine attachment in more detail.

Quick Quiz

1 Which of the following is not true of women's and men's stress responses?

    a. When under stress, women's brains secrete oxytocin, whereas men's brains secrete androgens.

    b. Females are less likely to respond to stress with fight-or-flight behavior.

    c. Researchers have found that oxytocin affects men differently than women and does not improve men's trust in or cooperation with others.

    d. In evolutionary terms, gender differences in responses to stress evolved because they maximized the survival of offspring.

2 When faced with stress from _____, people tend to respond by _____.

    a. fear of embarrassment, avoiding social support

    b. crowding, seeking social support

    c. impersonal dangers, avoiding social support

    d. social isolation, avoiding social support

3 Lonely people tend to _____

    a. think about themselves in self-defeating ways.

    b. spend excessive time inviting others to hang out with them.

    c. talk less about themselves and ask more questions about their conversational partners.

    d. All of the above

4 Which of the following is true regarding social support between children and parents?

    a. Adolescents increasingly turn to their peers, rather than their parents, for social support, but this trend tends to reverse when they enter college.

    b. Children who are securely attached to their mothers show less skill in dealing with their peers.

    c. The quality of college students' relationships with their parents has no significant impact on school performance.

    d. None of the above

Getting Information

LO 7.6 Summarize social comparison theory and how it relates to our tendency to be attracted to similar others.

LO 7.7 Discuss the type of person who is more likely to make self-disclosures and understand the consequences of self-disclosure.

LO 7.8 Explain how social comparisons are linked to self-evaluation and happiness.

How did Heinrich Harrer and Peter Aufschnaiter progress from ragged fugitives to insiders in the Forbidden City of Lhasa? The most plausible answer is that they had something the Tibetans needed: valuable information from the outside world. Aufschnaiter was an engineer, and Harrer was a trained educator who was able to help the Tibetans by translating foreign newspapers in several languages. Harrer also knew something about cinematography, a topic that fascinated the young Dalai Lama. Indeed, it was the Dalai Lama's hunger for knowledge that led their first meeting to last five hours. According to Harrer's account, the young monarch "poured out a flood of questions. He seemed to me like a person who had for years brooded in solitude over different problems, and now that he had at last someone to talk to, wanted to know all the answers at once." When the meeting came to an end, the Dalai Lama asked Harrer to become his tutor and to teach him English, geography, and arithmetic.

Although not all of our friends and acquaintances have heads full of exotic knowledge from faraway places, they can be great resources for potentially useful facts, ideas, and alternative opinions. If you want to find out quickly how to fix a leaky faucet, hem a pair of pants, or prepare a good spaghetti sauce, a friend or neighbor can be more helpful than any book in the public library. And when we put our heads together with others, our communal IQ often goes up (Thompson & Fine, 1999; Wegner, 1987). People working with friends tend to do better on any number of tasks, from memorizing words to solving complex problems (Andersson & Roennberg, 1997; Zajac & Hartup, 1997). One reason friends work well together is that they share a similar base of knowledge and are better equipped to "read" one another's feelings and intentions (Colvin, Vogt, & Ickes, 1997).

Besides being resources for facts about the physical world, other people's opinions are more or less all that matters when it comes to getting answers to questions about *social* realities (such as "How likable am I?"). When we seek out feedback about a personal decision, we tend to look for information that supports what we wanted to do anyway; other people advising us can give a more balanced opinion (Jonas, Schulz-Hardt, & Frey, 2005).

Social Comparison and Liking for Similar Others

In Chapter 3, we mentioned Leon Festinger's (1954) classic social comparison theory. According to Festinger, people have a drive to evaluate their opinions and abilities, and frequently the best way to do so is to compare themselves with others. Some questions (such as whether we can run a mile in five minutes) can be answered by checking the physical, rather than the social, world. However, to answer many questions about our abilities and opinions, we must turn to others. Are you being unreasonable in your relationship with your boyfriend or girlfriend? Do others perceive you as friendly or unfriendly? Are your opinions about the death penalty and abortion sensible ones, or do they make you seem eccentric?

Festinger's theory included an additional assumption—that we prefer to compare our opinions and abilities with those of similar rather than dissimilar others. To know whether you are a decent intramural basketball player, for instance, you wouldn't compare yourself to NBA all-stars. The relevant comparison group is other intramural players. Likewise, if you're a liberal Democrat and want to know whether your opinions about abortion and the death penalty are reasonable, you don't turn to members of the American Nazi Party for feedback but to other liberal Democrats. This aspect of Festinger's theory was an important historical influence on one of the most heavily researched topics in social psychology—the attraction toward similar others (Byrne, 1971; Hilmert, Kulik, & Christenfeld, 2006; Rushton & Bons, 2005).

Our motivation to obtain information from others is partly driven by a desire for accurate information. But most of us want our accurate information served with a spoonful of sugar, so we gravitate toward information that makes us feel good or that validates our view of the world (Bogart & Helgeson, 2000; Buckingham & Alicke, 2002; Suls, Lemos, & Stewart, 2002). Our attraction to similar others stems partly from the fact that they often agree with us, which makes us feel good (Clore & Byrne, 1974; Orive, 1988). Conversely, we tend to respond negatively to others who disagree with us (Chen & Kenrick, 2002; Norton, Frost, & Ariely, 2007; Rosenbaum, 1986). Part of the attraction to similar others is the simple expectation that they will like us more than dissimilar others (Condon & Crano, 1988). But another part is that they confirm our views about ourselves and the world (Boer et al., 2011; Pittman, 1998). When we compare ourselves with others, we tend to notice our similarities with more successful others, and how we are different from losers (Locke, 2005). Contrasting ourselves with others who are doing worse makes us feel good about ourselves; and narcissists feel a particularly strong boost from these downward social comparisons (Bogart, Benotsch, & Pavlovic, 2004).

Similarity and friendship. Research suggests that we like people whose looks and ages are similar to ours, who think like us, whose interests overlap with ours, and whose personal habits are similar to ours. Part of the appeal of similar others is that they affirm our beliefs and attitudes.

PERSON Self-Disclosers and Nondisclosers

Think for a minute about the people you know best. Do you know anyone who tends to "play it close to the chest," rarely disclosing information about herself or her feelings, and rarely consulting others for opinions about her personal life? Can you think of someone you know who, in contrast, wears her heart on her sleeve, always willing to disclose her personal feelings or experiences, happy to accept feedback from anyone who will listen?

Researchers have found robust individual differences in the tendency to exchange personal and social information with others. On the input side, some people need the feedback of others to come to decisions about appropriate behavior, whereas others seem happy making up their own minds. On the output side, some people openly disclose information about themselves, while others play it close to the vest. Indeed, a key aspect of being a friend is **self-disclosure**, sharing intimate information about oneself (Derlega et al., 1993; Harvey & Omarzu, 1997). Mutual disclosure is so important that complete strangers can be made to feel like friends after just half an hour of mutual disclosure of intimate details (Aron et al., 1997). You can often get others to like you just by opening up to them (Collins & Miller, 1994; Ensari & Miller, 2002). And disclosing our private inner thoughts and secrets can lead to new insights and make us feel better (Kelly et al., 2001).

But people differ widely in their inclination to self-disclose. While men are chatting impersonally about sports and politics, women are more likely to disclose information about themselves and their personal relationships (Martin, 1997; Salas & Ketzenberger, 2004; Sheets & Lugar, 2005). East Asians are less likely to self-disclose than are Americans, a difference that seems to be linked to the fact that Americans are more likely to change friends more frequently, which provides more incentives for self-disclosure (Schug, Yuki, & Maddux, 2010).

There can be downsides to self-disclosure. Entrusting another person with a personal secret can open the door to feelings of betrayal, to gossip, and to possible invasions of your privacy (Petronio, 2002). In hindsight, Monica Lewinsky's choice of Linda Tripp as a confidant was a very bad decision. The treacherous Tripp encouraged Lewinsky to tell all about her affair with President Bill Clinton, all the while taping the conversations in the hopes of making money from an exposé. The results not only humiliated Lewinsky and Clinton but also brought the U.S. Congress to a standstill, as Clinton's opponents used the disclosed secrets as grounds for an impeachment trial and further voyeuristic inquiries into the president's private life.

SITUATION Uncertainty about Important Issues

Are there circumstances that lead us to turn to others for social information? According to social comparison theory, the motivation to compare our opinions, abilities, or reactions with others will increase when we are feeling uncertain about something important (Marsh & Webb, 1996; Roney & Sorrentino, 1995). We don't need to check with others concerning topics about which we already know the answer (Is Christmas going to be on December 25 this year?) or about which we aren't very concerned (Was the 1992 fava bean harvest larger in Iran or Turkey?). And some circumstances are more likely to arouse uncertainty than others. For instance, rumors (like the stories about witches in Salem that spread during 1692) tend to spread more rapidly when an event is important and when actual facts are difficult to obtain (Allport & Postman, 1947). In one experimental study of uncertainty and affiliation, students were threatened with painful shock. Some saw physiological recording gauges informing them how other students were responding to the same threat. Other students watched their own physiological responses, and still others were given no information (Gerard & Rabbie, 1961). When the students thought they knew how other students were responding, they were less interested in affiliating than when they were given no information or information only about their own responses. This is consistent with the notion that part of the motivation for affiliation under fear is to compare one's own reactions with those of others. Later research finds the same effect among people facing various threats to their health (Buunk, Gibbons, & Visser, 2002).

SITUATION Similarity to Us

Another assumption of social comparison theory is that people in a state of uncertainty are especially motivated to make a particular kind of comparison. The theory assumes that we want to compare ourselves with others who are similar to us, either by virtue of being "in the same boat" or by virtue of having similar interests and personality

Self-disclosure The sharing of intimate information about oneself.

(Kulik & Mahler, 2000; Marsh & Webb, 1996). But people's need to compare with similar others has its limits. When the issue is highly important to our welfare, we prefer affiliating with others who can give us accurate information whether they are similar or not. For instance, patients awaiting coronary bypass surgery prefer the company of someone who has already had the operation over someone who is, like them, awaiting surgery (Kulik & Mahler, 1990). Likewise, students imagining waiting for a strong electric shock say that, if talking were allowed, they would rather wait with someone who has already experienced the shock (Kirkpatrick & Shaver, 1988).

The main goal of affiliation in truly threatening situations is often cognitive clarity: People whose physical well-being is on the line are not interested in affiliating simply to know whether their reactions are "socially appropriate"; they want to get the most useful information they possibly can (Kulik, Mahler, & Earnest, 1994).

When situations are not as threatening, however, we often affiliate with similar others to enable smoother interactions. Consider one intriguing study that suggests that the pull of similarity works at a nonverbal and even nonconscious level. Tanya Chartrand and John Bargh (1999) videotaped New York University students while they were talking with an experimental confederate who either shook his foot or rubbed his face. As shown in Figure 7.2, students showed a remarkable tendency to be nonverbal chameleons, mimicking the movements of the confederate. Later interviews indicated that people do this without even being aware of it. The researchers hypothesized that this apparently automatic nonverbal mimicry might serve to increase liking and to smooth social interactions. To test this idea, they did another study in which they reversed the process, by having a confederate nonverbally mimic the participant. Compared to a condition in which the confederate did not imitate their movements, students liked the mimic more and felt the interaction went more smoothly. It feels good to have things go smoothly in our nonverbal

Figure 7.2   Monkey see, monkey do, monkey like

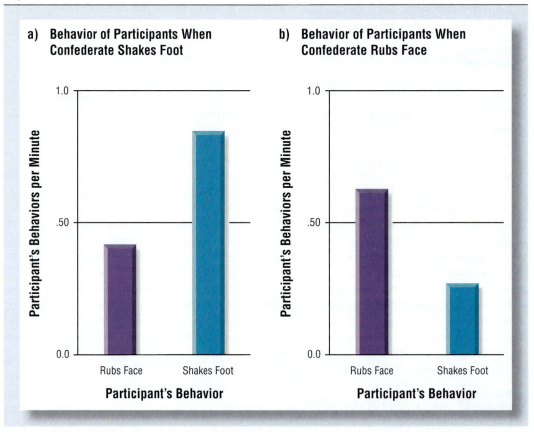

NYU students tended to imitate subtle nonverbal actions of an experimental confederate. When the confederate shook his or her foot a lot, students shook their feet more also (a). When the confederate instead rubbed his or her face, students likewise rubbed their faces (b).

interactions, and students whose nonverbal behaviors were mimicked actually became more helpful and generous (McIntosh, 2006; van Baaren et al., 2004).

INTERACTION When Dissimilarity Can Save Self-Esteem

Whether we seek information from similar others may depend on our self-concepts. Abe Tesser (2000) proposes that one important goal of social interaction is to maintain a positive evaluation of one's self. From the perspective of his *self-evaluation maintenance theory*, comparing oneself with similar others can be a double-edged sword. If a person is similar to you and very successful, you may be able to "bask in his or her glory" (Cialdini et al., 1976; Hirt et al., 1992). To say "My friend just won an award for his writing!" is to subtly suggest that you associate with geniuses. However, if the similar person's triumphant performance is in an area you regard as a special skill of your own, it may lead you to feel bad about your own performance (Beach et al., 1998). For instance, if you also fancy yourself a writer, your friend's prize may remind you that you have never won any writing awards. Campbell and Tesser (1985) note that, as a consequence, people prefer similar others whose performance is on par with their own but not better.

However, we aren't bothered if we find that another is better than us at something we don't regard as centrally relevant to how we define ourselves, or if we are primed to think about them as "family" (Gardner, Gabriel, & Hochschild, 2002). People are also very good at making fine distinctions to avoid comparisons that provoke envy in long-term relationships. A husband and wife in Campbell and Tesser's research were both political science professors, yet they expressed surprise when the researchers inquired whether there were problems of social comparison posed by their being in the same field. They were hardly in the same field, they pointed out, since one studied international relations while the other studied comparative politics!

One study suggests that the ignorance resulting from selective social comparisons may indeed be associated with bliss. Sonja Lyubomirsky and Lee Ross (1997) found that chronically unhappy students responded sensibly to social comparison information. As shown in Figure 7.3, the unhappy students raised their estimates of their own skill when they did better than a partner and lowered their estimates when they did worse. Happy students also raised their estimates when they outperformed the other student; but, when the other student outperformed them, they were oblivious to the feedback and raised their self-appraisals anyway!

Figure 7.3 Blissful ignorance of social comparison information

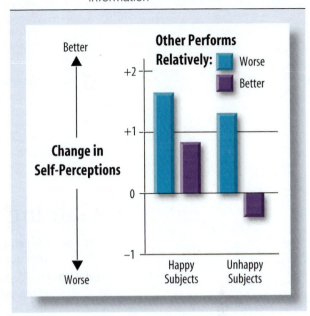

Students in one study estimated their skill at solving anagrams both before and after seeing another student do either worse or better than they had. Unhappy people upped their self-estimates after beating out the opponent and lowered them after being beaten. Happy people likewise upped their self-estimates after beating the other student, but they also raised self-estimates when the other student did better.

INVESTIGATION

Think of a time when you took pleasure from the news that someone you know had a smashing success and another time when it bugged you to hear about another's success. What was different? How do these two experiences fit with the research discussed in this section?

Quick Quiz

1 According to _____, people prefer to measure their opinions and abilities against _____ others.

    a. Social comparison theory, dissimilar

    b. Social comparison theory, similar

    c. Self-disclosure theory, dissimilar

    d. Self-disclosure theory, similar

2 Which of the following statements about *self-disclosure* is true?
   a. Men and women are equally likely to engage in self-disclosure.
   b. Socially anxious people tend to interpret others' feedback in the most positive light to protect their self-esteem.
   c. People low in the need for social approval are likely to reframe information into positive feedback for others.
   d. Women are more likely than men to engage in self-disclosure.

3 According to self-evaluation maintenance theory, we prefer to compare ourselves to:
   a. People who perform much less well than we do.
   b. People who perform slightly worse than we do.
   c. People who perform slightly better than we do.
   d. Similar others who perform well but only if their performance is not in an area we regard as our own special strength.

Gaining Status

LO 7.9 Describe the consequences of sex differences in seeking status versus affection on relationships.

LO 7.10 Understand how status motives contribute to our tendencies to approach or avoid others.

In pondering the question of why Heinrich Harrer and the Dalai Lama became friends, the interesting puzzle was why a monarch would want to rub elbows with a fugitive, not the reverse. There are few people who would turn down an invitation to chum around with the local monarch. Indeed, Harrer had been working for the Tibetan government before his audience with the Dalai Lama, grateful to have any form of employment. Shortly after his new friendship, he was given a big raise in salary, and his own status shot up in the eyes of the other Tibetans. It pays to have friends in high places.

Humans aren't the only ones who form bonds to increase their status—similar political power alliances are also found in other primate species (de Waal, 1989). For instance, social status in chimpanzee troupes, as in humans, is related to "who you know," and the top positions of dominance are often occupied by coalitions of friends, who, in tandem, can outrank even the largest and most domineering single chimps.

Teaming up for status. Whether or not individuals on the TV series *Survivor* get ahead in the game often depends on their ability to form connections with other people who are talented and socially powerful, but humans aren't the only primates who form alliances to gain power. The two male baboons at left have formed a coalition to compete for a female with the larger, more dominant, male at right. By forming this coalition, both of the less dominant males may gain access to mating opportunities that neither would have on his own.

PERSON Men's Friendships Are More Hierarchical

Interviews with college juniors and seniors suggest an interesting difference in the way men and women approach their friendships. Men are more likely to base their personal identity on career advancement, whereas women's identities are more likely to blend career and intimate relationships (Maines & Hardesty, 1987). Friendships among male adolescents are likely to avoid discussions of intimate topics, and instead focus on activities such as competitive sports (Martin, 1997; Shulman et al., 1997). In interactions with their parents, adolescent males are relatively more likely to discuss careers and colleges, whereas females are relatively more likely to discuss friends and family problems. In later life, women have more relationships with people outside work, whereas men have more relationships with coworkers (Rawlins, 1992).

Men also emphasize social hierarchy in their relationships more than women do (McWilliams & Howard, 1993). Testosterone—a hormone produced in much greater quantities by males than females—has been linked to competitive behavior in humans and a wide array of other animals (Frigerio et al., 2005; Schultheiss et al., 2005). Consistent with these findings, women (but not men) feel bad if they outperform their friends

(Benensen & Schinazi, 2004). Anita Barbee and her colleagues (1993) noted one consequence of gender differences in friendship styles: Because the male role deemphasizes nurturance and emotional expressiveness, men may have a more difficult time getting and giving emotional support. However, because the male role emphasizes achievement and independence, men may be better at exchanging instrumental support (such as helping a friend fix his car).

In sum, men's relationships are marked more by hierarchy and instrumentality—components of status-seeking. As we discussed earlier, women's relationships focus more on emotional support and intimacy. As a consequence, men may get more respect in their relationships, but women tend to get more affection.

SITUATION Status by Association

What circumstances might trigger the desire to affiliate with others for the sake of gaining status? When status is prominent in the situation, as in relationships on the job, people ought to try to associate with the higher-ups. On the other side of the coin, when another person has a socially undesirable characteristic that could lead to stigma by association, people may be motivated to distance themselves.

KISSING UP TO HIGH STATUS Concern about status in relationships comes to the fore when the social hierarchy is prominent. Indeed, relationships at work are likely to develop along status lines (Kanter, 1977). Graduate students who attend professional meetings become painfully aware of an annoying tendency of their conversational partners to break eye contact to read the name tags of passersby. The lowly graduate student is often deserted in mid-conversation if he or she is talking to a name-tag reader who spots a famous person walking by: "Excuse me. I need to run. . . . Ah, Doctor Zilstein, I noticed your name tag. I've read so many of your papers, and find them so inspiring." When people in organizations were surveyed about office politics, they frequently mentioned aligning themselves with powerful others as a way of getting ahead (Allen et al., 1979). And people in organizations commonly agree with their superiors in the hopes of getting the boss to like them (Greenberg & Baron, 1993; Liden & Mitchell, 1988). Indeed, when one person in a conversation acts nonverbally dominant, the other tends to automatically act submissive (Cheng & Chartrand, 2003; Markey, Funder, & Ozer, 2003).

This desire to form friendships with higher-ups is particularly strong in highly status-oriented cultures, such as in Japan. In one study, office workers in a U.S. organization and workers in a Japanese organization ranked the other office members and indicated how much they liked them. The Americans most liked workers at their own level, but the Japanese most liked those of higher status (Nakao, 1987).

KISSING OFF STIGMATIC ASSOCIATIONS On the other side of the coin, there is some evidence that people sometimes break social connections that could reflect poorly on them. For example, students in one experiment filled out the "Johnson Anger and Hostility Scale" and were later told their scores indicated a person who "has tendencies toward hostility and repressed anger but is usually unaware of these tendencies." Others filled out "Johnson's Dishonesty Scale" and were led to believe that they had high levels of "repressed dishonesty." Afterward, they saw another student's personality questionnaire and read a note from that student. In the note, the other person confessed either to becoming violent with a little nephew or to stealing some cash from a gym locker. Students who were feeling defensive about their own "repressed hostility" distanced themselves from the angry person, rating their own personality as very dissimilar. In contrast, students who had been made defensive about their own "repressed dishonesty" placed more distance between themselves and the thief (Schimel et al., 2000).

In a sense, this distancing phenomenon is the converse of "basking in reflected glory" (broadcasting one's associations with successful others), which we discussed in Chapter 4. C. R. Snyder, MaryAnne Lassegard, and Carol

Kissing up to the boss. Having a good relationship with one's superiors is a time-honored way of moving up in the hierarchy.

Figure 7.4 Cutting off reflected failure

Team Feedback

Students in one experiment were told that their team had done either splendidly or very poorly. Compared to those who got no information, those who thought the team had failed were substantially less likely to take a team badge.

Ford (1986) studied this distancing phenomenon in small groups of students assigned to "the Blue team" to work together on intellectual problems. Students were informed that their teams had either failed (scoring below 70% of people their age) or succeeded with flying colors (scoring above 90% of people their age). Afterward, students were told "there is a box of team badges by the door; you may take one and wear it if you like." Compared to students who got no information, those told their group had failed were far less likely to pick up the badge (see Figure 7.4). The researchers explained the results in terms of Heider's (1958) balance theory, which, as we discussed in Chapter 5, assumes that people manage their associations to maintain consistent (and preferably favorable) images of themselves.

INTERACTION ## Men's Status-Seeking May Erode Social Support

Overly zealous attempts to move up in the dominance hierarchy can defeat the goal of being liked. As Oscar Wilde put it, "Anybody can sympathise with the sufferings of a friend, but it requires a very fine nature to sympathise with a friend's success." Indeed, there may be an inherent conflict between the motive to get emotional support and the motive to gain status through friendship (Schneider et al., 2005). There is, in fact, some evidence that mixing work and play may, in the long run, damage one's social support networks. Highly motivated students, for example, often talk with their friends about how they're doing in school. Because your friends have only so much interest in what you're doing to get ahead, that may be a formula for losing friends. Less motivated students keep their support networks stronger in part by talking about things that their friends find more interesting (Harlow & Cantor, 1994).

Over the life span, men's status orientation may make them less desirable as friends. This has interesting implications for cross-sex friendships. As it turns out, men value the company of women, but women do not always reciprocate and would often rather hang out with other women (McWilliams & Howard, 1993). Women find their same-sex friendships more meaningful and more enjoyable than relationships with men (Reis, Senchak, & Solomon, 1985). As we noted earlier, women show their appreciation of their friends in very direct ways. Men are not so directly appreciative (Helgeson, Shaver, & Dyer, 1987). Women send a thank-you note, saying "That was really fun! I really value having you in my life! Let's have lunch again next Friday!" Men say, "I think I can find it in my heart to help you work on your pathetic golf swing again. Let's get together next Friday so you can watch how a master does it!" Small wonder that both sexes search for females in times of stress. This is an example of the person changing the situation. Males' sex-typical emphasis on status and competition often leads them to create a somewhat different (and less supportive) social environment than the one in which females dwell.

INVESTIGATION

Consider a friendship you have with someone of your own sex and one you have with someone of the opposite sex. In what ways do these two friends behave in ways consistent with, and inconsistent with, the research on sex differences discussed here and earlier in the chapter?

··

Once again, it's important not to exaggerate sex differences in social behavior. Although men are indeed more dominant and less agreeable in their same-sex friendships, things may reverse in romantic relationships, where women are more likely to start a quarrel or say something disagreeable (Suh, Moskowitz, Fournier, & Zuroff,

2004). Furthermore, people don't typically attain social dominance by being domineering and pushy. A study of adolescent males and females finds that both sexes use a combination of positive and coercive strategies to attain social dominance (Hawley, Little, & Card, 2008).

Quick Quiz

1 Which of the following claims is false?

    a. In later adulthood, women and men both tend to have more relationships with coworkers, as opposed to friends outside of work.

    b. Men, more than women, emphasize social hierarchy and instrumentality in their relationships.

    c. Men are more likely than women to base their personal identity on career advancement.

    d. None of the above

2 Which of the following claims is true?

    a. Men's status-seeking tends to create friendships that are less emotionally supportive than women's friendships.

    b. Women show their appreciation of friends more directly than men.

    c. Women find their same-sex friendships more meaningful and enjoyable than their friendships with men.

    d. All of the above

Exchanging Material Benefits

LO 7.11 Identify the four categories of social exchange rules used in different relationships.

LO 7.12 Explain the difference between a communal relationship and an exchange relationship and how exchange relationships differ between Western and non-Western cultures.

LO 7.13 Discuss how proximity is linked to social capital.

It was a bleak Christmas Eve during one of the worst periods of Heinrich Harrer's life as a fugitive. He and Aufschnaiter had just hiked 14 miles across frozen mountain terrain. Dressed in ragged clothes, they made a pitiful picture when they arrived at an isolated group of tents. The nomads living there, wary of local bandits, at first admonished the strangers to move along. But after a few minutes, they invited the two vagabonds to share their tent:

> We warmed ourselves by the fire and were given butter tea and a rare delicacy—a piece of white bread each. It was stale and hard as stone, but this little present on Christmas Eve in the wilds of Tibet meant more to us than a well-cooked Christmas dinner had ever done at home.

Harrer never forgot the kindness of these strangers, and his story of life in Tibet is full of many such episodes. Indeed, after being initially turned away in Lhasa, they were later treated to the warmest hospitality. When he and Aufschnaiter were finally permitted to stay in the Forbidden City, they immediately set about trying to repay the kindness by finding some work to do for the Tibetans. Harrer built a fountain and a new garden for his host, and Aufschnaiter used his engineering skills to build a canal and a new electrical generator for the city. A year after they had feasted on a mere bit of stale bread, Harrer threw a party for all the new friends he had made in Lhasa:

> I wanted to entertain my friends at a real Christmas party with a tree and presents. I had received so much kindness and hospitality that I wanted to give my friends some pleasure for a change.

Harrer's desire to treat his Tibetan hosts illustrates the powerful human drive to reciprocate favors. Reciprocating favors isn't just a polite custom; it may have been a key to our ancestors' survival through difficult times. Imagine you are living 1,000 years ago in a small group of people in the deepest jungles of South America. Imagine further that food is sometimes abundant but other times quite scarce. You have a lucky day at the local fishing hole and come home with a 12-pound fish. Do you hoard it for yourself and your immediate family, or do you share? For most of the history of the human species, our ancestors spent their time in just such small groups (Caporael, 1997; Sedikides & Skowronski, 1997). Research on modern hunter-gatherers reveals that if they did not share goods and services with one another, they would often perish (Hill & Hurtado, 1993).

Hunters in the Ache tribe, living in the Paraguayan jungle, for example, have a lot of ups and downs in their success at the hunt. Some days they bring home much more food than they could possibly eat; other days they come home empty-handed. If a man caught a wild pig and hoarded it for himself and his family, much of it would go to waste (there are no deep-freeze refrigerators in the Paraguayan jungle). During unlucky periods, individual hunters and their families would starve. Instead of living by a philosophy of "rugged individualism," however, hunters who have a lucky day share their meat with other families. And they don't just share a little; they share a lot—fully 90%. In exchange for this generosity, their neighbors share with them on days when the luck runs the other way (Hill & Hurtado, 1993). By exchanging resources, particularly those that are unpredictable and uncertain (like meat from the hunt, as opposed to vegetable crops), the group provides a mutual insurance policy against starvation (Kameda, Takezawa, & Hastie, 2003; Kameda et al., 2002).

Because of the importance of sharing resources, all societies have strong rules about who shares what with whom (Haslam, 1997). We discuss those rules in the next section.

Fundamental Patterns of Social Exchange

Although we may not have recently shared wild pig with our friends and neighbors, most of us frequently exchange material benefits, including rides to the store, Thanksgiving dinners, and inside tracks on job opportunities. The exchange of goods and services is so important to social life that some social psychologists believe it is at the very heart of our relationships with others (e.g., Brewer & Caporael, 2006; McCullough, Kimeldorf, & Cohen, 2008).

At the beginning of the chapter, we discussed social exchange theories, which presume that people are motivated to maximize their benefits in relationships with others. We also discussed equity, a form of exchange in which people strive not so much for selfish benefits but for fairness in their interactions with others. Which is it, are we driven toward fairness, or do we try to out-bargain others to our own benefit? It depends. Alan Fiske is a social psychologist who was also trained as a field anthropologist. On the basis of his studies of different human societies, Fiske suggested that people all around the world categorize relationships into four fundamental categories, each characterized by a different set of social exchange rules (see Table 7.1) (Fiske, 1992; Haslam & Fiske, 1999).

In **communal sharing** relationships, all members of a group share a pool of resources, taking when they are in need and giving when others are in need. Families often share according to a communal rule. In **authority ranking** relationships, goods are divided according to a person's status in the group. In a business, for instance, the boss gets a higher salary, a personal secretary, a reserved parking spot, and the freedom to come and go as she chooses. **Equality matching** involves exchange in which no one gets more than the others. Friends in a Chinese restaurant often share

Communal sharing A form of exchange in which members of a group share a pool of resources, taking when they are in need and giving when others are in need.

Authority ranking A form of exchange in which goods are divided according to a person's status in the group.

Equality matching A form of exchange in which each person gets the same as the others.

Table 7.1 Different Models of Social Exchange

Model of Social Relations	Rules of Exchange	Example of Relationship Using This Rule
Communal sharing	All members of a group share in the group's resources as needed and depend on one another for mutual care.	A tight-knit family
Authority ranking	Higher-ranking individuals are entitled to loyalty, respect, and deference; lower-ranking individuals are entitled to protection, advice, and leadership.	Military squad
Equality matching	No one gets more than others; people take turns, share equally, and reciprocate benefits.	Children playing a game at summer camp
Market pricing	Individuals trade according to rational rules of self-interest, taking goods and services in proportion to what they put in and seeking the best possible "deal."	Customer-shopkeeper

according to this sort of rule: Everyone gets one spring roll and a bowl of sweet and sour soup, and no one takes a second serving of the kung pao shrimp until everyone else has had their first. Finally, **market pricing** is a form of exchange in which everyone gets out in proportion to what they put in. If a waiter provides good service, he expects a good tip, and if you pay a lot for a meal, you expect cuisine that is above the ordinary. Market pricing is roughly equivalent to equity exchanges.

As implied by this more complicated view of social exchange, people aren't always motivated by the same exchange rules in their different relationships. The form of exchange depends on who's involved in the interaction and what type of interaction it is. We now turn to a consideration of some factors in the person and in the situation that affect decisions about exchange.

PERSON Individual Differences in Communal Orientation

When you think about the people you know, are there some who are always "counting"—keeping close tabs on what they give to and what they get from others? Whether someone is bothered by being underbenefitted or overbenefitted seems to depend in part on his or her personal orientation toward social exchange (Clark et al., 1987). People who take a communal orientation tend to believe that each person in a relationship should give whatever is necessary to satisfy the needs of the other (Clark & Jordan, 2002). Those low on this dimension, however, take a more market-oriented view—that what you give to another should be equal in value to what you get from him or her. As indicated in Figure 7.5, Bram Buunk and his colleagues (1993) found that people who are low in communal orientation (the market-value people) feel best when they are treated equitably and unhappy when they are getting either too much or too little. Those high in communal orientation, in contrast, are not particularly troubled if there is a discrepancy between what they are giving and what they are getting in a relationship.

Thus, people who have a communal orientation are less concerned with keeping careful track of inputs and outputs in their relationships with others. People who adopt an alternative exchange orientation, on the other hand, agree with items such as "When I give something to another person, I generally expect something in return" and "It's best to make sure things are always kept 'even' between two people in a relationship." When Serena Chen and her colleagues primed people to think about

Figure 7.5 When we get more—or less—than we deserve

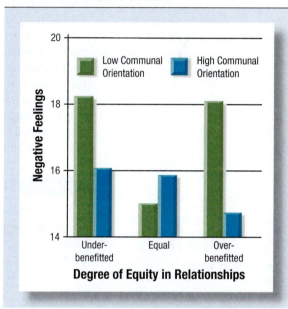

Bram Buunk and his colleagues found that people high in communal orientation are not particularly troubled by situations in which they are underbenefitted or overbenefitted. However, those who are low in communal orientation experience negative feelings if they are either under- or overbenefitted.

Source: From Bram P. Buunk et al. (1993). Perceived reciprocity, social support, and stress at work: The role of exchange and communal orientation. *Journal of Personality and Social Psychology, 65,* 801–811. Reprinted by permission of Bram P. Buunk.

Market pricing A form of exchange in which everyone gets out in proportion to what they put in.

power, they found that participants who had an exchange orientation (the "counters") become still more self-interested. People with a communal orientation, however, respond to thoughts of power by becoming more socially responsible, asking themselves what they can do for others rather than what others can do for them (Chen, Lee-Chai, & Bargh, 2001). As we discuss in the next section, a communal orientation can characterize not only people but also particular relationships and particular social situations.

SITUATION Communal and Exchange Relationships

In line with our discussion of the different orientations an individual might adopt toward others, Margaret Clark and Judson Mills and their colleagues have drawn a parallel distinction between different types of relationships between people (e.g., Clark & Chrisman, 1994; Clark & Mills, 2011). Exchange relationships are based on rewards and benefits traded in the past or that the person expects to trade in the future. Communal relationships, on the other hand, are relationships based on mutual concern for one another's welfare. A mother's relationship to her child is a good example of a communal relationship: The mother is likely to provide benefits based on the child's needs, not keep a mental checklist of benefits and costs to be used to decide whether to put the kid out on the street if the "deal" gets too costly for her.

A number of studies support the utility of a distinction between exchange and communal relationships. For instance, when young children share rewards with casual acquaintances, they use an equity principle—giving benefits depending on deservingness. When they share with friends, however, they are more inclined to distribute rewards equally—keeping less track of who deserves what (Pataki, Shapiro, & Clark, 1994; Xue & Silk, 2012). People in long-term relationships, or who want to establish long-term relationships, stop keeping track of the rewards they provide for the other. Instead, they pay closer attention to what the other person needs (Clark & Mills, 2011; Clark, Mills, & Corcoran, 1989).

SITUATION Proximity and Social Capital

One factor that reduces the cost of sharing is physical proximity. If you need a cup of sugar or an egg, for instance, it is a whole lot less costly to borrow one from your next-door neighbor than to go down the block to the house of someone you know better. The same principle holds if you want to invite someone to play a game of chess or to share a pizza.

Research conducted over several decades demonstrates a powerful **proximity-attraction principle**—we tend to choose our friends from those who live or work nearby. For instance, a classic study of friendships in a student housing project found that when residents were asked to name the person they most liked in the complex, the next-door neighbor headed the list (Festinger, Schachter, & Back, 1950). This was not because people had chosen to live near friends—residents were randomly assigned to apartments.

Neighbors are attractive not only because there are low costs to interacting with them, but also because they are simply more *familiar*. Whereas people are a bit wary of strange stimuli, including other people's faces, frequent exposure generally leads to liking (Bornstein, 1989; Zajonc, 1968). Although the Tibetans at first regarded Heinrich Harrer as an odd-looking alien, many of them, including the Dalai Lama, regarded him as a close friend at the end of his seven years in Tibet. The tendency to feel positively toward people, places, or things we've seen frequently is called the **mere exposure effect** (e.g., Harmon-Jones & Allen, 2001; Lee, 2001). Merely reading a list of names of people who belong to a group may lead us to implicitly feel like part

Proximity-attraction principle The tendency to become friends with those who live or work nearby.

Mere exposure effect The tendency to feel positively toward people, places, or things we have seen frequently.

Exposure and attraction. Before running for president, Barack Obama had already established a vivid public presence with a high-profile keynote speech at the Democratic convention in 2004, followed by numerous media appearances and a best-selling autobiographical book. Research supports the political intuition that mere exposure makes a person more attractive.

of the group and to like them more (Greenwald, Pickrell, & Farnham, 2002). The link between familiarity and preference is so strong that it can work in reverse; if we like a new person, we experience that person as more familiar (Monin, 2003). An impressive array of studies has demonstrated that people prefer not only other people with the same initials as theirs (people named Doug Kenrick like people named Dave Kenny) but also cities that sound like their names (people named Louis are more likely to live in St. Louis) and even occupations that sound like their names (people named Dennis or Denise are more likely to become dentists) (Pelham, Carvallo, & Jones, 2002).

Besides being familiar, neighbors have an even more obvious advantage. Physical proximity makes it easy to engage in those everyday social exchanges. Lynn Magdol and Diane Bessell (2003) found that people who live closer to their friends and relatives have more **social capital**—assets that could be drawn from their network of personal relationships. When these researchers examined people who had recently moved, they found that greater geographic distances meant less companionship and fewer favors from others. When people merely think about a mobile jet-setter lifestyle, they feel lonelier, and anticipate having fewer friends in the future (Oishi et al., 2013). When they move far away from their friends and relatives, women take it harder than men (Magdol, 2002). This fits with research we discussed earlier, suggesting that women are more intimately connected with their social support networks.

INVESTIGATION

How has proximity influenced the friendships you've formed, or ended, in your life?

INTERACTION **Distant Friends: Television, Facebook, and the Internet**

In recent years, many people have become increasingly distant from their friends and associates. Compared to the 1970s, in 2000 Americans were 58% less likely to attend club meetings, 33% less likely to have face-to-face dinners with other family members, and 45% less likely to have friends over for dinner. Robert Putnam (2000) reviewed a wealth of data to try to determine the factors responsible for this increasing social distance. One part of the problem is that Americans now spend more and more hours sitting silent in front of their television sets, watching actors and actresses interact with their friends instead of actually interacting with real people. Another important factor is mobility—people now live farther from their workplaces and so must spend much of their socializing time sitting alone in their cars on freeways.

Whereas some technological advances have increased the distance between us, others can help us maintain contact with the other members of our social networks (Bargh & McKenna, 2004). Social networking sites (such as Facebook), cell-phone text-messaging (☺ lol), and Internet connections at the local coffee shop have made it easier for people to stay in touch with distant friends (Buffardi & Campbell, 2008; Ellison, Steinfield, & Lampe, 2007; Igarashi, Takai, & Yoshida, 2005). Social psychologists originally expected to find that these technological innovations would yield the usual benefits found with face-to-face contacts, but results have been mixed (Kraut & Kiesler, 2003; McKenna, Green, & Gleason, 2002). One study suggested that increased use of the Internet comes at a cost to relationships with

Social capital Assets that can be drawn from one's network of personal relationships.

Face to Facebook. Kelly Huang, who works in Chicago, used Facebook to reconnect with her old friend, Tina Lee Naro, who works in New York. After graduating from high school in Texas, they had not seen one another for 10 years. As described in the text, Internet communication has social costs as well as benefits.

family and friends and results in increases in depression and loneliness (Kraut et al., 1998). Other researchers have found that using Facebook leads people to feel bad about their lives (Kross et al., 2013). Part of this may stem from the fact that so many Facebook posts show people eating fantastic meals at nice restaurants, announcing great things that have happened to them, and otherwise having a grand old time. This can lead to unfavorable social comparison, in which chronic Facebook users believe that other people are leading happier lives and that fate has dealt them an unfair hand (Chou & Edge, 2012).

Melanie Green and her colleagues note that people are drawn to Internet communication because it is easy, less risky than talking to real strangers, and immediately gratifying. Over the long haul, however, these researchers found that an increasing ratio of such "ersatz social engagements" to real conversations tended to decrease general life satisfaction (Green et al., 2005). However, other researchers have found some benefits of using Facebook (e.g. Deters & Mehl, 2012). One study found that Facebook users experienced an increase in social capital, and this was particularly true of those with low self-esteem—who might be less likely to initiate face-to-face encounters (Steinfeld, Ellison, & Lampe, 2008). So, like other technological advances, there may be benefits and costs to modern online communication. Nevertheless, virtual connections with friends do not substitute for actually being in the same room talking to your friends face-to-face (Kraut & Kiesler, 2003). And it's really hard to share wild pig over the Internet.

INTERACTION **Are Exchange Relationships Different in Western and Non-Western Cultures?**

Iris is eight years old and lives in a thatched hut with her parents and five brothers and sisters in a small village in Papua, New Guinea. Her grandparents live in a house 10 feet away, and her paternal uncles and their families live in the other neighboring houses. She refers to her cousins as brothers and sisters and plays with them every day. Each day, the family exchanges food with relatives, further strengthening the bonds between them. As part of her play, Iris learns to babysit her relatives. Iris knows that when she gets older, she will marry one of her more distant relatives, who lives in a nearby village.

Erika lives in an apartment with her parents and one younger brother in a suburb of a city in Sweden with a population of over a million. Her family has lived there for only two years, and although she has made several friends in the complex, they frequently move away and lose contact. Erika visits her mother's parents about six times a year and her other relatives twice a year. She is one of 90 second-graders in her school. After school, she goes into the city for music lessons, where she meets girls who live many miles away from her. When she grows up, she plans to study medicine at a university and perhaps live in another country (Tietjen, 1994).

The differences between the social lives of Iris and Erika illustrate three important distinctions noted by cross-cultural psychologists Fathali Moghaddam, Donald Taylor, and Stephen Wright (1993):

1. Relationships in Western society tend to be *freely chosen*; those in more traditional cultures tend to be *involuntary*. As the saying goes, "You can choose your friends, but you can't choose your family." In farming communities or jungle villages, there is little choice indeed. Your acquaintances are limited to members of your family and your tribal and religious group. Extended families may limit one another's freedom but also seem to buffer their members against extremes of stress (Diener, 2000).

2. Relationships in traditional cultures tend to be more *permanent* and *continuous* than those in Western cultures. In a modern urban setting, you may never see a first-time acquaintance again, many of your friends will move away and be replaced by new ones, and even your marriage may be temporary. In a small farming community or a jungle village, your relationships with the members of your small community will last your whole life.

3. Relationships in urban Western society tend to be *individualistic*; those in traditional societies tend to be *collectivistic*. Relationships with first-time acquaintances (like the person you talk to in the checkout line), with good friends, and with lovers are one to one, and the form of such relationships is determined by the personalities, attitudes, beliefs, and desires of the two individuals involved. In a small community, a person's relationships with neighbors and relatives are determined by the groups they belong to.

The extended family. Researchers studying relationships have generally emphasized voluntary, short-term relationships such as those found in large urban areas. But cross-cultural researchers note that involuntary extended family relationships are characteristic of people living in most of the world's rural cultures.

A number of features of traditional society disfavor voluntary, temporary, and individualistic relationships. Some are based simply on technology. A man living in the mountains of Tibet may be "only" 20 miles away from a potential friend in the next village; but to cover that 20 miles, he must hike along a footpath through the mountains, and it would take all day to travel just one way. In the same time it takes the Tibetan villager to hike the 20 miles up the mountain footpath, and with less effort, a New Yorker can visit a friend in Los Angeles, Seattle, or even London. And telephones, fax machines, and e-mail make it easy for modern urban dwellers to stay directly in touch with people all around the world.

Another source of such relationship differences comes from societal norms about collectivism versus individualism. As discussed in Chapter 2, collectively oriented societies see the social group as more important than the needs of the individual and value interdependence as opposed to independence (Hsu, 1983; Kitayama, Mesquita, & Karasawa, 2006). Individualistic societies such as the United States and Canada, however, place more emphasis on individual rights, freedom, equality, and personal independence (Hofstede, 1980; Iyengar & Lepper, 1999; Triandis, 1994). In this chapter's research video, Michael Varnum describes some research showing that whether you think about your friends in collectivist or individualist terms influences which areas of your brain light up when they win a reward (Varnum, et al., 2014).

WATCH THE VIDEO: *How Culture Influences Your Brain's Activity When Your Friends Win Rewards.*

The reason modern urban societies such as the United States and Canada are relatively more individualistic and less collectivist may be inherently connected to the types of relationships people have in these mobile and highly democratic societies. When one's network consists largely of short-term, interchangeable acquaintances, a market-based distribution of resources makes more sense than when one's network consists of close family members.

An understanding of cross-cultural differences in relationships again suggests an interaction between culture and the common evolved psychology that unites all human beings (Norenzayan & Heine, 2005). It is not so much that urban Europeans and residents of rural New Guinea have different natures or that they have arbitrarily constructed cultures out of thin air. Instead, people everywhere have different ways of relating to strangers, acquaintances, friends, and relatives (Haslam, 1997). Part of the reason modern cultures differ so greatly from traditional ones is that the structure of modern urban life has drastically changed the frequency of each of the different kinds of basic social interactions. In the next chapter, we focus on long-term love and family relationships. As we will see, those relationships hardly follow the same rules that apply to a business.

Quick Quiz

1   In _____, everyone takes resources from a common pool as needed, whereas in _____, resources are distributed according to status.

    a. Communal sharing, market pricing
    b. Communal, market
    c. Equality matching, authority ranking
    d. Equality matching, market pricing

2   _____ relationships are based on mutual concern for one another's welfare, whereas _____ relationships are based on rewards and benefits.

    a. Familial, market
    b. Market, exchange
    c. Exchange, communal
    d. Communal, exchange

3   Which of the following statements is false?

    a. The *proximity-attraction principle* states that we tend to become friends with those who live or work nearby.
    b. The *mere exposure effect* is the tendency to feel positively toward people, places, or things that are familiar.
    c. *Social capital* is a measure of one's cultural knowledge and ability to navigate many different social circles.
    d. None of the above

4   Which of the following statements is true?

    a. Traditional societies tend to favor voluntary relationships more than Western societies.
    b. Relationships in Western cultures tend to last just as long as those in non-Western cultures.
    c. Traditional societies tend to favor individualistic relationships more than Western societies.
    d. Relationships in traditional cultures tend to be more permanent and continuous than those in Western cultures.

Revisiting   The Fugitive Who Befriended the God-King

After reviewing the research on affiliation and friendship, the friendship between Heinrich Harrer and the Dalai Lama seems like less of a puzzle. As we noted, it is easy to understand why Harrer would have wanted to affiliate with the Dalai Lama. Having a friend in such a high place translates directly into status by association and indirectly into material rewards. Friendships all around the world are often motivated by material exchanges or the desire to gain or maintain status.

Although Harrer was in no position to increase the Dalai Lama's already sacred status and unlimited material resources, affiliating with the German appealed to the young king's other social motives. For one, the Dalai Lama's social position put him above all his own subjects, who could not dream of relating to him as just another human being.

It was lonely at the top of the world. As an outsider and non-Buddhist, Harrer was able to relate to the Dalai Lama in something closer to a normal way. And although his subjects could provide for all the Dalai Lama's material needs, Harrer was able to bring the brilliantly curious young boy something other Tibetans could not provide—a wealth of information about the world outside the Forbidden City.

In this chapter, we have again seen bridges between social psychology and other areas of knowledge. The findings on brain activity linking rejection and physical pain illustrate the link with cognitive neuroscience, for example, and the findings on loneliness and depression provide a bridge with clinical psychology. The research on different patterns of social exchange and on social capital illustrates the increasing bridges between social psychology and the field of economics. And the research on modern forms of communication, such as social networking websites, illustrates an interesting link between engineering and social psychology, demonstrating how the things we invent can re-invent our social lives.

The research on friendship suggests that the economic principle of selfish rational actors needs to be qualified for intimate relationships. For one, it seems as if it's better to give than to receive if you want to be liked. Treating others according to rules of selfish exchange—counting the value of what you gave them against what they gave you—is appropriate if you are conducting a business negotiation with complete strangers. But Clark and Mill's (2001) research indicates that this marketplace orientation keeps people at a distance, and acquaintances who want to become friends move toward a more communal orientation. Interestingly, after Harrer and Aufschnaiter were accepted by the Tibetans, they were treated more like family members, in line with the general tendency in collectivist societies. This inspired the Germans to want to give back.

What people want from their everyday friendships goes beyond material exchanges in other ways. Emotional support from friends is invaluable in times of stress, so offering your shoulder to a friend in need makes you a more valuable friend indeed. Being willing and ready to share your knowledge can also make you a better friend, particularly if you don't share it in a know-it-all way that makes your friends feel belittled. For men in particular, it would be useful to model their friendships after those of women, offering a little more admiration and kindness to their friends and showing off a little less competitively (unless your friend is a team member who can share your glory). Finally, it seems as though just being near others increases our attractiveness, so introverts in particular would increase their social capital if they made the effort to mingle and become a familiar face in the crowd. Thus, social psychological research on affiliation and friendship has provided clues for understanding friendships between foreigners and kings in the Forbidden City and for making and keeping friends in less remote places like Grand Rapids, Michigan, or Little Rock, Arkansas.

Chapter Summary

Summary of the Social Goals of Friendship and Affiliation

The Goal	Person	Situation	Interaction
Getting social support	• Gender—tend and befriend (often women), fight or take flight (often men)	• Impersonal threats • Feelings of social isolation	• Potential embarrassment or loss of face may lead people to reject social support. • Depressed or lonely people may act in ways that cut off needed support. • People often reject social support from parents as they grow older.
Getting information	• Self-disclosers (often women) and nondisclosers • Need for approval	• Uncertain situations • Similarity of others	• When someone close is better than us on a feature central to our self-concepts, we avoid comparing with them. • Happy people are oblivious to information that others have outperformed them.
Gaining status	• Men's friendships more hierarchical	• Prominence of social hierarchy • Importance of status in culture • Stigmatization of others	• Mixing work and play may weaken supportive relationships. • Because men are more hierarchical and less supportive, men tend to value friendships with women more than women value friendships with men.
Exchanging material benefits	• Communal orientation	• Anticipated length of relationship • Physical proximity builds social capital	• Virtual connections, while popular, are not as effective for most people as face-to-face friendships. • Voluntary, impermanent, and individualistic relationships in modern societies may favor equity over traditional communal exchange.

What Is a Friend?

1. Relationships with friends are voluntary, unlike those with relatives (although people often see relatives as friends). Relationships with friends differ from love relationships in the lack of romantic or passionate feelings.
2. According to the reinforcement-affect model, relationships have one overriding goal: to increase pleasant feelings and decrease unpleasant ones.
3. Social exchange theory presumes we are generally motivated to obtain good bargains in our relationships with others. Equity is a specific form of social exchange, involving a fair ratio of costs and benefits for both partners in a relationship.
4. Domain-specific models assume that different goals characterize different relationships at different times.

Getting Social Support

1. Social support is defined as the emotional, material, or informational assistance others provide.
2. Health psychology is the study of behavioral and psychological factors affecting illness. Having adequate social support is linked to reduced psychological and physical symptoms, better immune response, and quicker medical recoveries. Such support can come from pets as well as people.
3. Rather than the classic "fight or flight" response, women's more typical reaction to stress might better be described as "tend and befriend." Women are better at getting and giving support to their friends.
4. People seek out social support when threatened by impersonal dangers or social isolation but avoid social support if stress comes from crowding or fear of embarrassment.
5. Lonely and depressed people think and behave in ways that ultimately drive away the very support they seek.
6. For combating loneliness, college students find contact with their friends more useful than contact with family members. However, reassuring parents do have positive effects on grades and mood.

Getting Information

1. Other people can provide useful information about objective reality, social norms, and the self.
2. According to social comparison theory, people desire to measure themselves against similar others to evaluate their opinions and abilities.
3. Women are more likely to disclose personal information and elicit self-disclosures from others. Self-disclosure can have negative as well as positive consequences, in that disclosed secrets may be betrayed.
4. We seek information from others when we are uncertain about consequential issues and when the others are similar to us.
5. According to self-evaluation maintenance theory, we avoid comparisons with those who are very close to us when they excel in the same domains we do but take pleasure if their accomplishments reflect positively on our team.
6. Chronically happy people ignore information that others have outperformed them but are attentive to information that they have outperformed others.

Gaining Status

1. Compared to women, men place more emphasis on power and less emphasis on intimacy in their relationships. Consequently, men get more respect from their friends and acquaintances, whereas women get more affection.
2. People seek affiliations with high-status individuals in contexts in which status is salient, more so in some cultures than others. Conversely, people sometimes distance themselves from others who may damage their status.
3. Pursuing status in our relationships may reduce social support.

Exchanging Material Benefits

1. Different exchange rules apply in different relationships: In communal sharing, everyone takes freely from a common pool as they need. In authority ranking, resources are distributed according to status. In equality matching, everyone gets the same share. In market pricing, people trade goods and services according to rules of self-interest, seeking the best possible "deal."
2. Some people characteristically adopt a communal orientation and keep less careful track of inputs and outputs in relationships.
3. When people expect long-term interactions, they tend to adopt rules of communal exchange.
4. People living or working near one another are especially likely to become friends, partly because they share resources and rewarding experiences.
5. People have fewer face-to-face contacts in recent years, spending more time watching television and commuting to work. Social networking websites, text messaging, and Internet connections suggest mixed benefits and costs compared to face-to-face contact.
6. A person's typical orientation toward exchange may depend on cultural factors affecting who they spend time around. In cultures and places where relatives interact frequently, people adopt more communal norms.

Key Terms

Authority ranking, 232

Communal sharing, 232

Domain-general model, 214

Domain-specific model, 215

Equality matching, 232

Equity, 214

Friend, 213

Health psychology, 216

Market pricing, 233

Mere exposure effect, 234

Proximity-attraction
principle, 234

Reinforcement-affect
model, 213

Self-disclosure, 225

Social capital, 235

Social exchange, 214

Social support, 216

Chapter 8

Love and Romantic Relationships

Preference for Dominant Men

Day in Cycle

Martie Haselton, UCLA

Outline

Learning Objectives

LO 8.1   Identify and define Sternberg's three components of love.

LO 8.2   Describe the different varieties of love.

LO 8.3   Outline the three major goals of romantic relationships.

LO 8.4   Discuss the sex differences in a) the features that make women and men sexually attractive, b) attitudes toward sex, and c) hormones affecting sexual behavior.

LO 8.5   Describe the differences between people with restricted and unrestricted orientations.

LO 8.6   Describe two variations in cultural norms about sexual behavior.

LO 8.7   Identify the four attachment styles and explain how they later influence adult relationships.

LO 8.8   Explain the links between external threats, obsessive relationships, and normal processes of attachment.

LO 8.9   Discuss sex differences in jealousy and its possible adaptive function.

LO 8.10 Explain mate preferences for both men and women, and how gays, lesbians, and heterosexuals are similar and different in their choice of mates.

LO 8.11 Explain how polyandry and polygyny are linked to environmental factors.

LO 8.12 Describe the other factors that influence whether dominance is attractive.

LO 8.13 Summarize the factors in the person and the situation that affect people's likelihood of breaking up or staying together.

LO 8.14 Understand the communication rules used by happy vs. unhappy couples.

The Love Affair of "The Elephant and the Dove"

When Frida Kahlo married Diego Rivera, she was 22 years old; he was 42. Besides the age difference, there was a large discrepancy in their size, and her father dubbed them "the elephant and the dove" (Kettenman, 2008). Frida was also much more physically attractive than Diego. The fact that Diego was not as good-looking did not stop him from having numerous affairs. Frida tolerated Diego's notorious womanizing, but drew the line when he had an affair with Frida's younger sister. One of her paintings at the time reveals the depth of her pain, depicting a bloodied woman murdered by her own husband. Frida once compared her relationship with Diego to a near-fatal trolley accident that left her in pain for the rest of her life: "There have been two great accidents in my life. One was the trolley, and the other was Diego. Diego was by far the worst." After the affair with her sister, it was not surprising that Frida divorced Diego. But what was surprising was this: A year after their split, she remarried him.

The relationship between Frida Kahlo and Diego Rivera raises several questions about relationships. What is the nature of human love? Why are some people drawn into love affairs with partners often much younger or older than themselves? How different are men and women in their approaches to falling in love, to family life, and to sexual fidelity? There is a bit of controversy about this issue, with some researchers arguing that the sex differences in romance are very large and universal, and others arguing that they are small, and determined by arbitrary local norms (e.g., Conley et al., 2011; Schmitt et al., 2012; Kenrick, 2013; Stewart-Williams & Thomas, 2013). At the end of the chapter, we will consider a question of immense practical significance: What factors lead some couples to continue blissfully, whereas others end in painful breakups?

Defining Love and Romantic Attraction

LO 8.1 Identify and define Sternberg's three components of love.

LO 8.2 Describe the different varieties of love.

LO 8.3 Outline the three major goals of romantic relationships.

What is love? The answer is not as simple as one might think at first blush. For one thing, love is multifaceted, with no single characteristic defining it (Fletcher et al., 2000; Hendrick & Hendrick, 2006; Kenrick, 2006). For another, there's more than one variety of love (Campbell et al., 2002; Fehr, 2013).

The Defining Features of Love

What would you list as the defining features of love? For students at the University of British Columbia, "caring" topped the list, nominated by 44% of the participants (Fehr, 1988). Later studies have found caring, trust, and intimacy to be the features most people see as central to the definition of love (Fehr, 2013). However, students also listed dozens of other features of love, including some that don't necessarily fit the soft fuzzy prototype, such as "heart rate increases," "euphoria," and "sexual passion."

Can the dozens of different features of love be boiled down to a smaller set of feelings? Robert Sternberg (1986; 2006) proposed three essential components (see Figure 8.1):

Passion Factor on love scales composed of items tapping romantic attraction and sexual desire.

Intimacy Factor on love scales composed of items tapping feelings of close bonding with another.

Decision/commitment Factor on love scales composed of items tapping decision that one is in love with and committed to another.

Factor analysis A statistical technique for sorting test items or behaviors into conceptually similar groupings.

- **Passion:** physiological arousal and longing to be together (e.g., "sexual passion" and "heart rate increases")
- **Intimacy:** feelings promoting close bonds, including mutual sharing and emotional support
- **Decision/commitment:** in the short term, a decision to say you love the other person; in the long term, a commitment to maintain that love (see also Arriaga & Agnew, 2001)

How can we tell whether Sternberg's three-component theory is a valid one or whether there should really be six or seven or 10 components to love? To answer this question, Sternberg and other researchers have turned to **factor analysis**, which is a

Figure 8.1   Sternberg's triangular model of love

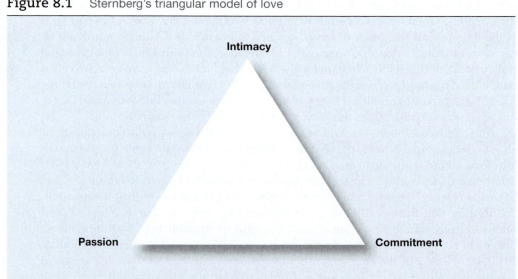

According to this model, love consists of three separable factors: passion, intimacy, and commitment.

statistical technique that sorts test items or behaviors into conceptually similar group-ings (Fletcher et al., 1999; Sternberg, 2006). If you describe your boss as agreeable, you would probably also describe her as warm and friendly. Hence, the words *warm*, *friendly*, and *agreeable* correlate with one another in descriptions of others, and factor analysis sorts them into a common category (or factor). Likewise, if you describe your cousin as conscientious, you are also likely to describe him as neat and hard working. So, a factor analysis sorts these words into another conceptual pile (Donahue, 1994; McCrae, Terraciano et al., 2005).

When Arthur Aron and Lori Westbay (1996) subjected 68 love features to factor analysis, the features sorted into three groups. One group included items such as trust, caring, honesty, and forgiveness. A second group included loyalty, devotion, and sacrifice. The third group included butterflies in the stomach, sexual passion, and excitement.

Aron and Westbay's factor analysis thus supported Sternberg's theory that love has three core ingredients: intimacy, decision/commitment, and passion. Some re-searchers find that feelings tapped by the intimacy factor often overlap quite a bit with feelings tapped by the other two (Acker & Davis, 1992; Fletcher, Simpson, & Thomas, 2000). That is, feelings of deep intimacy with another person are often closely linked to feelings of passion and commitment.

Are There Different Varieties of Love?

Research on the components of love (e.g., passion, intimacy, and commitment) asks the question: How do different feelings inside one person combine within one love relation-ship? Does Alicia's marriage to Alfredo have more commitment, but less passion, than her sister Brenda's marriage to Bob, for example? Research on the types of love addresses a different question: How do those different elements get combined in different kinds of re-lationships (e.g., Berscheid, 2010; Fehr, 2013; Hendrick & Hendrick, 1986; 2006; Sprecher & Regan, 1998)? How do Alicia's feelings of love for her husband Alfredo differ from her feelings of love for her sister Brenda?

To appreciate this distinction, think about different relationships for which you might use the word *love*. Not all of them involve equal parts of passion, intimacy, and commitment. If you are infatuated with an attractive stranger in your class, you may feel passion without in-timacy or commitment. In contrast, you may be committed to your sister but not experience increased heart rate in her presence.

In one study examining the different types of love, students were first given the example of different types of chairs, such as rocking chairs, lawn chairs, and stools, and then asked to list as many types of LOVE as they could bring to mind (Fehr & Russell, 1991). Students mentioned many different types of love, including love of pets and love of life, but the top 10 all included people: friendship, sexual love, parental love, brotherly love, sibling love, maternal love, passionate love, romantic love, familial love, and puppy love.

These types of love can be further divided into two broad groups, with parental love, maternal love, familial love, and brotherly love in one group, called **companionate love**, and another called **passion-ate love**, which involves romantic love and puppy love (Fehr, 2006; Sprecher & Regan, 1998). Hatfield and Rapson (1996) define passion-ate love as "a state of intense longing for union with another" and companionate love as "the affection and tenderness we feel for those with whom our lives are deeply entwined." Some evidence suggests that passionate and companionate love are controlled by distinct bi-ological systems (Diamond, 2004). In this chapter, we will consider passionate love extensively when we consider the goal of obtaining sexual gratification. We will consider companionate love in some depth when we consider the goal of establishing family bonds.

Companionate love Affection and tenderness felt for those whose lives are entwined with our own.

Passionate love A state of intense longing for union with another.

The goal of forming a family bond. Strong attach-ments between parents and children almost certainly contributed to the successful survival of our ancestors.

The distinction between passionate and companionate love is a central distinction, but it is possible to make additional distinctions (e.g., Fisher, 2006; Hendrick & Hendrick, 2006; Weis, 2006). For example, it is important to distinguish companionate love (between friends or long-term partners) from **nurturant love**—the feelings that inspire people to care for their children (Fitness & Williams, 2013; Shiota et al., 2011). And on the other side of that equation, there is **attachment love**, linked to the desire to be cared for or protected by another person.

INVESTIGATION

Think of two different people for whom you have felt different kinds of love and consider how they stand on Sternberg's three factors.

The Goals of Romantic Relationships

What purposes are served by falling in love and maintaining romantic relationships, and how are they different from friendships?

One important distinction between romantic relationships and friendships is the desire for sexual gratification. The passion factor is composed of interconnected feelings of physical attraction, romance, and the desire for sexual union. In fact, research suggests a great deal of overlap between passionate love and sexual attraction (Fehr, 2013; Fisher, Aron, & Brown, 2006; Lieberman & Hatfield, 2006). Hence, the first motive we consider in this chapter is the desire for sexual gratification.

Our ancestors needed more than sexual motivations to ensure the survival of their offspring. The survival of human children depended on parents who bonded together and shared their resources (Hazan & Diamond, 2000; Salmon & Shackelford, 2008). After carrying their offspring inside their bodies for nine months, human females spend years caring for them. And unlike males in most mammalian species, the human male generally stays around to help the female care for their young (Geary, 2008; Miller & Fishkin, 1997). Human offspring also profit from considerable investment by grandparents (Coall & Hertwig, 2011; Euler & Michalski, 2008; Laham, Gonsalkorale, & von Hippel, 2005). Hence, a second important goal of romantic relationships is to form a family bond.

Much of the research discussed in Chapter 7 regarding social exchanges between friends also applies to romantic relationships. A lover, like a friend, can provide information and social support, for example. In this chapter, we'll consider several unique ways in which romantic relationships serve the goal of gaining resources and social status. As we will see, there are interesting sex differences in the role of resources and social status in love relationships (Griskevicius, Tybur et al., 2008; Park et al., 2008).

Quick Quiz

1 Researchers using factor analysis found that feelings of love can be categorized into which of the following factors?

    a. Passion

    b. Intimacy

    c. Decision/commitment

    d. All of the above

2 Psychologists have distinguished several different varieties of love. Children's desire to be near their parents has been most closely linked to:

    a. Passionate love.

    b. Companionate love.

    c. Nurturant love.

    d. Attachment love.

3 The goal of obtaining sexual gratification is most closely linked to which of the following:

    a. Passion

    b. Intimacy

    c. Nurturance

    d. Attachment

Nurturant love Feelings of tenderness and concern, central to parents caring for their children.

Attachment love Desire to be cared for, and protected by, another person.

Obtaining Sexual Gratification

LO 8.4   Discuss the sex differences in a) the features that make women and men sexually attractive, b) attitudes toward sex, and c) hormones affecting sexual behavior.

LO 8.5   Describe the differences between people with restricted and unrestricted orientations.

LO 8.6   Describe two variations in cultural norms about sexual behavior.

Frida Kahlo and Diego Rivera were both notorious for their sexual appetites. Frida herself had affairs with women as well as men and told one friend that her view of life was "make love, take a bath, make love again" (Herrera, 1983). Both Frida and Diego were also inclined to fall passionately in love with their sexual partners. This is no coincidence, because sexual desire is usually listed as the most important ingredient in passionate love (Jacobs, 1992; Sprecher & Regan, 1998).

This sexual desire arises frequently in everyday life. The average college man or woman fantasizes about sex several times each day (Baumeister et al., 2001; Ellis & Symons, 1990). Not everyone is equally dominated by sexual motives, though. When Alfred Kinsey and his colleagues conducted their surveys of sexual activity, they encountered one man who had ejaculated only once in 30 years and another who claimed to have ejaculated over 30 times a week for 30 years (Kinsey et al., 1948).

We begin by considering which characteristics make people attractive as sexual partners. After that, we'll consider how gender, sex hormones, personality differences, and sexual orientation contribute to variations in sexual motivation. Then we'll consider how sexual behavior varies with aspects of a situation—from the transitory thrill of a roller-coaster ride to the shared norms of the wider culture.

`PERSON`   Who's Sexually Attractive?

Anyone who has lived through adolescence cannot help but notice the powerful role of physical appearance in determining who's regarded as sexy and who is not. Good-looking people are treated more warmly by the opposite sex, date more frequently, and are more sexually experienced (Feingold, 1992; Reis et al., 1982; Speed & Gangestad, 1997).

What is considered attractive? To some extent, the answer varies across times and places. For example, trends toward thinness in women have varied during this century in our culture and across cultures (Anderson et al., 1992). Compared with other

Is beauty universal? Although people adorn themselves in different ways in different cultures, a number of features, such as symmetry and health, are universally regarded as attractive.

ethnic groups, African American men prefer heavier women with relatively larger hips (Freedman et al., 2004).

At the same time, several features are universally considered attractive (Cunningham et al., 2002; Zebrowitz & Montepare, 2006). Despite variations in the preference for thinness versus fatness during the twentieth century, men generally preferred an average-weight woman with a low waist-to-hip ratio (large hips, small waist) to the other possibilities (Singh et al., 2010; Perriloux et al., 2010). Women with relatively low waist-to-hip ratios (around .7) tend to be healthier and more fertile, and to have healthier children (Lassek & Gaulin, 2008; Singh, 2002; Weeden & Sabini, 2005). Any shampoo ad will tell you that lustrous, shiny hair is attractive in women, and hair length and quality is associated with youth and health (Hinz et al., 2001). Large eyes and a small nose are also attractive in a woman, whereas a medium-sized nose and large jaw is more attractive in a man (Cunningham et al., 1997). Another sex-typed feature linked to attraction is vocal pitch. Men find women with relatively higher pitched voices more attractive, whereas women prefer men who are baritones rather than sopranos (Feinberg et al., 2005; Puts, 2005). In choosing sexual partners, women also prefer men who are muscular and athletic (Frederick & Haselton, 2007; Hönekopp et al., 2007; Li & Kenrick, 2006).

In several studies, researchers have used computer graphics to merge several faces into one "average" face. People generally judge these composite faces as better-looking than the individual faces that make them up (Jones, DeBruine, & Little, 2007; Langlois & Roggman, 1990). Why? Largely because composite faces are more symmetrical (Jones et al., 2007). Bodily symmetry—or the degree to which the left and right sides of a person's body are matched—is attractive to both sexes (e.g., Rhodes, 2006). Psychologist Steven Gangestad and biologist Randy Thornhill (1997) measured students' right feet, ankles, hands, wrists, elbows, and ears and compared those with the same measurements taken on their left sides. Bodily symmetry had different effects on the sexual behaviors of men and women. Symmetrical men began having sex earlier and had more partners than did asymmetrical men, whereas the effects were negligible for women. Gangestad and Thornhill suggest that women may choose symmetrical men as sexual partners because symmetry is partly linked to genes for disease resistance, which can be passed on to their offspring. Consistent with this hypothesis, symmetrical faces are perceived to be healthier (Jones et al., 2001; Rhodes et al., 2001).

Attractiveness can also be enhanced by positive expressions and behaviors, and we are more attracted to those who are familiar to us. So we all look better if we hang around for a while, particularly if we're smiling and being nice. After reviewing the literature on attractiveness, Leslie Zebrowitz and Gillian Rhodes (2002) note that being symmetrical or having sex-typical features is neither necessary nor sufficient to make a person attractive.

Figure 8.2 Minimum standards for partners

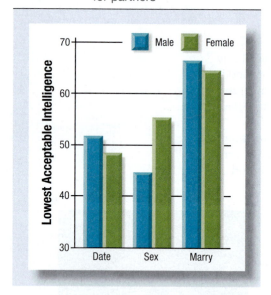

When asked about the minimum intelligence acceptable for a dating or marriage partner, men and women have similar standards. The sexes differ, however, in that men report that they are willing to have sex with someone who does not meet their intelligence criteria for a single date, whereas women are more particular about sexual partners.

Source: Based on Kenrick, D. T., Sadalla, E. K., Groth, G., & Trost, M. R. (1990). Evolution, traits, and the stages of human courtship: Qualifying the parental investment model. *Journal of Personality*, 58, 97–117.

PERSON ## Gender Differences in Sexuality

What is the lowest level of intelligence you would be willing to accept in a spouse? What about a single date? What if it were a one-night stand and you would never see the person again?

When students at Arizona State University were asked these questions, men and women often expressed similar standards (Kenrick et al., 1990). For a single date, for instance, both men and women wanted someone of at least average intelligence. For a marriage partner, both sexes wanted someone well above average in intelligence. But the two sexes diverged radically in their criteria for a sexual partner, as shown in Figure 8.2. Men were willing to have sex with a woman who did not meet their minimum standards for a date.

Numerous studies conducted in several different countries have replicated this tendency for men to be more interested in casual sex (e.g., Greitmeyer, 2005; Hald & Høgh-Olesen, 2010; Regan, 1998; Shackelford et al., 2004; Wiederman & Hurd, 1999). In fact, when asked about their life regrets, men are more likely to wish they'd slept with more partners, whereas women wish they'd tried harder to avoid getting involved with losers (Roese et al., 2006). A survey of 16,288 people from around the world suggests that the sex difference in the desire for sexual variety is universal (Schmitt et al., 2003).

Of course, attitudes are not always perfectly indicative of actual behaviors, and there is evidence that women are more likely than men to downplay their sexuality in a questionnaire (Alexander & Fisher, 2003). Would the two sexes really differ if offered an opportunity for a real one-night stand? In one field experiment, college women walked up to a man on campus and said, "I have been noticing you around campus. I find you to be very attractive." Then they asked the man one of three questions: "Would you go out tonight?" or "Will you come over to my apartment?" or "Would you go to bed with me?" (Clark & Hatfield, 1989).

As part of the same experiment, men walked up to women and asked the same questions. What do you think they said? As shown in Figure 8.3, about half of men and women said yes to a date, but the numbers diverged radically for the other requests. In fact, not one of the women agreed to an invitation to go to bed. Males, however, were even more willing to have sex than to go on a date. A later replication of this study in Denmark found that none of the single women, but 59% of the single men said "yes" to an offer to go to bed with a stranger. Danish men who said they were in relationships were less likely to say "yes" (only 18%), whereas of 23 women in relationships who were approached, one women did say "yes" (Hald & Høgh-Olesen, 2010).

There has been a controversy about what to make of the fact that men are much more likely to say "yes" to a sexual offer from a stranger (Conley 2011; Schmitt et al., 2012). Perhaps women are more frightened of a man who approaches them with an explicit sexual offer on the street, or do not expect that they would enjoy a sexual experience with such a man. This of course begs the question of why men are more willing to have sex with a strange woman than to go on a date with her.

Is it simply fear of pregnancy that leads women to prefer less wildly active sex lives? Studies of lesbians suggest the answer is no. Although sex with another woman presents no danger of becoming pregnant and no risk of dealing with potentially aggressive males, lesbians prefer to, and actually do, lead less active sex lives than do heterosexual women (Bailey et al., 1994; Schmitt et al., 2003).

For sexuality outside a committed relationship, then, sex differences are hard to miss. When it comes to long-term relationships, though, the two sexes are more similar (Kenrick et al., 2001; Kenrick, 2013; Li & Kenrick, 2006). Recall that although women were uninterested in sex with a stranger, they were as interested in going on a date as were males (Figure 8.3). And men and women were virtually identical in their selectiveness about intelligence in long-term partners (Figure 8.2). Although these gender similarities are less attention grabbing, they are just as important, and we will return to them when we discuss the motivation to form family bonds.

The meaning of sexual gratification itself is slightly different for men and women. At what age do men and women reach their "sexual peak"? When asked this question, adults of all ages tend to agree that it is substantially later for women than men (Barr, Bryan, & Kenrick, 2002). However, the same research also found that people define sexual peak for men in terms of *desire* and *frequency* of orgasm, whereas women's sexual peak is defined in terms of *satisfaction* with sex. Both men and women said they experienced their peak of sexual satisfaction later in life than their peak desire.

Figure 8.3 Men's and women's responses to a stranger's overtures

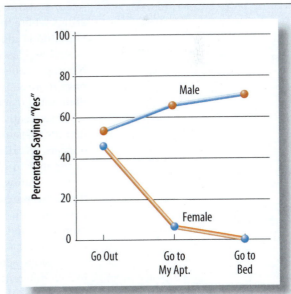

Students at Florida State University were approached by students of the opposite sex and invited to go out, to go to the other student's apartment, or to go to bed. Men and women were both equally receptive to offers to go out but differed greatly in their responses to sexually toned overtures.

Source: Based on Clark, R. & Hatfield, E. (1987). Gender Differences in Receptivity to Sexual Offers. *Journal of Psychology & Human Sexuality*, Vol. 2(1) 1989.

INVESTIGATION

We've discussed several ways in which men and women are similar and different in their approaches to sexuality. Can you think of any similarities or differences that were not covered in the preceding section?

PERSON ## Hormones and Sexual Desire

Hormones such as testosterone and estrogen play a critical role in people's experience of sexual desire, their behavior toward people they find attractive, and even who they find attractive (e.g., Gangestad et al., 2007; Gildersleeve, Haselton, & Fales, 2014; Miller et al., 2007).

Sexual desire in both men and women is linked to the hormone testosterone (Leitenberg & Henning, 1995; Regan, 1999; Sherwin et al., 1985). Consistent with our discussion of sex differences in sexuality, males produce several times more testosterone than females (Dabbs, 2000). Men involved in short-term relationships have relatively high levels of testosterone, whereas married men have low levels (Gray et al., 2004a, 2004b). Generally, a man's testosterone tends to drop as he settles into a relationship, but not if he is still interested in relationships with other women (McIntyre et al., 2006).

Whether someone is receptive to sex, and whether or not he or she has an orgasm, is linked to a different hormone—oxytocin, which also increases genital lubrication in women (Salonia et al., 2005). Women have higher levels of oxytocin, and this could help explain why women tend to see love and sex as more interconnected than do men (Diamond, 2004). For humans, most sexual experiences occur in the context of close loving relationships (Sprecher & Regan, 2000). By promoting feelings of attachment between lovers, oxytocin contributes to the powerful family bonds that characterize human mating relationships.

When women are ovulating (and likely to become pregnant), they tend to wear sexier and more fashionable clothes, groom themselves more, and attend social gatherings where they might meet men (Durante et al., 2008; Haselton & Gangestad, 2006; Haselton et al., 2007). They also feel sexier at such times, and men find them more desirable (Haselton et al., 2007; Pillsworth et al., 2004; Schwarz & Hassebrauck, 2008). Neuropsychological research using fMRI indicates that, around ovulation, women have more activation in the brain's reward centers, indicating a desire for more immediate satisfaction (Dreher et al., 2007).

In a creative field study, Geoffrey Miller, Josh Tybur, and Brent Jordan (2007) solicited the assistance of 18 "professional lap dancers working in gentlemen's clubs." The dancers recorded the size of their tips and information about their menstrual cycle. Compared to other phases, the women made significantly more money when they were ovulating. Why? One possibility is linked to the findings that women act more flirtatious when they are ovulating. Another possibility is that men respond differently to women who are ovulating. Indeed, women's faces, voices, and bodily odors become more attractive during the ovulatory phase of the cycle (Pipitone & Gallup, 2008; Roberts et al., 2004; Singh & Bronstad, 2001).

Besides sending out different signals when they are fertile, women are receptive to different kinds of men at different phases of the menstrual cycle (Gildersleeve et al., 2013, 2014). During the fertile phase, women are more attracted to highly masculine and symmetrical men (Feinberg et al., 2008; Gangestad et al., 2007; Gangestad et al., 2010; Little, Jones, & DeBruine, 2008). When less fertile, women respond more to warmth and faithfulness (Gangestad, Garver-Apgar et al., 2007). These effects are typically not found for women using oral contraceptives, suggesting that the changing preferences are products of hormonal variations. Indeed, heightened estrogen (highest during ovulation) is correlated with attraction toward signs of "good genes," whereas progesterone, highest around menstruation, is linked to preferences for men with features indicating that they are similar to the woman, and likely to invest in any offspring (DeBruine et al., 2005; Garver-Apgar et al., 2008; Jones, Little et al., 2005; Jones, Perrett et al., 2005).

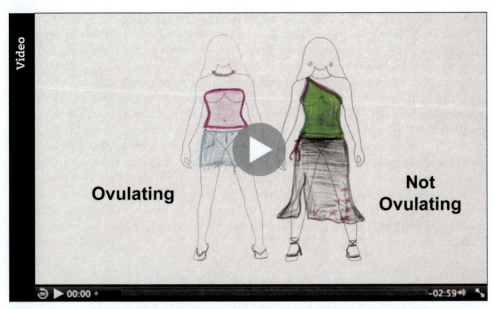

Video

Ovulating

Not Ovulating

00:00 ⬤ -02:59

WATCH THE VIDEO: *Click here to watch the research video for Chapter 8, in which we talk with Professors Martie Haselton of UCLA, and Kristina Durante of UT San Antonio about some of their research on ovulation and women's sexual behaviors.*

In sum, recent research using diverse methods, including studies of hormones, brain activity, and cyclic changes in women's behavior, indicate that our sexual behavior is influenced by biological events in our own bodies and in those of others, many of which occur outside our conscious awareness.

PERSON   ## Sociosexual Orientation

Traditional wedding vows in Europe and North America involve a commitment to forsake all others until death do us part. But although Frida Kahlo and Diego Rivera loved each other passionately, monogamous commitment was not part of their definition of a relationship. Before meeting Diego, Frida's relationship with her high school boyfriend was strained by a sexual tryst with her art teacher and another with a woman. After they were married, Diego encouraged her relationships with other women (some of whom were his lovers), and although he was jealous of her relationships with other men, he was in no position to demand sexual fidelity.

Frida and Diego were highly unconventional people in many ways, and their love lives certainly deviated from the North American societal "ideal." But research suggests that, although monogamous bonds are found in all human societies, humans also have more than one mating strategy. Besides cultural variations in sexual behavior, there is also evidence that within any society, different people adopt different approaches to mating (Jackson & Kirkpatrick, 2007; Webster & Bryan, 2007).

Jeffry Simpson and Steve Gangestad (1991, 1992) developed a scale to measure **sociosexual orientation**—the tendency to prefer either *unrestricted* sex (without the necessity of love) or *restricted* sex (only in the context of a long-term, loving relationship). The scale includes questions such as "How often do you fantasize about having sex with someone other than your current dating partner?" and "I would have to be closely attached to someone (both emotionally and psychologically) before I could feel comfortable and fully enjoy having sex with him or her."

People with an unrestricted orientation become interested in sex at an earlier age, have relatively more one-night stands, and are more likely to view their opposite-sex friends as potential sexual partners (Bleske-Rechek & Buss, 2001;

Sociosexual orientation Individual differences in the tendency to prefer either unrestricted sex (without the necessity of love) or restricted sex (only in the context of a long-term, loving relationship).

Ostovich & Sabini, 2005). They also begin having sex earlier in any given relationship and feel less commitment and love toward their current partners (Simpson & Gangestad, 1991). Moreover, unrestricted and restricted individuals seek different types of partners (e.g., Provost, Troje, & Quinsey, 2008). Restricted individuals prefer partners with traits linked to good parenting, such as responsibility, affection, and faithfulness (Gangestad & Simpson, 2000). Unrestricted people, on the other hand, choose partners who are socially visible and attractive, and focus their attention on physically attractive members of the opposite sex (Duncan et al., 2007; Maner et al., 2007). When primed to think about possible short-term sexual relationships, unrestricted men boost their tendency to engage in conspicuous consumption—to display their money in a flashy peacock-like manner (Sundie et al., 2011). Whereas most people prefer hearing "I love you" after they have sex, unrestricted men respond less positively. The researchers speculate that this is because unrestricted guys are hoping to take the sexual benefit without having to pay a commitment cost (Ackerman, Griskevicius, & Li, 2011).

PERSON Same-Sex Attraction

In their classic survey research, Kinsey and his colleagues (1948) found that over a third of men and 13% of the women in their sample had had at least one same-sex experience to orgasm. There were criticisms of Kinsey's sampling techniques, but a study of almost 5,000 twins in Australia found that although only 2.2% of the men and 0.6% of the women were exclusively attracted to the same sex, a much larger percentage—13% of men and 11% of women—had at least some sexual experience with, or attraction toward, the same sex (Zietsch et al., 2008).

Same-sex preference raises an interesting question: Given that natural selection works to promote successful reproduction, why is a substantial portion of the population attracted to members of the same sex? One possibility is that gay men and lesbians traditionally helped their relatives raise their offspring. An investigation of gay men in a traditional society (Samoa) finds support for this hypothesis (Vasey & VanderLaan, 2008, 2010). This explanation is also consistent with findings that gay men and lesbians are more likely to be later-born children in large families (Camperio-Ciani et al., 2004; King et al., 2005). Studies in modern urban contexts do not support this kin-support hypothesis, however, perhaps because people with exclusively same-sex preferences in modern societies tend to move away from family members (Bobrow & Bailey, 2001; Rahman & Hull, 2005; Vasey & VanderLaan, 2012).

Another possibility is that whatever genes predispose same-sex preference carry benefits in their heterosexual relatives (Zietsch et al., 2008; Barthes et al., 2013). This possibility is supported by findings that relatives of gay men and lesbians have more sexual partners, and more offspring, than relatives of a comparable sample of heterosexuals (Camperio-Ciani et al., 2004; VanderLaan et al., 2012). This puzzle is not yet resolved, however, and there is evidence that different explanations will apply to gay men and lesbians, and for those who, like Frida Kahlo, are bisexual (Diamond, 2007, 2008).

Most of the research discussed in this chapter involves studies done mainly on heterosexuals, who constitute the large majority of the population. However, we will return to consider differences and similarities between heterosexuals, gays, and lesbians later in the chapter. We will also consider nonmonogamous mating arrangements, common in other societies. An important lesson is this: Human beings engage in a more diverse set of sexual behaviors than specified by the norms of Western societies.

Same-sex attraction. One study, discussed in the text, suggested that although less than 1% of women are exclusively attracted to the same sex, a much higher percentage of women have, like Frida Kahlo, some sexual experience with, or attraction toward, other women.

SITUATION Arousing Settings

If you wanted to inspire romantic passion in a new dating partner, might it make sense to take that person to a horror movie? Maybe. Several studies suggest that any kind of arousing situation can fuel romantic passion (Foster et al., 1998; Lewandowski & Aron, 2004). For example, fear of electric shock, riding on a roller coaster, or standing on a shaky suspension bridge over a rocky canyon have been found to increase romantic attraction toward good-looking strangers (Dutton & Aron, 1974; Meston & Frohlich, 2003). Simply exercising strenuously for a few minutes can enhance a man's attraction to a good-looking woman (White et al., 1981; White & Kight, 1984).

How can scary movies or jumping jacks enhance passionate feelings for another person? According to **two-factor theory**, love, like other emotions, consists of general physiological arousal (racing heart, butterflies in the stomach) plus a label (love, fear, or excitement, depending on the situation in which you experience the

The Romeo and Juliet effect. Shakespeare intuitively understood a phenomenon that was corroborated by social psychological research centuries later. Obstacles to a love affair can produce arousal, which can sometimes fan the flames of love.

arousal) (Berscheid & Walster, 1974). The two-factor theory presumes any arousing situation can enhance passion to the extent that arousal from that situation is mistakenly attributed to a potential lover.

According to two-factor theory, if you are aroused for any reason, it may be attributed to someone you find attractive, but only if you think that person might in fact be the cause of your arousal. But other research suggests that students increase their attraction for someone they find attractive—*even when it is made perfectly clear to them that their arousal is not due to that person* (Allen et al., 1989). In that research, men aroused by strenuous exercise found an attractive woman more attractive, even when they were hooked up to a bulky blood-pressure cuff, and reminded about the exercise several times before rating their feelings toward the woman. What this suggests is that we do not need to make a cognitive error for arousal to intensify our passions. Just as the caffeine in a cup of coffee may cause a runner to run faster or a speaker to talk more rapidly, so any burst of physiological arousal can boost your attraction to someone you already find attractive.

SITUATION Cultural Norms about Sexuality

Did the unconventional sex lives of Frida Kahlo and Diego Rivera reflect cultural influences? Their relationship began during the "roaring twenties"—a period of sexual experimentation in Europe and North America (Martin, 1973). And Diego and Frida were members of an international set of radicals and free-thinkers who hoped to reinvent societal conventions (Herrera, 1983; Wolfe, 1991).

A half century later, during the 1960s and 1970s, a large proportion of European and North American society was swept up in another "sexual revolution." The effects lasted, and norms about premarital sexual behavior are still more liberal than they were during the 1950s (Regan, 2003).

Besides historical fluctuations, there are differences across societies in the extent to which premarital and extramarital sex are regarded as appropriate (Hatfield & Rapson, 1996; Lieberman & Hatfield, 2006). For instance, the Silwa of Egypt had strong taboos against premarital sex, which young people did not violate (Ammar, 1954). In contrast, on the Pacific island of Mangaia, young children openly practiced intercourse, and everyone had multiple premarital sex partners (Marshall & Suggs, 1971). North Americans are somewhere in between. Americans, on average, begin kissing at around age 13, and most have some sexual experience (heavy petting, oral sex, or intercourse) by age 16 (Regan & Joshi, 2003; Reynolds et al., 2003).

When asked: "How many sexual partners do you desire over the next 30 years?" women in Australia wanted about four on average, whereas women in Asian countries

Two-factor theory of love The theory that love consists of general arousal (factor 1), which is attributed to the presence of an attractive person and labeled as love (factor 2).

Culture and sexuality. Asian couples proceed through courtship at a much slower speed than do North Americans.

wanted fewer than two. Men in Australia also wanted more sexual partners than did Asian men, although men on both continents wanted twice as many partners as did women (Schmitt et al., 2003).

The norms about how love and marriage go together also vary from society to society. When asked whether they would marry someone who was otherwise desirable, but for whom they felt no romantic love, around 50% of Pakistanis and Indians, but less than 5% of Americans or Japanese, said "yes" (Sprecher et al., 1994).

There are also cultural variations within a country in the norms about appropriate sexual behavior. Americans who attend religious services regularly tend to have relatively negative attitudes about extramarital sex, pornography, same-sex preference, and abortion (Hood et al., 1996; Weeden, Cohen, & Kenrick, 2008; Weeden & Kurzban, 2013). Religious groups often encourage their members to live a high-fertility, monogamous lifestyle (go forth and multiply, but not with multiple partners). To people who marry early and begin having families, unrestricted sexual behavior is a threat because it can disrupt marital stability (Li et al., 2010; Weeden et al., 2008). A related line of research finds that opposition to recreational drugs such as marijuana is also driven by an aversion to sexual promiscuity (Kurzban et al., 2010). The same link between sexual attitudes and recreational drug use was also found in Belgium, the Netherlands, and Japan (Quintelier et al., 2013).

INTERACTION ## Sexual Situations Look Different to Men and Women

In one classic experiment, male and female participants watched a man and woman carry on a five-minute conversation. Afterward, the eavesdroppers and the conversationalists rated the interaction. Compared to females, males perceived the female actors as acting more seductively (Abbey, 1982). A later study finds these same biases in a speed-dating context: Where women underestimate men's sexual interest, and men overestimate women's sexual interest (Perilloux, Easton, & Buss, 2012). These perceptual differences can lead to unpleasant misunderstandings between the sexes (Abbey et al., 1996; Sheets & Braver, 1999; Perilloux et al., 2012).

Compared with women, men are more likely to interpret a woman's compliments, gifts, or touches as signals of sexual desire. Women, for their part, were more skeptical about interpreting a man's compliments, gifts, or touches as evidence of commitment. The authors interpreted these biases as adaptive. Because a woman can become pregnant, it is not in her interest to be uncritical about a man's honorable intentions. However, because women are reticent about jumping into bed, it is in a man's interest not to miss any possible signs of sexual interest (Haselton & Buss, 2000; Haselton & Funder, 2006).

In another study, participants were asked to judge whether faces in photographs showed subtle signs of "suppressing" any underlying feelings. In reality, all the faces had been carefully picked to be emotionally neutral. After watching a film clip that put them into a romantic frame of mind, men projected sexual feelings onto photos, but only the photos of beautiful women. Women's romantic feelings, however, did not cloud their judgment (Maner et al., 2005).

None of this should be interpreted to mean that women are not interested in sex. Instead, women and men are playing slightly different games when it comes to reproductive interests. As we noted, the rules change somewhat when women are in the fertile phase of their menstrual cycles (e.g., Gangestad et al., 2002). At these times, women become more interested in men with masculine features, such as a deep voice or taller stature (e.g., Pawlowski & Jasienska, 2005; Puts, 2005). Likewise, unrestricted women—who are inclined to have short-term sexual relationships—tend to prefer masculine men (Wayneforth et al., 2005). Women interested in "bad boys" (handsome, confident, and frivolous guys) are similar to men in preferring photos of the opposite sex whose eyes indicate sexual interest (Tombs & Silverman, 2004). Finally, when considering partners for short-term sexual relationships, women, like men, give priority to physical attractiveness over other characteristics they usually seek in a long-term mate (Fletcher et al., 2004; Li & Kenrick, 2006). Thus, some of the women some of the time play an alternative mating strategy—seeking a man whose characteristics signal good genes, even if that means compromising on getting a man who will stick around and make a high investment in offspring (Gangestad & Simpson, 2000; Penton-Voak et al., 2003).

INTERACTION Cultural Practices May Trick Evolved Mechanisms

When it comes to sexual attraction, the person and the situation interact on a broader cultural level. Consider one natural experiment, in which children on Israeli kibbutzim were raised in pods of several children from different families. When they grew up, the former podmates had stayed close friends but did not marry one another (Shepher, 1971). The lack of attraction is contradictory to classic findings that people tend to marry their neighbors (e.g., Bossard, 1932). It is especially interesting because there were no social norms prohibiting sexual attraction between podmates.

What happened? Shepher (1971) suggested the cause was an interaction between an unusual feature in the cultural environment (unrelated children living together) and an internal mechanism designed to reduce sexual feelings between brothers and sisters. Over the course of evolutionary history this would be a problem because harmful recessive genes show up more frequently when brothers and sisters mate (Lieberman et al., 2003; Tal & Lieberman, 2008; Walter, 1997). One way to prevent sexual attraction between siblings is to develop a natural aversion to sexual relationships between people raised under the same roof—who, in the past, were usually brothers and sisters (van den Berghe, 1983). Thus, the situation in the kibbutz seemed to trigger an innate mechanism normally invisible in other societies.

In another society in Taiwan, future brides live with their future husband's family during childhood. In this case, older children develop an aversion to younger siblings after seeing the younger child nursing at their mother's breast. Younger children (who obviously never see their older sibling nurse) instead develop aversion based on the number of years living in the same house with the older child (Lieberman & Smith, 2012). These findings remind us that asking whether sexual behavior is a function *either* of evolved genetic mechanisms *or* of sociocultural norms *or* of learning experiences is the wrong question (Kenrick & Gomez-Jacinto, 2013). Instead, the more productive questions are: How do biological influences interact with culture to affect learning, and how do those processes affect our thoughts and motivations?

Quick Quiz

1 Which of the following features is regarded as attractive in both sexes?

    a. Low waist-to-hip ratio
    b. Left-right symmetry
    c. Lower pitched voice
    d. Small nose
    e. All of the above

2 When asked about the minimum level of intelligence they would find acceptable in a date, a sexual partner, a steady date, or a marriage partner, a large difference between men and women was found for:

    a. Date.
    b. Sexual partner.
    c. Steady date.
    d. Marriage partner.
    e. There were large differences for sexual partners and long-term partners, but not for single dates.

3 Which of the following are true?

    a. In both women and men, sexual desire has been linked to the hormone testosterone.
    b. Contrary to stereotype, women's romantic behaviors do not seem to change across the menstrual cycle.

c. Men are more likely than women to adopt a "restricted" sociosexual orientation.

d. More women than men report exclusive same-sex attraction.

4. Which of the following phenomena was explained as due to a cultural practice tricking an evolved mechanism?

    a. People are more attracted to members of the opposite sex they meet after exercising or watching an exciting movie.

    b. Religious groups exert social pressures toward monogamous family bonds.

    c. Men are, compared to women, likely to attribute more sexual interest to interactions that women view as friendly.

    d. Children who are raised with children from other families are unlikely to feel strong romantic interest in one another.

Long-term relationships are good for your health. Research suggests that having a spouse is associated with disease resistance and longevity.

Need to belong The human need to form and maintain strong, stable interpersonal relationships.

Establishing Family Bonds

LO 8.7 Identify the four attachment styles and explain how they later influence adult relationships.

LO 8.8 Explain the links between external threats, obsessive relationships, and normal processes of attachment.

LO 8.9 Discuss sex differences in jealousy and its possible adaptive function.

A woman from the !Kung hunting and gathering society in the Kalahari desert observed, "When two people come together their hearts are on fire and their passion is very great. After a while, the fire cools and that's how it stays" (Jankowiak & Fischer, 1992). Research conducted in other societies also reveals that passionate sexual attraction is frequently intense at first but fades over time (Acker & Davis, 1992; Sprecher & Regan, 1998). Along with passionate feelings, sexual intercourse also declines over time (Hatfield & Rapson, 1996). After only a year, the average rate of intercourse between husbands and wives drops to half its original frequency.

If passion fades, what keeps people in long-term relationships? Sometimes married couples say they are staying together for the sake of the kids. But most frame the answer in a more positive light—our long-term partners become inextricable threads in our daily lives, and feelings of intimacy and commitment grow as passion fades (Cimbalo et al., 1976). Although sexual feelings contribute to the passionate component of love, prominent at the start of a relationship, people generally view feelings of commitment and intimacy as closer to the center of the definition of love (Fehr, 2013). In one recent experiment, people were either asked to think about their feelings of love for, or the sexual attraction for, their current romantic partner. Those who thought about love did well on a task requiring them to suppress thoughts about attractive alternative partners, those who thought about sex were unable to rein in their thoughts about attractive others (Gonzaga et al., 2008).

Losing a spouse to divorce or death wreaks more psychological and physical havoc than almost any other life event (Diener, 2000). After one spouse dies, the surviving partner's chance of dying skyrockets (Kaprio et al., 1987). Conversely, having a marriage partner around protects a person against major diseases, including cancer (Kiecolt-Glaser & Newton, 2001). Even short separations from long-term lovers can be emotionally distressing (Diamond et al., 2008).

Why are love relationships so much more intensely central to one's life, and painful to sever, than other relationships? After reviewing a host of studies on relationships of all types, Roy Baumeister and Mark Leary suggested that all humans have a general **need to belong** (Baumeister, 2012; Baumeister & Leary, 1995). They suggested that a desire for strong and stable relationships serves several functions. The same feeling that keeps a romantic couple bonded together to raise their children, they note, also keeps them attached to the children. Indeed, there is evidence that the bonds between committed lovers may be based on the same psychological mechanisms that link a mother and her infant (Zeifman & Hazan, 1997).

The Importance of Attachment

Strong bonds between mothers and offspring are characteristic of all mammalian species, serving to promote the newborn's survival (Bowlby, 1969). The bond leads young children to stay close to the mother and to cry out when the two are separated. The mother's presence reduces the child's stress and provides a **secure base** from which the child can safely explore the environment. Adult love relationships can also provide a secure base from which to explore the world and work productively (Elliot & Reis, 2003; Green & Campbell, 2000).

For most mammals, the adult male is out of the attachment loop, contributing little more than sperm to his offspring (Geary, 2000). But human males are different—they normally provide a great deal of care for their offspring. Husbands even mirror the hormonal changes of their expectant wives (Storey et al., 2000). Just before birth, fathers show increases in prolactin (a hormone linked to parenting in other animals). And just after birth, they decrease their secretion of testosterone (a hormone linked to dominant and sexual behaviors). The bond between parents may have evolved because human offspring are especially helpless. In species with helpless young, family bonds motivate both parents to merge their interests with those of their needy offspring (Bowlby, 1969; Brown & Brown, 2006).

PERSON Attachment Style

Like the desire to drink when we are thirsty or to bundle up against the cold, the need for deep attachments may be fundamental to the human condition (MacDonald & Leary, 2005). But not everyone finds it as simple to form a deep attachment as to reach for a glass of water or a warm jacket. Some people run from love, others drive potential lovers away by demanding too much affection too soon, and some seem to rush into casual affairs as a way to avoid long-term commitments (Brennan & Shaver, 1995; Del Giudice, 2011).

Consider the following descriptions:

1. I find it relatively easy to get close to others and am comfortable depending on them and having them depend on me. I don't often worry about being abandoned or about someone getting close to me.
2. I am somewhat uncomfortable being close to others; I find it difficult to trust them completely, difficult to allow myself to depend on them. I am nervous when anyone gets too close, and, often, love partners want me to be more intimate than I feel comfortable being.
3. I find that others are reluctant to get as close as I would like. I often worry that my partner doesn't really love me or won't want to stay with me. I want to merge completely with another person, and this desire sometimes scares people away.

Cindy Hazan and Phillip Shaver (1987) used those self-descriptions as part of their research on romantic love and attachment styles. They based the three categories on earlier studies of mother–infant relationships (Ainsworth et al., 1978; Bowlby, 1969; 1973). Developmental researchers had found that some children had a **secure attachment style**—easily expressing affection toward their mothers and unconcerned about being abandoned. Other children had an **anxious/ambivalent attachment style**—becoming visibly upset at any separation from their mothers and preoccupied with possible abandonment. Finally, children with an **avoidant attachment style** were defensively detached from their mothers, spurning affection if their mothers returned after a brief absence.

Some evidence suggests that early mother–infant experiences might translate into different styles of loving in adults (Fraley, 2002; Simpson et al., 2007, 2011). Adults who chose statement 1, for instance, were classified as *secure*; those who chose statement 2 were classified as *avoidant*; and those who chose statement 3 were classified as *anxious/ambivalent*. People who scored as secure reported staying in love relationships longer than those who scored themselves as either anxious/ambivalent or avoidant

Secure base Comfort provided by an attachment figure, which allows the person to venture forth more confidently to explore the environment.

Secure attachment style Attachments marked by trust that the other person will continue to provide love and support.

Anxious/ambivalent attachment style Attachments marked by fear of abandonment and the feeling that one's needs are not being met.

Avoidant attachment style Attachments marked by defensive detachment from the other.

(Hazan & Shaver, 1994a). Securely attached individuals have a number of pleasant personality characteristics: They are insightful and not self-enhancing, for example, and skilled at resolving relationship conflicts (Creasey & Ladd, 2005; Gjerde, Onishi, & Carlson, 2004).

Avoidant lovers adopt a different approach to relationships—they find intimacy unpleasant and they are uncomfortable with the level of sharing that tends to benefit long-term relationships (Bartz & Lydon, 2006). In stressful situations, avoidant individuals offer their partners less social support (Campbell et al., 2001; Collins & Feeney, 2000). And, unlike securely attached individuals, who focus on how they are similar to their intimate friends, avoidant individuals focus on how they are different from those close to them (Gabriel et al., 2005). Sexual intercourse often helps strengthen relationships, but compared to those who are securely attached, avoidant individuals are relatively more likely to experience sex as negative (Birnbaum et al., 2006).

Anxious/ambivalent lovers adopt yet a different approach to intimacy. Anxious lovers experience relationships like an emotional roller coaster, with more highs and lows, and relatively higher levels of sexual motivation (Davis et al., 2004). Anxious individuals often drive away the very partners they want so much to keep, by making excessive demands that the partner demonstrate love and commitment (Mikulincer & Shaver, 2013). Anxious/ambivalent lovers perceive their partners as less caring, and anxious/ambivalent women are prone to develop postpartum depression if they do not feel their partner is giving enough support (Campbell et al., 2005; Collins & Feeney, 2004; Kohn et al., 2012; Simpson et al., 2003).

Frida Kahlo's relationships with men fit the anxious/ambivalent style. Her letters to her high school boyfriend were full of pleas that he write more frequently and reassure her of his love. Several years later, she wrote similar letters to Diego Rivera: "All the rages I have gone through have served only to make me understand in the end that I love you more than my own skin, and that, though you may not love me in the same way, still you love me somewhat. Isn't that so?"

INVESTIGATION

Take a moment to think about your own affectionate relationships. Which one of the three different attachment styles seems to best describe you?

....

PERSON   Exchange/Communal Orientation

In Chapter 7, we discussed the difference between the *exchange* orientation found in relationships between strangers (in which costs and benefits are accounted carefully) and the *communal* orientation characterizing close relationships (in which benefits are given freely *according* to the partner's needs) (Clark & Aragón, 2013; Lemay & Clark, 2008; Mills et al., 2004).

Individuals high in *exchange orientation* agree with statements such as "I am apt to hold a grudge if I feel a friend or loved one has not fulfilled an obligation in our relationship." Given people's general tendency to make self-serving attributions— to view themselves in the best possible light—it is no surprise that people having high exchange orientations were generally more unhappy with their relationships (Buunk & Van Yperen, 1991). Conversely, those with a communal orientation find their relationships more satisfying (Mills et al., 2004; Peck et al., 2004). Communal individuals presume their partners are just as caring and supportive as they, and this tends to lead to a self-fulfilling prophecy (Lemay & Clark, 2008). Thus, when it comes to loving relationships, it is generally better to give than to keep track of what you're receiving.

The stability of our relationships isn't just a function of our personalities. Feelings of attachment wax and wane over time, as they did for Frida Kahlo and Diego Rivera. Are there certain factors in the situation that are linked to increases or decreases in the motivation to stay in deeply bonded relationships?

Attachment and threat. In young children and in adults, threats magnify the need to be near the one you love.

SITUATION Threats Magnify Attachment

On a moment-to-moment basis, situations that make us feel fear, anxiety, or insecurity intensify our feelings of attachment (Mikulincer et al., 2002). Thinking about your own death, for example, increases not only the desire to be near the one you love and your feelings of closeness to your partner, but also boosts the motivation to have children (Cox & Arndt, 2012; Mikulincer, Florian, & Hirschberger, 2003; Wisman & Goldenberg, 2005).

Partners in better functioning relationships are adept at responding quickly and effectively to one another in stressful times (Collins & Feeney, 2000). A recent neurophysiological study found that women whose partners hug them frequently show increases in oxytocin levels and reductions in blood pressure (Light, Grewen, & Amico, 2005).

The threat that may be most critical in sparking the need for togetherness is any danger to our relationships themselves. Indeed, the grief of separation feels very much like drug withdrawal, and is influenced by the same opiatelike chemicals in the body (Panksepp, Siviy, & Normansell, 1985).

The passionate drive to be reunited with a lost partner may be generally adaptive, helping us to maintain healthy relationships. But it may misfire in some cases, as we see next.

Erotomania A disorder involving the fixed (but incorrect) belief that one is loved by another, which persists in the face of strong evidence to the contrary.

Bridging Function and Dysfunction:
Obsessive Relationships and Unrequited Love

In Manhattan, a medical writer was imprisoned because, after eight arrests, she refused to stop pursuing a renowned surgeon. During her trial, she described the relationship as passionate and romantic, whereas the surgeon described a nightmare in which she appeared suddenly in the seat next to him on airline flights, unexpectedly showed up half-dressed at his apartment, and sent letters to his friends. She even threatened to kill him, saying, "I can't live while you are alive on this earth" (Anderson, 1993).

When such obsessions become extreme, they are labeled **erotomania**—a disorder characterized by fixed, delusional beliefs that one is passionately loved by another. The goal of erotomanic fantasies is typically an idealized romance or spiritual union rather than sexual desire (Anderson, 1993). Of 246 clinical erotomania cases reported between 1900 and 2000, 176 (or nearly 70%) were women (Brüne, 2001). The prototypical female with this disorder was single and in her mid-thirties, and the object of her passions was an older, higher-status man. The typical man afflicted with this disorder was in his late twenties, and his object tended to be a younger, physically attractive woman. About half of the men, but only 4% of the women, harassed their intended object to the point that the law became involved (Brüne, 2001).

More common than clinical erotomania are cases of former spouses or lovers who, though nonviolent, make their ex-partners miserable with incessant attempts to restore the relationship. Indeed, the large majority of stalking cases involve a terminated relationship or marriage (Anderson, 1993).

Most of us never become stalkers, but even well-functioning people can recognize the agony of unrequited love. In one study, 93% of participants recalled at least one experience of a strong romantic attraction to someone not attracted to them (Baumeister et al., 1993). The would-be lovers often felt the rejector had led them on, or had hidden stronger reciprocal feelings of attraction than they had admitted.

Why do people become enmeshed in nonreciprocal romances? Partly because the experiences were not completely negative. Both the rejected and the rejecter often retain warm feelings afterward. Some of the unpleasantness follows because an initially mutual attraction grows for one while it dies for the other. Because the target isn't always completely clear in breaking the bad news, the other may be left with false hopes. Finally, those being rejected often distort reality slightly to protect their own self-esteem (Baumeister et al., 1993; Sinclair & Frieze,

2005). It is hard to admit, even to ourselves, that another person finds us unacceptable as a love object.

Obsessive relationships, like other social dysfunctions, may be byproducts of otherwise adaptive psychological mechanisms. Obsessions with former lovers seem to reflect a misfiring of the mechanism that normally keeps people attached to their partners (Baumeister et al., 1993). Movies and literature frequently depict lovers persisting in the face of rejection to win their desired lovers in the end. Because relationships often experience their ups and downs, a tendency to stick together through thick and thin would have served to keep parents together. The frequency of feelings of unrequited love indicates that most people require some learning to know precisely when to turn off their attachment mechanism.

SITUATION **Jealousy and Same-Sex Competitors**

Despite their unconventional attitudes about monogamy, Diego Rivera and Frida Kahlo were extremely jealous of one another's other sexual indiscretions. Although Diego tolerated Frida's relationships with other women (some of whom were also involved with him), he threatened to kill at least one of Frida's male lovers (Herrera, 1983).

Imagine the person with whom you've been seriously involved has become interested in someone else. What would distress or upset you more:

1. Imagining your partner falling in love and forming a deep emotional attachment to that person.
2. Imagining your partner having sexual intercourse with that other person.

Most men answering that question say they would be more distressed by the sexual infidelity. However, approximately 80% of women said they would be more upset by the emotional attachment (Buss et al., 1992). Similar sex differences were found in Korea, Japan, Germany, the Netherlands, and Sweden (Buss, Shackelford, Kirkpatrick et al., 1999; Buunk et al., 1996; Wiederman & Kendall, 1999).

Why the sex difference? David Buss and his colleagues believe men's greater concern over sexual fidelity is rooted in a basic biological fact: Men cannot be 100% sure whether their wife's child is their own. If his partner had sex with another man, a man might unknowingly contribute substantial resources to raising another man's child (Mathes, 2005). Hence, a woman's sexual infidelity is more likely to lead to divorce than is a man's, even though men are more likely to be unfaithful (Drigotas & Barta, 2001; Shackelford, 1998). And around the world, men are, compared with women, more than four times as likely to kill over jealousy (Harris, 2003).

Why is a woman relatively more concerned about emotional attachments? Buss argues that this stems from the fact that the woman stands to lose her husband's contribution of resources to the offspring if he falls in love with another woman.

Feelings of jealousy boost people's attention to attractive members of their own sex (Maner, Galliot, Rouby, & Miller, 2007). People are sensitive to what their partners find desirable: Jealous women pay more attention to a potential rival's waist, hips, and hair, whereas men check out a rival's shoulders (Buunk & Dijkstra, 2005). There is a general tendency to overestimate the attractiveness of those potential competitors (Hill, 2007), but less masculine men are more jealous of rivals with masculine characteristics, and less feminine women are more jealous of highly feminine women (Park et al., 2008).

The sex differences in jealousy have been controversial. Some social psychologists suggest the difference may be an artifact of the particular method used to measure jealousy (e.g., DeSteno et al., 2002). But other researchers find the same sex difference using very different methods (Pietrzak et al., 2002; Sagarin et al., 2012; Schutzwohl,

2008; Shackelford et al., 2000; Tagler, 2010). On the other hand, Christine Harris (2003) argues that the sex difference in jealousy-linked homicides is just another manifestation of men's general tendency to be more violent. Although a greater absolute number of men kill their partners over jealousy, Harris notes that when women do commit murder, jealousy is the motive 16% of the time (compared to about 12% of the time for male perpetrators).

A recent neuropsychological study finds that men and women thinking about infidelity show brain activity in different regions, with men showing more activity in the amygdala, an area linked to aggressive behavior (Takahashi et al., 2006). Furthermore, clinical diagnoses of irrational and morbid jealousy find the same sex differences magnified. Men diagnosed with clinical jealousy are more worried about their partner's sexual infidelity and their imagined rival's status and resources; women are more focused on their partner's emotional infidelity and on their rival's youth and physical attractiveness (Easton, Schipper, & Shackelford, 2007).

The psychologists involved in this controversy agree that jealousy is a powerful emotion that is likely to have some adaptive function, but disagree as to whether there is a specific sex difference in the triggers for jealousy. One alternative is that both sexes are extremely upset by either sexual or emotional infidelity because, ancestrally, the survival of human infants required a close bond between both parents (DeSteno et al., 2002; Harris, 2003). Priming feelings of jealousy leads both men and women to be less interested in having children (Hill & DelPriore, 2012).

In reviewing this literature, social psychologist Brad Sagarin concludes that there is strong support for some differences in how and when men and women get jealous (Sagarin et al., 2012). In line with the emerging consensus that cultural and evolutionary factors interact to determine social behavior, Sagarin (2005) suggests that evolved mechanisms and societal norms interact in several ways to produce the observed sex differences in sexual jealousy.

INVESTIGATION

Considering the people you know, do you agree with the theory that men and women have different triggers for their jealousy or with the alternative view that the two sexes experience jealousy in similar ways for similar reasons?

INTERACTION Relationships Change Our Personalities

Our long-term relationships are situations that can eventually change our personalities (Cook, 2000; Scollon & Diener, 2006). Lee Kirkpatrick and Cindy Hazan (1994) found that some people switched from anxious/ambivalent to avoidant attachment styles over a four-year period. The switch to a standoffish approach may have been a way to control the unpleasant arousal of obsessing over whether she loves me or she loves me not.

Newlyweds rate their partners' personality traits more positively than the partners rate themselves. Two years later, people view themselves as becoming more agreeable and conscientious. Unfortunately, partners' ratings, once so positive, go in the reverse direction, and become more negative two years later (Watson & Humrichouse, 2006).

To some extent, we get along with our partners by simply overestimating our partner's similarity (Murray et al., 2002). Over the long haul, however, partners actually do change their attitudes, and their personalities, to fit with one another (Gonzaga, Campos, & Bradbury, 2007). The process of attitude alignment is strongest in well-adjusted couples, and for issues about which the partner really cares (Davis & Rusbult, 2001). People are more likely to change their personalities if they marry dissimilar partners (Caspi & Herbener, 1990). However, individuals who married partners with similar personality traits were happier in their marriages. The choice of a spouse is thus one of the more important ways in which we choose life situations to match our own dispositions. In the long run, those choices can also allow us to remain more like ourselves.

Quick Quiz

1 Which of the following are true?

    a. In healthy relationships, romantic passion persists unabated.

    b. Compared to most other species of mammals, human males contribute relatively less to the offspring.

    c. After a child is born, men show increases in testosterone production.

    d. Compared to people who have a communal orientation, people who have an exchange orientation are less happy with their relationships.

2 Researchers have suggested that attachment styles can be divided into which categories?

    a. Passionate, intimate, committed

    b. Secure, anxious/ambivalent, avoidant

    c. Communal, exchange, erotic

    d. Communal, detached, collective

3 Which of the following have been found with regard to variations in attachment?

    a. External threats (such as fear of death) tend to decrease feelings of love.

    b. Women are more likely than men to be diagnosed with a clinical case of erotomania.

    c. The sex difference in jealousy over sex vs. love is reversed in Asian cultures.

    d. Feelings of jealousy lead people to be more interested in having children.

Gaining Resources and Social Status

LO 8.10 Explain mate preferences for both men and women, and how gays, lesbians, and heterosexuals are similar and different in their choice of mates.

LO 8.11 Explain how polyandry and polygyny are linked to environmental factors.

LO 8.12 Describe the other factors that influence whether dominance is attractive.

As summer approaches in Central America, the male indigo bunting changes color, from brown to brilliant blue. After a 2,000-mile journey to North America, he immediately begins competing with other males for the richest breeding territories. Female buntings arrive several weeks later and choose from among the males. Males with poor territories attract no mates; those with rich territories attract multiple mates. Why do some females share the same mate when there are unattached males available? Because a resource-rich territory translates into surviving chicks (e.g., Pleszczynska & Hansell, 1980). In other species, when resources are so scarce that even dominant males cannot provide enough resources to feed the offspring, the rules of the game change, and one female may share several males (Gould & Gould, 1989). Some of the same harsh economics of status, resources, and mating found in birds also apply to human beings.

PERSON Gender and Sexual Orientation

Some evidence suggests men and women differ in ways that are similar to male and female indigo buntings. As in the case of indigo buntings, men with relatively more resources are attractive to women.

WOMEN'S PREFERENCE FOR STATUS Although he was physically unattractive, Diego Rivera was able to attract strikingly beautiful and talented women. Why? Diego had both fame and fortune going for him.

    Numerous studies reveal that women are, compared with men, more motivated to seek a mate high in social dominance or status (e.g., Badahdah & Tiemann, 2005; Li & Kenrick, 2006; Li, Yong et al., 2013). For instance, students in one study rated the attractiveness of potential partners dressed in either high-status attire (an upper-class

Who makes a more desirable date? Women presented with a man dressed in a suit and tie find him more desirable than the same man dressed as a fast-food clerk. Even if the man in the suit is unattractive, he is regarded as more desirable. Men pay less attention to the status of a woman's clothes and prefer a physically attractive woman in a fast-food outfit over a physically unattractive woman dressed in fancy clothes.

ensemble including a blue blazer and a gold Rolex wristwatch) or a low-status outfit (a blue baseball cap and a polo shirt displaying the Burger King employee logo). Sometimes the person was physically unattractive; sometimes he or she was good-looking. Men preferred the pretty woman regardless of her apparent social class, but women preferred a homely, well-dressed man to a handsome burger flipper (Townsend & Levy, 1990). Women in another study were more attracted to a man who made money in business over one who just got lucky, suggesting that women value the ability to generate future resources (Hanko, Master, & Sabini, 2004).

In singles' advertisements, men are more likely to advertise status or wealth, women to require status or wealth in a man (Rajecki et al., 1991; Wiederman, 1993). And women respond more to men who advertise their income and educational levels, whereas men reading women's ads pay no attention to a woman's status (Baize & Schroeder, 1995). A study of 37 different cultures found the same trends around the world (Buss, 1989). Like American women, Japanese, Zambian, and Yugoslavian women rate good financial prospects in a mate as more important than do men in those countries (Buss & Schmitt, 1993). Women living in a small-scale horticulturalist society in the Amazon jungle were more attracted to men whose high status was associated with being good hunters and warriors (Escasa, Gray, & Patton, 2010).

Besides his fame and fortune, Diego Rivera's creative abilities added to his desirability. Geoffrey Miller (2000) reviewed an array of evidence that creative displays, in humans and in other animals, are indications of "good genes." Given that females are generally more selective than males, ostentatious displays (such as a peacock's feathers) are a means by which males display their relative superiority over other males. Consistent with this account, men are more likely to display both resources and creativity when they have been primed to think about mating (Griskevicius, Cialdini, & Kenrick, 2006; Griskevicius et al., 2007).

MEN'S PREFERENCE FOR REPRODUCTIVE RESOURCES When Frida and Diego married, he was 42 and already wealthy and internationally famous; she was an unknown 22-year-old. Yet she approached him quite directly, yelling up to him as he was working on a mural: "Hey, Diego, come down here!" What gave a young woman the confidence to approach a famous and powerful middle-aged man as if she were his

Older men and younger women.
Why would two people separated by decades of age get together in a romantic relationship? The fact that women around the world are attracted to older men with status, and that very young men are attracted to relatively older women, is consistent with the different resources each sex contributes to the offspring.

equal? Part of the answer is that her youth and beauty did in fact equate her with him, at least in terms of value as a potential mate.

All around the world, women tend to seek and to marry somewhat older men, who generally have more resources and social status (Buss, 1989; Dunn, Brinton, & Clark, 2010; Kenrick & Keefe, 1992). Men, however, show a more complex pattern: Whereas older men are attracted to younger women, men in their twenties want women around their own age, and teenage boys are attracted to slightly older women (Buunk et al., 2001; Kenrick et al., 1996; Otta et al., 1999). Why do men pay so much less attention to the potential resources an older woman could provide and opt instead for women in their twenties? One part of the answer may come from a biological inequity between the resources males and females provide for their offspring.

Throughout the history of our species, females have always provided direct physical resources to the offspring—carrying them inside their bodies, nursing them, and taking primary care of them for years afterward. Hence, it would have been advantageous for ancestral men to seek health and reproductive potential in a mate (Cunningham et al., 1997). Age and physical attractiveness are cues to a woman's health and reproductive potential (Furnham et al., 2004; Pawlowski & Dunbar, 1999). Men evaluating potential dates place more emphasis on physical appearance (Li et al., 2002, 2013; Shaw & Steers, 1996). Attractive women are aware of their market value and are highly selective about the men they find acceptable (Buss & Shackelford, 2008).

Women are aware of the link between their attractiveness and bargaining power on the mating market. When times get economically tough, people generally stop spending, but women increase their expenditures on beauty products. This so-called "lipstick effect" is driven by women's desire to attract mates with resources (Hill et al., 2012).

Because men do not contribute their bodies to the offspring, biological theorists posit that ancestral females sought high-status men who could provide resources, protection, or "good genes"—signs of physical superiority over other males, including large size and dominant behavior (Gangestad & Thornhill, 1997). Indeed, to say that a man is physically attractive is to say he shows signs of social dominance, such as a strong chin and mature features, whereas a physically attractive woman shows signs not of dominance but of youthfulness and fertility (Cunningham et al., 1997; Li & Kenrick, 2006; Singh, 1993; Wade, 2000). Men's and women's ages are thus linked in a different way to the resources they provide for the offspring.

MATE PREFERENCES IN GAY MEN AND LESBIANS   Because gay men and lesbians are attracted to members of their own sex, they provide an ideal control group for examining some theories of mate choice (Bailey et al., 1994; VanderLaan & Vasey, 2008). Rather than mirroring heterosexuals' choices, preferences of gay men and lesbians are, in many ways, the same as those of heterosexuals of their own sex (Chivers et al., 2004; Groom & Pennebaker, 2005). Like heterosexual men, gay men are relatively uninterested in a partner's wealth and social status. They are more interested in physical attractiveness (Bailey et al., 1994). And instead of seeking older men, gay males have age preferences just like those of heterosexual men (Kenrick, Keefe, Bryan, Barr, & Brown, 1995). Older gay men are attracted to men in their twenties, despite the fact that the younger men are unlikely to reciprocate the older fellow's interest. Like the older men, young gay men are interested in young men.

These findings indicate that human mating behavior, like human vision, is not simply a one-switch mechanism (cf. Tooby & Cosmides, 1992). Although the switch for sexual orientation has a different setting in heterosexual and gay men, for whatever reason, gay men's whole pattern of preferences suggests most other switches are set at the same settings as in heterosexual men. Lesbians, however, show a complex combination of the preferences expressed by heterosexual men (some preference for youthful partners, for example) and heterosexual women (less emphasis on physical attractiveness and more inclination toward sexual fidelity, for example). Same-sex attraction is, thus, not simply an inverted form of heterosexuality but a complex pattern in which some aspects of mating behavior, but not others, are altered. As we noted earlier, different mechanisms seem to underlie male and female same-sex attraction (Diamond, 2007; VanderLaan & Vasey, 2008).

WHAT HAPPENS WHEN WOMEN GAIN STATUS AND RESOURCES?   Throughout most of history, women have had less access to status and resources than have men. Although sex differences remain, some modern women, including doctors, lawyers, and college professors, are wealthier and higher in status than most men. Do higher status women also shift to traditionally male preferences in a mate, such as a desire for youth or physical appearance?

In societies where women have little wealth or power, they desire more wealth in a man than in societies where women are relatively better off (Eagly et al., 2004). Nevertheless, the large sex differences described throughout this chapter were found in the world's most egalitarian societies, such as Holland, the United States, and Canada. Sex differences only get larger in third-world countries. And within American society, wealthy and high status women show the same interest in older, higher-status men shown by women with less power (Kenrick & Keefe, 1992; Townsend & Roberts, 1993; Wiederman & Allgeier, 1992).

The extent of the sex difference in mate preferences also varies with other factors (Kruger, Fitzgerald, & Peterson, 2010). Norm Li and his colleagues (2002) asked a group of adults waiting in an airport to design a mate under one of two experimental conditions. Some participants had an ample budget of "mate dollars" and could choose high levels of different desirable features (good looks, wealth, kindness, etc.). Other participants had lower budgets, so picking a mate with a lot of one characteristic (wealth, for example) meant sacrificing something else (getting someone less attractive, for instance). When women and men designed ideal mates without constraints on their choices, sex differences were relatively small: Both sexes wanted someone who was exceptionally personable, stunningly attractive, and wealthy. Brad Pitt and Angelina Jolie don't need to be realistic in choosing a mate; they can have it all. However, the rest of us mortals usually need to make compromises. Forced to compromise, men and women made very different choices. Women prioritized social status and gave up good looks; men prioritized attractiveness and gave up wealth. In choosing a casual sexual partner, however, women become more like men, shifting their priority to physical attractiveness (Fletcher et al., 2004; Li & Kenrick, 2006; Regan, Medina, & Joshi, 2001).

What do attractive, wealthy, and talented people want in a mate? People who have it all tend to demand partners who also have it all (and still may not be satisfied). Most of the rest of us need to compromise. Research discussed in the text indicates that men and women make very different compromises in what they are willing to accept in a mate.

SITUATION   Culture, Resources, and Polygamy

High in the Himalayan mountains along the border of Tibet and Kashmir, where cold winters and lack of rain make for rough survival conditions, a single woman may marry not one man but several. These men pool their resources to help raise the children as one family under the same roof. Things reverse themselves just a few hundred miles south, in the state of Patiala in northern India, where the powerful maharajah Rajinder Singh married over 350 women.

Faced with such variations, many social scientists in the early twentieth century concluded that human mating arrangements varied according to arbitrary and random historical factors. But later cross-cultural research suggests that this conclusion was premature. Marital arrangements have been linked to the distribution of status and resources within a society, which in turn links to the larger physical environment in which that society exists. A closer examination of the economics of marriage arrangements also teaches

A polyandrous family. One woman marries more than one man only rarely, and generally when resources are scarce.

A polygynous family. One man is likely to marry multiple women only when he is able to accumulate a relatively high level of wealth and status.

a broader lesson: When we go beyond gawking at how "they" are strangely different from "us," cross-cultural research can help us see the common threads that tie all humans together as a species.

Looking across cultures, the first thing we notice is that marriage patterns are not random at all. **Monogamy** is marriage between one man and one woman; **polygamy** includes both **polyandry** (one woman marrying more than one man) and **polygyny** (one man marrying more than one woman). The vast majority of societies allow men to marry multiple wives, whereas only about half of 1% allow polyandrous unions between a woman and multiple men. Whether a society permits polygamy or not, most individual marriages in all societies are monogamous. Why then, if our species is generally inclined toward monogamy, are some societies and some marriages nonmonogamous?

Let's take another look at the polyandrous Tibetans. A traditional Tibetan woman does not marry just any random group of men. Instead, like the two men depicted here in the photograph, the group of men is made up of brothers. Why does this happen? The answer is linked to environmental resources. The harsh conditions of life in the high Himalayas have made it difficult for a single man and a woman to survive alone. Even in modern times, Tibetan families in which one man marries one woman have fewer surviving children than do families in which brothers pool their resources (Crook & Crook, 1988). By sharing one wife, brothers preserve the family estate, which would not even support one family if it were subdivided each generation. If all the children are girls, the polyandrous pattern will switch to a polygynous one, and several sisters may marry one man, passing the family estate on to the sons of that marriage. Hence, Tibetan polyandry appears to be an economically based strategy by which a limited pool of resources gets channeled into a very focused family line.

Economic resources also provide a link between social status and polygynous marriage. Men are especially likely to take multiple wives when several conditions converge: (1) a steep social hierarchy, so some families have much higher status and wealth than others, (2) a generally rich environment, so the well-placed families can accumulate vast wealth, and (3) occasional famines, so the poor face possible danger of starvation (Crook & Crook, 1988). Under these circumstances, a woman joining a large wealthy family reaps benefits, even if she must share her husband with other women. Although a poor man might shower her with attention, a wealthy family provides a better buffer against famine and the chance of great wealth for her children in times of plenty. Interestingly, this is the same pattern found in birds like the indigo bunting; males who attract more than one female are those who control especially resource-rich territories (Orians, 1969).

Cross-cultural studies thus suggest that the links between marriage, wealth, and status have been forged by survival needs. How strong those links are in any particular society depends on the social and economic milieu.

Monogamy Marital custom in which one man marries one woman.

Polygamy Marital custom in which either one man marries more than one woman (polygyny) or one woman marries more than one man (polyandry).

Polyandry Marital arrangement involving one woman and more than one husband.

Polygyny Marital arrangement involving one man and more than one wife.

INVESTIGATION

How do the variations in polygamy and monogamy across cultures demonstrate the limitations of the old "nature versus nurture" dichotomy?

....

SITUATION Social Exchange in Committed Relationships

Status, resources, and social market value may have an important influence on who will be chosen as a partner in the first place. People initially seek partners whose mate value is similar to their own (Buss & Shackelford, 2008; Kenrick et al., 1993). But after a couple progresses into an intimate relationship, the accounting process may change. Studies in which partners are asked to count the benefits and costs they give and receive in their romantic relationships do not find such accounting to be a terribly important predictor of happiness (Clark & Monin, 2006; Clark & Reis, 1988). Once we have fallen in love, we may become as interested in our partner's benefits as in our own (Aron et al., 1992; VanLange & Rusbult, 1995).

Margaret Clark and Kathleen Chrisman (1994) suggested that, for people involved in communal relationships, they only start counting costs and rewards if there are gross violations of fair exchange. Consistent with this reasoning, Mikula and Schwinger (1978) found that the accounting process depended on the degree of good feeling between partners. Relationships in which people feel neutral about one another follow an **equity rule**: You get out benefits based on what you put in. Imagine a couple in which the man and woman kept separate groceries in the refrigerator and only gave back rubs when they received some monetary gift in return. Relationships in which people feel fairly positively about one another follow a slightly different rule: Everybody shares equally. Finally, those characterized by very positive feelings, as found in smoothly functioning marriages, follow a **need-based rule**: You give what your partner needs, without counting. In these couples, if the woman comes home from work with an aching back, her partner gives her a back rub without asking what he's going to get in return. Thus, increasing feelings of love lead to a decrease in nickel-and-dime accounting of who gave what to whom.

Indeed, paying undue attention to the accounting process can undermine intimate feelings. One experimental study found that simply asking romantic partners to think about the external benefits they get from one another led to a decrease in feelings of love (Seligman, Fazio, & Zanna, 1980). Hence, it seems wisest not to pay too much attention to the external resources you get from your partner once you have committed yourself.

INTERACTION   When Dominance Matters

Like most influences on social behavior, the importance of social dominance waxes and wanes depending on various interactions between the person and his or her situation. We'll consider two interesting types of interactions here. First, dominance may be desirable or undesirable in a mate, depending on other features of that person's personality. Second, our feelings about where we stand in the mating hierarchy depend on an interaction of our sex and the characteristics of other competitors.

DOMINANCE BY ITSELF ISN'T ENOUGH   We've discussed several findings suggesting that women seek socially dominant and competitive men. These characteristics are part of the traditional male role, which emphasizes attaining social rank over others, in contrast to the traditional female role, which emphasizes communal links with others (Sidanius, Cling, & Pratto, 1991). But what happens over the course of a relationship between a traditionally competitive male and a traditionally communal female?

After observing ongoing social interactions between traditional and nontraditional men and women, William Ickes (1993) suggested a paradoxical problem for traditional partners. Although women are initially attracted to socially dominant and competitive men, such men are not particularly pleasant to live with. Women are more satisfied in long-term relationships with more feminine or **androgynous** men (who combine traditionally masculine and feminine characteristics) (Antill, 1983). Although dominant men may be attractive to women, they are less likely to be loving, kind, and considerate. Indeed, highly dominant masculine men are relatively less attractive for long-term relationships (Kruger & Fitzgerald 2011). On the other hand, when women are worried about crime, they are more likely to make the trade-off, and boost their attraction toward aggressively dominant and physically formidable men, who are more likely to be able to protect them (Snyder et al., 2011).

Rather than being drawn to men who demonstrate pure machismo, women instead prefer partners high in *both* masculine assertiveness and feminine nurturance

Equity rule Each person's benefits and costs in a social relationship should be matched to the benefits and costs of the other.

Need-based rule Each person in a social relationship provides benefits as the other needs them, without keeping account of individual costs and benefits.

Androgynous Demonstrating a combination of masculine and feminine characteristics in one's behaviors.

Dominance and attraction. Women are attracted to dominant men, but only if they are also kind and understanding.

(Green & Kenrick, 1994). Indeed, both sexes will take a pass on competitive characteristics if it means settling for a partner who lacks nurturance or expressiveness. And whether a relationship will stand the test of time depends more on the man's agreeableness, and not his dominance (Bryan, Webster, & Mahaffey, 2011).

Another series of studies elucidated the interactive combination of masculine dominance and nurturant qualities (Jensen-Campbell et al., 1995). If you were a participant, you would have read a description of an opposite-sexed person who manifested one of four combinations of dominance and agreeableness. For example, you might read about someone who was both dominant (assertive, bold, talkative) and agreeable (considerate, cooperative, sympathetic). Or you might read about someone who was dominant but disagreeable (rude, selfish, uncooperative), and so on. Afterward, you would have rated the target person's desirability as a date.

For men rating women, it made no difference whether the woman was dominant, but they strongly preferred agreeable women to disagreeable women. Women preferred men who were dominant, but only if those men were also agreeable (see Figure 8.4). If a man was disagreeable, he was not desirable as a date, regardless of how dominant he was. This research further explains why women found Diego Rivera desirable. Frida Kahlo's biographer notes that besides being rich, powerful, and famous, he was tender, sensitive, charming, and appreciative of women: "he enjoyed talking with women: He valued their minds, and such an attitude was, in those days in Mexico, or anywhere else, a rare delight for most women" (Herrera, 1983).

Figure 8.4   Nice guys don't finish last, after all

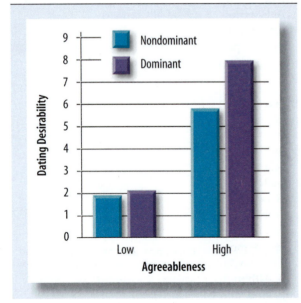

Female students judging men who are not agreeable pay little attention to whether the man is dominant or not. Dominance only matters when the man is agreeable.

Source: Based on Jensen-Campbell, L. A., Graziano, W. G., & West, S. G. (1995). Dominance, prosocial orientation, and female preferences: Do nice guys really finish last? *Journal of Personality and Social Psychology, 68,* 427–440.

WHO'S ON TOP?   Whether we can attract the mate we desire depends on the competition. Men and women in one series of studies were put into a mating frame of mind—by having them imagine an ideal date with a dream partner. Thinking about mating led men, but not women, to show off in several ways. For one, men in a mating frame of mind give more creative and interesting answers on various tests of creative ability (Griskevicius, Cialdini, & Kenrick, 2006). Men thinking about mating are more likely to disregard financial risks, to buy conspicuously expensive products, and to act aggressively (Griskevicius, Tybur et al., 2007, 2009; Li et al., 2012). Women in a mating frame of mind, on the other hand, are more likely to publicly display their cooperative and altruistic side—"Look how kind and agreeable I am!" (Griskevicius, Goldstein, Mortensen, Cialdini, & Kenrick, 2006; Griskevicius, Tybur et al., 2007).

Another team of social psychologists brought people into the lab and asked them to compete for partners. Symmetrical men with an unrestricted sociosexual orientation were more likely to use direct competitive tactics than were less symmetrical and restricted men. These sexy men tried to dominate opponents with statements like: "You'd have a lot more interesting time with me than with that other guy." Restricted men took a softer approach, focusing on their own positive qualities and presenting themselves as nice guys (Simpson et al., 1999).

Women were less likely to try to dominate their opponents (Simpson et al., 1999). But women are not immune to feelings of status competition in the mating arena. It simply shows up in different ways. Consider the findings of a study in which participants viewed profiles of eight members of their own sex who had presumably signed up for a campus dating service. In some cases, the other students were all highly socially dominant. One had been editor of a university newspaper and published articles in *Runner's World* on what it takes to achieve excellence; another was a youthful proprietor of a successful business. In other cases, the profiled students were low in dominance (one listed a letter to the editor of the campus newspaper as his major accomplishment, for example). Attached to each profile was a photograph. Half the students saw very attractive members of their sex (actually models from a local agency). The other half saw average-looking people. When later asked to rate their own desirability as marriage partners, men downgraded themselves after seeing a pool of potential competitors full of socially dominant high-rollers. Women, however, were affected by other women's physical attractiveness, downgrading their own mate value when those other women were all good-looking (Gutierres et al., 1999).

Using an eyetracker (a device that records exactly where a person looks on a computer screen), Jon Maner and colleagues (2003) found that women were highly attentive to beautiful women, whereas men were oblivious to handsome men. Women are also very good at remembering good-looking women they've seen before and are likely to overestimate the frequency of beautiful women in a crowd (Becker et al., 2005; Maner et al., 2003). These findings suggest that women are more attentive to physically attractive rivals.

Quick Quiz

1 Which of the following has been found with regard to the link between status and attractiveness?

    a. Both men and women prefer a physically attractive partner to one with higher status.

    b. The preference for high status partners is found in American women, but not women in Asian or African societies.

    c. Compared to men, women are more likely to mention their status or wealth in singles' advertisements.

    d. When men are primed to think about mating, they are more likely to display their resources.

2 Compared to mate preferences in heterosexual men and women:

    a. Preferences among those attracted to the same sex are reversed—gay men prefer status over attractiveness, and lesbian women prefer attractiveness over status.

    b. Both gay men and lesbians prefer attractiveness over status.

    c. Both gay men and lesbians prefer status over attractiveness.

    d. Gay men are interested in attractive partners in their twenties.

3 Which of the following is true with regard to polygamy and resources?

    a. A Tibetan woman marries multiple men only when she is wealthy.

    b. A Tibetan man enters a polyandrous marriage only when he is wealthy.

    c. Polygynous marriages in humans are found under opposite circumstances to those found in birds like indigo buntings.

    d. Polygynous marriages in humans are more likely when some families have much more.

4 Your romantic relationship is likely to be doing best if you and your partner divide benefits according to a(n) _____ rule.

    a. Equity

    b. Equanimity

    c. Need-based

    d. Status-based

Breaking Up (and Staying Together)

LO 8.13 Summarize the factors in the person and the situation that affect people's likelihood of breaking up or staying together.

LO 8.14 Understand the communication rules used by happy vs. unhappy couples.

So far, we've talked mostly about what draws people into relationships with one another. But getting together doesn't always lead to living happily ever after. Some relationships end after just one date, others after a few months. Some couples make it

Breaking up. George Clooney and Stacy Keibler broke up their two-year long relationship in 2013. Extraverted and unconventional people (such as many in the performing arts) are more inclined to change relationships than are conventional introverts, and being highly attractive no doubt increases the number of alternative temptations.

through all the stages of courtship, only to split after marriage. What causes people to break up? And have psychologists learned anything that can help keep relationships together and avoid the devastating consequences of divorce?

PERSON Some People Are Better at Getting Along

Marital stability and breakup depend in part on the person's ability and motivation to get along with his or her mate. A study of personality traits in 3,147 married twins found that problems maintaining long-term bonds may stem from genetically based differences in temperament (Jockin et al., 1996). First, twins in unstable marriages tended to be unconventional and extraverted. Unconventional and extraverted people, such as Diego Rivera, are likely to adopt an unrestricted sociosexual orientation, making their relationships less stable. Second, twins in unstable marriages were prone to negative moods. Although moody individuals may want to be in long-term relationships, their grouchiness leads their partners to feel more dissatisfied (Caughlin et al., 2000; Shackelford & Buss, 2000; McNulty, 2013).

Other research supports the idea that personality traits are intricately linked to skill in maintaining relationships (e.g., Assad et al., 2007). A longitudinal study tracked 300 couples who became engaged in the 1930s. Twenty-two broke their engagements, and 50 got divorced between 1935 and 1980. Among both men and women, emotional stability in the 1930s predicted a stable marriage over the next half century, whereas poor ability to control impulses predicted divorce (Kelly & Conley, 1987). Other research suggests that people high in self-control are better able to make accommodations to their partners, especially over the long haul (Finkel & Campbell, 2001; Kammrath & Peetz, 2011). And people who are securely attached are more likely to make choices that enhance their relationships (Turan and Vicary, 2010).

SITUATION Some Situations Pull Couples Apart

Situational factors from immediate stressors to broader social norms can also contribute to breakups (Fincham, 2003). Economic problems, for example, often play a role in driving couples apart (e.g., Notarius & Markman, 1993). Ready availability of alternative mates is another feature of the environment that can destabilize relationships (Greiling & Buss, 2000; Lydon et al., 2008; Lydon & Quinn, 2013; Mishra et al., 2007; Rusbult et al., 1982). But things go differently depending on whether there is an excess of men or women. Marcia Gutentag and Paul Secord (1983) found that when there was a surplus of marriageable women, men were less likely to commit, and societal norms shifted toward sexual permissiveness and delayed marriage. In contrast, when there were more marriageable men than women, norms shifted toward domestic values, with earlier marriages and less sexual permissiveness. Gutentag and Secord viewed the phenomenon in economic terms: A surplus of marriageable men allows women to demand that their suitors demonstrate more commitment and family values. Under those circumstances, women find it easier to find a man who will commit to marriage

(Kruger, Fitzgerald, & Peterson, 2010). A surplus of marriageable women, however, inspires women to compete with one another for men's affections.

Thomas Pollet and Daniel Nettle (2007, 2009) examined the economic consequences of sex ratios on marriages in different parts of the world, and found that when there is a relatively high number of men competing for a smaller number of women, women are less willing to settle down with a fellow unless he has money and/or property. Sex ratios have also been altering the economic relations between men and women in modern Asia (Belanger & Tran, 2011). In rural China, for example, there has been an increasing surplus of single men as young women have been migrating to the cities. This has had a negative effect on the psychological well-being of poor rural men, who feel increasingly hopeless about the prospects of finding a wife (Zhou et al., 2011).

Recent experiments have examined the effects of altering men's and women's perceptions of the local sex ratio and found results that fit with the population-level data. For example, when people are led to believe there are a lot of single men around, and fewer single women, both sexes say that men should spend more on dates and on engagement rings (Griskevicius et al., 2012). On the other hand, when women are led to believe that there are a lot of other desirable women in the neighborhood, and that it will hence be hard to find a good man, they are more likely to want a high-paying career—to choose a briefcase over a baby carriage (Durante et al., 2012).

INTERACTION Interactions: It Takes Two to Tango

Many of the factors contributing to relationship stability and termination involve interactions between the person and his or her environment (Finkel et al., 2007; McNulty et al., 2008; Overall et al., 2006). For example, low self-esteem or insecurity in one partner can affect relationship dynamics over time (Graham & Clark, 2006; Hellmuth & McNulty, 2008; Vasquez et al., 2002). People with low self-esteem tend to jump too quickly to the conclusion that their partners are losing interest. They then become cold and distant, which makes the relationship more costly for their partners. In the long run, their insecurities undermine the very relationships they need to feel better about themselves (Murray et al., 2002b).

Another person–situation interaction contributing to relationship stability involves changing our perceptions of the attractive alternatives out there (Johnson & Rusbult, 1989; Lydon, Fitzsimmons, & Naidoo, 2003). In one study of this phenomenon, students judged advertisements from magazines such as *Cosmopolitan*, *Gentleman's Quarterly*, and *Time*. The magazines included several photographs of attractive members of the opposite sex. Participants involved in dating relationships, in contrast to those not involved, found the models significantly less physically and sexually attractive (Simpson, Gangestad, & Lerma, 1990). In another study, participants saw a profile of a highly attractive and available member of the opposite sex (Lydon et al., 1999). Half were also told this person had expressed romantic interest in them. Less committed participants increased their attraction, but those who were more committed to their relationships became less attracted when the good-looking person expressed a romantic interest. Thus, being in a loving relationship can lead to defensive changes in perception—seeing potentially threatening alternatives as less desirable. And people who are inattentive to alternatives are, as you might expect, more content with what they've got (Miller, 1997).

Making sacrifices for your partner can have good or bad consequences, depending on why you do it. If you or your partner make sacrifices to promote positive goals— to make one another happy or to strengthen your bond—it makes you both feel better, and improves the quality of your relationship. If, however, you make sacrifices to avoid conflict or because you feel obligated, it tends to make you both miserable and undermine the relationship in the long run (Impett, Gable, & Peplau, 2005).

Perhaps the most important "environmental factor" for one member of a long-term couple is the behavior of the other. One partner's jokes, barbs, purrs, and growls creates the situation for the other, and ultimately for him or herself as well. If you express appreciation for you partner, for example, he or she is likely to appreciate you more in turn (Gordon et al., 2012).

Neuropsychological research indicates that relationship conflict can lead in the short-term to hormonal stress reactions and interfere with the immune system (Kiecolt-Glaser et al., 1993; Malarkey et al., 1994; Powers et al., 2006). In the long run, marital conflict can lead to violence and to dramatic negative effects on physical and mental health (Fincham, 2003).

Other research indicates that it's not only how you respond when things go wrong, but also how you respond when things go right. Relationships are happier when people react enthusiastically to their partner sharing good news, as compared to showing passive disinterest (Gable et al., 2006).

By studying precisely how different couples escalate and de-escalate conflicts, psychologists have developed some important insights about how to stay together in the face of life's inevitable ups and downs (Gottman, 1994; Gottman & Levenson, 1992; Markman & Rhoades, 2012).

Bridging Theory and Application:

Studying Healthy Communication to Save Marriages

Imagine you're married, and your spouse comes home from work in a foul mood. To cheer him or her up, you suggest dinner at your favorite restaurant, but get a testy response: "I really *don't* feel like eating Chinese again for the fifth time this month, thank you!" Do you drop the conversation and slam the door on your way out to eat alone? Or do you use the opportunity to bring up a few problems in the relationship that have been on your mind, pointing out parallels between your partner's behavior and that of his or her recently divorced parents? Though none of these responses sounds good on paper, it's often difficult not to strike back when our partner spews unpleasant feelings in our direction. Over time, though, such tit-for-tat, negative communications can destroy the fabric of a relationship. One team of psychologists working at the interface of social and clinical psychology has carefully studied the interaction styles of happy and unhappy couples and used their findings to help couples in trouble (Markman et al., 1988; Notarius & Pellegrini, 1984).

The research team began by videotaping couples discussing problems in their relationships. To learn how well-functioning couples resolve their differences, the researchers also videotaped happy couples discussing their problems. They then tracked couples over 10 years of marriage to discover what differentiated those who stayed together from those who eventually split. After many studies involving hundreds of couples, the researchers discovered some key differences between healthy and unhealthy communication patterns. They then used those discoveries to intervene in troubled marriages (Notarius & Markman, 1993; Markman & Rhoades, 2012).

Couples in the program began by listing potential problem areas, including alcohol, careers, money, relatives, and sex. They then discussed specific problems in their own relationships. Members of unhappy couples were likely to respond to conflict with "zingers"—negative statements about their partners that often trigger counterattacks. An irony of intimate relationships is that people who are normally polite toward strangers and acquaintances are often rude to the very people who expect tender

loving care from them. Thus, the researchers developed a guide to politeness for couples, including the following rules:

1. When your partner invites you to do something, say what you can do or want to do rather than what you can't or don't want to do. If your partner suggests a movie but you're feeling tired, say, "I'd love to go to the movies tomorrow," rather than "I'm too tired."
2. When your partner does a chore, don't focus on an aspect that didn't meet with your approval. Rather than saying, "You missed a spot," say, "Thanks for washing the counter." If you routinely don't like the way your partner does something, discuss it at a time specially set aside for the purpose.
3. Always greet each other with a warm hello and leave with a tender goodbye.
4. Avoid being a "psychopest," analyzing your partner's behavior under the guise of being helpful. Don't say things like: "Do you know you're being clinically obsessive-compulsive when you insist on keeping the kitchen so clean?"
5. Always speak for yourself, not your partner. Say, "I really want to go to the company picnic" rather than "I know you'll have a good time at the picnic."
6. If you have an opinion, say it rather than trying to get your partner to guess what it is. Say "I'm really dying to eat Mexican food tonight" instead of "Do you want to eat out tonight?"
7. If you don't have anything nice to say, try keeping quiet (based on Notarius & Markman, 1993, pp. 77–78).

These techniques can help couples stay together (Markman & Rhoades, 2012; Stanley et al., 2010). In one longitudinal study, premarital couples who learned these effective communication techniques had 50% fewer breakups than a comparison group of nonparticipant couples (Notarius & Markman, 1993).

For most people, it takes some effort to develop the skills to keep their relationship happy and healthy. Given the importance of strong relationships to mental and physical health, though, the investment is well worth it.

INVESTIGATION

Consider a couple you know who is happy and another who is unhappy (or already broken up). How do they differ in terms of the person, situation, and interactional factors that social psychologists have linked to relationship stability?

Quick Quiz

1 Which of the following personality traits has been found to reduce the likelihood of divorce?

    a. Emotional stability
    b. Extraversion
    c. Openness to Experience
    d. Unrestricted sociosexual orientation

2 When there are relatively few women and a larger number of men:

    a. Polygyny increases.
    b. Divorce increases.
    c. Women are more likely to value careers over families.
    d. Men are likely to spend more on engagement rings.

3 Research on communications between happy as opposed to unhappy couples suggests that happy couples:

    a. Feel more comfortable expressing their angry feelings openly.
    b. Are less concerned with being superficially "polite" to one another.
    c. Are more confident about standing their ground in an argument.
    d. Are less likely to counter-attack when their partner says something hostile.

The Love Affair of "The Elephant and the Dove"

Revisiting

We opened this chapter with some questions raised by the famous love relationship between Frida Kahlo and Diego Rivera. Why would an attractive and brilliantly talented young woman become involved with a much older, less attractive man? Research on mating decisions gives an easy answer to half of this question—Diego was rich, famous, and powerful, characteristics that boost men's attractiveness to women. Because men around the world tend to become more socially dominant and wealthier as they grow older, relationships between older men and younger women are found across human societies. Added to his wealth and social position, Diego could be highly sensitive and thoughtful, characteristics that combine with dominance to make men especially attractive.

Why did Diego have so many affairs? Part of the answer has to do with his personality—he was extraverted and unconventional, two characteristics associated with relationship instability. Another part of the answer has to do with his social situation—Frida was one of many young attractive women who offered themselves to him. As we saw, having many attractive alternatives is not good for fidelity (although some people are better at resisting temptation). The unconventionality of their relationship also made it easy for both Frida and Diego to respond to outside offers. Frida herself was attractive to men and women alike, and she, too, frequently had affairs.

We have seen that even though there are substantial universalities in human mating behavior, there are also important cultural variations. Cultural factors no doubt contributed to the unique relationship between Frida Kahlo and Diego Rivera. Frida and Diego were members of a group of unconventional thinkers, amongst whom sexually unrestricted behavior was normatively acceptable. In discussing the diversity of marital arrangements around the world, we noted that cultural and evolutionary factors often interact. Two revolutions had led to a dramatic change in the Mexican population, with many more women than men of marriageable age. As we have noted, sexual norms tend to become more unrestricted when there are more women than men.

Why, despite all the trials of their relationship, did Frida and Diego get back together and remain close until her death? As we have seen, love relationships often involve difficulties and conflicts. Yet we have also observed that people can learn to overcome their differences. Although their relationship did not fit the conventional mold in Western societies, it was in some ways a tribute to human flexibility and diversity and to the strength of human attachments. Despite their sexual attractions to others, Diego and Frida were deeply and positively bonded to one another. They encouraged and supported each other as artists, valued one another's opinions about their creative outputs, and provided social support through good and bad times. Indeed, their ability to maintain a lifelong relationship under such unconventional circumstances is a tribute to the positive inclinations of human beings.

In this chapter, we have again seen many bridges between social psychology and other disciplines. Neuropsychological studies have increasingly revealed a role for biological factors in human love, including hormonal influences on when we feel attraction, and to whom it is directed. The historical and cultural influences on relationships link the psychology of love with the fields of history, political science, and anthropology. And the different ways in which men and women make decisions in relationships with lovers and children raise interesting questions for economic psychology.

Chapter Summary

Summary of the Goals Served by Romantic Relationships and Factors Related to Each Goal

The Goal	Person	Situation	Interaction
Obtaining sexual gratification	• Opportunities provided by attractiveness • Gender • Levels of testosterone • Restricted vs. unrestricted sociosexual orientation • Sexual orientation	• Arousing settings • Societal permissiveness toward sexual expression	• Men may perceive sexuality in a situation women see as friendly. • Raising children under the same roof may trigger a mechanism designed to prevent incest.
Establishing family bonds	• Attachment style (secure, anxious/ambivalent, avoidant) • Exchange orientation	• Threats • Partner infidelity	• Over time, marital situation can affect partners' traits.
Gaining resources and social status	• Gender • Gay men have similar mate preferences to heterosexual men.	• Resources affect cultural rules about marriage. • Once involved, economics become less important.	• Social dominance is attractive to women only if it is combined with kindness. • Women's feelings about their position in the social hierarchy are linked to their appearance and that of their competitors; men's are based more on status and economic resources.

Defining Love and Romantic Attraction

1. The different components of love can be organized into three factors. Passion consists of romantic attraction and sexual desire. Intimacy consists of close bonding. Decision/commitment consists of a decision that one loves another and has made a commitment to maintain that love.

2. Feelings associated with love combine differently in different varieties of love, such as love for a family member or for a passionate lover. Passionate love is characterized by intense longing for another, whereas companionate love is composed of feelings of affection and tenderness. Nurturant love refers to the feelings parents have for their children, and attachment love refers to the desire to be cared for by another.

3. Major goals of romantic relationships include sexual gratification, forming family bonds, and gaining resources and social status.

Obtaining Sexual Gratification

1. Some features of physical attractiveness, including low waist-to-hip ratios in women and bodily symmetry in both sexes, are widely regarded as attractive across cultures.

2. Women are less interested in casual sexual opportunities and more selective about sexual partners. The two sexes are more similar in approaching long-term relationships.

3. Individual differences in sexual desire have been linked to the hormone testosterone in both sexes, and estrogen and progesterone have been found to influence women's sexual attractions in numerous ways.

4. Within each sex, individuals with an unrestricted sociosexual orientation have more sexual partners and choose partners who are socially attractive. Restricted individuals choose partners with traits linked to good parenting.

5. Attraction to the same sex raises interesting questions from an evolutionary perspective. It has been linked to tendencies to help brothers and sisters in traditional societies, and some evidence suggests it could be a byproduct of genetic inclinations that carry reproductive benefits in heterosexual relatives.

6. Situations that increase general physiological arousal can increase passionate attraction. According to two-factor theory, arousal from any source can be mistakenly attributed to the lover. However, arousal can boost attraction even when the person is aware the arousal did not come directly from the lover.

7. Norms for expressing sexual feelings before and after marriage vary across cultures, with Asian cultures being relatively restricted, and North Americans and Australians being less restricted. They also vary for different subcultural groups within a society, such as religious and nonreligious individuals.

8. Different people perceive potentially sexual situations differently. Compared to women, men generally

perceive more sexuality in interactions between men and women.

9. Culture and evolutionary mechanisms interact in influencing sexual attraction. Boys and girls raised under the same roof are less likely to later become passionately attracted, suggesting a mechanism blocking strong sexual attraction between siblings.

Establishing Family Bonds

1. Adult attachments share similarities with attachment bonds between mother and children. Unlike typical mammals, human adult males also bond with their offspring.
2. Individuals differ in their styles of attachment. Some are secure and confident of their lovers' support. Others are anxious/ambivalent; still others are avoidant.
3. People oriented to exchange rather than to communal benefits experience more dissatisfaction with their marriage partners.
4. Threatening situations increase the desire to be near those to whom we are attached.
5. Erotomania is a disorder in which the individual persists in believing that another person is deeply in love with him or her despite strong evidence to the contrary. It may involve a misfiring of a normal reaction to a threatened love bond.
6. Men are somewhat more upset by a partner's sexual relationship than by a deep emotional bond, whereas women tend to be relatively more troubled if their partners form a deep emotional bond with someone else.
7. Marriage itself is a situation that can affect personal traits over time.

Gaining Resources and Social Status

1. A mate's status, wealth, and dominance are more important to a woman considering a man than to a man considering a woman.
2. Signs of youthful maturity and attractiveness are universally valued by men as signs of reproductive potential.
3. Gay men act like heterosexual men in preferring relatively young attractive partners and paying relatively little attention to partners' status.
4. Sex differences in the desire for status in a mate are stronger in third world countries. However, even wealthy high status women in Western societies continue to seek male partners with status and wealth. Sex differences in mate choice are more pronounced when men and women are forced to choose which characteristics they most want in a mate.

5. Polyandry often involves a woman marrying brothers and is found in areas where resources are scarce and families would not survive if their land holdings were divided among children. Polygyny is more common and is more extreme when a steep social hierarchy combines with a generally rich environment to allow one family to accumulate vast wealth.
6. Both sexes seek long-term partners whose status and market value are similar to their own, but once people are involved in long-term relationships accounting of relative contributions decreases, and the partner's needs become more merged with one's own.
7. Dominance is only attractive in combination with kindness.
8. Women's feelings about their place in the social hierarchy are linked to their feelings about physical appearance; men's are linked to status and resources.

Breaking Up (and Staying Together)

1. Several person factors affect relationship stability. Individuals who are unconventional, extraverted, or moody tend to have less satisfying and stable marriages.
2. Some situations pull couples apart, including economic hardships and a societal excess of available mates. When there are relatively many available women and few men, norms shift toward sexual permissiveness and later marriage. When there is a relative surplus of men, societal norms shift toward earlier marriage and less permissiveness.
3. Harmonious relationships depend on more than a pleasant personality in one individual, because negative communications or insecurities in the other can change the situation and lead to an unpleasant cycle.
4. Commitment to a relationship changes perceptions of alternatives, leading people to see members of the opposite sex as less attractive.
5. Studies of happy couples have led to the discovery of communication principles that can help keep marriages together. Some involve simply communicating in a clear and considerate way and avoiding counterattacks to a partner's irritable barbs.

Key Terms

Androgynous, 267

Anxious/ambivalent attachment style, 257

Attachment love, 246

Avoidant attachment style, 257

Companionate love, 245

Decision/commitment, 244

Equity rule, 267

Erotomania, 259

Factor analysis, 244

Intimacy, 244

Monogamy, 266

Need-based rule, 267

Need to belong, 256

Nurturant love, 246

Passion, 244

Passionate love, 245

Polyandry, 266

Polygamy, 266

Polygyny, 266

Secure attachment style, 257

Secure base, 257

Sociosexual orientation, 251

Two-factor theory of love, 253

∨ Learning Objectives

LO 9.1 Define "pure" altruism and describe how it differs from other kinds of prosocial behavior.

LO 9.2 Outline the four major goals that prosocial actions can serve.

LO 9.3 Discuss the two insights provided by Hamilton (1964) and Trivers (1971) that help explain why giving might improve the giver's genetic well-being.

LO 9.4 Describe the two situational factors that expand a helper's sense of "we."

LO 9.5 Discuss what the social responsibility norm requires people to do.

LO 9.6 Identify three ways bystanders in emergencies influence the decision to help.

LO 9.7 Explain when and why men and women differ in their helping behavior.

LO 9.8 Understand how personal norms and religious and ethical codes influence helping.

LO 9.9 Explain how labeling and self-focus raise our motivation to help.

LO 9.10 Discuss why we sometimes decide not to offer help or receive help from others.

LO 9.11 Identify the three factors that, according to the arousal/cost–reward model, increase the chance that an observer will help a victim of an emergency.

LO 9.12 Describe when and why sadness leads to helping, according to the negative state relief model.

LO 9.13 Discuss when, according to the empathy–altruism hypothesis, pure altruism occurs.

LO 9.14 Summarize the evidence for and against the empathy–altruism hypothesis.

The Strange Case of Sempo Sugihara

The Years of Nazi ascendancy in Europe bear awful witness to the worst of human nature. More than 11 million civilians—including Jews, gypsies, homosexuals, and political dissidents—were uprooted, degraded, brutalized, and finally murdered in the Holocaust. Ironically, this period also gave evidence of the best of human nature: Remarkable acts of kindness, heroism, and self-sacrifice were undertaken on behalf of those victims by individuals who, for the most part, hardly knew them. However, the single most effective helping action taken during the Holocaust has gone virtually unrecognized.

It began near dawn on a summer day in 1940, when 200 Polish Jews crowded together outside the Japanese consulate in Lithuania to plead for help to escape the Nazi advance. Why they chose to seek the aid of Japanese officials is a puzzle. The governments of Nazi Germany and imperial Japan were strongly tied. Why would these Jews, the hated targets of the Third Reich, throw themselves on the mercy of one of Hitler's international partners?

The answer requires us to look back a few years, to the mid-1930s. Before its close strategic associations with Hitler's Germany developed, Japan had begun allowing displaced Jews easy access to its settlement in Shanghai, to attract the political goodwill and financial resources of the international Jewish community. The paradoxical result was that in the prewar years, as most of the countries of the world (the United States included) were turning away the desperate prey of Hitler's Final Solution, it was Japan—Hitler's ally—that was providing them sanctuary (Kranzler, 1976).

By July 1940, then, when 200 of the "prey" massed outside the door of the Japanese consulate in Lithuania, they knew that the man behind that door offered their best and perhaps last chance for to safety. His name was Sempo Sugihara. By all appearances,

Sugihara's lifeline. A line of men waits for life outside Sempo Sugihara's office while another line of men waits for death in a Nazi concentration camp. It's likely that without Sugihara's help, those in the first line would have soon become like those in the second.

Mr. Sugihara was an unlikely candidate for their savior. A midcareer diplomat, Sugihara was from a samurai family, Japan's warrior class known for loyalty, skill, and ferocity in battle. The son of a government official, he dreamed of becoming the Japanese ambassador to Russia some day. Sugihara was also a great lover of entertainments, parties, and music. On the surface, there was little to suggest that this fun-seeking, lifelong diplomat would risk his career, his reputation, and his future to try to save the Jews who woke him from a sound sleep one morning at 5:15. That, though, is precisely what he did—with full knowledge of the potential consequences for himself and for his family.

After speaking with members of the crowd outside his gate, Sugihara recognized the depths of their plight and wired Tokyo for permission to authorize travel visas for them. His request was summarily denied, as were his more urgent second and third petitions when he persisted in pressing the case for help. It was at this point in his life that this comfortable, professionally ambitious career official did what no one could have anticipated. He decided to begin writing the needed travel documents in outright defiance of his clearly stated, and twice restated, orders.

It was a choice that cost him his career. Within a month he was transferred from his consul general post to a lesser position in Berlin, where he could no longer maintain a free hand. Ultimately, he was expelled from the Foreign Ministry for his insubordination. In dishonor after the war, he was reduced to selling light bulbs for a living. But in the weeks before he had to close the consulate in Lithuania, he stayed the course he'd set for himself, interviewing applicants day and night and authoring the papers required for their escape. Even after the consulate had been shut and he'd taken up residence in a hotel, he continued to write visas. Although the stress of the situation had left him thin and exhausted and had rendered his wife incapable of nursing their infant child, he wrote without respite. Even on the platform for the train taking him to Berlin, even on the train itself, he wrote and thrust life-granting papers into life-grasping hands, eventually saving thousands of innocents. And at last, when the train began to draw him away, he bowed deeply and apologized to those he had to leave stranded—begging their forgiveness for his deficiencies as a helper (Watanabe, 1994).

To understand Sugihara's decision to help thousands of Jews escape to Shanghai, it's important to recognize a fundamental truth about prosocial action: It rarely arises from any single factor. A variety of forces act and interact to bring about help. Before we encounter these forces—and, in the process, try to solve the puzzle of Sempo Sugihara's actions—we should be clear about what prosocial behavior is. In addition, we should recognize that helping can serve the goals of the helper: There are advantages, both tangible and intangible, to giving aid. Therefore, in this chapter, after defining and illustrating what we mean by prosocial behavior, we identify the major goals of prosocial action and examine how they can account for various types of help-giving, including that of Sempo Sugihara.

The Goals of Prosocial Behavior

LO 9.1 Define "pure" altruism and describe how it differs from other kinds of prosocial behavior.

LO 9.2 Outline the four major goals that prosocial actions can serve.

Prosocial behavior comes in a wide range of sizes and forms. At its most basic level, **prosocial behavior** refers to any action intended to benefit another. This label applies even when the helper also stands to benefit. So, for example, if you put a $20 bill into a Salvation Army kettle to impress a friend, your action would still be prosocial. Although the motive to impress a friend might not be seen as especially praiseworthy, your behavior would still be considered prosocial. Now, suppose that instead of dropping $20 into a Salvation Army kettle to gain external reward or recognition, you sent it anonymously to that organization because you knew it would make you feel good

Prosocial behavior Action intended to benefit another.

inside. The crucial difference between these two kinds of assistance is whether you expected the reward to come from outside or inside yourself. Psychologists have long seen the importance of this distinction between external and internal sources of reward for helping and have assigned more moral value to prosocial acts that are motivated only by internal rewards. In fact, some theorists have defined such internally motivated helping as altruistic (Bar-Tal & Raviv, 1982; Eisenberg & Fabes, 1998).

Other theorists (Batson & Shaw, 1991), however, want to reserve the concept of altruism for a more limited type of prosocial behavior—something that we can label **pure (or true) altruism**. Pure altruism refers to conduct intended to benefit another for no other reason than to improve the other's welfare. In this category, helping is done without regard for external *or* internal rewards for the helper. There may well be rewards for helping; for the act to be purely altruistic, however, those rewards cannot have caused the decision to help. Thus, if you were to send $20 to the Salvation Army and you felt better about yourself afterward, you would have nonetheless engaged in pure altruism, provided you didn't make the donation *in order* to feel better or for any other self-oriented reason. At present the most controversial question confronting helping researchers is whether there ever is a purely altruistic act, untouched by self-interest. Toward the end of this chapter, we will review the results of research that has searched for the answer to this fundamental question.

Prosocial action occurs regularly in all human societies (Dovidio, Piliavin, Schroeder, & Penner, 2006) and helpfulness is a heritable trait, one that is passed on genetically (Rushton, Fulker, Neale, Nias, & Eysenck, 1986). It seems likely, then, that helping serves some valuable functions, not just for societies but for individuals as well. Indeed, research in social psychology points to several goals that prosocial action can serve. We can help (1) to improve our own basic welfare, (2) to increase social status and approval, (3) to manage our self-image, and (4) to manage our moods and emotions. Let's first consider the most basic of these reasons for helping someone else—to help ourselves.

Quick Quiz

1 Which of the following actions is closest to the definition of pure altruism?

    a. You drop $5 into a Salvation Army kettle outside a shopping mall because you feel guilty spending money on yourself that day.

    b. You buy groceries for your unemployed brother and leave them on his doorstep anonymously.

    c. Out of a sincere desire to help less fortunate people, you anonymously donate money to the Red Cross to be used for disaster relief in the Philippines.

    d. You surprise your best friend with an unexpected and costly gift.

2 Which of the following is one of the four major goals of prosocial action mentioned in the text:

    a. Managing our moods and emotions.

    b. Improving our own basic welfare.

    c. Increasing social status and approval.

    d. Managing our self-image.

    e. All of the above

Improving Our Basic Welfare: Gaining Genetic and Material Benefits

LO 9.3 Discuss the two insights provided by Hamilton (1964) and Trivers (1971) that help explain why giving might improve the giver's genetic well-being.

LO 9.4 Describe the two situational factors that expand a helper's sense of "we."

The question of why people help has always been a prickly one from the standpoint of the theory of evolution. On the surface, giving away resources to aid others presents a problem for the Darwinian view that we always operate to enhance our *own*

Pure (or true) altruism Action intended solely to benefit another.

survival. In seeming contradiction to this idea, we know that people help regularly in a variety of ways, from holding open a door to pulling a child from a burning building (McGuire, 1994; Pearce & Amato, 1980). Besides appearing in impressively varied ways, helping also appears impressively often in modern society. In the United States alone, 80% of adults donate money or volunteer time to a charity (Bello, 2008). Such other-oriented tendencies make more evolutionary sense when we add two insights to traditional evolutionary accounts of behavior.

Insights into the Evolution of Help

The first insight was provided by the biologist W. D. Hamilton (1964), who recognized that, from an evolutionary standpoint, the actions of an individual are designed not so much to ensure that the individual will survive as to ensure that the *genes* making up that individual will do so (Krebs, 2011; Tooby & Cosmides, 2005).

PROTECTING OUR KIN   This distinction between personal survival and genetic survival is incorporated in Hamilton's concept of **inclusive fitness**, defined as an individual's net success at getting his or her genes passed on not only in his or her own offspring but also in the offspring of any relatives. The distinction between personal and genetic survival is a profound one for understanding and predicting when helping will occur. It implies that people may well accept personal risks and losses if, in the process, they increase their inclusive fitness—the odds that their genes will survive. Consequently, we should be willing to risk even our own survival if it increases the chance that more copies of our genes will survive in any relatives we help.

The evidence is overwhelming that individuals prefer to help those to whom they are genetically related. Many animal species aid their relatives—feeding, defending, and sheltering them—in direct proportion to their degree of relatedness: An animal tends to help most those with which it is more likely to share genes through ancestry (Sherman, 1981). In large measure and in a large number of cultures, we humans show the same pattern (Cunningham et al., 1995; Curry et al., 2013; Neyer & Lang, 2003; Webster, 2003); see Figure 9.1. This tendency to help genetically close relatives holds true for such diverse forms of aid as donating a kidney in the United States or intervening in an ax fight in the jungles of Venezuela (Borgida, Conner, & Manteufal, 1992; Chagnon & Bugos, 1979).

Inclusive fitness The survival of one's genes in one's own offspring and in any relatives one helps.

Reciprocal aid Helping that occurs in return for prior help.

RECIPROCAL AID   Hamilton's notion of inclusive fitness gives us a way to understand self-sacrifice among kin. But how can the logic of evolution explain the fact that in both animal and human groups, nonrelatives also regularly help one another? The second important insight of modern evolutionary theory is the concept of **reciprocal aid**. Robert Trivers (1971) pointed out that helping is often mutual and cooperative, so that helpers benefit by being helped in return. Recall that in Chapter 6 you learned that all human societies have a norm for reciprocity that obligates people to give in return for the benefits they've received. Trivers showed that mutual helping often takes place among animals too. Those whose genes encouraged such interactions would have a survival advantage.

In the case of reciprocal aid among unrelated individuals, the survival advantage comes from the material advantage that cooperators would have over noncooperators. Indeed, cooperators do frequently enjoy this advantage in the long run because their mutual assistance gives them access to rewards and continuingly profitable relationships that wouldn't otherwise be available (Flynn, 2003). European economists found that when firms reciprocated by providing benefits to employees whose work helped the firm, the employees expended more effort and reduced the amount of shirking on the job. All of this greatly improved profits, ensuring

You delouse my back, and I'll delouse yours.   Reciprocal aid, in the form of mutual grooming, often occurs among animals. This cooperation benefits all involved.

Figure 9.1 Helping relatives and nonrelatives

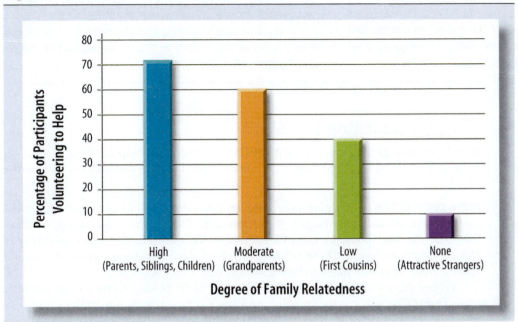

Participants indicated whether they would help certain others in a wide variety of situations. Their willingness to help closely reflected their genetic relatedness to the others.

Source: Adapted from the results of Cunningham, M. R., Jegerski, J., Gruder, C. L., & Barbee, A. P. (1995). Helping in different social relationships: Charity begins at home. Unpublished manuscript, University of Louisville, Department of Psychology, Louisville, KY.

the survival of the firm and the employees' jobs (Fehr, Gachter, & Kirchsteiger, 1997). In sum, the benefits of reciprocal helping can provide a material advantage to those who engage in it skillfully, making such individuals more likely to thrive and pass on their genes.

Using Behavioral Genetics to Study Helping

How much of human conduct can be explained by heredity, and how much by environment? The question has a long history in the annals of science (Bouchard, 2004; Galton, 1875). To disentangle these two fundamental causes of behavior, behavioral geneticists often contrast identical twins, who share all their genes, and nonidentical twins, who are born into the same family environment at the same time but share only half their genes. Studies of identical versus nonidentical twins have provided two streams of evidence about what motivates the tendency to help.

First, for both adults and children as young as 14 months, identical twins are more alike in their helping patterns than are nonidentical twins (Rushton et al., 1986; Zahn-Waxler, Robinson, & Emde, 1992). The size of the discrepancy has led geneticists to estimate that the tendency to help is due about equally to genetic and nongenetic factors.

Second, other studies have asked whether identical twins are especially likely to act prosocially toward each other. Nancy Segal found that on a task requiring subjects to earn points, identical twins worked harder to win points for each other than did nonidentical twins. Furthermore, on a puzzle-solving task 94% of the identical twins helped each other whereas only 46% of

Double duty. The special connection—genetic and otherwise—between identical twins makes them feel particularly helpful to one another.

nonidentical twins did so. Finally, in a bargaining game, the identical twins cooperated to benefit each other significantly more often than the nonidentical twins did (Segal, 2000). These results are consistent with the concept of inclusive fitness and the idea that individuals will act to increase the welfare of their genes, even if those genes are in someone else's body.

Studies of twins indicate a strong genetic impact on the tendency to help. At the same time, the fact that there is not perfect overlap between identical twins suggests that there is also a strong impact due to learning and environment—an optimistic finding for those who hope to be able to instill a prosocial orientation in others, especially children.

PERSON Learning to Help

Which features of the person might spur an individual to help in order to gain genetic and material benefits? Two stand out: instilled beliefs and an expanded sense of "we."

INSTILLED BELIEFS   If helping others—even unrelated others—can produce genetic and material gains for the helper, then those individuals who most strongly believe this to be the case should be most likely to help. This is precisely what one survey of U.S. corporations found: Those whose executives viewed self-interest as a reason for charity were especially likely to be big donors (Galaskiewicz, 1985).

Where does this view that helping is a way to promote one's own interests come from? One place is the learning process. Even relatively late in their development, people can be educated to believe that prosocial behavior is—or is not—personally prudent. Take, for instance, training in classical economic theory. A basic assumption is that people will neglect or exploit others to maximize their own outcomes. Researchers have found that economics students, more than students in other disciplines such as psychology, do follow the expectations of classical economic theory. They're more likely to demand a lopsided payment for themselves in a negotiation or when allocating funds (Kahneman, Knetsch, & Thaler, 1986; Marwell & Ames, 1981). And, especially pertinent to the topic of helping, they're less likely to make donations to charities—a reluctance that increases with greater training in economics (Frank, Gilovich, & Regan, 1993). On the other hand, poorer people, who have more to gain from sharing with one another, are more likely to develop egalitarian and compassionate values and to act generously toward others (Piff et al., 2010).

THE EXPANDED SENSE OF "WE"   There is another way a learned orientation to the world can influence the extent to which individuals act prosocially for a direct benefit. That learned orientation—an expanded sense of "we"—develops in the home, well before a person encounters a college curriculum, and it involves genetic rather than material benefit. As you've already seen, people prefer to help those to whom they're genetically related, presumably to enhance the survival of their own genes. It isn't really possible, though, for individuals to look inside one another and determine how many genes they share. Instead, people have to rely on *cues* of genetic relatedness—features normally associated with relatives (DeBruine, 2005; Krebs, 2012; Kurland & Gaulin, 2005). One such cue is the early presence of particular others or types of others in the home. Humans as well as animals react to those who were present while they were growing up as if they are relatives (Lieberman & Lobel, 2012). Although this clue to genetic relatedness can occasionally steer us wrong, it's normally accurate because people in the home typically *are* true family members—a group nearly everyone views as "we."

An interesting upshot of this logic is that those individuals whose parents regularly opened their homes to a wide range of people—of varying backgrounds, customs, and appearances—should be more likely, as adults, to help strangers. That would be so because their conception of "we" will have been broadened to include more than just the immediate or even the extended family. For them, the help-inspiring sense of "we-ness" should extend more fully to the *human* family (Burnstein, 2005; Piliavin, Dovidio, Gaertner, & Clark, 1981).

One source of support for this idea comes from cultures having different norms for inviting others, especially mere acquaintances, into the home. In many Asian societies, such invitations are rare, and an outsider who receives one should feel greatly honored. In Western society, however, get-togethers in the home with a variety of acquaintances—for casual dinners, to watch sporting events on TV, and so forth—are much more commonplace. Consistent with the notion that diverse home environments will lead to help for strangers, Americans are more willing to help people outside their own groups than are Japanese or Chinese individuals. But Japanese and Chinese individuals are more willing to help those from within their own groups than are Americans (Leung, 1988).

This further deepens the mystery of Sempo Sugihara. Why would a member of Japanese society, noted for its reluctance to embrace outsiders, be so dedicated to helping Jewish refugees, who were so clearly foreigners to him? Our first hint comes from an experience in Sugihara's youth. His father, a tax official who had been sent to Korea for a time, moved the family there and opened an inn. Sugihara recalled being greatly impressed by his parents' willingness to take in a broad mix of guests—tending to their basic needs for food and shelter, even cleaning their hair and clothing of lice—despite the fact that some were too impover-

The outsiders. This photo shows Sugihara's wife, son, and sister-in-law in Nazi-held territory some months after he'd been relieved of his duties in Lithuania. Note the sign on the park gate, which reads "No Jews allowed." It's unknown whether the sign was an incidental or purposive part of the picture. We do know, however, that Sugihara himself took the photograph and that he positioned his family outside the gate. What do you think? Was the sign an incidental feature of the shot or a consciously included piece of bitter irony? For a suggestive bit of evidence, see if you can locate the sister-in-law's right hand.

ished to pay (Watanabe, 1994). From this perspective, perhaps we can see one reason for Sugihara's later helping efforts toward thousands of European Jews—an expanded sense of "we" flowing from exposure to diverse individuals in the home. As he stated in an interview 45 years later, the nationality and religion of these victims didn't matter to him; it only mattered that "they were *human*, and they needed help" (Craig, 1985).

Of course, it's always risky to try to generalize from a single case to a broader conclusion. In this instance, however, we know that Sugihara wasn't the only notable rescuer of that era whose early home life incorporated human diversity. But Samuel and Pearl Oliner (1988) found that European Gentiles who harbored Jews from the Nazis were especially likely to report close childhood associations with people of different social classes and religions as they were growing up. Moreover, rescuers felt a sense of similarity to a wider and more varied group of people than did nonrescuers. This expanded sense of "we" related to the rescuers' helpfulness not only during the war but also half a century later, when they were still helping a greater variety of people and causes (Midlarsky & Nemeroff, 1995; Oliner & Oliner, 1988). All this suggests a piece of advice for prospective parents who want their children to develop a broadly charitable nature: Give them positive contact in the home with individuals from a wide spectrum of backgrounds.

SITUATION   Similarity and Familiarity

Just as prior learning history can influence one's sense of "we," so can certain features of the immediate situation. For example, according to an evolutionary account of helping motivation, those situational factors associated with an especially important category of "we"—relatives—should lead to increased helping. Evidence regarding two such factors, similarity and familiarity, is consistent with the evolutionary view (Berger et al., 2001).

SIMILARITY   One way two people can estimate their degree of genetic relatedness is by assessing their degree of similarity (DeBruine, 2005; Rushton et al., 1984). This is true not only for physical characteristics but also for certain personality traits and

All in the family. The tendency to benefit similar others occurs even within families, where greater helping occurs between family members who resemble one another (Leek & Smith, 1989, 1991). According to these results, when deciding which of several individuals to call on for help, all other things equal, your best choice would be the one most similar to you in personality and appearance.

attitudes (Park & Schaller, 2005; Uslaner, 2008). If prosocial action is motivated by a (no doubt nonconscious) desire to promote one's own genetic survival, then people ought to assist others who are similar to them in appearance, personality, and attitudes. For example, people report that they would assign higher priorities for life-saving medical treatment to those who share their political attitudes (Furnham, 1996). People are even more likely to help others who have adopted a similar posture to theirs (van Baaren et al., 2004).

If it's true that similarity leads to helping, then it ought to be possible to convince others to help us by convincing them that we're alike. Indeed, such an approach may have saved many lives in another mysterious incident from World War II. Despite their alliance with Germany, the Japanese military government decided, against the protests of their Nazi allies, to shelter and sustain the Jews within their borders for the length of the war. The events surrounding that decision, as described by a variety of scholars (Kranzler, 1976; Ross, 1994; Tokayer & Swartz, 1979), offer fascinating corroboration of the similarity-helping relationship and indicate how victims can—with great personal benefit—arrange to include themselves in the helper's sense of "we."

Bridging Theory and Application:

Getting Help by Adjusting the Helper's Sense of "We"

After Sugihara signed exit visas for thousands of Jews (Levine, 1997), they became part of an even larger contingent of Jewish refugees concentrated in the Japanese-controlled city of Shanghai. Following the attack on Pearl Harbor, though, all refugee passage in and out of Shanghai ended abruptly, and the situation of the Jewish community there quickly became precarious. Japan, after all, was by then a full-fledged wartime conspirator with Adolph Hitler and had to avoid steps that might threaten the solidarity of its alliance with this virulent anti-Semite. Nevertheless, the Japanese government resisted Nazi pressures to annihilate the Shanghai Jews in early 1942 and remained adamant in that resistance through the end of the war. Why?

According to Marvin Tokayer (Tokayer & Swartz, 1979, 178–181), the former chief rabbi of Tokyo, the answer is linked to a little-known set of events that took place several months earlier. The Nazis had sent to Tokyo Gestapo colonel Josef Meisinger, who began agitating for a policy of brutality toward the Jews under Japan's rule. Wanting to hear all sides, high-ranking members of Japan's military government called on the Jewish refugee community to send two leaders to a meeting that would significantly influence their future. The chosen representatives were both highly respected religious leaders, but they were respected in different ways. One, Rabbi Moses Shatzkes,

was renowned as an intensely studious man, one of the most brilliant religious scholars in Europe before the war. The other, Rabbi Shimon Kalisch, was much older and was known for his remarkable ability to understand basic human workings—a social psychologist of sorts.

When the two entered the meeting room, they and their translators found themselves in the company of some of the most powerful members of the Japanese High Command, who wasted little time in asking a pair of fateful questions: Why do our allies the Nazis hate you so much, and why should we resist their attempts to harm you? The scholar, Rabbi Shatzkes, was speechless. But Rabbi Kalisch's knowledge of human nature had equipped him to give, in one reply, the consummate answer to both questions. "Because," he said calmly, "we are Asian . . . *like you*."

Although brief, this assertion was inspired, because it made prominent two notions that stood to help the Jews by reshaping the Japanese officers' reigning sense of "we." First was a long-debated theory in Japan that tried to account for the remarkable resemblance between the characteristics of ancient Judaism and the Shinto religion of Japan. The theory was that at least some of the 10 "lost tribes" of Israel had traveled across Asia to Japan and had intermarried, mixing their beliefs and their blood, with the Japanese. The second point that Rabbi Kalisch's statement was designed to underscore was that, according to the Nazi's own racial claims, the German Master Race was genetically different from the "inferior" Asian peoples. With a single, penetrating observation, then, he sought to reframe the officers' conceptions of "we"—so that now it was the Jews who were included and the Nazis who were (self-proclaimedly) not.

Witnesses to the meeting report that the old rabbi's assertion had a powerful effect on the Japanese officers. After a lengthy silence, the most senior military official rose and granted the reassurance the rabbis had hoped to bring home to their community: "Go back to your people. Tell them . . . we will provide for their safety and peace. You have nothing to fear while in Japanese territory." And so it was.

The evolutionary perspective on helping also predicts some intricacies in the ways aid is provided. That is, the tendency to favor kin isn't expected to be equal under all circumstances. For instance, if people help closely related others to ensure the survival of more of their own genes, the preference for helping close kin should be strongest when survival is at issue. In a test of this hypothesis, Eugene Burnstein, Chris Crandall, and Shinobo Kitayama (1994) asked U.S. and Japanese college students how willing they would be to help others when the help involved either rescuing them from a burning building or picking up an item for them at the store. Generally, the closer the relative, the greater the willingness to help. However, in both cultures, this tendency to favor close relatives was much more pronounced when the need was life threatening.

Combatants in the battle to influence Japanese policy toward Jews. Nazi officials were unsuccessful in persuading the Japanese High Command to treat the Jews under its control as the Nazis wished. One reason may be the recognition, highlighted at a crucial meeting with Jewish leaders, of the common Asian origins of the Japanese and the Jews. Those Jewish leaders—Rabbis, Kalisches, and Shatzkes (pictured with their translators on the day of the meeting)—sought to include their people in the Japanese officials' sense of genetic "we" and to exclude the Nazis in this respect.

FAMILIARITY Because individuals typically live with their relatives or have had frequent contact with them, familiarity can also serve as a cue for similar heredity. Consider, for instance, that the word *familiar* is virtually the same as *familial*. The longer two siblings live together, the more likely they are to treat each other altruistically (Lieberman & Lobel, 2012). Of course, a great deal of prior exposure to another doesn't guarantee genetic overlap. But it doesn't have to. If familiarity with another is even roughly associated with shared genes, then, by the logic of evolutionary psychology, assisting that other should tend to benefit the helper's genes and should result in increased aid (Dovidio, Piliavin, Schroeder, & Penner, 2006; Rushton, 1989). Support for this idea exists on both fronts.

First, in both human and animal societies, the more related individuals are, the more contact they have with one another (Hames, 1979; Rushton, 1989). Second, people are more willing to help the others—even the *type* of others—with whom they are familiar (Burger et al., 2001). Once again, we can look for evidence in the rich data of Samuel and Pearl Oliner (1988) on rescuers of Jews during World War II. Compared to those who did not help, rescuers were more likely to have had contact with Jews before the war in their neighborhoods, at work, and in their friendships. Fundraisers report a similar phenomenon: People are much more willing to help with a problem if they know someone afflicted with it. As Thomas Schelling (1968, p. 130) has said, "If we know people, we care." This may be the case because, as social psychologists have shown, the more we know another, the more similarity we assume (Cunningham, 1986; Kenny & Kashy, 1994).

This relationship between familiarity and aid may provide another clue to the causes of Sempo Sugihara's helping actions. In the months before his decision to sacrifice his career to assist Jewish refugees, Sugihara came into contact with an 11-year-old Jewish boy, Solly Ganor, whose aunt owned a shop near the Japanese consulate. During those months, Sugihara befriended Solly, giving him a coin or contributing to the boy's stamp collection whenever they met. On one such occasion, Sugihara dismissed

Solly's expression of thanks, telling the boy, "Consider me your uncle." To this Solly responded, "Since you are my uncle, you should come Saturday to our Hanukkah party. The whole family will be there." At that party, Sugihara met not only Solly's immediate family but also a distant relative from Poland who described the horrors of Nazi occupation and asked for Sugihara's assistance in getting out of Europe. Sugihara replied that he was not then in a position to help but that perhaps he would be in the future. That opportunity to save his new friends came eight months later: The first exit visas Sugihara authorized were those of Solly's family (Ganor, 1995, p. 35).

INVESTIGATION

Consider the following terrible dilemma: Two people are drowning before your eyes, and you are able to rescue only one. The first is a close friend you have always liked and gotten along with. The other is a close relative—a brother or sister—with whom you've always had a difficult, conflict-filled relationship. Which would you save? Try to understand why.

Quick Quiz

1 Which of the following are actions that can improve one's own inclusive fitness?
   a. Taking in your brother's family after your brother loses his job and can no longer pay the rent.
   b. Making an anonymous donation to your local food bank.
   c. Giving your neighbor a ride to work on a cold morning after he was kind enough to lend you his snow blower.
   d. Donating a kidney to a sick little girl you saw featured on the nightly news.
   e. (a) and (c) only

2 A helper's sense of "we" can be expanded by:
   a. Physical attractiveness.
   b. Familiarity.
   c. Similarity.
   d. (b) and (c) only

Gaining Social Status and Approval

LO 9.5 Discuss what the social responsibility norm requires people to do.

LO 9.6 Identify three ways bystanders in emergencies influence the decision to help.

LO 9.7 Explain when and why men and women differ in their helping behavior.

Besides genetic and material advantages, a less direct kind of benefit can flow to helpers. Because helpfulness is viewed positively across human cultures (Dovidio, Piliavin, Schroeder, & Penner, 2006), those who help can elevate their image in the eyes of others. Donald Campbell (1975) argued that, in order to encourage assistance in situations that don't offer material or genetic rewards to the helper, all human societies provide *social* rewards to those who help. These social rewards usually take the form of increased liking and approval. In addition, prosocial acts can also enhance the helper's perceived power and status in the community (Hardy & Van Vugt, 2006). People who have been thinking about status are more likely to make sacrifices for the common good, such as choosing green products or hybrid cars, and they do so especially when they think other people will know about their beneficence (Griskevicius, Tybur, & van den Bergh, 2010).

The tactic of giving to increase social standing is not unique to corporate cultures. In his monumental work *The Gift*, French anthropologist Marcel Mauss (1967) detailed the importance and universality of gift giving in human social organization. However, despite the pervasiveness of the process, it can appear in a striking variety of forms. One of the most spectacular forms occurs in the practice of *potlatching*—a tribal ritual celebration in which the host gives away enormous quantities of goods to his guests, often going broke or into debt in the process.

What could account for this extreme form of gift giving? The answer currently favored by most anthropologists is that the custom functioned to establish and validate rank in the societies. That is, anyone who could accumulate and *expend* great wealth could rightfully assert a claim to distinguished social status (Cole & Chaikin, 1990; McAndrew, 2002). What was actually valued, then, was not wealth but social standing that could be claimed and legitimated by the giving away of wealth. When viewed in this light, the tribal chiefs of old were not so different from today's business chieftains who give generous corporate donations so that they and their companies will be perceived as more powerful and successful by their own rivals (Galaskiewicz, 1985).

Social Responsibility: The Helping Norm

The norms of a society often powerfully influence behavior. As we discussed in Chapter 6, there are two kinds of social norms: *descriptive norms* define what's typically done, whereas *injunctive norms* define what's typically approved and disapproved. Both kinds of norms affect helping: People are more likely to give assistance when they have evidence that others help and that others approve of help (Warburton & Terry, 2000). However, it's the approval of prosocial action that seems most relevant to the goal of gaining status and social approval. The Polish social psychologist Janusz Reykowski (1980) demonstrated the power of expected social approval in an experiment done on Bulgarian college students who were told, falsely, that admiration for altruists at their school was low. Later, when asked for assistance, they were far less likely to comply than those who had not received this information about their school's norms.

The most general helping norm is the **social responsibility norm** (Berkowitz, 1972). It states, rather broadly, that we should help those who are dependent on us for help. As we'll see, several factors affect when the social responsibility norm guides a person's decision to help. One of the most heavily researched factors is whether others (bystanders) are present when a helping opportunity arises, especially if the opportunity involves emergency aid. These bystanders can influence the action of the social responsibility norm—and, consequently, the decision to help—by serving in three ways: as sources of help, as sources of information about whether helping is required, and as sources of approval or disapproval of helping action. (See Figure 9.2.)

Potlatch power. By giving away vast stores of goods, highborn members of Northwest Pacific Coast tribes got something they wanted more—legitimacy for their claims to rank and status. At one potlatch, blankets were piled and ready for giving.

Social responsibility norm The societal rule that people should help those who need them to help.

Figure 9.2   Effects of onlookers on decisions to help

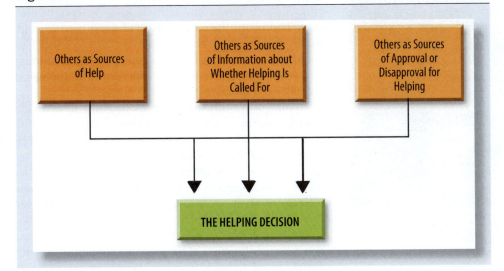

Others can affect the decision to provide assistance in three ways.

Catherine Genovese. Prior to Catherine Genovese's murder on a dark New York City street, social psychologists had spent relatively little time in the investigation of helping. But the special circumstances of her death—38 people had watched it occur over a span of 35 minutes without lifting a finger to help—brought a new research question into prominence: What are the factors that enhance and inhibit the tendency to help?

Bystander effect The tendency of a bystander to be less likely to help in an emergency if there are other onlookers present.

Diffusion of responsibility The tendency for each group member to dilute personal responsibility for acting by spreading it among all other group members.

BYSTANDERS AS SOURCES OF HELP In the early years of experimental social psychology, the study of antisocial behavior (prejudice, conflict, aggression) was given more weight than the study of prosocial activity. Perhaps because of the still-vivid horrors of World War II, social psychologists appeared more concerned with understanding and reducing the evil within human conduct than in understanding and enhancing the good. That changed decisively in the mid-1960s, however—due, in no small measure, to a single event. At 3 A.M. on March 13, 1964, a young woman named Catherine Genovese was knifed to death by a man she didn't know on the street outside her apartment in New York City. News of the killing created a national uproar (Rosenthal, 1964).

Why? Because, according to a front page story in the *New York Times*, the crime had been a long, loud, *public* event, observed by 38 of Genovese's neighbors who, roused from their beds by the commotion, peered down on it from the safety of their apartment windows. On the original account, not only had no one helped, no one had even bothered to call the police until after Ms. Genovese's attacker had done her in.

Later investigators cast doubt on details of the Kitty Genovese case (Manning, Levine, & Collins, 2007). Whether it was exaggerated or not, the story had an impact on the field of social psychology, and led to a whole line of research on bystander apathy. In the swirl of publicity that followed a front page *New York Times* story, social scientists found themselves pressed—by students in classrooms, by reporters in interviews, even by friends at cocktail parties—for an answer to the same question: Why don't people help one another? After one such party, two New York–based social psychologists, Bibb Latané and John Darley (1970), sat down to analyze the mystery. In the process, they hit upon an explanation that everyone else had missed: Although previous accounts had stressed that no action was taken *even though* several people had looked on, Latané and Darley suggested that no one had helped precisely *because* there were so many witnesses—something they labeled the **bystander effect** (Fischer et al., 2011). With so many observers on the scene, it was possible for each to think that someone else, perhaps someone more qualified, would help. According to Latané and Darley, responsibility for aid may be spread so thinly among a group of onlookers—a process called **diffusion of responsibility**—that none of them feels the obligation to act, and so no one does.

To test their idea, Darley and Latané (1968) did the first of many studies examining how the number of bystanders to an emergency affects the likelihood that anyone would help. Over an intercom system, New York City college students heard another student having what seemed to be an epileptic seizure. The percentage of subjects who left their private cubicles to give help declined dramatically with the number of other subjects who could help. If subjects thought they alone had heard the seizure, 85% of them tried to help. If they knew, however, that just one other subject had heard the seizure, assistance dropped to 62%; adding four fellow subjects to the intercom network suppressed helping even more, to 31%.

What does diffusion of responsibility have to do with the norm of social responsibility? Recall that the norm obliges us to help those who are dependent on *us* for help. So if the presence of others diffuses helping responsibility to those others, the victim automatically becomes less dependent on *us* for aid, which weakens our obligation to help according to the norm. Support for this view comes from research showing that imagining being with others not only reduced the tendency to help, it also reduced the sense of personal accountability among the potential helpers (Garcia, Weaver, Moskowitz, & Darley, 2002).

Victim? At times like this one, when the need for emergency aid is unclear, even genuine victims are unlikely to be helped in a crowd. Think how, if you were the next passerby in this situation, you might be influenced by the first passerby to believe that no aid was called for.

BYSTANDERS AS SOURCES OF INFORMATION ABOUT HELPING Besides diffusion of responsibility, Latané and Darley suggested another reason why onlookers might suppress emergency assistance: Their inaction may reduce the chance that a genuine emergency will be interpreted as one. In many cases, it is not clear to observers that an emergency is occurring; and when people are uncertain, they are reluctant to act (Bastardi & Shafir, 1998; Fischer et al., 2011; Tversky & Shafir, 1992a, 1992b). Instead, they look around for information to help them define the situation. In a developing emergency, bystanders become sources of information for one another. Each looks at the others for clues about how to react but does so rather quickly and subtly, with unconcerned glances, so as not to appear flustered or alarmist. As a result, everyone notices that everyone else is calmly *failing* to act, which leads all to the conclusion that there must be no real emergency. This, according to Latané and Darley (1968) is the phenomenon of **pluralistic ignorance**, in which each person in a grouping decides that because nobody is concerned, nothing's wrong. Could this state of affairs contribute to what—on the surface—appear to be shameful levels of bystander "apathy" in modern society? It appears so.

In one study, researchers pumped smoke through a vent into a laboratory where subjects were filling out a questionnaire (Latané & Darley, 1968). Subjects who were alone went to report the smoke 75% of the time, whereas subjects in groups of three did so only 38% of the time. But, by far, the danger was reported least often, only 10% of the time, by groups of three that contained one true subject and a pair of experimental confederates instructed to act as though there was no cause for alarm. The behavior of the true subjects was remarkable: Even as clouds of smoke filled the air, they worked dutifully at their questionnaires, coughing, rubbing their eyes, and waving the fumes away from their faces—but not reporting the problem. When asked why not, they indicated that they were sure the smoke signaled no fire, no real crisis. Instead, they defined the smoke in nonemergency terms: steam, smog, air conditioning vapor, or, in one case, "truth gas" intended to extract honest answers to the questionnaire!

It appears, then, that multiple bystanders, especially if they're passive, can reduce emergency aid by creating a shared illusion that nothing's wrong. Related support for this conclusion comes from studies showing that onlookers who act alarmed, rather than placid, increase the likelihood of such aid (Wilson, 1976). Consistently, later research finds that bystanders are more likely to help when it is clear that the victim is in danger, even when helping may mean more danger to the bystanders (Fischer et al., 2011).

BYSTANDERS AS SOURCES OF APPROVAL OR DISAPPROVAL There's a third way others can influence the workings of the social responsibility norm: by approving or disapproving of the decision to help. An individual who conforms to the norm and helps another in need usually gets the approval of observers. That is why in most cases, people assume that their helping acts will be socially rewarded (Bickman, 1971; Schwartz & Gottlieb, 1976). It is also why people are more likely to help when they think that others can identify them and their helping efforts (Schwartz & Gottlieb, 1976, 1980; van Bommel et al., 2012). But, as we've seen, some situations contain cues—for example, visibly passive bystanders—that make it appear that aid may not be appropriate. In these situations, helping is reduced, especially if the potential helper is identifiable to bystanders (Schwartz & Gottlieb, 1980). Thus being identifiable can either increase or decrease the tendency to help depending on whether others in the setting do or don't seem to favor the idea of aid.

Fear of social disapproval frequently suppresses assistance in one especially troubling type of potential emergency—a physical confrontation between a man and a woman. Lance Shotland and Margret Straw suspected that witnesses to such confrontations may not help because they think their intervention might be unwelcome interference in a "lovers' quarrel." Indeed, this was how some of the bystanders in the Catherine Genovese incident explained their inaction (Rosenthal, 1964). To test their hypothesis, Shotland and Straw exposed study participants to a staged fight between a man and a woman. When there were no cues as to the sort of relationship between the pair, the great majority of male and female participants (nearly 70%) assumed that the two were romantically involved; only 4% thought they were complete strangers.

Pluralistic ignorance The mistaken impression on the part of group members that, because no one else is acting concerned, there is no cause for alarm.

To get help, you have to say the right thing. Observers of male–female confrontations often assume that the pair is romantically involved and that intervention would be unwanted or inappropriate. To combat this perception and get aid, the woman needs to shout "I don't know you!"

In other experiments in which there were cues that defined the combatants' relationship—the woman shouted either "I don't know why I ever married you" or "I don't know you"—Shotland and Straw (1976) uncovered an ominous reaction on the part of participants. Although the severity of the fight was identical, observers were less willing to help the married woman because they thought it was a private matter in which their intervention would be unwanted and embarrassing to all concerned.

Thus a woman caught up in a physical confrontation with a man should not expect to get bystander aid by simply shouting for release. Observers are likely to define the event as a domestic squabble and, with that definition in place, may well assume that helping would be socially inappropriate. Fortunately, Shotland and Straw's data suggest a way to overcome this problem: By loudly labeling her attacker a stranger—"I don't know you!"—a woman should greatly increase her chances for aid.

A more general piece of advice for anyone in need of emergency assistance is to recall the fundamental lesson of bystander intervention research: Observers fail to help not so much because they are unkind as because they are unsure. They are often unsure of whether helping is appropriate. If they decide that it is, they are often unsure that they are responsible for providing it. And if they decide that they are, they are often unsure of how to help. If you were to find yourself in a crisis surrounded by onlookers, your best strategy would be to dispel these basic uncertainties for them. State clearly that you need aid, assign the principal responsibility for helping to one person, and describe the kind of assistance you require: "I need help! You, sir, in the blue jacket, call an ambulance."

PERSON Desire for Approval

If Campbell (1975) is right that human societies reward altruists with praise and honor to increase prosocial behavior, then those individuals who desire social approval should be more likely to help. In one study, college students first completed a personality scale measuring their need for approval and then had a chance to donate money to a good cause (Satow, 1975). Overall, the students who most desired approval from others gave more money. There was an important exception, however: When the donation was given in private, those who valued approval were no longer more generous. It seems that people having a high need for approval aren't especially kind. Rather, they are simply more desirous of the esteem that comes with the appearance of kindness.

SITUATION Effects of Those around Us

Although norms are said to be always in place within a culture, they're not always in mind. That is, an individual is more likely to obey a norm immediately after something has made the norm salient or prominent (Cialdini, 2012; Kallgren, Reno, & Cialdini, 2000). Several studies have shown this to be the case for helping: The more people are reminded of the social responsibility norm, the more they help (Harvey & Enzle, 1981; Nelson & Horton, 2005). Consistently, when people are made self-aware, by a camera or the use of their names, the presence of other bystanders can actually increase helping (van Bommel et al., 2012).

HELPING MODELS The sight of others acting in a socially responsible manner—by dropping money in a Salvation Army kettle, for instance—can spur an observer to help in two ways. First, the observation of others' behavior is frequently the way that people, especially children, learn appropriate conduct (Bandura, 1977). Exposing children to prosocial television programming, for example, teaches them to be more cooperative and generous (Forge & Phemister, 1987; Hearold, 1986). In addition to this teaching function, a prosocial model can also serve as a reminder, bringing the norm to consciousness in adults who may not have been thinking about helpfulness until they came across an instance of it. In a classic study by James Bryan and Mary Ann Test (1967), Los Angeles motorists were more likely to stop and help the driver of a disabled car if they'd witnessed another motorist doing so a quarter mile before.

POPULATION DENSITY Compared to rural areas, cities are decidedly less helpful places—a fact that is true around the world (Amato, 1983; Smith & Bond, 1998). Robert Levine (2003) assessed helping tendencies in 36 U.S. cities; see Table 9.1. He found that it was the density rather than the sheer size of a city that crucially affected helping. The more closely packed the population, the less assistance was given to strangers. One reason for this is that, to deal with the stimulus overload and stress caused by a dense population, urbanites often close themselves off and fail to see the needs of those around them (Evans & Lepore, 1993; Milgram, 1970). As a result, the helping norm, which requires them to give assistance to those *in need*, doesn't stimulate aid.

Let's role. Men are more likely to engage in heroic forms of aid, which are consistent with the masculine gender role.

INTERACTION Gender and Help

Helping often takes place as a result of interactions between factors in the person and in the situation that are associated with the goal of gaining status and approval. Research on gender and helping offers one such illustration.

Most people view women as the more helpful sex; they're rated as kinder, more compassionate, and more devoted to others' welfare than men (Ruble, 1983). What's more, there's good agreement on this point around the world; in over 90% of cultures studied, the traits of kindness, soft-heartedness, and helpfulness are more associated with women than with men (Williams & Best, 1990). It seems odd, then, that two sources of evidence suggest the reverse.

Table 9.1 Helping in Various U.S. Cities

Robert Levine (2003) assessed helping tendencies in 36 U.S. cities and ranked them on the basis of six separate measures of aid—willingness to: help a blind person cross a street, make change for a quarter, pick up a dropped pen, mail a lost letter, pick up magazines dropped by a disabled person, and contribute to the United Way. Population density, rather than size, of a city was crucially related to helping. The denser the population, the less the helping. The following table shows the five most helpful and the five least helpful cities.

Rank	Most helpful cities	Rank	Least helpful cities
1	Rochester, NY	32	Philadelphia, PA
2	Houston, TX	33	Fresno, CA
3	Nashville, TN	34	Los Angeles, CA
4	Memphis, TN	35	New York, NY
5	Knoxville, TN	36	Paterson, NJ

Source: Levine, R. V. (2003). The kindness of strangers. *American Scientist*, 91, 226–233.

The first type of evidence comes from the lists of helpers in our society who have exerted heroic efforts on behalf of others. For over a century, for instance, the Carnegie Hero Commission has regularly awarded medals to ordinary citizens who distinguish themselves "in saving, or attempting to save, the life of a fellow being." Although women have been eligible from the outset, more than 90% of the over 7,000 Carnegie medalists have been men. The second kind of evidence comes from social psychological studies of aid. Extensive reviews of these studies have found a decided tendency for men to help more often (Eagly & Crowley, 1986; Piliavin & Unger, 1985). What are we to make of the seeming inconsistency between what most people believe and what these two sources of information reveal about the helpfulness of men and women?

To solve the puzzle, we have to recognize first that, besides biological differences that may affect how helping takes place (Dabbs, 2000), males and females are socialized differently from one another (Burn, 1996; Gilligan, 1982). From childhood, men and women learn that different kinds of behavior are expected and admired in them—for example, men should be gallant and strong whereas women should be caring and gentle. These expectations about what's masculine and feminine constitute the gender roles of a society, and they can lead women and men to help under different sets of conditions. It's expected, for instance, that men will engage in typically male activities. This is one reason men are more likely to help others with car trouble (Penner, Dertke, & Achenbach, 1973), even when the aid only involves making a phone call for assistance (Gaertner & Bickman, 1971). Conversely, it is expected that women will engage in typically female activities. John Dovidio (1993) and his students provided a simple but telling illustration of this general point when, at a Laundromat, they asked for help either carrying or folding some clothes: Women were more willing to fold the laundry, and men were more willing to carry it.

Gender roles specify which *traits* are considered masculine and feminine, and these traits can affect when and how helping occurs. According to Alice Eagly and Maureen Crowley (1986), masculine helping traits are quite different from feminine helping traits. To fit with gender roles, masculine assistance should be daring, forceful, and directed toward anyone who's deserving—strangers included; feminine assistance, on the other hand, should be nurturing, supportive, and focused primarily on the needs of relationship partners such as family and friends. From this perspective, we can see why many more men than women are honored by the Carnegie Hero Commission: Heroism fits with the masculine—but not the feminine—gender role, as a hero is courageous and bold and willing to rescue nameless victims. Indeed, the Commission's bylaws specifically discriminate against anyone who saves a family member—that's not seen as heroic enough.

But does this gender-role explanation account for why men help more than women in social psychological experiments? Eagly and Crowley (1986) think it does. They point out that most helping experiments, especially those done in the early years, exposed subjects to emergency situations and victims with whom they had no prior relationship. No wonder, Eagly and Crowley say, that men help more than women in these studies: Assistance under these conditions requires bold, direct action on behalf of strangers, which is consistent principally with the masculine gender role.

Good support for this analysis comes from studies of types of aid more consistent with the feminine gender role, such as the willingness to provide emotional support and informal counseling on personal problems (Aries & Johnson, 1983; Johnson & Aries, 1983; Otten, Penner, & Waugh, 1988); in these studies, women helped more than men. Even studies of emergency aid—which show the usual tendency for men to help (strangers) more than do women—find the reverse when the person in need is a friend (McGuire, 1994) or when the help involves empathic tendencies (Becker & Eagly, 2004). However, the way that women provide emergency assistance is likely to be more indirect (summoning help) than it is for men, who tend to provide the help themselves (Senneker & Hendrick, 1983). Thus, the answer to the question "Who is likely to help more, women or men?" depends on whether the required help conforms to the socially approved feminine or masculine gender role.

Why do you suppose the gender roles regarding helping differ for men and women? Through what processes do you think these differences emerged?

Quick Quiz

1 According to anthropologists, what is the ultimate goal of potlatching?
   a. To take care of everyone in the tribe
   b. To make up for losses suffered from devastating floods and storms
   c. To increase the host's social standing
   d. To increase the host's chance of joining his ancestors in the afterlife

2 In what ways do bystanders influence the decision to help in emergencies?
   a. Bystanders are sources of approval or disapproval for helping.
   b. Bystanders tend to increase an individual's sense of personal responsibility to help.
   c. Bystanders act as sources of information about whether aid is required.
   d. All of the above
   e. (a) and (c)

3 Which of the following are true statements about differences in the helping behavior of men and women?
   a. Women are equally likely to help strangers, friends, and relatives, whereas men are slightly more likely to help strangers.
   b. Men are more likely to offer direct assistance to motorists with car trouble, whereas women are more likely to offer to call for assistance.
   c. Men are more likely to offer support that is direct, heroic, or otherwise consistent with the masculine gender role.
   d. All of the above

Managing Self-Image

LO 9.8 Understand how personal norms and religious and ethical codes influence helping.

LO 9.9 Explain how labeling and self-focus raise our motivation to help.

LO 9.10 Discuss why we sometimes decide not to offer help or receive help from others.

Any meaningful action we take can influence how we think of ourselves (Schlenker & Trudeau, 1990; Vallacher & Wegner, 1985). Prosocial action is no exception to this rule. For example, 50 years after the fact, Elizabeth Midlarsky and Robin Nemeroff (1995) found that the self-esteem of people who had been rescuers during the Holocaust was still being elevated by the help they had provided. Indeed, special or repeated acts of assistance cause people not just to have higher self-esteem but also to view themselves as more altruistic thereafter (Cialdini, Eisenberg, Shell, & McCreath, 1987). Perhaps this helps explain a puzzling, but welcome, turn of events observed by U.S. charity organizations at the end of 2005. During that year, an unprecedented series of disasters—including Hurricanes Katrina and Rita along the American Gulf Coast, a horrific earthquake in Pakistan, a tsunami in Southeast Asia that killed 230,000, and warfare in Sudan that left thousands homeless—generated an equally unprecedented outpouring of aid from the American people. Remarkably, none of this giving produced the usual "donor fatigue" that charities have come to expect immediately after a successful fundraising campaign when donors are reluctant to contribute again for a time (Strom, 2006). Instead, yearend holiday giving in 2005 proved as strong as or stronger than ever (Crary, 2005). How might we account for the lack of donor fatigue in this instance? Ironically, it may have been the *extended* string of tragedies draining American wallets that was key. At the end of this long series of helping acts, Americans considering a holiday donation may not have thought to themselves, "I've already given," but rather, "I'm a giver."

Because prosocial behavior can affect how we view ourselves, we can use it to manage self-image (self-concept) in two principal ways: We can use it both to *enhance* and to *verify* our self-definitions (Madon et al., 2008; Swann, 1990). If you felt in need of an ego boost, you could decide to do someone a good turn and—like those who helped during the Holocaust—you could improve your self-image in the process. Or if your sense of self already included an altruistic component—let's say you've always thought of yourself as charitable or generous—you might help a needy person to confirm that view; here, the goal would not be to enhance your self-concept but to verify it (Grube & Piliavin, 2000; Penner & Finkelstein, 1998). Beth Stark and Kay Deaux (1994) found support for this self-verification process in a study of volunteer workers in a prisoner rehabilitation program. The factor that best predicted whether a worker wanted to continue in the program was how much he or she felt volunteering was "an important reflection of who I am." In the following section, we explore a pair of factors in people that help them define who they are and that affect prosocial actions accordingly.

PERSON Personal Norms and Religious Codes

Helpful individuals frequently cite their personal beliefs and values as spurring their decisions to help. A study of charitable giving and volunteering in the United States found that 87% of the people surveyed said that a reason they contributed was that it was consistent with their existing personal values; no other factor was cited as often (Hodgkinson & Weitzman, 1990); see Figure 9.3. A similar pattern emerged when Mark Snyder and Allen Omoto (1992) asked 116 volunteer workers at an AIDS center why they decided to help; by far the largest number of volunteers (87%) cited the connection of the work to their existing personal values.

Personal norms The internalized beliefs and values that combine to form a person's inner standards for behavior.

If, as it appears, the beliefs and values that form a person's self-image can motivate that person toward prosocial behavior, it should be the case that those who have most fully internalized (incorporated) prosocial beliefs and values into their self-image should be most motivated to help (Reed & Aquino, 2003). For evidence in this regard, let's examine the influence of two kinds of internalized beliefs and values on helping: personal norms and religious codes.

PERSONAL NORMS According to Shalom Schwartz (1977), internalized beliefs and values link together to form an individual's **personal norms**, which represent the individual's internal standards for particular conduct. A personal norm differs from a social norm in two crucial ways. First, in the case of personal norms, the standards for what is appropriate behavior are inside the individual, not outside in moral rules of the culture. Second, approval and disapproval of relevant behavior also come from inside rather than outside the person; that is, the "pats on the back" (for behavior that meets the standards) and the "slaps on the wrist" (for behavior that violates the standards) are self-administered. So if your personal norm for helping influenced whether you gave a dollar to a homeless person, it would be because you first looked inside rather than outside yourself for guidance and, afterward, your reward would come from acting in accord with your own rules, not the society's. In general, research has supported Schwartz's thinking. People who have

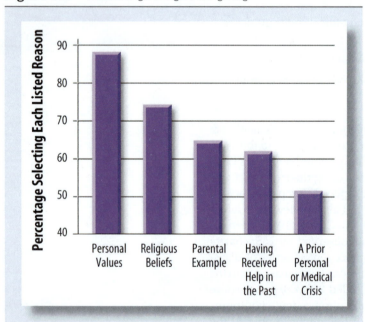

Figure 9.3 Reasons givers give for giving

Hodgkinson and Weitzman (1990) gave charitable individuals a list of personal background reasons for helping and asked them to indicate all that applied to them.

Source: Hodgkinson, V. A., & Weitzman, M. S. (1990). Giving and volunteering in the United States. Washington, DC: Independent Sector.

strong personal norms regarding such actions as giving blood, carpooling, or engaging in curbside recycling programs are more likely to engage in these behaviors (Harland, Staats, & Wilke, 2007; Hopper & Nielsen, 1991; Schwartz & Howard, 1982).

RELIGIOUS AND ETHICAL CODES Our self-images are sometimes influenced by the characteristics of the groups to which we belong (Turner, Hogg, Oakes, & Reicher, 1987). Certain of these groups have codes of conduct that encourage prosocial action. All the great religions of the world, for example, include concern and sacrifice for others as important moral principles (Dovidio, Piliavin, Schroeder, & Penner, 2006). We might expect, therefore, more helping on the part of individuals who define themselves as religious. National surveys typically find just this effect; moreover, people whose commitment reflects itself in regular attendance at religious services are more charitable than those who don't attend regularly (Penner, 2002; Volunteering in the U.S., 2005).

More dramatic evidence of the role that religious self-definition can play in the decision to help comes from the simultaneously sobering and uplifting story of Reginald Denny. On April 29, 1992, a Los Angeles jury acquitted of all charges four white police officers who had dealt a severe, much publicized, videotaped beating to a black man, Rodney King. The jury's decision hit the streets of South Central Los Angeles like a torch, igniting a 72-hour riot among the area's mostly minority-group residents, who felt that justice had been perverted. Roving gangs looted, burned, and terrorized. Especially targeted were white residents or motorists who had, unknowingly, driven into this violent, racially charged environment. Reginald Denny, a truck driver, was one. Pulled from his 18-wheel rig, he was relentlessly kicked and beaten by a group of young black men who left him lying unconscious in an intersection—all of which was recorded by a news helicopter team hovering directly above, beaming live pictures of the scene into thousands of homes.

Ten minutes' drive from that intersection, Lei Yuille, an African American woman, saw the televised events and rushed to Denny's aid. There she was joined by two other rescuers, both African American men, spurred to help by the same broadcast images. One, Titus Murphy, was a burly engineer, big enough to defend Denny from further battering. The other, Bobby Green, was a fellow trucker who knew he would be needed to drive Denny's 18-wheeler to the hospital—which he did at speeds up to 55 miles per hour with Yuille in the cab and Murphy clinging to the running board while holding Denny fast. If we can partially interpret Murphy's and Green's decisions to intervene in terms of their physical abilities (Cramer, McMaster, Bartell, & Dragra, 1988), how are we to account for the actions of Lei Yuille, a slender, 38-year-old dietitian? What could have caused her to transcend the us-versus-them antagonisms of that day and rush to the aid of one of "them"? When asked, she described something about herself and her family that she felt provided the only answer necessary: "We are Christians," she said (Deutsch, 1993).

The mobilizing power of self-definition also contributes to a deeper understanding of Sempo Sugihara's benevolence toward the victims of Nazi persecution. Like Lei Yuille, Sugihara was once asked by an interviewer to explain his noble actions; like her, he answered by identifying a group membership that helped define him. "You must remember," he told the interviewer, "I come from a samurai family." Perplexed, because the samurai tradition in Japan had always been a warrior tradition, the interviewer pressed Sugihara further. He conceded that the samurai were noted for the destructive fury of their attacks on battlefield combatants. The beleaguered Jews who appeared at his door in July 1940 hardly presented an occasion for such confrontation. In contrast, they were defenseless prey. But there was a rule in the samurai code of conduct, *bushido*, that applied in this case: "When a wounded bird flies into a samurai's coat, he is honor-bound to protect it. He must not throw it to the cat" (M. Tokayer, personal communication, May 19, 1994). In sum, our actions often flow from our conceptions of who we are or who we wish to be. When these existing or desired self-concepts require helpfulness, people in need frequently benefit (Shariff & Norenzayan, 2007).

Harm versus help—not a black-and-white choice. Reginald Denny is kicked and beaten beside his truck while a helicopter pilot records his plight. Lei Yuille is shown at a subsequent press conference, where she explained that her decision to help flowed from her religious self-conception.

SITUATION   Labeling and Self-focus

If it is true that a prosocial self-image spurs people to help, it ought to be the case that any situational factor that reminds or convinces people of their prosocial nature should raise their motivation to help. Two such factors have been shown to work in this fashion: labeling and self-focus.

LABELING EFFECTS   Social theorists have long recognized that one way we decide who we are on the inside is to look outside ourselves to the reactions of others. Charles Horton Cooley (1922) proposed the notion of the "looking glass self," the idea that our self-images are greatly influenced by how others see us. Sociologists have used this perspective to explain how negative social labels—calling someone a deviant or a criminal—could create future antisocial behavior (Becker, 1963; Schur, 1971). Psychologists, however, have been more interested in examining the impact of positive social labels on prosocial behavior. For example, Joan Grusec and her colleagues (1978) found that labeling children as kind and helpful led these children to donate, anonymously, more of their experimental prizes to other children; furthermore, three weeks later, children labeled in this manner were still more willing to aid others (Grusec & Redler, 1980). Prosocial labels work on adults, too. One to two weeks after hearing themselves described as generous and charitable, New Haven, Connecticut, residents were more willing to give a donation to the Multiple Sclerosis Society (Kraut, 1973).

SELF-FOCUS   Because most of us value helping (Dovidio, Piliavin, Schroeder, & Penner, 2006), it stands to reason that situational factors that focus us inside, on that personal value, should increase our helping efforts. Researchers have devised several creative techniques for getting subjects to focus on themselves—filling out a biographical questionnaire, posing for a photograph, watching themselves on closed-circuit TV, looking in a mirror—all of which have led these self-focused subjects to help more (Abbate et al., 2006; Gibbons & Wicklund, 1982; Verplanken & Holland, 2002). For instance, Claudia Hoover, Elizabeth Wood, and Eric Knowles (1983) found, first, that pedestrians who were stopped and asked to pose for a photograph (as part of a student's photography project) became more self-focused, as measured by the number of first-person pronouns (*I, me*) they used in an interview afterward. Second, pedestrians who had posed for the photograph were more helpful in picking up envelopes dropped by a passerby than participants who hadn't posed for the photograph.

Oddly, though, some research has shown that self-focusing procedures can also decrease helping (Gibbons & Wicklund, 1982; Rogers et al., 1982; Verplanken &

Holland, 2002). How can we explain this seeming contradiction? The key is to recognize that focusing on oneself doesn't guarantee that one's value for helping will stand out. Suppose you just failed a test and something—let's say the presence of a mirror—caused you to focus attention on yourself. Chances are that, even if a helping opportunity arose, your internal focus would not be concentrated on your personal value for helping; more likely, it would be concentrated on your concern and frustration at failing the test. Thus we might expect that when you're preoccupied with a personal problem, self-focus would orient you to your problem and away from your value for helping, making aid less likely. However, if you had no major personal problem to deal with while you were self-focused, and you encountered a salient, legitimate helping opportunity, you should orient to your internal helping values, making aid more likely (Froming, Nasby, & McManus, 1998). In fact, this is exactly the pattern of results found in a study done at the University of Texas by Frederick Gibbons and Robert Wicklund (1982). The presence of a mirror decreased the helpfulness of subjects who thought they had scored poorly on a test, but it increased the helpfulness of those who thought they had done fine and who, consequently, had no absorbing self-concern to distract them from helping issues.

Overall, what Gibbons and Wicklund's (1982) research demonstrates is that assistance is more frequent when self-focus is combined with the presence of a prominent, legitimate need for aid—because such a need will direct the internal focus toward one's helping values. When the need for aid is not salient or legitimate, however, or when there is some absorbing personal problem, self-focus will not lead to helping because the focus—although internal—will not be directed toward one's helping values (see Figure 9.4).

INTERACTION ## Deciding Not to Help Friends or to Seek Their Help

Frequently, to manage our self-images optimally through helping, we have to take into account features of the person we're helping and of the situation we're in. An illustration can be seen in a study done by Abraham Tesser and Jonathan Smith (1980), who

Figure 9.4   Self-focus and the decision to help

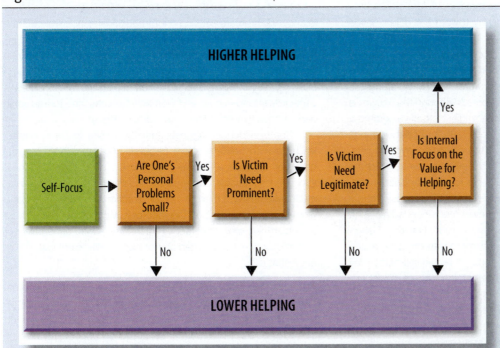

Self-focus is likely to lead to greater assistance primarily when that focus is directed to one's internal value for helping.

began with the hypothesis that we will try to help our friends succeed as long as that success doesn't damage how we view ourselves. They reasoned that our self-esteem is determined by comparing ourselves to those we feel are similar to us—friends rather than strangers. Therefore, although we won't mind if our friends do better than us on unimportant tasks, we won't want them to do better than us on dimensions that are important to our self-esteem.

To test this reasoning, Tesser and Smith first arranged for participants to do somewhat poorly on a verbal skills task, which was described either as a good indicator of "how well people can do in school" or as just a game "that doesn't tell us anything about the person." Next these participants got the chance to give clues to help a friend and a stranger perform the verbal skills task. As predicted, when the task was described as just a game—hence mostly irrelevant to participants' self-concepts—friends were given better clues than were strangers. Just the reverse occurred, however, when they thought the task measured intellectual ability and was relevant to self-esteem; in that case, friends got the poorer clues. Thus we don't always try to support a positive self-image by helping more. Depending on who the recipient is and on how we wish to view ourselves, we may actually try to maintain self-esteem by helping less (Pemberton & Sedikides, 2001).

As we see next, when taken to extremes, this desire to maintain self-esteem within the helping process can lead to self-damaging decisions.

Bridging Function and Dysfunction:

Failing to Seek Needed Help

Consider the following peculiar findings: In one study male participants were given the opportunity to request help on a mechanical task they could not solve, but fewer than 10% did (DePaulo, 1982). In Japan, Sweden, and the United States, individuals who received money from another liked that person more when he asked for repayment than when he did not (Gergen, Ellsworth, Maslach, & Seipel, 1975). Rather than appearing thankful, the citizens and governments of countries that receive foreign aid often respond with resentment and hostility toward the donor nation (Gergen & Gergen, 1983).

What are we to make of these curious tendencies to avoid asking for needed assistance, to prefer those who require repayment of their gifts, and to risk future help by criticizing the actions and intentions of current helpers? Although the answer is complex, much of it is captured in the single, instructive comment of French anthropologist Marcel Mauss (1967), "Charity wounds him who receives." The work of a trio of social psychologists, Jeffrey Fisher, Arie Nadler, and Bella DePaulo, has detailed the nature and location of the "wound"—it is to the self-concept and, more specifically, to the sense of self-esteem. These researchers have stressed that the receipt of aid, even much-needed aid, isn't always wholly positive (DePaulo & Fisher, 1980; Nadler & Fisher, 1986). In the process of relieving the immediate problem, assistance may, under certain circumstances, threaten self-esteem by implying that the recipient is incompetent, inadequate, or dependent. It is under these circumstances that—to maintain a positive self-concept—an individual may reject offers of needed help or minimize the value of that help (Bolger & Amarel, 2007). What are these circumstances? Nadler (1991) lists several.

Gender Beginning at an early age, in the majority of settings, males are less willing than females to request assistance (Addis

& Mahalik, 2003; Barbee et al., 1993; Barnett et al., 1990). Most observers explain this difference in terms of socialization rather than biology (Dovidio, Piliavin, Schroeder, & Penner, 2006; Nadler, 1991). That is, being independent and in control is more congruent with the traditional masculine (versus feminine) gender role. Differential training in self-sufficiency starts quite early, as a mother is typically less willing to respond to the cries of her own baby if it is a boy than if it is a girl (Ruddy & Adams, 1995). Thus, while still in infancy, children are socialized into traditional gender-role behavior, and little boys begin learning to be "little men." To avoid violating this learned conception of masculinity, then, males may refrain from requesting aid. Support for this view comes from research showing that the help-seeking difference between the sexes is especially strong in men and women who subscribe to traditional gender roles (Nadler, Maler, & Friedman, 1984).

Some evidence suggests that the desire to be in control leads men to perceive more frequently that they have no real need for assistance (Bruder-Mattson & Hovanitz, 1990); thus, they see less reason to request it. This may help explain the infamous reluctance of men to ask for directions when traveling and women's consternation in the face of it: What women define as a problem requiring assistance ("I think we're lost. Let's pull over and ask for directions"), men do not ("Lost? We're not lost. We're not lost at all").

Age The tendency to seek help drops at two points in our lives. The first occurs relatively early, around the age of seven or eight. According to Rita Shell and Nancy Eisenberg (1992), one reason for this shift is the development at that time of cognitive abilities that allow an enduring sense of self to be formed and threatened. It's not until after age seven or eight that children possess the mental capacity to recognize that the receipt of aid may imply lessened self-worth (Rholes & Ruble, 1986). Consequently, it's not until after that age that they begin protecting their self-worth by resisting some opportunities for help.

The second drop in help seeking occurs much later, after the age of 60. It seems strange that just as people enter a time when they may become more needful of assistance, they become particularly unwilling to ask for it (Brown, 1978; Veroff, 1981). Once again, however, we can solve the puzzle by recognizing the sometimes-threatening impact that assistance can have on self-esteem. The elderly report being especially concerned about maintaining personal control and self-sufficiency (Ryff, 1995). It makes sense, then, that they may reject opportunities for assistance that jeopardize their confidence that they still possess these qualities. Should you find yourself in the position of wishing to help the elderly, the existing research and thinking on the topic suggests that you do so in a way that preserves their independence and choice in the matter. Don't try to assume full control; instead, especially when their capacities are still intact, give elderly individuals responsibilities and options for managing the assistance (Reich & Zautra, 1995). Not only should they

be more likely to accept the aid but also they are likely to be happier and healthier as a result than those given little control (Heckhausen & Schulz, 1995; Langer, 1989a).

Self-esteem If you had to guess, would you say that high self-esteem or low self-esteem individuals are more reluctant to ask for assistance? Your first thought might be that people with low self-esteem would be more reluctant, to protect what little self-esteem they have. But research indicates the reverse. On academic tasks, in counseling groups, in alcohol treatment, and for a variety of other needs, it is high self-esteem people who avoid help seeking (Nadler, 1991; Wills & DePaulo, 1991). Why? Arie Nadler (1986) explains these findings in terms of the desire of such individuals to maintain their images of themselves as highly competent. In support of this explanation, studies have shown reduced help seeking among high self-esteem persons only in situations in which getting help would threaten a competent self-image—for example, when needing aid reflects low intelligence (Tessler & Schwartz, 1972).

Quick Quiz

1. Which of the following are examples of using prosocial behavior to verify one's self-definition?
   a. Sending out your monthly donation to the local children's hospital because you feel it's an important part of who you are.
   b. Refusing a charitable request because you do not feel the need to enhance your sense of generosity.
   c. Putting money in a Salvation Army pot because you want to be more generous around the holidays.
   d. None of the above

2. Which of the following statements about personal norms is not correct?
   a. Approval of relevant behavior comes from inside the individual.
   b. Personal norms are an individual's internal standards for appropriate behavior.
   c. Disapproval of one's behavior comes from inside the individual.
   d. Personal norms are correlated with initial intentions to contribute, but not with actual helping behavior.

3. Which of the following are factors that influence the likelihood that people will seek help?
   a. Low Self-Esteem—People with low self-esteem often avoid asking for help because they want to hold onto their remaining self-esteem.
   b. Adolescence—We see a sharp decrease in teenagers' tendency to seek help because during this period teenagers are most concerned with gaining independence.
   c. Gender—Males are less likely than females to request assistance, in line with traditional gender role socialization.
   d. All of the above

Managing Our Emotions and Moods

LO 9.11 Identify the three factors that, according to the arousal/cost–reward model, increase the chance that an observer will help a victim of an emergency.

LO 9.12 Describe when and why sadness leads to helping, according to the negative state relief model.

Help can be rewarding—and not just for the one who receives it. As we've seen, helpers can use it to produce material or genetic gain, to get social approval, and to support their self-image. There's another, even more direct way that help can benefit the helper—by removing the unpleasant state of arousal that comes from witnessing a victim's suffering. Think of the agitation and alarm you would feel if you came upon a family trapped and crying for rescue from the window of a burning building. The sight of their terrified faces, the sounds of their agonized pleas would no doubt trigger a powerful negative emotional reaction in you. For example, one brain-imaging study showed that observing another's pain activated the same regions of the brain governing emotional distress as are activated in the person actually experiencing the pain (Singer et al., 2004). Helping might be the most straightforward way for you to eliminate the emotional distress because it would eliminate the cause, the victims' plight.

Managing Emotional Arousal in Emergencies: The Arousal/Cost–Reward Model

This motivation for helping—to reduce the unpleasant arousal (distress) that we feel when observing substantial suffering or need—is the cornerstone of the **arousal/cost–reward model** developed by Jane Piliavin and her colleagues (Dovidio, Piliavin, Gaertner, Schroeder, & Clark, 1991; Piliavin et al., 1981) to explain helpfulness in emergencies. It proposes that observers of an emergency victim's plight will experience negative emotional arousal and will want to lend assistance in order to relieve this personal distress. According to the model, there are several conditions under which assistance should be most likely, all of which have received research support (see Figure 9.5).

Arousal/cost–reward model The view that observers of a victim's suffering will want to help to relieve their own personal distress.

1. *When the arousal is strong.* If negative arousal stimulates helping, the more an emergency generates such arousal in observers, the more helping it should produce. Several studies, using both physiological and verbal measures of arousal, have

Figure 9.5 The arousal/cost–reward model of emergency helping

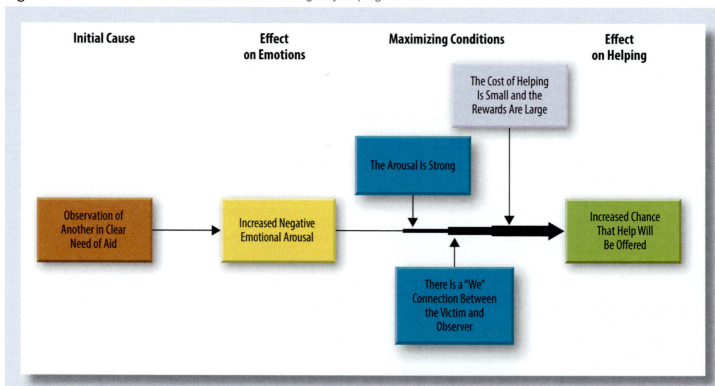

According to the arousal/cost–reward model, people who observe another in clear need of emergency aid will experience negative emotional arousal and will want to help to relieve this personal distress.

supported this prediction (Cramer et al., 1988; Gaertner & Dovidio, 1977; Krebs, 1975). In fact, when John Dovidio (1984) examined six studies of emergency aid that measured arousal, he found in each instance that as arousal rose in lone bystanders, so did their tendency to leap to the aid of victims.

2. *When there is a "we" connection between the victim and helper.* People are more willing to help those with whom they share an identity or similarity (a sense of "we-ness"), and this is especially so in life-and-death or emergency situations involving decisions about whom to rescue from a burning building (Burnstein, Crandall, & Kitayama, 1994). One reason this seems to be the case is that observers are more aroused by the plight of someone they feel connected with (Krebs, 1975).

3. *When reducing arousal through helping involves small costs and large rewards.* Because negative emotional arousal is unpleasant, those who can end it by helping will be motivated to do so. However, this should not be true, according to the model, if the helping act itself is even more unpleasant (costly) than the emotional distress—for example, if helping means having to make contact with the victim's blood (Piliavin & Piliavin, 1972). In sum, to the extent that helping is a low cost–high reward activity, people will relieve their negative emotional arousal prosocially. As the net cost of helping escalates, however, they are increasingly likely to choose other ways to reduce their emotional distress, such as leaving the scene (Dovidio et al., 1991; Fischer et al., 2011).

Managing Mood in Nonemergencies: The Negative State Relief Model

The arousal/cost–reward model has proven very successful at explaining how and why helping occurs in emergencies: Strong emotional arousal is typically part of an emergency, and thus helping can be used to manage that arousal. In nonemergency situations, in which such arousal is not normally present, individuals may still use helping to manage less intense emotional states: their moods. The idea that helping is a tactic that people sometimes use to influence their moods is called the **mood management hypothesis**, a part of the *negative state relief model* of helping (Cialdini, Kenrick, & Baumann, 1982; Schaller & Cialdini, 1990), which holds that people use helping to manage one particular mood—temporary sadness.

Mood management hypothesis The idea that people use helping tactically to manage their moods.

According to the negative state relief model, people often help to relieve their sadness because helping can be a reinforcing, mood-enhancing experience for them. One reason that prosocial activity may be reinforcing is that it has frequently been associated with reward in the past. Think about it. Hasn't it been the case that, since early childhood, you've gotten smiles, praise, or approval from your parents and teachers when you've shared with those around you? And hasn't it been the case as well that those you helped were more likely to do something nice for you in return? By virtue of the process of conditioning, this repeated pairing of prosocial activity with reward has likely worked to make you experience helping as pleasant and rewarding in itself (Grusec, 1991). As one brain-imaging experiment showed, when adults engaged in charitable giving the reward centers of their brains (associated with such pleasant activities as eating and sex) lit up (Moll et al., 2007).

Negative state relief. In a PBS fundraising drive, the most effective tactic was to sadden viewers and then give them a way to feel better by helping.

WATCH THE VIDEO: *Prof. Cialdini describing his research on sad mood and helping, and demonstrating how giving something to another person changes from a punishment to a reward as children grow older.*

Good support for the idea that giving assistance can pick up a person's spirits comes from laboratory studies showing that the act of helping can raise a helper's mood (Harris, 1977; Williamson & Clark, 1989; Williamson, Clark, Pegalis, & Behan, 1996) and from national surveys showing that, after the act, donors to charity feel better (Hodgkinson & Weitzman, 1994) and those who spend more on others than on themselves are happier for it (Dunn, Aknin, & Norton, 2008). Indeed, the positive emotion associated with giving assistance may be one reason that helpers tend to be healthier people who live longer (Brown, Nesse, Vinokur, & Smith, 2003). In the following sections, we examine the personal and situational factors that affect when people use aid to dispel their own sadness.

PERSON   **PRESENCE OF SADNESS**   The most basic principle of the negative state relief model is that, because prosocial action can raise one's mood, temporarily saddened individuals will use it to feel better again. If this is so, people who respond with sadness to another's plight should help more, as indeed they do. For instance, a study of the effectiveness of fund-raising appeals by a public broadcasting system station during four donation drives found that the most successful of the 4,868 individual appeals were those that evoked negative emotions in viewers and then gave them a way to relieve those emotions by helping others (Fisher, Vandenbosch, & Anita, 2008). In keeping with this logic, research has demonstrated that helping levels can jump significantly in people exposed to techniques that increase temporary sadness, such as reminiscing about unhappy events, reading a series of depressing statements, failing at a task, and doing or just witnessing harm to another (Cialdini, Kenrick, & Baumann, 1982).

SITUATION   **COSTS/BENEFITS OF HELPING**   It stands to reason that if you want to relieve a negative mood through helping, you should try to find the most painless route. After all, aid that costs you great amounts of time, energy, or resources might make you feel even worse rather than better for it. Therefore, those who start out in a saddened state ought to be especially sensitive to the cost/benefit aspects of helping opportunities.

James Weyant (1978) investigated this idea using a clever experimental procedure. First, he put Florida State University students into a happy, neutral, or sad mood. Then, he gave them a chance to volunteer for a nonprofit organization—either an organization that would generate a relatively large personal benefit by allowing them to feel they had supported an important cause (the American Cancer Society) or one that

Figure 9.6   Sad and selective

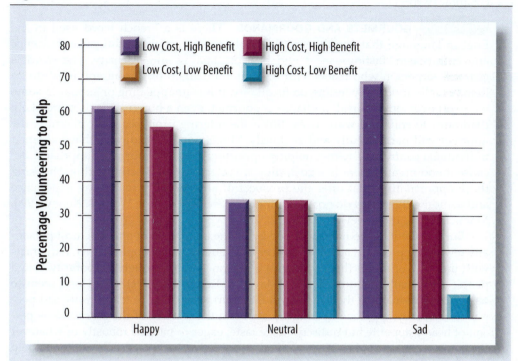

Saddened individuals seem to take a discriminating approach to helping opportunities, choosing sensitively among those likely to provide high-versus-low quality experiences.
Source: From Weyant, J. (1978). Effects of mood states, costs, and benefits on helping. *Journal of Personality and Social Psychology,* 10, 1169–1176.

would produce a relatively small such benefit (Little League Baseball). Finally, half of the students were told that if they decided to help they would have to collect donations in a personally costly fashion—by going door to door. The other half were told that they could collect donations in a way that didn't involve much personal cost—by sitting at a donations desk. Although students in a happy mood volunteered more than those in a neutral mood, these two kinds of participants weren't much affected by the costs and benefits of the helping opportunity. However, those in a sad mood were dramatically affected, helping most when the benefits outweighed the costs and helping least when the costs outweighed the benefits (see Figure 9.6). It appears, then, that saddened individuals are particularly choosy about the prosocial activities they select, volunteering for those likely to dispel their negative mood and avoiding those likely to deepen it.

SITUATION   **ABILITY OF THE HELPING ACT TO INFLUENCE MOOD**   For anyone interested in relieving sadness, a prosocial act should be attractive to the extent that it is able to change mood. However, if you were feeling so low that you thought nothing could cheer you up, helping wouldn't be especially likely because, under those circumstances, you couldn't use it to manage your mood. This is one reason that deeply depressed people, who don't believe that pleasurable activities can make them feel better, don't show high helping levels (Morris & Kanfer, 1983).

To test the idea that saddened individuals will help more only when they think their moods are changeable, one study put participants into a sad, neutral, or happy mood and then gave them a placebo drug (tonic water). Half were told the drug would "freeze" their current mood so that normal activities would not change it for the next 30 minutes. The other half thought their present mood was changeable. Finally, all got the chance to volunteer to contact blood donors by making phone calls. The placebo drug information didn't affect the helping decisions of those in a neutral or happy mood. It did lower helping among the saddened participants, however, whose helping increased solely when they thought it could alter their moods (Manucia, Baumann, & Cialdini, 1984).

INTERACTION **GOURMETS AND GOURMANDS** There is a French word used in the English language that simultaneously implies restraint and indulgence, reticence and enthusiasm, fastidiousness and passion, apathy and intensity. The word is *gourmet*—a person who reacts with uncommon disdain or uncommon relish to an item (usually food), depending on its quality. If it is unappealing or subpar in some way—an overcooked meal, perhaps—a gourmet, even a hungry one, is more likely than most to sniff and walk away. But if the offering promises great pleasure, the gourmet will partake fully and zealously. Much evidence indicates that saddened individuals confronted with a helping opportunity take a gourmet's approach: Because mood management is a goal, they are selective and discriminating, choosing those opportunities that offer the prospect of an especially rewarding experience and avoiding those that do not (Cunningham, Shaffer, Barbee, Wolff, & Kelley, 1990; Manucia et al., 1984; Weyant, 1978).

But this tendency to manage mood by taking advantage of only the most personally rewarding prosocial activities isn't equally strong in all people. In fact, it interacts with the kind of mood (happy or sad) a person is in. Although temporarily elated people are usually helpful (Salovey, Mayer, & Rosenhan, 1991), they don't seem to use helping to manage their moods in the gourmet fashion of temporarily sad people. Rather, they approach helping situations in the manner of the *gourmand*—a person of hearty appetite but indiscriminate taste, eager to partake robustly of whatever the environment provides. Thus, we find elated individuals especially willing to help whether the helping act promises to be rewarding or not. The same applies to elated consumers, who tend to choose the first buying opportunity they encounter rather than the most rewarding (Qiu & Yeung, 2008).

What is it about positive mood that increases a person's benevolence under various circumstances? The answer seems to lie in the tendency of elated people to see themselves and their environments in exceptionally rosy terms. They like and trust others more than do neutral mood individuals (Forgas & Bower, 1987; Forgas & East, 2008). In addition, they feel more competent (Alloy, Abramson, & Viscusi, 1981) and more optimistic about their future fortunes (Forgas & Moylan, 1987; Kiviat, 2003); it's perhaps for these reasons that a study of stock markets in 26 countries showed that stocks went up during periods of sunny weather (Hershleifer & Shumway, 2003). Finally, elated people tend to think about and remember the positive rather than negative features of almost anything they consider, including helping situations (Isen, Shalker, Clark, & Karp, 1978). That is, when encountering a helping opportunity, happy individuals will be especially likely to recall the positive aspects of past helping situations and to focus on the positive aspects of the present one (Clark & Waddell, 1983). With so upbeat a view of the rewards and costs of aid, it's not surprising that happy people are helpers. For each of these reasons, then, we can see why happy individuals would be willing to give some of their resources to a needy other.

Quick Quiz

1 Which of these is <u>not</u> a factor that increases helpfulness in emergencies?
   a. When there is little or no unpleasant arousal
   b. When the act of helping is a low cost–high reward activity
   c. When the helper shares a sense of identity or similarity with the victim
   d. When arousal is strong

2 According to the negative state relief model:
   a. Temporarily saddened individuals will use prosocial action to improve their mood.
   b. Saddened individuals prefer helping situations that yield high benefits, regardless of the costs of such help.
   c. Saddened individuals help more only when they think their moods are changeable.
   d. (a) and (c)
   e. All of the above

Does Pure Altruism Exist?

LO 9.13 Discuss when, according to the empathy–altruism hypothesis, pure altruism occurs.

LO 9.14 Summarize the evidence for and against the empathy-altruism hypothesis.

It is rare for a common English word to have been coined by a psychologist, but that is the case for *empathy*. Edward Bradford Titchener (1909), the great figure of American experimental psychology, first fashioned it out of a German art term that referred to the tendency of observers to project themselves into what they saw—the way we might mentally place ourselves in the scene of a painting or into the shoes of another. This process of putting oneself in the place of another is called **perspective taking**. It's one reason that most researchers find a strong connection between empathy and prosocial action, as people who assume the perspective of a needy other are more likely to help (Batson et al., 2007; Levy, Freitas, & Salovey, 2002: Penner, Harper, & Albrecht, 2012). It seems that when you put yourself in a victim's shoes, they are likely to take you to their owner's aid.

This appears to be true even among individuals who provide help for a living. In one study, those professional psychotherapists who possessed a strong, natural tendency for perspective taking were especially willing to help a young woman who needed assistance with an article she was writing on psychotherapy (Otten, Penner, & Altabe, 1991). Although perspective taking (a cognitive activity) has been seen as a feature of empathy from the time of Titchener, modern theorists have added a second component to the mix—an emotional component that involves sharing the feelings of another (Eisenberg & Miller, 1987). Hence, empathy is best viewed as including both the cognitive process of putting oneself in another's position and the emotional result of experiencing what the other is feeling (Davis, 1994).

What's noteworthy about empathy is the claim, made most forcefully by C. Daniel Batson and his associates, that when one empathizes with a suffering other a special form of helping can result that is purely altruistic. As noted at the beginning of the chapter, pure (true) altruism refers to prosocial action that is motivated only by a concern for the other's welfare. Although Batson (1991) concedes that help is often designed for personal gain—to make a good impression, to bolster self-concept, to relieve distress or sadness, and so on—he says that when empathy enters the picture, the basic motivation for helping can shift from self*fish* to self*less*. In other words, the goal of improving another's welfare can become dominant, suppressing—even supplanting—the goal of improving one's own welfare. This possibility is known as the **empathy–altruism hypothesis**.

Perspective taking: Putting yourself in another's blues. If you came upon this scene, what are the chances that you would help? They would jump significantly if you first imagined yourself in the needy person's position.

The Empathy–Altruism Sequence

What's the sequence of events that can turn us from egoistic (selfish) to altruistic (selfless)? Batson and Laura Shaw (1991) think it proceeds as follows: The process of perspective taking, in which we try to put ourselves in another's position, can first be stimulated by perceived similarity between ourselves and the other, or by an attachment (kinship, friendship, prior contact) we have to the other, or simply by instructions to take the other's perspective (Batson, Turk, Shaw, & Klein, 1995). Second, provided that the other is needy or suffering in some way, the perspective taking will cause us to experience **empathic concern**—feelings of warmth, tenderness, and compassion toward the other. Empathic concern is the key element of Batson's model because, unlike such emotional responses as personal distress and sadness, it is said to orient

Perspective taking The process of mentally putting oneself in another's position.

Empathy–altruism hypothesis The presumption that when one empathizes with the plight of another, one will want to help that other for purely altruistic reasons.

Empathic concern Compassionate feelings caused by taking the perspective of a needy other.

Figure 9.7   Batson's empathy–altruism hypothesis

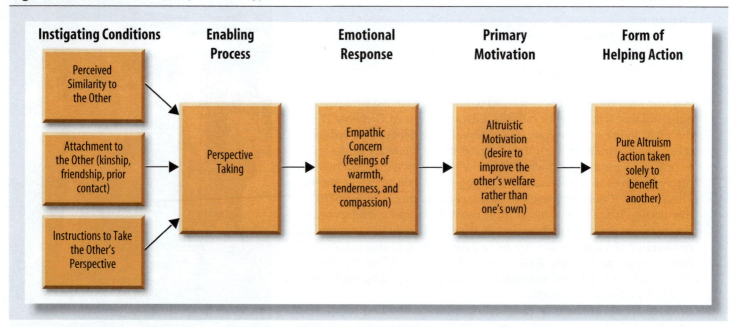

Pure altruism requires special circumstances, according to Batson's empathy–altruism model.

helpers away from a focus on their own welfare and onto a focus on the other's welfare. According to Batson, empathic concern leads directly to altruistic motivation—the desire to better another's welfare for its own sake—and, thus, to pure altruism (see Figure 9.7).

To support the idea of pure altruism, Batson and his associates did a series of experiments attempting to show that various egoistic motivations can't explain the pattern of helping that occurs when people feel empathic concern for another. In one study (Batson, Duncan, Ackerman, Buckley, & Birch, 1981), for instance, they wanted to demonstrate that participants experiencing empathic concern for a victim—"Elaine," a fellow participant who was receiving electric shocks—would help in a way that couldn't be explained simply as a selfish attempt to reduce their own unpleasant arousal at seeing her suffer.

Empathic concern was instilled in certain participants by telling them that they were very similar to Elaine in values and interests. Reasoning that individuals observing suffering could reduce their resulting arousal either by ending the victim's plight or by leaving the scene, the researchers gave subjects the chance to volunteer to take a set of eight remaining shocks for Elaine after they had seen her react badly to an initial pair of shocks. Half of the participants (Difficult Escape) were told that if they decided not to help, they would nonetheless have to stay and continue to watch Elaine suffer the remaining shocks; the rest (Easy Escape) were told that if they decided not to help, they could leave immediately. You would think that people motivated primarily to reduce their unpleasant arousal as painlessly as possible would help less in the Easy Escape condition, in which they could quickly leave the source of the arousal without having to endure any shocks. That is exactly what happened—*except* when they felt empathic concern for Elaine. Under those circumstances, it didn't matter whether escape was easy or difficult for them; they stayed and helped.

Batson (1991) interpreted these findings as indicating that egoistic motives, such as the desire to reduce unpleasant arousal, may often determine whether an individual helps but that these reasons may no longer play a decisive role once the individual feels empathic concern for the victim. This is because, then, the crucial motivation to help is no longer selfish but is truly altruistic. Using a similar logic, he and his coworkers have attempted to show that empathic concern overwhelms the influence of many of the other possible egoistic motives for helping: to gain social approval (Archer, 1984;

Fultz, Batson, Fortenbach, McCarthy, & Varney, 1986), to bolster self-concept (Batson et al., 1988), to relieve sadness (Batson et al., 1989; Cialdini et al., 1987b; Schroeder, Dovidio, Sibicky, Matthews, & Allen, 1988), and to make oneself feel happy (Batson et al., 1991; Smith, Keating, & Stotland, 1989). By examining and discounting the impact of each of these egoistic motives when empathy is present, Batson's research has added provocatively to the evidence suggesting that pure altruism can exist.

An Egoistic Interpretation

You might notice, however, that one important selfish reason for prosocial behavior hasn't been tested in Batson's work. It is the first motive we considered in this chapter—to ensure the survival of one's genes. Furthermore, in looking back at that section of the chapter, you might also notice that the factors that Batson says lead a person to feel empathic concern for another are identical to the factors that signal shared genes with another—similarity, kinship, friendship, and prior contact (familiarity). It may be, then, that feelings of empathic concern stimulate helping because they inform us that the recipient of that concern is likely to possess a greater-than-normal percentage of our genes (Kenrick, 1991; Tancredy & Fraley, 2006). This leads to the ironic possibility that when we feel empathy for another, we may be helpful not because of the most elevated motive—pure altruism—but because of the most primitive one—genetic advantage (Maner & Gailliot, 2007; Sturmer et al., 2006).

How can empathic feelings be associated with shared heredity? During the thousands of years when human behavior patterns were first developing, we lived in small bands—roving tribal villages—of genetically similar individuals who learned to communicate with one another in very basic ways, including the communication of emotion that comes from perspective taking (Buck & Ginzberg, 1991; Hoffman, 1984). Because this kind of empathic communication took place most frequently with members of one's family and tribe, the experience of empathy for another was linked with genetic similarity. What could have easily evolved, then, is a tendency to aid those with whom one empathizes (kin, friends, similar or familiar others) because they are likely to be one's relatives and that aid is therefore likely to increase the survival of one's own genes.

Of course, most people aren't likely to be conscious of such a process when deciding to help someone whose perspective they've taken. Instead, all they are likely to feel is a greater sense of identity or oneness with another (Galinsky & Moskowitz, 2000). This might explain why, in one study, college students who were asked to take the perspective of a fellow student came to see more of themselves in that person (Davis, Conklin, Smith, & Luce, 1996). Furthermore, neuroscientific studies find that we process other people's pain using the same neural circuits we use when we are ourselves in pain (Decety, 2012). This tendency to immerse ourselves in those with whom we empathize raises a crucial question about the existence of pure altruism: If empathy causes us to see our*selves* in another, can the decision to help that other be truly selfless?

Although there can be debate on that question (Batson et al., 1997b; 2012; Cialdini et al., 1997; Maner et al., 2002), there's little doubt that when we do take another's perspective the impact on helping can be dramatic.

INVESTIGATION

What do you think? Is there ever a purely altruistic act, one that was not caused by some form of gain to the helper?

Quick Quiz

 Which of these represents the correct sequence of events in the empathy-altruism model?

    a. Perceived similarity to other > empathic concern > perspective taking > altruistic motivation > pure altruism

    b. Perceived similarity to other > perspective taking > empathic concern > altruistic motivation > pure altruism

     c. Perspective taking > perceived similarity to other > empathic concern > primary motivation > pure altruism

     d. Empathic concern > attachment to the other > perspective taking > altruistic motivation > pure altruism

2 Which of the following are correct statements regarding the evidence for the empathy–altruism hypothesis?

     a. Research subjects take advantage of a chance to escape from watching another person suffer, unless they are feeling empathy.

     b. Empathy for another overwhelms several egoistic motives, such as the desire to gain approval or relieve sadness.

     c. Empathy causes us to see ourselves in others, which casts doubt on the notion that the decision to help is ever truly selfless (i.e., purely altruistic).

     d. All of the above

Revisiting

The Case of Sempo Sugihara

We began this chapter with an account of Sempo Sugihara's decision to assist Jewish refugees in Lithuania while knowing that this assistance would destroy his long-cherished diplomatic career. The decision was bewildering on its surface because there seemed nothing about the man that could have predicted his actions. But below the surface, as we saw, there were features of Sugihara and of his situation that, like uncovered clues, could resolve the mystery. Let's revisit and summarize those features, pointing in the process to bridges between his actions and existing research on helping decisions.

First, during his childhood, Sugihara witnessed memorable acts of kindness by his parents. Although such kindness probably had a general influence on his prosocial nature, there was something special about it that may have had a specific impact on his decision to help the Jews: Those whom his parents assisted were often foreigners—strangers and travelers given shelter and care. This early experience may well have led Sugihara to include a wider-than-normal range of individuals in his sense of "we," a concept that research has shown increases helping. Indeed, from his subsequent comments, it appears that he expanded the boundaries of "we" beyond the immediate or extended family to the human family.

Second, Sugihara developed a personal attachment to an 11-year-old Jewish boy, which provided the opportunity for social contact with the boy's family. If, as research evidence suggests (Batson et al., 1995; Mashek, Aron, & Boncimino, 2003), attachment and contact of this sort led him to empathize more readily with the plight of these individuals, it is not surprising that the boy's family received the first exit visa Sugihara wrote. Nor is it surprising that, after once committing himself to such a rescue effort, he would continue to assist similar others in a similar fashion

(see Chapter 6 for a discussion of the role of initial commitments in producing consistent later behavior).

Finally, Sugihara's willingness to sacrifice himself for the benefit of defenseless victims is consistent with his samurai background and self-image. To have "thrown a wounded bird to the cat" would have violated a code of conduct that was central to an important component of his self-definition. And, as considerable research has demonstrated, individuals will often go to great lengths to assure that their actions coincide with their preferred or existing self-concept.

When viewed beneath the surface, then, Sempo Sugihara's puzzling behavior seems not so puzzling after all. Rather, it appears quite compatible with the three bridging factors—an expanded sense of "we," a prior attachment to the victim, and a helping-relevant self-image—that have been shown to stimulate prosocial acts in a wide variety of individuals. Although one might be inclined to ask, "Well, which one of the three bridging factors did it? Which spurred him to begin writing the visas?" it is important to recognize that a helping decision as complex as Sugihara's—or most helping decisions, for that matter—cannot be attributed to a single cause. More likely, it was an interaction of factors—perhaps all three that we've described plus others we haven't uncovered—that pushed him to action.

One last question deserves consideration. Now that we think we know why Mr. Sugihara made his self-sacrificial choice, now that we can explain it in terms of ordinary influences on prosocial activity, should we find it any less awe-inspiring, any less noteworthy? Not in the least. Too often, observers treat human mysteries resolved like magic tricks revealed: Once the unknown is dispelled, wonder decays and attention drifts, as if there's nothing left to marvel at. But this is a superficial view, because what remains after the unknown is dispelled is the *known*, the marvelously systematic *known*. Perhaps the most awe-inspiring aspect of Sugihara's astonishing decision is that it can be traced to a set of recognized and rather commonplace motives for helping—the heavily trafficked bridges that consistently take helpers to the aid of victims.

Chapter Summary

Summary of the Goals Served by Prosocial Action and the Factors Related to Them

The Goal	Person	Situation	Interaction
Gaining genetic and material benefits	• Instilled beliefs regarding prosocial action • An expanded sense of "we"	• Similarity of victim to helper • Familiarity of victim to helper	• The tendency to aid relatives over nonrelatives is especially strong when the need is life-threatening.
Gaining social status and approval	• Desire for approval	• Helping models • Population density	• Whether males or females help more depends on whether the helping action fits more with the masculine or feminine gender role.
Managing self-image	• Personal norms • Religious and ethical codes	• Labeling • Self-focus	• The decision to help a friend over a stranger depends on the impact on one's self-concept. • Certain variables, including gender, age, and self-esteem, can impact whether one refuses needed aid if the aid threatens self-concept.
Managing our emotions and moods	• Sadness	• Costs/benefits of helping • Ability of helping to influence mood	• People in a sad mood approach helping selectively, choosing opportunities that appear rewarding; but people in a happy mood are much less selective, choosing to help in a wide range of situations.

The Goals of Prosocial Behavior

1. Prosocial behavior is action intended to benefit another.
2. There are two more limited types of prosocial behavior: the first is action intended to benefit another but not for external reward, and the second, called pure altruism, is action intended solely to benefit another, thus not for internal or external reward.

Improving Our Basic Welfare: Gaining Genetic and Material Benefits

1. People sometimes help to improve their own inclusive fitness (the survival of genes in offspring and relatives). This goal can be achieved by such means as aiding relatives or giving to nonrelatives who are likely to help in return (reciprocal aid).
2. Behavior geneticists, who use such methods as twin studies to determine how much of a behavior is due to heredity versus environment, typically find that both genetic and environmental factors are important causes.
3. People will be more likely to help another when early childhood experiences, similarity, and familiarity lead them to see the other in terms of family (the genetic "we").

Gaining Social Status and Approval

1. Because helping is typically valued in a culture, people may help to gain prestige and social approval.

2. The most general helping norm is the norm of social responsibility, which states that we should help those who are dependent on us for assistance.
3. Bystanders observing possible emergencies influence the decision to help in three ways: by serving as sources of potential aid, by serving as sources of information about whether aid is required, and by serving as sources of approval or disapproval for helping.
4. Individuals having a strong desire for approval are more likely to help under public circumstances.
5. Factors that draw attention to the social responsibility norm (e.g., helping models) lead to more helping.
6. Consistent with the socially approved masculine gender role, men help more when the situation requires heroic, direct assistance of the needy, including strangers. Consistent with the socially approved feminine gender role, women help more when the situation calls for nurturant, supportive help for relationship partners.

Managing Self-image

1. Because prosocial behavior can affect how people view themselves, they can use it to both enhance and verify their self-definitions.
2. Persons possessing strong religious codes and personal norms toward helping appear to help in order to act in accord with their self-images.
3. The labels others apply to us affect our self-images. Therefore, when we are labeled as generous or kind, we become more helpful.

4. Because most people value helping, they become more prosocial when they are made to focus inside on this value.

5. Not only does giving aid affect self-concept, so does accepting aid—by implying to the recipient that he or she may be incompetent, dependent, or inadequate.

Managing Our Emotions and Moods

1. Because helping is experienced as rewarding, it can be used to relieve an unpleasant state in the helper.

2. In emergencies, this unpleasant state is aversive arousal (distress), which, according to the arousal/cost–reward model, leads to assistance principally when (1) the arousal is strong, (2) there is a "we" connection between the victim and helper, and (3) reducing the arousal involves small costs and large rewards.

3. In nonemergency situations, helping can relieve the unpleasant state of sadness. According to the negative state relief model, temporarily saddened individuals help more when they (1) see the personal benefits of aid outweighing the costs and (2) view the help as able to influence their moods.

4. Elated individuals help in a wide range of situations, probably because they have an overly positive view of helping opportunities.

Does Pure Altruism Exist?

1. According to the empathy–altruism model, people who experience empathic concern for a needy other are willing to help simply to improve his or her welfare (pure altruism). Furthermore, perspective taking, which produces empathic concern, can be brought about by perceived attachments to another (similarity, kinship, friendship, familiarity).

2. In support of this model, those who take another's perspective do feel empathic concern and do appear—at least on the surface—to want to help for reasons having to do with the other's welfare rather than their own.

3. A nonaltruistic explanation exists, however, for why perspective taking leads to seemingly selfless aid: The factors that lead naturally to perspective taking (similarity, kinship, friendship, familiarity) are traditional cues of shared genetic makeup. Thus, perspective taking may spur feelings of shared heredity and the resultant helping may serve the goal of promoting one's own (genetic) welfare.

Key Terms

Arousal/cost–reward model, 300

Bystander effect, 288

Diffusion of responsibility, 288

Empathic concern, 305

Empathy–altruism hypothesis, 305

Inclusive fitness, 280

Mood management hypothesis, 301

Personal norms, 294

Perspective taking, 305

Pluralistic ignorance, 289

Prosocial behavior, 278

Pure (or true) altruism, 279

Reciprocal aid, 280

Social responsibility norm, 287

Chapter 10

Aggression

Video

Outline

Learning Objectives

LO 10.1 Identify the three criteria psychologists use for defining a behavior as aggression.

LO 10.2 Distinguish examples of direct and indirect, and instrumental versus emotional aggression.

LO 10.3 Describe how gender differences in aggression depend on one's definition.

LO 10.4 Explain the frustration–aggression hypothesis and Berkowitz's reformulation of the idea.

LO 10.5 Compare and contrast the excitation-transfer theory and cognitive neoassociation theory.

LO 10.6 Discuss which factors in the person and the situation affect frustration-driven aggression.

LO 10.7 Explain the social learning theory's assertion that aggressive behavior is caused by rewards for aggression.

LO 10.8 Identify who is most likely to find rewards in violence and explain why.

LO 10.9 Discuss how glamorization of violence in the media can influence our behavior.

LO 10.10 Explain how differential parental investment and sexual selection are connected to sex differences in status-linked aggression.

LO 10.11 Understand testosterone's links with aggression and dominance.

LO 10.12 Explain how age, sex, and culture link to status-driven aggression.

LO 10.13 Identify two features of the person that might contribute to a tendency toward self-defensive aggression.

LO 10.14 Explain why self-protective aggression can increase danger.

LO 10.15 Describe how parents can use rewards to *reduce* aggressive behavior in children.

LO 10.16 Understand how cognition can be used to reduce angry arousal.

LO 10.17 Explain specific ways that intervention at the societal level can reduce aggressive behavior.

A Wave of Senseless Violence

Susan Atkins, Patricia Krenwinkel, and Leslie Van Houten. Three young women involved in a notorious series of multiple murders described in the text.

In the comfortable, middle-class neighborhood where she grew up, Patricia Krenwinkel was described as a "very normal child" who was "very obedient." She had been a Camp Fire Girl and a singer in the church choir. After high school, she attended a Catholic college in Alabama. When she moved out to California to be with her sister, though, her life took a new turn. She moved into a commune, where drugs and free love were the everyday leisure activities and conventional society was scorned. And along with her newfound friends, the former Campfire Girl participated in events so shocking that, four decades later, they were still being explored in a television series on violence and evil.

Those events unfolded on a hot August night in 1969, when Krenwinkel accompanied three of her friends to a house in a wealthy area of Los Angeles. In the house were five people she had never before met. According to a diabolical premeditated plan, Krenwinkel and her friends brutally and ritualistically murdered these five total strangers (Bugliosi & Gentry, 1974).

One of Krenwinkel's accomplices was Charles Watson. In high school, Charles had been an A student and an all-around athletic star. After his arrest, folks back in his hometown refused to believe he was guilty, describing him as "the boy next door" and "a nice guy" who had "no temper." Yet on that August night, this nice hometown boy shot, stabbed, and beat four people. One of his victims was a pregnant woman, who he murdered despite her pleas for the life of her unborn child.

Unlike the clean-cut Krenwinkel and Watson, Susan Atkins seemed bound for trouble. She'd dropped out of high school to become a topless dancer and a prostitute. After a previous arrest, her own father had asked police not to let her back into society. After the killings, she wrote "Pig" on the wall in the victims' blood. She later bragged about the murders, claiming to have enjoyed them.

Linda Kasabian was the fourth person who drove to the scene of the murder. Like Susan Atkins, she had a troubled background, but unlike Atkins, she refused to participate in the killings. Instead, she stayed outside the house. When she heard screams, Linda ran to ask her friends to stop but was too late. She was met by a wounded victim staggering out of the house, to whom she said, "Oh, God, I'm so sorry." After unsuccessfully begging the others to stop, she ran back to the car.

On the very next night, the same group again drove together into a well-to-do neighborhood and murdered two more complete strangers in their home. This time, they were joined by their leader, Charles Manson, and two other members of his still-notorious "Family." Again, Linda Kasabian refused to participate. Soon afterward Kasabian escaped from the group, eventually becoming the chief witness for the prosecution. She was the only member of the group to show remorse during the trials.

Kasabian was even more shocked to hear the other Family members laughing as they watched the news reports of the killings. She reported that, "in my head I kept saying, 'Why would they do such a thing?'" This is a question people are still asking decades later. Were the killings completely random and senseless, or did the group have some motives that might connect these killings to the "everyday" violence that leaves tens of thousands of people dead or injured every year?

Most of us will never be involved with anything even remotely as violent as the Manson Family's mass murders. In the normal course of our lives, though, we may confront some family violence, purposeful shoves on the basketball court, heated arguments, or thinly veiled insults designed to do psychological harm. Adolescents in one study reported an average of 1.5 conflicts a day, ranging from verbal insults between friends to angry arguments with parents and fistfights with siblings (Jensen-Campbell & Graziano, 2000). What causes these outbursts of hostility? And why do people differ in their inclination toward such conflicts, with some managing to skillfully avoid any violence in their lives and others seeming to seek it out?

As you'll learn in this chapter, aggression, like other social behaviors, results from a decipherable pattern of interactions between the person and the situation. And you'll see that aggressive acts—from a mischievous taunt to a mass murder—make more sense when you understand the social psychological motives that underlie them.

What Is Aggression?

LO 10.1 Identify the three criteria psychologists use for defining a behavior as aggression.

LO 10.2 Distinguish examples of direct and indirect, and instrumental versus emotional aggression.

LO 10.3 Describe how gender differences in aggression depend on one's definition.

In everyday life, we use the word *aggression* to refer to a range of behaviors, from snide comments to violent murders, and even to describe assertive behavior, as when we talk of "an aggressive sales pitch." Most social psychologists, however, define **aggression** as behavior intended to injure another (e.g., Anderson & Bushman, 2002; Baron & Richardson, 1994). There are three crucial components of this definition:

1. Aggression is *behavior*. It is not the same as anger, an emotion that is often, but not always, associated with aggression. A person can feel angry and not act on those

Aggression Behavior intended to injure another.

feelings, or act aggressively without being angry. When Manson's followers later talked about their murderous spree, none of them mentioned any feelings of anger toward their victims.

2. The behavior is *intended*, or purposeful. You could hurt, even kill, someone else by accident, and it would not qualify as aggressive behavior. Indeed, people respond very differently to being hurt depending on whether they believe they were harmed on purpose or inadvertently (Barlett & Anderson, 2011). A teasing comment, for example, sometimes hurts the recipient even when the teaser meant only to make a friendly joke (Kowalski, 2000; Kruger et al., 2006). If the harm were truly unintended, this would not qualify as aggression.

3. The behavior is aimed at *hurting* another person. Social psychologists distinguish aggressiveness from **assertiveness**, which is behavior intended to express dominance or confidence. They also distinguish real aggression, with its malicious intent, from playful aggression (Boulton, 1994; Gergen, 1990). Play fighting can range from rough-and-tumble wrestling between children to pinching between lovers. It can be distinguished by frequent smiling and laughter, in contrast to the staring, frowning, and baring of the teeth that often accompany malicious aggression (Fry, 1990).

Different Types of Aggression

Social psychologists often distinguish between indirect and direct aggression (e.g., Bjorkvist et al., 1994; Griskevicius et al., 2009; Richardson & Green, 2006). **Indirect aggression** involves an attempt to hurt another person without obvious face-to-face conflict (malicious gossip is an example). **Direct aggression** is behavior aimed at hurting someone to his or her face. It may be either physical (striking, kicking, or shoving) or verbal (insulting or threatening another person).

Another distinction involves whether the aggression is emotional or instrumental. **Emotional aggression** is hurtful behavior that stems from angry feelings. If someone throws a chair at a coworker in a blind rage, that would be an example of emotional aggression. **Instrumental aggression** is hurting another person to accomplish some other goal—such as purposely tripping the star soccer player from the opposing team (Coulomb-Cabagno & Rascle, 2006). This distinction is not always crystal clear, as many angry behaviors serve goals such as retaliating for a blow to one's status, and an aggressive act may be simultaneously emotional and instrumental (Bushman & Anderson, 2001). Table 10.1 gives examples of each of the different types of aggressive behavior.

Gender Differences in Aggression May Depend on Your Definition

In 1974, Eleanor Maccoby and Carol Jacklin reviewed research that strongly supported a common assumption—that males are more aggressive than females. Twenty years later, Kaj Bjorkqvist argued instead that "the claim that human males are more aggressive than females . . . appears . . . to be false, and a consequence of narrow definitions and operationalizations of aggression in previous research" (Bjorkqvist et al., 1994,

Assertiveness Behavior intended to express dominance or confidence.

Indirect aggression Behavior intended to hurt someone without face-to-face confrontation.

Direct aggression Behavior intended to hurt someone to his or her face.

Emotional aggression Hurtful behavior that stems from angry feelings.

Instrumental aggression Hurting another to accomplish some other (nonaggressive) goal.

Table 10.1	Examples of Different Categories of Aggressive Behavior	
	Direct	**Indirect**
Emotional	An angry driver starts a fistfight with another driver who was tailgating him.	Under cover of night, an irritated tenant deflates the tires on the landlord's car.
Instrumental	A bank robber shoots a guard who attempts to thwart the robbery.	A woman interested in dating a man asks her sister to tell the man a vicious rumor about his current girlfriend's infidelity.

p. 28). Other researchers have found that, compared with men, women are actually *more* aggressive in some circumstances (Jenkins & Aube, 2002; Ramirez, 1993). So who's more aggressive—men, women, or neither?

Some researchers have noted that many sex-role stereotypes have changed since the 1960s and speculate that traditional gender differences in aggression have started disappearing as a consequence (Goldstein, 1986; Hyde, 1990). Back in the 1960s, women committed only about 15% of homicides. Was the first Manson Family murder, committed in 1969 by a group of three women and one man, part of the beginning of a trend toward "equal time" in the violent role? No. According to Bureau of Justice statistics depicted in Figure 10.1, the proportion of homicides committed by women has declined since the 1960s.

If historical change can't explain the contradictory evidence on sex differences in aggression, then what is the explanation? The answer seems to be that sex differences (or the lack thereof) depend on how you define and measure aggression (Hamby, 2009). If we focus on physical assault or murder, men are much more aggressive (Archer, 2000; Cross, Copping, & Campbell, 2011). From kindergarten until the nursing home, males are more likely than are females to hit, kick, knife, and shoot at one another (e.g., Archer & Coyne, 2005; Crick & Nelson, 2002; Walker, Richardson, & Green, 2000). However, girls are more likely than boys to use indirect aggression—hurting others through gossiping, spreading vicious rumors, and social rejection (Linder & Crick, 2002; Owens et al., 2000).

But there is one exception to the generalization that men are more likely to use direct physical aggression. Women are, compared with men, at least as likely to hit, kick, or otherwise physically attack their romantic partners (Archer, 2000; Jenkins & Aube, 2002; Strauss, 2012). But if that's true, why is it that

Sex differences in aggression.
Although women are somewhat more likely to hit a domestic partner, men generally do much more physical damage when they hit their wives or girlfriends. Singer Chris Brown repeatedly punched his girlfriend, Rihanna, drawing blood and producing visible injuries.

Figure 10.1   Percentage of homicides committed by each sex (1962–2012)

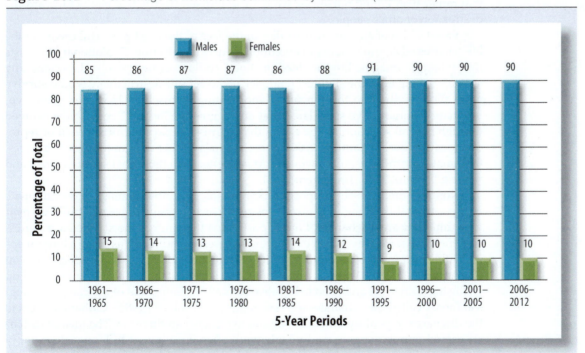

Males in the United States, as in all societies, commit most of the homicides. Changes in sex role norms since the 1960s have not been followed by a tendency for American women to commit a greater proportion of homicides.
Source: Statistics based on Department of Justice, FBI Uniform Crime Reports.

overwhelmingly more women than men show up at shelters for abused spouses? That is because a 120-pound woman striking a 180-pound man is simply not as physically damaging as when the reverse occurs, and hence a woman striking a man is less likely to be legally defined as violence (Archer, 1994; Strauss, 2012).

Thus, the size of the sex difference in aggressiveness depends on how you define aggression. Does this mean the sex difference is arbitrary or meaningless? Not quite. The difference between physical violence and indirect aggression is a real one, as real as the difference between being beaten with a baseball bat and being called a jerk behind your back (Harris, 1992). As you'll see, the differences between men's and women's aggressiveness are often linked to different motivations (Cross et al., 2011).

INVESTIGATION

Think of a time when a woman you know did something designed to hurt another person. Now think of a time when a man did something to hurt someone else. Which of these examples involved more direct and which more indirect aggression?

The Goals of Aggressive Behavior

Why are people aggressive? Social psychological research suggests that aggressive behavior may serve a wide range of motivations, including the desire to influence other people, to gain power and dominance over others, to create an impression of toughness, to gain money or social approval, or simply to discharge negative feelings (Berkowitz, 1993a; Campbell, 2005; Duntley, 2005; Kirkpatrick et al., 2002). Sigmund Freud suggested that aggressive behavior may serve as a goal in itself.

INSTINCTS: DRIVES TOWARD DEATH AND DESTRUCTION? Freud's view of human motivation originally included only "life instincts"—selfish drives that contributed to the individual's survival and reproduction. After viewing the ravages of World War I, though, he added a "death instinct"—an innate pull to end one's own life. Freud realized that a death instinct would conflict with the life instincts. So Freud postulated that rather than killing ourselves, we redirect our self-destructive instinct toward the destruction of other people.

Freud's idea of a death instinct flies in the face of the most powerful theory in the life sciences—Darwin's theory of evolution by natural selection. Evolutionary theorists find it hard to imagine how a "death instinct" could ever have evolved, because any animals having even the slightest tendency *not* to act self-destructively would survive more successfully than those bent on annihilating themselves. However, some evolutionary theorists have speculated that an "aggressive instinct" could have evolved through natural selection, to the extent that aggression pays off for survival or reproduction (e.g., Buss & Duntley, 2006). Those animals willing to fight for their territories, their mates, or their resources would survive better than those that simply turned and ran (e.g., Lorenz, 1966; Tinbergen, 1968).

Konrad Lorenz (1966) proposed that humans, like other animals, have an innate urge to attack. Like hunger or sexual desire, these aggressive urges will build up over time until they are discharged. Lorenz postulated that animals need to release aggressive energy in some way. When the energy is expressed indirectly, as when a bird preens its feathers during a face-to-face conflict with another bird, it is called **displacement** (Bushman et al., 2005; Vasquez et al., 2005). The idea that aggressive impulses build up inside the individual and need to be released is a key component of a social psychological theory called the catharsis-aggression theory (Feshbach, 1984). **Catharsis** refers to the discharge of pent-up emotion—aggressive energy in this case. The idea of catharsis gained popular appeal, and people were often encouraged to let out their angry feelings by hitting a punching bag, screaming, or otherwise acting out. Putting aside the consequences for other people, it feels better at a physiological level to respond to provocation with anger than with fear (Lerner et al., 2005). Members of the entertainment industry have often used the idea of catharsis to support their never-ending diet

Displacement Indirect expression of an aggressive impulse away from the person or animal that elicited it.

Catharsis Discharge of aggressive impulses.

of violent television and movies(Bushman & Anderson, 2001). The great film director Alfred Hitchcock once stated, "One of television's greatest contributions is that it brought murder back into the home where it belongs. Seeing a murder on television can be good therapy. It can help work off one's antagonism" (Myers, 1999). Contrary to the catharsis hypothesis, however, actually acting aggressively tends to increase rather than decrease later violent behavior (Anderson, Carnagy, & Eubanks, 2002; Verona & Sullivan, 2008). And decades of research, which we will discuss in detail, suggest that watching violence on television and in the movies increases rather than decrease violence in viewers (Bushman & Anderson, 2001).

Although Lorenz's evolutionary model of aggressive drive is like Freud's theory of the "death instinct" in assuming an inherent tendency to be aggressive, it is different in presuming an interaction between that drive and events in the environment (Tinbergen, 1968). Animals (including humans) will not be inclined to act aggressively unless the drive is triggered by something outside (such as a threat, an attack, or a frustration).

AGGRESSION AND ADAPTIVE GOALS   According to modern evolutionary analyses, humans are not "programmed" to be blindly aggressive (Campbell, 2005; Duntley, 2005). Aggressive behavior is one strategy for survival and reproduction, useful in some situations but not in most others. Across many different animal species, aggression has been found to serve a number of goals, allowing animals to control their territorial boundaries, to divide limited resources, and to defend their young (Scott, 1992). But because aggression always bears the risk of retaliation and could result in injury or death, pure hostility with no immediate, useful goal would probably hurt an animal's chance to survive and reproduce (Gilbert, 1994).

This analysis suggests that aggressive behavior is never a goal in itself. Instead, psychologists now assume that aggressive behavior is designed to serve some function. Because it may backfire and lead to injury and death for the perpetrator, psychologists also presume that people usually use aggressiveness only when other avenues have failed (Dabbs & Morris, 1990; Wilson & Daly, 1985).

What functions does aggression serve? We consider four in this chapter: to cope with feelings of annoyance, to gain material and social rewards, to gain or maintain social status, and to protect oneself or the members of one's group.

Quick Quiz

1 Which of the following is incorrect?

   a. If a man knocks over an old lady in a crowded mall because he was obsessing over an angry argument with his boss rather than paying attention, this would not be defined as aggression.

   b. A man who spreads a rumor about someone with whom he is competing for a job is engaging in indirect instrumental aggression.

   c. A military interrogator who punches a suspected terrorist to get him to turn in a collaborator is engaging in indirect instrumental aggression.

   d. A man who screams threats at his former boss because he is angry about losing his job is engaging in direct emotional aggression.

2 Which of the following is true of gender differences in aggression?

   a. Compared to men, women are more likely to attack their intimate partners in ways that require medical treatment.

   b. Men and women commit similar levels of violent crimes, but those for women are underreported.

   c. Men and women commit similar levels of violent crimes, but those for men are overreported.

   d. Men are more likely to engage in criminal violence.

3 Modern biologically oriented theorists believe:

   a. There is reasonable support for Freud's idea of a death instinct.

   b. Aggressive impulses, like hunger, tend to build up over time and require occasional catharsis

   c. Instinctive tendencies toward aggressive behavior are not possible.

   d. Instinctive tendencies toward aggressive behavior are only possible if they are linked to functional responses to threats and opportunities in the environment.

Coping with Feelings of Annoyance

LO 10.4 Explain the frustration–aggression hypothesis and Berkowitz's reformulation of the idea.

LO 10.5 Compare and contrast the excitation-transfer theory and cognitive neoassociation theory.

LO 10.6 Discuss which factors in the person and the situation affect frustration-driven aggression.

Before they began committing the mass murders they became notorious for, the Manson Family was living an impoverished lifestyle, making garbage runs to collect food from dumpsters behind supermarkets. For those like Krenwinkel and Watson, who came from middle-class backgrounds, the perception of hardship must have been magnified. To make the contrast even worse, Manson and several other members of the group had lived for a time in the elegant home of Brian Wilson (leader of the highly successful Beach Boys musical group), during which time they drove around in his Rolls Royce and lived quite splendidly.

Manson, having spent most of his life in prisons and foster homes, got his hopes up about joining in this wealthy lifestyle. He had come to believe that Wilson's friend Terry Melcher, a wealthy record producer, would sign him to a recording contract. Ultimately, however, Wilson put them out, Melcher spurned Manson, and the Family was reduced to stealing garbage. This detail is one clue to the first gruesome mass murder—the house that Manson and his Family picked was not a random choice, as it first seemed. In fact, it had belonged to Terry Melcher.

The Frustration–Aggression Hypothesis

In 1939, John Dollard and his colleagues proposed the **frustration–aggression hypothesis**—the theory that aggression is an automatic response to any blocking of goal-directed behavior. They argued that:

1. Whenever you see someone acting aggressively, you can assume the person was previously frustrated (if your boss yells at you when you arrive at the office, for instance, you might assume he was stuck in traffic on the way to work), and
2. Whenever someone is frustrated, some act of aggression will surely follow (if you get a flat tire that makes you an hour late for work, you'll need to take it out on someone, perhaps making an aggressive "hand signal" to another driver who fails to yield the right of way).

Social psychologists have raised a number of objections to the original frustration–aggression hypothesis (e.g., Baron & Richardson, 1994; Zillmann, 1994). One objection is that some aggressive acts, particularly those we would categorize as instrumental, don't seem to follow any particular frustration. During the 1930s and 1940s, a group of Brooklyn mobsters ran a business called Murder Incorporated, whose employees were paid handsome salaries to assassinate complete strangers—people who had not frustrated them in the least. A second objection is on the other side of the equation—frustration doesn't always lead to aggression. If a travel agent tells you that all the economy flights to Hawaii are booked and you believe she tried her best to help you, you may feel frustrated but are unlikely to get angry at her.

To deal with these objections, Leonard Berkowitz (1989, 1993a) postulated a **reformulated frustration–aggression hypothesis**. According to this revision, frustration is linked only to emotional (or anger-driven) aggression, not to instrumental aggression (of the Murder Incorporated type). Further, Berkowitz suggested that frustration leads to aggression only when it generates negative feelings. If you think the travel agent is purposefully frustrating you and you were strongly anticipating a low fare to Hawaii, then you'll feel a lot of negativity and be more prone to snap aggressively at her. There is another key implication of Berkowitz's reformulation: *Any* event that leads

Frustration–aggression hypothesis (original) The theory that aggression is an automatic response to any blocking of goal-directed behavior.

Frustration–aggression hypothesis (reformulated) The theory that any unpleasant stimulation will lead to emotional aggression to the extent that it generates unpleasant feelings.

Figure 10.2   The original and revised frustration–aggression hypotheses

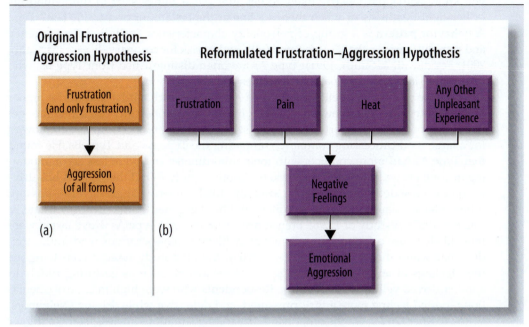

According to the original hypothesis (a), frustration always leads to aggression; and, conversely, aggression is always preceded by frustration (Dollard et al., 1939). According to the revised hypothesis (b), frustration is one of many unpleasant conditions that could lead to negative feelings and subsequent emotional aggression.

Source: Dollard, J., Miller, N. E., Doob, L. W.,Mowrer, O. H., & Sears, R. R. (1939). Frustration and aggression. New Haven, CT: Yale University Press.

to unpleasant feelings, including pain, heat, or psychological discomfort, can lead to aggression. The unpleasant feeling need not result from frustration per se. The original and reformulated frustration–aggression hypotheses are depicted in Figure 10.2.

According to the reformulated theory, unpleasant feelings may or may not lead to overtly aggressive behavior, depending on a number of factors—some in the person, some in the situation (Berkowitz, 1989, 1993a; 2012). We now turn to a consideration of these factors.

PERSON   Feelings of Arousal and Irritability

What internal factors stimulate people to act aggressively when they are annoyed? Two sets of factors have been examined, one related to temporary arousal states and the other to chronic irritability.

GENERAL AROUSAL   Berkowitz's (1989) modified frustration–aggression hypothesis assumed that aggression can be fueled by any form of unpleasant arousal, whether or not it results from frustration. Dolf Zillmann (1983, 1994) went one step further, arguing that any internal arousal state can enhance aggressive activity, including the arousal generated by exercising or even by watching an erotic film. According to Zillmann's **excitation-transfer theory**, the emotional reaction of anger produces the same symptoms that one feels during any arousing emotional state, including increased heart rate, sweaty palms, and elevated blood pressure. If a person is emotionally aroused for any reason and is later annoyed, or vice versa, the residual arousal may be mistaken for anger.

In one test of the excitation-transfer theory, women were first annoyed by another woman; some of them were then shown a nonviolent erotic film while others were shown a neutral control film (Cantor, Zillmann, & Einseidel, 1978). When they later got a chance to retaliate at their tormentor, women who had viewed erotica were more aggressive than those who had seen the control film. The researchers suggested that physiological arousal from the erotic film had been transferred into feelings of anger.

Excitation-transfer theory The theory that anger is physiologically similar to other emotional states and that any form of emotional arousal can enhance aggressive responses.

CHRONIC IRRITABILITY AND THE TYPE A PERSONALITY Can you think of someone you know who's particularly likely to get annoyed if things start to run behind his or her tight deadlines or when there's a line at the restaurant or a traffic jam? **Type A behavior pattern** is a group of personality characteristics, including time urgency and competitiveness, that is associated with higher risk for coronary disease (McCann, 2001; Rhodewalt & Smith, 1991). Type As are often distinguished from Type Bs, who take a more laid-back approach to deadlines and competition.

Because of their competitiveness, Type As tend to work harder and to rise higher in their professions (Matthews et al., 1980). However, their hostility can sometimes get in the way on the job. Robert Baron (1989) studied managers and technical employees for a large food-processing company, comparing the Type As and Type Bs. He found that Type As had more conflicts with their subordinates and were less accommodating in conflicts with their fellow workers. Another study found that Type A bus drivers on the crowded streets of India are more likely to drive aggressively—passing other vehicles, slamming on their brakes, and honking their horns (Evans, Palsane, & Carrere, 1987). A study of 11,965 French drivers found that Type As drove faster, were more likely to use cell phones, and were more likely to have a serious road-traffic accident than were other drivers (Nabi et al., 2005). A related study asked drivers to record their feelings of anger as well as aggressive behaviors (such as gesturing rudely to another driver, yelling, or tailgating). Respondents who were high in control orientation reported feeling more angry, pressured, and defensive while driving (Neighbors, Veitor, & Knee, 2002). On the other hand, frustrating situations are less likely to trigger hostility in people who are highly socially competent and thus able to choose a more effective course of action (Robinson et al., 2013).

SITUATION Unpleasant Situations

In one study, almost 1,000 Swedish teenagers described situations in which they had gotten angry (Torestad, 1990). Many of the anger-producing situations were directly connected to other people frustrating and annoying them (such as "My parents don't allow me to go out in the evening"). Consistent with the revised frustration–aggression hypothesis, researchers have found that many unpleasant situational factors, ranging from physical pain and unpleasant heat to long-term economic hardship, can fuel hostility (Berkowitz & Harmon-Jones, 2004; Dewall et al., 2007; Lindsay & Anderson, 2000).

PAIN In one series of experiments, students were assigned to the role of "supervisors," who administered shocks and rewards to other students working under them (Berkowitz, 1993b). They were asked to place a hand in a tank of water (presumably to investigate the influence of unpleasant conditions on supervision). In some cases, the water was painfully cold ice water; in other cases, it was closer to room temperature. When they were feeling pain, supervisors became more aggressive—recommending more shocks and fewer rewards for the students they were supervising (e.g., Berkowitz, Cochran, & Embree, 1981; Berkowitz & Thome, 1987). This research supports the folk wisdom that when the boss is having a bad day, you should stay out of his or her way.

SWELTERING HEAT The Manson Family murders were committed during an intense summer heat wave. During the previous night, the temperature hadn't dropped below 90 degrees Fahrenheit, and during the day it soared to over 100. Could this unpleasant weather have contributed to the Family members' violent inclinations? A reasonable amount of evidence suggests that the answer is yes—violent behaviors of all sorts are more likely during hot weather (Bushman, Wang, & Anderson, 2005; Kenrick & MacFarlane, 1986). Alan Reifman, Richard Larrick, and Steven Fein (1991) investigated how many times pitchers in major league baseball games threw balls that hit batters. Sometimes, pitchers hit batters on purpose—to intimidate them. This can be dangerous, because professionals fire a hardball at speeds approaching 100 miles per hour. The researchers found that as the weather got hotter, more batters got hit (see Figure 10.3).

Type A behavior pattern A group of personality characteristics, including time-urgency and competitiveness, that is associated with higher risk for coronary disease.

Were the pitchers really being intentionally aggressive, or did they just get less accurate as the temperature went up? Reifman and his colleagues statistically controlled for factors such as wild pitches, walks, and errors (related to inaccuracy). None of these factors could account for the relationship between temperature and the number of hit batters. The overheated pitchers weren't just throwing the ball anywhere; they were taking dead aim at the batters, and the hotter it got, the deadlier their aim got. A later analysis of over 50,000 Major League baseball games revealed another interesting twist: Sweltering heat is especially likely to inspire a pitcher to take aim at a batter if his teammates have been hit by the other pitcher earlier in the game (Larrick et al., 2011).

The effect of heat on aggression isn't limited to baseball pitches. Assaults, wife-beatings, rapes, murders, and even urban riots are all more likely to occur as temperature climbs (Anderson & DeNeve, 1992; Anderson et al., 1997). One contributing factor may be that there are simply more people (including violence-prone criminals and their potential victims) out on the streets when it gets warm. This would explain why crime is reliably found to drop when it gets very cold. Although people find cold weather to be unpleasant, most people stay home and huddle up by the fireplace. There is a controversy about whether aggression continues to increase, levels off, or perhaps even drops when the weather gets extremely hot (Bell, 2005; Cohn & Rotton, 2005). Under at least some circumstances, aggressive crimes may decrease at very high temperatures, when aggressors and potential victims are likely to stay indoors (and comfy) in front of the air conditioning vent (Rotton & Cohn, 2000). However, there is also evidence that unpleasantly hot weather fuels aggressive feelings, independent of the number of people out on the streets. Even within the same city, for example, aggressive crimes increase more than nonaggressive crimes as the mercury rises (Anderson, 1987).

Figure 10.3 Heated competition

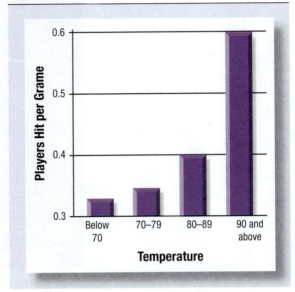

At temperatures above 90 degrees, pitchers hit almost twice as many batters as when the temperature is below 70 degrees. Analyses suggest that this is done purposely, and not due to heat-induced errors, or other confounding factors.

Source: Based on Reifman, A., Larrick, R. P., & Fein, S. (1991). Temper and temperature on the diamond: The heat-aggression relationship in major league baseball. *Personality and Social Psychology Bulletin, 17,* 580–585.

POVERTY A classic study by Carl Hovland and Robert Sears (1940) analyzed the price of cotton and the number of lynchings in 14 states of the American South during the years 1882 to 1930. They discovered a negative correlation: The lower the price (meaning worse times for the agricultural economy), the higher the number of lynchings. Using more sophisticated statistical techniques available four decades later, Joseph Hepworth and Stephen West (1988) found that the number of lynchings was highest when a recession followed a period of rising economic wellbeing. Hepworth and West linked this to the concept of **relative deprivation**, the feeling that I have less than the other people to whom I compare myself. Feelings of relative deprivation can result from dashed hopes, when good times encourage poor people to expect they'll soon be living like those on the good side of the tracks (Davies, 1962).

Downturns in the economy are most upsetting when they involve a downturn in your own personal finances, as they did for many during the "Great Recession" between 2007 and 2009. Indeed, a study of 815 unemployed people and their partners revealed that the financial strain of unemployment leads to a complex web of negative interactions in which both members of a couple become more depressed and more likely to get angry, criticize, and insult one another (Vinokur, Price, & Caplan, 1996). Another team of researchers interviewed 14,500 people twice over a yearlong period. Respondents were asked a number of questions about whether they'd been in a fight, used a weapon, struck their partner, or beaten their child in the two weeks prior to the interview. The odds of violence were fully six times higher among those who had lost their jobs during the intervening months, even among people who had no history of violent behavior (Catalano et al., 1993). In this chapter's research video, Martin Daly describes some fascinating links between unemployment, economic inequality and violent crimes.

Relative deprivation The feeling that one has less than the others to whom one compares oneself.

WATCH THE VIDEO: *Prof. Martin Daly of the University of Missouri describes his research on the deadly consequences of unemployment and economic inequality.*

INTERACTION   Annoyance Leads to Changes in Perception of Situations

When people get annoyed, they change their way of thinking. According to the **cognitive-neoassociation theory**, an unpleasant situation triggers a complex chain of internal events (see Figure 10.4). The first step in this process is that the unpleasant event unleashes negative feelings. For instance, you smash your shin on a cinderblock while searching for your lost car in a hot, humid parking lot, and it brings on a flood of negative feeling. Once you're in a negative mood, your thoughts turn to other negative experiences you've had in the past. The cognitive-neoassociation model envisions our memories as stored in interconnected networks of associated ideas, images, and feelings. When one negative feeling or thought occurs, it activates a host of related negative memories, feelings, and behaviors (Berkowitz, 1990; 2012; Berkowitz & Harmon-Jones, 2004).

Whether a negative chain of associations leads to aggressive behavior or to flight depends again on factors in the person that interact with factors in the situation. If you're in a negative mood on a dark street in a large city, for example, you may worry about your safety. However, the very same mood may contribute to angry thoughts if you're working in your yard and a cranky neighbor comes over to complain about your dog barking. Consider one study in which an obnoxious experimenter acted disgusted with students' performances on an anagram task. Following this, the students evaluated a woman who was being interviewed for a research assistant's position. Participants who had been insulted were kind in evaluating the assistant, unless she made a few mildly annoying mistakes. In this case, they seemed to unleash their resentment toward the obnoxious experimenter onto her (Pedersen et al., 2000). Other research suggests that we are more likely to displace our hostility from one person onto another when the second person provides any kind of triggering excuse to unleash the hostility, or when the second person resembles the first one in some way (Marcus-Newhall et al., 2000; Pedersen et al., 2008).

The **weapons effect** refers to the tendency for weapons, such as guns, to enhance aggressive thoughts and feelings (e.g., Bartholow et al., 2005; Crabb, 2000, 2005; Klinesmith, Kasser, & McAndrew, 2006). In the classic demonstration of this effect, male students were told they were participating in a study of physiological

Cognitive-neoassociation theory
Theory that any unpleasant situation triggers a complex chain of internal events, including negative emotions and negative thoughts. Depending on other cues in the situation (such as weapons), these negative feelings will be expressed as either aggression or flight.

Weapons effect The tendency for weapons, such as guns, to enhance aggressive thoughts, feelings, and actions.

Figure 10.4   Cognitive-neoassociation theory

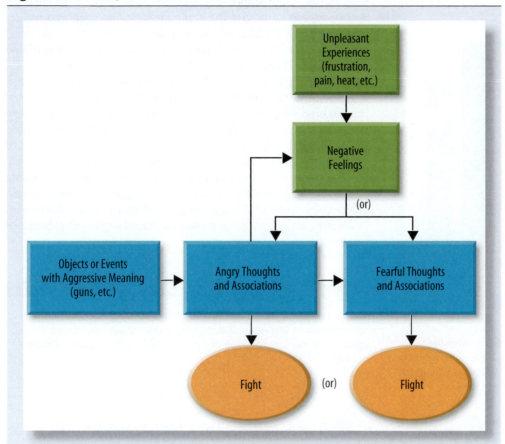

Negative thoughts follow negative feelings but can also feed back into increased negative feelings. Other cues in the situation, such as the presence of guns, may tilt these negative thoughts toward the consideration of aggressive behavior.

responses to stress (Berkowitz & LePage, 1967). If you were a subject in this experiment, the experimenter would explain that you were going to take turns with another student working on several problems. Your particular problem would be to list ideas a publicity agent might use to improve a popular singer's public image. Your fellow student would be asked to think of things a used car salesman might do to improve sales.

After you wrote down your ideas for the publicity campaign, the other student would give you feedback on the quality of your suggestions. This is where annoyance entered the picture—the "feedback" came in the form of electric shocks, anywhere from one to ten of them. If you were lucky, you would be in the nonangered condition—your partner would deliver only the minimum single shock (indicating your solutions were "very good"). If you were unlucky, your partner would blast you with not one, two, or three shocks but seven of them (simultaneously hurting you and expressing a harsh evaluation of your creativity). In that condition, as the experimenters planned, subjects tended to become angry.

Following this, though, you'd get a chance to retaliate. In one control condition, the experimenter would sit you down at an empty table with a shock key on it. In another, there were two badminton racquets on the table. In the crucial experimental condition, there was a 12-gauge shotgun and a .38 caliber revolver lying on the table. If there were sports equipment or weapons on the table, the experimenter would explain that it was part of another experiment and instruct you to disregard

Figure 10.5 The weapons effect

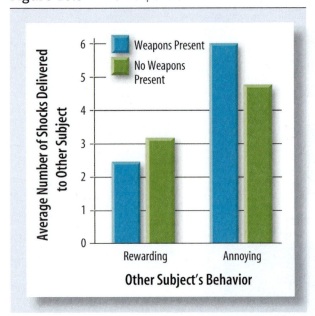

In one study, students were given the chance to deliver shocks to another student who had either treated them positively or annoyed them. As shown on the left, weapons didn't increase aggression when subjects weren't annoyed. As shown on the right, however, annoyed subjects delivered more shocks when guns were present.

them. Next, the experimenter would give you a sheet on which your partner had supposedly written his used-car sales ideas (in reality, all students saw the same suggestions prepared by the experimenter). Finally, you'd be asked to read the suggestions and to deliver "feedback" to the other student in the form of one to ten shocks. What do you do?

As Figure 10.5 shows, the presence of guns did not increase aggression if the person wasn't annoyed to begin with. In fact, nonangered subjects in the presence of weapons delivered very few shocks, and the shocks were very brief. But everything changed when the subjects were annoyed; now the presence of guns increased both the length and the number of shocks given. In line with his cognitive neoassociation theory, Berkowitz (1993a) believes that the mere presence of guns increases aggressiveness by "priming" aggressive associations. When the person is already angry, these associations increase the likelihood of retaliation.

INVESTIGATION

Think of a time when you felt particularly frustrated. Did you act aggressively to someone else, or not? How did your action, or inaction, fit the assumptions of the cognitive-neoassociation theory in Figure 10.4?

Figure 10.6 The cycle of frustration and aggression

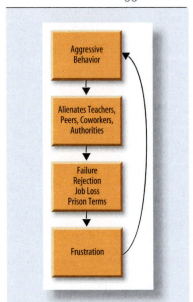

People who are aggressive elicit negative reactions from peers and authority figures. Consequently, they suffer more setbacks, including expulsion from school and incarcerations. These experiences increase frustration in their lives and lead to more aggressiveness.

INTERACTION **Some People Create Their Own Annoying Situations**

Another type of interaction occurs when people choose situations that match their personal characteristics. Would you enjoy working on the stock exchange, where traders need to stay constantly alert for the chance to win, or to avoid losing, hundreds of thousands of dollars? Or would you rather run a snowboarding shop, where you'd encounter laidback customers and no particular deadlines? If you are a Type A, it would be better for your health if you chose the less time-pressured job. However, research suggests that Type A students seem to go out of their way to choose the very situations that engage their competitiveness and time urgency (Westra & Kuiper, 1992).

Similarly, people who are prone to act aggressively may create life experiences that add to their own frustrations (Anderson, Buckley, & Carnagey, 2008). These, in turn, elicit more aggressiveness. For example, hot-tempered boys tend to alienate their teachers. Between frequent trips to the principal's office, they miss out on the opportunity to learn basic math and writing skills. As a consequence, they are later less qualified for jobs and suffer more unemployment. A history of violence in adolescence can lead to other irrevocable consequences, such as disfiguring injuries or time spent in prison. Partly because of persisting personality traits and partly because of the different environments they create for themselves, aggressive children get trapped in a cycle of frustration, which in turn leads to more aggression (Caspi, 2000; Moffitt, 1993). This cycle is depicted in Figure 10.6.

Quick Quiz

1 Which of the following is incorrect, according to the reformulated frustration–aggression hypothesis?

    a. Aggression must be preceded by frustration.
    b. Frustration is linked only to emotional aggression, not to instrumental aggression.
    c. Frustration leads to aggression only when it generates negative feelings.
    d. Any event that leads to unpleasant feelings can lead to aggression.

2   According to Zillman's excitation-transfer theory, which of the following types of arousal can lead to aggression?

    a. Arousal from physical exercise
    b. Arousal from watching a nonviolent erotic film
    c. Arousal from delivering a public speech
    d. All of the above

3   Which of the following personality and situational factors is not discussed in the text as increasing annoyance-related aggression?

    a. Type A personality
    b. Heat
    c. Type B personality
    d. Pain

4   Which of the following is incorrect regarding cognitive-neoassociation theory?

    a. Unpleasant stimulation can prime a network of negative thoughts and feelings.
    b. The presence of aggression-related cues, such as guns, can prime a network of negative thoughts and feelings.
    c. Pleasant stimulation, such as receiving a compliment, can sometimes prime a network of negative thoughts and feelings.
    d. (a), (b), and (c) are all incorrect

Gaining Material and Social Rewards

LO 10.7 Explain the social learning theory's assertion that aggressive behavior is caused by rewards for aggression.

LO 10.8 Identify who is most likely to find reward in violence and explain why.

LO 10.9 Discuss how glamorization of violence in the media can influence our behavior.

Vikings marauding across the countryside, urban gang members controlling lucrative drug territories, and schoolyard bullies taking children's lunch money have one thing in common—they reap rewards from aggressive behavior. Consider the case of America's most famous mobster.

Bridging Function and Dysfunction:

Gangland Violence

In a historically infamous episode of violence, Al Capone invited three of his fellow mobsters to a banquet in their honor. After wining and dining the men, Capone had his henchmen tie them to their chairs. He then personally proceeded to beat each of the three men to death with a baseball bat.

Despite his occasional capacity for extreme violence, though, many who knew him regarded Capone as a warm and benevolent friend. What, then, would prompt an otherwise friendly man to such extremes of violence? One answer is that it was part of his job description: Capone was an ambitious member of a profession that was, in his culture, a common path to material and social success.

Al Capone grew up just after the turn of the century in a poor immigrant family in Brooklyn. Because Capone was a tough and ambitious kid, he won the attention of a local mobster named Frankie Yale. When Capone was only 16, Yale put him to work

Al Capone. A man who used violence and antisocial behavior to gain immense material benefits, he came from a culture where this path to success had a long history.

collecting "protection" money from local businessmen. After killing a member of a rival gang, Capone was forced to move to Chicago, where he began to work his way to the top of the local mob. Capone killed several other men during his struggles to control lucrative alcohol-distribution territories. Once he rose to the top, he had his underlings do most of the murdering. However, he occasionally did his own killing to make a point. In the case of the men he beat with a baseball bat, Capone had learned that they were plotting against him, hoping to advance their own careers. To maintain his position as a powerful mafioso, he was expected to punish such disloyalty with death.

Capone's aggressiveness yielded big payoffs. By age 29, he controlled a syndicate reaping profits in the hundreds of millions of dollars, owned a beautiful estate in Florida, and wore diamonds that cost more than most men earned in a lifetime.

Capone wasn't the first, or the last, to play the role of Mafia don. Indeed, local thugs had wielded immense political and economic power in southern Italy and Sicily for centuries (Servadio, 1976). Because the region had been almost continually occupied, and exploited, by foreign armies, the native residents inherently disliked and distrusted government. Instead, they were loyal to local powerful men, who would protect them, get them jobs, and, at the same time, demand payment for that protection.

So, underneath what appears to outsiders to be a breakdown of societal structure is a clear and organized set of social structures and rules, derived from a particular military and political history. And like international conflict, a good deal of Mafia violence has been about controlling wealth and lucrative territories. Once again, then, we see that social dysfunctions are often rooted in otherwise functional processes.

The dangers of encouraging aggression in children. Andrew Golden, several years before he and Mitchell Johnson systematically massacred a teacher and four of their schoolmates.

Social Learning Theory: Rewarding Violence

According to the **social learning theory** model, aggressive behavior is caused by rewards for aggression (Bandura, 1973, 1983). Just as a Mafia don acts violently to maintain a lucrative drug, alcohol, or gambling business, so the local schoolyard bully acts violently to win some reward, if only a candy bar or praise from the other bullies.

Rewards for aggression can come directly, as when a boy's father buys him ice cream after the boy has been in a fight, or gives the boy a firearm as a Christmas present. The accompanying photo depicts young Andrew Golden posed in combat fatigues and holding a rifle. Several years later, Andrew, 11, and Mitchell Johnson, age 13, systematically gunned down four fellow students and a teacher. Like Andrew, Mitchell had been encouraged to shoot guns from earliest childhood by his parents and grandparents.

Rewards can also come indirectly, by observing others rewarded for aggression. From watching movies and television programs in which attractive characters punch, kick, beat, and shoot those who frustrate them, Bandura believes, children learn that violence is an acceptable way of handling conflicts with others. Just a few months before Johnson and Golden's killing spree, 14-year-old Michael Carneal similarly shot eight of his classmates in Paducah, Kentucky. Carneal had recently watched a movie in which movie star Leonardo DiCaprio committed a similar act of mayhem.

In a series of classic studies, Bandura and his colleagues examined the processes by which children come to imitate such depictions of violent behavior. In one study, children watched another person model a series of unusually violent acts toward a Bobo doll (an inflatable, life-size clown with a red nose that honks when a child punches it in the face). If the children observed the aggressive person receiving a reward, they were likely to spontaneously imitate the aggressive behavior later. They didn't do so if they'd watched the model being punished (Bandura, Ross, & Ross, 1963a, 1963b).

Bandura also notes that a person need not be particularly angry or upset to engage in reward-motivated aggressive behavior. Hired assassins and trained soldiers often act aggressively with no feelings of anger at all. Thus, social learning theory is particularly applicable to instrumental aggression.

PERSON ## Who Finds Rewards in Violence?

Are some people more likely to act aggressively for personal gain? Not every struggling immigrant could be as cold-blooded as Al Capone in his willingness to kill others who stood in the way of his business success. In contrast, it would be easier for a person who had little empathy for others and a magnified sense of self-worth to hurt

Social learning theory Theory that aggression is learned through direct reward or by watching others being rewarded for aggressiveness.

others for personal gain. Similarly, if a person were less sensitive to punishment, the potential costs of retaliation by victims or society would loom less large as deterrents.

PSYCHOPATHY A **psychopath** is an individual characterized by a lack of empathy for others, grandiose self-worth, and an insensitivity to punishment (Hare et al., 1990; Lalumiere et al., 2001). Psychopathy is also called antisocial personality disorder or sociopathy. Psychopaths' indifference to the pain of others is accompanied by impulsiveness and a tendency to deny responsibility for their own misdeeds. In a study comparing criminal violence in psychopaths and nonpsychopaths, researchers found that psychopaths' violent acts were three times more likely to be motivated by personal gain and over ten times less likely to have been motivated by emotion (Williamson, Hare, & Wong, 1987). Thus violence perpetrated by psychopaths is cool and calculated for personal reward. Recent evidence suggests that psychopaths' failure to learn from punishment may be linked to neurological deficits in the amygdala and orbital frontal cortex (Blair, 2004). Capone showed many of the classical characteristics of psychopathy, as in his coldhearted willingness to beat men to death and to assassinate his business competitors. And, like Capone, many psychopaths are quite socially charming (except to those who stand in their way).

EMPATHY If, like most people, you cannot help feeling distressed when you watch someone else in pain, you would probably take little pleasure in living the life of a henchman for the mob. Feelings of empathy—sharing the emotions of another—seem to make aggressive behavior unrewarding (Baumeister & Campbell, 1999; Zechmeister & Romero, 2002). Highly empathic people put themselves "in the other person's shoes" and tend to get consumed with guilt over hurting another (Leith & Baumeister, 1998). However, psychopaths, with their general tendency to feel less emotional arousal, and their particular lack of empathy (Harpur, 1993; Williamson et al., 1987), feel less compunction about hurting others in the course of committing other crimes, such as robbery.

ALCOHOL INTOXICATION Although empathy for another's pain can keep most nonpsychopaths from using violence, alcohol may temporarily turn off those normal empathic feelings. Participants in one study were given either an alcoholic or a nonalcoholic beverage to drink. Then they were asked to recall a conflict they had had in their romantic relationship. Those who were intoxicated were less able to see their partner's side of things—and they felt more anger at their partner (MacDonald, Zanna, & Holmes, 2000). This helps explain the strong association between spouse abuse and alcohol consumption (Coker et al., 2000; Thompson & Kingree, 2006).

One effect of alcohol is to remove the normal restraints against aggressive behavior—the concerns about the punishing negative consequences that will follow from hurting another. Fifty percent of the assailants in violent crime cases are drunk at the time they commit their misdeeds (Bushman, 1993). Indeed, alcohol leads to aggressiveness even in nonalcoholics, sometimes even when they're unprovoked (Gantner & Taylor, 1992; Gustafson, 1992). People are aware of the link between alcohol and aggression, and merely exposing participants to alcohol advertisements leads them to rate a stranger as more hostile (Bartholow & Heinz, 2006).

The lowered empathy and lack of concern about consequences may explain why alcohol is commonly involved in date rape (Abbey, Ross, McDuffie, & McAuslan, 1996). Antonia Abbey and her colleagues (1996) reviewed research suggesting that date rape may be increased by "alcohol myopia"—a narrow focus of attention on whatever seems most important to the person at that moment (Giancola & Corman, 2007; Steele & Josephs, 1988). Under the influence of alcohol, a sexually aroused man may become narrowly focused on his own sexual gratification and ignore or misinterpret his date's efforts to resist his advances.

SITUATION Glamorized Violence in the Media

One Manson Family member explained their violent spree by saying: "We were brought up on your TV" (Bugliosi & Gentry, 1974). Indeed, a key assumption of Bandura's (1983) social learning theory is that the media can teach us that aggressive

Psychopath Individual characterized by impulsivity, irresponsibility, low empathy, grandiose self-worth, and lack of sensitivity to punishment. Such individuals are inclined toward acting violently for personal gain.

Violence in the media. Movies and television programs expose children to thousands of acts of "justified" violence, from fistfights to murders.

Meta-analysis A statistical combination of results from different studies of the same topic.

behavior may lead to rewards. Turn on the television set during prime time, tune in to a children's cartoon show, or go to a movie theatre, and chances are that neither you, nor your innocent little niece or nephew, will have to wait long to witness mayhem. Over half of prime-time television shows contain violence, and it is usually presented in a way that makes it seem glamorous, trivial, and sanitized (Bushman & Phillips, 2001). Not only that; children are also exposed to violence in other media, from video games to song lyrics (Anderson, Carnegy, & Eubanks, 2003; Bushman & Anderson, 2002). To examine the effects of the multimedia onslaught of violence, researchers have taken several approaches.

CORRELATIONAL STUDIES Correlational studies ask whether watching more violence on a day-to-day basis is associated with acting more violently. Results of several correlational studies suggest that children, especially boys, who watch a lot of aggressive television are more aggressive toward other children (Belson, 1978; Friedrich-Cofer & Huston, 1986). For example, one longitudinal study revealed that children who watched a lot of violent television and who identified with aggressive characters were more likely to act aggressively in early adulthood (Huesmann et al., 2003).

Of course, such correlations do not prove causality. Perhaps children predisposed toward violence simply choose to watch more aggressive television. Or maybe some third factor, such as poverty, leads independently to both violent behavior and a preference for "shoot-'em-up" television programs. If so, poor people would continue to act violently even without the influence of violent television. One researcher investigated 22 different "third factors" that might have accidentally produced an association between violent behavior and television viewing. Yet even when all those other possible causes were measured and statistically removed, the connection between violent behavior and television watching still remained (Belson, 1978).

EXPERIMENTAL STUDIES Experimental studies randomly assign some participants to one or more doses of violent media and compare their reactions to those of people exposed to similar doses of nonviolent media. For example, college students in one study watched violent films for four nights in a row. Later, they participated in an unrelated experiment and were given the chance to harm the assistant. Compared to control participants, who had watched nonviolent shows, those who had been fed a diet of violent programming were more aggressive to the research assistant, regardless of whether or not she provoked them (Zillmann & Weaver, 1999). Other experimental studies have likewise suggested that more violent television leads to more aggressive behavior in children (Bushman & Anderson, 2001; Leyens et al., 1975; Parke et al., 1977).

Using Meta-analysis to Examine the Effects of Violent Media

Not all the research on media aggression yields the same conclusion (Friedrich-Cofer & Huston, 1986; Wiegman et al., 1992). What does a researcher do when studies contradict one another? Returning to the detective analogy used in Chapter 1, what would a detective do if a group of witnesses, none of them perfectly reliable, gave different versions of a crime they had witnessed? Rather than ignore all the testimony, a good detective would likely put all the accounts together and look for recurring themes or story elements common to several witnesses.

Meta-analysis is a statistical technique for discovering commonalities across a number of different studies. In the same way that variations between subjects in a single experiment are treated as random sources of error when an experimenter

conducts a test of statistical significance, so the variations between research studies on the same question are taken into account in a "meta-test" of statistical significance across all the studies. When one uses a number of studies, each with a large number of subjects, the chances increase dramatically that various random effects will cancel themselves out and that any true effects of the particular experimental variable will shine through.

Consider the imaginary findings depicted in Table 10.2. In both cases, subjects delivered an average of seven shocks in the nonviolent control conditions and ten shocks in the violent media conditions. On the left, the results are shown as they would be if there were absolutely no random factors affecting the results. On the right, the results are more like they would be in the real world,

Table 10.2 A Hypothetical Example of 10 Studies Measuring Number of Shocks Delivered by Subjects Exposed to Violent, as Opposed to Nonviolent, Media

RESULTS IF NO CHANCE FACTORS OPERATED		MORE TYPICAL RESULTS	
Violent Media	Nonviolent Media	Violent Media	Nonviolent Media
10	7	5	10
10	7	7	9
10	7	10	7
10	7	8	8
10	7	12	13
10	7	9	6
10	7	15	7
10	7	11	1
10	7	10	5
10	7	13	4
(Average) 10	7	10	7

complete with various sources of error. Note that in both cases the average results are the same. If one looked at only the first and second comparisons on the right side, one could mistakenly conclude that exposure to violent media *reduced* aggression. The comparison in row 4 would lead to a conclusion of no differences. Other comparisons, such as the last one, would exaggerate the size of the media effect. When one compares a large number of studies, however, the various sources of random error tend to cancel one another out and we're able to get a better idea of the "true" effect of violent media on the number of shocks delivered. In essence, this is what is involved in a meta-analysis—statistically averaging across a number of studies on the same question.

Because there have been many studies on the relationship between violent media and aggression, researchers have been able to conduct several meta-analyses on this question (e.g., Andison, 1977; Bushman & Anderson, 2001; Hearold, 1986). For example, one team of researchers considered 28 experimental studies in which children or adolescents who had just watched an aggressive (or a nonaggressive) film were observed and in which observers later recorded whether the subjects spontaneously acted aggressively (for instance, by hitting another child on the playground) (Wood, Wong, & Chachere, 1991). As expected, the data from the single experiments (which are plagued by various random factors) generated mixed results. In about a third of the

experiments, in fact, the control subjects were more aggressive than the experimental subjects, but in those reversals the effects tended to be relatively small. Many more studies found higher aggression in the subjects exposed to aggressive media, and more of those positive aggression effects were large. When the data were averaged across all the studies, the overall statistics were powerful enough for the researchers to conclude confidently that "media violence enhances children's and adolescents' aggression in interaction with strangers, classmates, and friends" (p. 380).

Although meta-analyses have led researchers to an increasingly confident consensus that exposure to violent media has harmful effects, the news media, which are owned by those making profits from violent television and movies, have used the mixed results to tell a different story to the public (Bushman & Anderson, 2001). But meta-analyses suggest that the correlation between watching violent television and later aggression is about .30—as strong as the relationship between smoking and cancer (Bushman & Philips, 2001). Not everyone who smokes will develop lung cancer, and not everyone who gets lung cancer was a smoker. Likewise, not everyone who watches violent television will later become violent. But just as your smoking is a major risk factor for your later health, your neighbor's kid watching a lot of violent media is a risk factor for the other kids in the neighborhood.

As you can see, then, conclusions from meta-analyses of media and aggression support Bandura's social learning theory of aggression. If people are exposed to models who act aggressively and get rewarded, they will learn to imitate the aggressive behavior of those models. The effects of aggressive media are not limited to prime-time television, though. Aggressive models are found in sources from children's video games to "adult" movies.

VIOLENT VIDEO GAMES Teenagers Eric Harris and Dylan Klebold enjoyed playing a graphically violent video game called *Doom*, which had been licensed by the U.S. military to train soldiers to kill effectively. On his Web site, Harris had a customized version

Practicing violence. Research suggests that violent video games can make violence toward real people more rewarding, and can desensitize players to the pain of others.

in which two shooters, equipped with extra weapons and unlimited ammunition, gun down helpless opponents. As a school project, they made a video in which they acted the game out, wearing trench coats and pretending to shoot school athletes. On April 20, 1999, Harris and Klebold turned their gory fantasies into reality, slaughtering 13 of their Columbine High School classmates and wounding 23 others. Did their experience winning points for killing opponents on the computer screen teach them that murder could be rewarding? Social psychologists Craig Anderson and Karen Dill (2000) gathered data suggesting the answer might be yes. In a correlational study, Anderson and Dill found that real-life video game play was associated with a record of aggressive and delinquent behaviors such as destroying property and hitting other students. A neuropsychological study examined patterns of brain wave activity while participants looked at violent images (such as a photo of a man holding a gun in another man's mouth). Compared with students who did not play violent video games, those with high exposure to violent video games showed a particular pattern of brain wave activity indicating that they had become desensitized to viewing violent images (Bartholow, Bushman, & Sestir, 2006).

As with all correlations, these findings do not establish cause and effect. Perhaps the violent video game choices merely reflect delinquent tendencies, rather than causing them. However, college students randomly assigned to play a graphically violent game (*Wolfenstein*) later had more aggressive thoughts and feelings than a comparable group who played a nonviolent game. The researchers concluded that violent video games can provide a forum in which youngsters learn and practice aggressive solutions to conflicts (Anderson et al., 2004; Carnagey & Anderson, 2005). Students in another experiment played the game *Mortal Kombat: Deadly Alliance* under varying conditions, from no blood to the maximum level of bloodiness. The bloodier the game, the more aroused, and more aggressive, the players became (Bartlett, Harris, & Bruey, 2008). Outside the laboratory, researchers have also found a relationship between violent video-game playing and antisocial delinquent behavior (DeLisi et al., 2013). Meta-analyses of studies on video game violence indicate a reliable effect of video games on aggressive thought, feelings, and behavior, about as strong as the effect of condom use on HIV infection (Anderson & Bushman, 2001; Anderson, Shibuya et al., 2010). Besides increasing aggressive behavior, experimental exposure to violent video games reduces normal physiological arousal to real violence, suggesting that young people who play those games become desensitized to other people's suffering (Carnegy, Anderson, & Bushman, 2007; Engelhardt et al., 2011).

VIOLENT PORNOGRAPHY Pornographic films and magazines often glamorize a particularly troubling form of violence—rape. In some such films, the victim is depicted as resisting the rapist at first but later rewarding the man's coerciveness by enjoying herself and wanting more sex. After watching such films, even nonangered men delivered more electric shocks to a woman (Donnerstein and Berkowitz, 1981). Another study found that after several nights of watching slasher films, participants were desensitized to violence toward women and later expressed less sympathy for a rape victim in a courtroom case (Mullin & Linz, 1995). Connecting with the research on video games, a recent study found that experimentally exposing men to video games with sex-stereotyped characters leads them to become more tolerant of sexual harassment (Dill, Brown, & Collins, 2008).

The effects of pornography on aggression are also controversial. Some researchers doubt that any clear relationship has been established (e.g., Brannigan, 1997; Fisher & Grenier, 1994). Others have pointed out that it is the violence, and not the sexual component, that seems to be responsible for any increases in aggression toward women (Malamuth & Donnerstein, 1984). In fact, earlier research using soft-core nonviolent erotica, such as *Playboy* centerfolds, found a decrease in aggression afterward (Baron, 1974). Neil Malamuth and his colleagues Tamara Addison and Mary Koss (2001) noted that this topic is a sensitive one because people, including the researchers themselves, often hold strong values on the topic. Conservatives believe that pornography undermines family values. Liberals believe that there is a negligible, and sometimes positive, effect and that censorship contradicts the First Amendment. Many feminists hold a third set of values, believing that pornography encourages men to hold demeaning and hostile attitudes toward women and often depicts rape as a positive experience for women.

On the basis of meta-analyses and some new data, Malamuth and his colleagues (2001) offered several conclusions. First, correlational and experimental data suggest that there is some relationship between men's hostility toward women and the use of pornography. The relationship is found particularly for violent (rather than nonviolent) pornography, and it is more likely among those who are exposed to very high levels and who have several risk factors for violence against women (such as being highly promiscuous). The available evidence does not clearly rule out the possibility that it is the men's aggressiveness that leads them to view pornography. However, the combination of experimental and correlational findings did lead the researchers to conclude that there is cause for concern that violent pornography may later lead some men to act violently toward women.

INTERACTION Violent Media Magnify Violent Inclinations

Glamorized violence may make aggression seem more rewarding, but it is not likely to affect everyone in the same way. Not everyone finds it rewarding to expose him- or herself to such depictions of violence. Many people will go well out of their way to avoid watching a violent movie or a bloody boxing match. Others seem to relish such experiences.

Researchers in Montreal asked moviegoers to fill out a short aggression questionnaire, either before or after they watched a violent film (which contained 61 depictions of death by machine guns, bayonets, knives, and explosions) or a nonviolent film (which contained no violent deaths). The researchers found that the violent film increased aggressive tendencies in viewers, whereas the nonviolent one produced no change. More interesting, though, is that those who chose the aggressive film were substantially more aggressive to begin with (Black & Bevan, 1992). A later series of laboratory experiments demonstrated this same relationship—aggressive films make people more violent, but it is violence-prone people who choose to expose themselves to the aggression in the first place (Bushman, 1995). Once again, we see a form of dynamic interaction between person and situation. Some people are prone to find violence pleasurable, and they choose situations in which violence is glamorized; others find it unpleasant, and they choose to avoid such situations. Over a series of such choices, small initial differences between people may get magnified.

INVESTIGATION

Think of someone you know who likes watching violent movies and television or who plays a lot of violent video games. Now think of someone who avoids violent media. Are these two people different in other ways that fit with the research we just discussed?

Quick Quiz

1 According to social learning theory, aggressive behavior is caused by:

    a. Direct rewards for violence.

    b. Observing others being reinforced for aggressive behavior of generosity.

    c. Either of the above

    d. None of the above

2 According to the text, which of the following factors are connected to rewards for violence?

    a. Psychopathy

    b. Alcohol

    c. Empathy

    d. All of the above

3 Which of the following is incorrect?

    a. Violence increases after playing graphic video games.

    b. Violent people choose to watch more violence, and their violent tendencies are increased by watching it.

    c. Contrary to expectation, watching a moderate amount of violent erotica actually decreases hostility toward women.

    d. Although not every study shows the same results, meta-analyses of many such studies demonstrate an increase in violence associated with violent media exposure.

Gaining or Maintaining Social Status

LO 10.10 Explain how differential parental investment and sexual selection are connected to sex differences in status-linked aggression.

LO 10.11 Understand testosterone's links with aggression and dominance.

LO 10.12 Explain how age, sex, and culture link to status-driven aggression.

Among the Dodoth of northern Uganda, a man isn't permitted to marry and have children until he has proven himself as a warrior. Societies around the world, from the Yanomamö of Brazil to the Masai of eastern Africa, proffer great respect on men who hold the "warrior status," which involves enjoyment of aggression and readiness to fight for one's "honor" (McCarthy, 1994).

At one level, acting aggressively to gain status is a subset of acting aggressively to gain material and social rewards. Al Capone used violence to maintain his status as a mob boss and to keep the bootleg profits rolling in. But the goal of gaining and maintaining status has another unique connection with aggression—people may fight for status even when it brings no tangible material rewards. Indeed, some people will fight for status even when they know they'll be punished for it. Some psychologists believe that the goal of gaining social status has a unique role in determining aggression, a role connected to our evolutionary past.

Differential parental investment The principle that animals making higher investment in their offspring (female as compared to male mammals, for instance) will be more careful in choosing mates.

Sexual selection A form of natural selection favoring characteristics that assist animals in attracting mates or in competing with members of their own sex.

Aggression and Sexual Selection

Why is the association between aggression and status so prevalent from the jungles of Brazil to the streets of Chicago and New York? Canadian psychologists Martin Daly and Margo Wilson (1988, 1994) traced the link to the powerful evolutionary principles of **differential parental investment** and sexual selection. According to the principle of differential parental investment, discussed in Chapter 8, females have more to lose from a rash mating decision (they can become pregnant). Hence they will take care in choosing the males with whom they mate, giving preference to those whose traits suggest better-quality genes.

What does female mating selectivity have to do with aggression? The answer lies in **sexual selection**—the process whereby any tendencies that help in reproduction are passed on to future generations (Miller, 2000). To win the attentions of selective females, males can do one of several things. They can display positive characteristics: a beautiful peacock's tail or an ability to build a sturdy nest or to defend a rich territory. Or they can beat out the competition directly—by fighting their way to the top of the local dominance hierarchy. Whether the game is defending a territory or winning a place at the top of the hierarchy, it helps to be larger and more aggressive (Alcock, 1993).

Hence, evolutionary theorists assume an inherent link between successful reproduction and competing

Status and aggression. These two high school boys are competing to win a state championship. Aggression, whether socially sanctioned or not, is one pathway to status.

for status. In this equation, aggression is only an incidental byproduct. Sexual selection theory makes several assumptions that apply to humans. Because humans are mammals and female mammals always invest heavily in their offspring, males will generally be more likely to compete for status and territory (Buss & Duntley, 2006; Campbell, 2005). We mentioned earlier that males committed the vast majority of U.S. homicides during recent decades. Consistent with the evolutionary perspective, the same gender difference holds up worldwide (see Figure 10.7).

If aggressive competition between males is about mating, then it should rise and fall with particular conditions. When males have little access to other resources with which to attract females, competition with other males should be harsher. Likewise, as males enter the years of reproductive competition, the aggressiveness should increase. Once a male has attracted a long-term mate, however, he has less need to butt heads with other males. We will consider the evidence for these predictions. In addition to the reproduction-based gender differences, assumed to hold up across cultures, there are also independent cultural differences in status-linked aggression, which we will also consider.

Figure 10.7 Percentage of same-sex homicides across various cultures and time periods

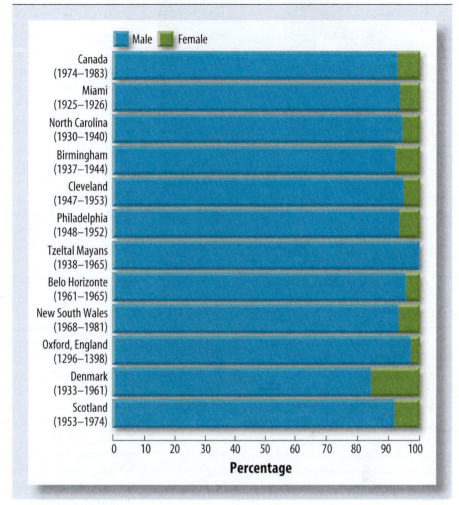

Homicides committed by adult members of the same sex (men killing men, women killing women) have been committed predominantly by men across different cultures and periods of history.

Source: Republished with permission of Transaction Publishers, from Homicide, Daly, M., & Wilson, M. 1988; permission conveyed through Copyright Clearance Center, Inc.

PERSON Sex and Testosterone

Zoologists have observed that the male proclivity for violent competitiveness is found widely among mammals (Boulton, 1994). You don't need to tromp off to study the antelopes of Uganda or the chimpanzees of Tanzania for evidence. Go out to the nearest farm and observe the differences between bulls and cows or stallions and mares, or stay in the neighborhood and observe the differences between male and female dogs.

The biological motivation to compete for status may be linked to the distant evolutionary past, but the driving mechanism is still in our bodies today. Testosterone is a hormone linked to masculine bodily development and behavior. It flows in greater quantities through male than female bloodstreams and has been directly linked to both aggressiveness and social dominance.

Social psychologist Jim Dabbs and his colleagues conducted an extensive series of investigations into the links between testosterone and social behavior. Some of their findings are:

- In boys aged 9 to 11, higher testosterone levels are associated with more aggressive behaviors (Chance, Brown, Dabbs, & Casey, 2000).
- Prison inmates with high testosterone levels have more confrontations with prison authorities. In addition, the crimes committed by these high-testosterone prisoners were, on average, more violent (Dabbs et al., 1987, 1991, 1995).

High-testosterone males. Researcher Jim Dabbs found that men with high testosterone are more likely to have showy tattoos and to engage in a variety of antisocial behaviors. Southern men with records of delinquency had higher testosterone levels than a comparison group of college students.

• Among 4,462 military veterans, those with high testosterone levels were more likely to have had trouble with the law, to have been violent, and to have an unusually large number of sexual partners (Dabbs & Morris, 1990).

All of these findings are correlational, making it difficult to determine whether high testosterone was a cause or a consequence of aggressive and antisocial behavior. The causal picture is muddied because testosterone levels can be raised by competition or sexual behavior (Mazur & Booth, 1998). For example, male college students in one study were insulted and pushed by another student (Cohen, Nisbett, Bowdle, & Schwarz, 1996). When subjects' testosterone levels were measured after this face-off, they had risen significantly.

Experimental studies, however, suggest that boosts in testosterone are a cause, and not just a correlate, of increased competitive behavior (Carré, McCormick, & Hariri, 2011). In one study, a small group of men were given increasingly higher doses of testosterone, doubling every two weeks over a six-week period (Kouri et al., 1995). During the course of the testosterone treatment, they were placed in a laboratory with another subject who they believed was penalizing them by pressing a button that would reduce cash paid to them. Those given the testosterone injections were more likely to retaliate than men given an inert placebo.

A fascinating series of studies by Dutch psychologists examined a group of 50 individuals as they were undergoing medical sex-change procedures. Stephanie VanGoozen and her colleagues (1995) were able to track changes in both directions. Thirty-five of the transsexuals were females receiving testosterone as part of their desired transformation into males. Fifteen were men receiving testosterone-suppressing drugs as part of their desired transformation into females. Women who received testosterone became more aggressive and more responsive to sexual arousal. Men deprived of testosterone showed dramatic changes in the opposite direction: decreases in aggressiveness and sexual arousability.

Both males and females produce testosterone, and it may affect both sexes in similar ways (Dabbs et al., 1996; Glickman et al., 1993). But adult males produce about seven times as much testosterone as do females (Mazur & Booth, 1998). Even in men, though, the effects of testosterone on aggression, like the effects of watching violent media, are not overwhelming, and researchers sometimes need to examine a large number of subjects to find clear effects (Dabbs & Morris, 1990).

In any individual, then, heightened testosterone is hardly an automatic trigger for violent or antisocial behavior. Instead, it may be more closely linked to competitive behaviors from rugby and tennis to chess and dominoes (Bateup et al., 2002; Mazur, Booth, & Dabbs, 1992; Wagner, Flinn, & England, 2002). After reviewing a number of studies, Allan Mazur and Alan Booth (1998) concluded that high levels of testosterone in humans encourage "behavior intended to dominate—to enhance one's status over—other people" (p. 353). Sometimes this behavior is aggressive, but sometimes it is not. Thus, testosterone may not have a direct effect on aggressiveness but an indirect one via its enhancement of the motivation to dominate others.

INVESTIGATION

There was an old song entitled "Ladies Love Outlaws." Have you ever seen evidence of a woman being attracted to a guy who seemed to be tough and/or antisocial? How might such examples fit with the research on testosterone and sexual selection?

SITUATION Insults and the Culture of Honor

Consistent with the assumption that status-linked aggression is more crucial to males than to females, a greater percentage of male murderers are motivated by a desire to retaliate for a previous insult or "put-down" (Daly & Wilson, 1988). Consider the brutal Manson Family murders with which we opened the chapter. Although the crime scene appeared at first to have been randomly chosen, further investigation revealed otherwise. Manson had been insulted several times by people connected to that house. Shortly before the murders, he had gone to the house looking for Terry Melcher, the Hollywood agent who had previously spurned him. It turned out that the property had been purchased by another Hollywood agent; when Manson tried to approach this man, he was again rebuffed, this time quite rudely.

The power of a personal put-down to elicit aggression has been harnessed in a number of laboratory studies of aggression. Experimental subjects are more likely to deliver electric shocks or other punishments to someone who insults them, compared to someone who treats them with respect (e.g., Buss, 1963; Carver & Glass, 1978). Outside the laboratory, college students' fantasies about killing others often follow incidents in which the other person humiliates them in some way (Duntley, 2005; Kenrick & Sheets, 1994).

The Southern culture of honor (and violence). William Anderson Hatfield (seated) was the patriarch whose family became enmeshed in a feud with the relatives of Ranel McCoy. The Hatfields and McCoys were agricultural families from the Kentucky/West Virginia border who showed many of the characteristics associated with the "Southern culture of violence."

Concern about saving face often gets carried to extreme lengths. In a classic study of homicides in Philadelphia, Marvin Wolfgang (1958) categorized 37% of the causes as "trivial altercations," disputes started over relatively petty issues, such as an insult or one person bumping into another. Though labeled "trivial," these altercations were the most common motives for murder. Only men seem to get involved in homicides over trivial altercations. Why? After an extensive examination of police reports of homicides, Wilson and Daly (1985) suggested that what was at stake was actually not trivial at all. Instead, violent disputes between males involve an escalating battle over status that begins when one man insults another in public.

Not every man responds to a put-down by running for the nearest gun. Whether such status confrontations turn violent depends on a feature of the broader situation—the culture in which a person is raised. According to Richard Nisbett (1993), those who reside in the southern and western United States are, compared to those living in the northern states, more likely to be socialized into a **culture of honor**, which involves a set of norms whose central idea is that people (particularly men) should be ready to use violence to defend their honor (Cohen & Nisbett, 1997).

In the Old South, it was difficult to get a conviction for murder if the victim had insulted the perpetrator and refused to retract the slur. And Southern laws still reflect that culture (Cohen, 1996). Southern states also have higher rates of homicides, but only for argument-related homicides—the sort that engage men's honor (Nisbett, Polly, & Lang, 1995). Southerners aren't generally more violent or more criminally oriented; they're simply more likely to kill as part of an argument. One team of social psychologists presented data to argue that the Southern culture of violence, and not the heat, may explain the high homicide rates in cities such as Houston (Cohn, Rotton, Peterson, & Tarr, 2004).

Dov Cohen, Brian Bowdle, and Norbert Schwarz joined Nisbett to conduct a fascinating, and slightly dangerous, series of experiments examining these regionally based differences in aggression (Cohen et al., 1996). The experimental setting was arranged so that the subject had to crowd past another student working at a filing cabinet, forcing that other student to move out of the way. The subject was then required to return past the same tight spot, at which point the other student slammed the file drawer shut, pushed his shoulder against the subject, and called the subject an "asshole." The confederate then quickly retreated behind a locked door—which turned out to

Culture of honor A set of societal norms whose central idea is that people (particularly men) should be ready to defend their honor with violent retaliation if necessary.

be a good idea, as one subject actually pursued him and aggressively tried to open the door. Two confederates were stationed nearby to record the subject's reactions to this insult. In response to this provocation, 65% of Northerners responded with more amusement than anger. This was true for only 15% of Southerners, however, who generally indicated much more outrage than humor.

Recent research has found that people who adhere to the "culture of honor" are also more likely to take potentially fatal risks, and also to favor more militant responses to terrorism (Barnes et al., 2012a, 2012b).

INTERACTION When Status Matters

Testosterone appears to stimulate a motivation toward dominance in men (Mazur & Booth, 1998). If that motivation can be satisfied without resort to violence, presumably it will. From the perspective of sexual selection theory, the male tendency to struggle for dominance is itself only a path to a more important goal—successful reproduction. This suggests that male status-linked aggressiveness will appear only in those circumstances when less dangerous paths to social status are blocked. Status-driven aggression should also be enhanced when females are hard to come by but reduced when a man has succeeded in the goal of attracting a mate. Research supports each of these interactive predictions.

BLOCKED PATHWAYS TO SUCCESS Using their sample of 4,462 U.S. military veterans, James Dabbs and Robin Morris (1990) examined the different correlates of high testosterone in high- and low-status men. Their results are depicted in Figure 10.8. Whereas high testosterone did not boost antisocial behaviors in men of high status, it substantially boosted the risk of adult delinquency in men of lower status.

Why the difference? Dabbs and Morris explain it in terms of the different paths to status. For men in both the upper- and the lower-class groups, testosterone probably stimulated the same drive for competition and dominance. However, upper-class men don't need to beat someone up to act on that drive—they can vent it during vigorous and risky activity on the tennis court, chessboard, or stock exchange. For lower-class men, though, who may be unemployed or working in menial jobs, these pathways to respect are not available, so they are more likely to answer the drive for respect and status by hitting someone or thwarting the law.

There is a popular claim that low self-esteem leads to aggressiveness. Although a number of studies do suggest that feelings of rejection can increase aggression (Gaertner, Iuzzini, & O'Mara, 2008; Leary, Twenge, & Quinlivan, 2006), people with generally *high* self-esteem (particularly men) are more likely to act aggressively than those with chronically low self-esteem (Baumeister, Bushman, & Campbell, 2000). It isn't people who are comfortable with themselves, or who are respected by others, that we most need to watch out for, though (Johnson, Burk, & Kirkpatrick, 2007). Instead, the most dangerous characters seem to be those with an overly inflated view of themselves, and a sense that other people don't give them enough respect (e.g., Johnson et al., 2007; Kernis, Grannemann, & Barclay, 1989; Twenge & Campbell, 2003).

COMPETITION FOR MATES Several lines of evidence suggest that status-linked aggressiveness ebbs and flows along with competition for mates. In other animal species, male aggressiveness increases just before the mating season, when territories and females are being contested (Gould & Gould, 1989). In humans, boys increase their dominance displays at puberty, when successful competitiveness (such as being a star athlete) begins to

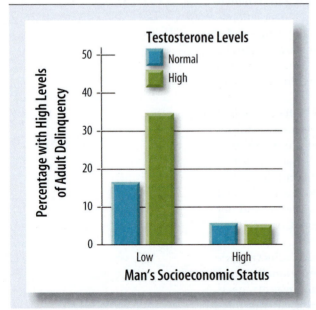

Figure 10.8 Testosterone contributes to risk of antisocial behavior only in lower-class men

High testosterone is associated with substantially greater risk in lower-class men, who presumably have limited resources with which to achieve social dominance.

lead to popularity with the opposite sex (Weisfeld, 1994). Men are most dangerous in their late teens and twenties, when their testosterone levels are highest, and when they are competing most vigorously for mates (Daly & Wilson, 1988; Palmer, 1993). Consistently, married men, particularly those who are committed to their wives or who have children, have lower testosterone levels than unmarried men (Gray et al., 2002; McIntyre et al., 2006).

Vlad Griskevicius and his colleagues conducted several studies of men's tendency to "aggress to impress" and its connections to mating and status. The researchers activated different social motives by having participants imagine themselves either beginning their first day on a high-powered job (status competition motive) or on a romantic date with someone they find highly attractive (mating motive). Afterwards, participants were asked what they would do if they were at a party and someone they knew rudely spilled a drink on them and did not apologize. Compared with the control condition, men primed to think about status were more likely to say they would do something directly aggressive; women were more likely to prefer an indirect retaliation, which did not get in their annoyer's face. When a mating motive was activated, however, men acted very differently, depending on the audience. If the audience was described as other males, the men again preferred to act in a directly aggressive manner; if the audience was composed of women, however, the men were more inclined to suppress their violent inclinations (see Figure 10.9). These findings are consistent with the idea that men realize that violence is not in itself attractive to women, but that it is linked to their perceived status among other men, which is what increases their attractiveness to women (Griskevicius, Tybur, Gangestad, Perea, Shapiro, & Kenrick, 2009).

Figure 10.9   Aggressing to impress

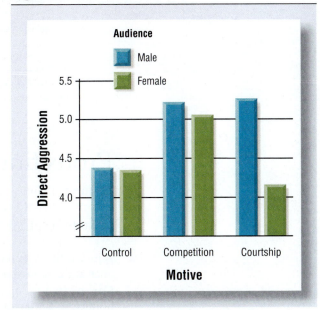

Whether men were inclined to react with direct aggression to an imagined insult depended on their current motivational state and the likely audience for the aggressive act. A courtship motive increased aggressive inclinations, but only if the audience was composed of other men.

Quick Quiz

1 According to the principles of differential parental investment and sexual selection, male aggressiveness:

a. Increases when males have offspring to protect.
b. Is linked to the fact that females are generally more selective about choosing mates.
c. Increases when a male successfully attracts a long-term mate to defend.
d. All of the above

2 Which of the following are true?

a. Experimental administrations of testosterone led to a slight decrease in aggressive impulses of transsexuals.
b. Experimental administrations of testosterone have been shown to increase aggressiveness in college women, but not men.
c. High testosterone typically increases antisocial behavior in high-status (but not low-status) males.
d. Correlational studies have found that higher testosterone levels are associated with more aggressive behaviors in boys, prison inmates, and military veterans.

3 Which of the following are true statements regarding the "culture of honor"?

a. It is a set of societal norms more prevalent in the southern and western regions of the U.S.
b. The central idea is that people (especially men) should be ready to use violent retaliation when their honor is insulted.
c. Laboratory studies have found a link, but the theory has received less support from studies conducted outside the lab.
d. Answers (a) and (b) are correct

4 Which of the following statements is incorrect?

a. There is a curvilinear relationship between age and status-driven aggression such that both younger and older males (but not middle-aged males) tend to commit the majority of status-linked violence.

b. High levels of testosterone are clearly associated with antisocial behavior only in men of low socioeconomic status.

c. Status-linked violence is more often found in men whose paths to success are blocked (i.e., younger, poorer men).

d. All of the above are incorrect

Protecting Oneself or Others

LO 10.13 Identify two features of the person that might contribute to a tendency toward self-defensive aggression.

LO 10.14 Explain why self-protective aggression can increase danger.

A jury is likely to have little sympathy for someone who murdered because of annoyance at the hot weather or a desire to win the respect of fellow gang members. But the final motive for aggression we'll consider can serve as a legitimate excuse, even for homicide. J. Martin Ramirez (1993) surveyed people in Spain, Finland, and Poland about the circumstances under which aggression might be justified. In all three countries, people rated "self-defense" and "protecting others" at the top of the list of justified causes of aggression. From an evolutionary perspective, it makes some sense that humans, like other animals, have an inclination to act aggressively if it is necessary to defend themselves or close relatives (Duntley, 2005).

Of course, not everyone protects himself or herself from violence by acting aggressively. As we discuss below, some people are especially likely to engage in self-defensive aggression, and some circumstances are more likely to turn defensive feelings into self-protective violence.

PERSON ## Self-Defenders

When Hans Toch (1984) set out to classify violent criminals, one of his murderous types was what he called the "self-defender." Such people "react to other persons as sources of physical danger. They are afraid that if they don't strike first, they'll become victims themselves" (Bertilson, 1990, p. 459).

Two features of the person might contribute to a tendency toward self-defensive aggression, one related to attributional style, the other related to one's relative size and strength.

DEFENSIVE ATTRIBUTIONAL STYLE Most aggressive children, rather than being heartless little psychopaths, are actually frightened of being attacked (Dodge et al., 1990). These little aggressors are often characterized by two key features: (1) a tendency to be overly emotional and (2) a tendency to believe that others are threatening them. Based on their studies of schoolyard aggressiveness, Kenneth Dodge and his colleagues have developed a social-information processing model of aggressive behavior in children (Dodge et al., 1990; Hubbard et al., 2001) (see Table 10.3).

Emotional children tend to have a **defensive attributional style**—a tendency to notice threats and to interpret other children's behavior as intentionally meant to harm them (Dodge & Coie, 1987). Because they are afraid of being hurt, defensive children are more likely to consider, and to choose, aggressive responses to situations that other children would ignore. Older children and adolescents who are incarcerated for violence often show the same defensive pattern. Rather than simply beating up others for the fun of it, these kids act aggressively in response to what

Defensive attributional style A tendency to notice threats and interpret other people's behavior as intended to do one harm.

Table 10.3	Differences in Social Information Processing by Defensive and Nondefensive Children			
			RESPONSE OF:	
			Nondefensive Child	**Defensive Child**
Step 1	Search the situation for possible threats.	Is anyone threatening me in any way?	Less likely to notice if another child bumps him or her in a game	More likely to notice another child bumping against him or her
Step 2	Interpret the cues.	Why did that kid bump into me?	More likely to interpret an ambiguous bump as an accident	More likely to interpret a bump as an attempt to push him or her around
Step 3	Consider possible ways to respond.	What should I do about the kid repeatedly bumping into me?	More likely to consider a peaceful solution, such as making a joke	More likely to consider an aggressive solution, such as hitting or retaliating in another way
Step 4	Select a response.	Which possibility will best solve the problem?	More likely to rule out an aggressive response even if he or she considers it	More likely to rule out a peaceful response
Step 5	Carry it out.	How do I do what I've decided on?	More skilled at carrying out peaceful options	More skilled at carrying out aggressive options

they perceive as threats from others (Hubbard et al., 2001). Indeed, the tendency to interpret ambiguous events as hostile, and to ruminate upon those perceived threats, contributes to feelings of anger and triggers reactive aggression in people of all ages (Wilkowski & Robinson, 2008).

THE EFFECT/DANGER RATIO AND ABUSIVE RELATIONSHIPS   Because of their relatively small physical size, females are more likely to be on the receiving end of bullying in their relationships with males (Ahmad & Smith, 1994). One survey of women waiting in doctors' offices revealed a startling fact: More than 40% had been physically abused by a husband or boyfriend at some time in their lives, and almost half that number were currently in an abusive relationship (Coker et al., 2000). Indeed, of the women killed in the United States, more than half are killed by their own partners.

Women also kill their partners, but for very different motives (Belknap et al., 2012; Browne, 1993; Daly & Wilson, 1988). Whereas men are likely to kill their partners as part of a pattern of harassment and attempted control, women are likely to kill their partners in self-defense. Thus, women typically resort to violence only in extreme circumstances—when they have been repeatedly threatened and abused.

Given that females feel angry as frequently as men do, why does it take more extreme circumstances to trigger serious physical violence in them? The answer may be linked to the **effect/danger ratio**—the person's assessment of the likely beneficial effect of aggressiveness, balanced against the likely dangers (Bjorkvist et al., 1994). If you are truly angry at another person, a punch in the face may deliver more of the desired effect than a verbal insult. However, there is a danger involved—the punch is more likely to elicit physical violence in return. So, if your opponent is 60 pounds heavier than you and has twice the upper body strength, you are likely to think twice about using physical aggression as a persuasive tool. Ironically, for women who live under constant threat from a larger, abusive man, killing him may seem less dangerous than a milder counterattack, which might just provoke more violence on his part.

SITUATION Perceived Threats

When one researcher asked teenagers what triggered their everyday feelings of anger, they most frequently mentioned someone else's intentionally acting unreasonably toward them, insulting them, teasing them, or physically harassing them (Torestad,

Effect/danger ratio Assessment of the likely beneficial effect of aggressiveness balanced against the likely dangers.

1990). And when college students were asked about homicidal fantasies, most could remember at least one, and it was often triggered by a threat to oneself or to a valued other (Kenrick & Sheets, 1994).

Simply showing up at school can be a threatening experience for some U.S. teenagers. The combination of being African American and being a teenager is particularly fraught with danger. Teenagers are 2.5 times more likely to be victims of violent crime than are people over 20 years of age, and blacks are much more likely to be murdered than whites (Hammock & Yung, 1993; Miniño, 2010). Among African American male adolescents, homicide is, in fact, the most common cause of death.

As we discussed in considering the effect/danger ratio, females may avoid acting aggressively because they fear an aggressive counterattack (Eagly & Steffen, 1986). What happens when the dangers of retaliation are removed? Jenifer Lightdale and Deborah Prentice (1994) conducted two studies in which men and women played an aggressive computer game under conditions of anonymity or identifiability. When they could be identified, women acted less aggressively than did men. However, when they could act aggressively without being identified, the gender difference disappeared. These experiments involved a relatively nonhostile form of aggressiveness—attacking another in a computer game. The female members of the Manson Family, however, demonstrated that there are circumstances under which women can lose their inhibitions, and even commit extreme violence toward strangers.

INTERACTION Self-protective Aggression Can Increase Danger

As we noted earlier, children who view the world in hostile terms are likely to strike out first (Dodge & Frame, 1982). When a child makes a preemptive strike against even an imagined threat, however, the world actually becomes more dangerous, as the child's preemptive strike is likely to elicit retaliation. In this case, a belief becomes a self-fulfilling prophecy—the child who views the world as more aggressive actually acts to create a world that is more aggressive.

Because of the real threats to their safety, adolescents in inner-city schools are highly fearful of attack, and some carry weapons to protect themselves. In fact, one survey found that one of every ten students in U.S. high schools reported having carried a weapon to school during the preceding 30 days (Cunningham et al., 2000). Unfortunately, as more young people carry dangerous weapons, the likelihood of serious violence goes up, and, in a vicious circle, so does the felt need to carry a weapon.

Like frightened teenagers, adults often purchase guns for self-defense (Kellermann et al., 1993). Unfortunately, those guns are much more likely to be used against friends or acquaintances than against criminals. In fact, compared to non–gun-owners, those who purchase guns increase, rather than decrease, their own likelihood of being killed. Having a gun in the home drastically increases one's chance of being killed (Cummings et al., 1997; Hepburn & Hemenway, 2004; Kellerman et al., 1993). Ironically, the increased danger comes from the fact that another person is now likely to use the gun-owner's own gun against him or her (Sugarmann & Rand, 1994).

There is another unintended cost of keeping a gun in the house for self-protection: Guns lead to more suicides than homicides (46 Americans a day commit suicide with a firearm, versus about 27 a day murdered with guns). The vast majority of people who attempt suicide consider it for less than an hour beforehand (after a temporary setback, such as a breakup or job loss). If they use a method other than firearms, most survive and do not go on to kill themselves. The most troubling statistic is that suicide among gun-owners' adolescent children is four times higher than in homes without firearms and is especially pronounced in homes where the guns are kept unlocked and loaded (Miller & Hemenway, 2008). So although owning a firearm may make one feel safe and may in some cases be used for self-protection, the potential benefits must be weighed against the increased risk the firearm itself poses for family members.

Quick Quiz

1 Which of the features below are characteristic of a defensive attributional style?

    a. Heightened tendency to notice threats from others
    b. Generally less emotional than the average child or adult
    c. Tendency to interpret other people's behavior as intended to do one harm
    d. Answers (a) and (c) are correct

2 Which of the following are true of female violence and the effect/danger ratio?

    a. Women are more likely to kill their partners in self-defense.
    b. Women generally resort to violence only in extreme circumstances, because the benefits of aggressing against a male partner are often outweighed by the dangers.
    c. Research indicates that women feel angry less frequently than men and thus are less likely to aggress against others.
    d. Answers (a) and (b) are correct

3 According to the text, which of the following is false?

    a. Guns lead to more suicides than homicides.
    b. Contrary to popular belief, White teenagers are statistically as likely as Black teenagers to be victims of homicide.
    c. Suicide among gun-owners' adolescent children is four times higher than in homes without firearms.
    d. People who purchase firearms to protect themselves actually increase, rather than decrease, their own chance of being killed.

Reducing Violence

LO 10.15 Describe how parents can use rewards to *reduce* aggressive behavior in children.

LO 10.16 Understand how cognition can be used to reduce angry arousal.

LO 10.17 Explain specific ways that intervention at the societal level can reduce aggressive behavior.

Given all we've learned about these environmental triggers of aggressive motivation and their connection to factors inside the person, is there anything we can do to reduce violence? A number of psychologists believe the answer is yes, and several have put their ideas into action by setting up programs to reduce and prevent violence (Meier & Wilkowski, 2013). One psychological program successfully reduced bullying in elementary school children (Olweus, 1991). Another reduced fighting and arrests among violent teenagers (Hammock & Yung, 1993). How do aggression-reduction programs work? There are several different approaches, each of which focuses on different motives for aggression. Some teach alternative techniques for gaining reward, some teach ways of handling annoyance and unpleasant arousal, others punish aggressive behavior, and still others propose to prevent aggression by reducing the threat of guns.

Rewarding Alternatives to Aggression

Gerald Patterson and his colleagues developed a program for aggressive children based on the assumption that the goal of aggressive behavior is often to attain rewards (Patterson, 1997; Patterson, Chamberlain, & Reid, 1982). From their social learning perspective, aggression can be reduced if the rewards that follow hostility are extinguished and if other means of attaining rewards are put into place. This program trains parents to recognize how they reward aggressive behavior in their children and encourages them to begin rewarding more acceptable alternative behaviors.

    As part of the program, the parent and child set up a contract in which the child wins points for appropriate behavior and loses points every time he or she acts aggressively. If a child earns enough points in a given day, he or she wins a reward. Depending on what the child finds most desirable, it might be staying up late to watch television, a special dessert, or having Mom read a story at bedtime. Patterson's group has conducted rigorous research on the program and concluded that this simple approach, of rewarding nonaggressiveness, is effective for most children.

Another approach to reducing aggression aims at cognition—by trying to teach people to control their own anger-arousing thoughts (Meier, Wilkowski, & Robinson, 2008). We discuss this approach next.

Bridging Theory and Application:

Using Cognition to Manage Angry Arousal

Earlier, we discussed Dolf Zillmann's (1983) theory of cognitive processes and aggressive feelings. Zillmann (1994) later expanded his theory to consider the mutual influence of angry feelings and thought processes in the escalation of hostility. According to this model (see Table 10.4), people go through three stages as they become progressively more angry. Imagine a woman discussing the volume of music with her hard-rock-loving upstairs neighbor. At stage 1, she is not highly emotionally aroused, her thought processes are careful and balanced, and her behaviors are cautiously assertive ("Sorry to bother you, but since it's after midnight, I wonder if you could turn down your Black Mega-Homicide album a few decibels?"). If the neighbor jokingly responds, "Hey, we're having a 'Thank God it's Wednesday party.' Try to loosen up a little bit!" she may move to stage 2, in which her arousal goes up, her thought processes are more selective and self-concerned, and her behaviors are more unyielding and hostile ("Turn the damn thing down or I'll call the police and get you and your drugged-out zombie friends evicted from this place!"). Because such hostile behaviors often trigger retaliations, the upstairs neighbor may simply slam the door in her face and turn the music up. At this point, she is likely to move to stage 3, in which her arousal levels are quite high, her cognitive processes are narrowly focused on spiteful counterattack, her capacity to empathize with the neighbor's reaction to her screaming insults is gone, and her choice of actions leans toward reckless and explosive behavior (perhaps returning with a baseball bat). In this cycle, the ability to think clearly becomes increasingly compromised as

emotional arousal increases. It's just when cool-headed rationality is most needed that it goes out the window.

One successful aggression reduction program trained people to short-circuit this escalating process by using cognition to block the runaway negative arousal. Raymond Novaco's (1975, 1995) cognitive approach focuses on training people to modify their own thoughts and feelings with well-rehearsed "self-statements."

Participants are taught to speak to themselves (silently) as they imagine situations that particularly annoy them. The self-statements deal with four stages of provocation:

1. *Preparing for provocation.* For times when they find themselves in situations likely to make them angry, participants rehearse such statements as "I can manage this situation. I know how to regulate my anger."
2. *Confronting the provocation.* For times when they're face-to-face with an upsetting event, they rehearse such statements as "You don't need to prove yourself" and "It's really a shame that this person is acting the way he is."
3. *Coping with the arousal and agitation.* If subjects find themselves getting upset, they are trained to say things such as "Time to relax and slow things down."
4. *Reflecting on the provocation.* After the subject has been in a provoking situation, during the time that people often continue to fume, he or she is taught to say things such as "These are difficult situations, and they take time to work out" and "It could have been a lot worse."

Table 10.4 Zillmann's Model of the Interdependencies between Cognition and Emotional Excitation in Escalating Aggressive Behavior

	STAGE 1	STAGE 2	STAGE 3
Cognition	Judgment is balanced.	Judgment begins to tip toward increased self-concern and lower empathy for the other's position.	Judgment becomes highly biased—excessive self-concern and illusions of invulnerability.
	The person appraises the situation carefully and exhaustively.	Appraisal of the situation is more selective.	Empathy for the other is gone. Spiteful thoughts predominate.
Affect (excitation)	Physiological arousal is low to moderate.	Arousal is in the moderate range.	Arousal is high.
Behavior	Cautious, but assertive	Unyielding and hostile	Impulsive, explosive, irresponsible, reckless, violent

Source: Based on Zillmann, D. (1994). Cognition–excitation interdependencies in the escalation of anger and angry aggression. In M. Potegal & J. F. Knutson (Eds.), Dynamics of aggression: Biological and social processes in dyads and groups (pp. 45–71). Hillsdale, NJ: Erlbaum.

The treatment was used for people who had problems controlling their anger. The cognitive approach was compared with two control conditions: One group was trained in deep-muscle relaxation techniques, and another was instructed only to pay attention to their anger experiences. Comparing the groups on feelings of anger and on physiological measures such as blood pressure, Novaco found that both relaxation and cognitive treatments had independent positive effects. Combining the two—teaching people both to control their thoughts and to relax—was the most effective treatment.

The cognitive and behavioral treatments we've discussed so far have met with some success in reducing aggression at the individual level (Del Vecchio & O'Leary, 2004). But some psychologists believe that to reduce aggressiveness in any true sense will require intervention at the societal level. Some researchers have therefore examined the effects of various legal punishments on aggressive behavior.

Legal Punishments

Punishment may not always be effective in training people to be nonaggressive (Gershoff, 2002). Punishing children often increases their feelings of anger and frustration, and physical punishment may teach a child that it's all right to be aggressive when in a position of power. Further, as we noted earlier, psychopaths, who are overrepresented among violent criminals, do not seem to learn from threats of punishment. Nevertheless, punishment, if it's immediate, strong, and consistent, may suppress some aggressive behavior (Berkowitz, 1993a).

Unfortunately, it is impossible for police and courts of law to catch every act of aggression and to punish it swiftly. Researchers have found no clear effects of capital punishment on murder rates. There are, for instance, no differences in homicide rates in states with and without capital punishment, and, comparing across different countries, those employing capital punishment actually have slightly higher homicide rates (Ellsworth, Haney, & Costanzo, 2001; Nathanson, 1987; Shin, 1978). David Phillips (1985) examined British press coverage of notorious executions between 1858 and 1921. He found that when an execution was intensively covered in the press, it was followed by a brief reduction in the number of homicides in London. Unfortunately, these brief downswings were followed by upswings about two weeks later. Hence, the bottom line is that capital punishment doesn't seem to have much effect on overall homicide rates (Levitt, 2004).

PREVENTION BY REMOVING THREATS If deterrence isn't an effective strategy in reducing violent crime, what about prevention? The FBI reported 450,369 homicides in the United States between 1980 and 2007. These tragedies cost society dearly, affecting relatives and friends as well as victims and making our society a scary place to live. Yet, compared with the amount of money and resources aimed at capturing and punishing violent criminals after they've done their harm, the investment our society makes in trying to prevent violence—that is, stop it before it happens—is almost nothing (Johnson, 1993).

One approach to prevention is simply to curfew young troublemakers, thereby keeping them off the streets at night—when violent altercations are most likely (Jones & Sigler, 2002). Another promising approach is to identify very young children as soon as they start showing signs of threatening or bullying other children and immediately intervene on several levels at once—individual, family, school, and neighborhood (Curtis, Ronan, & Borduin, 2004). In this multisystemic approach, psychologists go into the home and school environments and work not only with youthful offenders, but also with their parents, their peers, and their teachers. Because many violent youngsters hang out with other troublemakers, one key goal is to replace this network of delinquents with other friends who are involved in more prosocial activities. So, if the aggressive child is musically inclined or athletic, he might be encouraged to join the school band or an after-school athletic program. Parents are also instructed in techniques to encourage these prosocial activities and are themselves persuaded to spend more time with their child and to monitor his or her whereabouts at other times. A long-term follow-up found that troublesome teens who had participated in this multisystemic treatment were (compared to similar kids who had other conventional treatments) much less likely to have been arrested or to have spent time in jail over the next decade and a half (Schaeffer & Borduin, 2005).

Another form of prevention would be gun control. Opponents of gun control argue that "guns don't kill people, people kill people." That argument sounds sensible, until one checks the FBI Uniform Crime Reports to see exactly how people in the United States kill other people. Six times out of ten, people killing people use guns. Of the 450,369 people murdered in the United States between 1980 and 2007, 288,821 of them (64%) were done in with firearms, mostly handguns.

Another concern raised by opponents of gun control is that armed criminal types will terrorize unarmed citizens: "If guns are outlawed, only outlaws will have guns." But when nonoutlaws buy guns, rather than increasing their chances of protecting themselves against the bad guys, they dramatically increase their own chances of being killed or of having a family member killed (Cummings et al., 1997; Kellermann et al., 1993; Miller & Hemenway, 2008).

Americans are armed with more handguns and automatic weapons than the citizens of any other industrialized nation. Does that make Americans safer? Unfortunately not. Homicide rates in the United States are several times higher than those of any other major industrialized nation. If one compares the crime rates in Seattle, Washington, with those in nearby Vancouver, British Columbia (where handguns are rare), one finds that most crime statistics are similar in the two cities, with the exception of homicide, which is several times lower in Vancouver (Kellermann et al., 1993). Studies comparing homes with and without guns and countries with and without gun control suggest that serious gun-control interventions could result in dramatic decreases in the most frightful form of violence (Duke, Resnick, & Borowski, 2005). Indeed, when officials in Washington, D.C., passed a law that restricted handguns, there was no change in non-gun-related murders and suicides, but there was a 25% drop in gun-related deaths (Loftin et al., 1991).

INVESTIGATION

Imagine you were on a government task force whose goal was to reduce aggression in your town. Based on the research discussed in this chapter, what two pieces of advice would you offer as starters? Can you tap the research discussed earlier in the chapter to make a recommendation not covered in this last section?

Quick Quiz

1 What does Zillman's model of "escalating aggressive behavior" have in common with Novaco's cognitive approach to aggression reduction?

    a. Both models acknowledge the important role of physiological arousal in the escalation of hostility.

    b. Both models consider thought processes to be crucial to the escalation of hostility.

    c. Both models emphasize the important role of catharsis in venting angry feelings.

    d. Answers (a) and (b) are correct

2 As described, Patterson's program for reducing aggression in children includes which of the following:

    a. The child is awarded points for appropriate behavior.

    b. The child can trade in points for the privilege of engaging in a special activity in which he or she acts out pent-up aggression by punching a Bobo doll.

    c. The child loses points every time he or she acts aggressively.

    d. Answers (a) and (c) are correct

3　According to your text, which of these claims about legal punishments for violence is false?
  a. Capital punishment has a slight deterrence effect on murder rates within the U.S.
  b. Countries employing capital punishment have slightly higher homicide rates.
  c. There are no differences in homicide rates among U.S. states with and without capital punishment.
  d. Research found that when the British press covered notorious executions between 1858 and 1921, such coverage was followed by a short-lived reduction in homicides in London.

Revisiting Senseless Violence

Charles Manson, still unrepentant after three decades. Manson's aggressive behaviors, unlike those of his followers, seemed to stem more from deeply rooted personality characteristics than from transient situational factors.

Over forty years later, the Manson Family murders still fascinate the U.S. public. Logging onto the Internet, one finds several Charles Manson websites, complete with access to photos of Manson, paintings by Manson, recordings of his music, and updates about recent parole hearings for him and other Family members. In the transcript of his ninth parole hearing, Manson continues to express absolutely no remorse and to claim he is a victim, innocent of wrongdoing—on the legal technicality that he was never convicted of murdering anyone with his own hands. As of 2012, at age 77, Manson had committed 35 violent offenses in prison (Martinez, 2012). Manson's lifetime pattern of self-centered exploitation fits with the description of psychopaths—individuals who feel little remorse or empathy and who often use violence and other antisocial acts as instrumental means to an end (LaLumiere et al., 2001).

Manson's penchant for aggressiveness, social dominance, and sexuality fits with the picture of a high-testosterone male painted in our discussion of status-based aggression. Furthermore, Manson came from a poverty-stricken, low-opportunity background. His own mother deserted him; he never knew his father; and, while other children were getting a formal education, Manson was in and out of reform schools. That pattern is consistent with research findings that it is the combination of low social opportunity and high testosterone levels that is most deadly (Dabbs & Morris, 1990).

Patricia Krenwinkel, who began life as an obedient Campfire Girl, however, apparently returned to her former ways while serving a life sentence in prison. Now over 65 years old, she has reportedly been quiet, reclusive, and repentant for her crimes for decades. She has been described as "a model prisoner." Charles Watson, the former high school athlete and all-around "good guy" from Texas, went a step further in his repentance. He studied religion in prison, became ordained as a minister, and now works to save the souls of his fellow inmates. In 2009, Susan Atkins died in prison, at age 61. She had also repented for her former murderous ways and wrote about her love of Jesus on a Christian Web page for several years.

It's easy to attribute Manson's involvement in such awful crimes to a lifetime history of antisociality and lack of opportunity. But of Family members such as Krenwinkel and Watson, who were nonviolent before and after that period, we must still ask, with Linda Kasabian, "Why would they do such a thing?" Here the research literature on aggression provides some clues to make the murders seem a little less random. As we noted, aggression is increased by unpleasant circumstances, including heat and poverty. The gruesome murders occurred during a sweltering heat wave, following several months in which Manson's followers, many of whom came from middle-class backgrounds, had been reduced to scrounging for food in garbage cans.

In discussing the motive of self-protection, we considered how people's attributions can inspire aggressive behavior, even when they are wrong. If another person is perceived as a potential threat or the source of one's unpleasant experiences, aggression may follow. Manson apparently used the spirit of the times to create just the sort of embattled "us versus them" mentality found in cults such as those discussed in Chapter 6. In the late 1960s, U.S. society was clearly split into two embattled camps, characterized at one extreme by long-haired, drug-experimenting, free-loving hippie types (such as Manson and his group) and at the other by traditional and financially comfortable "establishment" types. During the year preceding the murders, young people were dying in increasing numbers in a war many regarded as unjust, police were brutally clashing with college students protesting that war, and two heroes of the counterculture (Martin Luther King Jr. and Robert Kennedy), both of whom had spoken out against that war, had been assassinated. Many young people talked openly of a revolution against a society perceived as materialistic, capitalistic, imperialistic, and downright evil. Manson, like many charismatic leaders, masterfully manipulated this sense of group threat and self-righteousness in his young hippie followers.

The central lesson of this chapter is this: Most aggression is "senseless" to the extent that it exploits others and is likely to elicit counter-aggression in return. But even acts as seemingly senseless as mass murder can be demystified by analyzing how factors in the person and the situation interact to trigger fundamental social motivations.

In trying to understand the social psychology of aggression, we have again seen many bridges with other areas of psychology, including developmental psychology (the findings on defensive children and on exposure to video games, for example), clinical psychology (the research on psychopathy and on aggression-control programs, for example), and cognitive neuroscience (the research on brain-wave responses to violent video games and on testosterone, for example). We have also seen bridges to other disciplines, including anthropology, biology, public health, and criminal justice. Because of the immense social impact of aggressive behavior on families, schools, neighborhoods, and even international relations, aggression is a topic on which researchers from many disciplines have joined forces.

Chapter Summary

A Summary of the Goals Served by Aggression and the Factors Related to Each Goal

The Goal	Person	Situation	Interaction
Coping with feelings of annoyance	• General physiological arousal • Type A tendencies toward time urgency and competitiveness	• Pain • Heat • Poverty (especially following short economic upswings)	• Unpleasant feelings or the presence of guns can prime a network of aggression-related thoughts and feelings. • Type As choose work situations that contribute to their own frustration. • Hot-tempered children get trapped in a lifetime cycle of missed opportunities and self-induced frustrations.
Gaining material and social rewards	• Psychopathic tendencies • Low empathy • Alcohol intoxication	• Factors that glamorize violence, including • Media violence • Violent computer games	• People who choose to watch violent media are more aggressive to begin with, and watching violent media further increases their aggressive proclivities.
Gaining or maintaining social status	• Gender • Testosterone	• Insults • Trivial altercations • Culture of honor	• Testosterone increases antisocial behavior only in low-status males. • Older males having mates and good social position become less hostile.
Protecting oneself or others	• Defensive attributional bias • Effect/danger ratio	• Perceived threats • Threatening neighborhoods • Proliferation of weapons	• Viewing the world in hostile terms leads to preemptive aggression, which in turn makes the world more hostile. • Possession of guns for self-protection increases one's chances of being killed.

What Is Aggression?

1. Aggression is defined as behavior intended to injure another. Angry feelings, unintentional harm, assertiveness, or playful aggression would not qualify as aggression under this definition.

2. Direct aggression involves an undisguised attempt to hurt another to his or her face. Indirect aggression is nonconfrontational and ambiguous.

3. Emotional aggression is hurtful behavior that stems from angry feelings. Instrumental aggression is hurting another to accomplish some other goal.

4. Men are more aggressive if one considers serious physical assault and homicide. Women are as aggressive as men if one is counting indirect aggression and mild physical aggression within relationships.

5. Freudian ideas about a "death instinct" don't fit with powerful general principles of evolution. Modern

evolutionary theorists believe that aggressive drives would only evolve if they were linked to adaptive survival or reproductive goals.

Coping with Feelings of Annoyance

1. The original frustration–aggression hypothesis presumed that (a) aggression was always a consequence of frustration and (b) all frustration always led to aggression. The reformulated hypothesis presumes that emotional aggression can be increased by any unpleasant stimulus.
2. According to the excitation-transfer theory, annoyance-linked aggression can be increased by any emotionally arousing experience that could be mistaken for anger, including watching an erotic film.
3. Type A behavior pattern is characterized by time urgency and competitiveness and an inclination to become angry at job-related frustrations.
4. In the short term, annoyance-linked aggression can be increased by unpleasant stimulation, including pain or heat. Over the long term, poverty is also associated with more violence.
5. According to the cognitive-neoassociation theory, either unpleasant stimulation or the presence of aggression-related cues (such as guns) can prime a network of negative thoughts and feelings.
6. Aggressive people, such as Type As, often make their own lives more frustrating.

Gaining Material and Social Rewards

1. In some subcultures, a willingness to act violently has been a ticket to wealth and success.
2. According to the social learning theory of aggression, rewards for violence can come either directly (from parents or friends) or indirectly (from watching other people get rewarded for aggression). Anger is not necessary when aggression is motivated by rewards.
3. Psychopaths have a lack of empathy for others, a high sense of self-worth, and an insensitivity to punishment. These individuals are especially likely to engage in cool and calculated aggression. Alcohol is likely to suppress feelings of empathy that normally make it unpleasant to hurt others.
4. Media such as television and movies often depict heroes being rewarded for violent behavior. Studies of the effects of violent media on observers don't always yield strong results, but meta-analyses of many studies lead to a clear conclusion: Across the many acts of violence shown in the media and the many people watching that violence, there is a reliable increase in aggression in viewers.
5. Violence also goes up after playing graphic video games.

6. Correlational and experimental studies suggest a relationship between watching violent erotica and hostility to women. The relationship is strongest for men who view very high levels of such violent pornography and who have other risk factors associated with violence toward women.
7. Violent people choose to watch more violence, and their violent tendencies are increased by watching it.

Gaining or Maintaining Social Status

1. According to sexual selection theory, female animals often choose to mate with males who have demonstrated their ability to compete successfully with other males. This selection led, over time, to increases in status-oriented aggressiveness in males.
2. Testosterone is associated with heightened aggressiveness and antisocial behavior in delinquents, prison inmates, and military veterans. Experimental administrations of this hormone increase aggressiveness in college students and transsexuals. Testosterone appears to motivate dominance-oriented behaviors, which may or may not turn into aggressiveness.
3. Even trivial insults to honor can lead to violence. In cultures of honor, such as the South, honor-related violence among men is more tolerated than in other regions.
4. Status-linked violence is found in men whose paths to success are blocked, such as younger, poorer men. Consistently high levels of testosterone are associated with aggressive and antisocial behavior only in men of lower socioeconomic status.

Protecting Oneself or Others

1. Across countries, aggression in the defense of oneself or others is considered justified.
2. Children with a defensive attributional style are more likely to perceive potential threats and often act aggressively as a preemptive defense. Women fear more dangers in response to their own aggressive behavior and are likely to resort to it only in situations of extreme self-defense.
3. Adolescents are more likely to be threatened, and the dangers go up for African American adolescents.
4. When the dangers of retaliation are removed, women may act more aggressively.
5. Preemptive or defensive aggression may actually increase threats in the long run. Simply buying a gun increases the chance of being killed.

Reducing Violence

1. Psychological interventions have had some success in reducing aggression at the individual and group levels.

One type of intervention teaches aggressive children non-aggressive alternative strategies for winning rewards.

2. Cognitive interventions teach aggressive people self-statements designed to short-circuit escalations of angry arousal and hostile thought patterns.

3. Punishment may suppress aggressive behavior in the short run but has the downside of teaching aggression over the long run. At the societal level, legal punishments have not been found to be particularly effective deterrents to violence.

4. Some psychologists have argued for preventive approaches, including reducing the numbers of guns. Other countries in which people have limited access to handguns, such as Canada, have substantially lower homicide rates than the United States, and a law limiting handguns in Washington, D.C., was followed by a substantial and specific reduction in gun-related murders.

Key Terms

Aggression, 313

Assertiveness, 314

Catharsis, 316

Cognitive-neoassociation theory, 322

Culture of honor, 335

Defensive attributional style, 338

Differential parental investment, 332

Direct aggression, 314

Displacement, 316

Effect/danger ratio, 339

Emotional aggression, 314

Excitation-transfer theory, 319

Frustration–aggression hypothesis (original), 318

Frustration–aggression hypothesis (reformulated), 318

Indirect aggression, 314

Instrumental aggression, 314

Meta-analysis, 328

Psychopath, 327

Relative deprivation, 321

Sexual selection, 332

Social learning theory, 326

Type A behavior pattern, 320

Weapons effect, 322

Chapter 11

Prejudice, Stereotyping, and Discrimination

Video

Learning Objectives

LO 11.1 Define the following terms and understand how they differ from one another: (a) prejudice, (b) stereotype, and (c) discrimination.

LO 11.2 Describe *stereotype threat* and discuss the costs and benefits of strategies people use to cope with stereotype threat.

LO 11.3 Define: (a) realistic group conflict theory, (b) social dominance orientation, and (c) minimal intergroup paradigm.

LO 11.4 Describe the Robbers Cave study and discuss what it may tell us about the causes of negative prejudices, stereotypes, and discrimination.

LO 11.5 Describe the self-fulfilling spiral of intergroup competition.

LO 11.6 Discuss how different forms of religiosity are linked to prejudice and discrimination.

LO 11.7 Describe which people are likely to express their groups' prejudice-relevant norms and the type of situation in which this inclination is especially likely to occur.

LO 11.8 Discuss how the desire to maintain favorable personal and social identities contributes to scapegoating.

LO 11.9 Describe the authoritarian personality and how this trait is related to negative prejudice.

LO 11.10 Explain how failure and threats to self-image threat can increase prejudice.

LO 11.11 Describe the "shooter bias" and explain how it reflects the process of stereotyping.

LO 11.12 Discuss the research on perceived outgroup homogeneity.

LO 11.13 Describe the circumstances that increase the likelihood of stereotyping.

LO 11.14 Describe the four types of strategies for reducing prejudice, stereotyping, and discrimination, and provide an example of each.

LO 11.15 Describe how the jigsaw classroom embodies the six principles of effective contact.

The Unlikely Journey of Ann Atwater and C. P. Ellis

The place was Durham, North Carolina, the year was 1971, and tensions were mounting. Challenging centuries-old institutions of racial discrimination, African Americans had taken to the streets, boycotting businesses that would not employ them, staging sit-down strikes in restaurants that refused to serve them, and marching to protest unfair housing practices. These protests angered many in Durham's white population, who considered their city a model of good race relations and fair treatment. On several occasions, demonstrators from the two sides clashed violently.

Against this backdrop of confrontation, officials called a public meeting to address perhaps the most contentious issue of all—school desegregation. A full 17 years after the Supreme Court had ruled that separate public schools for black and white children violated the U.S. Constitution, Durham's school system was still almost entirely segregated.

The meeting began quietly, but the peace wouldn't last. Claiborne Paul "C. P." Ellis and Ann Atwater were soon, once again, at each other's throats. "If we didn't have niggers in the schools, we wouldn't have any problems. The problem here today is niggers!" the white man shouted. The black woman leaped to her feet: "The problem is that we have stupid crackers like C. P. Ellis in Durham!"

Public showdowns were nothing new for these two (Davidson, 1996; Hochberg, 1996; Terkel, 1992). C. P. Ellis was the Exalted Cyclops of the Durham chapter of the Ku Klux Klan. He regularly attended city council and other public meetings and frequently rallied his members against the civil rights marchers. He distributed racist literature and taunted blacks on the streets. He threw an impromptu celebration party on the day of Martin Luther King Jr.'s murder, toasting the assassin. And Ellis had once shot a black youth.

Ann Atwater was a community activist who fought for everything C. P. Ellis opposed. Her expert knowledge of bureaucratic regulations made her an effective warrior against governmental discrimination. Her persuasive abilities and powerful personality made her a dynamic grassroots leader. And the sheer magnitude of her presence—she was a large woman, unafraid to throw her bulk around if necessary—made "Roughhouse Annie" a person to be reckoned with.

With their strong personalities and opposite goals, Ellis and Atwater collided often. Indeed, at one city council meeting, Ellis's racist epithets outraged Atwater to the point that she was ready to commit murder: Pulling a knife from her purse, she climbed over the rows of chairs toward her unsuspecting target. Fortunately—for both her and Ellis—she was intercepted without incident by several friends who quietly disarmed her. Not surprisingly, her animosity toward Ellis was matched by his toward her: He "hated her guts."

It seemed inevitable that Ellis and Atwater would always be at odds. So what followed the first school desegregation meeting was astonishing. Within just weeks of their shouting match, they developed a mutual respect. Within several months, they had become real friends—to the shock of both black and white communities. Decades later, the former leader of the Ku Klux Klan (KKK) and the militant civil rights activist continued to share a special bond. Said Ann Atwater, "I don't know of anything that could change us from being friends. . . . We don't shake hands. We hug and embrace." C. P. Ellis felt the same. And perhaps even more amazing, this former Klansman—this man who excitedly celebrated the assassination of Martin Luther King Jr.—came to claim as his greatest achievement his role in winning the first union contract in Durham to include Martin Luther King Jr.'s birthday as a paid holiday.

How do we explain the fascinating journey of these former foes? Why at one time were their lives so utterly consumed by powerful racial prejudices and stereotypes? And what changed their longstanding hatred into true respect and friendship? In this chapter, we explore the consequences of negative prejudices, stereotypes, and discrimination; why they exist so powerfully; when they come into play; and what we can do about them.

Planet Prejudice

LO 11.1 Define the following terms and understand how they differ from one another: (a) prejudice, (b) stereotype, and (c) discrimination.

LO 11.2 Describe *stereotype threat* and discuss the costs and benefits of strategies people use to cope with stereotype threat.

Open the newspaper or turn on the evening news, and you'll see no shortage of hostilities like those that once bound C. P. Ellis and Ann Atwater. The home of an interracial couple is firebombed. The Muslim prayer room at a prestigious university is vandalized. A man walks into a gay bar, has two drinks, and then attacks its patrons with a hatchet and gun. And on and on and on . . . .

This is not an American phenomenon, of course. Prejudice and its implications are universal. In Europe, powerful hostilities exist between "native" Europeans and immigrants from Africa, the Middle East, and Asia. In the usually tolerant city of Sydney, mobs of Anglo-Australian and Lebanese Australian youth riot and attack one another. In Japan, racism against *gaijin*—foreigners—is common. In India, parents are more likely to abort female than male fetuses. And, on a larger scale, conflicts between people of different ethnicities and religions litter the world's landscape—Jews and Arabs in

Planet Prejudice. Throughout all spheres of life, today, as in the past, negative prejudices, stereotypes, and discrimination exist all around us and all over the world.

the Middle East, Turks and Kurds in Turkey, Christians and Muslims in Indonesia, Muslims and Hindus in India . . . and on and on and on.

Many of us would like to believe that hate crimes are infrequent deviations from societal norms of intergroup respect and tolerance. We would like to believe that negative prejudices exist only in easily identifiable "rednecks" or "extremists" and that interethnic conflicts occur only elsewhere, in less "civilized" places. Unfortunately, as the research explored in this chapter suggests, nearly all of us hold at least a few negative prejudices and stereotypes, and these feelings and beliefs often lead us to discriminate against others.

"But aren't things getting better?" you ask. This is a fair question, especially in light of the 2008 election and 2012 re-election of President Barack Obama—the son of a black, foreign father and white, American mother. Indeed, compared to most of U.S. history, the present social atmosphere *is* more tolerant—at least toward some groups. Not only are most types of group-based discrimination now illegal, but fewer people are likely to express the simple, old-fashioned views common to past generations—that blacks are inherently lazier than whites, that women are genetically less intelligent than men, and so forth (e.g., Schuman et al., 1997). Instead, people's more modern reactions toward other groups tend to be more complex than in previous decades. For instance, racial prejudices held by whites are often accompanied by feelings of guilt, owing to the belief that blacks have been treated unfairly (Devine et al., 1991; Gaertner & Dovidio, 1986; Katz et al., 1986; Swim & Miller, 1999).

The movement away from old-fashioned views reflects, in part, an authentic shift toward tolerance. It also, however, reflects contemporary societal norms that frown on expressions of bigotry. As a result, people are less likely to *present themselves* as prejudiced, particularly to strangers (e.g., Dovidio & Gaertner, 2000; Plant & Devine, 1998). Instead, bigoted views are usually expressed more subtly, under the cover of arguments that can be defended on nonprejudicial grounds (e.g., Crandall & Eshleman, 2003; Saucier, Miller, & Doucet, 2005). "It's not that I'm sexist," a man might say, "I just think that affirmative action is discrimination in reverse." Because one *can* make ideological, nonprejudiced arguments for opposing policies like affirmative action, bigoted individuals may use such issues to mask their negative stereotypes and prejudices (Federico & Sidanius, 2002; Reyna et al., 2006) (see Table 11.1).

Table 11.1 Old-Fashioned Versus Modern Expressions of Racism and Sexism: Old Bigotries in New Bottles?

It has become less socially appropriate to blatantly express unfavorable views of African Americans and women. Consider the differences in how people with old-fashioned versus modern prejudices might express them:

Racism	Sexism
Old-Fashioned:	**Old-Fashioned:**
• Black people are generally not as smart as whites.	• Women are not as capable of thinking as logically as men.
• It's a bad idea for blacks and whites to marry one another.	• It is more important to encourage boys than to encourage girls to participate in athletics.
Modern:	**Modern:**
• Discrimination against blacks is no longer a problem in the United States.	• Society has reached the point where women and men have equal opportunities for achievement.
• Over the past few years, blacks have gotten more economically than they deserve.	• On average, people in our society treat husbands and wives equally.

Moreover, individuals who hold negative views of certain groups sometimes express them in apparently positive ways. Sexism, for example, can be of a benevolent nature (e.g., "women should be cherished and protected by men") or more hostile in its character (e.g., "women seek to gain power by getting control over men") (Glick & Fiske, 1996). Even benevolent sexism, though, can have negative implications—and sometimes be even worse than hostile sexism (Bair & Steele, 2010). In one set of experiments, women exposed to benevolent sexism performed less well on a problem-solving task than did those exposed to hostile sexism. This decrement occurred because thoughts related to self-doubt were especially likely to come to mind and disrupt problem-solving effectiveness (Dardenne, Dumont, & Bollier, 2007).

In sum, it's clear that bigoted feelings, beliefs, and behaviors still exist throughout our society and throughout the world. Nonetheless, many of them are more complex, and expressed more subtly, than in the past.

Prejudice and Stereotypes

The general attitude we have toward members of a particular group—how we *feel* about them—is known as **prejudice**. Ask yourself how you feel when you meet for the first time someone you know to be Muslim, homosexual, or Native American. If your initial reaction is one of dislike, you harbor a negative prejudice against that group. Negative prejudices differ in their intensity: You may really hate some groups but only feel a little unfavorably toward others. They also differ in their "quality": Thinking about some groups may make you angry, others may make you fearful, whereas others may disgust you, elicit pity, or make you feel sad. Different prejudices are "flavored" by different emotions (Brewer & Alexander, 2002; Cottrell & Neuberg, 2005; Devos et al., 2002).

Walter Lippmann (1922) used the term **stereotype** to refer to generalized *beliefs* we hold about groups—beliefs that reflect what we think members of a particular group are like. For instance, common stereotypes held by people in the United States include the beliefs that European Americans are achievement oriented, egotistical, and racist; that African Americans are loud, lazy, and antagonistic; that Asian Americans are shy, well-mannered, and intelligent; and that Mexican Americans are family oriented, lower-class, and hard-working (e.g., Niemann et al., 1994). Not only can stereotypes be positive or negative, but people can also hold positive stereotypes for groups against whom they are negatively prejudiced (Maddux et al., 2008). People who dislike Asians, for instance, may nonetheless believe them to be intelligent and well mannered.

Social psychologists often distinguish between *explicit* and *implicit* stereotypes and prejudices (e.g., Banaji & Greenwald, 1994; Devine, 1989; Fazio & Olson, 2003; Hutchings & Haddock, 2008; von Hippel, Sekaquaptewa, & Vargas, 1997). For example, if you ask yourself how you feel toward members of group X, the attitude you're aware of is your explicit prejudice toward the group. You can directly state this prejudice, and researchers measure it using surveys and questionnaires. But you may also have implicit attitudes toward group X—prejudices you may not be aware of and that you can't directly report. Implicit prejudices and stereotypes can only be measured indirectly, often by assessing how long it takes to make certain judgments.

The Implicit Association Test (IAT) (e.g., Greenwald, McGhee, & Schwartz, 1998; Rudman et al., 1999) is one technique researchers use to indirectly assess prejudice. Visit the following website and take the Race IAT for a spin: https://implicit.harvard.edu/implicit. When you receive your score, know that there is currently a debate over exactly what any individual's specific score means in terms of absolute levels of implicit prejudice (Blanton & Jaccard, 2006; Greenwald, Nosek, & Siriam, 2006). What is clear, however, is that those who score higher on the race IAT have stronger implicit preferences for whites than do those who receive lower scores.

Discrimination

Discrimination refers to *behaviors* directed toward others because of their group membership. If we treat two people differently although they're identical in all respects except for, say, the gender of their preferred romantic partners, we could rightly be

Prejudice A generalized attitude toward members of a social group.

Stereotype Generalized belief about members of social groups.

Discrimination Behaviors directed toward people on the basis of their group membership.

Discriminating preferences in Texas. When researchers went into retail stores seeking employment, the reception they received depended on their apparent sexual orientation: Job seekers wearing hats saying "Gay and Proud" were treated less favorably than those wearing hats saying "Texan and Proud."

accused of discriminating on the basis of sexual orientation. Consider, for instance, the following experiment conducted in a shopping mall in Texas: Trained student researchers went into stores ostensibly seeking jobs, with tape recorders hidden in their pockets and one of two baseball-type caps perched on their heads: One had the words *Gay and Proud* printed across the front; the other was identical except it said *Texan and Proud*. Through some clever stage managing, the students never knew which hat they wore into each store and followed the same predetermined script once inside. Nonetheless, clear evidence of discrimination emerged: When interacting with job-seekers presented as homosexual, potential employers spoke less and came across as less helpful and less interested (Hebl et al., 2002). Because everything about the students was otherwise the same, the different behaviors of the store managers in the presence of the different hats can be viewed as discrimination.

SEXUAL HARASSMENT AS GENDER DISCRIMINATION In a national sample, approximately 80% of high school students—girls and boys—report having been sexually harassed by their peers (*Hostile Hallways,* 2001). Other estimates suggest that as many as 50% of American women have been sexually harassed during their academic or working lives (Fitzgerald, 1993), including an estimated 70% of women who have served in the military (Street et al., 2007). Sexual harassment is a common form of discrimination.

In the eyes of the law, sexual harassment takes two forms. *Quid pro quo* (from the Latin for "something for something") *harassment* refers to attempts by the perpetrator to exchange something of value—a job, a good grade—for sexual favors. *Hostile environment harassment* refers to creating a professional setting that is sexually offensive, intimidating, or hostile. To qualify as illegal discrimination, sexual harassment must be directed at members of only one gender.

Behaviors can be harassing without qualifying as illegal, however. In these more ambiguous cases, and as with other forms of discrimination, labeling a behavior "sexual harassment" often depends on who's exhibiting the behavior, who's targeted by the behavior, and who's doing the labeling (Frazier et al., 1995). For instance, the same behaviors are generally viewed as more sexually harassing when performed by a person in power, such as a boss, and as less harassing when performed by an individual who is attractive and single (Pryor & Day, 1988; Sheets & Braver, 1993). Behaviors such as flirting and staring are seen as more harassing when directed at women than at men (e.g., U.S. Merit Systems Protections Board, 1988). And, although men and women tend to agree that sexual propositions and coercion are harassing, women—especially older women—are more likely than men to see unwanted requests for dates, physical contact, and behaviors that suggest derogatory attitudes as harassing (Ohse & Stockdale, 2008; Rotundo et al., 2001).

Situational factors also influence interpretations of sexual harassment. Male students in one experiment were exposed to sex stereotypical images taken from violent video games or to nonstereotypical images of professional men and women. Those exposed to the stereotypical images were less likely to interpret an ambiguous encounter between a professor and graduate student as harassing (Dill, Brown, & Collins, 2008).

Are some men more likely to harass than others? Yes: Men who view themselves as "hypermasculine," and who think that power and sex are closely connected, have a greater inclination to sexually harass (e.g., Bargh et al., 1995; Pryor & Stoller, 1994). Whether they actually *do* harass, however, depends on the situation. As Figure 11.1 reveals, sexual harassment is more likely to be perpetrated by men who see a strong connection between power and sex *and* who are placed in settings where harassing opportunities are available and implicitly condoned (Pryor et al., 1993).

INSTITUTIONALIZED DISCRIMINATION We've been discussing discrimination performed by individuals. Some discrimination, however, is performed not by individuals but by society's institutions. *Institutionalized discrimination* is discrimination that has been built into the legal, political, economic, and social institutions of a culture (e.g., Feagin & Feagin, 1999). It may be direct and hostile, as when laws prohibit certain groups of people from living in certain neighborhoods or working in certain occupations. Certainly, the United States has a long history of direct institutionalized discrimination (e.g., as in slavery-supporting laws and practices, and laws discriminating against women). Although direct institutionalized discrimination is generally illegal today, some forms of it remain. In most U.S. states, for instance, homosexuals cannot legally marry.

Institutionalized discrimination isn't always blatant, however, and sometimes it isn't even intentional. Consider, for example, that members of disadvantaged minority groups often have a more difficult time competing for employment because they have poorer educational backgrounds. Although the system that creates higher quality educational opportunities for wealthy white students in the suburbs isn't explicitly *designed* to make life difficult for poor black or Hispanic job seekers, this is one of its consequences. Individuals discriminate against members of other groups, and society's institutions do so, too.

In sum, *prejudices*, *stereotypes*, and *discrimination* refer to how we feel toward, think about, and behave in relation to members of groups. Often, negative prejudices, stereotypes, and discriminatory tendencies cluster together, forming syndromes we know as racism, sexism, anti-Semitism, heterosexism, ageism, and the like.

The Costs of Prejudice, Stereotyping, and Discrimination

The targets of negative prejudices often bear large material and psychological burdens. We discuss just some of these below.

MATERIAL COSTS Female musicians have traditionally been highly underrepresented in symphony orchestras. Explanations for this have included beliefs about women's supposed "unsuitable temperaments," "smaller techniques," and the like. To what extent, though, might a more simple bias against women play a role? One study explored this question by examining the hiring records of 11 major orchestras as a function of how they auditioned their applicants: Had the musicians been visible when they auditioned, making obvious their gender, or were they concealed behind screens, thereby masking their gender? Consistent with the gender discrimination hypothesis, female musicians fared better when judges were "blind" to their gender: Concealed auditions increased the likelihood that female musicians would advance from preliminary auditions into later rounds by around 50% and almost doubled the likelihood they would win the job (Goldin & Rouse, 2000). When their gender was known, female musicians were less likely to win these prestigious jobs.

This is just one example, of many, demonstrating the tangible costs of discrimination. Consider just a few others:

- The FBI reported that, in 2012, over 6,700 hate crimes were committed in the United States. About half of these were identified as racially motivated, 20% as motivated by sexual orientation bias, 19% by religious bias, 12% by ethnicity/national origin bias, and 1.5% by disability bias ("Hate Crime Statistics," 2012). And a study by the Department of Justice estimates that the number of hate crimes may actually be 19–31 times greater than the official statistics suggest (Harlow, 2005).
- Women and members of minority groups tend to receive less pay for the same work, even after controlling for job type, educational background, and the like (e.g., Blau & Kahn, 2000; Stroh, Brett, & Reilly, 1992).
- Overweight women, compared to thinner women, receive less financial help from their parents for attending college; overweight men do not face a similar

Figure 11.1 Who sexually harasses, and when?

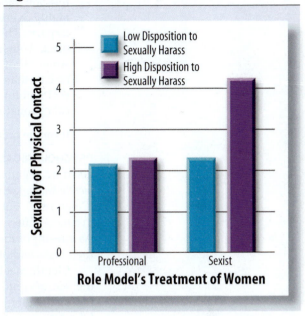

Sexually harassing behavior usually results from an interaction between personality dispositions and salient social norms. In one experiment, male participants predisposed toward sexual harassment were more likely to touch a female confederate in sexual ways, but only when they had first observed the male experimenter behave toward her in a sexist manner.

Source: Data from Pryor, J. B., LaVite, C., & Stoller, L. (1993). A social psychological analysis of sexual harassment: The person/situation interaction. *Journal of Vocational Behavior,* 42, 68-83. Figure 1.

discrimination (Crandall, 1995). Moreover, even after controlling for a host of relevant factors (e.g., education, intelligence, number of years in current job), highly overweight white women are paid about 7% less than their thinner counterparts. This bias was not present in the wages paid to heavyweight Hispanic or black women or to heavyweight men (Cawley, 2000).

- An audit of the auto industry revealed that white men were offered better deals on cars than were white women (who were asked to pay $109 more), black women ($318 more), and black men ($935 more)—even when they all adopted the identical negotiating strategy (Ayres & Siegelman, 1995).

It can be quite costly to be the victim of discrimination.

PSYCHOLOGICAL COSTS   There are also significant psychological costs of being targeted by negative prejudices, stereotypes, and discrimination. Consider the effects of *merely knowing* that others hold negative prejudices and stereotypes about one's group (Pinel, 1999). For example, "tokens" in a group—a lone woman in a group of men, for instance—often worry about being stereotyped by the others (Cohen & Swim, 1995). As a result of this increased self-consciousness, tokens are less able to concentrate on their tasks and often perform less well (e.g., Lord & Saenz, 1985; Saenz, 1994).

Claude Steele and Joshua Aronson (1995) hypothesized that **stereotype threat**—the fear of confirming others' negative stereotypes about one's group—also makes it more difficult for people to perform up to their potential, especially on difficult tasks. In a series of studies exploring this idea, undergraduate students answered tough questions taken from the verbal section of the Graduate Record Exam (GRE). Black students performed below their abilities—but only when race was made salient and they believed that a poor performance would confirm the cultural stereotype that blacks are less intelligent than whites (see Figure 11.2). Indeed, the findings of many studies reveal that individuals from many groups perform beneath their potential when they fear confirming the negative stereotypes held of their groups (Inzlicht & Schmader, 2012; Shapiro & Neuberg, 2007). For example:

- Women performed worse on math tests when gender was made salient than when it was not (e.g., McIntyre, Paulson, & Lord, 2003; Spencer, Steele, & Quinn, 1999).
- Latinos performed more poorly on an intelligence test when they believed the test was diagnostic of intellectual ability than when they thought it was unrelated to intellectual ability (Gonzales, Blanton, & Williams, 2002).
- White men performed relatively poorly on an athletic task when they thought it was related to "natural ability," whereas black men performed relatively poorly on the task when they thought it was related to "athletic intelligence" (Stone et al., 1999).
- Asian American women performed worse on a math test after their gender had been made salient but better on the same test after their Asian identity had been made salient (Shih, Pittinsky, & Ambady, 1999).
- White men performed worse on a math test when they thought they were being compared to Asian men than when they thought otherwise (Aronson et al., 1999).

When negative stereotypes about our group are "in the air," we are often less able to perform up to our potential. Stereotype threat may have these effects because it increases arousal, mental load, dejection, and negative thoughts while also decreasing effort and working memory capacity (e.g., Beilock, Rydell, & McConnell, 2007; Ben-Zeev, Fein, & Inzlicht, 2005; Jamieson & Harkins, 2007; Keller & Dauenheimer, 2003; Mazerolle et al., 2012; Schmader, Johns, & Forbes, 2008).

Stereotype threat The fear that one might confirm the negative stereotypes held by others about one's group.

Figure 11.2   When negative stereotypes are in the air

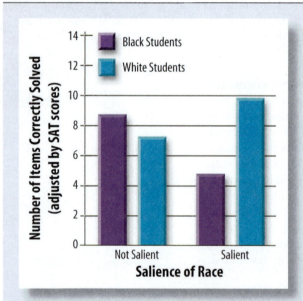

In one study, both black and white students performed well on a difficult exam (relative to their abilities, as assessed by SAT scores) except when asked beforehand to report their race. When race was made salient, black students underperformed whites.

Source: Adapted from C. M. Steele and J. Aronson (1995). Stereotype threat and the intellectual test performance of African Americans. *Journal of Personality and Social Psychology, 69,* 797–811. Reprinted by permission of Claude M. Steele.

How do people cope with the threats posed by negative prejudices, stereotypes, and discrimination? Some strategies are useful in the short run but create longer-term costs. For instance, confronted with stereotype threat, individuals sometimes self-handicap their performance—that is, put obstacles in the way of a successful performance (see Chapter 4) (Keller, 2002; Stone, 2002). Although this may provide them with an excuse for performing poorly—and thereby reduce anxiety about *really* confirming negative stereotypes ("after all, I didn't even try")—they have increased their chances of doing poorly on something that's important to them.

As a second example, stereotype threat sometimes leads people to **disidentify** with those arenas where society expects them to fail—to decide that the arena is no longer relevant to their self-concept and self-esteem (Crocker & Major, 1989; Steele, 1992). For instance, afraid of confirming the stereotype that they are unintelligent, African American students may, over time, disconnect academic performance from their self-images; afraid of confirming the stereotype that they aren't good at math, women may no longer see math as relevant to who they are; and so on (e.g., Major et al., 1998). Results from one study are consistent with this: The self-esteem of black children was less tied to school performance in the tenth grade than in the eighth grade—a pattern not found for white children (Osborne, 1995). In the short term, disidentifying with academics may be adaptive, helping these children maintain positive feelings about themselves in the face of negative social stereotypes. In the long run, however, distancing themselves from academic development leaves these children ill prepared to compete successfully in a world where knowledge and the ability to learn are critical.

There exist alternative strategies, however, that may be beneficial in both the short and long term. For example, women who use humor as a coping strategy are less likely to perform worse on a difficult math test after negative math stereotypes are made salient, because their use of humor apparently reduces the anxiety they experience during the test (Ford et al., 2004). In another experiment, researchers eliminated the negative effects of mathematics stereotype threat on female test performance by telling them about women who had been successful in the fields of architecture, medicine, and the like (McIntyre et al., 2003). By being reminded that the negative stereotypes don't apply to everyone, these women were better able to perform up to their personal potential. In another study, college students participated in a program designed to enhance their belief that intelligence can be enhanced—that, like a muscle, intelligence can grow if "exercised" via hard work. By the end of the semester, black program participants liked the academic process more, identified more with school, and earned higher grades than did students who had been randomly assigned to control conditions (Aronson, Fried, & Good, 2002). Believing that one can improve one's abilities through additional hard work can apparently reduce some of the damaging consequences of stereotype threat. Indeed, even just teaching people *about* stereotype threat before they take a difficult test can reduce its effects (Johns, Schmader, & Martens, 2005).

Even in the face of such efforts, however, negative prejudices, stereotypes, and discrimination can have serious material and psychological costs (Swim & Stangor, 1998). Moreover, these costs extend beyond those directly victimized. For instance, interracial interactions tax the cognitive resources of prejudiced individuals, which can have negative implications for performance on a variety of tasks (e.g., Bair & Steele, 2010; Richeson & Shelton, 2007). Nonbigoted individuals may be disliked for having friends who are themselves targets for prejudice (e.g., Neuberg et al., 1994; Sigelman et al., 1991). And when prejudices develop into aggression, the level of human tragedy can be staggering, as illustrated by interethnic and inter-religious conflicts and terrorist attacks occurring throughout the world.

INVESTIGATION

Imagine that you're interviewing for a job you really want and that your interviewer is a member of a group (e.g., ethnic, gender, sexual orientation) known to dislike members of your group. What kinds of thoughts are likely to go through your head as you're interviewing? How will they influence your performance in the interview?

Disidentify To reduce in one's mind the relevance of a particular domain (e.g., academic achievement) to one's self-esteem.

The Goals of Prejudice, Stereotyping, and Discrimination

In light of the great damage caused by negative stereotypes, prejudices, and discrimination, one might reasonably wonder *why* people think, feel, and behave in such ways. After all, to paraphrase Rodney King—the black Los Angeles motorist beaten by white police officers following a highly publicized car chase in 1991—wouldn't we all be better off if we could just get along?

If the answer to this question is yes, it's certainly not a simple yes. Prejudicial feelings, stereotypical thinking, and discriminatory actions serve several important goals. They can help support and protect one's own group, they can provide social approval, they can bolster personal and social identities, and they can help us navigate complex, information-rich social environments with an economy of mental effort. We explore each of these possibilities in turn.

Quick Quiz

1 Feeling negatively toward people who do not share your religious beliefs is an example of _____, whereas a generalized belief such as "all Asians are good at math" is an example of _____.
   a. prejudice, stereotype
   b. stereotype, prejudice
   c. stereotype, discrimination
   d. prejudice, discrimination

2 Which of the following examples are costs borne by targets of discrimination?
   a. Women and minority groups tend to be paid less for the same work.
   b. Women and minorities tend to receive worse deals on cars than White men.
   c. Stereotype threat
   d. All of the above

3 Which of the following strategies for coping with stereotype threat are beneficial in both the short and long term?
   a. Self-handicapping one's performance
   b. Reminding oneself that the negative stereotype does not apply to everyone
   c. Disidentifying with the domain (e.g., academic achievement) that is the source of the stereotype threat
   d. None of the above

Supporting and Protecting One's Group

LO 11.3 Define (a) realistic group conflict theory, (b) social dominance orientation, and (c) minimal intergroup paradigm.

LO 11.4 Describe the Robbers Cave study and discuss what it may tell us about the causes of negative prejudices, stereotypes, and discrimination.

LO 11.5 Describe the self-fulfilling spiral of intergroup competition.

Ann Atwater longed for her "piece of the pie." She and other members of the black community wanted to share in the American Dream. She wanted to obtain a well-paying job, live in a clean and safe neighborhood, and send her children to good schools. The laws and practices of white America denied her these opportunities.

C. P. Ellis wanted the same for his family. Although white, he was poor, like Ann Atwater. To Ellis, the black call for increased opportunity was a declaration of economic war. The pie is only so big, he thought. If the blacks get a piece, his thin slice, and the thin slices of whites like him, would become but slivers.

Like many others, Ellis believed that blacks and whites were competing for a limited pool of economic resources. Of course, logic tells us that Ellis's ability to get a well-paying job was obstructed as much by white competitors as by black competitors. Why, then, was it so easy for him to see blacks, but not whites, as the competition? Why wasn't Ellis equally resentful and antagonistic toward his white rivals? And why did he band together with other whites to hinder the progress made by blacks?

Creating and Maintaining Ingroup Advantage

Imagine yourself in the following laboratory experiment: You're seated with other students, and the researcher projects a series of dot patterns onto the screen at the front of the room. Each slide is presented for only a short time, and your task is to estimate the number of dots on each. You make your guesses privately. When the slide show is complete, the researcher ushers you into an individual cubicle where you're told that, on the basis of your guesses, you're an "overestimator." (Other participants are told instead that they are "underestimators." In reality, your designation is randomly assigned on the basis of a coin flip.) Of course, you have no preconceived notions of what it means to be an overestimator or underestimator, and the researcher explicitly tells you that neither type is better than the other.

You find the next task more interesting. You remain in your private cubicle, and your job is to allocate monetary rewards and penalties to the other people in your session. These other folks are identified in only two ways: by a code number, to hide each person's identity, and by a group designation that labels each person as either an overestimator or an underestimator. Your allocations will remain entirely confidential, and you'll never have any contact with the other participants. How would you split the money?

Henri Tajfel and his colleagues (1971) placed British teenagers in this very situation and labeled it the **minimal intergroup paradigm** because the groups (of overestimators and underestimators) were randomly determined, artificial, short term, and involved no contact between the members. Would participants allocate more money to members of their own groups (i.e., *ingroups*) than to members of other groups (i.e., *outgroups*)? The answer was yes. Indeed, even when groups are minimally defined, people often display an **ingroup bias**, benefiting members of their own groups over members of other groups (e.g., Brewer, 1979; Halevy et al., 2008; Mullen et al., 1992; Tajfel, 1982).

THE NATURE OF GROUP LIVING AND INTERGROUP CONFLICT   The roots of the ingroup bias likely lie in our evolutionary past (e.g., Campbell, 1965; Kurzban & Neuberg, 2005; Schaller, Park, & Faulkner, 2003). Group living was necessary for our ancestors' survival. Within small communities, humans cooperated with each other and developed norms of reciprocity to further strengthen the group bonds (Axelrod & Hamilton, 1981; Trivers, 1971). Moreover, because these communities consisted largely of biological relatives, behaviors that strengthened the group usually also benefited the genes of each individual member—increasing the likelihood that he or she (and his or her relatives) would survive and reproduce (Hamilton, 1964). It would have been advantageous, then, for humans both to think in terms of groups and to value the groups to which they belonged. Consistent with this, people display greater ingroup bias when they feel loyal to their groups and identify strongly with them (e.g., Hertel & Kerr, 2001; Jetten et al., 1997). Indeed, the ingroup bias seems to be a cross-cultural feature of human social life, and the inclination to favor one's own group may even operate automatically (Ashburn-Nardo, Voils, & Monteith, 2001; Otten & Moskowitz, 2000).

This alone does not explain, however, why people so often *dislike* members of other groups. Why, for instance, have Americans at times exhibited such fervent opposition to immigration? **Realistic group conflict theory** proposes that intergroup conflict emerges when groups find themselves competing for the same material resources (e.g., Bonacich, 1972; D. T. Campbell, 1965; Sherif et al., 1961/1988). Not only should such conflicts increase people's positive feelings of solidarity toward their own group but also they should lead people to develop strong dislikes for other groups. After all, "they" are trying to deny "us" the resources we need to survive and prosper. As a result, group members may act in ways that aid their group and harm other groups.

Minimal intergroup paradigm An experimental procedure in which short-term, arbitrary, artificial groups are created to explore the foundations of prejudice, stereotyping, and discrimination.

Ingroup bias The tendency to benefit members of one's own groups over members of other groups.

Realistic group conflict theory The proposal that intergroup conflict, and negative prejudices and stereotypes, emerge out of actual competition between groups for desired resources.

More recent approaches to understanding prejudice focus on a broader set of threats that humans have long dealt with as a social species, such as the possibilities of physical violence from others living within one's group or in close proximity, of becoming infected with others' contagious diseases, of having others take more from the group than they contribute, and the like (Schaller & Neuberg, 2012). As we learned in Chapter 2, different kinds of threats elicit different emotions—for example, the threat of physical harm evokes fear, whereas the threat of being ripped off elicits anger. This psychology, which partly evolved to deal with threats from within one's group, is employed to address threats from outside the group as well. One implication of this is that, to the extent that different groups are perceived to pose different threats, the emotional content of prejudices directed at these groups should differ as well—and they do (e.g., Cottrell & Neuberg, 2005; Tapias et al., 2007). In this chapter's research video, Prof. Mark Schaller of the University of British Columbia describes research on the special linkages between disease and intergroup prejudice.

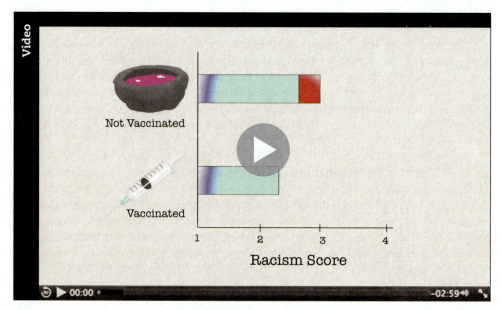

WATCH THE VIDEO: *How germs can make you prejudiced.*

Interestingly, the targets of threat stereotypes and prejudices have a nuanced understanding of the different ways in which they're viewed—and they seem to respond accordingly. For instance, Rebecca Neel and her colleagues (2013) found that young black men know that others are afraid of them and obese people know that others are disgusted by them. As a result, when wanting to create a favorable first impression, the young black men in her studies reported being especially likely to smile (which reduces perceptions of dangerousness) whereas the obese people report being especially likely to wear clean clothes (which reduces perceptions of dirtiness).

The threat-based perspective also suggests that people's prejudices toward a group should become more prominent when they feel particularly vulnerable to the threats typically associated with that group (e.g., Faulkner et al., 2004; Navarrete & Fessler, 2006). White American students who had just viewed clips from a frightening movie were especially likely to perceive the facial expressions of young black men to be angry (i.e., as threatening)—just as current American stereotypes would suggest (Maner et al., 2005), and a follow-up study found that fearful White participants were quicker to make avoidance movements in response to images of Black men (Miller, Zielaskowski, Maner, & Plant, 2012). In another study, white Canadians who believed that the world is a dangerous place rated black men (but not white men) as being particularly hostile when they made their ratings in a darkened, and thereby more fear-inducing, room

(Schaller, Park, & Mueller, 2003). The nature of people's stereotypes and prejudices are influenced by their current concerns and fears and by the specific threats they believe that members of other groups pose.

JUSTIFYING GROUP ADVANTAGE Whereas proponents of realistic group conflict theory propose that negative prejudices and stereotypes naturally *emerge* from economic conflict between groups, others have suggested that powerful people and institutions sometimes strategically *manipulate* stereotypes and prejudices to give themselves an advantage (Cox, 1959; Reich, 1971). For instance, some have argued that white Europeans invented the concept of black racial inferiority to justify their exploitative incursions into Africa. And C. P. Ellis eventually came to believe that Durham's businessmen encouraged and financed the KKK's racist activities to keep the poor whites and poor blacks fighting each other so that neither would notice the enormous wealth the town's leaders were accumulating.

Are systematic, economically motivated attempts like these to create or amplify negative stereotypes and prejudice common or powerful? Given that they would involve presumably secretive conspiracy, it's hard to know. Existing research does tell us, however, that most of us want to believe that the world is *just*—that good things happen to good people and bad things happen to bad people (Lerner, 1980). It makes sense, then, that successful individuals would want to believe that they're entitled to their economic successes—that they've earned their positions in life "fair and square." As a result, people may indeed use stereotypes and prejudices to justify existing social and economic inequalities (Jost & Burgess, 2000; Sidanius & Pratto, 1993). For instance, by stereotyping African Americans as unintelligent and lazy, white Americans can justify their own group's relatively high economic status.

In sum, the desire to support and protect the ingroup helps to create and maintain intergroup tensions. We see next that certain features of the person and situation increase this desire, thereby leading to negative stereotypes and prejudices.

Our resources for us, or our resources for them? Group competition for economic resources can create or magnify negative prejudices and discrimination. Over the past decade, citizens of the United States, Canada, and Western Europe have fought to curb new immigration, have sought to cut or eliminate expenditures for immigrants who've already arrived, and have stereotyped the potential competitors as inferior people who threaten their valued way of life.

PERSON Social Dominance Orientation

"Some groups of people are simply not the equals of others." "It's sometimes necessary to step on others to get ahead in life." "Some people are just more worthy than others." Such are the statements of persons high in social dominance orientation. **Social dominance orientation** describes the extent to which a person wants his or her own group to dominate and be superior to other groups (Kteily, Sidanius, & Levin, 2011; Sidanius & Pratto, 1999). Unlike individuals who believe that all people should be treated equally, individuals with a strong social dominance orientation prefer social systems in which groups are ordered according to their worth. They believe that superior groups (very often their own) ought to be wealthier and more powerful.

People having a strong social dominance orientation are particularly likely to hold negative stereotypes and prejudices against lower-status groups. For instance, white Americans with strong social dominance orientations are more prejudiced against blacks, allocate more group resources to white organizations than to black organizations, disapprove more of interracial marriages and gay and lesbian rights, are more sexist, and are more supportive of governmental policies through which the United States could dominate other nations (Pratto et al., 1994; Sidanius et al., 2007). Of course, the prejudice-creating influences of social dominance orientation are not limited to Americans. Felicia Pratto and her colleagues (1998; Sidanius & Pratto, 1999) measured

Social dominance orientation The extent to which a person desires that his or her own group dominate other groups and be socially and materially superior to them.

social dominance orientation in Canada, Taiwan, China, and Israel and asked citizens of these nations about their views toward women and their country's low-status groups. The commonality across nations was striking. In all nations, individuals having a strong social dominance orientation demonstrated greater levels of sexism, and, in most, social dominance orientation was associated with increased prejudices.

Where do high levels of social dominance orientation come from? Believing that your group is being threatened—especially if you highly identify with it—will increase your social dominance orientation (Morrison & Ybarra, 2008). Being a member of a dominant group, or even being *temporarily* assigned a position of power over others, also creates or enhances the acceptance of the belief that those who are better off deserve more than those who are not (e.g., Guimond et al., 2003). As we discussed above, such an ideology can help justify one's privileged position. And with a justification, it becomes easier to hold negative prejudices and stereotypes about those less well off than oneself and to discriminate against them.

SITUATION ## Intergroup Competition

When economic times are tough, acquiring resources for one's group takes on special urgency. We should thus expect increased ingroup favoritism and outgroup hostility when people believe they're competing with other groups for land, housing, jobs, and the like.

In a classic study, Carl Hovland and Robert Sears (1940) gathered data on the U.S. South between 1882 and 1930, correlating economic conditions with the number of lynchings—illegal hangings—of black people. As we noted in Chapter 10, economic pressures were clearly linked to outgroup hostility: When economic times were rough, white southerners lynched more blacks (Hepworth & West, 1988). This tendency wasn't confined to the South, as difficult economic times in northern cities also led to increased white violence against blacks, as well as to violence against immigrant Chinese (Olzak, 1992).

To explore the role of intergroup competition more closely, Muzafer Sherif and his colleagues (1961/1988) designed an intriguing field experiment. They began by selecting 22 well-adjusted, white fifth-grade boys with above-average intelligence, average-to-good school performance, and Protestant, middle-class, two-parent family backgrounds. All the boys attended different schools in the Oklahoma City area and didn't know each other prior to the study. The researchers then split the boys into two essentially identical groups and sent them to camp at Robbers Cave State Park in rural Oklahoma.

During the first days of the study, each group took part in typical camp activities—sports, hiking, swimming, and the like—unaware that the other group existed across the park. Soon, these two collections of strangers became real groups, with leaders, norms, favorite activities, and even names—the Rattlers and the Eagles. The experiment was now ready to proceed.

The researchers began a four-day tournament of contests—baseball games, tugs-of-war, touch football, tent pitching, a treasure hunt, and cabin inspections. To the winning group would go a trophy, individual medals, and highly appealing camping knives. To the losing group . . . nothing. Consistent with realistic group conflict theory, animosities between the groups grew quickly during the first baseball game and fiercely escalated throughout the competition. The Eagles burned the Rattlers' flag. The Rattlers raided the Eagles' cabin, turning over beds and scattering possessions. Derogatory name calling increased in frequency and intensity. Several fist fights broke out. And when the Eagles won the tournament and went off to celebrate their victory, the Rattlers raided their cabin and stole the hard-won camping knives. The Eagles confronted the Rattlers, the two groups began skirmishing, and the researchers had to physically separate the boys to avoid a full-scale fight.

Two days later, after a cooling-off period during which the Rattlers and Eagles were kept apart, the boys rated the characteristics of each group. These findings corroborated the researchers' observations. Whereas the campers saw members of their own group as brave, tough, and friendly, they viewed members of the other group as

Competition and animosity at Robbers Cave. The tug-of-war and other competitive events created powerful antagonisms between the Eagles and Rattlers, culminating in near-warfare.

sneaky, smart-alecky stinkers! These data are particularly striking when we recall that the boys had been selected for the study because of how similar they were to one another.

Indeed, whether it be the British disliking West Indians, the Dutch disliking Turks and Surinamers, or the French disliking North Africans, we see that negative prejudices and stereotypes often "target the competition": People direct their hostilities toward those groups they see themselves competing with at the moment (Pettigrew & Meertens, 1995). Moreover, competition may increase the salience of group distinctions, as demonstrated in one recent series of studies: White participants who had been primed with concerns about economic hardship and debt were, compared with control subjects, more likely to categorize a biracial face as Black (Rodeheffer, Hill, & Lord, 2012).

INTERACTION ## The Self-Fulfilling Spiral of Intergroup Competition

As blacks like Ann Atwater took to Durham's streets to protest the discrimination that confined them to inadequate housing, low-paying jobs, and lousy schools, poor whites like C. P. Ellis worried that any black gains would come at their expense. As the black calls for equal opportunity were generally dismissed by whites, blacks increased the frequency and vigor of their protests. In turn, the views of many of Durham's white citizens became harder and even more fixed. The conflict spiraled. Ann Atwater developed from a respectful housekeeper into "Roughhouse Annie," the militant civil rights activist. C. P. Ellis changed from being a quiet man struggling to keep his family afloat to the reactionary leader of the KKK.

Competition and hostility breed increased competition and hostility. As people view others as competitors, they themselves begin to compete, inadvertently bringing about or amplifying the competition they initially feared (Kelley & Stahelski, 1970) (see Figure 11.3). This *self-fulfilling prophecy* (see Chapter 3) can quickly spiral into increasingly intense forms of competition, as those involved become even more convinced of the others' malicious designs. This process is particularly pronounced at the group level, because groups compete more intensely against each other for resources than do individuals (e.g., Takemura & Yuki, 2007; Wildschut et al., 2003).

In this self-fulfilling spiral of intergroup competition, we see two fundamental forms of the person–situation interaction: First, competitive situations create competitive people and groups who possess little trust for one another, illustrating once again that *situations can change people* in important ways. Second, competitive, untrusting people and groups create ever more competitive and hostile situations, an example of how *people change their situations*. It's easy to see how such competitive spirals can create stubborn intergroup hatreds such as the ones between Israelis and Palestinians in the Middle East.

Figure 11.3   The competitive spiral

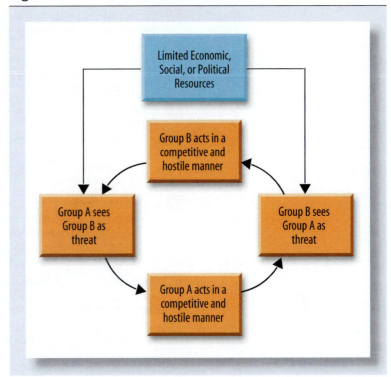

As groups see one another as competitors for common resources, they may begin to behave in ways that bring about or exaggerate the very competition they feared. This self-fulfilling spiral can rapidly escalate, creating stubborn and intense intergroup hostilities.

INVESTIGATION

In what ways did the September 11 attacks on the United States alter your sense of being "American"? Why? How did these changes influence your feelings and beliefs about different groups within the United States?

Quick Quiz

1 The evolutionary perspective suggests that humans' inclination toward prejudice evolved in part to deal with which of the following threats?

    a. The possibility of physical violence from others.

    b. The threat of becoming infected with others' contagious diseases.

    c. The threat of people taking more from the group than they contribute.

    d. All of the above

2 A person high in social dominance orientation would likely agree with which of the following statements?

    a. All groups should have access to equal opportunities in life.

    b. Treating people more equally would improve society's problems.

    c. Some groups of people are simply inferior to others.

    d. All of the above

3 _____ tends to _____ ingroup favoritism and outgroup hostility.

    a. Intergroup competition, decrease

    b. Intergroup competition, increase

    c. Social dominance orientation, decrease

    d. Outgroup identification, increase

4 Competitive situations create competitive people/groups, and competitive people/groups create increasingly more competitive and hostile situations. This description of the self-fulfilling spiral of intergroup competition illustrates which two forms of person–situation interactions?

    a. (1) Situations can change people and (2) people change their situations

    b. (1) People change their situations and (2) different people respond differently to the same situation

    c. (1) Persons choose their situations and (2) different situations prime different parts of the person

    d. (1) Situations choose the person and (2) situations can change people

Seeking Social Approval

LO 11.6 Discuss how different forms of religiosity are linked to prejudice and discrimination.

LO 11.7 Describe which people are likely to express their groups' prejudice-relevant norms and the type of situation in which this inclination is especially likely to occur.

Most of us can recall a conversation in which someone made a prejudiced remark or joke we privately found offensive. What did you do? Did you express your disapproval publicly? Perhaps you let it pass, perhaps even forcing a little smile? If so, you're not alone. In one experiment, for example, nonsexist women publicly conformed to the sexist opinions of three other participants, demonstrating that even nonprejudiced people may express prejudiced views (Swim, Ferguson, & Hyers, 1999). But why?

We suspect you feared social rejection. As we saw in Chapters 4 and 6, people want the approval of others and can get it by adjusting their opinions and behaviors to match those held by others. If those we care about view a particular group negatively, we may conform to those views in the hope of "fitting in" and gaining their approval (Blanchard et al., 1994; Zitek & Hebl, 2007). Because the benefits of social approval (and the costs of social rejection) are so powerful, even individuals who are usually motivated *not* to discriminate may discriminate anyway. For instance, black men in one set of experiments discriminated against Native American job candidates, but only when they believed their actions would be seen by people who would be evaluating them and were themselves bigoted against Native Americans (Shapiro & Neuberg, 2008).

Social norms and expectations may do more than just lead us to *pretend* that we hold certain stereotypes and prejudices. A prejudiced social environment may also give us permission to express the prejudices we already hold (Ford, Wentzel, & Lorion, 2001; Goodman et al., 2008; Wittenbrink & Henley, 1996). Participants in one study evaluated sexist events as being less offensive after hearing a series of sexist jokes—but only if they held sexist beliefs to begin with (Ford, 2000). Moreover, because social norms deeply infiltrate our everyday lives, and because we spend so much time around those from whom we seek approval, we can also internalize these messages and accept them as our own (e.g., Guimond, 2000). Just as it must have been quite easy for C. P. Ellis to pick up the racist messages of the pre-civil-rights South, it's easy for us today to internalize the stereotypic and prejudicial messages we hear at home, in the neighborhood, at work, and in the media.

PERSON   Religiosity and Prejudice

Many of the world's major faiths ascribe to the principle that people should accept others unconditionally, without regard to their race or ethnicity. It is thus puzzling that people who report being religious tend to be more prejudiced than those who do not (Allport & Kramer, 1946; Hunsberger & Jackson, 2005). Why might this be?

A long line of research has explored the possibility that, by understanding the different ways in which people are religious, we might be better able to understand the association between religion and prejudice (Allport & Ross, 1967; Batson & Burris, 1994; Hunsberger & Jackson, 2005). Some people possess an *extrinsic religiosity*—that is, they see religious worship as an opportunity to make friends, gain status, or find support during difficult times. From this perspective, religion is used to get something else and is merely a means to some other end; its messages are not adopted as a life standard. Research on individuals who are extrinsically religious suggests that they are more negatively prejudiced against racial outgroups and gays and lesbians than are nonreligious people (e.g., Batson & Ventis, 1982).

Alternatively, people may adhere to an *intrinsic religiosity*, hoping to live their religion and internalize its teachings (Allport & Ross, 1967). From this perspective, religion is not a means to some other goal but rather an end in itself. Because most organized religions teach tolerance, and because intrinsically religious people hope to integrate their religious creeds into their identities and actions, we might expect intrinsically religious individuals to be low on prejudice. Indeed, based on self-report data, intrinsically religious people seem less prejudiced. Other research using more subtle behavioral measures, however, suggests that intrinsically religious people may be more concerned with gaining the social approval that goes along with *appearing* tolerant than with actually *being* tolerant (Batson et al., 1986).

A third form of religiosity has been labeled *fundamentalism*, which is characterized by a certainty in the absolute truth of one's religious beliefs (Altemeyer & Hunsberger, 1992). Individuals who score high on fundamentalism scales tend to possess more negative views of racial and religious outgroups, gays and lesbians, and women than do nonreligious individuals (Hunsberger & Jackson, 2005).

Finally, a fourth form of religiosity has been labeled *quest religiosity* (Batson & Ventis, 1982). From this perspective, religion is a never-ending personal journey toward truth. People who are primarily quest-oriented are open-minded about spiritual matters and don't expect to find simple answers to complex spiritual and moral issues. Quest-oriented individuals are open-minded about other things as well, which may explain why they exhibit few prejudices in either their self-reports or their actions (Batson & Burris, 1994).

It seems, then, with the exception of those who view religion as a quest, that religiosity tends to enhance negative prejudices. This certainly seems to fit with quick and easy observations of conflicts across the world that appear to have religious roots—Hindus and Muslims in India, Jews and Muslims in the Middle East, Protestants and Catholics in Northern Ireland, and so forth. But a recent set of studies by Jeremy Ginges and his colleagues (2009) suggests a different interpretation.

These researchers were interested in whether religiosity affects support for suicide attacks on other groups, but thought it important to differentiate between two aspects of religiosity—*religious devotion* (measured with items that assessed, for instance, frequency of prayer) and *commitment to one's religious group* (measured with items that

The work of God? Across the globe, thousands have been killed by terrorists. Many of those planning and carrying out the attacks believe they're serving legitimate religious principles, as did Osama bin Laden (who was responsible for the September 11, 2001, attacks on New York and Washington). Are groups such as Al Qaeda cynically constructing façades of religiosity to justify a murderous political ideology that would otherwise seem reprehensible? Or do these groups truly believe they're doing the work of God? It seems puzzling, indeed, that people having strong religious beliefs can be so hateful toward other groups.

assessed frequency of attendance at formal religious services). These distinctions bear some resemblance to the intrinsic/extrinsic distinctions just discussed, with religious devotion perhaps being one aspect of intrinsic religiosity and commitment to one's religious group perhaps being one aspect of extrinsic religiosity.

Consider the researchers' reasoning: If religious beliefs, per se, increase prejudice against other groups, then people who are more religiously devoted should be especially likely to favor suicide attacks on members of other groups (even after controlling for their commitment to their religious group). If, however, commitment to one's religious group—and, relatedly, the extent to which one wants to be seen as a good group member—enhances prejudice, then people who are more committed to their religious groups should be especially likely to favor suicide attacks on other groups (even after controlling for their levels of religious devotion).

The researchers surveyed a wide range of groups to explore these alternative hypotheses—Palestinian Muslims, Israeli Jews, Indian Hindus, Russian Christian Orthodox, Indonesian Muslims, British Protestants, and Mexican Catholics—and the findings were clear: Commitment to one's religious group, as measured by attendance at religious services, uniquely predicted support for the killing of members of other groups; religious devotion, as measured by frequency of prayer, did not (Ginges, Hansen, & Norenzayan, 2009). Consistent with this, a global study of conflict found that groups that are religiously infused—whose religion is an important part of everyday group life—are more likely to be prejudiced and violently aggressive against other groups, even when those other groups are much more powerful (Neuberg et al., 2014). These findings suggest that, consistent with the mixed findings on intrinsic religiosity, it may be the extent to which religiosity is tied with social processes—a commitment to having one's group do well, the desire to be approved of by other ingroup members, and so forth—that helps account for the relationship between religion and negative prejudice and discrimination.

SITUATION ● Prejudice Norms Change Over Time

Because people have a need for social approval, they are willing to adopt a group's prejudicial norms. Norms, however, change over time. With these changes should come attendant shifts in people's expressions of stereotypes and prejudices.

Over the past 50 years, white Americans have reported increasingly favorable views toward issues such as racial integration, interracial marriage, and black presidential candidates (e.g., Ludwig, 2004). Do findings like these reflect actual changes in people's prejudices and stereotypes, or do they merely reveal people's desire to answer such surveys in socially appropriate ways? We've seen that the desire for social approval may lead people to adopt negative prejudices when they believe that others are bigoted. This same desire for social approval, however, may also lead people to adopt tolerant views when they believe that tolerance is the societal norm. For example, among high school students in North Carolina, white students' views of blacks were more favorable if they believed that their friends and parents approved of interracial friendships (Cox, Smith, & Insko, 1996).

If findings like these don't represent changes in actual attitudes, they surely reflect changes in the culture's injunctive and descriptive norms. As we discussed in earlier chapters, *injunctive norms* tell us what we *ought* to do and feel, and changes in U.S. laws and policies now communicate the message that discrimination against people on the bases of race, sex, ethnicity, religion, and age is inappropriate and counter to American beliefs. *Descriptive norms* tell us what people *actually* do and feel, and because the coercive power of the new laws has reduced the amount of observable discrimination, people are likely left with the impression that their peers are less bigoted now than before. Across the United States as a whole, then, changes over time in the injunctive norms have probably led to similar changes in the descriptive norms. As a result, people are not only less willing to express bigoted views in public but also actually may be less likely to hold them—as suggested by the actual election of Barack Obama to the U.S. presidency in 2008 and again in 2012.

INTERACTION Perceived Social Standing and Prejudice Expression

Recall a time when you were a newcomer—the new kid on the block, the new employee on the job, or the new student in the dorm. As a peripheral member of the group, you probably wanted to fit in and demonstrate your worth to the others. As a consequence, you were more likely to conform to the group's norms.

Jeffrey Noel, Daniel Wann, and Nyla Branscombe (1995) provided a nice demonstration of how the desire for social approval can lead peripheral group members to become especially hostile toward outgroups. Their subjects were fraternity and sorority members and pledges (members "in training"). As Figure 11.4 illustrates, full-fledged members exhibited similar amounts of prejudice against outgroup members regardless of whether their opinions were to be kept private or made public. In contrast, the pledges belittled other fraternities and sororities *only* when their evaluations were about to be made public to their fraternity brothers or sorority sisters. In an attempt to gain social approval, pledges strongly conformed to the norm of derogating other fraternities and sororities. These findings illustrate an important feature of the social approval process—approval-seekers conform to apparent group norms especially when these actions will be seen by potential approval-givers. They also illustrate one of the forms of person–situation interaction we've seen before—that certain people (in this case, pledges but not members) act in a particular ways (express prejudices), but only in specific situations (when those expressions are public).

In sum, because people seek social approval, they are likely to adopt and express negative prejudices when prejudices are the norm, and to be tolerant when tolerance is the norm. Because 1971 wasn't a popular time for tolerance in Durham, C. P. Ellis's membership in the KKK provided him with a great amount of social approval and respect within the white community. His friendship with Ann Atwater thus cost him dearly, because when Ellis stopped hating blacks his friends started hating him. The loss of his approving social network, and the loneliness it created, was unbearable: Ellis attempted suicide. Even 30 years later he stated, "there are a lot of people who hate me . . . I bet I could walk up to that corner right now and there wouldn't be two people who'd speak to me. That's how long it's lasted . . . I wish I had more friends" ("An Unlikely Friendship," 2003). The desire to gain social approval is powerful, indeed.

Figure 11.4 Pledging one's dislike for other groups . . . in public

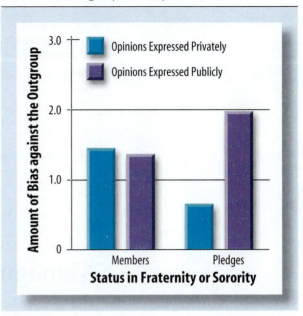

Fraternity and sorority pledges at the University of Kansas were especially disparaging of other fraternities and sororities, but only when they believed that members of their own groups would see their opinions. Peripheral members of groups such as pledges want to be accepted, even to the point of boldly proclaiming their outgroup prejudices.

Source: Data from Noel, J. G., Wann, D. L., & Branscombe, N. R. (1995). Peripheral ingroup membership status and public negativity toward outgroups. *Journal of Personality and Social Psychology, 68,* 127-137 Figure 3.

INVESTIGATION

Think of an incident in which you laughed at or "let pass" a statement you found to be prejudiced and offensive. If you were to confront a similar incident again, how would you respond? Why?

Quick Quiz

 1 Which of the following statements describes how social norms influence the expression and internalization of prejudice?

 a. People who find themselves in a prejudiced social environment may feel free to express the prejudices that they already hold.

 b. People may publicly conform to others' prejudiced views when they desire social approval, even if they wouldn't endorse such views privately.

 c. People may come to internalize the prejudiced views they are frequently exposed to in their everyday social environments.

 d. All of the above

2 _____ religious people strive to live their religion and internalize its teachings, whereas _____ religious people strive to use religious worship as an opportunity to make social connections or gain status.

    a. Fundamentalist, quest-oriented
    b. Quest-oriented, extrinsically
    c. Intrinsically, extrinsically
    d. Extrinsically, intrinsically

3 What accounts for the relationship between religiosity and negative prejudice and discrimination?

    a. Religious devotion
    b. Fundamentalism
    c. Intrinsic religiosity
    d. Commitment to one's religious group

4 People are especially likely to express their groups' prejudice-relevant norms when _____.

    a. they are new to the group and express their opinions privately
    b. they are new to the group and express their opinions publicly
    c. they are established group members and express their opinions privately
    d. they are established group members and express their opinions publicly

Managing Self-Image

LO 11.8 Discuss how the desire to maintain favorable personal and social identities contributes to scapegoating.

LO 11.9 Describe the authoritarian personality and how this trait is related to negative prejudice.

LO 11.10 Explain how failure and threats to self-image threat can increase prejudice.

C. P. Ellis was eight, playing football with his white neighbors against a team of black children from the other side of the railroad tracks. The black team won, and, as the kids wandered home, one of C. P.'s teammates, frustrated by the loss, yelled at the departing victors, "You niggers get back across the track." For the young C. P., this was an awakening. Although he recognized that he was poor and that his family was looked down upon by many, he knew in that instant that he could never be a "nigger"—that there would always be someone beneath him on the social ladder. He felt the security that comes from believing yourself better than someone else (Davidson, 1996, pp. 64–65).

Twenty-five years later, Ellis discovered a second, related sense of security as the Ku Klux Klan welcomed him into their fold. No longer an outsider, he felt he now belonged to something important—a brotherhood (Davidson, 1996, p. 123). Before the Klan ceremony, he could take refuge in knowing that he was not a "nigger"; afterward, he could also take pleasure and pride in knowing that he was a Klansman.

Personal and Social Identities

Social behavior is often motivated by the desire to feel good about oneself, and people are quite creative in the ways they accomplish this (see Chapter 3). For example, confronted by personal failure, we may attempt to preserve a favorable self-image by blaming other groups for our inadequacies—that is, by **scapegoating** them. Scapegoating is usually directed toward easily identifiable groups against whom socially acceptable prejudices already exist. It was a simple matter for C. P. Ellis to blame his financial failures on blacks. As he stated years later, "I had to hate somebody. Hatin' America is hard to do because you can't see it to hate it. You gotta have something to look at to hate. The natural person for me to hate would be black people, because my father before me was a member of the Klan" (Terkel, 1992). By blaming other groups for our own misfortunes and frustrations, we are better able to deal with our self-doubts and to feel good about ourselves.

Scapegoating The process of blaming members of other groups for one's frustrations and failures.

Alternatively, by linking ourselves to successful others and distancing ourselves from unsuccessful others—by *basking in reflected glory* and by *cutting off reflected failure*—we can boost our self-images (e.g., Cialdini et al., 1976; Snyder et al., 1986). These strategies reveal that self-image is influenced by more than just a sense of ourselves as individuals. Rather, self-image is also influenced by our **social identity**—by our opinions of, and feelings about, the social groups with which we identify. Like C. P. Ellis, whose self-image was elevated when he embraced the Klan and its white Christian heritage, many of our self-images are elevated by the pride we have in our groups and ethnic backgrounds.

The observation that social identities contribute to self-esteem forms the foundation of social identity theory (Tajfel & Turner, 1986). Just as individuals manage their personal identities by comparing themselves to other individuals, people manage their social identities by comparing their groups to other groups. Specifically, by positively differentiating your group from other groups—by engaging in *downward social comparison*, seeing your group as better than "them"—you can create a positive social identity, which in turn can increase your sense of self-worth (e.g., Hunter et al., 1996; Rubin & Hewstone, 1998). To create this positive differentiation, you might directly enhance your own group, perhaps through positive stereotypes. C. P. Ellis, for instance, was able to enhance his social identity by seeing the KKK as unique in its moral code of honor, chivalry, and desire to defend Christian America. Instead, you might actively derogate other groups, thereby making your own group look positive in contrast (Cialdini & Richardson, 1980). For example, by enthusiastically endorsing his culture's negative stereotypes of blacks as unintelligent and lazy, Ellis was better able to view the members of his own group as smart and hardworking. You might also discriminate against the other group by taking away its opportunities, thus giving your group a *real* advantage. Of course, you could do all of these things. By exaggerating the KKK's favorable characteristics, by labeling blacks with strong negative stereotypes, and by effectively fighting to block economic and educational gains by blacks, Ellis was able to boost his social identity and, thus, his broader self-image.

Ethnic pride. How we view the social groups to which we belong influences how we view ourselves. For this reason, we look to celebrate our social identities. Unfortunately, positive social identities sometimes come at the expense of other groups, because we derogate them so that our group can look good by comparison.

PERSON ## Ingroup Identification

C. P. Ellis immersed himself in Klan activities and soon established a reputation as an energetic and effective worker. Committed to the organization from the very beginning, Ellis became more and more identified with it as he rapidly moved up in the group's hierarchy, first to chaplain and then to Exalted Cyclops—the top position in the Durham klavern. His identity as a Klansman became an increasingly important part of his self-image, and his desire to act on his racist prejudices grew stronger as well. This is as we might expect. When people identify strongly with their groups, they have more to gain from their groups' favorable standings and more to lose should their groups' positions weaken.

Indeed, research indicates that people who are highly identified with their group are especially likely to advantage their group over others (Branscombe, Schmitt, & Schiffhauer, 2007; Hodson, Dovidio, & Esses, 2003). In one experiment, for example, students at a French Canadian university had the job of anonymously allocating extra-credit course points to fellow students. Some of the possible recipients were members of the students' own groups, and some were not. Students who felt no strong identification with their ingroups allocated points equally across the two groups. As predicted, however, high identifiers gave more points to their own groups (Gagnon & Bourhis, 1996). Ingroup identification leads to increased discrimination.

Social identity The beliefs and feelings we have toward the groups to which we see ourselves belonging.

PERSON ## Authoritarianism and Prejudice

Many believe that negative prejudices are produced by "sick" minds. After all, only a disturbed individual could feel negatively about others, and treat them badly, just because they look different or belong to another group. Right?

This idea that intergroup hostilities emerge from psychologically flawed personalities once formed the cutting-edge perspective on prejudice. Below, we explore this hypothesis more closely, focusing on the personality characteristic of **authoritarianism**— the tendency to submit to those having greater authority and to denigrate those having less authority.

Authoritarianism The tendency to submit to those having greater authority and to denigrate those having less authority.

Bridging Function and Dysfunction:

The Authoritarian Personality

As people around the world learned of the millions exterminated in the Nazi concentration camps, they confronted troubling questions: Where do prejudices this powerful come from? What kind of person participates in such killings? And what kind of person stands idly by and does nothing?

Emerging from these questions came the idea of an *authoritarian personality* (Adorno et al., 1950). Such individuals readily submit to authorities but are aggressive against those perceived to be lower on the social ladder; that is, they "kiss ass" above and "kick ass" below. They easily adopt and conform to society's conventions and rules. They are tough-minded toward people who challenge society's conventions. They view the world in simple black–white terms, abhorring shades of gray. And, most important for our purposes, they are hypothesized to be strongly prejudiced against members of minority groups.

According to Theodor Adorno and his colleagues, parents create the authoritarian personality by severely punishing and shaming their young children for even small transgressions. As a result, the children feel hostile toward their parents and other authority figures. But they do not want to express or acknowledge their hostility because doing so may (1) bring even more punishment and (2) create a powerful internal conflict between hating their punitive parents and believing that they ought instead to love and respect them. As a result, said the researchers, these children learn to repress their antagonisms toward their parents and other authorities and to displace their aggressive impulses onto weaker members of society. From these internal psychological conflicts emerge prejudices.

This view of prejudice quickly became prominent, perhaps because it seemed to explain why the German people—perceived to be very orderly, disciplined, and respectful of authority—not only allowed the dictatorial Adolf Hitler to come to power but also went along with his program to annihilate the Jews and others. But other researchers found weaknesses in the explanation offered by Adorno and his colleagues (e.g., Christie & Jahoda, 1954). For instance, people can become authoritarian through other means as well. According to one alternative view, adolescents simply learn to be authoritarian by observing their authoritarian parents (Altemeyer, 1998; Duriez et al., 2008). According to another account, tendencies toward authoritarianism are passed along genetically (Scarr, 1981). Indeed, all three views have received some empirical support.

Still, Adorno and his colleagues turned out to be quite correct about the relationship between authoritarianism and negative prejudice. People who view the world through authoritarian lenses *are* more negatively prejudiced toward outgroups than are people who do not (e.g., Haddock, Zanna, & Esses, 1993; Whitley & Lee, 2000). And this holds true for authoritarians in the United States, Canada, England, South Africa, Russia, and many other countries (e.g., Duckitt & Farre, 1994; Heaven & St. Quintin, 2003; Napier & Jost, 2008; Stephan et al., 1994).

It's psychologically comforting to believe that prejudices exist primarily in the minds of clearly dysfunctional, clearly authoritarian individuals. After all, because *we're* not like that, we can avoid having to own up to our own prejudices. But let's not deceive ourselves. Many of us have a greater tendency toward authoritarianism than we'd like to admit. We've seen, for example, how easy it is for ordinary folks to obey even extreme commands of others (Chapter 6). Moreover, the bulk of the studies demonstrating ties between authoritarianism and prejudice used college students as participants—people like you. Finally, authoritarianism can increase when we experience frustrating negative events or threatening events (e.g., Sales & Friend, 1973). For instance, after the terrorist attacks on the United States of September 11, 2001, Americans became more willing to trade some individual freedom for governmental power and became more critical of those who publicly disagreed with the president and official governmental policies. Because situations can arise that activate authoritarian attitudes and goals in almost anyone, most of us possess the capacity to do real damage to members of lesser-status groups.

There's another reason we should avoid holding the self-serving belief that strong negative prejudices exist only in the minds of people with dysfunctional personalities: It's just not true. Indeed, as we've seen throughout the chapter, and will see in the pages that follow, we *all* hold negative prejudices of some sorts, we *all* have negative stereotypes about certain groups, and we *all* discriminate against others at times. Yes, some types of people—such as authoritarians—are *more* prejudiced than others. But that does not let the "rest of us" off the hook for the consequences of our own negative prejudices, stereotypes, and discriminatory acts.

SITUATION Failure and Self-Image Threat

The bakery where C. P. Ellis worked as a deliveryman was closing down, and C. P. needed a job. It was a stroke of luck, then, that a local gas station was up for sale, and better luck yet that a neighboring store owner offered to co-sign the mortgage. Seeing this as his big chance to create a better life, Ellis jumped at the opportunity and put his heart, soul, and sweat into the business. Despite his considerable skills as an auto mechanic, however, his third-rate education left him woefully unprepared to run a business. With great disappointment and frustration, he would arrive at the end of each month only to discover that, after paying his bills, he was no better off than before. Around this time, C. P. Ellis attended his first KKK rally and just weeks later became a member. Was this a coincidence? Probably not.

When our self-images are shaken by frustration, failure, or other threats, we are more likely to derogate members of stigmatized groups (e.g., Allen & Sherman, 2011; Rudman, Dohn, & Fairchild, 2007; Shapiro, Mistler, & Neuberg, 2010; Sinclair & Kunda, 2000). Consider an experiment in which University of Michigan students first took an intelligence test and were given bogus feedback that they had either performed quite well or quite poorly (Fein & Spencer, 1997). They then went to a second study where they evaluated a job candidate's personality and job qualifications. Some subjects learned that the female job candidate was Jewish, activating for them stereotypes of the "Jewish American Princess." In contrast, other students learned that the candidate was Italian, activating no negative stereotypes for this population. Students who thought they did well on the intelligence test evaluated both candidates equally well. In contrast, students who thought they did poorly on the test evaluated the Jewish applicant much less favorably than the Italian candidate. Interestingly, the students who derogated the Jewish candidate subsequently showed increases in their personal self-esteem, suggesting that people can sometimes restore threatened self-esteem by derogating members of negatively stereotyped groups.

INVESTIGATION

We noted earlier that aggression against African Americans and immigrant Chinese increased as economic conditions worsened for America's white majority. We interpreted those findings in terms of the goal to support and protect one's ingroup. How might one reinterpret those findings in terms of the goal of managing self-image?

INTERACTION Self-Esteem and Threat

If boosting ingroups or derogating outgroups can help restore threatened self-esteem, a person with a chronically threatened sense of self—with relatively low self-esteem—should readily partake of such strategies (Wills, 1981; Wylie, 1979). This is indeed the case: Individuals having low self-esteem tend to be negatively prejudiced against outgroup members, and they show consistent favoritism toward the ingroup (Crocker & Schwartz, 1985; Crocker et al., 1987). You might be surprised to learn, however, that people who have high self-esteem also favor their own groups, often to an even greater extent than do people who have low self-esteem (Aberson et al., 2000; Guimond, Dif, & Aupy, 2002). The ingroup bias displayed by high self-esteem individuals may be especially pronounced when they are threatened by personal failure.

What happens, for example, when a woman who has high self-esteem ends up in a low-status sorority? Jennifer Crocker and her colleagues (1987) suspected that these women would find the low prestige of their sorority threatening to their self-regard. After all, these women likely believe that they deserve better. If so, the researchers reasoned, they should be especially likely to derogate members of other sororities. To explore this hypothesis, Crocker and her colleagues recruited sorority women from Northwestern University and assessed their views of sororities on campus.

Figure 11.5 Self-esteem and threat on sorority row

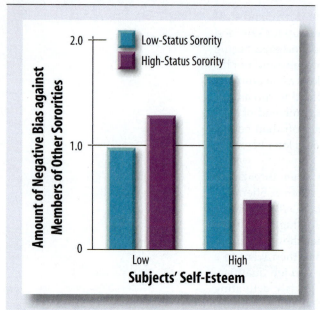

In a study of sorority women at Northwestern University, those with low self-regard derogated members of other sororities. The views of women who thought highly of themselves, however, depended on the prestige of their own affiliations: Those in a prestigious sorority showed little bias against other sororities, whereas those in a low-status sorority showed the greatest amount of bias of all. Apparently, belonging to a sorority "beneath them" was quite threatening, leading these women to derogate members of other houses in an attempt to restore their damaged self-image.

Source: Data from Crocker, J., Thompson, L. L., McGraw, K. M., & Ingerman, C. (1987). Downward comparison, prejudice, and evaluations of others: Effects of self-esteem and threat. *Journal of personality and Social Psychology, 52,* 907-916. Table 2, p. 913.

As Figure 11.5 reveals, most sorority women evaluated the members of other sororities more negatively than they did members of their own. For women who had low self-regard, the status of their own sororities made no difference: They derogated the members of other sororities, regardless. In contrast, sorority prestige made a large difference for women who had high self-esteem. Those in prestigious sororities showed little bias against other sorority women, whereas those in low-status sororities strongly derogated other sororities. Apparently, belonging to a low-status sorority threatened the positive self-image of these high-self-esteem women. Level of self-esteem and the presence of a social threat interact, then, to determine the amount of ingroup favoritism. Challenges to self-image are particularly threatening to people who hold themselves in high regard. As a result, these people are likely to demonstrate more pronounced ingroup favoritism.

Quick Quiz

1 Which of the following strategies contributes to negative prejudice and is used to maintain favorable personal and social identities?
- a. Disidentifying with one's favored group
- b. Upward social comparison
- c. Scapegoating
- d. All of the above

2 Which of the following is <u>not</u> a characteristic of the authoritarian personality?
- a. Authoritarians readily submit to authority figures.
- b. Authoritarians have trouble conforming to society's conventions and rules.
- c. Authoritarians view the world in simple black-white terms.
- d. Authoritarians are strongly prejudiced against members of minority groups.

3 Which of the following statements is true?
- a. People with low self-esteem do not tend to boost ingroups or derogate outgroups.
- b. The amount of ingroup favoritism displayed by people with high self-esteem is not affected significantly by whether they belong to a high or low status group.
- c. When our self-images are threatened by failure, we are more likely to derogate members of stigmatized groups.
- d. All of the above

Seeking Mental Efficiency

LO 11.11 Describe the "shooter bias," and explain how it reflects the process of stereotyping.

LO 11.12 Discuss the research on perceived outgroup homogeneity.

LO 11.13 Describe the circumstances that increase the likelihood of stereotyping.

It was near midnight in New York City, and undercover police officers in an unmarked car were patrolling the streets, hoping to catch a serial rapist who had been terrorizing the area for two years. They observed a black man pacing and fidgeting in front of a house, thought him suspicious, and stopped to question him. As the officers approached, the man—Amadou Diallo—turned into the house's dimly lit entry, either ignoring or not hearing the officers' instructions to stop. Suddenly, he turned back toward them, pulling a black object from his pocket. "Gun! He's got a gun," shouted one officer. Within seconds, 19 of the 41 shots fired had penetrated Diallo. As the officers moved closer to examine the body, they made a terrible discovery: Next to the dead man lay not a gun, but a *wallet*. They had killed an unarmed man.

Critics and the prosecutor claimed that the officers approached and shot Diallo because he was black, and that the death was thus not an accident but rather an act of homicide. The officers claimed that they had perceived themselves to be in mortal danger and had therefore made a horrible but understandable mistake. The jury's difficult task was to determine which interpretation was correct. "How would I have reacted had I been in the officers' shoes?" the jurors probably asked themselves. "Would I have mistaken the wallet for a gun? Would I have shot?"

Anthony Greenwald, Mark Oakes, and Hunter Hoffman (2003) gave college students a chance to enter a situation simulated to be similar to (but, of course, weaker than) the one that confronted the police officers that night. In a video game-like task, participants were asked to play the role of a plainclothes police officer and were given less than a second to react to individuals on the screen who popped out from behind a garbage dumpster. Sometimes the individual who appeared was a casually dressed undercover officer; when this was the case, the participant was to quickly hit the space bar on the keyboard to simulate a safety signal. Sometimes the individual was a casually dressed citizen carrying a harmless object; when this was the case, the participant was to do nothing. And sometimes the individual was a casually dressed criminal holding a gun; when this was the case, the participants were to use the computer mouse to point and click at the individual, thereby simulating the firing of their own weapon. The target individuals popping into view were sometimes black and sometimes white, and the researchers were interested in how race would influence the ability of the participants to make the correct decisions.

Their findings are troubling: Blacks were more likely to be incorrectly shot at than were whites, even when they were presented as plainclothes police officers. Why? First, participants were less able to quickly distinguish between guns and harmless objects when held by a black individual. Second, participants seemed to be more ready to treat an object held by blacks as if it were a gun, and "shoot." Other research studies corroborate and extend these findings: Under time pressure, stereotypical biases like these occur automatically, without conscious attention. They exist in people who are personally prejudiced and in those who are not. They exist in both whites and blacks. And they exist even when people are actively trying to avoid being influenced by race (Correll et al., 2002; Payne, 2001; Payne, Shimizu, & Jacoby, 2005). Indeed, it appears that just *knowing* the cultural stereotype—that just knowing that our culture views black men as dangerous—is enough to create these cognitive biases and the greater tendency to "shoot" unarmed black men than unarmed white men.

Joshua Correll, Geoffrey Urland, and Tiffany Ito (2006) examined the links between this "shooter bias" and brain activity. *Event-related brain potentials* (ERPs) are

What do your stereotypes see? Which of these two men is holding a gun and which a cell phone? When under time pressure, American college students—white and black, bigoted and not—are more likely to identify a harmless object as a weapon when it's in a black man's hand than in a white man's hand. Just knowing the cultural stereotype linking black men with aggression can be enough to create inaccurate, and sometimes fatal, judgments.

fluctuations in brain electrical activity that vary in response to specific events. Fortunately, for researchers interested in better understanding the shooter bias, different ERP components can distinguish between threat detection and cognitive control processes. For instance, threatening images such as angry faces activate an ERP component called the *P200*, whereas attempts to control initial inclinations activate an ERP component called the *N200*.

Correll and his colleagues hypothesized that, if black men are indeed believed to be especially threatening, they should elicit relatively large P200s (indicating the perception of danger, which should facilitate the decision to shoot) and relatively small N200s (indicating a relatively small inclination to control one's predisposition to shoot). The researchers asked participants to play a "shoot/don't shoot" game while wearing elastic caps containing electrodes that measured their brain activity. What did they find? First, replicating the previous findings, participants shot armed black targets more quickly than they shot armed white targets, and decided not to shoot unarmed white targets more quickly than they decided not to shoot unarmed black targets. Moreover, *both* processes appear to contribute to the shooter bias: P200 activity revealed that participants were indeed particularly quick to perceive black men as being threatening—within a quarter of a second!—and N200 activity indicated that participants were slower to inhibit their resulting "shoot" inclinations even when evidence indicated that shooting was the wrong decision (i.e., when the black targets were unarmed).

Findings like these illustrate just one implication of **stereotyping**—the process of categorizing an individual as a member of a particular group and then inferring that he or she possesses the characteristics generally held by members of that group. Stereotyping is ever-present because it is a cognitively inexpensive way of understanding others. By presuming that people are like other members of their groups, we avoid the effortful and time-consuming process of learning about them as individuals (Allport, 1954; Hamilton, 1981; Lippman, 1922; Tajfel, 1969). Moreover, because stereotypes are rich and vivid expectations for what group members will be like, we feel as though we know much about a person as soon as we identify the groups to which that person belongs. Stereotypes provide ready *interpretations* of ambiguous behaviors, leading the police officers to presume that Diallo was producing a gun, not a wallet (e.g., D'Agostino, 2000; Dunning & Sherman, 1997; Eberhardt et al., 2004). Stereotypes provide ready *explanations* for why certain events occur, leading people to guess that a boy's poor score on a math exam reflects bad luck or insufficient effort but that a girl's identically poor score reflects a lack of ability (Deaux & LaFrance, 1998; Frieze et al., 1978; Swim & Sanna, 1996). And stereotypes provide different *standards* for evaluating members of different groups, leading us to think little of a solid academic performance by an Asian American student but to assume that a similarly performing Native American student is highly talented (e.g., Biernat, Kobrynowicz, & Weber, 2003). Stereotyping provides a lot of information for little effort.

So did Amadou Diallo die because these police officers were prejudiced against blacks? It's certainly possible. But it's also possible that Diallo's death was truly a tragic mistake, one created by the all-too-human tendency to rapidly stereotype others combined with the readily available cultural belief that black men are dangerous. Unfortunately, we'll likely never know the truth in the heartbreaking case of Amadou Diallo. We do know, however, that the process of stereotyping is fundamental to human cognition and that its consequences can be severe.

The Characteristics of Efficient Stereotypes

In the long run, stereotypes are most useful as simplifying tools when they are reasonably accurate—when they do a pretty good job of describing what group members are truly like. Although many stereotypes are badly inaccurate—for example, women don't appear to talk more than men (Mehl et al., 2007)—others contain a substantial kernel of truth (e.g., Jussim, 2012; Oakes et al., 1994; Ottati & Lee, 1995; Ryan, 1996).

Stereotyping The process of categorizing an individual as a member of a particular group and then inferring that he or she possesses the characteristics generally held by members of that group.

Figure 11.6   Sharpening and softening to create efficient social categories

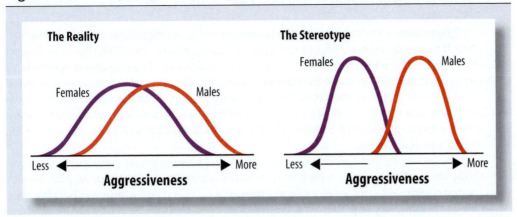

To save us time and cognitive effort, we often *sharpen* the distinctions between groups and *soften* the differences within groups. For example, although males and females do differ in their aggressiveness, we tend to exaggerate this difference in our minds.

For example, Janet Swim (1994) compared actual sex differences with college students' estimates of these sex differences. Although students' stereotypes sometimes underestimated the sex differences and sometimes overestimated them, Swim found that they were generally reasonably accurate. Most telling, the students rarely got the *direction* of the sex differences wrong. For example, they almost never erroneously believed that women are generally more aggressive than men.

Ironically, highly accurate stereotypes—those that fully reflect the complexity of real social groups—would be too complex to save us much time or effort. As a result, stereotypes tend to exaggerate the reality a bit by "sharpening"—exaggerating—the differences between groups and "softening"—reducing—the differences within groups, as we see in Figure 11.6 (e.g., Dijksterhuis & van Knippenberg, 1999; Krueger & Rothbart, 1990). This "softening" process leads people to see members of other groups as being overly *homogeneous*, or similar to each other (Boldry, Gaertner, & Quinn, 2007; Mullen & Hu, 1989; Park, Judd, & Ryan, 1991). For example, although women are on average less physically aggressive than men, some women are extremely aggressive, and others are extremely peaceful. Men in particular tend to underappreciate this variety, however, believing instead that most women are similar in their lack of aggressiveness.

The "they all look the same to me" phenomenon is one form of this **perceived outgroup homogeneity** effect—the tendency to overestimate the extent to which members of other groups are similar to one another. Because we generally fail to appreciate the variety of facial features possessed by members of other racial groups, often because we tend to categorize outgroup members instead of thinking of them as individuals, we are not very good at accurately recognizing them (e.g., Anthony, Copper, & Mullen, 1992; Brigham & Malpass, 1985; Hugenberg & Sacco, 2008). Consider, for instance, the case of Lenell Geter, a black man. Geter was a young engineer working at a research center in the Dallas area when he was identified from a photograph as the armed robber of a fast-food restaurant. There was no physical evidence linking Geter to the crime, he had no criminal record, and his coworkers testified that he had been working 50 miles away at the time of the theft. Nonetheless, convinced by the confident testimony of white and Hispanic eyewitnesses, the all-white jury found Geter guilty of the $615 robbery and sentenced him to life in prison. His case received a thorough second look only after persistent efforts by his coworkers and the NAACP brought it to the attention of local and national media. But only after the police arrested another man for the crime—a man implicated for a string of similar robberies and identified by the

Perceived outgroup homogeneity The phenomenon of overestimating the extent to which members within other groups are similar to each other.

same witnesses who fingered Geter—did the Dallas prosecutor's office declare Geter's innocence. After 16 months behind bars, Geter again became a free man (Applebome, 1983, 1984).

The tendency to overestimate the homogeneity of other groups serves a useful purpose: It makes it easier for us to stereotype others (Lambert et al., 2005; Spencer-Rogers et al., 2007). If a woman believes, for instance, that virtually all men are sports fans, she can comfortably assume that the next man she encounters will be sports-minded as well. If she believes, however, that men vary widely in this respect, she'll be less confident that the next man she encounters will be sports-minded, forcing her to form an effortful impression of him based on his individual characteristics (Linville et al., 1989; Ryan et al., 1996).

We see, then, that forming and using simple, homogeneous stereotypes is cognitively efficient, especially if they're reasonably accurate; it enables us to allocate our limited cognitive resources elsewhere. Stereotypes are even more efficient because they come to mind easily (e.g., Banaji & Greenwald, 1994; Devine, 1989; Macrae, Bodenhausen, Milne, & Jetten, 1994). That is, once you categorize an outgroup member, you'll quickly begin to see him or her as you see members of that group in general.

PERSON   Need for Structure

Some people like their lives to be relatively simple and well organized and dislike interruptions and unexpected events. These individuals have a high *need for structure* and, as we learned in Chapter 3, strive for simple ways to view the world (Thompson, Naccarato, & Parker, 1989). Because stereotypes are one way to simplify the world, such persons are more likely to use their existing stereotypes to understand others (Naccarato, 1988; Neuberg & Newsom, 1993), and are also more likely to form stereotypes of new groups (Schaller, Boyd, Yohannes, & O'Brien, 1995).

PERSON   Moods and Emotions

Feelings influence the motivation and ability to think about things thoroughly. They also influence which ideas come to mind. As a result, our moods and emotions can powerfully influence whether and how we stereotype others.

First, recall from Chapter 3 that people in good moods are less motivated to think about things thoroughly. Whereas certain negative moods, such as sadness, signal that we need to pay close attention to the people around us, positive moods signal that we can go about our business with relatively little worry that we'll be troubled in the near future (Schwarz, 1990b). People in positive moods, then, should be less concerned with being perfectly accurate and should be more willing to rely on simplifying cognitive shortcuts like stereotypes. Indeed, positive moods do increase stereotyping (e.g., Bodenhausen, Kramer, & Susser, 1994; Park & Banaji, 2000; Stroessner & Mackie, 1992). For example, Australian students who had been put in a positive mood—they had been given favorable feedback about a previous task—were more likely to exhibit a shooter bias against targets wearing Muslim headgear than were students in a neutral mood (Unkelbach, Forgas, & Denson, 2008).

Second, emotions that are arousing—like anger, fear, and euphoria—reduce the amount of cognitive resources available to us, limiting our ability to think about others thoroughly and thereby making stereotyping more likely. For instance, anger and anxiety make people particularly likely to stereotype others (Bodenhausen, Sheppard, & Kramer, 1994; Wilder, 1993). Indeed, even when physiological arousal is unrelated to feelings—as occurs after exercise—stereotyping is still more likely (Kim & Baron, 1988; Paulhus, Martin, & Murphy, 1992).

Moods and emotions also influence which social categories people use to understand others. Most of us fall into numerous categories, and how we are categorized by others may depend on how they're feeling at the time. One of this text's authors, for instance, is Jewish and a college professor. People who like college professors but dislike Jews are more likely to see him as a college professor if they're in a good mood

Figure 11.7   Feelings and stereotyping

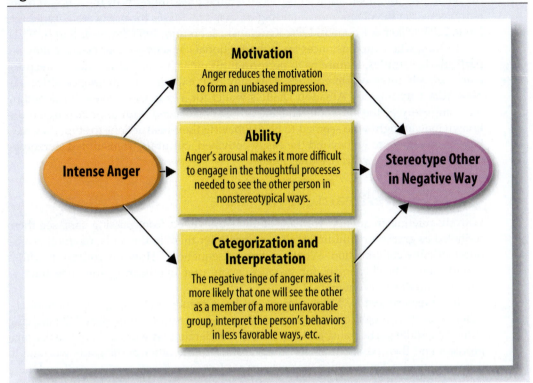

Our moods and emotions influence how we view others: They can alter (1) how motivated we are to go beyond our stereotypes and prejudices, (2) our ability to go beyond our stereotypes and prejudices, and (3) how we categorize and interpret the information available to us. For example, experiencing intense anger increases the likelihood that we will negatively stereotype others because it reduces our motivation to be fair, reduces our capacity to think carefully, and makes unfavorable social categories and interpretations more accessible.

when they meet him. If they're in a bad mood, however, they may be more likely to categorize him as a Jew.

Thus, both positive and negative moods can be problematic if one wants to avoid stereotyping others or evaluating them negatively (see Figure 11.7). Although people in negative moods are more motivated to go beyond their stereotypes to understand others, they tend to think about others in less favorable ways. Those in positive moods, on the other hand, view others more favorably, but they are also more likely to be cognitively lazy and to use their stereotypes. Finally, when highly aroused, either positively or negatively, people may not have the cognitive resources to go far beyond their stereotypes.

SITUATION   Cognitively Taxing Circumstances

Certain situations limit the amount of attention we have available for forming impressions of others, thereby increasing our reliance on simple, efficient thought processes such as stereotyping. We are more likely to stereotype in situations that are complex—that have many things going on (Bodenhausen & Lichtenstein, 1987; Miarmi & DeBono, 2007; Stangor & Duan, 1991). We are also more likely to stereotype when circumstances require us to perform other cognitive tasks at the same time. In one study, participants were asked to form an impression of an elderly woman. Even when they were motivated to form an accurate impression of "Hilda," participants who also had to keep in mind an eight-digit number were unable to avoid using their stereotypes of the elderly (Pendry & Macrae, 1994). Finally, sometimes we need to form impressions of others under time pressure, as when an interviewer knows that she has only 15 minutes to devote to each of 30 job applicants. Because time pressure reduces the amount of attention one can devote to understanding others, it increases the use of stereotypes (De Dreu, 2003; Dijker & Koomen, 1996; Kruglanski & Freund, 1983; Pratto & Bargh, 1991).

In sum, when circumstances tax our attentional capacity—either because they are particularly complex, require us to perform multiple tasks, or put us under time pressure—we rely more on stereotypes. This may help explain why the police officers in New York City mistook Amadou Diallo's wallet for a gun: Cognitively burdened by the complexity of the situation, and the arousal associated with approaching an unknown man at night who seemed to be disobeying their instructions to stop, they may have been unable to go beyond the easily activated, culturally transmitted stereotype that blacks are dangerous (Devine, 1989).

INTERACTION Overheard Ethnic Slurs

With disquieting frequency, we hear ethnic slurs yelled from passing cars, see them scribbled as graffiti on building walls, or encounter them in the midst of an otherwise unremarkable conversation. What are the consequences? How do you think whites would view a black person, for instance, soon after overhearing someone refer to African Americans as "niggers"?

In an experiment by Linda Simon and Jeff Greenberg (1996), groups of subjects, differing in their prejudices, participated in a study of "group processes." On arriving at the lab, white participants and one black confederate first worked individually on a problem and then passed their solutions around to the other participants working in different cubicles. Unknown to the participants, however, the researchers replaced these solutions with others, attaching to one either (1) a comment stating that "I can't believe they stuck us with this black person!" (2) a comment stating that "I can't believe they stuck us with this nigger!", or (3) no comment at all. Later, participants rated each other's characteristics.

As Figure 11.8 reveals, the ethnic slur had a negative effect on evaluations of the black team member, but only for participants who had strong negative prejudices to begin with. Participants who had strong pro-black attitudes were uninfluenced by the ethnic slur. And, perhaps most interesting, participants who had ambivalent feelings toward blacks—who held both strong positive and strong negative views—evaluated the black team member more *positively* after hearing the ethnic slur. For these ambivalent participants, the slur cast against a team member who had done nothing wrong may have reminded them of their own more virulent views—views inconsistent with their egalitarian self-images. Perhaps to protect themselves from an undesirable self-image, the ambivalent participants "bent over backward" to evaluate the team member positively (Katz, Wackenhut, & Hass, 1986).

These findings illustrate that not all people are influenced the same way by overheard ethnic slurs. In particular, ethnic slurs are more likely to lead negatively prejudiced people to use negative stereotypes than those who are not (Lepore & Brown, 1997; Wittenbrink et al., 1997). We see again, then, the interactive nature of persons and situations.

Figure 11.8 Overhearing an ethnic slur

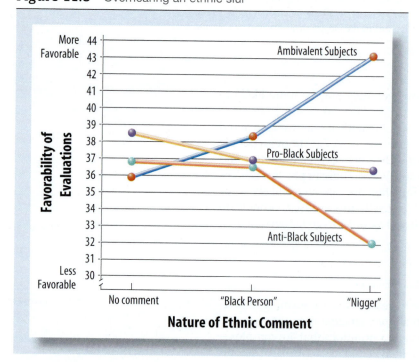

How does hearing or seeing an ethnic slur influence the way we judge those victimized by it? As the findings of this study reveal, the answer depends on our initial attitudes toward the victimized group.

Source: Data from Simon, L., & Greenberg, J. (1996). Further progress in understanding the effects of derogatory ethnic labels: The role of preexisting attitudes toward the targeted group. *Personality and Social Psychology Bulletin,* 22, 119-1204. Table 1.

To this point, we have seen that stereotypes, prejudices, and discrimination serve multiple functions. It's no wonder, then, that they are so resistant to change, a topic we explore next.

Quick Quiz

1 Which of the following research findings on the "shooter bias" is false?

> a. People are less able to distinguish between guns and harmless objects when held by a black individual.
> b. The shooter bias has only been found in white participants.
> c. The shooter bias has been found in people who are personally prejudiced and those who are not.
> d. This bias can occur even when people are actively trying to avoid being influenced by race.

2 Stereotypes tend to _____ the differences between groups and _____ the differences within groups.

> a. minimize, exaggerate
> b. soften, sharpen
> c. sharpen, soften
> d. homogenize, exaggerate

3 Which of the following factors increase the likelihood of stereotyping?

> a. Positive mood
> b. Arousing emotions (e.g., anger)
> c. Physiological arousal
> d. All of the above

Reducing Prejudice, Stereotyping, and Discrimination

LO 11.14 Describe the four types of strategies for reducing prejudice, stereotyping, and discrimination, and provide an example of each.

LO 11.15 Describe how the jigsaw classroom embodies the six principles of effective contact.

For Ann Atwater and C. P. Ellis, racial antagonism was a part of everyday life. It is thus remarkable that within just weeks of their hostile confrontation at the school meeting, they began to respect each other, and, within just months, had developed a true friendship. How can we explain such a dramatic turnaround? In this final section, we build on what we've learned to explore ways of effectively reducing negative prejudices, stereotyping, and discrimination.

Interventions Based on the Ignorance Hypothesis

If you ask passersby on the street to explain why negative prejudices and stereotypes exist, a good many will propose that people "just don't know any better." We might call this the *ignorance hypothesis*: If people only learned what members of other groups are truly like, they wouldn't stereotype, be prejudiced, or discriminate against them. This perspective suggests that after simply putting individuals from different groups together or simply teaching them what members of other groups are really like, they would discard their stereotypes and prejudices (Stephan & Stephan, 1984).

Indeed, there are some reasons to believe that simple contact and education could help reduce intergroup antagonisms. Both contact and education could teach people that they are similar to members of other groups. This should make outgroup members more likable, decrease the usefulness of the ingroup–outgroup distinction, and reduce the anxiety people sometimes feel when interacting with outsiders (Stephan & Stephan, 1985). People might also learn that members of other groups are *not* all the same, which would limit the usefulness of broad, simple stereotypes.

Unfortunately, research demonstrates that merely putting individuals from antagonistic groups in contact does little to reduce hostility (Miller & Brewer, 1984; Stephan & Stephan, 1996). Similarly, simply teaching people what other groups are like is an ineffective way to brush away intergroup hostilities (Bigler, 1999; Stephan, Renfro, & Stephan, 2004). Both simple contact and fact-based education alone are inadequate, for two reasons. First, such approaches assume that prejudices and conflict emerge from a straightforward logical assessment of outgroup characteristics. Although people may sometimes reason in this way, intergroup hostilities are generally linked less strongly to "facts" we have about other groups than to our emotional reactions to them (e.g., Haddock et al., 1994; Jussim et al., 1995; Stangor et al., 1991). Moreover, these approaches assume that people will easily accept information that disconfirms their stereotypes—an assumption that does not reflect the efforts most people go through to avoid changing their stereotypes (e.g., Kunda & Oleson, 1995; Pettigrew, 1979; Seta & Seta, 1993; Weber & Crocker, 1983).

By assuming, then, that prejudices and conflict emerge from a straightforward logical assessment of outgroup characteristics and that people actually want to rid themselves of erroneous stereotypes, the ignorance hypothesis fails to appreciate that stereotypes, prejudices, and discrimination serve important needs. Because of this, simple contact and fact-based education can play only a limited role in reducing intergroup conflict.

The Goal-Based Approach

A goal-based strategy for reducing prejudice, stereotyping, and discrimination, in contrast, may be more effective. Such an approach incorporates two established points: First, prejudice, stereotyping, and discrimination serve important goals for people. For example, discriminating against members of other groups can help us gain economic resources for our own group. Second, specific features of the person and situation bring these goals into prominence. For instance, the desire to benefit the ingroup is stronger for certain people (e.g., those high in social dominance orientation) and under certain circumstances (e.g., intergroup competition for limited economic resources).

This approach to understanding prejudice, stereotyping, and discrimination suggests several logical steps we might take to reduce them. First, we might attempt to *change features of the person*. For example, because people who are anxious are particularly likely to stereotype others, we might try to reduce their anxiety before they encounter members of easily stereotyped groups.

Second, we might try to *change features of the situation*. For instance, if people are more likely to form and express prejudices when it is socially acceptable to do so, a community concerned with intergroup conflict might focus some of its energies on creating and advertising social norms that disapprove of prejudice and approve of intergroup tolerance and appreciation.

Third, we might *give people alternative ways to satisfy their goals*. For instance, we've learned that people sometimes derogate members of other groups to boost their own self-regard. Steven Fein and Steven Spencer (1997) hypothesized that if people had other ways to feel good about themselves they would have less reason to derogate others. Participants in their study evaluated a female job candidate who was presented as either Jewish American or Italian American; in this particular student population, only the Jewish females were targets of unfavorable stereotypes. Before evaluating her, however, some of the participants had an opportunity to affirm their self-worth by writing about the things important to them; the other participants were not given this opportunity. The researchers' findings supported their predictions: The Jewish candidate was evaluated less favorably than the otherwise-identical Italian candidate *only* by participants given no chance to validate their self-worth. Findings like this suggest that interventions aimed at providing people with alternative ways of satisfying their needs may be effective in the fight against negative prejudices and stereotypes.

Finally, we might try to *activate goals incompatible with prejudice, stereotyping, and discrimination*. We learned in Chapter 3, for example, that people who are motivated to be accurate often go beyond their stereotypes and prejudices to form more individualized impressions of others (e.g., Neuberg & Fiske, 1987). Here, we focus on two other goals that have the potential to override the impact of our stereotypes and prejudices—to be fair and to empathize with members of the other groups.

EGALITARIAN VALUES AND THE SUPPRESSION OF NEGATIVE PREJUDICES We've seen that negative stereotypes and prejudices can come to mind automatically and lead us to discriminate against others. Many people, however, believe that it's important to be fair and egalitarian—to treat members of all groups equally. When such individuals notice a discrepancy between their ideals of fairness and their prejudiced feelings, thoughts, and behaviors, they are likely to feel guilt—and this guilt may motivate them to suppress, inhibit, or otherwise override their prejudicial biases (e.g., Monteith, Sherman, & Devine, 1998).

Milton Rokeach (1971) had a subset of white college freshmen at Michigan State University confront the inconsistency between their prejudices and their egalitarian values. The intervention was strikingly successful: Students in the self-confrontational conditions increased their support for black equal rights, were more likely to join the NAACP when solicited months later, and were even more likely to choose ethnic relations as their major. When the value of fairness becomes more salient, people become more tolerant and less prejudiced of others.

Unfortunately, it's not so easy to override one's negative prejudices. Prejudices often "leak" out in subtle ways, for example, in our facial expressions and body language—and if we're not aware of these expressions we will be unable to consciously control them (e.g., Vanman et al., 1997). Moreover, because controlling thoughts and feelings often requires focused attention, people in complex situations, in a rush, or otherwise cognitively taxed will be less able to suppress their unwanted prejudices and stereotypes (e.g., Gilbert & Hixon, 1991; Macrae, Hewstone, & Griffiths, 1993). Also, recall from Chapter 2 that our attempts to inhibit thoughts sometimes lead them to "rebound"; as a consequence, trying to inhibit stereotypical thoughts will sometimes lead them to return to mind later with even greater strength (e.g., Ko et al., 2008; Macrae et al., 1994a). Finally, people who haven't internalized the egalitarian norm and who thus feel forced to control their negative prejudices toward a certain group may later exhibit a negative backlash against that group—expressing even greater prejudices and perpetrating more discrimination than they had before (Plant & Devine, 2001).

Indeed, activating values of fairness is not enough for most people to override all the effects of their negative prejudices and stereotypes, in all circumstances. Recent research suggests, however, that people who possess extremely prominent egalitarian values are able to do so more effectively (Moskowitz, Salomon, & Taylor, 2000). The more central one's egalitarian goals, the less prejudiced one is likely to be.

TAKING THE PERSPECTIVE OF OTHERS People become more tolerant of other groups when they try to view the world from the other group's perspective (Galinsky & Moskowitz, 2000; Stephan & Finlay, 1999). Daniel Batson and his colleagues (1997a) found, for example, that people instructed to take the perspective of a particular person with AIDS subsequently viewed people with AIDS, as a group, more favorably.

By taking the perspective of members of stigmatized groups, we are more likely to recognize situational causes of their behavior, feel a sense of injustice for how they've been treated, and experience empathy for them (Dovidio et al., 2004; Vescio, Sechrist, & Paolucci, 2003). These new beliefs and feelings may underlie the success of some role-playing interventions (McGregor, 1993). For instance, in Jane Elliot's famous "Blue Eyes–Brown Eyes" technique for reducing racial prejudices, some participants are targeted for discrimination and humiliation because of their eye color. After a stressful few hours as a victim of discrimination, participants appear to be both less prejudiced (Byrnes & Kiger, 1990) and more sensitive to interracial issues. When circumstances lead us to see things from the perspective of unfairly disadvantaged groups, we are more likely to challenge our own stereotypes and prejudices.

In sum, the goal-based approach suggests four broad intervention strategies: change the person, change the situation, provide the person with an alternative way to

Figure 11.9   Goal-based strategies for reducing negative prejudices, stereotyping, and discrimination

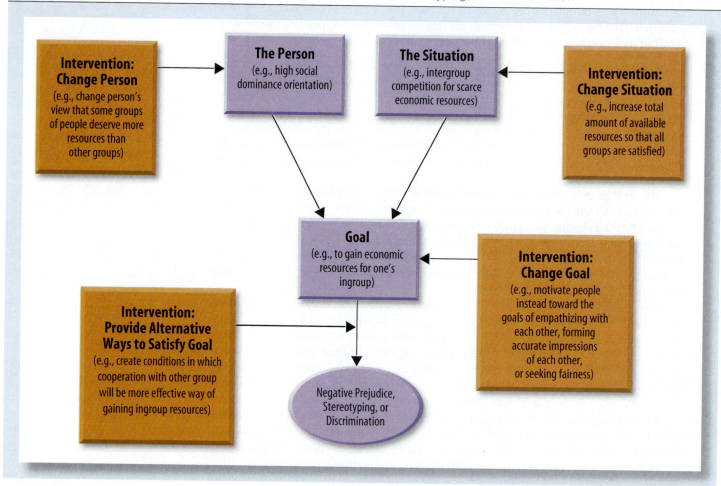

Features of the person and situation activate goals that may be satisfied by negative prejudices, stereotyping, or discrimination. Most effective interventions will thus include at least one of the following strategies: (1) change features of the person; (2) change features of the situation; (3) give people alternative ways to satisfy their goals; or (4) give people alternative goals incompatible with prejudice, stereotyping, and discrimination.

satisfy his or her goal, or change the goal (see Figure 11.9). We see next that the circumstances that improve the effectiveness of intergroup contact do so, in part, because they implement at least one of these four strategies.

When Contact Helps

In the landmark civil rights case *Brown v. Board of Education*, the Supreme Court heard arguments for and against desegregating the Topeka, Kansas, public schools. Many of the country's most well-respected social scientists proposed that schooling black and white children together would decrease racial prejudices and hostilities, particularly if certain conditions were met (e.g., Allport, 1954). By putting blacks and whites into everyday contact with one another, the thought was, these two groups may come to think more favorably about one another and get along better. Unfortunately, little attention was paid to these conditions, and many of the early desegregation attempts actually fueled racial tensions (Stephan, 1978).

We learned earlier that people's prejudices are sometimes based on their beliefs that members of other groups are threatening in some way. For example, whites who believe the stereotypes that blacks are physically dangerous, or that they get more than they deserve, may feel anxious while interacting with blacks. However, even whites who don't hold such stereotypes, and who may authentically be nonprejudiced, may still experience interracial encounters as stressful, given their desire to behave in ways, and to *be perceived* as behaving in ways, that are nonprejudiced (e.g., Plant, 2004; Plant & Devine, 2003; Stephan & Stephan, 2000; Vorauer & Turpie, 2004). Moreover, given white prejudices, it's difficult for blacks to determine whether a white person's friendly actions are driven by authentic feelings and beliefs or merely by a desire to avoid being labeled a racist (e.g., Crocker, Voelkl, Testa, & Major, 1991; Pinel, 1999; Shelton, Richeson, & Salvatore, 2005). On top of all this, many blacks hold negative stereotypes about whites and know that many whites are prejudiced against them. For both whites and blacks, then, interracial interactions can be complex, multi-layered, and difficult to navigate—especially for individuals inexperienced with them.

Fortunately, research has much to tell us about when intergroup contact—interracial or otherwise—is likely to reduce intergroup conflict (Dovidio, Gaertner, & Kawakami, 2003; Hodson, 2011; Pettigrew & Tropp. 2006):

- *Outgroup members must possess traits and abilities that challenge the negative stereotypes of their group* (Blanchard, Weigel, & Cook, 1975). For example, prejudice-reduction interventions such as school desegregation and equal employment programs will be most effective when they put men and whites in contact with high-performing women and members of minority groups.
- Because people are more likely to be accepting of other groups when they believe that tolerance is socially appropriate, intergroup *contact should be supported by local authorities and norms* (Cook, 1978). When school districts voluntarily hire more minority-group teachers, for example, and when teachers form interracial friendships, students will be more likely to view contact with students from other groups as legitimate.
- *The groups should be of equal status, at least within the contact setting* (Aronson et al., 1978; Weigel et al., 1975). If a teacher treats white students better than black students, or if a company hires women for only low-status clerical positions, there is little chance that intergroup contact will lead to changes in stereotypes and prejudices.
- *The contact should occur at the individual level*—person-to-person—thus allowing people to notice that they are similar in important ways to members of other groups and that the others *aren't* all alike (Herek & Capitanio, 1996; Pettigrew, 1997). For example, compared to those who do not personally know any people of Muslim faith, American teenagers who were acquainted with at least one Muslim were more likely to believe that most Muslims want peace and are accepting of those with other religious beliefs (Gallup, 2003). Person-to-person contact also makes possible the formation of friendships, and people with friends from other groups are more likely to feel favorably toward those groups and trust them more (van Laar et al., 2005; Paolini et al., 2004; Pettigrew et al., 2007; Tam et al., 2009). A lack of contact at the individual level—as when students in desegregated schools separate into race-based groups at lunchtime and during other free periods—makes it more difficult to reduce negative stereotypes and prejudices.
- *The contact should be rewarding* (Blanchard et al., 1975). If men and women work together on a project that fails, for instance, neither group is likely to change their negative stereotypes of the other.
- Finally, contact in which members of different groups *work together toward common goals* is especially likely to encourage intergroup tolerance (Cook, 1985).

This last point is illustrated nicely by the experience of the rival residents of the Oklahoma boys' camp we discussed earlier in this chapter. When we last visited the Rattlers and Eagles, the two groups were on the verge of warfare. And the situation progressively worsened, as contact between the two groups brought forth increasingly intense name calling, food fights, and physical skirmishes. Having successfully created intensely hostile groups, Muzafer Sherif and his colleagues (1961/1988) turned their attentions toward discovering a way to eliminate the hatreds. Their strategy was an elegantly straightforward one: If competition between groups creates hostility, they reasoned, then eliminating the competitive orientation and replacing it with a cooperative orientation should reduce hostility. And so the researchers placed the two groups in circumstances that required them to cooperate to get what they wanted. In one case,

Figure 11.10 From hostility to friendship

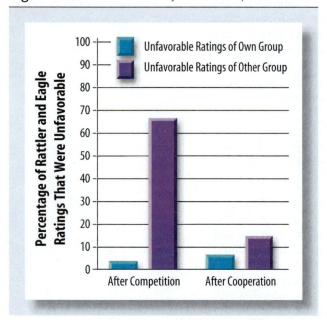

The hostility between the Rattlers and the Eagles eventually turned to friendship and acceptance after the two groups stopped competing and began cooperating with each other.
Source: Data from Sherif, M., Harvey, C. W. (1961/1988). The Robbers Cave experiment: Intergroup conflict and cooperation. Middletown, CT: Wesleyan University Press. Tables 7.5 and 7.6, pp. 194–195.

the engine of the truck used to transport the campers "broke down." The campers eventually realized that they could pull the truck to a rolling start, but only by working together. Through cooperative activities like this one, the two groups began to abandon their hostilities and, by the end of camp, had pooled their money and voted to share a bus on the return trip home (see Figure 11.10). By replacing a competitive orientation with a cooperative one, Sherif and his colleagues reduced the hostilities between the two groups.

Cooperation between members of different groups works for a variety of reasons. It replaces competition as a way of gaining economic and social resources. It motivates people to be more accurate in their understanding of outgroup members, reducing the tendency of competing groups to view each other in simplified ways (Ruscher et al., 1991). Working cooperatively with members of other groups may also lead us to see those groups is less homogeneous—to see members of those groups as different from one another—and this makes us less likely to apply our stereotypes and prejudices to them (Brauer & Er-Rafiy, 2011). And when we cooperate with others, we are more likely to include them in our sense of "we"—to see them as part of us (Dovidio et al., 1997a; Nier et al., 2001). As we discussed in Chapter 9, people sometimes expand their sense of "we" to include many others, and they sometimes contract it to include just a few (Allport, 1954; Brewer, 1991). Regardless of where people draw this boundary, however, they tend to prefer those inside the boundary to those outside it. So when working together with members of other groups—producing a "we are all in this together" mentality—people begin to see others as they see themselves, thus breaking down intergroup prejudices and stereotypes.

Sherif's intervention did more than just capitalize on the beneficial effects of cooperation, however. It also implemented the other five principles of effective contact. Because all the boys were selected to be highly similar to one another, the erroneous stereotypes held of the two groups were relatively easy to disconfirm. Cooperation between the groups was supported and approved by the camp authorities. The two groups were accorded equal status by the camp staff. The cooperative tasks required members of the two groups to interact with each other on an individual level. Finally, the cooperation was successful, making the contact a rewarding experience. By carefully crafting the correct set of conditions, Sherif and his colleagues were able to turn intergroup hostilities into acceptance and friendship.

Bridging Theory and Application:

Cooperation in the Classroom

Many early attempts to desegregate the schools did little to reduce negative prejudices and stereotypes. Confronted by this failure, several teams of researchers and educators imported the lessons learned from studies like Sherif's and began to restructure the classroom environment (DeVries, Edwards, & Slavin, 1978; Johnson & Johnson, 1975; Weigel et al., 1975).

Consider, for example, the *jigsaw classroom* designed by Elliot Aronson and his colleagues (1978) and first implemented in the Austin, Texas, school district. In it, each student is assigned to a mixed-race and mixed-gender team of six or so

students. Not coincidentally, the lessons are also divided into six parts (e.g., Lincoln's childhood, his career as a lawyer, and his election to the presidency). Each student is first given one part of the lesson and meets with an "expert" group made up of students from other teams who share the same assignment (e.g., Lincoln's childhood). Students then return to their home teams and convey their new knowledge to the other students. Because each student's information is only one piece of the puzzle, he or she depends on the five teammates to learn the whole lesson.

Piecing together the puzzle. By having students of different ethnicities and genders work and study together in coordinated, cooperative ways—as in the "jigsaw classroom"—schools can improve relations among students and enhance academic achievement.

Classroom structures like this take advantage of the six principles of effective contact. First, by splitting off into expert groups, all students are better prepared to teach their own teams effectively, which helps minority students disprove stereotypes of incompe-

tence. Second, because the teacher assigns students to teams, the interracial, cross-gender contact has the clear support and approval of an important authority. Third, the students are accorded equal status in the classroom—they're not segregated by race or gender, and they're all given equal responsibilities. Fourth, the contact is at the individual level, allowing students to see each other's favorable characteristics and to dispel illusions of outgroup homogeneity. Fifth, the students work cooperatively with each other toward the common goal of learning the day's lesson. And sixth, because the performance of students tends to improve within such structures—particularly the performance of students who had previously been doing poorly—the contact can be rewarding for all students if grades are designed to benefit from the improvement of teammates.

Indeed, students learning in cooperative classrooms are more likely to form close cross-ethnicity friendships, even with other students outside their classrooms (Johnson et al., 1984; Slavin & Cooper, 1999). Moreover, the achievement levels of students rise in such classrooms (Johnson & Johnson, 1994; Stevens & Slavin, 1995). Given the documented gains—reduced intergroup hostility and better overall educational achievement—cooperative classrooms can be an important weapon in the fight against negative prejudices, stereotypes, and discrimination.

INVESTIGATION

It's your first "real" job, and you find yourself managing an office in which racial and gender conflicts are common and widespread. Given what you've learned about reducing prejudices, stereotyping, and discrimination, how would you go about remedying the situation? Why?

Quick Quiz

1 Which of the following interventions is not an effective strategy for reducing prejudice, stereotyping, and discrimination?

   a. Activate goals incompatible with prejudice, stereotyping, and discrimination
   b. Taking the perspective of members of stigmatized groups
   c. Educating people about different groups so that they'll develop factual beliefs about stigmatized groups
   d. Change features of the situation

2 Which of the following is not a principle of effective intergroup contact?

   a. Contact should occur at the group-level so that the potential for interpersonal conflicts is minimized.
   b. Outgroup members must possess traits and abilities that challenge the negative stereotypes of their group.
   c. The groups should be of equal status, at least within the contact setting.
   d. The contact should be rewarding.

3 In which of the following ways does the jigsaw classroom design take advantage of the six principles of effective contact?

   a. The jigsaw method groups children according to race or ethnicity, which gives them the opportunity to demonstrate their competence and disprove negative stereotypes as a group.
   b. The students' grades do not depend on their classmates' performance, thus reducing the likelihood of interpersonal conflicts.
   c. The students work cooperatively with each other toward the common goal of learning the day's lesson.
   d. All of the above

Revisiting The Journey of Ann Atwater and C. P. Ellis

The conflict between Ann Atwater and C. P. Ellis was fierce and unwavering. They despised each other, and each would have been happy to see the other dead. How can the research we've explored help us explain the white-hot intensity of their hatred for each other and the power of the prejudices from which this hatred flowed?

Recall, first, that both were poor. Each needed more if their families were ever to realize the American Dream. As the Civil Rights movement gained momentum, the concerns and prejudices of poor whites like Ellis intensified: Black gains were likely to come out of poor white pockets, they thought, and this belief was reinforced by those who held the true wealth and power. At its core, then, the conflict between Atwater and Ellis rested on their common desire to gain economic and social resources for their own groups.

But this is only part of the reason for their hostilities, for prejudices and stereotyping serve other important functions as well. In light of the social norms of their time, Atwater and Ellis gained social approval for expressing their prejudices. In particular, the racist norms of the Old South influenced C. P. Ellis early in his life, his father being a member of the Ku Klux Klan. Moreover, negative prejudices and stereotypes helped Atwater and Ellis maintain favorable self-images. By viewing whites as immoral, Ann Atwater could better claim virtue for herself. By derogating blacks in response to personal frustrations and failure, C. P. Ellis could see himself as more worthy; and, by joining the Klan, he could associate himself with what he saw as a gallant and chivalrous attempt to preserve white Christian culture. Finally, the simplifying nature of stereotyping would certainly have been valuable for both Atwater and Ellis, given their work-filled, overwhelming, anxiety-laden lives.

So their prejudices grew. And as they found themselves working against each other with increasing frequency, Ellis came to represent for Atwater all that was wicked about whites, and Atwater came to represent for Ellis all that was base and threatening about blacks. It's astounding, then, that within weeks of the first school desegregation meeting the two began to respect each other and not long after became true friends. How do we explain such a dramatic turnaround?

It began when the organizer of the meetings—in a stroke of genius, or perhaps just by good fortune—convinced Atwater and Ellis to co-lead the group in its search for solutions to the desegregation problem. To say they were reluctant partners would be an understatement. But their agreement to work together—or perhaps, more accurately, to keep a wary eye on each other—provided a critical first step toward reconciliation, as their new responsibilities required that they *cooperate*. This step had been voluntary. Their second step was not. "How could she agree to work together with the Ku Klux Klan?" hissed the black community. "How could our leader even contemplate dealing with that woman?" spat Ellis's followers. For Ellis the rejection was devastating: He'd only wanted to protect the interests of the poor white community, and, in response, it would no longer accept him as one of its own. He was alone. And so Ellis and Atwater started drifting toward each other, pushed together by the very extremists who had hoped to keep them apart.

As they began to evaluate each other more closely, with an eye, this time, toward accuracy, they began to notice their many similarities. They were both hardworking but poor, both passionate in their desire to create better opportunities for their children, both brutally straightforward in their style, and both people of principle. Atwater was surprised to learn that Ellis feared entering black neighborhoods, just as she feared entering white neighborhoods. Ellis noticed that the black schools were in appalling condition, not because blacks didn't care about keeping them up, as he had once thought, but because, just like the school his children attended, they received little funding. It was natural for them to empathize with each other. Perhaps they were not one another's enemy, they began to think. Perhaps, instead, they had a common enemy—the rich who hoped to deny poor folks, black *and* white, a rightful "place to stand." Ellis's and Atwater's circles of "we" began to expand to include the other.

They'd never be the same. As the meetings continued their connection grew stronger and, until Ellis's death in 2005, they called each other "friend." At his funeral, Ann Atwater recalled the racial and personal tensions of the school desegregation meetings and the lifelong friendship they formed. "At the end of ten days, him and I fell in love and we've been in love ever since until he closed his eyes on Thursday" ("Activist mourns ex-KKK leader," 2005). Although the story of Ann Atwater and C. P. Ellis is extraordinary in one sense, it is unremarkable in another. For not only are the social forces that led them to hatred the very same forces that underlie our own prejudices and stereotypes, but the forces that inspired them to overcome their antagonisms are the very same ones that can help us do the same.

In studying the intertwined lives of Atwater and Ellis, we see how social psychological analyses of prejudice, stereotyping, and discrimination bridge to many domains of life. For instance, we have touched on constitutional law and public policy, sexual harassment in the military, racial discrimination in education, and consumer treatment in the shopping mall. We have seen that the effects of negative stereotyping and prejudice can hinder people's access to jobs, make it difficult for them to perform to their potential, and cause them to be misidentified as criminals. And, as in the jigsaw classroom, we've seen how an understanding of basic theory in social psychology can lead to reduced prejudices and increased tolerance.

We have also seen how social psychological analyses of prejudice serve to bridge and connect a wide range of

disciplines, from neuroscience to education, from cognitive science to cultural anthropology. As social animals, thinking of others in terms of group memberships is to be expected. It's not surprising, then, that stereotyping, prejudice, and discrimination are shaped by interacting systems spanning the depths of the brain to the reaches of culture.

Chapter Summary

A Summary of the Goals Served by Prejudice, Stereotyping, Discrimination, and the Factors Related to Them

The Goal	Person	Situation	Interaction
Supporting and protecting one's group	• Social dominance orientation	• Intergroup competition	• As groups view one another as potential competitors, they begin to compete, inadvertently bringing about the hostile competition they initially feared. This self-fulfilling prophecy can spiral into an increasingly intense conflict, as those involved become even more convinced that the others are hostile.
Seeking social approval	• Religiosity	• The times	• New or peripheral group members especially desire the group's approval. Because of this, they are particularly likely to publicly express the group's prejudices.
Managing self-image	• Ingroup identification • Authoritarianism	• Failure	• People with low self-esteem tend to devalue members of other groups. People with high self-esteem do so as well, but primarily when their self-image is threatened by failure.
Seeking mental efficiency	• Need for structure • Moods and emotions	• Cognitively taxing circumstance	• Overhearing an ethnic slur can lead a person to discriminate against the target of the slur, particularly when the slur fits with the listener's existing prejudices.

Planet Prejudice

1. Prejudice refers to the feelings we have about members of particular groups.
2. Stereotypes refer to the generalized beliefs we hold about what the members of particular group are like.
3. The Implicit Associations Test measures feelings and stereotypes that we may be unaware of, or unwilling to express in public.
4. Discrimination refers to positive or negative behaviors directed toward others because of their group membership.
5. Prejudice, stereotypes, and discrimination permeate the world's cultures and exact significant material and psychological costs from their targets.

Supporting and Protecting One's Group

1. To gain resources for our groups, we may create competitive advantages for our own groups and come to dislike and believe negative things about other groups.
2. People high in social dominance orientation want their own groups to dominate other groups and to be socially and materially superior to them. As a result, they are more likely to hold negative prejudices against and stereotypes of other groups.
3. When economic times are tough—when groups are competing for material resources—people are more likely to adopt and express negative prejudices and stereotypes.
4. By viewing one another as competitors, groups may bring about or amplify the competition they initially feared. This self-fulfilling prophecy can quickly spiral into increasingly intense forms of competition.

Seeking Social Approval

1. We often express or adopt the prejudices, stereotypes, and discriminatory tendencies held by those whose social approval we seek.
2. Religiosity has complex effects on prejudice and intergroup conflict. Only those who view religion as a quest for truth and meaning tend to be less prejudiced than those who consider themselves nonreligious. Strong social commitment to one's religious group tends to be associated with greater support for violence against other groups.
3. Because norms regarding prejudice and discrimination change over time, attitudes and behaviors—at least as they are publicly expressed—change as well.
4. New or peripheral group members especially desire the group's approval. For this reason, they are particularly likely to publicly express the group's prejudices.

Managing Self-Image

1. Negative prejudices, stereotypes, and discrimination can help us manage our personal and social identities. For example, by scapegoating members of weak minority groups or by elevating our groups over other groups, we can view ourselves in a more favorable light.
2. Those who strongly identify with their groups or who are high in authoritarianism are particularly likely to use prejudices and stereotypes to manage their self-images.
3. When people fail at something important to them, they are especially likely to demonstrate ingroup biases and discrimination.
4. Persons with high self-esteem are particularly likely to derogate members of outgroups, but only when their high self-regard is threatened.

Seeking Mental Efficiency

1. Stereotyping allows us to gain potentially useful information for relatively little cognitive effort.
2. Stereotyping others helps us interpret ambiguous behavior, provides ready explanations for why certain others act as they do, and suggests standards for how we should evaluate members of different groups.
3. The tendency to overestimate the homogeneity of other groups, called perceived outgroup homogeneity, makes it easier for us to stereotype others.
4. People are more likely to rely on their stereotypes when they have a high need for structure and when their moods and emotions leave them unmotivated or unable to process information about others thoroughly.
5. Situations that demand a lot of cognitive resources also make stereotyping more likely.
6. Negative stereotypes brought to mind by overhearing an ethnic slur can lead people to evaluate the targeted person less favorably, especially if they already possess strong, unfavorable stereotypes.

Reducing Prejudice, Stereotyping, and Discrimination

1. The ignorance hypothesis suggests that people would change their prejudices and stereotypes if only they knew the true facts about members of other groups. Facts alone, however, are not sufficient.
2. Because prejudice, stereotyping, and discrimination serve several useful functions, intervention strategies that take these functions and their causes into account will be most successful.
3. Under certain conditions, contact between members of different groups can create cross-group friendships and reduce intergroup conflict: Members of negatively stereotyped groups should behaviorally disconfirm these stereotypes; the contact should be supported by local norms and authorities; members of the different groups should interact as equal status participants; the contact should be at the individual, person-to-person level; the contact should be rewarding; and the contact should be cooperative, with members of the different groups working toward common goals.

Key Terms

Authoritarianism, 370

Discrimination, 353

Disidentify, 357

Ingroup bias, 359

Minimal intergroup paradigm, 359

Perceived outgroup homogeneity, 375

Prejudice, 353

Realistic group conflict theory, 359

Scapegoating, 368

Social dominance orientation, 361

Social identity, 369

Stereotype, 353

Stereotype threat, 356

Stereotyping, 374

Chapter 12

Groups

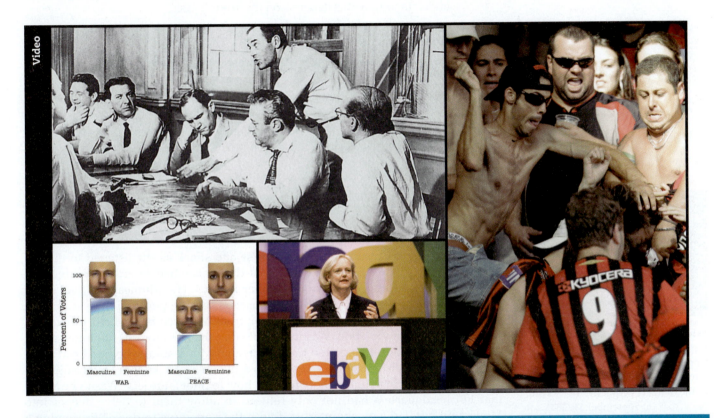

Outline

Learning Objectives

LO 12.1 Describe the characteristics of a "real" group.

LO 12.2 Define (a) *social facilitation*, (b) *deindividuation*, and (c) *dynamical systems*.

LO 12.3 Discuss the circumstances that make *social loafing* more likely to occur and describe what can be done to reduce social loafing.

LO 12.4 Discuss why people in individualistic societies tend to belong to more groups.

LO 12.5 Describe what kinds of people are best to have in performance groups and understand how this depends on the group's task.

LO 12.6 Define *transactive memory* and discuss how it might contribute to effective group decisions.

LO 12.7 Describe the circumstances that increase (a) *group polarization*, (b) *minority influence*, and (c) *groupthink*.

LO 12.8 Discuss the factors that determine (a) who wants to lead, (b) who is chosen to lead, and (c) who is an effective leader.

LO 12.9 Discuss how gender influences (1) whether one seeks leadership, (2) who gets chosen to lead, and (3) leadership effectiveness.

Whistleblower. Coleen Rowley testifies before the Senate Judiciary Committee about how the FBI bureaucracy failed to heed warnings of the dangers before the attacks on New York on September 11, 2001. Time magazine named her, along with Sherron Watkins and Cynthia Cooper, as "Persons of the Year" in 2002.

Blowing the Whistle on Hidden Group Pathologies

Imagine FBI agent Coleen Rowley's surprise and shock as she listened to the FBI director publicly state, time and again, that the agency had received no advanced warning of the terrorist attacks of September 11, 2001. Her Minneapolis field office had made repeated requests to FBI headquarters seeking permission to search the computer of Zacarias Moussaoui, a visitor from Morocco being held in custody for an immigration violation. Was it possible that the Director did not know about those requests? Hadn't he gotten the reports that Moussaoui, who had been identified by the French intelligence service as a member of a known terrorist group, had been enrolled in a flight school to learn how to pilot large jets? Wasn't he aware that FBI headquarters had not only refused to allow them to delve deeper into Moussaoui but had actively interfered with their attempts to do so? Presuming a horrible communication mix-up, Rowley and her colleagues tried, through multiple avenues, to get their messages past the many layers of bureaucracy and into the director's hands.

As weeks passed, however—and more and more evidence accumulated suggesting that Moussaoui had been the "missing" twentieth hijacker—the story from FBI headquarters remained the same: "We knew nothing." Reluctantly, Coleen Rowley came to what she later labeled a "sad realization"—that the leadership of one of the world's premier law enforcement agencies had decided to "circle the wagons . . . to protect the FBI from embarrassment and the relevant FBI officials from scrutiny." For an agent so dedicated to the Bureau, this realization was horrifying, and she was haunted by the question: If they had been allowed to dig deeper, could they have prevented the tragedy?

Rowley did not know the answer to this question. She did know, however, that her office's repeated requests to further the investigation had been dismissed as unimportant, and that FBI leaders were publicly stating something she knew to be false. Even so, the in-house memo she wrote to the FBI director was the act of a loyal agent, meant to help the FBI fix its organizational problems. She never expected that it would be leaked to the public or that she would become a star witness at congressional hearings. And she never expected that her attempts to improve the FBI would lead many within the organization to view her as a traitor.

Sherron Watkins and Cynthia Cooper did not work for the FBI, but rather for two of the highest flying American corporations of the 1990s. At its peak in 2000, Enron was the seventh-largest company in the United States; in 1999, WorldCom was worth $115 billion dollars and employed over 80,000 people worldwide. Both companies were known for their creative innovations and for defining the cutting edge of their respective fields. Enron had transformed itself from a natural gas pipeline company into a mega-corporation that traded everything from natural gas and electricity to bandwidth on the Internet. WorldCom had grown from a company that sold local telephone service to one that controlled a large part of the U.S. telephone, Internet, and wireless communication networks. Both companies had charismatic, "visionary" leaders—leaders who, according to Wall Street experts, had figured out new ways to bring American business into the twenty-first century. Their employees were willing to work extremely hard—challenged by high expectations and enticed by the rising value of the company stock options they received as part of their compensation. By most accounts, these were great, successful companies.

And so when Sherron Watkins went to Enron's CEO with concerns of major accounting irregularities, and Cynthia Cooper began investigating similar concerns she had at WorldCom, the responses of their colleagues and bosses were not what they expected. Indeed, Watkins now admits, she naively thought she was handing her CEO a "leadership moment," an opportunity to demonstrate his integrity and character. Instead, the reactions at both companies were dismissive and somewhat threatening: "There's nothing to it." "It's not how it looks." "Don't you have other work you ought to be doing?" But suspecting that things had turned terribly wrong, the two women ignored the pressures to "drop it" and, instead, dug deeper. Their suspicions turned out to be well grounded: Senior officers at both companies had been using illegal accounting tricks to create the appearance of profitability, thereby boosting the company's apparent worth on the stock market—and the value of their own considerable stock options and the sizes of their year-end bonuses. When the discoveries of Watkins and Cooper became known to the outside world, the stock values of the two companies plunged toward their actual worth, losing their once-enthusiastic investors tens of *billions* of dollars. The companies were forced into bankruptcy; thousands upon thousands of workers lost their jobs, and many lost their retirement nest eggs as well.

Coleen Rowley, Sherron Watkins, and Cynthia Cooper. The FBI, Enron, and WorldCom. Their stories, now intertwined, tell us much about the ways groups work—and sometimes don't. What led these three respected organizations, each possessing so much talent and experience, to make such poor decisions? What was it about the nature of these groups that made it difficult for the views of Rowley, Watkins, Cooper, and others to get fair and thoughtful hearings? What was it about the leadership of these organizations that contributed to their failures? And what more general lessons about decision making and leadership can we learn from these monumental failures?

We've seen throughout this textbook that people are "group beings" who are born into families, play with friends, learn with fellow students, cheer with strangers at sporting events, toil with coworkers to earn a living, and join forces with their comrades against common enemies. From the family room to the schoolyard, from the stadium to the workplace to the military base, we live in groups.

In this chapter, we examine how groups influence individuals and how individuals influence groups. We'll see that crowds often bring forth the worst and best of human propensities—aggression and compassion, indifference and help, and laziness and team spirit. We'll see how random collections of individuals can merge into unified groups. We'll see that groups are sometimes surprisingly effective and sometimes stunningly incompetent. And we'll explore the dynamic relationships between leaders and their followers, discovering how leaders are chosen, what makes them effective, and what makes them fail. In sum, we will take a close look at the group processes that influence your life each and every day.

The Nature of Groups

LO 12.1 Describe the characteristics of a "real" group.

LO 12.2 Define (a) *social facilitation,* (b) *deindividuation,* and (c) *dynamical systems.*

In its broadest sense, a **group** consists of two or more individuals who influence each other. This, of course, is a minimal definition, encompassing both collections of people who just happen to be in the same place at the same time (such as people waiting at a city bus stop) and highly structured organizations whose members share goals and identities (such as sororities and fraternities). Although a gathering of strangers awaiting the cross-town express seems like less of a "real" group than does a sorority, each can influence our actions. We begin, then, by exploring "groupings"—mere collections of individuals—and later turn our attentions to the characteristics and workings of "real" groups.

The Mere Presence of Others and Social Facilitation

Norman Triplett was a fan of bicycle racing. He also happened to be a psychologist. So when he observed that cyclists exhibited faster times competing against other cyclists than when competing singly against the clock, he headed for his laboratory to conduct one of the first experiments in social psychology. Triplett (1897–1898) asked children to wind fishing reels as quickly as possible. Like the bicycle racers, the children performed faster in the presence of others than when working alone.

Triplett attributed this phenomenon to a competitive instinct aroused by other people. What Triplett didn't know, however, was that performance can improve even when other people are not competitors and even when they just happen to be milling nearby. Why might the *mere presence* of others improve performance? Being around other people is physiologically arousing; their presence increases our heart rate, quickens our breathing, and so on. Moreover, people who are aroused are more likely to exhibit *dominant responses*—familiar, well-learned behaviors (Spence, 1956). Putting these together, the mere presence of others, by simply arousing us, should lead us to exhibit dominant responses (Zajonc, 1965).

If this logic is correct, being around others should sometimes improve performance and sometimes make it worse. When a dominant response advances a task, the presence of others should improve performance. Consider, for example, an experienced assembly-line autoworker who installs front-left fenders, a job that requires the worker to align the fender to the frame and then push it hard into place. For the autoworker, installing fenders is a well-mastered, simple task, meaning that the dominant response—first align, then push—enables the worker to complete the job successfully. As a result, as others wander the workfloor and increase the worker's arousal, he or she should become even more productive than usual.

But what would happen if a design change required a different installation procedure—first align the fender, then *hook* it into place? Would the presence of others still improve the worker's performance? Probably not, argued Zajonc, because the worker's dominant responses would no longer be appropriate to the task. As more people wander past the autoworker, the dominant response—pushing with enough force to pop the fender in—would interfere with the ability to hook the fender gently onto its fasteners. When our well-practiced, dominant responses don't advance a task—as with most new, unmastered tasks—the presence of others should impair performance.

Numerous studies support this theory of **social facilitation** (Zajonc, 1965): The presence of others indeed improves performance on well-mastered, simple tasks and hinders performance on unmastered, complex tasks (Bond & Titus, 1983; Guerin, 1993) (see Figure 12.1). As one example, consider the experiment performed by James Michaels and his colleagues (1982). After spying on pool players at Virginia Polytechnic Institute and assessing their shot-making ability, four confederates sauntered over to observe them. As predicted by social facilitation theory, the good players—for whom

Group Minimally, groups are two or more individuals who influence each other. Collections of individuals become increasingly "grouplike," however, when their members are interdependent and share a common identity, and when they possess structure.

Social facilitation The process through which the presence of others increases the likelihood of dominant responses, leading to better performance on well-mastered tasks and worse performance on unmastered tasks.

Figure 12.1   Performing in the presence of others

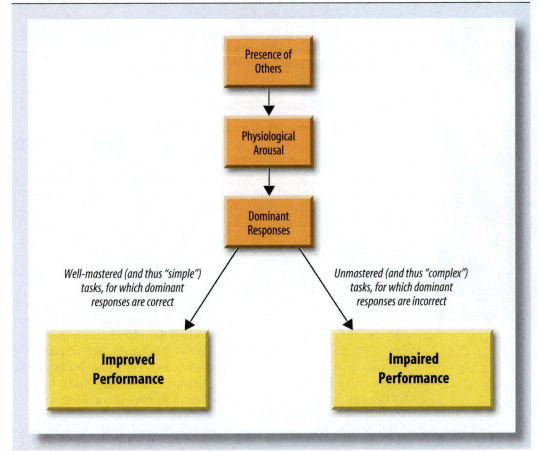

Being around other people is arousing and, when we are aroused, we are more likely to behave in well-learned, familiar ways. These dominant responses tend to be correct for well-mastered, "simple" tasks. As a result, we tend to perform better on mastered tasks when others are around. In contrast, dominant responses tend to be incorrect for unmastered, "complex" tasks. Consequently, we tend to perform more poorly on unmastered tasks when others are around.

pool was a relatively well-learned game—performed even better when watched, improving their shot-making rate from 71% to 80%. In contrast, the less talented players—who had not yet mastered the game—got worse, dropping from a 36% to 25% success rate. A more recent study brought this finding into the era of computer games, finding that an audience improved performance on videogames, but only when they were easy (Bowman et al., 2013).

The mere presence of others seems to be enough to facilitate dominant responses (e.g., Schmitt et al., 1986). Indeed, even the presence of a "virtual" other on a nearby computer screen facilitates dominant responses (Park & Catrambone, 2007). In humans, these effects are often intensified under certain conditions (Aiello & Douthitt, 2001). Consider, for instance, *evaluation apprehension*. When people believe that observers are explicitly assessing their performances, they become increasingly aroused, and this arousal further facilitates their dominant responses (Cottrell, 1968; Seta & Seta, 1992; Seta, Crisson, Seta, & Wang, 1989). For example, the dominant responses of autoworkers are likely to be boosted when someone is observing them, unless the observers are blindfolded and, hence, in no position to judge (Cottrell et al., 1968).

Distraction also seems to intensify social facilitation. As anyone studying for an exam in a busy dorm lounge knows all too well, being around others can be distracting, forcing people to struggle just to focus on the task at hand. Consider the arousal experienced by our autoworker as he or she tries to suppress now-obsolete dominant responses while also trying to ignore the hordes of noisy people wandering in and out

In a crowd, you can lose more than just your wallet. The presence of others may mask our identities and relax our inhibitions, leading us to lose contact with our values and to do things we would never consider doing otherwise.

of the workspace (Baron, 1986; Sanders, 1981). The distracting nature of people, and our tendency to believe that others are often evaluating us, together increase our arousal and thus facilitate our dominant responses.

In sum, just being around others makes it more likely that people will perform the behaviors they are most familiar with. As we see next, random groupings of individuals influence people in other ways as well.

Crowds and Deindividuation

"Be somebody . . . else," challenged Sims Online, as it advertised its simulated online communities in which thousands of subscribers pretend to live, work, and play as characters of their own choosing. In communities with names like Alphaville, the social atmosphere is generally friendly and cooperative. But not always. Groups of "griefers" sometimes roam these cyber-neighborhoods, descending on innocent fellow players to devastate the favorable reputations they've worked days and months to earn. Could you see yourself doing this to others? If you think not, you might want to think again. Actions that are rarely performed by a lone individual become more likely when that same individual is immersed in a group (Mann, 1981; Mullen, 1986). Why?

In groups, people may lose their senses of individual identity and, as a result, relax their inhibitions against behaving in ways inconsistent with their normal values—a process called **deindividuation** (Festinger et al., 1952; Le Bon, 1895/1960; Reimann & Zimbardo, 2011). Spectators who take part in a collective chant during a soccer game, for example, become more aggressive afterward (Bensimon & Bodner, 2011).

Groups deindividuate their members in two ways. First, crowds sometimes mask the identities of their individual members, making them anonymous and less accountable for their actions (Prentice-Dunn & Rogers, 1980). Consider the results of the classic clever field experiment we briefly described in Chapter 1 (Diener et al., 1976). One Halloween night in Seattle, as thousands of costumed children roamed the streets in search of candy and other treats (and perhaps some tricky mischief as well), researchers awaited their arrival at 27 homes scattered throughout the city. In the foyer of each home stood a table with two bowls—one filled with candy, the other with pennies and nickels. After greeting the children, the adult experimenter told the children to take *one* candy, and she then exited the room, leaving only the children and an observer hiding behind a colorful screen. Fifty-seven percent of the trick-or-treaters arriving in groups stole extra candy or money, as compared to only 21% of the children arriving alone. Consistent with hypotheses, the anonymity provided by being in a group clearly contributed to this increased theft: When children in groups were first asked their names and addresses by the researcher—thus eliminating their anonymity— they transgressed only 21% of the time.

Crowds also deindividuate by distracting members' attention away from their individual selves and their personal values (Prentice-Dunn & Rogers, 1982). In a second Halloween study, Arthur Beaman and his colleagues (1979) found that older children (aged nine and above) who had been asked their names and addresses were even less likely to steal extra candy when a mirror had been propped up behind the candy bowl. Apparently, seeing themselves in the mirror made these children *objectively self-aware* and thus less able to cast aside their personal values forbidding theft.

These studies illustrate one of the potentially problematic consequences of being among others: People may become deindividuated. These studies also tell us something about how "real" groups may begin to emerge out of mere collections of individuals. In each study, the behavior of the first group member had a large influence on the behaviors of those who followed: If the first child stole, the others were more likely to steal; if the first child took just the single allowed candy, the others followed this more positive example (Beaman et al., 1979; Diener et al., 1976). These findings support the conclusions drawn from a review of 60 studies of deindividuation. According to

Deindividuation The process of losing one's sense of personal identity, which makes it easier to behave in ways inconsistent with one's normal values.

Tom Postmes and Russell Spears (1998), people in crowds become increasingly sensitive to the actions of others in their immediate surroundings. In this way, *norms* begin to emerge, turning crowds into real groups.

Indeed, the actions of even a single individual can begin to provide structure to an initially haphazard collection of strangers. Just as one antisocial individual in a peaceful online community can be the seed from which sprouts a harassing mob, a prosocial individual can be the seed from which flower acts of community concern. The ways in which influence flows through groups are complex, however—a topic we turn to next.

INVESTIGATION

Recall a time you were in a group and behaved in a way very different from how you would have behaved alone. What was it about being in the group that led you to act that way?

Groups as Dynamic Systems: The Emergence of Norms

Imagine living in a freshman dorm with, say, 100 rooms. One day, you receive an email flyer announcing a meeting in two weeks to determine how to spend the dorm's social budget. There would likely be a wide range of initial opinions: Some students would want to throw one or two huge parties, others would want to have a greater number of small get-togethers spread across the year, and still others wouldn't care much either way. Regardless of your initial inclinations, however, most of you would remain at least slightly open to well-reasoned, persuasive arguments. So, as you discuss the issue with the other students, you might find yourself changing your mind a bit. Of course, your neighbors are in the same boat, so they, too, are probably being influenced by each other. In all, with each of 100 students interacting with a host of friends and acquaintances in the dorm, it is likely that opinions throughout the dorm will change in numerous, and seemingly chaotic, ways.

Under such circumstances, do you think you'd be able to predict your dorm's final decision or the patterns of preferences that would emerge? Although social psychologists know quite a bit about the general factors that determine influence in large groups, and have developed theories that appreciate the complexity underlying group processes (e.g., Arrow, McGrath, & Berdahl, 2000; Harton & Bourgeois, 2004; Latané et al., 1995), circumstances like these are stunningly complex, and it's extremely difficult to keep track of everything: There are just too many interconnected people having too many opinions influencing too many others over too long a time. But before you throw up your hands in despair, you should know about some fairly simple tools for studying complicated group interactions like these, tools as close as the nearest laptop computer.

Complex problems like these confront not just social psychologists trying to understand group influence but also meteorologists trying to predict global weather patterns, economists trying to understand the flow of money through the global economy, and animal biologists hoping to understand the link between predators and their prey on the African savannah. With the arrival of high-speed computers, however, these once-overwhelming tasks have become more manageable. Scientists not only have developed more complicated models of such **dynamical systems**—systems that possess many interconnected elements and that change and evolve over time—but also have discovered something quite unexpected: Order often emerges out of apparent chaos (Nowak et al., 2013; Waldrop, 1992).

To illustrate this, let's step back a moment to the days well before the advent of the personal computer. As World War II ended, American soldiers returned to the United States to begin or continue their college educations. To accommodate the rush of new students, the Massachusetts Institute of Technology (MIT) quickly constructed Westgate, the first university housing project dedicated to married veteran students and their families. For social psychologists, this was a unique opportunity to explore

Dynamical system A system (e.g., a group) made up of many interacting elements (e.g., people) that changes and evolves over time.

how real groups form and develop. And so, in the summer of 1946, Leon Festinger, Stanley Schachter, and Kurt Back (1950) of MIT's Research Center for Group Dynamics began what became a classic study in the psychology of groups.

For our purposes, one finding stands out: Over time, residents living near one another began to hold similar attitudes toward their community council. Westgate's 100 single-family homes were arranged in nine courts, with most houses within each court facing each other. Because MIT randomly assigned families to homes, it's safe to assume that attitudes toward housing associations were at first distributed haphazardly throughout the whole community. Over time, however, these scattered views began to cluster together—not because people relocated to be closer to those holding similar beliefs but because people influenced, and were influenced by, those living near them. Because residents communicated most often with members of their own courts, the courts began to emerge as unique groups, with their own attitudes toward the Westgate Council and their own norms either supporting or opposing it. From chaos, then, emerged organization.

Without the necessary tools, it was impossible for Festinger and his colleagues to explore in great depth how clustering of group attitudes like this might come about. But with the help of a modern computer and a simple spreadsheet program, we can watch structure emerge out of disorder (Harton & Bourgeois, 2004; Latané & Bourgeois, 1996). In Panel A of Figure 12.2, we approximate the layout of Westgate and randomly distribute across it opinions on the issue of a neighborhood council. We then let the computer "assume" that the 100 "residents" will communicate primarily with residents of their own courts, as Festinger and his colleagues found. We also add a second simple presumption—that residents will be influenced by the opinion of the majority of the neighbors they talk to. Finally, the computer has the residents communicate

Figure 12.2 The emerging group norms in Westgate

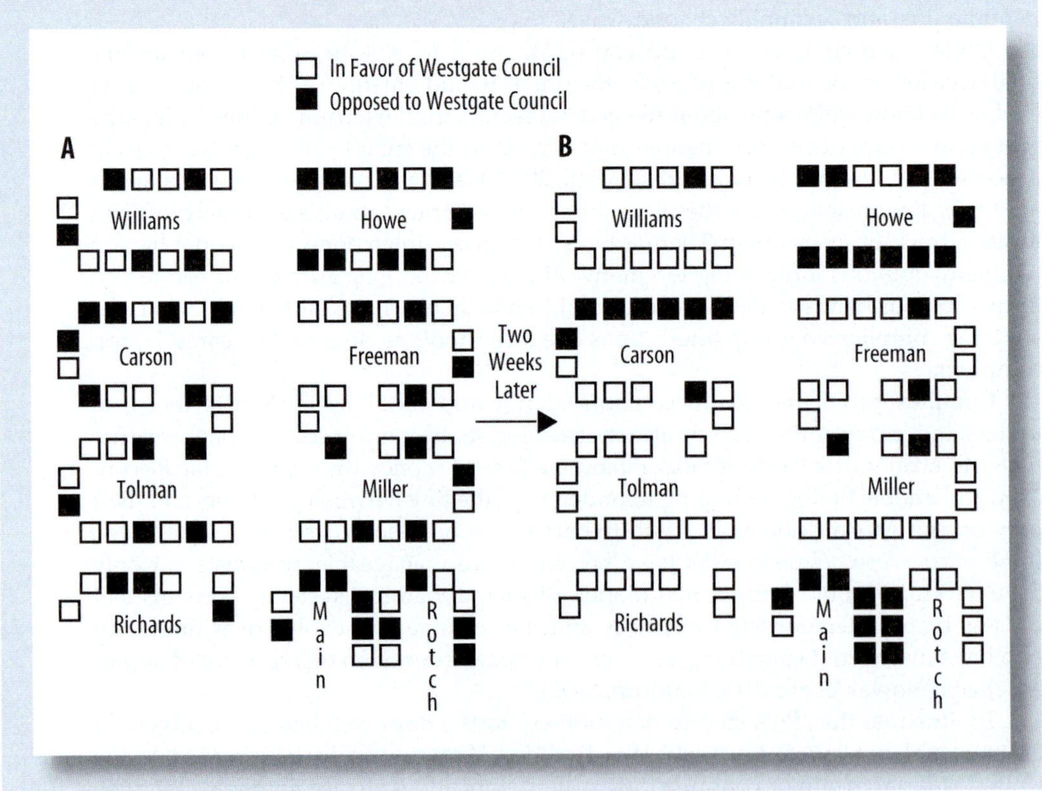

In our computer simulation of Westgate, we start with various attitudes toward the Westgate Council scattered throughout the community (Panel A) and see that most of the courts soon adopt common norms (Panel B).

with their immediate neighbors twice a "week" for two weeks. Although it would keep a chess grand master busy for some time trying to predict how residents in our make-believe community will mutually influence one another on a day-by-day basis, it is a simple matter to have a computer do the calculations.

In Figure 12.2, Panel B, we see that with just a few rounds of computer simulation, opinions toward the Westgate Council cluster together substantially. Whereas the Tolman and Richards Courts support the council unanimously, and the Miller, Freeman, Williams, and Rotch Courts are now generally supportive of the council, the Carson, Howe, and Main Courts are generally opposed. Although some individuals within most courts buck the trend, residents in the courts have generally come to agree with one another. From an initially scattered collection of individuals having equally scattered views emerge groups having coherent norms (e.g., Bourgeois & Bowen, 2001).

Dynamic computer simulations like these are valuable not only because they may help us explain existing findings but also because they can help us generate novel predictions. For example, what would have happened if a few residents holding opposing views had instead been assigned to each other's courts? One can test this by changing just a few of the initial values we give the computer. What we find is that even small changes can have large effects, with the norms in some courts changing dramatically.

Computer simulations are beginning to prove quite useful for understanding group dynamics and other areas of social psychology (e.g., Hastie & Stasser, 2000; Ilgen & Hulin, 2000; Rousseau & Van der Veen, 2005; Tesser & Achee, 1994; Vallacher, Read, & Nowak, 2002). These simulations become particularly valuable when researchers "go full cycle" to test the novel predictions created by the simulations against real human behavior (e.g., Latané & Bourgeois, 2001). So just as computer simulations help meteorologists predict weather patterns over Europe and economists comprehend stock market crashes on Wall Street, they assist social psychologists in clarifying the intriguing but complicated interactions that take place among people in groups.

"Real" Groups

A crowd of strangers dancing at a concert is different from a crowd of strangers streaming past one another on a busy street. The concertgoers influence one another, thereby showing the first signs of being a group. Mutual influence, however, is just one feature of "groupness." Indeed, when we think of corporations, social clubs, community associations, and families, it becomes clear that groups have other important features as well. In particular, real groups are likely to have members who are interdependent and share a common identity, and they are also likely to have a stable structure.

INTERDEPENDENCE   The members of "real" groups tend to be interdependent: They need each other to reach their shared goals. To say that group members are interdependent means more than just saying that they are all aimed in the same direction. For example, although the millions of U.S. citizens registered as members of the Democratic and Republican Parties share the goal of electing representatives to implement their preferred policies, these party members can independently do their business—by casting their ballots—without having much interaction with one another. In contrast, each party's elected members of Congress are interdependent: They need to work with one another each day to increase the likelihood that their party's policies become law. The Democratic and Republican caucuses within Congress each constitute more of a real group than do registered Democratic and Republican voters.

GROUP IDENTITY   Do the students at your college constitute a real group? The answer depends partly on whether you all *perceive yourselves* to be a group (Campbell, 1958; Hogg et al., 2004; Lickel, Hamilton, & Sherman, 2001). On an average day in the middle of the semester, as students on campus wander to and from class, probably few of you are aware that you share a common identity. On the day of the annual football contest against your cross-state rivals, however, this identity becomes salient, and interactions among students become more group-like. Although some group identities wax and wane in this way, others are a salient part of everyday life. Sorority members, who live,

Sororities are "real" groups. Sororities have all the features we commonly attribute to real groups. They have structure, in the form of roles (president, treasurer) and injunctive norms (not to date motorcycle gang members). Their members depend on one another to reach shared goals, as when they want to host social functions and philanthropic events for the community. And their members share a common group identity—they view themselves as being a group.

Role Expectation held by the group for how members in particular positions ought to behave.

Status hierarchy A ranking of group members by their power and influence over other members.

Communication network The pattern of information flow through a group.

Cohesiveness The strength of the bonds among group members.

eat, and party together, probably are conscious of their affiliation most days, often going so far as to advertise it proudly with big Greek letters emblazoned across their clothing.

People who strongly identify with a group often work harder on its behalf. For example, strong group identifiers tend to be very loyal: They are less likely to talk about the group's problems in public, especially when there are members of outgroups who might overhear (Packer, 2012), and they are relatively unlikely to abandon their groups for others even when leaving is personally advantageous (Blair & Jost, 2003; Van Vugt & Hart, 2004).

GROUP STRUCTURE Many groups develop stable structures. They may possess *injunctive norms*—shared expectations for how group members *ought* to behave if they wish to receive social approval and avoid disapproval (Levine & Moreland, 1998) (see Chapters 2 and 6). Members of a particular sorority may expect one another to dress conservatively, to stay away from men sporting nose rings, and to get good grades. Groups may also create **roles** for their members. Whereas injunctive norms describe how *all* members ought to behave, roles are shared expectations for how *particular* group members should behave. A sorority president may be expected to set the agenda for chapter meetings and confer regularly with other Greek organizations, whereas a treasurer may be expected to collect dues and balance the sorority's bank account. Roles often make groups more efficient, because it is rarely desirable for every member to contribute in the same way (Barley & Bechky, 1994; Strijbos et al., 2004). Just imagine, for example, the chaos that would reign if every sorority sister tried to run the weekly meetings or collect the dues.

A group may also have a **status hierarchy**, in which members are ranked in terms of their social power and the influence they have over other members (Kipnis, 1984). In a sorority, for instance, the president has more official status than the other officers, who in turn have more official status than the remaining members. A structured group usually also has a stable **communication network** through which information flows to its members. For example, in highly *centralized* networks, information tends to flow from one member (usually the leader) to all other members simultaneously, as when a sorority president makes an announcement during a chapter meeting. In *decentralized* networks, information passes among members without having to go through one particular person. In many businesses, instructions from senior officers are often passed, chainlike, through managerial layers until they finally reach the workers on the factory floor. It appears that the rigid status hierarchy and communication network of the FBI made it less responsive than it might have been to the requests of Coleen Rowley's Minneapolis field office to investigate Zacarias Moussaoui and his computer.

A final feature of group structure is **cohesiveness**, or the strength of the bonds among group members. Groups can be cohesive, or close-knit, because their members enjoy being with one another (*interpersonal cohesiveness*) or because they are all committed to the group's task (*task cohesiveness*). When a job requires communication and coordination, cohesive groups work particularly well (Gully et al., 1995; Mullen & Copper, 1994; Zaccaro, 1991). A recent meta-analysis found that cohesive groups perform, on average, 18 percentile points above the average noncohesive group (Evans & Dion, 2012). But cohesion isn't always good. Interpersonally cohesive teams sometimes have difficulty staying focused on their tasks (e.g., Zaccaro & Lowe, 1988) and are more susceptible to certain decision-making errors (e.g., Mullen et al., 1994), as we will see later.

In sum, stable groups are often structured by injunctive norms, roles, status hierarchies, stable communication networks, and cohesiveness. More broadly, we see that structure, interdependence, and a common group identity distinguish real groups from groupings—collections of individuals who merely influence one another. This

Figure 12.3 A continuum of groupness

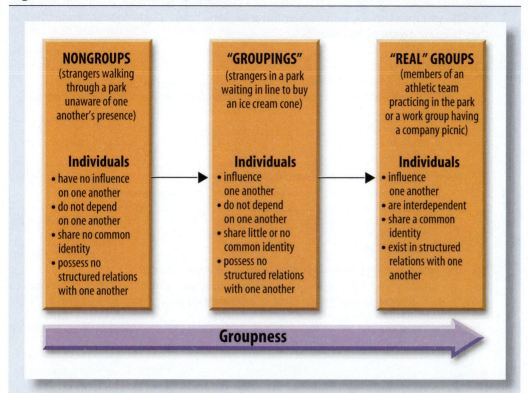

At the minimum, groups are two or more individuals who influence each other. Collections of individuals become increasingly "group-like," however, when their members are interdependent and share a common identity, and when they possess structure (injunctive norms, roles, status hierarchies, communication networks, cohesiveness).

distinction is a fuzzy one, however. For example, real groups can exist without having well-defined structures, as in the case of chanting fans at a football game. It seems best, then, to view "groupness" as a continuum (see Figure 12.3): Groups having structure, and in which members share a common identity and depend on one another to reach shared goals, are "groupier" than groups possessing fewer of these features (Levine & Moreland, 1998). In the remainder of this chapter, we focus primarily on these more "groupy" groups.

Why Do People Belong to Groups?

People seem to have a basic "need to belong" (Baumeister & Leary, 1995; McDougall, 1908), and group living is a universal feature of human life (Coon, 1946; Mann, 1980). Indeed, as we saw in Chapter 7, being excluded from a group is a horribly uncomfortable, even painful, experience, and people go to great lengths to be accepted by others (e.g., Pickett & Gardner, 2005; Williams, Forgas, & von Hippel, 2005). But *why* are groups so important that we seek to spend so much of our lives in them? What do groups do for us?

People seek groups for various reasons (Hogg, Hohman, & Rivera, 2008; Mackie & Goethals, 1987; Moreland, 1987). We may join groups because they allow us to express our values publicly, as when opponents of capital punishment pray together in candlelight vigils on the nights of planned executions. We may join groups because they help us define ourselves—help us "know who we are." Other times, we join groups because they provide needed emotional support, as when cancer patients attend support groups. This chapter focuses on two other primary reasons people belong to groups: to accomplish tasks they can't effectively accomplish otherwise and to acquire and share information in especially potent ways. We also explore a more secondary goal, that of gaining the material and social benefits of leadership. Although few people join groups with the aim of becoming leaders, many begin to seek leadership as they become aware of its rewards.

Quick Quiz

1 Which of the following factors contributes to a collection of individuals becoming a "real" group?

    a. Shared identity
    b. Interdependence
    c. Structure
    d. All of the above

2 Which of these statements about social facilitation is false?

    a. The presence of others impairs performance on unmastered tasks.
    b. The presence of others improves performance on well-mastered tasks.
    c. The presence of others improves performance on tasks for which dominant responses are incorrect.
    d. None of the above

3 The Halloween studies on deindividuation found which of the following?

    a. Trick-or-treaters arriving in groups were as likely to steal extra candy as those arriving alone.
    b. Theft among trick-or-treaters arriving in groups decreased significantly when they no longer felt anonymous.
    c. Placing a mirror behind the candy bowl decreased theft among those arriving in groups but did not affect those arriving alone.
    d. None of the above

4 What is a dynamical system?

    a. A system consisting of many interacting elements that changes and evolves over time.
    b. A system consisting of many interacting elements that have no discernible order.
    c. A social group with initially divergent opinions that converges over time on a single opinion.
    d. None of the above

Getting Things Done

LO 12.3 Discuss the circumstances that make *social loafing* more likely to occur and describe what can be done to reduce social loafing.

LO 12.4 Discuss why people in individualistic societies tend to belong to more groups.

LO 12.5 Describe what kinds of people are best to have in performance groups and understand how this depends on the group's task.

Your family and the FBI. Kappa Kappa Gamma sorority and the Westgate community council. The high school chess club and the United States of America. The Sierra Club and Enron. Although these groups differ in many ways, they have one important thing in common: They help their members accomplish tasks that would be difficult—if not impossible—to accomplish alone.

Lightening the Load, Dividing the Labor

Our ancestors discovered long ago that their chances of personal survival increased dramatically when they grouped themselves with others. In groups, they were better able to hunt, gather, and cultivate food; they were better able to build shelters and defend themselves; and they had others to care for them when they fell ill (Brewer, 1997; Caporael & Baron, 1997). The philosopher Baruch Spinoza was right when he noted that "because no one in solitude is strong enough to protect himself and procure the necessities of life, it follows that men by nature tend toward social organization" (Durant & Durant, 1963, 651).

Of course, the benefits of groups extend to less fundamental tasks as well. The chess club provides its members with practice partners and competition. Political parties and social action groups help people influence public policy. Even groups themselves often see advantages of banding together to get things done: Families join with other families to create small communities. These communities band together to form states, which form nations, and which work together in alliances and even larger organizations such as the United Nations.

Group performance is potentially more effective than individual performance for two reasons. First, "many hands make light work": In groups, individuals can share common burdens. In many agricultural communities, for example, families help one another bring in the crops, herd livestock to market, and build new barns. Although a single family alone might be able to raise a barn, helpful neighbors make the task much easier. Second, people in groups can divide their labor: With multiple people on the job, different people can perform different tasks. As a result, individuals can specialize—some becoming architects, others carpenters, and still others surveyors and landscapers. And because specialists are typically more proficient than generalists, groups often accomplish tasks better and faster than any individual could.

This is not to say that groups always outperform individuals. Moreover, groups rarely perform to their full potential (Davis, 1969; Laughlin, 1980; Steiner, 1972). Ironically, a major threat to efficient group performance is closely tied to one of the very reasons people belong to groups to begin with—their desire to lighten their personal loads.

Working together. People often pool their labor when tasks are too large for any individual or family to accomplish alone, as in this attempt to save a home from rising flood waters.

Social loafing Reducing one's personal efforts when in a group.

Bridging Function and Dysfunction:

The Social Disease of Social Loafing

The New England pickle factory was in . . . well, a pickle. It appeared that its pickle packers—the workers responsible for stuffing pickles into jars—had become a bit careless. Instead of stuffing only correct-sized pickles into the jars, some had begun to plop in pickles that were too short. Short pickles float and bob around unattractively in the brine, and the inspectors in quality control (the pickle police?) had to reject jar after jar of packed pickles. Pickle-packing productivity was proceeding poorly (Turner, 1978).

But why, you might ask, should you give a gherkin about pickle packing? To answer this question, let's step back to the late 1800s, to the laboratory of Max Ringelmann, a French agricultural engineer. Ringelmann researched farming productivity and observed that extra workers rarely increased output as much as one might expect. In one set of experiments, Ringelmann had men pull carts as hard as they could, either alone or working together in groups. He discovered something curious: As the number of men working together increased, the average pulling power of each man decreased. In two-person teams, each man was, on average, 93% as productive as he was working alone; in four-person teams, each man was only 77% as productive; and in eight-person teams, each man was merely 49% as productive (Kravitz & Martin, 1986; Ringelmann, 1913).

Ringelmann attributed part of the inefficiency to the difficulty of coordinating the efforts of many people, of getting them all to pull at the same time. Other research, however, has since revealed that decreased coordination is only one reason why groups can lose efficiency (Steiner, 1972). Most notably, as Ringelmann himself suspected, individual group members often exhibit **social loafing**: They decrease their personal efforts as their groups grow larger (Ingham et al., 1974; Latané, Williams, & Harkins, 1979).

For some tasks, social loafing isn't much of a problem: If five people could push a car out of a ditch, there seems little reason for a team of ten individuals to exert themselves fully. After all, the goal is not to break a sweat but merely to get the car rolling again. For other tasks, however, social loafing can be quite a problem. The goal of the pickle company, for instance, wasn't merely to produce some minimum number of jars each day. Instead, it wanted to pack as many pickles as possible. Managers probably didn't suspect, however, that by hiring many pickle packers to increase overall productivity, they also increased the propensity of each packer to *free-ride* on the efforts of the others—to take it easy and rely on the efforts of his or her coworkers (Kerr & Bruun, 1983). They probably also didn't realize that once employees saw able-bodied coworkers beginning to free-ride, they would reduce their own efforts so as not to be "suckered" into unfairly carrying the load for others (Kerr, 1983). The pickle company was paying individual workers for effort it never received, and consumers were paying for the factory's inefficiency. As Bibb Latané and his colleagues (1979) put it, social loafing can be a social disease.

Group members are more likely to loaf when their individual contributions can't be evaluated (Harkins, 1987). This can occur, for instance, when group members' contributions are unidentifiable—when they and others are unable to tell whose contributions are whose (e.g., Williams, Harkins, & Latané, 1981). It's worth noting that the pickle-packing assembly line was configured so that conveyer belts deposited the packed jars into a common hopper for inspection. Inspectors were thus unable to identify those particular pickle packers responsible for the poorly packed jars. There were few direct costs to those individual workers who chose to pack their pickles poorly.

How, then, is a pickle purveyor to promote productivity? What would *you* do to limit social loafing, say, when working on a group project? On the basis of a meta-analysis of almost 80 studies, Steven Karau and Kipling Williams (1993, 2001) provide several suggestions:

- *Make each group member's contributions identifiable* (Kerr & Bruun, 1981; Williams et al., 1981). Coaches of football teams typically film and score the performance of individual players. When other group members can evaluate our contributions, we are less likely to loaf, because we generally don't want to view ourselves—or to be viewed by others—as slackers (Harkins & Jackson, 1985; Szymanski & Harkins, 1987).
- *Make the task personally meaningful, challenging, or important* (Brickner, Harkins, & Ostrom, 1986; Smith et al., 2001; Zaccaro, 1984). In one experiment, for example, participants were less likely to loaf while wrapping bubble-gum when they believed that the gum would be put in care packages sent to U.S. soldiers stationed overseas (see Figure 12.4; Shepperd, 2001).
- *Make it clear to group members that their personal efforts will lead to a better group performance* (Shepperd & Taylor, 1999). Olympic swimmers swim faster in relay teams than alone, if their performance is seen as highly instrumental to a positive team outcome (Hüffmeier et al., 2012). Moreover, people are less likely to loaf when they believe they can make a unique contribution to the group goal; if group members each have a somewhat different job, they cannot easily presume that the work of others will hide their own laziness (Gockel et al., 2008).
- *Try to increase the interpersonal cohesiveness of your group.* For example, people loaf less when working with friends than with strangers. Of course, you can't always populate your groups with friends. You can, however, try to enhance how members of your groups feel about one another. For instance, treating fellow group members with respect increases their sense of group identity and their willingness to work on the group's behalf (Simon & Stürmer, 2003).
- *Recruit group members who tend toward being collectivistic in their interpersonal orientation.* People who are more collectivistic—such as women and residents of Eastern societies such as Japan—are less likely to loaf than are those who are more individualistic—men and residents of Western societies such as the United States (e.g., Earley, 1989; Gabrenya et al., 1985; Klehe & Anderson, 2007).

Figure 12.4   No loafing for a good cause

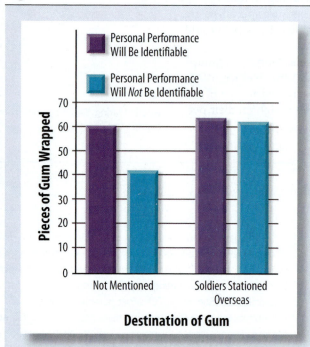

Participants in one experiment were asked to wrap pieces of bubblegum for 10 minutes—a less than exciting task! The two bars on the left illustrate a typical social loafing effect: Participants wrapped less gum when they believed their performance couldn't be evaluated—when they thought no one would know how much work they had done. When the task was given some extra meaning, however—when participants were told that the gum would be added to care packages sent to servicemen and servicewomen stationed overseas—social loafing disappeared: Participants wrapped as much gum even when they thought they were not being evaluated (Shepperd, 2001). By making performances meaningful and important to group members, we can reduce the likelihood of social loafing.

Source: Data from Shepperd, J. A. (2001). The desire to help and behavior in social dilemmas: Exploring responses to catastrophes. *Group Dynamics,* 5, 304–314. Table 1.

Although people have a strong urge to socially loaf when working in groups, the advantages of group action are great enough that many tasks can still get done more effectively by groups than by individuals working alone. And, on certain tasks, people sometimes even work harder when in the group than when working alone. For instance, when group members believe the task is important enough, they will often work harder to compensate for others' inadequate efforts (e.g., Liden et al., 2004; Williams & Karau, 1991). Moreover, when group members believe that their half-hearted efforts are holding back the group, they may increase their efforts to contribute (e.g., Hertel, Kerr, & Messé, 2000; Messé et al., 2002). After all, few of us want to be seen (or to see ourselves) as the "weakest link"—as the person who stops the group from getting things done.

PERSON   Expectations of Individual Failure
                and Group Success

Have you ever joined a study group? Why? We suspect that your decision to do so—or not—was influenced by two straightforward considerations: (1) how well you thought you'd do on the exam if you studied alone and (2) how well you thought you'd do on the exam if you studied with others. When you believe that you'll accomplish your tasks better when working with others than when working alone, you're more likely to form or join a group (Zander, 1985).

People are more likely to join a group when they worry that they may fail as individuals (Loher et al., 1994). For example, Jeffrey Vancouver and Daniel Ilgen (1989) allowed male and female students at Michigan State University to choose whether to work alone or with another student on six different tasks. Some of the tasks were stereotypically "male," such as changing a car's oil or designing a tool shed. The others were stereotypically "female," such as designing a store window or taking a quiz on flowers. Vancouver and Ilgen presumed that men would be less confident in their abilities to do well on the female tasks and that women would be less confident in their abilities to do well on the male tasks. As a result, they predicted that the students would much prefer to work alone on gender-consistent tasks and with others on gender-inconsistent tasks. This is indeed what they found. As students' expectations of individual success went down, their desire to work with others went up.

We suspect that these uncertain students preferred working with others because they also believed that their partners would be more skilled at the task, or that at least "two heads would be better than one." This brings us to the second part of the formula: People are more likely to join a group when they believe it will effectively move them toward their goals. In a study at the University of Delaware, Edgar Townsend (1973) found that students who viewed organizations as fruitful paths to their own personal and community goals were especially likely to be active in off-campus volunteer groups. Not surprisingly, people who've had success working in groups in the past are more likely to prefer working in groups in the future (Eby & Dobbins, 1997; Loher et al., 1994).

SITUATION   Current Needs, Individualistic Societies

Joining a group is a more attractive strategy for getting things done under some circumstances than others. Sometimes there is just no choice, as when a worker must join a labor union to get a job at the local factory. More frequently, however, people join performance groups when current circumstances make it hard to succeed alone. For example, just as workers have formed unions to gain increased control over their wages and working conditions, American citizens have formed groups such as the National Association for the Advancement of Colored People (NAACP) and the National Rifle Association (NRA) to further their preferred social causes. When interpersonal or societal circumstances become undesirable—when they make it difficult for people to reach their goals—individuals become more interested in working together to improve their lot (Tropp & Brown, 2004; Zander, 1985).

Some societies more than others seem to "breed" performance groups. Who participates in more performance groups—members of individualistic societies or members of collectivistic societies? You may have guessed collectivistic societies. After all, we've seen that collectivism is essentially *about* groups—about being interdependent with others, subordinating one's needs to the group's needs, and being loyal and committed. But, in an interesting paradox, people in these societies participate in fewer performance groups: People in collectivistic societies are generally so committed to their existing groups that they don't look elsewhere when they need help getting things done. Alternatively, consider prototypical individualists. Because they are less tied to their current groups, they feel free to "shop around" for other groups to fit their particular needs of the moment. In individualistic societies, then, people are quick to join many groups, although their commitment to these groups may often be transitory (Triandis, 1995).

Protecting the environment. Some needs are so great, and the task so large, that only coordinated effort by many individuals will be successful. Millions of people worldwide believe that the threats to the earth's natural ecology create such a need, and they have formed together into thousands of groups to clean parks and rivers, slow the harvesting of rain forests, reduce automobile and factory emissions, and encourage recycling.

Citizens of individualistic societies join multiple performance groups for other reasons as well. Individualistic societies tend to be wealthier and more literate and are often more urban than collectivistic societies, and these factors make it easier to join multiple groups (Meister, 1979; Stinchcombe, 1965). Urban living brings strangers together in the same place, providing a large pool of people who could work together for common goals. Moreover, residents of highly literate societies are exposed to many links with others—through newspapers, magazines, bulletin boards, and the Internet. Residents of nonliterate societies can only learn about potentially useful groups through personal contact, television and radio, or word of mouth.

INTERACTION When Are Groups Most Productive?

What are the characteristics of effective groups? Are group members who have certain personality types more valuable than others? Are groups composed of similar individuals more effective than groups of individuals who have varying backgrounds, experiences, or skills?

The answers to these and similar questions almost always come back the same: It depends. In particular, it depends on the type of task the group is hoping to accomplish (Davis, 1973; Hackman & Morris, 1975; Holland, 1985; McGrath, 1984; Steiner, 1972). Different tasks require different skills. What is needed to pull a bus from a ditch is different from what is needed to maintain a nation's security. In this section we explore how features of the group interact with requirements of the task to affect a group's productivity.

WHO SHOULD BE IN THE GROUP? Finding the right people for the right jobs is a challenge that faces managers of all sorts, from those leading government agencies and Fortune 500 corporations to those running fast food restaurants: What kinds of people work together best for what kinds of tasks? Robert Hogan and his colleagues (Driskell, Hogan, & Salas, 1987; Hogan et al., 1989) proposed a framework to explore this question. By classifying tasks by the skills required to complete them successfully and by classifying workers in terms of fundamental personality characteristics, they have hypothesized which people are best for different jobs. For example, team members who are prudent and conforming should perform well at conventional, routine tasks such as accounting but poorly at artistic tasks in which originality, nonconformity, and risk-taking are valuable. In contrast, a team made up of socially skilled individuals should do particularly well on tasks such as teaching but poorly on conventional tasks in which their desires to socialize would interfere with the need to follow routines carefully and pay close attention to detail.

Along similar lines, most problem-solving teams require at least one member who is achievement motivated and energetic (otherwise the team doesn't do any work), one member who is imaginative and curious (otherwise the team doesn't generate any good ideas), and one member who is agreeable and tolerant (otherwise the team doesn't get along) (Morrison, 1993). Moreover, teams that have too many highly sociable members often have problems staying on task, whereas teams that have too few sociable members never develop the rapport needed to generate new ideas freely (Barry & Stewart, 1997). The overall lesson, then, is this: Groups that are most productive tend to have members who complement one another and whose personality characteristics closely match the requirements of their tasks (Bell, 2007).

IS DIVERSITY VALUABLE? Consider two men's basketball teams whose starting players average 6 feet 8 inches in height. On Team A, all five starters are 6 feet 8 inches, making this team homogeneous on height. On Team B, one of the starters is 7 feet

1 inch, a second is 6 feet 10 inches, a third is 6 feet 9 inches, a fourth 6 feet 6 inches, and the fifth is 6 feet 2 inches; this team is diverse, or heterogeneous, on height. All else being equal, which team would you rather coach?

We suspect you'd choose Team B, because its greater diversity in height would make it easier for you to satisfy the functions of the different basketball positions—to find the right person for the job. The more heterogeneous Team B can better cover the different needs of the game of basketball. Indeed, not only is team heterogeneity often valuable in sports (Widmeyer, 1990) but heterogeneous groups also may have important advantages over homogeneous groups in other domains as well (e.g., Horwitz & Horwitz, 2007; Levine & Moreland, 1998; Schulz-Hardt et al., 2002; van Knippenberg & Schippers, 2007).

Like the value of different personalities, the value of group diversity depends greatly on the task (Laughlin, 1980; Steiner, 1972). Group heterogeneity helps on tasks in which a group needs only *one* member to get the correct answer. More generally, heterogeneous groups seem to do best on tasks requiring new solutions, flexibility, and quick adjustments to changing conditions (e.g., Nemeth, 1992). For example, scientists—whose jobs require innovation and creativity—perform better when their collaborators span a wider range of scientific disciplines (Pelz, 1956). Similarly, management teams whose members have different kinds of expertise and educational backgrounds are more innovative (Bantel & Jackson, 1989; Wiersema & Bantel, 1992).

This is not to say that diversity comes without costs. Diversity in experience can often hurt performance on tasks in which groups succeed only if *each* of their members performs his or her role well. Moreover, business teams varying widely in personalities, values, or backgrounds often have high turnover (Cohen & Bailey, 1997; McCain et al., 1983), and communication within highly diverse groups tends to be less frequent and more formal (Zenger & Lawrence, 1989). The benefits of heterogeneous groups must be weighed, then, against their costs.

CULTURAL DIVERSITY AND GROUP PERFORMANCE   The issue of group heterogeneity has crucial implications for today's U.S. workplaces, which are becoming more demographically diverse each year. As of 2013, 47% of U.S. workers were women, and about 32% were ethnic minorities (U.S. Department of Labor, 2014). Moreover, ethnic minorities provide a large proportion of the growth in the labor market. Given that today's businesses are more culturally diverse and more likely to operate globally, it is important to understand how cultural diversity influences business productivity.

Like other kinds of diversity, cultural diversity can have both advantages and disadvantages for group productivity (e.g., van Knippenberg, De Dreu, & Homan, 2004). On the plus side, research demonstrates that white students think about race-relevant and social-policy issues in more complex and thorough ways when they anticipate interacting in racially diverse groups (Antonio et al., 2004; Sommers, Warp, & Mahoney, 2008). Moreover, culturally diverse groups may generate a wider range of solutions to problems, especially if the diversity is related to the task (McLeod & Lobel, 1992).

As we saw earlier, however, diversity can have costs. These costs may be especially great when the diversity is racial or ethnic. People tend to be prejudiced against members of other racial and ethnic groups and often don't understand them very well. As a consequence, racially and ethnically diverse workplaces may be prone to communication problems and a lack of cohesion.

This need not be the case. Warren Watson, Kamalesh Kumar, and Larry Michaelsen (1993) created four- and five-member student work teams as part of an upper-level management course. About half of these teams were homogeneous, consisting only of white Americans. The remaining teams were culturally diverse, consisting of a white American, a black American, a Hispanic American, and a foreign national from a country in Asia, Latin America, Africa, or the Middle East (the five-member diverse teams had an additional Hispanic American or foreign national). The teams were challenged to generate solutions to four different business problems over the course of a semester. As Figure 12.5 reveals, the diverse groups initially had problems: Their performance was worse than that of the homogeneous groups and they had more difficulty getting along. As the semester wore on, however, the members of the diverse groups learned

Figure 12.5 Overcoming the potential difficulties of cultural diversity

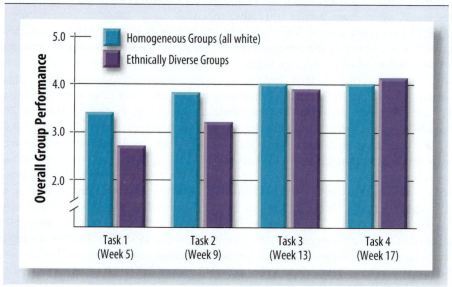

In a study of management students assigned to work together in either ethnically homogeneous (all white) or ethnically diverse groups, researchers found that diverse groups initially had problems getting along with one another and performed relatively poorly. By the end of the semester, however, these problems had disappeared, and performance had improved considerably.

Source: Data from Watson, W. E., Kumar, K., & Michaelsen, L. K. (1993). Cultural diversity's impact on interaction process and performance: Comparing homogeneous and diverse task groups. *Academy of Management Journal, 36,* 590–602. Table 2.

how to work with one another and, by the last assignment, were getting along as well as members of the homogeneous groups. More important, their overall performance was also as good by this last assignment.

These findings suggest that culturally diverse groups can overcome their initial difficulties and become more productive if they have sufficient motivation and opportunity. The benefits of cultural diversity can be great, if managers find ways to improve group communication, coordination, commitment, and cohesion.

INVESTIGATION

Think about a "task group" you recently worked with. Given what you now know about group productivity, what would you do next time to increase the group's effectiveness?

Quick Quiz

1 Which of the following is a strategy to decrease social loafing?

    a. Make each group member's contributions identifiable
    b. Try to increase the interpersonal cohesiveness of your group
    c. Recruit group members who tend toward being collectivistic in their interpersonal orientation
    d. All of the above

2 People in _____ societies tend to participate in performance groups more than those in _____ societies.

    a. collectivistic, individualistic
    b. individualistic, collectivistic
    c. egalitarian, individualistic
    d. hierarchical, individualistic

3 Effective problem-solving teams should typically consist of _____.

    a. At least one member who's agreeable and tolerant
    b. At least one member who is not achievement motivated and energetic
    c. Both of the above
    d. Neither of the above; effectiveness is not connected to individual group members' motivations

4 Group _____ helps on tasks in which a group needs only one member to get the correct answer, whereas group _____ is beneficial when group success depends on whether each of its members performs his or her role well.

    a. collectivism, individualism

    b. individualism, collectivism

    c. heterogeneity, homogeneity

    d. homogeneity, heterogeneity

Making Accurate Decisions

LO 12.6 Define *transactive memory* and discuss how it might contribute to effective group decisions.

LO 12.7 Describe the circumstances that increase (a) *group polarization,* (b) *minority influence*, and (c) *groupthink.*

Groups often possess a great deal of useful information. Even small, casual circles of friends can be extremely informative. They can recommend good pizza parlors, interesting psychology courses, or lucrative investment opportunities. They can tell you whether your political views are based on faulty information or whether you are as attractive, smart, and creative as you think you are.

Just as working with others can help with physical tasks, cooperating with others can help with cognitive, decision-making tasks (Laughlin, Carey, & Kerr, 2008). The advantages of cognitive cooperation grow larger as the tasks become more difficult for individual decision makers (Frings et al., 2008; Wilson, Timmel, & Miller, 2004), and when group members freely share information with one another (e.g., Resnick et al., 1991; Stasser, 1992; Thompson, Levine, & Messick, 1999; Tindale & Sheffen, 2002). Consider the top officers of any corporation. One may be an expert in manufacturing, another in marketing, and yet others in finance, sales, or the law. Because of this, chief executive officers—the bosses in charge—need not be experts themselves on everything. Rather, they just need to have access to people who possess the relevant knowledge and are willing to share it. In social psychological terms, a stable, well-functioning corporation has a **transactive memory**: knowledge located within the minds of its individual members and ways to spread it through communication (Wegner, 1987, 1995). Many groups have transactive memories, each possessing more knowledge as a group than any individual member has alone (e.g., Austin, 2003; Littlepage et al., 2008; Wegner, Erber, & Raymond, 1991; Zhang et al., 2007).

Because a transactive memory provides such rich information, group decisions can be more accurate than individual decisions. An experiment conducted by Larry Michaelsen, Warren Watson, and Robert Black (1989) illustrates this nicely. Students in 25 organizational behavior classes were assigned to small teams to work on various problems over the semester. In addition, students took six exams, first as individuals and then, after they had turned in their answer sheets, as a group. Both individual and group test scores contributed to students' course grades. Not only did the groups score higher than their average individual members but they also scored higher than their *best* individual members. Indeed, in only 3 of the 222 groups did the best member outperform the group. In certain circumstances, then, virtually all members gain from the group's knowledge (Watson et al., 1991).

Of course, groups don't always lead their members to make better decisions. Sometimes groups just don't possess accurate information. Moreover, useful information doesn't always get shared effectively, even when someone in the group does have it (Sargis & Larson, 2002; Wittenbaum & Stasser, 1996). Finally, even when knowledge is effectively shared within a group, that information may still be processed in a biased, unsatisfactory manner. Like individuals thinking alone, for example, groups may favor information confirming their initial views (Brownstein, 2003; Frey & Schulz-Hardt, 2001; Kray & Galinsky, 2003). Later, we explore how being in a group influences how people make decisions. First, however, we consider the factors in the person and the situation that lead people to use groups as sources of information and as aids to decision making.

Transactive memory A group memory system made up of (1) the knowledge held by individual group members and (2) a communication network for sharing this knowledge among the members.

From café society to the Internet. Just as writers and artists of nineteenth-century Paris gathered to share, discuss, and critique their art and the trends of the time, students today gather in "cyberspace" to share, discuss, and critique areas of current interest.

PERSON The Need to Know

Individuals with a thirst for knowledge often quench it in groups. Indeed, there are thousands of groups and organizations dedicated to providing information. Interested people gather in study groups to prepare for upcoming exams, in investment clubs to pool financial analyses, and in astronomy clubs to share notes on the cosmos. The computer revolution has created an explosion of chat rooms, blogs, and websites such as Facebook. Reminiscent of European "café society," where interested people would gather to discuss art, philosophy, literature, and the events of the day, cyber-groups now gather on the Internet to discuss topics of common interest. People who "need to know" often seek answers in groups.

This need to know may go well beyond intellectual curiosity. A person facing a lifetime illness, for example, may turn to a self-help support group for information. Although such groups can serve other functions—such as providing emotional support or friendship—some people join these groups primarily for information. A study of gay men who have HIV/AIDS, for example, revealed that a significant subset of members stopped attending meetings when their support groups stopped providing new information (Sandstrom, 1996).

SITUATION Uncertain Circumstances

Uncertain circumstances activate this need to know in most of us. It's not difficult to place yourself in the following scene: As your appointment nears its end, your physician reenters the examination room looking concerned and says, "I've got bad news. You have a brain tumor and need neurosurgery." In shock, you ask a few questions but, in the days that follow, new ones relentlessly interrupt your thoughts. You wonder what the operation will be like and how it's going to feel afterward. You wonder whether your fears are reasonable or whether you are overreacting. Faced with uncertainty, you want information.

A series of classic studies by Stanley Schachter (1959) investigated whether uncertain situations increase the desire to affiliate with others. Experimental participants anticipated electrical shocks that were either "quite painful" (the high-fear condition) or "not in any way painful" (the low-fear condition). While the equipment was ostensibly being readied, participants were allowed to choose whether to wait alone or with others. The high-fear participants generally preferred waiting with others, as long as the others were in the same boat—that is, as long as they were also waiting to be shocked. As Schachter put it, "misery doesn't love just any kind of company, it loves only miserable company" (p. 24). He proposed that this preference served an informational goal for his experimental participants: By being with these potentially "miserable" others and observing their behaviors, the fearful subjects could assess whether their own fears were reasonable. Uncertain circumstances motivate people to seek information from others—to engage in the *social comparison* processes (Festinger, 1954) we have explored in various chapters of this textbook.

As we discussed in Chapter 7, people facing uncertainty also want to know exactly what the upcoming event is going to be like. As a result, they often prefer to group themselves not just with others who are in the same boat but with those who have already completed the journey—those who have already experienced the event and who can thus reveal to them what lies ahead (e.g., Kirkpatrick & Shaver, 1988; Kulik & Mahler, 1989).

INTERACTION Discussion and Decision Making

We've seen that groups can provide people with information useful for making important decisions. For many decisions, however, information alone is not enough. Fortunately, groups can help in a second way—by providing opportunities to discuss the available information and ways of using it. Depending on a host of interacting factors, group discussions can influence individuals' decisions in various ways.

MAJORITY INFLUENCE AND GROUP POLARIZATION The issue of "same-sex marriage"—of whether homosexuals should be able to legally marry—is a controversial topic of conversation. Let's say you hadn't yet formed a strong opinion when you found yourself sitting with 10 friends or dorm-mates discussing the issue. Let's also say that seven of them believed that same-sex couples should be able to legally marry, whereas three of them thought they shouldn't be able to do so (this is about the actual ratio of supporters to nonsupporters among 18- to 39-year-olds; Washington Post-ABC News National Poll, 2014). We discussed in Chapter 5 how our desires to be accurate and to receive social approval often push our beliefs and attitudes toward the majority view (Wolf & Latané, 1985). The odds are pretty good, then, that your personal opinion would have shifted at least a little bit toward the pro-marriage side of the issue.

You wouldn't have been alone. The opinions of your friends would probably have shifted further toward the pro-marriage end of the continuum as well, resulting in what social psychologists call **group polarization**: After discussing an issue, the average judgment of group members tends to become more extreme than it was prior to the discussion (Brauer, Judd, & Jacquelin, 2001; Isenberg, 1986; Lamm & Myers, 1978). Because the members of your hypothetical group were, on average, pro–gay marriage prior to the discussion, they would likely become, on average, more extremely pro–gay marriage afterward (see Figure 12.6).

Early researchers observed that discussions led group members to make riskier decisions than they would as individuals, a phenomenon they labeled the *risky shift* (e.g., Stoner, 1961; Wallach et al., 1962). Subsequent studies discovered, however, that this shift toward risky decisions occurs only

Group polarization Occurs when group discussion leads members to make decisions that are more extremely on the side of the issue that the group initially favored.

Figure 12.6   The polarizing effects of group discussion

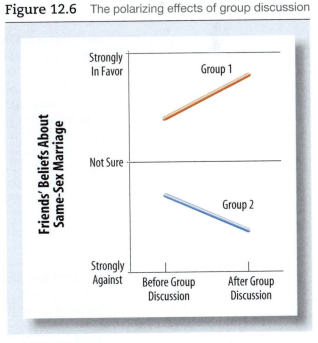

If one group of friends believes, on average, that same-sex marriage ought to be legal, they will believe so even more strongly after discussing it among themselves. In contrast, if a second group of friends believes, on average, that same-sex marriage ought to be illegal, they will be even less enthusiastic about it after discussing it among themselves.

Discussing same-sex marriage with similarly opinioned others.
What's your opinion of same-sex marriage? If you found yourself in a group of like-minded folks, how might your opinion change? Research on group polarization reveals that discussing issues with others who hold similar views often makes one's own views more extreme than they were prior to the conversation.

when the initial group tendency is toward risk taking; when the initial tendency favors caution, discussion leads to especially cautious decisions (e.g., Knox & Safford, 1976; Wallach et al., 1962). Group discussion thus *polarizes* decisions about risk. And it polarizes other kinds of decisions as well. Groups of relatively prejudiced individuals become even more prejudiced after discussing racial issues (Myers & Bishop, 1970), groups of moderately pro-feminist women become even more pro-feminist following discussion (Myers, 1975), and so on. Discussion exaggerates and enhances the group's pre-discussion views.

Why might this be? First, members of groups are likely to hear more arguments favoring the group inclination than arguments opposing it. If most of the people in your group favor same-sex marriage, you are going to hear a lot of arguments supporting it. Some of these arguments will be persuasive and new to you, pushing you further in the pro–gay marriage direction. Of course, others in the group will also hear new arguments favoring gay marriage, so they, too, will move even further toward that position. As a result of this *persuasive arguments* process, the group view, on the whole, becomes more extreme than it was prior to the discussion (e.g., Burnstein & Vinokur, 1977).

Second, discussion also illuminates the group norm. In your hypothetical group of friends, for instance, you would probably discover quite early the norm favoring same-sex marriage. If you liked the members of the group and were motivated to gain their positive regard, you would be tempted to shift your judgments toward theirs. Moreover, people tend to feel better about themselves when they compare favorably to others, and the group discussion provides a wonderful opportunity to boost yourself and social regard by adopting a strong position favoring same-sex marriage. After all, if the group supports same-sex marriage, you could become an even more treasured member of the group by becoming even more favorable toward it. If most group members are similarly motivated, the overall group position could quickly become extremely pro–gay marriage as each member tries to gain even more of the valued pro–gay marriage position. Through *social comparison* processes, too, then, groups tend to polarize during discussion (Baron & Roper, 1976; Blascovich et al., 1975; Goethals & Zanna, 1979; Myers, 1978).

The power of the majority to sway opinion probably accounted for the extremely aggressive deal making and accounting practices that eventually led to the demise of Enron. Enron hired individuals who believed in their "new way" of making money, and the norm they created became polarized as employees were exposed to one another's views. In the culture of Enron, where being among the best brought huge financial rewards, the desire to compare favorably was strong, leading to ever more risky deals and ever more "creative" accounting practices.

MINORITY INFLUENCE As we've just seen, and as we've seen throughout the book, the beliefs and attitudes of the majority can powerfully influence the judgments of others. But what about those who hold different, minority views? Don't they sometimes influence others? What about the views of those at Enron and WorldCom who believed that their business practices could harm their companies greatly? Or of those at the FBI who believed that the information about Zacarias Moussaoui warranted a thorough investigation? Were these individuals influential?

Minority influence is difficult to accomplish, for several reasons. First, opinion minorities are generally less able to exert social pressures on others. Because there

Minority influence Occurs when opinion minorities persuade others of their views.

are fewer of them, those in the minority can't provide as much social acceptance, and threaten as much social isolation, as can those in the majority. Indeed, at Enron, those who argued against the predominant view were generally either ignored or transferred to departments where they'd be less trouble. Second, as we discussed in Chapter 6, opinions expressed by larger numbers of people gain credibility and validity. "If most of my coworkers believe that this is the way to run a twenty-first-century business," an Enron employee might think, "perhaps it really *is* the right way to go."

Without the sway of the crowd on their side, individuals who want to convince others of minority opinions must marshall high-quality arguments and come across as especially credible. Consistent with this, opinion minorities are most persuasive when

- *They hold steadily to their views* (Maass & Clark, 1984; Moscovici et al., 1969). By consistently espousing their opinions, minorities demonstrate that these views are clearly convincing to them and should be to others as well. People presenting minority positions are especially persuasive when they are seen persisting in their view despite being harassed for doing so (Baron & Bellman, 2007).
- *They once held the majority position* (e.g., Clark, 1990; Levine & Ranelli, 1978). After all, "if *she* became convinced that the majority view was mistaken," one might think, "maybe there's something to it."
- *They're willing to compromise a bit.* Even while holding steadily to their views, minorities who are willing to negotiate will come across as reasonable and non-rigid (Mugny, 1982). Because no view is perfect, we find individuals who are rigid in their beliefs less credible and thus are persuaded less by them.
- *They have at least some support from others* (e.g., Asch, 1955; Clark, 2001; Gordijn et al., 2002; Mullen, 1983). Several individuals holding a minority position are more influential than a lone voice of dissent, partially because several dissenters can't be as easily dismissed as "out of touch."
- *They present their views as compatible with the majority view but as just a bit "ahead of the curve"* (e.g., Maass et al., 1982; Paicheler, 1977). By pointing out that their views are "in the same ballpark" as views held by most group members, opinion minorities make it easier for others to shift their opinions.
- *The audience wants to make an accurate decision.* This is when the audience will pay closest attention to the *quality* of arguments the two sides present (Laughlin & Ellis, 1986).

Even when minorities are persuasive, however, their influences may remain indirect or hidden (e.g., Crano & Seyranian, 2007; Gardikiotis, 2011). For instance, even when people are privately swayed by minority arguments, they may still go along with the majority in public (Maass & Clark, 1984). Why? By concealing their shifts toward the minority view, individuals may avoid social disapproval. In addition, movement toward the minority view doesn't always take the form of a dramatic, all-or-nothing conversion. Although well-presented minority arguments may not be immediately convincing, however, they do lead people to reassess their views and think harder and more creatively about the issues (e.g., DeDreu & West, 2001; Martin et al., 2002; Nemeth et al., 1990). Over time, this reevaluation may lead people to shift their opinions. Moreover, once shifted, opinions created via minority influence appear to be especially resistant to subsequent change (Martin, Hewstone, & Martin, 2008).

We see, then, that a host of interacting factors within group discussions influence members' decisions. Majority views are powerful, especially when people are worried about social approval, when the majority is big, or when people are making decisions about opinion rather than fact. In contrast, because people who hold minority views are less able to rely on the powers of social reward and punishment, they face an uphill battle: They must have strong arguments to make, *and* present these arguments credibly, *and* have an audience motivated to find the best answer.

Bridging Theory and Application:
Majority and Minority Influence in the Jury Room

Imagine for a moment that you're a prosecuting attorney about to present your closing arguments to a 12-person jury. To get a conviction, you need a unanimous verdict. How many jurors do you need to convince?

If you answered 12, you're formally correct; unanimity means "everyone agrees," and there are 12 members of this jury. In reality, however, a prosecuting attorney's case is a bit easier than that. Although estimates vary, a prosecutor who is able to convince just eight of the twelve jurors has as much as a 90% chance to win a conviction (Davis et al., 1975; Kalven & Zeisel, 1966; MacCoun & Kerr, 1988). How could this be?

What you need to remember is that the jury is a group—a group that deliberates before rendering its decision. Although jurors come to immediate consensus in around 30% of cases, the remaining 70% of decisions require conversation and debate (Kalven & Zeisel, 1966). And, like members of other decision-making groups, jurors try to persuade one another. So

The near-fiction of the lone, but persuasive, holdout.
Cultural myths and popular fiction bring us the rational and fiercely independent dissenter, able to withstand the arguments and pressures of the majority to persuade them of the truth, as Henry Fonda's character did in *Twelve Angry Men*. In reality, however, such steadfastness is unusual. Only in limited circumstances do single individuals holding minority views successfully convert majority members to their cause.

even when prosecuting attorneys can convince only eight jurors, they can be pretty confident that their side will be represented well in the jury room. After all, opinion majorities are powerful: Given their numerical advantage, they possess not only a greater arsenal of persuasive arguments but also the powers of social pressure.

Of course, majority views don't always win out. As the relative size of the minority faction increases, so does its resistance to majority influence and its ability to influence majority jurors (e.g., Tindale et al., 1990). Moreover, because jurors tend to exhibit a *leniency bias*—a greater willingness to acquit defendants than to convict them—a minority of jurors standing on the "not guilty" side of the issue has a somewhat easier time than does a minority voting to convict (MacCoun & Kerr, 1988; Tindale & Davis, 1983). Nonetheless, the power of minority jurors isn't great, and two legal trends appear to decrease it even further. First, in many jurisdictions, juries are getting smaller—down to as few as six members. This makes it more likely that a juror holding a minority position will be alone in his or her views, and we know that lone jurors are less able to hold fast to their positions (Kerr & MacCoun, 1985; Saks, 1977). Second, some courts no longer require juries to reach unanimous decisions but instead allow verdicts based on only three-quarters or two-thirds agreement. In such circumstances, jurors in the majority have less reason to take minority positions seriously (Hastie, Penrod, & Pennington, 1983; Kerr et al., 1976). The prospects of jurors holding minority views are not good.

Counter to the idealized notion that jury verdicts emerge from group discussion, then, we see instead that they are often determined before deliberations begin. When even a small majority of jurors initially shares a preferred verdict, it's very likely that the group's ultimate verdict will unanimously go that way. And the likelihood that a single disagreeing juror will persuade the rest toward his or her view is quite slim. In the classic film *Twelve Angry Men*, Henry Fonda plays a dedicated juror who converts all 11 others to his minority opinion. In North American cultures, we presume that a lone, rational juror will likewise stand fast against mistaken colleagues and perhaps even convert them to the truth. After all, jurors are the keepers of justice. Alas, such individuals are more likely to be found on your local movie screen than in your local courtroom.

GROUPTHINK AND DEFECTIVE DISCUSSION   The jury system exists because people believe that, through discussion, a group of individuals can better sift through the evidence to find truth and justice. Corporations and governmental agencies form managerial teams because they believe that, through discussion, such groups can create more effective business strategies. People discuss important problems with groups of friends because they believe that doing so leads to better personal decisions.

Unfortunately, groups don't always make better decisions than individuals. This is partly because discussion isn't always *discussion* as we like to think of it—as an open, thoughtful sharing of information and viewpoints. Irving Janis (1972, 1983) reviewed the history of presidential decision fiascoes, including John F. Kennedy's decision to launch the ill-fated Bay of Pigs attack on Cuba and Richard Nixon's decision to cover up the bungled Watergate break-in. Janis suggested that these and other disastrous decisions shared certain common features. Most fundamentally, these decisions were characterized by what he labeled **groupthink**—a style of making group decisions driven more by members' desires to get along than by their desires to evaluate potential solutions realistically. When group members feel strong pressure to agree with one another—to reach consensus—they often fail to engage each other in effective discussion (e.g., Postmes, Spears, & Cihangir, 2001; Quinn & Schlenker, 2002). This can lead to avoidable mistakes.

Figure 12.7 illustrates how certain characteristics of the group and circumstances can lead members to turn their focus toward agreeing with one another and maintaining group collegiality, which, in turn, can lead to poor decisions. For example, when powerful leaders reveal their own views at the beginning of the discussion, group

Figure 12.7 When group discussion interferes with good decision making

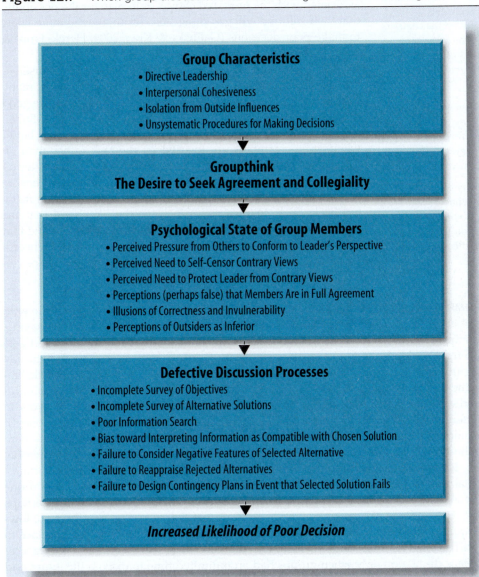

Inspired by Janis's (1972, 1983) classic research on "groupthink," social and decision scientists understand more about how the desire for group agreement can create discussion processes harmful to good decision making.

Source: Adapted from Janis, I. L., & Mann, L. (1977). Decision making: A psychological analysis of conflict, choice, and commitment. New York: Free Press.

Groupthink A style of group decision making characterized by a greater desire among members to get along and agree with one another than to generate and critically evaluate alternative viewpoints and positions.

Deadly decision making? Its wing badly damaged, the shuttle Columbia disintegrated upon re-entry into the earth's atmosphere, killing all seven astronauts aboard. The investigation into the disaster focused not only on technical failures of the shuttle but also on failures of the decision-making culture at NASA. Effective decision making requires a serious consideration of alternative views. In light of this, consider an investigator's interview with the chairwoman of the mission management team—the manager who overruled the request for satellite photos of the wing, which a group of lower-level engineers suspected had been damaged during lift-off:

Investigator: "As a manager, how do you seek out dissenting opinions?"
Manager: "Well, when I hear about them . . ."
Investigator: "By their very nature you may not hear about them . . . what techniques do you use to get them?"

She had no answer (Langewiesche, 2003, p. 82).

Would the detection of the damage have enabled a successful rescue of the astronauts? This issue is still in dispute. What's not in dispute is that, without the photographs that would have revealed the gaping damage to the wing, the astronauts never had a chance.

members are less likely to engage in the kinds of critical discussion needed to ferret out bad ideas (e.g., McCauley, 1989; Mullen et al., 1994; Shafer & Crichlow, 1996; Tetlock et al., 1992). Each of the cases we've discussed here—Enron, WorldCom, and the FBI—seem to have suffered from this problem: The preferences of the leaders were well known, and they appeared to have stifled debate among lower-level managers and agents, with calamitous results.

Moreover, when people make collaborative decisions in groups, as compared to alone, they are more likely to ignore information from outside the group (Minson & Mueller, 2012). And as group members get overconfident and begin to believe (perhaps falsely) that everyone agrees on the proper course of action, their discussions fall prey to a variety of defective processes (Tetlock et al., 1992). They fail to consider their objectives thoroughly, to survey alternative solutions, to examine the risks associated with the preferred choice, or to plan for the possibility that their solution will go wrong. As a result, they're more likely to make poor decisions (Galinsky & Kray, 2004; Herek, Janis, & Huth, 1987).

We see, then, that group discussions in and of themselves don't lead individuals to make better decisions. Rather, many factors *interact* to determine when group discussions create good decisions and when they create poor decisions (Aldag & Fuller, 1993; De Dreu et al., 2008; Whyte, 1989). Decisions are better when group members are focused on the task rather than on social harmony, when leaders encourage people to air alternative perspectives, and when groups have procedures to ensure that members critically evaluate all proposals and gather outside feedback. Such characteristics increase the likelihood that the group members will share the best available knowledge and that the perspectives of dissenting minority members will be heard. Under such circumstances, the information value of groups can be great indeed.

COMPUTER-MEDIATED DECISION MAKING More than ever, people communicate with one another via computer—through e-mail, live chat rooms, and instant messaging. Computer-mediated communication is not limited, however, to seeking the latest gossip from a friend, staying in touch with distant family members, or making Saturday night plans. Rather, it's used in organizations each day to bring groups of people "together" to make important decisions. The benefits of computer-mediated communication would seem obvious: By electronically connecting decision makers who work in different offices, cities, or even countries, businesses can save the time and money it would take to get everyone together in the same room. Indeed, corporations have spent billions of dollars creating and upgrading their computer systems, for this very reason.

Is this money well spent? If one is concerned about saving money on airfares, hotel rooms, meal allowances, and rental cars, perhaps the answer is *yes*. But if one is concerned about the quality of decisions that group members are making, perhaps not: The findings of a meta-analytic review suggest that groups generally make lower-quality decisions when communicating via computer than when speaking face to face (Baltes et al., 2002). Indeed, computer-mediated discussion worked as well as face-to-face discussion only when groups had an unlimited time to discuss the issues and were able to do so anonymously. Of course, because groups usually have to make decisions within a constrained time frame, and rarely discuss important issues anonymously, these exceptions may be of little consolation to those paying the bills.

So should these companies rip out their computer cables and send their decision makers back out on the road? Not so fast! Communication technologies are evolving at a fast rate, and experimental research into computer-mediated communication is still a young endeavor. Nonetheless, it's not yet clear that such technologies will, on their own, lead to decision making that is better than that found in face-to-face discussions.

INVESTIGATION

Think about a decision-making group you've recently been a part of. Given what you now know about group decision-making processes, what would you do next time to increase the quality of the group's decisions?

Quick Quiz

1 Which of the following is a reason that people seek out groups?
  a. To gain information by observing the behavior of people who are going through the same experience
  b. To gain knowledge from people with similar interests
  c. To glean information that will reduce feelings of uncertainty
  d. All of the above

2 Which of the following is NOT a factor that contributes to group polarization?
  a. Group members tend to hear more arguments supporting the majority view and thus are more likely to be authentically persuaded.
  b. Group members may try to make themselves look good by adopting a more extreme version of the group's preferred position.
  c. Group members in individualistic cultures don't want to appear like they're conforming to the majority so they will often polarize toward the minority view.
  d. None of the above

3 Which of the following factors helps make opinion minorities more persuasive?
  a. They display strength by showing unwillingness to compromise.
  b. They have at least some support from others.
  c. They present their views as incompatible with the majority view.
  d. The audience is not too concerned about making an accurate decision.

4 Which of the following techniques help counteract groupthink?
  a. Make group members interpersonally focused rather than task focused.
  b. Leaders reveal their own views at the beginning of the discussion rather than at the end.
  c. Insulate group members from criticism and outside feedback so as not to stifle the creative process.
  d. None of the above

Gaining Positions of Leadership

LO 12.8 Discuss the factors that determine (a) who wants to lead, (b) who is chosen to lead, and (c) who is an effective leader.

LO 12.9 Discuss how gender influences (1) whether one seeks leadership, (2) who gets chosen to lead, and (3) leadership effectiveness.

It seems clear why groups would want, even need, leaders. As they grow in size, groups tend to become unwieldy and disorganized. To combat this, groups select individuals to lead—to coordinate the group's multiple tasks, to channel relevant information appropriately, to inspire members to achieve the group's goals, and so on. Indeed, leadership is so important that all known societies have leaders as part of their social organizations (Van Vugt, 2006).

What is perhaps less clear is why people would *want* to lead. Leaders must invest large amounts of their time, take responsibility for the group's outcomes, and sometimes even put their personal security and life on the line. Prime ministers, presidents, and popes have all been targeted by assassins in recent years. Even when they're not

Table 12.1 The Top Ten Compensation Packages for Leaders of Major Corporations, 2012			
2012 Total Compensation			
1. Lawrence Ellison *Oracle*	$96.2 million	6. Richard Bracken *HCA*	$38.6 million
2. Robert A. Kotick *Activision Blizzard*	$64.9 million	7. Robert A. Iger *Walt Disney*	$37.1 million
3. Leslie Moonves *CBS*	$60.3 million	8. Paul A. Ricci *Nuance Communications*	$37.1 million
4. David M. Zaslav *Discovery Communications*	$49.9 million	9. Marissa A. Mayer *Yahoo*	$36.6 million
5. James Q. Crowe *Level 3 Communications*	$40.7 million	10. Mark G. Parker *Nike*	$35.2 million

Source: "Executive Pay by the Numbers," *The New York Times*, 6/29/13, available at http://www.nytimes.com/interactive/2013/06/30/business/executive-compensation-tables.html?_r=0

being shot at, leaders are often subjected to a barrage of criticisms, complaints, and personal intrusions.

If the costs of leadership are so great, why would anyone want the job? The simple answer is that the rewards of leadership are also great. When groups are successful, their leaders gain a great deal of personal satisfaction for a job well done. Moreover, groups tend to distribute many resources to their leaders, compensating them not only with recognition and high social status but also with the more material rewards of larger salaries, special business opportunities, and the like. Consider the case of Lawrence Ellison, CEO of Oracle, who was compensated in 2012 to the tune of $96 million ("Executive Pay by the Numbers," 2013). As Table 12.1 reveals, others in similar positions are compensated nicely as well; in fact, in 2004 the average CEO earned 430 *times* the wage of the average worker. Even people in small leadership positions—an assistant manager at a fast food restaurant, the president of a sorority—receive social or financial benefits greater than those received by individuals lower in the group's status hierarchy. When asked why he robbed banks, ace criminal Willie Sutton gave a straightforward answer: "Because that's where the money is." Why do people want to become leaders? To a large extent, the same holds: Because that's where the money and social status are.

For some people, acquiring the fruits of leadership is a primary reason for belonging to groups: They join (or create) groups so they may have followers to lead and resources to acquire. For others, however, gaining the benefits of leadership is only a secondary goal of group membership: People may first join a group to get things done, to acquire useful information, or to gain emotional support, but once inside they may see the benefits that accrue to leaders and pursue such positions for themselves.

We explore here two primary issues: (1) Who becomes a leader, and why? That is, what person and situation factors trigger an individual's desire to seek leadership, and what factors lead a group to accept that individual as its leader? And (2) when are leaders effective? When are they able to motivate their groups to follow their direction and perform well?

PERSON Who Wants to Lead?

Because leadership has significant costs as well as benefits, it makes sense that not everyone aspires to leadership (Anderson et al., 2012). What kind of person, then, is motivated to lead?

Leadership provides power and status, enables goal achievement, and is a sign of accomplishment. Logically, then, people ought to seek leadership when they are ambitious—when they have a strong desire to exercise power over others or when they have a strong urge to do great things (McClelland, 1984; Winter, 1973). *The need for power* is the desire to attain prestige, status, and influence over others. For example, as measured by their own public statements and the judgments of biographers, U.S. Presidents Harry S. Truman and John F. Kennedy rated particularly high in the need for power (Simonton, 1994), and such presidents have been more likely to lead the country into military conflict (Winter, 1987). In contrast, *achievement motivation*, introduced in Chapter 4, is the desire to do something exceptionally well for its own sake (McClelland, 1984). Jimmy Carter and Herbert Hoover were the presidents judged highest in the need for achievement, and achievement-oriented presidents are more likely to initiate new legislation or try out innovative approaches to leadership. Regardless of whether they are driven by power or achievement, however, leaders tend to be highly ambitious (Hogan & Hogan, 1991; Sorrentino & Field, 1986).

An exceptional leader. As CEO of online marketplace eBay, Meg Whitman led her company to huge financial heights and popularity. She proved herself exceptional in another way, too: Countering Thomas Carlyle's dictum that "the history of the world is but the biography of great men" (1841; in Simonton, 1994), Whitman burst through the "glass ceiling" into the top echelon of mostly male business leaders. As we'll soon learn, the fact that female leaders are relatively rare does not mean they are ineffective.

Ambition is not enough, however. Indeed, we all know individuals who have lofty ambitions who never ascend to positions of leadership. Beyond their ambitions, leaders tend to be highly energetic, which enables them to turn their ambitions into reality (Hogan & Hogan, 1991; Simonton, 1994). The self-made multimillionaire Andrew Carnegie, who ran steel mills and became one of America's great philanthropists, attested to the importance of effort when he observed that the average person "puts only 25 percent of his energy and ability into his work" and that the world "stands on its head for those few and far between souls who devote 100 percent." Systematic studies of leaders in many different fields bear out the importance of both ambition on the one hand and the ability and willingness to work hard on the other (Simonton, 1994).

Finally, it seems that men, in general, are somewhat more interested in becoming leaders than are women (Konrad et al., 2000). For example, in a cross-cultural study of IBM employees in 40 different countries, Hofstede (1980) found that male workers around the world tended to be interested in power, leadership, and self-realization, whereas female workers tended to stress quality of life and relationships between people. The male preference for leadership is no doubt influenced by the ways males and females are socialized (Geis, 1993). For instance, although men with dominant personalities tend to seek leadership positions more than do similarly dominant women, such women are more likely to seek leadership if they first observe a female leader (Carbonell & Castro, 2008). This general male preference may also be linked to a more fundamental sex difference, however: The hormone testosterone, present in higher concentrations in males, motivates competition for status (Mazur & Booth, 1998), as we saw in Chapter 10. Of course, the greater average desire that men have to lead says nothing about how *effective* men and women are as leaders, a topic we consider later.

SITUATION When Opportunity Knocks

What situational factors trigger one's desire to pursue a leadership role? Two seem especially important. The first we call "voids at the top." Leadership opportunities open up when current leaders die or depart the group. They also become available as groups grow larger (Hemphill, 1950; Mullen, Salas, & Driskell, 1989). As more people try to work together, problems of coordination, administration, and communication increase, and members seek leaders to organize them and pull things together. Furthermore, groups cry out for leadership more when they face a crisis than when things are calm (e.g., Helmreich & Collins, 1967). Admiral William Halsey, referring to military leadership during World War II, noted that "there are no great men, only great challenges that ordinary men are forced by circumstances to meet" (Simonton, 1994, 404). Important problems lead groups to call out for leaders, and such calls are more likely to inspire ambitious or responsible individuals.

Second, people sometimes just happen to be well situated for leadership—they're in the right place at the right time. For example, by virtue of being at the center of a communication network or at the head of a table, some individuals have more links to others and are thus more likely to be asked to lead (Forsyth, 1990; Nemeth & Wachtler, 1974). Connections of a more personal sort are also important. Indeed, many would argue that "it's not what you know, but who you know" that determines getting ahead in this world. Whether it be the son of Enron CEO Kenneth Lay getting a cushy job at his father's company, or the sons of former President George H. W. Bush and Senator Albert Gore Sr. having the opportunity to run against each other for U.S. president in 2000, connections matter.

INTERACTION **Who Gets to Lead?**

Before becoming U.S. president, Barack Obama had a vision of how the United States ought to be governed. But so did a lot of other people, and the political ambitions of most never got beyond debating current events with their spouses over supper. Not every energetic individual having a high need for achievement gets to be a president, corporate CEO, or even captain of the local field hockey team. Groups don't give the same opportunity to everyone who wants to lead. Instead, they try to choose individuals who possess the characteristics that fit best with the group's needs (Fiedler, 1993; Hollander, 1993).

People have images and beliefs of what good leaders are like and try to find leaders who fit those images (Chemers, 1997; Lord et al., 1984). First, good leaders are usually seen as possessing relevant skills. Not surprisingly, individuals who are seen as being intelligent or as having high levels of expertise are more likely to be chosen to lead (e.g., Rice et al., 1984; Rubin, Bartels, & Bommer, 2002). Second, good leaders are expected to be invested in the group, which may be why people who speak a lot and participate during group meetings are especially likely to be chosen to lead—even when the quality of their participation isn't particularly high (e.g., Jones & Kelly, 2007; Mullen et al., 1989). Third, group members pick as their leaders individuals whose "styles" seem to fit well with current circumstances. In one experiment, for instance, reminders of death increased people's preferences for charismatic, visionary political candidates—for the kinds of leaders who create a larger sense of meaning for their followers (Cohen et al., 2004).

Finally, in people's minds, leaders have a certain "look" to them. For instance, leaders are expected to have physically mature facial features—narrow eyes, a broad jaw, and an angular face; people with "baby-faced" features—large eyes, a small chin, and a round face—are seen as more submissive and naive, and therefore less well suited for certain kinds of leadership (Zebrowitz, 1994; Zebrowitz et al., 1991). And in U.S. society, the right look also means being tall. For example, the five greatest presidents, according to historians, were Lincoln (6 feet 4 inches), Washington, Jefferson, and Franklin D. Roosevelt (all around 6 feet 2 inches), and Andrew Jackson, the shortest of the bunch at only 6 feet 1 inch (Simonton, 1994). And the shorter of the candidates in U.S. presidential elections since 1900 have won only 13 of the 39 contests.

This tendency to evaluate potential leaders against our stereotyped images of what good leaders are like can have unfortunate consequences, because our images may be shallow and only partially attuned to the characteristics that actually make for effective leadership. For example, otherwise highly qualified individuals who don't fit our images are likely to be passed over for important leadership positions. This may partially explain why women are so underrepresented as leaders (Bartol & Martin, 1986; Hoyt, 2010). It's not simply that men are more motivated to seek positions of leadership, as we discussed before. Rather, women just don't "look" like leaders in the stereotypical sense and so are less likely to be chosen to lead (Eagly & Karau, 2002; Koenig et al., 2011). Indeed, even when highly qualified women step forward as candidates, men are, on average, more likely to win (Eagly & Karau, 1991). As we'll see next, however, these stereotypes of male and female leaders may be misleading.

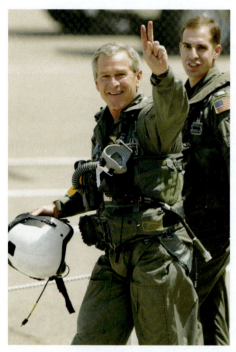

Trying to look the part. During the U.S. war with Iraq, former President George W. Bush donned a Navy flight suit and made a highly televised visit to an aircraft carrier at sea. Understanding that appearances matter, and perhaps cognizant of his own lack of military experience, Bush likely knew that looking the part would enhance his ability to be a wartime leader.

INTERACTION **When Are Leaders Effective?**

Just because a person is a leader doesn't mean he or she is an *effective* leader. Indeed, the histories of nations, corporations, and athletic teams—virtually all kinds of groups—are littered with the ruins of poor leadership. What factors, then, influence whether a leader will successfully move a group toward its goals? The answer depends on how the personal characteristics of the leader mesh with, and engage, the motivations of the group members. Just as people with certain personalities are better equipped for some tasks than for others, some leadership styles are more effective in some groups than are others. Leadership success is thus *contingent* on the group's needs (Fiedler, 1993). For example, workers in conventional occupations (such as accountants) respond well to task-oriented and authoritative leadership, whereas workers in investigative occupations (such as college professors) much prefer to manage themselves (Hogan, Curphy, & Hogan, 1994).

Moreover, as a group's circumstances change, the leader's style usually must change as well if he or she hopes to remain effective (Fiedler, 1993; Hersey & Blanchard, 1982). Whereas new workers tend to appreciate leaders who assign them to clear, structured tasks, more expert workers do not take as well to directive leadership. Finally, whether a particular leadership style is effective may depend on the other resources available to the leader. In a classic early experiment conducted by Kurt Lewin, Ronald Lippitt, and Ralph White (1939; White & Lippitt, 1960), children meeting in groups to work on hobbies were led by adults who adopted either autocratic or democratic leadership styles. The autocratic leaders were instructed to decide dictatorially what the groups would do and how they would do it. The democratic leaders were instructed to encourage the groups to make their own decisions. When the leaders were there to watch over them, groups having autocratic leaders spent more time working than did groups having democratic leaders. Does this mean that a dictatorial leadership style is more effective than a more democratic one? Not necessarily. When the leaders were absent, the groups with autocratic leaders decreased their efforts, whereas the groups with democratic leaders did not. Autocratic leadership may be effective only when leaders can supervise their members closely (see Figure 12.8). The effectiveness of leaders depends on the nature of the task.

Figure 12.8 Autocratic and democratic leadership

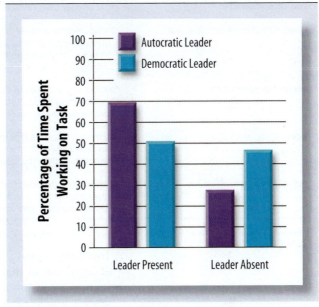

Children working on hobbies were supervised by either autocratic or democratic leaders (Lewin, Lippitt, & White, 1939; White & Lippitt, 1960). Groups assigned to autocratic leaders spent more time working than groups with democratic leaders, but only when their leaders were there to supervise their activities. When their leaders were absent, they drastically decreased their efforts. Autocratic leaders may be effective only when they can keep their group members under close surveillance.

Source: Data from White, R. K., & Lippitt, R. (1960). Autocracy and democracy: An experimental inquiry. New York: Harper & Brothers. p. 65.

TRANSFORMATIONAL LEADERS Leaders can be effective by matching their styles to the needs of the group. There are special exceptions to this rule, however: Some leaders are effective not because they change themselves but because they transform the group (e.g., Bass, 1998; Burns, 1978). Have you ever had a teacher, a coach, or a boss who inspired you to rise above your everyday personal concerns, to put forth your best efforts for the good of your group or even of your whole society? Bernard Bass and Bruce Avolio of the Center for Leadership Studies at the State University of New York began an extensive program of research by addressing a similar question to South African business executives and U.S. Army colonels. From the participants' responses, they developed the Multifactor Leadership Questionnaire (MLQ) and, in the years since, have tested it on numerous groups around the world, including managers in New Zealand, India, and Japan; executives and middle managers in a Fortune 500 firm; and military officers in Canada and Germany. On the basis of this research, they have concluded that there are certain characteristics of leaders that inspire not only high satisfaction among followers but also high productivity (Center for Leadership Studies, 2000). They label individuals who have several of these characteristics **transformational leaders**, because, like John F. Kennedy, Martin Luther King Jr., and even Adolph Hitler, these leaders significantly altered the motivations, outlooks, and behaviors of their followers.

Transformational leadership
Leadership that changes the motivations, outlooks, and behaviors of followers, enabling the group to reach its goals better.

Table 12.2	The Characteristics of Transformational Leadership
The Characteristic	**How Leader Manifests It**
Idealized influence or "charisma"	Communicates a sense of a "joint mission" in followers Expresses dedication to his or her followers Appeals to the hopes and desires of followers Is willing to sacrifice his or her self-gain for the good of the group
Intellectual stimulation	Creates an openness to new ways of thinking Creates a "big picture" that connects different views of the problem Is willing to entertain even seemingly foolish ideas
Inspirational motivation	Convinces followers that they have the ability to accomplish more than they previously thought possible Sets an example for others to strive for Presents an optimistic view of the future
Individualized consideration	Recognizes individual strengths and weaknesses Shows interest in the well-being of others Supports worker's efforts to better themselves on the job

Source: This article was published in Leardership theory and research: Perspectives and directions, M. M. Chemers & R. Ayman, Transformational leardership: A response to critiques, 49-80, Copyright Academic Press (1983).

Transformational leaders are charismatic and engage the aspirations and self-concepts of followers so that the successes of the group become the followers' own personal successes and the leader's mission becomes their own (House & Shamir, 1993). Such leaders intellectually stimulate their followers, getting them to examine their values and approaches to life, and make them feel that they are personally important and have important contributions to make (see Table 12.2). Transformational leaders help group members with diverse sets of skills better take advantage of this potential strength (e.g., Shin & Zhou, 2007). They are also particularly effective when the group faces challenging tasks, uncertainty about its future, or pressures to change (De Hoogh, Den Hartog, & Koopman, 2005; Shamir & Howell, 1999). By creating a psychologically safe climate, they encourage people not to go along with the majority, but instead to propose novel innovations (Nijstad et al., 2012). For example, as we saw in Chapter 2, the difficult challenges faced by African Americans as they sought their civil rights not only called for a transformational leader like Martin Luther King Jr. but also provided a context in which his style of leadership would be particularly effective.

We've seen, then, that leaders can be effective in two general ways: They can fit their styles to the existing needs of the group or they can inspire the group toward their own goals.

GENDER AND LEADERSHIP   For much of history, the division of labor was fairly clear-cut: Women raised the kids, and the men went off "to work." This began to change during World War II, and women now make up nearly 50% of the American workforce. Although women in positions of world leadership and top management are still the exception, more and more women are leading their groups, and this trend is likely to continue. How do women fare in leadership positions? The question has practical importance. If women are as effective as men in leadership roles but are denied access to those roles because they don't match people's images of what a leader should be, then organizations are losing a valuable pool of talent, and women are being unfairly treated.

We learned that leaders tend to be more effective when they match their leadership style to their groups' tasks. With this in mind, Alice Eagly, Steven Karau, and Mona Makhijani (1995) gathered 74 organizational studies and 22 laboratory studies that compared male and female leadership effectiveness. Combining these results using the technique of meta-analysis, they discovered that the average sex difference in leadership was *zero*—men and women did not differ in their effectiveness as leaders. They delved a bit deeper, however, and rated each occupation in terms of its compatibility with the male and female gender role. That is, positions such as grade-school principal were coded as "female," whereas jobs such as drill sergeant were coded as "male." They also rated whether the position required the ability to connect well with others and whether it required an ability to control and influence others. Considering these additional factors, a sex difference emerged from the data: Women were more effective in jobs that were viewed as feminine or that required interpersonal skills; men were more effective in jobs that were viewed as masculine or that required a hard-nosed task orientation.

Eagly and her colleagues (1995) explained their results in terms of *social role theory*. According to this perspective, we are all encouraged to behave in ways that are congruent with culturally defined gender roles. Because the culturally appropriate behavior for a man is to be controlling and directive, men will tend to be particularly effective leaders when the group's task requires someone to ride its members hard. In contrast, because the culturally appropriate behavior for a woman is to be relationship oriented, women will tend to be particularly effective leaders when the group's task requires someone to attend to members' needs and feelings. One team of researchers in Great Britain found that when group members were focused on competition with other groups (other English universities), they chose male leaders. On the other hand, when they were focused on competition and cooperation within their own group, they overwhelmingly chose female leaders (Van Vugt & Spisak, 2008). In this chapter's research video, Prof. Mark Van Vugt of Amsterdam's Free University describes in more detail when people prefer women versus men as group leaders.

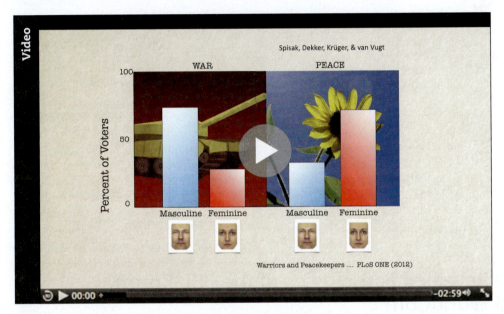

WATCH THE VIDEO: *When do people prefer women as leaders?*

As we saw, transformational leaders can engage the desires and needs of their followers and thereby alter the group's path toward success. Although the differences are relatively small, women leaders tend to exhibit more of this transformational style than do men (Eagly, Johannesen-Schmidt, & Van Engen, 2003). Given the demonstrated effectiveness of transformational leadership, it seems that stereotypes about (ineffective) female leadership are problematically reducing the pool of talented individuals from which groups select their leaders.

In sum, when one takes into account the requirements of the leadership situation, we see that the typically male orientation toward leadership may be more effective for some tasks whereas the typically female orientation toward leadership may be more effective for others. Moreover, because they tend to be somewhat more transformational in style, women may be in a somewhat better position to lead effectively. The bottom line, thus, seems to be this: The most effective leaders—male and female—are those who are able to adjust their strategies as circumstances warrant. Like the emergence of leadership itself, we see that leadership effectiveness is determined by an interaction between the person (the potential leader) and the situation (the group).

INVESTIGATION

Earlier, you recalled "task" and "decision-making" groups you've participated in. Who emerged as the leaders of these groups? Why them and not the others?

Quick Quiz

1 Which of the following person and situation factors increase the likelihood that an individual becomes a leader?

    a. Being male

    b. Being highly ambitious

    c. A void at the top presents a new leadership opportunity

    d. All of the above

2 Which of the following claims about leadership effectiveness is *true*?

    a. Leadership success tends to be independent of a group's specific needs or the nature of the task.

    b. New workers tend to prefer more directive leadership than expert workers.

    c. Groups with autocratic leaders tend to be more productive regardless of whether the group leader is present to supervise their tasks.

    d. None of the above

3 Which of the following claims about transformational leadership is false?

    a. Transformational leaders are better at adapting themselves to fit the group's needs rather than adapting the group to fit their own style.

    b. Transformational leaders inspire followers to feel like the group's successes are also the followers' personal successes.

    c. Transformational leaders help group members with diverse sets of skills better take advantage of this potential strength.

    d. Transformational leadership is particularly effective when a group faces uncertainty about its future.

4 Which of the following claims about gender and leadership is true?

    a. Studies show that men and women do not differ in their effectiveness as leaders.

    b. Men tend to exhibit slightly more transformational leadership than women.

    c. Men are equally effective leaders regardless of whether the group's task requires stereotypically "female" or "male" skills.

    d. All of the above

Revisiting

The Revealed Pathologies of the FBI, Enron, and WorldCom

Enron and WorldCom once sat perched atop the corporate world, and the FBI was respected around the globe for its advanced investigative techniques. What caused the horrible mistakes made by these organizations? How do we explain the actions that eventually destroyed two of them, and badly damaged the reputation of the third?

U.S. president Harry S. Truman kept a small sign on his desk that stated, simply, "The buck stops here." It communicated a straightforward idea: "As leader, I'm ultimately responsible for all that occurs on my watch." Perhaps, then, we should begin our analysis here. After all, leaders have the potential to instill their goals and visions in their followers, to create group norms, and to shape the culture in which their groups make decisions.

Together, Kenneth Lay and Jeffrey Skilling turned Enron into a powerhouse. Lay was the "player" who formed political connections, cultivated powerful people in powerful places, and became a renowned philanthropist. His job was to nurture the magical aura of Enron.

Skilling ran the company from the inside. For the impatient Skilling, every problem had a solution, and every goal could be reached if one were creative and gutsy enough. His brash and competitive style came to characterize the company. If an employee was squeamish about taking risks and unwilling to do what was necessary to get things done, his or her days were numbered. "Losers" would have to leave the fast lane of Enron for the slower pedestrian pace of jobs and lifestyles elsewhere.

There were some advantages to Skilling's approach. In particular, it inspired innovation. Some of the creative ideas he and his protégés generated greatly benefited the energy industry. But there was also a downside: With his emphasis on working on the edge, on creating opportunities where none before existed, there would be inevitable failures. For businesses with reasonable expectations, occasional failures are manageable. But Enron wanted to be the "World's Leading Company," and Skilling couldn't afford failures. So when the economy began to slow, and others started competing more effectively, Enron began to struggle. Fortunately, or so it seemed at the time, a clever financial officer created a new solution (after all, as every good Enron employee knew, every problem has a solution!). He began creating complex "partnerships" to hide Enron's losses, enabling the company's balance sheets to show healthy profits.

A few questioned the appropriateness of this tricky accounting. However, the swashbuckling norm of adventure that Enron had cultivated, combined with the belief that the people of Enron were smarter than those elsewhere, interfered with the organization's ability to accurately assess its risk and make well-reasoned decisions. Moreover, mechanisms of group pressure—"everyone else seems to think it's OK," "I'll be labeled a loser if I'm the one who points out the inappropriateness of it all"—made successful minority influence impossible. Enron soon became an unstable house of cards created by too many risky business ventures and held together only by an increasing number of accounting tricks. And so as Sherron Watkins' internal memo to Kenneth Lay came to public light, Enron quickly collapsed. The power of transformational leadership can yield great things, as charismatic leaders like Martin Luther King Jr. have taught us. But this power can also lead groups down dangerous paths.

WorldCom was also run by a charismatic leader— Bernard Ebbers—who believed that the way to grow in the telecommunications field was to purchase related companies and link them together into ever-larger networks. Indeed, this strategy worked quite well for a while, and WorldCom quickly became an international force. Ebbers, however, valued making his deals more than actually operating the company and providing good customer service, an attitude that filtered its way down through the layers of management. Those who thought differently found little support, and many left the company. And so when there were no more big deals to be made, WorldCom's inefficient operations and unsatisfied customer base made it difficult to meet the elevated investor expectations for profit and growth. Like Enron, WorldCom employed questionable accounting practices to hide its losses. And, as at Enron, when Cynthia Cooper approached WorldCom's board of directors with her suspicions, this once-powerful company, now also a house of cards, collapsed as well. Again, we see how an organization that fails to appreciate dissent and seriously contemplate minority viewpoints can fail in its aims.

The FBI's leadership problem was less an instance of misguided transformational leadership at the top than a lack of control given to agents in the field. The FBI is a highly structured, hierarchical organization—one in which the flow of information and authorization proceeds through pre-ordained, lock-step procedures. Agents were afraid of offending their superiors, who were afraid of offending those above them. As Coleen Rowley stated in her congressional testimony, the hesitation of career-minded agents to make decisions for which they could be later criticized stifled their ability to take direct and quick action. We've seen this pattern all too often: When group members are so concerned with fitting in, getting along, being accepted, or maintaining their

Kenneth Lay of Enron. A jury convicted Lay of ten counts of fraud for his role in the Enron scandal. With recommended sentences of 5 to 10 years for each count, these guilty verdicts were likely to put him in prison for the rest of his life. Lay died of a heart attack prior to sentencing.

positions, the ability of groups to take advantage of one of their strengths—all the information and wisdom that potentially can be shared among its members—is seriously hindered. And so, just as the dissent-muffling decision-making cultures of Enron and WorldCom contributed to their downfalls, the hesitant decision-making culture at FBI headquarters squashed the requests of Rowley's Minneapolis field office to further its investigation of Zacarias Moussaoui.

When the problematic features of the FBI, Enron, and WorldCom cultures came to light, did their well-paid leaders adopt President Truman's rule for themselves and accept responsibility for their groups' failures? Did they take the next step and assume responsibility for curing the pathologies plaguing their organizations? "The buck stops somewhere else," they seemed to be saying.

The buck did indeed stop somewhere else. It stopped at the desks of Coleen Rowley, Sherron Watkins, Cynthia Cooper, and others, too, who attempted to fix the problems they saw in their organizations. Did their leaders appreciate their efforts? Hardly. Moreover, even some of their coworkers saw them more as traitors than as heroes. After all, isn't loyalty to one's group a fundamental value, necessary to maintain a good working cohesion? To some extent, yes. Of course, these women believed they were being loyal to their organizations, in a truly fundamental way. Thought Coleen Rowley: The purpose of the FBI is to protect the American people, which is much more important than protecting the reputation of the agency itself. Thought Sherron Watkins and Cynthia Cooper: Corporations are fundamentally responsible to their shareholders, and so rooting out problems that defraud these shareholders is more important than maintaining a positive corporate image. By acting as they did, all three believed they were working in their organizations' best long-term interests. By putting themselves and their careers on the line to point out what was wrong with their organizations, they reaffirmed what can be right about organizations and demonstrated that authentic, courageous leadership can emerge even under the most difficult of circumstances.

We've seen in this chapter that social psychology bridges to the organization sciences—to the study of large companies and federal bureaucracies, to communities and friendship networks, to social clubs and criminal juries. As social animals, much of our daily lives are spent in groups, so it's not surprising that the findings and theories of social psychology have much to offer those interested in improving management practices, jury decision-making processes, community engagement and participation, team performance, and the like. As we move to the next chapter, we see that social psychology has much to contribute not only to the understanding of individuals and their interactions with one another but also to the understanding of much larger groups and, indeed, of societies.

Chapter Summary

Summary of the Goals Served by Belonging to Groups and the Factors Related to Them

The Goal	Person	Situation	Interaction
Getting things done	• Expectations of individual failure and group success	• Current needs • Individualistic societies	• Groups are particularly productive when certain characteristics—member personalities and diversity—fit well with the demands of their tasks.
Making accurate decisions	• The need to know	• Uncertain circumstances	• Group discussion often leads members to adopt the majority view. In limited circumstances, however, group members holding minority views are influential. • When group members are more concerned with maintaining their social relationships than with generating and critically evaluating alternative decisions, group discussion can lead to very poor decisions.
Gaining positions of leadership	• Ambition (need for power and need for achievement) • Energy • Gender	• Voids at the top • Connections	• Groups select leaders who fit their "prototype" of what a good leader is for the circumstances they face. • When a leadership style fits well with the current needs of the group, groups perform better.

The Nature of Groups

1. The mere presence of others can facilitate performance on well-mastered tasks and impair performance on unmastered tasks. Social facilitation is enhanced when task performers think others are evaluating them and when the others are distracting.

2. People can become deindividuated in groups, losing their sense of identity and relaxing their inhibitions against behaving counter to their normal values.

3. Although the flow of influence within groups is complex, order generally emerges from the chaos, as communicating group members begin to share attitudes and beliefs. Computer simulations help investigators explore complex group interactions.

4. Minimally, groups are two or more individuals who influence one another. Collections of individuals become increasingly "grouplike" when their members are interdependent and share a common identity and when they develop structure (i.e., injunctive norms, roles, status hierarchies, communication networks, and cohesiveness).

Getting Things Done

1. Performance groups help people accomplish tasks that would be difficult to accomplish alone.

2. Although groups are frequently more productive than individuals, they are rarely as productive as they could be. People often loaf, decreasing their personal efforts as their groups grow larger.

3. People who expect to have difficulty reaching their goals as individuals or who expect to reach their goals easily as group members are particularly likely to join groups to accomplish their tasks.

4. When societal circumstances are difficult, people are particularly likely to create or join performance groups.

5. Although members of both collectivistic and individualistic societies join together to get things done, people in individualistic cultures belong to more performance groups, albeit with less commitment to each.

6. Productive groups have members whose personalities closely match the requirements of their tasks.

7. Diverse groups are especially productive on tasks in which a group needs only one member to get the correct answer, and on tasks requiring new solutions, flexibility, and quick adjustments to changing conditions. They are less productive on tasks in which a group needs all of its members to perform their role well, and on tasks in which interpersonal cohesion and communication are important.

Making Accurate Decisions

1. When groups effectively share useful information, members usually make better decisions.

2. Individuals who need to know about things are especially likely to create and join information groups.

3. Uncertain, threatening circumstances lead people to seek others for informational purposes.

4. Group discussions frequently influence members toward the majority view. One implication of this is group polarization, which occurs for two reasons: Group members tend to hear more arguments supporting the majority view of the issue and thus are more likely to be authentically persuaded, and group members may try to make themselves look good by adopting a more extreme version of the group's preferred position.

5. Minority influence is difficult because individuals holding minority views are less able to rely on the powers of social reward and punishment. To be persuasive, minorities must possess quality arguments, present these arguments credibly, and have an audience motivated to find the best answer.

6. Group decisions are better when members are task focused and not excessively interpersonally focused, when leaders encourage alternative perspectives, and when groups have explicit procedures to ensure that members critically evaluate all proposals and gather outside feedback. Such features reduce "groupthink" and increase the likelihood that decisions will be informed by the best available knowledge.

7. Although holding great promise for saving time and money, computer-mediated discussion appears to reduce the quality of group decisions.

Gaining Positions of Leadership

1. Because leading a group often requires personal sacrifices, groups reward leaders with social status and material gain.

2. People who want to lead tend to be ambitious, energetic, and male.

3. People are more likely to seek leadership when there is a void at the top. People also become interested in leadership by virtue of being "in the right place at the right time" or of having personal connections.

4. Leaders emerge through an interactive process in which groups try to select leaders whose characteristics match their needs. Partly because women often don't fit people's stereotypes of what an effective leader is, they are underrepresented in high-level leadership positions.

5. Effective leadership depends on how the personal characteristics and style of the leader mesh with the group's needs.

6. Certain leaders are transformational, changing the motivations, outlooks, and behaviors of their followers.

7. Men tend to be more effective leading jobs requiring "masculine" skills and a hard-nosed task orientation; women are more effective leading jobs requiring "feminine" skills and interpersonal sensitivities. More generally, women are slightly more transformational in leadership style, which may put them in a somewhat better position to lead effectively.

Key Terms

Cohesiveness, 398

Communication network, 398

Deindividuation, 394

Dynamical system, 395

Group, 392

Groupthink, 413

Group polarization, 409

Minority influence, 410

Role, 398

Social facilitation, 392

Social loafing, 401

Status hierarchy, 398

Transactive memory, 407

Transformational leadership, 419

Chapter 13

Social Dilemmas: Cooperation versus Conflict

Outline

Learning Objectives

LO 13.1 Define *social dilemma* and explain how it is linked to the prisoner's dilemma and the tragedy of the commons.

LO 13.2 Explain how public goods dilemmas and replenishing resource dilemmas differ.

LO 13.3 Define the term *social trap* and explain how the costs of social traps are hidden.

LO 13.4 Describe the four specific social value orientations and explain how they fit with the more general egoistic and prosocial distinction.

LO 13.5 Describe the techniques that can be used to change the consequences of selfishness in social dilemmas.

LO 13.6 Discuss the difference between the deterrence and conflict spiral views.

LO 13.7 Discuss how different kinds of threats affect nationalism and ethnocentrism.

LO 13.8 Explain how tit-for-tat strategies, the dollar game, perceptual dilemmas, and the GRIT strategy are linked to the reciprocal dynamics of conflict.

Contrasting Future Worlds

In 1971, Italy and Bangladesh were both densely populated countries. Italy, with a population of about 54 million, had 50 people for every one in the state of New Mexico (whose area is similar to Italy). Bangladesh, in contrast, had an even denser population, with 66 million people crammed into an area less than half Italy's size (see Figure 13.1).

By 2014, there were 2.5 people in Bangladesh for every person who lived there in 1971. This tiny country is now home to 166 million human beings. Although Bangladesh is a fertile country, its farms are insufficient to feed so many people, and things are getting worse. Indeed, the country ranks near the bottom of the list of the world's countries in terms of percentage of starving children, with over a third of the children in Bangladesh underweight (*CIA World Factbook*, 2014). And illiteracy helps keep Bangladeshis down, with 43% of the adult population unable to read and write (compared to only 1% of Americans).

In response to these dismal conditions, Bangladesh's Bengali people have flocked into neighboring India, where they've hardly been welcome. In 1983, 1,700 Bengalis were slaughtered in five hours when the residents of one Indian village went on a rampage against them. These days, Bangladesh and India are still bickering over India's attempts to fence off its border with Bangladesh.

Italians, on the other hand, have gone in a completely different direction. The Italian population has grown only 13% in 45 years, and its growth rate has hovered close to zero in recent years. During the same time, Italy has moved from the status of a third-world country to one of the world's wealthiest. At 99%, Italy's literacy rate is equivalent to that of the United States.

Meanwhile, Italy's alliances with fellow European countries have completely reversed the conflicts of the early twentieth century. Indeed, the Italians have joined with their former foes in the European Union, or EU, which is the European equivalent of the United States, where common passports and a shared currency are erasing old national boundaries. Like Italy, the other Western European nations have seen a decrease in population growth along with an increase in economic prosperity. And European countries are leading the rest of the world in efforts to protect the environment.

Figure 13.1 The People's Republic of Bangladesh is about the size of Wisconsin

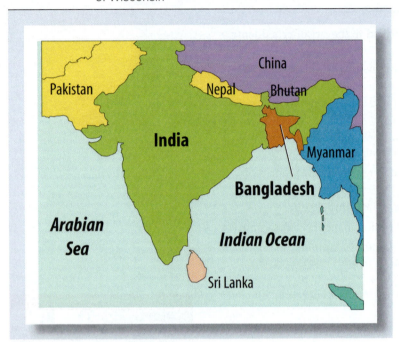

If everyone in California, New York, Texas, Pennsylvania, Illinois, Ohio, Florida, Michigan, New Jersey, and Indiana (the 10 most heavily populated states of the United States) were suddenly to migrate to Wisconsin, it would then have a population roughly equivalent to that of Bangladesh.

The Indian and European subcontinents paint two contrasting images of the world's future. If the population explosion in third-world countries like Bangladesh and India continues, the world's forests, oceans, and rivers will continue to be depleted, other species will continue to be driven to extinction, and international conflicts will continue to increase. If, however, the revolutionary changes now taking place in Italy and the rest of Europe spread to the rest of the globe, the human population explosion and its vast toll on the earth's fragile ecosystems could be halted, or even reversed. Indeed, some economic theorists envision a coming revolution in which quiet and efficient vehicles exhaust only water vapor, industrial waste is nearly eliminated, unemployment disappears, efficient houses produce their own energy, the world's disappearing forests are renewed, and the waste from coal, nuclear reactors, and petroleum is largely eradicated.

So why isn't the whole world following the European example? With overpopulation, environmental degradation, and international conflict placing such obvious costs on the people in Bangladesh, India, and Pakistan, why don't they do something about it?

The puzzles of unrestrained population growth, destruction of the earth's resources, and international conflict are probably the most important questions facing humankind today. We consider these puzzles together in this chapter for two related reasons. First, these group-level social phenomena complete our progression from the psychology of the individual through ever more complex interactions of the person and the environment. Second, these global social dilemmas vividly demonstrate how thoughts and feelings within single individuals can combine into unexpected patterns at the group level. Indeed, the problems of overpopulation, environmental destruction, and international conflict emerge only at the level of very large groups.

First, we define social dilemmas and examine what these three social problems have in common. Then we analyze the goals that underlie these grand dilemmas and the factors in the person and situation that may tell us how to resolve them.

Defining Social Dilemmas

LO 13.1 Define *social dilemma* and explain how it is linked to the prisoner's dilemma and the tragedy of the commons.

LO 13.2 Explain how public goods dilemmas and replenishing resource dilemmas differ.

The modern problems of overpopulation, environmental destruction, and international conflict all build on self-serving psychological mechanisms originally designed for life in small groups. Unfortunately, these same mechanisms have disastrous consequences at the global level. Indeed, each global problem pits single individuals, with all their self-serving and self-deceiving tendencies, against the greater good of their larger groups. As such, each problem qualifies as a form of **social dilemma**—a situation in which an individual profits from selfishness unless everyone chooses the selfish alternative, in which case the whole group loses

Social dilemma A situation in which an individual profits from selfishness unless everyone chooses the selfish alternative, in which case the whole group loses.

(Allison, Beggan, & Midgley, 1996; Parks, Rumble, & Posey, 2002; Dovidio, Piliavin, Penner, & Schroeder, 2006).

Research on social dilemmas is rooted in a very simple game called the *prisoner's dilemma* (Axelrod, Riolo, & Cohen, 2002; Van Vugt & Van Lange, 2006). Imagine that you're a professional crook and that you and your partner in crime have been arrested for trespassing and suspicion of a recent string of heists. Your lawyer confronts you with the dilemma depicted in Figure 13.2. What would you do? When students in laboratory experiments play variants of this game, the best outcome for player A, but the worst for B, comes if A chooses to defect (confess) and B chooses to cooperate (stay silent). If they both choose to defect (as when both burglars agree to testify against one another), there are slightly negative outcomes for both. Finally, if they both choose to cooperate (as when both burglars agree to keep mum), the result is that they both do moderately well (Sheldon, 1999; Tenbrunsel & Messick, 1999).

International conflicts sometimes take the one-on-one character of the prisoner's dilemma, as the leaders of two opposing nations try to face each other down. However, global problems more often involve group-level dilemmas—which pit the individual's immediate interests against those of the larger group (Foddy et al., 1999; Koole, et al.,

---

Figure 13.2 The prisoner's dilemma

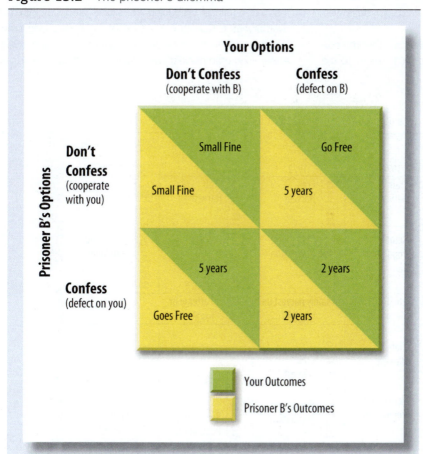

Imagine you are one of two burglars who have been arrested while trespassing at the scene of a potential heist, and you are being held on suspicion for a string of burglaries. You have two options: Remain silent (thereby cooperating with the other crook in evading prosecution) or confess to the district attorney (thereby defecting on your pact of silence with the other burglar). If only one person confesses, thereby providing the District Attorney with solid evidence against the other, he or she goes free. For the pair of you, the best outcome is if you both remain silent. But the decision poses a dilemma: If you remain silent, while the other crook confesses, things will turn out really badly for you.

2001). These group-level dilemmas confront billions of human beings every day and underlie the problems of overpopulation and environmental destruction. The prototype of these insidious social dilemmas is the "tragedy of the commons," which we discuss next.

Bridging Function and Dysfunction:

The Tragedy of the Commons

When it comes to protecting the environment, individual selfishness can lead to ruinous consequences for the group. To illustrate this, ecologist Garrett Hardin (1968) described the overgrazing of common pastures in New England. Those pastures were public areas where sheepherders could freely graze their animals. On their own private pastures, herders grazed only as many animals as the land could support, aware that overgrazing would destroy the grass and starve their whole herd. On the commonly shared areas, however, herders showed no such restraint. Consequently, the commons were frequently destroyed by overgrazing.

What caused the tragedy of the commons? The immediate benefit of adding one more animal was paid directly to the individual sheepherder. However, the cost of that surplus animal was shared by all users of the commons. Thus, the most self-interested action an individual could take, in the short run, was to add an additional animal. When large numbers of herders followed that short-sighted strategy, the long-range cost was the destruction of the grazing area for the whole group.

The commons dilemma is an example of a **replenishing resource management dilemma** (Schroeder, 1995a). In this type of dilemma, group members share a renewable resource that will continue producing benefits if group members don't overharvest it. Consider the case of the Alaska king crab (see Figure 13.3). In the four years between 1980 and 1984, the Alaska king crab harvest went down 92%, despite an increasing

Figure 13.3   When taking a little extra leads to a lot less

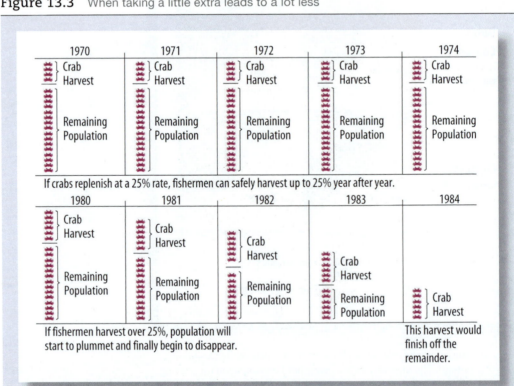

If crab fishermen harvest slowly, the population continues to replenish itself, allowing continued profit in the future. Although conservation is in the interest of the industry as a whole, the immediate interest of individual crab fishermen tempts them to take as many as they can now. But if all do so, they destroy most of the breeding population, as happened during the 1980s. This is an example of a replenishing resource management dilemma.

number of boats searching for crabs with more and more sophisticated equipment. As illustrated in Figure 13.3, if all individuals try to maximize their profits in a given year, there won't be enough crabs to replenish the population, and the remainder will quickly disappear. The same dilemma has led to the near depletion of many fish species, including the red snapper, Atlantic cod, and bluefin tuna (Hayden, 2003).

Social psychologist Kevin Brechner (1977) simulated the commons dilemma in the laboratory. He offered groups of three students a chance to earn a semester's worth of experimental credit (normally three hours) in just half an hour if they could succeed in winning 150 points in a game. To win the points, students simply pressed a button that took a point from a common pool and put it into their own personal accounts. The common pool was displayed on a board with 24 lights. When any of the players took a point, one of the lights in the common pool went out. Like a field of grass for common grazing or a breeding population of king crabs, the pool of points replenished itself. When the pool was near the top, it replenished rapidly—every two seconds. If it went below three-quarters full, it replenished more slowly (every four seconds). Below half, the replacement rate slowed to every six seconds. And if it was "grazed" down to one-fourth of its original size, points were replaced only every eight seconds. Once the last point was "grazed," the game was over, and the pool stopped replenishing completely (see Figure 13.4).

To succeed, students needed to cooperate in keeping the pool at a high level so it could replenish itself at the maximum rate. When students were not allowed to communicate, they tended to do very poorly. In fact, most noncommunicating groups ran the pool dry in less than one minute. Those students earned an average of only 14 points each. When students were allowed to communicate with one another, they did quite a bit better, although they still usually failed to optimize, averaging about 70 points per person. Like the disappearing crab problem, controlled laboratory research shows that people often have great difficulty maintaining common resources (e.g., Seijts & Latham, 2000). Even

Figure 13.4 Social traps in the laboratory

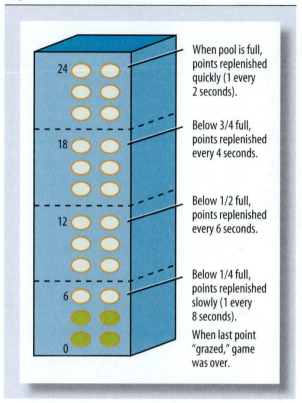

Groups in Kevin Brechner's (1977) experiment were faced with a resource that, like a crab population, replenished more rapidly if harvested slowly. Because of individual selfishness, the pools were very rapidly depleted, especially when group members could not communicate with one another.

though the whole group benefits when its individual members restrain themselves from taking too much too quickly, individual temptations to be selfish often lead to group ruin.

In dilemmas like the tragedy of the commons, each individual can *take* something from a limited common pool. It's worth distinguishing this type of dilemma from a **public goods dilemma**. A public goods dilemma is a situation in which the whole group can benefit if some individuals *give* something for the common good but in which individuals profit from "free-riding" if enough others contribute (Abele & Ehrhardt, 2005; Allison & Kerr, 1994; Kurzban & DeScioli, 2008). An example is when public broadcasting stations appeal for money. If some minimum number of listeners contributes, the station can continue to provide broadcasts for all to enjoy. If too few people contribute, though, the public good will be lost. The dilemma arises because no single individual is essential to providing the public good. The most self-serving thing to do, from a purely economic perspective, is to ignore the requests and hope someone else will be more socially responsible. In this way, an individual gets the benefits without incurring any of the costs.

The key global problems are all grand-scale social dilemmas. As we'll describe in detail throughout this chapter, each pits simple mechanisms of individual self-interest against the good of the global community. Those global problems are also linked to one another (Howard, 2000; Oskamp, 2000).

Replenishing resource management dilemma A situation in which group members share a renewable resource that will continue to produce benefits if group members do not overharvest it but in which any single individual profits from harvesting as much as possible.

Public goods dilemma A situation in which (1) the whole group can benefit if some of the individuals give something for the common good but (2) individuals profit from "free riding" if enough others contribute.

Figure 13.5   The population explosion

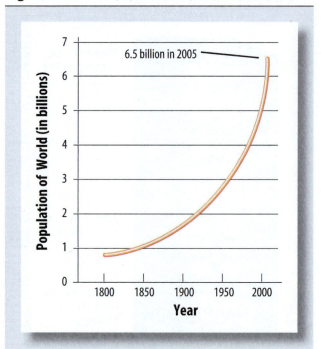

For over 1 million years, the human population was relatively low (below 10 million). There have been dramatic increases in the last 200 years, however, and a population of almost 10 billion is projected within the next several decades. This increase is leading to serious environmental damage and, in turn, to international political conflicts.

Interlocking Problems and Solutions

What could possibly have led villagers in Assam, India, to go on a five-hour rampage and massacre 1,700 Bengali immigrants? A team of 30 researchers was assembled to study this and similar incidents around the world (Homer-Dixon et al., 1993). They found a common pattern: Overpopulation is leading to dwindling natural resources in many countries, which in turn puts a tremendous strain on their economies. Short-term solutions to these economic problems (such as extensive logging of rainforests for quick profits) only make the problems worse in the long run.

Given the dramatic increases in world population (see Figure 13.5), the research team concluded that more environmental destruction and international conflict will likely follow. Population growth in areas such as Bangladesh, Central America, or Africa, for example, has damaged local environments and food sources, leading local residents to migrate away in search of livable habitats. This migration in turn leads to international conflicts as whole populations fight over the remaining valuable lands and resources. The murderous spree against Bengali immigrants wasn't a historical anomaly. Such genocidal incidents have become more common in Africa, Central America, and the Middle East in recent years.

What Goals Underlie Global Social Dilemmas?

Why do people get trapped in these escalating dilemmas? Few of us wake up in the morning with the intentional goal of contributing to global overpopulation, environmental destruction, or international conflict. Instead, most of us contribute unintentionally, simply by going about our lives with the goals that have always served human beings well. Indeed, global problems are "dilemmas" partly because each is rooted in motivations that were useful for our ancestors living in small groups (Penn, 2003; Van Vugt, Griskevicius, & Schultz, 2014). Many of the motivations we've discussed throughout this book come into play in influencing the individual decisions that add up to global social problems. For example, the goal of reproduction, discussed in Chapter 8, underlies the population problem. And the general goal of simplifying complex information, discussed in depth in Chapters 2 and 3, often causes people to cling to a simple political or economic solution without analyzing how it would play out in the complexities of the real world (Gardner & Stern, 1996). However, our discussion of global social problems will focus on two goals that take on very special characteristics in large groups of people—the desire to gain immediate satisfaction and the desire to defend ourselves and valued others.

The desire to gain immediate satisfaction is a good example of a goal that serves individual needs but leads to problems at the group level. Our ancestors didn't stand around helpless in the rain and snow or search for the most difficult way to catch a fish or cut down a tree. Instead, they survived because they always had an eye out for special advantages: warmth in the winter and coolness in the summer; more abundant supplies of fruit, fish, and meat; and technologies to save time and labor. The irony is that our ancestors' skills at "conquering" the environment may result in our destroying the environment for our descendants.

Fortunately, another feature of human beings is our capacity to (at least occasionally) delay short-term gratification for long-term benefits (Insko et al., 1998; Yamagishi & Cook, 1993). Furthermore, humans survived by cooperating with other group members, and many people are motivated to sacrifice for the good of the group (Van Vugt & Van Lange, 2006). Understanding the circumstances under which we seek short-term selfish rewards as opposed to long-term group benefits could suggest solutions to the great problems of the modern age (Van Vugt et al., 2014).

One variable that may influence our selfishness and how much we cooperate is the degree of contact we have with relatives. Our ancestors spent most of their time around others with whom they shared family ties and long-term cooperative relationships. People today may come into contact with hundreds of nonrelatives every day, many of them total strangers. In line with our earlier discussion of genetic self-interest and helping (see Chapter 9), several experimental studies suggest that people are more cooperative toward kin, or with people who look like their relatives, than toward unrelated strangers (Ackerman, Kenrick, & Schaller, 2007; Krupp, DeBruine, & Barclay, 2008).

Another feature of modern life creates a hurdle to cooperativeness. The goal most directly related to international conflict is the desire to defend ourselves and valued others. There are again opposing forces at work here, and protecting our special interests may require a delicate balance. As we learned in Chapter 11, groups sometimes compete with one another over scarce resources, and this competition escalates as those resources become scarcer. Hence, nations and groups within those nations have inherent conflicts of interest (Mitchell, 1999). If that competition leads to outright warfare, the competitors place themselves and those they value in great danger, particularly in a world armed with abundant and dangerous weapons.

We will thus organize our discussion of global social dilemmas around these two basic goals: to satisfy drives for immediate comfort and resources and to protect ourselves and those we value.

Quick Quiz

1 A social dilemma is best defined as _____.
- a. A situation in which two "prisoners" must choose simultaneously whether to confess to a crime, with different consequences depending on the selfishness of each player
- b. A situation in which group members share a renewable resource that continues producing benefits unless members overharvest it
- c. A situation in which an individual profits from seeking personal benefits, unless everyone chooses selfishly, in which case the whole group loses
- d. A situation in which the whole group benefits from individuals contributing something for the common good, but in which the public good will be lost if too few people contribute

2 In a _____, group members share a renewable resource that will continue producing benefits if group members don't overharvest it, whereas in a _____, the whole group benefits if some members *give* something for the common good but individuals profit from free-riding if enough others contribute.
- a. public goods dilemma, replenishing resource dilemmas
- b. replenishing resource dilemmas, public goods dilemma
- c. public goods dilemma, prisoner's dilemma
- d. replenishing resource dilemmas, prisoner's dilemma

3 These two basic goals underlie global social dilemmas:
- a. The goal of reproduction and the goal of simplifying complex information.
- b. The goal of reproduction and the desire to gain immediate satisfaction.
- c. The desire to gain immediate satisfaction and the desire to defend ourselves and valued others.
- d. The goal of simplifying complex information and the desire to defend ourselves and valued others.

Gaining Immediate Satisfaction

LO 13.3 Define the term *social trap* and explain how the costs of social traps are hidden.

LO 13.4 Describe the four specific social value orientations and explain how they fit with the more general egoistic and prosocial distinction.

LO 13.5 Describe the techniques that can be used to change the consequences of selfishness in social dilemmas.

During the 1960s, a popular expression was "If it feels good, do it!" Physiological psychologists actually discovered an area of the mammalian brain that seemed to be especially designed to control "feeling good." Olds and Milner (1954) implanted

Sliding into smogland. For years, Los Angeles has had record high levels of smog. When only a few Los Angelitos drove cars, they were simply a convenient means of transportation and made no substantial contribution to air quality problems. However, the millions of automobiles on the road now bring relatively fewer rewards, and many greater punishments, including massive traffic jams and a perennial cloud of smog.

electrodes into a region of the brain's hypothalamus that was later dubbed the "pleasure center." Animals would press a lever for hour after hour just for a jolt of stimulation there. Since that time, research from neuropsychological studies of the human brain have revealed that humans likewise have particular brain areas, and a set of interlinked neurochemical and hormonal systems, that become active whenever we experience pleasure (Kelley, 2005). These systems seem to be designed as the brain's way of saying to the body: "Whatever you just did, do it again!" But the desire for short-term satisfaction can sometimes lead us into traps, as you'll see next.

Social Traps

Several decades ago, behavioral psychologist John Platt (1973) provided some fascinating insights into how the drive for immediate self-gratification could lead to social dilemmas. According to Platt, the desire for quick gratification leads to **social traps**—situations in which individuals or groups are drawn toward immediate rewards that later prove to have unpleasant or lethal consequences. Platt noted that social traps, far from being mysterious, operate according to the most basic of reinforcement principles: We repeat those behaviors that lead to immediate reward. Unfortunately, the trap occurs when behaviors that are reinforcing in the moment have hidden costs. Those costs can be hidden for several reasons.

DIFFERENCES BETWEEN SHORT-TERM AND LONG-TERM CONSEQUENCES Sometimes, the short-term consequences of our behaviors are positive, but the long-term consequences are negative. If you drive to work alone or adjust your household thermostat to 75 degrees Fahrenheit regardless of the outside temperature, you get immediate and personal payoff. The costs of shrinking energy supplies come only after years, and most of us don't think about them when we take the comfortable short-cut today. In the opposite direction, the costs of spending an extra half hour on the bus, wearing sweaters indoors, or sweating a bit in the summer are also immediate and personal. Although these behaviors could ultimately promote the benefits of more abundant fuel and cleaner air, these payoffs are far removed.

IGNORANCE OF LONG-TERM CONSEQUENCES Automobiles produce emissions that contribute to lung cancer, cardiovascular disease, hypertension, and mental retardation (Doyle, 1997). The original designers of internal combustion engines had no idea of these consequences and probably never envisioned eight-lane highways jammed with commuters driving SUVs. Thus, we sometimes get trapped in behavior patterns because they provide great rewards in the short term and costs that do not become obvious until much later.

SLIDING REINFORCERS A **sliding reinforcer** is a stimulus that brings rewards when used in small doses but punishments when used in large doses. For some time, Los Angeles ranked at or near the top among major metropolitan areas having the most polluted air in the United States. A substantial portion of that pollution came from automobile exhaust fumes. When the first automobiles were introduced into the Los Angeles area, though, they provided convenience without much impact on air quality. If there were only a few cars on the road, there would still be no atmospheric problem in Los Angeles. Unfortunately, when several million of them went on the road, the machines turned the city's sunny skies into a cloud of gray smog.

Thus, social traps are based on rules that are, in other circumstances, adaptive. The individuals who get trapped aren't pathological or abnormal in their behavior. Indeed, each individual is making a rational decision—to seek immediate self-interest! The problem arises when individuals join together in groups, and individual selfishness becomes a problem for the group as a whole. The idea of a social trap can help us

Social trap A situation in which individuals or groups are drawn toward immediate rewards that later prove to have unpleasant or lethal consequences.

Sliding reinforcer A stimulus that brings rewards when used in small doses, but punishments when used in large doses.

understand not only the destruction of the environment but also overpopulation and international conflict, each of which gets worse as individuals or groups seek short-term selfish rewards that sometimes mask long-term shared costs (Howard, 2000; Lynn & Oldenquist, 1986).

What factors influence people to seek immediate personal self-gratification over long-term benefits to the group? These tendencies should be related to personal and situational factors that (1) enhance egoistic self-centeredness, (2) focus the person on immediate gratification versus long-haul benefits, (3) decrease feelings of social responsibility and interdependence, and (4) promote competitiveness rather than cooperation. We will now consider research that has explored these factors.

PERSON Egoistic versus Prosocial Orientations

What factors within the person are likely to lead him or her to look out for "number one" instead of the group's long-term benefits? A great deal of research in recent years has attempted to distinguish people who have different values about benefiting themselves versus others (e.g., Chen, Mannix, & Okamura, 2003; DeCremer & Van Dijk, 2002; Sagiv et al., 2011).

DISTINGUISHING DIFFERENT VALUE ORIENTATIONS Imagine that you're playing a game in which you and the other players can earn real money. Which of the following four outcomes would you prefer?

1. You sacrifice your own rewards, enabling the other people in the group to make a lot more money.
2. You and the other players work together so that, though none of you get the highest possible reward, you all do slightly better than most would do on their own.
3. You cooperate with the group if it is in your personal interest but compete if you see a way to make more profits.
4. You compete to win, even sacrificing some of your own winnings if it helps you do better than the other players.

After presenting people in different countries with a standard series of questions in which they allocate benefits to themselves and their groups, social psychologists have concluded that people tend to take one of these four approaches to these problems (e.g., Liebrand & Van Run, 1985; McClintock et al., 1973). **Altruists** value the group benefits, even if it means that they must make personal sacrifices. **Cooperators** value working together to maximize the joint benefits to themselves and the group. **Individualists** try to maximize their own personal gains, without regard to the rest of the group. Finally, **competitors** strive to come out relatively better than other players—to "win" regardless of whether their personal winnings are high or low in an absolute sense. Most people fall into the cooperative and individualistic categories, with smaller numbers falling into the altruistic and competitive types (Liebrand & VanRun, 1985; Van Lange et al., 1997a). Some researchers conveniently categorize altruistic and cooperative people into a "prosocial" category and individualists and competitors into an "egoistic" category (Biel & Garling, 1995; Chen et al., 2003). See Table 13.1.

Altruist Someone oriented toward bringing the group benefits, even if it means personal sacrifice.

Cooperator Someone oriented toward working together to maximize the joint benefits to the self and the group.

Individualist Someone oriented toward maximizing personal gains, without regard to the rest of the group.

Competitor Someone oriented to come out relatively better than other players, regardless of whether personal winnings are high or low in an absolute sense.

Table 13.1	Social Value Orientations	
General Orientation	**Specific Approach**	**Description**
Prosocial	Altruists	Motivated to help others, even at a cost to themselves
	Cooperators	Motivated to maximize joint profits for themselves and group members
Egoistic	Individualists	Motivated to maximize their own outcomes, with no regard for the costs or benefits to others
	Competitors	Motivated to do relatively better than others, even if it increases their costs

In one experiment, students played a game involving "energy conservation." Groups of seven students started with a shared pool of about $100. Over five rounds, each player could win the amount of money he had taken for himself, provided the total taken by the whole group did not exceed what was left in the pool. If the pool went below 0, the game was over. Subjects could choose to take money for themselves in $1.50 increments ranging from $1.50 to $9. With seven people playing the game across five trials, the group could win only if most people took very small amounts on any trial (choosing $1.50 or $3 would usually be the safest strategy).

On the first trial of the game, altruists were the only ones even close to the mark for obtaining the group good, taking just over $3 for themselves. Cooperators took around $4, individualists around $5, and competitors over $5. As the game progressed, all subjects realized that the money would run out, and so tended to reduce the amounts they took. However, competitors and individualists, even though they got information that they had taken far too much on the first trial, never reduced their takings enough to make up for their big initial self-helpings. Even on the last trial, when resources were nearly gone, competitors still took slightly more than anyone else (Liebrand & Van Run, 1985).

Consistent with these results, other studies also find that people having egoistic orientations cooperate less than those having prosocial orientations (Allison & Messick, 1990; Utz, Ouwerkerk, & Van Lange, 2004). In a related line of research, one recent study compared narcissistic and nonnarcissistic students' performance in a social dilemma game. Narcissistic people tend to have inflated views of themselves, to view themselves as more deserving than others, and to respond positively to questions such as: "If I ruled the world, it would be a much better place." In the game, players worked together to manage a forest, in which the remaining trees increased by 10% after each round (each round represents an imaginary year of foresting). At first, narcissists did better than their opponents because they took more on the early rounds of play. In the long run, however, their self-centered behaviors brought the whole group down, because groups with higher percentages of narcissists were more likely to exhaust the pool of resources and end the game early (Campbell, Bush, Brunell, & Shelton, 2005). There is another self-defeating consequence of self-serving behavior: Other group members are on the look-out for people who are uncooperative and may take steps to punish selfish individuals (Kurzban, DeScioli, & O'Brien, 2007; Vanneste et al., 2007).

DEVELOPMENT OF PROSOCIAL AND EGOISTIC ORIENTATIONS Why do people differ in their social-value orientations? Paul Van Lange and his colleagues speculated that the differences are rooted in experiences of interdependence with others, beginning in childhood and further shaped by interactions during adulthood and old age (Van Lange et al., 1997b). The researchers examined these hypotheses in several ways. In one study, they asked 631 Dutch men and women about their families: How many brothers and sisters did they have, and what was their position in the family? Prosocial individuals (altruists and cooperators) had more siblings than egoists (individualists and competitors). In particular, prosocial individuals had more *older* siblings. Van Lange and his colleagues reasoned that growing up in a home with several siblings required people to develop norms of sharing and that older siblings were better at modeling and enforcing those sharing rules. These researchers and others have also uncovered some good news in the developmental psychology of cooperation: People generally become more prosocial as they age (Benenson, Pascoe, & Radmore, 2007).

The researchers also examined the relationship between prosocial orientation and attachment style (as discussed in Chapter 8). They found that prosocially oriented people were more likely to have a secure attachment style in their romantic relationships. In other words, prosocials, compared with egoists, feel relatively less fear of abandonment in their relationships and are

Sisterhood and prosocial orientation. Researchers in the Netherlands found that growing up in a home with several siblings was associated with a more cooperative orientation, particularly when those siblings were older sisters.

comfortable being close to others. Related research suggests that individual differences in trust are important in a social dilemma (Van Lange & Semin-Goosens, 1998). In laboratory social dilemmas, people who generally trust others are more likely to cooperate with other group members (Parks, Henager, & Scamahorn, 1996; Yamagishi, 1988b).

INVESTIGATION

Where do you fit in the classification of value orientations discussed in Table 13.1? Considering how many sisters and brothers you have, to what extent does your value orientation fit with the research just discussed?

SITUATION Changing the Consequences of Short-Sighted Selfishness

What factors in the social situation can reverse people's tendency to go for quick self-gratification over long-term benefits to the group? Platt (1973) suggested that the timing of rewards and punishments for selfish versus group-oriented behaviors was crucial. Other research suggests that the activation of social norms may also play a key role.

TIMING REWARDS AND PUNISHMENTS John Platt (1973) suggested several ways to capitalize on our selfish reward-seeking tendencies to draw us out of social traps:

1. *Using alternative technologies to change long-term negative consequences.* The 2014 Honda Civic Hybrid gets 47 miles per gallon on the highway; the Toyota Prius does even better, getting 51 miles to the gallon. The more luxurious Tesla, on the hand, is a totally electric car that never uses a single gallon of gasoline and can go over 250 miles between charges.

   Buying one of the new hyper-efficient cars is just one of the things you can do to enjoy the conveniences of modern life with less destructive impact on the environment. Solar panels, which extract free energy from the sun, likewise allow low-impact comfort seeking. Insulating one's home is another such solution. Although home insulation seems less futuristic than solar panels and electric cars, it's one of the most important changes people can make to cut down energy waste (Gardner & Stern, 1996). In fact, using solar panels, insulating, covering windows, and tuning furnaces could save more than 75% of the energy used to heat homes (Yates & Aronson, 1983). Technological changes are often quite effective because they can be done on a "one-shot" basis—buying an energy-efficient car, for example, will lead to energy conservation for years to come (Stern, 2000).

2. *Moving future negative consequences into the present.* If you turn your air conditioner to a chilly 68 degrees during the first week in August, meanwhile leaving your back door open for the cat, you might not have to pay any consequences for your inefficient decisions until the second week in September, when the August electric bill arrives. Alternatively, a household thermostat could be fitted with a bright, digital printout that gave household members continual feedback in dollars and cents about how much energy they were using. In this way, keeping doors tightly closed and covering the windows during the day would have a visible and immediate rewarding effect—whereas turning the air conditioner on would have a visible and immediate punishing effect. Indeed, research supports Platt's suggestion that immediate feedback about energy consumption is an effective

Using new technology to save the environment. New technologies, like this all-electric Tesla hybrid, can sometimes reduce the long-term negative consequences of previously damaging reward-seeking behaviors. One obstacle is that people must be convinced to adopt new technologies, many of which, like better home insulation and solar panels, are not as glamorous as sleek new cars.

means to encourage conservation (Seligman, Becker, & Darley, 1981; Van Vugt & Samuelson, 1999).

3. *Adding immediate punishments for undesirable behaviors.* If an individual gets a stiff fine for littering, or if a company is penalized for pollution, that takes away the immediate pleasure of environmentally destructive behaviors. Administered under the right circumstances, punishments can spur people to act in the collective interest (Balliet, Mulder, & Van Lange, 2011). If punishments are large enough, for example, and if people believe they will get caught, aversive consequences could work to decrease environmentally destructive behaviors (DiMento, 1989; Yamagishi, 1988a). On a broader level, environmental psychologists believe that dramatic benefits would follow from simply requiring industrial polluters to pay the costs of cleaning up their own toxic and harmful waste products instead of spewing them out into the air and water (Howard, 2000; Winter, 2000). As things are currently done, most polluting industries leave their mess for the public to clean up after they have already damaged the environment. Indeed, industries now pollute vastly more than all private citizens combined, and technologically developed countries like the United States are the worst offenders (Stern, 2000). However, in countries like Denmark industrial leaders are discovering that by emulating the recycling loops found throughout nature's ecosystems, they can dramatically reduce costs and consequently increase profits (Hawken et al., 1999).

4. *Reinforcing more desirable environmental alternatives.* Rewards for desirable behaviors work without triggering negative emotional reactions. Many North American cities now support recycling programs that allow people to conveniently place all their glass, plastic, and paper in bins for curbside pickup. A similar approach is to offer rewards (such as lottery tickets) for using public transportation or for reducing energy use (Geller, 1992). Research suggests that such approaches, though sometimes expensive, can be successful (Balliet et al., 2011; Gardner & Stern, 1996; McKenzie-Mohr, 2000).

Besides these techniques designed to appeal to selfish motivations in single individuals, Platt (1973) also suggested the use of social pressures. These socially based solutions often involve the activation of social norms about proper behavior (Kerr, 1995; Oskamp, 2000).

ACTIVATING SOCIAL NORMS   As we've noted, norms can be *descriptive* or *injunctive* (Kallgren, Reno, & Cialdini, 2000). A descriptive norm, as described in Chapter 6, is simply what most people do in a given situation, with no necessary implication of right or wrong. For example, the majority of Mexican Americans living in New Mexico eat more spicy food than do the majority of Swedish Americans living in North Dakota. There would be nothing immoral about a Swede who ate spicy foods, or a Chicano who preferred bland mashed potatoes to salsa. In contrast, an injunctive norm is a social expectation about what people *should* do in a particular situation. Throwing litter in a trash receptacle rather than out the car window is considered right and proper, regardless of how many other people do or don't behave that way. Both descriptive and injunctive norms influence people's inclinations to act unselfishly in social dilemmas.

DESCRIPTIVE NORMS—"EVERYBODY'S DOING IT."   Demonstrating the importance of descriptive norms, people adjust their own cooperativeness to match the rest of their group (Parks, Sanna, & Berd, 2001). For instance, students in one social dilemma study contributed more to the public good when a greater percentage of the rest of the group did so (Komorita, Parks, & Hulbert, 1992). Moreover, our beliefs about what others would do in the same situation influence our cooperativeness in social dilemmas. For example, economists, whose models of human behavior assume rampant individual selfishness, are substantially more selfish than other groups (Braver, 1995; Miller, 1999). If you expect that everyone else will do the selfish thing, it may make sense to act selfishly (Caruso, Epley, & Bazerman, 2006). However, when students in the Netherlands and the United States were led to expect that the other parties involved in a social dilemma were highly moral, they were more likely to cooperate

(Van Lange & Liebrand, 1991). Likewise, communication between participants in a social dilemma helps increase cooperation, particularly for those who are not generally inclined to trust others (Tazelaar, Van Lange, & Ouwerkerk, 2004).

INJUNCTIVE NORMS—"DOING THE RIGHT THING." Several types of injunctive norms influence people to act more or less selfishly in social dilemmas. These include the norms of commitment, reciprocity, fairness, and social responsibility (Kerr, 1995; Lynn & Oldenquist, 1986; Stern, Dietz, & Kalof, 1993). According to the norm of commitment, for example, if you say you will do something, the proper thing to do is to carry through with it. Indeed, people do stick by their commitments to work for the group good, even when it turns out to be costly to them personally (e.g., Kerr & Kaufman-Gilliland, 1994; Neidert & Linder, 1990).

If injunctive norms control greediness in social dilemmas, people ought to act more responsibly when they can be identified. Indeed, people cooperate more when they think that other group members will be able to observe their individual choices (Messick & Brewer, 1983; Neidert & Linder, 1990). These findings, based on studies of U.S. college students, suggest that even in an individualistic and capitalistic society, people are aware

The norm of social responsibility. One powerful injunctive norm in society specifies that individuals are responsible for helping solve the world's problems. Organizations such as Greenpeace and the Nature Conservancy try to appeal to that sense of social responsibility.

that "looking out for number one" is socially undesirable. There are, however, cultural differences in the norms about appropriate behavior. Craig Parks and Anh Vu (1994) found that Vietnamese were more cooperative in a social dilemma than were Americans, a tendency the authors attributed to the contrast between collectivist norms in Vietnamese society and individualist norms in American society. At the same time, a recent study compared Americans' generosity in social dilemmas to that of 15 different small-scale traditional societies (such as the Machiguenga, who live in the forests of Peru). Two very encouraging findings emerged: First, across all the different societies, people were more generous than the standard economic models would predict. Second, Americans were generally more generous than people living in traditional societies (Henrich et al., 2006).

One social dilemma study indicates that groups that contain individual members who consistently make contributions to the public good can change the group norms, so that formerly selfish members begin to contribute as well (Weber & Murnighan, 2008). Other research suggests that group members are often quite willing to go out of their way to reward others who contribute to the group good (Kiyonari & Barclay, 2008). Thus, cooperativeness can become contagious.

Several other studies find situational cues can radically change people's mental set about what is normatively appropriate in a social dilemma. For example, different groups of students in one study played a dilemma game according to identical rules, with only the name of the game varying. Students were much more generous and cooperative when the game was called the "Community Game" than when the same game was labeled the "Wall Street Game" (Liberman, Samuels, & Ross, 2004). In an even more subtle manipulation of social norms, half the students in one experiment were primed for interdependence (by completing sentences containing words such as "group," "friendships," or "together") while the other half were primed for *independence* (by completing sentences containing words such as "independent," "individual," or "self-contained"). The students who were primed for interdependence were later more cooperative and trusting in a public-goods dilemma (Utz, 2004a).

INTERACTION ## Matching Interventions with Motives

In designing social interventions to prevent the environmental damages of wholesale selfishness, it is important to consider how different motivations within individuals interact with different types of intervention policies. An intervention that increases

Table 13.2 Interaction Between Different Environmental Interventions and Different Motivations Within Individuals		
Type of Intervention	**Motive Activated**	**Example**
Command-and-control	Fear	Penalties for automobile manufacturers who produce too many gas-guzzling cars Loss of educational benefits for families having too many children (as in China)
Market-based	Greed	Tax rebates for consumers who purchase solar heating panels Payments for voluntary sterilization (as in India)
Voluntarist	Social responsibility	Sierra Club's appeal to members to write to Congress in favor of a new wilderness area Planned Parenthood's appeals for volunteers to work delivering birth control in poor countries

cooperation in one type of person can actually decrease cooperation in others (Bogaert, Boone, & Declerck, 2008; Utz, 2004b). Table 13.2 organizes environmental interventions into three categories (Karp & Galding, 1995).

Command-and-control policies are prescriptive legal regulations that use police power to punish violators. For example, the U.S. Environmental Protection Agency (EPA) threatens automobile manufacturers with fines if they don't produce enough fuel-efficient cars. **Market-based policies**, in contrast, offer rewards to those who reduce their environmentally destructive behaviors (such as financial rebates for installing solar panels). Finally, **voluntarist policies** use neither threats nor economic rewards, but rather appeal directly to people's intrinsic sense of social responsibility. Not all people feel the same obligation to do their part for the common good. For example, public transit is widely available in the Netherlands, but some people still prefer to use automobiles to get around. The preference for public transit is high among those who both (1) believe cars hurt the environment and (2) are concerned about the future (Joireman, Van Lange, & Van Vugt, 2004).

There are different societal implications of policies that appeal to these different motives. For instance, command-and-control policies are likely to elicit resistance. Automobile manufacturers and oil companies, for example, have fought punitive regulations every step of the way. Market-based approaches, such as tax rebates for energy efficiency, can be expensive, but they don't trigger resistance and don't require policing (people readily identify themselves if they get goodies for doing so). Voluntarist approaches don't require coercive governmental laws or costly administration and policing agencies. In fact, contrary to the economic model of self-interest, people often voluntarily act in cooperative and helpful ways (Buchan et al., 2011; Henrich et al., 2006). For example, many people anonymously send food to starving people halfway around the world, and others recycle because they think it's the "right thing to do," regardless of what others are doing (Clinton, 2007; Weber & Murnighan, 2008).

INVESTIGATION

Your assignment: Save the planet. Or at least your local chunk of it. Think of a way you could use the different findings in this section to help officials in your city or state get the citizens to clean up their environmental acts.

Quick Quiz

Command-and-control policy A prescriptive legal regulation that uses police power to punish violators.

Market-based policy An offer of rewards to those who reduce their socially harmful behaviors.

Voluntarist policy An appeal to people's intrinsic sense of social responsibility.

1 Which of the following are causes of social traps?

   a. Behaviors with positive short-term consequences but negative long-term consequences
   b. Ignorance of long-term consequences
   c. Sliding reinforcers
   d. All of the above

2 _____ are motivated to maximize their own outcomes with no regard for the costs or benefits to others, whereas _____ are motivated to maximize joint profits for themselves and group members.

   a. Competitors, altruists
   b. Competitors, cooperators
   c. Individualists, altruists
   d. Individualists, cooperators

3 Which of the statements about the development of prosocial orientation is *true*?

    a. People generally become more prosocial as they age.

    b. Prosocial individuals have more *younger* siblings.

    c. Prosocial individuals are more likely to have an anxious/ambivalent attachment style.

    d. None of the above

4 Which of the following strategies utilizes our reward-seeking tendencies to draw us out of social traps?

    a. Moving present negative consequences into the future.

    b. Reinforcing more desirable environmental alternatives.

    c. Adding delayed punishments for undesirable behaviors.

    d. All of the above

5 _____ policies appeal to social responsibility norms and work well with people who have a _____ orientation; in contrast, _____ policies appeal to individual self-interest.

    a. Voluntarist, prosocial, command-and-control

    b. Voluntarist, prosocial, market-based

    c. Market-based, egoistic, command-and-control

    d. Market-based, egoistic, voluntarist

Defending Ourselves and Valued Others

LO 13.6 Discuss the difference between the deterrence and conflict spiral views.

LO 13.7 Discuss how different kinds of threats affect nationalism and ethnocentrism.

LO 13.8 Explain how tit-for-tat strategies, the dollar game, perceptual dilemmas, and the GRIT strategy are linked to the reciprocal dynamics of conflict.

Thus far, we've been discussing how large-scale problems can flow from primitive urges to seek positive gratification. On the other side of the coin, serious social problems can also stem from a primitive motivation to avoid being exploited or harmed by members of outgroups.

Outgroup Bias and International Conflict

In 1913, an anthropologist described a curious custom he'd observed in the aboriginal tribes of Australia (Radcliffe-Brown, 1913). Before entering a camp, the anthropologist's native interpreter would stand on the outskirts until the village elders approached him. The elderly men would inquire about the interpreter's father's father and then discuss his genealogy for a few minutes. When they could find a common relative, he would enter. In one case, however, the interpreter could find absolutely no links. Frightened by this turn of events, he slept far outside the village that night. The interpreter explained that he was a Talainji and that these men, members of the Karieria tribe, were not his relatives. In this land, he explained to the puzzled anthropologist, "the other must be my relative or my enemy. If he is my enemy, I shall take the first opportunity of killing him, for fear he will kill me" (p. 164).

Unfortunately, the tendency to favor the members of one's own group and dislike outsiders is universal (LeVine & Campbell, 1972). Experimental research indicates that people regard members of outgroups as less truly human than the members of their own groups, attributing simpler emotional reactions to "them" and a more complex array of human emotions to "us" (Cortes et al., 2005). Ironically, raising awareness of how one's own group has mistreated another group (as in reminding British people of the mass killing of Australian Aborigines or reminding White Americans of the mass killing of Native Americans) only serves to make this bias even stronger (Castano & Giner-Sorolla, 2006).

Outgroup hatred and distrust. Around the world, people tend to distrust other groups and regard them as inferior. These Arab protesters are defacing an American flag, which they regard as a symbol of evil. On the other side, many Americans regard Arabs and their culture as vastly inferior to that of the United States.

In Chapter 11, we considered how this outgroup bias creates local problems within modern society, such as the conflicts between civil rights workers and Klan members in North Carolina. When the outgroup is made up of people from a foreign country competing with our own, it can seem especially alien and threatening. During the Cold War, for instance, President Ronald Reagan referred to the Soviet Union as an "Evil Empire." Conversely, Soviets at the time viewed Americans as evil and greedy imperialists who used their power to prop up dictators around the world.

All the factors discussed in Chapter 11 concerning prejudice against other racial and ethnic groups apply to international outgroups as well. Different countries, for example, are often in conflict over real benefits, including territory and natural resources, and disdain of foreigners may be one way to raise group self-esteem. In this section, we will explore the larger political arena but remain grounded in psychological processes, examining specifically how factors in the person and situation trigger the motivation to defend ourselves and those we value.

PERSON   Some of Us Are More Defensive Than Others

What factors inside the person might lead to a tendency to be alert to threats from an international outgroup? This question is important for two reasons. Knowing which individuals are especially sensitive to such threats could help individual leaders deal with each other and perhaps help them tailor negotiation tactics to avoid triggering dangerous feelings of outgroup hostility. Second, examining such individual differences might help us understand decision making by both powerful citizens and the less powerful people who indirectly affect international policy through "public opinion."

SOCIAL DOMINANCE ORIENTATION   As discussed in Chapter 11, social dominance orientation refers to the desire that one's ingroup dominate other groups (Haley & Sidanius, 2005; Levin et al., 2002; Sidanius et al., 2000). In addition to its links to intergroup prejudice within a society, social dominance orientation is also tied to attitudes about military strength and international conflict (Nelson & Milburn, 1999).

People who score high on social dominance orientation tend to favor increased military spending and more aggressive approaches to international conflict. In 1990, Iraq's leader, Saddam Hussein, invaded neighboring Kuwait. The United States led a massive military counterattack in which tens of thousands of Iraqis were killed. During the conflict, Felicia Pratto and her colleagues (1994) measured Stanford undergraduates' social dominance orientation and asked the students how they thought Iraq should be handled. Compared to those having low scores, students high in social dominance orientation said they were more willing to sacrifice personally for the war and favored more military force and restriction of civil liberties (such as freedom of the press) for the war effort.

GENDER DIFFERENCES IN ETHNOCENTRISM AND MILITARISM   Would there be fewer international conflicts if more women were world leaders? Some research suggests that the answer might be yes. The researchers who developed the social dominance scale have found that it is centrally linked to a person's gender. In a wide range of countries, including Sweden, India, England, and the United States, men are more militaristic, politically conservative, ethnocentric, and punitive than are women (Sidanius et al., 1994).

In one study, Jim Sidanius, Felicia Pratto, and Lawrence Bobo (1994) surveyed a random sample of 1,897 men and women from Los Angeles about their social dominance orientation. Because Los Angeles is a very culturally diverse city, the sample included people of different ethnicities, religions, and places of origin. The researchers found that men were more dominance oriented than women across all of the social groupings they investigated. Whether young or old; rich or poor; well

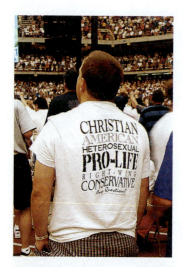

Gender and social dominance orientation. Men across groups tend to score higher in the motivation for social dominance. This man's T-shirt suggests that he believes that his groups—Christians, Americans, heterosexuals, and conservatives—are superior to the alternatives.

Gender-typed cultural roles. Across cultures, men are likely to choose roles emphasizing social dominance, such as military and warrior roles. According to the biocultural interactionist theory, ancient inclinations interact with the roles and norms created by current societies (which are themselves built around those ancient inclinations).

educated or poorly educated; Republican or Democrat; Asian, European, or Latino, men tended to have higher social dominance scores. And a larger sample of 7,000 respondents from six different countries corroborated the sex differences (Sidanius et al., 2000).

What accounts for this gender difference in social dominance orientation? Sidanius and Pratto think neither biological nor sociocultural factors tell the whole story. They instead favor a *biocultural interactionist* position. Pratto (1996) observes that the distinction between natural and cultural factors is a false dichotomy because humans evolved to live in social groups in the first place. According to their biocultural perspective, men in all human cultures have tended to gravitate to positions involving "ranking" (such as chiefs, lords, and in modern times, government officials) and competition with outgroups (warriors or, in modern times, soldiers).

The researchers believe that this difference in social dominance orientation is cross-culturally universal because in all ancestral societies, there was a correlation between a man's social status and his reproductive success. Because, as discussed in Chapter 8, females are often more selective in choosing mates, males must compete among themselves for females' attentions. In human groups throughout history, men who were successful as warriors, protecting the group against opposing groups, reaped direct and indirect rewards.

Sidanius and Pratto's biocultural interactionist theory of social dominance doesn't assume that it is "all in our genes" (Sidanius & Pratto, 2003). Instead, they note how males' competitive tendencies influence their choices of occupations and political groups. For instance, 84% of police officers are men, as are 80% of people in the military. At the highest levels of such occupations, the sex differences are even greater—the vast majority of the highest ranking people in the U.S. Department of Defense are men. This is partly because of the choices made by men and women and partly because of the aspects of the culture that encourage the existing sex differences. In most countries, women still aren't permitted in the military, and female police officers are rare (Pratto et al., 1997). This is a key insight of research at the interface of anthropology, biology, and social psychology—that there is continual interplay between evolved human predispositions and the complex cultures that we construct around those predispositions (Cohen, 2001; Kenrick, Nieuweboer, & Buunk, 2010; Krebs & Janicki, 2004; Norenzayan, Schaller, & Heine, 2006).

AUTHORITARIANISM AND SENSE OF THREAT   As discussed in Chapter 11, authoritarianism reflects the tendency to respect power, obey authority, and rigidly cohere to society's conventions (Feather, 1998; Jost et al., 2003). In the international arena, authoritarians are generally more favorable toward a strong military and more hostile toward foreigners (Doty, Peterson, & Winter, 1991; Tibon & Blumberg, 1999). Students scoring high in authoritarianism wanted more use of force against Iraq during the 1990 war in the Persian Gulf, even to the point of using nuclear weapons. And afterward, they expressed less regret about the deaths of Iraqi civilians and more gloating over the U.S. victory (Doty et al., 1997).

Timothy McVeigh, the man convicted of killing 168 people in the 1995 bombing of the federal building in Oklahoma City, demonstrated a number of features of the authoritarian personality. He was reportedly strongly racist and suspicious of a "New World Order" undermining the U.S. government, and he reputedly believed that his bombing was morally justified as a retaliation for offenses by the federal government. He quit the National Rifle Association because he thought them "too soft," and his favorite piece of literature was a racist and anti-Semitic book popular among the far right (Morganthau & Annin, 1997). McVeigh's profile fits with findings of a study by Marina Abalakina-Paap and her colleagues Walter Stephan, Traci Craig, and Larry Gregory (1999). These researchers studied the distinctive characteristics of people who accept conspiracy theories. The typical believer in conspiracy theories tends to be high in authoritarianism and in feelings of alienation, powerlessness, and hostility.

Other studies corroborate that authoritarians are especially prone to feeling threatened (Lambert, Burroughs, & Nguyen, 1999; Lavine et al., 1999). Consequently, they tend to be low in openness to new experiences and to strike observers as defensive and prejudiced (Butler, 2000; Lippa & Arad, 1999; Saucier, 2000). An interesting study of 1,600 South Africans corroborated that prejudice is associated with feeling relatively worse off than others, but also revealed high prejudice in those who are substantially better off than others (Dambrun et al., 2006). One possibility is that deprivation may contribute to authoritarian defensiveness, whereas being especially well-off may contribute to feelings of social dominance.

Although social dominance orientation and authoritarianism are both linked to nationalism and prejudice against foreigners, there are some important distinctions (Altemeyer, 2004; Roccato & Ricolfi, 2005). People high in authoritarianism tend, in general, to be socially submissive and to have the desire to follow a strong leader; whereas those high in social dominance generally want to lead others. Social dominance orientation also lacks the rigid morality associated with authoritarianism (Altemeyer, 2004; Whitley, 1999). One researcher studied a small subgroup of the Canadian population that is high on both authoritarianism and social dominance orientation. These people tended to be dogmatically religious, like authoritarians, but to be more power-hungry, manipulative, and opposed to equality than the typical authoritarian. The researcher suggested that such people may be potentially dangerous to society, in that the leaders of prejudiced militant organizations are likely to be drawn from their ranks (Altemeyer, 2004).

SIMPLIFIED IMAGES OF INTERNATIONAL CONFLICT Political psychologist Philip Tetlock (1983b) examined the speeches made by policymakers involved in international conflicts. He noted that, in making important decisions, national leaders often fall back on overly simplified images of the world. During the Cold War between the United States and the Soviet Union, for example, two very simple images of the conflict were dominant. One of these was the **deterrence view**—that any sign of weakness would be exploited by the opponent and that leaders needed to show their willingness to use military force. From a deterrence perspective, some demonstration of aggressiveness is often necessary as a preventive measure to stop the other side from aggressing against one's group. People who hold a deterrence view—that demonstrations of weakness would be exploited—were less likely to support nuclear disarmament (Chibnall & Wiener, 1988). The other prominent view was a **conflict spiral view**, which presumed that every escalation of international threat leads the opponent to feel more threatened and that leaders need to demonstrate peaceful intentions in order to reduce the opponent's own defensive hostilities.

Deterrence view The belief that signs of weakness will be exploited by the opponent and that leaders need to show their willingness to use military force.

Conflict spiral view The belief that escalations of international threat lead an opponent to feel more threatened and that leaders should thus demonstrate peaceful intentions to reduce the opponent's own defensive hostilities.

INVESTIGATION

Look at a recent newspaper or magazine or go on the Internet to find one or two statements by people currently involved in international conflicts (heads of state, military leaders, or political activists in Palestine or Israel, for example). Do their statements indicate a deterrence or a conflict spiral view?

Tetlock (1983b) noted that each of these cognitive frames was correct in some circumstances and incorrect in others. Against an opponent such as Hitler, a deterrence viewpoint might have been more effective than a view that led to conciliation. On the other hand, international policy experts estimate that the U.S. invasion of Iraq, argued by President G. W. Bush to be the centerpiece of the war on terror, seems to have spurred increases in the membership of Al-Qaeda (the group responsible for the terrorist attacks of September 11, 2001) (Karon, 2004).

SITUATION ## Competition and Threat

During the first half of the twentieth century, the citizens of Italy, Germany, France, and England were twice embroiled in massive world wars that killed millions. Those same nations are now joined in a cooperative union. Not only are the former opponents from the two world wars now united, but the European Union was later expanded to include several countries (such as Czechoslovakia, Lithuania, and Poland) that were formerly part of the Soviet Union. How did mutual cooperation replace mutual threat and hostility? Examining the situational factors that trigger the motivation to protect one's ingroup may provide part of the answer.

In this section, we consider two related factors linked to escalations and de-escalations in outgroup hostility—competition over resources and threat. We discussed how these factors relate to intergroup prejudice in Chapter 11; we now consider how they extend beyond local prejudices to international conflicts.

GROUP COMPETITION OVER RESOURCES At the chapter's opening, we discussed the bloody conflict between Bengali immigrants and the natives of Assam, India. This incident was linked to competition over scarce resources—fertile land in areas of rapid population growth. It demonstrates how realistic group conflict theory can be directly applied to international relations.

Although international conflicts sometimes trace directly to realistic conflict, the economic motivations aren't always clearly recognized by the participants. Instead, if we compete with the members of another group, that may simply change our perceptions of that group in a generally negative manner, and lower our thresholds for becoming angry with them (Butz & Plant, 2006; Wann & Grieve, 2005). As we discussed in Chapter 11, the boys in the Rattlers and the Eagles at the Robbers Cave summer camp came to perceive outgroup members more negatively after competing for scarce rewards. But the former enemies shifted to a more positive view after the groups joined together to work toward common goals (Sherif et al., 1961).

Within the broader society, militaristic and punitive authoritarian tendencies tend to increase when the economy turns down and people face unemployment and hunger (McCann, 1999; Sales, 1973). For example, one study compared the period of 1978 through 1982 (a time of increasing unemployment, rising interest rates, and economic dissatisfaction) with the period 1983 through 1987 (a time of increasing personal income, decreasing interest

Economic threat and authoritarianism. Historically, the clearest example of increased authoritarianism following economic hard times was the rise of Nazism in Germany after the terrible depression and international humiliation Germans suffered following their loss in World War I. During such difficult times, Hitler's plans to expand German territory and simultaneously restore international respect for Germany fell on receptive ears among the German populace.

rates, and economic hopefulness). This study revealed higher levels of racial prejudice and some signs of a heightened emphasis on power and toughness (such as more registrations for attack dogs) during the economic hard times (Doty et al., 1991). In this chapter's research video, Prof. Sarah Hill describes her research showing how economic threats can even change our basic perceptions of other people, altering people's thresholds for seeing a mixed race person as a member of their racial group.

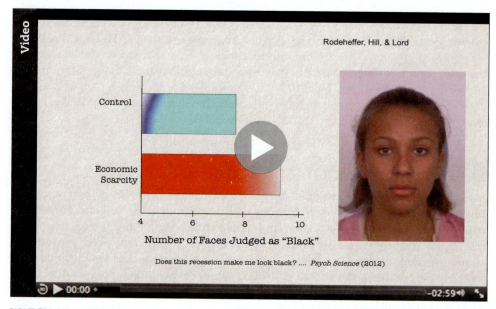

WATCH THE VIDEO: *Does this economic recession make me look Black? Watch Sarah Hill describe her research showing how economic threats can alter racial discrimination at the simplest cognitive level.*

Figure 13.6 Group competitiveness in everyday life

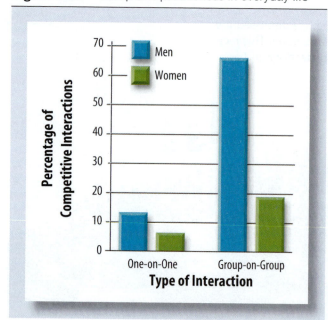

Michael Pemberton, Chester Insko, and John Schopler asked students to record and categorize their daily interactions. Students recorded more competitive interactions involving groups than during one-on-one meetings with others. The pattern held for both sexes, but women were less likely to have competitive interactions, even in groups, whereas men in groups had predominantly competitive interactions.

A number of researchers have found that simply placing people into groups increases competitiveness, even though that competition may result in losses for all concerned (e.g., Bornstein, 2003; Insko et al., 1990, 1994; Wildschut et al., 2003). For example, students in one study recorded their daily interactions and categorized them as either group or individual activities. More of the interactions involving groups were competitive, particularly when males were involved (Pemberton, Insko, & Schopler, 1996) (see Figure 13.6). Other research supports this general pattern; people in groups are more likely to respond to annoyances by escalating from mild complaints through threats and physical harassment (Mikolic, Parker, & Pruitt, 1997).

Why are group interactions more competitive? Part of the problem is that individuals, assuming that large groups bring out the worst in people, simply expect the members of the *other* group to act more competitively, which leads both sides to act competitively in a self-perpetuating cycle (Winquist & Larson, 2004). When the researchers analyzed the content of discussions between group members, they found a positive relationship between competitiveness and distrust of the other side's intentions (Pemberton et al., 1996).

How can groups move from distrust to trust? For one thing, individual experiences that encourage two groups to cooperate with each other can reduce outgroup biases (Gaertner, Iuzzini, Witt, & Oriña, 2006; Gaertner et al., 1990; Thompson, 1999). If an individual in group A is given the chance to negotiate one-to-one with an individual in group B, and they manage to come to a satisfactory settlement, both individuals walk away with more positive opinions of the other group as a whole (Thompson, 1993). These positive one-on-one experiences teach group members that the individuals on the other side have motivations similar to those of the individuals on "our side." Simply reminding people that their two groups are interconnected in some way can also reduce the "us versus them" mentality (Kramer & Brewer, 1984; Levine et al., 2005; Wit & Kerr, 2002). When the members of the U.S. Olympic team play against other countries, for example, they forget the former rivalries between their "home teams" in Michigan, Nebraska, and California.

Herbert Kelman and his associates directly applied many of the social psychological findings on intergroup competition and cooperation to international conflict resolution (Kelman, 1998, 1999; Rouhana & Kelman, 1994). During official negotiations, both sides often face pressures that enhance competition. These include the need to bargain for terms that benefit one's own side, to satisfy sometimes angry constituencies who will read about the negotiations in the newspapers, and so on. Kelman brought together groups of influential Israelis and Palestinians for noncompetitive, interactive problem-solving workshops. These workshops involved political leaders, parliament members, influential journalists, former military officers, and government officials from the two sides. Participants get together not to negotiate but simply to familiarize one another with the viewpoints of the other side and to brainstorm potential solutions that could later be brought to official negotiations. In these noncompetitive group settings, participants developed more complex images of the other side. This helped them overcome their prejudicial oversimplifications. The nonhostile norms of the group settings also promoted new ideas for solutions. And the participants formed new coalitions that cut across the lines of conflict (Kelman, 1998).

THREATS Indian prime minister Atal Bihari Vajpayee apparently believed that nuclear weapons could prevent wars between India and its neighbors. In response to world outrage over India's renewed underground nuclear tests in May 1998, he claimed that the weapons had been developed solely to promote peaceful coexistence and not to attack Pakistan. Unfortunately, Pakistan took it as a threat and exploded its own nuclear weapons as a counterthreat. This should be no surprise, given that research suggests that threats tend to increase, rather than decrease, conflict.

Consider the results of one typical study, in which students were told by the experimenter:

> There are two of you who are going to play a game in which you can either win money or lose money. I want you to earn as much money as you can regardless of how much the other earns. This money is real and you will keep whatever you earn. (Deutsch, 1986, p. 164)

The game consisted of a series of trials. Players picked one of several plays on any trial, ranging from cooperation to attack or defense.

Unbeknownst to the real subjects, their opponents were actually confederates of the experimenter. The experimental confederates tried out several different strategies for inducing cooperation from a partner. One of these was a *punitive deterrent* strategy, in which the accomplice used a cooperative reward strategy on the first trial and responded with an attack if the real player did not cooperate. Another strategy was the *nonpunitive deterrent* strategy. In this case, the accomplice responded to an attack with a defense and otherwise cooperated. Finally, some accomplices used a *turn the other cheek* strategy. In this case, the accomplice started out playing cooperatively and kept cooperating. If attacked by the opponent, he would get even more cooperative.

Figure 13.7 shows the results from this experiment (Deutsch, 1986). Note that the most successful strategy was the nonpunitive deterrence approach. The least successful was the totally cooperative turning of the other cheek. The punitive deterrence strategy started out somewhat successfully but dropped in effectiveness as it made the opponent increasingly angry and elicited counterattacks.

Figure 13.7 Winning and losing strategies

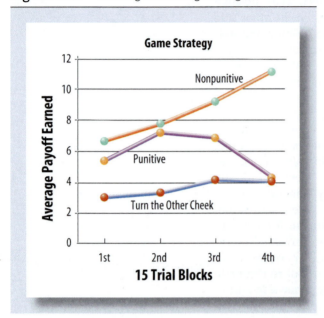

In Morton Deutsch's laboratory dilemma game, confederates of an experimenter played one of three strategies against subjects in a laboratory dilemma. A punitive deterrent strategy was less effective over time, often eliciting angry retaliations. A strategy of turning the other cheek was consistently exploited by opponents. A nonpunitive deterrent strategy won the most points over the course of the game.

Source: Deutsch, M. (1986). Strategies for inducing cooperation. In R. K. White (Ed.), Psychology and the prevention of nuclear war (pp. 162–170). New York: New York University Press.

Integrative complexity The extent to which a person demonstrates simplified "black-and-white" categorical thinking, as opposed to acknowledgment of all sides of an issue.

The researcher argued that the principles of conflict and cooperation found in these laboratory dilemmas apply to interactions between nations (Deutsch, 1986). When one nation uses coercive pressure on another, as when the United States started a war with Iraq, it tends to elicit anger and counterattacks from the opponent. When one nation consistently "turns its other cheek" to another nation's aggressions, as when the Allies "appeased" Hitler when he first began invading his neighbors, it is likely to lead to exploitation. The best approach for a country is generally to choose cooperation unless it is attacked.

Results of these classic laboratory studies are also consistent with more recent research indicating that several types of threats increase nationalist and militarist sentiments in various ways. For example, one series of studies found that either contemplating one's own death or thinking about the terrorist attacks of September 11, 2001, led American students to increase their support for President George W. Bush (Landau et al., 2004). Other laboratory studies find that people become more cooperative with their own groups when they are competing with other groups (Burton-Chellew, Ross-Gillespie, & West, 2010), and this tendency may be especially pronounced among men (Van Vugt, De Cremer, & Janssen, 2007). A cross-cultural study of this phenomenon found that American students responded to thoughts of death or of losing their resources by becoming more patriotically pro-American; whereas Costa Ricans were more complacent in the face of thoughts about death, but became more patriotically pro–Costa Rica when they thought about being isolated from other people (Navarrete, Kurzban, Fessler, & Kirkpatrick, 2004). Another study examined Gallup ratings of U.S. president George W. Bush and found that the American public had a tendency to approve of Bush more strongly whenever there had been a government-issued terror warning during the preceding week (Willer, 2004).

Threats of invasion or terrorism are not the only kinds of threats that feed the venomous sentiments of nationalism and ethnocentrism. Jay Faulkner, Mark Schaller, Justin Park, and Leslie Duncan (2004) found that concerns about disease (aroused by viewing someone with a disfigured face, for example) led Canadian students to feel more prejudice toward foreigners from third-world countries (such as Sri Lanka), and to favor stronger anti-immigration laws to keep foreigners out of Canada. Presumably, people from third-world countries are more likely to be seen as carrying dangerous diseases.

Another fascinating series of investigations at the interface of psychology and political science examined how international threat affects decision making in national leaders and their political constituencies (e.g., Mandel, Axelrod, & Lehman, 1993; Satterfield, 1998; Tibon, 2000; Winter, 2007). In one study, Canadian psychologists Peter Suedfeld, Michael Wallace, and Kimberly Thachuk (1993) analyzed over 1,200 statements made by national leaders before, during, and after the Persian Gulf crisis of 1990. Suedfeld and his colleagues examined the "integrative complexity" of leaders' public statements. **Integrative complexity** is the extent to which the leaders' statements demonstrate simplified "black-and-white" categorical thinking as opposed to acknowledgment of all sides of a conflict. A simple statement, for example, might affirm repeatedly that Iraq acted in an evil way and describe the evils of Iraq's leader, Saddam Hussein. A complex statement might express disapproval of Iraq while discussing the different historical facets of the conflict, including Kuwait's refusal to negotiate with Iraq about a secure Persian Gulf outlet and Kuwait's violation of

OPEC price-control agreements. The researchers found that leaders of the nations most directly involved in the conflict (such as U.S. president George H. W. Bush and Iraqi president Saddam Hussein) made less complex statements than those who were less involved. Furthermore, the statements got simpler and simpler as the stressfulness of the situation increased.

The problems of simplified thinking are further exaggerated when members of different nations don't even understand their opponents' view of the world, as we discuss next.

INTERACTION Intercultural Misperception and International Conflict

In 1991, American president George H. W. Bush had initially believed that Iraqi leader Saddam Hussein was bluffing when he threatened to invade Kuwait. But Hussein did in fact invade Kuwait. A short while later, a news report observed that Saddam thought Bush was bluffing about his threat carry out his threat to invade Iraq if they did not withdraw from Kuwait (McDaniel & Thomas, 1991). But a few days after that news report, Bush unleashed the force of more than 500,000 troops and a massive technological attack on Iraq.

According to social psychologist Paul Kimmel (1997), George H. W. Bush and Saddam Hussein both misunderstood the threats made by the other side because of gaps in intercultural communication. Before Saddam Hussein invaded Kuwait, he had met with U.S. ambassador April Glaspie and indicated his intentions. On the basis of his interactions with the U.S. ambassador, he believed that Washington wouldn't get involved if he invaded. Later, he apparently didn't believe that the United States would lead a counterattack but instead interpreted the military preparations as a bluff.

These misunderstandings were costly ones, eventually leading to the deaths of thousands of Iraqis and hundreds of Americans and setting the stage for another United States–Iraq war in 2003. What could have caused such miscommunication? Part of the problem is that communications between Westerners and Arabs are often confusing for both sides. According to one Western diplomat stationed in the region at the time of the war, "In the Middle East everyone lies. If you tell the truth you are considered hopelessly naive and even dangerous because people find the truth the most difficult of options to understand" (Lane, 1991, p. 18).

When U.S. troops were dispatched to Saudi Arabia, they were given a training booklet to help them avoid insulting local Arabs. It included the advice that "it is natural for an Arab to speak with double meanings—and the American who fails to watch for these can make foolish mistakes" (Dickey, 1991, p. 27).

Arabs themselves apparently experience frequent difficulties with communications from the other side. Hussein's negotiators reported feeling that U.S. leaders were insulting them rather than negotiating sincerely. After those negotiators refused even to accept a letter from Bush to Hussein, which they said contained "language that is not compatible with language between heads of state," one Iraqi negotiator said, "I never thought that you Americans could be so arrogant. Such a free and open country you have and still you refuse to see our viewpoint" (quoted in Kimmel, 1997, p. 408).

Based on his own work with international negotiators, Kimmel (1997) recommends that they include a period of "intercultural exploration" in their negotiations. Intercultural exploration involves identifying each side's cultural assumptions and communicating them clearly before moving on to collaborate in finding a solution. He notes, for instance, several basic differences between the assumptions of American and Iraqi negotiators. Americans were task oriented, impersonal, definite in their demands, and fast paced. Iraqis, however, prefer slower-paced, personal negotiations in which the two groups get to know one another. Another important difference is that Americans tend to focus on the future, whereas Arabs have a much stronger sense that

Saddam Hussein. This Iraqi leader led the invasion of Kuwait in 1990 and elicited a costly counterattack by the United Nations. An analysis of statements made by leaders, including Saddam Hussein and U.S. then-president George Bush, revealed more simplistic thinking at times of intense conflict. Peter Suedfeld and his colleagues (1993) suggest that anxiety puts a strain on cognitive resources and leads to simplified, heuristic thinking.

the past should be considered. An Egyptian diplomat observed: "You have to remember you're in a region where people talk about the Crusades as if they were yesterday" (quoted in McGrath, 1991, p. 24).

Kimmel distinguishes several levels of cultural awareness, including

- *Cultural chauvinism*: A complete unawareness of other cultures, which leads negotiators to attribute ignorance and bad intentions to the other side.
- *Ethnocentrism*: An awareness of ethnic, religious, racial, or national differences, accompanied by a conviction that one's own way is the "right" one.
- *Tolerance*: Awareness of, and appreciation of, differences but still accompanied by a feeling that one's own culture is more effective and realistic; leads negotiators to try to "educate" or "develop" those who differ.
- *Minimization*: Awareness of cultural differences but with a focus on the many similarities across human cultures, which could lead to ignoring important differences at critical points in negotiation.
- *Understanding*: Realization that one's own way of doing things is only one of many and that others are not abnormal in any way.

Kimmel notes that most negotiators have a hard time operating consistently at the level of "understanding." This is partly because negotiators prefer the familiar norms of their own group and partly because the constituents back home may not trust them if they seem too chummy with the other side. Nevertheless, negotiations based on an awareness of the important differences in cultural assumptions are bound to go more smoothly.

One of the key goals of intercultural awareness on the part of international negotiators, according to Kimmel (1997), is to move from a focus on "us" versus "them" to "we." When two groups focus on their shared goals, deception and threats become less necessary.

INTERACTION The Reciprocal Dynamics of Cooperation and Conflict

Negotiation dilemmas involve dynamic interactions—complex interconnected patterns of change over time. Looking back at Figure 13.7, we can see the effects of a punitive strategy getting worse over time, whereas the effects of a nonpunitive deterrence strategy tended to improve (Deutsch, 1986). Opponents in laboratory dilemmas often "lock in" on either a cooperative or a competitive pattern (Rapoport, Diekmann, & Franzen, 1995). The real world provides a never-ending stream of examples, such as the recent escalation in the long conflict between Israel and Palestine. We will now examine several areas of research on these processes and consider what lessons this research can teach about how to wind down these escalating conflicts.

TIT-FOR-TAT STRATEGIES The most "stable" strategy in reciprocal negotiations over time is called a **tit-for-tat strategy** (Axelrod, 1984; Komorita, Hilty, & Parks, 1991; Nowak, Sasaki, Taylor, & Fundenberg, 2004). A player using the tit-for-tat strategy responds cooperatively when the opponent is cooperative. When the opponent is competitive, the player responds competitively and then switches back to a cooperative strategy to "bait" the opponent back to the mutually beneficial cooperative pattern. According to social psychologist Samuel Komorita and his colleagues (1991), the tit-for-tat strategy works by doubly relying on the powerful norm of reciprocity (discussed in detail in Chapter 9). It reciprocates cooperation with cooperation and returns competition for competition. It thus combines the "you scratch my back, I'll scratch yours" reciprocation with "an eye for an eye" retaliation. Indeed, experience playing against someone who uses a tit-for-tat strategy can even lead intrinsically competitive people to get the message, and begin cooperating (Sheldon, 1999).

Tit-for-tat strategy A negotiating tactic in which the individual responds to competitiveness with competitiveness and to cooperation with cooperation.

THE DOLLAR GAME The conflicts between Israel and Palestine, India and Pakistan, and the United States and Iraq all illustrate a special type of social trap. The entrapping quality of this type of competitive escalation is shown nicely in a dilemma called the "dollar game" (Teger, 1980).

Could you imagine otherwise intelligent college students bidding several dollars to win a $1 prize? Each of the authors of this textbook has played the game in class and watched it happen again and again. The game begins by offering a dollar to the highest bidder. The game initially appeals to greed—if the highest bid is 4 cents, then the dollar would go for 4 cents, and the bidder would gain 96 cents. However, other students who see someone else about to get a dollar practically for free join the fray with higher bids. The feature of the game that makes it a social trap is this: The second-highest bidder must also pay up. Thus if one student bids 4 cents, and another bids a dime, the top bidder wins 90 cents, but the second bidder loses 4 cents. Because of this feature, no one wants to come in second, so it may actually become profitable to bid over a dollar if you have made the second-highest bid (of say 90 cents) and your opponent bids the full dollar. As the game progresses, the initial greed motivation is replaced with increasing fear of loss. In classes, we have often watched students get caught up in the action and once saw the bidding go over $20. Those same excessive bids have repeatedly been found in laboratory subjects playing the game in smaller groups (Teger, 1980). International conflicts often demonstrate the features of this type of social trap, where an initial desire for what seems like a good outcome (winning a dollar or scaring off a potential adversary) is replaced by fear of losing face and an escalating commitment of resources.

PERCEPTUAL DILEMMAS   Despite all the evidence that hostility will be reciprocated with hostility, history keeps repeating itself with failed attempts to use aggressive coercion as a negotiating technique. For example, the Nazi bombing of civilian areas in London was designed to force the British to surrender. Instead, it had the effect of strengthening the British determination to fight. Nevertheless, when the Americans joined with the English against the Germans, they repeated history by bombing German civilian areas in the hopes of weakening German resolve. Again, the bombing did little to weaken the German will to resist (Rothbart & Hallmark, 1988). If threats and coercive manipulations fail so often in the laboratory and in the real world, why are they used so frequently? Social psychologists Myron Rothbart and William Hallmark (1988) suggest that part of the answer has to do with simple cognitive tendencies toward "ingroup favorability" and "outgroup bias."

In a pair of laboratory experiments, Rothbart and Hallmark asked students to role-play a defense minister from either "Takonia" or "Navalia"—two hypothetical nations sharing the same island and a history of conflict. "Defense ministers" were asked to judge the effectiveness of several strategies for dealing with the opponent. The strategies ranged from cooperative (for example, unilaterally cutting back your production of submarines by 20%, with the expectation that your opponent will then make similar cutbacks in artillery) to coercive (building more submarines and threatening to use them if your opponent does not cut back its long-range artillery forces). Although Takonian and Navalian ministers read about the same conflict, their ideas about effective strategies were the mirror-opposite of one another. Students acting as Takonian ministers believed that their own country would respond to cooperative strategies but that the Navalian opponents would probably have to be coerced. Navalians, however, believed that Navalia would respond best to cooperative overtures but that those Takonians would require coercion to bring them into line.

Because students role-playing Navalian and Takonian ministers couldn't have felt the same sort of punitive anger that might have motivated the bombings of North Vietnam or Germany, Rothbart and Hallmark (1988) argue that their results are a simple extension of the "minimal group" findings, discussed in Chapter 11 on prejudice. Merely putting people into two groups leads them to judge their own side in positive terms (as generally "cooperative," for example) and the other side in negative terms (as "stubborn" and "noncompliant").

Perceptual dilemma The combination of a social dilemma and an outgroup bias, in which each side in a conflict believes that it is best for both sides to cooperate, while simultaneously believing that the other side would prefer that "we" cooperated while "they" defected.

Ingroup biases of students role-playing Takonians and Navalians in a laboratory simulation are harmless. However, similar ingroup biases show up in the real world of international relations, where they can have disastrous consequences. Scott Plous (1985) found evidence that American and Soviet leaders during the Cold War wanted mutual disarmament but perceived the other side as wanting nuclear superiority. Plous argued that both sides were locked in a **perceptual dilemma**—an unfortunate combination of a social dilemma and an outgroup bias. In a perceptual dilemma, each side in a conflict believes that its best outcome would be for both sides to cooperate, while simultaneously believing that the other side will gladly exploit, but not offer, cooperative gestures.

To test his idea that Soviet and American leaders during the 1980s were locked in a perceptual dilemma, Plous sent questionnaires to U.S. senators. He asked the senators to rate the desirability of America's continued arming or disarming if the Soviets either armed or disarmed. The senators were also asked what they thought the Soviets would prefer. The results (shown in Figure 13.8) show that U.S. senators thought it best for the United States if both sides disarmed. They strongly opposed either continued escalation or U.S. disarmament in the face of continued Soviet armament. Unfortunately, the senators thought that Soviet leaders viewed things very differently. Although they believed that the Soviets would also like mutual disarmament, they thought the Soviets would most prefer to continue arming while the United States disarmed. Under those circumstances, the United States would be left with no alternative but to keep building arms reluctantly. A survey of Soviet leaders, however, showed that Soviets thought exactly the opposite (Guroff & Grant, 1981). The Soviets themselves viewed arms control as essential but firmly believed that the Americans preferred to keep building the U.S. arsenal.

Figure 13.8   A perceptual dilemma

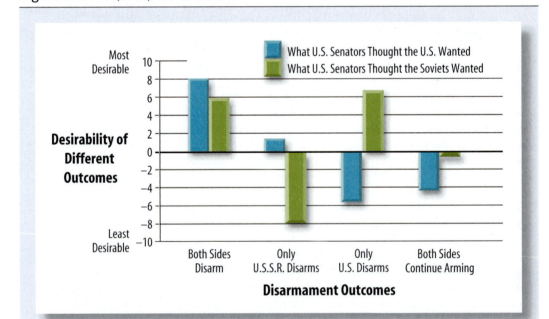

U.S. senators surveyed during the Cold War correctly perceived that neither side wanted to disarm while the other side continued to get stronger. However, they believed that the "ingroup" (the United States) most wanted mutual disarmament while the "outgroup" (the Soviet Union) slightly preferred the "sneaky" alternative of continuing to prepare for nuclear war while the United States disarmed. Analyses of Soviet leaders' statements indicated that the Soviets wanted to disarm but believed that the United States most wanted to continue building nuclear weapons while the Soviets got weaker.

These findings suggest that neither the Soviets nor the Americans had purely aggressive intentions in stockpiling nuclear weapons. Instead, they were mainly trying to communicate their threat potential to the other side. Unfortunately, coercive threats take on a life of their own when two sides use them against one another. One analysis of 99 serious international disputes (involving troop movements, port blockades, withdrawn ambassadors, and so on) found that, if they were not preceded by an arms race, only 4% led to war. Of those that were preceded by an arms race, on the other hand, fully 82% resulted in war (Wallace, 1979).

Although the Cold War is over and the Soviet Union has been largely disbanded, most of the nuclear weapons built by the Soviets and Americans still exist. Because they are so abundant, there is a remaining danger of an accidental nuclear war. In addition, several other countries, such as China, India, Israel, Iran, Pakistan, and South Korea, now have their own nuclear weapons or the technology to build them. Can advances in social science help us solve the problems that advances in physical science have wrought in the field of military technology?

GRIT (graduated and reciprocated initiatives in tension reduction)
A strategy for breaking conflict spirals by publicly challenging the opponent to match de-escalations.

Bridging Theory and Application:

Increasing Intergroup Cooperation with the GRIT Strategy

We have considered several obstacles to international cooperation. People naturally divide themselves into beloved ingroups and despised outgroups (Krebs & Denton, 1997; Tajfel & Turner, 1979). Once conflicts begin, they tend to escalate (Deutsch, 1986). Arms races between nations often lead to war (Wallace, 1979). Fortunately, though, the upward spiral of conflict isn't inevitable: It can be reversed.

In Chapter 11, we discussed the warring summer campers at Robbers Cave (Sherif et al., 1961). When forced to work together toward common goals, the Rattlers and Eagles overcame their rivalry and even started to like one another. These findings suggest that countries in conflict could promote peace by working together toward mutually beneficial goals (such as finding a cure for cancer or AIDS). Replacing international competition with cooperation may be easier said than done, however. While two sides are still locked in conflict, each side distrusts the other's motives and fears exploitation. And, as we mentioned earlier, laboratory studies do show that unconditional cooperation will often be exploited (Deutsch, 1986).

As a way out of the two-sided dilemma of increasing threat versus exploited appeasement, psychologist Charles Osgood (1962) suggested the **graduated and reciprocated initiatives in tension reduction (GRIT)** strategy for breaking conflict spirals by publicly challenging the opponent to match de-escalations. To break a conflict spiral, Osgood proposed that one side of the conflict begin with a peaceful initiative. To avoid appearing or actually becoming weaker with such a conciliatory move, Osgood suggested the first step be a small one. Along with the small initial peace offering, the peace-promoter using GRIT makes a public statement that larger and larger reductions in conflict will follow if the other side follows suit with peaceful initiatives of its own. By reciprocating gradually larger reductions in armaments, both sides can thereby avoid ever getting into a highly disadvantaged position. The beauty of the GRIT strategy is that, instead

Grit and the end of the cold war. Soviet premier Gorbachev used a variation of the GRIT strategy—graduated and reciprocated initiatives in tension reduction—to help spin down the conflict spiral of nuclear weapons production. He won the Nobel Peace Prize for his efforts. He is pictured here with former U.S. president Reagan.

of challenging one another toward increasing competition, the opponents begin to challenge one another toward increased cooperation.

The GRIT strategy has been effective in laboratory conflict simulations (Lindskold, 1983). Additional encouragement comes from studies of a very similar strategy that evolutionary economists call "raising the stakes" (Van den Bergh & Dewitte, 2006). Do these strategies work in the real world of international relations? During the 1980s, Soviet premier Mikhail Gorbachev used a very similar strategy to bring U.S. president Ronald Reagan to the bargaining table. Gorbachev first proposed a one-sided weapons test ban in the Soviet Union and offered to continue it if the United States would follow suit. When the United States didn't reciprocate,

Gorbachev showed his resolve by beginning weapons tests again. However, his first gesture had warmed up American public opinion, so Gorbachev tried again the following year by offering to have American inspectors verify Soviet arms reductions. This time he was successful, and Reagan agreed to a treaty that required reductions in nuclear armaments on both sides. Gorbachev's policy of reciprocal concessions had indeed led to a happy outcome and may have been a key to ending the Cold War.

The GRIT strategy, like the tit-for-tat and the punitive deterrence strategies, leads competitors into a pattern of dynamic interaction. It differs in a very important way, however. Instead of stimulating conflict or stabilizing an already peaceful situation, it leads to a pattern of escalating peacemaking.

INVESTIGATION

You've been appointed secretary of state, and your job is to peruse the material in this chapter to come up with two positive moves that our government (or one of our allies) could use to ease current world tensions and two negative things to avoid. What would you select?

Quick Quiz

1 Which of the following statements is *false*?

    a. Social dominance orientation refers to the desire that one's ingroup dominates others groups.

    b. Men and women are equally likely to be high in social dominance.

    c. Authoritarianism refers to the tendency to be deferential to authority, moralistically aggressive, and ethnocentric.

    d. People high in authoritarianism have the desire to follow a strong leader, whereas those high in social dominance generally want to lead others.

2 Leaders holding a _____ view believe that demonstrations of peaceful intent reduce opponents' defensiveness, whereas leaders holding a _____ view believe that signs of weakness will be exploited and that one must show willingness to use military power.

    a. conflict spiral, deterrence

    b. deterrence, conflict spiral

    c. conflict spiral, command-and-control

    d. cooperator, command-and-control

3 Which of the following statements is *true*?

    a. Political leaders' integrative complexity tends to increase when faced with the stress of international threats.

    b. In laboratory studies, punitive deterrent strategies were the most effective strategies for inducing cooperation.

    c. Threats such as mortality salience, loss of valuable resources, and dangerous diseases tend to increase nationalism and ethnocentrism.

    d. All of the above

4 According to Kimmel, the _____ level of cultural awareness is _____, which is the realization that one's own way of doing things is only one of many and that others are not abnormal in any way; in contrast, the _____ level is _____, which is a complete unawareness of other cultures that leads negotiators to attribute ignorance and bad intentions to the other side.

    a. optimal, tolerance; sub-optimal, cultural chauvinism

    b. optimal, minimization; sub-optimal, ethnocentrism

    c. highest, understanding; lowest, ethnocentrism

    d. highest, understanding; lowest, cultural chauvinism

5 The _____ strategy leads to a pattern of escalating peacemaking, whereas the _____ strategy may escalate conflict by responding to competitiveness with further competitiveness.

    a. tit-for-tat, GRIT

    b. GRIT, tit-for-tat

    c. punitive deterrence, GRIT

    d. punitive deterrence, tit-for-tat

Revisiting   The Future

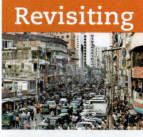

We opened this chapter with the contrast between two possible pathways for the world's future. One is unfolding on the Indian subcontinent, as Bengalis, East Indians, and Pakistanis continue to multiply their numbers and magnify the conflicts that have driven them apart for most of the last century. Another is unfolding in Western Europe, where population growth has slowed to a standstill, environmental consciousness has blossomed, and former foes have united into a cooperative union. Down one path, humans will continue to destroy the planet's resources, fight over the dwindling remainders, and do irreversible damage to the oceans, the atmosphere, and the earth's other species. Down the other, humans will live in quieter, greener, and more harmonious conditions, and literally save the planet.

In this chapter, we saw how overpopulation, environmental destruction, and international conflict are all conceptually linked to the phenomenon of social traps—situations in which immediate selfishness leads, in the long run, to group disaster. In the case of overpopulation, individuals act on the most primary of individual selfish motives—the inclination to reproduce one's genes. As the growing population demands more food, those who harvest the oceans and the forests are daily drawn into a classic social dilemma: Despite the long-term disastrous consequences for the greater good, it is in the selfish interest of each individual fisherman or logger to take as much as possible now. Likewise, international conflicts often demonstrate the features of another sort of trap, as illustrated in the "dollar game." In this type of trap, an initial desire for what seems like a good outcome (winning a dollar or scaring off a potential adversary) is replaced by a fear of losing face and an escalating commitment of resources. Once again, we see the importance of social psychology's bridges with other

disciplines. Economists, biologists, and political scientists are intensively studying social dilemmas as well, as scientists in different disciplines begin to realize the implications of these processes for the world's most pressing problems.

Although the momentum of overpopulation and international conflict sometimes seems unstoppable, the example of Italy and Western Europe suggests that the tide could be turned. Demographers suggest one very simple solution—the wide dissemination of family planning knowledge and technology. Family planning technology could provide an elegant solution, because it does not require convincing billions of people to suppress their sexual desires. Instead it short-circuits the natural system and simultaneously appeals to another general human motivation—to control family size when density goes up. The remaining problem, however, is not a technical one, but a social one: People need to use existing knowledge and technologies to limit their family sizes and use the world's resources more wisely (e.g., Bryan, Aiken, & West, 1996; Oskamp, 2000).

Social traps are intellectually fascinating because they illustrate how order can emerge in complex systems. "Locked-in" cyclic patterns emerge from the individual motivations of a handful of international leaders, or thousands of crab fishermen, or billions of individuals making decisions about family planning or recycling. One of the most fascinating features of such complex systems is that they can often be pulled in a completely different direction by a small input (Cohen, 2001; Kenrick, Li, & Butner, 2003; Nowak & Vallacher, 1998). Just as a few threats can lead to a locked-in pattern of conflict, a few trusting acts done as part of a GRIT strategy can get two nations locked into a pattern of cooperation.

The discovery of the simple dynamics of social traps underlying these complex global problems raises an optimistic possibility. Hopefully, psychologists, biologists, and economists will work together to uncover solutions to problems that cannot be solved simply by new technology. These great problems are rooted in behavior, emotion, and cognition, and their solution may well stimulate the most important and exciting scientific discoveries of the dawning century.

Chapter Summary

Summary of Goals Affecting Social Dilemmas and of Related Person, Situation, and Interactional Factors

The Goal	Person	Situation	Interaction
Gaining immediate satisfaction	• Personal value orientation: prosocial (altruistic and cooperative) versus egoistic (individualist and competitive)	• Timing of positive and negative consequences for selfishness • Descriptive and injunctive norms about selfish versus group-oriented behavior	• Command-and-control policies appeal to fear. They may trigger resistance and only work if violators expect to get caught. • Market-based policies appeal to greed. They elicit less resistance but may be economically infeasible. • Voluntarist policies appeal to social responsibility. They require no government policing but fail if people are truly selfish.

(continued)

The Goal	Person	Situation	Interaction
Defending ourselves and valued others	• Social dominance orientation • Gender • Authoritarianism • Simplified images of conflict: deterrence versus conflict spiral	• Competition over scarce resources • Interacting at group versus individual level • Threats • Stressful decision-making context for leaders	• Communication between people from different cultures can be misinterpreted at several levels. • Groups and individuals can "lock in" to repeated cooperative or competitive patterns. • Tit-for-tat strategy reciprocates cooperation and competition and stabilizes interactions. • Escalating competitions such as "dollar game" are a form of social trap. • Outgroup biases create perceptual dilemmas in which opponents are seen to desire more competitive outcomes. • GRIT strategy replaces escalating competition cycle with escalating cooperation cycle.

Defining Social Dilemmas

1. A social dilemma is a situation in which an individual profits from seeking personal benefits, unless everyone chooses selfishly, in which case the whole group loses.
2. The "tragedy of the commons" is an example of a replenishing resource management dilemma, in which group members share a renewable resource that continues producing benefits unless members overharvest it.
3. A public goods dilemma is a situation in which the whole group can benefit if some of the individuals give something for the common good, but in which the public good will be lost if too few people contribute.
4. Overpopulation, environmental destruction, and international conflict are special dilemmas emerging at the level of nations and global populations. Each pits short-term individual interests against the long-term good of humankind. The global dilemmas are interconnected and contribute to one another.

Gaining Immediate Satisfaction

1. A social trap is a situation in which individuals or groups are drawn in by immediate rewards but ultimately get caught in unpleasant or lethal consequences. Social traps are caused by differences between short-term and long-term consequences, ignorance of long-term consequences, or sliding reinforcers.
2. Person factors affecting the goal of immediate satisfaction include value orientations. Altruists and cooperators have a prosocial orientation, whereas competitors and individualists have an egoistic orientation. Egoists tend to have fewer siblings, whereas prosocial individuals have more older siblings, particularly sisters. Egoistic orientation in adulthood is associated with less trust and less relationship security.
3. Situation factors affecting this goal include short-term and long-term consequences of conservation or wasteful behaviors. To increase conservation, one could change

long-term negative consequences with alternative technologies, move future negative consequences to the present, add immediate punishments for undesirable behaviors, and reinforce desirable alternatives. Social solutions include the activation of descriptive and injunctive norms.
4. Command-and-control policies appeal to fear of punishment to coerce less shortsighted behavior. Market-based policies appeal to individual self-interest. Voluntarist policies appeal to norms of social responsibility and work better with people who have a prosocial orientation.

Defending Ourselves and Valued Others

1. Social dominance orientation refers to desires that one's own group dominate other groups. Across cultures, men tend to have higher social dominance orientations than do women. Authoritarians are deferential to authority, highly respectful of power, moralistically aggressive, and ethnocentric. Leaders adopting a deterrence view believe that signs of weakness will be exploited and that one must show willingness to use military power. Those holding a conflict spiral view believe that demonstrations of peaceful intent reduce opponents' defensiveness.
2. Authoritarian tendencies tend to increase under conditions of economic threat. Simply placing people into groups can trigger competitiveness. Intergroup cooperation can lead to decreases in outgroup prejudices.
3. Threats increase competition in laboratory conflicts. Although unconditional cooperation is exploited, punitive deterrent strategies anger opponents and escalate conflict. Nonpunitive deterrence strategies seem to minimize conflict and help players maximize gains. International leaders show decreased cognitive complexity during conflicts, perhaps because anxiety strains cognitive resources.
4. Threats and cooperative gestures between nations are sometimes misinterpreted because of cultural differences in communication.

5. The tit-for-tat strategy, which reciprocates both competition and cooperation, is most effective in stabilizing conflict situations. The dollar game is a social trap that mimics international conflicts. International conflicts are worsened by perceptual dilemmas, in which opponents believe the other side desires not a reduction in conflict but an unfair and one-sided solution.

6. The GRIT strategy is a technique that replaces conflict escalation with cooperative escalation.

Key Terms

Altruist, 435

Command-and-control policy, 440

Competitor, 435

Conflict spiral view, 444

Cooperator, 435

Deterrence view, 444

GRIT (graduated and reciprocated initiatives in tension reduction), 453

Individualist, 435

Integrative complexity, 448

Market-based policy, 440

Perceptual dilemma, 451

Public goods dilemma, 431

Replenishing resource management dilemma, 431

Sliding reinforcer, 434

Social dilemma, 428

Social trap, 434

Tit-for-tat strategy, 450

Voluntarist policy, 440

Chapter 14

Integrating Social Psychology

Video

AIG 22.19 +0.52   GOOG 574.02 -0.15   MSFT 25.04 +0.15

Learning Objectives

LO 14.1 Explain why our discussion of research in social psychology proceeded from social cognition to social dilemmas.

LO 14.2 Identify at least one theoretical connection between the research findings in the list of Findings and Theories.

LO 14.3 Describe the proximate–ultimate continuum, and explain where each of the major theoretical perspectives fit along that continuum.

LO 14.4 Describe the connections between the evolutionary, sociocultural, social learning, and social cognitive perspectives.

LO 14.5 Explain how culture, learning, and cognition contribute to gender differences in social behavior.

LO 14.6 Name the five broad fundamental motives underlying social behavior, and connect each one to at least one or two topics in social psychology.

LO 14.7 Discuss the connection between dysfunctional social behavior and normal behavior.

LO 14.8 Describe the different types of interaction between person and situation.

LO 14.9 Explain why research methods matter, even if you're not going to be a researcher.

LO 14.10 Discuss the four take-home messages about research methods from this text.

LO 14.11 Describe three connections between social psychology and (a) other areas of psychology, (b) other basic sciences, and (c) applied sciences such as business, medicine, and law.

Public Spectacles, Hidden Conspiracies, and Multiple Motives

On January 20, 2009, Barack Obama delivered his first inaugural address to a crowd of over a million people. In that speech, he noted how far the United States had come—electing as president a man whose own father might not have been served in a restaurant. Being an African American from a family of modest means, Obama's election was an uphill battle. He did, however, have one advantage: Both his parents were highly educated. His father, a black man born in rural Kenya, went on to earn a graduate degree in economics from Harvard. His mother, a white woman born in Kansas, earned a Ph.D. in anthropology. Barack himself did well in school and graduated from Harvard Law School with honors. After graduation, he passed up lucrative offers at law firms to work as a poorly paid civil rights lawyer in the downtrodden urban areas of Chicago. When he later entered politics, Obama impressed observers with his ability to communicate comfortably and effectively to so many different groups—from African American inner-city kids to middle-aged conservative rural whites. With his dual roots in white and black culture, Obama has been a glowing testament to, even a personification of, racial integration. Yet despite Barack Obama's many talents and qualifications, he might never have had the chance to deliver his inaugural address if not for another rousing speech that was delivered near that same spot in Washington, D.C., almost 50 years before.

In 1963, on a sweltering August day, 200,000 Americans had gathered at the Lincoln Memorial to protest racial discrimination. At that time, public schools were still segregated throughout the South, blacks were routinely denied the right to vote, and civil rights workers were being attacked by police dogs.

The giant crowd stood as Reverend Martin Luther King Jr. stepped onto the podium to deliver what is now regarded as one of history's greatest speeches. King

Top, Barack Obama at his inauguration; bottom, Martin Luther King Jr. at the March on Washington.

Self-presentation and public life. John and Robert Kennedy were caught in a self-presentational dilemma involving Martin Luther King Jr. and FBI director J. Edgar Hoover (who was conducting a vicious vendetta against King).

began with a reference to Abraham Lincoln's Emancipation Proclamation, but went on to declare that Lincoln's words of Emancipation, along with the Declaration of Independence, were like bad checks when black Americans tried to cash them in for their promised guarantees of freedom. King described his famous dream, in which his four children would live in a world where the descendants of slaves could walk hand in hand with the descendants of slave-owners. He closed his great speech with words borrowed from an old spiritual song, looking forward to the day when people of all colors could finally declare that we are "free at last."

Behind the scenes of this great unifying event, however, King's personal world was being torn apart. Just before the march, President John F. Kennedy and his brother Robert, the attorney general, had persuaded King to break off his friendships with Stanley Levison and Jack O'Dell, two whites prominent in the Civil Rights movement. Just before the march, between friendly meetings with King, Robert Kennedy had secretly approved FBI wiretaps of King's phone. The electronic eavesdropping caught King bragging about his extramarital sexual exploits, unwittingly providing ammunition for Hoover's vicious crusade against the black preacher. Why would the Kennedys, who were becoming more committed to solving the race problem, try to split up the movement's leaders? This is a mystery linked to another prominent man—FBI Director J. Edgar Hoover. Hoover had informed the Kennedys that Levison and O'Dell were affiliated with the Communist Party.

Why would the FBI director mastermind such a strong personal attack on King? Why would the Kennedys cooperate with Hoover's plotting? Why would King yield to Hoover's plot to tear him from his close friends? And how could immense societal change arise out of all the self-focused personal motivations of everyone involved in this intrigue, from the handful of great leaders to the many thousands of marchers torn between a spirit of revolt and the dream of interracial peace and harmony?

The social interactions surrounding the historic march on Washington illustrate many of the mysteries of social life. In this chapter, we'll try to integrate the pieces of the puzzle that we've discussed throughout this book. We'll see that the many separate clues do fit together to yield some "take home" lessons about gender, about culture, about dysfunctional social behavior, and about how to apply the findings and methods of social psychology to everyday life. In the course of fitting these puzzle pieces together, we'll reconsider the fundamental motives underlying social behavior and the ever-important interactions between the person and the social situation.

What Ground Have We Covered?

LO 14.1 Explain why our discussion of research in social psychology proceeded from social cognition to social dilemmas.

LO 14.2 Identify at least one theoretical connection between the research findings in the list presented in this section.

We began this book by defining social psychology as the scientific study of how people's thoughts, feelings, and behaviors are influenced by other people. We proceeded from the simplest level, considering the individual person's motives, feelings, and thought processes and how these parts fit together with his or her situation. In discussing the person and the situation in Chapter 2, we used the example of Martin Luther King Jr. Around the time of the march on Washington, we can see King's different motives again coming sharply into conflict as he faced a very difficult situation: The choice between personal friendships and the good of the Civil Rights movement. In Chapter 3, we examined social cognition—the mental processes people use to understand themselves and others, where we highlighted the vastly differing perceptions people hold of Senator Hillary Rodham Clinton. Like Clinton, King was viewed as a hero by some and a scoundrel by others. To FBI director Hoover, King was a dangerous troublemaker.

We went on to reflect on how people present themselves to others, considering the case of the great imposter Ferdinand DeMara and noting that we all manage our self-presentations to help meet important personal goals. At the time of the march on Washington, John and Robert Kennedy were caught in a complex self-presentational dilemma. Their goal of being seen by the U.S. public as promoting civil rights inspired them to befriend King, but their goal of being seen as hard on Communism worked at cross-purposes by motivating them to cooperate in Hoover's attack on King.

In Chapters 5 and 6, we examined how people persuade and influence one another. King's 15-minute speech to the marchers in Washington was certainly one of history's masterpieces of social influence. Borrowing the credibility of Abraham Lincoln and the U.S. Constitution, he conjured up images of freedom and justice that eventually led millions of people to reconsider their attitudes about race relations.

We next considered affiliation and friendship. With the support of social networks, people can climb Mount Everest or go to the moon. Without them, it would be impossible to get almost anywhere in life. Even with his great rhetorical powers, Martin Luther King Jr. couldn't have brought hundreds of thousands of people to Washington. He needed the support of powerful politicians and an army of civil rights workers.

From friendship, we moved on to consider love and romantic relationships—social interactions that have the power to change the course of history, as the secrets on King's extramarital affairs may have done. We noted how our own personal satisfactions in relationships with lovers and family members are often served by promoting another's well-being. This theme continued in Chapter 9, where we considered such prosocial behaviors as Sempo Sugihara's great personal sacrifices on behalf of the Jews in Nazi Germany—not unlike King's dedication to the cause of civil rights.

In Chapter 10, we discussed a troubling side of human social life—aggression. We saw how brutality could arise even in otherwise normal people and also how it could, ironically, be triggered by some of the same positive group-based motives that stimulated the march on Washington. Some of these themes came up again in Chapter 11, in which we considered stereotyping, prejudice, and discrimination, using the case of the Klansman and the civil rights worker to demonstrate how normal processes of cognition and motivation can lead either to bitter bigotries or sweet harmonies.

Finally, we moved beyond the individual level to consider processes that arise only in groups, such as the FBI, Enron, or the great crowd of marchers on Washington. It would seem that the interactions of so many people, with so many individual motives, would lead to an unpredictable and chaotic state of affairs, but we saw instead that a more regular pattern of dynamic self-organization often emerges within the group. We discussed how one set of those self-organizational patterns—social dilemmas—may underlie global social problems such as overpopulation, environmental destruction, and international conflict—processes that came together in the five-hour-long massacre of 1,700 Bengali immigrants by the residents of Assam, India.

Thus, we began our exploration by searching inside the individual's head. Step by step, we've moved outward to explore increasingly complex interactions—people presenting themselves to others, negotiating webs of social influences, loves and hatreds, and finally coming together in organizations, crowds, and nations.

Findings and Theories

In our broad survey of social psychology, we encountered a great many intriguing research findings on a wide range of topics. Here are just a few examples of findings from recent social psychological investigations:

- Giving to other people can make you happier and healthier (Brown et al., 2003; Dunn, Aknin, & Norton, 2013).
- Being excluded from a social interaction activates the same neurological circuits as does physical pain (MacDonald & Leary, 2005; Williams & Nida, 2011).

- Whether or not a woman is inclined to be unfaithful, and which characteristics she finds attractive in a man, is linked to her hormone levels (Durante, Li, & Haselton, 2008; Gangestad, Garver-Apgar, Simpson, & Cousins, 2007; Gildersleeve, Haselton, & Fales, 2014).
- It is difficult to extinguish fear toward a member of a racial outgroup, but only if the outgroup member is a man (Navarrete, McDonald, Molina, & Sidanius, 2012; Olsson, Ebert, Banaji, & Phelps, 2005).
- Athletes who are blind from birth nevertheless make the same facial expressions as sighted athletes when they win or lose a contest (Matsumoto & Willingham, 2009).
- People's political attitudes are connected to their mating strategies and to their religious beliefs, but the connection can change depending on whether the people are black or white (Cohen et al., 2009; Weeden, Cohen, & Kenrick, 2008).
- A woman's self-esteem drops if she thinks a man rejected her because of appearance, a man's self-esteem drops if he thinks the rejection was based on his insufficient status (Pass, Lindenberg, & Park, 2010).
- When Asian Americans experience the feeling of love, it is more likely to include a blend of negative and positive feelings, whereas European Americans are more likely to experience love in unmitigated positive terms (Shiota et al., 2010).

Social psychologists have uncovered thousands of other research "facts," but as Jules Henri Poincaré observed in 1905, "a collection of facts is no more a science than a heap of stones is a house." Instead of finishing your study of social psychology with a loose heap of colorful trivia nuggets, you should come away with an interconnected set of theoretical principles that lay a foundation for understanding your social interactions on the job, in your family, out on the streets, or during your travels.

Quick Quiz

1 Which of the following is *true*?

  a. Social cognition is the process of thinking about and making sense of oneself and others.
  b. Social cognition unfolds at the level of the *individual*, whereas social dilemmas involve complex social interactions at the group and global level.
  c. Social dilemmas are dynamic processes that may underlie major social problems such as international conflict.
  d. All of the above

2 Which of the following is true?

  a. A woman's self-esteem drops if she thinks a man rejected her because of her status, whereas a man's self-esteem drops if he thinks the rejection was based on his appearance.
  b. A woman's inclination toward sexual infidelity is linked to her hormone levels.
  c. Giving away money activates the same brain regions that are associated with physical pain.
  d. Asian Americans view love as an unmitigated positive experience; Euro-Americans are more likely to see love as involving a blend of negative and positive feelings.

Major Theoretical Perspectives of Social Psychology

LO 14.3 Describe the proximate–ultimate continuum, and explain where each of the major theoretical perspectives fit along that continuum.

LO 14.4 Describe the connections between the evolutionary, sociocultural, social learning, and social cognitive perspectives.

LO 14.5 Explain how culture, learning, and cognition contribute to gender differences in social behavior.

In Chapter 1, we described four historically important theoretical perspectives. Let's revisit those perspectives to see how they are woven through the field of social psychology. More important, let's explore the links among them.

The different perspectives are not incompatible alternatives. Instead, they're interlinked views of the same social phenomena. One way to appreciate these links is to look at the perspectives along a continuum of **proximate** to **ultimate** levels of explanation (see Figure 14.1). A proximate explanation focuses on immediate causes in the here and now (an accusation of Communist ties led Robert Kennedy to approve the FBI wiretap of King). By contrast, a relatively more ultimate explanation focuses on background or historical causes (Communists had been secretly involved in major social movements in the United States for decades). Proximate and ultimate explanations aren't alternatives. Instead, they're intimately woven together— the historical background factors, for example, affect the perception of the immediate situation (fear of Communist ties only made sense when considered in historical context).

As we indicate in Figure 14.1, relatively proximate questions are narrower in focus (Why does the mass media devote so much space to the love lives of people most of us will never even meet— Kim Kardashian and Kanye West for instance?), and those questions are nested within broader, more ultimate, questions (Why are people generally so concerned about other people's mating behaviors?). Now let's explore the connections among these different levels of explanation.

Figure 14.1   Theoretical perspectives are interconnected

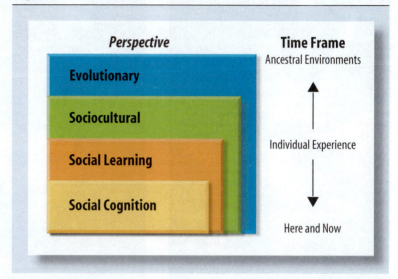

The different theoretical perspectives are not incompatible but instead provide different perspectives on the same phenomena. Cognitive approaches tend to take very "proximate" glimpses of behavior, examining causes in the immediate present, but also connecting ongoing experience to long-term memory and the individual's past experiences with reward and punishment (the focus of the social learning perspective). Sociocultural and evolutionary perspectives consider how background factors in the broader culture and the evolutionary past affect learning and ongoing thought and perception.

The Sociocultural Perspective

In Chapter 1, you read about E. A. Ross (1908), who viewed social psychology as the study of fads, crazes, riots, and other group phenomena. In surveying social psychology, you've seen many social processes that emerge only in groups. One example is minority influence, a process in which a small part of a group changes the opinions of the larger group (Kerr, 2002; Phillips, 2003; Tormala & DeSensi, 2009). The Civil Rights movement is a good example: An initially small band of people eventually brought together hundreds of thousands of others who hailed from locations as geographically and politically distant as Massachusetts and Mississippi. Those efforts eventually changed the norms of U.S. society, making it possible for the son of a white woman from Kansas and a black man from Kenya to rise to the status of U.S. president.

Until recently, these mutual influences between several hundred individuals in a mob or several hundred thousand individuals in a larger society seemed too complex to study scientifically. In the last few years, however, scientists working in fields from ecology to economics have begun to develop powerful new mathematical and conceptual tools for studying complex dynamical systems, such as crowds and social movements, which involve many mutually interacting elements (Harton & Bourgeois, 2004; Kenrick et al., 2002; Nowak, Vallacher Stawinska, & Bree, 2013). Why aren't hairstyles and attitudes more randomly distributed across different groups instead of clustered together? It is, for example, as unlikely that you'll see someone with multiple tattoos and purple hair at the Republican women's luncheon as that you'll see a clean-cut man wearing a business suit dancing at a Megadeth concert. The new conceptual tools are allowing researchers to study *how* attitudes and behaviors spread and cluster within large groups (Latané, 1996; Latané & Bourgeois, 2001).

A central legacy of the sociocultural approach is the focus on norms—social expectations about appropriate behavior that vary between and within different societies

Proximate explanation A focus on relatively immediate causes.

Ultimate explanation A focus on background or historical causes.

(Conway, Sexton, & Tweed, 2006; Kaplan, 2003; Lalwani, Shavitt, & Johnson, 2006). In the late 1990s, business organizations and their employees sometimes clashed over different norms for multiple body piercings (one Canadian woman was fired by a Starbucks coffeehouse for wearing a tiny barbell through her tongue). In the corporate business subculture of North American society today, it's socially appropriate to sport body piercings only on one's earlobes. In other subcultures (artistically oriented youth, for example), it's considered socially desirable to pierce multiple chunks of metal through ears, noses, eyebrows, tongues, nipples, and even genitalia. In yet other societies, people have indulged in even more extreme forms of bodily mutilation, placing giant objects in their lips and ears, stretching their necks to twice their normal length, and wrapping the bones of their feet so tightly that they crippled themselves. These wide variations illustrate the powerful influence of norms on social behavior.

Cultural influences on bodily ornamentation. In different cultures, at different times in history, the norms about the appropriateness and placement of body piercings have varied widely for women and for men.

In each chapter of this book, we've discussed the influences of culture, such as the individualistic norms of North American society and the collectivist norms of Asian or Latin American countries (e.g., Galin & Avraham, 2009; Navarrete, 2005; Oishi, Wyer, & Colcombe, 2000). Taking a cross-cultural focus helps us to notice things that might otherwise be difficult to understand, such as why Japanese people are so much more uncomfortable with answering machines than Americans are. Whereas American communication tends to be focused on getting the information across, Japanese conversations are more concerned with being polite and considerate. As a consequence, Japanese people speaking to an answering machine feel compelled to spend more time on social niceties that Americans might regard as dispensable (Miyamoto & Schwarz, 2006). Cultural differences don't stop at national boundaries, but can help us see and understand interesting differences within a country based on ethnic, religious, or regional variations. Americans raised in Boston in an Italian Catholic family may have very different norms for appropriate behavior than Americans raised in New York in a Jewish family, or southern Baptists from Alabama (e.g., Cohen, 2009; Cohen et al., 2006; Vandello & Cohen, 2003).

The Evolutionary Perspective

The evolutionary perspective views social behavior through the lens of Darwin's theory of evolution by natural selection (Kenrick & Cohen, 2012; Ketelaar & Ellis, 2000). The central assumption is that, along with an upright posture and the ability to walk on two feet, we inherited a brain designed partly to help us deal with the problems of living in human social groups. Researchers are beginning to adopt this perspective in examining many topics in social psychology, including altruism, love, family relationships, friendship, aggression, and prejudice (e.g., Campbell & Ellis, 2005; Cottrell & Neuberg, 2005; McCullough, 2008; Sagarin et al., 2003; Tybur, Lieberman, & Griskevicius, 2009).

Like sociocultural theorists, evolutionary psychologists look across cultures, but they search more for human commonalities than for differences between people

Universals and particulars. The particular norms about marriage vary from culture to culture, but long-term bonds between parents are a universal feature, found across all human societies.

(e.g., Daly & Wilson, 1988; Kenrick & Gomez-Jacinto, 2014; Schmitt et al., 2003). Explorations of varying cultures reveal not only fascinating differences but also fundamental similarities in humans around the globe.

SEEING OUR COMMONALITY THROUGH THE MANY SOCIETAL DIFFERENCES We've discussed many differences in social rules from culture to culture. Bringing along dessert or gently refusing another helping of the main course may indicate graceful manners in Toledo but boorish rudeness in Tokyo. A woman marrying two brothers at the same time would be loathsome in Topeka but wholesome in Tibet. Learning about such cultural differences can reduce our ethnocentrism by making us aware that there are many other ways of being social than the one we learned as children. And an even closer look at other cultures can teach us another lesson: Beneath all the cultural differences, there is a core of similarity connecting all human beings with one another.

We've encountered many such similarities through the course of this book. Recall, for example, that although societies vary widely in their homicide rates and in their cultural norms about the appropriateness of violence (e.g., Vandello & Cohen, 2003), males commit over 80% of the homicides in every society. Further, these homicides are often committed for similar reasons, such as men's competition for status and mating opportunities (Daly & Wilson, 1988; Minkov, 2009). Similarly, despite wide variations in marriage patterns around the world, including one woman marrying several men and one man marrying several women, we also saw that these differences are accompanied by some underlying universals (Kenrick, Nieuweboer, & Buunk, 2010; Shackelford, Schmitt, & Buss, 2005). All human cultures have some form of marriage, for example, and even in societies that allow multiple spouses, most people nevertheless pair up monogamously, with one woman marrying one man (Daly & Wilson, 1983).

Likewise, we've seen cross-cultural variations in rules for gift giving alongside universal rules about reciprocity, cross-cultural variations in individualism alongside a universal tendency toward communalism in family groups, and so on. Thus, as we meet people from different societies and from different subcultures within our society, we should expect that these people will play by rules that are sometimes shockingly different from ours. But we also expect to find that, beneath sometimes dazzling differences, human beings everywhere have basic goals and concerns much like our own.

CULTURE AND EVOLUTION INTERACTING Although evolutionary psychologists and sociocultural theorists have differed in their emphasis on universals versus differences, it would be an oversimplification to say that sociocultural theorists have ignored universals or that evolutionary psychologists have ignored differences (Kenrick & Gomez-Jacinto, 2014; Triandis, 1994). Indeed, the two perspectives are looking at two sides of the same coin, and it would be a mistake to try to draw a line between culture and evolution (Janicki & Krebs, 1998; Norenzayan, Schaller, & Heine, 2006). For a long time, psychologists conceptualized the mind as a "blank slate" (Pinker, 2002). We would suggest that a better metaphor is a coloring book (Kenrick, Nieuweboer, & Buunk, 2010). For example, the human mind is designed to learn a language and a set of cultural norms (Fiske et al., 1998; MacNeilage & Davis, 2005). Just as human language is, in turn, shaped by the human mind, so, too, is human culture. That is, culture develops within the potentialities and limits set by human evolution, and human evolution develops within the possibilities and limits set by culture (see Figure 14.2).

In addition to observing similarities across cultures, evolutionary researchers have searched for parallels in social behavior across different species (e.g., Kurland & Gaulin, 2005; Salmon, 2005). For example, the behavior of males and females is generally more similar in species in which males help care for the offspring—as do many birds and human beings—than in species in which males make minimal investments—as do baboons (Geary, 2000). Paying attention to similarities across cultures and species in amorous, aggressive, and altruistic behaviors can help us see our own social behavior in broader perspective.

Figure 14.2 Evolutionary and sociocultural factors are not independent

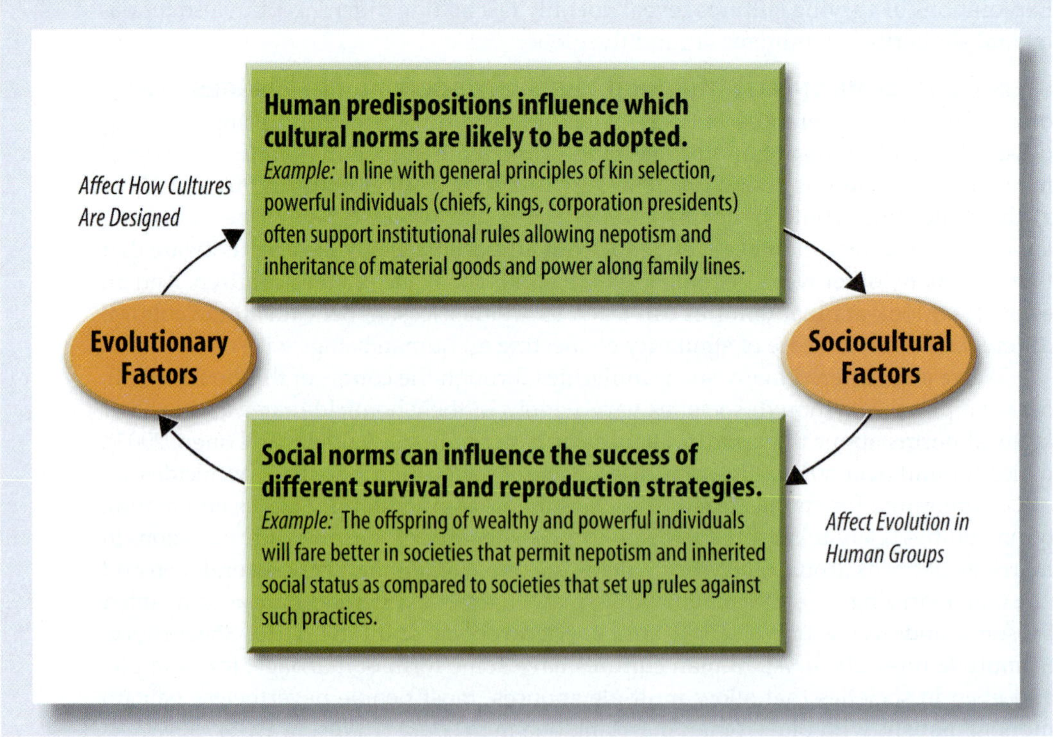

Human beings have always lived in cultural groups, and the norms of those groups have affected the evolution of our species. Conversely, cultural norms are adopted or changed based on how successfully they fit human nature. The process is a continual loop of biological and cultural forces.

Social psychologists who adopt an evolutionary perspective don't buy pith helmets and set off for Africa to dig up hominid bones or live among gorillas. Such studies are relevant to human evolution, but they fall into the domain of anthropology and zoology. Instead, social psychologists use evolutionary principles to derive hypotheses about ongoing social interactions that can be tested in laboratory or field experiments, surveys, or behavioral archives (e.g., Faulkner, Schaller, Park, & Duncan, 2004; Haselton & Nettle, 2006; Schmitt, Jonason et al., 2012). For example, we discussed in Chapter 8 how researchers used evolutionary models to make different predictions about how men and women would evaluate their relationships after viewing attractive or socially dominant members of the opposite sex (Dijkstra & Buunk, 1998; Kenrick et al., 1994). The "fossils" that psychologists hunt for are not bones buried in the ground but the inherited psychological mechanisms we still carry around inside our heads (Buss & Kenrick, 1998; Todd, Hertwig, & Hoffrage, 2005).

The Social Learning Perspective

The social learning perspective brings us down from the grand levels of society and evolutionary history to a smaller scale—that of the individual person responding to rewards and punishments in his or her environment. We saw, for example, that people feel positively about another person or group if first exposed to that person or group while their mood is boosted by something as simple as eating tasty food. Martin Luther King Jr.'s speech at the march on Washington masterfully used this principle of association to connect his cause to powerful patriotic symbols and images of happy little children. Barack Obama profited not only from King's ability to change Americans' associations to African Americans, but also from other critical learning experiences that contributed to his individual success, including exposure to two highly educated parents. In Chapter 10, we saw a negative consequence of social learning experiences in findings that graphic video games can reward violent thoughts and impulses and desensitize normal neuropsychological reactions to seeing other people suffer (Anderson et al., 2010; Bartholow et al., 2006).

There's a direct linkage between the social learning and the sociocultural perspectives (Navarrete et al., 2010; Ohman & Mineka, 2001). Indeed, we learn different cultural norms (whether to feel uncomfortable about eating beef or horse or dog, for example) from years of such conditioning and modeling experiences. We've also discussed evidence that social learning sometimes follows tracks laid down by the evolutionary history of our species. For example, children raised together in a kibbutz pod learn to like one another, yet they don't marry each other. Apparently, the normal processes leading to sexual attraction among people in the same neighborhood are inhibited by being raised under the same roof. This suggests that a mechanism may have evolved to prevent siblings from learning to feel strong, passionate attraction to each other (Lieberman & Smith, 2012; Shepher, 1971). In this case, a unique cultural learning environment may have "tricked" that mechanism.

INVESTIGATION

Think of one social norm that is designed to control people's individual genetic self-interest and another social norm that is more compatible with people's self-interest. Is there a harsher societal punishment for violating the first or the second? Why?

The Social Cognitive Perspective

The social learning perspective is concerned with events in the objective world, such as a parent threatening to take away a misbehaving child's dessert. But what if the rowdy child doesn't hear the parent's threat or doesn't believe it? Our reactions to the social world depend on the mental processes of noticing, interpreting, judging, and remembering—processes that are the focus of the social cognitive perspective, probably the most influential perspective in modern social psychology (e.g., Hamilton & Carlston, 2013; Malle, 2004; Sherman et al., 2009; Tesser & Bau, 2002).

Adopting a social cognitive perspective helps us make sense of one FBI agent's response to King's speech at the march on Washington. The agent stated that the "powerful demagogic speech" convinced him "that Communist influence is being exerted on Martin Luther King, Jr.," and that "we must mark him . . . as the most dangerous Negro . . . from the standpoint of Communism . . . and national security." How could a speech full of references to the U.S. Constitution and the Battle Hymn of the Republic be so interpreted? A social cognitive perspective would focus on the cognitive cues made salient by the FBI investigation of possible Communist connections to the Civil Rights movement and by Director Hoover's almost obsessive concern with Communist conspiracies.

Because it forms a crucial part of our own interactionist model, a social cognitive perspective has been woven throughout every chapter of this book. For example, the distinction between "automatic" and "thoughtful" cognitive processing has been central in research on persuasion and attitude change (e.g., Chaiken & Ledgerwood, 2012; Gregg, Seibt, & Banaji, 2006; Petty & Briñol, 2012). Processes of social attribution (as in deciding whether a compliment is sincere or manipulative) were central to our discussion of friendship, love, prosocial behavior, aggression, and stereotyping. Indeed, the goal of seeking information is one that we found to underlie a great many social interactions.

The social cognitive perspective has important links to the other perspectives (e.g., Alter & Kwan, 2009; Chiu, Ng, & Au, 2013; Neuberg, Becker, & Kenrick, 2013). Without cognitive processing on a moment-to-moment basis, there would be no learning, and without past learning or a brain that evolved to organize complex information about the social world, there would be no causal attributions, social schemas, heuristic judgments, or group stereotypes. Factors in the cultural environment also have important influences on what a person pays attention to in a social situation, and how that person interprets what he or she sees (e.g., Miyamoto, Nisbett, & Masuda, 2006). Figure 14.3 depicts just one example of such links by highlighting some of the interconnections between social cognition and social learning.

INVESTIGATION

Think back to a social psychological research finding you remember from earlier in the semester. What makes this finding stand out in your memory? Connect that finding to social norms, evolutionary self-interest, and/or social rewards and punishments.

There's a similar two-way street between any of the perspectives (as shown in the earlier connection between the sociocultural and evolutionary perspectives). The importance of considering more than a single perspective reveals itself in different approaches to gender.

Are Gender Differences in Our Genes, in Our Cultural Learning Experiences, or All in Our Minds?

If you can't tell from the accent whether a person is from Boston or New York, you may not care enough to even comment on it. If you can't immediately tell whether the person is a man or a woman, however, this uncertainty will probably capture your attention and interest.

Why are people so fascinated by these rare gender ambiguities? Social psychologists Susan Cross and Hazel Markus (1993) suggest that it's because gender is such a vivid social category. Whether someone is a male or a female is immediately visible to the naked eye and relevant in many everyday situations. These researchers adopted the cognitive perspective that gender stereotypes function like other categories, including racial stereotypes. Once we put someone into a simple category, we don't need to expend extra cognitive effort to understand or interact with him or her.

Consistent with this perspective, young children who see someone act out of line with their gender stereotypes may mentally distort the behavior to bring it back into

Figure 14.3   The interplay of cognition and learning

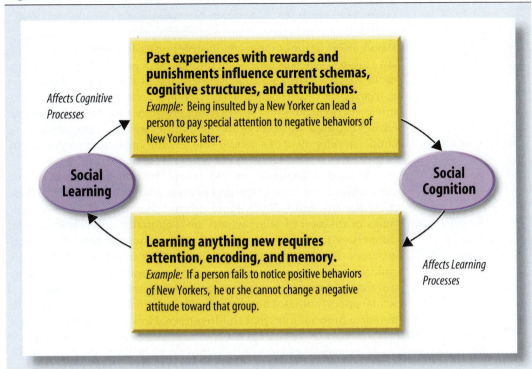

To learn to like or dislike another group, we must notice that group and register our experience with them in long-term memory. Once we have learned a habitual way of responding to others, it will affect our later tendency to notice and remember them. This is one example of how learning and cognition go hand in hand.

line. For instance, five- and six-year-old children shown a girl sawing a piece of wood may misremember it as a boy doing the sawing (Martin & Halverson, 1983). And adults also bend their perceptions to fit gender-role schemas. Adults in one study judged a baby's reaction when a jack-in-the-box pops open. Was the baby's cry fearful or angry? Observers who thought the baby was a girl were more likely to see fear; those who thought it was a boy were more likely to see anger (Condry & Condry, 1976). People who rapidly view an angry face next to a neutral face are more likely to perceive the anger on the man's face (when it was really on the woman's) than the reverse (see anger "jump" from a man to a woman) (Neel et al., 2012).

Findings such as these suggest that our judgments have some built-in gender biases. But do they mean that gender is "all in the head"? Carol Martin (1987, 2000) suggested that gender stereotypes, like some other stereotypes, are based on at least a kernel of truth. Canadian subjects reported large gender differences between the typical "North American male" and the typical "North American female." Men were perceived as substantially higher in dominance, aggressiveness, and willingness to take a stand; women were perceived as much more gentle, tender, compassionate, and warm. People rating themselves on the same dimensions reported the same stereotypical differences, but to a much lesser degree. They see a "typical man" as highly aggressive, pushy, and cold, but men see themselves as only moderately aggressive, a little less pushy, and not so cold. Thus, cognitive biases can lead us to magnify small actual gender differences (Martin, 1987).

Alice Eagly (1995) reviewed a large number of studies examining actual gender differences in behavior as well as stereotypes about those differences and concluded that laypeople have a reasonably good feel for which differences are large (such as physical violence and attitudes about premarital sex) and which are small (such as feelings of anger and attitudes about long-term relationships). Why do people, despite all their cognitive biases, still end up with a fairly good idea about the magnitude of gender differences? Eagly suggests that it is precisely because gender is such a salient cognitive category—people pay a lot of attention to the similarities and differences between men and women.

Gender schemas. Our attention is easily drawn to people who cannot be easily classified as male or female, in line with research suggesting that gender schemas are powerful and primary mental categories.

Why do men and women act in line with gender stereotypes? That's still a controversial question to be resolved by research. Undoubtedly, young children learn that certain behaviors are more appropriate for men, and certain behaviors are more appropriate for women (Eagly & Wood, 1999). Some of these gender-role norms are similar across different cultures, whereas others are different (Archer, 2009). For example, more women than men practice medicine in Russia, but the reverse is true in the United States. Women in both countries, however, commit fewer homicides and spend relatively more time caring for infants. Observing these differences and similarities no doubt contributes to a child's development of a gender-role schema and informs a young boy or girl about how to act.

At another level, we can ask where the societal differences and similarities come from in the first place (Gangestad, Haselton, & Buss, 2006; Kenrick & Li, 2000). From an evolutionary perspective, some types of division of labor would have naturally arisen from gender differences in reproductive biology; others would have been more arbitrary. The fact that our female ancestors carried and nursed their children may help account for women's generally greater nurturance toward children and for their generally lower enthusiasm about casual sexual opportunities. Thus, basic biological differences may contribute to the gender differences in social roles that children learn. However, our reproductive history is irrelevant for many of the roles that are nowadays arbitrarily assigned to one sex or the other, such as medical practice, accounting, or social work. In short, asking whether gender differences are in our genes, our cultural learning experiences, *or* our minds may be the wrong question. All these forces work together to produce social behavior (Kenrick & Gomez-Jacinto, 2014).

As our discussion of gender illustrates, each of the different perspectives helps us understand social behavior, and putting the different perspectives together elucidates more of the whole picture (see Figure 14.4). The interactionist framework we've used to organize this book is a synthesis of the different historically important perspectives. In the next section, we reprise the main points of our framework.

Figure 14.4 Different perspectives on gender

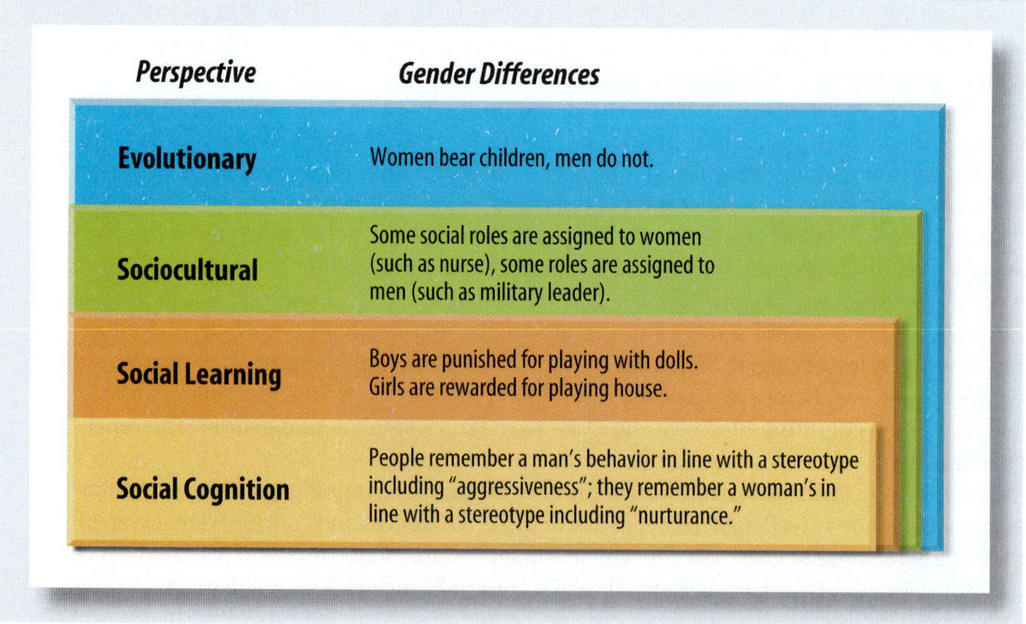

Perspective	Gender Differences
Evolutionary	Women bear children, men do not.
Sociocultural	Some social roles are assigned to women (such as nurse), some roles are assigned to men (such as military leader).
Social Learning	Boys are punished for playing with dolls. Girls are rewarded for playing house.
Social Cognition	People remember a man's behavior in line with a stereotype including "aggressiveness"; they remember a woman's in line with a stereotype including "nurturance."

The similarities and differences between men and women can be considered from each of the different major perspectives, and doing so helps us to see the connections between those perspectives.

Quick Quiz

1 A (n) _____ explanation focuses on background or historical causes, whereas a(n) _____ explanation focuses on relatively immediate causes.

    a. proximate, ultimate

    b. ultimate, proximate

    c. evolutionary, proximate

    d. sociocultural, ultimate

2 Which of the following statements about the evolutionary perspective is *false*?

    a. The evolutionary perspective is linked to the sociocultural perspective in that evolutionary psychologists also look across cultures, but they search more for fundamental differences rather than similarities between people.

    b. The evolutionary perspective's central assumption is that humans inherited a brain designed partly to help us deal with the problems of living in social groups.

    c. The evolutionary and social learning perspectives are sometimes linked, in that social learning processes can reflect evolved behavioral mechanisms.

    d. The evolutionary perspective focuses on general principles of survival and reproduction that apply across cultures and species.

3 Which of the following scenarios is NOT an example of the link between the social cognitive and social learning perspectives?

    a. A person is insulted by a member of a stigmatized group; after this occurrence, she pays special attention to the negative behaviors of that group.

    b. A person fails to notice the positive behaviors of a stigmatized group and as a result never changes her attitude toward that group.

    c. A person adheres to a society's social norms by greeting new business partners with gifts.

    d. None of the above

4 The _____ perspective shows that some sex differences and similarities have biological roots, whereas the _____ perspective suggests that sex differences sometimes get exaggerated through stereotypes.

    a. evolutionary, cognitive

    b. evolutionary, sociocultural

    c. sociocultural, cognitive

    d. sociocultural, social learning

Combining the Different Perspectives

LO 14.6 Name the five broad fundamental motives underlying social behavior, and connect each one to at least one or two topics in social psychology.

LO 14.7 Discuss the connection between dysfunctional social behavior and normal behavior.

LO 14.8 Describe the different types of interaction between person and situation.

In Chapter 1, we derived two broad principles from the different historical perspectives: (1) Social behavior is goal oriented and (2) social behavior represents a continual interaction between the person and the situation. Now that we've reviewed the field of social psychology, let's revisit these two broad principles and the essential lessons about them that have emerged.

Social Behavior Is Goal Oriented

For each topic in social psychology, we began with a simple question: What goals or motives underlie this particular sort of behavior? Why did Sempo Sugihara, a Japanese civil servant, risk his own career to help hundreds of Lithuanian Jews escape from the Nazis when their own neighbors were unwilling to help? What makes some people, like Al Capone or Charles Manson, become murderously violent? Why did the Dalai Lama, regarded as a god by his Tibetan subjects, befriend someone most Tibetans looked down on? And what clues about everyday motivation can we draw from these exceptional cases?

With regard to the question of why people like Sugihara help others, for example, we considered four general goals: gaining genetic and material benefits, gaining social status and approval, managing self-image, and managing emotions and moods. We discussed the question of why people like Charles Manson and Al Capone act violently in terms of four likely goals: coping with feelings of annoyance, gaining material or social rewards, gaining or maintaining social status, and protecting themselves and others. And we considered the question of why people like Heinrich Harrer and the Dalai Lama affiliate with their friends in terms of four goals: getting social support, getting information, gaining status, and exchanging material benefits.

In looking back over the different goals, we can see that the same goals sometimes underlie very different social behaviors (Griskevicius, Goldstein, Mortensen et al., 2006; Griskevicius, Tybur et al., 2007, 2009; Horowitz et al., 2006). For example, we discussed how the goal of improving or maintaining status influenced self-presentation, friendship, helping, love, aggression, and prejudice. With our discussion of the broad range of social behavior behind us, it's time to consider the commonalities between the goals behind different social behaviors. Can we derive a smaller number of fundamental motivations that, taken together, underlie most of our social interactions?

In Chapter 1, we discussed several examples of broad motives underlying social behavior: (1) to establish social ties, (2) to understand ourselves and others, (3) to gain and maintain status, (4) to defend ourselves and those we value, and (5) to attract and retain mates. We chose these particular motives for a reason. After looking over the broad field of social psychology, we concluded that one or more of these motives are related directly or indirectly to almost all the social behaviors discussed throughout this book. In a sense, these broad motives give us hints about the ultimate function of many of the things we do with, to, and for other people.

Let's consider these fundamental motives again, with an eye to two questions: How do these broad motives shed light on the function of social behaviors ranging from altruism to xenophobia? And how do these broad motives connect to more specific day-to-day and moment-to-moment goals that arise in our interactions with other people?

TO ESTABLISH SOCIAL TIES A central purpose of social behavior is to form and maintain friendly associations with other people (Deci & Ryan, 2000; MacDonald & Leary, 2005; Maner et al., 2007). With other people on our side, we can accomplish tasks we would never dream of on our own, as Barack Obama drew strength from the millions of individuals who contributed time and money and labor to his presidential campaign. And with others against us, the simplest task can turn into a nightmare In looking back, we see that the motivation to establish social ties reveals itself in various forms: In Chapter 4, we discussed the goal of appearing likeable, and in Chapters 5, 6, 9, and 11 we considered many different social behaviors that are motivated by the goal of gaining social approval. Indeed, Chapter 7 was dedicated entirely to the topic of affiliation and friendship. The list of goals we discussed in Chapter 7 (getting social support and information, improving one's social status, and exchanging material benefits) tells us something important about the different goals of social behavior. They are often interdependent. In particular, when you establish connections with other people, you open the gate to satisfying your other social goals. To understand ourselves and others, to gain and maintain status, to attract and retain mates, and to defend ourselves and those we value, it is crucial that we seek and maintain the company of others.

Mark Leary and his colleagues (1995) argued that social ties underlie another important goal—to maintain

Only the well-connected survive. Participants on the popular *Survivor* television series are placed in an isolated part of the world with one or two groups of strangers. The groups compete with one another for food, shelter, and other essentials, and the losing group is forced to vote one of its members off the island. At the end, only one individual survives, and he or she goes home with a million dollars. As in real life, those who succeed in this game are those who have been able to form strong cooperative alliances.

self-esteem. When students were excluded from a work group, for instance, or when they merely thought about doing something likely to lead to social rejection (causing an accident or cheating on an exam), they reported feelings of lowered self-esteem. Several studies conducted by Leary and others have supported the hypothesis that self-esteem is a *sociometer*—an index of whether we feel included or excluded by other people (e.g., Anthony, Holmes, & Wood, 2007; Denissen, Penke, & Schmitt, 2008).

TO UNDERSTAND OURSELVES AND OTHERS Was Martin Luther King Jr. really a Communist-influenced, rabble-rousing hypocrite, as J. Edgar Hoover claimed? Are you charming and likable, as your best friend says you are, or a socially awkward klutz, as you felt when you went on that blind date? It's hard to get through any social interaction without giving some thought to who the players are, why they're doing what they're doing, and what they're thinking and expecting of you (Fiske, 2004; Stevens & Fiske, 1995). Hence, the motivation to understand ourselves and others has come up again and again throughout this book. It was the focus of Chapter 3, and it was central to several other chapters. For instance, we included goals linked to gaining or organizing social information in our discussions of attitudes, friendship, prejudice, and groups, and we discussed the goal of developing and managing self-concept in one form or another in the chapters on attitudes, self-presentation, social influence, prosocial behavior, and prejudice.

There is another important point about broad social motives: They can be broken down into component subgoals. Sometimes we search for information to simplify the world, sometimes to protect our views of ourselves, and sometimes to gain a detailed and accurate picture of ourselves and others (Eibach & Ehrlinger, 2006; Griskevicius, Goldstein, Mortensen et al., 2006; Pittman, 1998). Which informational goal is active depends on other aspects of the situation. Sometimes it's enough to take a cognitive shortcut, as when we assume that the next person driving a yellow car with a light on top will give us a ride to the airport. Sometimes we need to search more deeply for accurate information, as when we lose a game of chess to someone we classified as a ditzy airhead. And sometimes we need to protect our self-regard, as when we refuse a phone call from a former lover who's calling to read us a long list of our personal flaws.

TO GAIN AND MAINTAIN STATUS As we noted earlier, the goal of gaining and maintaining status was central to several topics, including self-presentation, affiliation and friendship, love and romantic relationships, aggression, prejudice, and group dynamics. Self-esteem is linked not only to whether we feel liked by others but also to whether we feel respected by others. We feel better about ourselves when others look up to us. As we noted in Chapter 3, for example, North Americans and Europeans are motivated to see themselves as, compared to others, more competent, more intelligent, and otherwise more worthy of respect (e.g., Steele, 1988; Tesser, 1988). Likewise, in Chapter 11, we saw that people sometimes make themselves feel better by focusing on how another person or group is below them in status (Hogg, 2003).

Status carries not only the benefits of direct access to rewards. As we discussed in Chapter 8, it also brings the indirect benefits of attracting mates and promoting the survival of our offspring. As we discussed in Chapter 7, people all around the world think about themselves and others along two prominent dimensions—agreeableness and social dominance (White, 1980; Wiggins & Broughton, 1985). We want to know not only whether someone else is nice, but also whether he or she is above or below us in the status hierarchy.

Psychologists Robert and Joyce Hogan (1991) note the occasional conflict between the two basic motives to be liked and to gain status. If you're too eager to move ahead

Basking in reflected glory. Obama supporters demonstrate their personal sense of victory on the night their candidate won the presidential election.

of others in the social hierarchy, you may lose points for agreeableness. At the same time, if others like you, trust you, and feel like part of your family or team, they will not only help you succeed but also share in your glory (Tesser, 1988). For example, on the night that Barack Obama won his bid for the presidency, his supporters around the country could be seen raising their arms in victory.

TO DEFEND OURSELVES AND THOSE WE VALUE Violence and prejudice, as we saw in Chapters 10, 11, and 13, are often triggered by the goal of defending ourselves and our group members. We've seen how concerns raised by thinking about death or disease or even being in the dark can lead people to dislike and distrust outsiders (Faulkner et al., 2004; Navarrete et al., 2004; Pyszczynski, Solomon, & Greenberg, 2002). However, this same motive can contribute to prosocial behaviors, because risking ourselves to save another often means fighting for him or her. King's interwoven images of angry, unsatisfied blacks and children victimized by prejudice made it clear that he believed his quest was, in some way, a battle for his own children's future. A study of justice-based aggression suggests another fascinating link between social psychology, behavioral economics, and neurobiology. Rose McDermott and her colleagues found that the monoamine oxidase A gene (MAOA, sometimes called the "warrior gene") was connected to people's willingness to spend their own money to punish other game players who they believed had acted unfairly (McDermott et al., 2009).

At the beginning of the chapter, we discussed J. Edgar Hoover's vendetta against King. On closer examination, Hoover's antagonism toward King and the Civil Rights movement was linked to an exaggerated goal of self- and group defense. In the next section, we discuss the fine line between paranoid suspicion and normal social skepticism and self-protection.

Bridging Function and Dysfunction:
The Thin Line between Normal and Abnormal Social Functioning

Historian Arthur Schlesinger (1978), a former special assistant to President Kennedy, described J. Edgar Hoover as suffering from "incipient paranoia." Likewise, another biography of Hoover described him on the book's jacket as "paranoid" (Gentry, 1991). Was the man who headed the FBI for almost 50 years actually paranoid?

Hoover certainly did not suffer from the hallucinations or disorganized speech patterns that qualify a person for a diagnosis of paranoid schizophrenia. However, he did have beliefs that others regarded as delusions, and he met several of the criteria for the milder diagnosis of paranoid personality disorder. The symptoms of paranoid personality disorder include unjustified suspicion that others are deceiving you; preoccupation with unjustified doubts about the loyalty of friends or associates; a tendency to bear grudges; hypersensitivity to being slighted by others; an obsession with sexual infidelity; and a tendency to counterattack against perceived slights or assaults (based on Barlow & Durand, 1995).

Hoover kept a list of personal enemies, and Martin Luther King Jr. was prominent on that list. King had angered Hoover by speaking out against the FBI. King's slight was merely to mention to a reporter that he agreed with a *New York Times* article critical of the FBI's handling of one particular civil rights case. Hoover kept detailed information about his enemies' sex lives, which he released to the press whenever he felt anyone might become a threat to him. Former agents who disagreed with Hoover about policy were referred to as "Judases." One former assistant to

Hoover stated that, "If he didn't like you, he destroyed you." When a book critical of the FBI was published in 1950, Hoover had the publisher called before the House Un-American Activities Committee and slandered as having links with Communists.

Hoover was unquestionably a defensive, suspicious, and hostile man, but was he insane? In fact, his behaviors indicate the sometimes fine line between normal and abnormal social processes. Consider a few other facts about his situation. Most observers, including Attorney General Kennedy and many members of the FBI, believed that the Communist Party had very little influence on the Civil Rights movement. Communist Party membership in the United States had been dwindling for decades and virtually disappeared after revelations about Stalin's reign of terror. However, the Party had been popular around the time of the Great Depression. Socialists and Communists were active in the growth of organized labor unions, and they helped promote poverty-buffering policies such as unemployment insurance. Several of Martin Luther King Jr.'s associates, including Jack O'Dell, Stanley Levison, and Bayard Rustin, had indeed been members of Communist or socialist groups at that time. Hoover had uncovered many such associations and released a book, *Masters of Deceit*, discussing how Communists had infiltrated social action groups. And there was, in fact, a true "Communist conspiracy" to incite worldwide revolution, which included spies and covert Communist operations that Hoover and the FBI had uncovered inside the United States.

J. Edgar Hoover and Clyde Tolson. Hoover was alleged to have had a homosexual relationship with his assistant, Clyde Tolson. Here they are shown on one of their semi-annual vacations together. Hoover's inclination to collect secrets about other people's sex lives may have been motivated in part by the knowledge of the damage he would suffer if his own private life were made public.

Hence, Hoover's tendency to interpret ambiguous associations as links to the Communist conspiracy demonstrates normal cognitive biases discussed in earlier chapters, such as the availability heuristic (overestimating the probability of events that come easily to mind) and the confirmation bias (seeking to affirm the truth of our theories without considering other possibilities). These types of cognitive biases plague us all, so it makes sense that a man who spent most of his life searching for hidden conspiracies would be on red alert for any remotely suspicious ties between people. Because Hoover saw Communism as a serious threat to the United States, his defensive attitude toward anything associated with Communism is a natural outgrowth of in-group protective tendencies.

Hoover's particular proclivity for collecting damaging evidence about his enemies' sex lives also makes a bit more sense when considered in light of reports of another allegation—that Hoover was himself a homosexual. At the time, if the U.S. public had been informed that the crime-fighting defender of American values was a homosexual, his powerful position (which depended on continual reappointment by elected politicians) would have been seriously jeopardized. By maintaining extensive intelligence on the sex lives of powerful people, including senators, congressmen, presidents, and their wives, and by demonstrating a willingness to use that information, he managed to hold his position as head of the FBI for five decades.

Hoover's case thus demonstrates the central lesson of the Bridging Function and Dysfunction features throughout this book. Disordered social behavior often reveals normal psychological mechanisms in bolder relief. Conversely, understanding normal psychological mechanisms can often help us understand the function of apparently disordered behavior.

TO ATTRACT AND RETAIN MATES From an evolutionary perspective, the social behavior of all animals, including humans, is influenced by behavioral mechanisms that ultimately serve one central motive—successful reproduction. As we noted in Chapter 8's discussion of love and romantic relationships, however, to say that animals are designed to reproduce doesn't mean simply that everything they do is ultimately designed to result in sex (Kenrick, Griskevicius, Neuberg, & Schaller, 2010). Reproduction involves much more than just sexual intercourse. All mammals, and humans in particular, are designed to have only a few offspring, on which they lavish a great deal of care (Zeifman & Hazan, 1997). Whereas some species of fish produce hundreds of offspring every season, more than five human children is considered a large family. So, compared with most other species, humans demonstrate very strong "family values" and devote tremendous resources to child care.

Humans differ from most mammals in another important way. Good parenting is a goal not only of the human female but also of the male (Geary, 2005). And human mothers and fathers give their offspring not only food and shelter but also years of psychological support and social survival training. In many cases, parents even set their children up with jobs and marriages when they reach adulthood. As we discussed in Chapter 8, men and women join together to raise the children in every human culture. These parental bonds are a part of our biological heritage, although, like language, they are flexible and sensitive to the environment.

The goal of attracting and retaining mates demonstrates two other important points. First, goals aren't necessarily conscious. Second, they involve imperfectly tuned mechanisms. Biological theorists assume that all animals in the world today, including modern humans, are here because their ancestors reproduced more efficiently than their competitors. But biologists don't assume that ants or geese or humans had ancestors that were conscious of the goal of reproducing their genes (Haselton & Nettle, 2006). Nor were those ancestors infallible in making the most adaptive choices. Ants sometimes commit mindless suicide by attacking a human who has a can of insect spray in hand, and geese raised by humans sometimes try to mate with the wrong species. In so doing, these animals are enacting programs that, in most other circumstances, helped their ancestors survive and reproduce. In the case of human beings, we saw that our choices of mates are, in many cases, motivated neither by a conscious drive to reproduce nor by any other obvious "rational" strategy. The avoidance of unrelated members of the opposite sex raised together in a kibbutz "family," for example, wasn't based on a conscious adaptive choice. Instead, it seemed to reflect a mechanism that helped most of our ancestors avoid the harmful genetic consequences of incest (Lieberman, Tooby, & Cosmides, 2007).

ARE THERE OTHER BASIC MOTIVES UNDERLYING SOCIAL BEHAVIOR?   We believe most of the particular goals we've addressed in this book can be linked to one of five basic social motives: to form alliances, to gather social information, to gain status, to protect oneself and one's group, and to mate. In many cases, a particular social behavior can simultaneously serve more than one motive—joining a group can result in social support, social information, increased status, and self-protection, for instance, and finding a mate can likewise further many objectives besides the direct goal of starting a family.

On a moment-to-moment basis, however, our movement through the social world is rarely driven by an awareness of these grand-scale "ultimate" motives. Instead, we guide our life toward shorter-term, proximate goals (Little, 1989). When Martin Luther King Jr. and J. Edgar Hoover finally met, the two were quite cordial to each other (Gentry, 1991). King probably turned on the charm with the very narrow goal of getting this potentially dangerous man to form a more favorable impression of him, not the goal of benefitting his children or of promoting racial equality. Likewise, each of the fundamental motives we've discussed can be subdivided into several more immediate goals. Attracting a mate, forming a relationship, responding to a competitor's flirtation with one's partner, and sharing child care are all part of the ultimate goal of successful reproduction, but we need to do very different things to achieve the various subgoals (Kenrick, Sundie, & Kurzban, 2008).

In several cases, we discussed social goals that don't serve social ends but instead serve the more general motivation to seek rewards or avoid unpleasant feelings. For some time, psychologists tried to reduce all behavior to one or two broad motivations, such as "seeking reward." However, many psychologists now search for more specific goals aimed at solving particular problems (Neuberg, Kenrick, & Schaller, 2010; Sedikides & Skowronski, 1997; Tooby & Cosmides, 2005). There are no doubt certain categories of resources that are generally rewarding, such as increases in status or access to food. But particular social situations may change everything. Whether an M & M, a handshake, a bit of gossip, a kiss, a compliment, or a victory is reinforcing, punishing, or neutral critically depends on the social context in which it occurs and on the goals that are activated at the time. A handshake from someone we desire as a mate, a kiss from someone we regard as an enemy, or a smashing victory in a game of chess against one of our own children, for instance, may be more punishment than reward. Hence, when we want to understand the root causes of social behavior, it's often more fruitful to consider goals at a more specific level and to consider how those goals interact with the situation the person is in, as we discuss in the next section.

INVESTIGATION

List two issues involving your relationships with other people that have been on your mind recently. How do they connect with the motives we just discussed?

··

INTERACTION   ## The Interaction between the Person and the Situation

As we've seen, people differ in their desires for social support, social information, status, sex, and personal security. They also vary in other ways that affect social relationships—in their beliefs, in their attributional strategies, in their self-esteem, and

Figure 14.5 Different perspectives on the person and situation

Perspective	Person	Situation
Evolutionary	• Genetic predispositions • Human nature	• Features in our ancestors' environments linked to survival or reproduction
Sociocultural	• Internal social standards	• Societal norms
Social Learning	• Habits • Conditioned preferences	• Rewards • Punishments
Social Cognition	• Schemas • Remembered episodes • Attributional strategies	• Attention-grabbing features of the social environment

Each of the theoretical perspectives takes a slightly different (but compatible) view of factors in the person and in the situation.

so on. Some people, like Hoover, are defensively hostile much of the time; others, like King, are more often self-sacrificially altruistic. These differences between people have been studied from all the different perspectives (see Figure 14.5).

We've also seen that situations vary in the extent to which they trigger different motivations. Some situations, such as a personal insult or another person's flirting with one's lover, bring out the defensive vindictiveness in most of us. Other situations, such as the sight of a starving child, bring out the altruistic tendencies in most of us. These situational factors range from momentary changes in the social situation to childhood experiences to broad cultural norms about appropriate behavior.

Finally, we have seen that there is a continual interaction between those factors inside the person and those in the social situation. The many ways in which person and situation factors interact can be summarized in terms of six general principles that follow.

DIFFERENT PERSONS RESPOND DIFFERENTLY TO THE SAME SITUATION As we noted in Chapter 2, Gordon Allport observed that "the same fire that melts the butter, hardens the egg." Two people may focus on the same details of the same situation and nevertheless respond differently to it. For example, when their self-worth is threatened, people with high self-esteem seek out the company of others, whereas people with low self-esteem avoid other people (Park & Maner, 2009). Threats to our lives would stop many of us from persisting in most courses of action, but for Martin Luther King Jr., who had built his life around the teachings of dedicated martyrs such as Jesus Christ and Mahatma Gandhi, such threats seemed to make him fight harder. Likewise, we've seen that how people respond to persuasive arguments, orders from authority, hostile insults, and attractive members of the opposite sex can vary as a function of differences in their personalities.

SITUATIONS CHOOSE THE PERSON Other people could have led the Montgomery bus boycott, but Martin Luther King Jr. was drafted by his peers. Other people would have loved to direct the FBI, but J. Edgar Hoover was appointed. And other people dreamed of becoming president of the United States in 2009, but Barack Obama was the one elected. Obviously, not everyone gets to enter every situation he or she would like. We are sometimes chosen, sometimes overlooked, and sometimes rejected by potential

Situations choose people. Someone like Jennifer Lawrence, who is beautiful and talented, and who has won numerous awards, is chosen to enter situations (such as parties, relationships, and acting jobs) from which many others would be excluded.

dates, potential friends, potential athletic teams, potential colleges, and potential jobs. Those choices are themselves a function of our enduring characteristics and our self-presentations—how others perceive our likability, our competence, and our social dominance. Ultimately, then, the social situation and the person become inseparable from each other, so that it becomes meaningless to ask where one ends and the other begins. Our personalities and our situations can truly be said to cause one another.

PERSONS CHOOSE THEIR SITUATIONS Most of us are aware of the power of the situation. Parents warn their children to beware of the bad influences of unsavory friends and lovers, high school counselors advise students to select just the right college, and religious leaders counsel us to avoid places of temptation. Although we don't always follow such counsel, most of us do avoid certain situations and actively seek out others. For example, masculine males will volunteer to watch erotic films whereas feminine females will not. Likewise, violence-prone people are more likely to choose a violent film to watch, whereas those having a more pacific nature won't. In this way, the relationship between person and situation gets magnified—delinquent teens choose to hang out with other ruffians; well-behaved teens choose the church group; and intellectuals choose the science club. As a consequence, their respective delinquent, well-behaved, and highbrow tendencies will be further enhanced.

DIFFERENT SITUATIONS PRIME DIFFERENT PARTS OF THE PERSON Sometimes we want people to like us; other times we want them to respect us; and still other times we want them to fear us. In some circumstances, we want another person to be completely frank with us; in others, we prefer the person be polite and diplomatic. These motives rarely just pop out of thin air—they are more often triggered by the situations in which we find ourselves. When other people reject us, for example, we are motivated to avoid further hurt, and we withdraw from social contact. When other people ignore us, however, we are motivated to promote ourselves and try to reengage with others (Molden et al., 2009).

PERSONS CHANGE THE SITUATION In our discussion of groups, we saw that a single individual could change the direction of a whole group, either from the top down, in the case of leaders such as FBI director J. Edgar Hoover, or from the bottom up, as in the case of minority influence. During the course of his years as director, Hoover transformed the FBI into a much more powerful, and more paranoid, organization than it had been before. These changes influenced the behaviors not only of several presidential administrations, but also of thousands of other U.S. citizens, including Martin Luther King Jr.

SITUATIONS CHANGE THE PERSON Although we may do our best to choose situations that match our personal dispositions, we often end up in circumstances we couldn't perfectly predict. A reserved woman may have chosen a certain liberal arts college because she wanted to avoid the crowds of a large, urban university and found an unexpectedly nonconformist social climate. At the end of the college experience, that person is more likely to be politically liberal (Newcomb, 1961). Some of these changes can happen quickly. For example, Japanese people generally tend to focus more on a person's situation than do Americans, who are more likely to ignore context and zero in on the person in center stage. However, Americans begin to think more in the Japanese style if they are simply exposed to Japanese street scenes, which are more complex than American street scenes (Miyamoto et al., 2006).

These interactions often run in multiple directions. For example, emotional people are less likely to become parents in the first place, but if they do have children, they become still more emotional (Jokela et al., 2009). These interactions can also compound over time (e.g., Rusbult, Kumashiro, Kubacka, & Finkel, 2009). For example, young children trying out for sports teams have a disadvantage if they were born shortly before the birthday cut-off. If the cut-off is January 1, then at try-out time children born in December are 11 months younger than those

Different situations activate different parts of the self. Like the rest of us, even public figures like President Barack Obama show different parts of themselves depending on the goals activated by different situations.

born the previous January (when you are six years old, 11 months can make a big difference in maturity, coordination, and experience). As a consequence, the relatively older children are more likely to make the teams, get more practice and high-level coaching, and be selected for teams again in the later grades. Over time, then, initially small differences get magnified, and years later the accident of birthdates turns into real differences in skill and self-confidence and uneven distributions on professional sports teams (Musch & Grondin, 2001).

Why delve so deeply into the complex interactions between persons and situations? Why not just keep our explanations simple? The answer is that simplistic explanations are often incorrect. Although the cognitive misers within us are often satisfied with simple black or white answers, the truth is usually a much more thought-provoking blend of checkerboards and swirls in various shades of gray. Searching carefully through these complexities helps us avoid placing too much blame on the single individual or making the converse error of viewing people as passive pawns of their situations. Charles Manson's neglect by a delinquent mother and Martin Luther King Jr.'s happy childhood in the home of a successful Baptist minister were different enough to have shaped them in important ways. But not every neglected child turns out to be a vicious mass murderer, and not every child of a happy religious home turns out to be a great social crusader.

INVESTIGATION

Link your major in college, where you are going to school, and/or an important relationship to the different types of interactions we've just discussed.

Quick Quiz

1 Which of the following is NOT one of the five broad fundamental motives underlying human social behavior?

    a. To attract and retain mates
    b. To attain economic wealth
    c. To gain and maintain status
    d. To understand ourselves and others
    e. To defend ourselves and those we value

2 Which of the following statements is *false*?

    a. Even psychologically healthy people are susceptible to cognitive biases such as the availability heuristic and the confirmation bias.
    b. Disordered social behavior often arises from normal psychological mechanisms.
    c. Understanding normal psychological mechanisms can help us understand the function of disordered behavior.
    d. None of the above

3 The _____ perspective focuses on person factors such as habits and conditioned preferences, whereas the _____ perspective focuses on person factors such as schemas and attributional strategies.

    a. social cognition, sociocultural
    b. social cognition, social learning
    c. social learning, social cognition
    d. social learning, sociocultural

4 Which of the following examples demonstrates how *the situation changes the person*?

    a. A reserved person attends a liberal arts college and by the end of his college experience he has become an activist for politically liberal causes.
    b. A person motivated to make an accurate decision about which laptop to buy for school conducts a great deal of unbiased research before the purchase; after the purchase, however, she does not want to hear any information that may suggest she made the wrong choice.
    c. Violence-prone people are more likely to choose violent media entertainment.
    d. All of the above

Why Research Methods Matter

LO 14.9 Explain why research methods matter, even if you're not going to be a researcher.

LO 14.10 Discuss the four take-home messages about research methods from this text.

If the social world were simpler, we could just trust our eyes and ears to tell us why people act the way they do. But research on self-presentation and social cognition teaches us that our eyes and ears don't always take in the full story. Not only do other people try to hide their own motives in very skillful ways, but in turn our own minds often distort, oversimplify, or deny what we see and hear. If we could clear away all these cognitive and motivational biases, there would still be our limited perceptual capacities and the constraints of reality to add confusion (Fiedler & Wänke, 2009; Kenrick, Delton et al., 2007). Even a microscope won't allow us to see how different genes interact with one another and with earlier life experiences to affect how different people respond to their everyday social encounters. As we've just discussed, persons and situations interact in highly complex and reciprocal ways that can make the search for causal relationships boggling to the unaided mind.

The search for scientific explanations of social behavior, then, requires a very special sort of detective work. Research methods are the tools that allow that detective work to be done. For this reason, understanding research methods is important not only to the social scientist but also to every one of us. After all, we're all the consumers of social science information. Can we trust the conclusions of a magazine article or a television documentary about the causes of gang violence or teen pregnancy or racial conflict? Just because a conclusion is confidently asserted by a well-spoken, attractive news commentator doesn't mean it's right. Without research to back up his or her conclusion, the expert's opinion is subject to all the same biases of social perception and social cognition that can lead you or your father or your great-aunt Ginger astray.

Research methods help overcome a number of problems, including people's biases and limitations in reporting their own social behaviors. As consumers of social science information about how to win friends, influence lovers, pacify potential enemies, and raise happy children, we should all take care before accepting the unsubstantiated opinions of experts. In the Bridging Method and Evidence feature, we discuss four useful take-home messages worth keeping in mind whenever you are consuming expert opinion about scientific evidence.

Bridging Method and Evidence:
Some Conclusions for Consumers of Social Science Information

Throughout this book, we've discussed a number of detective tools that psychologists use to overcome their own perceptual and cognitive limitations. These include general-purpose tools, such as meta-analysis and unobtrusive measures, and specialized tools, such as facial action coding and behavior genetic studies of twins separated at birth. Social psychologists continue to develop creative new research methods for studying social behavior. For example, one team of social psychologists has been using the wonders of modern computer technology to study social interactions in virtual reality (Bailenson, Blascovich, & Guadagno, 2008; Bailenson et al., 2005). As we've seen throughout the book, modern neuroscientific methods are now being used to help us begin to understand the link between processes in the brain and social experiences ranging from rejection to love to prejudice (e.g., Bartholow et al., 2006; Eisenberger, Lieberman, & Williams, 2003; Phelps et al., 2000).

Looking over these methods yields some general conclusions for amateur and professional social psychological detective work.

1. *Look for good descriptions to accompany explanations.* Before considering motives for a crime, a detective needs an accurate picture of what happened at the crime scene. Experiments help uncover cause-and-effect relationships but cannot paint a complete picture of real-world behavior. Descriptive methods such as surveys and archives help fill out the picture. Ideally, research programs go "full cycle" between experimentation—used to unravel causal mechanisms—and field work—used to keep the researcher tracking phenomena that really matter in the outside world (Cialdini, 1995).

   Good observation requires more than just the naked eye. Like a telescope to an astronomer, some techniques can help psychologists examine otherwise invisible social phenomena. For example, factor analysis taps the capacities of computers to help researchers discern statistical patterns among attitudes, feelings, and behaviors, such as the five factors of personality or the three factors of love (Lemieux & Hale, 2002; Pytlik-Zillig, Hemenover, & Dienstbier, 2002). Not all such methods require fancy technology. Analyses of emotional expression exploit simple, slow-motion videotape technology, and thought-listing techniques involve merely asking people to make their private ruminations public (Ekman & Friesen, 1971; Vohs & Schmeichel, 2003).

2. *Don't trust everything people say.* The butler may claim innocence with an earnest face, but the jury should still review the evidence. As we noted, people's reports can be biased or dead wrong. You may not be willing or able to say if your angry outburst was affected by feelings of insecurity, for example, or if your empathy for a hungry child was based on a general human inclination toward nurturance. Several techniques, including unobtrusive measurement

and behavior genetic methods, are designed to help us see beyond people's limited views.

As an information consumer, you don't need to be a methodological expert, but when you hear about research relevant to you, you ought to ask if the conclusions are based on people's reports about things they cannot, or will not, describe accurately. Again, like a good detective, you must examine the whole picture. When survey respondents admit behaviors such as masturbation or homicidal fantasies, we can guess that, if anything, they are underestimating. But if they describe themselves in desirable ways—that they harbor no racial prejudices, for example—it's best to look for covert measures to corroborate their stories.

3. *Beware of confounds.* Just because the butler was at the crime scene and owned a gun doesn't mean he did it. In experiments, confounding variables are factors accidentally varied along with the independent variable, as when children who watch an aggressive film encounter a hostile looking male experimenter with a large tattoo, while children in the control condition encounter a saintly looking, grandmotherly experimenter. Maybe the grandma in this poorly designed imaginary study suppressed children's expressions of hostility or the tattooed man instigated them, or maybe not. But if the same experimenters didn't run both conditions, we can't tease apart the effects of the film, versus the experimenter's demeanor, on the children's aggression.

Confounds also plague descriptive studies, as when a researcher finds a correlation between property crimes and ethnicity but fails to consider social class. Social class is a potential confound because it's systematically linked with both race and property crimes (the wealthy have less need to burglarize hubcaps). Without measuring social class, we can't tease out (or unconfound) its effects.

Behavior genetic methods, discussed in Chapter 9, incorporate several techniques for teasing apart confounds. Children resemble their parents and siblings in social behaviors ranging from altruism to violence. These similarities could be due to either shared family environment or shared genes. Without special methods, we can't tell. By examining adopted siblings (who share an environment but not genes) or identical twins separated at birth (who share genes but not an environment), we can begin to pull apart the normally confounded factors (e.g., Abrahamson, Baker, & Caspi, 2002).

4. *Ask for converging evidence.* Just as a detective wouldn't trust an individual witness without checking other sources, so we shouldn't place too much confidence in any lone research finding (McGrath, Martin, & Kukla, 1982; Simpson & Campbell, 2005). Chance or unintended error may have led to erroneous conclusions. One tool for dealing with this problem is meta-analysis. For example, numerous studies, mentioned in Chapter 10, examined how violent media affect aggression in viewers (Wood, Wong, & Chachere, 1991). Some found positive results, some negative results, and some no results at all. The different results are due to random error, variations

in the independent and dependent variables, and so on. Meta-analysis statistically combines studies to reduce dangers from these chance factors and to allow more confident conclusions.

Meta-analysis cannot rule out a systematic bias across different studies. For example, if 100 studies examined college students delivering electric shock to other students in laboratories, we're not sure whether the results apply to aggression outside the lab. To deal with this problem, researchers use *triangulation*—examining the same problem using different research methods, each having different biases. Field studies suggesting that children who watch more violent television are more aggressive cannot separate cause and effect, because violence-prone children may choose violent television shows. Laboratory experiments in which children are randomly assigned to watch violent or nonviolent programs solve that problem but raise questions of artificiality that field studies do not. Surveys of parents can ask about more natural everyday aggression but are subject to biased parental memory. If all these studies nevertheless point in the same direction, despite opposite strengths and weaknesses, we can make more confident conclusions (Anderson & Bushman, 2001). As discussed in Chapter 1, the situation is like that of a detective confronted with several imperfect witnesses: One witness loves the butler and is hard of hearing, one hates the butler but wasn't wearing his glasses, and another has intact vision and hearing but doesn't know the butler well enough to make an airtight identification. If they all agree that he did it, though, the detective can draw a more confident conclusion about the butler's culpability.

Quick Quiz

1 Which of the following statements best describes *triangulation*?

    a. The extent to which the findings of a particular research study extend to other similar circumstances or cases.

    b. The technique of using three different theoretical perspectives to analyze the same problem.

    c. The technique of examining the same problem using different research methods, each having different biases.

    d. A focus on background or historical causes.

2 Which of the following statements is a sound recommendation for consumers of social science?

    a. Don't trust everything people say.

    b. Don't trust converging evidence.

    c. Look for good descriptions to accompany explanations.

    d. Beware of confounds.

    e. All of the above

How Does Social Psychology Fit into the Network of Knowledge?

LO 14.13 Describe three connections between social psychology and (a) other areas of psychology, (b) other basic sciences, and (c) applied sciences such as business, medicine, and law.

In Chapter 1, we noted social psychology's many bridges with other areas of psychology. In later chapters, we've seen numerous connections with *developmental psychology*, observing how adult patterns of aggression, altruism, and love, for instance, grow out of basic predispositions and early learning (see Table 14.1). Connections with *personality psychology* were incorporated into every chapter, as we considered how traits inside the individual continually interact with the social environment. Links to *environmental psychology* showed up in our discussions of heat and aggression, overcrowding, and environmental destruction. In every chapter, we saw connections with *clinical psychology* in the *Bridging Function and Dysfunction* features, which considered topics from mild obsessiveness to paranoia. Likewise, we drew links with *cognitive psychology* in every chapter of this book, as we explored how mental processes of attention, perception, memory, and decision making are

Triangulation Technique of examining the same problem using different research methods, each having different biases.

Table 14.1 Social Psychology's Connections with Other Areas of Psychology

Area of Psychology	Example of Overlapping Question
Developmental	Does the early attachment between mother and infant influence love relationships in later life?
Personality	What individual differences predict aggressive behavior?
Environmental	What social conditions lead people to recycle?
Clinical	How is paranoia connected to normal group defensiveness?
Cognitive	How does the limited human attention span affect stereotypes?
Neuroscience	How does testosterone affect human relationships?

intertwined with person–situation interactions. *Neuroscience* was essential to our discussions of hormonal effects on sexual and aggressive behavior, and of differential brain activity associated with diverse social reactions such as feeling love or trying to remember the faces of outgroup members (Golby et al., 2001; Gray et al., 2004a; Hamann et al., 2004). Given the view of some cognitive psychologists that many of the unique features of the human brain evolved to deal with problems of living in social groups (Schaller et al., 2007; Tooby & Cosmides, 2005), it makes sense that we human beings devote many of our mental capacities to dealing with other people. Social psychology is thus centrally linked to all the other areas of brain and behavioral science (Brewer, Kenny, & Norem, 2000; Cacioppo, 2002; Harmon-Jones & Devine, 2003).

At a still broader level, social psychology has bridges to other disciplines outside psychology's loose boundaries. At the most basic level, research on altruism, aggression, and love has been linked to developments in *genetics* and *biochemistry*. At a broader level, research on groups, organizations, and societies weaves social psychology together with the social sciences—*sociology, anthropology, economics*, and *political science*. At this level, social psychology is also linked to those areas of biological research on complex relationships between groups of animals and their natural environments—*ethology* and *ecology*. Table 14.2 lists some examples of the kinds of questions that link social psychology and other basic sciences.

Table 14.2 Social Psychology's Connections with Other Basic Sciences

Area of Study	Example of Overlapping Question
Genetics	Is altruism linked to common genes shared within families?
Biochemistry	Does testosterone similarly affect male and female behavior?
Sociology	How do groups choose leaders?
Anthropology	Are there universal patterns to human marriage?
Economics	Are there circumstances when people sharing a common resource (such as a forest or an ocean) will restrain their selfish tendencies that lead to overexploitation?
Political science	How do group processes affect policy decisions in international conflict situations?
Ethology	Do the mating rituals of peacocks shed any light on human courtship?
Ecology	How does the dynamic balance between predators and prey in a forest link with the behavior of students playing a prisoner's dilemma game in a laboratory?

Bridging Theory and Application:

Social Psychology's Usefulness for Business, Medicine, and Law

One goal of research is simply to satisfy our curiosity. The human mind craves knowledge about the causes and purposes of human love, self-sacrificial altruism, prejudice, and violence. We want to understand what makes ourselves and others tick. But basic science has always gone hand in hand with application. The discoveries of ancient astronomers gazing at the stars allowed explorers and entrepreneurs to sail around the globe and find their way back to where they started; the discoveries of early biologists curious about the human body and about the tiny animals moving under their microscopes eventually led to modern medicine; and the discoveries of physicists interested in abstract principles of gravity and motion eventually made it possible to land a human being on the moon (Boorstin, 1983). Indeed, the philosophical questions that stimulate research in basic science often intrigue us because they deal with puzzling practical problems. The more we can understand about love or friendship or in-group favoritism, the better chance we have to prevent divorce or loneliness or destructive prejudice.

In every chapter of this textbook, we've spotlighted bridges between social psychology and applied sciences. For example, we saw a number of links with business, as in our feature on person–situation fit in the workplace in Chapter 2. Unpleasant relationships on the job can fill our days with misery, damage our bodies, and even disrupt our home lives (Barling & Rosenbaum, 1986). J. Edgar Hoover wasn't the only boss whose employees lived in constant fear of his wrath.

Social relationships aren't just the icing on our work lives; they're very often the cake itself. Most jobs require some degree of negotiating, persuading, teaching, disciplining, advising, and cooperating with other people. Hence, there is an inherently close connection between social psychology and business fields such as organizational behavior, marketing, and management (e.g., Griskevicius, Goldstein, Mortensen et al., 2009; Thaler & Sunstein, 2008). A glance at textbooks in any of these fields reveals considerable overlap with the topics in this textbook. Students who have studied social psychology frequently pursue careers in the business world, and conversely, business students frequently study social psychology as part of their training.

In this chapter's research video, we discuss some research by Jessica Li, who has a Ph.D. in social psychology and is now a professor of marketing at the University of Kansas. Her research demonstrates linkages between economics, evolutionary biology, and the social psychology of decision-making.

Social psychologists have also built bridges with medicine and other health sciences (Salovey et al., 1998; Taylor,

WATCH THE VIDEO: *How mating and self-protection motives can alter your economic decisions.*

2002). Health psychology interventions were explored in many places throughout this book. Doctors, nurses, and public health officials often find that their persuasive appeals fail to move patients to stop smoking, change unhealthy diets, increase exercise or contraceptive use, or even just take their prescribed medications. Some experts estimate that public health would benefit far more from simple changes in behavior than from dramatic medical discoveries (Matarazzo, 1980). Imagine, for example, the effects on sexually transmitted diseases if all unmarried sexual partners could be convinced to use condoms or the effects on lung cancer if a whole generation of youth could be convinced not to smoke. Without a single advance in medical technology, two of the major health concerns of Western society would practically disappear. Thus, increasing numbers of social psychologists are conducting research on preventive medicine (e.g., Bryan, Aiken, & West, 1999).

A third area in which social psychological principles have been extensively applied is the law (e.g., Ellsworth & Mauro, 1998; Wells & Olson, 2003). We considered these applications in discussing topics such as lie detection, false confessions, and techniques to reduce violence at the societal level. Social

psychologists have also conducted research on jury decision making and eyewitness testimony (Leippe, 1995; Wells, Olsen, & Charman, 2002). Obviously, legal argumentation and jury decision making involve attribution, persuasion, and group interaction—processes social psychologists have studied for decades. In recent years, a number of social psychologists have taken positions teaching in law schools. Increasingly, social psychology students are taking advanced degrees in organizational psychology, health psychology, and legal psychology.

Table 14.3 Social Psychology's Connections with Applied Sciences

Area of Application	Example of Overlapping Question
Law	How do social pressures within a jury influence the decisions of individual jury members?
Medicine	Can doctors and nurses interact with patients in ways that promote compliance with health recommendations?
Business	Are there ways for management to decrease employee dishonesty?
Education	How do teacher expectancies influence a child's performance in the classroom?
Engineering	How can computer networks be designed to facilitate communication between electronically linked employees?

In addition to business, medicine, and law, social psychology has obvious implications for education (which involves many of the processes we've discussed throughout this book) and even for engineering (as social communication becomes more and more technologically based). Although social psychological research is often concerned with basic theoretical questions, there are a great number of applications for its theoretical findings. As the pioneering social psychologist Kurt Lewin once said, "There is nothing so practical as a good theory." He would probably be pleased to see the numerous practical applications of the field to which he made such influential theoretical contributions (see Table 14.3).

INVESTIGATION

Think of at least one other question connecting social psychology and another discipline (besides the ones listed in Tables 14.2 and 14.3).

Quick Quiz

1 Which of the following questions demonstrates the link between social psychology and other areas of psychology?

    a. Does attachment between mother and infant affect later relationships?
    b. What individual differences predict prosocial behavior?
    c. How does testosterone affect aggressive behavior?
    d. All of the above

2 Social psychology is linked with the social sciences such as _____ as well as areas of biology such as _____.

    a. economics, genetics
    b. ecology, genetics
    c. sociology, anthropology
    d. ecology, ethology

3   Which of the following questions is NOT an example of social psychology's connection with applied sciences?

    a. How do group processes within a jury influence individual jury members' decisions?
    b. What psychological tools can managers use to increase employee productivity?
    c. How are brain activity patterns linked to processing rapidly presented faces?
    d. How do teacher expectancies influence a child's performance in the classroom?

The Future of Social Psychology

A popular science writer recently suggested that scientists might soon run out of questions to answer. That writer was clearly not familiar with social psychology. Researchers have only begun to understand the complex interactions between person and situation underlying our thoughts and feelings about altruism, racial prejudice, aggression, and group behavior. Indeed, the frontier here is as vast as a great continent, and researchers have so far managed to map only a few intermittent points along the shoreline. As social psychologists explore these questions, they are increasingly joining forces with new integrative disciplines such as cognitive science, evolutionary psychology, and dynamical systems (Haselton & Funder, 2006; Kenrick, Li, & Butner, 2003). Cognitive science connects work on social cognition with other research on the workings of the human brain, evolutionary theory provides insights into the ultimate goals of social behavior, and dynamical systems research holds the promise of understanding how the thoughts and motivations of individuals add up to monumental group-level processes

From individual psychology to society. Decisions made by single individuals can interact to produce complex, and sometimes unexpected, phenomena at the group level. The Civil Rights movement provided a grand example of the two-way interaction between individual and society.

from civil rights marches to international conflicts. Because our human ancestors always lived in groups, the eventual integration of the various behavioral and brain sciences will almost certainly have social psychological questions at the fore (Schaller, Park, & Kenrick, 2007). Accordingly, the study of social psychological processes is yielding new understanding of the links between the evolution of simple mechanisms in the human brain and the emergence of human culture (e.g., Gangestad, Haselton, & Buss, 2006; Kenrick, Nieuweboer, & Buunk, 2010; Norenzayan et al., 2006).

The movement toward a more integrated science of the mind and social behavior isn't only of philosophical interest. It's also laden with immense practical potential. On the one hand, the increasing emphasis on positive social psychology is beginning to provide insights about how to make people happy with their social relationships, and what contributes to the emergence of heroism, kindness, and love (e.g., Gable & Haidt, 2005; Lyubomirsky, King, & Diener, 2005; Penner, Dovidio, Piliavin, & Schroeder, 2005). On the other hand, a truly scientific understanding of the motivating forces behind negative social behaviors such as aggression, prejudice, and narcissistic selfishness may provide the keys to solving some of the most important problems in the world today. Perhaps the human ingenuity that made it possible to chat with someone on the other side of the globe, to fly from New York to London in an afternoon, and to take close-up photographs of other planets will enable us to solve the great social problems of overpopulation, international conflict, and the destruction of our planet (Oskamp, 2000; Penn, 2003).

Although such hopes may seem unrealistic now, it's worth keeping in mind that in the few decades since J. Edgar Hoover worried about Communist links to the crowd that marched on Washington, the nuclear weapons race between the Soviet Union and the United States has ended and the population explosion has slowed. And when Martin Luther King Jr.

started the fight for civil rights, it still seemed like only a dream that legalized racial discrimination could be erased from U.S. lawbooks. At that time, few would have believed that a two-year-old black boy in Hawaii would someday grow up to become president of the United States. However, the concerted efforts of a committed few made the realization of that dream possible. Perhaps the twenty-first century will see advances in the science of social behavior that make it possible for little boys and little girls of different skin colors to walk together in a world that is free not only of racial intolerance but also of fears of overpopulation, pollution, and warfare. Perhaps the scientific curiosity of your generation will lead to discoveries that one day allow us all to say that we are, finally, free at last!

Chapter Summary

What Ground Have We Covered?

1. We began our investigation of the mysteries of social life with individual motives, feelings, and thoughts. We proceeded to consider how individuals think about, present themselves to, and interact with others. Finally, we explored social processes at the group and global level.

2. The numerous findings of social psychology are best understood not as discrete bits of information but in terms of their implications for broader theoretical perspectives.

Major Theoretical Perspectives of Social Psychology

1. The *sociocultural* perspective focuses on group-level processes such as varying norms across societies.

2. The *evolutionary* perspective focuses on general principles of survival and reproduction that apply across cultures and species.

3. Linking the sociocultural and evolutionary perspectives, we discover common features of human nature underneath sometimes dazzling sociocultural differences.

4. The *social learning* perspective focuses on rewards and punishments in particular environments. Learning processes reflect sociocultural norms and evolved behavioral mechanisms.

5. The *social cognitive* perspective considers processes involved in noticing, interpreting, judging, and remembering social events. Cognitive scientists and evolutionary psychologists are beginning to search for clues about how evolved brain and behavioral mechanisms are designed to function in the social environment.

6. Examining gender differences and similarities from a variety of perspectives, we see that evolutionary perspectives reveal the biological roots of some sex differences and similarities, sociocultural and social learning perspectives show how sometimes small biological differences can be enhanced by experience, and

cognitive perspectives suggest how sex differences sometimes get exaggerated through stereotypes.

Combining the Different Perspectives

1. Our exploration of social life was guided by two broad principles: (1) social behavior is goal oriented and (2) social behavior represents a continual interaction between person and situation.

2. Several broad motives underlie a wide range of social behavior: (1) to establish social ties, (2) to understand ourselves and others, (3) to gain and maintain status, (4) to defend ourselves and those we value, and (5) to attract and retain mates. These motives are often interdependent and can be subdivided into long-term and immediate subgoals.

3. Studying dysfunctional social behavior can sometimes elucidate normal psychological mechanisms.

4. Some social behaviors serve general, nonsocial motives such as reward seeking. But the search for nonspecific, content-free goals may not be as informative as a search for specific goals aimed at solving particular problems.

5. Person–situation interactions involve six general principles: (1) Different people respond differently to the same situation, (2) situations choose people, (3) people choose their situations, (4) different situations prime different parts of the person, (5) people change their situations, and (6) situations change people.

Why Research Methods Matter

1. Research methods are tools that help scientists avoid biased descriptions and explanations.

2. Research methods are the detective tools used by social psychologists. As consumers of scientific results, we should (1) look for good descriptions to accompany explanations, (2) not trust everything people say, (3) watch for confounds, and (4) ask for converging evidence from different studies and different methods.

How Does Social Psychology Fit into the Network of Knowledge?

1. Social psychology is interconnected with other areas of psychology exploring cognitive and neurological processes, learning and development, individual differences, and disordered behavior.
2. Social psychology links to more molecular sciences such as genetics and molecular biology and to more broadly focused sciences such as ethology, ecology, and other social sciences.
3. Social psychological research has important implications for applied fields such as business, medicine, law, education, and engineering.

The Future of Social Psychology

1. Social psychology increasingly connects with integrative disciplines of cognitive science, evolutionary psychology, and dynamical systems. Because the human mind is designed to promote survival in social groups, social psychological questions are central to an integrated behavioral and brain science.
2. Advances in understanding social behavior could help solve global problems, including overpopulation, international conflict, and environmental destruction.

Key Terms

Proximate explanation, 463

Triangulation, 482

Ultimate explanation, 463

Glossary

Adaptation   A characteristic that is well designed for survival and reproduction in a particular environment.

Affordance   An opportunity or threat provided by a situation.

Aggression   Behavior intended to injure another.

Altruist   Someone oriented toward bringing the group benefits, even if it means personal sacrifice.

Anchoring and adjustment heuristic   A mental shortcut through which people begin with a rough estimation as a starting point and then adjust this estimate to take into account unique characteristics of the present situation.

Androgynous   Demonstrating a combination of masculine and feminine characteristics in one's behaviors.

Anxious/ambivalent attachment style   Attachments marked by fear of abandonment and the feeling that one's needs are not being met.

Archival method   Examination of systematic data originally collected for other purposes (such as marriage licenses or arrest records).

Arousal/cost-reward model   The view that observers of a victim's suffering will want to help to relieve their own personal distress.

Assertiveness   Behavior intended to express dominance or confidence.

Attachment love   Desire to be cared for, and protected by, another person.

Attention   The process of consciously focusing on aspects of our environment or ourselves.

Attitudes   Favorable or unfavorable evaluations of a particular person, object, event, or idea.

Attribution theories   Theories designed to explain how people determine the causes of behavior.

Augmenting principle   The judgmental rule that states that if an event occurs despite the presence of strong opposing forces, we should give more weight to those possible causes that lead toward the event.

Authoritarianism   The tendency to submit to those having greater authority and to denigrate those having less authority.

Authority ranking   A form of exchange in which goods are divided according to a person's status in the group.

Automaticity   The ability of a behavior or cognitive process to operate without conscious guidance once it's put into motion.

Availability heuristic   A mental shortcut people use to estimate the likelihood of an event by the ease with which instances of that event come to mind.

Avoidant attachment style   Attachments marked by defensive detachment from the other.

Bait-and-switch technique   Gaining a commitment to an arrangement, then making the arrangement unavailable or unappealing and offering a more costly arrangement.

Balance theory   Heider's theory that people prefer harmony and consistency in their views of the world.

Basking in reflected glory   The process of associating ourselves with successful, high-status others or events.

Body language   The popular term for nonverbal behaviors like facial expressions, posture, body orientation, and hand gestures.

Bystander effect   The tendency of a bystander to be less likely to help in an emergency if there are other onlookers present.

Case study   An intensive examination of an individual or group.

Catharsis   Discharge of aggressive impulses.

Central route to persuasion   The way people are persuaded when they focus on the quality of the arguments in a message.

Chronically accessible   The state of being easily activated, or primed, for use.

Cognitive dissonance   The unpleasant state of psychological arousal resulting from an inconsistency within one's important attitudes, beliefs, or behaviors.

Cognitive heuristic   A mental shortcut used to make a judgment.

Cognitive response model   A theory that locates the most direct cause of persuasion in the self-talk of the persuasion target.

Cognitive-neoassociation theory   Theory that any unpleasant situation triggers a complex chain of internal events, including negative emotions and negative thoughts. Depending on other cues in the situation (such as weapons), these negative feelings will be expressed as either aggression or flight.

Cohesiveness   The strength of the bonds among group members.

Collectivistic culture   A culture that socializes its members to think of themselves in terms of their relationships and as members of the larger social group, and to prioritize the concerns of their relationship partners and groups before their own.

Command-and-control policy   A prescriptive legal regulation that uses police power to punish violators.

Communal sharing   A form of exchange in which members of a group share a pool of resources, taking when they are in need and giving when others are in need.

Communication network   The pattern of information flow through a group.

Companionate love   Affection and tenderness felt for those whose lives are entwined with our own.

Competence motivation   The desire to perform effectively.

Competitor   Someone oriented to come out relatively better than other players, regardless of whether personal winnings are high or low in an absolute sense.

Compliance   Behavior change that occurs as a result of a direct request.

Conflict spiral view   The belief that escalations of international threat lead an opponent to feel more threatened and that leaders should thus demonstrate peaceful intentions to reduce the opponent's own defensive hostilities.

Conformity   Behavior change designed to match the actions of others.

Confound   A variable that systematically changes along with the independent variable, potentially leading to a mistaken conclusion about the effect of the independent variable.

Consistency principle   The principle that people will change their attitudes, beliefs, perceptions, and actions to make them consistent with each other.

Cooperator   Someone oriented toward working together to maximize the joint benefits to the self and the group.

Correlation   The extent to which two or more variables are associated with one another.

Correlation coefficient   A mathematical expression of the relationship between two variables.

Correspondence bias (fundamental attribution error)   The tendency for observers to overestimate the causal influence of personality factors on behavior and to underestimate the causal role of situational influences.

Correspondent inference theory   The theory that proposes that people determine whether a behavior corresponds to an actor's internal disposition by asking whether (1) the behavior was intended, (2) the behavior's consequences were foreseeable, (3) the behavior was freely chosen, and (4) the behavior occurred despite countervailing forces.

Counterargument   An argument that challenges and opposes other arguments.

Counterattitudinal action   A behavior that is inconsistent with an existing attitude.

Counterfactual thinking   The process of imagining alternative, "might have been" versions of actual events.

Covariation model   The theory that proposes that people determine the cause of an actor's behavior by assessing whether other people act in similar ways (consensus), the actor behaves similarly in similar situations (distinctiveness), and the actor behaves similarly across time in the same situation (consistency).

Culture   The beliefs, customs, habits, and languages shared by the people living in a particular time and place.

Culture of honor   A set of societal norms whose central idea is that people (particularly men) should be ready to defend their honor with violent retaliation if necessary.

Cutting off reflected failure   The process of distancing ourselves from unsuccessful, low-status others or events.

Debriefing   A discussion of procedures, hypotheses, and participant reactions at the completion of the study.

Decision/commitment   Factor on love scales composed of items tapping decision that one is in love with and committed to another.

Defensive attributional style   A tendency to notice threats and interpret other people's behavior as intended to do one harm.

Deindividuation   The process of losing one's sense of personal identity, which makes it easier to behave in ways inconsistent with one's normal values.

Demand characteristic   Cue that makes participants aware of how the experimenter expects them to behave.

Dependent variable   The variable measured by the experimenter.

Descriptive method   Procedure for measuring or recording behaviors, thoughts, and feelings in their natural state (including naturalistic observations, case studies, archival studies, surveys, and psychological tests).

Descriptive norm   A norm that defines what behaviors are typically performed.

Descriptive norm   A norm that defines what is commonly done in a situation.

Deterrence view   The belief that signs of weakness will be exploited by the opponent and that leaders need to show their willingness to use military force.

Differential parental investment   The principle that animals making higher investment in their offspring (female as compared to male mammals, for instance) will be more careful in choosing mates.

Diffusion of responsibility   The tendency for each group member to dilute personal responsibility for acting by spreading it among all other group members.

Direct aggression   Behavior intended to hurt someone to his or her face.

Discounting principle   The judgmental rule that states that as the number of possible causes for an event increases, our confidence that any particular cause is the true one should decrease.

Discrimination   Behaviors directed toward people on the basis of their group membership.

Disidentify   To reduce in one's mind the relevance of a particular domain (e.g., academic achievement) to one's self-esteem.

Displacement   Indirect expression of an aggressive impulse away from the person or animal that elicited it.

Dispositional inference   The judgment that a person's behavior has been caused by an aspect of that person's personality.

Disrupt-then-reframe technique   A tactic that operates to increase compliance by disrupting one's initial, resistance-laden view of a request and quickly reframing the request in more favorable terms.

Domain-general model   A model that attempts to explain a wide range of different behaviors according to a simple general rule (such as: do it if it's rewarding).

Domain-specific model   A model that presumes that the governing principles vary from one domain of behavior to another (such as friendship versus romance versus parent–child relationships).

Door-in-the-face technique   A technique that increases compliance by beginning with a large favor likely to be rejected and then retreating to a more moderate favor.

Downward social comparison   The process of comparing ourselves with those who are less well off.

Dramaturgical perspective   The perspective that much of social interaction can be thought of as a play, with actors, performances, settings, scripts, props, roles, and so forth.

Dual process model of persuasion   A model that accounts for the two basic ways that attitude change occurs—with and without much thought.

Dynamical system   A system (e.g., a group) made up of many interacting elements (e.g., people) that changes and evolves over time.

Effect/danger ratio   Assessment of the likely beneficial effect of aggressiveness balanced against the likely dangers.

Elaboration likelihood model   A model of persuasive communication that holds that there are two routes to attitude change—the central route and the peripheral route.

Emotional aggression   Hurtful behavior that stems from angry feelings.

Emotions   Relatively intense feelings characterized by physiological arousal and complex cognitions.

Empathic concern   Compassionate feelings caused by taking the perspective of a needy other.

Empathy–altruism hypothesis   The presumption that when one empathizes with the plight of another, one will want to help that other for purely altruistic reasons.

Equality matching   A form of exchange in which each person gets the same as the others.

Equity   A state of affairs in which one person's benefits and costs from a relationship are proportional to the benefits and costs incurred by his or her partner.

Equity rule   Each person's benefits and costs in a social relationship should be matched to the benefits and costs of the other.

Erotomania   A disorder involving the fixed (but incorrect) belief that one is loved by another, which persists in the face of strong evidence to the contrary.

Evolutionary perspective   A theoretical viewpoint that searches for the causes of social behavior in the physical and psychological predispositions that helped our ancestors survive and reproduce.

Excitation-transfer theory   The theory that anger is physiologically similar to other emotional states and that any form of emotional arousal can enhance aggressive responses.

Exemplar   A mental representation of a specific episode, event, or individual.

Experiment   A research method in which the researcher sets out to systematically manipulate one source of influence while holding others constant.

Experimental method   Procedure for uncovering causal processes by systematically manipulating some aspect of a situation.

Expert power   The capacity to influence other people as a function of a person's presumed wisdom or knowledge.

External validity   The extent to which the results of an experiment can be generalized to other circumstances.

Factor analysis   A statistical technique for sorting test items or behaviors into conceptually similar groupings.

False consensus effect   The tendency to overestimate the extent to which others agree with us.

Field experimentation   The manipulation of independent variables using unknowing participants in natural settings.

Foot-in-the door technique   A technique that increases compliance with a large request by first getting compliance with a smaller, related request.

Friend   Someone with whom we have an affectionate relationship.

Frustration–aggression hypothesis (original)   The theory that aggression is an automatic response to any blocking of goal-directed behavior.

Frustration–aggression hypothesis (reformulated)   The theory that any unpleasant stimulation will lead to emotional aggression to the extent that it generates unpleasant feelings.

Generalizability   The extent to which the findings of a particular research study extend to other similar circumstances or cases.

Goal   A desired outcome; something one wishes to achieve or accomplish.

GRIT (graduated and reciprocated initiatives in tension reduction)   A strategy for breaking conflict spirals by publicly challenging the opponent to match de-escalations.

Group   Minimally, groups are two or more individuals who influence each other. Collections of individuals become increasingly "grouplike," however, when their members are interdependent and share a common identity, and when they possess structure.

Group polarization   Occurs when group discussion leads members to make decisions that are more extremely on the side of the issue that the group initially favored.

Groupthink   A style of group decision making characterized by a greater desire among members to get along and agree with one another than to generate and critically evaluate alternative viewpoints and positions.

Health psychology   The study of behavioral and psychological factors that affect illness.

Hypothesis   A researcher's prediction about what he or she will find.

Impression motivation   The motivation to achieve approval by making a good impression on others.

Inclusive fitness   The survival of one's genes in one's own offspring and in any relatives one helps.

Independent variable   The variable manipulated by the experimenter.

Indirect aggression   Behavior intended to hurt someone without face-to-face confrontation.

Individualist   Someone oriented toward maximizing personal gains, without regard to the rest of the group.

Individualistic culture   A culture that socializes its members to think of themselves as individuals and to give priority to their personal goals.

Ingratiation   An attempt to get others to like us.

Ingroup bias   The tendency to benefit members of one's own groups over members of other groups.

Injunctive norm   A norm that defines what behaviors are typically approved or disapproved.

Injunctive norm   A norm that describes what is commonly approved or disapproved in a situation.

Inoculation procedure   A technique for increasing individuals' resistance to a strong argument by first giving them weak, easily defeated versions of it.

Instrumental aggression   Hurting another to accomplish some other (nonaggressive) goal.

Integrative complexity   The extent to which a person demonstrates simplified "black-and-white" categorical thinking, as opposed to acknowledgment of all sides of an issue.

Internal validity   The extent to which an experiment allows confident statements about cause and effect.

Intimacy   Factor on love scales composed of items tapping feelings of close bonding with another.

Labeling technique   Assigning a label to an individual and then requesting a favor that is consistent with the label.

Low-ball technique   Gaining a commitment to an arrangement and then raising the cost of carrying out the arrangement.

Market pricing   A form of exchange in which everyone gets out in proportion to what they put in.

Market-based policy   An offer of rewards to those who reduce their socially harmful behaviors.

Mere exposure effect   The tendency to feel positively toward people, places, or things we have seen frequently.

Meta-analysis   A statistical combination of results from different studies of the same topic.

Minimal intergroup paradigm   An experimental procedure in which short-term, arbitrary, artificial groups are created to explore the foundations of prejudice, stereotyping, and discrimination.

Minority influence   Occurs when opinion minorities persuade others of their views.

Monogamy   Marital custom in which one man marries one woman.

Mood management hypothesis   The idea that people use helping tactically to manage their moods.

Moods   Relatively long-lasting feelings that are diffuse and not directed toward particular targets.

Motivation   The force that moves people toward desired outcomes.

Motive   A high-level goal fundamental to social survival.

Multiple audience dilemma   A situation in which a person needs to present different images to different audiences, often at the same time.

Natural selection   The process by which characteristics that help animals survive and reproduce are passed on to their offspring.

Naturalistic observation   Recording everyday behaviors as they unfold in their natural settings.

Need for cognition   The tendency to enjoy and engage in deliberative thought.

Need to belong   The human need to form and maintain strong, stable interpersonal relationships.

Need-based rule   Each person in a social relationship provides benefits as the other needs them, without keeping account of individual costs and benefits.

Nonreactive measurement   Measurement that does not change a subject's responses while recording them.

Norm of reciprocity   The norm that requires that we repay others with the form of behavior they have given us.

Nurturant love   Feelings of tenderness and concern, central to parents caring for their children.

Obedience   Compliance that occurs in response to a directive from an authority figure.

Observer bias   Error introduced into measurement when an observer overemphasizes behaviors he or she expects to find and fails to notice behaviors he or she does not expect.

Participant observation   A research approach in which the researcher infiltrates the setting to be studied and observes its workings from within.

Passion   Factor on love scales composed of items tapping romantic attraction and sexual desire.

Passionate love   A state of intense longing for union with another.

Perceived outgroup homogeneity   The phenomenon of overestimating the extent to which members within other groups are similar to each other.

Perceptual dilemma   The combination of a social dilemma and an outgroup bias, in which each side in a conflict believes that it is best for both sides to cooperate, while simultaneously believing that the other side would prefer that "we" cooperated while "they" defected.

Peripheral route to persuasion   The way people are persuaded when they focus on factors other than the quality of the arguments in a message, such as the number of arguments.

Person   Features or characteristics that individuals carry into social situations.

Personal commitment   Anything that connects an individual's identity more closely to a position or course of action.

Personal norms   The internalized beliefs and values that combine to form a person's inner standards for behavior.

Person–situation fit   The extent to which a person and a situation are compatible.

Perspective taking   The process of mentally putting oneself in another's position.

Persuasion   Change in a private attitude or belief as a result of receiving a message.

Pluralistic ignorance   The mistaken impression on the part of group members that, because no one else is acting concerned, there is no cause for alarm.

Pluralistic ignorance   The phenomenon in which people in a group misperceive the beliefs of others because everyone acts inconsistently with their beliefs.

Polyandry   Marital arrangement involving one woman and more than one husband.

Polygamy   Marital custom in which either one man marries more than one woman (polygyny) or one woman marries more than one man (polyandry).

Polygyny   Marital arrangement involving one man and more than one wife.

Postdecisional dissonance   The conflict one feels about a decision that could possibly be wrong.

Prejudice   A generalized attitude toward members of a social group.

Priming   The process of activating knowledge or goals, of making them ready for use.

Prosocial behavior   Action intended to benefit another.

Proximate explanation   A focus on relatively immediate causes.

Proximity-attraction principle   The tendency to become friends with those who live or work nearby.

Psychological test   Instrument for assessing a person's abilities, cognitions, or motivations.

Psychopath   Individual characterized by impulsivity, irresponsibility, low empathy, grandiose self-worth, and lack of sensitivity to punishment. Such individuals are inclined toward acting violently for personal gain.

Public goods dilemma   A situation in which (1) the whole group can benefit if some of the individuals give something for the common good but (2) individuals profit from "free riding" if enough others contribute.

Public self-consciousness   The tendency to have a chronic awareness of oneself as being in the public eye.

Pure (true) altruism   Action intended solely to benefit another.

Random assignment   The practice of assigning participants to treatments so each person has an equal chance of being in any condition.

Reactance theory   Brehm's theory that we react against threats to our freedoms by reasserting those freedoms, often by doing the opposite of what we are being pressured to do.

Realistic group conflict theory   The proposal that intergroup conflict, and negative prejudices and stereotypes, emerge out of actual competition between groups for desired resources.

Reciprocal aid   Helping that occurs in return for prior help.

Reflected appraisal process   The process through which people come to know themselves by observing or imagining how others view them.

Reinforcement-affect model   The theory that we like people with whom we associate positive feelings and dislike those with whom we associate negative feelings.

Relative deprivation   The feeling that one has less than the others to whom one compares oneself.

Reliability   The consistency of the score yielded by a psychological test.

Replenishing resource management dilemma   A situation in which group members share a renewable resource that will continue to produce benefits if group members do not overharvest it but in which any single individual profits from harvesting as much as possible.

Representative sample   A group of respondents having characteristics that match those of the larger population the researcher wants to describe.

Representativeness heuristic   A mental shortcut people use to classify something as belonging to a certain category to the extent that it is similar to a typical case from that category.

Role   Expectation held by the group for how members in particular positions ought to behave.

Scapegoating   The process of blaming members of other groups for one's frustrations and failures.

Schema   A mental representation capturing the general characteristics of a particular class of episodes, events, or individuals.

Scripted situation   A situation in which certain events are expected to occur in a particular sequence.

Secure attachment style   Attachments marked by trust that the other person will continue to provide love and support.

Secure base   Comfort provided by an attachment figure, which allows the person to venture forth more confidently to explore the environment.

Self-concept   A mental representation capturing our views and beliefs about ourselves.

Self-disclosure   The sharing of intimate information about oneself.

Self-esteem   Our attitude toward ourselves.

Self-fulfilling prophecy   When an initially inaccurate expectation leads to actions that cause the expectation to come true.

Self-handicapping   The behavior of withdrawing effort or creating obstacles to one's future successes.

Self-monitoring   The tendency to be chronically concerned with one's public image and to adjust one's actions to fit the needs of the current situation.

Self-perception process   The process through which people observe their own behavior to infer internal characteristics such as traits, abilities, and attitudes.

Self-presentation   The process through which we try to control the impressions people form of us; synonymous with impression management.

Self-promotion   An attempt to get others to see us as competent.

Self-regulation   The process through which people select, monitor, and adjust their strategies in an attempt to reach their goals.

Self-serving bias   The tendency to take personal credit for our successes and to blame external factors for our failures.

Sexual selection   A form of natural selection favoring characteristics that assist animals in attracting mates or in competing with members of their own sex.

Shyness   The tendency to feel tense, worried, or awkward in novel social situations and with unfamiliar people.

Situation   Environmental events or circumstances outside the person.

Sliding reinforcer   A stimulus that brings rewards when used in small doses, but punishments when used in large doses.

Social anxiety   The fear people experience while doubting that they'll be able to create a desired impression.

Social capital   Assets that can be drawn from one's network of personal relationships.

Social cognition   The process of thinking about and making sense of oneself and others.

Social cognitive perspective   A theoretical viewpoint that focuses on the mental processes involved in paying attention to, interpreting, and remembering social experiences.

Social comparison   The process through which people come to know themselves by comparing their abilities, attitudes, and beliefs with those of others.

Social desirability bias   The tendency for people to say what they believe is appropriate or acceptable.

Social dilemma   A situation in which an individual profits from selfishness unless everyone chooses the selfish alternative, in which case the whole group loses.

Social dominance orientation   The extent to which a person desires that his or her own group dominate other groups and be socially and materially superior to them.

Social exchange   The trading of benefits within relationships.

Social facilitation   The process through which the presence of others increases the likelihood of dominant responses, leading to better performance on well-mastered tasks and worse performance on unmastered tasks.

Social identity   The beliefs and feelings we have toward the groups to which we see ourselves belonging.

Social influence   A change in overt behavior caused by real or imagined pressure from others.

Social learning perspective   A theoretical viewpoint that focuses on past learning experiences as determinants of a person's social behaviors.

Social learning theory   Theory that aggression is learned through direct reward or by watching others being rewarded for aggressiveness.

Social loafing   Reducing one's personal efforts when in a group.

Social norm   A rule or expectation for appropriate social behavior.

Social psychology   The scientific study of how people's thoughts, feelings, and behaviors are influenced by other people.

Social responsibility norm   The societal rule that people should help those who need them to help.

Social support   Emotional, material, or informational assistance provided by other people.

Social trap   A situation in which individuals or groups are drawn toward immediate rewards that later prove to have unpleasant or lethal consequences.

Social validation   An interpersonal way to locate and validate the correct choice.

Socialization   The process whereby a culture teaches its members about its beliefs, customs, habits, and language.

Sociocultural perspective   The theoretical viewpoint that searches for the causes of social behavior in influences from larger social groups.

Sociosexual orientation   Individual differences in the tendency to prefer either unrestricted sex (without the necessity of love) or restricted sex (only in the context of a long-term, loving relationship).

Status hierarchy   A ranking of group members by their power and influence over other members.

Stereotype   Generalized belief about members of social groups.

Stereotype threat   The fear that one might confirm the negative stereotypes held by others about one's group.

Stereotyping   The process of categorizing an individual as a member of a particular group and then inferring that he or she possesses the characteristics generally held by members of that group.

Survey method   A technique in which the researcher asks people to report on their beliefs, feelings, or behaviors.

That's-not-all technique   A technique that increases compliance by "sweetening" an offer with additional benefits.

Theory   Scientific explanation that connects and organizes existing observations and suggests fruitful paths for future research.

Theory of planned behavior   A theory stating that the best predictor of a behavior is one's behavioral intention, which is influenced by one's attitude toward the specific behavior, the subjective norms regarding the behavior, and one's perceived control over the behavior.

Tit-for-tat strategy   A negotiating tactic in which the individual responds to competitiveness with competitiveness and to cooperation with cooperation.

Transactive memory   A group memory system made up of (1) the knowledge held by individual group members and (2) a communication network for sharing this knowledge among the members.

Transformational leadership Leadership that changes the motivations, outlooks, and behaviors of followers, enabling the group to reach its goals better.

Triangulation Technique of examining the same problem using different research methods, each having different biases.

Two-factor theory of love The theory that love consists of general arousal (factor 1), which is attributed to the presence of an attractive person and labeled as love (factor 2).

Type A behavior pattern A group of personality characteristics, including time-urgency and competitiveness, that is associated with higher risk for coronary disease.

Ultimate explanation A focus on background or historical causes.

Upward social comparison The process of comparing ourselves with those who are better off.

Validity The extent to which a test measures what it is designed to measure.

Voluntarist policy An appeal to people's intrinsic sense of social responsibility.

Weapons effect The tendency for weapons, such as guns, to enhance aggressive thoughts, feelings, and actions.

References

Aarts, H., & Dijksterhuis, A. (2003). The silence of the library: Environment, situational norm, and social behavior. *Journal of Personality and Social Psychology, 84,* 18–28.

Abalakina-Paap, M., Stephan, W. G., Craig, T., & Gregory, W. L. (1999). Beliefs in conspiracies. *Political Psychology, 20,* 637–647.

Abatte, S. S., Isgro, A., Wicklund, R. A., & Boca, S. (2006). A field experiment on perspective-taking, helping, and self awareness. *Basic and Applied Social Psychology, 28,* 283–287.

Abbey, A. (1982). Sex differences in attributions for friendly behavior: Do males misperceive females' friendliness? *Journal of Personality and Social Psychology, 42,* 830–838.

Abbey, A., Ross, L. T., McDuffie, D., & McAuslan, P. (1996). Alcohol, misperception, and sexual assault: How and why are they linked? In D. M. Buss & N. M. Malamuth (Eds.), *Sex, power, conflict* (pp. 138–161). New York: Oxford University Press.

Abele, S., & Ehrhart, K. M. (2005). The timing effect in public good games. *Journal of Experimental Social Psychology, 41,* 470–481.

Abelson, R. P. (1981). Psychological status of the script concept. *American Psychologist, 36,* 715–729.

Abend, T. A., & Williamson, G. M. (2002). Feeling attractive in the wake of breast cancer: Optimism matters, and so do interpersonal relationships. *Personality & Social Psychology Bulletin, 28,* 427–436.

Aberson, C. L., Healy, M., & Romero, V. (2000). Ingroup bias and self-esteem: A meta-analysis. *Personality and Social Psychology Review, 4,* 157–173.

Abrahamson, A. C., Baker, L. A., & Caspi, A. (2002). Rebellious teens? Genetic and environmental influences on the social attitudes of adolescents. *Journal of Personality and Social Psychology, 83,* 1392–1408.

Abu-Lughod, L. (1986). *Veiled sentiments: Honor and poetry in a Bedouin society.* Berkeley: University of California Press.

Acker, M., & Davis, M. H. (1992). Intimacy, passion, and commitment in adult romantic relationships: A test of the triangular theory of love. *Journal of Social and Personal Relationships, 9,* 21–50.

Ackerman, J. M., Griskevicius, V., & Li, N. P. (2011). Let's get serious: Communicating commitment in romantic relationships. *Journal of Personality and Social Psychology, 100*(6), 1079.

Ackerman, J. M., & Kenrick, D. T. (2008). The costs of benefits: Help-refusals highlight key trade-offs of social life. *Personality and Social Psychology Review, 12,* 118–140.

Ackerman, J. M., Kenrick, D. T., & Schaller, M. (2007). Is friendship akin to kinship? *Evolution and Human Behavior, 28,* 365–374.

Activist Mourns Ex-KKK leader. (2005, November 8). *The News & Observer.* Retrieved from www .newsobserver.com/102/v-print/story/362297 .html

Adams, G. (2005). The cultural grounding of personal relationships: Enemyship in North American and West African worlds. *Journal of Personality and Social Psychology, 88,* 948–968.

Adams, J. (1995). *Sellout: Aldrich Ames and the corruption of the CIA.* New York: Viking.

Adams, R. G., & Bleiszner, R. (1994). An integrative conceptual framework for friendship research. *Journal of Social and Personal Relationships, 11,* 163–184.

Addis, M. E., & Mahalik, J. R. (2003). Men, masculinity, and the context of help seeking. *American Psychologist, 58,* 5–14.

Adkins, B., & Caldwell, D. (2004). Firm or subgroup culture: Where does fitting in matter most? *Journal of Organizational Behavior, 25,* 969–978.

Adorno, T. W., Frenkel-Brunswik, E., Levinson, D. J., & Sanford, R. N. (1950). *The authoritarian personality.* New York: Harper and Row.

Affleck, G., Tennen, H., Pfeiffer, C., & Fifield, C. (1987). Appraisals of control and predictability in adapting to a chronic disease. *Journal of Personality and Social Psychology, 53,* 273–279.

Ahmad, Y., & Smith, P. K. (1994). Bullying in schools and the issue of sex differences. In J. Archer (Ed.), *Male violence* (pp. 70–86). New York: Routledge.

Aiello, J. R., & Douthitt, E. A. (2001). Social facilitation from Triplett to electronic performance monitoring. *Group Dynamics, 5,* 163–180.

Ainsworth, M. D. S., Blehar, M. C., Waters, E., & Wall, S. (1978). *Patterns of attachment: Assessed in the strange situation and at home.* Hillsdale, NJ: Erlbaum.

Ajzen, I. (2011). The theory of planned behaviour: Reactions and reflections. *Psychology & Health, 26*(9), 1113–1127.

Akimoto, S. A., Sanbonmatsu, D. M., & Ho, E. A. (2000). Manipulating personal salience: The effects of performance expectations on physical positioning. *Personality and Social Psychology Bulletin, 26,* 755–761.

Aknin, L. B., Barrington-Leigh, C. P., Dunn, E. W., Helliwell, J. F., Burns, J., Biswas-Diener, R., et al. (2013). Prosocial spending and well-being: Cross-cultural evidence for a psychological universal. *Journal of Personality & Social Psychology, 104,* 635–652.

Alba, J. W., & Marmorstein, H. (1987). The effects of frequency knowledge on consumer decision making. *Journal of Consumer Research, 14,* 14–25.

Albarracin, D., Johnston, B. T., Fishbein, M., & Muellerleile, P. A. (2001). Theories of reasoned action and planned behavior as models of condom use: A meta-analysis. *Psychological Bulletin, 127,* 142–161.

Albarracin, D., & Mitchell, A. L. (2004). The role of defensive confidence in preference for proattitudinal information: How believing that one is strong can sometimes be a defensive weakness. *Personality and Social Psychology Bulletin, 30,* 1565–1584.

Albarracin, D., & Wyer, R. S. (2000). The cognitive impact of past behavior: Influences on beliefs, attitudes, and future behavioral decisions. *Journal of Personality and Social Psychology, 79,* 5–22.

Albarracin, D., & Wyer, R. S. (2001). Elaborative and nonelaborative processing of a behavior-related communication. *Personality and Social Psychology Bulletin, 27,* 691–705.

Alcock, J. (1989). *Animal behavior: An evolutionary approach* (4th ed.). Sunderland, MA: Sinauer Associates.

Alcock, J. (1993). *Animal behavior: An evolutionary approach* (5th ed.). Sunderland, MA: Sinauer Associates.

Aldag, R. J., & Fuller, S. R. (1993). Beyond fiasco: A reappraisal of the groupthink phenomenon and a new model of group decision processes. *Psychological Bulletin, 113,* 533–552.

Alexander, M. G., & Fisher, T. D. (2003). Truth and consequences: Using the bogus pipeline to examine sex differences in self-reported sexuality. *Journal of Sex Research, 40,* 27–35.

Alicke, M. D., & Govorun, O. (2005). The better-than-average effect. In M. D. Alicke, D. Dunning, & J. I. Krueger (Eds.), *The self in social perception* (pp. 85–106). New York: Psychology Press.

Alicke, M. D., & Largo, E. (1995). The role of the self in the false consensus effect. *Journal of Experimental Social Psychology, 31,* 28–47.

Allcott, H. (2011). Social norms and energy conservation. *Journal of Public Economics, 95*(9), 1082–1095.

Allen, J., Kenrick, D. T., Linder, D. E., & McCall, M. A. (1989). Arousal and attraction: A response facilitation alternative to misattribution and negative reinforcement models. *Journal of Personality and Social Psychology, 57,* 261–270.

Allen, K. M., Blascovich, J., Tomaka, J., & Kelsey, R. M. (1991). Presence of human friends and pet dogs as moderators of autonomic responses to stress in women. *Journal of Personality and Social Psychology, 61,* 582–589.

Allen, M. (1989). The man who broke North Haven's heart. *Yankee, 53,* 52.

Allen, R. W., Madison, D. L., Porter, L. W., Renwick, P. A., & Mayes, B. T. (1979). Organizational politics: Tactics and characteristics of its actors. *California Management Review, 22,* 77–83.

Allen, T. J., & Sherman, J. W. (2011). Ego threat and intergroup bias: A test of motivated-activation versus self-regulatory accounts. *Psychological Science, 22*(3), 331–333.

Allen, V. L., & Levine, J. M. (1969). Consensus and conformity. *Journal of Experimental Social Psychology, 5,* 389–399.

Allgeier, A. R., Byrne, D., Brooks, B., & Reeves, D. (1979). The waffle phenomenon: Negative evaluations of those who shift attitudinally. *Journal of Applied Social Psychology, 9,* 170–182.

Allison, S. T., Beggan, J. K., & Midgley, E. H. (1996). The quest for "similar instances" and "simultaneous possibilities": Metaphors in social dilemma research. *Journal of Personality and Social Psychology, 71,* 479–497.

Allison, S. T., & Kerr, N. L. (1994). Group correspondence biases and the provision of public goods. *Journal of Personality and Social Psychology, 66,* 688–698.

Allison, S. T., & Messick, D. M. (1988). The feature-positive effect, attitude strength, and degree of perceived consensus. *Personality and Social Psychology Bulletin, 14,* 231–241.

Allison, S. T., & Messick, D. M. (1990). Social decision heuristics in the use of shared resources. *Journal of Behavioral Decision Making, 3,* 195–204.

Alloy, L. B., & Abramson, L. Y. (1979). Judgment of contingency in depressed and nondepressed students: Sadder but wiser? *Journal of Experimental Psychology, 108,* 441–485.

Alloy, L. B., Abramson, L. Y., & Viscusi, D. (1981). Induced mood and the illusion of control. *Journal of Personality and Social Psychology, 41,* 1129–1140.

Allport, F. H. (1924). *Social psychology.* Boston: Houghton Mifflin.

Allport, G. W. (1954). *The nature of prejudice.* Reading, MA: Addison-Wesley.

Allport, G. W., & Kramer, B. M. (1946). Some roots of prejudice. *Journal of Psychology, 22,* 9–39.

Allport, G. W., & Postman, L. (1947). *The psychology of rumor.* New York: Henry Holt.

Allport, G. W., & Ross, J. M. (1967). Personal religious orientation and prejudice. *Journal of Personality and Social Psychology, 5,* 432–443.

Altemeyer, B. (1998). The other "authoritarian personality." In M. P. Zanna (Ed.), *Advances in experimental social psychology* (Vol. 30, pp. 48–92). New York: Academic Press.

Altemeyer, B. (2004). Highly dominating, highly authoritarian personalities. *Journal of Social Psychology, 144,* 421–447.

Altemeyer, B., & Hunsberger, B. (1992). Authoritarianism, religious fundamentalism, quest, and prejudice. *The International Journal for the Psychology of Religion, 2*(2), 113–133.

Alter, A. L., & Forgas, J. P. (2007). On being happy but fearing failure: The effects of mood on self-handicapping strategies. *Journal of Experimental Social Psychology, 43,* 947–954.

Alter, A. L., & Kwan, V. S. Y. (2009). Cultural sharing in a global village: Evidence for extracultural cognition in European Americans. *Journal of Personality and Social Psychology, 96,* 742–760.

Amato, P. R. (1983). Helping behavior in urban and rural environments. *Journal of Personality and Social Psychology, 45,* 571–586.

Ambady, N., Bernieri, F. J., & Richeson, J. A. (2000). Toward a histology of social behavior: Judgmental accuracy from thin slices of the behavioral stream. In M. P. Zanna (Ed.), *Advances in experimental social psychology* (Vol. 32, pp. 201–271). San Diego, CA: Academic Press.

Ambady, N., & Rosenthal, R. (1993). Half a minute: Predicting teacher evaluations from thin slices of nonverbal behavior and physical attractiveness. *Journal of Personality and Social Psychology, 64,* 431–441.

Ambrose, M. L., Arnaud, A., & Schminke, M. (2008). Individual moral development and ethical climate: The influence of person-organization fit on job attitudes. *Journal of Business Ethics, 77,* 323–333.

American Society for Aesthetic Plastic Surgery. (2009). *Cosmetic procedures in 2007.* Retrieved January 19, 2009, from http://www.surgery .org/public/consumer/trends/cosmetic_ procedures_in_2007

Ammar, H. (1954). *Growing up in an Egyptian village: Silwa, Province of Aswan.* London: Routledge & Kegan Paul.

Amodio, D. M., Harmon-Jones, E., & Devine, P. G. (2003). Individual differences in the activation and control of affective race bias as assessed by startle eyeblink response and self-report. *Journal of Personality & Social Psychology, 84,* 738–753.

Anderson, C. A. (1987). Temperature and aggression: Effects on quarterly, yearly, and city rates of violent and nonviolent crime. *Journal of Personality and Social Psychology, 52,* 1161–1173.

Anderson, C. A., Buckley, K. E., & Carnagey, N. L. (2008). Creating your own hostile environment: A laboratory examination of trait aggressiveness and the violence escalation cycle. *Personality and Social Psychology Bulletin, 34,* 462–473.

Anderson, C. A., & Bushman, B. J. (1997). External validity of "trivial" experiments: The case of laboratory aggression. *Review of General Psychology, 1,* 19–41.

Anderson, C. A., & Bushman, B. J. (2001). Effects of violent video games on aggressive behavior, aggressive cognition, aggressive affect, physiological arousal, and prosocial behavior. A meta-analytic review of the literature. *Psychological Science, 12,* 353–359.

Anderson, C. A., & Bushman, B. J. (2002). Human aggression. *Annual Review of Psychology, 53,* 27–51.

Anderson, C. A., Bushman, B. J., & Groom, R. W. (1997). Hot years and serious and deadly assault: Empirical tests of the heat hypothesis. *Journal of Personality and Social Psychology, 73,* 1213–1223.

Anderson, C. A., Carnagey, N. L., & Eubanks, J. (2003). Exposure to violent media: Effects of songs with violent lyrics on aggressive thoughts and feelings. *Journal of Personality & Social Psychology, 84,* 960–971.

Anderson, C. A., Carnagey, N. L., Flanagan, M., Benjamin, A. J., Eubanks, J., & Valentine, J. C.

(2004). Violent video games: Specific effects of violent content on aggressive thoughts and behavior. In M. Zanna (Ed.), *Advances in experimental social psychology* (Vol. 36, pp. 199–249). New York: Elsevier.

Anderson, C. A., & DeNeve, K. M. (1992). Temperature, aggression, and the negative affect escape model. *Psychological Bulletin, 111,* 347–351.

Anderson, C. A., & Dill, K. E. (2000). Video games and aggressive thoughts, feelings, and behavior in the laboratory and in life. *Journal of Personality & Social Psychology, 78,* 772–790.

Anderson, C. A., Shibuya, A., Ihori, N., Swing, E. L., Bushman, B. J., Sakamoto, A., et al. (2010). Violent video game effects on aggression, empathy, and prosocial behavior in Eastern and Western countries: A meta-analytic review. *Psychological Bulletin, 136*(2), 151–173.

Anderson, C. A., Willer, R., Kilduff, G. J., & Brown, C. E. (2012). The origins of deference: When do people prefer lower status? *Journal of Personality and Social Psychology, 102*(5), 1077.

Anderson, D. E., DePaulo, B. M., & Ansfield, M. E. (2002). The development of deception detection skill: A longitudinal study of same sex friends. *Personality and Social Psychology Bulletin, 28,* 536–545.

Anderson, J. L., Crawford, C. B., Nadeau, J., & Lindberg, T. (1992). Was the Duchess of Windsor right? A crosscultural review of the sociobiology of ideals of female body shape. *Ethology and Sociobiology, 13,* 197–227.

Anderson, N. H. (Ed.). (1991). *Contributions to information integration theory* (Vols. 1, 2, and 3). Hillsdale, NJ: Erlbaum.

Anderson, S. C. (1993). Anti-stalking laws: Will they curb the erotomanic's obsessive pursuit? *Law and Psychology Review, 17,* 171–191.

Anderson, S. M., & Chen, S. (2002). The relational self: An interpersonal socialcognitive theory. *Psychological Review, 109,* 619–645.

Andersson, J., & Roennberg, J. (1997). Cued memory collaboration: Effects of friendship and type of retrieval cue. *European Journal of Cognitive Psychology, 9,* 273–287.

Andison, F. S. (1977). TV violence and viewer aggression: A cumulation of study results. *Public Opinion Quarterly, 41,* 314–331.

Anthony, D. B., Holmes, J. G., & Wood, J. V. (2007). Social acceptance and selfesteem: Tuning the sociometer to interpersonal value. *Journal of Personality and Social Psychology, 92,* 1024–1039.

Anthony, T., Copper, C., & Mullen, B. (1992). Cross-racial facial identification: A social cognitive integration. *Personality and Social Psychology Bulletin, 18,* 296–301.

Antill, J. K. (1983). Sex role complementarity versus similarity in married couples. *Journal of Personality and Social Psychology, 45,* 145–155.

Antonio, A. L., Chang, M. J., Hakuta, K., Kenny, D. A., Levin, S., & Milem, J. F. (2004). Effects of racial diversity on complex thinking in college students. *Psychological Science, 15,* 507–510.

Apicella, C. L., Dreber, A., Campbell, B., Gray, P. B., Hoffman, M., & Little, A. C. (2008). Testosterone and financial risk preference. *Evolution and Human Behavior, 29,* 384–390.

Applebome, P. (1983, May 31). Racial issues raised in robbery case. *New York Times,* p. A14.

Applebome, P. (1984, March 22). Black is cleared by new arrest in Texas holdup. *New York Times,* p. A16.

Archer, J. (1994). Introduction: Male violence in perspective. In J. Archer (Ed.), *Male violence* (pp. 1–22). New York: Routledge.

Archer, J. (2000). Sex differences in aggression between heterosexual partners: A meta-analytic review. *Psychological Bulletin, 126,* 651–680.

Archer, J. (2009). Does sexual selection explain human sex differences in aggression? *Behavioral and Brain Sciences, 32*(3–4), 249–266.

Archer, J., & Coyne, S. M. (2005). An integrated review of indirect, relational, and social aggres-

sion. *Personality & Social Psychology Review, 9,* 212–230.

Archer, R. L. (1984). The farmer and the cowman should be friends: An attempt at reconciliation with Batson, Coke, and Pych. *Journal of Personality and Social Psychology, 46,* 709–711.

Aries, E. J., & Johnson, F. L. (1983). Close friendship in adulthood: Conversational content between same-sex friends. *Sex Roles, 9,* 1183–1197.

Arkes, H. R., Hackett, C., & Boehm, L. (1989). The generality of the relation between familiarity and judged validity. *Journal of Behavioral Decision Making, 2,* 81–94.

Arkin, R. M., & Baumgardner, A. H. (1985). Self-handicapping. In J. H. Harvey & G. Weary (Eds.), *Basic issues in attribution theory and research* (pp. 169–202). New York: Academic Press.

Arkin, R. M., & Baumgardner, A. H. (1988). *Social anxiety and self-presentation: Protective and acquisitive tendencies in safe versus threatening encounters.* Unpublished manuscript, University of Missouri, Columbia.

Armitage, C. J., & Connor, M. (2001). Efficacy of the theory of planned behaviour: A meta-analytic review. *British Journal of Social Psychology, 40,* 471–499.

Armor, D. A., & Taylor, S. E. (1998). Situated optimism: Specific outcome expectancies and self-regulation. In M. P. Zanna (Ed.), *Advances in experimental social psychology* (Vol. 30, pp. 309–379). New York: Academic Press.

Armor, D. A., & Taylor, S. E. (2003). The effects of mindset on behavior: Selfregulation in deliberative and implemental frames of mind. *Personality and Social Psychology Bulletin, 29,* 86–95.

Aron, A., Aron, E. N., & Smollan, D. (1992). Inclusion of other in the self scale and the structure of interpersonal closeness. *Journal of Personality and Social Psychology, 63,* 596–612.

Aron, A., Melinat, E., Aron, E. N., Vallone, R. D., & Bator, R. J. (1997). The experimental generation of interpersonal closeness: A procedure and some preliminary findings. *Personality and Social Psychology Bulletin, 23,* 363–377.

Aron, A., & Westbay, L. (1996). Dimensions of the prototype of love. *Journal of Personality and Social Psychology, 70,* 535–551.

Aron, E. N., & Aron, A. (1997). Sensory-processing sensitivity and its relation to introversion and emotionality. *Journal of Personality and Social Psychology, 73,* 345–368.

Aronson, E. (1969). The theory of cognitive dissonance. A current perspective. In L. Berkowitz (Ed.), *Advances in experimental social psychology* (Vol. 4, pp. 1–34). San Diego, CA: Academic Press.

Aronson, E., Blaney, N., Stephan, C., Sikes, J., & Snapp, M. (1978). *The jigsaw classroom.* Beverly Hills, CA: Sage.

Aronson, E., Turner, J. A., & Carlsmith, J. M. (1963). Communicator credibility and communication discrepancy as determinates of opinion change. *Journal of Abnormal and Social Psychology, 67,* 31–36.

Aronson, E., Wilson, T. D., & Brewer, M. (1998). Experimentation in social psychology. In G. Lindzey & E. Aronson (Eds.), *Handbook of social psychology* (4th ed., pp. 99–142). New York: McGraw-Hill.

Aronson, J., Fried, C. B., & Good, C. (2002). Reducing the effects of stereotype threat on African American college students by shaping theories of intelligence. *Journal of Experimental Social Psychology, 38,* 113–125.

Aronson, J., Lustina, M. J., Good, C., Keough, K., Steele, C. M., & Brown, J. (1999). When white men can't do math: Necessary and sufficient factors in stereotype threat. *Journal of Experimental Social Psychology, 35,* 29–46.

Arriaga, X. B., & Agnew, C. R. (2001). Being committed: Affective, cognitive, and conative components of relationship commitment. *Personality & Social Psychology Bulletin, 27,* 1190–1203.

Arrow, H., McGrath, J. E., & Berdahl, J. L. (2000). *Small groups as complex systems: Formation, coordination, development, and adaptation.* Thousand Oaks, CA: Sage.

Asch, S. E. (1955). Opinions and social pressures. *Scientific American, 193*, 31–35.

Asch, S. E. (1956). Studies of independence and conformity: A minority of one against a unanimous majority. *Psychological Monographs, 70*(9, Whole number 416).

Aseltine, R. H., Jr., Gore, S., & Colten, M. E. (1994). Depression and the social developmental context of adolescence. *Journal of Personality and Social Psychology, 67*, 252–263.

Ashburn-Nardo, L., Voils, C. I., & Monteith, M. J. (2001). Implicit associations as the seeds of intergroup bias: How easily do they take root? *Journal of Personality and Social Psychology, 81*, 789–799.

Assad, K. K., Donnellan, M. B., & Conger, R. D. (2007). Optimism: An enduring resource for romantic relationships. *Journal of Personality and Social Psychology, 93*, 285–297.

Aune, R. K., & Basil, M. C. (1994). A relational obligations approach to the foot-in-the-mouth effect. *Journal of Applied Social Psychology, 24*, 546–556.

Austin, J. R. (2003). Transactive memory in organizational groups: The effects of content, consensus, specialization, and accuracy on group performance. *Journal of Applied Psychology, 88*, 866–878.

Axelrod, R. (1984). *The evolution of cooperation.* New York: Basic Books.

Axelrod, R., & Hamilton, W. D. (1981). The evolution of cooperation. *Science, 211*, 1390–1396.

Axelrod, R., Riolo, R. L., & Cohen, M. D. (2002). Beyond geography: Cooperation with persistent links in the absence of clustered neighborhoods. *Personality & Social Psychology Review, 6*, 341–346.

Axsom, D., Yates, S., & Chaiken, S. (1987). Audience response as a heuristic cue in persuasion. *Journal of Personality and Social Psychology, 53*, 30–40.

Ayduk, Ö., Gyurak, A., Akinola, M., & Mendes, W. B. (2013). Consistency over flattery self-verification processes revealed in implicit and behavioral responses to feedback. *Social Psychological and Personality Science, 4*(5), 538–545.

Ayres, I., & Siegelman, P. (1995). Race and gender discrimination in bargaining for a new car. *American Economic Review, 85*, 304–321.

Bacon, F. T. (1979). Credibility of repeated statements. *Journal of Experimental Psychology: Human Learning and Memory, 5*, 241–252.

Badahdah, A. M., & Tiemann, K. A. (2005). Mate selection criteria among Muslims living in America. *Evolution and Human Behavior, 26*, 432–440.

Bailensen, J. N., Blascovich, J., & Guadagno, R. E. (2008). Self-representations in immersive virtual environments. *Journal of Applied Social Psychology, 38*, 2673–2690.

Bailenson, J. N., Beall, A. C., Loomis, J., Blascovich, J., & Turk, M. (2005). Transformed social interaction, augmented gaze, and social influence in immersive virtual environments. *Human Communication Research, 31*, 511–537.

Bailenson, J. N., & Yee, N. (2005). Digital chameleons. Automatic assimilation of nonverbal gestures in immersive virtual reality environments. *Psychological Science, 16*, 814–819.

Bailey, J. M., Gaulin, S., Agyei, Y., & Gladue, B. A. (1994). Effects of gender and sexual orientation on evolutionarily relevant aspects of human mating psychology. *Journal of Personality and Social Psychology, 66*, 1081–1093.

Bair, A. N., & Steele, J. R. (2010). Examining the consequences of exposure to racism for the executive functioning of Black students. *Journal of Experimental Social Psychology, 46*, 127–132.

Baize, H. R., & Schroeder, J. E. (1995). Personality and mate selection in personal ads: Evolutionary preferences in a public mate selection process. *Journal of Social Behavior and Personality, 10*, 517–536.

Baker, L. A., Pearcey, S. M., & Dabbs, J. M., Jr. (2002). Testosterone, alcohol, and civil and rough conflict resolution strategies in lesbian couples. *Journal of Homosexuality, 42*, 1637–1647.

Baldwin, M. W., & Main, K. J. (2001). Social anxiety and the cued activation of relational knowledge. *Personality and Social Psychology Bulletin, 27*, 1637–1647.

Ball, A. D., & Tasaki, L. H. (1992). The role and measurement of attachment in consumer behavior. *Journal of Consumer Psychology, 1*, 155–172.

Balliet, D., Mulder, L. B., & Van Lange, P. A. M. (2011). Reward, punishment, and cooperation: A meta-analysis. *Psychological Bulletin, 137*(4), 594–615.

Baltes, B. B., Dickson, M. W., Sherman, M. P., Bauer, C. C., & LaGanke, J. (2002). Computer-mediated communication and group decision making: A meta-analysis. *Organizational Behavior and Human Decision Processes, 87*, 156–179.

Banaji, M. R., & Greenwald, A. G. (1994). Implicit social cognition: Attitudes, self-esteem, and stereotypes. *Psychological Review, 102*, 4–27.

Bandura, A. (1973). *Aggression: A social learning analysis.* Englewood Cliffs, NJ: Prentice-Hall.

Bandura, A. (1977). Toward a unifying theory of behavioral change. *Psychological Review, 84*, 191–215.

Bandura, A. (1983). Psychological mechanisms of aggression. In R. G. Geen & E. I. Donnerstein (Eds.), *Aggression: Theoretical and empirical reviews* (Vol. 1, pp. 1–40). New York: Academic Press.

Bandura, A., & Menlove, F. L. (1968). Factors determining vicarious extinction of avoidance behavior through symbolic modeling. *Journal of Personality and Social Psychology, 8*, 99–108.

Bandura, A., Ross, D., & Ross, S. A. (1961). Transmission of aggression through imitation of aggressive models. *Journal of Abnormal and Social Psychology, 63*, 575–582.

Bandura, A., Ross, D., & Ross, S. A. (1963a). Imitation of film-mediated aggressive models. *Journal of Abnormal and Social Psychology, 66*, 3–11.

Bandura, A., Ross, D., & Ross, S. A. (1963b). Vicarious reinforcement of imitative learning. *Journal of Abnormal and Social Psychology, 67*, 601–607.

Bank, B. J., & Hansford, S. L. (2000). Gender and friendship: Why are men's best same-sex friendships less intimate and supportive? *Personal Relationship, 7*, 63–78.

Bantel, K. A., & Jackson, S. E. (1989). Top management and innovations in banking: Does the composition of the top team make a difference? *Strategic Management Journal, 10*, 107–124.

Barbee, A. P., Cunningham, M. R., Winstead, B. A., Derlega, V. J., Gulley, M. R., Yankeelov, P. A., et al. (1993). Effects of gender role expectations on the social support process. *Journal of Social Issues, 49*, 175–190.

Bargh, J. A., Chen, M., & Burrows, L. (1996). Automaticity of social behavior: Direct effects of trait construct and stereotype activation on action. *Journal of Personality and Social Psychology, 71*, 230–244.

Bargh, J., & McKenna, K. (2004). The Internet and social life. *Annual Review of Psychology, 55*, 573–590.

Bargh, J. A., & Pratto, F. (1986). Individual construct accessibility and perceptual selection. *Journal of Experimental Social Psychology, 22*, 293–311.

Bargh, J. A., Raymond, P., Pryor, J. B., & Strack, F. (1995). The attractiveness of the underling: An automatic power (R) sex association and its consequences for sexual harassment. *Journal of Personality and Social Psychology, 68*, 768–781.

Bargh, J. A., & Williams, E. L. (2006). The automaticity of social life. *Psychological Science, 15*, 1–4.

Barker, R. G., & Gump, P. V. (1964). *Big school, small school: High school size and student behavior.* Stanford, CA: Stanford University Press.

Barlett, C. P., & Anderson, C. A. (2011). Reappraising the situation and its impact on aggressive be-

havior. *Personality and Social Psychology Bulletin, 37*(12), 1564–1573.

Barlett, C. P., Harris, R. J., & Bruey, C. (2008). The effect of the amount of blood in a violent video game on aggression, hostility, and arousal. *Journal of Experimental Social Psychology, 44*, 539–546.

Barley, S. R., & Bechky, B. A. (1994). In the backrooms of science: The work of technicians in science labs. *Work and Occupations, 21*, 85–126.

Barling, J., & Rosenbaum, A. (1986). Work stressors and wife abuse. *Journal of Applied Psychology, 71*, 346–348.

Barlow, D. H., & Durand, V. M. (1995). *Abnormal psychology: An integrative approach.* Pacific Grove, CA: Brooks/Cole.

Barnes, C. D., Brown, R. P., & Osterman, L. L. (2012). Don't tread on me masculine honor ideology in the US and militant responses to terrorism. *Personality and Social Psychology Bulletin, 38*(8), 1018–1029.

Barnes, C. D., Brown, R. P., &Tamborski, M. (2012). Living dangerously culture of honor, risk-taking, and the nonrandomness of "accidental" deaths. *Social Psychological and Personality Science, 3*(1), 100–107.

Barnett, M. A., Sinisi, C. S., Jaet, B. P., Bealer, R., Rodell, P., & Saunders, L. C. (1990). Perceiving gender differences in children's help-seeking. *Journal of Genetic Psychology, 151*, 451–460.

Baron, R. A. (1974). The aggression inhibiting influence of heightened sexual arousal. *Journal of Personality & Social Psychology, 30*, 318–322.

Baron, R. A. (1989). Personality and organizational conflict: Effects of Type A behavior pattern and self-monitoring. *Organizational Behavior and Human Decision Processes, 44*, 281–296.

Baron, R. A., & Richardson, D. R. (1994). *Human aggression* (2nd ed.). New York: Plenum.

Baron, R. M., & Boudreau, L. A. (1987). An ecological perspective on integrating personality and social psychology. *Journal of Personality and Social Psychology, 53*, 1222–1228.

Baron, R. M., & Misovich, S. J. (1993). Dispositional knowing from an ecological perspective. *Personality and Social Psychology Bulletin, 19*, 541–552.

Baron, R. S. (1986). Distraction-conflict theory: Progress and problems. In L. Berkowitz (Ed.), *Advances in experimental social psychology* (pp. 1–40). Orlando, FL: Academic Press.

Baron, R. S. (2000). Arousal, capacity, and intense indoctrination. *Personality and Social Psychology Review, 4*, 238–254.

Baron, R. S., & Bellman, S. B. (2007). No guts, no glory: Courage, harassment and minority influence. *European Journal of Social Psychology, 37*, 101–124.

Baron, R. S., & Roper, G. (1976). Reaffirmation of social comparison views of choice shifts: Averaging and extremity effects in an autokinetic situation. *Journal of Personality and Social Psychology, 33*, 521–530.

Baron, R. S., Hoppe, S. I., Kao, C. F., Brunsman, B., Linneweh, B., & Rogers, D. (1996). Social corroboration and opinion extremity. *Journal of Experimental Social Psychology, 32*, 537–560.

Baron, R. S., Vandello, J., & Brunsman, B. (1996). The forgotten variable in conformity research: Impact of task importance on social influence. *Journal of Personality and Social Psychology, 71*, 915–927.

Barr, A., Bryan, A., & Kenrick, D. T. (2002). Socially shared cognitions about desire, frequency, and satisfaction in men and women. *Personal Relationships, 9*, 287–300.

Barreto, M., Spears, R., Ellemers, N., & Shahinper, K. (2003). Who wants to know? The effect of audience on identity expression among minority group members. *British Journal of Social Psychology, 42*, 299–318.

Barry, B., & Stewart, G. L. (1997). Composition, process, and performance in self-managed groups: The role of personality. *Journal of Applied Psychology, 82*, 62–78.

Bar-Tal, D., & Raviv, A. (1982). A cognitive-learning model of helping behavior development: Possible implications and applications. In N. Eisenberg (Ed.), *The development of prosocial behavior* (pp. 199–217). New York: Academic Press.

Barthes, J., Godelle, B., & Raymond, M. (2013). Human social stratification and hypergyny: Toward an understanding of male homosexual preference. *Evolution and Human Behavior, 34*(3), 155–163.

Bartholow, B. D., Anderson, C. A., Carnagey, N. L., & Benjamin, A. J. (2005). Interactive effects of life experience and situational cues on aggression: The weapons priming effect in hunters and nonhunters. *Journal of Experimental Social Psychology, 41*, 48–60.

Bartholow, B. D., Bushman, B. J., & Sestir, M. A. (2006). Chronic violent video game exposure and desensitization to violence: Behavioral and event-related brain potential data. *Journal of Experimental Social Psychology, 42*, 532–539.

Bartholow, B. D., & Heinz, A. (2006). Alcohol and aggression without consumption: Alcohol cues, aggressive thoughts, and hostile perception bias. *Psychological Science, 17*, 30–37.

Bartholow, B. D., Sestir, M. A., & Davis, E. B. (2005). Correlates and consequences of exposure to video game violence: Hostile personality, empathy, and aggressive behavior. *Personality and Social Psychology Bulletin, 31*, 1573–1586.

Bartlett, F. A. (1932). *A study in experimental and social psychology.* New York: Cambridge University Press.

Bartol, K. M., & Martin, D. C. (1986). Women and men in task groups. In R. D. Ashmore & F. K. Del Boca (Eds.), *The social psychology of female-male relations: A critical analysis of central concepts* (pp. 259–310). New York: Academic Press.

Barton, J. (1794). *Lectures on female education.* New York: Gaine.

Bartz, J. A., & Lydon, J. E. (2006). Navigating the interdependence dilemma: Attachment goals and the use of communal norms with potential close others. *Journal of Personality and Social Psychology, 91*, 77–96.

Bass, B. M. (1998). *Transformational leadership: Industry, military, and educational impact.* Mahwah, NJ: Erlbaum.

Bass, B. M., & Avolio, B. J. (1993). Transformational leadership: A response to critiques. In M. M. Chemers & R. Ayman (Eds.), *Leadership theory and research: Perspectives and directions* (pp. 49–80). San Diego, CA: Academic Press.

Bassili, J. N. (1996). Meta-judgmental versus operative indexes of psychological attributes: The case of measures of attitude strength. *Journal of Personality and Social Psychology, 71*, 637–653.

Bastardi, A., & Shafir, E. (1998). On the pursuit and misuse of useless information. *Journal of Personality and Social Psychology, 75*, 19–32.

Bateup, H. S., Booth, A., Shirtcliff, E. A., & Granger, D. A. (2002). Testosterone, cortisol, and women's competition. *Evolution & Human Behavior, 23*, 181–192.

Bator, R. J., & Cialdini, R. B. (2006). The nature of consistency motivation: Consistency, aconsistency, and anticonsistency in a dissonance paradigm. *Social Influence, 1*, 208–233.

Batson, C. D. (1991). *The altruism question: Toward a social-psychological answer.* Hillsdale, NJ: Erlbaum.

Batson, C. D., & Burris, C. T. (1994). Personal religion: Depressant or stimulant of prejudice and discrimination. In M. P. Zanna & J. M. Olson (Eds.), *The psychology of prejudice: The Ontario symposium* (Vol. 7, pp. 149–169). Hillsdale, NJ: Erlbaum.

Batson, C. D., Batson, J. G., Griffitt, C. A., Barrientos, S., Brandt, J. R., Sprengelmeyer, P., et al. (1989). Negative-state relief and the empathy-altruism hypothesis. *Journal of Personality and Social Psychology, 56*, 922–933.

Batson, C. D., Duncan, B. D., Ackerman, P., Buckley, T., & Birch, K. (1981). Is empathic emotion a source of altruistic motivation? *Journal of Personality and Social Psychology, 40*, 290–302.

Batson, C. D., Dyck, J. L., Brandt, J. R., Batson, J. G., Powell, A. L., McMaster, M. R., et al. (1988). Five studies testing two new egoistic alternatives to the empathy-altruism hypothesis. *Journal of Personality and Social Psychology, 55*, 52–77.

Batson, C. D., Eklund, J. H., Chermok, V. L., Hoyt, J. L., & Ortiz, B. G. (2007). An additional antecedent of empathic concern: Valuing the welfare of the person in need. *Journal of Personality and Social Psychology, 93*, 65–74.

Batson, C. D., Flink, C. H., Schoenrade, P. A., Fultz, J., & Pych, V. (1986). Religious orientation and overt versus covert racial prejudice. *Journal of Personality and Social Psychology, 50*, 175–181.

Batson, C. D., Polycarpou, M. P., Harmon-Jones, E., Imhoff, H. J., Mitchener, E. C., Bednar, L. L., et al. (1997). Empathy and attitudes: Can feeling for a member of a stigmatized group improve feelings toward the group? *Journal of Personality and Social Psychology, 72*, 105–118.

Batson, C. D., Sager, K., Garst, E., Kang, M., Rubchinsky, K., & Dawson, K. (1997). Is empathy-induced helping due to self-other merging? *Journal of Personality and Social Psychology, 73*, 495–509.

Batson, C. D., & Shaw, L. L. (1991). Evidence for altruism: Toward a pluralism of prosocial motives. *Psychological Inquiry, 2*, 107–122.

Batson, C. D., Turk, C. L., Shaw, L. L., & Klein, T. R. (1995). Information function of empathic emotion: Learning that we value the other's welfare. *Journal of Personality and Social Psychology, 68*, 300–313.

Batson, C. D., & Ventis, W. L. (1982). *The religious experience: A social-psychological perspective.* New York: Oxford University Press.

Baum, A., & Davis, G. E. (1980). Reducing the stress of high-density living: An architectural intervention. *Journal of Personality and Social Psychology, 38*, 471–481.

Baumeister, R. F. (1982). A self-presentational view of social phenomena. *Psychological Bulletin, 91*, 3–26.

Baumeister, R. F. (1993). Understanding the inner nature of low self-esteem: Uncertain, fragile, protective, and conflicted. In R. F. Baumeister (Ed.), *Self-esteem: The puzzle of low self-regard* (pp. 201–218). New York: Plenum.

Baumeister, R. F. (2012). Need-to-Belong theory. In P. A. M. Van Lange, A. W. Kruglanski, & E. T. Higgins (Eds.), *Handbook of theories of social psychology* (pp. 121–140). Los Angeles, CA: Sage Press.

Baumeister, R. F., Bushman, B. J., & Campbell, W. K. (2000). Self-esteem, narcissism, and aggression: Does violence result from low self-esteem or from threatened egotism? *Current Directions in Psychological Science, 9*, 26–29.

Baumeister, R. F., & Campbell, W. K. (1999). The intrinsic appeal of evil: Sadism, sensational thrills, and threatened egotism. *Personality & Social Psychology Review, 3*, 210–221.

Baumeister, R. F., Campbell, J. D., Kreuger, J. I., & Vohs, K. D. (2003). Does high self-esteem cause better performance, interpersonal success, happiness, or healthier lifestyles? *Psychological Science in the Public Interest, 4*, 1–44.

Baumeister, R. F., Catanese, K. R., & Vohs, K. D. (2001). Is there a gender difference in strength of sex drive? Theoretical views, conceptual distinctions, and a review of relevant evidence. *Personality & Social Psychology Review, 5*, 242–273.

Baumeister, R. F., DeWall, C. N., Ciarocco, N. H., & Twenge, J. M. (2005). Social exclusion impairs self-regulation. *Journal of Personality & Social Psychology, 88*, 589–604.

Baumeister, R. F., Hutton, D. G., & Tice, D. M. (1989). Cognitive processes during deliberate self-presentation: How self-presenters alter and misinterpret the behavior of their interaction partners. *Journal of Experimental Social Psychology, 25*, 59–78.

Baumeister, R. F., & Ilko, S. A. (1995). Shallow gratitude: Public and private acknowledgment of external help in accounts of success. *Basic and Applied Social Psychology, 16*, 191–209.

Baumeister, R. F., & Leary, M. R. (1995). The need to belong: Desire for interpersonal attachments as a fundamental human motivation. *Psychological Bulletin, 117*, 497–529.

Baumeister, R. F., & Showers, C. J. (1986). A review of paradoxical performance effects: Choking under pressure in sports and mental tests. *European Journal of Social Psychology, 16*, 361–383.

Baumeister, R. F., Smart, L., & Boden, J. M. (1996). Relation of threatened egotism to violence and aggression: The dark side of high self-esteem. *Psychological Review, 103*, 5–33.

Baumeister, R. F., & Sommer, K. L. (1997). What do men want? Gender differences and two spheres of belongingness. *Psychological Bulletin, 122*, 38–44.

Baumeister, R. F., Wotman, S. R., & Stillwell, A. M. (1993). Unrequited love: On heartbreak, anger, guilt, scriptlessness, and humiliation. *Journal of Personality and Social Psychology, 64*, 377–394.

Baumgardner, A. H., & Brownlee, E. A. (1987). Strategic failure in social interaction: Evidence for expectancy disconfirmation processes. *Journal of Personality and Social Psychology, 52*, 525–535.

Beach, S. R. H., Tesser, A., Fincham, F. D., Jones, D. J., Johnson, D., & Whitaker, D. J. (1998). Pleasure and pain in doing well, together: An investigation of performance-related affect in close relationships. *Journal of Personality and Social Psychology, 74*, 923–938.

Beaman, A. L., Klentz, B., Diener, E., & Svanum, S. (1979). Self-awareness and transgression in children: Two field studies. *Journal of Personality and Social Psychology, 37*, 1835–1846.

Bearman, P. S., & Moody, J. (2004). Suicide and friendships among American adolescents. *American Journal of Public Health, 94*, 89–95.

Becker, B. J. (1988). Influence again: An examination of reviews and studies of gender differences in social influence. In J. S. Hyde & M. C. Linn (Eds.), *The psychology of gender: Advances through meta-analysis* (pp. 178–209). New York: Academic Press.

Becker, D. V., Kenrick, D. T., Guerin, S., & Maner, J. K. (2005). Concentrating on beauty: Sexual selection and sociospatial memory. *Personality and Social Psychology Bulletin, 31*, 1643–1652.

Becker, D. V., Kenrick, D. T., Neuberg, S. L., Blackwell, K. C., & Smith, D. M. (2007). The confounded nature of angry men and happy women. *Journal of Personality and Social Psychology, 92*, 179–190.

Becker, D. V., Neel, R., & Anderson, U. S. (2010). Illusory conjunctions of angry facial expressions follow intergroup biases. *Psychological Science, 21*(7), 938–940.

Becker, H. S. (1963). *Outsiders.* New York: Free Press.

Becker, M., Vignoles, V. L., Owe, E., Brown, R., Smith, P. B., Easterbrook, M., et al. (2012). Culture and the distinctiveness motive: Constructing identity in individualistic and collectivistic contexts. *Journal of Personality and Social Psychology, 102*(4), 833.

Becker, S. W., & Eagly, A. H. (2004). The heroism of women and men. *American Psychologist, 59*, 163–178.

Becoming Barbie. (1995, December 8). *20/20.* American Broadcasting Company.

Beggan, J. K., & Allison, S. T. (1997). More there than meets the eyes: Support for the mere-ownership effect. *Journal of Consumer Psychology, 6*, 285–297.

Beilock, S. L., & Carr, T. H. (2001). On the fragility of skilled performance: What governs choking under pressure? *Journal of Experimental Psychology: General, 130*, 701–725.

Beilock, S. L., Rydell, R. J., & McConnell, A. R. (2007). Stereotype threat and working memory: Mechanisms, alleviation, and spillover. *Journal of Experimental Psychology: General, 136*, 256–276.

Belanger, D., & Tran, G. L. (2011). The impact of transnational migration on gender and marriage in sending communities of Vietnam. *Current Sociology, 59*, 59–77.

Belknap, J., Larson, D. L., Abrams, M. L., Garcia, C., & Anderson-Block, K. (2012). Types of intimate partner homicides committed by women self-defense, proxy/retaliation, and sexual proprietariness. *Homicide Studies, 16*(4), 359–379.

Bell, P. A. (2005). Reanalysis and perspective in the heat-aggression debate. *Journal of Personality and Social Psychology, 88*, 71–73.

Bell, S. T. (2007). Deep-level composition variables as predictors of team performance: A meta-analysis. *Journal of Applied Psychology, 92*, 595–615.

Bello, M. (2008, October 7). Poll: Donors feel fiscal squeeze. *USA Today*, p. 15E.

Belson, W. A. (1978). *Television violence and the adolescent boy*. Westmead, UK: Saxon House, Teakfield.

Bem, D. J. (1967). Self-perception: An alternative explanation of cognitive dissonance phenomena. *Psychological Review, 74*, 183–200.

Bem, D. J. (1972). Self-perception theory. In L. Berkowitz (Ed.), *Advances in experimental social psychology* (Vol. 6, pp. 1–62). New York: Academic Press.

Benensen, J. F., & Alavi, K. (2004). Sex differences in children's investment in same-sex peers. *Evolution and Human Behavior, 25*, 258–266.

Benenson, J. F., & Koulnazarian, M. (2008). Sex differences in help-seeking appear in early childhood. *British Journal of Developmental Psychology, 26*, 163–169.

Benenson, J. F., & Schinazi, J. (2004). Sex differences in reactions to outperforming same-sex friends. *British Journal of Developmental Psychology, 22*, 317–333.

Benenson, J. F., Pascoe, J., & Radmore, N. (2007). Children's altruistic behavior in the dictator game. *Evolution and Human Behavior, 28*, 168–175.

Bennett, B. (2005, December 12). True confessions? *Time, 166*, 45–46.

Bensimon, M., & Bodner, E. (2011). Playing with fire: The impact of football game chanting on level of aggression. *Journal of Applied Social Psychology, 41*(10), 2421–2433.

Benzeval, M., Green, M. J., & Macintyre, S. (2013). Does perceived physical attractiveness in adolescence predict better socioeconomic position in adulthood? Evidence from 20 years of follow up in a population cohort study. *PLoS One, 8*(5), e63975.

Ben-Zeev, T., Fein, S., & Inzlicht, M. (2005). Stereotype threat and arousal. *Journal of Experimental Social Psychology, 41*, 174–181.

Berg, J. H., Stephan, W. G., & Dodson, M. (1981). Attributional modesty in women. *Psychology of Women Quarterly, 5*, 711–727.

Berglas, S., & Jones, E. E. (1978). Drug choice as a self-handicapping strategy in response to noncontingent success. *Journal of Personality and Social Psychology, 36*, 405–417.

Berkowitz, L. (1972). Social norms, feelings, and other factors affecting helping behavior and altruism. In L. Berkowitz (Ed.), *Advances in experimental social psychology* (Vol. 6, pp. 63–108). New York: Academic Press.

Berkowitz, L. (1989). Frustration-aggression hypothesis: Examination and reformulation. *Psychological Bulletin, 106*, 59–73.

Berkowitz, L. (1990). On the formation and regulation of anger and aggression: A cognitive-neoassociationistic analysis. *American Psychologist, 45*, 494–503.

Berkowitz, L. (1993a). *Aggression*. New York: McGraw-Hill.

Berkowitz, L. (1993b). Pain and aggression: Some findings and implications. *Motivation and Emotion, 17*, 277–293.

Berkowitz, L. (2012). A different view of anger: The cognitive-neoassociation conception of the relation of anger to aggression. *Aggressive Behavior, 38*(4), 322–333.

Berkowitz, L., Cochran, S., & Embree, M. (1981). Physical pain and the goal of aversively stimulated aggression. *Journal of Personality and Social Psychology, 40*, 687–700.

Berkowitz, L., & Harmon-Jones, E. (2004). Toward an understanding of the determinants of anger. *Emotion, 4*, 107–130.

Berkowitz, L., & LePage, A. (1967). Weapons as aggression-eliciting stimuli. *Journal of Personality and Social Psychology, 7*, 202–207.

Berkowitz, L., & Thome, P. R. (1987). Pain expectation, negative affect, and angry aggression. *Motivation and Emotion, 11*, 183–193.

Bernard, M. M., Maio, G. R., & Olson, J. M. (2003). The vulnerability of values to attack: Inoculation of values and value-relevant attitudes. *Personality and Social Psychology Bulletin, 29*, 63–75.

Bernichon, T., Cook, K. E., & Brown, J. D. (2003). Seeking self-evaluative feedback: The interactive role of global self-esteem and specific self-views. *Journal of Personality and Social Psychology, 84*, 194–204.

Berns, G. S., Chappelow, J., Zink, C. F., Pagnoni, G., Martin-Skurski, M. E., & Richards, J. (2005). Neurobiological correlates of social conformity and independence during mental rotation. *Biological Psychiatry, 58*, 245–253.

Bernstein, D. A. (1993). Excuses, excuses. *APS Observer, 6*, 4.

Berntson, G. G., & Cacioppo, J. T. (2000). Psychobiology and social psychology: Past, present, and future. *Personality & Social Psychology Review, 4*, 3–15.

Berry, D. S., & Landry, J. C. (1997). Facial maturity and daily social interaction. *Journal of Personality and Social Psychology, 72*, 570–580.

Berscheid, E. (1983). Emotion. In H. H. Kelley, E. Berscheid, A. Christensen, J. Harvey, T. Huston, G. Loevinger, E. McClintock, L. A. Peplau, & D. Peterson (Eds.), *Close relationships* (pp. 110–168). San Francisco: Freeman.

Berscheid, E. (2010). Love in the fourth dimension. *Annual Review of Psychology, 61*, 1–25.

Berscheid, E., & Walster, E. (1974). A little bit about love. In T. Huston (Ed.), *Foundations of interpersonal attraction* (pp. 355–381). New York: Academic Press.

Bertilson, H. S. (1990). Aggression. In V. J. Derlega, B. A. Winstead, & W. H. Jones (Eds.), *Personality: Contemporary theory and research* (pp. 458–480). Chicago: Nelson-Hall.

Besag, V. (1989). *Bullies and victims in school*. Philadelphia, PA: Open University Press.

Betz, A. L., Skowronski, J. J., & Ostrom, T. M. (1996). Shared realities: Social influence and stimulus memory. *Social Cognition, 14*, 113–140.

Bickman, L. (1971). The effect of another bystander's ability to help on bystander intervention in an emergency. *Journal of Experimental Social Psychology, 7*, 367–379.

Bickman, L. (1974). The social power of a uniform. *Journal of Applied Social Psychology, 4*, 47–61.

Biek, M., Wood, W., & Chaiken, S. (1996). Working knowledge, cognitive processing, and attitudes: On the determinants of bias. *Personality and Social Psychology Bulletin, 22*, 547–556.

Biel, A., & Garling, T. (1995). The role of uncertainty in resource dilemmas. *Journal of Environmental Psychology, 15*, 221–233.

Biernat, M., Kobrynowicz, D., & Weber, D. L. (2003). Stereotypes and shifting standards: Some paradoxical effects of cognitive load. *Journal of Applied Social Psychology, 33*, 2060–2079.

Biernat, M., & Manis, M. (1994). Shifting standards and stereotype-based judgments. *Journal of Personality and Social Psychology, 66*, 5–20.

Biesanz, J. C., Neuberg, S. L., Smith, D. M., Asher, T., & Judice, T. N. (2001). When accuracy-motivated perceivers fail: Limited attentional capacity and the reemerging self-fulfilling prophecy. *Personality and Social Psychology Bulletin, 27*, 621–629.

Biesanz, J. C., West, S. G., & Millevoi, A. (2007). What do you learn about someone over time? The relationship between length of acquaintance and consensus and self-other agreement in judgments of personality. *Journal of Personality and Social Psychology, 92*, 119–135.

Bigler, R. S. (1999). The use of multicultural curricula and materials to counter racism in children. *Journal of Social Issues, 55*, 687–705.

Biner, P. M., Angle, S. T., Park, J. H., Mellinger, A. E., & Barber, B. C. (1995). Need state and the illusion of control. *Personality and Social Psychology Bulletin, 21*, 899–907.

Birnbaum, G. E., Reis, H. T., Mikulincer, M., Gillath, O., & Orpaz, A. (2006). When sex is more than just sex: Attachment orientations, sexual experience, and relationship quality. *Journal of Personality and Social Psychology, 91*, 929–943.

Bizer, G. Y., Larsen, J. T., & Petty, R. E. (2011). Exploring the valence-framing effect: Negative framing enhances attitude strength. *Political Psychology, 32*(1), 59–80.

Bjorkvist, K., Osterman, K., & Lagerspetz, K. M. J. (1994). Sex differences in covert aggression among adults. *Aggressive Behavior, 20*, 27–33.

Black, S. L., & Bevan, S. (1992). At the movies with Buss and Durkee: A natural experiment on film violence. *Aggressive Behavior, 18*, 37–45.

Blaine, B., & Crocker, J. (1993). Self-esteem and self-serving biases in reactions to positive and negative events: An integrative review. In R. Baumeister (Ed.), *Self-esteem: The puzzle of low self-regard* (pp. 55–86). New York: Plenum.

Blair, I. V., & Jost, J. T. (2003). Exit, loyalty, and collective action among workers in a simulated business environment: Interactive effects of group identification and boundary permeability. *Social Justice Research, 16*, 95–108.

Blair, R. J. R. (2004). The roles of orbital frontal cortex in the modulation of antisocial behavior. *Brain and Cognition, 55*, 198–208.

Blais, J. (2005, 9 July). Harry Potter has been very good to J.K. Rowling. *USA Today*. Retrieved 26 May 2009.

Blanchard, F. A., Crandall, C. S., Brigham, J. C., & Vaughn, L. A. (1994). Condemning and condoning racism: A social context approach to interracial settings. *Journal of Applied Psychology, 79*, 993–997.

Blanchard, F. A., Lilly, T., & Vaughn, L. A. (1991). Reducing the expression of racial prejudice. *Psychological Science, 2*, 101–105.

Blanchard, F. A., Weigel, R. H., & Cook, S. W. (1975). The effect of relative competence of group members upon interpersonal attraction in cooperating interracial groups. *Journal of Personality and Social Psychology, 32*, 519–530.

Blanck, P. D., Rosenthal, R., Snodgrass, S. E., DePaulo, B. M., & Zuckerman, M. (1981). Sex differences in eavesdropping on nonverbal cues: Developmental changes. *Journal of Personality and Social Psychology, 41*, 391–396.

Blanton, H., Buunk, B. P., Gibbons, F. X., & Kuyper, H. (1999). When better-than-others compare upward: Choice of comparison and comparative evaluation as independent predictors of academic performance. *Journal of Personality and Social Psychology, 76*, 420–430.

Blanton, H., & Jaccard, J. (2006). Arbitrary metrics in psychology. *American Psychologist, 61*, 27–41.

Blanton, H., Cooper, J., Skurnik, I., & Aronson, J. (1997). When bad things happen to good feedback: Exacerbating the need for self-justification with self-affirmations. *Personality and Social Psychology Bulletin, 23*, 684–692.

Blascovich, J., Ginsberg, G. P., & Howe, R. C. (1975). Blackjack and the risky shift, II: Monetary stakes. *Journal of Experimental Social Psychology, 11*, 224–232.

Blascovich, J., & Kelsey, R. M. (1990). Using electrodermal and cardiovascular measures of arousal in social psychological research. In C. Hendrick & M. S. Clark (Eds.), *Review of personality and social psychology: Research methods in personality and social psychology* (Vol. 11, pp. 45–73). Newbury Park, CA: Sage.

Blascovich, J., Mendes, W. B., Hunter, S. B., & Salomon, K. (1999). Social "facilitation" as challenge and threat. *Journal of Personality & Social Psychology, 77*, 68–77.

Blass, T. (1999). The Milgram paradigm after 35 years. *Journal of Applied Social Psychology, 29*, 955–978.

Blau, F. D., & Kahn, L. M. (2000). *Gender differences in pay* (National Bureau of Economic Research Working Paper: 7732). Cambridge, MA: National Bureau of Economic Research.

Bleske-Rechek, A. L., & Buss, D. M. (2001). Opposite-sex friendship: Sex differences and similarities in initiation, selection, and dissolution. *Personality & Social Psychology Bulletin, 27*, 1310–1323.

Bly, B., Pierce, M., & Prendergast, J. (1986, January). Twenty-two rules for successful self-promotion. *Direct Marketing, 48*, 74.

Bobrow, D., & Bailey, J. M. (2001). Is male homosexuality maintained via kin selection? *Evolution and Human Behavior, 22*, 361–368.

Bocchiaro, P., Zimbardo, P. G., & Van Lange, P. A. M. (2012). To defy or not to defy: An experimental study of the dynamics of disobedience and whistle-blowing. *Social Influence, 7*(1), 35–50. Retrieved from http://dx.doi.org/10.1080/155 34510.2011.648421

Bodenhausen, G. V. (1990). Stereotypes as judgmental heuristics: Evidence of circadian variations in discrimination. *Psychological Science, 1*, 319–322.

Bodenhausen, G. V., Kramer, G. P., & Süsser, K. (1994). Happiness and stereotypic thinking in social judgment. *Journal of Personality and Social Psychology, 66*, 621–632.

Bodenhausen, G. V., & Lichtenstein, M. (1987). Social stereotypes and information-processing strategies: The impact of task complexity. *Journal of Personality and Social Psychology, 52*, 871–880.

Bodenhausen, G. V., Sheppard, L. A., & Kramer, G. P. (1994). Negative affect and social judgment: The differential impact of anger and sadness. *European Journal of Social Psychology, 24*, 45–62.

Boehm, L. E. (1994). The validity affect: A search for mediating variables. *Personality and Social Psychology Bulletin, 20*, 285–293.

Boen, F., Vanbeselaere, N., Pandelaere, M., Dewitte, S., Duriez, B., Snauwaert, B., et al. (2002). Politics and basking-inreflected-glory. *Basic and Applied Social Psychology, 24*, 204–213.

Boer, D., Fischer, R., Strack, M., Bond, M. H., Lo, E., & Lam, J. (2011). How shared preferences in music create bonds between people: Values as the missing link. *Personality and Social Psychology Bulletin, 37*(9), 1159–1171.

Bogaert, S., Boone, C., & Declerck, C. (2008). Social value orientation and cooperation in social dilemmas: A review and conceptual model. *British Journal of Social Psychology, 47*, 453–480.

Bogart, L. M., Benotsch, E. G., & Pavlovic, J. D. (2004). Feeling superior but threatened: The relation of narcissism to social comparison. *Basic and Applied Social Psychology, 26*, 35–44.

Bogart, L. M., & Helgeson, V. S. (2000). Social comparisons among women with breast cancer: A longitudinal investigation. *Journal of Applied Social Psychology, 30*, 547–575.

Bohner, G., & Dickel, N. (2011). Attitudes and attitude change. *Annual Review of Psychology, 62*, 391–417.

Bohra, K. A., & Pandey, J. (1984). Ingratiation toward strangers, friends, and bosses. *Journal of Social Psychology, 122*, 217–222.

Boldry, J. G., Gaertner, L., & Quinn, J. (2007). Measuring the measures: A meta-analytic investigation of the measures of outgroup homogeneity. *Group Processes and Intergroup Relations, 10*, 157–178.

Bolger, N., & Amarel, D. (2007). Effects of social support visibility on adjustment to stress. *Journal of Personality and Social Psychology, 92*, 458–475.

Bolger, N., & Eckenrode, J. (1991). Social relationships, personality, and anxiety during a major

stressful event. *Journal of Personality and Social Psychology, 61*, 440–449.

Bonacich, E. (1972). A theory of ethnic antagonism: The split labor market. *American Sociological Review, 37*, 547–559.

Bonanno, G. A., Rennicke, C., & Dekel, S. (2005). Self-enhancement among high-exposure survivors of the September 11th terrorist attack: Resilience or social maladjustment? *Journal of Personality and Social Psychology, 88*, 984–998.

Bond, C. F., Jr., & DePaulo, B. M. (2006). Accuracy of deception judgments. *Personality and Social Psychology Review, 10*, 214–234.

Bond, C. F., Jr., & DePaulo, B. M. (2008). Individual differences in judging deception: Accuracy and bias. *Psychological Bulletin, 134*, 477–492.

Bond, C. F., Jr., Thomas, B. J., & Paulson, R. M. (2004). Maintaining lies: The multiple-audience problem. *Journal of Experimental Social Psychology, 40*, 29–48.

Bond, C. F., & Titus, L. J. (1983). Social facilitation: A meta-analysis of 241 studies. *Psychological Bulletin, 94*, 265–292.

Bond, M. H. (2004). Culture and aggression: From context to coercion. *Personality and Social Psychology Review, 8*, 62–78.

Bond, R., & Smith, P. B. (1996). Culture and conformity: A meta-analysis of studies using Asch's line judgment task. *Psychological Bulletin, 119*, 111–137.

Boninger, D. S., Krosnick, J. A., & Berent, M. K. (1995). Origins of attitude importance: Self-interest, social identification, and value relevance. *Journal of Personality and Social Psychology, 68*, 61–80.

Boorstin, D. J. (1983). *The discoverers.* New York: Random House.

Boothroyd, L. G., Jones, B. C., Burt, D. M., DeBruine, L. M., & Perrett, D. I. (2008). Facial correlates of sociosexuality. *Evolution and Human Behavior, 29*, 211–218.

Borden, R. J. (1975). Witnessed aggression: Influence of an observer's sex and values on aggressive responding. *Journal of Personality and Social Psychology, 31*, 567–573.

Borgida, E., Conner, C., & Manteufal, L. (1992). Understanding living kidney donation: A behavioral decision-making perspective. In S. Spacapan & S. Oskamp (Eds.), *Helping and being helped* (pp. 183–212). Newbury Park, CA: Sage.

Bornstein, G. (2003). Intergroup conflict: Individual, group, and collective interests. *Personality & Social Psychology Review, 7*, 129–145.

Bornstein, R. F. (1989). Exposure and affect: Overview and meta-analysis of research, 1968–1987. *Psychological Bulletin, 106*, 265–289.

Borsari, B., & Carey, K. B. (2003). Decriptive and injunctive norms in college drinking: A meta-analytic integration. *Journal of Studies on Alcohol, 64*, 331–341.

Boski, P. (1983). A study of person perception in Nigeria: Ethnicity and self versus other attributions for achievement-related outcomes. *Journal of Cross-Cultural Psychology, 14*, 85–108.

Bossard, J. H. S. (1932). Residential propinquity as a factor in marriage selection. *American Journal of Sociology, 38*, 219–224.

Bosson, J. K., & Swann, W. B., Jr. (1999). Self-liking, self-competence, and the quest for self-verification. *Personality and Social Psychology Bulletin, 25*, 1230–1241.

Boster, F. J., & Mongeau, P. (1984). Fear-arousing persuasive messages. In R. Bostrom (Ed.), *Communications yearbook* (Vol. 8, pp. 330–375). Beverly Hills, CA: Sage.

Bouchard, T. J., Jr. (2004). Genetic influences on human psychological traits. *Current Directions in Psychological Science, 13*, 148–151.

Boulton, M. J. (1994). The relationship between playful and aggressive fighting in children, adolescents, and adults. In J. Archer (Ed.), *Male violence* (pp. 23–41). New York: Routledge.

Bourgeois, M. J., & Bowen, A. M. (2001). Self-organization of alcohol-related attitudes and

beliefs in a campus housing complex: An initial investigation. *Health Psychology, 20*, 434–437.

Bowlby, J. (1969). *Attachment and loss: Vol. 1: Attachment.* New York: Basic Books.

Bowlby, J. (1973). *Attachment and loss: Vol. II: Separation.* New York: Basic Books.

Bowman, N. D., Weber, R., Tamborini, R., & Sherry, J. (2013). Facilitating game play: How others affect performance at and enjoyment of video games. *Media Psychology, 16*(1), 39–64.

Bowles, H. R., Babcock, L., & Lai, L. (2007). Social incentives for gender differences in the propensity to initiate negotiations: Sometimes it does hurt to ask. *Organizational Behavior and Human Decision Processes, 103*, 84–103.

Brüne, M. (2001). De Clerambault's syndrome (erotomania) in an evolutionary perspective. *Evolution and Human Behavior, 22*, 409–415.

Branch, T. (1988). *Parting the waters: America in the King years 1954–63.* New York: Simon & Schuster.

Brandis, S. G. (2004). *Servant of the lotus feet: A Hare Krishna odyssey.* New York: Universe.

Brandt, M. J., & Wetherell, G. A. (2012). What attitudes are moral attitudes? The case of attitude heritability. *Social Psychological and Personality Science, 3*(2), 172–179.

Brannigan, A. (1997). The postmodern experiment: Science and ontology in experimental social psychology. *British Journal of Sociology, 48*, 594–610.

Branscombe, N. R., Schmitt, M. T., & Schiffhauer, K. (2007). Racial attitudes in response to thoughts of White privilege. *European Journal of Social Psychology, 37*, 203–215.

Brauer, M., & Er-rafiy, A. (2011). Increasing perceived variability reduces prejudice and discrimination. *Journal of Experimental Social Psychology, 47*, 871–881.

Brauer, M., Judd, C. M., & Jacquelin, V. (2001). The communication of social stereotypes: The effects of group discussion and information distribution on stereotypic appraisals. *Journal of Personality and Social Psychology, 81*, 463–475.

Braver, S. L. (1995). Social contracts and the provision of public goods. In D. A. Schroeder (Ed.), *Social dilemmas: Perspectives on individuals and groups* (pp. 69–86). Westport, CT: Praeger.

Braver, S. L., Linder, D. E., Corwin, T. T., & Cialdini, R. B. (1977). Some conditions that affect admissions of attitude change. *Journal of Experimental Social Psychology, 13*, 565–576.

Brechner, K. C. (1977). An experimental analysis of social traps. *Journal of Experimental Social Psychology, 13*, 552–564.

Brehm, J. W. (1966). *A theory of psychological reactance.* New York: Academic Press.

Brehm, J. W., & Cohen, A. R. (1962). *Explorations in cognitive dissonance.* New York: Wiley.

Brehm, S. S., & Brehm, J. W. (1981). *Psychological reactance.* New York: Academic Press.

Brennan, K. A., & Shaver, P. R. (1995). Dimensions of adult attachment, affect regulation, and romantic relationship functioning. *Personality and Social Bulletin, 21*, 267–283.

Brescoll, V. L., & Uhlmann, E. L. (2008). Can an angry woman get ahead? Status conferral, gender, and expression of emotion in the workplace. *Psychological Science, 19*, 268–275.

Brewer, M. B. (1979). In-group bias in the minimal intergroup situation: A cognitive-motivational analysis. *Psychological Bulletin, 86*, 307–324.

Brewer, M. B. (1988). A dual-process model of impression formation. In T. K. Srull & R. S. Wyer, Jr. (Eds.), *Advances in social cognition* (Vol. 1, pp. 1–36). Hillsdale, NJ: Erlbaum.

Brewer, M. B. (1991). The social self: On being the same and different at the same time. *Personality and Social Psychology Bulletin, 17*, 475–482.

Brewer, M. B. (1997). On the social origins of human nature. In C. McGarty & S. A. Haslam (Eds.), *The message of social psychology: Perspectives on mind in society* (pp. 54–62). Oxford, UK: Blackwell.

Brewer, M. B., & Alexander, M. G. (2002). Intergroup emotions and images. In D. M. Mackie & E.

R. Smith (Eds.), *From prejudice to intergroup relations: Differentiated reactions to social groups* (pp. 209–225). New York: Psychology Press.

Brewer, M. B., & Caporael, L. R. (2006). An evolutionary perspective on social identity: Revisiting groups. In M. Schaller, J. Simpson, & D. T. Kenrick (Eds.), *Evolution and social psychology* (pp. 143–161). New York: Psychology Press.

Brewer, M. B., & Chen, Y.-R. (2007). Where (who) are collectives in collectivism? Toward conceptual clarification of individualism and collectivism. *Psychological Review, 114,* 133–151.

Brewer, M. B., Kenny, D. A., & Norem, J. K. (2000). Personality and social psychology at the interface: New directions for interdisciplinary research. *Personality & Social Psychology Review, 4,* 2.

Brickner, M. A., Harkins, S. G., & Ostrom, T. M. (1986). Effects of personal involvement: Thought-provoking implications for social loafing. *Journal of Personality and Social Psychology, 51,* 763–770.

Briggs, J. L. (1970). *Never in anger: Portrait of an Eskimo family.* Cambridge, MA: Harvard University Press.

Briggs, S. R., Cheek, J. M., & Buss, A. H. (1980). An analysis of the Self-Monitoring Scale. *Journal of Personality and Social Psychology, 38,* 679–686.

Brigham, J. C., & Malpass, R. S. (1985). The role of experience and contact in the recognition of faces of own- and other-race persons. *Journal of Social Issues, 41,* 139–155.

Brissette, I. S., Scheier, M. S., & Carver, C. S. (2002). The role of optimism in social network development, coping, and psychological adjustment during a life transition. *Journal of Personality & Social Psychology, 82,* 102–111.

Brown, R. B. (1978). Social and psychological correlates of help seeking behavior among urban adults. *American Journal of Community Psychology, 6,* 425–439.

Brown, S. L., & Brown, R. M. (2006). Selective investment theory: Recasting the functional significance of close relationships. *Psychological Inquiry, 17,* 1–29.

Brown, S. L., Nesse, R. M., Vinokur, A. D., & Smith, D. M. (2003). Providing social support may be more beneficial than receiving it: Results from a prospective study of mortality. *Psychological Science, 14,* 320–327.

Browne, A. (1993). Violence against women by male partners. *American Psychologist, 48,* 1077–1087.

Brownstein, A. L. (2003). Biased predecision processing. *Psychological Bulletin, 129,* 545–568.

Bruder-Mattson, S. F., & Hovanitz, C. A. (1990). Coping and attributional styles as predictors of depression. *Journal of Clinical Psychology, 46,* 557–565.

Bruner, J. S. (1957). On perceptual readiness. *Psychological Review, 64,* 123–152.

Bryan, A. D., Aiken, L. S., & West, S. G. (1996). Increasing condom use: Evaluation of a theory-based intervention to prevent sexually transmitted diseases in young women. *Health Psychology, 15,* 371–382.

Bryan, A. D., Aiken, L. S., & West, S. G. (1999). The impact of males proposing condom use on perceptions of an initial sexual encounter. *Personality & Social Psychology Bulletin, 25,* 275–286.

Bryan, A. D., Aiken, L. S., & West, S. G. (2004). HIV/STD risk among incarcerated adolescents: Optimism about the future and self-esteem as predictors of condom use self-efficacy. *Journal of Applied Social Psychology, 34,* 912–936.

Bryan, A. D., Webster, G. D., & Mahaffey, A. L. (2011). The big, the rich, and the powerful: Physical, financial, and social dimensions of dominance in mating and attraction. *Personality and Social Psychology Bulletin, 37*(3), 365–382.

Bryan, J. H., & Test, M. A. (1967). Models and helping: Naturalistic studies in aiding behavior. *Journal of Personality and Social Psychology, 6,* 400–407.

Buchan, N. R., Brewer, M. B., Grimalda, G., Wilson, R. K., Fatas, E., & Foddy, M. (2011). Global social identity and global cooperation. *Psychological Science, 22*(6), 821–828.

Buckingham, J. T., & Alicke, M. D. (2002). The influence of individual versus aggregate social comparison and the presence of others on self-evaluations. *Journal of Personality & Social Psychology, 83,* 1117–1130.

Budesheim, T. L., & DePaola, S. J. (1994). Beauty of the beast? The effects of appearance, personality, and issue information on evaluations of political candidates. *Personality and Social Psychology Bulletin, 20,* 339–348.

Buffardi, L. E., & Campbell, W. K. (2008). Narcissism and social networking web sites. *Personality and Social Psychology Bulletin, 34,* 1303–1314.

Bugental, D. B. (2000). Acquisition of the algorithms of social life: A domain-based approach. *Psychological Bulletin, 126,* 187–219.

Bugliosi, V., & Gentry, C. (1974). *Helter skelter.* New York: Bantam.

Bukowski, W. M., Hoza, B., & Boivin, M. (1994). Measuring friendship quality during pre- and early adolescence: The development and psychometric properties of the friendship qualities scale. *Journal of Personal and Personal Relationships, 11,* 471–484.

Burger, J. M. (1986). Increasing compliance by improving the deal: The that's-not-all technique. *Journal of Personality and Social Psychology, 51,* 277–283.

Burger, J. M. (2009). Replicating Milgram: Would people still obey today? *American Psychologist, 64,* 1–11.

Burger, J. M., & Caldwell, D. F. (2003). The effects of monetary incentives and labeling on the foot-in-the-door effect: Evidence for a self-perception process. *Basic and Applied Social Psychology, 25,* 235–231.

Burger, J. M., & Guadagno, R. E. (2003). Self-concept clarity and the foot-in-thedoor procedure. *Basic and Applied Social Psychology, 25,* 79–86.

Burger, J. M., Soroka, S., Gonzago, K., Murphy, E., & Smervell, E. (2001). The effect of fleeting attraction on compliance to requests. *Personality and Social Psychology Bulletin, 27,* 1578–1586.

Burger King fire-walkers burn feet. (2001, October 7). *Arizona Republic,* p. A12.

Burkley, E. (2008). The role of self-control in resistance to persuasion. *Personality and Social Psychology Bulletin, 34,* 419–431.

Burleson, K., Leach, C. W., & Harrington, D. M. (2005). Upward social comparison and self-concept: Inspiration and inferiority among art students in an advanced programme. *British Journal of Social Psychology, 44,* 109–123.

Burn, S. H. (1996). *The social psychology of gender.* New York: McGraw-Hill.

Burn, S. W. (1991). Social psychology and the stimulation of recycling behaviors: The block leader approach. *Journal of Applied Social Psychology, 21,* 611–629.

Burnkrant, R. E., & Unnava, H. R. (1989). Self-referencing: A strategy for increasing processing of message content. *Personality and Social Psychology Bulletin, 15,* 628–638.

Burns, J. M. (1978). *Leadership.* New York: Harper & Row.

Burnstein, E. (2005). Altruism and genetic relatedness. In D. M. Buss (Ed.), *The handbook of evolutionary psychology* (pp. 528–551). Hoboken, NJ: Wiley.

Burnstein, E., Crandall, C., & Kitayama, S. (1994). Some neo-Darwin decision rules for altruism: Weighing cues for inclusive fitness as a function of the biological importance of the decision. *Journal of Personality and Social Psychology, 67,* 773–789.

Burnstein, E., & Vinokur, A. (1977). Persuasive argumentation and social comparison as determinants of attitude polarization. *Journal of Experimental Social Psychology, 13,* 315–332.

Burstein, K. (2000). *Quoted from panel discussion titled "Hillary Rodham Clinton as feminist heroine."* Retrieved July 4, 2003, from http://www.theamericanenterprise.org/taeja00i.htm

Burton-Chellew, M. N., Ross-Gillespie, A., & West, S. A. (2010). Cooperation in humans: Competition between groups and proximate emotions. *Evolution and Human Behavior, 32,* 104–108.

Bushman, B. J. (1984). Perceived symbols of authority and their influence on compliance. *Journal of Applied Social Psychology, 14,* 501–508.

Bushman, B. J. (1993). Human aggression while under the influence of alcohol and other drugs: An integrative research review. *Current Directions in Psychological Science, 2,* 148–152.

Bushman, B. J. (1995). Moderating role of trait aggressiveness in the effects of violent media on aggression. *Journal of Personality & Social Psychology, 69,* 950–960.

Bushman, B. J., & Anderson, C. A. (2002). Violent video games and hostile expectations: A test of the general aggression model. *Personality & Social Psychology Bulletin, 28,* 1679–1686.

Bushman, B. J., & Baumeister, R. F. (1998). Threatened egotism, narcissism, self-esteem, and direct and displaced aggression: Does self-love or self-hate lead to violence? *Journal of Personality and Social Psychology, 75,* 219–229.

Bushman, B. J., Bonacci, A. M., Pedersen, W. C., Vasquez, E. A., & Miller, N. (2005). Chewing on it can chew you up: Effects of rumination on triggered displaced aggression. *Journal of Personality and Social Psychology, 88,* 969–983.

Bushman, B. J., & Phillips, C. M. (2001). If the television program bleeds, memory for the advertisement recedes. *Current Directions in Psychological Science, 10,* 43–47.

Bushman, B. J., & Stack, A. D. (1996). Forbidden fruit versus tainted fruit: Effects of warning labels on attraction to television violence. *Journal of Experimental Psychology: Applied, 2,* 207–226.

Buss, A. H. (1963). Physical aggression in relation to different frustrations. *Journal of Abnormal and Social Psychology, 67,* 1–7.

Buss, D. M. (1987). Selection, evocation, and manipulation. *Journal of Personality and Social Psychology, 53,* 1214–1221.

Buss, D. M. (1989). Sex differences in human mate preference: Evolutionary hypothesis tested in 37 cultures. *Behavioral and Brain Sciences, 12,* 1–49.

Buss, D. M., & Duntley, J. D. (2006). The evolution of aggression. In M. Schaller, J. A. Simpson, & D. T. Kenrick (Eds.), *Evolution and social psychology* (pp. 263–285). New York: Psychology Press.

Buss, D. M., & Kenrick, D. T. (1998). Evolutionary social psychology. In D. T. Gilbert, S. T. Fiske, & G. Lindzey (Eds.), *The handbook of social psychology* (4th ed., Vol. 2, pp. 982–1026). Boston: McGraw-Hill.

Buss, D. M., Larsen, R. J., Westen, D., & Semmelroth, J. (1992). Sex differences in jealousy: Evolution, physiology, and psychology. *Psychological Science, 3,* 251–255.

Buss, D. M., & Schmitt, D. P. (1993). Sexual strategies theory: An evolutionary perspective on human mating. *Psychological Review, 2,* 204–232.

Buss, D. M., & Shackelford, T. K. (2008). Attractive women want it all: Good genes, economic investment, parenting proclivities, and emotional commitment. *Evolutionary Psychology, 6,* 134–146.

Butler, J. C. (2000). Personality and emotional correlates of right-wing authoritarianism. *Social Behavior & Personality, 28,* 1–14.

Butz, D. A., & Plant, E. A. (2006). Perceiving outgroup members as unresponsive: Implications for approach-related emotions, intentions, and behavior. *Journal of Personality and Social Psychology, 91*(6), 1066–1079.

Buunk, B. P., & Baker, A. B. (1995). Extradyadic sex: The role of descriptive and injunctive norms. *Journal of Sex Research, 32,* 313–318.

Buunk, B. P., Angleitner, A., Oubaid, V., & Buss, D. M. (1996). Sex differences in jealousy in evolutionary and cultural perspective: Tests from the Netherlands, Germany, and the United States. *Psychological Science, 7,* 359–363.

Buunk, B. P., Collins, R. L., Taylor, S. E., VanYperen, N. W., & Dakof, G. A. (1990). The affective consequences of social comparison: Either direction has its ups and downs. *Journal of Personality and Social Psychology, 59*, 1238–1249.

Buunk, B. P., & Dijkstra, P. (2005). A narrow waist versus broad shoulders: Sex and age differences in the jealousy-evoking characteristics of a rival's body build. *Personality and Individual Differences, 39*, 379–389.

Buunk, B. P., Dijkstra, P., Kenrick, D. T., & Warntjes, A. (2001). Age preferences for mates as related to gender, own age, and involvement level. *Evolution & Human Behavior, 22*, 241–250.

Buunk, B. P., Doosje, B. J., Jans, L. G. J. M., & Hopstaken, L. E. M. (1993). Perceived reciprocity, social support, and stress at work: The role of exchange and communal orientation. *Journal of Personality and Social Psychology, 65*, 801–811.

Buunk, B. P., Gibbons, F. X., & Visser, A. (2002). The relevance of social comparison processes for prevention and health care. *Patient Education and Counseling, 47*, 1–3.

Buunk, B. P., & VanYperen, N. (1991). Referential comparisons, relational comparisons, and exchange orientation: Their relation to marital satisfaction. *Personality and Social Psychology Bulletin, 17*, 709–717.

Buunk, B. P., & Verhoeven, K. (1991). Companionship and support in organizations: A microanalysis of the stress-reducing features of social interaction. *Basic and Applied Social Psychology, 12*, 242–258.

Byrne, D. (1971). *The attraction paradigm.* New York: Academic Press.

Byrne, D., & Clore, G. L. (1970). A reinforcement-affect model of evaluative responses. *Personality: An International Journal, 1*, 103–128.

Byrne, D., London, O., & Reeves, K. (1968). The effects of physical attractiveness, sex, and attitude similarity on interpersonal attraction. *Journal of Personality, 36*, 259–271.

Byrnes, D. A., & Kiger, G. (1990). The effect of a prejudice-reduction simulation on attitude change. *Journal of Applied Social Psychology, 20*, 341–356.

Cacioppo, J. T. (2002). Social neuroscience: Understanding the pieces fosters understanding the whole and vice-versa. *American Psychologist, 57*, 819–831.

Cacioppo, J. T., Gardner, W. L., & Berntson, G. G. (1999). The affect system has parallel and integrative processing components: Form follows function. *Journal of Personality and Social Psychology, 76*, 839–855.

Cacioppo, J. T., Hawkley, L. C., Rickett, E. M., & Masi, C. M. (2005). Sociality, spirituality, and meaning making: Chicago health, aging, and social relations study. *Review of General Psychology, 9*, 143–155.

Cacioppo, J. T., Klein, D. J., Berntson, G. G., & Hatfield, E. (1993). The psychophysiology of emotion. In M. Lewis & J. M. Haviland (Eds.), *Handbook of emotions* (pp. 119–142). New York: Guilford Press.

Cacioppo, J. T., Petty, R. E., Feinstein, J. A., & Jarvis, W. B. G. (1996). Dispositional differences in cognitive motivation: The life and times of individuals varying in need for cognition. *Psychological Bulletin, 119*, 197–253.

Cacioppo, J. T., Petty, R. E., Kao, C. F., & Rodriguez, R. (1986). Central and peripheral routes to persuasion: An individual differences perspective. *Journal of Personality and Social Psychology, 51*, 1032–1043.

Campbell, A. (1999). Staying alive: Evolution, culture, and women's intrasexual aggression. *Behavioral & Brain Sciences, 22*, 203–252.

Campbell, A. (2005). Aggression. In D. M. Buss (Ed.), *Handbook of evolutionary psychology* (pp. 628–652). Hoboken, NJ: Wiley & Sons.

Campbell, D. T. (1958). Common fate, similarity, and other indices of the status of aggregates of persons as social entities. *Behavioral Science, 3*, 14–25.

Campbell, D. T. (1965). Ethnocentric and other altruistic motives. In D. LeVine (Ed.), *Nebraska symposium on motivation: 1965* (pp. 283–311). Lincoln: University of Nebraska Press.

Campbell, D. T. (1975). On the conflicts between biological and social evolution and between psychology and oral tradition. *American Psychologist, 30*, 1103–1126.

Campbell, J. D., & Fairey, P. J. (1989). Informational and normative routes to conformity. *Journal of Personality and Social Psychology, 57*, 457–468.

Campbell, J. D., & Tesser, A. (1985). Self-evaluation maintenance processes in relationships. In S. Duck & D. Perlman (Eds.), *Understanding personal relationships: An interdisciplinary approach* (pp. 107–135). Beverly Hills, CA: Sage.

Campbell, L., & Ellis, B. J. (2005). Commitment, love, and mate retention. In D. M. Buss (Ed.), *The handbook of evolutionary psychology* (pp. 419–446). New York: Wiley.

Campbell, L., Simpson, J. A., Boldry, J., & Kashy, D. A. (2005). Perceptions of conflict and support in romantic relationships: The role of attachment anxiety. *Journal of Personality and Social Psychology, 88*, 510–531.

Campbell, L., Simpson, J. A., Kashy, D. A., & Rholes, W. S. (2001). Attachment orientations, dependence, and behavior in a stressful situation: An application of the actor-partner interdependence model. *Journal of Social and Personal Relationships, 8*, 821–843.

Campbell, M. C. (1995). When attention-getting advertising tactics elicit consumer inferences of manipulative intent. *Journal of Consumer Research, 4*, 225–254.

Campbell, W. K., Bush, C. P., Brunell, A. B., & Shelton, J. (2005). Understanding the social costs of narcissism: The case of the tragedy of the commons. *Personality & Social Psychology Bulletin, 31*, 1358–1368.

Campbell, W. K., Foster, C. A., & Finkel, E. J. (2002). Does self-love lead to love for others? A story of narcissistic game playing. *Journal of Personality & Social Psychology, 83*, 340–354.

Campero-Ciani, A., Corna, F., & Capiluppi, C. (2004). Evidence for maternally inherited factors favouring male homosexuality and promoting female fecundity. *Proceedings of the Royal Society B, 271*, 2217–2221.

Campos, L. D. S., Otta, A., & Siqueira, J. D. E. (2002). Sex differences in mate selection strategies: Content analyses and responses to personal advertisements in Brazil. *Evolution and Human Behavior, 23*, 395–406.

Cann, A. (2004). Rated importance of personal qualities across four relationships. *Journal of Social Psychology, 144*, 322–334.

Cannon, W. B. (1929). *Bodily changes in pain, hunger, fear and rage: An account of recent research into the function of emotional excitement* (2nd ed.). New York: Appleton-Century-Crofts.

Cannon, W. B. (1932). *The wisdom of the body.* New York: Norton.

Cantor, J. R., Zillmann, D., & Einseidel, E. F. (1978). Female responses to provocation after exposure to aggressive and erotic films. *Communication Research, 5*, 395–411.

Cantril, H. (1940). *The invasion from Mars.* Princeton, NJ: Princeton University Press.

Cantú, S. M., Simpson, J. A., Griskevicius, V., Weisberg, Y. J., Durante, K. M., & Beal, D. J. (2014). Fertile and selectively flirty women's behavior toward men changes across the ovulatory cycle. *Psychological Science, 25*(2), 431–438.

Caporael, L. R. (1997). The evolution of truly social cognition: The core configurations model. *Personality and Social Psychology Review, 1*, 276–298.

Caporael, L. R., & Baron, R. M. (1997). Groups as the mind's natural environment. In J. A. Simpson & D. T. Kenrick (Eds.), *Evolutionary social psychology* (pp. 317–344). Hillsdale, NJ: Erlbaum.

Caprara, G. V., Barbanelli, C., Consiglio, C., Picconi, L., & Zimbardo, P. G. (2003). Personalities of politicians and voters: Unique and synergis-tic relationships. *Journal of Personality & Social Psychology, 84*, 849–856.

Carbonell, J. L., & Castro, Y. (2008). The impact of a leader model on highdominant women's self-selection for leadership. *Sex Roles, 58*, 776–783.

Carducci, B. J., Deuser, P. S., Bauer, A., Large, M., & Ramaekers, M. (1989). An application of the foot in the door technique to organ donation. *Journal of Business and Psychology, 4*, 245–249.

Carli, L. L. (1989). Gender differences in interaction style and influence. *Journal of Personality and Social Psychology, 56*, 565–576.

Carli, L. L. (2001). Gender and social influence. *Journal of Social Issues, 57*, 725–741.

Carlston, D. E. (2013). *Oxford handbook of social cognition.* New York: Oxford University Press.

Carlston, D. E., Skowronski, J. J., & Sparks, C. (1995). Savings in relearning: II. On the formation of behavior-based trait associations and inferences. *Journal of Personality and Social Psychology, 69*, 420–436.

Carnagey, N. I., & Anderson, C. A. (2005). The effects of reward and punishment in violent video games on aggressive affect, cognition, and behavior. *Psychological Science, 16*, 882–889.

Carnegie, D. (1936/1981). *How to win friends and influence people.* New York: Pocket Books.

Carney, D. R., Cuddy, A. J., & Yap, A. J. (2010). Power posing brief nonverbal displays affect neuroendocrine levels and risk tolerance. *Psychological Science, 21*(10), 1363–1368.

Carré, J. M., McCormick, C. M., & Hariri, A. R. (2011). The social neuroendocrinology of human aggression. *Psychoneuroendocrinology, 36*(7), 935–944.

Caruso, E. M. (2008). Use of experienced retrieval ease in self and social judgments. *Journal of Experimental Social Psychology, 44*, 148–155.

Caruso, E. M., Epley, N., & Bazerman, M. H. (2006). The costs and benefits of undoing egocentric responsibility assessments in groups. *Journal of Personality and Social Psychology, 91*, 857–871.

Carver, C. S., & Glass, D. C. (1978). Coronary-prone behavior and interpersonal aggression. *Journal of Personality and Social Psychology, 58*, 622–633.

Carver, C. S., & Scheier, M. F. (1985). Aspects of the self and control of behavior. In B. R. Schlenker (Ed.), *The self and social life* (pp. 146–174). New York: McGraw-Hill.

Carver, C. S., & Scheier, M. F. (1998). *On the self-regulation of behavior.* Cambridge, UK: Cambridge University Press.

Carver, C. S., Scheier, M. F., & Segerstrom, S. C. (2010). Optimism. *Clinical Psychology Review, 30*(7), 879–889.

Case, R. B., Moss, A. J., & and Case, N. (1992). Living alone after myocardial infarction: Impact on prognosis. *Journal of the American Medical Association, 267*, 575–585.

Cashdan, E. (1995). Hormones, sex, and status in women. *Hormones and Behavior, 29*, 345–366.

Caspi, A. (2000). The child is father of the man: Personality continuities from childhood to adulthood. *Journal of Personality & Social Psychology, 78*, 158–172.

Caspi, A., & Bem, D. J. (1990). Personality continuity and change across the life course. In L. A. Pervin (Ed.), *Handbook of personality: Theory and research* (pp. 549–575). New York: Guilford.

Caspi, A., Elder, G. H., & Bem, D. J. (1988). Moving away from the world: Life-course patterns of shy children. *Developmental Psychology, 24*, 824–831.

Caspi, A., & Herbener, E. S. (1990). Continuity and change: Assortative marriage and the consistency of personality in adulthood. *Journal of Personality and Social Psychology, 58*, 250–258.

Castano, E., & Giner-Sorolla, R. (2006). Not quite human: Infrahumanization in response to collective responsibility for intergroup killing. *Journal of Personality and Social Psychology, 90*, 804–818.

Catalano, R., Dooley, D., Novaco, R., Wilson, G., & Hough, R. (1993). Using ECA survey data to examine the effect of job layoffs on violent behavior. *Hospital and Community Psychiatry, 44,* 874–878.

Caughlin, J. P., Huston, T. L., & Houts, R. M. (2000). How does personality matter in marriage? An examination of trait anxiety, interpersonal negativity, and marital satisfaction. *Journal of Personality & Social Psychology, 78,* 326–336.

Cawley, J. (2000). *Body weight and women's labor market outcomes* (National Bureau of Economic Research Working Paper: 7841). Cambridge, MA: National Bureau of Economic Research.

Center for Leadership Studies. (2000). *CLS library.* Retrieved June 15, 2000, from http://cls.binghamton.edu/library.htm. Web site now located at www.gallupleadershipinstitute.org

Centers for Disease Control. (1991). Weapon-carrying among high school students. *Journal of the American Medical Association, 266,* 225–253.

Chagnon, N. A., & Bugos, P. E. (1979). Kin selection and conflict: An analysis of a Yanomano ax fight. In N. A. Chagnon & W. Irons (Eds.), *Evolutionary biology and social behavior* (pp. 213–238). North Scituate, MA: Duxbury Press.

Chaiken, S., & Eagly, A. H. (1983). Communication modality as a determinant of persuasion: The role of communicator salience. *Journal of Personality and Social Psychology, 45,* 241–256.

Chaiken, S., Giner-Sorolla, R., & Chen, S. (1996). Beyond accuracy: Defense and impression motives in heuristic and systematic processing. In P. M. Gollwitzer & J. A. Bargh (Eds.), *The psychology of action* (pp. 553–578). New York: Guilford.

Chaiken, S., & Ledgerwood, A. (2011). A theory of heuristic and systematic information processing. In P. A. M. Van Lange, A. W. Kruglanski, & E. T. Higgins (Eds.), *Handbook of theories of social psychology* (Vol. 1, pp. 246–266). Thousand Oaks, CA: Sage.

Chaiken, S., & Maheswaran, D. (1994). Heuristic processing can bias systematic processing. *Journal of Personality and Social Psychology, 66,* 460–473.

Chaiken, S., & Trope, Y. (Eds.). (1999). *Dual-process theories in social psychology.* New York: Guilford.

Chance, S. E., Brown, R. T., Dabbs, J. M., & Casey, R. (2000). Testosterone, intelligence and behavior disorders in young boys. *Personality & Individual Differences, 28,* 437–445.

Chang, E. C., & Asakawa, K. (2003). Cultural variations on optimistic and pessimistic bias for self versus a sibling: Is there evidence for self-enhancement in the West and for self-criticism in the East when the referent group is specified? *Journal of Personality and Social Psychology, 84,* 569–581.

Chartrand, T. L., & Bargh, J. A. (1999). The chameleon effect: The perception-behavior link and social interaction. *Journal of Personality and Social Psychology, 76,* 893–910.

Chartrand, T. L., & Lakin, J. L. (2013). The antecedents and consequences of human behavioral mimicry. *Annual Review of Psychology, 64,* 285–308.

Chatman, J. A. (1991). Matching people and organizations. *Administrative Science Quarterly, 36,* 459–484.

Chatman, J. A., Caldwell, D. F., & O'Reilly, C. A. (1999). Managerial personality and performance: A semi-idiographic approach. *Journal of Research in Personality, 33,* 514–545.

Cheek, J. M., & Briggs, S. R. (1990). Shyness as a personality trait. In W. R. Crozier (Ed.), *Shyness and embarrassment: Perspectives from social psychology* (pp. 315–337). Cambridge, UK: Cambridge University Press.

Cheek, J. M., & Melchior, L. A. (1990). Shyness, self-esteem, and self-consciousness. In H. Leitenberg (Ed.), *Handbook of social and evaluation anxiety* (pp. 47–82). New York: Plenum.

Cheek, J. M., Melchior, L. A., & Carpentieri, A. M. (1986). Shyness and self-concept. In L. M. Hartman & K. R. Blankenstein (Eds.), *Perception*

of self in emotional disorder and psychotherapy (pp. 113–131). New York: Plenum Press.

Chemers, M. M. (1997). *An integrative theory of leadership.* Mahwah, NJ: Erlbaum.

Chen, F. F. (2008). What happens if we compare chopsticks with forks? The impact of making inappropriate comparisons in cross-cultural research. *Journal of Personality and Social Psychology, 95,* 1005–1018.

Chen, F. F., & Kenrick, D. T. (2002). Repulsion or attraction: Group membership and assumed attitude similarity. *Journal of Personality & Social Psychology, 83,* 111–125.

Chen, M., & Bargh, J. A. (1999). Consequences of automatic evaluation: Immediate behavioral predispositions to approach or avoid the stimulus. *Personality and Social Psychology Bulletin, 25,* 215–224.

Chen, S., Boucher, H. C., & Tapias, M. P. (2006). The relational self revealed: Integrative conceptualization and implications for interpersonal life. *Psychological Bulletin, 132,* 151–179.

Chen, S., Lee-Chai, A. Y., & Bargh, J. A. (2001). Relationship orientation as a moderator of the effects of social power. *Journal of Personality & Social Psychology, 80,* 173–187.

Chen, S., Schechter, D., & Chaiken, S. (1996). Getting at the truth or getting along: Accuracy-versus impressionmotivated heuristic and systematic processing. *Journal of Personality and Social Psychology, 71,* 262–275.

Chen, Y. R., Mannix, E. A., & Okamura, T. (2003). The importance of who you meet: Effects of self-versus otherconcerns among negotiators in the United States, the People's Republic of China, and Japan. *Journal of Experimental Social Psychology, 39,* 1–15.

Cheng, C., Cheung, S., Chio, J. H., & Chan, M. S. (2013). Cultural meaning of perceived control: A meta-analysis of locus of control and psychological symptoms across 18 cultural regions. *Psychological Bulletin, 139*(1), 152–188.

Cheng, C. M., & Chartrand, T. L. (2003). Self-monitoring without awareness: Using mimicry as a nonconscious affiliation strategy. *Journal of Personality and Social Psychology, 85,* 1170–1179.

Chesler, E. (1999, August 9–16). "Hillary Clinton: New York progressive," *The Nation.* In S. K. Flinn (2000) (Ed.), *Speaking of Hillary: A reader's guide to the most controversial woman in America* (pp. 298–301). Ashland, OR: White Cloud Press.

Chibnall, J. T., & Wiener, R. L. (1988). Disarmament decisions as social dilemmas. *Journal of Applied Social Psychology, 18,* 867–879.

China: Olympics help Tsingtao Sales. (2008, August 20). *The New York Times,* p. C5.

Chinese Cultural Connection. (1987). Chinese values and the search for culture-free dimensions of culture. *Journal of Cross-Cultural Psychology, 18,* 143–164.

Chivers, M. L., Rieger, G., Latty, E., & Bailey, J. M. (2004). A sex difference in the specificity of sexual arousal. *Psychological Science, 15,* 736–744.

Chou, H. T. G., & Edge, N. (2012). "They are happier and having better lives than I am": The impact of using Facebook on perceptions of others' lives. *Cyberpsychology, Behavior, and Social Networking, 15*(2), 117–121.

Christakis, N. A., & Fowler, J. M. (2008). The collective dynamics of smoking in a large social network. *New England Journal of Medicine, 358,* 2249–2258.

Christensen, P. N., & Kashy, D. A. (1998). Perceptions of and by lonely people in initial social interaction. *Personality and Social Psychology Bulletin, 24,* 322–329.

Christie, R., & Jahoda, M. (1954). *Studies in the scope and method of "The Authoritarian Personality."* Glencoe, IL: Free Press.

Chulef, A. S., Read, S. J., & Walsh, D. A. (2001). A hierarchical taxonomy of human goals. *Motivation and Emotion, 25,* 191–232.

CIA World Factbook (2014). Retrieved from https://www.cia.gov/library/publications /the-world-factbook/rankorder/2224rank.html

Cialdini, R. B. (1995). A full-cycle approach to social psychology. In G. C. Brannigan & M. R. Merrens (Eds.), *The social psychologists: Research adventures* (pp. 52–73). New York: McGraw-Hill.

Cialdini, R. B. (2008). *Influence: Science and practice* (5th ed.). Boston: Allyn & Bacon.

Cialdini, R. B. (2012). The focus theory of normative conduct. In P. A. M. VanLange, A. W. Kruglanski, & T. T. Higgins (Eds.), *Handbook of theory in social psychology* (Vol. II, pp. 295–312). Thousand Oaks, CA: Sage.

Cialdini, R. B., & Ascani, K. (1976). Test of a concession procedure for inducing verbal, behavioral, and further compliance with a request to give blood. *Journal of Applied Psychology, 61,* 295–300.

Cialdini, R. B., & Baumann, D. J. (1981). Littering: A new unobtrusive measure of attitude. *Social Psychology Quarterly, 44,* 254–259.

Cialdini, R. B., Borden, R., Thorne, A., Walker, M., Freeman, S., & Sloane, L. T. (1976). Basking in reflected glory: Three (football) field studies. *Journal of Personality and Social Psychology, 34,* 366–375.

Cialdini, R. B., Brown, S. L., Lewis, B. P., Luce, C., & Neuberg, S. L. (1997). Reinterpreting the empathy-altruism relationship: When one into one equals oneness. *Journal of Personality and Social Psychology, 73,* 481–494.

Cialdini, R. B., Cacioppo, J. T., Bassett, R., & Miller, J. A. (1978). Low-ball procedure for producing compliance: Commitment then cost. *Journal of Personality and Social Psychology, 36,* 463–476.

Cialdini, R. B., Eisenberg, N., Green, B. L., Rhoads, K., & Bator, R. (1998). Undermining the undermining effect of reward on sustained interest. *Journal of Applied Social Psychology, 28,* 253–267.

Cialdini, R. B., Eisenberg, N., Shell, R., & McCreath, H. (1987a). Commitments to help by children: Effects on subsequent prosocial self-attributions. *British Journal of Social Psychology, 26,* 237–245.

Cialdini, R. B., Kallgren, C. A., & Reno, R. R. (1991). A focus theory of normative conduct: A theoretical refinement and reevaluation of the role of norms in human conduct. In M. P. Zanna (Ed.), *Advances in experimental social psychology* (Vol. 24, pp. 201–234). New York: Academic Press.

Cialdini, R. B., Kenrick, D. T., & Baumann, D. J. (1982). Effects of mood on prosocial behavior in children and adults. In N. Eisenberg (Ed.), *The development of prosocial behavior* (pp. 339–359). New York: Academic Press.

Cialdini, R. B., Levy, A., Herman, C. P., Kozlowski, L. T., & Petty, R. E. (1976). Elastic shifts of opinion: Determinants of direction and durability. *Journal of Personality and Social Psychology, 34,* 663–672.

Cialdini, R. B., & Richardson, K. D. (1980). Two indirect tactics of image management: Basking and blasting. *Journal of Personality and Social Psychology, 39,* 406–415.

Cialdini, R. B., Schaller, M., Houlihan, D., Arps, K., Fultz, J., & Beaman, A. L. (1987b). Empathy-based helping: Is it selflessly or selfishly motivated? *Journal of Personality and Social Psychology, 52,* 749–758.

Cialdini, R. B., Trost, M. R., & Newsom, J. T. (1995). Preference for consistency: The development of a valid measure and the discovery of surprising behavioral implications. *Journal of Personality and Social Psychology, 69,* 318–328.

Cialdini, R. B., Vincent, J. E., Lewis, S. K., Catalan, J., Wheeler, D., & Darby, B. L. (1975). Reciprocal concessions procedure for inducing compliance: The door-in-the-face technique. *Journal of Personality and Social Psychology, 31,* 206–215.

Cicerello, A., & Sheehan, E. P. (1995). Personal advertisements: A content analysis. *Journal of Social Behavior and Personality, 10,* 751–756.

Cimbalo, R. S., Faling, V., & Mousaw, P. (1976). The course of love: A crosssectional design. *Psychological Reports, 38,* 1292–1294.

Cioffi, D., & Garner, R. (1996). On doing the decision: The effects of active versus passive choice on commitment and selfperception. *Personality and Social Psychology Bulletin, 22*, 133–147.

Clark, M. S., & Aragón, O. R. (2013). Communal (and other) relationships: History, theory development, recent findings, and future directions. In J. A. Simpson & L. Campbell (Eds.), *Oxford handbook of close relationships* (pp. 255–280). New York: Oxford University Press.

Clark, M. S., & Chrisman, K. (1994). Resource allocation in intimate relationships. In A. H. Weber & J. H. Harvey (Eds.), *Perspectives on close relationships* (pp. 176–192). Boston: Allyn & Bacon.

Clark, M. S., & Jordan, S. D. (2002). Adherence to communal norms: What it means, when it occurs, and some thoughts on how it develops. In B. Laursen & W. G. Graziano (Eds.), *Social exchange in development. New directions for child and adolescent development* (pp. 3–25). San Francisco: Jossey-Bass/Pfeiffer.

Clark, M. S., & Mills, J. R. (2011). A theory of communal (and exchange) relationships. In *Handbook of Theories of Social Psychology* (pp. 232–250). Los Angeles, CA: Sage Publications.

Clark, M. S., & Reis, H. T. (1988). Interpersonal processes in close relationships. *Annual Review of Psychology, 39*, 609–672.

Clark, M. S., Mills, J. R., & Corcoran, D. M. (1989). Keeping track of needs and inputs of friends and strangers. *Personality and Social Psychology Bulletin, 15*, 533–542.

Clark, M. S., & Monin, J. K. (2006). Giving and receiving communal responsiveness as love. In R. J. Sternberg & K. Weis (Eds.), *The new psychology of love* (pp. 200–224). New Haven, CT: Yale University Press.

Clark, M. S., Ouellette, R., Powell, M. C., & Milberg, S. (1987). Recipient's mood, relationship type, and helping. *Journal of Personality and Social Psychology, 53*, 94–103.

Clark, M. S., & Waddell, B. A. (1983). Effects of moods on thoughts about helping, attraction and information acquisition. *Social Psychology Quarterly, 46*, 31–35.

Clark, R. D., III. (1990). Minority influence: The role of argument refutation of the majority position and social support for the minority position. *European Journal of Social Psychology, 20*, 489–497.

Clark, R. D., III. (2001). Effects of majority defection and multiple minority sources on minority influence. *Group Dynamics, 5*, 57–62.

Clark, R. D., III, & Hatfield, E. (1989). Gender differences in receptivity to sexual offers. *Journal of Psychology and Human Sexuality, 2*, 39–55.

Clary, E. G., & Tesser, A. (1983). Reactions to unexpected events: The naive scientist and interpretive activity. *Personality and Social Psychology Bulletin, 9*, 609–620.

Clinton, B. (2007). *Giving: How each of us can change the world*. New York: Knopf.

Clobert, M., & Saroglou, V. (2012). Intercultural non-conscious influences: Prosocial effects of Buddhist priming on Westerners of Christian tradition. *International Journal of Intercultural Relations.*

Clore, G. L., & Byrne, D. (1974). A reinforcement-affect model of attraction. In T. L. Huston (Ed.), *Foundations of interpersonal attraction* (pp. 143–170). New York: Academic Press.

Coall, D. A., & Hertwig, R. (2011). Grandparental investment: A relic of the past or a resource for the future? *Current Directions in Psychological Science, 20*, 93–98.

Cody, M. J., Seiter, J., & Montagne-Miller, Y. (1995). Men and women in the marketplace. In P. J. Kalbfleish & M. J. Cody (Eds.), *Gender, power, and communication in human relationships* (pp. 305–330). Hillsdale, NJ: Erlbaum.

Cohen, A. B. (2009). Many forms of culture. *American Psychologist, 64*, 194–204.

Cohen, A. B., Malka, A., Hill, E. D., Thoemmes, F., Hill, P. C., & Sundie, J. M. (2009). Race as a moderator of the relationship between religiosity and political alignment. *Personality and Social Psychology Bulletin, 35*, 271–282.

Cohen, A. B., Malka, A., Rozin, P., & Cherfas, L. (2006). Religion and unforgivable offenses. *Journal of Personality, 74*, 85–118.

Cohen, D. (1996). Law, social policy, and violence: The impact of regional cultures. *Journal of Personality and Social Psychology, 70*, 961–978.

Cohen, D. (2001). Cultural variation: Considerations and implications. *Psychological Bulletin, 127*, 451–471.

Cohen, D., & Gunz, A. (2002). As seen by the other . . . : Perceptions of the self in the memories and emotional perceptions of Easterners and Westerners. *Psychological Science, 13*, 55–59.

Cohen, D., & Nisbett, R. E. (1997). Field experiments examining the culture of honor: The role of institutions in perpetuating norms about violence. *Personality and Social Psychology Bulletin, 23*, 1188–1199.

Cohen, D., Nisbett, R. E., Bowdle, B. F., & Schwarz, N. (1996). Insult, aggression, and the Southern culture of honor: An "experimental ethnography." *Journal of Personality and Social Psychology, 70*, 945–960.

Cohen, F., Solomon, S., Maxfield, M., Pyszczynski, T., & Greenberg, J. (2004). Fatal attraction: The effects of mortality salience on evaluations of charismatic, task-oriented, and relationship-oriented leaders. *Psychological Science, 15*, 846–851.

Cohen, J., & Blake, A. (2013, January 23). Hillary Clinton reaches new heights of political popularity. *Washington Post.*

Cohen, J., & Golden, E. (1972). Informational social influence and product evaluation. *Journal of Applied Psychology, 56*, 54–59.

Cohen, L. L., & Swim, J. K. (1995). The differential impact of gender ratios on women and men: Tokenism, self-confidence, and expectations. *Personality and Social Psychology Bulletin, 21*, 876–884.

Cohen, S. G., & Bailey, D. E. (1997). What makes teams work: Group effectiveness research from the shop floor to the executive suite. *Journal of Management, 23*, 239–290.

Cohn, E. G., & Rotton, J. (2005). The curve is still out there: A reply to Bushman, Wang, & Anderson's (2005) "Is the curve relating temperature to aggression linear or curvilinear?" *Journal of Personality and Social Psychology, 89*, 67–70.

Cohn, E. G., Rotton, J., Peterson, A. G., & Tarr, D. B. (2004). Temperature, city size, and the Southern subculture of violence. *Journal of Applied Social Psychology, 34*, 1652–1674.

Coker, A. L., Smith, P. H., McKeown, R. E., & King, M. J. (2000). Frequency and correlates of intimate partner violence by type: Physical, sexual, and psychological battering. *American Journal of Public Health, 90*, 553–559.

Cole, D., & Chaikin, I. (1990). *An iron hand upon the people*. Seattle: University of Washington Press.

Collins, N. L., & Feeney, B. C. (2000). A safe haven: An attachment theory perspective on support seeking and caregiving in intimate relationships. *Journal of Personality & Social Psychology, 78*, 1053–1073.

Collins, N. L., & Feeney, B. C. (2004). Working models of attachment shape perceptions of social support: Evidence from experimental and observational studies. *Journal of Personality and Social Psychology, 87*, 363–383.

Collins, N. L., & Miller, L. C. (1994). Self-disclosure and liking: A meta-analytic review. *Psychological Bulletin, 116*, 457–475.

Collins, R. L. (1996). For better or worse: The impact of upward social comparison on self-evaluations. *Psychological Bulletin, 119*, 51–69.

Colvin, C. R., & Block, J. (1994). Do positive illusions foster mental health? An examination of the Taylor and Brown formulation. *Psychological Bulletin, 116*, 3–20.

Colvin, C. R., Block, J., & Funder, D. C. (1995). Overly positive self-evaluations and personality: Negative implications for mental health. *Journal of Personality and Social Psychology, 68*, 1152–1162.

Colvin, C. R., Vogt, D., & Ickes, W. (1997). Why do friends understand each other better than strangers do? In W. J. Ickes (Ed.), *Empathic accuracy* (pp. 169–193). New York: Guilford Press.

Condon, J. W., & Crano, W. D. (1988). Inferred evaluation and the relation between attitude similarity and interpersonal attraction. *Journal of Personality and Social Psychology, 54*, 789–797.

Condry, J. C., & Condry, S. (1976). Sex differences: A study of the eye of the beholder. *Child Development, 47*, 812–819.

Conley, T. D., Moors, A. C., Matsick, J. L., Ziegler, A., & Valentine, B. A. (2011). Women, men, and the bedroom: Methodological and conceptual insights that narrow, reframe, and eliminate gender differences in sexuality. *Current Direction in Psychological Science, 20*(5), 296–300.

Connery, D. S. (1977). *Guilty until proven innocent*. New York: Putnam's Sons.

Connery, D. S. (1995). *Convicting the innocent*. Cambridge, MA: Brookline.

Conway, L. G., Sexton, S. M., & Tweed, R. G. (2006). Collectivism and governmentally initiated restrictions: A cross-sectional and longitudinal analysis across nations and within a nation. *Journal of Cross-Cultural Psychology, 37*, 20–41.

Cook, S. W. (1978). Interpersonal and attitudinal outcomes in cooperating interracial groups. *Journal of Research and Development in Education, 12*, 97–113.

Cook, W. L. (2000). Understanding attachment security in family context. *Journal of Personality & Social Psychology, 78*, 285–294.

Cooley, C. H. (1922). *Human nature and the social order*. New York: Charles Scribner's Sons.

Coon, C. S. (1946). The universality of natural groupings in human societies. *Journal of Educational Sociology, 20*, 163–168.

Cooper, J., Bennett, E. A., & Sukel, H. L. (1996). Complex scientific testimony: How do jurors make decisions? *Law and Human Behavior, 20*, 379–394.

Cooper, J., Mirabile, R., & Scher, S. J. (2005). Actions and attitudes: The theory of cognitive dissonance. In T. C. Brock & M. C. Green (Eds.), *Persuasion: Psychological insights and perspectives* (pp. 63–79). Thousand Oaks, CA: Sage.

Copeland, J. T. (1994). Prophecies of power: Motivational implications of social power for behavioral confirmation. *Journal of Personality and Social Psychology, 67*, 264–277.

Correll, J., Park, B., Judd, C. M., & Wittenbrink, B. (2002). The police officer's dilemma: Using ethnicity to disambiguate potentially threatening individuals. *Journal of Personality and Social Psychology, 83*, 1314–1329.

Correll, J., Urland, G. R., & Ito, T. A. (2006). Shooting straight from the brain: Early attention to race promotes bias in the decision to shoot. *Journal of Experimental Social Psychology, 42*, 120–128.

Cortes, B. P., Demoulin, S., Rodriguez, R. T., Rodriguez, A. P., & Leyens, J. (2005). Infrahumanization or familiarity? Attribution of uniquely human emotions to the self, the ingroup, and the outgroup. *Personality and Social Psychology Bulletin, 31*, 243–253.

Cotterell, N., Eisenberger, R., & Speicher, H. (1992). Inhibiting effects of reciprocation wariness on interpersonal relationships. *Journal of Personality and Social Psychology, 62*, 658–668.

Cottrell, C. A., & Neuberg, S. L. (2005). Different emotional reactions to different groups: A sociofunctional threat-based approach to "prejudice." *Journal of Personality and Social Psychology, 88*, 770–789.

Cottrell, N. B. (1968). Performance in the presence of others: Mere presence, audience, and affiliation effects. In E. C. Simmel, R. A. Hoppe, & G. A. Milton (Eds.), *Social facilitation and imitative behavior* (pp. 91–110). Boston: Allyn & Bacon.

Cottrell, N. B., Wack, D. L., Sekerak, G. J., & Rittle, R. H. (1968). Social facilitation of dominant responses by the presence of an audience and the mere presence of others. *Journal of Personality and Social Psychology, 9*, 245–250.

Coudevylle, G., Ginis, K. A. M., & Famose, J.-P. (2008). Determinants of self-handicapping strategies in sport and their effects on athletic performance. *Social Behavior and Personality, 36*, 391–398.

Coulomb-Cabagno, G., & Rascle, O. (2006). Team sports players' observed aggression as a function of gender, competitive level, and sport type. *Journal of Applied Social Psychology, 36*, 1980–2000.

Coulomb-Cabagno, G., Rascle, O., & Souchen, N. (2005). Players' gender and male referees' decisions about aggression in French soccer: A preliminary study. *Sex Roles, 52*, 547–553.

Cox, C. L., Smith, S. L., & Insko, C. A. (1996). Categorical race versus individuating belief as determinants of discrimination: A study of Southern adolescents in 1966, 1979, and 1993. *Journal of Experimental Social Psychology, 32*, 39–70.

Cox, C. R., & Arndt, J. (2012). How sweet it is to be loved by you: The role of perceived regard in the terror management of close relationships. *Journal of Personality and Social Psychology, 102*(3), 616–632.

Cox, O. C. (1959). *Caste, class, and race: A study in social dynamics*. New York: Monthly Review Press.

Crabb, P. B. (1996a). Answering machines take the "answering" out of telephone interactions. *Journal of Social Behavior & Personality, 11*, 387–397.

Crabb, P. B. (1996b). Video camcorders and civil inattention. *Journal of Social Behavior & Personality, 11*, 805–816.

Crabb, P. B. (1999). The use of answering machines and caller ID to regulate home privacy. *Environment & Behavior, 31*, 657–670.

Crabb, P. B. (2000). The material culture of homicidal fantasies. *Aggressive Behavior, 26*, 225–234.

Crabb, P. B. (2005). The material culture of suicidal fantasies. *Journal of Psychology, 139*, 211–220.

Craig, B. (1985, July 30). A story of human kindness. *Pacific Stars and Stripes*, 13–16.

Cramer, R. E., McMaster, M. R., Bartell, P. A., & Dragna, M. (1988). Subject competence and the minimization of the bystander effect. *Journal of Applied Social Psychology, 18*, 1133–1148.

Crandall, C. S. (1995). Do parents discriminate against their heavyweight daughters? *Personality and Social Psychology Bulletin, 21*, 724–735.

Crandall, C. S., & Eshleman, A. (2003). A justification-suppression of the expression and experience of prejudice. *Psychological Bulletin, 129*, 414–446.

Crandall, C. S., Eshleman, A., & O'Brien, L. (2002). Social norms and the expression and suppression of prejudice. *Journal of Personality and Social Psychology, 82*, 359–378.

Crano, W. D., & Seyranian, V. (2007). Majority and minority influence. *Social and Personality Psychology Compass, 1*, 572–589.

Crary, D. (2005, December 15). Donor zeal impresses charities: Giving may be record for U.S. *Arizona Republic*, p. A28.

Creasey, G., & Ladd, A. (2005). Generalized and specific attachment representations: Unique and interactive roles in predicting conflict behaviors in close relationships. *Personality and Social Psychology Bulletin, 31*, 1026–1038.

Crichton, R. (1959). *The great impostor*. New York: Random House.

Crichton, R. (1961). *The rascal and the road*. New York: Random House.

Crick, N. R., & Nelson, D. A. (2002). Relational and physical victimization within friendships: Nobody told me there'd be friends like these. *Journal of Abnormal Child Psychology, 30*, 599–607.

Crocker, J., & Major, B. (1989). Social stigma and self-esteem: The selfprotective properties of stigma. *Psychological Review, 96*, 608–630.

Crocker, J., & Park, L. E. (2003). Seeking self-esteem: Construction, maintenance, and protection of self-worth. In M. R. Leary & J. P. Tangney (Eds.),

Handbook of self and identity (pp. 291–313). New York: Guilford Press.

Crocker, J., & Park, L. E. (2004). The costly pursuit of self-esteem. *Psychological Bulletin, 130*(3), 392–414.

Crocker, J., & Schwartz, I. (1985). Prejudice and in-group favoritism in a minimal intergroup situation: Effects of self-esteem. *Personality and Social Psychology Bulletin, 11*, 379–386.

Crocker, J., Thompson, L. L., McGraw, K. M., & Ingerman, C. (1987). Downward comparison, prejudice, and evaluations of others: Effects of self-esteem and threat. *Journal of Personality and Social Psychology, 52*, 907–916.

Crocker, J., Voelkl, K., Testa, M., & Major, B. M. (1991). Social stigma: Affective consequences of attributional ambiguity. *Journal of Personality and Social Psychology, 60*, 218–228.

Crook, J. H., & Crook, S. J. (1988). Tibetan polyandry: Problems of adaptation and fitness. In L. Betzig, M. Borgerhoff Mulder, & P. Turke (Eds.), *Human reproductive behavior: A Darwinian perspective* (pp. 97–114). Cambridge, UK: Cambridge University Press.

Cross, C. P., Copping, L. T., & Campbell, A. (2011). Sex differences in impulsivity: A meta-analysis. *Psychological Bulletin, 137*(1), 97–130.

Cross, S. E., & Markus, H. R. (1993). Gender in thought, belief, and action: A cognitive approach. In A. E. Beall & R. J. Sternberg (Eds.), *The psychology of gender* (pp. 55–98). New York: Guilford Press.

Croyle, R., & Cooper, J. (1983). Dissonance arousal: Physiological evidence. *Journal of Personality and Social Psychology, 45*, 782–791.

Cullum, J., O'Grady, M., Sandoval, P., Armeli, S., & Tennen, H. (2013). Ignoring norms with a little help from my friends: Social support reduces normative influence on drinking behavior. *Journal of Social and Clinical Psychology, 32*(1), 17–33.

Culos-Reed, S. N., Brawley, L. R., Martin, K. A., & Leary, M. R. (2002). Self-presentation concerns and health behaviors among cosmetic surgery patients. *Journal of Applied Social Psychology, 32*, 560–569.

Cummings, P., Koepsell, T. D., Grossman, D. C., Savarino, J., & Thompson, R. S. (1997). The association between the purchase of a handgun and homicide or suicide. *American Journal of Public Health, 87*, 974–978.

Cunningham, M. R. (1986). Levites and brother's keepers: A sociobiological perspective on prosocial behavior. *Humboldt Journal of Social Relations, 13*, 35–67.

Cunningham, M. R., Barbee, A. P., & Philhower, C. L. (2002). Dimensions of facial physical attractiveness: The intersection of biology and culture. In G. Rhodes & L. R. Zebrowitz (Eds.), *Facial attractiveness: Evolutionary, cognitive, and social perspectives* (pp. 193–238). Westport, CT: Ablex Publishing.

Cunningham, M. R., Druen, P. B., & Barbee, A. P. (1997). Angels, mentors, and friends: Tradeoffs among evolutionary, social, and individual variables in physical appearance. In J. Simpson & D. T. Kenrick (Eds.), *Evolutionary social psychology* (pp. 109–141). Hillsdale, NJ: Erlbaum.

Cunningham, M. R., Jegerski, J., Gruder, C. L., & Barbee, A. P. (1995). *Helping in different social relationships: Charity begins at home.* Unpublished manuscript, University of Louisville, Department of Psychology, Louisville, KY.

Cunningham, M. R., Shaffer, D. R., Barbee, A. P., Wolff, P. L., & Kelley, D. J. (1990). Separate processes in the relation of elation and depression to helping. *Journal of Experimental Social Psychology, 26*, 13–33.

Cunningham, P. B., Henggeler, S. W., Limber, S. P., Melton, G. B., & Nation, M. A. (2000). Patterns and correlates of gun ownership among nonmetropolitan and rural middle school students. *Journal of Clinical Child Psychology, 29*, 432–442.

Curran, J. (1977). Skills training as an approach to the treatment of heterosexual-social anxiety: A review. *Psychological Bulletin, 84*, 140–157.

Curry, O., Roberts, S. G., & Dunbar, R. I. M. (2013). Altruism in social networks: Evidence for a 'kinship premium'. *British Journal of Psychology, 104*, 283–295.

Curtis, N. M., Ronan, K. R., & Borduin, C. M. (2004). Multisystemic treatment: A meta-analysis of outcome studies. *Journal of Family Psychology, 18*, 411–419.

Cutrona, C. E. (1982). Transition to college: Loneliness and the process of social adjustment. In L. A. Peplau & D. Perlman (Eds.), *Loneliness: A sourcebook of current theory, research, and therapy* (pp. 291–309). New York: Wiley-Interscience.

Cutrona, C. E., Cole, V., Colangelo, N., Assouline, S. G., & Russell, D. W. (1994). Perceived parental social support and academic achievement: An attachment theory perspective. *Journal of Personality and Social Psychology, 66*, 369–378.

D'Agostino, P. R. (2000). The encoding and transfer of stereotype-driven inferences. *Social Cognition, 18*, 281–291.

D'Agostino, P. R., & Fincher-Kiefer, R. (1992). Need for cognition and the correspondence bias. *Social Cognition, 10*, 151–163.

Dabbs, J. M., Jr. (1996). Testosterone, aggression, and delinquency. In S. Bhasin, H. L. Gabelnick, J. M. Spieler, R. S. Swerdloff, C. Wang, & C. Kelly (Eds.), *Pharmacology, biology, and clinical applications of androgens: Current status and future prospects* (pp. 179–189). New York: Wiley-Liss.

Dabbs, J. M., Jr. (2000). *Heroes, rogues, and lovers: Testosterone and behavior*. New York: McGraw-Hill.

Dabbs, J. M., Jr., Bernieri, F. J., Strong, R. K., Campo, R., & Milun, R. (2001). Going on stage: Testosterone in greetings and meetings. *Journal of Research in Personality, 35*, 27–40.

Dabbs, J. M., Jr., Carr, S., Frady, R., & Riad, J. (1995). Testosterone, crime, and misbehavior among 692 male prison inmates. *Personality and Individual Differences, 18*, 627–633.

Dabbs, J. M., Jr., Frady, R., Carr, T., & Besch, N. (1987). Saliva testosterone and criminal violence in young prison inmates. *Psychosomatic Medicine, 49*, 174–182.

Dabbs, J. M., Jr., Hargrove, M. F., & Heusel, C. (1996). Testosterone differences among college fraternities: Well-behaved versus rambunctious. *Personality and Individual Differences, 20*, 157–161.

Dabbs, J. M., Jr., Jurkovic, G., & Frady, R. (1991). Salivary testosterone and cortisol among late adolescent male offenders. *Journal of Abnormal Child Psychology, 19*, 469–478.

Dabbs, J. M., Jr., & Morris, R. (1990). Testosterone, social class, and anti-social behavior in a sample of 4462 men. *Psychological Science, 1*, 209–211.

Dalsky, D., Gohm, C. L., Noguchi, K., & Shiomura, K. (2008). Mutual self-enhancement in Japan and the United States. *Journal of Cross-Cultural Psychology, 39*, 215–223.

Daly, J. A., Hogg, E., Sacks, D., Smith, M., & Zimring, L. (1983). Sex and relationship affect social self-grooming. *Journal of Nonverbal Behavior, 7*, 183–189.

Daly, M., Salmon, C., & Wilson, M. (1997). Kinship: The conceptual hole in psychological studies of social cognition and close relationships. In J. A. Simpson & D. T. Kenrick (Eds.), *Evolutionary social psychology* (pp. 265–296). Mahwah, NJ: Erlbaum.

Daly, M., & Wilson, M. (1994). Evolutionary psychology of male violence. In J. Archer (Ed.), *Male violence* (pp. 253–288). New York: Routledge.

Dambrun, M., Taylor, D. M., McDonald, D. A., Crush, J., & Méot, A. (2006). The relative deprivation-gratification continuum and the attitudes of South Africans toward immigrants: A test of the V-curve hypothesis. *Journal of Personality and Social Psychology, 91*, 1032–1044.

Dandeneau, S. D., Baldwin, M. W., Baccus, J. R., Sakellaropoulo, M., & Pruessner, J. C. (2007). Cutting stress off at the pass: Reducing vigilance and responsiveness to social threat by manipulating attention. *Journal of Personality and Social Psychology, 93*, 651–666.

Dardenne, B., Dumont, M., & Bollier, T. (2007). Insidious dangers of benevolent sexism: Consequences for women's performance. *Journal of Personality and Social Psychology, 93*, 764–779.

Darley, J. M., Fleming, J. H., Hilton, J. L., & Swann, W. B., Jr. (1988). Dispelling negative expectancies: The impact of interaction goals and target characteristics on the expectancy confirmation process. *Journal of Experimental Social Psychology, 24*, 19–36.

Darley, J. M., & Latané, B. (1968). Bystander intervention in emergencies: Diffusion of responsibility. *Journal of Personality and Social Psychology, 8*, 377–383.

Das, E. H. H. J., de Wit, J. B. F., & Stroebe, W. (2003). Fear appeals motivate acceptance of action recommendations. *Personality and Social Psychology Bulletin, 29*, 650–664.

Daubman, K. A., Heatherington, L., & Ahn, A. (1992). Gender and the selfpresentation of academic achievement. *Sex Roles, 27*, 187–204.

Dauten, D. (2004, July 22). How to be a good waiter, and other innovative ideas. *Arizona Republic*, p. D3.

Davidson, A. R., Yantis, S., Norwood, M., & Montano, D. E. (1985). Amount of information about the attitude object and attitude-behavior consistency. *Journal of Personality and Social Psychology, 49*, 1184–1198.

Davidson, K., & Prkachin, K. (1997). Optimism and unrealistic optimism have an interacting impact on health-promoting behavior and knowledge changes. *Personality and Social Psychology Bulletin, 23*(6), 617–625.

Davidson, O. G. (1996). *The best of enemies: Race and redemption in the New South*. New York: Scribner.

Davidson, R. J., Ekman, P., Saron, C. D., Senulis, J. A., & Friesen, W. V. (1990). Approach/withdrawal and cerebral asymmetry: Emotional expression and brain physiology. *Journal of Personality and Social Psychology, 58*, 330–341.

Davies, J. C. (1962). Toward a theory of revolution. *American Sociological Review, 27*, 5–19.

Davis, B. P., & Knowles, E. S. (1999). A disrupt-then-reframe technique of social influence. *Journal of Personality and Social Psychology, 76*, 192–199.

Davis, D., & Follette, W. C. (2001). Foibles of witness memory in high profile/traumatic cases. *Journal of Air Law and Commerce, 66*, 1421–1449.

Davis, D., & Leo, R. A. (2006). Psychological weapons of influence: Applications in the interrogation room. *Nevada Lawyer, 14*, 14–19.

Davis, D., & O'Donohue, W. T. (2004). The road to perdition: "Extreme influence" tactics in the interrogation room. In W. T. O'Donohue, P. R. Laws, & C. Hollin (Eds.), *Handbook of forensic psychology* (pp. 897–996). New York: Basic Books.

Davis, D., Shaver, P. R., & Vernon, M. L. (2004). Attachment style and subjective motivations for sex. *Personality and Social Psychology Bulletin, 30*, 1076–1090.

Davis, J. H. (1969). *Group performance*. New York: Addison-Wesley.

Davis, J. H. (1973). Group decision and social interaction: A theory of social decision schemes. *Psychological Review, 80*, 97–125.

Davis, J. H., Kerr, N. L., Atkin, R. S., Holt, R., & Meek, D. (1975). The decision processes of 6- and 12-person mock juries assigned unanimous and twothirds majority rules. *Journal of Personality and Social Psychology, 32*, 1–14.

Davis, J. L., & Rusbult, C. E. (2001). Attitude alignment in close relationships. *Journal of Personality & Social Psychology, 81*, 65–84.

Davis, K. E., & Todd, M. J. (1985). Assessing friendship: Prototypes, paradigm cases and relationship description. In S. Duck & D. Perlman (Eds.), *Understanding personal relationships: An interdisciplinary approach* (pp. 17–38). Beverly Hills, CA: Sage.

Davis, M. H. (1994). *Empathy: A social psychological approach*. Madison, WI: Brown and Benchmark.

Davis, M. H. (2000, April 8). Tempe teens brawl in "Fight Club." *Arizona Republic*, p. B1.

Davis, M. H., Conklin, L., Smith, A., & Luce, C. (1996). The effect of perspective taking on the cognitive representation of persons: A merging of self and other. *Journal of Personality and Social Psychology, 70*, 213–226.

Davis, M. H., Morris, M. M., & Kraus, L. A. (1998). Relationship-specific and global perceptions of social support: Associations with well-being and attachment. *Journal of Personality and Social Psychology, 74*, 468–481.

Dawes, R. M. (1989). Statistical criteria for establishing a truly false consensus effect. *Journal of Experimental Social Psychology, 25*, 1–17.

Day, D. V., Shleicher, D. J., Unckless, A. L., & Hiller, N. J. (2002). Self-monitoring personality at work: A meta-analytic investigation of construct validity. *Journal of Applied Psychology, 87*, 390–401.

Deaux, K., & Hanna, R. (1984). Courtship in the personal column: The influence of gender and sexual orientation. *Sex Roles, 11*, 363–375.

Deaux, K., & LaFrance, M. (1998). Gender. In D. T. Gilbert, S. T. Fiske, & G. Lindzey (Eds.), *The handbook of social psychology* (4th ed., Vol. 1, pp. 788–827). New York: McGraw-Hill.

Deaux, K., & Lewis, L. L. (1984). The structure of gender stereotypes: Interrelationships among components and gender label. *Journal of Personality and Social Psychology, 46*, 991–1004.

Deaux, K., & Major, B. (1987). Putting gender into context: An interactive model of gender-related behavior. *Psychological Review, 94*, 369–389.

Deaux, K., Reid, A., Mizrahi, K., & Ethier, K. A. (1995). Parameters of social identity. *Journal of Personality and Social Psychology, 68*, 280–291.

DeBono, K. G. (1987). Investigating the social-adjustive and value-expressive functions of attitude: Implications for persuasion processes. *Journal of Personality and Social Psychology, 52*, 279–287.

DeBruine, L. M. (2005). Trustworthy but not lustworthy: Context-specific effects of facial resemblance. *Proceedings of the Royal Society of London B, 272*, 919–922.

DeBruine, L. M., Jones, B. C., & Perrett, D. I. (2005). Women's attractiveness judgments of self-resembling faces change across the menstrual cycle. *Hormones and Behavior, 47*, 379–383.

Decety, J. (2012). Neuroscience of empathic responding. In S. L. Brown, R. M. Brown, & L. A. Penner (Eds.), *Moving beyond self-interest: Perspectives from evolutionary biology, neuroscience, and the social sciences* (pp. 109–132). New York: Oxford University Press.

Deci, E. L., Koestner, R., & Ryan, R. M. (1999). A meta-analytic review of experiments examining the effects of extrinsic rewards on intrinsic motivation. *Psychological Bulletin, 125*, 627–668.

Deci, E. L., Koestner, R., & Ryan, R. M. (2001). Extrinsic rewards and intrinsic motivation in education: Reconsidered once again. *Review of Educational Research, 71*, 1–27.

Deci, E. L., & Ryan, R. M. (1985). *Intrinsic motivation and self-determination in human behavior*. New York: Plenum.

Deci, E. L., & Ryan, R. M. (2000). The "what" and "why" of goal pursuits: Human needs and the self-determination of behavior. *Psychological Inquiry, 11*, 227–268.

DeCremer, D., & VanDijk, E. (2002). Reactions to group success and failure as a function of identification level: A test of the goal-transformation hypothesis in social dilemmas. *Journal of Experimental Social Psychology, 38*, 435–442.

DeDreu, C. K. W. (2003). Time pressure and closing of the mind in negotiation. *Organizational Behavior and Human Decision Processes, 91*, 280–295.

De Dreu, C. K. W., Nijstad, B. A., & van Knippenberg, D. (2008). Motivated information processing in group judgment and decision making. *Personality and Social Psychology Review, 12*, 22–49.

DeDreu, C. K. W., & West, M. A. (2001). Minority dissent and team innovation: The importance of participation in decision making. *Journal of Applied Psychology, 86*, 1191–1201.

De Hoogh, A. H. B., Den Hartog, D. N., & Koopman, P. L. (2005). Linking the Big Five factors of personality to charismatic and transactional leadership: Perceived dynamic work environment as a moderator. *Journal of Organizational Behavior, 26*, 839–865.

Del Giudice, M. (2009). Sex, attachment, and the development of reproductive strategies. *Behavioral & Brain Sciences, 32*, 1–68.

Del Guidice, M. (2011). Sex differences in romantic attachment: A meta-analysis. *Personality and Social Psychology Bulletin, 37*(2), 193–214.

DeLisi, M., Vaughn, M. G., Gentile, D. A., Anderson, C. A., & Shook, J. J. (2013). Violent video games, delinquency, and youth violence new evidence. *Youth Violence and Juvenile Justice, 11*(2), 132–142.

Deluga, R. J., & Perry, J. T. (1994). The role of subordinate performance and ingratiation in leader-member exchanges. *Group and Organization Management, 19*, 67–86.

Del Vecchio, T., & O'Leary, K. D. (2004). Effectiveness of anger treatments for specific anger problems: A meta-analytic review. *Clinical Psychology Review, 24*(1), 15–34.

Denissen, J. J. A., Penke, L., & Schmitt, D. P. (2008). Self-esteem reactions to social interactions: Evidence for sociometer mechanisms across days, people, and nations. *Journal of Personality and Social Psychology, 95*, 181–196.

DePaulo, B. M. (1982). Social-psychological processes in informal help seeking. In T. A. Wills (Ed.), *Basic processes in helping relationships* (pp. 255–277). New York: Academic Press.

DePaulo, B. M. (1992). Nonverbal behavior and self-presentation. *Psychological Bulletin, 111*, 203–243.

DePaulo, B. M., Epstein, J. A., & LeMay, C. S. (1990). Responses of the socially anxious to the prospect of interpersonal evaluation. *Journal of Personality, 58*, 623–640.

DePaulo, B. M., & Fisher, J. D. (1980). The costs of asking for help. *Basic and Applied Social Psychology, 1*, 23–35.

DePaulo, B. M., Kashy, D. A., Kirkendol, S. E., Wyer, M. M., & Epstein, J. A. (1996). Lying in everyday life. *Journal of Personality and Social Psychology, 70*, 979–995.

DePaulo, B. M., Lindsay, J. J., Malone, B. E., Muhlenbruck, L., Charlton, K., & Cooper, H. (2003). Cues to deception. *Psychological Bulletin, 129*, 74–112.

Derlega, V. J., Metts, S., Petronio, S., & Margulis, S. J. (1993). *Self-disclosure*. Newbury Park, CA: Sage.

DeSteno, D., Bartlett, M. Y., Braverman, J., & Salovey, P. (2002). Evolutionary mechanism or artifact of measurement? *Journal of Personality & Social Psychology, 83*, 1103–1116.

Deters, F. G., & Mehl, M. R. (2012). Does posting Facebook status updates increase or decrease loneliness? An online social networking experiment. *Social Psychological and Personality Science, 4*(5), 579–586.

Deutsch, L. (1993, August 27). 4 tell jury how they ran from TVs to help Denny. *San Francisco Examiner*, p. A11.

Deutsch, M. (1986). Strategies for inducing cooperation. In R. K. White (Ed.), *Psychology and the prevention of nuclear war* (pp. 162–170). New York: New York University Press.

Deutsch, M., & Gerard, H. B. (1955). A study of normative and informational social influences upon individual judgment. *Journal of Abnormal and Social Psychology, 51*, 629–636.

Devine, P. G. (1989). Stereotypes and prejudice: Their automatic and controlled components. *Journal of Personality and Social Psychology, 56*, 5–18.

Devine, P. G., Monteith, M. J., Zuwerink, J. R., & Elliot, A. J. (1991). Prejudice with and without compunction. *Journal of Personality and Social Psychology, 60*, 817–830.

Devos, T., Silver, L. A., Mackie, D. M., & Smith, E. R. (2002). Experiencing intergroup emotions. In D. M. Mackie & E. R. Smith (Eds.), *From prejudice to intergroup emotions: Differentiated reactions to social groups* (pp. 111–134). New York: Psychology Press.

DeVries, D. L., Edwards, K. J., & Slavin, R. E. (1978). Biracial learning teams and race relations in the classroom: Four field experiments using teams-games-tournament. *Journal of Educational Psychology, 70*(3), 356–362.

de Waal, F. B. M. (1989). *Chimpanzee politics: Power and sex among apes*. Baltimore: Johns Hopkins University Press.

Dewall, C. N., Baumeister, R. F., Stillman, T. F., & Gailliot, M. T. (2007). Violence restrained: Effects of self-regulation and its depletion on aggression. *Journal of Experimental Social Psychology, 43*, 62–76.

Diamond, L. M. (2003). What does sexual orientation orient? A biobehavioral model distinguishing romantic love and sexual desire. *Psychological Review, 110*, 173–192.

Diamond, L. M. (2004). Emerging perspectives on distinctions between romantic love and sexual desire. *Current Directions in Psychological Science, 13*, 116–119.

Diamond, L. M. (2007). A dynamical systems approach to female same-sex sexuality. *Perspectives on Psychological Science, 2*, 142–161.

Diamond, L. M. (2008). Female bisexuality from adolescence to adulthood: Results from a 10-year longitudinal study. *Developmental Psychology, 44*, 5–14.

Diamond, L. M., Hicks, A. M., & Otter-Henderson, K. D. (2008). Every time you go away: Changes in affect, behavior, and physiology associated with travel-related separations from romantic partners. *Journal of Personality and Social Psychology, 95*, 385–403.

Dickerson, S. S., Gruenewald, T. L., & Kemeny, M. E. (2004). When the social self is threatened: Shame, physiology, and health. *Journal of Personality, 72*, 1191–1216.

Dickey, C. (1991, January 7). Why we can't seem to understand the Arabs. *Newsweek*, pp. 26–27.

Diener, E. (2000). Subjective well-being: The science of happiness and a proposal for a national index. *American Psychologist, 55*, 34–43.

Diener, E., & Biswas-Diener, R. (2008). *Happiness: Unlocking the mysteries of psychological wealth*. Malden, MA: Blackwell/Wiley.

Diener, E., Fraser, S. C., Beaman, A. L., & Kelem, R. T. (1976). Effects of deindividuation variables on stealing among Halloween trick-or-treaters. *Journal of Personality and Social Psychology, 33*, 178–183.

Dijker, A. J., & Koomen, W. (1996). Stereotyping and attitudinal effects under time pressure. *European Journal of Social Psychology, 26*, 61–74.

Dijksterhuis, A., & van Knippenberg, A. (1999). On the parameters of associative strength: Central tendency and variability as determinants of stereotype accessibility. *Personality and Social Psychology Bulletin, 25*, 527–536.

Dijkstra, P., & Buunk, B. P. (1998). Jealousy as a function of rival characteristics: An evolutionary perspective. *Personality & Social Psychology Bulletin, 24*, 1158–1166.

Dill, K. E., Brown, B. P., & Collins, M. A. (2008). Effects of exposure to sex-stereotyped video game characters on tolerance of sexual harassment. *Journal of Experimental Social Psychology, 44*, 1402–1408.

DiMento, J. F. (1989). Can social science explain organizational noncompliance with environmental law? *Journal of Social Issues, 45*, 109–133.

Dion, K. L., Dion, K. K., & Keelan, J. P. (1990). Appearance anxiety as a dimension of social-evaluative anxiety: Exploring the ugly duckling syndrome.*Contemporary Social Psychology, 14*, 220–224.

Ditto, P. H., & Lopez, D. F. (1992). Motivated skepticism: Use of differential decision criteria for preferred and nonpreferred conclusions. *Journal of Personality and Social Psychology, 63*, 568–584.

Dodd, E. H., Giuliano, T. A., Boutell, J. M., & Moran, B. E. (2001). Respected or rejected: Perceptions of women who confront sexist remarks. *Sex Roles, 45*, 567–577.

Dodge, K. A., & Coie, J. D. (1987). Social information processing factors in reactive and proactive aggression in children's peer groups. *Journal of Personality and Social Psychology, 53*, 1146–1158.

Dodge, K. A., & Frame, C. L. (1982). Social cognitive biases and deficits in aggressive boys. *Child Development, 53*, 1146–1158.

Dodge, K. A., Price, J. M., Bachorowski, J. A., & Newman, J. P. (1990). Hostile attributional biases in severely aggressive adolescents. *Journal of Abnormal Psychology, 99*, 385–392.

Doherty, K., & Schlenker, B. R. (1991). Self-consciousness and strategic self-presentation. *Journal of Personality, 59*, 1–18.

Dolinski, D. (2000). On inferring one's beliefs from one's attempt and its consequences for subsequent compliance. *Journal of Personality and Social Psychology, 78*, 260–272.

Dolinski, D. (2012). The nature of the first small request as a decisive factor in the effectiveness of the foot-in-the-door technique. *Applied Psychology, 61*(3), 437–453.

Dollard, J., Miller, N. E., Doob, L. W., Mowrer, O. H., & Sears, R. R. (1939). *Frustration and aggression*. New Haven, CT: Yale University Press.

Donahue, E. M. (1994). Do children use the Big Five, too? Content and structural form in personality description. *Journal of Personality, 62*, 45–66.

Donaldson, S. I., Graham, J. W., Piccinin, A. M., & Hansen, W. B. (1995). Resistance-skills training and onset of alcohol use. *Health Psychology, 14*, 291–300.

Donders, N. C., Correll, J., & Wittenbrink, B. (2008). Danger stereotypes predict racially biased attentional processing. *Journal of Experimental Social Psychology, 44*, 1328–1333.

Donnerstein, E., & Berkowitz, L. (1981). Victim reactions to aggressive erotic films as a factor in violence against women. *Journal of Personality and Social Psychology, 41*, 710–724.

Doty, R. M., Peterson, B. E., & Winter, D. G. (1991). Threat and authoritarianism in the United States, 1978–1987. *Journal of Personality and Social Psychology, 61*, 629–640.

Doty, R. M., Winter, D. G., Peterson, B. E., & Kemmelmeier, M. (1997). Authoritarianism and American students' attitudes about the Gulf War. *Personality and Social Psychology Bulletin, 23*, 1133–1143.

Dovidio, J. F. (1984). Helping behavior and altruism: An empirical and conceptual overview. In L. Berkowitz (Ed.), *Advances in experimental social psychology* (Vol. 17, pp. 361–427). New York: Academic Press.

Dovidio, J. F. (1993, October). *Androgyny, sex roles, and helping*. Paper presented at the meetings of the Society of Experimental Social Psychology, Santa Barbara, CA.

Dovidio, J. F., Ellyson, S. L., Keating, C. F., Heltman, K., & Brown, C. E. (1988). The relationship of social power to visual displays of dominance between men and women. *Journal of Personality and Social Psychology, 54*, 233–242.

Dovidio, J. F., & Gaertner, S. L. (2000). Aversive racism and selection decisions: 1989 and 1999. *Psychological Science, 11*, 315–319.

Dovidio, J. F., Gaertner, S. L., & Kawakami, K. (2003). Intergroup contact: The past, present, and the future. *Group Processes and Intergroup Relations, 6*, 5–20.

Dovidio, J. F., Gaertner, S. L., Validzic, A., Matoka, K., Johnson, B., & Frazier, S. (1997a). Extending the benefits of recategorization: Evaluations, self-disclosure, and helping. *Journal of Experimental Social Psychology, 33*, 401–420.

Dovidio, J. F., Piliavin, J. A., Gaertner, S. L., Schroeder, D. A., & Clark, R. D., III. (1991). The arousal: Cost-Reward Model and the process of intervention: A review of the evidence. In M. S. Clark (Ed.), *Review of personality and social psychology* (Vol. 12, pp. 86–118). Newbury Park, CA: Sage.

Dovidio, J. F., Piliavin, J. A., Schroeder, D. A., & Penner, L. A. (2006). *The social psychology of prosocial behavior*. Mahwah, NJ: Erlbaum.

Dovidio, J. F., ten Vergert, M., Stewart, T. L., Gaertner, S. L., Johnson, J. D., Esses, V. M., et al. (2004). Perspective and prejudice: Antecedents and mediating mechanism. *Personality and Social Psychology Bulletin, 30*, 1537–1549.

Dowd, E. T., Hughes, S., Brockbank, L., Halpain, D., Seibel, C., & Seibel, P. (1988). Compliance-based and defiance-based intervention strategies and psychological reactance in the treatment of free and unfree behavior. *Journal of Counseling Psychology, 35*, 363–369.

Dowd, E. T., Milne, C. R., & Wise, S. L. (1991). The therapeutic reactance scale: A measure of psychological reactance. *Journal of Counseling and Development, 69*, 541–545.

Downs, A. C., & Lyons, P. M. (1991). Natural observations of the links between attractiveness and initial legal judgments. *Personality and Social Psychology Bulletin, 17*, 541–547.

Doyle, R. (1997, April). By the numbers: Air pollution in the U.S. *Scientific American, 27*.

Dreher, J., Schmidt, P. J., Kohn, P., Furman, D., Rubinow, D., & Berman, K. F. (2007). Menstrual cycle phase modulates reward-related neural function in women. *Proceedings of the National Academy of Sciences, 104*, 2465–2470.

Drigotas, S. M., & Barta, W. (2001). The cheating heart: Scientific explorations of infidelity. *Current Directions in Psychological Science, 10*, 177–180.

Driskell, J. E., Hogan, R., & Salas, E. (1987). Personality and group performance. In C. Hendrick (Ed.), *Group processes and intergroup relations* (pp. 91–112). Newbury Park, CA: Sage.

Duckitt, J., & Farre, B. (1994). Right-wing authoritarianism and political intolerance among whites in the future majority-rule South Africa. *Journal of Social Psychology, 134*, 735–741.

Duke, N., Resnick, M. D., & Borowsky, I. W. (2005). Adolescent firearm violence: Position paper of the society for adolescent medicine. *Journal of Adolescent Health, 37*, 171–174.

Du Maurier, D. (1977). *Myself when young: The shaping of a writer*. Garden City, NY: Doubleday.

Duncan, L. A., Park, J. H., Faulkner, J., Schaller, M., Neuberg, S. L., & Kenrick, D. T. (2007). Adaptive allocation of attention: Effects of sex and sociosexuality on visual attention to attractive opposite-sex faces. *Evolution and Human Behavior, 28*, 359–364.

Dunn, E. W., Aknin, L. B., & Norton, M. I. (2008). Spending money on others promotes happiness. *Science, 319*, 1687–1688.

Dunn, E. W., & Norton, M. (2013). *Happy money: The science of smarter spending*. New York: Simon & Schuster.

Dunn, M. J., Brinton, S., & Clark, L. (2010). Universal sex differences in online advertisers age preferences: Comparing data from 14 cultural groups and 2 religious groups. *Evolution and Human Behavior, 31*, 383–393.

Dunning, D., & Balcetis, E. (2013). Wishful seeing: How preferences shape visual perception. *Current Directions in Psychological Science, 22*, 33–37.

Dunning, D., Leuenberger, A., & Sherman, D. A. (1995). A new look at motivated inference: Are self-serving theories of success a product of motivational forces? *Journal of Personality and Social Psychology, 69*, 58–68.

Dunning, D., Perie, M., & Story, A. L. (1991). Self-serving prototypes of social categories. *Journal of Personality and Social Psychology, 61*, 957–968.

Dunning, D., & Sherman, D. A. (1997). Stereotypes and tacit inference. *Journal of Personality and Social Psychology, 73*, 459–471.

Duntley, J. D. (2005). Adaptations to dangers from humans. In D. M. Buss (Ed.), *Handbook of evolutionary psychology* (pp. 224–254). Hoboken, NJ: Wiley.

Dunton, B. C., & Fazio, R. H. (1997). An individual difference measure of motivation to control prejudiced reactions. *Personality and Social Psychology Bulletin, 23,* 316–326.

Durant, W., & Durant, A. (1963). *The age of Louis XIV.* New York: Simon & Schuster.

Durante, K. M., Griskevicius, V., Simpson, J. A., Cantú, S. M., & Tybur, J. M. (2012). Sex ratio and women's career choice: Does a scarcity of men lead women to choose briefcase over baby? *Journal of Personality and Social Psychology, 103*(1), 121–134.

Durante, K. M., Li, N. P., & Haselton, M. G. (2008). Changes in women's choice of dress across the ovulatory cycle: Naturalistic and laboratory taskbased evidence. *Personality and Social Psychology Bulletin, 34,* 1451–1460.

Duriez, B., Soenens, B., & Vansteenkiste, M. (2008). The intergenerational transmission of authoritarianism: The mediating role of parental goal promotion. *Journal of Research in Personality, 42,* 622–642.

Dutton, A., & Aron, A. (1974). Some evidence for heightened sexual attraction under conditions of high anxiety. *Journal of Personality and Social Psychology, 30,* 510–517.

Duval, S., & Wicklund, R. A. (1972). *A theory of objective self-awareness.* New York: Academic Press.

Dykas, M. J., & Cassidy, J. (2011). Attachment and the processing of social information across the life span: Theory and evidence. *Psychological Bulletin, 137*(1), 19–46.

Dykman, B., & Reis, H. T. (1979). Personality correlates of classroom seating position. *Journal of Educational Psychology, 71,* 346–354.

Eagly, A. H. (1987). *Sex differences in social behavior: A social-role interpretation.* Hillsdale, NJ: Erlbaum.

Eagly, A. H. (1995). The science and politics of comparing women and men. *American Psychologist, 50*(3), 145–158.

Eagly, A. H., Ashmore, R. D., Makhijani, M. G., & Longo, L. C. (1991). What is beautiful is good, but . . . : A metaanalytic review of research on the physical attractiveness stereotype. *Psychological Bulletin, 110,* 109–128.

Eagly, A. H., & Carli, L. L. (1981). Sex of researchers and sex-typed communications as determinants of sex differences in influencability: A meta-analysis of social influence studies. *Psychological Bulletin, 90,* 1–20.

Eagly, A. H., & Chaiken, S. (1993). *The psychology of attitudes.* Fort Worth, TX: Harcourt Brace Jovanovich.

Eagly, A. H., & Chaiken, S. (1998). Attitude structure and function. In D. Gilbert, S. T. Fiske, & G. Lindzey (Eds.), *Handbook of social psychology* (4th ed., Vol. 2, pp. 269–322). Boston: McGraw-Hill.

Eagly, A. H., & Chrvala, C. (1986). Sex differences in conformity: Status and gender role interpretations. *Psychology of Women Quarterly, 10,* 203–220.

Eagly, A. H., & Crowley, M. (1986). Gender and helping behavior: A metaanalytic view of the social psychological literature. *Psychological Bulletin, 100,* 283–308.

Eagly, A. H., Johannesen-Schmidt, M. C., & Van Engen, M. L. (2003). Transformational, transactional, and laissez-faire leadership styles: A meta-analysis comparing women and men. *Psychological Bulletin, 129,* 569–591.

Eagly, A. H., & Karau, S. J. (1991). Gender and the emergence of leaders: A metaanalysis. *Journal of Personality and Social Psychology, 60,* 685–710.

Eagly, A. H., & Karau, S. J. (2002). Role congruity theory of prejudice toward female leaders. *Psychological Review, 109,* 573–598.

Eagly, A. H., Karau, S. J., & Makhijani, M. G. (1995). Gender and the effectiveness of leaders: A meta-analysis. *Psychological Bulletin, 117,* 125–145.

Eagly, A. H., & Steffen, V. J. (1986). Gender and aggressive behavior: A meta-analytic review of the social psychological literature. *Psychological Bulletin, 100,* 309–330.

Eagly, A. H., & Wood, W. (1999). The origins of sex differences in human behavior: Evolved dispositions versus social roles. *American Psychologist, 54,* 408–423.

Eagly, A. H., Wood, W., & Chaiken, S. (1978). Causal inferences about communicators and their effect on opinion change. *Journal of Personality and Social Psychology, 36,* 424–435.

Eagly, A. H., Wood, W., & Fishbaugh, L. (1981). Sex differences in conformity: Surveillance by the group as a determinant of male nonconformity. *Journal of Personality and Social Psychology, 40,* 384–394.

Eagly, A. H., Wood, W., & Johannesen- Schmidt, M. C. (2004). Social role theory of sex differences and similarities: Implications for the partner preferences of women and men. In A. H. Eagly, A. E. Beall, & R. Sternberg (Eds.), *Psychology of gender* (2nd ed., pp. 269–295). New York: Guilford Press.

Earley, P. C. (1989). Social loafing and collectivism: A comparison of the United States and the People's Republic of China. *Administrative Science Quarterly, 34,* 565–581.

Eberhardt, J. L., Goff, P. A., Purdie, V. J., & Davies, P. G. (2004). Seeing black: Race, crime, and visual processing. *Journal of Personality and Social Psychology, 87,* 876–893.

Eby, L. T., & Dobbins, G. H. (1997). Collectivistic orientation in teams: An individual and group-level analysis. *Journal of Organizational Behavior, 18,* 275–295.

Edinger, J. A., & Patterson, M. L. (1983). Nonverbal involvement and social control. *Psychological Bulletin, 93,* 30–56.

Edwards, J. A., & Weary, G. (1993). Depression and the impression formation continuum: Piecemeal processing despite the availability of category information. *Journal of Personality and Social Psychology, 64,* 636–645.

Edwards, K., & Smith, E. E. (1996). A disconfirmation bias in the evaluation of arguments. *Journal of Personality and Social Psychology, 71,* 5–24.

Efran, M. G., & Patterson, E. W. J. (1974). Voters vote beautiful: The effects of physical appearance on a national election. *Canadian Journal of Behavioral Science, 6,* 352–356.

Efran, M. G., & Patterson, E. W. J. (1976). *The politics of appearance.* Unpublished manuscript, University of Toronto, ON.

Egan, K. J. (1990). What does it mean to a patient to be "in control"? In F. M. Ferrante, G. W. Ostheimer, & B. G. Covino (Eds.), *Patient-controlled analgesia* (pp. 17–26). Boston: Blackwell.

Eibach, R. P., & Ehrlinger, J. (2006). "Keep your eyes on the prize": Reference points and racial differences in assessing progress toward equality. *Personality and Social Psychology Bulletin, 32,* 66–77.

Eibl-Eibesfeldt, I. (1973). The expressive behavior of the deaf-and-blind-born. In M. von Cranach & I. Vine (Eds.), *Social communication and movement* (pp. 163–194). New York: Academic Press.

Eid, M., & Diener, E. (2001). Norms for experiencing emotions in different cultures: Inter- and intra-national differences. *Journal of Personality and Social Psychology, 81,* 869–885.

Einon, D. (1994). Are men more promiscuous than women? *Ethology and Sociobiology, 15,* 131–143.

Eisenberg, N., & Fabes, R. A. (1998). Prosocial development. In W. Damon (Ed.), *Handbook of child psychology* (5th ed., Vol. 3, pp. 701–798). New York: Wiley.

Eisenberg, N., & Miller, P. (1987). The relation of empathy to prosocial and related behaviors. *Psychological Bulletin, 101,* 91–119.

Eisenberger, N. I., Lieberman, M. D., & Williams, K. D. (2003). Does rejection hurt? An fMRI study of social exclusion. *Science, 302,* 290–292.

Eisenstadt, D., Leippe, M. R., Stambush, M. A., Rauch, S. M., & Rivers, J. A. (2005). Dissonance and prejudice. *Basic and Applied Social Psychology, 27,* 127–141.

Ekman, P. (1982). *Emotion in the human face* (2nd ed.). Cambridge, UK: Cambridge University Press.

Ekman, P. (1985). *Telling lies: Clues to deceit in the marketplace, politics, and marriage.* New York: W.W. Norton.

Ekman, P., & Friesen, W. V. (1971). Constants across cultures in the face and emotion. *Journal of Personality and Social Psychology, 17,* 124–129.

Ekman, P., & Friesen, W. V. (1978). *The facial-action coding system.* Palo Alto, CA: Consulting Psychologists Press.

Elfenbein, H. A., & Ambady, N. (2002). On the universality and cultural specificity of emotion recognition: A meta-analysis. *Psychological Bulletin, 128,* 203–235.

Elkin, R. A., & Leippe, M. R. (1986). Physiological arousal, dissonance, and attitude change. *Journal of Personality and Social Psychology, 51,* 55–65.

Elliot, A. J., & Church, M. A. (2003). A motivational analysis of defensive pessimism and self-handicapping. *Journal of Personality, 71,* 369–396.

Elliot, A. J., & Devine, P. G. (1994). On the motivational nature of cognitive dissonance: Dissonance as psychological discomfort. *Journal of Personality and Social Psychology, 67,* 382–394.

Elliot, A. J., & Reis, H. T. (2003). Attachment and exploration in adulthood. *Journal of Personality & Social Psychology, 85,* 317–331.

Ellis, B. J., & Symons, D. (1990). Sex differences in sexual fantasy: An evolutionary psychological approach. *Journal of Sex Research, 27,* 527–555.

Ellis, L. (1986). Evidence of neuroandrogenic etiology of sex roles from a combined analysis of human, nonhuman primate and nonprimate mammalian studies. *Personality and Individual Differences, 7,* 519–552.

Ellsworth, P. C., Haney, C., & Costanzo, M. (2001). Society for the Psychological Study of Social Issues (SPSSI) position statement on the death penalty. *Society for Psychological Study of Social Issues.* Retrieved from www.spssi.org/position-statements.html

Ellsworth, P. C., & Mauro, R. (1998). Psychology and law. In D. T. Gilbert, S. T. Fiske, & G. Lindzey (Eds.), *Handbook of social psychology* (4th ed., Vol. 2, pp. 684–732). New York: McGraw-Hill/Oxford University Press.

Emert, C. (2000, September 2). Olympic seal of approval. *San Francisco Chronicle,* pp. D1–D2.

Emmons, R. A. (1989). The personal striving approach to personality. In L. A. Pervin (Ed.), *Goals concepts in personality and social psychology* (pp. 87–126). Hillsdale, NJ: Erlbaum.

Emmons, R. A., Diener, E., & Larsen, R. J. (1986). Choice and avoidance of everyday situations and affect congruence: Two models of reciprocal interactionism. *Journal of Personality and Social Psychology, 51,* 815–826.

End, C. M., Dietz-Uhler, B., Harrick, E. A., & Jacquemotte, L. (2002). Identifying with winners: A reexamination of sport fans' tendency to BIRG. *Journal of Applied Social Psychology, 32,* 1017–1030.

Engelhardt, C. R., Bartholow, B. D., Kerr, G. T., & Bushman, B. J. (2011). This is your brain on violent video games: Neural desensitization to violence predicts increased aggression following violent video game exposure. *Journal of Experimental Social Psychology, 47*(5), 1033–1036.

English, T., & Chen, S. (2011). Self-concept consistency and culture: The differential impact of two forms of consistency. *Personality and Social Psychology Bulletin, 37*(6), 838–849.

Ensari, N., & Miller, N. (2002). The outgroup must not be so bad after all: The effects of disclosure, typicality, and salience on intergroup bias. *Journal of Personality & Social Psychology, 83,* 313–329.

Epley, N., & Gilovich, T. (2004). Are adjustments insufficient? *Personality and Social Psychology Bulletin, 30,* 447–460.

Epley, N., Keysar, B., Van Boven, L., & Gilovich, T. (2004). Perspective taking as egocentric anchoring and adjustment. *Journal of Personality and Social Psychology, 87,* 327–339.

Epstude, K., & Roese, N. J. (2008). The functional theory of counterfactual thinking. *Personality and Social Psychology Review, 12*, 168–192.

Erber, J. T., & Prager, I. G. (2000). Age and excuses for forgetting: Self-handicapping versus damage-control strategies. *International Journal of Aging and Human Development, 50*, 201–214.

Erber, R., & Fiske, S. T. (1984). Outcome dependency and attention to inconsistent information. *Journal of Personality and Social Psychology, 47*, 709–726.

Ericksen, M. K., & Sirgy, M. J. (1989). Achievement motivation and clothing behavior: A self-image congruence analysis. *Journal of Social Behavior and Personality, 4*, 307–326.

Escasa, M., Gray, P. B., & Patton, J. Q. (2010). Male traits associated with attractiveness in Conambo, Ecuador. *Evolution and Human Behavior, 31*, 193–200.

Estow, S., Jamieson, J. P., & Yates, J. R. (2007). Self-monitoring and mimicry of positive and negative social behaviors. *Journal of Research in Personality, 41*, 425–433.

Evans, A. T., & Clark, J. K. (2012). Source characteristics and persuasion: The role of self-monitoring in self-validation. *Journal of Experimental Social Psychology, 48*(1), 383–386.

Evans, C. R., & Dion, K. L. (2012). Group cohesion and performance a meta-analysis. *Small Group Research, 43*(6), 690–701.

Evans, G. W., & Lepore, S. J. (1993). Household crowding and social support: A quasiexperimental analysis. *Journal of Personality and Social Psychology, 65*, 308–316.

Evans, G. W., Lepore, S. J., & Schroeder, A. (1996). The role of interior design elements in human responses to crowding. *Journal of Personality and Social Psychology, 70*, 41–46.

Evans, G. W., Palsane, M. N., & Carrere, S. (1987). Type A behavior and occupational stress: A cross-cultural study of blue-collar workers. *Journal of Personality and Social Psychology, 52*, 1002–1007.

Evans, G. W., & Wener, R. E. (2007). Crowding and personal space invasion on the train: Please don't make me sit in the middle. *Journal of Environmental Psychology, 27*, 90–94.

Evans, J. S. B. T. (2008). Dual-processing accounts of reasoning, judgment, and social cognition. *Annual Review of Psychology, 59*, 255–278.

Executive Pay by the Numbers. (2013). *The New York Times*. Retrieved June 29, from http://www.nytimes.com/interactive/2013/06/30/business/executive-compensation-tables.html?_r=0

Exline, R. V. (1972). Visual interaction: The glances of power and preference. In J. K. Cole (Ed.), *Nebraska symposium on motivation* (Vol. 19, pp. 163–206). Lincoln: University of Nebraska Press.

Farc, M.-M., & Sagarin, B. S. (2009). Using attitude strength to predict registration and voting behavior in 2004 U. S. presidential elections. *Basic and Applied Social Psychology, 31*, 106–173.

Farrar, E. W. R. (1838). *The young lady's friend; A manual of practical advice and instruction to young females on their entering upon the duties of life after quitting school*. London: John W. Parker.

Fast, J. (1970). *Body language*. New York: M. Evans and Company.

Faulkner, J., Schaller, M., Park, J. H., & Duncan, L. A. (2004). Evolved disease-avoidance mechanisms and contemporary xenophobic attitudes. *Group Processes and Intergroup Relations, 7*, 333–353.

Fazio, R. H. (1987). Self-perception theory: A current perspective. In M. P. Zanna, J. M. Olson, & C. P. Herman (Eds.), *Ontario symposium on personality and social psychology* (pp. 129–150). Hillsdale, NJ: Erlbaum.

Fazio, R. H., Jackson, J. R., Dunton, B. C., & Williams, C. J. (1995). Variability in automatic activation as an unobtrusive measure of racial attitudes: A bona fide pipeline? *Journal of Personality and Social Psychology, 69*, 1013–1027.

Fazio, R. H., & Olson, M. A. (2003). Implicit measures in social cognition research: Their mean-

ing and uses. *Annual Review of Psychology, 54*, 297–327.

Fazio, R. H., & Williams, C. J. (1986). Attitude accessibility as a moderator of the attitude-perception and attitude-behavior relations. *Journal of Personality and Social Psychology, 51*, 505–514.

Fazio, R. H., Zanna, M. P., & Cooper, J. (1977). Dissonance and self-perception. *Journal of Experimental Social Psychology, 13*, 464–479.

Feagin, J. R., & Feagin, C. B. (1999). *Racial and ethnic relations* (6th ed.). Upper Saddle River, NJ: Prentice-Hall.

Feather, N. T. (1998). Reactions to penalties for offenses committed by the police and public citizens: Testing a social-cognitive process model of retributive justice. *Journal of Personality & Social Psychology, 75*, 528–544.

Fehr, B. (1988). Prototype analysis of the concepts of love and commitment. *Journal of Personality and Social Psychology, 55*, 557–579.

Fehr, B. (2006). A prototype approach to studying love. In R. J. Sternberg & K. Weis (Eds.), *The new psychology of love* (pp. 225–248). New Haven, CT: Yale University Press.

Fehr, B., & Russell, J. A. (1991). The concept of love viewed from a prototype perspective. *Journal of Personality and Social Psychology, 60*, 425–438.

Fehr, E., Gachter, S., & Kirchsteiger, G. (1997). Reciprocity as a contract enforcement device. *Econometrica, 65*, 833–860.

Fein, S., & Spencer, S. J. (1997). Prejudice as self-image maintenance: Affirming the self through derogating others. *Journal of Personality and Social Psychology, 73*, 31–44.

Feinberg, D. R., DeBruine, L. M., Jones, B. C., & Little, A. C. (2008, April). Correlated preferences for men's facial and vocal masculinity. *Evolution and Human Behavior, 29*, 233–241.

Feinberg, D. R., Jones, B. C., DeBruine, L. M., Moore, E. R., Smith, M. J. L., Cornwell, R. E., et al. (2005). The voice and face of woman: One ornament that signals quality? *Evolution and Human Behavior, 26*, 398–408.

Feingold, A. (1992). Good-looking people are not what we think. *Psychological Bulletin, 111*, 304–341.

Feldman, R. S., Forrest, J. A., & Happ, B. R. (2002). Self-presentation and verbal deception: Do self-presenters lie more? *Basic and Applied Social Psychology, 24*, 163–170.

Felson, R. B. (1982). Impression management and the escalation of aggression and violence. *Social Psychology Quarterly, 45*, 245–254.

Felson, R. B., & Tedeschi, J. T. (1993). A social interactionist approach to violence: Cross-cultural implications. *Violence and Victims, 8*, 295–310.

Fenigstein, A. (1979). Self-consciousness, self-attention, and social interaction. *Journal of Personality and Social Psychology, 37*, 75–86.

Fenigstein, A., & Abrams, D. (1993). Self-attention and the egocentric assumption of shared perspectives. *Journal of Experimental Social Psychology, 29*, 287–303.

Ferguson, M. J., & Bargh, J. A. (2004). Liking is for doing: The effects of goal pursuit on automatic evaluation. *Journal of Personality and Social Psychology, 87*, 557–572.

Ferrante, F. M., Ostheimer, G. W., & Covino, B. G. (1990). *Patient-controlled analgesia*. Boston: Blackwell Scientific.

Ferrari, J. R. (1991). A second look at behavioral self-handicapping among women. *Journal of Social Behavior and Personality, 6*, 195–206.

Ferris, T. (1997, April 14). The wrong stuff. *The New Yorker*, p. 31.

Feshbach, S. (1984). The catharsis hypothesis, aggressive drive, and the reduction of aggression. *Aggressive Behavior, 10*, 91–101.

Festinger, L. (1954). A theory of social comparison processes. *Human Relations, 7*, 117–140.

Festinger, L. (1957). *A theory of cognitive dissonance*. Stanford, CA: Stanford University Press.

Festinger, L., & Carlsmith, J. M. (1959). Cognitive consequences of forced compliance. *Journal of Abnormal and Social Psychology, 58*, 202–210.

Festinger, L., Pepitone, A., & Newcomb, T. (1952). Some consequences of deindividuation in a group. *Journal of Abnormal and Social Psychology, 47*(#2 Supp.), 382–389.

Festinger, L., Reicken, H. W., & Schachter, S. (1956). *When prophesy fails*. Minneapolis: University of Minnesota Press.

Festinger, L., Schachter, S., & Back, K. (1950). *Social pressures in informal groups*. Stanford, CA: Stanford University Press.

Fiedler, F. E. (1993). The leadership situation and the black box in contingency theories. In M. M. Chemers & R. Ayman (Eds.), *Leadership theory and research: Perspectives and directions* (pp. 1–28). San Diego, CA: Academic Press.

Fiedler, K., Schmid, J., & Stahl, T. (2002). What is the current truth about polygraph lie detection? *Basic and Applied Social Psychology, 24*, 313–324.

Fiedler, K., & Wänke, M. (2009). The cognitive-ecological approach to rationality in social psychology. *Social Cognition, 27*, 699–732.

Fincham, F. D. (2003). Marital conflict: Correlates, structure, and context. *Current Directions in Psychological Science, 12*, 23–27.

Finkel, E. J., Burnette, J. L., & Scissors, L. E. (2007). Vengefully ever after: Destiny beliefs, state attachment anxiety, and forgiveness. *Journal of Personality and Social Psychology, 92*, 871–886.

Finkel, E. J., & Campbell, W. K. (2001). Self-control and accommodation in close relationships: An interdependence analysis. *Journal of Personality & Social Psychology, 81*, 263–277.

Fishbein, M., & Ajzen, I. (1975). *Beliefs, attitude, intention, and behavior: An introduction to theory and research*. Reading, MA: Addison-Wesley.

Fisher, H. (2006). The drive to love: The neural mechanism for mate selection. In R. J. Sternberg & K. Weis (Eds.), *New psychology of love* (pp. 87–115). New Haven: Yale University Press.

Fisher, R. J., Vandenbosch, M., & Anita, K. A. (2008). An empathy-helping perspective on consumers' responses to fund-raising appeals. *Journal of Consumer Research, 35*, 519–531.

Fisher, W. A., & Grenier, G. (1994). Violent pornography, antiwoman thoughts, and antiwoman acts: In search of reliable effects. *Journal of Sex Research, 31*, 23–38.

Fiske, A. P. (1992). The four elementary forms of sociality: Framework for a unified theory of social relations. *Psychological Review, 99*, 689–723.

Fiske, A. P. (2000). Complementarity theory: Why human social capacities evolved to require cultural complements. *Personality & Social Psychology Review, 4*, 76–94.

Fiske, A. P. (2002). Using individualism and collectivism to compare cultures—a critique of the validity and measurement of the constructs: Comment on Oyserman et al. (2002). *Psychological Bulletin, 128*, 78–88.

Fiske, A. P., Kitayama, S., Markus, H. R., & Nisbett, R. E. (1998). The cultural matrix of social psychology. In D. Gilbert, S. T. Fiske, & G. Lindzey (Eds.), *Handbook of social psychology* (4th ed., Vol. 2, pp. 915–981). Boston: McGraw-Hill.

Fiske, S. T. (2004). *Social beings: A core motives approach to social psychology*. Hoboken, NJ: Wiley.

Fiske, S. T., Cuddy, A. J., Glick, P., & Xu, J. (2002). A model of (often mixed) stereotype content: Competence and warmth respectively follow from perceived status and competition. *Journal of Personality and Social Psychology, 82*, 878–902.

Fiske, S. T., & Neuberg, S. L. (1990). A continuum of impression formation, from category-based to individuating processes: Influences of information and motivation on attention and interpretation. In M. P. Zanna (Ed.), *Advances in experimental social psychology* (Vol. 23, pp. 1–74). New York: Academic Press.

Fiske, S. T., & Taylor, S. E. (1991). *Social cognition* (2nd ed.). New York: McGraw-Hill.

Fitzgerald, L. F. (1993). Sexual harassment: Violence against women in the workplace. *American Psychologist, 48*, 1070–1076.

Fleming, J. H., & Darley, J. M. (1991). Mixed messages: The multiple audience problem and strategic communication. *Social Cognition, 9,* 25–46.

Fleming, J. H., & Rudman, L. A. (1993). Between a rock and a hard place: Self-concept regulating and communicative properties of distancing behaviors. *Journal of Personality and Social Psychology, 64,* 44–59.

Fletcher, G. J. O., Simpson, J. A., & Thomas, G. (2000). The measurement of perceived relationship quality components: A confirmatory factor analytic approach. *Personality & Social Psychology Bulletin, 26,* 340–354.

Fletcher, G. J. O., Simpson, J. A., Thomas, G., & Giles, L. (1999). Ideals in intimate relationships. *Journal of Personality & Social Psychology, 76,* 72–89.

Fletcher, G. J. O., Tither, J. M., O'Loughlin, C., Friesen, M., & Overall, N. (2004). Warm and homely or cold and beautiful? Sex differences in trading off traits in mate selection. *Personality and Social Psychology Bulletin, 30,* 659–672.

Flynn, F. J. (2003). How much should I give and how often? The effects of generosity and frequency of favor exchange on social status and productivity. *Academy of Management Journal, 46,* 539–553.

Foddy, M., Smithson, M., Schneider, S., & Hogg, M. (1999). *Resolving social dilemmas: Dynamic, structural, and intergroup aspects.* Philadelphia: Psychology Press.

Ford, C. V. (1996). *Lies! Lies!! Lies!!!: The psychology of deceit.* Washington, DC: American Psychiatric Press.

Ford, T. E. (2000). Effects of sexist humor on tolerance of sexist events. *Personality and Social Psychology Bulletin, 26,* 1094–1107.

Ford, T. E., Ferguson, M. A., Brooks, J. L., & Hagadone, K. M. (2004). Coping sense of humor reduces effects of stereotype threat on women's math performance. *Personality and Social Psychology Bulletin, 30,* 643–653.

Ford, T. E., Wentzel, E. R., & Lorion, J. (2001). Effects of exposure to sexist humor on perceptions of normative tolerance of sexism. *European Journal of Social Psychology, 31,* 677–691.

Forgas, J. P. (1979). *Social episodes: The study of interaction routines.* London: Academic Press.

Forgas, J. P. (1995). The Affect-Infusion Model (AIM). *Psychological Bulletin, 117,* 39–66.

Forgas, J. P., & Bower, G. H. (1987). Mood effects on person perception judgments. *Journal of Personality and Social Psychology, 53,* 53–60.

Forgas, J. P., & East, R. (2008). On being happy and gullible: Mood effects on skepticism and the detection of deception. *Journal of Experimental Social Psychology, 44,* 1362–1367.

Forgas, J. P., & Moylan, S. (1987). After the movies: Transient mood and social judgments. *Personality and Social Psychology Bulletin, 13,* 467–477.

Forge, K. L., & Phemister, S. (1987). The effect of prosocial cartoons on preschool children. *Child Development Journal, 17,* 83–88.

Forsyth, D. R. (1990). *Group dynamics* (2nd ed.). Pacific Grove, CA: Brooks/Cole.

Forsyth, D. R., Schlenker, B. R., Leary, M. R., & McCown, N. E. (1985). Self-presentational determinants of sex differences in leadership behavior. *Small Group Behavior, 16,* 197–210.

Foster, C. A., Witcher, B. S., Campbell, W. K., & Green, J. D. (1998). Arousal and attraction: Evidence for automatic and controlled processes. *Journal of Personality and Social Psychology, 74,* 86–101.

Foushee, M. C. (1984). Dyads and triads at 35,000 feet. *American Psychologist, 39,* 885–893.

Frable, D. E. S., Blackstone, T., & Scherbaum, C. (1990). Marginal and mindful: Deviants in social interaction. *Journal of Personality and Social Psychology, 59,* 140–149.

Fraley, R. C. (2002). Attachment stability from infancy to adulthood: Meta-analysis and dynamic modeling of developmental mechanisms. *Personality & Social Psychology Review, 6,* 123–151.

Fraley, R. C., & Davis, K. E. (1997). Attachment formation and transfer in young adults' close friendships and romantic relationships. *Personal Relationships, 4,* 131–144.

Frank, M. G., & Ekman, P. (1993). Not all smiles are created equal: The differences between enjoyment and nonenjoyment smiles. *Humor, 6,* 9–26.

Frank, R. H., Gilovich, T., & Regan, D. T. (1993). Does studying economics inhibit cooperation? *Journal of Economic Perspectives, 7,* 159–171.

Frazier, P. A., Cochran, C. C., & Olson, A. M. (1995). Social science research on lay definitions of sexual harassment. *Journal of Social Issues, 51,* 21–38.

Fredrickson, B. L. (2001). The role of positive emotions in positive psychology: The broaden-and-build theory of positive emotions. *American Psychologist, 56,* 218–226.

Fredrickson, B. L., & Levenson, R. W. (1998). Positive emotions speed recovery from the cardiovascular sequelae of negative emotions. *Cognition and Emotion, 12,* 191–220.

Fredrickson, B. L., Tugade, M. M., Waugh, C. E., & Larkin, G. R. (2003). What good are positive emotions in crisis? A prospective study of resilience and emotions following the terrorist attacks on the United States on September 11th, 2001. *Journal of Personality and Social Psychology, 84,* 365–376.

Frederico, C. M., & Sidanius, J. (2002). Racism, ideology, and affirmative action revisited: The antecedents and consequences of "principled objections" to affirmative action. *Journal of Personality and Social Psychology, 82*(4), 488–502.

Fehr, B. (2013). The social psychology of love. In J. A. Simpson & L. Campbell (Eds.), *Oxford handbook of close relationships* (pp. 201–288). New York: Oxford University Press.

Ferreira, M., Garcia-Marques, L., Hamilton, D., Ramos, T., Uleman, J. S., & Jerónimo, R. (2012). On the relation between spontaneous inferences and intentional inferences: An inference monitoring hypothesis. *Journal of Experimental Social Psychology, 48,* 1–11.

Fischer, P., Krueger, J. I., Greitemeyer, T., Vogrincic, C., Kastenmüller, A., Frey, D., et al. (2011). The bystander-effect: A meta-analytic review on bystander intervention in dangerous and non-dangerous emergencies. *Psychological Bulletin, 137*(4), 517–537.

Fisher, H. E., Aron, A., & Brown, L. L. (2006). Romantic love: A mammalian brain system for mate choice. *Philosophical Transactions of the Royal Society B: Biological Sciences, 361*(1476), 2173–2186.

Fitness, J., & Williams, V. (2013). The features and functions of positive emotions in close relationships. *Positive Psychology of Love, 44.*

Forgas, J. P. (2013). Don't worry, be sad! On the cognitive, motivational, and interpersonal benefits of negative mood. *Current Directions in Psychological Science, 22*(3), 225–232.

Freedman, J. L., & Fraser, S. C. (1966). Compliance without pressure: The foot-in-the-door technique. *Journal of Personality and Social Psychology, 4,* 195–203.

Freedman, R. E. K., Carter, M. M., Sbrocco, T., & Gray, J. J. (2004). Ethnic differences in preferences for female weight and waist-to-hip ratio: A comparison of African-American and White American college and community samples. *Eating Behaviors, 5,* 191–198.

French, J. R. P., Jr., & Raven, B. (1959). The bases of social power. In D. Cartwright (Ed.), *Studies in social power* (pp. 150–167). Ann Arbor, MI: Institute for Social Research.

Frey, D., & Schulz-Hardt, S. (2001). Confirmation bias in group information seeking and its implications for decision making in administration, business and politics. In F. Butera & G. Mugny (Eds.), *Social influence in social reality: Promoting individual and social change* (pp. 53–73). Ashland, OH: Hogrefe & Huber Publishers.

Friedmann, E., Katcher, A. H., Lynch, J. J., & Thomas, S. A. (1980). Animal companions and one-year survival of patients after discharge from a coronary care unit. *Public Health Reports, 95,* 307–312.

Friedrich-Cofer, L., & Huston, A. (1986). Television violence and aggression: The debate continues. *Psychological Bulletin, 100,* 364–371.

Frieze, I. H., Fisher, J. R., Hanusa, B. H., McHugh, M. C., & Valle, V. H. (1978). Attributions of the causes of success and failure as internal and external barriers to achievement. In J. L. Sherman & F. L. Denmark (Eds.), *The psychology of women: Future directions in research* (pp. 519–552). New York: Psychological Dimensions.

Frieze, I. H., & Ramsey, S. J. (1976). Nonverbal maintenance of traditional sex roles. *Journal of Social Issues, 32,* 133–141.

Frigerio, D., Hirschenhauser, K., Mostl, E., Dittami, J., & Kotrschal, K. (2005). Experimentally elevated testosterone increase status signaling in male Greylag geese (Anser anser). *Acta Ethologica, 7,* 9–18.

Frijda, N. H. (1986). *The emotions.* Cambridge, UK: Cambridge University Press.

Frijda, N. H. (1988). The laws of emotion. *American Psychologist, 43,* 349–358.

Frings, D., Hopthrow, T., Abrams, D., Hulbert, L., & Gutierrez, R. (2008). Groupdrink: The effects of alcohol and group process on vigilance errors. *Group Dynamics: Theory, Research, and Practice, 12,* 179–190.

Fritschler, A. L. (1975). *Smoking and politics.* Englewood Cliffs, NJ: Prentice-Hall.

Fritz, H. L., Nagurney, A. J., & Helgeson, V. S. (2003). Social interactions and cardiovascular reactivity during problem disclosure among friends. *Personality & Social Psychology Bulletin, 29,* 713–725.

Froming, W. J., Nasby, W., & McManus, J. (1998). Prosocial self-schemas, self-awareness, and children's prosocial behavior. *Journal of Personality and Social Psychology, 75,* 766–777.

Fry, D. P. (1990). Play aggression among Zapotec children: Implications for the practice hypothesis. *Aggressive Behavior, 16,* 321–340.

Fry, P. S., & Ghosh, R. (1980). Attributions of success and failure: Comparison of attributional differences between Asian and Caucasian children. *Journal of Cross-Cultural Psychology, 11,* 343–363.

Frye, G. J., Lord, C. G., & Brady, S. E. (2012). Attitude change following imagined positive actions toward a social group: Do memories change attitudes, or attitudes change memories? *Social Cognition, 30*(3), 307–322.

Fu, G., & Lee, K. (2007). Social grooming in the kindergarten: The emergence of flattery behavior. *Developmental Science, 10,* 255–265.

Fu, G., Lee, K., Cameron, C. A., & Xu, F. (2001). Chinese and Canadian adults' categorization and evaluation of lie- and truth-telling about prosocial and antisocial behaviors. *Journal of Cross-Cultural Psychology, 32,* 720–727.

Fultz, J., Batson, C. D., Fortenbach, V. A., McCarthy, P. M., & Varney, L. L. (1986). Social evaluation and the empathy-altruism hypothesis. *Journal of Personality and Social Psychology, 50,* 761–769.

Funder, D. C. (1999). *Personality judgment: A realistic approach to person perception.* San Diego, CA: Academic Press.

Furnham, A. (1996). Factors relating to the allocation of medical resources. *Journal of Social Behavior and Personality, 11,* 615–624.

Furnham, A., Hosoe, T., & Tang, T. L. P. (2002). Male hubris and female humility? A cross-cultural study of ratings of self, parental, and sibling multiple intelligence in America, Britain, and Japan. *Intelligence, 30,* 101–115.

Furnham, A., Mistry, D., & McClelland, A. (2004). The influence of age of the face and the waist to hip ratio on judgments of female attractiveness and traits. *Personality and Individual Differences, 36,* 1171–1185.

Fussell, P. (1983). *Class.* New York: Ballentine.

Gabbay, F. H. (1992). Behavior-genetic strategies in the study of emotion. *Psychological Science, 3,* 50–55.

Gable, S. L., Gonzaga, G. C., & Strachman, A. (2006). Will you be there for me when things go right? Supportive responses to positive event disclosures. *Journal of Personality and Social Psychology, 91,* 904–917.

Gable, S. L., & Haidt, J. (2005). What (and why) is positive psychology? *Review of General Psychology, 9,* 103–110.

Gable, S. L., & Reis, H. T. (1999). Now and then, them and us, this and that: Studying relationships across time, partner, context, and person. *Personal Relationships, 6,* 415–432.

Gabrenya, W. K., Jr., Wang, Y. E., & Latané, B. (1985). Social loafing on an optimizing task: Cross-cultural differences among Chinese and Americans. *Journal of Cross-Cultural Psychology, 16,* 223–242.

Gabriel, S., Carvallo, M., Dean, K. K., Tippin, B., & Renaud, J. (2005). How I see me depends on how I see we: The role of attachment style in social comparison. *Personality and Social Psychology Bulletin, 31,* 1561–1572.

Gaertner, L., Iuzzini, J., & O'Mara, E. M. (2008). When rejection by one fosters aggression against many: Multiplevictim aggression as a consequence of social rejection and perceived groupness. *Journal of Experimental Social Psychology, 44,* 958–970.

Gaertner, L., Iuzzini, J., Witt, M. G., & Oriña, M. M. (2006). Us without them: Evidence for an intragroup origin of positive in-group regard. *Journal of Personality and Social Psychology, 90,* 426–439.

Gaertner, S. L., & Bickman, L. (1971). Effects of race on the elicitation of helping behavior. *Journal of Personality and Social Psychology, 20,* 218–222.

Gaertner, S. L., & Dovidio, J. F. (1977). The subtlety of white racism, arousal, and helping behavior. *Journal of Personality and Social Psychology, 35,* 691–707.

Gaertner, S. L., & Dovidio, J. F. (1986). The aversive form of racism. In J. F. Dovidio & S. L. Gaertner (Eds.), *Prejudice, discrimination, and racism* (pp. 61–89). Orlando, FL: Academic Press.

Gaertner, S. L., Mann, J. A., Dovidio, J. F., Murrell, A. J., & Pomare, M. (1990). How does cooperation reduce intergroup bias? *Journal of Personality and Social Psychology, 59,* 692–704.

Gagnon, A., & Bourhis, R. Y. (1996). Discrimination in the minimal group paradigm: Social identity of self-interest. *Personality and Social Psychology Bulletin, 22,* 1289–1301.

Galanti, G. A. (1993). Reflections on brainwashing. In M. D. Langone (Ed.), *Recovery from cults* (pp. 85–103). New York: Norton.

Galaskiewicz, J. (1985). *Social organization of an urban grants economy: A study of business philanthropy and nonprofit organizations.* New York: Academic Press.

Galin, A., & Avraham, S. (2009). A crosscultural perspective on aggressiveness in the workplace: A comparison between Jews and Arabs in Israel. *Cross-Cultural Research, 43,* 30–45.

Galinsky, A. D., & Kray, L. J. (2004). From thinking about what might have been to sharing what we know: The effects of counterfactual mindsets on information sharing in groups. *Journal of Experimental Social Psychology, 40,* 606–618.

Galinsky, A. D., & Moskowitz, G. B. (2000). Perspective-taking: Decreasing stereotype expression, stereotype accessibility, and in-group favoritism. *Journal of Personality and Social Psychology, 78,* 708–724.

Gallup, G. H., Jr. (2003, October 7). *Personal contact affects teen views of Muslims.* Princeton, NJ: Gallup Organization.

Galton, F. (1875). The history of twins as a criterion of the relative power of nature and nurture. *Journal of the Anthropological Institute, 5,* 391–406.

Gangestad, S. W., Garver-Apgar, C. E., Simpson, J. A., & Cousins, A. J. (2007). Changes in women's mate preferences across the ovulatory cycle. *Journal of Personality and Social Psychology, 92,* 151–163.

Gangestad, S. W., Haselton, M. G., & Buss, D. M. (2006). Evolutionary foundations of cultural variation: Evoked culture and mate preferences. *Psychological Inquiry, 17,* 75–95.

Gangestad, S. W., & Simpson, J. A. (2000). The evolution of human mating: Tradeoffs and strategic pluralism. *Behavioral & Brain Sciences, 23,* 573–587.

Gangestad, S. W., Simpson, J. A., Cousins, A. J., Garver-Apgar, C. E., & Christensen, P. N. (2004). Women's preferences for male behavioral displays change across the menstrual cycle. *Psychological Science, 15,* 203–206.

Gangestad, S. W., & Snyder, M. (1985). To carve nature at its joints: On the existence of discrete classes in personality. *Psychological Review, 92,* 317–349.

Gangestad, S. W., & Snyder, M. (2000). Self-monitoring: Appraisal and reappraisal. *Psychological Bulletin, 126,* 530–555.

Gangestad, S. W., & Thornhill, R. (1997). Human sexual selection and developmental stability. In J. A. Simpson & D. T. Kenrick (Eds.), *Evolutionary social psychology* (pp. 169–196). Hillsdale, NJ: Erlbaum.

Gangestad, S. W., Thornhill, R., & Garver-Apgar, C. E. (2002). Changes in women's sexual interests and their partners' mate retention tactics across the menstrual cycle: Evidence for shifting conflicts of interest. *Proceedings of the Royal Society of London, B, 269,* 975–982.

Gangestad, S. W., Thornhill, R., & Garver-Apgar, C. E. (2010). Men's facial masculinity predicts changes in their female partners' sexual interests across the ovulatory cycle, whereas men's intelligence does not. *Evolution and Human Behavior, 31,* 412–424.

Gannon, K. M., Skowronski, J. J., & Betz, A. L. (1994). Depressive diligence in social information processing: Implications for order effects in impressions and for social memory. *Social Cognition, 12,* 263–280.

Ganor, S. (1995). *Light one candle.* New York: Kodansha.

Gantner, A. B., & Taylor, S. P. (1992). Human physical aggression as a function of alcohol and threat of harm. *Aggressive Behavior, 18,* 29–36.

Garcia, S. M., Weaver, K., Moskowitz, G. B., & Darley, J. M. (2002). Crowded minds: The implicit bystander effect. *Journal of Personality and Social Psychology, 83,* 843–853.

Gardikiotis, A. (2011). Minority influence. *Social and Personality Psychology Compass, 5(9),* 679–693.

Gardner, G. T., & Stern, P. C. (1996). *Environmental problems and human behavior.* Boston: Allyn & Bacon.

Gardner, W. L., Gabriel, S., & Hochschild, L. (2002). When you and I are "we," you are not threatening: The role of self-expansion in social comparison. *Journal of Personality & Social Psychology, 82,* 239–251.

Gardner, W. L., Pickett, C. L., & Brewer, M. B. (2000). Social exclusion and selective memory: How the need to belong influences memory for social events. *Personality & Social Psychology Bulletin, 26,* 486–496.

Gardner, W. L., Reithel, B. J., Cogliser, C. C., Walumbwa, F. O., & Foley, R. T. (2012). Matching personality and organizational culture effects of recruitment strategy and the five-factor model on subjective person-organization fit. *Management Communication Quarterly, 26(4),* 585–622.

Garner, R. L. (2005). Post-it note persuasion: A sticky influence. *Journal of Consumer Psychology, 15,* 230–237.

Garrow, D. J. (1986). *Bearing the cross: Martin Luther King, Jr., and the Southern Christian Leadership Conference.* New York: Vintage Books.

Garry, M., & Polaschek, D. L. L. (2000). Imagination and memory. *Current Directions in Psychological Science, 9,* 6–10.

Garver-Apgar, C. E., Gangestad, S. W., & Thornhill, R. (2008). Hormonal correlates of women's mid-cycle preference for the scent of symmetry. *Evolution and Human Behavior, 29,* 223–232.

Gawronski, B. (2012). Back to the future of dissonance theory: Cognitive consistency as a core motive. *Social Cognition, 30(6),* 652–668.

Gawronski, B., Walther, E., & Blank, H. (2005). Cognitive consistency and the formation of interpersonal attitudes: Cognitive balance affects the encoding of social information. *Journal of Experimental Social Psychology, 41,* 618–626.

Geary, D. C. (2000). Evolution and proximate expression of human paternal investment. *Psychological Bulletin, 126,* 55–77.

Geary, D. C. (2005). Evolution of paternal investment. In D. M. Buss (Ed.), *Handbook of evolutionary psychology* (pp. 483–505). New York: Wiley.

Geary, D. C. (2008). Evolution of fatherhood. In C. A. Salmon & T. K. Shackelford (Eds.), *Family relationships: An evolutionary perspective* (pp. 115–144). New York: Oxford University Press.

Geary, D. C., & Flinn, M. V. (2002). Sex differences in behavioral and hormonal response to social threat: Commentary on Taylor et al. (2000). *Psychological Review, 109,* 745–750.

Geis, F. L. (1993). Self-fulfilling prophecies: A social psychological view of gender. In A. E. Beall & R. J. Sternberg (Eds.), *The psychology of gender* (pp. 9–54). New York: Guilford Press.

Geizer, R. S., Rarick, D. L., & Soldow, G. F. (1977). Deception and judgment accuracy: A study in person perception. *Personality and Social Psychology Bulletin, 3,* 446–449.

Gelfand, M. J., Chiu, C. Y., & Hong, Y. Y. (2014). *Advances in culture and psychology* (Vol. 3). New York: Oxford University Press.

Gelfand, M. J., Raver, J. L., Nishii, L., Leslie, L. M., Lun, J., Lim, B. C., et al. (2011). Differences between tight and loose cultures: A 33-nation study. *Science, 332(6033),* 1100–1104.

Geller, E. S. (1992). Applied behavior analysis and social marketing: An integration for environmental preservation. *Journal of Social Issues, 45(1),* 17–36.

Gentry, C. (1991). *J. Edgar Hoover: The man and his secrets.* New York: W.W. Norton.

Gerard, H. B., & Rabbie, J. M. (1961). Fear and social comparison. *Journal of Abnormal and Social Psychology, 62,* 586–592.

Gergen, K. J., Ellsworth, P., Maslach, C., & Seipel, M. (1975). Obligation, donor resources, and reactions to aid in three cultures. *Journal of Personality and Social Psychology, 31,* 390–400.

Gergen, M. (1990). Beyond the evil empire: Horseplay and aggression. *Aggressive Behaviour, 16,* 381–398.

Gergen, M., & Gergen, K. (1983). Interpretive dimensions of international aid. In A. Nadler, J. D. Fisher, & B. M. DePaulo (Eds.), *New directions in helping* (Vol. 3, pp. 32–348). New York: Academic Press.

Gershoff, E. T. (2002). Corporal punishment by parents and associated child behaviors and experiences: A meta-analytic and theoretical review. *Psychological Bulletin, 128,* 539–579.

Giacalone, R. A. (1985). On slipping when you thought you had put your best foot forward: Self-promotion, selfdestruction, and entitlements. *Group and Organization Studies, 10,* 61–80.

Giacalone, R. A., & Riordan, C. A. (1990). Effect of self-presentation on perceptions and recognition in an organization. *The Journal of Psychology, 124,* 25–38.

Giancola, P. R., & Corman, M. D. (2007). Alcohol and aggression: A test of the attention-allocation model. *Psychological Science, 18,* 649–655.

Gibbons, F. X., Benbow, C. P., & Gerrard, M. (1994). From top dog to bottom half: Social comparison strategies in response to poor performance. *Journal of Personality and Social Psychology, 67,* 638–652.

Gibbons, F. X., & Gerrard, M. (1989). Effects of upward and downward social comparison on mood states. *Journal of Social and Clinical Psychology, 8,* 14–31.

Gibbons, F. X., & McCoy, S. B. (1991). Self-esteem, similarity, and reactions to active versus downward social comparison. *Journal of Personality and Social Psychology, 60,* 414–424.

Gibbons, F. X., & Wicklund, R. A. (1982). Self-focused attention and helping behavior. *Journal of Personality and Social Psychology, 43,* 462–474.

Gibson, B. (2008). Can evaluative conditioning change attitudes toward mature brands? New evidence from the implicit association test. *Journal of Consumer Research, 35,* 178–188.

Gibson, B., & Sachau, D. (2000). Sandbagging as a self-presentational strategy: Claiming to be less than you are. *Personality and Social Psychology Bulletin, 26,* 56–70.

Gibson, J. J. (1979). *The ecological approach to visual perception.* Boston: Houghton Mifflin.

Gilbert, D. T., & Hixon, J. G. (1991). The trouble of thinking: Activation and application of stereotypic beliefs. *Journal of Personality and Social Psychology, 60,* 509–517.

Gilbert, D. T., & Malone, P. S. (1995). The correspondence bias. *Psychological Bulletin, 117,* 21–38.

Gilbert, D. T., Pelham, B. W., & Krull, D. S. (1988). On cognitive busyness: When person perceivers meet persons perceived. *Journal of Personality and Social Psychology, 54,* 733–740.

Gilbert, D. T., Tafarodi, R. W., & Malone, P. S. (1993). You can't not believe everything you read. *Journal of Personality and Social Psychology, 65,* 221–233.

Gilbert, P. (1994). Male violence: Towards an integration. In J. Archer (Ed.), *Male violence* (pp. 352–389). New York: Routledge.

Gildersleeve, K. A., DeBruine, L., Haselton, M. G., Frederick, D. A., Penton-Voak, I. S., Jones, B. C., et al. (2013). Shifts in women's mate preferences across the ovulatory cycle: A critique of Harris (2011) and Harris (2012). *Sex Roles, 69,* 516–524.

Gildersleeve, K. A., Haselton, M. G., & Fales, M. (2014). Do women's mate preferences change across the ovulatory cycle? A meta-analytic review. *Psychological Bulletin.* Retrieved from http://dx.doi.org/10.1037/a0035438

Gilligan, C. (1982). *In a different voice.* Cambridge, MA: Harvard University Press.

Gilmartin, B. G. (1987). *Shyness and love: Causes, consequences, and treatment.* Lanham, MD: University Press of America.

Gilovich, T., Medvec, V. H., & Savitsky, K. (2000). The spotlight effect in social judgment: An egocentric bias in estimates of the salience of one's own actions and appearance. *Journal of Personality & Social Psychology, 78,* 211–222.

Giner-Sorolla, R., & Chaiken, S. (1994). The causes of hostile media judgments. *Journal of Experimental Social Psychology, 30,* 165–180.

Ginges, J., Hansen, I., & Norenzayan, A. (2009). Religion and support for suicide attacks. *Psychological Science, 20,* 224–230.

Gjerde, P. F., Onishi, M., & Carlson, K. S. (2004). Personality characteristics associated with romantic attachment: A comparison of interview and self-report methodologies. *Personality and Social Psychology Bulletin, 30,* 1402–1415.

Gladis, M. M., Michela, J. L., Walter, H. J., & Vaughan, R. D. (1992). High school students' perceptions of AIDS risk: Realistic appraisal or motivated denial? *Health Psychology, 11,* 307–316.

Glasman, L. R., & Albarracin, D. (2006). Forming attitudes that predict future behavior. *Psychological Bulletin, 132,* 778–822.

Glick, P., & Fiske, S. T. (1996). The Ambivalent Sexism Inventory: Differentiating hostile and benevolent sexism. *Journal of Personality and Social Psychology, 70,* 491–512.

Glickman, S. E., Frank, L. G., Holekamp, K. E., & Licht, P. (1993). Costs and benefits of "androgenization" in the female spotted hyena. In P. Bateson & P. H. Klopfer (Eds.), *Behavior and evolution: Perspectives in ethology* (Vol. 10, pp. 87–117). New York: Plenum.

Gockel, C., Kerr, N. L., Seok, D.-H., & Harris, D. W. (2008). Indispensability and group identification as sources of task motivation. *Journal of Experimental Social Psychology, 44,* 1316–1321.

Godfrey, D. K., Jones, E. E., & Lord, C. G. (1986). Self-promotion is not ingratiating. *Journal of Personality and Social Psychology, 50,* 106–115.

Goethals, G. R., & Zanna, M. P. (1979). The role of social comparison in choice shifts. *Journal of Personality and Social Psychology, 37,* 1469–1476.

Goffman, E. (1959). *The presentation of self in everyday life.* New York: Anchor Books.

Golby, A. J., Gabrieli, J. D. E., Chiao, J. Y., & Eberhardt, J. L. (2001). Differential responses in the fusiform region to same-race and other-race faces. *Nature Neuroscience, 4,* 845–850.

Goldberg, J. A. (1990). Interrupting the discourse on interruptions: An analysis in terms of relationally neutral, power- and rapport-oriented acts. *Journal of Pragmatics, 14,* 883–903.

Goldin, C., & Rouse, C. (2000). Orchestrating impartiality: The impact of "blind" auditions on female musicians. *American Economic Review, 90,* 715–741.

Goldstein, D. G., & Gigerenzer, G. (2002). Models of ecological rationality: The recognition heuristic. *Psychological Review, 109,* 75–90.

Goldstein, J. H. (1986). *Aggression and crimes of violence* (2nd ed.). New York: Oxford University Press.

Goldstein, N. J., Cialdini, R. B., & Griskevicius, V. (2008). A room with a viewpoint: Using normative appeals to motivate environmental conservation in a hotel setting. *Journal of Consumer Research, 35,* 472–482.

Gollwitzer, P. M., Heckhausen, H., & Steller, B. (1990). Deliberative versus implemental mindsets. *Journal of Personality and Social Psychology, 59,* 1119–1127.

Gonnerman, M. E., Jr., Parker, C. P., Lavine, H., & Huff, J. (2000). The relationship between self-discrepancies and affective states: The moderating roles of self-monitoring and standpoints on the self. *Personality and Social Psychology Bulletin, 26,* 810–819.

Gonzaga, G. C., Campos, B., & Bradbury, T. (2007). Similarity, convergence, and relationship satisfaction in dating and married couples. *Journal of Personality and Social Psychology, 93,* 34–48.

Gonzaga, G. C., Haselton, M. G., Smurda, J., Davies, M., & Poore, J. C. (2008). Love, desire, and the suppression of thoughts of romantic alternatives. *Evolution and Human Behavior, 29,* 119–126.

Gonzales, M. H., & Meyers, S. A. (1993). "Your mother would like me": Self-presentation in the personal ads of heterosexual and homosexual men and women. *Personality and Social Psychology Bulletin, 19,* 131–142.

Gonzales, P. M., Blanton, H., & Williams, K. J. (2002). The effects of stereotype threat and double-minority status on the test performance of Latino women. *Personality and Social Psychology Bulletin, 28,* 659–670.

Goodman, J. A., Schell, J., Alexander, M. G., & Eidelman, S. (2008). The impact of a derogatory remark on prejudice toward a gay male leader. *Journal of Applied Social Psychology, 38,* 542–555.

Gordijn, E., De Vries, N. K., & De Dreu, C. K. W. (2002). Minority influence on focal and related attitudes: Change in size, attributions, and information processing. *Personality and Social Psychology Bulletin, 28,* 1315–1326.

Gordon, A. M., Impett, E. A., Kogan, A., Oveis, C., & Keltner, D. (2012). To have and to hold: Gratitude promotes relationship maintenance in intimate bonds. *Journal of Personality and Social Psychology, 103*(2), 257–274.

Gordon, R. A. (1996). Impact of ingratiation on judgments and evaluations: A meta-analytic investigation. *Journal of Personality and Social Psychology, 71,* 54–70.

Gottlieb, B. H. (1994). Social support. In A. L. Weber & J. H. Harvey (Eds.), *Perspectives on close relationships* (pp. 307–324). Boston: Allyn & Bacon.

Gottman, J. M., & Levenson, R. W. (1992). Marital processes predictive of later dissolution: Behavior, physiology, and health. *Journal of Personality and Social Psychology, 63*(2), 221.

Gould, J. L., & Gould, C. L. (1989). *Sexual selection.* New York: Scientific American Library.

Gouldner, A. W. (1960). The norm of reciprocity: A preliminary statement. *American Sociological Review, 25,* 161–178.

Gracia, E., & Herrero, J. (2004). Personal and situational determinants of relationship-specific perceptions of social support. *Social Behavior and Personality, 32,* 459–447.

Gracian, B. (1649/1945). *The art of worldly wisdom.* New York: Charles Thomas.

Graham, S. M., & Clark, M. S. (2006). Self-esteem and organization of valenced information about others: The "Jekyll and Hyde"-ing of relationship partners. *Journal of Personality and Social Psychology, 90,* 652–665.

Gray, P. B., Campbell, B. C., Marlowe, F. W., Lipson, S. F., & Ellison, P. T. (2004a). Social variables predict between-subject but not day-to-day variation in the testosterone of U.S. men. *Psychoneuroendocrinology, 29,* 1153–1162.

Gray, P. B., Chapman, J. F., Burnham, T. C., McIntyre, M. H., Lipson, S. F., & Ellison, P. T. (2004b). Human male pair bonding and testosterone. *Human Nature, 15,* 119–131.

Gray, P. B., Kahlenberg, S. M., Barrett, E. S., Lipson, S. F., & Ellison, P. T. (2002). Marriage and fatherhood are associated with lower testosterone in males. *Evolution & Human Behavior, 23,* 193–201.

Graybar, S. R., Antonuccio, D. O., Boutilier, L. R., & Varble, D. L. (1989). Psychological reactance as a factor affecting patient compliance to physician advice. *Scandinavian Journal of Behaviour Therapy, 18,* 43–51.

Graziano, W. G., & Eisenberg, N. (1997). Agreeableness: A dimension of personality. In R. Hogan, J. Johnson, & S. Briggs (Eds.), *Handbook of personality psychology* (pp. 795–824). San Diego, CA: Academic Press.

Graziano, W. G., Habashi, M. M., Sheese, B. E., & Tobin, R. M. (2007). Agreeableness, empathy, and helping: A person X situation perspective. *Journal of Personality and Social Psychology, 93,* 583–599.

Graziano, W. G., Hair, E. C., & Finch, J. F. (1997). Competitiveness mediates the link between personality and group performance. *Journal of Personality and Social Psychology, 73,* 1394–1408.

Green, B. L., & Kenrick, D. T. (1994). The attractiveness of gender-typed traits at different relationship levels: Androgynous characteristics may be desirable after all. *Personality and Social Psychology Bulletin, 20,* 244–253.

Green, J. D., & Campbell, W. K. (2000). Attachment and exploration in adults: Chronic and contextual accessibility. *Personality & Social Psychology Bulletin, 26,* 452–461.

Green, M. C., Hilken, J., Friedman, H., Grossman, K., Gasiewski, J., Adler, R., et al. (2005). Communication via instant messenger: Short- and long-term effects. *Journal of Applied Social Psychology, 35,* 487–507.

Greenberg, J. (1985). Unattainable goal choice as a self-handicapping strategy. *Journal of Applied Social Psychology, 15,* 140–152.

Greenberg, J., & Baron, R. A. (1993). *Behavior in organizations* (4th ed.). Boston: Allyn & Bacon.

Greenberg, J., Pyszczynski, T., & Solomon, S. (1982). The self-serving attributional bias: Beyond self-presentation. *Journal of Experimental Social Psychology, 18,* 56–67.

Greenberg, J., Pyszczynski, T., Solomon, S., Rosenblatt, A., Veeder, M., Kirkland, S., et al. (1990). Evidence for Terror Management Theory II: The effects of mortality salience on reactions to those who threaten or bolster the cultural worldview. *Journal of Personality and Social Psychology, 58,* 308–318.

Greenberg, J., Schimel, J., Martens, A., Pyszczynski, T., & Solomon, S. (2001). Sympathy for the devil: Evidence that reminding whites of their mortality promotes more favorable reactions to white racists. *Motivation and Emotion, 25,* 113–133.

Greenberg, M. S., & Westcott, D. R. (1983). Indebtedness as a mediator of reactions to aid. In J. D. Fisher, A. Nadler, & B. M. DePaulo (Eds.), *New directions in helping behavior* (Vol. 1, pp. 113–141). San Diego, CA: Academic Press.

Greenwald, A. G. (1968). Cognitive learning, cognitive response to persuasion, and attitude change. In A. G. Greenwald, T. C. Brock, & T. M. Ostrom (Eds.), *Psychological foundations of attitudes* (pp. 147–170). New York: Academic Press.

Greenwald, A. G., Banaji, M. R., Rudman, L. A., Farnham, S. D., Nosek, B. A., & Mellott, D. S. (2002). A unified theory of implicit attitudes, stereotypes, self-esteem, and self-concept. *Psychological Review, 109,* 3–25.

Greenwald, A. G., McGhee, D. E., & Schwartz, J. L. K. (1998). Measuring individual differences in implicit cognition: The implicit association test. *Journal of Personality and Social Psychology, 74,* 1464–1480.

Greenwald, A. G., Nosek, B. A., & Sriram, N. (2006). Consequential validity of the implicit association test: Comment on Blanton and Jaccard (2006). *American Psychologist, 61,* 56–61.

Greenwald, A. G., Oakes, M. A., & Hoffman, H. G. (2003). Targets of discrimination: Effects of race on responses to weapons holders. *Journal of Experimental Social Psychology, 39,* 399–405.

Greenwald, A. G., Pickrell, J. E., & Farnham, S. D. (2002). Implicit partisanship: Taking sides for no reason. *Journal of Personality & Social Psychology, 83,* 367–379.

Gregg, A. P., Seibt, B., & Banaji, M. R. (2006). Easier done than undone: Asymmetry in the malleability of implicit preferences. *Journal of Personality and Social Psychology, 90,* 1–20.

Gregory, S. W., & Webster, S. (1996). A nonverbal signal in voices of interview partners effectively predicts communication accommodation and social status perceptions. *Journal of Personality and Social Psychology, 70,* 1231–1240.

Gregory, W. L., Burroughs, W. J., & Ainslie, F. M. (1985). Self-relevant scenarios as indirect means of attitude change. *Personality and Social Psychology Bulletin, 11,* 435–444.

Greiling, H., & Buss, D. M. (2000). Women's sexual strategies: The hidden dimension of extra-pair mating. *Personality & Individual Differences, 28,* 929–963.

Greitemeyer, T. (2005). Receptivity to sexual offers as a function of sex, socioeconomic status, physical attractiveness, and intimacy of the offer. *Personal Relationships, 12,* 373–386.

Greve, W., & Wentura, D. (2003). Immunizing the self: Self-concept stabilization through reality-adaptive self-definitions. *Personality and Social Psychology Bulletin, 29,* 39–50.

Griffitt, W. (1970). Environmental effects on interpersonal behavior: Ambient effective temperature and attraction. *Journal of Personality and Social Psychology, 15,* 240–244.

Grimes, W. (1997, October 15). In the war against no-shows, restaurants get together. *New York Times,* p. f11.

Griskevicius, V., Cialdini, R. B., & Kenrick, D. T. (2006). Peacocks, Picasso, and parental investment: The effects of romantic motives on creativity. *Journal of Personality & Social Psychology, 91,* 63–76.

Griskevicius, V., Delton, A. W., Robertson, T. E., & Tybur, J. M. (2011). Environmental contingency in life history strategies: The influence of mortality and socioeconomic status on reproductive timing. *Journal of Personality and Social Psychology, 100,* 241–254.

Griskevicius, V., Goldstein, N., Mortensen, C., Cialdini, R. B., & Kenrick, D. T. (2006). Going along versus going alone: When fundamental motives facilitate strategic (non)conformity. *Journal of Personality and Social Psychology, 91,* 281–294.

Griskevicius, V., Goldstein, N. J., Mortensen, C. R., Sundie, J. M., Cialdini, R. B., & Kenrick, D. T.

(2009). Fear and loving in Las Vegas: Evolution, emotion, and persuasion. *Journal of Marketing Research, 46*(3), 384–395.

Griskevicius, V., Tybur, J. M., Ackerman, J. M., Delton, A. W., Robertson, T. E., & White, A. E. (2012). The financial consequences of too many men: Sex ratio effects on saving, borrowing, and spending. *Journal of Personality and Social Psychology, 102*(1), 69.

Griskevicius, V., Tybur, J. M., Gangestad, S. W., Perea, E. F., Shapiro, J. R., & Kenrick, D. T. (2009). Aggress to impress: Hostility as an evolved context-dependent strategy. *Journal of Personality and Social Psychology, 96,* 980–994.

Griskevicius, V., Tybur, J. M., Sundie, J. M., Cialdini, R. B., Miller, G. F., & Kenrick, D. T. (2007). Blatant benevolence and conspicuous consumption: When romantic motives elicit strategic costly signals. *Journal of Personality and Social Psychology, 93,* 85–102.

Griskevicius, V., Tybur, J. M., & van den Bergh, B. (2010). Going green to be seen: Status, reputation, and conspicuous conservation. *Journal of Personality and Social Psychology, 98*(3), 392–404.

Groom, C. J., & Pennebaker, J. W. (2005). The language of love: Sex, sexual orientation, and language use in online personal advertisements. *Sex Roles, 52,* 447–461.

Gross, J. J., John, O. P., & Richards, J. M. (2000). The dissociation of emotion expression from emotion experience: A personality perspective. *Personality and Social Psychology Bulletin, 26,* 712–726.

Grube, J. A., & Piliavin, J. A. (2000). Role identity, organizational experiences, and volunteer performance. *Personality and Social Psychology Bulletin, 26,* 1108–1119.

Gruner, S. L. (1996, November). Reward good consumers. *Inc.,* p. 84.

Grusec, J. E. (1991). The socialization of empathy. In M. S. Clark (Ed.), *Review of personality and social psychology* (Vol. 12, pp. 9–33). Newbury Park, CA: Sage.

Grusec, J. E., Kuczynski, L., Rushton, J. P., & Simutis, Z. M. (1978). Modeling, direct instruction, and attributions: Effects on altruism. *Developmental Psychology, 14,* 51–57.

Grusec, J. E., & Redler, E. (1980). Attribution, reinforcement, and altruism: A developmental analysis. *Developmental Psychology, 16,* 525–534.

Guadagno, R. E., Okdie, B. M., & Eno, C. A. (2008). Who blogs: Personality predictors of blogging. *Computers in Human Behavior, 24,* 1993–2004.

Gudjonsson, G. H. (1988). How to defeat the polygraph tests. In A. Gale (Ed.), *The polygraph test: Lies, truth and science* (pp. 126–136). London: Sage.

Gudjonsson, G. H. (2003). *The psychology of interrogations and confessions: A handbook.* New York: Wiley.

Guadagno, R. E., Muscanell, N. L., Rice, L. M., & Roberts, N. (2013). Social influence online: The impact of social validation and likability on compliance. *Psychology of Popular Media Culture, 2*(1), 51–60. Retrieved from http://dx.doi .org/10.1037/a0030592

Guéguen, N., Meineri, S., Martin, A., & Grandjean, I. (2010). The combined effect of the foot-in-the-door technique and the "but you are free" technique: An evaluation on the selective sorting of household wastes. *Ecopsychology, 2*(4), 231–237.

Gueguen, N., & Pascual, A. (2000). Evocation of freedom and compliance: The "but you are free of . . ." technique. *Current Research in Social Psychology, 5,* 264–270.

Guéguen, N., & Pascual, A. (2013). Low-ball and compliance: Commitment even if the request is a deviant one. *Social Influence,* (ahead-of-print), 1–10.

Guenther, C. L., & Alicke, M. D. (2008). Self-enhancement and belief perseverance. *Journal of Experimental Social Psychology, 44,* 706–712.

Guerin, B. (1993). *Social facilitation.* Paris: Cambridge University Press.

Guerin, B. (1994). What do people think about the risks of driving? *Journal of Applied Social Psychology, 24,* 994–1021.

Guimond, S. (2000). Group socialization and prejudice: The social transmission of intergroup attitudes and beliefs. *European Journal of Social Psychology, 30,* 335–354.

Guimond, S., Dambrun, M., Michinov, N., & Duarte, S. (2003). Does social dominance generate prejudice? Integrating individual and contextual determinants of intergroup cognitions. *Journal of Personality and Social Psychology, 84,* 697–721.

Guimond, S., Dif, S., & Aupy, A. (2002). Social identity, relative group status and intergroup attitudes: When favourable outcomes change intergroup relations . . . for the worse. *European Journal of Social Psychology, 32,* 739–760.

Guinote, A. (2008). Power and affordances: When the situation has more power over powerful than powerless individuals. *Journal of Personality and Social Psychology, 95,* 237–252.

Gully, S. M., Devine, D. J., & Whitney, D. J. (1995). A meta-analysis of cohesion and performance: Effects of level of analysis and task interdependence. *Small Group Research, 26,* 497–520.

Gump, B. B., & Kulik, J. A. (1997). Stress, affiliation, and emotional contagion. *Journal of Personality and Social Psychology, 72,* 305–319.

Guroff, G., & Grant, S. (1981). *Soviet elites: World view and perceptions of the U.S.* (USICA Report No. R-18-81). Washington, DC: Office of Research, United States International Communication Agency.

Gustafson, R. (1992). Alcohol and aggression: A replication study controlling for potential confounding variables. *Aggressive Behavior, 18,* 21–28.

Gutentag, M., & Secord, P. F. (1983). *Too many women? The sex ratio question.* Beverly Hills, CA: Sage.

Gutierres, S. E., Kenrick, D. T., & Partch, J. J. (1999). Beauty, dominance, and the mating game: Contrast effects in selfassessment reflect gender differences in mate selection. *Personality & Social Psychology Bulletin, 25,* 1126–1134.

Hackman, J. R., & Morris, C. G. (1975). Group tasks, group interaction process, and group performance effectiveness: A review and proposed integration. In L. Berkowitz (Ed.), *Advances in experimental social psychology* (Vol. 8, pp. 47–99). New York: Academic Press.

Hackman, J. R., & Oldham, G. R. (1980). *Work redesign.* Reading, MA: Addison-Wesley.

Haddock, G., Zanna, M. P., & Esses, V. M. (1993). Assessing the structure of prejudicial attitudes: The case of attitudes toward homosexuals. *Journal of Personality and Social Psychology, 65,* 1105–1118.

Haddock, G., Zanna, M. P., & Esses, V. M. (1994). The (limited) role of trait-laden stereotypes in predicting attitudes toward Native peoples. *British Journal of Social Psychology, 33,* 83–106.

Haidt, J. (2001). The emotional dog and its rational tail: A social intuitionist approach to moral judgment. *Psychological Review, 108,* 814–834.

Hald, G. M., & Høgh-Olesen, H. (2010). Receptivity to sexual invitations from strangers of the opposite gender. *Evolution and Human Behavior, 31,* 453–458.

Halevy, N., Bornstein, G., & Sagiv, L. (2008). "In-group love" and "out-group hate" as motives for individual participation in intergroup conflict: A new game paradigm. *Psychological Science, 19,* 405–411.

Haley, H., & Sidanius, J. (2005). Person-organization congruence and the maintenance of group-based social hierarchy: A social dominance perspective. *Group Processes and Intergroup Relations, 8,* 187–203.

Hall, J. A., Carter, J. D., & Horgan, T. G. (2001). Status roles and recall of nonverbal cues. *Journal of Nonverbal Behavior, 25,* 79–100.

Hall, J. A., Coats, E. J., & LeBeau, L. S. (2005). Nonverbal behavior and the vertical dimension of social relations: A meta-analysis. *Psychological Bulletin, 131,* 898–924.

Hall, J. A., & Friedman, G. B. (1999). Status, gender, and nonverbal behavior: A study of structured interactions between employees of a company. *Personality and Social Psychology Bulletin, 25*(9), 1082–1091.

Hall, J. A., & Halberstadt, A. G. (1986). Smiling and gazing. In J. S. Hyde & M. C. Linn (Eds.), *The psychology of gender: Advances through meta-analysis* (pp. 136–158). Baltimore: Johns Hopkins University Press.

Hamann, S., Herman, R. A., Nolan, C. L., & Wallen, K. (2004). Men and women differ in amygdala response to visual sexual stimuli. *Nature Neuroscience, 7*, 411–416.

Hamby, S. (2009). The gender debate about intimate partner violence: Solutions and dead ends. *Psychological Trauma: Theory, Research, Practice, and Policy, 1*(1), 24.

Hamermesh, D., & Biddle, J. E. (1994). Beauty and the labor market. *The American Economic Review, 84*, 1174–1194.

Hames, J. L., Hagan, C. R., & Joiner, T. E. (2013). Interpersonal processes in depression. *Annual Review of Clinical Psychology, 9*, 355–377.

Hames, R. B. (1979). Relatedness and interaction among the Ye'kwana. In N. S. Chagnon & W. Irons (Eds.), *Evolutionary biology and human social behavior* (pp. 128–141). North Scituate, MA: Duxbury Press.

Hamilton, D. L. (1981). *Cognitive processes in stereotyping and intergroup behavior*. Hillsdale, NJ: Erlbaum.

Hamilton, V. L., Sanders, J., & McKearney, S. J. (1995). Orientations toward authority in an authoritarian state: Moscow in 1990. *Personality and Social Psychology Bulletin, 21*, 356–365.

Hamilton, W. D. (1964). The genetical evolution of social behavior. *Journal of Theoretical Biology, 7*, 1–52.

Hammock, W. R., & Yung, B. (1993). Psychology's role in the public health response to assaultive violence among young African-American men. *American Psychologist, 48*, 142–154.

Han, S.-P., & Shavitt, S. (1994). Persuasion and culture: Advertising appeals in individualistic and collectivistic societies. *Journal of Experimental Social Psychology, 30*, 326–350.

Hanko, K., Master, S., & Sabini, J. (2004). Some evidence about character and mate selection. *Personality and Social Psychology Bulletin, 30*, 732–742.

Harackiewicz, J. M., Sansone, C., & Manderlink, G. (1985). Competence, achievement orientation, and intrinsic motivation: A process analysis. *Journal of Personality and Social Psychology, 48*, 493–508.

Hardin, G. (1968). The tragedy of the commons. *Science, 162*, 1243–1248.

Hardy, C. L., & Van Vugt, M. (2006). Nice guys finish first: The competitive altruism hypothesis. *Personality and Social Psychology Bulletin, 10*, 1402–1413.

Hare, R. D., Harpur, T. J., Hakstein, A. R., Forth, A. E., Hart, S. D., & Newman, J. P. (1990). The revised psychopathy checklist: Descriptive statistics, reliability, and factor structure. *Psychological Assessment, 2*, 338.

Harkins, S. G. (1987). Social facilitation and social loafing. *Journal of Experimental Social Psychology, 23*, 1–18.

Harkins, S. G., & Jackson, J. M. (1985). The role of evaluation in eliminating social loafing. *Personality and Social Psychology Bulletin, 11*, 457–465.

Harland, P., Staats, H., & Wilke, H. A. M. (2007). Situational and personality factors as direct or personal norm mediated predictors of pro-environmental behavior. *Basic and Applied Social Psychology, 29*, 323–334.

Harlow, C.W. (2005, November). *Hate crime reported by victims and police* (Bureau of Justice Statistics Special Report, NCJ 209911). Retrieved from www.ojp.usdoj.gov/bjs/pub/pdf/hcrvp.pdf

Harlow, R. E., & Cantor, N. (1994). Social pursuit of academics: Side effects and spillover of strategic reassurance seeking. *Journal of Personality and Social Psychology, 66*, 386–397.

Harmon-Jones, E., & Allen, J. J. B. (2001). The role of affect in the mere exposure effect: Evidence from psychophysiological and individual differences approaches. *Personality & Social Psychology Bulletin, 27*, 889–898.

Harmon-Jones, E., Brehm, J. W., Greenberg, J., Simon, L., & Nelson, D. E. (1996). Evidence that production of aversive consequences is not necessary to create cognitive dissonance. *Journal of Personality and Social Psychology, 70*, 5–16.

Harmon-Jones, E., & Devine, P. G. (2003). Introduction to the special section on social neuroscience: Promise and caveats. *Journal of Personality & Social Psychology, 85*, 589–593.

Harmon-Jones, E., & Harmon-Jones, C. (2002). Testing the action-based model of cognitive dissonance: The effect of action orientation on postdecisional attitudes. *Personality and Social Psychology Bulletin, 28*, 711–723.

Harmon-Jones, E., Peterson, H., & Vaughn, K. (2003). The dissonance-inducing effects of an inconsistency between experienced empathy and knowledge of past failures to help. *Basic and Applied Social Psychology, 25*, 69–78.

Harpur, T. (1993). Cognitive and biological factors contributing to the abnormal perception of emotional material in psychopathic criminals [Abstract]. *Violent Crime and Its Victims: Proceedings of American Society of Criminology, 45*, 86–87.

Harrer, H. (1996). *Seven years in Tibet*. New York: Tarcher/Putnam.

Harris, C. R. (2003). A review of sex differences in sexual jealousy, including self-report data, psychophysiological responses, interpersonal violence, and morbid jealousy. *Personality & Social Psychology Review, 7*, 102–128.

Harris, M. B. (1992). Sex, race, and experiences of aggression. *Aggressive Behavior, 18*, 201–217.

Harris, M. D. (1977). The effects of altruism on mood. *Journal of Social Psychology, 102*, 197–208.

Harris, M. J., & Rosenthal, R. (1985). Mediation of interpersonal expectancy effects: 31 meta-analyses. *Psychological Bulletin, 97*, 363–386.

Harris, R. N., & Snyder, C. R. (1986). The role of uncertain self-esteem in self-handicapping. *Journal of Personality and Social Psychology, 51*, 451–458.

Hart, E. A., Leary, M. R., & Rejeski, W. J. (1989). The measurement of social physique anxiety. *Journal of Sport and Exercise Psychology, 11*, 94–104.

Harter, S. (1993). Causes and consequences of low self-esteem in children and adolescents. In R. Baumeister (Ed.), *Self-esteem: The puzzle of low self-regard* (pp. 87–116). New York: Plenum.

Harton, H. C., & Bourgeois, M. J. (2004). Cultural elements emerge from dynamic social impact. In M. Schaller & C. S. Crandall (Eds.), *The psychological foundations of culture* (pp. 41–75). Mahwah, NJ: Erlbaum.

Hartwig, M., & Bond, C. F., Jr. (2011). Why do lie-catchers fail? A lens model meta-analysis of human lie judgments. *Psychological Bulletin, 137*(4), 643.

Harvey, J. H., & Omarzu, J. (1997). Minding the close relationship. *Personality and Social Psychology Review, 1*, 224–240.

Harvey, M. D., & Enzle, M. E. (1981). A cognitive model of social norms for understanding the transgression-helping effect. *Journal of Personality and Social Psychology, 41*, 866–888.

Haselton, M. G., & Buss, D. M. (2000). Error management theory: A new perspective on biases in cross-sex mind reading. *Journal of Personality & Social Psychology, 78*, 81–91.

Haselton, M. G., & Funder, D. C. (2006). The evolution of accuracy and bias in social judgment. In M. Schaller, J. A. Simpson, & D. T. Kenrick (Eds.), *Evolution and social psychology* (pp. 16–37). New York: Psychology Press.

Haselton, M. G., & Gangestad, S. W. (2006). Conditional expression of women's desires and men's mate guarding across the ovulatory cycle. *Hormones and Behavior, 49*, 509–518.

Haselton, M. G., Mortezaie, M., Pillsworth, E. G., Bleske, A. E., & Frederick, D. A. (2007). Ovulatory shifts in human female ornamentation: Near ovulation, women dress to impress. *Hormones and Behavior, 51*, 40–45.

Haselton, M. G., & Nettle, D. (2006). The paranoid optimist: An integrative evolutionary model of cognitive biases. *Personality and Social Psychology Review, 10*, 47–66.

Haslam, N. (1997). Four grammars for primate social relations. In J. A. Simpson & D. T. Kenrick (Eds.), *Evolutionary social psychology* (pp. 297–316). Mahwah, NJ: Erlbaum.

Haslam, N., & Fiske, A. P. (1999). Relational models theory: A confirmatory factor analysis. *Personal Relationships, 6*(2), 241–250.

Hassan, S. (1990). *Combatting cult mind control*. Rochester, VT: Park Street Press.

Hassan, S. (2000). *Releasing the bonds: Empowering people to think for themselves*. Boston, MA: Freedom of Mind Press.

Hastie, R., Penrod, S. D., & Pennington, N. (1983). *Inside the jury*. Cambridge, MA: Harvard University Press.

Hastie, R., & Stasser, G. (2000). Computer simulation methods for social psychology. In H. T. Reis & C. M. Judd (Eds.), *Handbook of research methods in social and personality psychology* (pp. 85–114). New York: Cambridge University Press.

Hatfield, E., Greenberger, E., Traupmann, J., & Lambert, P. (1982). Equity and sexual satisfaction in recently married couples. *Journal of Sex Research, 18*, 18–32.

Hatfield, E., & Rapson, R. L. (1996). *Love and sex: Cross-cultural perspectives*. Boston: Allyn & Bacon.

Hatfield, E., Traupmann, J., Sprecher, S., Utne, M., & Hay, J. (1985). Equity and intimate relationships: Recent research. In W. Ickes (Ed.), *Compatible and incompatible relationships* (pp. 1–27). New York: Springer-Verlag.

Haugtvedt, C. P., & Petty, R. E. (1992). Personality and persuasion: Need for cognition moderates the persistence and resistance of attitude changes. *Journal of Personality and Social Psychology, 63*, 308–319.

Hawken, P., Lovins, A., & Lovins, L. H. (1999). *Natural capitalism: Creating the next industrial revolution*. Boston: Little Brown.

Hawley, P. H., Little, T. D., & Card, N. A. (2008). The myth of the alpha male: A new look at dominance-related beliefs and behaviors among adolescent males and females. *International Journal of Behavioral Development, 32*, 76–88.

Hayden, T. (2003, June 9). Fished out. *U.S. News & World Report*, pp. 38–45.

Hazan, C., & Diamond, L. M. (2000). The place of attachment in human mating. *Review of General Psychology, 4*, 186–204.

Hazan, C., & Shaver, P. R. (1987). Romantic love conceptualized as an attachment process. *Journal of Personality and Social Psychology, 52*, 511–524.

Hazan, C., & Shaver, P. R. (1994a). Attachment as an organizational framework for research on close relationships. *Psychological Inquiry, 5*, 1–22.

Hazan, C., & Shaver, P. R. (1994b). Deeper into attachment theory. *Psychological Inquiry, 5*, 68–79.

Hearold, S. (1986). A synthesis of 1043 effects of television on social behavior. In G. Comstock (Ed.), *Public communications and behavior* (Vol. I, pp. 65–133). New York: Academic Press.

Heatherton, T. F. (2011). Neuroscience of self and self-regulation. *Annual Review of Psychology, 62*, 363.

Heaven, P. C. L., & St. Quintin, D. (2003). Personality factors predict racial prejudice. *Personality and Individual Differences, 34*, 625–634.

Hebl, M. R., Foster, J. B., Mannix, L. M., & Dovidio, J. F. (2002). Formal and interpersonal discrimination: A field study of bias toward homosexual applicants. *Personality and Social Psychology Bulletin, 28*, 815–825.

Heckel, R. V. (1973). Leadership and voluntary seating choice. *Psychological Reports, 32*, 141–142.

Heckhausen, J., & Schultz, R. (1995). A life-span theory of control. *Psychological Review, 102,* 284–304.

Heider, F. (1946). Attitudes and cognitive organization. *Journal of Psychology, 21,* 107–112.

Heider, F. (1958). *The psychology of interpersonal relations.* New York: Wiley.

Heilman, M. E., Block, C. J., & Martell, R. F. (1995). Sex stereotypes: Do they influence perceptions of managers? *Journal of Social Behavior and Personality, 10,* 237–252.

Heilman, M. E., & Okimoto, T. G. (2007). Why are women penalized for success at male tasks? The implied communality deficit. *Journal of Applied Psychology, 92,* 81–92.

Heilman, M. E., Wallen, A. S., Fuchs, D., & Tamkins, M. M. (2004). Penalties for success: Reactions to women who succeed at male gender-typed tasks. *Journal of Applied Psychology, 89,* 416–427.

Heine, S. J., & Hamamura, T. (2007). In search of East Asian self-enhancement. *Personality and Social Psychology Review, 11,* 1–24.

Heine, S. J., & Lehman, D. R. (1995). Cultural variation in unrealistic optimism: Does the West feel more invulnerable than the East? *Journal of Personality and Social Psychology, 68,* 595–607.

Heine, S. J., & Lehman, D. R. (1997). Culture, dissonance, and self-affirmation. *Personality and Social Psychology Bulletin, 23,* 389–400.

Hejmadi, A., Davidson, R. J., & Rozin, P. (2000). Exploring Hindu Indian emotion expressions: Evidence for accurate recognition by Americans and Indians. *Psychological Science, 11,* 183–187.

Helgeson, V. S. (1992). Moderators of the relation between perceived control and adjustment to chronic illness. *Journal of Personality and Social Psychology, 63,* 656–666.

Helgeson, V. S., Shaver, P., & Dyer, M. (1987). Prototypes of intimacy and distance in same-sex and opposite-sex relationships. *Journal of Social and Personal Relationships, 4,* 195–234.

Helgeson, V. S., & Taylor, S. E. (1993). Self-generated feelings of control and adjustment to physical illness. *Journal of Social Issues, 47,* 91–103.

Hellmuth, J. C., & McNulty, J. K. (2008). Neuroticism, marital violence, and the moderating role of stress and behavioral skills. *Journal of Personality and Social Psychology, 95,* 166–180.

Helmreich, R. L., & Collins, B. E. (1967). Situational determinants of affiliative preference under stress. *Journal of Personality and Social Psychology, 6,* 79–85.

Helweg-Larsen, M., & Shepperd, J. A. (2001). Do moderators of the optimistic bias affect personal or target risk estimates? A review of the literature. *Personality and Social Psychology Review, 5,* 74–95.

Hemphill, J. K. (1950). Relations between the size of the group and the behavior of "superior" leaders. *Journal of Social Psychology, 32,* 11–22.

Henderlong, J., & Lepper, M. R. (2002). The effects of praise on children's intrinsic motivation: A review and synthesis. *Psychological Bulletin, 128,* 774–795.

Hendrick, C., & Hendrick, S. S. (1986). A theory and method of love. *Journal of Personality and Social Psychology, 50,* 392–402.

Hendrick, C., & Hendrick, S. S. (2006). Styles of romantic love. In R. J. Sternberg & K. Weis (Eds.), *The new psychology of love* (pp. 149–170). New Haven, CT: Yale University Press.

Hendricks, M., & Brickman, P. (1974). Effects of status and knowledgeability of audience on self-presentation. *Sociometry, 37,* 440–449.

Hendry, J. (1993). *Wrapping culture: Politeness, presentation, and power in Japan and other societies.* Oxford, UK: Clarendon Press.

Henley, N. M. (1973). Status and sex: Some touching observations. *Bulletin of the Psychonomic Society, 2,* 91–93.

Henley, N. M., & Harmon, S. (1985). The nonverbal semantics of power and gender: A perceptual study. In S. L. Ellyson & J. F. Dovidio (Eds.), *Power, dominance, and nonverbal behavior* (pp. 151–164). New York: Springer-Verlag.

Henrich, J., Ensminger, J., Boyd, R., Henrich, N. S., Bowles, S., Hill, K., et al. (2006). "Economic man" in cross-cultural perspective: Behavioral experiments in 15 small-scale societies. *Behavioral and Brain Sciences, 28,* 795–855.

Henrich, J., & Gil-White, F. J. (2001). The evolution of prestige: Freely conferred status as a mechanism for enhancing the benefits of cultural transmission. *Evolution and Human Behavior, 22,* 165–196.

Hepburn, L. M., & Hemenway, D. (2004). Firearm availability and homicide: A review of the literature. *Aggression and Violent Behavior, 9,* 417–440.

Hepworth, J. T., & West, S. G. (1988). Lynching and the economy: A time-series reanalysis of Hovland and Sears (1940). *Journal of Personality and Social Psychology, 55,* 239–247.

Herek, G. M. (1986). The instrumentality of attitudes. Toward a neofunctional theory. *Journal of Social Issues, 42,* 99–114.

Herek, G. M., & Capitanio, J. P. (1996). "Some of my best friends": Intergroup contact, concealable stigma, and heterosexuals' attitudes toward gay men and lesbians. *Personality and Social Psychology Bulletin, 22,* 412–424.

Herek, G. M., Janis, I. L., & Huth, P. (1987). Decision making during international crises: Is quality of process related to outcome? *Journal of Conflict Resolution, 31,* 203–226.

Herrera, H. (1983). *Frida: A biography of Frida Kahlo.* New York: Harper Collins.

Hershleifer, D., & Shumway, T. (2003, June). Good day sunshine: Stock returns and the weather. *Journal of Finance,* 1009–1032.

Hertel, G., & Kerr, N. L. (2001). Priming in-group favoritism: The impact of normative scripts in the minimal group paradigm. *Journal of Experimental Social Psychology, 37,* 316–324.

Hertel, G., Kerr, N. L., & Messé, L. A. (2000). Motivation gains in performance groups: Paradigmatic and theoretical developments on the Kohler effect. *Journal of Personality and Social Psychology, 79,* 580–601.

Hertwig, R., Gigerenzer, G., & Hoffrage, U. (1997). The reiteration effect in hindsight bias. *Psychological Review, 104,* 194–202.

Hidi, S., & Harackiewicz, J. M. (2000). Motivating the academically unmotivated: A critical issue for the 21st century. *Review of Educational Research, 70,* 151–179.

Higgins, E. T. (1996). Knowledge activation: Accessibility, applicability, and salience. In E. T. Higgins & A. W. Kruglanski (Eds.), *Social psychology: Handbook of basic principles* (pp. 133–168). New York: Guilford.

Higgins, E. T. (1997). Beyond pleasure and pain. *American Psychologist, 52,* 1280–1300.

Higgins, E. T., King, G. A., & Mavin, G. H. (1982). Individual construct accessibility and subjective impressions and recall. *Journal of Personality and Social Psychology, 43,* 35–47.

Higgins, E. T., Rholes, W. S., & Jones, C. R. (1977). Category accessibility and impression formation. *Journal of Experimental Social Psychology, 13,* 141–154.

Higgins, R. L., & Harris, R. N. (1988). Strategic "alcohol" use: Drinking to selfhandicap. *Journal of Social and Clinical Psychology, 6,* 191–202.

Hill, K., & Hurtado, A. M. (1993). Hunter-gatherers in the New World. In P. Sherman & J. Alcock (Eds.), *Exploring animal behavior* (pp. 154–160). Sunderland, MA: Sinauer.

Hill, K., & Hurtado, M. (1996). *Ache life history.* Hawthorne, NY: Aldine-deGruyter.

Hill, S. E. (2007). Overestimation bias in mate competition. *Evolution and Human Behavior, 28,* 118–123.

Hill, S. E., & DelPriore, D. J. (2012). (Not) bringing up baby: The effects of jealousy on the desire to have and invest in children. *Personality and Social Psychology Bulletin, 39*(2), 206–218.

Hill, S. E., Rodeheffer, C. D., Griskevicius, V., Durante, K., & White, A. E. (2012). Boosting beauty in an economic decline: Mating, spending, and the lipstick effect. *Journal of Personality and Social Psychology, 103*(2), 275–291.

Hilmert, C. J., Kulik, J. A., & Christenfeld, N. J. S. (2006). Positive and negative opinion modeling: The influence of another's similarity and dissimilarity. *Journal of Personality and Social Psychology, 90,* 440–452.

Hinz, V. B., Matz, D. C., & Patience, R. A. (2001). Does women's hair signal reproductive potential? *Journal of Experimental Social Psychology, 37,* 166–172.

Hirt, E. R., Deppe, R. K., & Gordon, L. J. (1991). Self-reported versus behavioral self-handicapping: Empirical evidence for a theoretical distinction. *Journal of Personality and Social Psychology, 61,* 981–991.

Hirt, E. R., & Markman, K. D. (1995). Multiple explanation: A consider-an-alternative strategy for debiasing judgments. *Journal of Personality and Social Psychology, 69,* 1069–1086.

Hirt, E. R., McDonald, H. E., & Erickson, G. A. (1995). How do I remember thee? The role of encoding set and delay in reconstructive memory processes. *Journal of Experimental Social Psychology, 31,* 379–409.

Hirt, E. R., Zillman, D., Erickson, G. A., & Kennedy, C. (1992). Costs and benefits of allegiance: Changes in fans' self-ascribed competencies after team victory versus defeat. *Journal of Personality and Social Psychology, 63,* 724–738.

Hochberg, A. (1996, April 19). 1971 School desegregation made friends out of enemies. *National Public Radio All Things Considered.*

Hodges, B. H., & Geyer, A. L. (2006). A nonconformist account of the Asch experiments. *Personality and Social Psychology Review, 10,* 2–19.

Hodgkinson, V. A., & Weitzman, M. S. (1990). *Giving and volunteering in the United States.* Washington, DC: Independent Sector.

Hodgkinson, V. A., & Weitzman, M. S. (1994). *Giving and volunteering in the United States.* Washington, DC: Independent Sector.

Hodson, G. (2011). Do ideologically intolerant people benefit from intergroup contact? *Current Directions in Psychological Science, 20,* 154–159.

Hodson, G., Dovidio, J. F., & Esses, V. M. (2003). Ingroup identification as a moderator of positive-negative asymmetry in social discrimination. *European Journal of Social Psychology, 33,* 215–233.

Hoffman, M. L. (1984). Interaction of affect and cognition in empathy. In C. E. Izard, J. Kagan, & R. B. Zajonc (Eds.), *Emotions, cognitions, and behavior* (pp. 103–131). Cambridge, UK: Cambridge University Press.

Hofling, C. K., Brotzman, E., Dalrymple, S., Graves, N., & Pierce, C. M. (1966). An experimental study in nurse-physician relationships. *Journal of Nervous and Mental Disease, 143,* 171–180.

Hofstede, G. (1980/2001). *Culture's consequences: International differences in workrelated values.* Thousand Oaks, CA: Sage.

Hogan, R. (1993). A socioanalytic theory of personality. In M. Page (Ed.), *Nebraska symposium on motivation: Personality—Current theory and research* (pp. 58–89). Lincoln: University of Nebraska Press.

Hogan, R., & Hogan, J. (1991). Personality and status. In D. Gilbert & J. J. Connolly (Eds.), *Personality, social skills, and psychopathology: An individual differences approach* (pp. 137–154). New York: Plenum Press.

Hogan, R., Curphy, G. J., & Hogan, J. (1994). What we know about leadership: Effectiveness and personality. *American Psychologist, 49,* 493–504.

Hogan, R., Jones, W. H., & Cheek, J. M. (1985). Socioanalytic theory: An alternative to armadillo psychology. In B. R. Schlenker (Ed.), *The self and social life* (pp. 175–198). New York: McGraw-Hill.

Hogan, R., & Kaiser, R. B. (2005). What we know about leadership. *Review of General Psychology, 9,* 169–180.

Hogan, R., Raza, S., Sampson, D., Miller, C., & Salas, E. (1989). *The impact of personality on team performance* (Report to the Office of Naval Research). Tulsa, OK: University of Tulsa.

Hogg, M. A. (2003). Intergroup relations. In J. DeLamater (Ed.), *Handbook of social psychology* (pp. 479–501). New York: Kluwer.

Hogg, M. A., Abrams, D., Otten, S., & Hinkle, S. (2004). The social identity perspective: Intergroup relations, self-conception, and small groups. *Small Group Research, 35,* 246–276.

Hogg, M. A., Hohman, Z. P., & Rivera, J. E. (2008). Why do people join groups? Three motivational accounts from social psychology. *Social and Personality Psychology Compass, 2/3,* 1269–1280.

Holland, J. L. (1985). *Making vocational choices: A theory of vocational personalities and work environments* (2nd ed.). Englewood Cliffs, NJ: Prentice-Hall.

Holland, J. L. (1997). *Making vocational choices: A theory of vocation personalities and work environments* (3rd ed.). Lutz, FL: Psychological Assessment Resources.

Hollander, E. P. (1993). Legitimacy, power, and influence: A perspective on relational features of leadership. In M. M. Chemers & R. Ayman (Eds.), *Leadership theory and research: Perspectives and directions* (pp. 29–47). San Diego, CA: Academic Press.

Holmberg, D., & MacKenzie, S. (2002). So far so good: Scripts for romantic relationship development as predictors of relational well-being. *Journal of Social and Personal Relationships, 19,* 777–796.

Holoien, D. S., & Fiske, S. T. (2013). Downplaying positive impressions: Compensation between warmth and competence in impression management. *Journal of Experimental Social Psychology, 49*(1), 33–41.

Holtgraves, T., & Dulin, J. (1994). The Muhammad Ali effect: Differences between African Americans and European Americans in their perceptions of a truthful bragger. *Language and Communication, 14,* 275–285.

Holtgraves, T., & Srull, T. K. (1989). The effects of positive self-descriptions on impressions: General principles and individual differences. *Personality and Social Psychology Bulletin, 15,* 452–462.

Holtgraves, T., & Yang, J.-N. (1990). Politeness as universal: Cross-cultural perceptions of request strategies and inferences based on their use. *Journal of Personality and Social Psychology, 59,* 719–729.

Homer-Dixon, T. F., Boutwell, J. H., & Rathjens, G. W. (1993, February). Environmental change and violent conflict. *Scientific American,* 38–45.

Hönekopp, J., Rudolph, U., Beier, L., Liebert, A., & Müller, C. (2007). Physical attractiveness of face and body as indicators of physical fitness in men. *Evolution and Human Behavior, 28,* 106–111.

Hong, Y. Y., Chiu, C. Y., & Kung, T. M. (1997). Bringing culture out in front: Effects of cultural meaning system activation on social cognition. In K. Leung, Y. Kashima, U. Kim, & S. Yamaguchi (Eds.), *Progress in Asian social psychology* (Vol. 1, pp. 135–146). Singapore: Wiley.

Honts, C. R., Raskin, D. C., & Kircher, D. C. (1994). Mental and physical countermeasures reduce the accuracy of polygraph tests. *Journal of Applied Psychology, 79,* 252–259.

Hood, R. W., Jr., Spilka, B., Hunsberger, B., & Gorsuch, R. (1996). *The psychology of religion: An empirical approach* (2nd ed.). New York: Guilford.

Hooper, N., Davies, N., Davies, L., & McHugh, L. (2011). Comparing thought suppression and mindfulness as coping techniques for spider fear. *Consciousness and Cognition, 20*(4), 1824–1830.

Hopper, J. R., & Nielsen, J. M. (1991). Recycling as altruistic behavior: Normative and behavioral strategies to expand participation in a community recycling program. *Environment and Behavior, 23,* 195–220.

Horowitz, L. M., Wilson, K. R., Turan, B., Zolotsev, P., Constantino, M. J., & Henderson, L. (2006). How interpersonal motives clarify the meaning of interpersonal behavior: A revised circumflex model. *Personality and Social Psychology Review, 10,* 67–86.

Horwitz, S. K., & Horwitz, I. B. (2007). The effects of team diversity on team outcomes: A meta-analytic review of team demography. *Journal of Management, 33,* 987–1015.

Hoshino-Browne, E., Zanna, A. S., Spencer, S. J., Zanna, M. P., & Kitayama, S. (2005). On the cultural guises of cognitive dissonance: The case of Easterners and Westerners. *Journal of Personality and Social Psychology, 89,* 294–310.

American Association of University Women Educational Foundation. *Hostile hallways: Bullying, teasing, and sexual harassment in school.* (2001). Report of the American Association of University Women. Washington, DC: Author.

House, R. J., & Shamir, B. (1993). Toward the integration of transformational, charismatic, and visionary theories. In M. M. Chemers & R. Ayman (Eds.), *Leadership theory and research: Perspectives and directions* (pp. 81–108). San Diego, CA: Academic Press.

Hovland, C. I., Janis, I. L., & Kelley, H. H. (1953). *Communication and persuasion: Psychological studies of opinion change.* New Haven, CT: Yale University Press.

Hovland, C. I., Lumsdaine, A. A., & Sheffield, F. D. (1949). *Experiments on mass communication.* Princeton, NJ: Princeton University Press.

Hovland, C. I., & Sears, R. (1940). Minor studies in aggression: VI. Correlation of lynchings with economic indices. *Journal of Psychology, 9,* 301–310.

Howard, G. S. (2000). Adapting human lifestyles for the 21st century. *American Psychologist, 55,* 509–515.

Hoyt, C. L. (2010). Women, men, and leadership: Exploring the gender gap at the top. *Social and Personality Psychology Compass, 4*(7), 484–498.

Hrdy, S. B. (1999). *Mother nature: A history of mothers, infants, and natural selection.* New York: Pantheon Books.

Hsu, F. L. K. (1983). *Rugged individualism reconsidered.* Knoxville: University of Tennessee Press.

Huang, J. Y., & Bargh, J. A. (2014). The Selfish Goal: Autonomously operating motivational structures as the proximate cause of human judgment and behavior. *Behavioral & Brain Sciences, 37*(2), 121–135.

Hubbard, J. A., Dodge, K. A., Cillessen, A. H. N., Coie, J. D., & Schwartz, D. (2001). The dyadic nature of social information processing in boys' reactive and proactive aggression. *Journal of Personality & Social Psychology, 80,* 268–280.

Huesmann, L. R., Moise-Titus, J., Podolski, C. L., & Eron, L. D. (2003). Longitudinal relations between children's exposure to TV violence and their aggressive and violent behavior in young adulthood. *Developmental Psychology, 39,* 201–221.

Hüffmeier, J., Krumm, S., Kanthak, J., & Hertel, G. (2012). "Don't let the group down": Facets of instrumentality moderate the motivating effects of groups in a field experiment. *European Journal of Social Psychology, 42*(5), 533–538.

Hugenberg, K., & Sacco, D. F. (2008). Social categorization and stereotyping: How social categorization biases person perception and face memory. *Social and Personality Psychology Compass, 2,* 1052–1072.

Hull, C. L. (1934). *Hypnosis and suggestibility.* New York: D. Appleton- Century.

Human, L. J., Biesanz, J. C., Parisotto, K. L., & Dunn, E. W. (2012). Your best self helps reveal your true self: Positive self-presentation leads to more accurate personality impressions. *Social Psychological and Personality Science, 3*(1), 23–30.

Hunsberger, B., & Jackson, L. M. (2005). Religion, meaning, and prejudice. *Journal of Social Issues, 61,* 807–826.

Hunter, J. A., Platow, M. J., Howard, M. L., & Stringer, M. (1996). Social identity and intergroup evaluation bias: Realistic categories and domain specific self-esteem in a conflict setting. *European Journal of Social Psychology, 26,* 631–647.

Hutchings, P. B., & Haddock, G. (2008). Look black in anger: The role of implicit prejudice in the categorization and perceived emotional intensity of racially ambiguous faces. *Journal of Experimental Social Psychology, 44,* 1418–1420.

Hyde, J. S. (1990). Meta-analysis and the psychology of gender differences. *Signs, 16,* 55–73.

Hyde, J. S. (1996). Where are the gender differences? Where are the gender similarities? In D. M. Buss & N. M. Malamuth (Eds.), *Sex, power, conflict: Evolutionary and feminist perspectives* (pp. 107–118). New York: Oxford University Press.

Ickes, W. (1993). Traditional gender roles: Do they make, and then break, our relationships? *Journal of Social Issues, 49,* 71–85.

Igarashi, T., Takai, J., & Yoshida, T. (2005). Gender differences in social network development via mobile phone text messages: A longitudinal study. *Journal of Social and Personal Relationships, 22,* 691–713.

Ilgen, D. R., & Hulin, C. L. (2000). *Computational modeling of behavior in organizations: The third scientific discipline.* Washington, DC: American Psychological Association.

Impett, E. A., Gable, S. L., & Peplau, L. A. (2005). Giving up and giving in: The costs and benefits of daily sacrifice in intimate relationships. *Journal of Personality and Social Psychology, 89,* 327–344.

Inbau, F. E., Reid, J. E., Buckley, J. P., & Jayne, B. C. (2001). *Criminal interrogation and confessions* (4th ed.). Gaithersburg, MD: Aspen Publishers.

Ingham, A. G., Levinger, G., Graves, J., & Peckham, V. (1974). The Ringelmann effect: Studies of group size and group performance. *Journal of Personality and Social Psychology, 10,* 371–384.

Insko, C. A. (1965). Verbal reinforcement of attitude. *Journal of Personality and Social Psychology, 2,* 621–623.

Insko, C. A., Drenan, S., Solomon, M. R., Smith, R., & Wade, T. J. (1983). Conformity as a function of the consistency of positive self-evaluation with being liked and being right. *Journal of Experimental Social Psychology, 19,* 341–358.

Insko, C. A., Schopler, J., Graetz, K. A., Drigotas, S. M., Currey, D. P., Smith, S. L., et al. (1994). Individual-intergroup discontinuity in the Prisoner's Dilemma Game. *Journal of Conflict Resolution, 38,* 87–116.

Insko, C. A., Schopler, J., Hoyle, R. H., Dardis, G. J., & Graetz, K. A. (1990). Individual-group discontinuity as a function of fear and greed. *Journal of Personality and Social Psychology, 58,* 68–79.

Insko, C. A., Schopler, J., Pemberton, M. B., Wieselquist, J., McIlraith, S. A., Currey, D. P., et al. (1998). Long-term outcome maximization and the reduction of interindividual-intergroup discontinuity. *Journal of Personality & Social Psychology, 75,* 695–711.

Insko, C. A., Smith, R. H., Alicke, M. D., Wade, J., & Taylor, S. (1985). Conformity and group size: The concern with being right and the concern with being liked. *Personality and Social Psychology Bulletin, 11,* 41–50.

Inzlicht, M., & Schmader, T. (2012). *Stereotype threat: Theory, process, and application.* New York: Oxford University Press.

Isbell, L. (2004). Not all happy people are lazy or stupid: Evidence of systematic processing in happy moods. *Journal of Experimental Social Psychology, 40,* 341–349.

Isen, A. M. (2002). Missing in action in the AIM: Positive affect's facilitation of cognitive flexibility, innovation, and problem solving. *Psychological Inquiry, 13,* 57–65.

Isen, A. M., Shalker, T. E., Clark, M., & Karp, L. (1978). Affect, accessibility of material in memory, and behavior. *Journal of Personality and Social Psychology, 36,* 1–12.

Isenberg, D. J. (1986). Group polarization: A critical review and meta-analysis. *Journal of Personality and Social Psychology, 50,* 1141–1151.

Iyengar, S. S., & Lepper, M. R. (1999). Rethinking the value of choice: A cultural perspective on intrinsic motivation. *Journal of Personality & Social Psychology, 76,* 349–366.

Izard, C. E. (2007). Basic emotions, natural kinds, emotion schemas, and a new paradigm. *Perspectives on Psychological Science, 2,* 260–280.

Jacks, J. Z., & Cameron, K. A. (2003). Strategies for resisting persuasion. *Basic and Applied Social Psychology, 25,* 145–161.

Jackson, J. J., & Kirkpatrick, L. A. (2007). The structure and measurement of human mating strategies: Toward a multidimensional model of sociosexuality. *Evolution and Human Behavior, 28,* 382–391.

Jackson, J. J., & Kirkpatrick, L. A. (2008). The structure and measurement of human mating strategies: Toward a multidimensional model of sociosexuality. *Evolution and Human Behavior, 28,* 382–391.

Jackson, L. M., & Esses, V. M. (1997). Of scripture and ascription: The relation between religious fundamentalism and intergroup helping. *Personality and Social Psychology Bulletin, 23,* 893–906.

Jacobs, J. R. (1992). Facilitators of romantic attraction and their relation to lovestyle. *Social Behavior and Personality, 20,* 227–234.

Jacobson, R. P., Mortensen, C. R., & Cialdini, R. B. (2011). Bodies obliged and unbound: Differentiated response tendencies for injunctive and descriptive social norms. *Journal of Personality and Social Psychology, 100*(3), 433–448. Retrieved from http://dx.doi.org/10.1037/a0021470

James, W. (1890). *Principles of psychology.* New York: Henry Holt.

Jamieson, J. P., & Harkins, S. G. (2007). Mere effort and stereotype threat performance effects. *Journal of Personality and Social Psychology, 93,* 544–564.

Janicki, M., & Krebs, D. L. (1998). Evolutionary approaches to culture. In C. Crawford & D. L. Krebs (Eds.), *Handbook of evolutionary psychology: Ideas, issues, and applications* (pp. 163–208). Mahwah, NJ: Erlbaum.

Janis, I. L. (1972). *Victims of groupthink.* Boston: Houghton Mifflin.

Janis, I. L. (1983). *Groupthink: Psychological studies of policy decisions and fiascoes* (2nd ed.). Boston: Houghton Mifflin.

Janis, I. L. (1997). Groupthink. In W. A. Lesko (Ed.), *Readings in social psychology* (3rd ed., pp. 333–337). Boston: Allyn & Bacon.

Janis, I. L., & Mann, L. (1977). *Decision making: A psychological analysis of conflict, choice, and commitment.* New York: Free Press.

Janiszewski, C., & Uy, D. (2008). Precision of the anchor influences the amount of adjustment. *Psychological Science, 19,* 121–127.

Jankowiak, W. R., & Fischer, E. F. (1992). A cross-cultural perspective on romantic love. *Ethnology, 31,* 149–155.

Janoff-Bulman, R., & Wade, M. B. (1996). The dilemma of self-advocacy for women: Another case of blaming the victim? *Journal of Social and Clinical Psychology, 15,* 143–152.

Jaremka, L. M., Fagundes, C. P., Peng, J., Bennett, J. M., Glaser, R., Malarkey, W. B., et al. (2013). Loneliness promotes inflammation during acute stress. *Psychological Science, 24,* 1089–1097.

Jemmott, J. B., III, Ditto, P. H., & Croyle, R. T. (1986). Judging health status: Effects of perceived prevalence and personal relevance. *Journal of Personality and Social Psychology, 50,* 899–905.

Jenkins, S. S., & Aube, J. (2002). Gender differences and gender-related constructs in dating aggression. *Personality & Social Psychology Bulletin, 28,* 1106–1118.

Jensen-Campbell, L. A., & Graziano, W. G. (2000). Beyond the schoolyard: Relationships as moderators of daily interpersonal conflict. *Personality & Social Psychology Bulletin, 26,* 923–935.

Jensen-Campbell, L. A., & Graziano, W. G., & West, S. G. (1995). Dominance, prosocial orientation, and female preferences: Do nice guys really finish last? *Journal of Personality and Social Psychology, 68,* 427–440.

Jetten, J., Spears, R., & Manstead, A. S. R. (1997). Strength of identification and intergroup differentiation: The influence of group norms. *European Journal of Social Psychology, 27,* 603–609.

Jockin, V., McGue, M., & Lykken, D. T. (1996). Personality and divorce: A genetic analysis. *Journal of Personality and Social Psychology, 71,* 288–299.

Johns, M., Schmader, T., & Martens, A. (2005). Knowing is half the battle: Teaching stereotype threat as a means of improving women's math performance. *Psychological Science, 16,* 175–179.

Johnson, B. T., & Eagly, A. H. (1989). The effect of involvement on persuasion: A meta-analysis. *Psychological Bulletin, 106,* 290–314.

Johnson, D. (1993). The politics of violence research. *Psychological Science, 4,* 131–133.

Johnson, D. J., & Rusbult, C. E. (1989). Resisting temptation: Devaluation of alternative partners as a means of maintaining commitment in close relationships. *Journal of Personality and Social Psychology, 57,* 967–980.

Johnson, D. W., & Johnson, R. T. (1975). *Learning together and alone: Cooperation, competition, and individualization.* Englewood Cliffs, NJ: Prentice-Hall.

Johnson, D. W., & Johnson, R. T. (1994). Cooperative learning in the culturally diverse classroom. In R. DeVillar, C. Fultis, & J. Cummings (Eds.), *Cultural diversity in schools* (pp. 57–74). New York: SUNY Press.

Johnson, D. W., Johnson, R. T., & Maruyama, G. (1984). Goal interdependence and interpersonal attraction in heterogeneous classrooms: A meta-analysis. In N. Miller & M. B. Brewer (Eds.), *Groups in contact* (pp. 187–213). New York: Academic Press.

Johnson, F. L., & Aries, E. J. (1983). Conversational patterns among same-sex pairs of late adolescent close friends. *Journal of Genetic Psychology, 142,* 225–238.

Johnson, K. A., White, A. E., Boyd, B. M., & Cohen, A. B. (2011). Matzah, meat, milk, and mana: Psychological influences on religio-cultural food practices. *Journal of Cross-Cultural Psychology, 14,* 1421–1436.

Johnson, K. L., Gill, S., Reichman, V., & Tassinary, L. G. (2007). Swagger, sway, and sexuality: Judging sexual orientation from body motion and morphology. *Journal of Personality and Social Psychology, 93,* 321–334.

Johnson, R. T., Burk, J. A., & Kirkpatrick, L. A. (2007). Dominance and prestige as differential predictors of aggression and testosterone levels in men. *Evolution and Human Behavior, 28,* 345–351.

Johnson, R. W., Kelly, R. J., & LeBlanc, B. A. (1995). Motivational basis of dissonance: Aversive consequences or inconsistency. *Personality and Social Psychology Bulletin, 21,* 850–855.

Joiner, T. E., Jr. (1994). Contagious depression: Existence, specificity to depressed symptoms, and the role of reassurance seeking. *Journal of Personality and Social Psychology, 67,* 287–296.

Joiner, T. E., Alfano, M. S., & Metalsky, G. I. (1992). When depression breeds contempt: Reassurance seeking, self-esteem, and rejection of depressed college students by their roommates. *Journal of Abnormal Psychology, 101,* 165–173.

Joireman, J., Anderson, J., & Strathman, A. (2003). The aggression paradox: Understanding links among aggression, sensation seeking, and the consideration of future consequences. *Journal of Personality & Social Psychology, 84,* 1287–1302.

Joireman, J. A., Van Lange, P. A. M., & Van Vugt, M. (2004). Who cares about the environmental impact of cars? Those with an eye toward the future. *Environment and Behavior, 36,* 187–206.

Jokela, M., Kivimäki, M., Elovainio, M., & Keltikangas-Järvinen, L. (2009). Personality and having children: A two-way relationship. *Journal of Personality and Social Psychology, 96,* 218–230.

Jonas, E., Graupmann, V., & Frey, D. (2006). The influence of mood on the search for supporting versus conflicting information. *Personality and Social Psychology Bulletin, 32,* 3–15.

Jonas, E., Schulz-Hardt, S., & Frey, D. (2005). Giving advice or making decisions in someone else's place: The influence of impression, defense, and accuracy motivation on the search for new information. *Personality and Social Psychology Bulletin, 31,* 977–990.

Jonason, P. K. (2007). An evolutionary psychology perspective on sex differences in exercise behaviors and motivations. *Journal of Social Psychology, 147,* 5–14.

Jones, B. C., DeBruine, L. M., & Little, A. C. (2007). The role of symmetry in attraction to average faces. *Perception and Psychophysics, 69,* 1273–1277.

Jones, B. C., Little, A. C., Boothroyd, L. G., DeBruine, L. M., Feinberg, D. R., Law Smith, M. J., et al. (2005). Commitment to relationships and preferences for femininity and apparent health in faces are strongest on days of the menstrual cycle when progesterone level is high. *Hormones and Behavior, 48,* 283–290.

Jones, B. C., Little, A. C., Penton-Voak, I. S., Tiddeman, B. P., Burt, D. M., & Perrett, D. I. (2001). Facial symmetry and judgements of apparent health: Support for a "good genes" explanation of the attractiveness-symmetry relationship. *Evolution and Human Behavior, 22,* 417–429.

Jones, B. C., Perrett, D. I., Little, A. C., Boothroyd, L. G., Cornwell, R. E., Feinberg, D. R., et al. (2005). Menstrual cycle, pregnancy and oral contraceptive use alter attraction to apparent health in faces. *Proceedings of the Royal Society of London B, 272,* 347–354.

Jones, E. E. (1990). *Interpersonal perception.* New York: Freeman.

Jones, E. E., & Davis, K. E. (1965). From acts to dispositions the attribution process in person perception. *Advances in Experimental Social Psychology, 2,* 219–266.

Jones, E. E., & Harris, V. A. (1967). The attribution of attitudes. *Journal of Experimental Social Psychology, 3,* 1–24.

Jones, E. E., & Kelly, J. R. (2007). Contributions to a group discussion and perceptions of leadership: Does quantity always count more than quality? *Group Dynamics: Theory, Research, and Practice, 11,* 15–30.

Jones, E. E., & Pittman, T. S. (1982). Toward a general theory of strategic self-presentation. In J. Suls (Ed.), *Psychological perspectives on the self* (Vol. 1, pp. 231–262). Hills-dale, NJ: Erlbaum.

Jones, E. E., & Wortman, C. (1973). *Ingratiation: An attributional approach.* Morristown, NJ: General Learning Corporation.

Jones, J. T., Pelham, B. W., Carvallo, M., & Mirenberg, M. C. (2004). How do I love thee? Let me count the Js: Implicit egotism and interpersonal attraction. *Journal of Personality and Social Psychology, 87,* 665–683.

Jones, M. A., & Sigler, R. T. (2002). Law enforcement partnership in community corrections: An evaluation of juvenile offender curfew checks. *Journal of Criminal Justice, 30,* 245–256.

Jones, W. H., & Carver, M. D. (1991). Adjustment and coping implications of loneliness. In C. R. Snyder & D. R. Forsyth (Eds.), *Handbook of social and clinical psychology* (pp. 395–410). New York: Pergamon.

Jones, W. H., Cavert, C. W., Snider, R. L., & Bruce, T. (1985). Relational stress: An analysis of situations and events associated with loneliness. In S. Duck & D. Perlman (Eds.), *Understanding personal relationships: An interdisciplinary approach* (pp. 221–242). Beverly Hills, CA: Sage.

Jones, W. H., Freemon, J. E., & Goswick, R. A. (1981). The persistence of loneliness: Self and other determinants. *Journal of Personality, 49,* 27–48.

Jones, W. H., Hobbs, S. A., & Hockenbury, D. (1982). Loneliness and social skill deficits. *Journal of Personality and Social Psychology, 42,* 682–689.

Jones, W. H., Sansone, C., & Helm, B. (1983). Loneliness and interpersonal judgments. *Personality and Social Psychology Bulletin, 9,* 437–441.

Jordan, A. H., & Monin, B. (2008). From sucker to saint: Moralization in response to self-threat. *Psychological Science, 19,* 809–815.

Jorden, D. L. (1993). Newspaper effects on policy preferences. *Public Opinion Quarterly, 57,* 191–204.

Josephs, R. A., Markus, H. R., & Tarafodi, R. W. (1992). Gender and self-esteem. *Journal of Personality and Social Psychology, 63,* 391–402.

Jost, J. T., & Burgess, D. (2000). Attitudinal ambivalence and the conflict between group and system justification motives in low status groups. *Personality and Social Psychology Bulletin, 26,* 293–305.

Jost, J. T., Glaser, J., Kruglanski, A. W., & Sulloway, F. J. (2003). Political conservatism as motivated social cognition. *Psychological Bulletin, 129,* 339–375.

Joule, R. V. (1987). Tobacco deprivation: The foot-in-the-door technique versus the low-ball technique. *European Journal of Social Psychology, 17,* 361–365.

Joule, R. V., Gouilloux, F., & Weber, F. (1989). The lure: A new compliance procedure. *Journal of Social Psychology, 129,* 741–749.

Judge, T. A., & Bretz, R. D., Jr. (1994). Political influence behavior and career success. *Journal of Management, 20,* 43–65.

Jussim, L. (1991). Social perception and social reality: A reflection-construction model. *Psychological Review, 98,* 54–73.

Jussim, L. (2012). *Social perception and social reality: Why accuracy dominates bias and self-fulfilling prophecy.* New York: Oxford University Press.

Jussim, L., Eccles, J., & Madon, S. (1995). Social perception, social stereotypes, and teacher expectations: Accuracy and the quest for the powerful self-fulfilling prophecy. In M. P. Zanna (Ed.), *Advances in experimental social psychology* (Vol. 27, pp. 215–255). New York: Academic Press.

Kacmar, K. M., Carlson, D. S., & Bratton, V. K. (2004). Situational and dispositional factors as antecedents of ingratiatory behaviors in organizational settings. *Journal of Vocational Behavior, 65,* 309–331.

Kacmar, K. M., Delery, J. E., & Ferris, G. R. (1992). Differential effectiveness of applicant impression management tactics on employment interview decisions. *Journal of Applied Social Psychology, 22*(16), 1250–1272.

Kadlec, D. (1997, May 5). The new world of giving. *Time, 149,* 62–64.

Kafetsios, K., & Nezlek, J. B. (2002). Attachment styles in everyday social interaction. *European Journal of Social Psychology, 32,* 719–735.

Kahan, D. M. (1997). Social influence, social meaning, and deterrence. *Virginia Law Review, 83,* 349–395.

Kahneman, D., Knetsch, J. L., & Thaler, R. (1986). Fairness and the assumptions of economics. *Journal of Business, 59,* S285–S300.

Kahneman, D., Knetsch, J. L., & Thaler, R. H. (1991). The endowment effect, loss aversion, and status quo bias. *Journal of Economic Perspectives, 5,* 193–206.

Kahneman, D., & Tversky, A. (1972). Subjective probability: A judgment of representativeness. *Cognitive Psychology, 3,* 430–454.

Kallgren, C. A., Reno, R. R., & Cialdini, R. B. (2000). A focus theory of normative conduct: When norms do and do not affect behavior. *Personality & Social Psychology Bulletin, 26,* 1002–1012.

Kallgren, C. A., & Wood, W. (1986). Access to attitude-relevant information in memory as a determinant of attitude–behavior consistency. *Journal of Experimental Social Psychology, 22,* 328–338.

Kalven, H., Jr., & Zeisel, H. (1966). *The American jury.* Boston: Little, Brown.

Kammrath, L. K., & Peetz, J. (2011). The limits of love: Predicting immediate versus sustained caring behaviors in close relationships. *Journal of Experimental Social Psychology, 47,* 414–417.

Kanazawa, S. (1992). Outcome or expectancy? Antecedent of spontaneous causal attribution. *Personality and Social Psychology Bulletin, 18,* 659–668.

Kanter, R. M. (1977). *Men and women of the corporation.* New York: Basic Books.

Kantola, S. J., Syme, G. J., & Campbell, N. A. (1984). Cognitive dissonance and energy conservation. *Journal of Applied Psychology, 69,* 416–421.

Kaplan, H. B. (2003). Social psychological perspectives on deviance. In J. DeLamater (Ed.), *Handbook of social psychology* (pp. 479–502). New York: Kluwer.

Kaprio, J., Koskenvuo, M., & Rita, H. (1987). Mortality after bereavement: A prospective study of 95,647 widowed persons. *American Journal of Public Health, 77,* 283–287.

Karau, S. J., & Williams, K. D. (1993). Social loafing: A meta-analytic review and theoretical integration. *Journal of Personality and Social Psychology, 65,* 681–706.

Karau, S. J., & Williams, K. D. (2001). Understanding individual mutation in groups: The collective effort model. In M. E. Turner (Ed.), *Groups at work: Theory and research* (pp. 113–141). Mahwah, NJ: Erlbaum.

Karon, T. (2004, May 26). Why al-Qaeda thrives. *Time Online Edition.* Retrieved from www.time.com/time/world/article/0,8599,642825,00.html

Karp, D. R., & Gaulding, C. L. (1995). Motivational underpinning of command-and-control, market-based, and voluntarist environmental policies. *Human Relations, 48,* 439–465.

Kasser, T., & Sheldon, K. M. (2000). Of wealth and death: Materialism, mortality salience, and consumption behavior. *Psychological Science, 11,* 348–351.

Kassin, S. M. (2008). False confessions: Causes, consequences, and implications for reform. *Current Directions in Psychological Science, 17,* 249–253.

Kassin, S. M., & Kiechel, K. L. (1996). The social psychology of false confessions: Compliance, internalization, and confabulation. *Psychological Science, 7,* 125–128.

Katz, I., Wackenhut, J., & Hass, R. G. (1986). Racial ambivalence, value duality, and behavior. In J. F. Dovidio & S. L. Gaertner (Eds.), *Prejudice, discrimination, and racism* (pp. 35–59). Orlando, FL: Academic Press.

Kay, A. C., Gaucher, D., Napier, J. L., Callan, M. J., & Laurin, K. (2008). God and the government: Testing a compensatory control mechanism for the support of external systems. *Journal of Personality and Social Psychology, 95,* 18–35.

Keating, C. F., Mazur, A., & Segall, M. H. (1977). Facial gestures which influence the perception of status. *Sociometry, 40,* 374–378.

Keinan, G. (1987). Decision making under stress: Scanning of alternatives under controllable and uncontrollable threats. *Journal of Personality and Social Psychology, 52,* 639–644.

Keller, J. (2002). Blatant stereotype threat and women's math performance: Self-handicapping as a strategic means to cope with obtrusive negative performance expectations. *Sex Roles, 47,* 193–198.

Keller, J., & Dauenheimer, D. (2003). Stereotype threat in the classroom: Dejection mediates the disrupting threat effect on women's math performance. *Personality and Social Psychology Bulletin, 29,* 371–381.

Kellermann, A. L., Rivara, F. P., Rushforth, N. B., Banton, J. B., Reay, O. T., Francisco, J. T., et al. (1993). Gun ownership as a risk factor for homicide in the home. *New England Journal of Medicine, 329,* 1084–1091.

Kelley, A. E. (2005). Neurochemical networks encoding emotion and motivation: An evolutionary perspective. In J. M. Fellous & M. A. Arbib (Eds.), *Who needs emotions? The brain meets the robot* (pp. 29–77). New York: Oxford University Press.

Kelley, H. H. (1950). The warm-cold variable in first impressions of persons. *Journal of Personality, 18,* 431–439.

Kelley, H. H. (1973). The processes of causal attribution. *American Psychologist, 28,* 107–128.

Kelley, H. H., & Stahelski, A. J. (1970). Social interaction basis of cooperators' and competitors' beliefs about others. *Journal of Personality and Social Psychology, 16,* 66–91.

Kelly, A. E. (1998). Clients' secret keeping in outpatient therapy. *Journal of Counseling Psychology, 45,* 50–57.

Kelly, A. E., & McKillop, K. J. (1996). Consequences of revealing personal secrets. *Psychological Bulletin, 120,* 450–465.

Kelly, A. M., Klusas, J. A., vonWeiss, R. T., & Kenny, C. (2001). What is it about revealing secrets that is beneficial? *Personality & Social Psychology Bulletin, 27,* 651–665.

Kelly, E. L., & Conley, J. J. (1987). Personality and compatibility: A prospective analysis of marital stability and marital satisfaction. *Journal of Personality and Social Psychology, 52,* 27–40.

Kelly, M. (1993, May 23). "Saint Hillary," *New York Times.* In S. K. Flinn (2000) (Ed.), *Speaking of Hillary: A reader's guide to the most controversial woman in America* (pp. 89–103). Ashland, OR: White Cloud Press.

Kelman, H. C. (1998). Social-psychological contributions to peace making and peacebuilding in the Middle East. *Applied Psychology: An International Review, 47,* 5–28.

Kelman, H. C. (1999). Interactive problem solving as a metaphor for international conflict resolution: Lessons for the policy process. *Peace and Conflict: Journal of Peace Psychology, 5,* 201–218.

Keltner, D., & Ekman, P. (1994). Facial expressions in emotion. In V. S. Ramachandran (Ed.), *Encyclopedia of human behavior* (Vol. 2, pp. 361–369). San Diego, CA: Academic Press.

Keltner, D., Haidt, J., & Shiota, M. N. (2006). Social functionalism and the evolution of emotions. In M. Schaller, J. A. Simpson, & D. T. Kenrick (Eds.), *Evolution and social psychology* (pp. 115–142). New York: Psychology Press.

Kemmelmeier, M., & Winter, D. G. (2000). Putting threat into perspective: Experimental studies on perceptual distortion in international conflict. *Personality & Social Psychology Bulletin, 26,* 795–809.

Kenny, D. A. (1994). *Interpersonal perception: A social relations analysis.* New York: Guilford.

Kenny, D. A., Albright, L., Malloy, T. E., & Kashy, D. A. (1994). Consensus in interpersonal perception: Acquaintance and the big five. *Psychological Bulletin, 116,* 245–258.

Kenny, D. A., & DePaulo, B. M. (1993). Do people know how others view them? An empirical and theoretical account. *Psychological Bulletin, 114,* 145–161.

Kenny, D. A., & Kashy, D. A. (1994). Enhanced co-orientation in the perception of friends: A social relations analysis. *Journal of Personality and Social Psychology, 67,* 1024–1033.

Kenrick, D. T. (1991). Proximate altruism and ultimate selfishness. *Psychological Inquiry, 2,* 135–137.

Kenrick, D. T. (2006a). A dynamical evolutionary view of love. In R. J. Sternberg & K. Weis (Eds.), *Psychology of love* (2nd ed., pp. 15–34). New Haven, CT: Yale University Press.

Kenrick, D. T. (2006b). Evolutionary psychology: Resistance is futile. *Psychological Inquiry, 17,* 102–108.

Kenrick, D. T. (2013). Men and women are only as different as they look! *Psychological Inquiry, 24,* 202–206.

Kenrick, D. T., Ackerman, J., & Ledlow, S. (2003). Evolutionary social psychology: Adaptive predispositions and human culture. In J. DeLamater (Ed.), *Handbook of social psychology* (pp. 103–124). New York: Kluwer.

Kenrick, D. T., Becker, D. V., Butner, J., Li, N. P., & Maner, J. K. (2004). Evolutionary cognitive science: Adding what and why to how the mind works. In K. Sterelney & J. Fitness (Eds.), *From mating to mentality: Evaluating evolutionary psychology.* New York: Psychology Press.

Kenrick, D. T., Delton, A. W., Robertson, T., Becker, D. V., & Neuberg, S. L. (2007). How the mind warps: A social evolutionary perspective on cognitive processing disjunctions. In J. P. Forgas, M. G. Haselton, & W. Von Hippel (Eds.), *The evolution of the social mind: Evolution and social cognition* (pp. 49–68). New York: Psychology Press.

Kenrick, D. T., & Funder, D. C. (1988). Profiting from controversy: Lessons from the person-situation debate. *American Psychologist, 43,* 23–34.

Kenrick, D. T., & Gomez-Jacinto, L. (2014). Economics, sex, and the emergence of society: A dynamic life history model of cultural variation. In M. J. Gelfand, C. Y. Chiu, & Y. Y. Hong (Eds.), *Advances in culture and psychology* (Vol. 3, pp. 78–123). New York: Oxford University Press.

Kenrick, D. T., & Griskevicius, V. (2013). *The rational animal: How evolution made us smarter than we think.* New York: Basic Books.

Kenrick, D. T., Griskevicius, V., Neuberg, S. L., & Schaller, M. (2010). Renovating the pyramid of needs: Contemporary extensions built upon ancient foundations. *Perspectives on Psychological Science, 5,* 292–314.

Kenrick, D. T., Groth, G. R., Trost, M. R., & Sadalla, E. K. (1993). Integrating evolutionary and social exchange perspectives on relationships: Effects of gender, self-appraisal, and involvement level on mate selection criteria. *Journal of Personality and Social Psychology, 64,* 951–969.

Kenrick, D. T., & Johnson, G. A. (1979). Interpersonal attraction in aversive environments: A problem for the classical conditioning paradigm? *Journal of Personality and Social Psychology, 37,* 572–579.

Kenrick, D. T., & Keefe, R. C. (1992). Age preferences in mates reflect sex differences in human reproductive strategies. *Behavioral and Brain Sciences, 15,* 75–133.

Kenrick, D. T., Keefe, R. C., Bryan, A., Barr, A., & Brown, S. (1995). Age preferences and mate choice among homosexuals and heterosexuals: A case for modular psychological mechanisms. *Journal of Personality and Social Psychology, 69,* 1166–1172.

Kenrick, D. T., & Li, N. (2000). The Darwin is in the details. *American Psychologist, 5,* 1060–1061.

Kenrick, D. T., Li, N. P., & Butner, J. (2003). Dynamical evolutionary psychology: Individual decision-rules and emergent social norms. *Psychological Review, 110,* 3–28.

Kenrick, D. T., & MacFarlane, S. (1986). Ambient temperature and horn honking: A field study of interpersonal hostility. *Environment and Behavior, 18,* 179–191.

Kenrick, D. T., Maner, J. K., Butner, J., Li, N. P., Becker, D. V., & Schaller, M. (2002). Dynamic evolutionary psychology: Mapping the domains of the new interactionist paradigm. *Personality and Social Psychology Review, 6,* 347–356.

Kenrick, D. T., Maner, J. K., & Li, N. L. (2014). Evolutionary social psychology. In D. M. Buss (Ed.), *Handbook of evolutionary psychology* (2nd ed.). New York: Wiley.

Kenrick, D. T., Montello, D. R., Gutierres, S. E., & Trost, M. R. (1993). Effects of physical attractiveness on affect and perceptual judgment: When social comparison overrides social reinforcement. *Personality and Social Psychology Bulletin, 19,* 195–199.

Kenrick, D. T., Neuberg, S. L., Zierk, K., & Krones, J. (1994). Evolution and social cognition: Contrast effects as a function of sex, dominance, and physical attractiveness. *Personality and Social Psychology Bulletin, 20,* 210–217.

Kenrick, D. T., Nieuweboer, S., & Buunk, A. P. (2010). Universal mechanisms and cultural diversity: Replacing the blank slate with a coloring book. In M. Schaller, S. Heine, A. Norenzayan, T. Yamagishi, & T. Kameda (Eds.), *Evolution, culture, and the human mind* (pp. 257–272). Mahwah, NJ: Lawrence Erlbaum Associates.

Kenrick, D. T., Sadalla, E. K., Groth, G., & Trost, M. R. (1990). Evolution, traits, and the stages of human courtship: Qualifying the parental investment model. *Journal of Personality, 58,* 97–117.

Kenrick, D. T., & Sheets, V. (1994). Homicidal fantasies. *Ethology and Sociobiology, 14,* 231–246.

Kenrick, D. T., Sundie, J. M., & Kurzban, R. (2008). Cooperation and conflict between kith, kin, and strangers: Game theory by domains. In C. Crawford & D. Krebs (Eds.), *Foundations of evolutionary psychology.* Mahwah, NJ: Lawrence Erlbaum Associates.

Kenrick, D. T., Sundie, J. M., Nicastle, L. D., & Stone, G. O. (2001). Can one ever be too wealthy or too chaste? Searching for nonlinearities in mate judgment. *Journal of Personality & Social Psychology, 80,* 462–471.

Kenrick, D. T., Trost, M. R., & Sheets, V. L. (1996). The feminist advantages of an evolutionary perspective. In D. M. Buss & N. Malamuth (Eds.), *Sex, power, conflict: Feminist and evolutionary perspectives* (pp. 29–53). New York: Oxford University Press.

Kernis, M. H., Cornell, D. P., Sun, C.-R., Berry, A., & Harlow, T. (1993). There's more to self-esteem than whether it is high or low: The importance of stability of self-esteem. *Journal of Personality and Social Psychology, 65,* 1190–1204.

Kernis, M. H., Grannemann, B. D., & Barclay, L. C. (1992). Stability of self-esteem: Assessment, correlates, and excuse making. *Journal of Personality, 60,* 621–644.

Kernis, M. H., Paradise, A. W., Whitaker, D., Wheatman, S., & Goldman, B. (2000). Master of one's "Psychological Domain"? Not likely if one's self-esteem is unstable. *Personality and Social Psychology Bulletin, 26,* 1297–1305.

Kerr, N. L. (1983). Motivation losses in small groups: A social dilemma analysis. *Journal of Personality and Social Psychology, 45,* 819–828.

Kerr, N. L. (1995). Norms in social dilemmas. In D. A. Schroeder (Ed.), *Social dilemmas: Perspectives on individuals and groups* (pp. 31–47). Westport, CT: Praeger.

Kerr, N. L. (2002). When is a minority a minority? Active versus passive minority advocacy and social influence. *European Journal of Social Psychology, 32,* 471–483.

Kerr, N. L., Atkin, R. S., Stasser, G., Meek, D., Holt, R. W., & Davis, J. H. (1976). Guilt beyond a reasonable doubt: Effects of concept definition and assigned decision rule on the judgments of mock jurors. *Journal of Personality and Social Psychology, 34,* 282–294.

Kerr, N. L., & Bruun, S. E. (1981). Ringelman revisited: Alternative explanations for the social loafing effect. *Personality and Social Psychology Bulletin, 7,* 224–231.

Kerr, N. L., & Bruun, S. E. (1983). Dispensability of member effort and group motivation losses: Free-rider effects. *Journal of Personality and Social Psychology, 44,* 78–94.

Kerr, N. L., Garst, J., Lewandowski, D. A., & Harris, S. E. (1997). That still small voice: Commitment to cooperate as an internalized versus a social norm. *Personality and Social Psychology Bulletin, 23,* 1300–1311.

Kerr, N. L., & Kaufman-Gilliland, C. M. (1994). Communication, commitment, and cooperation in social dilemmas. *Journal of Personality and Social Psychology, 66,* 513–529.

Kerr, N. L., & MacCoun, R. J. (1985). The effects of jury size and polling method on the process and product of jury deliberation. *Journal of Personality and Social Psychology, 48,* 349–363.

Kerr, N. L., & Tindale, R. S. (2004). Group performance and decision making. *Annual Review of Psychology, 55,* 623–655.

Ketelaar, T., & Ellis, B. J. (2000). Are evolutionary explanations unfalsifiable? Evolutionary psychology and the Lakatosian philosophy of science. *Psychological Inquiry, 11,* 1–21.

Kettenmann, A. (2008). *Kahlo.* Los Angeles: Taschen.

Kiecolt-Glaser, J. K., Malarkey, W. B., Chee, M., Newton, T., Cacioppo, J. T., Mao, H., et al. (1993). Negative behavior during marital conflict is associated with immunological down-regulation. *Psychosomatic Medicine, 55,* 395–409.

Kiecolt-Glaser, J. K., & Newton, T. L. (2001). Marriage and health: His and hers. *Psychological Bulletin, 127,* 472–503.

Killeya, L. A., & Johnson, B. T. (1998). Experimental induction of biased systematic processing: The directed thought technique. *Personality and Social Psychology Bulletin, 24,* 17–33.

Kim, H. S. (2002). We talk, therefore we think? A cultural analysis of the effect of talking on thinking. *Journal of Personality & Social Psychology, 83,* 828–842.

Kim, H. S., & Baron, R. S. (1988). Exercise and the illusory correlation: Does arousal heighten stereotypic processing? *Journal of Experimental Social Psychology, 24,* 366–380.

Kim, H. S., & Sherman, D. K. (2007). "Express yourself": Culture and the effect of self-expression on choice. *Journal of Personality and Social Psychology, 92,* 1–11.

Kim, H. S., Sherman, D. K., Mojaverian, T., Sasaki, J. Y., Park, J., Suh, E. M., et al. (2011). Gene-culture interaction oxytocin receptor polymorphism (OXTR) and emotion regulation. *Social Psychological and Personality Science, 2*(6), 665–672.

Kimmel, P. R. (1997). Cultural perspectives on international negotiations. In L. A. Peplau & S. E. Taylor (Eds.), *Sociocultural perspectives in social psychology* (pp. 395–411). New York: Prentice-Hall.

King, M., Green, J., Osborn, D. P. J., Arkell, J., Hetherton, J., & Pereira, E. (2005). Family size in white gay and heterosexual men. *Archives of Sexual Behavior, 34,* 117–122.

Kinsey, A. C., Pomeroy, W. B., & Martin, C. E. (1948). *Sexual behavior in the human male.* Philadelphia: Saunders.

Kipnis, D. (1984). The use of power in organizations and in interpersonal settings. In S. Oskamp (Ed.), *Applied social psychology annual* (Vol. 5, pp. 179–210). Newbury Park, CA: Sage.

Kirkcaldy, B. D., Shephard, R. J., & Siefen, R. G. (2002). The relationship between physical activity and self-image and problem behavior among adolescents. *Social Psychiatry and Psychiatric Epidemiology, 37,* 544–550.

Kirkpatrick, L. A., & Hazan, C. (1994). Attachment styles and close relationships: A four-year prospective study. *Personal Relationships, 1,* 123–142.

Kirkpatrick, L. A., & Shaver, P. (1988). Fear and affiliation reconsidered from a stress and coping perspective: The importance of cognitive clarity and fear reduction. *Journal of Social and Clinical Psychology, 7,* 214–233.

Kirkpatrick, L. A., Waugh, C. E., Valencia, A., & Webster, G. D. (2002). The functional domain specificity of self-esteem and the differential prediction of aggression. *Journal of Personality & Social Psychology, 82,* 756–767.

Kirmani, A. (1990). The effect of perceived advertising cost on brand perceptions. *Journal of Consumer Research, 17,* 160–171.

Kirmani, A., & Wright, P. (1989). Money talks: Perceived advertising expense and expected product quality. *Journal of Consumer Research, 16,* 344–353.

Kitayama, S., & Cohen, D. (2007). *Handbook of cultural psychology.* New York: Guilford Press.

Kitayama, S., Mesquita, B., & Karasawa, M. (2006). Cultural affordances and emotional experience: Socially engaging and disengaging emotions in Japan and the United States. *Journal of Personality and Social Psychology, 91,* 890–903.

Kitayama, S., Takagi, H., & Matsumoto, H. (1995). Cultural psychology of Japanese self: I. Causal attribution of success and failure [in Japanese]. *Japanese Psychological Review, 38,* 247–280.

Kiviat, B. (2003, July 28). Sunny money on Wall Street. *Time,* p. 70.

Kiyonari, T., & Barclay, P. (2008). Cooperation in social dilemmas: Free riding may be thwarted by second-order reward rather than by punishment. *Journal of Personality and Social Psychology, 95,* 826–842.

Kleck, R. E., Vaughan, R. C., Cartwright-Smith, J., Vaughan, K. B., Colby, C., & Lanzetta, J. T. (1976). Effects of being observed on expressive subjective and physical responses to painful stimuli. *Journal of Personality and Social Psychology, 34,* 1211–1218.

Klehe, U.-C., & Anderson, N. (2007). The moderating influence of personality and culture on social loafing in typical versus maximum performance situations. *International Journal of Selection and Assessment, 15,* 250–262.

Klein, K., & Hodges, S. D. (2001). Gender differences, motivation, and empathic accuracy: When it pays to understand. *Personality & Social Psychology Bulletin, 27,* 720–730.

Klein, S. B., Cosmides, L., Tooby, J., & Chance, S. (2002). Decisions and the evolution of memory: Multiple systems, multiple functions. *Psychological Review, 109,* 306–329.

Klein, O., Snyder, M., & Livingston, R. W. (2004). Prejudice on the stage: Self-monitoring and the public expression of group attitudes. *British Journal of Social Psychology, 43*(2), 299–314.

Klinesmith, J., Kasser, T., & McAndrew, F. T. (2006). Guns, testosterone, and aggression: An experimental test of a mediational hypothesis. *Psychological Science, 17,* 568–571.

Knox, R. E., & Inkster, J. A. (1968). Postdecisional dissonance at post time. *Journal of Personality and Social Psychology, 8,* 319–323.

Knox, R. E., & Safford, R. K. (1976). Group caution at the race track. *Journal of Experimental Social Psychology, 12,* 317–324.

Ko, S. J., Muller, D., Judd, C. M., & Stapel, D. A. (2008). Sneaking in through the back door: How category-based stereotype suppression leads to rebound in feature-based effects. *Journal of Experimental Social Psychology, 44,* 833–839.

Kobayashi, F., Schallert, D. L., & Ogren, H. A. (2003). Japanese and American "folk" vocabularies for emotions. *Journal of Social Psychology, 143,* 451–478.

Koenig, A. M., Eagly, A. H., Mitchell, A. A., & Ristikari, T. (2011). Are leader stereotypes masculine? A meta-analysis of three research paradigms. *Psychological Bulletin, 137*(4), 616.

Koestner, R., & McClelland, D. C. (1990). Perspectives on competence motivation. In L. A. Pervin (Ed.), *Handbook of personality: Theory and research* (pp. 527–548). New York: Guilford.

Koestner, R., & Wheeler, L. (1988). Self-presentation in personal relationships: The influence of implicit notions of attraction and role expectations. *Journal of Social and Personal Relationships, 5,* 149–160.

Kohn, J. L., Rholes, W. S., Simpson, J. A., Martin, A. M., III, Tran, S., & Wilson, C. L. (2012). Changes in marital satisfaction across the transition to parenthood: The role of adult attachment orientations. *Personality and Social Psychology Bulletin, 38*(11), 1506–1522.

Kolditz, T. A., & Arkin, R. M. (1982). An impression management interpretation of the self-handicapping strategy. *Journal of Personality and Social Psychology, 43,* 492–502.

Komorita, S. S., Hilty, J. A., & Parks, C. D. (1991). Reciprocity and cooperation in social dilemmas. *Journal of Conflict Resolution, 35,* 494–518.

Komorita, S. S., Parks, C. D., & Hulbert, L. G. (1992). Reciprocity and the induction of cooperation in social dilemmas. *Journal of Personality and Social Psychology, 62,* 607–617.

Konrad, A. M., Ritchie, J. E., Jr., Lieb, P., & Corrigall, E. (2000). Sex differences and similarities in job attribute preferences: A meta-analysis. *Psychological Bulletin, 126,* 593–641.

Koole, S. L., Jager, W., VanDenBerg, A. E., Vlek, C. A. J., & Hofstee, W. K. B. (2001). On the social nature of personality: Effects of extraversion, agreeableness, and feedback about collective resource use on cooperation in a resource dilemma. *Personality & Social Psychology Bulletin, 27,* 289–301.

Kors, D. J., Linden, W., & Gerin, W. (1997). Evaluation interferes with social support: Effects of cardiovascular stress reactivity in women. *Journal of Social and Clinical Psychology, 16,* 1–23.

Kosfeld, M., Heinrichs, M., Zak, P. J., Fischbacher, U., & Fehr, E. (2005). Oxytocin increases trust in humans. *Nature, 435,* 673–676.

Kouri, E., Lukas, S., Pope, H., & Oliva, P. (1995). Increased aggressive responding in male volunteers following the administration of gradually increasing doses of testosterone cypionate. *Drug and Alcohol Dependence, 40,* 73–79.

Kowalski, R. M. (2000). "I was only kidding!": Victims' and perpetrators' perceptions of teasing. *Personality & Social Psychology Bulletin, 26,* 231–241.

Kowalski, R. M., & Leary, M. R. (1990). Strategic self-presentation and the avoidance of aversive events: Antecedents and consequences of self-enhancement and self-depreciation. *Journal of Experimental Social Psychology, 26,* 322–336.

Krackow, A., & Blass, T. (1995). When nurses obey or defy inappropriate physician orders: Attributional differences. *Journal of Social Behavior and Personality, 10,* 585–594.

Kramer, R. M., & Brewer, M. B. (1984). Effects of group identity on resource use in a simulated commons dilemma. *Journal of Personality and Social Psychology, 46*(5), 1044–1057.

Kranzler, D. (1976). *Japanese, Nazis, and Jews: The Jewish refugee community of Shanghai, 1938–1945.* New York: Yeshiva University Press.

Krauss, M. W., Piff, P. K., & Keltner, D. (2011). Social class as culture : The convergence of resources and rank in the social realm. *Current Directions in Psychological Science, 20,* 246–250.

Kraut, R. E. (1973). Effects of social labeling on giving to charity. *Journal of Experimental Social Psychology, 9,* 551–562.

Kraut, R., & Kiesler, S. (2003). The social impact of internet use. *Psychological Science Agenda, 16*(3), 8–10.

Kraut, R., Patterson, M., Lundmark, V., Kiesler, S., Mukhopadhyay, T., & Scherlis, W. (1998). Internet paradox: A social technology that reduces social involvement and psychological wellbeing? *American Psychologist, 53,* 1017–1031.

Kravitz, D. A., & Martin, B. (1986). Ringelmann rediscovered: The original article. *Journal of Personality and Social Psychology, 50,* 936–941.

Kray, L. J., & Galinsky, A. D. (2003). The debiasing effect of counterfactual mindsets: Increasing the search for disconfirmatory information in group decisions. *Organizational Behavior and Human Decision Processes, 91,* 69–81.

Krebs, D. (1975). Empathy and altruism. *Journal of Personality and Social Psychology, 32,* 1134–1146.

Krebs, D. L. (2011). *The origins of morality: An evolutionary account.* New York: Oxford University Press.

Krebs, D. L. (2012). How altruistic by nature? In S. L. Brown, R. M. Brown, & L. A. Penner (Eds.), *Moving beyond self-interest: Perspectives from evolutionary biology, neuroscience, and the social sciences* (pp. 25–38). New York: Oxford University Press.

Krebs, D. L., & Denton, K. (1997). Social illusions and self-deception: The evolution of biases in person perception. In J. A. Simpson & D. T. Kenrick (Eds.), *Evolutionary social psychology* (pp. 21–48). Mahwah, NJ: Erlbaum.

Krebs, D. L., & Janicki, M. (2004). Biological foundations of moral norms. In M. Schaller & C. S. Crandall (Eds.), *The psychological foundations of culture* (pp. 125–148). Mahwah, NJ: Erlbaum.

Kressel, L. M., & Uleman, J. S. (2010). Personality traits function as causal concepts. *Journal of Experimental Social Psychology, 46,* 213–216.

Krosnick, J. A., Betz, A. L., Jussim, L. J., & Lynn, A. R. (1992). Subliminal conditioning of attitudes. *Personality and Social Psychology Bulletin, 18,* 152–162.

Kross, E., Verduyn, P., Demiralp, E., Park, J., Lee, D. S., et al. (2013). Facebook use predicts declines in subjective well-being in young adults. *PLos ONE, 8*(8), e69841. doi:10.1371/journal.pone.0069841

Kruger, D. J., & Fitzgerald, C. J. (2011). Reproductive strategies and relationship preferences associated with prestigious and dominant men. *Personality and Individual Differences, 50*(3), 365–369.

Kruger, D. J., Fitzgerald, C. J., & Peterson, T. (2010). Female scarcity reduces women's marital ages and increases variance in men's marital ages. *Evolutionary Psychology, 8*(3), 420–431.

Krueger, J. I. (2007). From social projection to social behaviour. *European Review of Social Psychology, 18,* 1–35.

Krueger, J., & Rothbart, M. (1990). Contrast and accentuation effects in category learning. *Journal of Personality and Social Psychology, 59,* 651–663.

Kruger, J., Gordon, C. L., & Kuban, J. (2006). Intentions in teasing: When "just kidding" just isn't good enough. *Journal of Personality and Social Psychology, 90,* 412–425.

Kruger, J. S. (1999). *Egocentrism in self and social judgment.* Unpublished doctoral dissertation, Cornell University.

Kruglanski, A. W., & Freund, T. (1983). The freezing and unfreezing of lay inferences: Effects on impressional primacy, ethnic stereotyping, and numerical anchoring. *Journal of Experimental Social Psychology, 19,* 448–468.

Kruglanski, A. W., & Mayseless, O. (1988). Contextual effects in hypothesis testing: The role of competing alternatives and epistemic motivations. *Social Cognition, 6,* 1–20.

Krull, D. S., Loy, M. H., Lin, J., Wang, C. F., Chen, S., & Zhao, X. (1999). The fundamental attribution error: Correspondence bias in individualist and collectivist cultures. *Personality and Social Psychology Bulletin, 25,* 1208–1219.

Krumhuber, E., & Kappas, A. (2005). Moving smiles: The role of dynamic components for the perception of the genuineness of smiles. *Journal of Nonverbal Behavior, 29,* 3–24.

Krupp, D. B., Debruine, L. M., & Barclay, P. (2008). A cue of kinship promotes cooperation for the public good. *Evolution and Human Behavior, 29,* 49–55.

Krusemark, E. A., Campbell, W. K., & Clementz, B. (2008). Attributions, deception, and event-related potentials: An investigation of the self-serving bias. *Psychophysiology, 45,* 511–515.

Kteily, N. S., Sidanius, J., & Levin, S. (2011). Social dominance orientation: Cause or 'mere effect'? Evidence for SDO as a causal predictor of prejudice and discrimination against ethnic and racial outgroups. *Journal of Experimental Social Psychology, 47,* 208–214.

Kudo, E., & Numazaki, M. (2003). Explicit and direct self-serving bias in Japan: Reexamination of self-serving bias for success and failure. *Journal of Cross-Cultural Psychology, 34,* 511–521.

Kukla, A. (1972). Attributional determinants of achievement-related behavior. *Journal of Personality and Social Psychology, 21,* 166–174.

Kulig, J. W. (2000). Effects of forced exposure to a hypothetical population on false consensus. *Personality and Social Psychology Bulletin, 26,* 629–636.

Kulik, J. A., & Mahler, H. I. M. (1989). Stress and affiliation in a hospital setting: Preoperative roommate preferences. *Personality and Social Psychology Bulletin, 15,* 183–193.

Kulik, J. A., & Mahler, H. I. M. (1990). Stress and affiliation research: On taking the laboratory to health field settings. *Annals of Behavioral Medicine, 12,* 106–111.

Kulik, J. A., & Mahler, H. I. M. (2000). Social comparison, affiliation, and emotional contagion under threat. In J. Suls & L. Wheeler (Eds.), *Handbook of social comparison: Theory and research* (pp. 295–320). New York: Kluwer Academic Publishers.

Kulik, J. A., Mahler, H. I. M., & Earnest, A. (1994). Social comparison and affiliation under threat: Going beyond the affiliate-choice paradigm.

Journal of Personality and Social Psychology, 66(2), 301–309.

Kunda, Z. (1987). Motivation and inference: Self-serving generation and evaluation of evidence. *Journal of Personality and Social Psychology, 53,* 636–647.

Kunda, Z. (1999). *Social cognition: Making sense of people.* Cambridge, MA: MIT Press.

Kunda, Z., Miller, D. T., & Claire, T. (1990). Combining social concepts: The role of causal reasoning. *Cognitive Science, 14,* 551–577.

Kunda, Z., & Oleson, K. C. (1995). Maintaining stereotypes in the face of disconfirmation: Constructing grounds for subtyping deviants. *Journal of Personality and Social Psychology, 68,* 565–579.

Kurland, J. A., & Gaulin, S. J. C. (2005). Cooperation and conflict among kin. In D. M. Buss (Ed.), *The handbook of evolutionary psychology* (pp. 447–482). Hoboken, NJ: Wiley.

Kurman, J. (2001). Self-enhancement: Is it restricted to individualistic cultures? *Personality and Social Psychology Bulletin, 27,* 1705–1716.

Kurzban, R. (2012). *Why everyone (else) is a hypocrite: Evolution and the modular mind.* Princeton, NJ: Princeton University Press.

Kurzban, R., & Descioli, P. (2008). Reciprocal cooperation in groups: Information-seeking in a public goods game. *European Journal of Social Psychology, 38,* 139–158.

Kurzban, R., DeScioli, P., & O'Brien, E. (2007). Audience effects on moralistic punishment. *Evolution & Human Behavior, 28,* 75–84.

Kurzban, R., Dukes, A., & Weeden, J. (2010). Sex, drugs and moral goals: Reproductive strategies and views about recreational drugs. *Proceedings of the Royal Society B: Biological Sciences, 277*(1699), 3501–3508.

Kurzban, R., & Leary, M. R. (2001). Evolutionary origins of stigmatization: The functions of social exclusion. *Psychological Bulletin, 127,* 187–208.

Kurzban, R., & Neuberg, S. L. (2005). Managing ingroup and outgroup relationships. In D. Buss (Ed.), *Handbook of evolutionary psychology* (pp. 653–675). New York: Wiley.

LaFramboise, T., Coleman, H. L., & Gerton, J. (1993). Psychological impact of biculturalism: Evidence and theory. *Psychological Bulletin, 114,* 395–412.

LaFrance, M., Hecht, M. A., & Paluck, E. L. (2003). The contingent smile: A meta-analysis of sex differences in smiling. *Psychological Bulletin, 129,* 305–334.

Laham, S. M., Gonsalkorale, K., & von Hippel, W. (2005). Darwinian grandparenting: Preferential investment in more certain kin. *Personality and Social Psychology Bulletin, 31,* 63–72.

Lakin, J. L., & Chartrand, T. L. (2003). Using nonconscious behavioral mimicry to create affiliation and rapport. *Psychological Science, 14,* 334–339.

Lalumiere, M. L., Harris, G. T., & Rice, M. E. (2001). Psychopathy and developmental instability. *Evolution & Human Behavior, 22,* 75–92.

Lalwani, A. K., Shavitt, S., & Johnson, T. (2006). What is the relation between cultural orientation and socially desirable responding? *Journal of Personality and Social Psychology, 90,* 165–178.

Lambert, A. J., Burroughs, T., & Nguyen, T. (1999). Perceptions of risk and the buffering hypothesis: The role of just world beliefs and right-wing authoritarianism. *Personality & Social Psychology Bulletin, 25,* 643–656.

Lambert, A. J., Payne, B. K., Ramsey, S., & Shatter, L. M. (2005). On the predictive validity of implicit attitude measures: The moderating effect of perceived group variability. *Journal of Experimental Social Psychology, 41,* 114–128.

Lamm, H., & Myers, D. G. (1978). Group-induced polarization of attitudes and behavior. In L. Berkowitz (Ed.), *Advances in experimental social psychology* (Vol. 11, pp. 145–195). Orlando, FL: Academic Press.

Landau, M. J., Solomon, S., Greenberg, J., Cohen, F., Pyszczynski, T., Arndt, J., et al. (2004). Deliver us from evil: The effects of mortality salience and reminders of 9/11 on support for President George W. Bush. *Personality and Social Psychology Bulletin, 30,* 1136–1150.

Lane, C. (1991, January 7). Saddam's Endgame. *Newsweek,* pp. 14–18.

Langer, E. J. (1975). The illusion of control. *Journal of Personality and Social Psychology, 32,* 311–328.

Langer, E. J. (1989). *Mindfulness.* Reading, MA: Addison-Wesley.

Langer, E. J., Blank, A., & Chanowitz, B. (1978). The mindlessness of ostensibly thoughtful action: The role of placebic information in interpersonal interaction. *Journal of Personality and Social Psychology, 36,* 635–642.

Langer, E. J., & Moldoveanu, M. (2000). Mindfulness research and the future. *Journal of Social Issues, 56,* 129–139.

Langewiesche, W. (2003). Columbia's last flight. *The Atlantic Monthly, 292,* 58–87.

Langleben, D., Schroeder, L., Maldjian, J., Gur, R., McDonald, S., Ragland, J., et al. (2002). Brain activity during simulated deception: An event-related functional magnetic resonance study. *NeuroImage, 15,* 727–732.

Langlois, J. H., Kalakanis, L., Rubenstein, A. J., Larson, A., Hallam, M., & Smoot, M. (2000). Maxims or myths of beauty? A meta-analytic and theoretical review. *Psychological Bulletin, 126,* 390–423.

Langlois, J. H., Ritter, J. M., Casey, R. J., & Sawin, D. B. (1995). Infant attractiveness predicts maternal behaviors and attitudes. *Developmental Psychology, 31,* 464–472.

Langlois, J. H., & Roggman, L. A. (1990). Attractive faces are only average. *Psychological Science, 1,* 115–121.

Larimer, M. E., & Neighbors, C. (2003). The impact of social norms on gambling behavior among college students. *Psychology of Addictive Behaviors, 17,* 235–243.

Larrick, R. P., Timmerman, T. A., Carton, A. M., & Abrevaya, J. (2011). Temper, temperature, and temptation heat-related retaliation in baseball. *Psychological Science, 22*(4), 423–428.

Lassek, W. D., & Gaulin, S. J. C. (2008). Waist-hip ratio and cognitive ability: Is gluteofemoral fat a privileged store of neurodevelopmental resources? *Evolution and Human Behavior, 29,* 26–34.

Latané, B. (1996). Dynamic social impact: The creation of culture by communication. *Journal of Communication, 46,* 13–25.

Latané, B., & Bourgeois, M. J. (1996). Experimental evidence for dynamic social impact: The emergence of subcultures in electronic groups. *Journal of Communication, 46,* 35–47.

Latané, B., & Bourgeois, M. J. (2001). Simulating dynamic social impact: Three levels of prediction. In J. Forgas & K. Williams (Eds.), *Social influence: Direct and indirect processes* (pp. 61–76). Philadelphia: Psychology Press.

Latané, B., & Bourgeois, M. J. (2001). Successfully simulating dynamic social impact: Three levels of prediction. In J. P. Forgas & K. D. Williams (Eds.), *Social influence: Direct and indirect processes* (pp. 61–76). Sydney Symposium of Social Psychology. New York: Psychology Press.

Latané, B., & Darley, J. M. (1968). Group inhibition of bystander intervention in emergencies. *Journal of Personality and Social Psychology, 10,* 215–221.

Latané, B., & Darley, J. M. (1970). *The unresponsive bystander: Why doesn't he help?* New York: Appleton-Century-Croft.

Latané, B., Liu, J. H., Nowak, A., Bonevento, M., & Zheng, L. (1995). Distance matters: Physical space and social impact. *Personality and Social Psychology Bulletin, 21,* 795–805.

Latané, B., Williams, K., & Harkins, S. (1979). Many hands make light the work: The causes and consequences of social loafing. *Journal of Personality and Social Psychology, 37,* 822–832.

Laughlin, P. R. (1980). Social combination process of cooperative problem-solving groups at verbal intellective tasks. In M. Fishbein (Ed.), *Progress in social psychology* (Vol. 1, pp. 127–155). Hillsdale, NJ: Erlbaum.

Laughlin, P. R., Carey, H. R., & Kerr, N. L. (2008). Group-to-individual problem-solving transfer. *Group Processes & Intergroup Relations, 11,* 319–330.

Laughlin, P. R., & Ellis, A. L. (1986). Demonstrability and social combination processes on mathematical intellective tasks. *Journal of Experimental Social Psychology, 22,* 177–189.

Lavine, H., Burgess, D., Snyder, M., Transue, J., Sullivan, J. L., Haney, B., et al. (1999). Threat, authoritarianism, and voting: An investigation of personality and persuasion. *Personality & Social Psychology Bulletin, 25,* 337–347.

Lazarus, R. S. (1983). The costs and benefits of denial. In S. Breznitz (Ed.), *The denial of stress* (pp. 1–30). Madison, CT: International Universities Press.

Lazarus, R. S., & Folkman, S. (1984). *Stress, appraisal, and coping.* New York: Springer.

Le Bon, G. (1895/1960). *Psychologie des foules (the crowd).* New York: Viking Press.

Leary, M. R. (1986a). The impact of interactional impediments on social anxiety and self-presentation. *Journal of Experimental Social Psychology, 22,* 122–135.

Leary, M. R. (1986b). Affective and behavioral components of shyness. In W. H. Jones, J. M. Cheek, & S. R. Briggs (Eds.), *Shyness: Perspectives on research and treatment* (pp. 27–38). New York: Plenum Press.

Leary, M. R. (1995). *Self-presentation: Impression management and interpersonal behavior.* Madison, WI: Brown & Benchmark.

Leary, M. R., Allen, A. B., & Terry, M. L. (2011). Managing social images in naturalistic versus laboratory settings: Implications for understanding and studying self-presentation. *European Journal of Social Psychology, 41*(4), 411–421.

Leary, M. R., & Baumeister, R. F. (2000). The nature and function of self-esteem: Sociometer theory. *Advances in Experimental Social Psychology, 32,* 1–62.

Leary, M. R., & Kowalski, R. M. (1990). Impression management: A literature review and two-component model. *Psychological Bulletin, 107,* 34–47.

Leary, M. R., & Shepperd, J. A. (1986). Behavioral self-handicaps versus self-reported handicaps: A conceptual note. *Journal of Personality and Social Psychology, 51,* 1265–1268.

Leary, M. R., Tambor, E. S., Terdal, E. S., & Downs, D. L. (1995). Self-esteem as an interpersonal monitor: The sociometer hypothesis. *Journal of Personality and Social Psychology, 68,* 518–530.

Leary, M. R., & Tangney, J. P. (2003). The self as an organizing construct in the behavioral and social sciences. In M. R. Leary & J. P. Tangney (Eds.), *Handbook of self and identity* (pp. 3–14). New York: Guilford Press.

Leary, M. R., Tchividjian, L. R., & Kraxberger, B. E. (1994). Self-presentation can be hazardous to your health: Impression management and health risk. *Health Psychology, 13,* 461–470.

Leary, M. R., Toner, K., & Gan, M. (2011). Self, identity, and reactions to distal threats: The case of environmental behavior. *Psychological Studies, 56*(1), 159–166.

Leary, M. R., Twenge, J. M., & Quinlivan, E. (2006). Interpersonal rejection as a determinant of anger and aggression. *Personality and Social Psychology Review, 10,* 111–132.

Lee, A. Y. (2001). The mere exposure effect: An uncertainty reduction explanation revisited. *Journal of Personality & Social Psychology, 83,* 1255–1266.

Lee, T. M. C., Liu, H. L., Tan, L. H., Chan, C. C. H., Mahankali, S., Feng, C. M., et al. (2002). Lie detection by functional magnetic resonance imaging. *Human Brain Mapping, 15,* 157–164.

Leek, M., & Smith, P. K. (1989). Phenotypic matching human altruism, and mate selection. *Behavioral and Brain Sciences, 12,* 534–535.

Leek, M., & Smith, P. K. (1991). Cooperation and conflict in threegeneration families. In P. K.

Smith (Ed.), *The psychology of grandparent-hood: An international perspective* (pp. 177–194). London: Routledge.

Lefebvre, L. M. (1975). Encoding and decoding of ingratiation in modes of smiling and gaze. *British Journal of Social and Clinical Psychology, 14,* 33–42.

Lehman, B. J., & Crano, W. D. (2002). The pervasive effects of vested interest on attitude-criterion consistency in political judgment. *Journal of Experimental Social Psychology, 38,* 101–112.

Lehman, D. R., Chiu, C. Y., & Schaller, M. (2004). Psychology and culture. *Annual Review of Psychology, 55,* 689–714.

Leibman, M. (1970). The effects of sex and race norms on personal space. *Environment and Behavior, 2,* 208–246.

Leippe, M. R. (1995). The case for expert testimony about eyewitness memory. *Psychology, Public Policy, & Law, 1,* 909–959.

Leippe, M. R., & Elkin, R. A. (1987). When motives clash: Issue involvement and response involvement as determinants of persuasion. *Journal of Personality and Social Psychology, 52,* 269–278.

Leitenberg, H., & Henning, K. (1995). Sexual fantasy. *Psychological Bulletin, 117,* 469–496.

Leith, K. P., & Baumeister, R. F. (1998). Empathy, shame, guilt, and narratives of interpersonal conflict: Guilt-prone people are better at perspective-taking. *Journal of Personality, 66,* 1–37.

Lemay, E. P., Jr., & Clark, M. S. (2008). How the head liberates the heart: Projection of communal responsiveness guides relationship promotion. *Journal of Personality and Social Psychology, 94,* 647–671.

Lemieux, R., & Hale, J. L. (2002). Cross-sectional analysis of intimacy, passion, and commitment: Testing the assumptions of the triangular theory of love. *Psychological Reports, 90,* 1009–1014.

Lemyre, L., & Smith, P. M. (1985). Intergroup discrimination and self-esteem in the minimal group paradigm. *Journal of Personality and Social Psychology, 49,* 660–670.

Lench, H. C., & Ditto, P. H. (2008). Automatic optimism: Biased use of base rate information for positive and negative events. *Journal of Experimental Social Psychology, 44,* 631–639.

Leo, R. A. (1996). Inside the interrogation room. *The Journal of Criminal Law and Criminology, 86,* 266–303.

Leo, R. A. (2008). *Police interrogation and American justice.* Cambridge, MA: Harvard University Press.

Lepore, L., & Brown, R. (1997). Category and stereotype activation: Is prejudice inevitable? *Journal of Personality and Social Psychology, 72,* 275–287.

Lepore, S. J., Ragan, J. D., & Jones, S. (2000). Talking facilitates cognitive-emotional processes of adaptation to an acute stressor. *Journal of Personality & Social Psychology, 78,* 499–508.

Lepper, M. R., Greene, D., & Nisbett, R. E. (1973). Undermining children's intrinsic interest with extrinsic reward: A test of the 'overjustification' hypothesis. *Journal of Personality and Social Psychology, 28,* 129–137.

Lerner, J. S., Gonzalez, R. M., Dahl, R. E., Hariri, A. R., & Taylor, S. E. (2005). Facial expressions of emotion reveal neuroendocrine and cardiovascular stress responses. *Biological Psychiatry, 58,* 743–750.

Lerner, M. J. (1980). *The belief in a just world: A fundamental delusion.* New York: Plenum.

Leung, K. (1988). Theoretical advances in justice behavior: Some cross-cultural inputs. In M. H. Bond (Ed.), *The cross-cultural challenge to social psychology* (pp. 218–239). Newbury Park, CA: Sage.

Leventhal, H., & Cameron, L. (1994). Persuasion and health attitudes. In S. Shavitt & T. C. Brock (Eds.), *Persuasion* (pp. 219–249). Boston: Allyn & Bacon.

Levin, S., Federico, C. M., Sidanius, J., & Rabinowitz, J. L. (2002). Social dominance orientation and intergroup bias: The legitimation of favoritism for high-status groups. *Personality & Social Psychology Bulletin, 28,* 144–157.

Levine, H. (1997). *In search of Sugihara.* New York: Free Press.

Levine, J. M., & Moreland, R. L. (1998). Small groups. In D. T. Gilbert, S. T. Fiske, & G. Lindzey (Eds.), *The handbook of social psychology* (4th ed., Vol. 2, pp. 415–469). Boston: McGraw-Hill.

Levine, J. M., & Ranelli, C. J. (1978). Majority reaction to shifting and stable attitudinal deviates. *European Journal of Social Psychology, 8,* 55–70.

Levine, M., Prosser, A., Evans, D., & Reicher, S. (2005). Identity and emergency intervention: How social group membership and inclusiveness of group boundaries shape helping behavior. *Personality and Social Psychology Bulletin, 3,* 443–453.

Levine, R. A., & Campbell, D. T. (1972). *Ethnocentrism: Theories of conflict, ethnic attitudes, and group behavior.* New York: Wiley.

Levine, R. V. (2003). The kindness of strangers. *American Scientist, 91,* 226–233.

Levitt, S. D. (2004). Understanding why crime fell in the 1990s: Four factors that explain the decline and six that do not. *Journal of Economic Perspectives, 18,* 163–190.

Levy-Leboyer, C. (1988). Success and failure in applying psychology. *American Psychologist, 43,* 779–785.

Lewandowski, G. W., & Aron, A. P. (2004). Distinguishing arousal from novelty and challenge in initial romantic attraction between strangers. *Social Behavior and Personality, 32,* 361–372.

Lewin, K., Lippitt, R., & White, R. K. (1939). Patterns of aggressive behavior in experimentally created "social climates." *Journal of Social Psychology, 10,* 271–279.

Lewis, M. (1993). The emergence of human emotions. In M. Lewis & J. M. Haviland (Eds.), *Handbook of emotions* (pp. 223–236). New York: Guilford.

Lewis, M. (2000). *Handbook of emotions.* New York: Guilford.

Leyens, J. P., Camino, L., Parke, R. D., & Berkowitz, L. (1975). Effects of movie violence on aggression in a field setting as a function of group dominance and cohesion. *Journal of Personality and Social Psychology, 32,* 346–360.

Li, N. P., Bailey, J. M., Kenrick, D. T., & Linsenmeier, J. A. (2002). The necessities and luxuries of mate preferences: Testing the trade-offs. *Journal of Personality & Social Psychology, 82,* 947–955.

Li, N. P., Halterman, R. A., Cason, M. J., Knight, G. P., & Maner, J. K. (2008). The stress-affiliation paradigm revisited: Do people prefer the kindness of strangers or their attractiveness? *Personality and Individual Differences, 44,* 382–391.

Li, N. P., & Kenrick, D. T. (2006). Sex similarities and differences in preferences for short-term mates: What, whether, and why. *Journal of Personality and Social Psychology, 90,* 468–489.

Li, N. P., Yong, J. C., Tov, W., Sng, O., Fletcher, G. J. O., Valentine, K. A., et al. (2013). Mate preferences do predict attraction and choices in the early stages of mate selection. *Journal of Personality & Social Psychology, 105*(5), 757–776.

Li, Y. J., Cohen, A. B., Weeden, J., & Kenrick, D. T. (2010). Mating competitors increase religious beliefs. *Journal of Experimental Social Psychology, 46,* 428–431.

Li, Y. J., Johnson, K. A., Cohen, A. B., Williams, M. J., Knowles, E. D., & Chen, Z. (2012). Fundamental(ist) attribution error: U.S. Protestants are dispositionally focused. *Journal of Personality and Social Psychology, 102*(2), 281–290.

Li, Y. J., Kenrick, D. T., Griskevicius, V., & Neuberg, S. L. (2012). Economic decision biases and fundamental motivations: How mating and self-protection alter loss aversion. *Journal of Personality and Social Psychology, 102*(3), 550–561.

Liberman, V., Samuels, S. M., & Ross, L. (2004). The name of the game: Predictive power of reputa-tions versus situational labels in determining prisoner's dilemma game moves. *Personality and Social Psychology Bulletin, 30,* 1175–1185.

Lickel, B., Hamilton, D. L., & Sherman, S. J. (2001). Elements of a lay theory of groups: Types of groups, relationship styles, and the perception of group entitavity. *Personality and Social Psychology Review, 5,* 129–140.

Liden, R. C., & Mitchell, T. R. (1988). Ingratiatory behaviors in organizational settings. *Academy of Management Review, 12,* 572–587.

Liden, R. C., Wayne, S. J., Jaworski, R. A., & Bennett, N. (2004). Social loafing: A field investigation. *Journal of Management, 30,* 285–304.

Lieberman, D., & Hatfield, E. (2006). Passionate love: Cross-cultural and evolutionary perspectives. In R. J. Sternberg & K. Weis (Eds.), *The new psychology of love* (pp. 274–297). New Haven, CT: Yale University Press.

Lieberman, D., & Lobel, T. (2012). Kinship on the kibbutz: Coresidence duration predicts altruism, personal sexual aversions, and moral attitudes among communally reared peers. *Evolution and Human Behavior, 33*(1), 26–34.

Lieberman, D., & Smith, A. (2012). It's all relative sexual aversions and moral judgments regarding sex among siblings. *Current Directions in Psychological Science, 21*(4), 243–247.

Lieberman, D., Tooby, J., & Cosmides, L. (2003). Does morality have a biological basis? An empirical test of the factors governing moral sentiments relating to incest. *Proceedings of the Royal Society of London, B, 270,* 819–826.

Lieberman, D., Tooby, J., & Cosmides, L. (2007). The architecture of human kin detection. *Nature, 445,* 727–731.

Lieberman, M. D. (2007). Social cognitive neuroscience: A review of core processes. *Annual Review of Psychology, 58,* 259–289.

Lieberman, M. D., Jarcho, J. M., & Obayashi, J. (2005). Attributional inference across cultures: Similar automatic attributions and different controlled corrections. *Personality and Social Psychology Bulletin, 31,* 889–901.

Liebrand, W. B., & VanRun, G. J. (1985). The effects of social motives on behavior in social dilemmas in two cultures. *Journal of Experimental Social Psychology, 21,* 86–102.

Light, K. C., Grewen, K. M., & Amico, J. A. (2005). More frequent partner hugs and higher oxytocin levels are linked to lower blood pressure and heart rate in premenopausal women. *Biological Psychology, 69,* 5–21.

Lightdale, J. R., & Prentice, D. A. (1994). Rethinking sex differences in aggression: Aggressive behavior in the absence of social roles. *Personality and Social Psychology Bulletin, 20,* 34–44.

Likowski, K., Mühlberger, A., Seibt, B., Pauli, P., & Weyers, P. (2008). Modulation of facial mimicry by attitudes. *Journal of Experimental Social Psychology, 44,* 1065–1072.

Lindsay, J. J., & Anderson, C. A. (2000). From antecedent conditions to violent actions: A general affective aggression model. *Personality & Social Psychology Bulletin, 26,* 533–547.

Lindskold, S. (1983). Cooperators, competitors, and response to GRIT. *Journal of Conflict Resolution, 27,* 521–532.

Linville, P. W., Fischer, G. W., & Salovey, P. (1989). Perceived distributions of the characteristics of in-group and out-group members: Empirical evidence and a computer simulation. *Journal of Personality and Social Psychology, 57,* 165–188.

Lippa, R., & Arad, S. (1999). Gender, personality, and prejudice: The display of authoritarianism and social dominance in interviews with college men and women. *Journal of Research in Personality, 33,* 463–493.

Lippmann, W. (1922). *Public opinion.* New York: Harcourt Brace.

Little, B. R. (1989). Personal projects analysis: Trivial pursuits, magnificent obsessions, and the search for coherence. In D. M. Buss & N. Cantor (Eds.), *Personality psychology: Recent trends and emerging directions* (pp. 15–31). New York: Springer-Verlag.

Little, A. C., Jones, B. C., & DeBruine, L. M. (2008). Preferences for variation in masculinity in real male faces change across the menstrual cycle: Women prefer more masculine faces when they are more fertile. *Personality and Individual Differences, 45,* 478–482.

Littlepage, G. E., Hollingshead, A. B., Drake, L. R., & Littlepage, A. M. (2008). Transactive memory and performance in work groups: Specificity, communication, ability differences, and work allocation. *Group Dynamics: Theory, Research, and Practice, 12,* 223–241.

Locke, K. D. (2005). Connecting the horizontal dimension of social comparison with self-worth and self-confidence. *Personality and Social Psychology Bulletin, 31,* 795–803.

Lockwood, P., Shaughnessy, S. C., Fortune, J. L., & Tong, M. (2012). Social comparisons in novel situations: Finding inspiration during life transitions. *Personality and Social Psychology Bulletin, 38*(8), 985–996.

Loftin, C., McDowall, D., Wiersema, B., & Cottey, T. J. (1991). Effects of restrictive licensing of handguns on homicide and suicide in the District of Columbia. *New England Journal of Medicine, 325,* 1615–1620.

Loftus, E. M., & Ketcham, K. (1994). *The myth of repressed memory: False memories and allegations of sexual abuse.* New York: St. Martin's Press.

Loher, B. T., Vancouver, J. B., & Czajka, J. (1994, April). *Preferences and reactions to teams.* Presented at the 9th annual conference of the Society for Industrial and Organizational Psychology, Nashville, TN.

Lord, C. G., Lepper, M. R., & Preston, E. (1984). Considering the opposite: A corrective strategy for social judgment. *Journal of Personality and Social Psychology, 47,* 1231–1243.

Lord, C. G., Ross, L., & Lepper, M. R. (1979). Biased assimilation and attitude polarization. *Journal of Personality and Social Psychology, 37,* 2098–2109.

Lord, C. G., & Saenz, D. S. (1985). Memory deficits and memory surfeits: Differential cognitive consequences of tokenism for tokens and observers. *Journal of Personality and Social Psychology, 49,* 918–926.

Lord, C. G., Saenz, D. S., & Godfrey, D. K. (1987). Effects of perceived scrutiny on participant memory for social interactions. *Journal of Experimental Social Psychology, 23,* 498–517.

Lord, R. G., Foti, R. J., & de Vader, C. L. (1984). A test of leadership categorization theory: Internal structure, information processing, and leadership perceptions. *Organizational Behavior and Human Decision Processes, 34,* 343–378.

Lorenz, K. (1966). *On aggression.* New York: Harcourt-Brace-Jovanovich.

Losch, M., & Cacioppo, J. (1990). Cognitive dissonance may enhance sympathetic tonis, but attitudes are changed to reduce negative affect rather than arousal. *Journal of Experimental Social Psychology, 26,* 289–304.

Loucks, E. B., Berkman, L. F., Gruenewald, T. L., & Seeman, T. E. (2005). Social integration is associated with fibrinogen concentration in elderly men. *Psychosomatic Medicine, 67,* 353–358.

Lucas, T., Alexander, S., Firestone, I. J., & Baltes, B. B. (2006). Self-efficacy and independence from social influence: Discovery of an efficacy-difficulty effect. *Social Influence, 1,* 58–80.

Ludwig, J. (2004, June 1). *Acceptance of interracial marriage at record high.* Report of the Gallup Organization, Princeton, NJ.

Lundgren, S. R., & Prislin, R. (1998). Motivated cognitive processing and attitude change. *Personality and Social Psychology Bulletin, 24,* 715–726.

Lydon, J. E., Fitzsimons, G. M., & Naidoo, L. (2003). Devaluation versus enhancement of attractive alternatives: A critical test using the calibration paradigm. *Personality & Social Psychology Bulletin, 29,* 349–359.

Lydon, J. E., Jamieson, D. W., & Holmes, J. G. (1997). The meaning of social interactions in the transition from acquaintanceship to friendship. *Journal of Personality and Social Psychology, 73,* 536–548.

Lydon, J. E., Menzies-Toman, D., Burton, K., & Bell, C. (2008). If-then contingencies and the differential effects of the availability of an attractive alternative on relationship maintenance for men and women. *Journal of Personality and Social Psychology, 95,* 50–65.

Lydon, J. E., & Quinn, S. K. (2013). Relationship maintenance processes. In J. A. Simpson & L. Campbell (Eds.), *Oxford handbook of close relationships* (pp. 573–588). New York: Oxford University Press.

Lydon, J. E., & Zanna, M. P. (1990). Commitment in the face of adversity: A value-affirmation approach. *Journal of Personality and Social Psychology, 58,* 1040–1057.

Lykken, D., & Tellegen, A. (1996). Happiness is a stochastic phenomenon. *Psychological Science, 7,* 186–189.

Lynn, M., & McCall, M. (1998). *Beyond gratitude and gratuity: A meta-analytic review of the determinants of restaurant tipping.* Unpublished manuscript, Cornell University, School of Hotel Administration, Ithaca, NY.

Lynn, M., & Oldenquist, A. (1986). Egoistic and nonegoistic motives in social dilemmas. *American Psychologist, 41,* 529–534.

Lyubomirsky, S., King, L., & Diener, E. (2005). The benefits of frequent positive affect: Does happiness lead to success? *Psychological Bulletin, 131,* 803–855.

Lyubomirsky, S., & Ross, L. (1998). Hedonic consequences of social comparison: A contrast of happy and unhappy people. *Journal of Personality and Social Psychology, 73,* 1141–1157.

Lyubomirsky, S., Sheldon, K. M., & Schkade, D. (2005). Pursuing happiness: The architecture of sustainable change. *Review of General Psychology, 9,* 111–131.

Maass, A., & Clark, R. D. (1984). Hidden impact of minorities: Fifteen years of minority influence. *Psychological Bulletin, 95,* 428–450.

Maass, A., Clark, R. D., III., & Haberkorn, G. (1982). The effects of differential ascribed category membership and norms on minority influence. *European Journal of Social Psychology, 12,* 89–104.

MacCoun, R. J., & Kerr, N. L. (1988). Asymmetric influence in mock jury deliberation: Jurors' bias for leniency. *Journal of Personality and Social Psychology, 54,* 21–33.

MacDonald, G., & Leary, M. R. (2005). Why does social exclusion hurt? The relationship between social and physical pain. *Psychological Bulletin, 131,* 202–223.

MacDonald, G., Zanna, M. P., & Holmes, J. G. (2000). An experimental test of the role of alcohol in relationship conflict. *Journal of Experimental Social Psychology, 36,* 182–193.

MacDonald, T. K., Fong, G. T., Zanna, M. P., & Martineau, A. M. (2000). Alcohol myopia and condom use: Can alcohol intoxication be associated with more prudent behavior? *Journal of Personality & Social Psychology, 78,* 605–619.

Mack, D., & Rainey, D. (1990). Female applicants' grooming and personnel selection. *Journal of Social Behavior and Personality, 5,* 399–407.

MacKay, C. (1841/1932). *Popular delusions and the madness of crowds.* New York: Farrar, Straus, and Giroux.

Mackie, D. M., & Goethals, G. R. (1987). Individual and group goals. In C. Hendrick (Ed.), *Group processes* (pp. 144–166). Newbury Park, CA: Sage.

MacNeilage, P. F., & Davis, B. L. (2005). The evolution of language. In D. M. Buss (Ed.), *The handbook of evolutionary psychology* (pp. 653–675). New York: Wiley.

Macrae, C. N., Bodenhausen, G. V., Milne, A. B., & Jetten, J. (1994). Out of mind but back in sight: Stereotypes on the rebound. *Journal of Personality and Social Psychology, 67,* 808–817.

Macrae, C. N., Bodenhausen, G. V., Milne, A. B., & Wheeler, V. (1996). On resisting the temptation for simplification: Counterintentional effects of stereotype suppression on social memory. *Social Cognition, 14,* 1–20.

Macrae, C. N., Hewstone, M., & Griffiths, R. J. (1993). Processing load and memory for stereotype-based information. *European Journal of Social Psychology, 23,* 77–87.

Macrae, C. N., Milne, A. B., & Bodenhausen, G. V. (1994). Stereotypes as energy-saving devices: A peek inside the cognitive toolbox. *Journal of Personality and Social Psychology, 66,* 37–47.

Maddux, W. W., Galinsky, A. D., Cuddy, A. J. C., & Polifroni, M. (2008). When being a model minority is good . . . and bad: Realistic threat explains negativity toward Asian Americans. *Personality and Social Psychology Bulletin, 34,* 74–89.

Madon, S., Guyll, M., Buller, A. A., Scherr, K. C., Willard, J., & Spoth, R. (2008). The mediation of mothers' self-fulfilling effects on their children's alcohol use: Self-verification, informational consistency, and modeling processes. *Journal of Personality and Social Psychology, 95,* 369–384.

Madon, S., Smith, A., Jussim, L., Russell, D. W., Eccles, J., Palumbo, P., et al. (2001). Am I as you see me or do you see me as I am? Self-fulfilling prophecies and self-verification. *Personality and Social Psychology Bulletin, 27,* 1214–1224.

Magdol, L. (2002). Is moving gendered? The effects of residential mobility on the psychological well-being of men and women. *Sex Roles, 47,* 553–560.

Magdol, L., & Bessell, D. R. (2003). Social capital, social currency, and portable assets: The impact of residential mobility on exchanges of social support. *Personal Relationships, 10,* 1149–1169.

Maines, D. R., & Hardesty, M. J. (1987). Temporality and gender: Young adults' career and family plans. *Social Forces, 66,* 102–120.

Maio, G. R., & Olson, J. M. (1995). Relations between values, attitudes, and behavioral intentions: The moderating role of attitude function. *Journal of Experimental Social Psychology, 31,* 266–285.

Major, B., Spencer, S., Schmader, T., Wolfe, C., & Crocker, J. (1998). Coping with negative stereotypes about intellectual performance: The role of psychological disengagement. *Personality and Social Psychology Bulletin, 24,* 34–50.

Malamuth, N. M., Addison, T., & Koss, M. (2001). Pornography and sexual aggression: Are there reliable effects and can we understand them? *Annual Review of Sex Research, 11,* 26–91.

Malamuth, N. M., & Donnerstein, E. (1984). *Pornography and sexual aggression.* Orlando, FL: Academic Press.

Malarkey, W., Kiecolt-Glaser, J. K., Pearl, D., & Glaser, R. (1994). Hostile behavior during marital conflict alters pituitary and adrenal hormones. *Psychosomatic Medicine, 56,* 41–51.

Malle, B. F. (1999). How people explain behavior: A new theoretical framework. *Personality & Social Psychology Review, 3,* 23–48.

Malle, B. F. (2004). *How the mind explains behavior: Folk explanations, meaning, and social interaction.* Cambridge, MA: MIT Press.

Malle, B. F. (2006). The actor-observer asymmetry in causal attribution: A (surprising) meta-analysis. *Psychological Bulletin, 132,* 895–919.

Mandel, D. R. (2003). Counterfactuals, emotion, and context. *Cognition and Emotion, 17,* 139–159.

Mandel, D. R., Axelrod, L. J., & Lehman, D. R. (1993). Integrative complexity in reasoning about the Persian Gulf War and the accountability to skeptical audience hypothesis. *Journal of Social Issues, 49,* 201–215.

Mandel, N., & Johnson, E. J. (2002). When Web pages influence choice: Effects of visual primes on experts and novices. *Journal of Consumer Research, 29,* 235–245.

Maner, J. K., DeWall, C. N., Baumeister, R. F., & Schaller, M. (2007). Does social exclusion motivate interpersonal reconnection? Resolving the "porcupine problem." *Journal of Personality and Social Psychology, 92,* 42–55.

Maner, J. K., & Gailliot, M. T. (2007). Altruism and egoism: Prosocial motivations for helping depend on the relationship context. *European Journal of Social Psychology, 37,* 347–358.

Maner, J. K., Gailliot, M. T., Rouby, D. A., & Miller, S. L. (2007). Can't take my eyes off you: Attentional adhesion to mates and rivals. *Journal of Personality and Social Psychology, 93,* 389–401.

Maner, J. K., & Gerend, M. A. (2007). Motivationally selective risk judgments: Do fear and curiosity boost the boons or the banes? *Organizational Behavior and Human Decision Processes, 103,* 256–267.

Maner, J. K., Kenrick, D. T., Becker, D. V., Delton, A. W., Hofer, B., Wilbur, C. J., et al. (2003). Sexually selective cognition: Beauty captures the mind of the beholder. *Journal of Personality and Social Psychology, 6,* 1107–1120.

Maner, J. K., Kenrick, D. T., Becker, D. V., Robertson, T. E., Hofer, B., Neuberg, S. L., et al. (2005). Functional projection: How fundamental social motives can bias interpersonal perception. *Journal of Personality and Social Psychology, 88,* 63–78.

Maner, J. K., Luce, C. L., Neuberg, S. L., Cialdini, R. B., Brown, S., Sagarin, B. J., et al. (2002). The effects of perspective taking on motivations for helping: Still no evidence for altruism. *Personality and Social Psychology Bulletin, 28,* 1601–1610.

Maner, J. K., & Mead, N. (2010). The essential tension between leadership and power: When leaders sacrifice group goals for the sake of self-interest. *Journal of Personality and Social Psychology, 99,* 482–497.

Manis, M., Cornell, S. D., & Moore, J. C. (1974). Transmission of attitude relevant information through a communication chain. *Journal of Personality and Social Psychology, 30,* 81–94.

Mann, L. (1980). Cross-cultural studies of small groups. In H. Triandis & R. Brislin (Eds.), *Handbook of cross-cultural psychology: Social psychology* (Vol. 5, pp. 155–209). Boston: Allyn & Bacon.

Mann, L. (1981). The baiting crowd in episodes of threatened suicide. *Journal of Personality and Social Psychology, 41,* 703–709.

Mann, T., Nolen-Hoeksema, S., Huang, K., Burgard, D., Wright, A., & Hansen, K. (1997). Are two interventions worse than none? Joint primary and secondary prevention of eating disorders in college females. *Health Psychology, 16,* 215–225.

Manning, R., Levine, M., & Collins, A. (2007). The Kitty Genovese murder and the social psychology of helping: The parable of the 38 witnesses. *American Psychologist, 62*(6), 555.

Manucia, G. K., Baumann, D. J., & Cialdini, R. B. (1984). Mood influences in helping: Direct effects or side effects? *Journal of Personality and Social Psychology, 46,* 357–364.

Marcus-Newhall, A., Pedersen, W. C., Carlson, M., & Miller, N. (2000). Displaced aggression is alive and well: A meta-analytic review. *Journal of Personality & Social Psychology, 78,* 670–689.

Markey, P. M., Funder, D. C., & Ozer, D. J. (2003). Complementarity of interpersonal behaviors in dyadic interactions. *Personality & Social Psychology Bulletin, 29,* 1082–1090.

Markman, H. J., Floyd, F., Stanley, S., & Storaasli, R. (1988). The prevention of marital distress: A longitudinal investigation. *Journal of Consulting and Clinical Psychology, 56,* 210–217.

Markman, H. J., & Rhoades, G. K. (2012). Relationship education research: Current status and future directions. *Journal of Marital and Family Therapy, 38,* 169–200.

Markus, H., & Kitayama, S. (1991). Culture and the self: Implications for cognition, emotion, and motivation. *Psychological Bulletin, 98,* 224–253.

Markus, H., & Nurius, P. (1986). Possible selves. *American Psychologist, 41,* 954–969.

Markus, H., & Wurf, E. (1987). The dynamic self-concept: A social psychological perspective. *Annual Review of Psychology, 38,* 299–337.

Marsh, A. A., Elfenbein, H. A., & Ambady, N. (2003). Nonverbal "accents": Cultural differences in facial expressions of emotion. *Psychological Science, 14,* 373–376.

Marsh, K. L., & Webb, W. M. (1996). Mood uncertainty and social comparison: Implications for mood management. *Journal of Social Behavior and Personality, 11,* 1–26.

Marshall, D. S., & Suggs, R. G. (1971). *Human sexual behavior: Variations in the ethnographic spectrum.* New York: Basic Books.

Martin, C. L. (1987). A ratio measure of sex stereotyping. *Journal of Personality and Social Psychology, 52,* 489–499.

Martin, C. L. (2000). Cognitive theories of gender development. In T. Eckes & H. M. Trautner (Eds.), *The developmental psychology of gender* (pp. 91–121). Mahwah, NJ: Erlbaum.

Martin, C. L., & Halverson, C. F., Jr. (1983). The effects of sex-typing schemas on young children's memory. *Child Development, 54,* 563–574.

Martin, K. A., & Leary, M. R. (1999). Would you drink after a stranger? The influence of self-presentational motives on willingness to take a health risk. *Personality and Social Psychology Bulletin, 25,* 1092–1100.

Martin, K. A., & Leary, M. R. (2001). Self-presentational determinants of health risk behavior among college freshmen. *Psychology and Health, 16,* 17–27.

Martin, R. (1997). "Girls don't talk about garages!": Perceptions of conversations in same- and cross-sex friendships. *Personal Relationships, 4,* 115–130.

Martin, R., Gardikiotis, A., & Hewstone, M. (2002). Levels of consensus and majority and minority influence. *European Journal of Social Psychology, 32,* 645–665.

Martin, R., Hewstone, M., & Martin, P. Y. (2008). Majority versus minority influence: The role of message processing in determining resistance to counter-persuasion. *European Journal of Social Psychology, 38,* 16–34.

Martin, R. G. (1973). *The woman he loved.* New York: Simon & Schuster.

Martinez, M. (2012). *Charles Manson denied parole, with next parole hearing set for 2027. CNN Justice.* Retrieved from http://www.cnn.com/2012/04/11/justice/california-charles-manson/

Marwell, G., & Ames, R. (1981). Economists free ride, does anyone else? Experiments on the provision of public goods, IV. *Journal of Public Economics, 15,* 295–310.

Marx, E. M., Williams, J. M. G., & Claridge, G. C. (1992). Depression and social problem solving. *Journal of Abnormal Psychology, 101,* 78–86.

Mashek, D. J., Aron, A., & Boncimino, M. (2003). Confusions of self with close others. *Personality and Social Psychology Bulletin, 29,* 382–392.

Massing, M. (1996, July 11). How to win the tobacco war. *New York Review of Books,* pp. 32–36.

Masuda, T., Ellsworth, P. C., Mesquita, B., Leu, J., Tanida, S., & Van de Veerdonk, E. (2008). Placing the face in context: Cultural differences in the perception of facial emotion. *Journal of Personality and Social Psychology, 94,* 365–381.

Matarazzo, J. D. (1980). Behavioral health and behavioral medicine: Frontiers for a new health psychology. *American Psychologist, 35,* 807–817.

Mather, M., & Sutherland, M. R. (2011). Arousal-biased competition in perception and memory. *Perspectives on Psychological Science, 6,* 114–133.

Mathes, E. W. (2005). Men's desire for children carrying their genes and sexual jealousy: A test of paternity uncertainty as an explanation of male sexual jealousy. *Psychological Reports, 96,* 791–798.

Matheson, K., & Dursun, S. (2001). Social identity precursors to the hostile media phenomenon: Partisan perceptions of coverage of the Bosnian conflict. *Group Processes and Intergroup Relations, 4,* 116–125.

Matsumoto, D., & Hwang, H. S. (2011). Judgments of facial expressions of emotion in profile. *Emotion, 11*(5), 1223.

Matsumoto, D., & Willingham, B. (2006). The thrill of victory and the agony of defeat: Spontaneous expressions of medal winners of the 2004 Athens Olympic Games. *Journal of Personality and Social Psychology, 91,* 568–581.

Matsumoto, D., & Willingham, B. (2009). Spontaneous facial expressions of emotion of congenitally and non-congenitally blind individuals. *Journal of Personality and Social Psychology, 96*(1), 1–10.

Matsumoto, D., Yoo, S. H., Nakagawa, S., Altarriba, J., Alexandre, J., Anguas-Wong, A. M., et al. (2008). Culture, emotion regulation, and adjustment. *Journal of Personality and Social Psychology, 94,* 925–937.

Matsunami, K. (1998). *International handbook of funeral customs.* Westport, CT: Greenwood Press.

Matthews, K. A., Scheier, M. F., Brunson, B. I., & Carducci, B. (1980). Attention, unpredictability, and reports of physical symptoms: Eliminating the benefits of unpredictability. *Journal of Personality and Social Psychology, 38,* 525–537.

Mauro, R., Sato, K., & Tucker, J. (1992). The role of appraisal in human emotions: A cross-cultural study. *Journal of Personality and Social Psychology, 62,* 301–317.

Mauss, M. (1967). *The gift.* New York: W. W. Norton.

Maxwell, L. E., & Evans, G. W. (2000). The effects of noise on pre-school children's pre-reading skills. *Journal of Environmental Psychology, 20,* 91–97.

Mazerolle, M., Régner, I., Morisset, P., Rigalleau, F., & Huguet, P. (2012). Stereotype threat threatens automatic recall and undermines controlled processes in older adults. *Psychological Science, 23*(7), 723–727.

Mazur, A., & Booth, A. (1998). Testerosterone and dominance in men. *Behavioral and Brain Sciences, 21,* 353–397.

Mazur, A., Booth, A., & Dabbs, J. M., Jr. (1992). Testosterone and chess competition. *Social Psychology Quarterly, 55,* 70–77.

McAdams, D. P. (1990). *The person.* San Diego, CA: Harcourt Brace Jovanovich.

McAlister, A. L., Ramirez, A. G., Galavotti, C., & Gallion, K. J. (1989). In R. E. Rice & C. K. Atkin (Eds.), *Public communication campaigns* (pp. 291–307). Newbury Park, CA: Sage.

McAndrew, F. T. (2002). New evolutionary perspectives on altruism. *Current Directions in Psychological Science, 11,* 79–82.

McArthur, L. A. (1972). The how and what of why: Some determinants and consequences of causal attribution. *Journal of Personality and Social Psychology, 22,* 171–193.

McArthur, L. Z., & Baron, R. M. (1983). Toward an ecological theory of social perception. *Psychological Review, 90,* 215–238.

McCain, B. E., O'Reilly, C. A., III., & Pfeffer, J. (1983). The effects of departmental demography on turnover: The case of a university. *Academy of Management Journal, 26,* 626–641.

McCann, S. J. H. (1997). Threatening times, "strong" presidential popular vote winners, and the victory margin, 1824–1964. *Journal of Personality and Social Psychology, 73,* 160–170.

McCann, S. J. H. (1999). Threatening times and fluctuations in American church memberships. *Personality & Social Psychology Bulletin, 25,* 325–336.

McCann, S. J. H. (2001). The precocity-longevity hypothesis: Earlier peaks in career achievement predict shorter lives. *Personality & Social Psychology Bulletin, 27,* 1429–1439.

McCanne, T. R., & Anderson, J. A. (1987). Emotional responding following experimental manipulation of facial electromyographic activity. *Journal of Personality and Social Psychology, 52,* 759–768.

McCarthy, B. (1994). Warrior values: A socio-historical survey. In J. Archer (Ed.), *Male violence* (pp. 105–120). New York: Routledge.

McCarthy, J. (1952). The master impostor: An incredible tale. *Life, 32,* 79–89.

McCauley, C. (1989). The nature of social influence in groupthink: Compliance and internalization. *Journal of Personality and Social Psychology, 57,* 250–260.

McClelland, D. C. (1984). *Human motivation.* Glenview, IL: Scott, Foresman.

McClelland, D. C., Atkinson, J. W., Clark, R. A., & Lowell, E. L. (1953). *The achievement motive.* New York: Appleton-Century-Crofts.

McClintock, C. G., Messick, D. M., Kuhlman, D. M., & Campos, F. T. (1973). Motivational basis of choice in three choice decomposed games. *Journal of Experimental Social Psychology, 9,* 572–590.

McConahay, J. B. (1986). Modern racism, ambivalence, and the modern racism scale. In J. F. Dovidio & S. L. Gaertner (Eds.), *Prejudice, discrimination, and racism* (pp. 91–125). Orlando, FL: Academic Press.

McCornack, S. A., & Levine, T. R. (1990). When lovers become leery: The relationship between suspiciousness and accuracy in detecting deception. *Communication Monographs, 57,* 219–230.

McCrae, R. R., Terraciano, A., & 79 members of the personality profiles of cultures project (2005). Personality profiles of cultures: Aggregate personality traits. *Journal of Personality and Social Psychology, 89,* 407–425.

McCrea, S. M., & Hirt, E. R. (2001). The role of ability judgments in self-handicapping. *Personality and Social Psychology Bulletin, 27,* 1378–1389.

McCrea, S. M., Hirt, E. R., & Milner, B. (2008). She works hard for the money: Valuing effort underlies gender differences in behavioral self-handicapping. *Journal of Experimental Social Psychology, 44,* 292–311.

McCullough, M. E. (2008). *Beyond revenge: The evolution of the forgiveness instinct.* San Francisco: Jossey-Bass.

McCullough, M. E., Kimeldorf, M. B., & Cohen, A. D. (2008). An adaptation for altruism? The social causes, social effects, and social evolution of gratitude. *Current Directions in Psychological Science, 17,* 281–285.

McDaniel, A., & Thomas, E. (1991, September 30). Playing chicken in Iraq. *Newsweek,* p. 40.

McDermott, R., Tingley, D., Cowden, J., Frazzetto, G., & Johnson, D. D. P. (2009). Monoamine oxidase A gene (MAOA) predicts behavioral aggression following provocation. *PNAS, 106,* 2118–2123.

McDougall, W. (1908). *Social psychology: An introduction.* London: Methuen.

McFarland, C., Ross, M., & Conway, M. (1984). Self-persuasion and self-presentation as mediators of anticipatory attitude change. *Journal of Personality and Social Psychology, 46,* 529–540.

McFarlin, D. B., Baumeister, R. F., & Blascovich, J. (1984). On knowing when to quit: Task failure, self-esteem, advice, and nonproductive persistence. *Journal of Personality, 52,* 138–155.

McGowan, S. (2002). Mental representations in stressful situations: The calming and distressing effects of significant others. *Journal of Experimental Social Psychology, 38,* 152–161.

McGrath, J. E. (1984). *Groups: Interaction and performance.* Englewood Cliffs, NJ: Prentice-Hall.

McGrath, J. E., Martin, J., & Kukla, R. A. (1982). *Judgment calls in research.* Beverly Hills, CA: Sage.

McGrath, P. (1991, January 7). More than a madman. *Newsweek,* pp. 20–24.

McGregor, I. (1993). Effectiveness of role playing and antiracist teaching in reducing student prejudice. *Journal of Education Research, 86*(4), 215–226.

McGuire, A. M. (1994). Helping behaviors in the natural environment: Dimensions and correlates of helping. *Personality and Social Psychology Bulletin, 20,* 45–56.

McGuire, W. J. (1966). Attitudes and opinions. *Annual Review of Psychology, 17,* 475–514.

McGuire, W. J. (1997). Creative hypothesis generating in psychology. *Annual Review of Psychology, 48,* 1–30.

McGuire, W. J., & McGuire, C. V. (1996). Enhancing self-esteem by directed-thinking tasks: Cognitive and affective positivity asymmetries. *Journal of Personality and Social Psychology, 70,* 1117–1125.

McIntosh, D. N. (2006). Spontaneous facial mimicry, liking and emotional contagion. *Polish Psychological Bulletin, 37,* 31–42.

McIntyre, M., Gangestad, S. W., Gray, P. B., Chapman, J. F., Burnham, T. C., O'Rourke, M. T., et al. (2006). Romantic involvement often reduces men's testosterone levels—but not always: The moderating role of extrapair sexual interest. *Journal of Personality and Social Psychology, 91,* 642–651.

McIntyre, R. B., Paulson, R. M., & Lord, C. G. (2003). Alleviating women's mathematics stereotype threat through salience of group achievements. *Journal of Experimental Social Psychology, 39,* 83–90.

McKenna, K. Y. A., & Bargh, J. A. (2000). Plan 9 from cyberspace: The implications of the internet for personality and social psychology. *Personality & Social Psychology Review, 4,* 57–75.

McKenna, K. Y. A., Green, A. S., & Gleason, M. E. J. (2002). Relationship formation on the internet: What's the big attraction? *Journal of Social Issues, 58,* 9–31.

McKenzie-Mohr, D. (2000). Fostering sustainable behavior through community-based social marketing. *American Psychologist, 55,* 531–537.

McKimmie, B. M., Newton, S. A., Schuller, R. A., & Terry, D. J. (2013). It's not what she says, it's how she says it: The influence of language complexity and cognitive load on the persuasiveness of expert testimony. *Psychiatry, Psychology and Law, 20*(4), 578–589.

McLachlan, S., & Hagger, M. S. (2011). The influence of chronically accessible autonomous and controlling motives on physical activity within an extended theory of planned behavior. *Journal of Applied Social Psychology, 41*(2), 445–470.

McLeod, P. L., & Lobel, S. A. (1992, August). *The effects of ethnic diversity on idea generation in small groups.* Presented at the 52nd annual meeting of the Academy of Management, Las Vegas, Nevada.

McMullen, M. N., & Markman, K. D. (2002). Affective impact of close counterfactuals: Implications of possible futures for possible pasts. *Journal of Experimental Social Psychology, 38,* 64–70.

McNulty, J. K. (2013). Personality and relationships. In J. A. Simpson & L. Campbell (Eds.), *Oxford handbook of close relationships* (pp. 535–552). New York: Oxford University Press.

McNulty, J. K., O'Mara, E. M., & Karney, B. R. (2008). Benevolent cognitions as a strategy of relationship maintenance: "Don't sweat the small stuff". . . But it is not all small stuff. *Journal of Personality and Social Psychology, 94,* 631–646.

McNulty, S. E., & Swann, W. B., Jr. (1994). Identity negotiation in roommate relationships: The self as architect and consequence of social reality. *Journal of Personality and Social Psychology, 67,* 1012–1023.

McWilliams, S., & Howard, J. A. (1993). Solidarity and hierarchy in cross-sex friendships. *Journal of Social Issues, 49,* 191–202.

Mead, G. H. (1934). *Mind, self, and society.* Chicago: University of Chicago Press.

Medvec, V. H., Madey, S. F., & Gilovich, T. (1995). When less is more: Counterfactual thinking and satisfaction among Olympic medalists. *Journal of Personality and Social Psychology, 69,* 603–610.

Mehl, M. R., Vazire, S., Ramírez-Esparza, N., Slatcher, R. B., & Pennebaker, J. W. (2007). Are women really more talkative than men? *Science, 317*(5834), 82.

Mehu, M., Grammer, K., & Dunbar, R. (2007). Smiles when sharing. *Evolution and Human Behavior, 28,* 415–422.

Meier, B. P., & Wilkowski, B. M. (2013). Reducing the tendency to aggress: Insights from social and personality psychology. *Social and Personality Psychology Compass, 7*(6), 343–354.

Meier, B. P., Wilkowski, B. M., & Robinson, M. D. (2008). Bringing out the agreeableness in everyone: Using a cognitive self-regulation model to reduce aggression. *Journal of Experimental Social Psychology, 44,* 1383–1387.

Meister, A. (1979). Personal and social factors of social participation. *Journal of Voluntary Action Research, 8,* 6–11.

Meleshko, K. G. A., & Alden, L. E. (1993). Anxiety and self-disclosure: Toward a motivational model. *Journal of Personality and Social Psychology, 64,* 1000–1009.

Mendes, W. B., Reis, H. T., Seery, M. D., & Blascovich, J. (2003). Cardiovascular correlates of emotional expression and suppression: Do content and gender context matter? *Journal of Personality & Social Psychology, 84,* 771–792.

Merton, R. K. (1948). The self-fulfilling prophecy. *Antioch Review, 8,* 193–210.

Mesquita, B. (2001). Emotions in collectivist and individualist contexts. *Journal of Personality and Social Psychology, 80,* 68–74.

Messé, L. A., Hertel, G., Kerr, N. L., Lount, R. B., Jr., & Park, E. S. (2002). Knowledge of partner's ability as a moderator of group motivation gains: An exploration of the Koehler discrepancy effect. *Journal of Personality and Social Psychology, 82,* 935–946.

Messick, D. M., & Brewer, M. B. (1983). Solving social dilemmas: A review. *Review of Personality and Social Psychology, 4,* 11–44.

Meston, C. M., & Frohlich, P. F. (2003). Love at first fright: Partner salience moderates roller-coaster-induced excitation transfer. *Archives of Sexual Behavior, 32,* 537–544.

Metcalf, P., & Huntington, R. (1991). *Celebrations of death: The anthropology of mortuary ritual* (2nd ed.). Cambridge, UK: Cambridge University Press.

Miarmi, L., & Evans, K. G. (2007). The impact of distractions on heuristic processing: Internet advertisements and stereotype use. *Journal of Applied Social Psychology, 37,* 539–548.

Michaels, J. W., Blommel, J. M., Brocato, R. M., Linkous, R. A., & Rowe, J. S. (1982). Social facilitation and inhibition in a natural setting. *Replications in Social Psychology, 2,* 21–24.

Michaelsen, L. K., Watson, W. E., & Black, R. H. (1989). A realistic test of individual versus group consensus decision making. *Journal of Applied Psychology, 74,* 834–839.

Midlarsky, E., & Nemeroff, R. (1995, July). *Heroes of the Holocaust: Predictors of their well-being in later life.* Poster presented at the American Psychological Society meetings, New York.

Mikolic, J. M., Parker, J. C., & Pruitt, D. G. (1997). Escalation in response to persistent annoyance: Groups versus individuals and gender effects. *Journal of Personality and Social Psychology, 72,* 151–163.

Mikula, G., & Schwinger, T. (1978). Affective inter-member relations and reward allocation in groups: Some theoretical considerations. In H. Brandstatter, H. J. Davis, & H. Schuller (Eds.), *Dynamics of group decisions* (pp. 229–250). Beverly Hills, CA: Sage.

Mikulincer, M., & Florian, V. (2002). The effects of mortality salience on self-serving attributions—Evidence for the function of self-esteem as a terror management mechanism. *Basic and Applied Social Psychology, 24,* 261–271.

Mikulincer, M., Florian, V., & Hirschberger, G. (2003). The existential function of close relationships: Introducing death into the science of love. *Personality & Social Psychology Review, 7,* 20–40.

Mikulincer, M., Gillath, O., & Shaver, P. R. (2002). Activation of the attachment system in adulthood: Threat-related primes increase the accessibility of mental representations of attachment figures. *Journal of Personality & Social Psychology, 83*, 881–895.

Mikulincer, M., & Shaver, P. R. (2013). The role of attachment security in adolescent and adult close relationships. In J. A. Simpson & L. Campbell (Eds.), *Oxford handbook of close relationships* (pp. 66–89). New York: Oxford University Press.

Milgram, S. (1963). Behavioral study of obedience. *Journal of Abnormal and Social Psychology, 67*, 371–378.

Milgram, S. (1964). Issues in the study of obedience: A reply to Baumrind. *American Psychologist, 19*, 848–852.

Milgram, S. (1965). Some conditions of obedience and disobedience to authority. *Human Relations, 18*, 57–76.

Milgram, S. (1970). The experience of living in cities. *Science, 167*, 1461–1468.

Milgram, S. (1974). *Obedience to authority: An experimental view.* New York: Harper & Row.

Milgram, S., Bickman, L., & Berkowitz, L. (1969). Note on the drawing power of crowds of different size. *Journal of Personality and Social Psychology, 13*(2), 79.

Millar, M. G., & Millar, K. U. (1996). The effect of direct and indirect experiences on affective and cognitive responses and the attitude-behavior relation. *Journal of Experimental Social Psychology, 32*, 561–579.

Miller, A. G., Collins, B. E., & Brief, D. E. (Eds.). (1995). Perspectives on obedience to authority: The legacy of the Milgram experiments. *Journal of Social Issues, 51*(3), 1–19.

Miller, D. T. (1976). Ego involvement and attributions for success and failure. *Journal of Personality and Social Psychology, 34*, 901–906.

Miller, D. T. (1999). The norm of self-interest. *American Psychologist, 54*(12), 1053–1060.

Miller, D. T., & McFarland, C. (1987). Pluralistic ignorance: When similarity is interpreted as dissimilarity. *Journal of Personality and Social Psychology, 53*, 298–305.

Miller, D. T., & Nelson, L. D. (2002). Seeing approach motivation in the avoidance behavior of others: Implications for an understanding of pluralistic ignorance. *Journal of Personality and Social Psychology, 83*, 1066–1075.

Miller, D. T., & Ross, M. (1975). Self-serving biases in attribution of causality: Fact or fiction? *Psychological Bulletin, 82*, 213–255.

Miller, G. F. (2000). *The mating mind: How sexual choice shaped the evolution of human nature.* New York: Doubleday.

Miller, G. F., Tybur, J. M., & Jordan, B. D. (2007). Ovulatory cycle effects on tip earnings by lap dancers: Economic evidence for human estrus? *Evolution and Human Behavior, 28*, 375–381.

Miller, L. (2002, March 19). Charities hop 9/11 inspires "e-philanthropy." *USA Today*, p. 4D.

Miller, L. C., & Fishkin, S. A. (1997). On the dynamics of human bonding and reproductive success: Seeking windows on the adapted-for-human-environmental interface. In J. A. Simpson & D. T. Kenrick (Eds.), *Evolutionary social psychology* (pp. 169–196). Hillsdale, NJ: Erlbaum.

Miller, M., & Hemenway, D. (2008). Guns and suicide in the United States. *New England Journal of Medicine, 359*, 989–991.

Miller, N., & Brewer, M. B. (1984). *Groups in contact.* New York: Academic Press.

Miller, N. H., Pedersen, W. H., Earleywine, M., & Pollock, V. E. (2003). A theoretical model of triggered displaced aggression. *Personality & Social Psychology Review, 7*, 75–97.

Miller, N., & Zimbardo, P. (1966). Motive for fear-induced affiliation: Emotional comparison or interpersonal similarity? *Journal of Personality, 34*, 481–503.

Miller, P. J., Fung, H., & Mintz, J. (1996). Self-construction through narrative practices: A Chinese and American comparison of early socialization. *Ethos, 24*, 237–280.

Miller, R. S. (1995). On the nature of embarrassability: Shyness, social evaluation, and social skill. *Journal of Personality, 63*, 315–339.

Miller, R. S. (1997). Inattentive and contented: Relationship commitment and attention to alternatives. *Journal of Personality and Social Psychology, 73*, 758–766.

Miller, R. S., & Schlenker, B. R. (1985). Egotism in group members: Public and private attributions of responsibility for group performance. *Social Psychology Quarterly, 48*, 85–89.

Miller, S. L., Zielaskowski, K., Maner, J. K., & Plant, E. A. (2012). Self-protective motivation and avoidance of heuristically threatening outgroups. *Evolution and Human Behavior, 33*, 726–735.

Mills, C. M., & Keil, F. C. (2005). The development of cynicism. *Psychological Science, 16*, 385–390.

Mills, J., Clark, M. S., Ford, T. E., & Johnson, M. (2004). Measurement of communal strength. *Personal Relationships, 11*, 213–230.

Miniño, A. M. (2010). Mortality among teenagers aged 12–19 years: United States, 1999–2006 (NCHS data brief, no 37). Hyattsville, MD: National Center for Health Statistics.

Minkov, M. (2009). Risk-taking reproductive competition explains national murder rates better than socioeconomic inequality. *Cross-Cultural Research, 43*, 3–29.

Minson, J. A., & Mueller, J. S. (2012). The cost of collaboration why joint decision making exacerbates rejection of outside information. *Psychological Science, 23*(3), 219–224.

Mischel, W., Cantor, N., & Feldman, S. (1996). In E. T. Higgins & A. W. Kruglanski (Eds.), *Social psychology: Handbook of basic principles* (pp. 329–360). New York: Guilford.

Mischel, W., Shoda, Y., & Mendoza-Denton, R. (2002). Situation-behavior profiles as a locus of consistency in personality. *Current Directions in Psychological Science, 11*, 50–54.

Mishra, S., Clark, S., & Daly, M. (2007). One woman's behavior affects the attractiveness of others. *Evolution and Human Behavior, 28*, 145–149.

Mitchell, C. (1999). Negotiation as problem solving: Challenging the dominant metaphor. *Peace and Conflict: Journal of Peace Psychology, 5*, 219–224.

Miyamoto, Y., & Kitayama, S. (2002). Cultural variation in correspondence bias: The critical role of attitude diagnosticity of socially constrained behavior. *Journal of Personality & Social Psychology, 83*, 1239–1248.

Miyamoto, Y., Nisbett, R. E., & Masuda, T. (2006). Culture and the physical environment: Holistic versus analytic perceptual affordances. *Psychological Science, 17*, 113–119.

Miyamoto, Y., & Schwarz, N. (2006). When conveying a message may hurt the relationship: Cultural differences in the difficulty of using an answering machine. *Journal of Experimental Social Psychology, 42*, 540–547.

Moffitt, T. E. (1993). Adolescence-limited and life-course-persistent antisocial behavior: A developmental taxonomy. *Psychological Review, 100*, 674–701.

Moghaddam, F. M., Taylor, D. M., & Wright, S. C. (1993). *Social psychology in cross-cultural perspective.* New York: W. H. Freeman.

Molden, D. C., Lucas, G. M., Gardner, W. L., Dean, K., & Knowles, M. L. (2009). Motivations for prevention or promotion following social exclusion: Being rejected versus being ignored. *Journal of Personality and Social Psychology, 96*, 415–431.

Moll, J., Krueger, F., Zahn, R., Pardini, M., Oliveira-Souza, R., & Grafman, J. (2007). Human fronto-mesolimbic networks guide decisions about charitable donation. *Proceedings of the National Academy of Sciences, 103*, 15623–15628.

Monin, B. (2003). The warm glow heuristic: When liking leads to familiarity. *Journal of Personality and Social Psychology, 85*, 1035–1048.

Monteith, M. J., Sherman, J. W., & Devine, P. G. (1998). Suppression as a stereotype control strategy. *Personality and Social Psychology Review, 2*, 63–82.

Moore, M. M. (1985). Nonverbal courtship patterns in women: Context and consequences. *Ethology and Sociobiology, 6*, 237–247.

Moreland, R. L. (1987). The formation of small groups. In C. Hendrick (Ed.), *Group processes* (pp. 80–110). Newbury Park, CA: Sage.

Morganthau, T., & Annin, P. (1997, June 16). Should McVeigh die? *Newsweek*, pp. 20–27.

Mori, K., & Arai, M. (2010). No need to fake it: Reproduction of the Asch experiment without confederates. *International Journal of Psychology, 45*(5), 390–397. Retrieved from http://dx.doi.org/10.1080/00207591003774485

Morier, D., & Seroy, C. (1994). The effects of interpersonal expectancies on men's self-presentation of gender-role attitudes to women. *Sex Roles, 31*, 493–504.

Morling, B., Kitayama, S., & Miyamoto, Y. (2002). Cultural practices emphasize influence in the United States and adjustment in Japan. *Personality and Social Psychology Bulletin, 28*, 311–323.

Morling, D., & Lamoreaux, M. (2008). Measuring culture outside the head: A meta-analysis of individualism-collectivism in cultural products. *Personality and Social Psychology Review, 12*, 199–221.

Morr Serewicz, M. C., & Gale, E. (2008). First-date scripts: Gender roles, context, and relationship. *Sex Roles, 58*, 149–164.

Morris, D. (1999, June 15). The first lady's little problem. *New York Post.*

Morris, M. W., & Peng, K. (1994). Culture and cause: American and Chinese attributions for social and physical events. *Journal of Personality and Social Psychology, 67*, 949–971.

Morris, M. W., Podolny, J. M., & Ariel, S. (2001). Culture, norms, and obligations: Cross-national differences in patterns of interpersonal norms and felt obligations toward co-workers. In W. Wosinska, R. B. Cialdini, D. W. Barrett, & J. Reykowski (Eds.), *The practice of social influence in multiple cultures* (pp. 97–124). Mahwah, NJ: Erlbaum.

Morris, S. J., & Kanfer, F. H. (1983). Altruism and depression. *Personality and Social Psychology Bulletin, 9*, 567–577.

Morris, W. N., & Miller, R. S. (1975). The effects of consensus-breaking and consensus-preempting partners on reduction of conformity. *Journal of Experimental Social Psychology, 11*, 215–223.

Morrison, J. D. (1993). *Group composition and creative performance.* Unpublished doctoral dissertation, University of Tulsa, Tulsa, OK.

Morrison, K. R., & Ybarra, O. (2008). The effects of realistic threat and group identification on social dominance orientation. *Journal of Experimental Social Psychology, 44*, 156–163.

Moscovici, S., Lage, E., & Naffrechoux, M. (1969). Influence of a consistent minority on the responses of a majority in a color perception task. *Sociometry, 32*, 365–380.

Moskowitz, G. B. (1993). Individual differences in social categorization: The influence of personal need for structure on spontaneous trait inferences. *Journal of Personality and Social Psychology, 65*, 132–142.

Moskowitz, G. B. (2002). Preconscious effects of temporary goals on attention. *Journal of Experimental Social Psychology, 38*, 397–404.

Moskowitz, G. B., & Roman, R. J. (1992). Spontaneous trait inferences as self-generated primes: Implications for conscious social judgment. *Journal of Personality and Social Psychology, 62*, 728–738.

Moskowitz, G. B., Salomon, A. R., & Taylor, C. M. (2000). Preconsciously controlling stereotyping: Implicitly activated egalitarian goals prevent the activation of stereotypes. *Social Cognition, 18*, 151–177.

Mugny, G. (1982). *The power of minorities*. New York: Academic Press.

Mullen, B. (1983). Operationalizing the effect of the group on the individual: A self-attention perspective. *Journal of Experimental Social Psychology, 19,* 295–322.

Mullen, B. (1986). Atrocity as a function of lynch mob composition: A self-attention perspective. *Personality and Social Psychology Bulletin, 12,* 187–197.

Mullen, B., Anthony, T., Salas, E., & Driskell, J. E. (1994). Group cohesiveness and quality of decision making: An integration of tests of the groupthink hypothesis. *Small Group Research, 25,* 189–204.

Mullen, B., Brown, R., & Smith, C. (1992). Ingroup bias as a function of salience, relevance, and status: An integration. *European Journal of Social Psychology, 22,* 103–122.

Mullen, B., & Copper, C. (1994). The relation between group cohesiveness and performance: An integration. *Psychological Bulletin, 115,* 210–227.

Mullen, B., & Hu, L. T. (1989). Perceptions of ingroup and outgroup variability: A meta-analytic integration. *Basic and Applied Social Psychology, 10,* 233–252.

Mullen, B., Salas, E., & Driskell, J. E. (1989). Salience, motivation, and artifact as contributions to the relation between participation rate and leadership. *Journal of Experimental Social Psychology, 25,* 545–559.

Mullin, C. R., & Linz, D. (1995). Desensitization and resensitization to violence against women: Effects of exposure to sexually violent films on judgments of domestic violence victims. *Journal of Personality & Social Psychology, 69,* 449–459.

Munro, G. D., & Ditto, P. H. (1997). Biased assimilation, attitude polarization, and affect in reactions to stereotype-relevant scientific information. *Personality and Social Psychology Bulletin, 23*(6), 636–653.

Murdock, G. P. (1923/1970). Rank and potlatch among the Haida. In *Yale University publications in anthropology* (Vol. 13). New Haven, CT: Human Relations Area Files Press.

Murray, D. R., Trudeau, R., & Schaller, M. (2010). On the origins of cultural differences in conformity: Four tests of the pathogen prevalence hypothesis. *Personality and Social Psychology Bulletin, 37,* 318–329.

Murray, H. A. (1938). *Explorations in personality.* New York: Oxford University Press.

Murray, S. L., Rose, P., Bellavia, G. M., Holmes, J. G., & Kusche, A. G. (2002). When rejection stings: How self-esteem constrains relationship-enhancement processes. *Journal of Personality & Social Psychology, 83,* 557–573.

Musch, J., & Grondin, S. (2001). Unequal competition as an impediment to personal development: A review of the relative age effect in sport. *Developmental Review, 21,* 147–167.

Mussweiler, T., & Strack, F. (2000). The use of category and exemplar knowledge in the solution of anchoring tasks. *Journal of Personality and Social Psychology, 78,* 1038–1052.

Mussweiler, T., Strack, F., & Pfeiffer, T. (2000). Overcoming the inevitable anchoring effect: Considering the opposite compensates for selective accessibility. *Personality and Social Psychology Bulletin, 26,* 1142–1150.

Myers, D. G. (1975). Discussion-induced attitude polarization. *Human Relations, 28,* 699–714.

Myers, D. G. (1978). Polarizing effects of social comparison. *Journal of Experimental Social Psychology, 14,* 554–563.

Myers, D. G. (2000). The funds, friends, and faith of happy people. *American Psychologist, 55,* 56–67.

Myers, D. G., & Bishop, G. D. (1970). Discussion effects on racial attitudes. *Science, 169,* 778–789.

Nabi, H., Consoli, S. M., Chastang, J. F., Chiron, M., Lafont, S., & Lagarde, E. (2005). Type A behavior pattern, risky driving behaviors, and serious road traffic accidents: A prospective study of the GAZEL cohort. *American Journal of Epidemiology, 161,* 864–870.

Naccarato, M. E. (1988). *The impact of need for structure on stereotyping and discrimination.* Unpublished master's thesis, University of Waterloo, Ontario.

Nadler, A. (1986). Self-esteem and the seeking and receiving of help: Theoretical and empirical perspectives. In B. Maher & W. Maher (Eds.), *Progress in experimental personality research* (Vol. 14, pp. 115–163). New York: Academic Press.

Nadler, A. (1991). Help-seeking behavior: Psychological costs and instrumental benefits. In M. S. Clark (Ed.), *Review of personality and social psychology* (Vol. 12, pp. 290–311). Newbury Park, CA: Sage.

Nadler, A., & Fisher, J. D. (1986). The role of threat to self-esteem and perceived control in recipient reaction to help: Theory development and empirical validation. In L. Berkowitz (Ed.), *Advances in experimental social psychology* (Vol. 19, pp. 81–122). San Diego, CA: Academic Press.

Nadler, A., Maler, S., & Friedman, A. (1984). Effects of helper's sex, subject's sex, subject's androgyny and self-evaluation on males' and females' willingness to seek and receive help. *Sex Roles, 10,* 327–339.

Nail, P. R., Correll, J. S., Drake, C. E., Glenn, S. B., Scott, G. M., & Stuckey, C. (2001). A validation study of the preference for consistency scale. *Personality and Individual Differences, 31,* 1193–1202.

Nail, P. R., MacDonald, G., & Levy, D. A. (2000). Proposal of a four-dimensional model of social response. *Psychological Bulletin, 126,* 454–470.

Nail, P. R., & Van Leeuwen, M. D. (1993). An analysis and restructuring of the diamond model of social response. *Personality and Social Psychology Bulletin, 19,* 106–116.

Nakao, K. (1987). Analyzing sociometric preferences: An example of Japanese and U.S. business groups. *Journal of Social Behavior and Personality, 2,* 523–534.

Nathanson, S. (1987). *An eye for an eye? The morality of punishing by death.* Totowa, NJ: Rowman & Littlefield.

National Research Council. (2003). *The polygraph and lie detection.* Washington, DC: National Academic Press.

Navarrete, C. D. (2005). Death concerns and other adaptive challenges: The effects of coalition-relevant challenges on worldview defense in the U.S. and Costa Rica. *Group Processes and Intergroup Relations, 8,* 411–427.

Navarrete, C. D., & Fessler, D. M. T. (2006). Disease avoidance and ethnocentrism: The effects of disease vulnerability and disgust sensitivity on intergroup attitudes. *Evolution and Human Behavior, 27,* 270–282.

Navarrete, C. D., Fessler, D. M. T., & Eng, S. J. (2007). Elevated ethnocentrism in the first trimester of pregnancy. *Evolution and Human Behavior, 28,* 60–65.

Navarrete, C. D., Kurzban, R., Fessler, D. M. T., & Kirkpatrick, L. A. (2004). Anxiety and intergroup bias: Terror management or coalitional psychology? *Group Processes & Intergroup Relations, 7,* 370–397.

Navarrete, C. D., Olsson, A., Ho, A. K., Mendes, W. B., Thomsen, L., & Sidanius, J. (2009). Fear extinction to an outgroup face: The role of target gender. *Psychological Science, 20,* 155–158.

Neel, R., Becker, D. V., Neuberg, S. L., & Kenrick, D. T. (2012). Who expressed what emotion? Men grab anger, women grab happiness. *Journal of Experimental Social Psychology, 48,* 583–586.

Neel, R., Neufeld, S. L., & Neuberg, S. L. (2013). Would an obese person whistle Vivaldi? Targets of prejudice self-present to minimize appearance of specific threats. *Psychological Science, 24*(5), 678–687.

Neidert, G. P., & Linder, D. E. (1990). Avoiding social traps: Some conditions that maintain adherence to restricted consumption. *Social Behaviour, 5,* 261–284.

Neighbors, C., Vietor, N. A., & Knee, C. R. (2002). A motivational model of driving anger and aggression. *Personality & Social Psychology Bulletin, 28,* 324–335.

Nelson, L. L., & Milburn, T. W. (1999). Relationships between problem-solving competencies and militaristic attitudes: Implications for peace education. *Peace and Conflict: Journal of Peace Psychology, 5,* 149–168.

Nemeth, C. J. (1992). Minority dissent as a stimulant to group performance. In S. Worchel, W. Wood, & J. A. Simpson (Eds.), *Group process and productivity* (pp. 95–111). Newbury Park, CA: Sage.

Nemeth, C. J., Mayseless, O., Sherman, J., & Brown, Y. (1990). Improving recall by exposure to consistent dissent. *Journal of Personality and Social Psychology, 58,* 429–437.

Nemeth, C. J., & Wachtler, J. (1974). Creating perceptions of consistency and confidence: A necessary condition for minority influence. *Sociometry, 37,* 529–540.

Neuberg, S. L. (1989). The goal of forming accurate impressions during social interactions: Attenuating the impact of negative expectancies. *Journal of Personality and Social Psychology, 56,* 374–386.

Neuberg, S. L., & Fiske, S. T. (1987). Motivational influences on impression formation: Outcome dependency, accuracy-driven attention, and individuating processes. *Journal of Personality and Social Psychology, 53,* 431–444.

Neuberg, S. L., Kenrick, D. T., & Schaller, M. (2010). Evolutionary social psychology. In S. T. Fiske, D. T. Gilbert, & G. Lindzey (Eds.), *Handbook of social psychology* (5th ed., Vol. II, pp. 761–796). New York: John Wiley & Sons.

Neuberg, S. L., & Newsom, J. T. (1993). Personal need for structure: Individual differences in the desire for simple structure. *Journal of Personality and Social Psychology, 65,* 113–131.

Neuberg, S. L., Schaller, M., & Kenrick, D. T. (2009). Evolutionary social psychology. In S. T. Fiske, D. T. Gilbert, & G. Lindzey (Eds.), *Handbook of social psychology* (5th ed.). New York: John Wiley & Sons.

Neuberg, S. L., Smith, D. M., Hoffman, J. C., & Russell, F. J. (1994). When we observe stigmatized and "normal" individuals interacting: Stigma by association. *Personality and Social Psychology Bulletin, 20,* 196–209.

Neuberg, S. L., Warner, C. M., Mistler, S. A., Berlin, A., Hill, E. D., Johnson, J. D., et al. (2014). Religion and intergroup conflict: Findings from the global group relations project. *Psychological Science, 25,* 198–206.

Neumann, R. (2000). The causal influences of attributions on emotions: A procedural priming approach. *Psychological Science, 11,* 179–182.

Newby-Clark, I. R., McGregor, I., & Zanna, M. P. (2002). Thinking and caring about cognitive inconsistency. *Journal of Personality and Social Psychology, 82,* 157–166.

Newcomb, T. M. (1961). *The acquaintance process.* New York: Holt, Rinehart and Winston.

Neyer, F. J., & Lang, F. R. (2003). Blood is thicker than water: Kinship orientation across adulthood. *Journal of Personality and Social Psychology, 84,* 310–321.

Nezlek, J. B. (1993). The stability of social interaction. *Journal of Personality and Social Psychology, 65,* 930–941.

Nezlek, J. B., & Derks, P. (2001). Use of humor as a coping mechanism, psychological adjustment, and social interaction. *Humor: International Journal of Humor Research, 14,* 395–413.

Nezlek, J. B., Hampton, C. P., & Shean, G. D. (2000). Clinical depression and day-to-day social interaction in a community sample. *Journal of Abnormal Psychology, 109,* 11–19.

Nezlek, J. B., & Leary, M. R. (2002). Individual differences in self-presentational motives in daily social interaction. *Personality and Social Psychology Bulletin, 28,* 211–223.

Niedenthal, P. M., Tangney, J. P., & Gavanski, I. (1994). "If only I weren't" versus "If only I hadn't": Distinguishing shame and guilt in counterfactual thinking. *Journal of Personality and Social Psychology, 67*, 585–595.

Niemann, Y. F., Jennings, L., Rozelle, R. M., Baxter, J. C., & Sullivan, E. (1994). Use of free responses and cluster analysis to determine stereotypes of eight groups. *Personality and Social Psychology Bulletin, 20*, 379–390.

Nier, J. A., Gaertner, S. L., Dovidio, J. F., Banker, B. S., Ward, C. M., & Rust, M. C. (2001). Changing interracial evaluations and behavior: The effects of a common group identity. *Group Processes and Intergroup Relations, 4*, 299–316.

Nijstad, B. A., Berger-Selman, F., & De Dreu, C. K. (2014). Innovation in top management teams: Minority dissent, transformational leadership, and radical innovations. *European Journal of Work and Organizational Psychology, 23*(2), 310–322.

Nisbett, R. E. (1993). Violence and U.S. regional culture. *American Psychologist, 48*, 441–449.

Nisbett, R. E., Polly, G., & Lang, S. (1995). Homicide and regional U.S. culture. In R. B. Ruback & N. A. Weiner (Eds.), *Interpersonal violent behaviors* (pp. 135–151). New York: Springer.

Nisbett, R. E., & Ross, L. (1980). *Human inference*. Englewood Cliffs, NJ: Prentice Hall.

Noel, J. G., Wann, D. L., & Branscombe, N. R. (1995). Peripheral ingroup membership status and public negativity toward outgroups. *Journal of Personality and Social Psychology, 68*, 127–137.

Nolan, J. M., Schultz, P. W., Cialdini, R. B., Goldstein, N. J., & Griskevicius, V. (2008). Normative social influence is underdetected. *Personality and Social Psychology Bulletin, 34*, 913–923.

Norenzayan, A., Choi, I., & Nisbett, R. E. (2002). Cultural similarities and differences in social inference: Evidence from behavioral predictions and lay theories of behavior. *Personality and Social Psychology Bulletin, 28*, 109–120.

Norenzayan, A., & Heine, S. J. (2005). Psychological universals: What are they and how can we know? *Psychological Bulletin, 131*, 763–784.

Norenzayan, A., & Nisbett, R. E. (2000). Culture and causal cognition. *Current Directions in Psychological Science, 9*, 132–135.

Norenzayan, A., Schaller, M., & Heine, S. J. (2006). Evolution and culture. In M. Schaller, J. A. Simpson, & D. T. Kenrick (Eds.), *Evolution and social psychology* (pp. 343–364). New York: Psychology Press.

Norrander, B. (1997). The independence gap and the gender gap. *Public Opinion Quarterly, 61*, 464–476.

Norton, M. I., Frost, J. H., & Ariely, D. (2007). Less is more: The lure of ambiguity, or why familiarity breeds contempt. *Journal of Personality and Social Psychology, 92*, 97–105.

Notarius, C., & Markman, H. (1993). *We can work it out: Making sense of marital conflict*. New York: G. P. Putnam's Sons.

Notarius, C., & Pellegrini, D. (1984). Marital processes as stressors and stress mediators: Implications for marital repair. In S. Duck (Ed.), *Personal relationship, Vol. 5: Repairing personal relationships* (pp. 67–88). London: Academic Press.

Novaco, R. W. (1975). *Anger control: The development and evaluation of an experimental treatment*. Lexington, MA: Lexington Books.

Novaco, R. W. (1995). Clinical problems of anger and its assessment and regulation through a stress coping skills approach. In W. O'Connor & L. Krasner (Eds.), *Handbook of psychological skills training: Clinical techniques and applications* (pp. 320–338). Boston: Allyn & Bacon.

Nowak, M. A., Sasaki, A., Taylor, C., & Fudenberg, D. (2004). Emergence of cooperation and evolutionary stability in finite populations. *Nature, 428*, 646–650.

Nowak, A., & Vallacher, R. R. (1998). *Dynamical social psychology*. New York: Guilford.

Nowak, A., Vallacher, R., Strawinska, U., & Brée, D. S. (2013). Dynamical social psychology: An introduction. In A. Nowak, K. Winkowska-Nowak, & D. Bree (Eds.), *Complex human dynamics: From mind to societies* (pp. 1–19). Berlin Heidelberg: Springer.

Nowicki, S., & Manheim, S. (1991). Interpersonal complementarity and time of interaction in female relationships. *Journal of Research in Personality, 322*–333.

O'Brian, M. E., & Jacks, J. Z. (2000, February). *Values, self, and resistance to persuasion*. Poster session presented at the annual meeting of the Society of Personality and Social Psychology, Nashville, Tennessee.

O'Brien, J. A. (1993, September 23). Mother's killing still unresolved, but Peter Reilly puts past behind. *The Hartford Courant*, p. A1.

O'Gorman, R., Wilson, D. S., & Miller, R. R. (2008). An evolved cognitive bias for social norms. *Evolution and Human Behavior, 29*, 71–78.

O'Grady, M. A. (2013). Alcohol self-presentation: The role of impression motivation and impression construction. *Journal of Applied Social Psychology, 43*(4), 854–869.

Oishi, S., Kesebir, S., Miao, F. F., Talhelm, T., Endo, Y., Uchida, Y., et al. (2013). Residential mobility increases motivation to expand social network: But why? *Journal of Experimental Social Psychology, 49*, 217–223.

O'Sullivan, M. (2008). Home runs and humbugs: Comment on Bond and DePaulo (2008). *Psychological Bulletin, 134*, 493–497.

O'Sullivan, M., Ekman, P., & Friesen, W. V. (1988). The effect of comparisons on detecting deceit. *Journal of Nonverbal Behavior, 12*, 203–215.

Oakes, P. J., Haslam, S. A., & Turner, J. C. (1994). *Stereotyping and social reality*. Oxford, UK: Blackwell.

Ohman, A., Lundqvist, D., & Esteves, F. (2001). The face in the crowd revisited: A threat advantage with schematic stimuli. *Journal of Personality & Social Psychology, 80*, 381–396.

Ohman, A., & Mineka, S. (2001). Fears, phobias, and preparedness: Toward an evolved module of fear and fear learning. *Psychological Review, 108*, 483–522.

Ohse, D. M., & Stockdale, M. S. (2008). Age comparisons in workplace sexual harassment perceptions. *Sex Roles, 59*, 240–253.

Oishi, S., Wyer, R. S., & Colcombe, S. J. (2000). Cultural variation in the use of current life satisfaction to predict the future. *Journal of Personality & Social Psychology, 78*, 434–445.

Okimoto, D. I., & Rohlen, T. P. (1988). *Inside the Japanese system: Readings on contemporary society and political economy*. Stanford, CA: Stanford University Press.

Olds, J. M., & Milner, P. M. (1954). Positive reinforcement produced by electrical stimulation of the septal area and other areas of the rat brain. *Journal of Comparative and Physiological Psychology, 47*, 419–427.

Oliner, S. P., & Oliner, P. M. (1988). *The altruistic personality: Rescuers of Jews in Nazi Europe*. New York: The Free Press.

Olson, J. M., Hafer, C. L., & Taylor, L. (2001). I'm mad as hell, and I'm not going to take it anymore: Reports of negative emotions as a self-preservation tactic. *Journal of Applied Social Psychology, 31*, 981–999.

Olson, J. M., Vernon, P. A., Harris, J. A., & Jang, K. L. (2001). The heritability of attitudes: A study of twins. *Journal of Personality and Social Psychology, 80*, 845–860.

Olson, M. A., & Fazio, R. H. (2002). Implicit acquisition and manifestation of classically conditioned attitudes. *Social Cognition, 20*, 89–104.

Olsson, A., Ebert, J. P., Banaji, M. R., & Phelps, E. A. (2005). The role of social groups in the persistence of learned fear. *Science, 309*, 785–787.

Olweus, D. (1978). *Aggression in schools*. New York: Wiley.

Olweus, D. (1991). Bully/victim problems among school children: Basic facts and effects of a school-based intervention program. In D. Pepler & K. Rubin (Eds.), *The development and treatment of childhood aggression* (pp. 411–448). Hillsdale, NJ: Erlbaum.

Olzak, S. (1992). *The dynamics of ethnic competition and conflict*. Stanford, CA: Stanford University Press.

Oppenheimer, D. M. (2004). Spontaneous discounting of availability in frequency judgment tasks. *Psychological Science, 15*, 100–105.

Orians, G. H. (1969). On the evolution of mating systems in birds and mammals. *American Naturalist, 103*, 589–603.

Orive, R. (1988). Social projection and social comparison of opinions. *Journal of Personality and Social Psychology, 54*, 953–964.

Osborne, J. W. (1995). Academics, self-esteem, and race: A look at the underlying assumptions of the disidentification hypothesis. *Personality and Social Psychology Bulletin, 21*, 449–455.

Osborne, R. E., & Gilbert, D. T. (1992). The preoccupational hazards of social life. *Journal of Personality and Social Psychology, 62*, 219–228.

Osgood, C. E. (1962). *An alternative to war or surrender*. Urbana: University of Illinois Press.

Oskamp, S. (2000). A sustainable future for humanity: How can psychology help? *American Psychologist, 55*, 496–508.

Ostovich, J. M., & Sabini, J. (2005). Timing of puberty and sexuality in men and women. *Archives of Sexual Behavior, 34*, 197–206.

Oswald, D. L., & Clark, E. M. (2003). Best friends forever? High school friendships and the transition to college. *Personal Relationships, 10*, 187–205.

Oswald, D. L., Clark, E. M., & Kelly, C. M. (2004). Friendship maintenance: An analysis of individual and dyad behaviors. *Journal of Social and Clinical Psychology, 23*, 413–441.

Otta, E., Queiroz, R. D., Campos, L. D., daSilva, M., & Silveira, M. T. (1999). Age differences between spouses in a Brazilian marriage sample. *Evolution and Human Behavior, 20*, 99–104.

Ottati, V., & Lee, Y.-T. (1995). Accuracy: A neglected component of stereotype research. In Y.-T. Lee, L. J. Jussim, & C. R. McCauley (Eds.), *Stereotype accuracy: Toward appreciating group differences* (pp. 29–59). Washington, DC: American Psychological Association.

Otten, C. A., Penner, L. A., & Altabe, M. N. (1991). An examination of therapists' and college students' willingness to help a psychologically distressed person. *Journal of Social and Clinical Psychology, 10*, 102–120.

Otten, C. A., Penner, L. A., & Waugh, G. (1988). What are friends for: The determinants of psychological helping. *Journal of Social and Clinical Psychology, 7*, 34–41.

Otten, S., & Moskowitz, G. B. (2000). Evidence for implicit evaluative in-group bias: Affect-biased spontaneous trait inference in a minimal group paradigm. *Journal of Experimental Social Psychology, 36*, 77–89.

Overall, N. C., Fletcher, G. J. O., & Friesen, M. D. (2003). Mapping the intimate relationship mind: Comparisons between three models of attachment representations. *Personality and Social Psychology Bulletin, 29*, 1479–1493.

Overall, N. C., Fletcher, G. J. O., & Simpson, J. A. (2006). Regulation processes in intimate relationships: The role of ideal standards. *Journal of Personality and Social Psychology, 91*, 662–685.

Ovitz and out at disney. (1996, December 13). *New York Daily News*, p. 7.

Ovitz, Hollywood power broker, resigns from no. 2 job at Disney. (1996, December 13). *New York Times*, p. 1.

Owens, L., Shute, R., & Slee, P. (2000). "Guess what I just heard!": Indirect aggression among teenage girls in Australia. *Aggressive Behavior, 26*, 67–83.

Oyserman, D., Bybee, D., Terry, K., & Hart-Johnson, T. (2004). Possible selves as roadmaps. *Journal of Research in Personality, 38*, 130–149.

Oyserman, D., & Lee, S. W. S. (2008). Does culture influence what and how we think? Effects of priming individualism and collectivism. *Psychological Bulletin, 134*, 311–342.

Ozer, D. J. (1986). *Consistency in personality: A methodological framework*. New York: Springer-Verlag.

Packer, D. J. (2008). Identifying systematic disobedience in Milgram's experiments: A meta-analytic review. *Perspectives on Psychological Science, 3,* 301–304.

Packer, D. J. (2012). On not airing our dirty laundry: Intergroup contexts suppress ingroup criticism among strongly identified group members. *British Journal of Social Psychology, 53*(1), 93–111.

Padilla, A. M. (1994). Bicultural development: A theoretical and empirical examination. In R. G. Malgady & O. Rodriguez (Eds.), *Theoretical and conceptual issues in Hispanic mental health* (pp. 20–51). Malabar, FL: Krieger.

Page, B. I., Shapiro, R. Y., & Dempsey, G. (1987). What moves public opinion? *American Political Science Review, 81,* 23–43.

Paicheler, G. (1977). Norms and attitude change II: The phenomenon of bipolarization. *European Journal of Social Psychology, 7,* 5–14.

Palmer, C. T. (1993). Anger, aggression, and humor in Newfoundland floor hockey: An evolutionary analysis. *Aggressive Behavior, 19,* 167–173.

Paloutzian, R. F., & Ellison, C. W. (1982). Loneliness, spiritual well-being and the quality of life. In L. A. Peplau & D. Perlman (Eds.), *Loneliness: A sourcebook of current theory, research, and therapy* (pp. 224–237). New York: Wiley.

Pandey, J., & Rastagi, R. (1979). Machiavellianism and ingratiation. *Journal of Social Psychology, 108,* 221–225.

Panksepp, J. (2003). Can anthropomorphic analyses of separation cries in other animals inform us about the emotional nature of social loss in humans? Comment on Blumberg and Sokoloff (2001). *Psychological Review, 100,* 376–388.

Panksepp, J. (2005). Why does separation distress hurt? Comment on MacDonald and Leary (2005). *Psychological Bulletin, 131,* 224–230.

Panksepp, J., Siviy, S. M., & Normansell, L. A. (1985). Brain opioids and social emotions. In M. Reite & T. Field (Eds.), *The psychobiology of attachment and separation* (pp. 3–50). London: Academic Press.

Paolini, S., Hewstone, M., Cairns, E., & Voci, A. (2004). Effects of direct and indirect cross-group friendships on judgments of Catholics and Protestants in Northern Ireland: The mediating role of an anxiety-reduction mechanism. *Personality and Social Psychology Bulletin, 30,* 770–786.

Park, B., Judd, C. M., & Ryan, C. S. (1991). Social categorization and the representation of variability information. In W. Stroebe & M. Hewstone (Eds.), *European review of social psychology* (Vol. 2, pp. 211–245). New York: Wiley.

Park, J., & Banaji, M. R. (2000). Mood and heuristics: The influence of happy and sad states on sensitivity and bias in stereotyping. *Journal of Personality and Social Psychology, 78,* 1005–1023.

Park, J. H., & Schaller, M. (2005). Does attitude similarity serve as a heuristic cue for kinship? Evidence of an implicit cognitive association. *Evolution and Human Behavior, 26,* 158–170.

Park, J. H., Wieling, M. B., Buunk, A. P., & Massar, K. (2008). Sex-specific relationship between digit ratio (2D:4D) and romantic jealousy. *Personality and Individual Differences, 44,* 1039–1045.

Park, L. E., Crocker, J., & Mickelson, K. D. (2004). Attachment styles and contingencies of self-worth. *Personality and Social Psychology Bulletin, 30,* 1243–1254.

Park, L., & Maner, J. K. (2009). Does self-threat promote social connection? The role of self-esteem and contingencies of self-worth. *Journal of Personality & Social Psychology, 96,* 203–217.

Park, S., & Catrambone, R. (2007). Social facilitation effects of virtual humans. *Human Factors, 49,* 1054–1060.

Parke, R. D., Berkowitz, L., Leyens, J. P., West, S. G., & Sebastian, J. (1977). Some effects of violent and nonviolent movies on the behavior of juvenile delinquents. In L. Berkowitz (Ed.), *Advances in experimental social psychology* (Vol. 10, pp. 135–172). New York: Academic Press.

Parks, C. D., Henager, R. F., & Scamahorn, S. D. (1996). Trust and reactions to messages of intent in social dilemmas. *Journal of Conflict Resolution, 40,* 134–151.

Parks, C. D., Rumble, A. C., & Posey, D. C. (2002). The effects of envy on reciprocation in a social dilemma. *Personality & Social Psychology Bulletin, 28,* 509–520.

Parks, C. D., Sanna, L. J., & Berel, S. R. (2001). Actions of similar others as inducements to cooperate in social dilemmas. *Personality and Social Psychology Bulletin, 27*(3), 345–354.

Parks, C. D., & Vu, A. D. (1994). Social dilemma behavior of individuals from highly individualistic and collectivist cultures. *Journal of Conflict Resolution, 38,* 708–718.

Parks-Stamm, E. J., Heilman, M. E., & Hearns, K. A. (2008). Motivated to penalize: Women's strategic rejection of successful women. *Personality and Social Psychology Bulletin, 34,* 237–247.

Parrott, W. G. (2002). The functional utility of negative emotions. In L. F. Barrett & P. Salovey (Eds.), *The wisdom in feeling: Psychological processes in emotional intelligence* (pp. 341–359). New York: Guilford Press.

Pashler, H. (1994). Dual-task interference in simple tasks: Data and theory. *Psychological Bulletin, 116,* 220–244.

Pass, J. A., Lindenberg, S. M., & Park, J. H. (2010). All you need is love: Is the sociometer especially sensitive to one's mating capacity? *European Journal of Social Psychology, 40,* 221–234.

Pataki, S. P., Shapiro, C., & Clark, M. S. (1994). Children's acquisition of appropriate norms for friendships and acquaintances. *Journal of Personal Relationships, 11,* 427–442.

Patterson, G. R. (1997). Performance models for parenting: A social interactional perspective. In J. E. Gruser & L. Kuczynski (Eds.), *Parenting and children's internalization of values: A handbook of contemporary theory* (pp. 193–226). New York: John Wiley & Sons.

Patterson, G. R., Chamberlain, P., & Reid, J. B. (1982). A comparative evaluation of parent training procedures. *Behavior Therapy, 13,* 638–650.

Paulhus, D. L., Martin, C. L., & Murphy, G. K. (1992). Some effects of arousal on sex stereotyping. *Personality and Social Psychology Bulletin, 18,* 325–330.

Pavlidis, I., Eberhardt, N. L., & Levine, J. A. (2002). Seeing through the face of deception. *Nature, 415,* 35.

Pawlowski, B., & Dunbar, R. I. M. (1999). Withholding age as putative deception in mate search tactics. *Evolution & Human Behavior, 20,* 53–69.

Pawlowski, B., & Jasienska, G. (2005). Women's preferences for sexual dimorphism in height depend on menstrual cycle phase and expected duration of relationship. *Biological Psychology, 70,* 38–43.

Payne, B. K. (2001). Prejudice and perception: The role of automatic and controlled processes in misperceiving a weapon. *Journal of Personality and Social Psychology, 81,* 181–192.

Payne, B. K., Shimizu, Y., & Jacoby, L. L. (2005). Mental control and visual illusions: Toward explaining race-biased weapon misidentifications. *Journal of Experimental Social Psychology, 41,* 36–47.

Pearce, P. L., & Amato, P. R. (1980). A taxonomy of helping: A multidimensional scaling analysis. *Social Psychology Quarterly, 43,* 363–371.

Peck, S. R., Shaffer, D. R., & Williamson, G. M. (2004). Sexual satisfaction and relationship satisfaction in dating couples: The contributions of relationships communality and favorability of sexual exchanges. *Journal of Psychology and Human Sexuality, 16,* 17–37.

Pedersen, W. C., Bushman, B. J., Vasquez, E. A., & Miller, N. (2008). Kicking the (barking) dog effect: The moderating role of target attributes on triggered displaced aggression. *Personality and Social Psychology Bulletin, 34,* 1382–1395.

Pedersen, W. C., Gonzales, C., & Miller, N. (2000). The moderating effect of trivial triggering provocation on displaced aggression. *Journal of Personality & Social Psychology, 78,* 913–927.

Pelham, B. W. (1993). On the highly positive thoughts of the highly depressed. In R. Baumeister (Ed.), *Self-esteem: The puzzle of low self-regard* (pp. 183–200). New York: Plenum.

Pelto, P. J. (1968). The difference between "tight" and "loose" societies. *Transaction, 5,* 37–40.

Pelz, D. C. (1956). Some social factors related to performance in a research organization. *Administrative Science Quarterly, 1,* 310–325.

Pemberton, M. B., Insko, C. A., & Schopler, J. (1996). Memory for and experience of differential competitive behavior of individuals and groups. *Journal of Personality and Social Psychology, 71,* 953–966.

Pemberton, M., & Sedikides, C. (2001). When do individuals help close others improve? The role of information diagnosticity. *Journal of Personality and Social Psychology, 81,* 234–246.

Pendry, L. F., & Macrae, C. N. (1994). Stereotypes and mental life: The case of the motivated but thwarted tactician. *Journal of Experimental Social Psychology, 30,* 303–325.

Pendry, L. F., & Macrae, C. N. (1996). What the disinterested perceiver overlooks: Goal-directed social categorization. *Personality and Social Psychology Bulletin, 22,* 249–256.

Penn, D. J. (2003). The evolutionary roots of our environmental problems: Toward a Darwinian ecology. *Quarterly Review of Biology, 78,* 275–301.

Pennebaker, J. W., Barger, S. D., & Tiebout, J. (1989). Disclosure of traumas and health among holocaust survivors. *Psychosomatic Medicine, 51,* 577–589.

Pennebaker, J. W., Hughes, C. F., & O'Heeron, R. C. (1987). The psychophysiology of confession: Linking inhibitory and psychosomatic processes. *Journal of Personality and Social Psychology, 52,* 781–793.

Penner, L. A. (2002). The causes of sustained volunteerism: An interactionist perspective. *Journal of Social Issues, 58,* 447–467.

Penner, L. A., Dertke, M. C., & Achenbach, C. J. (1973). The flash system: A field study of altruism. *Journal of Applied Social Psychology, 3,* 362–373.

Penner, L. A., Dovidio, J. F., Piliavin, J. A., & Schroeder, D. A. (2005). Prosocial behavior: Multilevel perspectives. *Annual Review of Psychology, 56,* 365–392.

Penner, L. A., & Finkelstein, M. A. (1998). Dispositional and structural determinants of volunteerism. *Journal of Personality and Social Psychology, 74,* 525–537.

Penner, L. A., Harper, F. W. K., & Albrecht, T. L. (2012). The role of emotions in caregiving: Caring for the pediatric cancer patients. In S. L. Brown, R. M. Brown, & L. A. Penner (Eds.), *Moving beyond self-interest: Perspectives from evolutionary biology, neuroscience, and the social sciences* (pp. 166–177). New York: Oxford University Press.

Penninx, B. W. J. H., Rejeski, W. J., Pandya, J., Miller, M. E., DiBari, M., Applegate, W. B., et al. (2002). Exercise and depressive symptoms: A comparison of aerobic and resistance exercise effects on emotional and physical function in older persons with high and low depressive symptomatology. *Journals of Gerontology B: Psychological Sciences and Social Sciences, 57B,* 124–132.

Penton-Voak, I. S., Little, A. C., Jones, B. C., Burt, D. M., Tiddeman, B. P., & Perrett, D. J. (2003). Female condition influences preferences for sexual dimorphism in faces of male humans (*Homo sapiens*). *Journal of Comparative Psychology, 117,* 264–271.

Peplau, L. A., Russell, D., & Heim, M. (1979). The experience of loneliness. In I. H. Frieze, D. Bar-Tal, & J. S. Carroll (Eds.), *New approaches to social problems: Applications of attribution theory.* San Francisco: Jossey-Bass.

Perilloux, C., Easton, J. A., & Buss, D. M. (2012). The misperception of sexual interest. *Psychological Science, 23*(2), 146–151.

Perloff, R. M. (1993). *The dynamics of persuasion.* Hillsdale, NJ: Erlbaum.

Perriloux, H. K., Webster, G. D., & Gaulin, S. J. C. (2010). Signals of genetic quality and maternal investment capacity: The dynamic effects of fluctuating asymmetry and waist-to-hip ratio on men's rating of women's attractiveness. *Social Psychological and Personality Science, 1*(1), 34–42.

Pervin, L. A., & Rubin, D. B. (1967). Student dissatisfaction with college and the college dropout: A transactional approach. *Journal of Social Psychology, 72,* 285–295.

Pessiglione, M., Petrovic, P., Daunizeau, J., Palminteri, S., Dolan, R. J., & Frith, C. D. (2008). Subliminal instrumental conditioning demonstrated in the human brain. *Neuron, 59,* 561–567.

Petrocelli, J. V., Tormala, Z. L., & Rucker, D. D. (2007). Unpacking attitude certainty: Attitude certainty and attitude correctness. *Journal of Personality and Social Psychology, 92,* 30–41.

Petronio, S. (2002). *Boundaries of privacy: Dialectics of disclosure.* Albany: State University of New York Press.

Pettigrew, T. F. (1979). The ultimate attribution error: Extending Allport's cognitive analysis of prejudice. *Personality and Social Psychology Bulletin, 5,* 461–476.

Pettigrew, T. F. (1997). Generalized intergroup contact effects on prejudice. *Personality and Social Psychology Bulletin, 23,* 173–185.

Pettigrew, T. F., Christ, O., Wagner, U., & Stellmacher, J. (2007). Direct and indirect intergroup contact effects on prejudice: A normative interpretation. *International Journal of Intercultural Relations, 31,* 411–425.

Pettigrew, T. F., & Meertens, R. W. (1995). Subtle and blatant prejudice in Western Europe. *European Journal of Social Psychology, 25,* 57–75.

Pettigrew, T. F., & Tropp, L. R. (2006). A meta-analytic test of intergroup contact theory. *Journal of Personality and Social Psychology, 90*(5), 751–783.

Petty, R. E., Brinol, P., & Tormala, Z. L. (2002). Thought confidence as a determinant of persuasion. *Journal of Personality and Social Psychology, 82,* 722–741.

Petty, R. E., & Cacioppo, J. T. (1979). Issue involvement can increase or decrease persuasion by enhancing messagerelevant cognitive responses. *Journal of Personality and Social Psychology, 37,* 1915–1926.

Petty, R. E., & Cacioppo, J. T. (1984). The effects of involvement on responses to argument quantity and quality: Central and peripheral routes to persuasion. *Journal of Personality and Social Psychology, 46,* 69–81.

Petty, R. E., & Cacioppo, J. T. (1986). *Communication and persuasion: Central and peripheral routes to attitude change.* New York: Springer-Verlag.

Petty, R. E., Cacioppo, J. T., Strathman, A. J., & Priester, J. R. (2005). To think or not to think. In T. C. Brock & M. C. Green (Eds.), *Persuasion: Psychological insights and perspectives* (pp. 81–116). Thousand Oaks, CA: Sage.

Petty, R. E., & Wegener, D. T. (1998). Matching versus mismatching attitude functions: Implications for scrutiny of persuasive messages. *Personality and Social Psychology Bulletin, 24,* 227–240.

Pfeffer, J. (1998). Understanding organizations: Concepts and controversies. In D. T. Gilbert, S. T. Fiske, & G. Lindzey (Eds.), *Handbook of social psychology* (4th ed., Vol. 2, pp. 733–777). New York: McGraw-Hill.

Phelan, J. E., & Rudman, L. A. (2010). Prejudice toward female leaders: Backlash effects and women's impression management dilemma. *Social and Personality Psychology Compass, 4*(10), 807–820.

Phelps, E. A., O'Connor, K. J., Cunningham, W. A., Funayama, E. S., Gatenby, J. C., Gore, J. C., et al. (2000). Performance on indirect measures of race evaluation predicts amygdala activation. *Journal of Cognitive Neuroscience, 12,* 729–738.

Phillips, D. P. (1985). Natural experiments on the effects of mass media violence on fatal aggression: Strengths and weaknesses of a new approach. In L. Berkowitz (Ed.), *Advances in experimental social psychology* (Vol. 19, pp. 207–250). Orlando, FL: Academic Press.

Phillips, D. P. (1989). Recent advances in suicidology: The study of imitative suicide. In R. F. W. Diekstra, R. Maris, S. Platt, A. Schmidtke, & G. Sonneck (Eds.), *Suicide and its prevention: The role of attitude and imitation* (pp. 299–312). Leiden, Netherlands: E. J. Brill.

Phillips, K. W. (2003). The effects of categorically based expectations on minority influence: The importance of congruence. *Personality & Social Psychology Bulletin, 29,* 3–13.

Phinney, J., & Devich-Navarro, M. (1997). Variations in bicultural identification among African American and Mexican American adolescents. *Journal of Research on Adolescence, 7,* 3–32.

Pickett, C. L., & Gardner, W. L. (2005). The social monitoring system: Enhanced sensitivity to social cues as an adaptive response to social exclusion. In K. Williams, J. Forgas, & W. von Hippel (Eds.), *The social outcast: Ostracism, social exclusion, rejection, and bullying* (pp. 213–226). New York: Psychology Press.

Pietrzak, R. H., Laird, J. D., Stevens, D. A., & Thompson, N. S. (2002). Sex differences in human jealousy: A coordinated study of forced-choice, continuous rating- scale, and physiological responses on the same subjects. *Evolution and Human Behavior, 23,* 83–94.

Piff, P. K., Kraus, M. W., Côté, S., Cheng, B. H., & Keltner, D. (2010). Having less, giving more: The influence of social class on prosocial behavior. *Journal of Personality and Social Psychology, 99*(5), 771–784.

Piliavin, J. A., Dovidio, J. F., Gaertner, S. L., & Clark, R. D., III. (1981). *Emergency intervention.* New York: Academic Press.

Piliavin, J. A., & Piliavin, I. M. (1972). Effect of blood on reactions to a victim. *Journal of Personality and Social Psychology, 23,* 353–361.

Piliavin, J. A., & Unger, R. K. (1985). The helpful but helpless female: Myth or reality? In V. O'Leary, R. K. Unger, & B. S. Wallston (Eds.), *Women, gender and social psychology* (pp. 149–186). Hillsdale, NJ: Erlbaum.

Pillsworth, E. G., Haselton, M. G., & Buss, D. M. (2004). Ovulatory shifts in female sexual desire. *Journal of Sex Research, 41,* 55–65.

Pilluta, M. M., Malhotra, D., & Murnighan, K. (2003). Attributions of trust and the calculus of reciprocity. *Journal of Experimental Social Psychology, 39,* 448–455.

Pin, E. J., & Turndorf, J. (1990). Staging one's ideal self. In D. Brisset & C. Edgley (Eds.), *Life as theatre* (pp. 163–181). Hawthorne, NY: Aldine de Gruyter.

Pinel, E. (1999). Stigma consciousness: The psychological legacy of social stereotypes. *Journal of Personality and Social Psychology, 76,* 114–128.

Pinker, S. (2002). *The blank slate: The modern denial of human nature.* New York: Viking.

Pipitone, R. N., & Gallup, G. G. (2008). Women's voice attractiveness varies across the menstrual cycle. *Evolution and Human Behavior, 29,* 268–274.

Pittam, J. (1994). *Voice in social interaction: An interdisciplinary approach.* Thousand Oaks, CA: Sage.

Pittman, T. S. (1998). Motivation. In D. T. Gilbert, S. T. Fiske, & G. Lindzey (Eds.), *Handbook of social psychology* (4th ed., Vol. 1, pp. 549–590). New York: McGraw-Hill/Oxford University Press.

Pittman, T. S., & D'Agostino, P. R. (1985). Motivation and attribution: The effects of control deprivation on subsequent information processing. In J. H. Harvey & G. Weary (Eds.), *Attribution: Basic issues and applications* (pp. 117–141). New York: Academic Press.

Plant, E. A. (2004). Responses to interracial interactions over time. *Personality and Social Psychology Bulletin, 30,* 1458–1471.

Plant, E. A., & Devine, P. G. (1998). Internal and external motivation to respond without prejudice. *Journal of Personality and Social Psychology, 75,* 811–832.

Plant, E. A., & Devine, P. G. (2003). Antecedents and implications of intergroup anxiety. *Personality and Social Psychology Bulletin, 29,* 790–801.

Plant, E. A., Peruche, B. M., & Butz, D. A. (2004). Eliminating automatic racial bias: Making race non-diagnostic for responses to criminal suspects. *Journal of Experimental Social Psychology, 41,* 141–156.

Platow, M. J., Haslam, S. A., Both, B., Chew, I., Cuddon, M., Goharpey, N., et al. (2005). "It's not funny if *they're* laughing": Self-categorization, social influence, and responses to canned laughter. *Journal of Experimental Social Psychology, 41,* 542–550.

Platt, J. (1973). Social traps. *American Psychologist, 28,* 641–651.

Pleszczynska, W. K., & Hansell, R. I. C. (1980). Polygyny and decision theory: Testing of a model in lark buntings (*Calamospiza malanocorys*). *American Naturalist, 116,* 821–830.

Plomin, R., DeFries, J. C., & McClearn, G. E. (1990). *Behavioral genetics: A primer.* New York: W. H. Freeman.

Plous, S. (1985). Perceptual illusions and military realities the nuclear arms race. *Journal of Conflict Resolution, 29*(3), 363–389.

Plutchik, R. (1994). *The psychology and biology of emotion.* New York: HarperCollins.

Pollard, C. A., & Henderson, J. G. (1988). Four types of social phobia in a community sample. *Journal of Nervous and Mental Disease, 176,* 440–445.

Pollet, T. V., & Nettle, D. (2007). Driving a hard bargain: sex ratio and male marriage success in a historical US population. *Biology Letters, 4,* 31–33.

Pollet, T. V., & Nettle, D. (2009). Market forces affect patterns of polygyny in Uganda. *Proceedings of the National Academy of Sciences of the USA, 106,* 2114–2117.

Pomeranz, E. M., Chaiken, S., & Tordesillas, R. S. (1995). Attitude strength and resistance processes. *Journal of Personality and Social Psychology, 69,* 408–419.

Postmes, T., & Spears, R. (1998). Deindividuation and antinormative behavior: A meta-analysis. *Psychological Bulletin, 123,* 238–259.

Postmes, T., Spears, R., & Cihangir, S. (2001). Quality of decision making and group norms. *Journal of Personality and Social Psychology, 80,* 918–930.

Powers, S. I., Pietromonaco, P. R., Gunlicks, M., & Sayer, A. (2006). Dating couples' attachment styles and patterns of cortisol reactivity and recovery in response to a relationship conflict. *Journal of Personality & Social Psychology, 90,* 613–628.

Pratkanis, A. R. (Ed.). (2007). *Science of social influence.* New York: Psychology Press.

Pratto, F. (1996). Sexual politics: The gender gap in the bedroom, the cupboard, and the cabinet. In D. M. Buss & N. M. Malamuth (Eds.), *Sex, power, conflict: Evolutionary and feminist perspectives* (pp. 179–230). New York: Oxford University Press.

Pratto, F., & Bargh, J. A. (1991). Stereotyping based on apparently individuating information: Trait and global components of sex stereotypes under attentional overload. *Journal of Experimental Social Psychology, 27,* 26–47.

Pratto, F., Liu, J. H., Levin, S., Sidanius, J., Shih, M., & Bachrach, H. (1998). *Social dominance orientation and legitimization of inequality across cultures.* Unpublished manuscript, Stanford University.

Pratto, F., Saguy, T., Stewart, A. L., Morselli, D., Foels, R., Aiello, A., et al. (2013). Attitudes toward global ascendance: Israeli and global perspectives. *Psychological Science, 25*(1), 85–94.

Pratto, F., Sidanius, J., Stallworth, L. M., & Malle, B. F. (1994). Social dominance orientation: A personality variable predicting social and political attitudes. *Journal of Personality and Social Psychology, 67,* 741–763.

Pratto, F., Stallworth, L. M., Sidanius, J., & Siers, B. (1997). The gender gap in occupational role attainment: A social dominance approach. *Journal of Personality and Social Psychology, 72,* 37–53.

Prentice, D. A., & Miller, D. T. (1993). Pluralistic ignorance and alcohol use on campus: Some consequences of misperceiving the social norm. *Journal of Personality and Social Psychology, 64,* 243–256.

Prentice-Dunn, S., & Rogers, R. W. (1980). Effects of deindividuating situational cues and aggressive models on subjective deindividuation and aggression. *Journal of Personality and Social Psychology, 39,* 104–113.

Prentice-Dunn, S., & Rogers, R. W. (1982). Effects of public and private self-awareness on deindividuation and aggression. *Journal of Personality and Social Psychology, 43,* 503–513.

Price, R. H., & Bouffard, D. L. (1974). Behavioral appropriateness and situational constraint as dimensions of social behavior. *Journal of Personality and Social Psychology, 30,* 579–586.

Priester, J. R., & Petty, R. E. (2001). Extending the bases of subjective attitudinal ambivalence. *Journal of Personality and Social Psychology, 80,* 19–34.

Provost, M. P., Troje, N. F., & Quinsey, V. L. (2008). Short-term mating strategies and attraction to masculinity in point-light walkers. *Evolution and Human Behavior, 29,* 65–69.

Pryor, J. B., & Day, J. D. (1988). Interpretations of sexual harassment: An attributional analysis. *Sex Roles, 18,* 405–417.

Pryor, J. B., LaVite, C., & Stoller, L. (1993). A social psychological analysis of sexual harassment: The person/situation interaction. *Journal of Vocational Behavior, 42,* 68–83.

Pryor, J. B., & Merluzzi, T. V. (1985). The role of expertise in processing social interaction scripts. *Journal of Experimental Social Psychology, 21,* 362–379.

Pryor, J. B., & Stoller, L. (1994). Sexual cognition processes in men who are high in the likelihood to sexually harass. *Personality and Social Psychology Bulletin, 20,* 163–169.

Purvis, J. A., Dabbs, J. M., & Hopper, C. H. (1984). The "opener": Skilled user of facial expression and speech pattern. *Personality and Social Psychology Bulletin, 10,* 61–66.

Putnam, R. D. (2000). *Bowling alone: The collapse and revival of American community.* New York: Simon & Schuster.

Puts, D. A. (2005). Mating context and menstrual phase affect women's preferences for male voice pitch. *Evolution and Human Behavior, 26,* 388–397.

Pyszczynski, T., Greenberg, J., & Solomon, S. (1999). A dual-process model of defense against conscious and unconscious death-related thoughts: An extension of terror management theory. *Psychological Review, 106,* 835–845.

Pyszczynski, T., Greenberg, J., Solomon, S., Arndt, J., & Schimel, J. (2004). Why do people need self-esteem? A theoretical and empirical review. *Psychological Bulletin, 130,* 435–468.

Pyszczynski, T., Solomon, S., & Greenberg, J. (2002). *In the wake of 9/11: The psychology of terror.* New York: American Psychological Association.

Pytlik-Zillig, L. M., Hemenover, S. H., & Dienstbier, R. A. (2002). What do we assess when we assess a Big 5 trait? A content analysis of the affective, behavioral and cognitive processes represented in the Big 5 personality inventories. *Personality & Social Psychology Bulletin, 28,* 847–858.

Qiu, C., & Yeung, W. M. (2008). Mood and comparative judgment: Does mood influence everything and finally nothing? *Journal of Consumer Research, 34,* 657–669.

Quinn, A., & Schlenker, B. R. (2002). Can accountability produce independence? Goals as determinants of the impact of accountability on conformity. *Personality and Social Psychology Bulletin, 28,* 472–483.

Quintelier, K. J., Ishii, K., Weeden, J., Kurzban, R., & Braeckman, J. (2013). Individual differences in reproductive strategy are related to views about recreational drug use in Belgium, The Netherlands, and Japan. *Human Nature, 24*(2), 196–217

Radcliffe, N. M., & Klein, W. M. P. (2002). Dispositional, unrealistic, and comparative optimism. *Personality and Social Psychology Bulletin, 28,* 836–846.

Radcliffe-Brown, A. (1913). Three tribes of Western Australia. *Journal of the Royal Anthropological Institute, 43,* 143–194.

Radice, S. (2010). J.K. Rowling: A moral responsibility to give. *Philanthropy Impact.* Retrieved from http://www.philanthropy-impact.org/article/jk-rowling-moral-responsibility-give

Rahman, Q., & Hull, M. S. (2005). An empirical test of the kin selection hypothesis for male homosexuality. *Archives of Sexual Behavior, 34,* 461–467.

Rajecki, D. W., Bledsoe, S. B., & Rasmussen, J. L. (1991). Successful personal ads: Gender differences and similarities in offers, stipulations, and outcomes. *Basic and Applied Social Psychology, 12,* 457–469.

Ramirez, J. M. (1993). Acceptability of aggression in four Spanish regions and a comparison with other European countries. *Aggressive Behavior, 19,* 185–197.

Rampton, S., & Stauber, J. (2001). *Trust us, we're experts.* New York: Tarcher/Putnam.

Rapoport, A., Diekmann, A., & Franzen, A. (1995). Experiments with social traps IV: Reputation effects in the evolution of cooperation. *Rationality and Society, 7,* 431–441.

Ratneswar, S., & Chaiken, S. (1991). Comprehension's role in persuasion: The case of its moderating effect on the impact of source cues. *Journal of Consumer Psychology, 18,* 52–62.

Rausch, H. L. (1977). Paradox, levels, and junctures in person-situation systems. In D. Magnusson & N. S. Endler (Eds.), *Personality at the crossroads* (pp. 287–304). Hillsdale, NJ: Erlbaum.

Rawlins, W. K. (1992). *Friendship matters: Communication, dialectics, and the life course.* New York: Aldine DeGruyter.

Reed, A., & Aquino, K. F. (2003). Moral identity and the expanding circle of moral regard toward out-groups. *Journal of Personality and Social Psychology, 84,* 1270–1286.

Reed, M. B., Lange, J. E., Ketchie, J. M., & Clapp, J. D. (2007). The relationship between social identity and college student drinking. *Social Influence, 2,* 269–294.

Regan, D. T., & Kilduff, M. (1988). Optimism about elections: Dissonance reduction at the ballot box. *Political Psychology, 9,* 101–107.

Regan, P. C. (1998). What if you can't get what you want? Willingness to compromise ideal mate selection standards as a function of sex, mate value, and relationship context. *Personality & Social Psychology Bulletin, 24,* 1294–1303.

Regan, P. C. (1999). Hormonal correlates and causes of sexual desire: A review. *Canadian Journal of Human Sexuality, 8,* 1–16.

Regan, P. C. (2003). *The mating game: A primer on love, sex, and marriage.* Thousand Oaks, CA: Sage.

Regan, P. C., & Joshi, A. (2003). Ideal partner preferences among adolescents. *Social Behavior and Personality, 31,* 13–20.

Regan, P. C., Medina, R., & Joshi, A. (2001). Partner preferences among homosexual men and women: What is desirable in a sex partner is not necessarily desirable in a romantic partner. *Social Behavior and Personality, 29,* 625–634.

Reich, J. W., & Zautra, A. J. (1995). Spouse encouragement of self-reliance and other-reliance in rheumatoid arthritis couples. *Journal of Behavioral Medicine, 18,* 249–260.

Reich, M. (1971). The economics of racism. In D. M. Gordon (Ed.), *Problems in political economy* (pp. 107–113). Lexington, MA: Heath.

Reif, C. D., & Singer, B. (2000). Interpersonal flourishing: A positive health agenda for the new millennium. *Personality & Social Psychology Review, 4,* 30–44.

Reifman, A., Larrick, R. P., & Fein, S. (1991). Temper and temperature on the diamond: The heat-aggression relationship in major league baseball. *Personality and Social Psychology Bulletin, 17,* 580–585.

Reilly, P. (1995). When will it ever end? In D. S. Connery (Ed.), *Convicting the innocent* (pp. 84–86). Cambridge, MA: Brookline.

Reimann, M., & Zimbardo, P. G. (2011). The dark side of social encounters: Prospects for a neuroscience of human evil. *Journal of Neuroscience, Psychology, and Economics, 4*(3), 174.

Reingen, P. H., & Kernan, J. B. (1993). Social perception and interpersonal influence: Some consequences of the physical attractiveness stereotype in a personal selling setting. *Journal of Consumer Psychology, 2,* 25–38.

Reinhard, M. (2010). Need for cognition and the process of lie detection. *Journal of Experimental Social Psychology, 46,* 961–971.

Reis, H. T., Collins, W. A., & Berscheid, E. (2000). The relationship context of human behavior and development. *Psychological Bulletin, 126,* 844–872.

Reis, H. T., Senchak, M., & Solomon, B. (1985). Sex differences in the intimacy of social interaction: Further examination of potential explanations. *Journal of Personality and Social Psychology, 48,* 1204–1217.

Reis, H. T., Sheldon, K. M., Gable, S. L., Roscoe, J., & Ryan, R. M. (2000). Daily well-being: The role of autonomy, competence, and relatedness. *Personality & Social Psychology Bulletin, 26,* 419–435.

Reis, H. T., Wheeler, L., Spiegel, N., Kernis, M. H., Nezlek, J., & Perri, M. (1982). Physical attractiveness in social interaction: II. Why does appearance affect social experience. *Journal of Personality and Social Psychology, 43,* 979–996.

Reiss, M., & Rosenfeld, P. (1980). Seating preferences as nonverbal communication: A self-presentational analysis. *Journal of Applied Communication Research, 8,* 22–30.

Renninger, L. A., Wade, T. J., & Grammer, K. (2004). Getting that female glance: Patterns and consequences of male nonverbal behavior in courtship contexts. *Evolution and Human Behavior, 25,* 416–431.

Resnick, L. B., Levine, J. M., & Teasley, S. D. (1991). *Perspectives on socially shared cognition.* Washington, DC: American Psychological Association.

Reykowski, J. (1980). Origin of pro-social motivation: Heterogeneity of personality development. *Studia Psychologica, 22,* 91–106.

Reyna, C., Henry, P. J., Korfmacher, W., & Tucker, A. (2006). Examining the principles in principled conservatism: The role of responsibility stereotypes as cues for deservingness in racial policy decisions. *Journal of Personality and Social Psychology, 90,* 109–128.

Reynolds, M. A., Herbenick, M. A., & Bancroft, J. H. (2003). The nature of childhood sexual experiences: Two studies 50 years apart. In J. H. Bancroft (Ed.), *Sexual development in childhood.* Bloomington: Indiana University Press.

Rhodes, G. (2006). The evolution of facial attractiveness. *Annual Review of Psychology, 57,* 199–226.

Rhodes, G., Zebrowitz, L. A., Clark, A., Kalick, S. M., Hightower, A., & McKay, R. (2001). Do facial averageness and symmetry signal health? *Evolution and Human Behavior, 22,* 31–46.

Rhodewalt, F., & Agustsdottir, S. (1986). Effects of self-presentation on the phenomenal self. *Journal of Personality and Social Psychology, 50,* 47–55.

Rhodewalt, F., & Hill, S. K. (1995). Self-handicapping in the classroom: The effects of claimed self-handicaps on responses to academic failure. *Basic and Applied Social Psychology, 16,* 397–416.

Rhodewalt, F., & Smith, T. W. (1991). Current issues in Type A behavior, coronary proneness, and coronary heart disease. In C. R. Snyder & D.

R. Forsyth (Eds.), *Handbook of social and clinical psychology* (pp. 197–220). New York: Pergamon.

Rholes, W. S., & Ruble, D. N. (1986). Children's impressions of other persons. *Child Development, 57*, 872–878.

Rice, R. W., Instone, D., & Adams, J. (1984). Leader sex, leader success, and leadership process: Two field studies. *Journal of Applied Psychology, 69*, 12–31.

Richardson, D. S., & Green, L. R. (2006). Direct and indirect aggression: Relationships as social context. *Journal of Applied Social Psychology, 36*, 2492–2508.

Richeson, J. A., & Shelton, J. N. (2007). Negotiating interracial interactions: Costs, consequences, and possibilities. *Current Directions in Psychological Science, 16*, 316–320.

Rieskamp, J., & Hoffrage, U. (2008). Inferences under time pressure: How opportunity costs affect strategy selection. *Acta Psychologica, 127*, 258–276.

Rind, B., & Benjamin, D. (1994). Effects of public image concerns and self-image on compliance. *Journal of Social Psychology, 134*, 19–25.

Ringelmann, M. (1913). Recherches sur les moteurs animés: Travail de l'homme [Research on animate sources of power: The work of man]. *Annales de l'Institute National Agronomique, 2e série—tome, XII*, 1–40.

Robberson, M. R., & Rogers, R. W. (1988). Beyond fear appeals: Negative and positive persuasive appeals to health and self-esteem. *Journal of Applied Social Psychology*, 277–287.

Roberts, B. W., Caspi, A., & Moffitt, T. E. (2003). Work experiences and personality development in young adulthood. *Journal of Personality & Social Psychology, 84*, 582–593.

Roberts, S. C., Havlicek, J., Flegr, J., Hruskova, M., Little, A. C., Jones, B. C., et al. (2004). Female facial attractiveness increases during the fertile phase of the menstrual cycle. *Proceedings of the Royal Society of London B (Suppl.), 271*, S270–S272.

Robins, R. W., & Beer, J. S. (2001). Positive illusions about the self: Short-term benefits and long-term costs. *Journal of Personality and Social Psychology, 80*, 340–352.

Robinson, G. E., Fernals, R. D., & Clayton, D. F. (2008). Genes and social behavior. *Science, 322*, 896–900.

Robinson, M. D., Fetterman, A. K., Hopkins, K., & Krishnakumar, S. (2013). Losing one's cool: Social competence as a novel inverse predictor of provocation-related aggression. *Personality and Social Psychology Bulletin, 39*, 1268–1279.

Robinson, M. D., Johnson, J. T., & Shields, S. A. (1995). On the advantages of modesty: The benefits of a balanced self-presentation. *Communication Research, 22*, 575–591.

Roccato, M., & Ricolfi, L. (2005). On the correlation between right-wing authoritarianism and social dominance orientation. *Basic and Applied Social Psychology, 27*, 187–200.

Rodeheffer, C. D., Hill, S. E., & Lord, C. G. (2012). Does this recession make me look Black? The effect of resource scarcity on the categorization on biracial faces. *Psychological Science, 23*(12), 1476–1478.

Rodin, J. (1986). Aging and health: Effects of the sense of control. *Science, 233*, 1271–1276.

Rodin, J., & Langer, E. J. (1977). Long-term effects of a control-relevant intervention with the institutionalized aged. *Journal of Personality and Social Psychology, 35*, 897–902.

Rodkin, P. C., Farmer, T. W., Pearl, R., & Van Acker, R. (2000). Heterogeneity of popular boys: Antisocial and prosocial configurations. *Developmental Psychology, 36*, 14–24.

Roese, N. J., Pennington, G. L., Coleman, J., Janicki, M., Li, N. P., & Kenrick, D. T. (2006). Sex differences in regret: All for love or some for lust? *Personality and Social Psychology Bulletin, 32*, 770–780.

Roese, N. J., & Summerville, A. (2005). What we regret most . . . and why. *Personality and Social Psychology Bulletin, 31*, 1273–1285.

Rogers, M., Miller, N., Mayer, F. S., & Duval, S. (1982). Personal responsibility and salience of the request for help. *Journal of Personality and Social Psychology, 43*, 956–970.

Rogers, R. W., & Mewborn, C. R. (1976). Fear appeals and attitude change: Effects of a threat's noxiousness, probability of occurrence, and the efficacy of coping responses. *Journal of Personality and Social Psychology, 34*, 54–61.

Rohner, R. P., Khaleque, A., & Cournoyer, D. E. (2005). Parental acceptance-rejection: Theory, methods, cross-cultural evidence, and implications. *Ethos, 33*, 299–334.

Rokeach, M. (1971). Long-range experimental modification of values, attitudes, and behavior. *American Psychologist, 26*, 453–459.

Rom, E., & Mikulincer, M. (2003). Attachment theory and group processes: The association between attachment style and group-related representations, goals, memories, and functioning. *Journal of Personality & Social Psychology, 84*, 1220–1237.

Romero, A. A., Agnew, C. R., & Insko, C. A. (1996). The cognitive mediation hypothesis revisited. *Personality and Social Psychology Bulletin, 22*, 651–665.

Roney, C. J. R., & Sorrentino, R. M. (1995). Uncertainty orientation, the self, and others: Individual differences in values and social comparison. *Canadian Journal of Behavioural Science, 27*, 157–170.

Roney, J. R. (2003). Effects of visual exposure to the opposite sex: Cognitive aspects of mate attraction in human males. *Personality & Social Psychology Bulletin, 29*, 393–404.

Rose, S., & Frieze, I. H. (1993). Young singles' contemporary dating scripts. *Sex Roles, 28*, 499–509.

Rosen, S., Cochran, W., & Musser, L. M. (1990). Reactions to a match versus mismatch between applicant's self-presentational style and work reputation. *Basic and Applied Social Psychology, 11*, 117–129.

Rosenbaum, M. E. (1986). The repulsion hypothesis: On the nondevelopment of relationships. *Journal of Personality and Social Psychology, 61*, 1156–1166.

Rosenfeld, J. P. (2002). Event-related potentials in the detection of deception, malingering, and false memories. In M. Kleiner (Ed.), *Handbook of polygraph testing* (pp. 265–286). San Diego, CA: Academic Press.

Rosenthal, A. M. (1964). *Thirty-eight witnesses*. New York: McGraw-Hill.

Ross, C. E., & Mirowsky, J. (1983). The worse place and the best face. *Social Forces, 62*, 529–536.

Ross, E. A. (1908). *Social psychology*. New York: Macmillan.

Ross, J. R. (1994). *Escape to Shanghai: A Jewish community in China*. New York: Free Press.

Ross, L. (1977). The intuitive psychologist and his shortcomings: Distortions in the attribution process. In L. Berkowitz (Ed.), *Advances in experimental social psychology* (Vol. 10, pp. 174–221). New York: Academic Press.

Ross, L., Greene, D., & House, P. (1977). The "false consensus effect": An egocentric bias in social perception and attribution processes. *Journal of Experimental Social Psychology, 13*, 279–301.

Ross, L., Lepper, M., & Ward, A. (2010). History of social psychology: Insights, challenges, and contributions to theory and application. In S. T. Fiske, D. T. Gilbert, & G. Lindsey (Eds.), *Handbook of social psychology* (5th ed., Vol. 2, pp. 3–50). Hoboken, NJ: John Wiley & Sons, Inc.

Ross, M., Heine, S. J., Wilson, A. E., & Sugimori, S. (2005). Cross-cultural discrepancies in self-appraisals. *Personality and Social Psychology Bulletin, 31*, 1175–1188.

Ross, M., Xun, W. Q. E., & Wilson, A. E. (2002). Language and the bicultural self. *Personality and Social Psychology Bulletin, 28*, 1040–1050.

Rossion, B., Caldara, R., Seghier, M., Schuller, A. M., Lazeyras, F., & Mayer, E. (2003). A network of occipito-temporal face-sensitive areas besides the right middle fusiform gyrus is necessary for normal face processing. *Brain, 126*, 2381–2395.

Rothbart, M., & Hallmark, W. (1988). Ingroup-out-group differences in the perceived efficacy of coercion and conciliation in resolving social conflict. *Journal of Personality and Social Psychology, 55*, 248–257.

Rotton, J., & Cohn, E. G. (2000). Violence is a curvilinear function of temperature in Dallas: A replication. *Journal of Personality & Social Psychology, 78*, 1074–1081.

Rotundo, M., Nguyen, D. H., & Sackett, P. R. (2001). A meta-analytic review of gender differences in perceptions of sexual harassment. *Journal of Applied Psychology, 86*, 914–922.

Rouhana, N. N., & Kelman, H. C. (1994). Promoting joint thinking in international conflicts: An Israeli-Palestinian continuing workshop. *Journal of Social Issues, 50*, 157–178.

Rousseau, D., & van der Veen, A. M. (2005). The emergence of a shared identity: An agent-based computer simulation of idea diffusion. *Journal of Conflict Resolution, 49*, 686–712.

Rozin, P., & Cohen, A. B. (2003). High frequency of facial expressions corresponding to confusion, concentration, and worry in an analysis of naturally occurring facial expressions of Americans. *Emotion, 3*, 68–75.

Ruback, B. R., & Juing, D. (1997). Territorial defense in parking lots: Retaliation against waiting drivers. *Journal of Applied Social Psychology, 27*, 821–834.

Rubin, M., & Hewstone, M. (1998). Social identity theory's self-esteem hypothesis: A review and some suggestions for clarification. *Personality and Social Psychology Review, 2*, 40–62.

Rubin, R. S., Bartels, L. K., & Bommer, W. H. (2002). Are leaders smarter or do they just seem that way? Exploring perceived intellectual competence and leadership emergence. *Social Behavior and Personality, 30*, 105–118.

Ruddy, M. G., & Adams, S. R. (1995). *Responsiveness to crying: How mothers' beliefs vary with infant's sex*. Poster presented at the American Psychological Society meetings, New York.

Ruder, M., & Bless, H. (2003). Mood and the reliance on the ease of retrieval heuristic. *Journal of Personality and Social Psychology, 85*, 20–32.

Rudman, L. A. (1998). Self-promotion as a risk factor for women: The costs and benefits of counterstereotypical impression management. *Journal of Personality and Social Psychology, 74*, 629–645.

Rudman, L. A., Dohn, M. C., & Fairchild, K. (2007). Implicit self-esteem compensation: Automatic threat defense. *Journal of Personality and Social Psychology, 93*, 798–813.

Rudman, L. A., & Glick, P. (2001). Prescriptive gender stereotypes and backlash toward agentic women. *Journal of Social Issues, 57*, 743–762.

Rudman, L. A., Greenwald, A. G., Mellott, D. S., & Schwartz, J. L. K. (1999). Measuring the automatic components of prejudice: Flexibility and generality of the implicit association test. *Social Cognition, 17*, 437–465.

Rule, B. G., Taylor, B. R., & Dobbs, A. R. (1987). Priming effects of heat on aggressive thoughts. *Social Cognition, 5*, 131–143.

Runyan, W. M. (1981). Why did Van Gogh cut off his ear? The problem of alternative explanations in psychobiography. *Journal of Personality & Social Psychology, 40*, 1070–1077.

Rusbult, C. E., Kumashiro, M., Kubacka, K. E., & Finkel, E. J. (2009). "The part of me that you bring out": Ideal similarity and the Michaelangelo phenomenon. *Journal of Personality and Social Psychology, 96*, 61–82.

Rusbult, C. E., Zembrodt, I. M., & Gunn, L. K. (1982). Exit, voice, loyalty, and neglect: Responses to dissatisfaction in romantic relationships. *Journal of Personality and Social Psychology, 43*, 1230–1242.

Ruscher, J. B., & Fiske, S. T. (1990). Interpersonal competition can cause individuating impression formation. *Journal of Personality and Social Psychology, 58*, 832–842.

Ruscher, J. B., Fiske, S. T., Miki, H., & Van Manen, S. (1991). Individuating processes in competition: Interpersonal versus intergroup. *Personality and Social Psychology Bulletin, 17,* 595–605.

Rushton, J. P. (1989). Genetic similarity, human altruism and group selection. *Behavioral and Brain Science, 12,* 503–518.

Rushton, J. P., & Bons, T. A. (2005). Mate choice and friendship in twins: Evidence for genetic similarity. *Psychological Science, 16,* 555–559.

Rushton, J. P., Fulker, D. W., Neale, M. C., Nias, D. K. B., & Esyenck, H. J. (1986). Altruism and aggression: The heritability of individual differences. *Journal of Personality and Social Psychology, 50,* 1192–1198.

Rushton, J. P., Russell, R. J. H., & Wells, P. A. (1984). Genetic similarity theory: Beyond kin selection altruism. *Behavioral Genetics, 14,* 179–193.

Russell, D., Peplau, L. A., & Cutrona, C. E. (1980). The revised UCLA loneliness scale: Concurrent and discriminant validity evidence. *Journal of Personality and Social Psychology, 39,* 472–480.

Russell, J. A. (1994). Is there universal recognition of emotion from facial expression? A review of the cross-cultural studies. *Psychological Bulletin, 115,* 102–141.

Russell, J. A. (1995). Facial expressions of emotion: What lies beyond minimal universality? *Psychological Bulletin, 118,* 379–391.

Russo, N. F. (1966). Connotations of seating arrangements. *Cornell Journal of Social Relations, 2,* 37–44.

Ryan, C. S. (1996). Accuracy of black and white college students' ingroup and outgroup stereotypes. *Personality and Social Psychology Bulletin, 22,* 1114–1127.

Ryan, C. S., Judd, C. M., & Park, B. (1996). Effects of racial stereotypes on judgments of individuals: The moderating role of perceived group variability. *Journal of Experimental Social Psychology, 32,* 71–103.

Ryff, C. D. (1995). Psychological well-being in adult life. *Current Directions in Psychological Science, 4,* 99–104.

Ryff, C. D., & Singer, B. (2000). Interpersonal flourishing: A positive health agenda for the new millennium. *Personality and Social Psychology Review, 4,* 30–44.

Saarni, C. (1993). Socialization of emotion. In M. Lewis & J. M. Haviland (Eds.), *Handbook of emotions* (pp. 435–446). New York: Guilford.

Sadalla, E. K., Kenrick, D. T., & Vershure, B. (1987). Dominance and heterosexual attraction. *Journal of Personality and Social Psychology, 52,* 730–738.

Saenz, D. S. (1994). Token status and problem-solving deficits: Detrimental effects of distinctiveness and performance monitoring. *Social Cognition, 12,* 61–74.

Safire, W. (1996, January 8). "Blizzard of lies," *New York Times.* In S. K. Flinn (2000) (Ed.), *Speaking of Hillary: A reader's guide to the most controversial woman in America* (pp. 146–148). Ashland, OR: White Cloud Press.

Sagarin, B. J. (2005). Reconsidering evolved sex differences in jealousy: Comment on Harris (2003). *Personality and Social Psychology Review, 9,* 62–75.

Sagarin, B. J., Becker, D. V., Guadagno, R. E., Nicastle, L. D., & Millevoi, A. (2003). Sex differences (and similarities) in jealousy: The moderating influence of infidelity experience and sexual orientation of the infidelity. *Evolution & Human Behavior, 24,* 17–23.

Sagarin, B. J., Cialdini, R. B., Rice, W. E., & Serna, S. B. (2002). Dispelling the illusion of invulnerability: The motivations and mechanisms of resistance to persuasion. *Journal of Personality and Social Psychology, 83,* 526–541.

Sagarin, B. J., Martin, A. L., Coutinho, S. A., Edlund, J. E., Patel, L., Skowronski, J. J., & Zengel, B. (2012). Sex-differences in jealousy: A meta-analytic examination. *Evolution and Human Behavior, 33,* 595–614.

Sagiv, L., & Schwartz, S. H. (2000). Value priorities and subjective well-being: Direct relations

and congruity effects. *European Journal of Social Psychology, 30,* 177–198.

Sagiv, L., Sverdlik, N., & Schwarz, N. (2011). To compete or to cooperate? Values' impact on perception and action in social dilemma games. *European Journal of Social Psychology, 41*(1), 64–77.

Saks, M. (1977). *Jury verdicts.* Lexington, MA: D.C. Heath.

Salas, D., & Ketzenberger, K. E. (2004). Associations of sex and type of relationship on intimacy. *Psychological Reports, 94,* 1322–1324.

Sales, S. M. (1973). Threat as a factor in authoritarianism: An analysis of archival data. *Journal of Personality and Social Psychology, 28,* 44–57.

Sales, S. M., & Friend, K. E. (1973). Success and failure as determinants of level of authoritarianism. *Behavioral Sciences, 18,* 163–172.

Salmon, C. (2005). Parental investment and parent-offspring conflict. In D. M. Buss (Ed.), *The handbook of evolutionary psychology* (pp. 506–527). New York: Wiley.

Salmon, C. A., & Shackelford, T. K. (2008). Toward an evolutionary psychology of the family. In C. A. Salmon & T. K. Shackelford (Eds.), *Family relationships: An evolutionary perspective* (pp. 3–15). New York: Oxford University Press.

Salmon, P. (2001). Effects of physical exercise on anxiety, depression, and sensitivity to stress: A unifying theory. *Clinical Psychology Review, 21,* 33–61.

Salonia, A., Nappi, R. E., Pontillo, M., Daverio, R., Smeraldi, A., Briganti, A., et al. (2005). Menstrual cycle-related changes in plasma oxytocin are relevant to normal sexual function in healthy women. *Hormones and Behavior, 47*(2), 164–169.

Salovey, P., & Birnbaum, D. (1989). Influence of mood on health-relevant cognitions. *Journal of Personality and Social Psychology, 57,* 539–551.

Salovey, P., Mayer, J. D., & Rosenhan, D. L. (1991). Mood and helping: Mood as a motivator of helping and helping as a regulator of mood. In M. S. Clark (Ed.), *Review of personality and social psychology* (Vol. 12, pp. 215–237). Newbury Park, CA: Sage.

Salovey, P., Rothman, A. J., & Rodin, J. (1998). Health behavior. In D. T. Gilbert, S. T. Fiske, & G. Lindzey (Eds.), *Handbook of social psychology* (4th ed., Vol. 2, pp. 633–683). New York: McGraw-Hill.

Sanbonmatsu, D. M., Akimoto, S. A., & Biggs, E. (1993). Overestimating causality: Attributional effects of confirmatory processing. *Journal of Personality and Social Psychology, 65,* 892–903.

Sanchez-Burks, J. (2002). Protestant relational ideology and (in)attention to relational cues in work settings. *Journal of Personality and Social Psychology, 83,* 919–929.

Sanders, G. S. (1981). Driven by distraction: An integrative review of social facilitation theory and research. *Journal of Experimental Social Psychology, 17,* 227–251.

Sandstrom, K. L. (1996). Searching for information, understanding, and self-value: The utilization of peer support groups by gay men with HIV/AIDS. *Social Work in Health Care, 23,* 51–74.

Sapolsky, R. M. (2001). *A primate's memoir.* New York: Scribner.

Saporito, B. (2005, October 24). Place your bets. *Time,* p. 76.

Sarason, B. R., Sarason, I. G., & Gurung, R. A. R. (1997). Close personal relationships and health outcomes: A key to the role of social support. In S. Duck (Ed.), *Handbook of personal relationships* (2nd ed., pp. 547–573). New York: Wiley.

Sargis, E. G., & Larson, J. R., Jr. (2002). Informational centrality and member participation during group decision making. *Group Processes and Intergroup Relations, 5,* 333–347.

Sarnoff, I., & Zimbardo, P. (1961). Anxiety, fear, and social affiliation. *Journal of Abnormal and Social Psychology, 62,* 356–363.

Satow, K. L. (1975). Social approval and helping. *Journal of Experimental Social Psychology, 11,* 501–509.

Satterfield, J. M. (1998). Cognitive-affective states predict military and political aggression and risk taking. *Journal of Conflict Resolution, 42,* 667–690.

Saucier, D. A., Miller, C. T., & Doucet, N. (2005). Differences in helping whites and blacks: A meta-analysis. *Personality and Social Psychology Review, 9,* 2–16.

Saucier, G. (2000). Isms and the structure of social attitudes. *Journal of Personality & Social Psychology, 78,* 366–385.

Saxe, L. (1994). Detection of deception: Polygraph and integrity tests. *Current Directions in Psychological Science, 3,* 69–73.

Scarr, S. (1981). The transmission of authoritarian attitudes in families: Genetic resemblance in social-political attitudes? In S. Scarr (Ed.), *Race, social class, and individual differences* (pp. 399–427). Hillsdale, NJ: Erlbaum.

Schachter, S. (1951). Deviation, rejection, and communication. *Journal of Abnormal and Social Psychology, 46,* 190–207.

Schachter, S. (1959). *The psychology of affiliation: Experimental studies of the sources of gregariousness.* Stanford, CA: Stanford University Press.

Schachter, S., & Singer, J. E. (1962). Cognitive, social, and psychological determinants of emotional state. *Psychological Review, 69,* 379–399.

Schaeffer, C. M., & Borduin, C. M. (2005). Long-term follow-up to a randomized clinical of multisystemic therapy with serious and violent juvenile offenders. *Journal of Consulting and Clinical Psychology, 73,* 445–453.

Schaller, M. (1997). The psychological consequences of fame: Three tests of the self-consciousness hypothesis. *Journal of Personality, 65,* 291–309.

Schaller, M., Boyd, C., Yohannes, J., & O'Brien, M. (1995). The prejudiced personality revisited: Personal need for structure and formation of erroneous group stereotypes. *Journal of Personality and Social Psychology, 68,* 544–555.

Schaller, M., & Cialdini, R. B. (1990). Happiness, sadness, and helping: A motivational integration. In E. T. Higgins & R. M. Sorrentino (Eds.), *Handbook of motivation and cognition* (Vol. 2, pp. 265–296). New York: Guilford.

Schaller, M., & Murray, D. R. (2008). Pathogens, personality, and culture: Disease prevalence predicts worldwide variability in sociosexuality, extraversion, and openness to experience. *Journal of Personality and Social Psychology, 95,* 212–221.

Schaller, M., & Neuberg, S. L. (2012). Danger, disease, and the nature of prejudice(s). In J. Olson & M. P. Zanna (Eds.), *Advances in experimental social psychology* (Vol. 46, pp. 1–55). Burlington, VT: Academic Press.

Schaller, M., & Park, J. H. (2011). The behavioral immune system (and why it matters). *Current Directions in Psychological Science, 20*(2), 99–103.

Schaller, M., Park, J. H., & Faulkner, J. (2003). Prehistoric dangers and contemporary prejudices. *European Review of Social Psychology, 14,* 105–137.

Schaller, M., Park, J. H., & Kenrick, D. T. (2007). Human evolution and social cognition. In R. I. M. Dunbar & L. Barrett (Eds.), *Oxford handbook of evolutionary psychology.* Oxford, England: Oxford University Press.

Schaller, M., Park, J. H., & Mueller, A. (2003). Fear of the dark: Interactive effects of beliefs about danger and ambient darkness on ethnic stereotypes. *Personality & Social Psychology Bulletin, 29,* 637–646.

Schank, R. C., & Abelson, R. P. (1977). *Scripts, plans, goals, and understanding.* Hillsdale, NJ: Erlbaum.

Scheier, M. F., & Carver, C. S. (1988). A model of behavioral self-regulation: Translating intention into action. In L. Berkowitz (Ed.), *Advances in experimental social psychology* (Vol. 21, pp. 303–346). San Diego, CA: Academic Press.

Schelling, T. C. (1968). The life you save may be your own. In S. Chase (Ed.), *Problems in public expenditure analysis.* Washington, DC: The Brookings Institute.

Scherer, K. R., & Wallbott, H. G. (1994). Evidence for universality and cultural variation of differential emotion response patterning. *Journal of Personality and Social Psychology, 66,* 310–328.

Schimel, J., Pyszczynski, T., Greenberg, J., O'Mahen, H., & Arndt, J. (2000). Running from the shadow: Psychological distancing from others to deny characteristics people fear in themselves. *Journal of Personality and Social Psychology, 78,* 446–462.

Schlenker, B. R. (1980). *Impression management: The self-concept, social identity, and interpersonal relationships.* Monterey, CA: Brooks/Cole.

Schlenker, B. R. (2003). Self-presentation. In M. R. Leary & J. P. Tangney (Eds.), *Handbook of self and identity* (pp. 492–518). New York: Guilford Press.

Schlenker, B. R., Dlugolecki, D. W., & Doherty, K. (1994). The impact of self-presentations on self-appraisals and behavior: The power of public commitment. *Personality and Social Psychology Bulletin, 20,* 20–33.

Schlenker, B. R., & Pontari, B. A. (2000). The strategic control of information: Impression management and self-presentation in daily life. In A. Tesser, R. B. Felson, & J. M. Suls (Eds.), *Psychological perspectives on self and identity* (pp. 199–232). Washington, DC: American Psychological Association.

Schlenker, B. R., Pontari, B. A., & Christopher, A. N. (2001). Excuses and character: Personal and social implications of excuses. *Personality and Social Psychology Review, 5,* 15–32.

Schlenker, B. R., & Trudeau, J. V. (1990). The impact of self-presentations on private self-beliefs: Effects of prior self-beliefs and misattribution. *Journal of Personality and Social Psychology, 58,* 22–32.

Schlenker, B. R., & Weigold, M. F. (1992). Interpersonal processes involving impression regulation and management. *Annual Review of Psychology, 43,* 133–168.

Schlesinger, A. M. (1978). *Robert Kennedy and his times.* New York: Ballantine Books.

Schmader, T., Johns, M., & Forbes, C. (2008). An integrated process model of stereotype threat effects on performance. *Psychological Review, 115,* 336–356.

Schmader, T., & Major, B. (1999). The impact of ingroup vs. outgroup performance on personal values. *Journal of Experimental Social Psychology, 35,* 47–67.

Schmidtke, A., & Hafner, H. (1988). The Werther effect after television films: New evidence for an old hypothesis. *Psychological Medicine, 18,* 665–676.

Schmitt, B. H., Gilovich, T., Goore, N., & Joseph, L. (1986). Mere presence and social facilitation: One more time. *Journal of Experimental Social Psychology, 22,* 242–248.

Schmitt, D. P. (2005a). Fundamentals of human mating strategies. In D. M. Buss (Ed.), *Handbook of evolutionary psychology* (pp. 258–291). New York: Wiley.

Schmitt, D. P. (2005b). Is short-term mating the maladaptive result of insecure attachment? A test of competing evolutionary perspectives. *Personality and Social Psychology Bulletin, 31,* 747–768.

Schmitt, D. P. (2006a). Evolutionary and cross-cultural perspectives on love. In R. J. Sternberg & K. Weis (Eds.), *The new psychology of love* (pp. 249–273). New Haven, CT: Yale University Press.

Schmitt, D. P. (2006b). Sociosexuality from Argentina to Zimbabwe: A 48-nation study of sex, culture, and strategies of human mating. *Behavioral and Brain Sciences, 28,* 247–311.

Schmitt, D. P., Jonason, P. K., Byerley, G. J, Flores, S. D., Illbeck, B. E., O'Leary, K. N., & Qudrat, A. (2012). A reexamination of sex differences in sexuality: New studies reveal old truths. *Current Directions in Psychological Science, 21*(2), 135–139.

Schmitt, D. P., and 118 Members of International Sexuality Description Project. (2003). Universal sex differences in the desire for sexual variety: Tests from 52 nations, 6 continents, and 13 islands. *Journal of Personality & Social Psychology, 85,* 85–104.

Schneider, B. H., Woodburn, S., del Pilar Soteras, M., & Udvari, S. J. (2005). Cultural and gender differences in the implications of competition for early adolescent friendship. *Merrill Palmer Quarterly, 51,* 163–191.

Schneider, D. J. (1969). Tactical self-presentation after success and failure. *Journal of Personality and Social Psychology, 13,* 262–268.

Schroeder, D. A. (1995a). An introduction to social dilemmas. In D. A. Schroeder (Ed.), *Social dilemmas: Perspectives on individuals and groups* (pp. 1–14). Westport, CT: Praeger.

Schroeder, D. A. (1995b). *Social dilemmas: Perspectives on individuals and groups.* Westport, CT: Praeger.

Schroeder, D. A., Dovidio, J. F., Sibicky, M. E., Matthews, L. L., & Allen, J. L. (1988). Empathy and helping behavior: Egoism or altruism. *Journal of Experimental Social Psychology, 24,* 333–353.

Schug, J., Yuki, M., & Maddux, W. (2010). Relational mobility explains between- and within-culture differences in self-disclosure to close friends. *Psychological Science, 21*(10), 1471–1478.

Schulte, B. (1998, March 8). Sleep research focusing on mind's effectiveness. *The Arizona Republic,* p. A33.

Schultheiss, O. C., Wirth, M. M., Torges, C. M., Pang, J. S., Villacorta, M. A., & Welsh, K. M. (2005). Effects of implicit power motivation on men's and women's implicit learning and testosterone changes after social victory or defeat. *Journal of Personality and Social Psychology, 88,* 174–188.

Schultz, P. W. (1999). Changing behavior with normative feedback interventions: A field experiment on curbside recycling. *Basic and Applied Social Psychology, 21,* 25–36.

Schulz, R. (1976). Effects of control and predictability on the physical and psychological well-being of the institutionalized aged. *Journal of Personality and Social Psychology, 33,* 563–573.

Schulz-Hardt, S., Jochims, M., & Frey, D. (2002). Productive conflict in group decision making: Genuine and contrived dissent as strategies to counteract biased information seeking. *Organizational Behavior and Human Decision Processes, 88,* 563–586.

Schuman, H., Steeh, C., Bobo, L., & Krysan, M. (1997). *Racial attitudes in America: Trends and interpretations.* Cambridge, MA: Harvard University Press.

Schur, E. M. (1971). *Labeling deviant behavior: Its sociological implications.* New York: Harper & Row.

Schützwohl, A. (2008). The crux of cognitive load: Constraining deliberate and effortful decision processes in romantic jealousy. *Evolution and Human Behavior, 29,* 127–132.

Schwartz, B., Tesser, A., & Powell, E. (1982). Dominance cues in nonverbal behavior. *Social Psychology Quarterly, 45,* 114–120.

Schwartz, S. H. (1977). Normative influences on altruism. In L. Berkowitz (Ed.), *Advances in experimental social psychology* (Vol. 10, pp. 222–280). New York: Academic Press.

Schwartz, S. H., & Gottlieb, A. (1976). Bystander reactions to a violent theft: Crime in Jerusalem. *Journal of Personality and Social Psychology, 34,* 1188–1199.

Schwartz, S. H., & Gottlieb, A. (1980). Bystander anonymity and reactions to emergencies. *Journal of Personality and Social Psychology, 39,* 418–430.

Schwartz, S. H., & Howard, J. A. (1982). Helping and cooperation: A self-based motivational model. In V. J. Derlega & J. Grelak (Eds.), *Cooperation and helping behavior: Theories and research* (pp. 327–353). New York: Academic Press.

Schwartzwald, J., Bizman, A., & Raz, M. (1983). The foot-in-the-door paradigm: Effects of second request size on donation probability and do-nor generosity. *Personality and Social Psychology Bulletin, 9,* 443–450.

Schwarz, N. (1990a). Assessing frequency reports of mundane behaviors: Contributions of cognitive psychology to questionnaire construction. In C. Hendrick & M. S. Clark (Eds.), *Research methods in personality and social psychology* (pp. 98–119). Newbury Park, CA: Sage.

Schwarz, N. (1990b). Feelings as information: Informational and motivational functions of affective states. In R. Sorrentino & E. T. Higgins (Eds.), *Handbook of motivation and cognition* (Vol. 2, pp. 527–561). New York: Guilford.

Schwarz, N., Bless, H., & Bohner, G. (1991). Mood and persuasion: Affective states influence the processing of persuasive communications. In M. P. Zanna (Ed.), *Advances in experimental social psychology* (Vol. 24, pp. 161–197). New York: Academic Press.

Schwarz, N., Bless, H., Strack, F., Klumpp, G., Rittenauer-Schatka, H., & Simons, A. (1991). Ease of retrieval as information: Another look at the availability heuristic. *Journal of Personality and Social Psychology, 61,* 195–202.

Schwarz, N., & Clore, G. L. (1996). Feelings and phenomenal experiences. In E. T. Higgins & A. W. Kruglanski (Eds.), *Social psychology: Handbook of basic principles* (pp. 433–465). New York: Guilford.

Schwarz, N., & Clore, G. L. (2003). Mood as information: 20 years later. *Psychological Inquiry, 14,* 296–303.

Schwarz, S., & Hassebrauck, M. (2008). Self-perceived and observed variations in women's attractiveness throughout the menstrual cycle—a diary study. *Evolution and Human Behavior, 29,* 282–288.

Scollon, C. N., & Diener, E. (2006). Love, work, and changes in extraversion and neuroticism over time. *Journal of Personality and Social Psychology, 91,* 1152–1165.

Scott, J. P. (1992). Aggression: Functions and control in social systems. *Aggressive Behavior, 18,* 1–20.

Seal, D. W., Smith, M., Coley, B., Perry, J., & Gamez, M. (2008). Urban heterosexual couples' sexual scripts for three shared sexual experiences. *Sex Roles, 58,* 626–638.

Sedikides, C., & Anderson, C. A. (1994). Causal perceptions of intertrait relations: The glue that holds person types together. *Personality and Social Psychology Bulletin, 20,* 294–302.

Sedikides, C., Gaertner, L., & Toguchi, Y. (2003). Pancultural self-enhancement. *Journal of Personality & Social Psychology, 84,* 60–79.

Sedikides, C., Gaertner, L., & Vevea, J. L. (2005). Pancultural self-enhancement reloaded: A meta-analytic reply to Heine. *Journal of Personality and Social Psychology, 4,* 539–551.

Sedikides, C., & Gregg, A. P. (2008). Self-enhancement: Food for thought. *Perspectives on Psychological Science, 3,* 102–116.

Sedikides, C., & Luke, M. (2008). On when self-enhancement and self-criticism function adaptively and maladaptively. In E. C. Chang (Ed.), *Self-criticism and self-enhancement: Theory, research, and clinical implications* (pp. 181–198). Washington, DC: American Psychological Association.

Sedikides, C., & Skowronski, J. J. (1991). The law of cognitive structure activation. *Psychological Inquiry, 2,* 169–184.

Sedikides, C., & Skowronski, J. J. (1997). The symbolic self in evolutionary context. *Personality and Social Psychology Review, 1,* 80–102.

Sedikides, C., & Skowronski, J. J. (2000). On the evolutionary functions of the symbolic self: The emergence of self-evaluation motives. In A. Tesser, R. B. Felson, & J. M. Suls (Eds.), *Psychological perspectives on self and identity* (pp. 91–117). Washington, DC: American Psychological Association.

Sedikides, C., Skowronski, J. J., & Gaertner, L. (2004). Self-enhancement and self-protection motivation: From the laboratory to an evolutionary context. *Journal of Cultural and Evolutionary Psychology, 2,* 61–79.

Segal, N. L. (2000). *Entwined lives: Twins and what they tell us about human behavior*. New York: Plume.

Segrist, D. J., Corcoran, K. J., Jordan- Fleming, M. K., & Rose, P. (2007). Yeah, I drink . . . but not as much as other guys: The majority fallacy among male adolescents. *North American Journal of Psychology, 9,* 307–320.

Seijts, G. H., & Latham, G. P. (2000). The effects of goal setting and group size on performance in a social dilemma. *Canadian Journal of Behavioural Science, 32,* 104–116.

Seiter, J. S. (2007). Ingratiation and gratuity: The effect of complimenting customers on tipping behavior in restaurants. *Journal of Applied Social Psychology, 37,* 478–485.

Seligman, C., Becker, L., & Darley, J. (1981). Encouraging residential energy conservation through feedback. In A. Baum & J. Singer (Eds.), *Advances in environmental psychology* (Vol. 3, pp. 93–114). Hillsdale, NJ: Erlbaum.

Seligman, C., Fazio, R. H., & Zanna, M. P. (1980). Effects of salience of extrinsic rewards on liking and loving. *Journal of Personality and Social Psychology, 38,* 453–460.

Seligman, M. E. P., Steen, T. A., Park, N., & Peterson, C. (2005). Positive psychology progress: Empirical validation of interventions. *American Psychologist, 60,* 410–421.

Sell, A., Cosmides, L., Tooby, J., Sznycer, D., von Rueden, C., & Gurven, M. (2008). Human adaptations for the visual assessment of strength and fighting ability from the body and face. *Proceedings of the Royal Society B, 27,* 575–584.

Senneker, P., & Hendrick, C. (1983). Androgyny and helping behavior. *Journal of Personality and Social Psychology, 45,* 916–925.

Servadio, G. (1976). *Mafioso: A history of the mafia from its origins to the present day*. New York: Stein & Day.

Seta, C. E., & Seta, J. J. (1992). Increments and decrements in mean arterial pressure as a function of audience composition: An averaging and summation analysis. *Personality and Social Psychology Bulletin, 18,* 173–181.

Seta, J. J., Crisson, J. E., Seta, C. E., & Wang, M. E. (1989). Task performance and perceptions of anxiety: Averaging and summation in an evaluative setting. *Journal of Personality and Social Psychology, 56,* 387–396.

Seta, J. J., & Seta, C. E. (1993). Stereotypes and the generation of compensatory and noncompensatory expectancies of group members. *Personality and Social Psychology Bulletin, 19,* 722–731.

Shackelford, T. (1998). Divorce as a consequence of spousal infidelity. In V. De Munck (Ed.), *Romantic love and sexual behavior* (pp. 135–153). Westport, CT: Praeger.

Shackelford, T. K., & Buss, D. M. (2000). Marital satisfaction and spousal costinfliction. *Personality & Individual Differences, 28,* 917–928.

Shackelford, T. K., Goetz, A. T., LaMunyon, C. W., Quintus, B. J., & Weekes-Shackelford, V. A. (2004). Sex differences in sexual psychology produce sex-similar preferences for a short-term mate. *Archives of Sexual Behavior, 33,* 405–412.

Shackelford, T. K., LeBlanc, G. J., & Drass, E. (2000). Emotional reactions to infidelity. *Cognition and Emotion, 14,* 643–659.

Shackelford, T. K., Schmitt, D. P., & Buss, D. M. (2005). Universal dimensions of human mate preferences. *Personality and Individual Differences, 39,* 447–458.

Shafer, M., & Crichlow, S. (1996). Antecedents of groupthink: A quantitative study. *Journal of Conflict Resolution, 40,* 415–435.

Shaffer, D., Garland, A., Vieland, V., Underwood, M., & Busner, C. (1991). The impact of curriculum-based suicide prevention programs for teenagers. *Journal of the American Academy of Child and Adolescent Psychiatry, 30,* 588–596.

Shaffer, J. W., Graves-Pirrko, L., Swank, R., & Pearson, T. A. (1987). Clustering of personality traits in youth and the subsequent development of cancer among physicians. *Journal of Behavioral Medicine, 10,* 441–447.

Shamir, B., & Howell, J. M. (1999). Organizational and contextual influences on the emergence and effectiveness of charismatic leadership.*Leadership Quarterly, 10,* 257–283.

Shapiro, J. R., Mistler, S. A., & Neuberg, S. L. (2010). Threatened selves and differential prejudice expression by White and Black perceivers. *Journal of Experimental Social Psychology, 46,* 469–473.

Shapiro, J. S., & Neuberg, S. L. (2007). From stereotype threat to stereotype threats: Implications of a multi-threat framework for causes, moderators, mediators, consequences, and interventions. *Personality and Social Psychology Review, 11,* 107–130.

Shapiro, J. S., & Neuberg, S. L. (2008). When do the stigmatized stigmatize? The ironic effects of being accountable to (perceived) majority group prejudiceexpression norms. *Journal of Personality and Social Psychology, 95,* 877–898.

Sharif, A. F., & Norenzayan, A. (2007). God is watching you: Priming God concepts increases prosocial behavior in an anonymous economic game. *Psychological Science, 18,* 803–809.

Sharpsteen, D. J., & Kirkpatrick, L. A. (1997). Romantic jealousy and adult romantic attachment. *Journal of Personality and Social Psychology, 72,* 627–640.

Shavitt, S. (1990). The role of attitude objects in attitude function. *Journal of Experimental Social Psychology, 26,* 124–148.

Shaw, J. I., & Steers, W. N. (1996). Effects of perceiver sex, search goal, and target person attributes on information search in impression formation. *Journal of Social Behavior & Personality, 11,* 209–227.

Sheets, V. L., & Braver, S. L. (1993, April). *Perceptions of sexual harassment: Effects of a harasser's attractiveness*. Paper presented to the Western Psychological Association, Phoenix, Arizona.

Sheets, V. L., & Braver, S. L. (1999). Organizational status and perceived sexual harassment: Detecting the mediators of a null effect. *Personality & Social Psychology Bulletin, 25,* 1159–1171.

Sheets, V. L., & Lugar, R. (2005). Friendship and gender in Russia and the United States. *Sex Roles, 52,* 131–140.

Sheldon, K. M. (1999). Learning the lessons of tit-for-tat: Even competitors can get the message. *Journal of Personality & Social Psychology, 77,* 1245–1253.

Sheldon, K. M., & Elliot, A. J. (1999). Goal-striving, need satisfaction, and longitudinal well-being: The self-concordance model. *Journal of Personality and Social Psychology, 76,* 482–497.

Shell, R., & Eisenberg, N. (1992). A developmental model of recipients' reactions to aid. *Psychological Bulletin, 111,* 413–433.

Shelton, J. N., Richeson, J. A., & Salvatore, J. (2005). Expecting to be the target of prejudice. Implications for interethnic interactions. *Personality and Social Psychology Bulletin, 31,* 1189–1202.

Shen, H., Wan, F., & Wyer, R. S., Jr. (2011). Cross-cultural differences in the refusal to accept a small gift: The differential influence of reciprocity norms on Asians and North Americans. *Journal of Personality and Social Psychology, 100*(2), 271.

Shepher, J. (1971). Mate selection among second generation kibbutz adolescents and adults: Incest avoidance and negative imprinting. *Archives of Sexual Behavior, 1,* 293–307.

Shepperd, J. A. (1993a). Productivity loss in performance groups: A motivation analysis. *Psychological Bulletin, 113,* 67–81.

Shepperd, J. A. (1993b). Student derogation of the Scholastic Aptitude Test: Biases in perceptions and presentations of College Board scores. *Basic and Applied Social Psychology, 14,* 455–473.

Shepperd, J. A. (2001). The desire to help and behavior in social dilemmas: Exploring responses to catastrophes. *Group Dynamics, 5,* 304–314.

Shepperd, J. A., & Arkin, R. M. (1989). Self-handicapping: The moderating roles of public self-consciousness and task importance. *Personality and Social Psychology Bulletin, 15,* 252–265.

Shepperd, J. A., & Arkin, R. M. (1990). Shyness and self-presentation. In W. R. Crozier (Ed.), *Shyness and embarrassment: Perspectives from social psychology* (pp. 286–314). Cambridge, UK: Cambridge University Press.

Shepperd, J. A., Arkin, R. M., & Slaughter, J. (1995). Constraints on excuse making: The deterring effects of shyness and anticipated retest. *Personality and Social Psychology Bulletin, 21,* 1061–1072.

Shepperd, J. A., Ouellette, J. A., & Fernandez, J. K. (1996). Abandoning unrealistic optimism: Performance estimates and the temporal proximity of self-relevant feedback. *Journal of Personality and Social Psychology, 70,* 844–855.

Shepperd, J. A., & Socherman, R. E. (1997). On the manipulative behavior of low Machiavellians: Feigning incompetence to "sandbag" an opponent. *Journal of Personality and Social Psychology, 72,* 1448–1459.

Shepperd, J. A., & Taylor, K. M. (1999). Social loafing and expectancy-value theory. *Personality and Social Psychology Bulletin, 25,* 1147–1158.

Shepperd, J., Malone, W., & Sweeny, K. (2008). Exploring causes of the self-serving bias. *Social and Personality Psychology Compass, 2,* 895–908.

Sherif, M. (1936). *The psychology of social norms*. New York: Harper.

Sherif, M., Harvey, O. J., White, B. J., Hood, W. R., & Sherif, C. W. (1961/1988). *The Robbers Cave experiment: Intergroup conflict and cooperation*. Middletown, CT: Wesleyan University Press.

Sherman, J. W., & Frost, L. A. (2000). On the encoding of stereotype-relevant information under cognitive load. *Personality and Social Psychology Bulletin, 26,* 26–34.

Sherman, J. W., Kruschke, J. K., Sherman, S. J., Percy, E. J., Petrocelli, J. V., & Conrey, F. R. (2009). Attentional processes in stereotype formation: A common model for category accentuation and illusory correlation. *Journal of Personality and Social Psychology, 96,* 305–323.

Sherman, P. W. (1981). Kinship demography, and Belding's ground squirrel nepotism. *Behavioral Ecology and Sociology, 8,* 604–606.

Sherwin, B. B., Gelfand, M. M., & Brender, W. (1985). Androgen enhances sexual motivation in females: A prospective, crossover study of sex steroid administration in the surgical menopause. *Psychosomatic Medicine, 47,* 339–351.

Shih, M., Pittinsky, T. L., & Ambady, N. (1999). Stereotype susceptibility: Identity salience and shifts in quantitative performance. *Psychological Science, 10,* 80–83.

Shin, K. (1978). *Death penalty and crime: Empirical studies*. Fairfax, Va: Center for Economic Analysis, George Mason University.

Shin, S. J., & Zhou, J. (2007). When is educational specialization heterogeneity related to creativity in research and development teams? Transformational leadership as a moderator. *Journal of Applied Psychology, 92,* 1709–1721.

Shiota, M. N., Campos, B., Gonzaga, G. C., Keltner, D., & Peng, K. (2010). I love you but...: Cultural differences in complexity of emotional experience during interaction with a romantic partner. *Cognition and Emotion, 24*(5), 786–799.

Shiota, M. N., Keltner, D., & John, O. P. (2006). Positive emotion dispositions differentially associated with Big Five personality and attachment style. *Journal of Positive Psychology, 1,* 61–71.

Shiota, M. N., Neufeld, S. L., Yeung, W. H., Moser, S. E., & Perea, E. F. (2011). Feeling good: Autonomic nervous system responding in five positive emotions. *Emotion, 11*(6), 1368.

Shoda, Y., LeeTiernan, S., & Mischel, W. (2002). Personality as a dynamical system: Emergency of stability and distinctiveness from intra- and interpersonal interactions. *Personality and Social Psychology Review, 6,* 316–325.

Shotland, R. L., & Straw, M. (1976). Bystander response to an assault: When a man attacks a woman. *Journal of Personality and Social Psychology, 34,* 990–999.

Shulman, S., Elicker, J., & Sroufe, L. A. (1994). Stages of friendship growth in preadolescence as related to attachment history. *Journal of Personal and Personal Relationships, 11,* 341–361.

Shulman, S., Laursen, B., Kalman, Z., & Karpovsky, S. (1997). Adolescent intimacy revisited. *Journal of Youth and Adolescence, 26,* 597–617.

Sicoly, F., & Ross, M. (1979). Facilitation of ego-biased attributions by means of self-serving observer feedback. *Journal of Personality and Social Psychology, 35,* 734–741.

Sidanius, J., Cling, B. J., & Pratto, F. (1991). Ranking and linking as a function of sex and gender role attitudes. *Journal of Social Issues, 47,* 131–149.

Sidanius, J., Haley, H., Molina, L., & Pratto, F. (2007). Vladimir's choice and the distribution of social resources: A group dominance perspective. *Group Processes and Intergroup Relations, 10,* 257–265.

Sidanius, J., Levin, S., Liu, J., & Pratto, F. (2000). Social dominance orientation, anti-egalitarianism and the political psychology of gender: An extension and cross-cultural replication. *European Journal of Social Psychology, 30,* 41–67.

Sidanius, J., & Pratto, F. (1993). The inevitability of oppression and the dynamics of social dominance. In P. Sniderman & P. Tetlock (Eds.), *Prejudice, politics, and the American dilemma* (pp. 173–211). Stanford, CA: Stanford University Press.

Sidanius, J., & Pratto, F. (1999). *Social dominance: An intergroup theory of social hierarchy and oppression.* New York: Cambridge University Press.

Sidanius, J., & Pratto, F. (2003). Social dominance theory and the dynamics of inequality: A reply to Schmitt, Branscombe, & Kappen and Wilson & Liu. *British Journal of Social Psychology, 42,* 207–213.

Sidanius, J., Pratto, F., & Bobo, L. (1994). Social dominance orientation and the political psychology of gender: A case of invariance? *Journal of Personality and Social Psychology, 67,* 998–1011.

Siegel, J. M. (1990). Stressful life events and use of physician services among the elderly. *Journal of Personality and Social Psychology, 58,* 1081–1086.

Siemer, M., Mauss, I., & Gross, J. J. (2007). Same situation, different emotions: How appraisals shape our emotions. *Emotion, 7,* 592–600.

Sigelman, C. K., Howell, J. L., Cornell, D. P., Cutright, J. D., & Dewey, J. C. (1991). Courtesy stigma: The social implications of associating with a gay person. *Journal of Social Psychology, 131,* 45–56.

Silva, N. D., Hutcheson, J., & Wahl, G. D. (2010). Organizational strategy and employee outcomes: A person-organization fit perspective. *The Journal of Psychology, 144*(2), 145–161.

Simon, B., & Stürmer, S. (2003). Respect for group members: Intragroup determinants of collective identification and group-serving behavior. *Personality and Social Psychology Bulletin, 29,* 183–193.

Simon, L., & Greenberg, J. (1996). Further progress in understanding the effects of derogatory ethnic labels: The role of preexisting attitudes toward the targeted group. *Personality and Social Psychology Bulletin, 22,* 1195–1204.

Simonton, D. K. (1994). *Greatness: Who makes history and why.* New York: Guilford.

Simpson, J. A., & Campbell, L. (2005). Methods of evolutionary sciences. In D. M. Buss (Ed.), *The handbook of evolutionary psychology* (pp. 119–145). New York: Wiley.

Simpson, J. A., Collins, W. A., & Salvatore, J. E. (2011). The impact of early interpersonal experience on adult romantic relationship functioning: Recent findings from the Minnesota Longitudinal Study of Risk and Adaptation. *Current Directions in Psychological Science, 20*(6), 355–359.

Simpson, J. A., Collins, W. A., Tran, S., & Haydon, K. C. (2007). Attachment and the experience and

expression of emotions in romantic relationships: A developmental perspective. *Journal of Personality and Social Psychology, 92,* 355–367.

Simpson, J. A., & Gangestad, S. W. (1991). Individual differences in sociosexuality: Evidence for convergent and discriminant validity. *Journal of Personality and Social Psychology, 67,* 870–883.

Simpson, J. A., & Gangestad, S. W. (1992). Sociosexuality and romantic partner choice. *Journal of Personality, 60,* 31–51.

Simpson, J. A., Gangestad, S. W., Christensen, P. N., & Leck, K. (1999). Fluctuating asymmetry, sociosexuality, and intrasexual competitive tactics. *Journal of Personality & Social Psychology, 76,* 159–172.

Simpson, J. A., Rholes, W. S., Campbell, L., Tran, S., & Wilson, C. L. (2003). Adult attachment, the transition to parenthood, and depressive symptoms. *Journal of Personality & Social Psychology, 84,* 1172–1187.

Sinclair, H. C., & Frieze, I. H. (2005). When courtship persistence becomes intrusive pursuit: Comparing rejecter and pursuer perspectives of unrequited attraction. *Sex Roles, 52,* 839–852.

Sinclair, L., & Kunda, Z. (2000). Motivated stereotyping of women: She's fine if she praised me but incompetent if she criticized me. *Personality and Social Psychology Bulletin, 26,* 1329–1342.

Sinclair, R. C., Hoffman, C., Mark, M. M., Martin, L. L., & Pickering, T. L. (1994). Construct accessibility and the misattribution of arousal: Schachter and Singer revisited. *Psychological Science, 5,* 15–19.

Sinclair, R. C., Mark, M. M., & Shotland, R. L. (1987). Construct accessibility and generalizability across response categories. *Personality and Social Psychology Bulletin, 13,* 239–252.

Singer, M. T., & Lalich, J. (1995). *Cults in our midst.* San Francisco: Jossey-Bass.

Singer, T., Seymour, B., O'Doherty, J., Kaube, H., Dolan, R. J., & Frith, C. D. (2004, February 20). Empathy for pain involves the affective but not sensory components of pain. *Science,* 1157–1162.

Singh, D. (1993). Adaptive significance of female physical attractiveness: Role of waist-to-hip ratio. *Journal of Personality and Social Psychology, 65,* 293–307.

Singh, D. (2002). Female mate value at a glance: Relationship of waist-to-hip ratio to health, fecundity and attractiveness. *Neuroendocrinology Letters, 23,* 65–75.

Singh, D., & Bronstad, P. M. (2001). Female body odor is a potential cue to ovulation. *Proceedings of the Royal Society of London, Biology, 268,* 797–801.

Singh, D., Dixson, B. J., Jessop, T. S., Morgan, B., & Dixson, A. F. (2010). Cross-cultural consensus for waist-hip ratio and women's attractiveness. *Evolution and Human Behavior, 31,* 176–181.

Sip, K. E., Roepstorff, A., McGregor, W., & Frith, C. D. (2008). Detecting deception: The scope and limits. *Trends in Cognitive Sciences, 12,* 48–53.

Sisask, M., & Värnik, A. (2012). Media roles in suicide prevention: A systematic review. *International Journal of Environmental Research and Public Health, 9,* 123–138.

Sivacek, J., & Crano, W. D. (1982). Vested interest as a moderator of attitudebehavior consistency. *Journal of Personality and Social Psychology, 43,* 210–221.

Slavin, R. E., & Cooper, R. (1999). Improving intergroup relations: Lessons learned from cooperative learning programs. *Journal of Social Issues, 55,* 647–663.

Smidt, K. E., & DeBono, K. G. (2011). On the effects of product name on product evaluation: An individual difference perspective. *Social Influence, 6*(3), 131–141.

Smith, A. N., Watkins, M. B., Burke, M. J., Christian, M. S., Smith, C. E., Hall, A., et al. (2013). Gendered influence: A gender role perspective on the use and effectiveness of influence tactics. *Journal of Management, 39*(5), 1156–1183.

Smith, B. N., Kerr, N. A., Markus, M. J., & Stasson, M. F. (2001). Individual differences in social

loafing: Need for cognition as a motivator in collective performance. *Group Dynamics, 5,* 150–158.

Smith, C. T., De Houwer, J., & Nosek, B. A. (2013). Consider the source persuasion of implicit evaluations is moderated by source credibility. *Personality and Social Psychology Bulletin, 39*(2), 193–205.

Smith, D. M., Neuberg, S. L., Judice, T. N., & Biesanz, J. C. (1997). Target complicity in the confirmation and disconfirmation of erroneous perceiver expectations: Immediate and longer term implications. *Journal of Personality and Social Psychology, 73,* 974–991.

Smith, E. R., & DeCoster, J. (2000). Dual process models in social and cognitive psychology. *Personality and Social Psychology Review, 4,* 108–131.

Smith, E. R., & Semin, G. R. (2007). Situated social cognition. *Current Directions in Psychological Science, 16,* 132–135.

Smith, E. R., & Zárate, M. A. (1992). Exemplar-based model of social judgment. *Psychological Review, 99,* 3–21.

Smith, K. D., Keating, J. P., & Stotland, E. (1989). Altruism reconsidered: The effect of denying feedback on a victim's status to witnesses. *Journal of Personality and Social Psychology, 57,* 641–650.

Smith, P. B., & Bond, M. H. (1994). *Social psychology across cultures.* Boston: Allyn & Bacon.

Smith, P. B., & Bond, M. H. (1998). *Social psychology across cultures* (2nd ed.). Boston: Allyn & Bacon.

Smith, P. B., Bond, M. H., & Kagitcibasi, C. (2006). *Understanding social psychology across cultures: Living and working in a changing world.* London: Sage.

Smolowe, J. (1990, November 26). Contents require immediate attention. *Time,* p. 64.

Snibbe, A. C., & Markus, H. R. (2005). You can't always get what you want: Educational attainment, agency, and choice. *Journal of Personality and Social Psychology, 88,* 703–720.

Snow, D. A., Robinson, C., & McCall, P. L. (1991). "Cooling out" men in singles bars and nightclubs: Observations on the interpersonal survival strategies of women in public places. *Journal of Contemporary Ethnography, 19,* 423–449.

Snyder, C. R., & Forsyth, D. R. (1991). *Handbook of social and clinical psychology.* New York: Pergamon.

Snyder, C. R., & Higgins, R. L. (1988). Excuses: Their effective role in the negotiation of reality. *Psychological Bulletin, 104,* 23–35.

Snyder, C. R., Lassegard, M., & Ford, C. E. (1986). Distancing after group success and failure: Basking in reflected glory and cutting off reflected failure. *Journal of Personality and Social Psychology, 51*(2), 382–388.

Snyder, C. R., Tennen, H., Affleck, G., & Cheavens, J. (2000). Social, personality, clinical, and health psychology tributaries: The merging of a scholarly "River of dreams." *Personality and Social Psychology Review, 4,* 16–29.

Snyder, J. K., Fessler, D. M. T., Tiokhin, L., Frederick, D. A., Lee, S. W., & Navarette, C. D. (2011). Trade-offs in a dangerous world: women's fear of crime predicts preference for aggressive and formidable mates. *Evolution and Human Behavior, 32,* 127–137.

Snyder, M. (1974). Self-monitoring of expressive behavior. *Journal of Personality and Social Psychology, 30,* 526–537.

Snyder, M. (1987). *Public appearances, private realities: The psychology of self-monitoring.* New York: Freeman.

Snyder, M., & Cantor, N. (1998). Understanding personality and social behavior: A functionalist strategy. In D. T. Gilbert, S. T. Fiske, & G. Lindzey (Eds.), *The handbook of social psychology* (4th ed., Vol. 1, pp. 635–679). Boston: McGraw-Hill.

Snyder, M., & DeBono, K. G. (1985). Appeals to image and claims about quality: Understanding the psychology of advertising. *Journal of Personality and Social Psychology, 49,* 586–597.

Snyder, M., & DeBono, K. G. (1989). Understanding the functions of attitudes. In A. R. Pratkanis, S. J. Breckler, & A. G. Greenwald (Eds.), *Attitude structure and function* (pp. 339–359). Hillsdale, NJ: Erlbaum.

Snyder, M., & Haugen, J. A. (1995). Why does behavioral confirmation occur? A functional perspective on the role of the target. *Personality and Social Psychology Bulletin, 21,* 963–974.

Snyder, M., & Ickes, W. (1985). Personality and social behavior. In G. Lindzey & E. Aronson (Eds.), *Handbook of social psychology* (3rd ed., Vol. 2, pp. 883–948). New York: Random House.

Snyder, M., & Omoto, A. M. (1992). Who helps and why? In S. Spacapan & S. Oskamp (Eds.), *Helping and being helped: Naturalistic studies* (pp. 213–239). Newbury Park, CA: Sage.

Snyder, M., & Swann, W. B., Jr. (1976). When actions reflect attitudes: The politics of impression management. *Journal of Personality and Social Psychology, 34,* 1034–1042.

Solano, A., Batten, P. G., & Parish, E. A. (1982). Loneliness and patterns of self-disclosure. *Journal of Personality and Social Psychology, 43,* 524–531.

Sommers, S. R., Warp, L. S., & Mahoney, C. C. (2008). Cognitive effects of racial diversity: White individuals' information processing in heterogeneous groups. *Journal of Experimental Social Psychology, 44,* 1129–1136.

Sorrentino, R. M., & Field, N. (1986). Emergent leadership over time: The functional value of positive motivation. *Journal of Personality and Social Psychology, 50,* 1091–1099.

Speed, A., & Gangestad, S. W. (1997). Romantic popularity and mate preferences: A peer nomination study. *Personality & Social Psychology Bulletin, 9,* 928–935.

Spence, K. W. (1956). *Behavior theory and conditioning.* New Haven, CT: Yale University Press.

Spence, S. A. (2008). Playing Devil's advocate: The case against fMRI lie detection. *Legal and Criminological Psychology, 13,* 11–25.

Spencer, S. J., Josephs, R. A., & Steele, C. M. (1993). Low self-esteem: The uphill struggle for self-integrity. In R. Baumeister (Ed.), *Self-esteem: The puzzle of low self-regard* (pp. 21–36). New York: Plenum.

Spencer, S. J., Steele, C. M., & Quinn, D. (1999). Stereotype threat and women's math performance. *Journal of Experimental and Social Psychology, 35,* 4–28.

Spencer-Rodgers, J., Hamilton, D. L., & Sherman, S. J. (2007). The central role of entitativity in stereotypes of social categories and task groups. *Journal of Personality and Social Psychology, 92,* 369–388.

Sprecher, S., Aron, A., Hatfield, E., Cortese, A., Potapova, E., & Levitskaya, A. (1994). Love: American style, Russian style, and Japanese style. *Personal Relationships, 1,* 349–369.

Sprecher, S., & Regan, P. C. (1998). Passionate and companionate love in courting and young married couples. *Sociological Inquiry, 68,* 163–185.

Sprecher, S., & Regan, P. C. (2000). Sexuality in a relational context. In C. Hendrick & S. Hendrick (Eds.), *Close relationships: A sourcebook* (pp. 217–227). Thousand Oaks, CA: Sage.

Stacy, A., Sussman, S., Dent, C. W., Burton, D., & Flay, B. R. (1992). Moderators of social influence in adolescent smoking. *Personality and Social Psychology Bulletin, 18,* 163–172.

Stangor, C., & Duan, C. (1991). Effects of multiple task demands upon memory for information about social groups. *Journal of Experimental Social Psychology, 27,* 357–378.

Stangor, C., & McMillan, D. (1992). Memory for expectancy-congruent and expectancy-incongruent information: A review of the social and social developmental literatures. *Psychological Bulletin, 111,* 42–61.

Stangor, C., Sullivan, L. A., & Ford, T. E. (1991). Affective and cognitive determinants of prejudice. *Social Cognition, 9,* 359–380.

Stanley, S. M., Allen, E. S., Markman, H. J., Rhoades, G. K., & Prentice, D. L. (2010). Decreasing divorce in U.S. Army couples: Results from a randomized controlled trial using PREP for Strong Bonds. *Journal of Couple and Relationship Therapy, 9,* 149–160.

Stapel, D. A., & Johnson, C. S. (2007). When nothing compares to me: How defensive motivations and similarity shape social comparison effects. *European Journal of Social Psychology, 37,* 824–838.

Stark, B., & Deaux, K. (1994, July 2). *Integrating motivational and identity theories of volunteerism.* Poster presented at the annual meeting of the American Psychological Society, Washington, DC.

Stasser, G. (1992). Information salience and the discovery of hidden profiles by decision-making groups: A "thought experiment." *Organizational Behavior and Human Decision Processes, 52(1),* 156–181.

Staw, B. M., & Ross, J. (1980). Commitment in an experimenting society. *Journal of Applied Psychology, 65,* 249–260.

Steele, C. M. (1988). The psychology of self-affirmation: Sustaining the integrity of the self. In L. Berkowitz (Ed.), *Advances in experimental social psychology* (Vol. 21, pp. 261–302). New York: Academic Press.

Steele, C. M. (1992, April). Race and the schooling of black Americans. *The Atlantic Monthly,* pp. 68–78.

Steele, C. M., & Aronson, J. (1995). Stereotype threat and the intellectual test performance of African Americans. *Journal of Personality and Social Psychology, 69,* 797–811.

Steele, C. M., & Josephs, R. A. (1988). Drinking your troubles away II: An attention-allocation model of alcohol's effect on psychological stress. *Journal of Abnormal Psychology, 97,* 196–205.

Steiner, I. D. (1972). *Group process and productivity.* New York: Academic Press.

Steinfield, C., Ellison, N. B., & Lampe, C. (2008). Social capital, self-esteem, and use of online social network sites: A longitudinal analysis. *Journal of Applied Developmental Psychology, 29,* 434–445.

Stephan, C. W., Renfro, L., & Stephan, W. G. (2004). The evaluation of multicultural education programs: Techniques and a meta-analysis. In W. G. Stephan & W. P. Vogt (Eds.), *Education programs for improving intergroup relations, theory, research, and practice* (pp. 227–242). New York: Teachers College Press.

Stephan, W. G. (1978). School desegregation: An evaluation of predictions made in *Brown v. Board of Education. Psychological Bulletin, 85,* 217–238.

Stephan, W. G., Ageyev, V., Coates-Shrider, L., Stephan, C. W., & Abalakina, M. (1994). On the relationship between stereotypes and prejudice: An international study. *Personality and Social Psychology Bulletin, 20,* 277–284.

Stephan, W. G., & Finlay, K. (1999). The role of empathy in improving intergroup relations. *Journal of Social Issues, 55,* 729–743.

Stephan, W. G., & Stephan, C. W. (1984). The role of ignorance in intergroup relations. In N. Miller & M. B. Brewer (Eds.), *Groups in contact* (pp. 229–255). New York: Academic Press.

Stephan, W. G., & Stephan, C. W. (1985). Intergroup anxiety. *Social Issues, 41,* 157–175.

Stephan, W. G., & Stephan, C. W. (1996). *Intergroup relations.* Madison, WI: Brown & Benchmark.

Stephan, W. G., & Stephan, C. W. (2000). An integrated threat theory of prejudice. In S. Oskamp (Ed.), *Reducing prejudice and discrimination* (pp. 23–46). Hillsdale, NJ: Erlbaum.

Stern, P. C. (2000). Psychology and the science of human-environment interactions. *American Psychologist, 55,* 523–530.

Stern, P. C., Diet, T., & Kalof, L. (1993). Value orientations, gender, and environmental concern. *Environment and Behavior, 25,* 322–348.

Sternberg, R. J. (1986). A triangular theory of love. *Psychological Review, 93,* 119–135.

Sternberg, R. J. (2006). A duplex theory of love. In R. J. Sternberg & K. Weis (Eds.), *The new psychology of love* (pp. 184–199). New Haven, CT: Yale University Press.

Sternthal, B., Dholakia, R., & Leavitt, C. (1978). The persuasive effect of source credibility: Tests of cognitive response. *Journal of Consumer Research, 4,* 252–260.

Stevens, L. E., & Fiske, S. T. (1995). Motivation and cognition in social life: A social survival perspective. *Social Cognition, 13,* 189–214.

Stevens, R., & Slavin, R. (1995). The cooperative elementary school: Effects on student's achievement, attitudes, and social relations. *American Educational Research Journal, 32,* 321–351.

Stewart, J. E. (1980). Defendant's attractiveness as a factor in the outcome of criminal trials: An observational study. *Journal of Applied Social Psychology, 10,* 348–361.

Stewart, J. E. (1985). Appearance and punishment: The attraction-leniency effect. *Journal of Social Psychology, 125,* 373–378.

Stewart-Williams, S., & Thomas, A. G. (2013). The ape that thought it was a peacock: Does evolutionary psychology exaggerate human sex differences? *Psychological Inquiry, 24(3),* 137–168.

Stiles, W. B., Lyall, L. M., Knight, D. P., Ickes, W., Waung, M., Hall, C., et al. (1997). Gender differences in verbal presumptuousness and attentiveness. *Personality and Social Psychology Bulletin, 23,* 759–772.

Stinchcombe, A. L. (1965). Social structure and organizations. In J. G. March (Ed.), *Handbook of organizations* (pp. 142–193). Chicago: Rand McNally.

Stinson, D. A., Logel, C., Zanna, M. P., Holmes, J. G., Cameron, J. J., Wood, J. V., et al. (2008). The cost of lower self-esteem: Testing a self- and social-bonds model of health. *Journal of Personality and Social Psychology, 94,* 412–428.

Stone, J. (2002). Battling doubt by avoiding practice: The effects of stereotype threat on self-handicapping in white athletes. *Personality and Social Psychology Bulletin, 28,* 1667–1678.

Stone, J. (2003). Self-consistency for low self-esteem in dissonance processes: The role of self-standards. *Personality and Social Psychology Bulletin, 29,* 446–858.

Stone, J., & Cooper, J. (2001). A self-standards model of cognitive dissonance. *Journal of Experimental Social Psychology, 37,* 228–243.

Stone, J., & Fernandez, N. C. (2008). To practice what we preach: The use of hypocrisy and cognitive dissonance to motivate behavior change. *Social and Personality Psychology Compass, 2,* 1024–1051.

Stone, J., Lynch, C. I., Sjomeling, M., & Darley, J. M. (1999). Stereotype threat effects on black and white athletic performance. *Journal of Personality and Social Psychology, 77,* 1213–1227.

Stone, V. E., Cosmides, L., Tooby, J., Kroll, N., & Knight, R. T. (2002). Selective impairment of reasoning about social exchange in a patient with bilateral limbic system damage. *Proceedings of National Academy of Science, 99,* 11531–11536.

Stoner, J. A. F. (1961). *A comparison of individual and group decisions involving risk.* Unpublished master's thesis, Massachusetts Institute of Technology.

Storey, A. E., Walsh, C. J., Quinton, R. L., & Wynne-Edwards, K. E. (2000). Hormonal correlates of paternal responsiveness in new and expectant fathers. *Evolution & Human Behavior, 21,* 79–95.

Stouffer, S. A., Suchman, E., DeVinney, S. A., Star, S., & Williams, R. M. (Eds.). (1949). *The American soldier: Adjustment during army life.* Princeton, NJ: Princeton University Press.

Strack, F., Martin, L. L., & Stepper, S. (1988). Inhibiting and facilitating conditions of the human smile: A nonobtrusive test of the facial feedback hypothesis. *Journal of Personality and Social Psychology, 54,* 768–777.

Strack, F., Werth, L., & Deutsch, R. (2006). Reflective and impulsive determinants of consumer behavior. *Journal of Consumer Psychology, 16,* 205–216.

Strack, S., & Coyne, J. C. (1983). Social confirmation of dysphoria: Shared and private reactions to depression. *Journal of Personality and Social Psychology, 44,* 798–806.

Straus, M. A. (2012). Blaming the messenger for the bad news about partner violence by women: The methodological, theoretical, and value basis of the purported invalidity of the conflict tactics scales. *Behavioral Sciences & the Law, 30*(5), 538–556.

Street, A. E., Gradus, J. L., Stafford, J., & Kelly, K. (2007). Gender differences in experiences of sexual harassment: Data from a male-dominated environment. *Journal of Consulting and Clinical Psychology, 75,* 464–474.

Strickland, B. R., & Crowne, D. P. (1962). Conformity under conditions of simulated group pressure as a function of need for social approval. *Journal of Social Psychology, 58,* 171–181.

Strijbos, J. W., Martens, R. L., Jochems, W. M. G., & Broers, N. J. (2004). The effect of functional roles on group efficiency: Using multilevel modeling and content analysis to investigate computer-supported collaboration in small groups. *Small Group Research, 35,* 195–229.

Stroessner, S. J., & Mackie, D. M. (1992). The impact of induced affect on the perception of social variability in social groups. *Personality and Social Psychology Bulletin, 18,* 546–554.

Stroh, L. K., Brett, J. M., & Reilly, A. H. (1992). All the right stuff: A comparison of female and male managers' career progression. *Journal of Applied Psychology, 77,* 251–260.

Strohmetz, D. B., Rind, B., Fisher, R., & Lynn, M. (2002). Sweetening the till: The use of candy to increase restaurant tipping. *Journal of Applied Social Psychology, 32,* 300–309.

Strom, S. (2006, April 30). Donor fatigue wasn't a problem in '05, charities say. *Arizona Republic,* p. A13.

Stukas, A. A., Jr., & Snyder, M. (2002). Targets' awareness of expectations and behavioral confirmation in ongoing interactions. *Journal of Experimental Social Psychology, 38,* 31–40.

Sturmer, S., Snyder, M., Kropp, A., & Siem, B. (2006). Empathy-mediated helping: The moderating role of group membership. *Personality and Social Psychology Bulletin, 32,* 943–956.

Suedfeld, P., Wallace, M. D., & Thachuk, K. L. (1993). Changes in integrative complexity among Middle East leaders during the Persian Gulf crisis. *Journal of Social Issues, 49,* 183–191.

Sugarman, J., & Rand, K. (1994, March 10). Cease fire. *Rolling Stone,* pp. 30–42.

Suh, E. J., Moskowitz, D. S., Fournier, M. A., & Zuroff, D. C. (2004). Gender and relationships: Influences on agentic and communal behaviors. *Personal Relationships, 11,* 41–59.

Suls, J., & Green, P. J. (2003). Pluralistic ignorance and college student perceptions of gender-specific alcohol norms. *Health Psychology, 22,* 479–486.

Suls, J., Lemos, K., & Stewart, H. L. (2002). Self-esteem, construal, and comparisons with the self, friends, and peers. *Journal of Personality & Social Psychology, 82,* 252–261.

Suls, J., Martin, R., & David, J. P. (1998). Person-environment fit and its limits: Agreeableness, neuroticism, and emotional reactivity to interpersonal conflict. *Personality and Social Psychology Bulletin, 24,* 88–98.

Suls, J., Martin, R., & Wheeler, L. (2002). Social comparison: Why, with whom, and with what effect? *Current Directions in Psychological Science, 11,* 159–163.

Sumner, W. G. (1906). *Folkways.* New York: New American Library.

Sundie, J. M., Kenrick, D. T., Griskevicius, V., Tybur, J. M., Vohs, K. D., & Beal, D. J. (2011). Peacocks, Porsches, and Thorstein Veblen: Conspicuous consumption as a sexual signaling system. *Journal of Personality and Social Psychology, 100*(4), 664–680.

Surowiecki, J. (2004). *The wisdom of crowds.* New York: Doubleday.

Sussman, S., Dent, C. W., Flay, B. R., Hansen, W. B., & Johnson, C. A. (1986). Psychosocial predictors of cigarette smoking onset by white, black, Hispanic, and Asian adolescents in Southern California. *Morbidity and Mortality Weekly Report Supplement, 36,* 3–10.

Swann, W. B., Jr. (1990). To be adored or to be known? The interplay of self-enhancement and self-verification. In R. M. Sorrentino & E. T. Higgins (Eds.), *Foundations of social behavior* (Vol. 2, pp. 404–448). New York: Guilford.

Swann, W. B., Jr., Hixon, J. G., & De La Ronde, C. (1992). Embracing the bitter "truth": Negative self-concepts and marital commitment. *Psychological Science, 3,* 118–121.

Swann, W. B., Jr., Rentfrow, P. J., & Guinn, J. S. (2003). Self-verification: The search for coherence. In M. R. Leary & J. P. Tangney (Eds.), *Handbook of self and identity* (pp. 367–383). New York: Guilford Press.

Swann, W. B., Stein-Seroussi, A., & Giesler, R. B. (1992). Why people self-verify. *Journal of Personality and Social Psychology, 62*(3), 392–401.

Swann, W. B., Jr., Stephenson, B., & Pittman, T. S. (1981). Curiosity and control: On the determinants of the search for social knowledge. *Journal of Personality and Social Psychology, 40,* 635–642.

Swim, J. K. (1994). Perceived versus meta-analytic effect sizes: An assessment of the accuracy of gender stereotypes. *Journal of Personality and Social Psychology, 66,* 21–36.

Swim, J. K., Aikin, K. J., Hall, W. S., & Hunter, B. A. (1995). Sexism and racism: Old-fashioned and modern prejudices. *Journal of Personality and Social Psychology, 68,* 199–214.

Swim, J. K., Ferguson, M. J., & Hyers, L. L. (1999). Avoiding stigma by association: Subtle prejudice against lesbians in the form of social distancing. *Basic and Applied Social Psychology, 21,* 61–68.

Swim, J. K., & Hyers, L. L. (1999). Excuse me—What did you just say? Women's public and private responses to sexist remarks. *Journal of Experimental Social Psychology, 35,* 68–88.

Swim, J. K., & Miller, D. L. (1999). White guilt: Its antecedents and consequences for attitudes toward affirmative action. *Personality and Social Psychology Bulletin, 25,* 500–514.

Swim, J. K., & Sanna, L. J. (1996). He's skilled, she's lucky: A meta-analysis of observers' attributions for women's and men's successes and failures. *Personality and Social Psychology Bulletin, 22,* 507–519.

Swim, J. K., & Stangor, C. (1998). *Prejudice: The target's perspective.* San Diego, CA: Academic Press.

Szymanski, K., & Harkins, S. G. (1987). Social loafing and self-evaluation with a social standard. *Journal of Personality and Social Psychology, 53,* 891–897.

Tagler, M. J. (2010). Sex differences in jealousy: Comparing the influences of previous infidelity among college students and adults. *Social Psychological and Personality Science, 1*(4), 353–360.

Tajfel, H. (1969). Cognitive aspects of prejudice. *Journal of Social Issues, 25,* 79–97.

Tajfel, H. (1982). Social psychology of intergroup relations. *Annual Review of Psychology, 33,* 1–39.

Tajfel, H., Billig, M. G., Bundy, R. P., & Flament, C. (1971). Social categorization and intergroup behavior. *Journal of Social Psychology, 1,* 149–178.

Tajfel, H., & Turner, J. (1979). An integrative theory of intergroup conflict. In W. G. Austin & S. Worchel (Eds.), *The social psychology of intergroup relations* (pp. 33–47). Monterey, CA: Brooks-Cole.

Tajfel, H., & Turner, J. C. (1986). The social identity theory of intergroup behavior. In S. Worchel & W. G. Austin (Eds.), *Psychology of intergroup relations* (2nd ed., pp. 7–24). Chicago: Nelson-Hall.

Takahashi, H., Matsuura, M., Yahata, N., Koeda, M., Suhara, T., & Okubo, Y. (2006). Men and women show distinct brain activations during imagery of sexual and emotional infidelity. *Neuroimage, 32,* 1299–1307.

Takemura, K., & Yuki, M. (2007). Are Japanese groups more competitive than Japanese individuals? A cross-cultural validation of the interindividual–intergroup discontinuity effect. *International Journal of Psychology, 42,* 27–35.

Tal, I., & Lieberman, D. (2008). Kin detection and the development of sexual aversions: Toward an integration of theories on family sexual abuse. In C. A. Salmon & T. K. Shackelford (Eds.), *Family relationships: An evolutionary perspective* (pp. 205–229). New York: Oxford University Press.

Tam, T., Hewstone, M., Kenworthy, J., & Cairns, E. (2009). Intergroup trust in Northern Ireland. *Personality and Social Psychology Bulletin, 35,* 45–59.

Tamres, L. K., Janicki, D., & Helgeson, V. S. (2002). Sex differences in coping behavior: A meta-analytic review and an examination of relative coping. *Personality & Social Psychology Bulletin, 6,* 2–30.

Tancredy, C. M., & Fraley, R. C. (2006). The nature of adult twin relationships: An attachment-theoretical perspective. *Journal of Personality and Social Psychology, 90,* 78–93.

Tangney, J. P. (1992). Situational determinants of shame and guilt in young adulthood. *Personality and Social Psychology Bulletin, 18,* 199–206.

Tapias, M. P., Glaser, J., Keltner, D., Vasquez, K., & Wickens, T. (2007). Emotion and prejudice: Specific emotions toward outgroups. *Group Processes and Intergroup Relations, 10,* 27–39.

Taylor, S. E. (2006). Tend and befriend: Biobehavioral bases of affiliation under stress. *Current Directions in Psychological Science, 15,* 273–277.

Taylor, S. E., & Brown, J. D. (1988). Illusion and well-being: A social psychological perspective on mental health. *Psychological Bulletin, 103,* 193–210.

Taylor, S. E., Burklund, L., Eisenberger, N. I., Lehman, B. J., Hilmert, C. J., & Lieberman, M. D. (2008). Neural bases of moderation of cortisol stress responses by psychosocial resources. *Journal of Personality and Social Psychology, 95,* 197–211.

Taylor, S. E., Collins, R. L., Skolan, L. A., & Aspinwall, L. G. (1989). Maintaining positive illusions in the face of getting negative information: Getting the facts without letting them get to you. *Journal of Social and Clinical Psychology, 8,* 114–129.

Taylor, S. E., & Crocker, J. (1981). Schematic bases of social information processing. In E. T. Higgins, C. P. Herman, & M. P. Zanna (Eds.), *Social cognition: The Ontario Symposium* (Vol. 1, pp. 89–134). Hillsdale, NJ: Erlbaum.

Taylor, S. E., & Fiske, S. T. (1978). Salience, attention, and attribution: Top of the head phenomena. In L. Berkowitz (Ed.), *Advances in experimental social psychology* (Vol. 11, pp. 249–288). New York: Academic Press.

Taylor, S. E., & Gollwitzer, P. M. (1995). Effects of mindset on positive illusions. *Journal of Personality and Social Psychology, 69,* 213–226.

Taylor, S. E., & Gonzaga, G. C. (2006). Evolution, relationships, and health: The social shaping hypothesis. In M. Schaller, J. Simpson, & D. T. Kenrick (Eds.), *Evolution and social psychology* (pp. 211–236). New York: Psychology Press.

Taylor, S. E., Klein, L. C., Lewis, B. P., Gruenwald, T. L., Gurung, R. A. R., & Updegraff, J. A. (2000b). Biobehavioral responses to stress in females: Tend-and-befriend, not fight-or-flight. *Psychological Review, 107,* 411–429.

Taylor, S. E., Lerner, J. S., Sherman, D. K., Sage, R. M., & McDowell, N. K. (2003a). Are self-enhancing cognitions associated with healthy or unhealthy biological profiles? *Journal of Personality & Social Psychology, 85,* 605–616.

Taylor, S. E., Lerner, J. S., Sherman, D. K., Sage, R. M., & McDowell, N. K. (2003b). Portrait of the self-enhancer: Well adjusted and well liked or maladjusted and friendless? *Journal of Personality & Social Psychology, 84,* 165–176.

Taylor, S. E., Lichtman, R. R., & Wood, J. V. (1984). Attributions, beliefs about control, and adjustment to breast cancer. *Journal of Personality and Social Psychology, 46,* 489–502.

Tazelaar, M. J. A., Van Lange, P. A. M., & Ouwerkerk, J. W. (2004). How to cope with "noise" in social dilemmas: The benefits of communication. *Journal of Personality and Social Psychology, 87,* 845–859.

Teenager got doctors' messages, ordered treatment. (2000, December 17). *St. Louis Post-Dispatch,* p. A7.

Teger, A. (1980). *Too much invested to quit.* New York: Pergamon.

Tenbrunsel, A. E., & Messick, D. M. (1999). Sanctioning systems, decision frames, and cooperation. *Administrative Science Quarterly, 44,* 684–707.

Terkel, S. (1992). *Race: How blacks and whites think and feel about the American obsession.* New York: Anchor.

Terry, D. J., & Hogg, M. A. (1996). Group norms and the attitude-behavior relationship: A role for group identification. *Personality and Social Psychology Bulletin, 22,* 776–793.

Tesser, A. (1988). Toward a self-evaluation maintenance model of social behavior. In L. Berkowitz (Ed.), *Advances in experimental social psychology* (Vol. 21, pp. 181–227). San Diego, CA: Academic Press.

Tesser, A. (1993). The importance of heritability in psychological research: The case of attitudes. *Psychological Review, 100,* 129–142.

Tesser, A. (2000). On the confluence of self-esteem maintenance mechanisms. *Personality & Social Psychology Review, 4,* 290–299.

Tesser, A., & Achee, J. (1994). Aggression, love, conformity, and other social psychological catastrophes. In R. R. Vallacher & A. Nowak (Eds.), *Dynamical systems in social psychology* (pp. 95–109). San Diego, CA: Academic Press.

Tesser, A., & Bau, J. J. (2002). Social psychology: Who we are and what we do. *Personality & Social Psychology Review, 6,* 72–85.

Tesser, A., Campbell, J., & Mickler, S. (1983). The role of social pressure, attention to the stimulus, and self-doubt in conformity. *European Journal of Social Psychology, 13,* 217–233.

Tesser, A., & Smith, J. (1980). Some effects of task relevance and friendship on helping. *Journal of Experimental Social Psychology, 16,* 582–590.

Tessler, R. C., & Schwartz, S. H. (1972). Help-seeking, self-esteem, and achievement motivation: An attributional analysis. *Journal of Personality and Social Psychology, 21,* 318–326.

Tetlock, P. E. (1983). Policy-makers' images of international conflict. *Journal of Social Issues, 39,* 67–86.

Tetlock, P. E., Peterson, R. S., McGuire, C., Chang, S. J., & Feld, P. (1992). Assessing political group dynamics: A test of the groupthink model. *Journal of Personality and Social Psychology, 63,* 403–425.

Thaler, R. H., & Sunstein, C. R. (2008). *Nudge: Improving decisions about health, wealth, and happiness.* New Haven: Yale University Press.

Thibaut, J., & Kelley, H. H. (1959). *The social psychology of groups.* New York: Wiley.

Thompson, E. P., Roman, R. J., Moskowitz, G. B., Chaiken, S., & Bargh, J. A. (1994). Accuracy motivation attenuates covert priming: The systematic reprocessing of social information. *Journal of Personality and Social Psychology, 66,* 474–489.

Thompson, L. (1993). The impact of negotiation on intergroup relations. *Journal of Experimental Social Psychology, 29,* 304–325.

Thompson, L., & Fine, G. A. (1999). Socially shared cognition, affect, and behavior: A review and integration. *Personality & Social Psychology Review, 3,* 278–302.

Thompson, L. L., Levine, J. M., & Messick, D. M. (1999). *Shared cognition in organizations: The management of knowledge.* Mahwah, NJ: Erlbaum.

Thompson, M. M., Naccarato, M. E., & Parker, K. E. (1989). *Assessing cognitive need: The development of the Personal Need for Structure (PNS) and Personal Fear of Invalidity (PFI) measures.* Paper presented at the annual meeting of the Canadian Psychological Association, Halifax, Nova Scotia.

Thompson, M. P., & Kingree, J. B. (2006). The roles of victim and perpetrator alcohol use in intimate partner violence outcomes. *Journal of Interpersonal Violence, 21,* 163–177.

Thompson, S. (1999). Illusions of control: How we overestimate our personal influence. *Current Directions in Psychological Science, 8,* 187–190.

Thompson, S. C., & Schlehofer, M. M. (2008). Control, denial, and heightened sensitivity to personal threat: Testing the generality of the threat orientation approach. *Personality and Social Psychology Bulletin, 34,* 1070–1083.

Thompson, S. C., Sobolow-Shubin, A., Galbraith, M. E., Schwankovsky, L., & Cruzen, D. (1993). Maintaining perceptions of control: Finding control in low-control circumstances. *Journal of Personality and Social Psychology, 64,* 293–304.

Tibon, S. (2000). Personality traits and peace negotiations: Integrative complexity and attitudes toward the Middle East peace process. *Group Decision and Negotiation, 9,* 1–15.

Tibon, S., & Blumberg, H. H. (1999). Authoritarianism and political socialization in the context of the Arab-Israeli conflict. *Political Psychology, 20,* 581–591.

Tice, D. M. (1991). Esteem protection or enhancement? Self-handicapping motives and attributions differ by trait self-esteem. *Journal of Personality and Social Psychology, 60,* 711–725.

Tice, D. M. (1992). Self-concept change and self-presentation: The looking glass self is also a magnifying glass. *Journal of Personality and Social Psychology, 63,* 435–451.

Tice, D. M. (1993). The social motivations of people with low self-esteem. In R. Baumeister (Ed.), *Self-esteem: The puzzle of low self-regard* (pp. 37–54). New York: Plenum.

Tice, D. M., Butler, J. L., Muraven, M. B., & Stillwell, A. M. (1995). When modesty prevails: Differential favorability of self-presentation to friends and strangers. *Journal of Personality and Social Psychology, 69,* 1120–1138.

Tice, D. M., & Wallace, H. M. (2003). The reflected self: Creating yourself as (you think) others see you. In M. R. Leary & J. P. Tangney (Eds.), *Handbook of self identity* (pp. 91–105). New York: Guilford Press.

Tiedens, L. Z., & Fragale, A. R. (2003). Power moves: Complementarity in dominant and submissive nonverbal behavior. *Journal of Personality and Social Psychology, 84,* 558–568.

Tietjen, A. M. (1994). Children's social networks and social supports in cultural context. In W. J. Lonner & R. Malpass (Eds.), *Psychology and culture* (pp. 101–106). Boston: Allyn & Bacon.

Tinbergen, N. (1968). On war and peace in animals and man. *Science, 160,* 1411–1418.

Tindale, R. S., & Davis, J. H. (1983). Group decision making and jury verdicts. In H. H. Blumberg, A. P. Hare, V. Kent, & M. F. Davies (Eds.), *Small groups and social interaction* (Vol. 2, pp. 9–38). Chichester, UK: Wiley.

Tindale, R. S., Davis, J. H., Vollrath, D. A., Nagao, D. H., & Hinsz, V. B. (1990). Asymmetrical social influence in freely interacting groups: A test of three models. *Journal of Personality and Social Psychology, 58,* 438–449.

Tindale, R. S., & Sheffen, S. (2002). Shared information, cognitive load, and group memory. *Group Processes and Intergroup Relations, 5,* 5–18.

Tinsley, C., & Weldon, E. (2003). Responses to a normative conflict among American and Chinese managers. *International Journal of Cross-Cultural Management, 3,* 181–192.

Titchener, E. B. (1909). *Elementary psychology of the thought processes.* New York: Macmillan.

Toch, H. (1969). *Violent men: An inquiry into the psychology of violence.* Chicago, IL: Aldine.

Toch, H. (1984). *Violent men.* Cambridge: Schenkman.

Todd, P. M., Hertwig, R., & Hoffrage, U. (2005). Evolutionary cognitive psychology. In D. M. Buss (Ed.), *The handbook of evolutionary psychology* (pp. 776–802). New York: Wiley.

Tokayer, M., & Swartz, M. (1979). *The Fugu plan: The untold story of the Japanese and the Jews during World War II.* New York: Paddington.

Tolmacz, R. (2004). Attachment style and willingness to compromise when choosing a mate. *Journal of Social and Personal Relationships, 21,* 267–272.

Toma, C. L., Hancock, J. T., & Ellison, N. B. (2008). Separating fact from fiction: An examination of deceptive self-presentation in online dating profiles. *Personality and Social Psychology Bulletin, 34,* 1023–1036.

Tombs, S., & Silverman, I. (2004). Pupillometry: A sexual selection approach. *Evolution and Human Behavior, 25,* 221–228.

Tomkins, S. S. (1980). Affect as amplification: Some modifications in theory. In R. Plutchik & H. Kellerman (Eds.), *Emotion: Theory, research and experience: Vol. 1: Theories of emotion* (pp. 141–164). New York: Academic Press.

Tooby, J., & Cosmides, L. (1992). The psychological foundations of culture. In J. H. Barkow, L. Cosmides, & J. Tooby (Eds.), *The adapted mind: Evolutionary psychology and the generation of culture* (pp. 19–136). New York: Oxford University Press.

Tooby, J., & Cosmides, L. (2005). Conceptual foundations of evolutionary psychology. In D. M. Buss (Ed.), *The handbook of evolutionary psychology* (pp. 5–67). New York: Wiley.

Toppe, C. M., Kirsch, A. D., & Michel, J. (2001). *Giving and volunteering in the United States.* Washington, DC: Independent Sector.

Torestad, B. (1990). What is anger provoking? A psychophysical study of perceived causes of anger. *Aggressive Behavior, 16,* 9–26.

Tormala, Z. L., & DeSensi, V. L. (2009). The effects of minority/majority source status on attitude certainty: A matching perspective. *Personality and Social Psychology Bulletin, 35,* 114–125.

Tormala, Z. L., & Petty, R. E. (2002). What doesn't kill me makes me stronger: The effects of resisting persuasion on attitude certainty. *Journal of Personality and Social Psychology, 83,* 1298–1313.

Townsend, E. J. (1973). An examination of participants in organizational, political, informational, and interpersonal activities. *Journal of Voluntary Action Research, 2,* 200–211.

Townsend, J. M., & Levy, G. D. (1990). Effects of potential partner's costume and physical attractiveness on sexuality and partner selection: Sex differences in reported preferences of university students. *Journal of Psychology, 124,* 371–376.

Townsend, J. M., & Roberts, L. W. (1993). Gender differences in mate preferences among law students: Diverging and converging criteria. *Journal of Psychology, 127,* 507–528.

Townsend, M. A., McCracken, H. E., & Wilton, K. M. (1988). Popularity and intimacy as determinants of psychological well-being in adolescent friendships. *Journal of Early Adolescence, 8,* 421–436.

Trafimow, D., & Finlay, K. A. (1996). The importance of subjective norms for a majority of people: Between-subjects and within-subjects. *Personality and Social Psychology Bulletin, 22,* 820–828.

Trautmann-Lengsfeld, S., & Herrmann, C. S. (2013). EEG reveals an early influence of social conformity on visual processing in group pressure situations. *Social Neuroscience, 8*(1), 75–89. Retrieved from http://dx.doi.org/10.1080/17470919.2012.742927

Trawalter, S., Todd, A. R., Baird, A. A., & Richeson, J. A. (2008). Attending to threat: Race-based patterns of selective attention. *Journal of Experimental Social Psychology, 44,* 1322–1327.

Triandis, H. C. (1989). The self and social behavior in differing cultural contexts. *Psychological Review, 96,* 506–520.

Triandis, H. C. (1994). *Culture and social behavior.* New York: McGraw-Hill.

Triplett, N. (1897–1898). The dynamogenic factors in pacemaking and competition. *American Journal of Psychology, 9,* 507–533.

Trivers, R. L. (1971). The evolution of reciprocal altruism. *Quarterly Review of Biology, 46,* 35–37.

Trope, Y., & Thompson, E. P. (1997). Looking for truth in all the wrong places? Asymmetric search of individuating information about stereotypes group members. *Journal of Personality and Social Psychology, 73,* 229–241.

Tropp, L. R., & Brown, A. C. (2004). What benefits the group can also benefit the individual: Group enhancing and individual-enhancing motives for collective action. *Group Processes and Intergroup Relations, 7,* 267–282.

Tsai, J. L., Knutson, B., & Fung, H. H. (2006). Cultural variation in affect valuation. *Journal of Personality and Social Psychology, 90,* 288–307.

Turan, B., & Vicary, A. M. (2010). Who recognizes and choose behaviors that are best for a relationship? The separate roles of knowledge, attachment, and motivation. *Personality and Social Bulletin, 36*(1), 119–131.

Turner, J. C. (1991). *Social influence.* Pacific Grove, CA: Brooks/Cole.

Turner, S. (1978, January 8). The life and times of a pickle packer. *Boston Globe Magazine,* p. 10.

Turnley, W. H., & Bolino, M. C. (2001). Achieving desired images while avoiding undesired images: Exploring the role of self-monitoring in impression management. *Journal of Applied Psychology, 86,* 351–360.

Tversky, A., & Kahneman, D. (1973). Availability: A heuristic for judging frequency and probability. *Cognitive Psychology, 5,* 207–232.

Tversky, A., & Kahneman, D. (1974). Judgment under uncertainty: Heuristics and biases. *Science, 185,* 1124–1131.

Tversky, A., & Shafir, E. (1992a). The disjunction effect in choice under uncertainty. *Psychological Science, 3,* 305–309.

Tversky, A., & Shafir, E. (1992b). Choice under conflict: The dynamics of deferred decision. *Psychological Science, 3,* 358–361.

Twenge, J. M., & Campbell, W. K. (2003). "Isn't it fun to get the respect that we're going to deserve?" Narcissism, social rejection, and aggression. *Personality & Social Psychology Bulletin, 29,* 261–272.

Twenge, J. M., Catanese, K. R., & Baumeister, R. F. (2002). Social exclusion causes self-defeating behavior. *Journal of Personality & Social Psychology, 83,* 606–615.

Twenge, J. M., Zhang, L., & Im, C. (2004). It's beyond my control: A cross-temporal meta-analysis of increasing externality in locus of control, 1960–2002. *Personality and Social Psychology Review, 8,* 308–319.

Tybout, A. M., & Yalch, R. F. (1980). The effect of experience: A matter of salience? *Journal of Consumer Research, 6,* 406–413.

Tybur, J. M., Lieberman, D. L., & Griskevicius, V. G. (2009). Microbes, mating, and morality: Individual differences in three functional domains of disgust. *Journal of Personality and Social Psychology, 29,* 103–122.

Tykocinski, O. E., & Steinberg, N. (2005). Coping with disappointing outcomes: Retroactive pessimism and motivated inhibition of counterfactuals. *Journal of Experimental Social Psychology, 41,* 551–558.

Tyler, J. M. (2012). Triggering self-presentation efforts outside of people's conscious awareness. *Personality and Social Psychology Bulletin, 38*(5), 619–627.

Tyler, J. M., & Feldman, R. S. (2005). Deflecting threat to one's image: Dissembling personal information as a self-presentation strategy. *Basic and Applied Social Psychology, 27,* 371–378.

Tyler, J. M., & Feldman, R. S. (2007). The double-edged sword of excuses: When do they help, when do they hurt. *Journal of Social and Clinical Psychology, 26,* 659–688.

Tyler, T. R., & Degoey, P. (1995). Trust in organizational authorities: The influence of motive attributions on willingness to accept decisions. In R. Kramer & T. R. Tyler (Eds.), *Trust in organizational authorities* (pp. 331–356). Beverly Hills, CA: Sage.

U.S. Department of Labor. (2014). *Labor force statistics from the Current Population Survey.* Retrieved April 28, 2014, from http://www.bls.gov/cps/cpsaat11.htm

U.S. Merit Systems Protection Board. (1988). *Sexual harassment in the federal workplace: An update.* Washington, DC: U.S. Government Printing Office.

Udry, J. R., Billy, J. O. G., Morris, N. M., Groff, T. R., & Raj, M. H. (1985). Serum androgenic hormones motivate sexual behavior in adolescent boys. *Fertility and Sterility, 43,* 90–94.

Uleman, J. S., Saribay, S. A., & Gonzalez, C. M. (2008). Spontaneous inferences, implicit impressions, and implicit theories. *Annual Review of Psychology, 59,* 329–360.

Unkelbach, C., Forgas, J. P., & Denson, T. F. (2008). The turban effect: The influence of Muslim headgear and induced affect on aggressive responses in the shooter bias paradigm. *Journal of Experimental Social Psychology, 44,* 1409–1413.

Unlikely Friendship Curriculum Development and Planning Team. (2003). *An unlikely friendship: Curriculum and video guide.* Chapel Hill, NC: FPG Child Development Institute.

U.S. Federal Bureau of Investigation. (2007). *Hate crime statistics.* Retrieved February 10, 2009, from www.fbi.gov/ucr/hc2007/incidents.htm

U.S. Federal Bureau of Investigation. (2012). *Hate crime statistics.* Retrieved April 28, 2014, from http://www.fbi.gov/news/pressrel/press-releases/fbi-releases-2012-hate-crime-statistics

Uskul, A. K., Kitayama, S., & Nisbett, R. E. (2008). Ecocultural basis of cognition: Farmers and fishermen are more holistic than herders. *PNAS, 105,* 8552–8556.

Uslaner, E. M. (2008). Where you stand depends on where you grandparents sat. *Public Opinion Quarterly, 72,* 725–740.

Utz, S. (2004a). Self-construal and cooperation: Is the interdependent self more cooperative than the independent self. *Self and Identity, 3,* 177–190.

Utz, S. (2004b). Self-activation is a twoedged sword: The effects of I primes on cooperation. *Journal of Experimental Social Psychology, 40,* 769–776.

Utz, S., Ouwerkerk, J. W., & Van Lange, P. A. M. (2004). What is smart in a social dilemma? Differential effects of priming competence on cooperation. *European Journal of Social Psychology, 34,* 317–332.

Väänänen, A., Buunk, B. P., Kiyimäki, M., Pentti, J., & Vahtera, J. (2005). When it is better to give than to receive: Long-term effects of perceived reciprocity in support exchange. *Journal of Personality and Social Psychology, 89,* 176–193.

Vallacher, R. R., Read, S. J., & Nowak, A. (2002). The dynamical perspective in personality and social psychology. *Personality & Social Psychology Review, 6,* 264–273.

Vallacher, R. R., & Wegner, D. M. (1985). *A theory of action identification.* Hillsdale, NJ: Erlbaum.

Vallacher, R. R., & Wegner, D. M. (1987). What do people think they're doing? Action identification and human behavior. *Psychological Review, 94,* 3–15.

Vallone, R. P., Ross, L., & Lepper, M. R. (1985). The hostile media phenomenon: Biased perception and perceptions of media bias coverage of the Beirut massacre. *Journal of Personality and Social Psychology, 49,* 577–585.

Van Baaren, R. B., Holland, R. W., Kawakami, K., & van Knippenberg, A. (2004). Mimicry and prosocial behavior. *Psychological Science, 15,* 71–74.

van Beest, I., & Williams, K. D. (2006). When inclusion costs and ostracism pays, ostracism still hurts. *Journal of Personality and Social Psychology, 91,* 918–928.

van Bommel, M., van Prooijen, J., Elfers, H., & van Lange, P. A. M. (2012). Be aware to care: Public self-awareness leads to a reversal of the bystander effect. *Journal of Experimental Social Psychology, 48*(4), 926–930.

Van Boven, L. (2005). Experientialism, materialism, and the pursuit of happiness. *Review of General Psychology, 9,* 132–142.

Van Boven, L., Kruger, J., Savitsky, K., & Gilovich, T. (2000). When social worlds collide: Overconfidence in the multiple audience problem. *Personality and Social Psychology Bulletin, 26,* 619–628.

van den Bergh, B., & Dewitte, S. (2006). The robustness of the "raise-the-stakes" strategy: Coping with exploitation in noisy Prisoner's Dilemma games. *Evolution and Human Behavior, 27,* 19–28.

van den Berghe, P. L. (1983). Human inbreeding avoidance: Culture in nature. *Behavioral and Brain Sciences, 6,* 91–123.

van der Plight, J., & Eiser, J. R. (1984). Dimensional salience, judgment, and attitudes. In J. R. Eiser (Ed.), *Attitudinal judgment* (pp. 161–177). New York: Springer-Verlag.

Van Goozen, S. H. M., Cohen-Kettenis, P. T., Gooren, L. J. G., Frijda, N. H., & VandePoll, N. E. (1995). Gender differences in behaviour: Activating effects of cross-sex hormones. *Psychoneuroendocrinology, 20,* 343–363.

van Knippenberg, D., De Dreu, C. K. W., & Homan, A. C. (2004). Work group diversity and group performance: An integrative model and research agenda. *Journal of Applied Psychology, 89,* 1008–1022.

van Knippenberg, D., & Schippers, M. C. (2007). Work group diversity. *Annual Review of Psychology, 58,* 515–541.

Van Laar, C., Levin, S., Sinclair, S., & Sidanius, J. (2005). The effect of college roommate contact on ethnic attitudes and behaviors. *Journal of Experimental Social Psychology, 41,* 329–345.

Van Lange, P. A. M., Agnew, C. R., Harinck, F., & Steemers, G. E. M. (1997). From game theory to real life: How social value orientation affects willingness to sacrifice in ongoing close relationships. *Journal of Personality and Social Psychology, 73,* 1330–1344.

Van Lange, P. A. M., & Liebrand, W. B. (1991). The influence of other's morality and own social value orientation on cooperation in the Netherlands and the U.S.A. *International Journal of Psychology, 26,* 429–449.

Van Lange, P. A. M., Otten, W., DeBruin, E. M. N., & Joireman, J. A. (1997). Development of prosocial, individualistic, and competitive orientations: Theory and preliminary evidence. *Journal of Personality and Social Psychology, 73,* 733–746.

Van Lange, P. A. M., & Rusbult, C. E. (1995). My relationship is better than— and not as bad as— yours is: The perception of superiority in close relationships. *Personality and Social Psychology Bulletin, 21,* 32–44.

Van Lange, P. A. M., & Semin-Goosens, A. (1998). The boundaries of reciprocal cooperation. *European Journal of Social Psychology, 28,* 847–854.

Van Overwalle, F., & Heylighen, F. (2006). Talking nets: A multiagent connectionist approach to communication and trust between individuals. *Psychological Review, 113,* 606–627.

Van Vugt, M. (2006). The evolutionary origins of leadership and followership. *Personality and Social Psychology Review, 10,* 354–372.

Van Vugt, M. (2009). Averting the tragedy of the commons: Using social psychological science to protect the environment. *Current Directions in Psychological Science, 18,* 169–173.

Van Vugt, M., De Cremer, D., & Janssen, D. P. (2007). Gender differences in cooperation and competition: The male-warrior hypothesis. *Psychological Science, 18,* 19–23.

Van Vugt, M., Griskevicius, V., & Schultz, P. (2014). Naturally green: Harnessing stone age psychological biases to foster environmental behavior. *Social Issues and Policy Review, 8,* 1–32.

Van Vugt, M., & Hart, C. M. (2004). Social identity as social glue: The origins of group loyalty. *Journal of Personality and Social Psychology, 86,* 585–598.

Van Vugt, M., Hogan, R., & Kaiser, R. B. (2008). Leadership, followership, and evolution: Some lessons from the past. *American Psychologist, 63,* 182–196.

Van Vugt, M., & Samuelson, C. D. (1999). The impact of personal metering in the management of a natural resource crisis: A social dilemma analysis. *Personality & Social Psychology Bulletin, 25,* 731–745.

Van Vugt, M., & Spisak, B. R. (2008). Sex differences in the emergence of leadership during competitions within and between groups. *Psychological Science, 19*(9), 854–858.

Van Vugt, M., & Van Lange, P. A. M. (2006). Psychological adaptations for prosocial behavior: The altruism puzzle. In M. Schaller, J. A. Simpson, & D. T. Kenrick (Eds.), *Evolution and social psychology* (pp. 237–261). New York: Psychology Press.

Vancouver, J. B., & Ilgen, D. R. (1989). Effects of interpersonal orientation and the sex-type of the task on choosing to work alone or in groups. *Journal of Applied Psychology, 74,* 927–934.

Vandello, J. A., & Cohen, D. (2003). Male honor and female fidelity: Implicit cultural scripts that perpetuate domestic violence. *Journal of Personality & Social Psychology, 84,* 997–1010.

VanderLaan, D. P., Forrester, D. L., Petterson, L. J., & Vasey, P. L. (2012). Offspring production among the extended relatives of Samoan men and fa'afafine. *PLoS One, 7*(4), e36088.

VanderLaan, D. P., & Vasey, P. L. (2008). Mate retention behavior of men and women in heterosexual and homosexual relationships. *Archives of Sexual Behavior, 37,* 572–585.

Vanman, E. J., Paul, B. Y., Ito, T. A., & Miller, N. (1997). The modern face of prejudice and structural features that moderate the effect of cooperation on affect. *Journal of Personality and Social Psychology, 73,* 941–959.

Vanneste, S., Verplaetse, J., Van Hiel, A., & Braeckman, J. (2007). Attention bias toward noncooperative people. A dot probe classification study in cheating detection. *Evolution and Human Behavior, 28,* 272–276.

Varnum, M. E. W., Na, J., Murata, A., & Kitayama, S. (2012). Social class differences in N400 indicate differences in spontaneous trait inference. *Journal of Experimental Psychology: General, 141,* 518–526.

Varnum, M. E. W., Shi, Z., Chen, A., Qiu, J., & Han, S. (2014). When "Your" reward is the same as "My" reward: Self-construal priming shifts neural responses to own vs. friend's rewards. *NeuroImage, 87,* 164–169.

Vasey, P. L., & VanderLaan, D. P. (2008). Avuncular tendencies and the evolution of male androphilia in Samoan. *Fa'afafine. Archives of Sexual Behavior, 37,* 572–585.

Vasey, P. L., & VanderLaan, D. P. (2010). Avuncular tendencies and the evolution of male androphilia in Samoan fa'afafine. *Archives of Sexual Behavior, 39*(4), 821–830.

Vasey, P. L., & VanderLaan, D. P. (2012). Sexual orientation in men and avuncularity in Japan: Implications for the Kin Selection Hypothesis. *Archives of Sexual Behavior, 41*(1), 209–215.

Vasquez, E. A., Denson, T. F., Pedersen, W. C., Stenstrom, D. M., & Miller, N. (2005). The moderating effect of trigger intensity on triggered displaced aggression. *Journal of Experimental Social Psychology, 41,* 61–67.

Vasquez, K., Durik, A. M., & Hyde, J. S. (2002). Family and work: Implications of adult attachment styles. *Personality & Social Psychology Bulletin, 28,* 874–886.

Veblen, T. (1899). *The theory of the leisure class: An economic study of institutions.* New York: MacMillan.

Veitch, R., & Griffitt, W. (1976). Good news, bad news: Affective and interpersonal effects. *Journal of Applied Social Psychology, 6,* 69–75.

Veroff, J. B. (1981). The dynamics of helpseeking in men and women: A national survey study. *Psychiatry, 44,* 189–200.

Verona, E., & Sullivan, E. A. (2008). Emotional catharsis and aggression revisited: Heart rate reduction following aggressive responding. *Emotion, 8,* 331–340.

Verplanken, B., & Holland, R. W. (2002). Motivated decision making: Effects of activation of self-centrality of values on choices and behavior. *Journal of Personality and Social Psychology, 82,* 434–437.

Verschuere, B., Crombez, G., De Clercq, A., & Koster, E. H. W. (2005). Psychopathic traits and autonomic responding to concealed information in a prison sample. *Psychophysiology, 42,* 239–245.

Vescio, T. K., Sechrist, G. B., & Paolucci, M. P. (2003). Perspective taking and prejudice reduction: The mediational role of empathy arousal and situational attributions. *European Journal of Social Psychology, 33,* 455–472.

Vilela, B. B., González, J. A. V., Ferrín, P. F., & del Río Araújo, M. (2007). Impression management tactics and affective context: Influence on sales performance appraisal. *European Journal of Marketing, 41,* 624–639.

Vinokur, A. D., Price, R. H., & Caplan, R. D. (1996). Hard times and hurtful partners: How financial strain affects depression and relationship satisfaction of unemployed persons and their spouses. *Journal of Personality & Social Psychology, 71,* 166–179.

Visser, P. S., & Krosnick, J. A. (1998). Development of attitude strength over the life cycle: Surge and decline. *Journal of Personality and Social Psychology, 75,* 1389–1410.

Visser, P. S., & Mirabile, R. R. (2004). Attitudes in the social context: The impact of social network composition on individual-level attitude strength. *Journal of Personality and Social Psychology, 87,* 779–795.

Vohs, K. D., Baumeister, R. F., & Ciarocco, N. J. (2005). Self-regulation and self-presentation: Regulatory resource depletion impairs impression management and effortful self-presentation depletes regulatory resources. *Journal of Personality and Social Psychology, 88,* 632–657.

Vohs, K. D., & Schmeichel, B. J. (2003). Self-regulation and extended now: Controlling the self alters the subjective experience of time. *Journal of Personality & Social Psychology, 85,* 217–230.

von Baeyer, C. L., Sherk, D. L., & Zanna, M. P. (1981). Impression management in the job interview: When the female applicant meets the male (chauvinist) interviewer. *Personality and Social Psychology Bulletin, 7,* 45–51.

von Hippel, W., & Gonsalkorale, K. (2005). "That is bloody revolting!": Inhibitory control of thoughts better left unsaid. *Psychological Science, 16,* 497–500.

von Hippel, W., Sekaquaptewa, D., & Vargas, P. (1997). The linguistic intergroup bias as an implicit indicator of prejudice. *Journal of Experimental Social Psychology, 33,* 490–509.

Vonk, R. (2002). Self-serving interpretations of flattery: Why ingratiation works. *Journal of Personality and Social Psychology, 82,* 515–526.

Vorauer, J. D., & Turpie, C. (2004). Disruptive effects of vigilance on dominant group members' treatment of outgroup members: Choking versus shining under pressure. *Journal of Personality and Social Psychology, 87,* 384–399.

Vrugt, A., & Koenis, S. (2002). Perceived self-efficacy, personal goals, social comparison, and scientific productivity. *Applied Psychology: An International Review, 51,* 593–607.

Vrugt, A., & Van Eechoud, M. (2002). Smiling and self-presentation of men and women for job photographs. *European Journal of Social Psychology, 32,* 419–431.

Wade, T. J. (2000). Evolutionary theory and self-perception: Sex differences in body esteem predictors of self-perceived physical and sexual attractiveness and self-esteem. *International Journal of Psychology, 35,* 36–45.

Wagner, J. D., Flinn, M. V., & England, B. G. (2002). Hormonal response to competition among male coalitions. *Evolution and Human Behavior, 23,* 437–442.

Wakefield, M. (2002, June 22). *The spectator.* Retrieved from http://www.spectator.co.uk /article.php3?table=old&section=current&issue=2002-06-22&id=1978

Waldrop, M. M. (1992). *Complexity: The emerging science at the edge of order and chaos.* New York: Simon & Schuster.

Walker, S., Richardson, D. S., & Green, L. R. (2000). Aggression among older adults: The relationship of interaction networks and gender role to direct and indirect responses. *Aggressive Behavior, 26,* 145–154.

Wallace, M. D. (1979). Arms races and escalations: Some new evidence. In J. D. Singer (Ed.), *Explaining war: Selected papers from the correlates of war project* (pp. 240–252). Beverly Hills, CA: Sage.

Wallach, M. A., Kogan, N., & Bem, D. J. (1962). Group influence on individual risk taking. *Journal of Abnormal and Social Psychology, 65,* 75–86.

Waller, N. G., Kojetin, B. A., Bouchard, T. J., Jr., Lykken, D. T., & Tellegen, A. (1990). Genetic and environmental influences on religious interests, attitudes, and values: A study of twins reared apart and together. *Psychological Science, 1,* 138–142.

Walter, A. (1997). The evolutionary psychology of mate selection in Morocco—A multivariate analysis. *Human Nature, 8,* 113–137.

Wann, D. L., & Grieve, F. G. (2005). Biased evaluations of in-group and outgroup spectator behavior at sporting events: The importance of team identification and threats to social identity. *Journal of Social Psychology, 145,* 531–545.

Warburton, J., & Terry, D. J. (2000). Volunteer decision making by older people. *Basic and Applied Social Psychology, 22,* 245–257.

Washington Post-ABC News National Poll. (2014). *March 2014 Post-ABC national poll: Politics, 2014 midterms, gay marriage.* Retrieved April 28, 2014, from http://www.washingtonpost.com /page/2010-2019/WashingtonPost/2014/03/05 /National-Politics/Polling/question_13288.xml?uuid=VWqBHKQjEeO4ZTiyVNkgYw

Watanabe, T. (1994, March 20). An unsung "Schindler" from Japan. *Los Angeles Times,* p. 1.

Watson, D., & Humrichouse, J. (2006). Personality development in emerging adulthood: Integrating evidence from self-ratings and spouse ratings. *Journal of Personality and Social Psychology, 91,* 904–917.

Watson, W. E., Kumar, K., & Michaelsen, L. K. (1993). Cultural diversity's impact on interaction process and performance: Comparing homogeneous and diverse task groups. *Academy of Management Journal, 36,* 590–602.

Watson, W., Michaelsen, L. K., & Sharp, W. (1991). Member competence, group interaction, and group decision making: A longitudinal study. *Journal of Applied Psychology, 76,* 803–809.

Wayne, S. J., & Ferris, G. R. (1990). Influence tactics, affect, and exchange quality in supervisor-subordinate interactions: A laboratory experiment and field study. *Journal of Applied Psychology, 75,* 487–499.

Wayneforth, D., Delwadia, S., & Camm, M. (2005). The influence of women's mating strategies on preference for masculine facial architecture. *Evolution and Human Behavior, 26,* 409–416.

Weary, G. (1980). Examination of affect and egotism as mediators of bias in causal attributions. *Journal of Personality and Social Psychology, 38,* 348–357.

Weary, G., Marsh, K. L., Gleicher, F., & Edwards, J. A. (1993). Depression, control motivation, and the processing of information about others. In G. Weary, F. Gleicher, & K. L. Marsh (Eds.), *Control motivation and social cognition* (pp. 255–287). New York: Springer-Verlag.

Weber, J. M., & Murnighan, J. K. (2008). Suckers or saviors? Consistent contributors in social dilemmas. *Journal of Personality and Social Psychology, 95,* 1340–1353.

Weber, R., & Crocker, J. (1983). Cognitive processes in the revision of stereotypic beliefs. *Journal of Personality and Social Psychology, 45,* 961–977.

Webster, D. M. (1993). Motivated augmentation and reduction of the overattribution bias. *Journal of Personality and Social Psychology, 65,* 261–271.

Webster, G. D. (2003). Prosocial behavior in families: Moderators of resource sharing. *Journal of Experimental Social Psychology, 39,* 644–652.

Webster, G. D., & Bryan, A. (2007). Sociosexual attitudes and behaviors: Why two factors are better than one. *Journal of Research in Personality, 41,* 917–922.

Wechsler, H., Lee, J. E., Kuo, M., & Lee, H. (2000). College binge drinking in the 1990s: A continuing problem: Results of the Harvard School of Public Health 1999 College Alcohol Study. *Journal of American College Health, 48,* 199–210.

Wechsler, H., & Nelson, T. F. (2008). What we have learned from the Harvard School of Public Health College Alcohol Study: Focusing attention on college student alcohol consumption and the environmental conditions that promote it. *Journal of Studies on Alcohol and Drugs, 69,* 481–490.

Weeden, J., Cohen, A. B., & Kenrick, D. T. (2008). Religious attendance as reproductive support. *Evolution and Human Behavior, 29,* 327–334.

Weeden, J., & Kurzban, R. (2013). What predicts religiosity? A multinational analysis of reproductive and cooperative morals. *Evolution and Human Behavior, 34*(6), 440–445.

Weeden, J., & Sabini, J. (2005). Physical attractiveness and health in Western societies: A review. *Psychological Bulletin, 131,* 635–653.

Wegner, D. M. (1987). Transactive memory: A contemporary analysis of the group mind. In B. Mullen & G. R. Goethals (Eds.), *Theories of group behavior* (pp. 185–208). New York: Springer-Verlag.

Wegner, D. M. (1995). A computer network model of human transactive memory. *Social Cognition, 13,* 319–339.

Wegner, D. M., & Erber, R. (1992). The hyperaccessibility of suppressed thoughts. *Journal of Personality and Social Psychology, 63,* 903–912.

Wegner, D. M., Erber, R., & Raymond, P. (1991). Transactive memory in close relationships. *Journal of Personality and Social Psychology, 61,* 923–929.

Wegner, D. M., Schneider, D. J., Carter, S., III, & Whire, L. (1987). Paradoxical effects of thought suppression. *Journal of Personality and Social Psychology, 58,* 409–418.

Weigel, R. H., Wiser, P. L., & Cook, S. W. (1975). The impact of cooperative learning experiences on cross-ethnic relations and attitudes. *Journal of Social Issues, 31,* 219–244.

Weiner, T., Johnston, D., & Lewis, N. A. (1995). *Betrayal: The story of Aldrich Ames, an American spy.* New York: Random House.

Weinstein, N. D., & Klein, W. M. (1996). Unrealistic optimism: Present and future. *Journal of Social and Clinical Psychology, 15,* 1–8.

Weis, K. (2006). Individualism, collectivism, and the psychology of love. In R. J. Sternberg & K. Weis (Eds.), *New psychology of love* (pp. 313–326). New Haven, CT: Yale University Press.

Weisfeld, G. (1994). Aggression and dominance in the social world of boys. In J. Archer (Ed.), *Male violence* (pp. 43–69). New York: Routledge.

Wells, G. L., & Olsen, E. A. (2003). Eyewitness testimony. *Annual Review of Psychology, 54,* 277–295.

Wells, G. L., Olson, E. A., & Charman, S. D. (2002). The confidence of eyewitnesses in their identifications from lineups. *Current Directions in Psychological Science, 11,* 151–154.

Wenzlaff, R. M., & Wegner, D. M. (2000). Thought suppression. *Annual Review of Psychology, 51,* 93–120.

West, S. G., Gunn, S. P., & Chernicky, P. (1975). Ubiquitous Watergate: An attributional analysis. *Journal of Personality and Social Psychology, 32,* 55–66.

West, S. L., & O'Neal, K. K. (2004). Project D.A.R.E. outcome effectiveness revisited. *American Journal of Public Health, 94,* 1027–1029.

Westerwick, A. (2013). Effects of sponsorship, web site design, and google ranking on the credibility of online information. *Journal of Computer-Mediated Communication, 18*(2), 80–97.

Westra, H. A., & Kuiper, N. A. (1992). Type A, irrational cognitions, and situational factors relating to stress. *Journal of Research in Personality, 26,* 1–20.

Weyant, J. (1978). Effects of mood states, costs, and benefits on helping. *Journal of Personality and Social Psychology, 10,* 1169–1176.

Wheeler, L., Reis, H., & Nezlek, J. (1983). Loneliness, social interaction, and sex roles. *Journal of Personality and Social Psychology, 45,* 943–953.

Wheeler, S. C., & DeMarree, K. G. (2009). Multiple mechanisms of prime-to-behavior effects. *Social and Personality Psychology Compass, 3*(4), 566–581.

White, A. E., Kenrick, D. T., & Neuberg, S. L. (2013). Beauty at the ballot box: Disease threats predict preferences for physically attractive leaders. *Psychological Science, 24*(12), 2429–2436.

White, G. L., Fishbein, S., & Rutstein, J. (1981). Passionate love: The misattribution of arousal. *Journal of Personality and Social Psychology, 41,* 56–62.

White, G. L., & Kight, T. D. (1984). Misattribution of arousal and attraction: Effects of salience of explanation of arousal. *Journal of Experimental Social Psychology, 20,* 55–64.

White, G. M. (1980). Conceptual universals in interpersonal language. *American Anthropologist, 82,* 759–781.

White, L. C. (1988). *Merchants of death.* New York: Morrow.

White, R. K., & Lippitt, R. (1960). *Autocracy and democracy: An experimental inquiry.* New York: Harper & Brothers.

White, R. W. (1959). Motivation reconsidered: The concept of competence. *Psychological Review, 66,* 297–333.

Whitley, B. E., Jr. (1999). Right-wing authoritarianism, social dominance orientation, and prejudice. *Journal of Personality & Social Psychology, 77,* 126–134.

Whitley, B. E., & Lee, S. E. (2000). The relationship of authoritarianism and related constructs to attitudes toward homosexuality. *Journal of Applied Social Psychology, 30,* 144–170.

Whyte, G. (1989). Groupthink reconsidered. *Academy of Management Review, 14,* 40–56.

Widmeyer, W. N. (1990). Group composition in sport. *International Journal of Sport Psychology, 21,* 264–285.

Wiederman, M. W. (1993). Evolved gender differences in mate preferences: Evidence from personal advertisements. *Ethology and Sociobiology, 14,* 331–352.

Wiederman, M. W., & Allgeier, E. R. (1992). Gender differences in mate selection criteria: Sociobiological or socioeconomic explanation? *Ethology and Sociobiology, 13,* 115–124.

Wiederman, M. W., & Hurd, C. (1999). Extradyadic involvement during dating. *Journal of Social & Personal Relationships, 16,* 265–274.

Wiederman, M. W., & Kendall, E. (1999). Evolution, sex, and jealousy: Investigation with a sample from Sweden. *Evolution & Human Behavior, 20,* 121–128.

Wiegman, O., Kuttschreuter, M., & Baarda, B. (1992). A longitudinal study of the effects of television viewing on aggressive and prosocial behaviors. *British Journal of Social Psychology, 31,* 147–164.

Wiersema, M. F., & Bantel, K. A. (1992). Top management team demography and corporate strategic change. *Academy of Management Journal, 35,* 91–121.

Wiggins, J. S., & Broughton, R. (1985). The interpersonal circle: A structural model for the integration of personality research. In R. Hogan & W. H. Jones (Eds.), *Perspectives in personality* (Vol. 1, pp. 1–48). Greenwich, CT: JAI Press.

Wilder, D. A. (1993). The role of anxiety in facilitating stereotypic judgments of outgroup behavior. In D. M. Mackie & D. L. Hamilton (Eds.), *Affect, cognition, and stereotyping: Interactive processes in intergroup perception* (pp. 87–109). New York: Academic Press.

Wilder, D. A., & Shapiro, P. (1989). The role of competition-induced anxiety in limiting the beneficial impact of positive behavior by an outgroup member. *Journal of Personality and Social Psychology, 56,* 60–69.

Wildschut, T., Pinter, B., Vevea, J. L., Insko, C. A., & Schopler, J. (2003). Beyond the group mind: A quantitative review of the interindividual-intergroup discontinuity effect. *Psychological Bulletin, 129,* 698–722.

Wilkowski, B. M., & Robinson, M. D. (2008). The cognitive basis of trait anger and reactive aggression: An integrative analysis. *Personality and Social Psychology Review, 12,* 3–21.

Willer, R. (2004). The effects of government-issued terror warnings on presidential approval ratings. *Current Research in Social Psychology, 10*(1), 1–12.

Williams, E. F., & Gilovich, T. (2008). Do people really believe they are above average? *Journal of Experimental Social Psychology, 44,* 1121–1128.

Williams, J. E., & Best, D. L. (1990). *Measuring sex stereotypes: A multination study.* Newbury Park, CA: Sage.

Williams, K. D. (2007). Ostracism. *Annual Review of Psychology, 58,* 425–452.

Williams, K. D., Bourgeois, M., & Croyle, R. T. (1993). The effects of stealing thunder in criminal and civil trials. *Law and Human Behavior, 17,* 597–609.

Williams, K. D., Cheung, D. K., & Choi, W. (2000). Cyberostracism: Effects of being ignored over the internet. *Journal of Personality and Social Psychology, 79,* 748–762.

Williams, K. D., Harkins, S., & Latané, B. (1981). Identifiability as a deterrent to social loafing: Two cheering experiments. *Journal of Personality and Social Psychology, 40,* 303–311.

Williams, K. D., & Karau, S. J. (1991). Social loafing and social compensation: The effects of expectations of co-worker performance. *Journal of Personality and Social Psychology, 61,* 570–581.

Williams, K. D., & Nida, S. A. (2011). Ostracism: Consequences and coping. *Current Directions in Psychological Science, 20,* 71–75.

Williams, K., Forgas, J., & von Hippel, W. (2005). *The social outcast: Ostracism, social exclusion, rejection, and bullying.* New York: Psychology Press.

Williams-Avery, R. M., & MacKinnon, D. P. (1996). Injuries and use of protective equipment among college in-line skaters. *Accident Analysis and Prevention, 28,* 779–784.

Williamson, G., & Clark, M. S. (1989). Effects of providing help to another and of relationship type on the provider's mood and self-evaluation. *Journal of Personality and Social Psychology, 56,* 722–734.

Williamson, G., Clark, M. S., Pegalis, L. J., & Behan, A. (1996). Affective consequences of refusing to help in communal and exchange relationships. *Personality and Social Psychology Bulletin, 22,* 34–47.

Williamson, S., Hare, R. D., & Wong, S. (1987). Violence: Criminal psychopaths and their victims. *Canadian Journal of Behavioral Science, 19,* 454–462.

Wills, T. A. (1981). Downward comparison principles in social psychology. *Psychological Bulletin, 90,* 245–271.

Wills, T. A., & DePaulo, B. M. (1991). Interpersonal analysis of the help-seeking process. In C. R. Snyder & D. R. Forsyth (Eds.), *Handbook of social and clinical psychology: The health perspective* (pp. 350–375). Elmsford, NY: Pergamon.

Wilson, A. E., & Ross, M. (2001). From chump to champ: People's appraisals of their earlier and present selves. *Journal of Personality & Social Psychology, 80,* 572–584.

Wilson, D. S., Timmel, J. J., & Miller, R. R. (2004). Cognitive cooperation: When the going gets tough, think as a group. *Human Nature, 15,* 225–250.

Wilson, J. P. (1976). Motivation, modeling, and altruism: A person x situation analysis. *Journal of Personality and Social Psychology, 34,* 1078–1086.

Wilson, M., & Daly, M. (1985). Competitiveness, risk taking, and violence: The young male syndrome. *Ethology and Sociobiology, 6,* 59–73.

Wilson, T. D., & LaFleur, S. J. (1995). Knowing what you'll do: Effects of analyzing reasons on self-prediction. *Journal of Personality and Social Psychology, 68,* 21–35.

Winquist, J. R., & Larson, J. R. (2004). Sources of the discontinuity effect: Playing against a group versus being in a group. *Journal of Experimental Social Psychology, 40,* 675–682.

Winter, D. G. (1973). *The power motive.* New York: Free Press.

Winter, D. G. (1987). Leader appeal, leader performance, and the motive profiles of leaders and followers: A study of American presidents and elections. *Journal of Personality and Social Psychology, 52,* 196–202.

Winter, D. D. (2000). Some big ideas for some big problems. *American Psychologist, 55,* 516–522.

Winter, D. G. (2007). The role of motivation, responsibility, and integrative complexity in crisis escalation: Comparative studies of war and peace crises. *Journal of Personality and Social Psychology, 92,* 920–937.

Wisman, A., & Goldenberg, J. L. (2005). From the grave to the cradle: Evidence that mortality salience engenders a desire for offspring. *Journal of Personality and Social Psychology, 89,* 46–61.

Wisman, A., & Koole, S. L. (2003). Hiding in the crowd: Can mortality salience promote affiliation with others who oppose one's world views? *Journal of Personality & Social Psychology, 84,* 511–526.

Wit, A. P., & Kerr, N. L. (2002). "Me versus just us versus us all" categorization and cooperation in nested social dilemmas. *Journal of Personality & Social Psychology, 83,* 616–637.

Wittenbaum, G. M., & Stasser, G. (1996). Management of information in small groups. In J. L. Nye & A. M. Brower (Eds.), *What's social about social cognition? Research on socially shared cognition in small groups* (pp. 3–28). Thousand Oaks, CA: Sage.

Wittenbrink, B., & Henly, J. R. (1996). Creating social reality: Informational social influence and the content of stereotypic beliefs. *Personality and Social Psychology Bulletin, 22,* 598–610.

Wittenbrink, B., Judd, C. M., & Park, B. (1997). Evidence for racial prejudice at the implicit level and its relationship with questionnaire measures. *Journal of Personality and Social Psychology, 72,* 262–274.

Wolf, S., & Latané, B. (1985). Conformity, innovation, and the psychosocial law. In S. Moscovici, G. Mugny, & E. Van Avermaet (Eds.), *Perspectives on minority influence* (pp. 201–215). Cambridge, UK: Cambridge University Press.

Wolfe, B. D. (1991). *The fabulous life of Diego Rivera.* New York: Cooper Square Press.

Wolfgang, M. E. (1958). *Patterns in criminal homicide.* Philadelphia: University of Pennsylvania Press.

Wong, S., Bond, M. H., & Rodriguez, P. M. (2008). The influence of cultural value orientations on self-reported emotional expression across cultures. *Journal of Cross-Cultural Psychology, 39,* 224–229.

Wood, J. V. (1989). Theory and research concerning social comparisons of personal attributes. *Psychological Bulletin, 106,* 231–248.

Wood, J. V., Giordano-Beech, M., & Ducharme, M. J. (1999). Compensating for failure through social comparison. *Personality and Social Psychology Bulletin, 25,* 1370–1386.

Wood, W., Kallgren, C. A., & Preisler, R. M. (1985). Access to attitude-relevant information in memory as a determinant of persuasion. *Journal of Experimental Social Psychology, 21,* 73–85.

Wood, W., & Neal, D. T. (2007). A new look at habits and the habit-goal interface. *Psychological Review, 114,* 843–863.

Wood, W., & Quinn, J. M. (2003). Forewarned and forearmed? Two meta-analytic syntheses of forewarnings of influence appeals. *Psychological Bulletin, 129,* 119–138.

Wood, W., & Stagner, B. (1994). Why are some people easier to influence than others? In S. Shavitt & T. C. Brock (Eds.), *Persuasion* (pp. 149–174). Boston: Allyn & Bacon.

Wood, J. V., Taylor, S. E., & Lichtman, R. R. (1985). Social comparison in adjustment to breast cancer. *Journal of Personality and Social Psychology, 49,* 1169–1183.

Wood, J. V., & Wilson, A. E. (2003). How important is social comparison? In M. R. Leary & J. P. Tangney (Eds.), *Handbook of self and identity* (pp. 344–366). New York: Guilford Press.

Wood, W., Wong, F. Y., & Chachere, J. G. (1991). Effects of media violence on viewer's aggression in unconstrained social interaction. *Psychological Bulletin, 109,* 371–383.

Wooten, D. B., & Reed, A. (1998). Informational influence and the ambiguity of product experience: Order effects on the weighting of evidence. *Journal of Consumer Psychology, 7,* 79–99.

Word, C. O., Zanna, M. P., & Cooper, J. (1974). The nonverbal mediation of self-fulfilling prophecies in interracial interaction. *Journal of Experimental Social Psychology, 10,* 109–120.

Wortman, C. B., & Linsenmeier, J. (1977). Interpersonal attraction and techniques of ingratiation. In B. Staw & G. Salancik (Eds.), *New directions in organizational behavior* (pp. 133–179). Chicago: St. Clair.

Wosinska, W., Dabul, A. J., Whetstone-Dion, R., & Cialdini, R. B. (1996). Self-presentational responses to success in the organization: The costs and benefits of modesty. *Basic and Applied Social Psychology, 18,* 229–242.

Wyer, N., Sherman, J. W., & Stroessner, S. J. (2000). The roles of motivation and ability in controlling the consequences of stereotype suppression. *Personality and Social Psychology Bulletin, 26,* 13–25.

Wyer, R. S. (2008). The role of knowledge accessibility in cognition and behavior. In C. P. Haugtvedt, P. M. Herr, & F. R. Kardes (Eds.), *Handbook of consumer psychology* (pp. 31–76). New York: Lawrence Erlbaum Associates.

Wyer, R. S., Jr., & Srull, T. K. (1986). Human cognition in its social context. *Psychological Review, 93,* 322–359.

Wylie, R. (1979). *The self-concept* (Vol. 2). Lincoln: University of Nebraska Press.

Xue, M., & Silk, J. B. (2012). The role of tracking and tolerance in relationship among friends. *Evolution and Human Behavior, 33,* 17–25.

Yamagishi, T. (1988a). Seriousness of a social dilemma and the provision of a sanctioning system. *Social Psychology Quarterly, 51,* 32–42.

Yamagishi, T. (1988b). The provision of a sanctioning system in the United States and Japan. *Social Psychology Quarterly, 51,* 264–270.

Yamagishi, T., & Cook, K. S. (1993). Generalized exchange and social dilemmas. *Social Psychology Quarterly, 56,* 235–248.

Yamagishi, T., Hashimoto, H., Cook, K. S., Kiyonari, T., Shinada, M., Mifune, N., et al. (2012). Modesty in self-presentation: A comparison between the USA and Japan. *Asian Journal of Social Psychology, 15*(1), 60–68.

Yamagishi, T., Tanida, S., Mashima, R., Shimoma, E., & Kanazawa, S. (2003). You can judge a book by its cover: Evidence that cheaters may look different from cooperators. *Evolution and Human Behavior, 24,* 290–301.

Yamaguchi, S., Greenwald, A. G., Banaji, M. R., Murakami, F., Chen, D., Shiomura, K., et al. (2007). Apparent universality of positive implicit self-esteem. *Psychological Science, 18,* 498–500.

Yates, S. M., & Aronson, E. (1983). A social psychological perspective on energy conservation in residential buildings. *American Psychologist, 38*(4), 435–444.

Yuki, M., Maddux, W. W., & Masuda, T. (2007). Are the windows to the soul the same in the East and West? Cultural differences in using the eyes and mouth as cues to recognize emotions in Japan and the United States. *Journal of Experimental Social Psychology, 43,* 303–311.

Yun, S., Takeuchi, R., & Liu, W. (2007). Employee self-enhancement motives and job performance behaviors: Investigating the moderating effects of employee role ambiguity and managerial perceptions of employee commitment. *Journal of Applied Psychology, 92,* 745–756.

Zaccaro, S. J. (1984). Social loafing: The role of task attractiveness. *Personality and Social Psychology Bulletin, 10,* 99–106.

Zaccaro, S. J. (1991). Nonequivalent associations between forms of cohesiveness and group-related outcomes: Evidence for multidimensionality. *Journal of Social Psychology, 131,* 387–399.

Zaccaro, S. J., & Lowe, C. A. (1988). Cohesiveness and performance on an additive task: Evidence for multidimensionality. *Journal of Social Psychology, 128,* 547–558.

Zahn-Waxler, C., Robinson, J. L., & Emde, R. N. (1992). The development of empathy in twins. *Developmental Psychology, 28,* 1038–1047.

Zajac, R. J., & Hartup, W. W. (1997). Friends as co-workers: Research review and classroom implications. *Elementary School Journal, 98,* 3–13.

Zajonc, R. B. (1965). Social facilitation. *Science, 149,* 269–274.

Zajonc, R. B. (1968). Attitudinal effects of mere exposure. *Journal of Personality and Social Psychology Monographs, 9*(2, part 2), 1–27.

Zajonc, R. B. (1980). Feeling and thinking: Preferences need no inferences. *American Psychologist, 35,* 151–175.

Zander, A. (1985). *The purposes of groups and organizations.* San Francisco: Jossey-Bass.

Zanna, M. P., & Pack, S. J. (1975). On the self-fulfilling nature of apparent sex differences in behavior. *Journal of Experimental Social Psychology, 11,* 583–591.

Zautra, A. J., Johnson, L. M., & Davis, M. C. (2005). Positive affect as a source of resilience for women in chronic pain. *Journal of Consulting and Clinical Psychology, 73,* 212–220.

Zebrowitz, L. A. (1994). Facial maturity and political prospects: Persuasive, culpable, and powerful faces. In R. C. Schank & E. Langer (Eds.), *Beliefs, reasoning, and decision making: Psychologic in honor of Bob Abelson* (pp. 315–346). Hillsdale, NJ: Erlbaum.

Zebrowitz, L. A., & Collins, M. A. (1997). Accurate social perception at zero acquaintance: The affordances of a Gibsonian approach. *Personality and Social Psychology Review, 1,* 204–223.

Zebrowitz, L. A., & Montepare, J. M. (2006). The ecological approach to person perception: Evolutionary roots and contemporary offshoots. In M. Schaller, J. A. Simpson, & D. T. Kenrick (Eds.), *Evolution and social psychology* (pp. 81–113). New York: Psychology Press.

Zebrowitz, L. A., & Rhodes, G. (2002). Nature let a hundred flowers bloom: The multiple ways and wherefores of attractiveness. In G. Rhodes & L. A. Zebrowitz (Eds.), *Facial attractiveness: Evolutionary, cognitive, and social perspectives: Advances in visual cognition* (Vol. 1, pp. 261–293). Westport, CT: Ablex Publishing.

Zebrowitz, L. A., Tenenbaum, D. R., & Goldstein, L. H. (1991). The impact of job applicants' facial maturity, gender, and academic achievement on hiring recommendations. *Journal of Applied Social Psychology, 21,* 525–548.

Zebrowitz, L. A., Voinescu, L., & Collins, M. A. (1996). "Wide-eyed" and "crooked-faced": Determinants of perceived and real honesty across the life span. *Personality and Social Psychology Bulletin, 22,* 1258–1269.

Zechmeister, J. S., & Romero, C. (2002). Victim and offender accounts of interpersonal conflict: Autobiographical narratives of forgiveness and unforgiveness. *Journal of Personality & Social Psychology, 82,* 675–686.

Zeifman, D., & Hazan, C. (1997). Attachment: The pair in pair-bonds. In J. A. Simpson & D. T.

Kenrick (Eds.), *Evolutionary social psychology* (pp. 237–264). Mahwah, NJ: LEA.

Zenger, T. R., & Lawrence, B. S. (1989). Organizational demography: The differential effects of age and tenure distributions on technical communication. *Academy of Management Journal, 32,* 353–376.

Zhang, S., Morris, M. W., Cheng, C. Y., & Yap, A. J. (2013). Heritage-culture images disrupt immigrants' second-language processing through triggering first-language interference. *Proceedings of the National Academy of Sciences, 110*(28), 11272–11277.

Zhang, Z.-X., Hempel, P. S., Han, Y.-L., & Tjosvold, D. (2007). Transactive memory system links work team characteristics and performance. *Journal of Applied Psychology, 92,* 1722–1730.

Zhou, X. D., Wang, X. L., Lu, L., & Hesketh, T. (2011). The very high sex ratio in rural China: Impact on the psychosocial wellbeing of unmarried men. *Social Science & Medicine, 73,* 1422–1427.

Ziegler, R. (2013). Mood and processing of proattitudinal and counterattitudinal messages. *Personality and Social Psychology Bulletin, 39,* 482–495.

Zietsch, B. P., Morley, K. I., Shekar, S. N., Verweij, K. J. H., Keller, M. C., MacGregor, S., et al. (2008). Genetic factors predisposing to homosexuality may increase mating success in heterosexuals. *Evolution and Human Behavior, 29,* 424–433.

Zillmann, D. (1983). Transfer of excitation in emotional behavior. In J. Cacioppo & R. E. Petty (Eds.), *Social psychophysiology* (pp. 215–240). New York: Guilford.

Zillmann, D. (1994). Cognition-excitation interdependencies in the escalation of anger and angry aggression. In M. Potegal & J. F. Knutson (Eds.), *Dynamics of aggression: Biological and social processes in dyads and groups* (pp. 45–71). Hillsdale, NJ: Erlbaum.

Zillmann, D., & Weaver, J. B., III. (1999). Effects of prolonged exposure to gratuitous violence on provoked and unprovoked hostile behavior. *Journal of Applied Social Psychology, 29,* 145–165.

Zimbardo, P. G. (1969). The human choice: Individuation, reason, and order versus deindividuation, impulse, and chaos. In W. J. Arnold & D. Levine (Eds.), *Nebraska Symposium on Motivation, 1969* (Vol. 17, pp. 237–307). Lincoln: University of Nebraska.

Zimbardo, P. G. (1997, May). What messages are behind today's cults? *APA Monitor,* p. 14.

Zitek, E. M., & Hebl, M. R. (2007). The role of social norm clarity in the influenced expression of prejudice over time. *Journal of Experimental Social Psychology, 43,* 867–876.

Zou, X., Morris, M. W., & Benet-Martínez, V. (2008). Identity motives and cultural priming: Cultural (dis)identification in assimilative and contrastive responses. *Journal of Experimental Social Psychology, 44,* 1151–1159.

Zuckerman, M., Kieffer, S. C., & Knee, C. R. (1998). Consequences of self-handicapping: Effects on coping, academic performance, and adjustment. *Journal of Personality and Social Psychology, 74,* 1619–1628.

Zuckerman, M., & Tsai, F.-F. (2005). Costs of self-handicapping. *Journal of Personality, 73,* 411–442.

Text Credits

Chapter 1   Page 3: J.K. Rowling, The Fringe Benefits of Failure, and the Importance of Imagination, acceptance speech for honorary degree, Harvard, June 5, 2008; 3: Blais, J. (2005). Harry Potter has been very good to J.K. Rowling. *USA Today*. July 9; 6: Ross, Edward Alsworth. (1908). *Social Psychology*: pp. 1–2; 6: Ross, Edward Alsworth. (1908). *Social Psychology*: p. 65; 16: James, W. (1890). *Principles of psychology*. New York: Henry Holt. p. 294; 19–20: Wilson, M., & Daly, M. (1985). Competitiveness, risk taking, and violence: The young male syndrome. *Ethology and Sociobiology*, 6, 59–73. p. 64; 27: Cialdini, R. B., & Ascani, K. (1976). Test of a concession procedure for inducing verbal, behavioral, and further compliance with a request to give blood. *Journal of Applied Psychology*, 61, 295–300; 28: Milgram, S. (1964). Issues in the study of obedience: A reply to Baumrind. *American Psychologist*, 19, 848–852. p. 850

Chapter 2   Page 41: Kelley, H. H. (1950). The warm–cold variable in first impressions of persons. *Journal of Personality*, 18, 431–439; 55: Pryor, J. B., & Merluzzi, T. V. (1985). The role of expertise in processing social interaction scripts. *Journal of Experimental Social Psychology*, 21, 362–379; 59: Miller, P. J., Fung, H., & Mintz, J. (1996). Self-construction through narrative practices: A Chinese and American comparison of early socialization. *Ethos*, 24, 237–280; Okimoto, D. I., & Rohlen, T. P. (1988). *Inside the Japanese system: Readings on contemporary society and political economy*. Stanford, CA: Stanford University Press; 63: Padilla, A. M. (1994). Bicultural development: A theoretical and empirical examination. In R. G. Malgady & O. Rodriguez (Eds.), *Theoretical and conceptual issues in Hispanic mental health* (pp. 20–51). Malabar, FL: Krieger. p. 30; 48: Based on Burger, J. M., & Caldwell, D. F. (2003). Table 3, p. 239. The effects of monetary incentives and labeling on the foot-in-the-door effect: Evidence for a self-perception process. *Basic and Applied Social Psychology*, 25, 235–231; 51: Baum, A., & Davis, G. E. (1980). Reducing the stress of high-density living: An architectural intervention. *Journal of Personality and Social Psychology*, 38, 471–481. Fig. 1, p. 475; 55: Adapted Price, R. H., & Bouffard, D. L. (1974). Behavioral appropriateness and situational constraint as dimensions of social behavior. *Journal of Personality and Social Psychology*, 30, 579–586. p. 581; 58: Based on J. Deregewski et al. (1983), *Expications in Cross-Cultural Psychology*, pp. 335–355, Fig. 2 © Swets & Zeitlinger Publishers; 61: Based on Bartholow, B. D., Sestir, M. A., & Davis, E. B. (2005). Correlates and consequences of exposure to video game violence: Hostile personality, empathy, and aggressive behavior. *Personality and Social Psychology Bulletin*, 31, 1573–1586. Figure 2, p. 1581

Chapter 3   Page 71: Obama, Barack. Press conference in Chicago. December 1, 2008; 71: Peggy Noonan, former speech writer for Presidents Ronald Reagan and George H. W. Bush, cited in Wakefield, 2002; 71: Hillary Rodham Clinton as a Feminist Heroine. *American Enterprise* 11, 5 (July–August 2000): 32–37; 72: Safire, William. "Blizzard of Lies". *New York Times*, Jan. 8, 1999; 72: Dick Morris, 1999, former Bill Clinton political strategist; 72: Chesler, Ellen. Nation, Volume 269, August 9–16. Nation Company; 73: Maner, J. K., Gailliot, M. T., Rouby, D. A., &

Miller, S. L. (2007). Can't take my eyes off you: Attentional adhesion to mates and rivals. *Journal of Personality and Social Psychology*, 93, 389–401; 80: Estimates based on 2010 U.S. Cause of Death data, reported by the Centers for Disease Control; 86: Miller, D. T., & Ross, M. (1975). Self serving biases in attribution of causality: Fact or fiction? *Psychological Bulletin*, 82, 213–255; 94: Lord, C. G., Lepper, M. R., & Preston, E. (1984). Considering the opposite: A corrective strategy for social judgment. *Journal of Personality and Social Psychology*, 47, 1231–1243. p. 1233; 91: Based on data reported in Sedikides, C., Gaertner, L., & Toguchi, Y. (2003). Pancultural self-enhancement. *Journal of Personality & Social Psychology*, 84, 60–79. Table 3; 97: McArthur, L. A. (1972). The how and what of why: Some determinants and consequences of causal attribution. *Journal of Personality and Social Psychology*, 22, 171–193; 99: Adapted from Pendry, L. F., & Macrae, C. N. (1994). Stereotypes and mental life: The case of the motivated but thwarted tactician. *Journal of Experimental Social Psychology*, 30, 303–325. Table 1; 101: Du Maurier, D. (1977). *Myself when young: The shaping of a writer*. Garden City, NY: Doubleday

Chapter 4   Page 109: From Snyder, M. (1974). Self-monitoring of expressive behavior. *Journal of Personality and Social Psychology*, 30, 526–537. Reprinted by permission of Mark Snyder; 114: Carnegie, Dale. (1936/1981). *How to win friends and influence people*. New York: Pocket Books. p. 66; 116: Becoming Barbie. (1995, December 8). 20/20, American Broadcasting Company; 118: Barton, J. (1794). *Lectures on female education*. New York: Gaine. p. 72; 116: Reprinted from *Journal of Experimental Social Psychology*, 11, Mark P. Zanna1, Susan J. Pack, On the self-fulfilling nature of a apparent sex differences in behavior, 583–591, 1975, with permission from Elsevier; 118: Barton, J. (1794). *Lectures on female education*. New York: Gaine. p. 162; 135: Crichton, R. (1959). *The great impostor*. New York: Random House. p. 10

Chapter 5   Page 149: L. C. White, (1988), *Merchants of death*. New York: Morrow, p. 145; 151: Adapted from Petty, R. E., & Cacioppo, J. T. (1984). The effects of involvement on responses to argument quantity and quality: Central and peripheral routes to persuasion. *Journal of Personality and Social Psychology*, 46, 69–81; 157: Inbau, F. E., Reid, J.E., Buckley, J. P., & Jayne, B. C. (2001). *Criminal interrogation and confessions* (4th ed.). Gaithersburg, MD: Aspen Publishers; 159: Napoleon Bonaparte. Clive Shearer, *Everyday Excellence: Creating A Better Workplace Through Attitude, Action, And Appreciation* (ASQ Quality Press, 2006: 22); 161: Cooper, Joel; Bennett, Elizabeth A.; Sukel, Holly L. Complex scientific testimony: How do jurors make decisions? *Law and Human Behavior*, Vol 20(4), Aug 1996, 379–394; 161: Based on Leventhal, H., & Cameron, L. (1994). Persuasion and health attitudes. In S. Shavitt & T. C. Brock (Eds.), *Persuasion* (pp. 219–249). Boston: Allyn & Bacon; 162: Michael Faraday. Douglas T. Kenrick; Steven L. Neuberg; Robert B. Cialdini, *Social Psychology: Unraveling the Mystery*, 3e; Allyn & Bacon, 2004: 162; 166: Ralph Waldo Emerson. Martin H. Manser, *The Facts on File Dictionary of Proverbs*. Infobase Publishing, 2007; 166: Wilde, Oscar. The Relation of Dress to Art, *The Pall Mall Gazette*

(February 28, 1885); 166: Aldous Huxley, Wordsworth in the Tropics, Do What You Will (Chatto & Windus, London, 1929); 167: Cialdini, R. B., Trost, M. R., & Newsom, J. T. (1995). Preference for consistency: The development of a valid measure and the discovery of surprising behavioral implications. *Journal of Personality and Social Psychology*, 69, 318–328; 169: Adapted from Han, S-P., & Shavitt, S. (1994). Persuasion and culture: Advertising appeals in individualistic and collectivistic societies. *Journal of Experimental Social Psychology*, 30, 326–350; 173: Reilly, P. (1995). When will it ever end? In D. S. Connery (Ed.), *Convicting the innocent* (pp. 84–86). Cambridge, MA: Brookline. p. 93; 173: Connery, D. S. (1995). *Convicting the innocent*. Cambridge, MA: Brookline. p. 92

Chapter 6   Page 178: Hassan, S. (1990). *Combatting cult mind control*. Rochester, VT: Park Street Press. p. 24; 179: Hassan, S. (1990). *Combatting cult mind control*. Rochester, VT: Park Street Press. p. 24; 180: Adapted from Asch, S. E. (1956). Studies of independence and conformity: A minority of one against a unanimous majority. *Psychological Monographs*, 70 (9, Whole number 416); 184: Based on data from Milgram, S. (1963). Behavioral study of obedience. *Journal of Abnormal and Social Psychology*, 67, 371–378; 186: Galanti, G. A. (1993). Reflections on brainwashing. In M. D. Langone (Ed.), *Recovery from cults* (pp. 85–103). New York: Norton. p. 91; 187: Milgram, S. (1965). Some conditions of obedience and disobedience to authority. *Human Relations*, 18, 57–56. p. 74; 189: Gracian, B. (1649/1945). *The art of worldly wisdom*. New York: Charles Thomas. p. 142; 189: MacKay, C. (1841/1932). *Popular delusions and the madness of crowds*. New York: Farrar, Straus, and Giroux., p. 260; 190: Singer, M. T., & Lalich, J. (1995). *Cults in our midst*. San Francisco: Jossey-Bass., 1995, p. 273; 190: Based on data from Milgram, S., Bickman, L., & Berkowitz, L. (1969). Note on the drawing power of crowds of different size. *Journal of Personality and Social Psychology*, Vol. 13(2), Oct. 1969, 79–82; 191: Sherif, M. (1936). *The Psychology of Social Norms*. New York: Harper & Row. p. 111; 192: Hassan, S. (1990). *Combatting cult mind control*. Rochester, VT: Park Street Press. p. 68; 192: Adapted from Baron, R. S., Vandello, J., & Brunsman, B. (1996). The forgotten variable in conformity research: Impact of task importance on social influence. *Journal of Personality and Social Psychology*, 71, 915–927; 193: Janis, I. L. (1997). Groupthink. In W. A. Lesko (Ed.), *Readings in social psychology* (3rd ed., pp. 333–337). Boston: Allyn & Bacon. (p. 334); 195: Cialdini, Robert B. (2009). *Influence: Science and Practice*. Boston: Allyn and Bacon. p. 36; 198: Dowd, E. T., Milne, C. R., & Wise, S. L. (1991). The therapeutic reactance scale: A measure of psychological reactance. *Journal of Counseling and Development*, 69, 541–545: 543: 198: Guéguen, N., Meineri, S., Martin, A., & Grandjean, I. (2010). The combined effect of the foot-in-the-door technique and the "but you are free" technique: An evaluation on the selective sorting of household wastes. *Ecopsychology*, 2(4), 231–237; 201–202: WILLIAM GRIMES, In War Against No-Shows, Restaurants Get Tougher, October 15, 1997, *The New York Times Company*; 204: Cialdini, R. B., Eisenberg, N., Green, B. L., Rhoads, K., & Bator, R. (1998). Undermining the undermining effect of reward on sustained interest. *Journal of Applied Social Psychology*, 28, 253–267; 205: Hassan, S. (1990). *Combatting cult mind control*. Rochester, VT: Park Street Press, p. 13; 206: Adapted from Deutsch, M., & Gerard, H. B. (1955). A study of normative and informational social influences upon individual judgment. *Journal of Abnormal and Social Psychology*, 51, 629–636

Chapter 7   Page 213: Bukowski, W.M., Hoza, B., & Boivin, M. (1994). Measuring friendship quality during pre and early adolescence: The development and psychometric properties of the friendship qualities scale. *Journal of Personal and Personal Relationships*, 11, 471–484; 217: Cannon, W. B. (1932). *The wisdom of the body*. New York: Norton; 219: James, W. (1890). *Principles of psychology*. New York: Henry Holt; 219: William James; 227: Cialdini, R. B., & Ascani, K. (1976). Test of a concession procedure for inducing verbal, behavioral, and further compliance with a request to give blood. *Journal of Applied Psychology*, 61, 295–300; 227: Beach, S. R. H., Tesser, A., Fincham, F. D., Jones, D. J., Johnson, D., & Whitaker, D. J. (1998). Pleasure and pain in doing well, together: An investigation of performance-related affect in close relationships. *Journal of Personaltiy and Social Psychology*, 74, 923–938; 229: Allen, R. W., Madison, D. L., Porter, L. W., Renwick, P. A., & Mayes, B. T. (1979). Organizational politics: Tactics and characteristics of its actors. *California Management Review*, 22, 77–83; 230: Oscar Wilde, *The Prose of Oscar Wilde*, Cosimo, Inc., 2005; 233: From Bram P. Buunk et al. (1993). Perceived reciprocity, social support, and stress at work: The role of exchange and communal orientation. *Journal of Personality and Social Psychology*, 65, 801–811. Reprinted by permission of Bram P. Buunk; 236: Green, M. C., Hilkenm J., Friedman, H., Grossman, K., Gasiewski, J., Adler, R., & Sabini, J. (2005). Communication via instant messenger: Short and long-term effects. *Journal of Applied Social Psychology*, 35, 487–507

Chapter 8   Page 243: Kettenmann, A. (2008). *Kahlo*. Los Angeles: Taschen; 245: Hatfield, E., & Rapson, R. L. (1996). *Love and sex: Cross-cultural perspectives*. Boston: Allyn & Bacon; 247: Herrera, H. (1983). *Frida: A biography of Frida Kahlo*. New York: Harper Collins; 248: Based on Kenrick, D. T., Sadalla, E. K., Groth, G., & Trost, M. R. (1990). Evolution, traits, and the stages of human courtship: Qualifying the parental investment model. *Journal of Personality*, 58, 97–117; 249: Clark, R. D., & Hatfield, E. (1989). Gender differences in receptivity to sexual offers. *Journal of Psychology and Human Sexuality*, 2, 39–55; 249: Based on Clark, R. & Hatfield, E. (1987). Gender Differences in Receptivity to Sexual Offers. *Journal of Psychology & Human Sexuality*, Vol. 2(1) 1989; 251: Simpson, J. A., & Gangestad, S. W. (1992). Sociosexuality and romantic partner choice. *Journal of Personality*, 60, 31–51; 256: Jankowiak, W. R., & Fischer, E. F. (1992). A cross-cultural perspective on romantic love. *Ethnology*, 31, 149–155; 259: Anderson, S. C. (1993). Anti-stalking laws: Will they curb the erotomanic's obsessive pursuit? *Law and Psychology Review*, 17, 171–191; 268: Herrera, H. (1983). *Frida: A biography of Frida Kahlo*. New York: Harper Collins / Based on Griskevicius, V., Goldstein, N., Mortensen, C., Cialdini, R. B., & Kenrick, D. T. (2006). Going along versus going alone: When fundamental motives facilitate strategic (non)conformity. *Journal of Personality and Social Psychology*, 91, 281–294; Griskevicius, V., Tybur, J. M., Sundie, J. M., Cialdini, R. B., Miller, G. F., & Kenrick, D. T. (2007). Blatant benevolence and conspicuous consumption: When romantic motives elicit strategic costly signals. *Journal of Personality and Social Psychology*, 93, 85–102; 268: Based on Jensen-Campbell, L. A., Graziano, W. G., & West, S. G. (1995). Dominance, prosocial orientation, and female preferences: Do nice guys really finish last? *Journal of Personality and Social Psychology*, 68, 427–440

Chapter 9   Page 283: Craig, B. (1985, July 30). A story of human kindness. *Pacific Stars and Stripes*, 13–16; 285: Schelling, T. C. (1968). The life you save may be your own. In S. Chase (Ed.),

Problems in public expenditure analysis. Washington, DC: The Brookings Institute. p.130; 290: Shotland, R. L., & Straw, M. (1976). Bystander response to an assault: When a man attacks a woman. *Journal of Personality and Social Psychology, 34,* 990–999; 295: Deutsch, L. (1993, August 27). 4 tell jury how they ran from TVs to help Denny. *San Francisco Examiner,* p. A11; 295: M. Tokayer, personal communication, May 19, 1994; 298: Mauss, M. (1967). *The gift.* New York: W. W. Norton; 281: Adapted from the results of Cunningham, M. R., Jegerski, J., Gruder, C. L., & Barbee, A. P. (1995). Helping in different social relationships: Charity begins at home. Unpublished manuscript, University of Louisville, Department of Psychology, Louisville, KY; 291: Levine, R. V. (2003). The kindness of strangers. *American Scientist, 91,* 226–233; 294: Hodgkinson, V. A., & Weitzman, M. S. (1990). *Giving and volunteering in the United States.* Washington, DC: Independent Sector; 303: From Weyant, J. (1978). Effects of mood states, costs, and benefits on helping. *Journal of Personality and Social Psychology, 10,* 1169–1176

Chapter 10   Page 314: Bjorkvist, K., Osterman, K., & Lagerspetz, K. M. J. (1994). Sex differences in covert aggression among adults. *Aggressive Behavior, 20,* 27–33. p. 28; 315: Statistics based on Department of Justice, FBI Uniform Crime Reports; 317: Alfred Hitchcock, acceptance speech for Milestone Award, Screen Producers Guild dinner, March 7th, 1965; 319: Dollard, J., Miller, N. E., Doob, L. W.,Mowrer, O. H., & Sears, R. R. (1939). *Frustration and aggression.* New Haven, CT: Yale University Press; 321: Based on Reifman, A., Larrick, R. P., & Fein, S. (1991). Temper and temperature on the diamond: The heat-aggression relationship in major league baseball. *Personality and Social Psychology Bulletin, 17,* 580–585; 327: Bugliosi, V., & Gentry, C. (1974). *Helter skelter.* New York: Bantam; 329: Wood, W., Wong, F. Y., & Chachere, J. G. (1991). Effects of media violence on viewer's aggression in unconstrained social interaction. *Psychological Bulletin, 109,* 371–383. p. 380; 334: Mazur, A., & Booth, A. (1998). Testerosterone and dominance in men. *Behavioral and Brain Sciences, 21,* 353–397; 338: Bertilson, H. S. (1990). Aggression. In V. J. Derlega, B. A. Winstead, & W. H. Jones (Eds.), *Personality: Contemporary theory and research* (pp. 458–480). Chicago: Nelson-Hall; 342: Based on Zillmann, D. (1994). Cognition–excitation interdependencies in the escalation of anger and angry aggression. In M. Potegal & J. F. Knutson (Eds.), *Dynamics of aggression: Biological and social processes in dyads and groups* (pp. 45–71). Hillsdale, NJ: Erlbaum

Chapter 11   Page 351: Hochberg, A. (1996, April 19). 1971 School desegregation made friends out of enemies. National Public Radio All Things Considered; 352: Items adapted from McConahay (1986) and Swim et al. (1995); 355: Data from Pryor, J. B., LaVite, C., & Stoller, L. (1993). A social psychological analysis of sexual harassment: The person/situation interaction. *Journal of Vocational Behavior, 42,* 68–83. Figure 1; 356: Adapted from C. M. Steele and J. Aronson (1995). Stereotype threat and the intellectual test performance of African Americans. *Journal of Personality and Social Psychology, 69,* 797–811. Reprinted by permission of Claude M. Steele; 367: Unlikely Friendship Curriculum Development and Planning Team. (2003). *An unlikely friendship: Curriculum and video guide.* Chapel Hill, NC: FPG Child Development Institute; 367: Data from Noel, J. G.,

Wann, D. L., & Branscombe, N. R. (1995). Peripheral ingroup membership status and public negativity toward outgroups. *Journal of Personality and Social Psychology, 68,* 127–137 Figure 3; 368: Terkel, S. (1992). *Race: How blacks and whites think and feel about the American obsession,* New York: Anchor; 372: Data from Crocker, J., Thompson, L. L., McGraw, K. M., & Ingerman, C. (1987). Downward comparison, prejudice, and evaluations of others: Effects of self-esteem and threat. *Journal of personality and Social Psychology, 52,* 907–916. Table 2, p. 913; 378: Data from Simon, L., & Greenberg, J. (1996). Further progress in understanding the effects of derogatory ethnic labels: The role of preexisting attitudes toward the targeted group. *Personality and Social Psychology Bulletin, 22,* 119–1204. Table 1; 384: Data from Sherif, M., Harvey, C. W. (1961/1988). *The Robbers Cave experiment: Intergroup conflict and cooperation.* Middletown, CT: Wesleyan University Press. Tables 7.5 and 7.6, pp. 194–195

Chapter 12   Page 400: Durant, W., & Durant, A. (1963). *The age of Louis XIV.* New York: Simon & Schuster.651; 402: Data from Shepperd, J. A. (2001). The desire to help and behavior in social dilemmas: Exploring responses to catastrophes. *Group Dynamics, 5,* 304–314. Table 1; 406: Data from Watson, W. E., Kumar, K., & Michaelsen, L. K. (1993). Cultural diversity's impact on interaction process and performance: Comparing homogeneous and diverse task groups. *Academy of Management Journal, 36,* 590–602. Table 2; 409: Schachter, S. (1959). *The psychology of affiliation: Experimental studies of the sources of gregariousness.* Stanford, CA: Stanford University Press. p. 24; 413: Adapted from Janis, I. L., & Mann, L. (1977). *Decision making: A psychological analysis of conflict, choice, and commitment.* New York: Free Press; 416: "Executive Pay by the Numbers," *The New York Times,* 6/29/13, available at http://www.nytimes.com/interactive/2013/06/30/business/executive-compensation-tables.html?_r=0; 417: Simonton, D. K. (1994). *Greatness: Who makes history and why.* New York: Guilford.404; 419: Data from White, R. K., & Lippitt, R. (1960). *Autocracy and democracy: An experimental inquiry.* New York: Harper & Brothers. p. 65

Chapter 13   Page 441: Radcliffe-Brown, A. (1913). Three tribes of Western Australia. *Journal of the Royal Anthropological Institute, 43,* 143–194. (p. 164); 443: Sidanius, J., & Pratto, F. (2003). Social dominance theory and the dynamics of inequality: A reply to Schmitt, Branscombe, & Kappen and Wilson & Liu. *British Journal of Social Psychology, 42,* 207–213; 447: Deutsch, M. (1986). Strategies for inducing cooperation. In R. K. White (Ed.), *Psychology and the prevention of nuclear war* (pp. 162–170). New York: New York University Press. p. 164; 448: Deutsch, M. (1986). Strategies for inducing cooperation. In R. K. White (Ed.), *Psychology and the prevention of nuclear war* (pp. 162–170). New York: New York University Press; 449: Lane, C. (1991, January 7). Saddam's Endgame. *Newsweek,* p. 14–18. p. 18; 449: Dickey, C. (1991, January 7). Why we can't seem to understand the Arabs. *Newsweek,* p. 26–27. p. 27; 449: Kimmel, P. R. (1997). Cultural perspectives on international negotiations. In L. A. Peplau & S. E. Taylor (Eds.), *Sociocultural perspectives in social psychology* (pp. 395–411). New York: Prentice-Hall. p. 408; 450: McGrath, P. (1991, January 7). More than a madman. *Newsweek,* pp. 20–24. p. 24

Chapter 14   Page 462: Poincare, J. H. (1905). *Science and hypothesis.* London: Walter Scott

Photo Credits

Chapter 1 Page 3: Jeremy sutton-hibbert/Alamy; 8(l): David Keith Jones/Images of Africa Photobank/Alamy; 8(c): v.s.anandhakrishna/Shutterstock; 8(r): rusty426/Shutterstock; 9: Dave Kenrick; 10: Ken Levine/Getty Images; 15: Lucy Nicholson/AFP/Getty Images; 18: absolutimages/Shutterstock; 19: Peter Barritt/Alamy; 23: Philip G. Zimbardo; 28: Alexandra Milgram; 30: Matthew Healey/UPI Photo/Newscom

Chapter 2 Page 37(l): Bettmann/CORBIS; 37(r): Flip Schulke/Historical/Corbis; 43: Dr. Fritz Strack; 45(b): ZUMA Press, Inc./Alamy; 47: PHANIE/Photo Researchers, Inc; 52: Milan 54; 53: Ricard Lord/The Image Works; 54: Imagesource/Glow Images; 64(l): © Maxwell Irish Government Pool/Xinhua Press/Corbis; 64(r): White House Photo/Alamy; 67: Bettmann/CORBIS; Library of Congress Prints and Photographs Division [LC-USZ62-126559]; 45: Dr. Fritz Strack

Chapter 3 Page 71: Arnold Gold/New Haven Register/The Image Works; 77: Wavebreakmedia/Shutterstock; 81: Focus Pocus LTD/Fotolia; 88: Budimir Jevtic/Shutterstock; 90: Russell Underwood/Flirt/Corbis; 98: Igor Mojzes/Fotolia; 100: Arnold Gold/New Haven Register/The Image Works

Chapter 4 Page 104: AP Images; 106: Tracy Whiteside/Shutterstock; 107: © Robbie Jack/Corbis; 111(l): Rob Rich/Everett Collection/Newscom; 111(r): Allstar Picture Library/Alamy; 112: RIA-Novosti/The Image Works; 115(l): Dacher Keltner; 115(r): Dacher Keltner; 116: Europics/Newscom; 117: AP Photo; 119: © CORBIS; 123: Vibe Images/Alamy; 126: Christine Langer-Pueschel/Shutterstock; 129: Splash News/Newscom; 132: Karin Cooper/Getty Images; 134: AP Images

Chapter 5 Page 139: Subconscious Prime Products; 146: Mitchell Funk/Getty Images; 148: Doug Kenrick; 149: Gilles Mingasson/Getty Images; 152: Naypong/Shutterstock; 153: The Image Bank; 158: Ryan McVay/Getty Images; 160: Patti McConville/Alamy; 163: Jemal Countess/Getty Images; 168(l): Principal Financial Group; 168(r): Principal Financial Group; 171: Bonnie Kamin/PhotoEdit

Chapter 6 Page 177: Bettina Cirone/Photo Researchers, Inc; 181: © Kim Kulish/Corbis; 182: Lynne Sutherland/Alamy; 186: AP Photo/Barry Thumma; 194(t): Stefano Lunardi/Olive/IML Image Group Ltd/Alamy; 194(b): Jeff Greenberg/PhotoEdit—All rights reserved; 203: James Schnepf/Getty Images; 208(t): Bettina Cirone/Photo Researchers, Inc; 208(b): Steve Hassan

Chapter 7 Page 212(t): AP Photo/Gert Eggenberger; 212(b): Everett Collection; 213: Blend Images/Alamy; 216: Darren McCollester/Getty Images; 217: © Ted Horowitz/CORBIS; 218(t): Mario Tama/Getty Images; 218(b) Ace Stock Limited/Alamy; 224: Dennis MacDonald/PhotoEdit; 228: Anthro-Photo File; 229: Spencer Grant/PhotoEdit; 234: AP Photo/Gerald Herbert; 235: AP Photo/Charles Rex Arbogast; 237: Sean Sprague/The Image Works; 238: AP Photo/Gert Eggenberger

Chapter 8 Page 243: Everett Collection Historical/Alamy; 245: Sergey Mostovoy/Fotolia; 247(l): erichon/Fotolia; 247(c): Sheldan Collins/Encyclopedia/Corbis; 247(r): Kevin Parry/WireImage/Getty Images; 252: Miramax/courtesy Everett Collection; 253: United Archives GmbH/IFTN Cinema Collection/Alamy; 254(t): Michael S. Yamashita/Documentary/Corbis; 254(b): Yeko Photo Studio/Shutterstock; 256: Xalanx/Fotolia; 259(l): Tom Grill/JGI/Blend Images/Getty Images; 259(r): blickwinkel/Alamy; 263: Pearson Education; 264: Paul Skipper/ARROYO/AP images; 265(t): TM & Copyright 20th Century Fox Film Corp/Everett Collection; 265(b): John Henshall/Alamy; 266: Jenny Matthews/Alamy; 268: Lionsgate/Photos 12/Alamy; 270: George Pimentel/Getty Images; 273: Everett Collection Historical/Alamy

Chapter 9 Page 277(t): United States Holocaust Memorial Museum; 277(b): United States Holocaust Memorial Museum; 280: Chuck Pefley/Alamy; 281: Teake Zuidema/The Image Works; 283: United States Holocaust Memorial Museum Yad Vashem Photo Archives, courtesy of Hiroki Sugihara Dr. Zorah Warhaftig; 284: IS-200608/Image Source/Alamy; 285: Rabbi Shimon Kalisch & Moshe Shatzkes working with Japanese officials in the 1940s; 287: American Museum of Natural History; 288(t): New York Times Text and Pictures – PARS; 288(b): Jack Maguire/Alamy; 290: Tatagatta/Fotolia; 291: JGI/Blend Images/Getty Images; 296(l): Alan Levenson/Time and Life Pictures/Getty Images; 296(r): Bob Galbraith/AP Images; 301: Lon C. Diehl/PhotoEdit; 305: Credit/Alamy; 308: United States Holocaust Memorial Museum Yad Vashem Photo Archives, courtesy of Hiroki Sugihara Dr. Zorah Warhaftig

Chapter 10 Page 312: AP Photo; 315: AFP/Getty Images; 325: AF archive/Alamy; 326: © Najlah Feanny/CORBIS SABA; 328: Warner Bros./courtesy Everett Collection; 330: Joe Raedle/Newsmakers/Getty Images; 332: Enigma/Alamy; 334: blickwinkel/Alamy; 335: © CORBIS; 345: Handout/Getty Images

Chapter 11 Page 350: AP Images; 352: Mike Stewart/Sygma/Corbis; 354(t): Dr. Eden B. King; 354(b): Dr. Eden B. King; 361: Gary Williams/Getty Images; 362: Archives of the History of American Psychology; 365: Reuters/CORBIS; 369: Richard Cummins/CORBIS; 373: Joshua Correll; 385: Robin Nelson/PhotoEdit; 386: AP Photo/Grant Halverson

Chapter 12 390: MIKE THEILER/AFP/Getty Images; 394: CESAR FERRARI/Reuters /Landov; 398: Syracuse Newspapers/Gary Walts/The Image Works; 401: RICHARD TSONG-TAATARII/MCT /Landov; 404: ANTONIO SCORZA/Getty Images; 408(l): INTERFOTO/Alamy; 408(r): CJG—Technology/Alamy; 410: David McNew/Getty Images; 412: Everett Collection; 414: AP Photo/Dr. Scott Lieberman, File; 417: David McNew/Getty Images; 418: Mike Blake/Reuters/Corbis

Chapter 13 Page 427(t): Tips Images/Tips Italia Srl a socio unico/Alamy; 427(b): Catarina Belova/Shutterstock; 434: Andy Ennis./Alamy; 436: Myrleen Pearson/PhotoEdit;

437: EpicStockMedia/Alamy; 439: AP Photo/John McConnico; 441: AP Photo/Alaa al-Marjani; 442: Mike Greenlar/The Image Works; 443(l): AP Photo/Jim MacMillan; 443(r): © Jim Zuckerman/CORBIS; 445: World History Archive/Image Asset Management Ltd./Alamy; 449: © Handout/CNP/Corbis; 453: RIA Novosti/Alamy

Chapter 14 Page 459(t): HARRY E. WALKER/MCT /Landov; 459(b): AP Photo/File; 460: AP Photo/Henry Burroughs; 464(l): Topham/The Image Works; 464(r): Bill Bachmann/The Image Works; 465(l): Kent Meireis/The Image Works; 465(r): Trevor Thompson/Alamy; 470: © ER Productions/CORBIS; 472: MONTY BRINTON/CBS /Landov; 473: JOSE M. OSO-RIO/MCT /Landov; 475: © CORBIS; 478: Celebrity Monitor, PacificCoastN/Newscom; 479(l): AP Photo/Rob Carr; 479(r): AP Photo/M. Spencer Green; 486: AP Photo/File

Name Index

Mueller, J. S., 414
Mugny, G., 411
Mulder, L. B., 438
Mullen, B., 359, 375, 394, 398, 411, 417, 418
Mullin, C. R., 330
Munro, G. D., 160
Murakami, F., 91
Murdock, G. P., 130
Murnighan, J. K., 439, 440
Murnighan, K., 194
Murphy, G. K., 376
Murray, H. A., 38
Murray, S. L., 261
Musch, J., 479
Musser, L. M., 117
Mussweiler, T., 80, 94
Myers, D. G., 30, 213, 409, 410

N

Nabi, H., 320
Naccarato, M. E., 82, 376
Nadler, A., 298, 299
Naffrechoux, M., 411
Nagurney, A. J., 30
Naidoo, L., 271
Nail, P. R., 167, 198
Nakao, K., 229
Napier, J. L., 370
Nasby, W., 297
Nathanson, S., 343
Navarrete, C. D., 8, 360, 448, 464, 474
Neal, D. T., 38
Neale, M. C., 281
Neel, R., 15, 73, 82, 119, 360, 469
Neidert, G. P., 439
Neighbors, C., 53, 320
Nelson, D. A., 315
Nelson, L. D., 53
Nelson, L. L., 442
Nelson, T. F., 54
Nemeroff, R., 283
Nemeth, C. J., 405, 411, 418
Nesse, R. M., 302
Nettle, D., 271, 467, 475
Neuberg, S. L., 9, 14–15, 27, 73, 77, 82–83, 93, 98,
    119, 198, 254, 307, 353, 356–357, 360, 364, 366, 371,
    376, 381, 464, 468, 469, 475–476
Neufeld, S. L., 119, 360
Neumann, R., 45
Newby-Clark, I. R., 167
Newcomb, T. M., 478
Newsom, J. T., 376
Newton, S. A., 162
Newton, T. L., 256
Neyer, F. J., 280
Nezlek, J., 218, 247
Nezlek, J. B., 109, 218, 220
Nguyen, D. H., 354
Nguyen, T., 444
Nias, D. K. B., 281
Nida, S. A., 461
Niedenthal, P. M., 46
Nielsen, J. M., 295
Niemann, Y. F., 353
Nier, J. A., 384

Nijstad, B. A., 420
Nisbett, R. E., 5, 18, 79, 88, 205, 334, 335, 468
Noel, J. G., 367
Nolan, J. M., 53
Nolen-Hoeksema, S., 200
Norem, J. K., 483
Norenzayan, A., 11, 79, 238, 295, 366, 433, 443, 466, 486
Normansell, L. A., 259
Norrander, B., 207
Norton, M. I., 26, 224, 302, 461
Nosek, B. A., 155, 353
Notarius, C., 270, 272
Novaco, R. W., 343
Nowak, A., 31, 397, 455, 463
Nowak, M. A., 450
Nowicki, S., 146
Numazaki, M., 91
Nurius, P., 47

O

Oakes, M. A., 373
Oakes, P. J., 374
Obayashi, J., 79
O'Brian, M. E., 143
O'Brien, E., 436
O'Brien, J. A., 173
O'Brien, L., 352
O'Brien, M., 376
O'Connor, K. J., 13, 30, 481
O'Donohue, W. T., 156
O'Gorman, R., 8
O'Grady, M. A., 116
O'Heeron, R. C., 217
Ohman, A., 8, 44, 467
Ohse, D. M., 354
Oishi, S., 235, 464
Okamura, T., 435
Okimoto, D. I., 59
Okimoto, T. G., 132
Oldenquist, A., 435, 439
Oldham, G. R., 62
Olds, J. M., 433
O'Leary, K. D., 343
Oleson, K. C., 380
Oliner, P. M., 283
Oliner, S. P., 283
Oliveira-Souza, R., 301
Olsen, E. A., 485
Olson, J. M., 141, 147, 148, 154
Olson, M. A., 141, 353
Olsson, A., 8, 462
Olweus, D., 341
Olzak, S., 362
O'Mara, E. M., 271, 336
Omarzu, J., 225
Omoto, A. M., 294
O'Neal, K. K., 30
Onishi, M., 258
Oppenheimer, D. M., 95
O'Reilly, C. A., III., 405
Orians, G. H., 266
Orive, R., 224
O'Rourke, M. T., 250, 337
Osborne, J. W., 357
Osborne, R. E., 122

Subject Index

Answer Key

Chapter 1:

Quick Quiz 1.1
1. b; **2.** d; **3.** d

Quick Quiz 1.2
1. c; **2.** e

Quick Quiz 1.3
1. d; **2.** c

Quick Quiz 1.4
1. d; **2.** e; **3.** b; **4.** d; **5.** c

Quick Quiz 1.5
1. d; **2.** d

Chapter 2:

Quick Quiz 2.1
1. c; **2.** b; **3.** d; **4.** c

Quick Quiz 2.2
1. d; **2.** b; **3.** a; **4.** c

Quick Quiz 2.3
1. b; **2.** d; **3.** a

Chapter 3:

Quick Quiz 3.1
1. d; **2.** c

Quick Quiz 3.2
1. d; **2.** b; **3.** b; **4.** c

Quick Quiz 3.3
1. a; **2.** b; **3.** b; **4.** d

Quick Quiz 3.4
1. d; **2.** c; **3.** d; **4.** e; **5.** a

Chapter 4:

Quick Quiz 4.1
1. d; **2.** b; **3.** d

Quick Quiz 4.2
1. d; **2.** a; **3.** b; **4.** a

Quick Quiz 4.3
1. c; **2.** b; **3.** b; **4.** c

Quick Quiz 4.4
1. d; **2.** b; **3.** c

Chapter 5:

Quick Quiz 5.1
1. c; **2.** b; **3.** d

Quick Quiz 5.2
1. b; **2.** c; **3.** d; **4.** e

Quick Quiz 5.3
1. b; **2.** a; **3.** d

Quick Quiz 5.4
1. a; **2.** a; **3.** c; **4.** d

Quick Quiz 5.5
1. b; **2.** a; **3.** d

Chapter 6:

Quick Quiz 6.1
1. d; **2.** d; **3.** b

Quick Quiz 6.2
1. b; **2.** d; **3.** c

Quick Quiz 6.3
1. d; **2.** a; **3.** a

Quick Quiz 6.4
1. c; **2.** b; **3.** d

Chapter 7:

Quick Quiz 7.1
1. d; **2.** c; **3.** a

Quick Quiz 7.2
1. c; **2.** a; **3.** a; **4.** d

Quick Quiz 7.3
1. b; **2.** d; **3.** d

Quick Quiz 7.4
1. a; **2.** d

Quick Quiz 7.5
1. b; **2.** d; **3.** c; **4.** d

Chapter 8:

Quick Quiz 8.1
1. d; **2.** d; **3.** a

Quick Quiz 8.2
1. b; **2.** b; **3.** a; **4.** d

Quick Quiz 8.3
1. d; **2.** b; **3.** b

Quick Quiz 8.4
1. d; **2.** d; **3.** d; **4.** c

Quick Quiz 8.5
1. a; **2.** d; **3.** d

Chapter 9:

Quick Quiz 9.1
1. c; **2.** e

Quick Quiz 9.2
1. e; **2.** d

Quick Quiz 9.3
1. c; **2.** e; **3.** c

Quick Quiz 9.4
1. a; **2.** d; **3.** c

Quick Quiz 9.5
1. a; **2.** d

Quick Quiz 9.6
1. b; **2.** d

Chapter 10:

Quick Quiz 10.1
1. c; **2.** d; **3.** d

Quick Quiz 10.2
1. a; **2.** d; **3.** c; **4.** c

Quick Quiz 10.3
1. c; **2.** d; **3.** c

Quick Quiz 10.4
1. b; **2.** d; **3.** d; **4.** a

Quick Quiz 10.5
1. d; **2.** d; **3.** b

Quick Quiz 10.6
1. d; **2.** d; **3.** a

Chapter 11:

Quick Quiz 11.1
1. a; **2.** d; **3.** b

Quick Quiz 11.2
1. d; **2.** c; **3.** b; **4.** a

Quick Quiz 11.3
1. d; **2.** c; **3.** d; **4.** b

Quick Quiz 11.4
1. c; **2.** b; **3.** c

Quick Quiz 11.5
1. b; **2.** c; **3.** d

Quick Quiz 11.6
1. c; **2.** a; **3.** c

Chapter 12:

Quick Quiz 12.1
1. d; **2.** c; **3.** b; **4.** a

Quick Quiz 12.2
1. d; **2.** b; **3.** c; **4.** c

Quick Quiz 12.3
1. d; **2.** c; **3.** b; **4.** d

Quick Quiz 12.4
1. d; **2.** b; **3.** a; **4.** a

Chapter 13:

Quick Quiz 13.1
1. c; **2.** b; **3.** c

Quick Quiz 13.2
1. d; **2.** d; **3.** a; **4.** b; **5.** b

Quick Quiz 13.3
1. b; **2.** a; **3.** c; **4.** d; **5.** b

Chapter 14:

Quick Quiz 14.1
1. d; **2.** b

Quick Quiz 14.2
1. b; **2.** a; **3.** c; **4.** a

Quick Quiz 14.3
1. b; **2.** d; **3.** c; **4.** a

Quick Quiz 14.4
1. c; **2.** b

Quick Quiz 14.5
1. d; **2.** a; **3.** c